TO THE STUDENT

This text was created to provide you with a high-quality educational resource. As a publisher specializing in college texts for business and economics, our goal is to provide you with learning materials that will serve you well in your college studies and throughout your career.

The educational process involves learning, retention, and the application of concepts and principles. You can accelerate your learning efforts, utilizing the supplements accompanying this text:

Study Guide for use with FUNDAMENTALS OF FINANCIAL ACCOUNTING by *Glenn A. Welsch and Charlotte W. Heywood* ISBN 0-256-07539-5

SmartAccount II: Analytical Financial Accounting Software by *Michael Gibbins, Richard Chandler, and Christine Newton* ISBN 0-256-07066-0

These learning aids are designed to improve your performance and the course by highlighting key points in the text and providing you with assistance in mastering basic concepts.

Check your campus bookstore, or ask the manager to place an order for you today.

We at Irwin sincerely hope that this text package will assist you in reaching your goals both now and in the future.

1800668-2253

0 66721 01281 4

uncalt

4509

Bm455

FUNDAMENTALS OF
FINANCIAL ACCOUNTING

FUNDAMENTALS OF FINANCIAL ACCOUNTING

Glenn A. Welsch
College of Business Administration
The University of Texas at Austin

George Richard Chesley
Faculty of Commerce
Saint Mary's University

Second Canadian Edition

IRWIN
Homewood, IL 60430
Boston, MA 02116

This symbol indicates that the paper in this book is made from recycled paper. Its fiber content exceeds the recommended minimum of 50% waste paper fibers as specified by the EPA.

Cover photo: *Franco Fontana/Image Bank/Chicago*

© RICHARD D. IRWIN, INC., 1987 and 1990

Sponsoring editor: *Roderick T. Banister*
Project editor: *Karen Smith*
Production manager: *Irene H. Sotiroff*
Designer: *Michael Warrell*
Cover design: *Sailor and Cook*
Compositor: *Better Graphics, Inc.*
Typeface: *10/12 Palatino*
Printer: *R. R. Donnelley & Sons Company*

ISBN 0-256-07538-7
Library of Congress Catalog Card No. 89–85749

Printed in the United States of America
3 4 5 6 7 8 9 0 DO 7 6 5 4 3 2

To
Dianna, Christy, and Allison

PREFACE

This second Canadian edition of *Fundamentals of Financial Accounting* is a revision of a successful first edition and is based on the experience and academic integrity of the fifth United States edition. Canadian readers are provided with the latest Canadian rules, practices, and material to reflect the uniqueness of Canadian accounting while at the same time enabling an appreciation of the accounting practices of an increasingly relevant financial scene in the United States.

Chapter discussions present a comprehensive, modern, and readable introduction to financial accounting, the accounting that communicates financial information to the financial markets and private investors. Chapter discussions are divided into sections (called parts) and supplements to assist readers in digesting the concepts and procedures involved. Questions, exercises, problems, and cases provide the opportunity to gain the proficiency so necessary for the subsequent study of accounting and the subsequent use of accounting in future courses and careers. The "whys" and the "hows" are presented in an integrated manner throughout the book so that completion of a program of study will provide an appropriate understanding to accounting majors and other students alike.

The sectioning of the discussions and the comprehensive assignment materials should enable the book to suit the various pedagogical philosophies present in Canadian academic circles. Sufficient discussions are available for a two-semester sequence of courses even though the book is primarily focused for the most usual one-semester course. The readability of the text discussions will permit instructors the rare opportunity to enrich their classroom presentations. Responses to the use of the first edition in distance education situations have been so outstanding that they provide testimony to this conclusion. Enriching discussions can be motivated or focused by the case materials available and the interesting annual report of Consolidated-Bathurst Inc. provided in Appendix B and referenced in nearly every set of chapter cases. The Consolidated-Bathurst report is one that is comprehensive yet understandable, and it features a company that has been in the financial news recently.

The second edition contains more than the usual editorial revisions. The difficult introduction to accounting information processing and financial reporting has been reorganized to ease the beginning few weeks for students.

A number of chapters were redesigned to make the discussions more consistent with current commercial practices and modern accounting and academic approaches. For example, sales discounts are now rare but sales taxes are not. Worksheets are now computer spreadsheets, and classroom instruction has moved toward more specific types of analyses. Pensions and estimated liabilities have been included for the first time in the text to reflect their importance in current financial reporting. Income taxes, the key to cash flows for decision making, have been revised consistent with the new Canadian terminology and practices. Accounting practices for property, buildings, equipment, and intangibles have been described in a manner that reflects new Canadian reporting standards. Cash flow discussions have been revised to make them more consistent with new practices both in Canada and the United States. One chapter that may appear to reverse this modernization trend is the current cost and inflation discussions in Chapter 17. Practice has moved away from the suggestions made here, but the chapter has been retained because of its importance to earlier discussions on business valuations and the continuing world importance of price inflation. Only a narrow North American view and a decision to restrict earlier conceptual presentations could justify omission of this material.

Readers of this book should find a clear—and conceptually relevant—discussion of the issues of financial accounting. Instructors and students should find materials that are appropriate to challenge their intellect while at the same time relevant to the topic and level of the audience we are addressing.

Acknowledgements

The second edition has benefited from the detailed reviews done by Brian Duggan, the University of Manitoba; Maureen Fizzel, the University of Saskatchewan; John Heaphy, McGill University; Darrell Herauf, Carleton University; and Jacqueline Thachuk, Kwantlen College. Their suggestions about the first edition and the drafts of the second edition were carefully analyzed for the final presentation of this new volume. While all their comments could not be adopted, they represented major improvements incorporated into this edition. Reviews, comments, and suggestions by numerous adopters of the first edition are too many to acknowledge individually, but they were most appreciated. I also had the benefit of detailed reviews done for the U.S. fifth edition, which I found most helpful. Unfortunately they are simply too numerous to acknowledge individually.

Materials were made available for the problems and cases through the kindness of the Canadian Institute of Chartered Accountants, the Society of Management Accountants of Canada, and the Certified General Accountants of Canada. *The Globe and Mail, The Bottom Line,* John Wiley and Sons Canada Limited, and Que Corporation kindly provided permission to reprint some of their materials. They, of course, are not responsible for the editorial and content changes I made to their material. Consolidated-Bathurst, Inc. kindly permitted the reprint of an extensive portion of their 1987 annual report.

A special thank you is extended to my former colleagues Edgar Scott and Chuck Dirkson for their efforts in preparing the income tax materials and some of the computer assignment cases. Teresa Durant and Greg Taylor provided individual assistance with typing the drafts and preparing the computer supplements available with the instructor's manual. The drafts of this edition were done while I was a member of the School of Business Administration at Dalhousie University. Their financial and administrative support was crucial to the writing of this edition.

The U.S. author, Glenn Welsch, wishes to acknowledge the support and assistance of the following students at The University of Texas at Austin: Vicky Conway, Annick Barton, Jody Daughtler, Melissa Gan, Erica Peters, and Lynette Broaders. Also he acknowledges the valuable editorial suggestions provided by Petria Sandlin and Kathy Springer and Professors Janet Daniels, University of Hartford; Harry Dickinson, University of Virginia; Ralph Drtina, Lehigh University; Sandra and David Byrd, Southwest Missouri State University; Stuart Webster, Lehigh; and LaVern Krueger, University of Missouri.

Appreciation is given to the American Institute of Certified Public Accountants, American Accounting Association, Financial Accounting Standards Board, and the authors identified by citations for permission to quote from their publications.

Professor Welsch, as author of the fifth U.S. edition, provided me with the fruits of his labour and the opportunity to include my ideas with his output. The extent of his trust can only be appreciated by one who has received it. I, of course, accept responsibility for the results contained between these covers.

Suggestions and comments on this text and its related materials by its readers would be most welcome.

G. R. (Dick) Chesley

CONTENTS

CHAPTER FIVE

Information Processing in an Accounting System   210

CHAPTER SIX

Accounting for Sales Revenue and Cost of Goods Sold   272

CHAPTER SEVEN

Costing Methods for Measuring Inventory and Cost of Goods Sold 360

CHAPTER EIGHT

Cash, Short-Term Investments in Securities, and Receivables 430

CHAPTER NINE

Operational Assets—Property, Plant, and Equipment; Natural Resources; and Intangibles 496

CHAPTER TEN

Measuring and Reporting Liabilities 562

FUNDAMENTALS OF
FINANCIAL ACCOUNTING

ONE

PERSPECTIVES— ACCOUNTING OBJECTIVES AND COMMUNICATION

PURPOSE

In our environment, people need information to make rational economic decisions. Most consumers use product and price information prior to purchasing a specific item. Investors and creditors need financial information before they provide funds to a business entity. A primary source of financial information is the periodic financial statements provided by a business entity. The primary purpose of this chapter is to define accounting, review the environment in which accounting is done, and describe how accounting serves our society.

Shown on the facing page are selected summary financial data communicated by one large company in its annual report. The ratios, physical data, and graphical presentation are interesting. Appendix B at the end of this book contains the full version of these statements.

LEARNING OBJECTIVES

1. Write and explain the objectives of accounting.
2. Explain how accounting reports help decision makers.
3. Tell how the business environment influences accounting.
4. Give an overview of the financial statements used to communicate information.
5. Expand your business vocabulary by learning the "Important Terms Defined in This Chapter."
6. Apply the knowledge learned from this chapter.

ORGANIZATION

Part A—objectives and environment of accounting
1. Accounting defined.
2. Use of accounting information by decision makers.
3. Historical accounting perspectives.
4. Groups involved in accounting innovation.

Part B—communication of accounting information
1. Communication concepts.
2. Overview of external financial reports.

Consolidated-Bathurst Inc.

Highlights

		1987	1986	1985
Operations	Net sales	$2,261	$2,018	$1,727
(millions of dollars)	Earnings before extraordinary items	182	104	80
	Net earnings	214	49	78
	Cash flow from operations	360	257	196
	Additions to property and plant	$ 261	$ 231	$ 176
Balance sheet	Total assets	$2,265	$2,031	$1,863
(millions of dollars)	Working capital	394	339	320
	Property and plant — net	$1,339	$1,191	$1,037
Per common share	Earnings before extraordinary items	$ 1.63	$ 0.87	$ 0.70
(dollars)	Net earnings	1.95	0.34	0.68
	Cash flow from operations	3.38	2.37	1.88
	Dividends	0.54	0.30	0.30
	Book value	$ 8.33	$ 6.76	$ 6.54
Ratios and other data	Ratio of current assets to current liabilities	2.0 to 1	2.1 to 1	2.1 to 1
	Ratio of short- and long-term debt to shareholders' equity	31/69	40/60	38/62
	Return on common shareholders' equity—%	19.6	12.8	10.3
	Number of issued common shares	102,318,399	102,266,100	101,999,614
	Number of employees	15,111	14,619	14,413

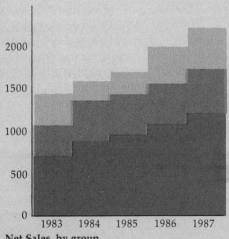

Net Sales, by group
(millions of dollars)

- Packaging, Europa Carton
- North American Packaging
- Pulp and Paper

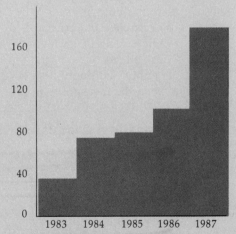

Earnings before extraordinary items
(millions of dollars)

PART A—OBJECTIVES AND ENVIRONMENT OF ACCOUNTING

Accounting Defined

Accounting can be defined as the collection of financial data about an organization and the analysis, measurement, recording, and reporting of that information to decision makers. An accounting system processes the (*a*) flows of resources into (inflows) and out (outflows) of an organization, (*b*) resources controlled (i.e., assets) by the organization, and (*c*) claims against those resources (i.e., debts). Accounting requires judgment and interpretation in analyzing, reporting, and using the reported financial results. The flow of accounting information of an entity can be summarized as in Exhibit 1–1, which shows that the end products of an accounting system are **financial statements** that are prepared for decision makers.

Economics has a special relationship with accounting. Economics has been defined as the study of how people and society choose to employ scarce productive resources that could have alternative uses to produce various commodities and distribute them for consumption, now or in the future, among various persons and groups in society.[1] Like economics, accounting has a conceptual foundation that provides guidelines for the collection, measurement, and communication of financial information about an organization. In general, accounting reports how an entity has allocated its scarce resources. Thus, accounting collects, measures, interprets, and reports financial information on the same activities that are the focus of economics. Economics explains economic relationships on a conceptual level, whereas accounting reports the economic relationships primarily on a practical level. However, accounting measurements are as consistent with economic concepts as is possible. Accounting must cope with the complex and practical problems of measuring in monetary terms the economic effects of **exchange transactions** (i.e., resource inflows and outflows). These effects relate to the resources held and the claims against the resources of an entity. Throughout this textbook, the theoretical and practical issues that arise in the measurement process are discussed from the accounting viewpoint.

Accounting Operates in a Complex Environment

The environment in which accounting operates is affected by such forces as the type of (*a*) government (e.g., democracy versus dictatorship), (*b*) economic system (e.g., free enterprise versus socialism), (*c*) industry (e.g., technological versus agrarian), (*d*) organizations within that society (e.g., labour unions), and (*e*) regulatory controls (i.e., private sector versus governmental). Accounting is influenced significantly by the educational level and economic development of the society.

---

[1] Paul A. Samuelson, *Economics*, 9th ed. (New York: McGraw-Hill, 1973).

Exhibit 1–1 Flow of economic information in an accounting system

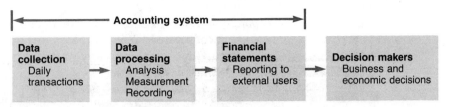

Note: Financial statements should be prepared in such form and use such terminology and classification of items that significant information is readily understandable (*CICA Handbook*, Section 1500, para. 08).

Each of us is associated with social, political, and economic organizations such as businesses, churches, fraternal organizations, political parties, provinces, environmental groups, and professional associations. These organizations face important resource allocation decisions. Organizations are essential to the workings of a society; in fact, they constitute much of society.

Fundamental to a dynamic and successful society is the ability of each organization to measure and report its accomplishments, to undergo critical self-analysis, and, through sound decisions, to renew itself and grow. In this way, individual and societal objectives are served best. Essentially, society, and the various organizations that comprise it, thrive in direct proportion to the efficiency with which scarce resources of human talent, materials, services, and capital are allocated. To achieve this goal, organizations need information about how the resources are obtained and used. Accounting information is designed to meet this need.

Accounting is a management information system that is continuously changed to meet the evolving needs of society. The environmental characteristics of a society are diverse and complex; therefore, accounting is always facing new challenges. For example, an inflationary spiral necessitates the development of accounting concepts and procedures that will report "real" effects separately from purely inflationary effects (discussed in Chapter 17).

Throughout this textbook you will study how accounting responds to the environment of Canada. In the next few paragraphs we will discuss two environmental characteristics—types of business entities and measurement in dollars. These characteristics have pervasive effects on accounting concepts and procedures.

Types of Business Entities

This textbook emphasizes **accounting for profit-making entities.** In our environment there are three main types of business entities—sole proprietorship, partnership, and corporation. Their primary characteristics are given in the paragraphs that follow.

A **sole proprietorship** is an unincorporated business owned by one person. This type of business entity is common in the services, retailing, and farming industries. Usually, the owner is the manager. Legally, the business and the owner are not separate entities—they are the same. However, accounting views the business as a separate entity to be accounted for separate from its owner.

A **partnership** is an unincorporated business that is owned by two or more persons known as partners. The agreements between the owners are specified in a partnership contract. This contract deals with such matters as division of income each reporting period and distribution of resources of the business upon termination of its operations. A partnership is not legally separate from its owners. Legally, each partner in a general partnership is responsible for the debts of the business. This means that each general partner has **unlimited liability.** However, accounting views the partnership as a separate business entity to be accounted for separately from its several owners.

A **corporation** is a business that is incorporated under the laws of a particular province or the Government of Canada. The owners are shareholders or stockholders. Ownership is represented by shares of capital stock that usually can be bought and sold freely. When an approved application is filed by the organizers, the government issues a charter. This charter gives the corporation the right to operate as a separate legal entity, separate and apart from its owners. The owners enjoy **limited liability.** That is, the owners are liable for the debts of the corporation only to the extent of their investments. The charter specifies the types and amounts of capital stock that can be issued. The shareholders elect a governing board of directors, which in turn employs managers and exercises general supervision of the corporation.[2] Accounting for the business entity focuses on the corporation, not on the directors and managers as individuals.

In terms of economic importance, the corporation is the dominant form of business organization in Canada. The advantages of the corporate form include (*a*) limited liability for the shareholders, (*b*) continuity of life, (*c*) ease in transferring ownership (shares), and (*d*) opportunities to raise large amounts of money by selling shares to a large number of people. The primary disadvantages of a corporation are that (*a*) they tend to be impersonal and (*b*) their income is subject to two different taxes. First, corporate income is taxed when earned and then again when shareholders receive dividends. Because of several advantages, most large and medium-sized businesses (and many small ones) are organized as corporations. Therefore, we shall emphasize this form of business. Nevertheless, the accounting concepts, standards, and measurement procedures that we will discuss also apply to the other types of businesses.

Measurement in Dollars

A monetary system provides the primary way to measure and communicate economic information about the flow of resources in and out of an organization. In a monetary system, the unit of exchange (dollars in our case) is the common

---

[2] There are a number of specialized types of entities that we do not discuss, such as joint ventures, mutual funds, cooperatives, investment trusts, and syndicates. Consideration of these entities is appropriate for advanced accounting courses.

denominator used to measure value. Thus, the monetary unit provides a means for expressing the available resources and the resource flows of an entity.

Accounting uses the monetary system of each country within which it operates. One of the critical problems in accounting is the conversion of financial amounts from one monetary system to another monetary system in measuring resources and resource flows for multinational activities.

Measurement Fundamentals

Essential in any measurement process is a precise definition of what is to be measured. Examples of specific items often measured are the population of Ontario, the rainfall in Nova Scotia, the voter registrations in Newfoundland, and the bank deposits in Alberta (each for a stipulated time). Similarly, in the measurement of resources and debts of a business, accounting requires precise definition of the specific entity for which financial data are to be collected, measured, and reported. When a specific entity is defined for financial reporting purposes, it often is referred to as an **accounting entity.** In any measurement scheme, the definition of what should be measured often involves problems. For example, in measuring the population of Ontario, should the total include military personnel? university students? prison inmates? long-term visitors? hotel guests? Similarly, in defining an accounting entity, important problems must be resolved. First, we must define a separate and specific accounting entity. An accounting entity has a specialized definition that is known as the separate-entity assumption.[3] The separate-entity assumption requires that for accounting measurement purposes, the particular entity being accounted for be distinguished carefully from all similar and related entities and persons. Under this assumption, an accounting entity is separate and distinct from its owner(s). Such an entity is viewed as owning the resources (i.e., assets) used by it and as owing the claims (i.e., debts) against those resources. For measurement purposes, the assets, debts, and activities of the entity are kept separate from those of the owners and other entities.

The Use of Accounting Information by Decision Makers

Your role as a decision maker is significant, whether you are a manager, investor, professional person, owner of a business, or an interested citizen. [Decision makers use various approaches to select one solution to a given problem from among a set of several alternative solutions. Selection of the best alternative is the basic decision.] In making decisions, a decision maker is concerned about the future because a decision cannot change the past. However, an effective decision maker should not neglect to consider past events and their outcomes. Knowledge and interpretation of what has happened in the past can aid in making decisions because history may shed considerable light on what the future is likely to hold. Thus, one of the fundamental inputs to decision making

---

[3] A list of the fundamental assumptions and principles underlying accounting is summarized in Exhibit 4–5.

is dependable and relevant historical data. A large portion of historical data that are relevant to business decisions is expressed in monetary terms. They include costs (i.e., resources expended), revenues (i.e., resources earned), assets (i.e., things owned), liabilities (i.e., amounts owed), and owners' equity (i.e., total assets less total liabilities of the entity). Thus, accounting provides important information for decision making. The information provided by financial reports must be understandable and relevant to the decision. This is a primary reason why measurements in accounting must adhere to acceptable standards and concepts.

Accounting reports (i.e., financial statements) serve those who use the reported information in three related ways:

1. Accounting provides information that is helpful in making decisions. Most important decisions, regardless of the type of endeavour involved, are based, in part, upon complex financial considerations. Accounting provides an important base and a particular analytical orientation that help the decision maker assess the future financial implications and potential outcomes of various alternatives that are considered.

2. Accounting reports the economic effects of past decisions on the entity. Once a decision is made and implementation starts, significant and often subtle financial economic effects on the entity occur. These economic effects often are critical to the success of the endeavour. The evolving effects of past decisions must be measured continuously and periodically reported so that the decision maker can be informed of continuing and newly developing problems, and of successes, over time. Accounting provides a continuing feedback of the economic effects of a series of decisions already made, the results of which are communicated to the decision maker by means of periodic financial statements.

3. Accounting keeps track of a wide range of items to meet the financial scorekeeping and safeguarding responsibilities that must be assumed by all organizations. These include how much cash is available for use; how much customers owe the company; what debts are owed by the organization; what items are owned by the company, such as machinery and office equipment; and inventory levels on hand.

Accounting Information in Decision Making

Most organizations engage in activities for an extended period of time. During this time, resources are committed and used with the expectation that there will be desirable results in the future. During the period of continuing activities, those involved in the organization need information about the continuing amounts of resources committed, resources used, resources on hand, and outputs (goods and services). This information should be reported, interpreted, and

Exhibit 1–2 Accounting information flows in a decision and implementation cycle

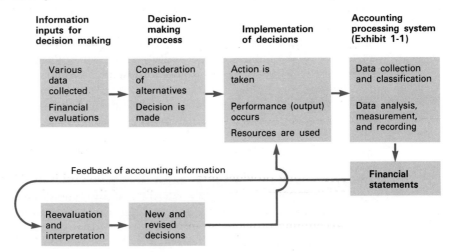

evaluated periodically. The accounting process is designed to provide a continuing flow of such information to all interested parties. A typical flow of accounting information in an entity is diagrammed in Exhibit 1–2. The financial statements constitute the primary source of relevant information on a continuing basis. This information is important feedback concerning the outcome of particular decisions.

Now we will examine two different entities—a business and a hospital.

A Business

The objectives of a business are determined by the organizers. Initially, the owners provide the funds, which often are supplemented by funds provided by creditors. These funds are used by the managers of the business to acquire equipment, inventory, services, and other assets. Assume you are the manager of the entity and that you develop a **business plan** for operating the business. As the business operates, additional resources flow in from the sale of goods and services and flow out for expenses. As the manager of the business, you need information, on a continuing basis, about sources and amounts of funds, revenues (products and services sold), expenses, the amounts invested in equipment and inventory, the cash situation, the amount spent for research and development, and the amount of money used in the sales efforts.

As the manager, you need such information for two reasons. First, accounting information will help you to make sound decisions about the entity that can improve its effectiveness and efficiency. Second, accounting information reports what the score was during the immediate past periods. This scorekeeping is important to the evaluation and control of performance. Exhibit 1–2 shows financial evaluations and interpretations as important information inputs to the decision-making process.

Now, assume instead that you are a shareholder (an owner) of the business. You have a substantial amount of money invested in the business. As a shareholder, you must continuously select from among three alternatives: (1) retain your ownership interest, (2) expand or contract it, or (3) dispose of it completely. As a shareholder, you also are interested in management decisions that will expand the business and make it more profitable. Therefore, you, and the other shareholders, need financial information about the trend of sales, the level of expenses, the amount of earnings, the amount invested by the entity in various assets (such as inventory and machinery), the debts of the business, and cash flows. As an investor, you need to know how the management is allocating the scarce resources provided by the shareholders and the creditors. The primary objective of periodic financial statements is to provide, on a continuing basis, information bearing on the three alternatives listed. The accounting information provided should be an important part of the decision-making process of the shareholders in ways similar to those depicted in Exhibit 1–2.

A Hospital

Assume you are on the board of governors of a hospital. Therefore, you share the responsibility for the basic decisions and guidelines for its continued operation at an efficient level. Like the owner of a business, you have a wide variety of questions about its revenues, expenses, funds tied up in buildings and equipment, cost of charity services, and so on, that are in the scorekeeping category. Also, you are concerned with whether enough resources are being allocated to such activities as emergency care, sanitation, and nursing services. To make sound decisions in these areas, you need information about prior allocation of resources and about the quality and quantity of resulting output or benefits. Thus, as a member of the board, you have many information needs that are important to your decisions.

Consider the administration of the hospital. The administration needs accounting information about the operations of the hospital similar to that discussed above for the manager of a business, and for the same reasons. Typically, the administrator will need more detailed accounting information than the governor. However, whether one is a governor or administrator of the hospital, financial measurement and the reported results should be continuing inputs to the decision-making process.

The following summary from *The Bottom Line* illustrates the importance attached to the personal financial advice provided by accountants to one group of Canadians.

High rollers lean on accountants

Toronto—When asked to evaluate various personal financial planning advisors, affluent Canadians place most confidence in their accountants, according to a *Financial Times*/Decima Poll published February 15.

The poll, based on interviews with a random sample of 1,200 Canadians with an average $112,000 annual household income, found that 79% rely on their accountants for financial planning advice; only 28% were guided by the advice of insurance agents.

Between those extremes, respondents placed the following levels of confidence: stockbroker—61%; bank manager—59%; lawyer—42%; trust company manager—41%. Among those with the most confidence in accountants are Quebecers (88%), people earning $150,000 a year or more (85%) and those 40 to 49 years of age (83%).[4]

Historical Perspectives

Accounting is as old as the exchange processes (whether barter or monetary) that gradually developed with civilization. The earliest written records, including the Scriptures, contain references to what now is called accounting.

Accounting evolved in response to the economic needs of society. Prior to the 15th century, accounting had no well-defined pattern except that it developed in answer to governing and trading needs of the era. The first known treatment of the subject of accounting was written in 1494, two years after Christopher Columbus discovered America. An Italian monk and mathematician, Fr. Luca Pacioli, described an approach developed by Italian merchants to account for their activities as owner-managers of business ventures. Pacioli laid the foundations of the basic "accounting model" that is used to this day. As economic activity progressed from the feudal system to agriculture and then to the Industrial Revolution, accounting continued to adapt to the needs of society. As business units became more complex and broader in scope, accounting evolved in response to the increased planning and control responsibilities of management. As governments grew in size and became more centralized, accounting was developed to meet the increased accountabilities.

In the 17th and 18th centuries, the Industrial Revolution in England provided the impetus for developing new approaches in accounting. That impetus was on the accumulation of data about the cost of manufacturing each product. In the latter half of the 19th century, English accountants, small in numbers but large in competence, appeared on the North American scene. By 1900, the lead in accounting developments, provided earlier by the English, began to shift to North Americans. Since the turn of this century, spearheaded by the accounting profession in the United States, accounting has experienced dynamic growth.

The Accounting Profession Today

Since 1900, accounting has attained the stature of such professions as law, medicine, engineering, and architecture. As with all recognized professions, accounting is subject to licensing, observes a code of professional ethics, requires a high level of professional competence, is dedicated to service to the public, requires a high level of academic study, and rests on a "common body of knowledge." In addition to meeting specified academic requirements, the accountant may be licensed to be a **public accountant** or **PA.** It is granted only upon completion of requirements specified by provincial statutes. Although the

---

[4] *The Bottom Line,* March 1988, p. 9.

requirements vary among provinces, they include good character, experience, and successful completion of an examination. The professional examinations are designed by one of three professional accounting associations in Canada according to their examination syllabus. These examinations cover such topics as accounting theory and practice, auditing, and taxation.[5]

As with physicians, engineers, lawyers, and architects, accountants commonly are employed by businesses, government entities, nonprofit organizations, and so on. Accountants employed in these activities often take and pass professional examinations.

Practice of Public Accounting

A public accountant (PA) can offer professional services to the public for a fee, as does the lawyer and physician. In this posture, the accountant is known appropriately as an independent PA because certain responsibilities also extend to the general public (third parties) rather than being limited to the specific business or other entity that pays for the services. Independent PAs, although paid by their clients, are not employees of their clients. This concept of independence from the client is a unique characteristic of the accounting profession. The consequences of this uniqueness are not as widely understood as perhaps they should be. For example, the lawyer and the physician, in case of malpractice or incompetence, generally are subject to potential liability (lawsuits) that may extend only to the client or patient involved (and the family). In contrast, the independent PA, in case of malpractice or negligence in the audit function, is subject to potential liability that may extend to all parties (whether known to the PA or not) who have suffered loss or failed to make a profit through reliance on financial statements "approved" by the PA.

While a single individual may practice public accounting, usually two or more individuals organize an accounting firm in the form of a partnership. Firms vary in size from a one-person office, to regional firms, to the national firms, some of which have hundreds of offices located around the world. Nearly all accounting firms render three types of services: auditing, management advisory services, and tax services.

Auditing
One important function performed by the PA in public practice is the audit or attest function. Its purpose is to lend reliability to the financial reports; that is, to assure that they are believable (i.e., relevant, accurate, and not biased). Primarily, this function involves an examination of the financial reports prepared by the management of the entity in order to assure that they are in conformance with **generally accepted accounting concepts and standards** (discussed in Part B). In carrying out this function, the independent PA examines the underlying

---

[5] To facilitate subsequent presentation, the initials PA will often be used to designate a professional public accountant, regardless of the particular professional designation actually used by the accountant.

transactions, including the collection, classification, and assembly of the financial data incorporated in the financial reports. In performing these tasks, established professional standards must be maintained and the information reported must conform to **generally accepted accounting principles** (often referred to as **GAAP**) appropriate for the entity involved. Additionally, the PA is responsible for verifying that the financial reports "fairly present" the resource inflows and outflows and the financial position of the entity. The magnitude of these responsibilities may be appreciated when it is realized that the number of transactions involved in a major enterprise runs into the billions each year. The PA does not examine each one of these transactions; rather, professional approaches are used to ascertain beyond reasonable doubt that they were measured and reported properly.

Occasionally, the auditor may encounter attempts to manipulate accounting reports, for example, to increase reported profit by omitting certain expenses or to overstate financial position by omitting certain debts. There are many intentional and unintentional opportunities for preparing misleading financial reports. The audit function performed by an independent PA is the best protection available to the public in this respect. Many investors have learned the pitfalls of making investments in enterprises that do not have their financial reports examined by an independent PA.

At the conclusion of an audit, the independent PA is required to provide an **auditor's opinion** that indicates whether the financial statements are appropriate and not misleading. For example, a recent auditor's opinion was presented as follows:

SUNCOR INC.

Auditor's Report—opinion paragraph

In our opinion, these consolidated statements present fairly the financial position of the Company as at December 31, 1986 and the results of its operations and the changes in its financial position for the year then ended in accordance with generally accepted accounting principles which, after giving retroactive effect to the change in method of accounting for oil and gas operations in the exploration, production and resources development segment as explained in Note 1(a) to the financial statements, have been applied on a basis consistent with that of the preceding year.[6]

Management Advisory Services

Many independent PA firms also offer advisory or consulting services. These services usually are accounting based and encompass such activities as the design and installation of accounting, data processing, profit planning (i.e., budget), and control systems; financial advice; forecasting; inventory controls; cost-effectiveness studies; and operational analyses. This facet of public practice is experiencing rapid growth.

---

[6] *Financial Reporting in Canada,* 17th ed. (Toronto: Canadian Institute of Chartered Accountants, 1987), p. 233. Retroactive changes in accounting procedures are discussed in Chapter 12.

Tax Services

PAs in public practice usually are involved in rendering income tax services to their clients. These services include both tax planning as a part of the decision-making process, tax compliance, and also determination of the income tax liability (reported on the annual tax return). Because of the increasing complexity of provincial and federal tax laws, particularly income tax laws, a high level of competence in this area is required. PAs specializing in taxation can provide this competence. The PA's involvement in tax planning often is quite significant. Virtually every major business decision carries with it significant tax impacts; so much so, in fact, that tax-planning considerations frequently govern the decision.

Employment by Organizations

Many accountants are employed by profit-making and nonprofit organizations. A company or other organization, depending upon its size and complexity, may employ from one up to hundreds of accountants. In a business enterprise, the chief financial officer (usually a vice president or controller—sometimes comptroller) is a member of the management team. This responsibility usually entails a wide range of management, financial, and accounting duties. Exhibit 1–3 shows a typical organizational arrangement of the financial function in a business enterprise. In the business entity, accountants typically are engaged in a wide variety of activities, such as general management, general accounting, cost accounting, profit planning (i.e., budgeting) and control, internal auditing, and electronic data processing. A common pattern in recent years has been the selection of a "financial expert" as the chief executive or president of the company. One primary function of the accountants in organizations is **management accounting;** that is, to provide data that are useful for **internal** managerial decision making and for controlling operations. In addition, the functions of external reporting, tax planning, control of assets, and a host of related responsibilities normally are performed by accountants in industry. The role of accountants within organizations is emphasized in management accounting texts.

Employment in the Public Sector

The vast and complex operations of governmental units, from the local to the international level, create a great need for accountants. Accountants employed in the public sector perform functions similar to those performed by their counterparts in private organizations. Additionally, various provincial and federal regulatory agencies and their auditing departments utilize the services of accountants in carrying out their regulatory duties.

Finally, accountants are involved in varying capacities in the evolving programs of pollution control, health care, minority enterprises, and other socially oriented programs, whether sponsored by private industry or by government.

Exhibit 1-3 Typical organization of the financial function

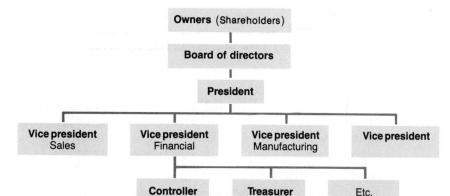

Groups Involved in Accounting Innovation

The designation PA used in the previous section is a generic designation that will be used in this text to denote all accountants (particularly professionally designated ones) engaged in public accounting practice. In Canada, three professional groups dominate the practice of public accounting and thus the development of accounting thought. The role of each is described briefly.

The Canadian Institute of Chartered Accountants (CICA)

Of the three professional groups in Canada, the predominant group is the CICA through its Accounting Standards Committee. In addition to chartered accountants (CAs) from across Canada, membership of this committee is made up from members of the Canadian Council of Financial Analysts, Financial Executives Institute of Canada, and the Society of Management Accountants. This committee is charged with the responsibility of issuing pronouncements which are incorporated in the *CICA Handbook*. This *Handbook* constitutes the official source of generally accepted accounting principles for most profit-oriented enterprises in Canada. Part of the acceptance of this predominance for the committee's pronouncements comes from the legal sanction given to the *Handbook* in the Canada Business Corporations Act and various provincial statutes involved with incorporation or regulation of profit-oriented enterprises.

In addition to the *Handbook* pronouncements, other CICA committees sponsor research studies of accounting issues and publish the *Public Sector Accounting*

Statements. The Public Sector Statements represent an attempt to improve the financial accounting practice of governments in Canada.

The Certified General Accountants of Canada (CGAC)

The CGAC has recently begun a loose-leaf book entitled the *GAAP Guide.* This book provides a summary of *CICA Handbook* pronouncements and highlights differences between Canadian standards and the various ones in the United States and those of the International Accounting Standards Committee (IASC). In addition, the CGAC Research Foundation publishes research monographs on various topics of interest to practitioners and academics.

The Society of Management Accountants of Canada (SMAC)

Members of the Society of Management Accountants (designated Certified Management Accountants or CMAs)[7] serve as members of the Accounting Standards Committee who issue *Handbook* pronouncements. The society sponsors on its own a number of research studies that concentrate on management accounting issues, but a few provide background research for financial accounting problems. In addition, the Society of Management Accountants of Canada, through its Accounting Principles and Practices Committee, issues *Management Accounting Guidelines.* These guidelines present authoritative statements of operating practices, information, and implementation procedures for management accountants.

The Canadian Academic Accounting Association (CAAA)

The CAAA is an association of academic and professional accountants. While it does not certify professional competence like the other three groups, it does provide a forum for the discussion of issues in financial accounting through their annual meeting, their research monographs, and their journal, *Contemporary Accounting Research.* CAAA committees and individual members also provide analyses of various recommendations and publications of the other associations.

Other Groups

In Canada, securities regulation traditionally has been a provincial matter. Each province regulates securities sold to the public in its jurisdiction. Securities regulators in Canada have delegated, for the most part, accounting and disclosure standards to the Accounting Standards Committee of CICA through

---

[7] The CMA designation replaced the RIA (Registered Industrial Accountant) designation on July 1, 1985.

their acceptance of the *CICA Handbook* as generally accepted accounting principles. Exceptions to this cooperation under various companies' acts and *National Policy Statement No. 27* of the securities regulators in Canada result from federal government control over banks, insurance, and trust companies. Some federal provincial friction has arisen over who will regulate some types of security sales for these institutions. Organizations that sell their securities in the United States do have to comply with the rules of the Securities and Exchange Commission (SEC) in addition to those of their Canadian jurisdiction.

Many Canadian organizations have operations or engage in financing throughout the world. To help harmonize financial reporting among various sovereign jurisdictions, the International Accounting Standards Committee (IASC) was founded in 1973. In Canada, CICA, SMAC, and CGAC are all members of this private group and agree to work toward the objectives of the IASC as set forth in its *International Accounting Standards (IASs)*. The three Canadian associations work, along with 90 others, for the recognition of the usefulness of *IASs*. For example, Canadian accounting standards state it is desirable for firms reporting in the international environment to disclose their conformity with *IASs*.[8]

Because of the close ties of Canadian business to the United States, research and pronouncements in that country are important to Canadian accountants.

At the present time, four important groups in the United States predominate in the development of financial accounting concepts and practice. These groups are the American Institute of Certified Public Accountants, the Financial Accounting Standards Board, the U.S. Securities and Exchange Commission, and the American Accounting Association. The past and present roles of each group are reviewed briefly below.

American Institute of Certified Public Accountants (AICPA)

This institute was organized a few years prior to the turn of the century by a group of accountants engaged in public and industrial accounting. Membership currently is limited to certified public accountants (CPAs). It carries on a wide-ranging program encompassing professional development, publications, and the development and communication of accounting standards and procedures through its Committee on Accounting Procedure. At one time, these *Accounting Research Bulletins (ARBs)* enunciated certain **recommended** financial accounting principles and procedures. Later the AICPA organized the Accounting Principles Board (APB) to replace the former committee. The APB issued 31 numbered *Opinions* during its existence from 1959 through mid-1973. The *Opinions* dealt with many of the difficult issues of financial accounting; as a consequence, many of them were highly controversial. Throughout this volume you will encounter a few references to the *ARBs* and numerous references to APB *Opinions*.

---

[8] *CICA Handbook*, Section 1501, para. 05.

Financial Accounting Standards Board (FASB)

Accounting is a complex and frequently controversial professional activity. In the light of these controversies, the AICPA in 1972 decided to reassess the approaches to establishing financial accounting concepts and standards. As a consequence of this reassessment, the APB was discontinued, and in its place the Financial Accounting Standards Board was established and continues to function. The seven FASB members are appointed by an independent board of trustees and serve on a full-time basis (in contrast to the previous groups, each member receives full-time compensation). The FASB was organized to be independent. It has as its sole function the **establishment and improvement of accounting concepts and standards.**

Securities and Exchange Commission (SEC)

This government regulatory agency operates under authority granted by the Securities Acts of 1933 and 1934. These acts were in response to the manipulations, irrational speculation, and lack of credible financial information that existed when the stock market crash occurred in 1929–30. The acts gave the SEC authority to **prescribe accounting guidelines for the financial reports required to be submitted by corporations that sell their securities in interstate commerce** (i.e., registered companies, which primarily are those listed on the stock exchanges). This list includes most of the large, and some medium-sized, corporations. The SEC requires these corporations to submit periodic financial reports, which are maintained in the files of the Commission as a matter of public record. Also, a prospectus, which is a preliminary statement presented to prospective buyers or investors, is required before the sale of securities. From the beginning, the SEC, as a matter of policy, usually has followed the accounting concepts, standards, and procedures established by the accounting profession. The SEC publishes *Regulation S-X* and issues *Accounting Series Releases* (*ASRs*), which prescribe the special guidelines to be followed by registered companies in preparing the financial reports submitted in conformance with the Securities Acts. Its staff also has worked closely with the accounting profession on the evolution and improvement of accounting standards.

American Accounting Association (AAA)

This association was organized during the World War I period by a group of university accounting professors. The association sponsors and encourages the improvement of accounting teaching and accounting research (primarily on a theoretical plane), and publishes a magazine, *The Accounting Review*. Its committees issue reports that, coupled with the research activities of individual academicians, exert a pervasive influence on the development of accounting theory and standards.

Summary of Part A

The prior discussions of the environment in which accounting operates suggest the importance of competitive and successful businesses (from the smallest to the largest) to an economy. Economic success in a competitive business economy means earning reasonable profits and providing funds (cash) to meet broad reinvestment needs. Adequate reinvestment in businesses means more jobs, better wages, continuing technological advances, expansion of efficient productive capacity, adequate dividends for investors, and more tax revenue to the government (to support socially desirable programs and other governmental activities). The economic dimensions of this success by individual businesses are communicated in accounting reports.

PART B—COMMUNICATION OF ACCOUNTING INFORMATION

This part of the chapter presents an overview of the end product of the accounting processing system—the **periodic financial statements** of a business. These statements are viewed as the primary way to communicate financial information about an entity. Chapter 2 will continue this overview of the basic financial statements.

The remaining chapters will discuss and illustrate how the financial statements are derived. Therefore, those chapters will focus on the economic analyses, measurements, and recording of transactions that precede the preparation of financial statements.

Communication Concepts and Approaches

Communication is a flow of information from one party to one or more other parties. **Effective communication** means that the recipient understands what the sender intends to convey. Communication involves problems in understanding the words, symbols, and sounds used by the parties involved. Accounting uses words and symbols to communicate financial information that is relevant to the decisions made by investors, creditors, and other interested parties. As decisions are made, reliance is placed upon certain information that often is unique to the issue involved. Often, decisions are made without adequate information. Either the needed information is not available in time or the cost of developing it is too high when compared to its potential usefulness.[9] The form in which information is "packaged" and the avenues used to communicate it sometimes affect the decision. For example, some individuals are more influ-

---

[9] This sentence suggests the concept of cost-benefit analysis; that is, a comparison of the cost of pursuing a particular course of action compared with the economic benefits or advantages derived from that course of action.

enced by graphic than by quantitative presentations. However, others find narrative preferable to tabular expression, while some prefer summaries rather than details. Still others are not interested in technical presentations.

Financial information and the means used to communicate it often have strong and pervasive behavioral impacts on decision makers.[10] The behavioral impacts of accounting extend to both positive and negative motivations of people. The frequency, form, and quality of one's communications with others are often important to the recipients.

The terminology of accounting was developed to communicate financial information effectively. As is common with other professions, such as law and medicine, the terminology of accounting is technical because precision is essential. Accounting has developed in direct response to the needs of its environment. Therefore, accounting is continuously evolving new concepts, terminology, procedures, and means of communication. In the chapters to follow, you should learn the basic terminology of accounting. That terminology is referred to as the "language of business."

Overview of External Financial Statements

Financial statements often are classified as (1) internal (i.e., management accounting) statements and (2) external (i.e., financial accounting) statements. **Internal financial statements** are not given to parties outside the entity. They are used exclusively by, and are prepared under the direction of, the managers of the entity; therefore, they are prepared to meet specific internal policies and guidelines established by those managers.

External financial statements are the end product of an accounting system. They are given to parties (i.e., external decision makers) outside the entity (which include shareholders and creditors). External parties are unable to specify guidelines for preparation of the statements. The information presented on external financial statements helps investors and others make better economic decisions about the entity. Thus, financial statements must present information that is relevant to economic decisions. That is, they must be useful for predicting the future successes (and failures) of the business. **Relevance** is an important qualitative characteristic of financial statements.

To ensure that external parties can rely on the information reported in financial statements, the entity is required to conform to specific and well-known **generally accepted accounting principles (GAAP)** that are developed by the accounting profession. GAAP will be discussed in the remaining chapters.

---

[10] A behavioral impact is an individual's response to external forces. An individual may be motivated toward or away from certain courses of action by information or observations that come to his or her attention. For example, one may be motivated to purchase a large automobile rather than a small one because of prestige. However, a financial report showing the relative costs of operating the two automobiles may motivate the individual to purchase the small automobile. Thus, the financial report exerted a significant behavioral impact on the decision maker.

This textbook discusses the **preparation and interpretation** of external financial reports only. The following pages present an overview of the external financial statements required by GAAP.

A general understanding of financial statements at the outset helps you to understand the accounting process when it is discussed in later chapters. Three required financial statements for a profit-making entity for **external reporting** to owners, potential investors, creditors, and other decision makers are the—

1. **Income statement** (also called the statement of revenues, expenses, and income).
2. **Balance sheet** (also called the statement of assets, liabilities, and owners' equity and statement of financial position).
3. **Statement of changes in financial position,** abbreviated SCFP (also called the statement of cash flow).

These three required statements summarize the financial activities of the business entity for each specific period of time. They can be prepared at any time (such as end of the year, quarter, or month) and can apply to any time span (such as 10 years, 1 year, 1 quarter, or 1 month). The heading of each statement has a specific statement of the **time dimension** of the report. Although these three statements directly relate to each other, for instructional convenience, they are considered separately. First, we will illustrate these statements for a simple business case. The next chapter discusses and illustrates them in a more complex case.

The Income Statement

The income statement reports the **profit performance** of a business entity. The term profit is used widely in our language, but accountants prefer to use the technical term income. The **accounting model** for the income statement is:

$$\text{REVENUES} - \text{EXPENSES} = \text{INCOME}$$

An income statement reports the revenues and expenses for a specified period. Revenues cause inflows of resources into a business, and expenses cause outflows of resources. Income statements present the results of operations for a specific period of time, which is called the **time-period assumption** (e.g., "For the Year Ended December 31, 19A"). Results of operations include **revenues, expenses,** and the resulting **income.**

Illustration. The income statement of Business Supports, Inc., is presented in Exhibit 1–4. Business Supports is a company that provides professional secretarial, reproduction, and mailing services for a fee. Business Supports was organized by three individuals as a **corporation.** Each owner (called a shareholder) received 1,000 shares of capital stock as proof of ownership. The **heading**

Exhibit 1–4 Income statement (simplified)

BUSINESS SUPPORTS, INC.	←Name of entity	
Income Statement	←Title of report	HEADING
For the Year Ended December 31, 19A	←Time period	

Revenues:

Stenographic revenue	$30,000	
Printing revenue	20,000	
Mailing revenue	13,000	
Total revenues		$63,000

Expenses:

Salary expense	30,750	
Payroll benefits expense	1,100	
Rent expense for office space	2,400	
Rental payments for copiers	6,600	
Utilities expense	400	
Advertising expense	960	
Supplies expense	90	
Interest expense	100	
Depreciation expense on office equipment	600	
Total expenses (excluding income tax)		43,000
Pretax income		20,000
Income tax expense ($20,000 × 17%)		3,400
Net income		$16,600
Earnings per share (EPS) ($16,600 ÷ 3,000 shares)		$5.53

of the statement specifically identifies the name of the entity, the title of the report, and the **time period** over which the net income was earned (one year). Notice that there are three major captions: **revenues, expenses,** and **net income.** The detail given under each caption meets the needs of decision makers interested in Business Supports, Inc. This latter point is significant because the composition and the detail of a financial statement vary, depending on the characteristics of the business entity and the needs of the decision makers.

Next we will discuss the four primary elements on an income statement—revenues, expenses, net income, and earnings per share.

Revenues

Revenues are earned from the sale of goods or services rendered by the entity to others for which the entity will receive (or has received) cash or something else of value. When a business sells goods or renders services, it usually receives cash immediately. If goods or services are sold on credit, the business receives an **account receivable,** which is collected in cash later. In either case, the business recognizes revenue for the period as the sum of sales of goods and services for cash and on credit. Revenue is measured in dollars as the bargained

cash-equivalent price agreed on by the two parties to the transaction.[11] Various terms are used in financial statements to describe revenue, such as sales revenue, service revenue, rental revenue, and interest revenue. Revenues are discussed in more detail in Chapter 4.

Expenses

Expenses represent the dollar amount of resources expended or used up by the entity during a period of time to earn revenues. Expenses may require the immediate payment of cash and/or some other resource such as services or inventory items. The payment may be on credit so that cash or some other resource is paid after the expense is incurred. For accounting purposes, the **period in which an expense is incurred[12] is the period in which the goods are used or the services are received.** The expense may be incurred in one period, and the payment made in another period.

An expense may represent the cost of **using** equipment or buildings that were purchased earlier for continuing use in operating the business rather than for sale. Such items often have a high acquisition cost. Through use, each one is worn out (or becomes obsolete) over an extended period of time known as useful life. As such items are used in operating the business, a portion of their cost becomes an expense. This kind of expense is called **depreciation expense.** For example, on January 1, 19A, Business Supports purchased office equipment for its own use at a cash cost of $6,000. It was estimated that the office equipment would have a useful life of 10 years. Therefore, the depreciation expense each year for using the equipment is measured as $6,000 \div 10$ years $= \$600$. The income statement for 19A (Exhibit 1–4) reports this amount as a noncash expense.[13]

Business Supports also reported **interest expense** for one year on the $1,000, 10% note payable (i.e., $1,000 \times 10\% = \$100$) because this debt was outstanding for all of 19A.

As a corporation, Business Supports has a 17% income tax rate on income. Therefore, Business Supports incurred **income tax expense** of $3,400 (i.e., $20,000 \times 17\% = \$3,400$).

Net Income

Net income (often called profit by nonaccountants) is the excess of total revenues over total expenses. If the total expenses exceed the total revenues, a **net loss** is reported. When revenues and expenses are equal for the period, the business has operated at **break even.**

---

[11] Revenue sometimes is called income, such as rent income, interest income, and royalty income, but this practice causes confusion. Ideally, **income should be used to refer only to the difference between revenues and expenses.**

[12] Incurred, as used in this context, means that the amount involved should be accounted for (i.e., recorded in the accounting system) during the specific period.

[13] Accounting for depreciation is discussed in detail in Chapter 9.

Notice that Business Supports reported (*a*) pretax income, (*b*) income tax expense, and (*c*) net income, which is an **aftertax** amount.[14]

Earnings per Share (EPS)

The amount of earnings per share (EPS) is reported immediately below net income on the income statement of corporations. EPS is computed by dividing net income by the number of shares of **common** stock outstanding. Because Business Supports had 3,000 shares of common stock outstanding (i.e., 1,000 shares were owned by each of the three shareholders) and a net income of $16,600, EPS was computed as $16,600 ÷ 3,000 shares = $5.53 per share for the year. EPS is given extensive attention by security analysts and investors.

The importance of EPS to investors and thus to the financial press results because EPS provides a means of relating net income to the market price per share. EPS relates net income, a total conception, to the number of shares outstanding to present a unit conception. The unit amount, EPS, can then be related to market price per share so certain types of comparisons can be made by investors. Concern exists, however, that reducing a complex income statement to a single EPS can be misleading. As a result, specific guidelines are provided by the *CICA Handbook*, Section 3500, for computing and reporting EPS. Even though EPS is required only for certain companies, the number will be shown for all illustrations until the specific rules are specified in later chapters.

Some people view the income statement as the most important of the three required financial statements because it is designed to report the amount of **net income** and the details of how that amount was earned.

The Balance Sheet

The purpose of the balance sheet is to report the financial position of a business at a particular point in time. Financial position is the amount of resources (i.e., assets) and the liabilities (i.e., debts) of a business. Therefore, the balance sheet is frequently called the statement of financial position. The **accounting model** for the balance sheet is:[15]

$$\text{ASSETS} = \text{LIABILITIES} + \text{OWNERS' EQUITY}$$

Assets represent resources owned by the entity, liabilities are the debts (obligations) of the entity, and owners' equity represents the interests of the owners.[16]

---

[14] Most corporations are subject to income taxes at rates that vary provincially and by nature of the business conducted. Some of these specifics will be discussed in Appendix A at end of this book. Sole proprietorships and partnerships, as business entities, are not subject to income taxes. In each of these situations, the owner, or owners, must report the income of the entity on their own individual income tax returns. For illustration purposes, an average tax rate is used herein to ease the arithmetic.

[15] The accounting model is an algebraic equation that can be rearranged. For example, it frequently is expressed as: Assets − Liabilities = Owners' Equity.

[16] Owners' equity for a corporation usually is called shareholders' equity.

Exhibit 1-5   Balance sheet (simplified)

<table>
<tr><td colspan="4" align="center">**BUSINESS SUPPORTS, INC.**
Balance Sheet
At December 31, 19A</td></tr>
<tr><td align="center">**Assets**</td><td></td><td align="center">**Liabilities**</td><td></td></tr>
<tr><td>Cash . . . .</td><td>$13,600</td><td>Accounts payable . . . . $ 900</td><td></td></tr>
<tr><td>Accounts receivable . . . .</td><td>13,000</td><td>Income taxes payable . . . .   500</td><td></td></tr>
<tr><td>Land . . . .</td><td>20,000</td><td>Notes payable,</td><td></td></tr>
<tr><td>Office equipment . . . . $6,000</td><td></td><td>   short term, 10% . . . . <u>1,000</u></td><td></td></tr>
<tr><td>   Less: Accumulated</td><td></td><td>   Total liabilities . . . .</td><td>$ 2,400</td></tr>
<tr><td>   depreciation . . . . <u>600</u></td><td>5,400*</td><td></td><td></td></tr>
<tr><td></td><td></td><td align="center">**Shareholders' Equity**</td><td></td></tr>
<tr><td></td><td></td><td>Contributed capital:</td><td></td></tr>
<tr><td></td><td></td><td>   Capital stock (3,000 no-par</td><td></td></tr>
<tr><td></td><td></td><td>   shares) . . . . $33,000</td><td></td></tr>
<tr><td></td><td></td><td>   Retained earnings . . . . <u>16,600</u></td><td></td></tr>
<tr><td></td><td></td><td>   Total shareholders'</td><td></td></tr>
<tr><td></td><td></td><td>   equity . . . .</td><td>49,600</td></tr>
<tr><td></td><td></td><td>Total liabilities and</td><td></td></tr>
<tr><td>Total assets . . . .</td><td>$52,000</td><td>   shareholders' equity . . . .</td><td>$52,000</td></tr>
</table>

* This is the **undepreciated** cost; it is usually called the "book value" of the asset.

Illustration. The balance sheet of Business Supports, Inc., is presented in Exhibit 1-5. Notice that the **heading** specifically identifies the name of the entity, the title of the report, and the specific date of the statement. Note that the specific point in time—in this case, December 31, 19A—is stated clearly on the balance sheet. This contrasts with the dating on the income statement, which indicates a period of time (such as one year). After the statement heading, the **assets** are listed on the left and the **liabilities** and **owners' equity** (called shareholders' equity for a corporation) on the right. The result is that the two sides "balance" in conformity with the accounting model given above. In the following chapters we will learn that the accounting model for the balance sheet is the basic building block for the entire accounting process.

Next we will discuss the three elements reported on a balance sheet—assets, liabilities, and owners' equity.

Assets

Assets are the resources owned by the entity. Assets may be tangible (physical in character) such as land, buildings, and machinery. Or they may be intangible (characterized by legal claims or rights) such as amounts due from customers (legal claims called accounts receivable) and patents (legal right to exclusive use).

Notice in the balance sheet given in Exhibit 1-5 that each **asset** listed has an assigned dollar amount. An asset should be measured on the basis of the total cost incurred to acquire it. For example, the balance sheet for Business Supports reports "Land, $20,000"; this is the amount of resources paid for the land when it was acquired. It may be that because of market changes, the market value of the land at December 31, 19A (date of the balance sheet), actually was more or less than $20,000. Nevertheless, the balance sheet reports the land at its **original acquisition cost.** It follows that the balance sheet does not purport to show the **current market value** of the assets listed.

Notice that the balance sheet reports "Office equipment, $6,000," which was its **acquisition cost. Accumulated depreciation** of $600 is subtracted from the original cost. This $600 is the same as the amount of depreciation expense on the income statement (Exhibit 1–4). This amount is deducted because it represents the portion of the original cost that is "worn out or used up" to earn the revenues. This is a cumulative amount; therefore, at the end of the next year (19B) the deduction for accumulated depreciation will be $1,200 (i.e., $600 × 2 years).

You may ask why accountants do not change the measurement of each asset for each subsequent balance sheet to reflect the new market values. This revaluation is not done because the acquisition cost is factually objective (i.e., not an estimate), whereas the current market value of the assets owned by the entity would have to be estimated at the end of each year. The estimate would be subjective because the assets are not sold each year-end. Such subjectivity could reduce the reliability of the financial statements.

Liabilities

Liabilities are the debts or obligations of the entity. They arise primarily because of the purchase of goods or services from others on credit and through cash borrowings to finance the business.

If a business does not pay its creditors, the law may give the creditors the right to force the sale of assets sufficient to meet their claims.

Business entities often borrow money by entering into a formal note contract. In this case, a liability called **notes payable** is created. A note payable, which may be short term or long term, specifies a definite maturity or payment date and the rate or amount of interest charged by the lender. Also, many businesses purchase goods and services on credit that do not involve notes. This transaction creates a liability known as **accounts payable.** Another type of liability arises because income taxes often are paid, at least in part, several months after the end of the year. Therefore, a liability to the government, **income taxes payable,** must be reported until the taxes are fully paid. Notice in Exhibit 1–5 that Business Supports listed three liabilities and the amount of each.

Owners' Equity

The accounting model states (see footnote 15) that owners' equity is equal to total assets minus total liabilities of the business. Because creditors' claims legally come first, owners' equity represents a **residual interest** or claim of the owners to the assets. Owners' equity sometimes is called net worth or capital. However, the preferable designations are (*a*) "owner's equity" for a sole proprietorship; (*b*) "partners' equity" for a partnership; and (*c*) "shareholders' equity" for a corporation. Owners' equity in a business comes from two sources: (1) **contributed capital,** which equals the investment of cash and other assets in the business by the owners; and (2) **retained earnings,** which is the amount of accumulated earnings kept in the business.[17]

In Exhibit 1–5, the shareholders' equity section reports the following:

1. **Contributed capital**—The three shareholders invested a total of $33,000 in the business. Each shareholder received 1,000 shares of no-par capital stock. They invested an average price of $11 per share. The 3,000 shares issued are reported at their contributed value (3,000 × $11) as "Capital stock."

Shares have been traditionally of two types, par value and no-par value. The introduction of the Canada Business Corporations Act (CBCA) in 1975 has promoted the use of no-par shares by companies incorporated under the federal act and in those provinces that amended their companies act to conform to the CBCA. Both par and no-par shares can still be seen in Canada. If Business Supports had $10 par value shares, the disclosure of the 3,000 shares issued for $11 each would appear as follows:

Contributed capital:
Capital stock (3,000 shares, par value $10 per
   share) $30,000
Contributed surplus   3,000
      Total contributed capital $33,000

Both par and no-par shares will appear in illustrations to follow. Chapter 12 will provide a more extensive discussion of this topic.

2. **Retained earnings**—The accumulated amount of earnings less all losses and dividends paid to the shareholders since formation of the corporation is reported as "Retained earnings." During the first year, Business Supports, Inc., earned $16,600, as shown on the income statement (Exhibit 1–4). This amount is reported as retained earnings on the balance sheet for Business Supports at this date because no dividends were declared or paid to the shareholders during the first year (since organization).

3. **Total shareholders' equity**—The sum of the owners' investment ($33,000) plus the retained earnings ($16,600) equals $49,600. This amount may be verified in terms of the basic accounting model: Assets ($52,000) − Liabilities ($2,400) = Shareholders' equity ($49,600).

---

[17] The term **retained earnings** usually is used by businesses organized as corporations. In contrast, sole proprietorships and partnerships usually do not use this term because it is included in the owners' capital account(s). These distinctions are discussed later.

A cash dividend is the payment by a corporation of an equal amount to each share of capital stock outstanding. For example, if a cash dividend of $6,000 had been declared and paid by Business Supports to the three shareholders during the year, the balance sheet would have reflected cash of $7,600 (i.e., $13,600 − $6,000) and retained earnings of $10,600 (i.e., $16,600 − $6,000). Dividend payments should not be shown as an expense but rather as a reduction of retained earnings. In later chapters, a fourth statement, A Statement of Retained Earnings, will show specifically how dividends reduce retained earnings.

Statement of Changes in Financial Position (SCFP)

A business requires substantial cash for operations and expansion. Cash comes primarily from four sources: (1) owner investments, (2) borrowings, (3) earnings, and (4) selling noncash assets. Users of financial statements need information about the sources and uses of cash because such information helps them project their own future cash flows. Therefore, a **statement of changes in financial position (SCFP)** is required.

The objective of the SCFP is to communicate to decision makers information about the sources (inflows) and uses (outflows) of cash. The **accounting model** for the SCFP is:

$$\text{CASH SOURCES} \underset{\text{(inflows)}}{} - \text{CASH USES} \underset{\text{(outflows)}}{} = \text{NET CHANGE IN CASH} \underset{\text{(increase or decrease)}}{}$$

Specifically sources and uses are reclassified into three categories that may contain either sources or uses: operations, financing, and investing. Exhibit 1–6 will provide an illustration of what is commonly included in each of the three subcategories.

Illustration. The SCFP of Business Supports, Inc., is presented in Exhibit 1–6. Notice that the heading is dated the same as the income statement because it covers a period of time (i.e., "For the Year Ended December 31, 19A"). At this point you do not need to be concerned about the derivation of the amounts illustrated. Rather, you should notice the detailed information about the cash inflows and cash outflows for the year. This information is relevant to investors and creditors in projecting the future cash flows of the business.[18]

The SCFP is derived from an analysis of the balance sheet and the income statement. For example, total revenue reported on Exhibit 1–4 (the income

---

[18] Some companies prepare the SCFP using "funds" defined as working capital, rather than as cash. The current Canadian standards define cash as cash plus short-term investments minus short-term borrowings. At these early stages it is more convenient to avoid this additional complexity. Chapter 15 will present a more complete discussion of these issues.

Exhibit 1–6 Statement of changes in financial position (SCFP) (simplified)

BUSINESS SUPPORTS, INC.
Statement of Changes in Financial Position, Cash Basis
For the Year Ended December 31, 19A

Sources of cash (inflows):		
From operations:		
From cash revenues	$50,000	
Less: Cash used for expenses	44,400	
Cash inflow from operations		$ 5,600
From financing:		
Investment by owners (shares issued for cash)	33,000	
Loan—note payable	1,000	
Cash inflow from financing		34,000
Total cash inflow during the year		39,600
Uses of cash (outflows):		
For investing:		
To purchase office equipment	6,000	
To purchase land	20,000	
Total cash used during the year (for investing)		26,000
Change—increase in cash during the year		$13,600

statement) of $63,000, less $13,000 of the revenue (mailing) extended on credit, equals $50,000. This amount represents the cash inflow from revenue in Exhibit 1–6. Total expenses of $46,400 (including income tax expense), shown on Exhibit 1–4 (income statement), less the **noncash expenses** of $600 for depreciation, $900 for accounts payable, and $500 for income taxes payable, equals the $44,400 reported in Exhibit 1–6 as the cash used for expenses. Thus, the earned net income of $16,600 caused a cash inflow of $5,600. Shares of capital stock were sold and caused a cash inflow of $33,000. Also, a loan was obtained to secure another $1,000, giving a total cash inflow during the year of $39,600. During the year, $26,000 cash was expended for office equipment and land. Therefore, the statement reports that $13,600 more cash was received than was spent during the year.

A detailed discussion of the SCFP is deferred to Chapter 15 because its preparation requires special procedures that are best understood after your knowledge of accounting is substantial.

The financial statements of Business Supports, Inc., have been simplified so that the key points are clearly evident. Throughout the remaining chapters various cases will reference the 1987 Annual Report of Consolidated-Bathurst Inc. presented in Appendix B at the end of the textbook just preceding the

Index. This Annual Report includes the financial statements of a large Canadian corporation and much of the supplementary financial and other information companies typically include in their published annual reports. Periodic reference to this report when various topics are introduced throughout the textbook will provide a comprehensive look at how one company has treated the particular material. Specifically the required financial statements and their accompanying notes will serve as useful illustrations of various matters.

DEMONSTRATION CASE

At the end of most chapters, one or more demonstration cases are presented. These cases provide an overview of the primary issues discussed in the chapter. Each demonstration case is followed by a recommended solution. The case should be read carefully; then you should prepare your own solution before you study the recommended solution. This self-evaluation is highly recommended.

The introductory case presented below will start you thinking in monetary terms of some of the resource inflows and outflows of a business. (Note: The case will test your comprehension of Part B of the chapter and also your analytical skills.)

ABC Service Corporation was organized by Able, Baker, and Cain on January 1, 19A. On that date each investor bought 1,000 shares of no-par capital stock at $12 cash per share. On the same day, the corporation borrowed $10,000 from a local bank and signed a three-year, 15%, note payable. The interest is payable each December 31. On January 1, 19A, the corporation purchased two service trucks for $20,000 cash. Operations started immediately.

At the end of 19A, the corporation had completed the following additional business transactions (summarized):

a. Performed services and billed customers for $100,500, of which $94,500 was collected in cash by year-end.   *1500*

b. Paid $55,500 cash for expenses (including the annual interest on the note payable).

c. Paid $7,000 cash to the Revenue Canada Taxation for income taxes. At the end of the year, ABC still owed the government $1,000 (the average income tax rate was 20%).

d. Depreciated the cost of the two service trucks on the basis of a four-year useful life (disregard any residual value at the end of the four-year life).

Required:
Complete the two 19A financial statements shown in Exhibit 1–7 by entering the correct amounts. The suggested solution is given in Exhibit 1–8.

Exhibit 1-7 Format of financial statements—demonstration case

---

ABC SERVICE CORPORATION
Income Statement

Date _____

			Computations
Revenues:			
Service revenue		$ _____	_____
Expenses:			
Various expenses*	$ _____		_____
Interest expense	_____		_____
Depreciation expense . . .	_____		_____
Total expenses		_____	
Pretax income		_____	
Income tax expense		_____	_____
Net income		$ _____	
Earnings per share		$ _____	_____

*Includes all expenses other than those specifically noted separately.

ABC SERVICE CORPORATION
Balance Sheet

Date _____

Assets:			
Cash		$ _____	_____
Accounts receivable		_____	_____
Service trucks	$ _____		_____
Less: Accumulated			
depreciation	_____	_____	_____
Total assets		$ _____	
Liabilities:			
Note payable	$ _____		_____
Income taxes payable . . .	_____		_____
Total liabilities		$ _____	
Shareholders' equity:			
Capital stock, no-par			
shares	_____		_____
Retained earnings	_____		_____
Total shareholders'			
equity		_____	_____
Total liabilities and			
shareholders' equity . . .		$ _____	

Exhibit 1–8 Suggested solution—demonstration case

ABC SERVICE CORPORATION
Income Statement

Date _For the Year Ended December 31, 19A_

Revenues:			**Computations**
Service revenue		$100,500	*Given*
Expenses:			
Various expenses	$54,000		*Given (minus interest)*
Interest expense	1,500		*$10,000 × 15%*
Depreciation expense . . .	5,000		*$20,000 ÷ 4 years*
Total expenses		$ 60,500	
Pretax income		40,000	
Income tax expense		8,000	*$40,000 × 20%*
Net income		$ 32,000	
Earnings per share		$ 10.67	*$32,000 ÷ 3,000 shares*

ABC SERVICE CORPORATION
Balance Sheet

Date _At December 31, 19A_

Assets:			
Cash		$58,000	*$36,000 + $10,000 + $94,500*
			− $55,500 − $7,000 − $20,000
Accounts receivable		6,000	*$100,500 − $94,500*
Service trucks	$20,000		*Given, cost of trucks*
Less: Accumulated			
depreciation	5,000	15,000	*$20,000 ÷ 4 years = $5,000*
Total assets		$79,000	
Liabilities:			
Note payable	$10,000		*Given, bank loan*
Income taxes payable . . .	1,000		*Given, amount unpaid*
Total liabilities		$11,000	
Shareholders' equity:			
Capital stock, 3,000			
no-par shares	36,000		*3,000 × $12*
Retained earnings	32,000		*From income statement**
Total shareholders'			
equity		68,000	
Total liabilities and			
shareholders' equity . . .		$79,000	

* Beginning RE ($-0-) + Net income ($32,000) − Dividends ($-0-) = Ending RE ($32,000).

SUMMARY OF CHAPTER

Accounting interacts with almost all aspects of the environment: social, economic, and political. Any open society is complex and is characterized by a large number of organizations. Each organization, whether local, national, or international, can be an **accounting entity.** The essence of accounting is the measurement and reporting of financial information for an accounting entity. **Measurement** and **reporting** of the financial effects of transactions on accounting entities are relevant to interested decision makers. Your decision-making potential is enhanced if you understand the financial impacts of alternative solutions to particular problems.

Part B of the chapter explained and illustrated the basic features of the three required external financial reports—the income statement, the balance sheet, and the statement of changes in financial position (SCFP).

The income statement is a statement of operations that reports revenues, expenses, and net income for a stated period of time. Earnings per share (EPS), which gives the relationship between net income and the number of common shares outstanding, was illustrated.

The balance sheet is a statement of **financial position** that reports dollar amounts for the assets, liabilities, and owners' equity at a specific point in time.

The statement of changes in financial position (SCFP) is a statement of the inflows and outflows of cash that reports those flows for a specific period of time.

The accounting model for the balance sheet, **Assets = Liabilities + Owners' Equity,** is the **foundation for the entire accounting process.**

The financial statements for a small company were illustrated. In the next chapters, you will move one step forward by learning more about the basic accounting model and the analysis of business transactions.

IMPORTANT TERMS DEFINED IN THIS CHAPTER

AAA American Accounting Association. *p. 18*

Accounting Entity A business or other organization; one that is separate and distinct from its owners. *p. 7*

AICPA American Institute of Certified Public Accountants. *p. 17*

Assets Items owned; have value. *p. 25*

Auditing Attest function; reliability; auditor's opinion. *p. 12*

Balance Sheet Position statement; Assets = Liabilities + Owners' Equity. *p. 21*

CAAA Canadian Academic Accounting Association. *p. 16*

Canada Business Corporations Act Act of Government of Canada regulating the incorporation and operation of corporations. *p. 15*

Cash Inflows Cash received; increase Cash. *p. 28*

Cash Outflows Cash paid; decrease Cash. *p. 28*

CGAC Certified General Accountants of Canada. *p. 16*

CICA Canadian Institute of Chartered Accountants. *p. 15*

CICA Handbook Source of GAAP published by the Accounting Standards Committee of CICA. *p. 15*

CMA Certified Management Accountant; designation used by members of the Society of Management Accountants. *p. 16*

Contributed Capital Total amount invested by shareholders. *p. 27*

Corporation A separate legal entity; shares represent ownership. *p. 6*

Depreciation Allocation of the cost of operational assets; based on use. *p. 23*

Dividend (Cash) A cash payment from a corporation to its shareholders based on the number of shares held. *p. 28*

EPS Earnings per share; common stock. *p. 24*

Expenses Outflow of resources; for goods and services used. *p. 23*

FASB Financial Accounting Standards Board. *p. 18*

GAAP Generally accepted accounting principles. *p. 20*

IASC International Accounting Standards Committee. *p. 17*

Income Statement Required report; operations; income; EPS. *p. 21*

Liabilities Obligations; debts; promises to pay. *p. 26*

Management Advisory Services Service rendered by PA firms; consulting; complements audit and tax services (MAS). *p. 13*

Net Income Revenues − Expenses = Income. *p. 23*

Owners' Equity Assets − Liabilities = Owners' Equity. *p. 26*

Partnership No capital stock; two or more owners. *p. 6*

Retained Earnings Accumulated earnings; reduced by dividends. *p. 27*

Revenues Inflow of resources from sale of goods and services. *p. 22*

SCFP Statement of changes in financial position. *p. 28*

SEC Securities and Exchange Commission. *p. 18*

Separate-Entity Assumption An entity must be accounted for separately and apart from its owners. *p. 7*

Shareholders' Equity Assets − Liabilities = Shareholders' Equity. *p. 27*

SMAC Society of Management Accountants of Canada. *p. 16*

Sole Proprietorship No shares; one owner. *p. 5*

QUESTIONS

Part A: Questions 1–7

1. Define accounting.
2. Explain the use of the monetary unit in accounting.

3. Briefly distinguish among a sole proprietorship, partnership, and corporation.
4. What is an accounting entity? Why is a business treated as a separate entity for accounting purposes?
5. Briefly explain the three ways that financial statements serve statement users.
6. List and briefly explain the three primary services provided by PAs.
7. Briefly explain the role of the:
   a. FASB.
   b. CICA.
   c. CAAA.

Part B: Questions 8–23

8. Financial statements are the end products of the accounting process. Explain.
9. Define communication.
10. The accounting process generates financial reports for both "internal" and "external" users. Identify some of the groups of the users.
11. Complete the following:

Name of statement		**A more descriptive name**
a. Income statement	*a.*	_____
b. Balance sheet	*b.*	_____
c. Statement of changes in financial position (SCFP)	*c.*	_____

12. What information should be included in the heading of each of the required financial statements?
13. Explain why the income statement and the SCFP are dated "For the Year Ended December 31, 19X," whereas the balance sheet is dated "At December 31, 19X."
14. Define revenue.
15. Define expense.
16. Briefly define the following: net income, net loss, and break even.
17. What are the purposes of (*a*) the income statement, (*b*) the balance sheet, and (*c*) the SCFP?
18. Explain the accounting model for the income statement. What are the three major items reported on the income statement?
19. Explain the accounting model for the balance sheet. Define the three major components reported on the balance sheet.
20. Explain the accounting model for the SCFP. Explain the three major components reported on the statement.
21. Why is owners' equity referred to frequently as a residual interest?
22. What are the two primary sources of owners' equity in a business?
23. What are the appropriate titles for owners' equity for (*a*) sole proprietorship, (*b*) partnership, and (*c*) corporation?

EXERCISES

Part A: Exercises 1–1 and 1–2

E1–1   **(Identifying Important Accounting Organizations)**
Below is a list of important abbreviations used in Part A of the chapter. These abbreviations also are used widely in business. For each abbreviation give the full designation. The first one is an example.

Abbreviation	Full designation
(1) PA	Public Accountant
(2) APB	
(3) CICA	
(4) AAA	
(5) CMA	
(6) AICPA	
(7) IASC	
(8) FASB	
(9) CGA	

E1–2   **(Characteristics of the Environment of Accounting)**
Match each description with its related term or abbreviation by entering the appropriate letter in the blanks provided.

Related term or abbreviation	Description
_____ (1) CGA	A. The collection, analysis, measurement, recording, and reporting information about an entity to decision makers.
_____ (2) Auditing	
_____ (3) Sole proprietorship	
_____ (4) Corporation	B. Measurement of information about an entity in the monetary unit—dollars.
_____ (5) Accounting	
_____ (6) Separate entity	C. An unincorporated business owned by two or more persons.
_____ (7) Auditor's report	
_____ (8) CMA	D. An entity defined for accounting purposes, separate from its owners.
_____ (9) Partnership	
_____ (10) CICA	E. An incorporated entity that issues shares as evidence of ownership.
_____ (11) FASB	
_____ (12) CA	F. A Certified Management Accountant.
_____ (13) Unit of measure	G. Attest function by an independent PA.

Related term or abbreviation	Description
_____ (14) CAAA	H. Chartered Accountant.
_____ (15) American Accounting Association	I. An unincorporated business owned by one person.
	J. Independent PA's statement that indicates whether the financial statements are appropriate and not misleading.
	K. Certified General Accountant.
	L. Financial Accounting Standards Board.
	M. American Accounting Association.
	N. Canadian Academic Accounting Association.
	O. Encourages improvement of accounting teaching and accounting research.
	P. Canadian Institute of Chartered Accountants.

Part B: Exercises 1–3 to 1–11

E1–3 (Using the Income Statement and Balance Sheet Models)

Review the chapter explanations of the income statement and the balance sheet models. Apply these models in each independent case below to compute the two missing amounts for each case. Assume it is the end of 19A, the first full year of operations for the company.

Independent Cases	Total Revenues	Total Assets	Total Expenses	Total Liabilities	Net Income (Loss)	Shareholders' Equity
A	$95,000	$150,000	$88,000	$92,000	$ 3000	$ 58000
B	76 000	112,000	61,000	42 000	10,000	70,000
C	80,000	92,000	86,000	26,000		
D	50,000			40,000	9,000	77,000
E			81,000	73,000	(6,000)	88,000

E1–4 (Analyzing an Income Statement)

Rose Corporation was organized by three individuals on January 1, 19A, to provide electronic repair services. At the end of 19A, the following income statement was prepared:

ROSE CORPORATION
Income Statement
For the Year Ended December 31, 19A

Revenues:		
Service sales (cash)	$178,000	
Service sales (credit)	12,000	
Total revenues		$190,000
Expenses:		
Salaries	71,000	
Rent	12,000	
Utilities	10,000	
Advertising	11,000	
Supplies	18,000	
Interest	3,000	
Depreciation	5,000	
Total expenses		130,000
Pretax income		60,000
Income tax expense		13,200
Net income		$ 46,800
EPS		$2.34

Required:

a. What was the average monthly revenue amount?

b. What was the monthly rent amount?

c. Explain why "Supplies, $18,000" is an expense.

d. Explain why "Interest, $3,000" is reported as an expense.

e. Explain what is meant by "Depreciation, $5,000."

f. What was the average income tax rate for Rose Corporation?

g. How many shares of capital stock were outstanding?

h. Can you determine how much cash the company had on December 31, 19A? Explain.

E1–5   **(Preparing a Simple Income Statement)**

Assume you are the owner of "The Drop-In Shop," which specializes in items that interest university students. At the end of January 19A you find that (for January only):

a. Sales, per the cash register tapes, totaled $80,000, plus one sale on credit (a special situation) of $1,000.

b. With the help of a friend (who majored in accounting), you determined that all of the goods sold during January had cost you $30,000 when they were purchased.

c. During the month, according to the chequebook, you paid $35,000 for salaries, utilities, supplies, advertising, and other expenses; however, you have not yet paid the $600 monthly rent for January on the store and fixtures.

On the basis of the data given, what was the amount of income for January (disregard income taxes)? Show computations. (Hint: A convenient form to use would have the following major side captions: revenue from sales, expenses, and the difference—income.)

E1-6   **(Analysis of Cash Inflow from Operations)**

SuperServ Company, a service organization, prepared the following special report for the month of January 19A:

Service Revenues, Expenses, and Income

Service revenues:

Cash services (per cash register tape)	$95,000	
Credit services (per charge bills; not yet collected by end of January)	30,000	$125,000

Expenses:

Salaries and wages (paid by cheque)	50,000	
Salary for January not yet paid	2,000	
Supplies used (taken from those on hand, purchased for cash during December)	1,000	
Estimated cost of wear and tear on used delivery truck for the month (depreciation)	500	
Other expenses (paid by cheque)	21,500	75,000
Pretax income		50,000
Income tax expense (not yet paid)		10,000
Income for January		$ 40,000

Required:

a. The owner (who knows very little about the financial part of the business) asked you to compute the "amount that cash increased in January 19A from the operations of the company." You decided to prepare a detailed report for the owner with the following major side captions: cash inflows (collections), cash outflows (payments), and the difference—net increase (or decrease) in cash.

b. What was the average income tax rate?

c. See if you can reconcile the "difference—net increase (or decrease) in cash" you computed in (a) with the income for January 19A.

E1-7   **(Preparing a Simple Income Statement and Balance Sheet)**

Dusty Corporation was organized by five individuals on January 1, 19A. At the end of January 19A, the following monthly financial data are available:

Total revenues	$110,000
Total expenses (excluding income taxes)	80,000
Cash balance, January 31, 19A	18,000
Receivables from customers (all considered collectible)	12,000
Merchandise inventory (by inventory count at cost)	35,000
Payables to suppliers for merchandise purchased from them (will be paid during February 19A)	9,000
Capital stock, par $10, 2,600 shares	26,000

No dividends were declared or paid during 19A.

Assume a 20% tax rate on the income of this corporation; the income taxes will be paid during the first quarter of 19B.

Required:

Complete the following two statements:

DUSTY CORPORATION
Income Statement
For the Month of January 19A

Total revenues . . . . $_____
  Less: Total expenses (excluding income tax) . . . . _____
Pretax income . . . . _____
  Less: Income tax expense . . . . _____
Net income . . . . $_____

DUSTY CORPORATION
Balance Sheet
At January 31, 19A

Assets:
  Cash . . . . $_____
  Receivables from customers . . . . _____
  Merchandise inventory . . . . _____
Total assets . . . . $_____
Liabilities:
  Payables to suppliers . . . . $_____
  Income taxes payable . . . . _____
    Total liabilities . . . . _____
Shareholders' equity:
  Capital stock . . . . $_____
  Retained earnings . . . . _____
Total liabilities and shareholders' equity . . . . $_____

E1–8   (Completing a Simple Balance Sheet)

Cutrate Bookstore was organized as a corporation by Mary Newell and Joe Owens; each contributed $40,000 cash to start the business. Each received 3,000 no-par common shares. The store completed its first year of operations on December 31, 19A. On that date, the following financial items for the year were determined: December 31, 19A, cash on hand and in the bank, $41,100; December 31,19A, amounts due from customers from sales of books, $19,000; store and office equipment, purchased January 1, 19A, for $50,000 (estimated useful life 10 years; depreciate an equal amount each year); December 31, 19A, amounts owed to publishers for books purchased, $7,000; and a note payable, 10%, one year, dated July 1, 19A, to a local bank for $2,000. No dividends were declared or paid to the shareholders during the year.

Required:

a. Complete the following balance sheet at the end of 19A.

b. What was the amount of net income for the year?

c. Show how the $100 liability for interest payable was computed. Why is it shown as a liability on this date?

		_____	
		_____	
		_____	

Assets		**Liabilities**	
Cash	$ ____	Accounts payable	$ ____
Accounts receivable	____	Note payable	____
Store and office equipment . . . $ ____		Interest payable	100
Less: Accumulated		Total liabilities	$ ____
depreciation to date . . . . . ____	____		
		Shareholders' Equity	
		Common shares, no-par	____
		Retained earnings	16,000
		Total shareholders' equity	____
		Total liabilities and	
Total assets	$ ====	shareholders' equity	$ ====

E1–9 **(Preparing a Simple SCFP, Cash Basis)**

Blue Manufacturing Corporation is preparing the annual financial statements for the shareholders. A SCFP, cash basis, must be prepared. The following data on cash flows were developed for the entire year ended December 31, 19D; cash inflow from operating revenues, $250,000; cash expended for operating expenses, $190,000; sale of unissued Blue shares for cash, $20,000; cash dividends declared and paid to shareholders during the year, $15,000; and payments on long-term notes payable, $50,000. During the year, a tract of land was sold for $10,000 cash (which was the same price that Blue had paid for the land in 19C), and $33,000 cash was expended for two new machines. The machines were used in the factory.

Required:

Prepare a SCFP, cash basis, for 19D. Follow the format illustrated in the chapter.

E1–10 **(Completing a Simple Income Statement)**

Quality Realty Corporation has been operating for five years and is owned by three investors. J. Doe owns 60% of the total 9,000 issued shares and is the managing executive in charge. On December 31, 19C, the following financial items for the entire year were determined: commissions earned and collected in cash, $140,000, plus $14,000 uncollected; rental service fees earned and collected, $16,000; salaries expense paid, $56,700; commissions expense paid, $40,000; employee benefits paid, $3,000; rent paid, $2,200 (not including December rent yet to be paid); utilities expense paid, $900; promotion and advertising paid, $6,000; and miscellaneous expenses paid, $400. There were no other unpaid expenses at December 31. Quality Realty rents its office space but owns the furniture therein. The furniture cost $6,000 when acquired and has an estimated life of 10 years (depreciate an equal amount each year). The average income tax rate for this corporation is 30%. Also during the year, the company paid the owners "out of profit" cash dividends amounting to $10,000.

Required:

Complete the following income statement.

_____

_____

_____

Revenues:
  Commissions earned . . . . $ _____
  Rental service fees . . . . _____
    Total revenues . . . . $ _____
Expenses:
  Salaries expense . . . . _____
  Commission expense . . . . _____
  Employee benefits expense . . . . _____
  Rent expense . . . . _____
  Utilities expense . . . . _____
  Promotion and advertising . . . . _____
  Miscellaneous expenses . . . . _____
  Depreciation expense . . . . _____
    Total expenses (excluding income taxes) . . . . . . _____
Pretax income . . . . _____
  Income tax expense . . . . _____
Net income . . . . $ 42,000

Earnings per share (EPS) . . . . $ _____

E1–11   **(Applying the Balance Sheet Model)**

On June 1, 19F, Rand Corporation prepared a balance sheet just prior to going out of business. The balance sheet totals showed the following:

        Assets (no cash) $100,000
        Liabilities 60,000
        Shareholders' equity 40,000

Shortly thereafter, all of the assets were sold for cash.

Required:

a. How would the balance sheet appear immediately after the sale of the assets for cash for each of the following cases? Use the format given below.

	Cash received for the assets	Assets	− Liabilities =	Shareholders' Equity
		Balances immediately after sale		
Case A	$110,000	$ _____	$ _____	$ _____
Case B	100,000	_____	_____	_____
Case C	90,000	_____	_____	_____

b. How should the cash be distributed in each separate case? (Hint: Creditors have a priority claim over owners upon dissolution.) Use the format given below.

	To creditors	To shareholders	Total
Case A	$_____	$_____	$_____
Case B	_____	_____	_____
Case C	_____	_____	_____

PROBLEMS

Part A: Problems 1–1 to 1–3

P1–1   **(Analyzing Transactions)**

Below are listed five transactions completed by VT Company during the year 19A:

a. Sold services for cash, $40,000.

b. Purchased a microcomputer for use in performing the accounting function of the company: cost, $6,000; paid cash.

c. Paid salaries, $20,000 cash.

d. Borrowed cash, $15,000 on a 12% interest-bearing note.

e. The owner of VT Company purchased a special pickup for his personal use: cost, $16,000; paid cash from his personal funds.

Required:

Complete the tabulation given below. Indicate the effects (in dollars) of each of the above transactions on the balance sheet, income statement, and SCFP of VT Company. Consider only the effects on the date the transactions were completed. Provide explanatory comments to support your response for each transaction. Use "+" for increase and "−" for decrease on the income statement and balance sheet.

Financial Statements	Transaction (a)	(b)	(c)	(d)	(e)
Income statement:					
Revenues	$⁺40,000	$	$⁺20,000	$	$
Expenses		+20,000			
Balance sheet:		+6000	−20,000	+15,000	
Assets	+40,000	−6000		+15,000	—
Liabilities	−6,000				—
Owners' equity	−20,000				—
SCFP:					
Cash inflow	+40,000			15,000	—
Cash outflow		6000	20,000		—

Explanations:

P1–2   **(Analysis of Data to Support a Loan Application)**

On January 1, 19A, three individuals organized Quick Service Company. Each individual invested $10,000 cash in the business. On December 31, 19A, they prepared a list of resources (assets) owned and a list of the debts (liabilities) to support a company loan request of $50,000 submitted to a local bank. None of the three investors had studied accounting. The two lists prepared were as follows:

Company resources:

Cash	$ 8,000
Service supplies inventory (on hand)	5,000
Service trucks (four practically new)	64,000
Personal residences of organizers (three houses)	190,000
Service equipment used in the business (practically new)	24,000
Bills due from customers (for services already completed)	13,000
Total	$304,000

Obligations of the company:

Unpaid wages to employees	$ 18,000
Unpaid taxes	6,000
Owed to suppliers	8,000
Owed on service trucks and equipment (to a finance company)	40,000
Loan from organizer	15,000
Total	$ 87,000

Required:

a. If you were advising the local bank about the two lists, what issues would you raise? Explain the basis for each question and include any recommendations that you have (consider the separate-entity assumption).

b. In view of your response to (*a*), what do you think the amount of **net resources** (i.e., assets minus liabilities) of the company would be? Show your computations.

P1–3   **(Comparison of Income with Cash Flow)**

Rush Service Company was organized on January 1, 19A. At the end of the first quarter (three months) of operations, the owner prepared a summary of its operations as shown in the first column of the following tabulation:

[handwritten: only expenses affects the income]

[handwritten in left margin: not income. income is earned. all wage earned reduce reduce affect income. all wage earned reduce income. does not affect income]

Summary of Transactions	Computation of—	
	Income	Cash
1. Services performed for customers, $66,000, of which one sixth remained uncollected at the end of the quarter.	$ +66,000	$ +55,000
2. Cash borrowed from the local bank, $20,000 (one-year note).	0	+20,000
3. Purchased a small service truck for use in the business; cost, $8,000; paid 20% down, balance on credit.	0	-1600
4. Expenses, $42,000, of which one fifth remained unpaid at the end of the quarter. *[handwritten: 33,600 collected]*	-33,600	-33,600
5. Purchased service supplies for use in the business, $2,000, of which one fourth remained unpaid (on credit) at the end of the quarter. Also, one fifth of these supplies were unused (still on hand) at the end of the quarter.		-1500
6. Wages earned by employees, $18,000, of which one sixth remained unpaid at the end of the quarter.	-18,000	-15,000
7. Purchased land for future use for $20,000 cash.		-20,000
Based only on the above transactions, compute the following for the quarter: Income (or loss) Cash inflow (or outflow)	$ _____	$ _____

[handwritten above table: 66,000 / 1÷6 - 11,000 / 55,000 / + //]

Required:

a. For each of the seven transactions given in the tabulation above, enter what you consider the correct amounts. Enter a zero when appropriate. The first transaction is illustrated.

b. For each transaction, explain the basis of your dollar responses. (Hint: Income and cash flow totals are not the same.)

Part B: Problems 1–4 to 1–8

P1–4 **(Completing a Simple Balance Sheet)**

DC Corporation was organized by Donald Dunn and Cynthia Cummings; they had previously operated the company as a partnership. Each owner has 10,000 shares of capital stock of DC Corporation. At the end of the accounting year, 19H, the company bookkeeper prepared the following incomplete balance sheet (amounts simplified for problem purposes):

DC CORPORATION
Balance Sheet

(1)	Assets:			
(2)	Cash			$28,000
(3)	Accounts receivable			15,000
(4)	Equipment*		$	
(5)	Less: Accumulated depreciation		10,000	40,000
(6)	Total _____			$83,000
(7)	_____			
(8)	Accounts payable		8,000	
(9)	Income tax payable		1,000	
(10)	Note payable, short term, 15%†		4,000	
(11)	_____			
(12)	_____			_____
(13)	Capital stock, $_____ par value		20,000	
(14)	Contributed surplus		10,000	
(15)	Retained earnings		40,000	
(16)	_____			70,000
(17)	Total liabilities and shareholders' equity			$

* Equipment has a 10-year estimated life; equal amounts expensed each year.
† Note dated July 1, 19H, time to maturity, 12 months.

Required (the lines are numbered above for problem reference purposes):

1. Define the term *assets* as used on the balance sheet.
2. What would be DC's cash balance in the bank assuming the company has $500 cash on hand on December 31, 19H?
3. Explain why "Accounts receivable" represents an asset.
4. Compute the amount that the equipment cost when it was acquired by DC Corporation.
5. Explain "Accumulated depreciation." What does the $10,000 indicate?
6. Enter the correct caption.
7. Enter the correct caption.
8. Explain why "Accounts payable" is a liability.
9. Explain what this liability represents.
10. What amount of interest expense applies to the year 19H? Note that the amount computed will be shown on the income statement as "Interest expense."
11. Enter the appropriate caption and amount.
12. Enter the appropriate caption.
13. Enter the amount of the par value per share of capital stock.
14. What was the total issue price per share of capital stock?
15. Explain what the $40,000 amount means.
16. Enter appropriate caption.
17. Enter correct amount.
18. Do you have any suggestions about the heading of the statement?

P1-5   (Redraft an Incorrect Income Statement)

Surfir Realty Company was organized early in 19A as a corporation by four investors, each of whom invested $6,000 cash. The company has been moderately successful, even though internal financial controls are inadequate. Although financial reports have been prepared each year (primarily in response to income tax requirements), sound accounting procedures have not been followed. Therefore, the financial performance of the company is known only vaguely by the four shareholders. Recently, one of the shareholders, with the agreement of the others, sold his shares to a local accountant. The new shareholder was amazed when handed the report below. This report was prepared by an employee for the last meeting of the board of directors. The accountant could tell immediately that the reported profit was wrong. She quickly observed that no interest expense was shown on a $10,000, 12%, note payable that had been outstanding throughout the year. Also, no recognition had been given to depreciation expense of office equipment that was purchased on January 1, 19D, at a cost of $12,000 with an estimated six-year useful life.

SURFIR REALTY
Profit Statement ⟶ Income statement
year ended **December 31, 19D**

— Rev.

Commissions earned (all collected)	$155,400
Property management revenue (exclusive of $1,200 not collected)	9,000
Total	164,400
Expenses Salaries paid	35,000
Commissions paid	36,000
Employee benefits paid	3,200
Office supplies expense	150
Rent paid	3,000
Utilities paid	600
Advertising (excluding the December bill for advertising of $4,000 not yet paid)	26,000 30,000
Miscellaneous expenses	450
Exp Total	104,400
Net Inc Profit for the year (pretax)	$ 60,000

EPS: $60,000 ÷ 10,000 shares = $6.

Required:

You were asked to redraft the income statement, including corrections. Assume an average income tax rate of 30%. (Hint: The correct EPS is $3.78)

P1-6   (Prepare a Simple Income Statement and Balance Sheet)

Assume you are president of Great Lakes Company. At the end of the first year (December 31, 19A) of operations, the following financial data are available for the company:

Cash	$ 35,000
Receivables from customers (all considered collectible)	15,000
Inventory of merchandise (based on physical count and priced at cost)	80,000
Equipment owned, at cost	25,000
Depreciation expense (equipment)	2,500
Note payable, one year, 12% annual interest, owed to the bank (dated July 1, 19A)	30,000
Interest on the note through December 31, 19A (due to be paid to the bank on June 30, 19B; $30,000 × 12% × 6/12)	1,800
Salary payable for 19A (on December 31, 19A, this was owed to an employee who was away because of an emergency; will return around January 10, 19B, at which time the payment will be made)	1,000

Total sales revenue $120,000
Expenses paid, including the cost of the merchandise sold (excluding income taxes
   at a 30% rate; the taxes will be paid during the first quarter of 19B)   75,000
Capital stock, 10,000 shares outstanding   80,000
No dividends were declared or paid during 19A.

Required (show computations):

a. Prepare a summarized income statement for the year 19A. (Hint: EPS is $2.78, rounded.)

b. Prepare a balance sheet at December 31, 19A.

P1-7 (Analyze a Student's Business and Prepare a Simple Income Statement)

During the summer between her junior and senior years, Jeri Brown needed to earn sufficient money for the coming academic year. Unable to obtain a job with a reasonable salary, she decided to try the lawn-care business for three months. After a survey of the market potential, Jeri bought a used pickup truck on June 1 for $1,200. On each door she painted "Jeri's Lawn Service, Ph. XX." Also, she spent $600 for mowers, trimmers, and tools. To acquire these items she borrowed $2,000 cash on a note (endorsed by a friend) at 15% interest per annum, payable at the end of the three months (ending August 31).

At the end of the summer, Jeri realized that she had "done a lot of work, and her bank account looked good." This fact prompted her to become concerned about how much profit the business had earned.

A review of the cheque stubs showed the following: Deposits in the bank of collections from customers totaled $11,400. The following cheques were written: gas, oil, and lubrication, $830; pickup repairs, $175; repair of mowers, $80; miscellaneous supplies used, $100; helpers, $4,400; employee benefits, $175; payment for assistance in preparing payroll forms, $25; insurance, $150; telephone, $90; and $2,075 to pay off the note including interest (on August 31). A notebook kept in the pickup, plus some unpaid bills, reflected that customers still owed her $600 for lawn services rendered and that she owed $100 for gas and oil (credit card charges). She estimated that the "wear and tear" for use of the truck and the other equipment for three months amounted to $300.

Required:

a. Prepare a quarterly income statement for Jeri's Lawn Service for the months June, July, and August 19A. Use the following main captions: revenues from services, expenses, and net income. Because this is a sole proprietorship, the business will not be subject to income tax. (Hint: Total revenues amounted to $12,000.)

b. Do you see a need for one or more additional financial reports for this business for 19A and thereafter? Explain.

P1-8 (Analyze a Student's Business and Prepare a Simple Income Statement)

Upon graduation from high school, Jack Kane immediately accepted a job as a plumber's helper for a large local plumbing company. After three years of hard work, Jack received a plumber's license and decided to start his own business. He had saved $5,000 which he invested in the business. First, he transferred this amount from his savings account to a business bank account for "Kane Plumbing Company, Incorporated." His lawyer had advised him to start as a corporation. He then purchased a used panel truck for $3,000 cash and secondhand tools for $800; rented space in a small building; inserted an ad in the local paper; and opened the doors on October 1, 19A. Immediately, Jack was very busy, and after one month, he employed a helper. Although Jack knew practically nothing about the financial side of the business, he realized that a number of reports were required and that costs and collections had to be controlled carefully. At the end of the year, prompted in part by concern about his income tax situation (previously he only had to report salary), he recognized the need for financial statements. His wife, Jane, "developed some financial statements for the business." On December 31, 19A, with the help of a friend, she gathered the following data for the three months just ended: Deposits in the bank account of collections for plumbing services totaled $30,000. The following cheques were written: plumber's helper, $7,550; employee benefits paid, $150; supplies purchased and used on jobs, $9,000; oil, gas, and maintenance on truck, $1,100; insurance, $300; rent, $500; utilities and telephone, $650; and miscellaneous expenses, $400 (including advertising). Also, there were uncollected bills to customers for plumbing services amounting to $2,000. The rent for December amounting to $100 had not been paid. The average income tax rate is 20%. The "wear and tear on the truck and tools due to use during the three months" was estimated by Jack to be $250.

Required:

a. Prepare a quarterly income statement for Kane Plumbing for the three months of October–December 19A. Use the following main captions: revenue from services, expenses, pretax income, and net income. (Hint: Expenses, excluding income taxes, totaled $20,000.)

b. Do you think that Jack may have a need for one or more additional financial reports for 19A and thereafter? Explain.

CASES

Part A: Cases 1–1 and 1–2

C1–1   **(Analysis of the Assets and Liabilities of a Business)**
D. X. Jones owns and operates the DXJ Sporting Goods (a sole proprietorship). An employee prepares a financial report for the business at each year-end. This report lists all of the resources (assets) owned by Jones (including such personal items as the home owned and occupied by Jones). It also lists all of the debts of the business (but not the "personal" debts of Jones).

Required:

a. From the accounting point of view, in what ways do you disagree with what is being included in and excluded from the report of business assets and liabilities?

b. Upon questioning, Jones responded, "Don't worry about it, we use it only to support a loan from the bank." How would you respond to this comment?

C1–2   **(A Decision about a Proposed Audit)**
You are one of three partners who own and operate the Triple X Refreshments. The business has been operating for seven years. One of the other partners has always prepared the annual financial statements. Recently you proposed that "the statements should be audited each year because it would benefit the partners and preclude possible

disagreements about the division of profits." The partner that prepares the statements proposed that his "Uncle Ray, who has a lot of financial experience can do the job and at little cost." Your other partner remained silent.

Required:

a. What position would you take on the proposal? Justify your response.

b. What would you strongly recommend? Give the basis for your recommendation.

Part B: Cases 1–3 to 1–5

C1–3   **(Identifying Deficiencies in an Income Statement and Balance Sheet)**
Slack Corporation was organized on January 1, 19A. At the end of 19A, the company had not yet employed an accountant. However, an employee who was "good with numbers" prepared the following statements at that date:

SLACK CORPORATION
December 31, 19A

Income from sales of merchandise	$180,000
Total amount paid for goods sold during 19A	(95,000)
Selling costs	(30,000)
Depreciation (on service vehicles used)	(15,000)
Income from services rendered	50,000
Salaries and wages paid	(60,000)
Income taxes (at tax rate of 20%)	(6,000)
Profit for the year 19A	$ 24,000

SLACK CORPORATION
December 31, 19A

Resources:		
Cash		$ 31,000
Merchandise inventory (held for resale)		44,000
Service vehicles		45,000
Retained earnings (profit earned in 19A)		24,000
Grand total		$144,000
Debts:		
Payables to suppliers		$ 15,000
Note owed to bank		20,000
Due from customers		12,000
Total		47,000
Supplies on hand (to be used in rendering services)	$12,000	
Accumulated depreciation (on service vehicles)	15,000	
Capital stock, 10,000 no-par shares	70,000	
Total		97,000
Grand total		$144,000

The above amounts, except for some totals, are correct.

Required:

a. List all of the deficiencies in the above statements that you can identify. Give a brief explanation on each one.

b. Prepare a proper income statement (correct net income is $24,000) and balance sheet (correct balance sheet total is $129,000).

C1–4   (Introduction to an Actual Set of Financial Statements)

A complete set of financial statements is given in Appendix B immediately preceding the Index. Throughout this course you may be asked to examine those statements to become familiar with actual financial statements that you will encounter in other courses and after you graduate.

Required:

a. What is the full name of this company?

b. What is the ending date of the current reporting year?

c. Give the exact title and date that the company uses for the income statement, balance sheet, and statement of changes in financial position.

d. What is the amount of net income reported by the company for the current year?

e. What is the amount of total assets reported by the company for the current year?

f. There is a section in the financial statements titled "Notes to Consolidated Financial Statements." How many numbered notes are given?

g. What is the name of the independent Public Accountants (the audit firm)?

C1–5   (Concepts and Recognition)

As an individual who is reading this book, you are an accounting entity. You are not a sole proprietorship, a partnership, or a corporation but you are an entity. As such you can represent yourself by financial statements and you may have to for purposes of obtaining a bank loan or to provide financial information for one purpose or another. You have assets, liabilities, and owner's equity. The question is what are they, how can they be valued, and should they be included in your statement of financial position?

Required:

a. List all your attributes that you believe to be assets. Determine how you might value these assets. Use costs, benefits, or resale value of these assets. You may disguise your personal fortune if you feel better about it.

b. List your liabilities. Consider those for which you will have to use assets to extinguish. Value those you can and consider how you determined the value.

c. What is your owner's equity? Where did it come from? List the total amount and as many sources as possible including what you were born with.

TWO

THE FUNDAMENTAL ACCOUNTING MODEL AND TRANSACTION ANALYSIS

PURPOSE

Chapter 1 emphasized the importance of the communication of accounting information to certain decision makers. It also presented an overview of external financial statements. The purpose of Chapter 2 is to begin our discussions of how the accounting function collects data about business transactions and how those data are processed to provide the periodic financial statements. To accomplish this purpose, this chapter discusses the fundamental accounting model, transaction analysis, and how the results of transaction analysis are recorded in an accounting system.

A diagram showing how all companies apply the fundamental model is presented on the facing page.

LEARNING OBJECTIVES

1. Explain what constitutes a business transaction.
2. Analyze some simple business transactions in terms of the fundamental accounting model: Assets = Liabilities + Owners' Equity, and Debits = Credits.
3. Record the results of transaction analysis in two basic ways: (a) journal entries and (b) T-accounts.
4. Use the T-account balances to prepare a simple income statement and balance sheet.
5. Expand your business vocabulary by learning about the "Important Terms Defined in This Chapter."
6. Apply the knowledge learned from this chapter.

ORGANIZATION

1. The fundamental accounting model.
2. Nature of transactions.
3. Debits = Credits.
4. Transaction analysis.
5. Journal entries and T-accounts.

Balance Sheet (fundamental model)

Assets	=	Liabilities	+	Owners' Equity
Cash $29,300		Notes payable $5,000		Capital stock $20,000
Accounts receivable.. 3,000		Accounts payable 1,500		Retained
Delivery truck 8,000				earnings 12,200
Less: Accumulated				
depreciation ...... (1,600)				
Totals $38,700		$6,500		$32,000

- Typical transaction that affects **only** the balance sheet:
  (a) Sold (issued) capital stock:
  >   Debit: Cash 20,000
  >   Credit: Capital stock 20,000

- Typical transaction that affects **both** the balance sheet and income statement:
  (b) Incurred operating expenses on credit:
  >   Debit: Operating expenses 2,000
  >   Credit: Accounts payable 2,000

Income Statement

Revenue	$44,000
Operating expenses	(29,400)
Interest expense...	(600)
Net income	$14,000

- Note: When you complete this chapter, you will know how all companies record transactions in journal entries such as these.

The Fundamental Accounting Model

Chapter 1 presented the accounting model:

ASSETS = LIABILITIES + OWNERS' EQUITY

It is both an algebraic model and an economic model. As an **algebraic model,** it can be rearranged in various ways, such as Assets − Liabilities = Owners' Equity. As an **economic model,** it expresses an economic truism: "What I own less what I owe equals my net worth." For example, if on December 31 you own assets of $100,000 and owe debts of $30,000, your net worth (i.e., "owners' equity") is $70,000. All of us measure our **net** resources in this way.

Let's carry our personal example one step further to see how you stand at the end of the next month. To do this you must **record each and every transaction** that you complete. The amounts for assets, liabilities, and owners' equity will change as follows:

Recording transactions in terms of the fundamental accounting model (personal), month of January:

Transactions	Owns Assets	=	Owes Liabilities	+	net worth Owners' Equity
Your beginning financial situation	$100,000		$30,000		$70,000
a. Received a $3,000 salary	+3,000		-0-		+3,000
Revised situation	103,000		30,000		73,000
b. Paid monthly bills, $2,000	-2,000		-0-		-2,000
Revised situation	101,000		30,000		71,000
c. Paid a debt, $10,000 (no interest now)	-10,000		-10,000		-0-
Revised situation	91,000		20,000		71,000
d. Paid cash for ABC shares as an investment, $5,000 . . .	-5,000 +5,000				
Your ending financial situation	$ 91,000		$20,000		$71,000

Notice two important points in the above schedule: (1) Each transaction had a **dual** effect in the model; and (2) after each transaction is recorded, the model is in balance (i.e., A = L + OE).

Now, let's apply the fundamental accounting model to a business. The model is used to **analyze and record** each and every transaction completed by the business entity. Assume that B. Bass and three friends organized a corporation called Bass Cleaners, Inc.

The **separate-entity assumption** (Chapter 1) requires that this business be accounted for as an entity separate and apart from its owners (i.e., shareholders). From the previous personal illustration, we see that (a) revenues **increase** shareholders' equity, (b) expenses **decrease** shareholders' equity, and (c) dividends (i.e., withdrawals) paid by the corporation to shareholders **decrease** shareholders' equity in the company. Therefore, for a business, we can elaborate on the fundamental accounting model as follows:

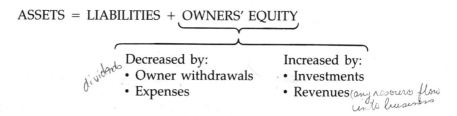

ASSETS = LIABILITIES + OWNERS' EQUITY

dividends

Decreased by:
• Owner withdrawals
• Expenses

Increased by:
• Investments
• Revenues *(any resource flow into business)*

The elaboration of the fundamental accounting model includes two items, revenues and expenses that increase or decrease Owners' Equity. In Chapter 1, revenues were described as cash or something else of value received from the sale of goods or services. Expenses were described as the using up of resources during a period of time to earn revenues. A potential confusion can exist when these descriptions are related to the fact that revenues increase owners' equity while expenses decrease it. Remembering that owners' equity was alternatively defined as net worth suggests that an increase in owners' equity is an increase in net worth which is an increase in the resources of the entity, revenue. A decrease in Owners' Equity is a decrease in net worth which in turn is a using up of the resources of the entity. If the increase in resources or the decrease in resources occur because of the business operations then it is likely revenues or expenses exist as opposed to investments or owner withdrawals. For reasons of later clarity, accountants have chosen to define revenues and expenses in terms of resources rather than Owners' Equity.

The fundamental accounting model applied to a business is a broad economic description of an accounting entity that accommodates the recording of each transaction that directly affects the entity. The **dual economic effect** of each transaction is recorded in terms of this expanded accounting model. The dual effect is recorded in terms of this model regardless of whether the accounting system is handwritten, mechanized, or computerized. Before illustrating our hypothetical business situation, we will examine the nature of business transactions.

Nature of Transactions

Accounting focuses on certain events that have an economic impact on the entity. Those events are recorded as a part of the accounting process and generally are referred to as **transactions.** A broad definition of transactions includes (1) exchanges of resources (assets) and/or obligations (liabilities) between the business (i.e., the accounting entity) and one or more parties other than the entity; and (2) certain events (or economic occurrences) that are not between the entity and one or more parties but have a direct and measurable effect on the accounting entity. Examples of the first category of transactions include the purchase of a machine, the sale of merchandise, the borrowing of cash, and the investment in the business by the owners. Examples of the second category of transactions include: (1) **economic events,** such as a drop in the replacement cost of an item held in inventory and a flood loss; and (2) **time adjustments,** such as depreciation of an operational asset (as a result of use) and the "using up" of prepaid insurance. Throughout this textbook, the word **transaction** will be used in the broad sense to include both types of events.[1]

Most transactions are evidenced by a **business document.** In the case of a sale on credit, a charge ticket is prepared, and in the case of a purchase of goods for resale, an invoice is received. In other transactions, such as a cash sale, the only document may be the cash register tape. The documents that underlie, or support, transactions usually are called **source documents.** From the accounting point of view, the important requirement is that procedures be established to capture the data on each transaction as it occurs. Once this is done, the accounting system transfers and summarizes the economic impact of each transaction on the entity from its initial recording to the end product—the **periodic financial statements.**

The fundamental feature of most transactions with external parties is an exchange where the business entity both gives up something and receives something in return. In the case of a sale of merchandise for cash, the entity gives up resources (the goods sold) and receives in return another resource (cash). In the case of a credit sale of merchandise, the resource received at the time of sale is an account receivable (an asset). Later, another transaction occurs when the account receivable is collected; here, the resource relinquished is the receivable, and the resource received is cash. In the purchase of an asset (either merchandise for resale or a truck purchased for use in the business), the entity acquires the noncash asset and gives up cash, or in the case of a credit purchase, the entity incurs a liability. Another transaction occurs later when the debt is paid. At that time, the entity gives up a resource (cash) and "receives" satisfaction of the debt. The sale or purchase of services can be analyzed in the same way.

The Fundamental Accounting Model Illustrated

B. Bass and three others organized Bass Cleaners, Inc., on January 1, 19A. Each of the four organizers invested $5,000 cash, and each received 200 shares of capital stock. The company immediately started operations. Therefore, each transaction completed by the business must be recorded in the company's accounting system in terms of the fundamental accounting model:

$$\text{Assets} = \text{Liabilities} + \text{Shareholders' Equity}$$

---

[1] A narrow definition of a transaction limits it to the first category; that is, events between the entity and one or more parties other than the entity. This definition is useful in certain circumstances and is conceptually correct. However, accounting recognizes a number of events that are not transactions in the strict sense. Therefore, we have defined the term in the broader sense to generalize our terminology.

Exhibit 2–1 lists a series of transactions completed during the year 19A. The exhibit shows how each transaction is recorded in terms of the fundamental accounting model for Bass Cleaners, Inc. You should study it carefully and notice that (1) each transaction is recorded separately; (2) in recording each transaction, the equality of the fundamental accounting model is maintained (i.e., assets will always equal liabilities plus owners' equity); and (3) the dual effect, as discussed in the preceding section, is recorded for each transaction.

Each transaction is **analyzed,** then entered in terms of the accounting model. The last line of Exhibit 2–1 shows the financial position of the business at December 31, 19A (end of Year 1):

Assets, $38,700 = Liabilities, $6,500 + Shareholders' Equity, $32,200

Exhibit 2–1 shows what is done in an accounting system. However, it does not show how the 19A **periodic financial statements** are prepared. Exhibit 2–2 shows the 19A **income statement** and **balance sheet** for Bass Cleaners. These statements were explained in Chapter 1, Part B.

Three of the required financial statements for external parties are the income statement, balance sheet, and statement of changes in financial position. The primary categories (often termed elements) of items reported on the financial statements are:

Income statement—revenues, expenses, gains, and losses.
Balance sheet—assets, liabilities, and owners' equity.[2]

The terms gains and losses have not been defined in previous pages. Their procedural treatment is the same as that of revenues and expenses. Conceptually they are much the same as revenues and expenses except that they are not a result of the normal business activities. Rather they are ancillary or incidental to the normal revenues and expenses. Typically they are classified according to their source so that accounting reports are more comprehensive and more useful for readers. These financial statements and their elements are discussed throughout this textbook.

The 19A income statement and balance sheet for Bass Cleaners were prepared by selecting data from Exhibit 2–1 for each element reported. The financial statement elements for Bass Cleaners are:

Income statement:
• Revenues
• Expenses

---

[2] The elements of financial statements are discussed in detail in Chapter 4 of this textbook.

Exhibit 2–1   Transaction analysis illustrated

BASS CLEANERS, INC.
Transaction Analysis—19A

	Dual effect of each transaction on the entity			
	Assets	= Liabilities	+	Shareholders' Equity
Transactions				
a. Bass Cleaners received $20,000 cash invested by owners; 800 shares (no-par value) issued to the four owners	Cash + $20,000	=		Capital stock (800 shares) + $20,000
b. Borrowed $5,000 cash on 12% note payable	Cash + 5,000	Note payable + $5,000		
c. Purchased delivery truck for cash at cost of $8,000	Cash − 8,000; Delivery truck + 8,000			
d. Cleaning revenue collected in cash, $40,000	Cash + 40,000			Cleaning revenue + 40,000
e. Cleaning revenue earned in 19A, but the bill is not collected, $4,000	Accounts receivable + 4,000			Cleaning revenue +, 4,000
f. Operating expenses paid in cash, $25,800	Cash − 25,800			Operating expenses − 25,800

g. Operating expenses incurred in 19A but not paid, $2,000		Accounts payable + 2,000	Operating expenses	–	2,000
h. Paid 12% interest on the $5,000 note payable, (b) above, with cash ($5,000 × 12% = $600) ...	Cash	– 600	Interest expense	–	600
i. Depreciation expense for one year on truck ($8,000 ÷ 5 years = $1,600) ...	Truck	– 1,600	Operating expenses, depreciation	–	1,600
j. Cash dividend of $1,800 declared and paid to shareholders*	Cash	– 1,800	Retained earnings (or dividends paid)	–	1,800
k. Collected $1,000 cash on accounts receivable in (e)	Cash + Accounts receivable –	1,000 1,000			
l. Paid $500 cash on accounts payable in (g)	Cash	– 500	Accounts payable –		500
Totals (end of accounting period) ...	Total assets	$38,700	= Total liabilities	$6,500 + Total shareholders' equity	$32,200

no change

Observe how these items and their respective ending balances flow into the financial statements, Exhibit 2–2.

* A cash dividend is not an expense; it is a withdrawal of resources from the business and is paid to the owners.

Exhibit 2–2 Income statement and balance sheet illustrated

Observe that these items and their respective amounts were developed in the transaction analysis illustrated in Exhibit 2–1.

BASS CLEANERS, INC.
Income Statement
For the Year Ended December 31, 19A

Cleaning revenue ($40,000 + $4,000)		$44,000
Operating expenses ($25,800 + $2,000 + $1,600)	$29,400	
Interest expense	600	30,000
Net income		$14,000

Note: To simplify the illustration, income taxes are disregarded and operating expenses are not itemized.

BASS CLEANERS, INC.
Balance Sheet
At December 31, 19A

Assets

Cash ($20,000 + $5,000 − $8,000 + $40,000 − $25,800 − $600 − $1,800 + $1,000 − $500)		$29,300
Accounts receivable ($4,000 − $1,000)		3,000
Delivery truck		$ 8,000
Less: Accumulated depreciation		1,600	6,400
Total assets		$38,700

Liabilities

Notes payable		$ 5,000
Accounts payable ($2,000 − $500)		1,500
Total liabilities		$ 6,500

Shareholders' Equity

Contributed capital:		
Capital stock (800 no-par shares)		20,000
Retained earnings (beginning retained earnings, $–0–, plus net income, $14,000, minus dividends declared and paid, $1,800)		12,200
Total shareholders' equity		32,200
Total liabilities and shareholders' equity		$38,700

(handwritten annotations: "rightaway billed", "shows at orig. purchase")

Income statement first
then balance sheet.

Balance sheet:
- Asset
  Accounts:
    Cash
    Accounts receivable
    Delivery truck
       Accumulated depreciation

- Liability
  Accounts:
    Notes payable
    Accounts payable

- Owners' equity
  Accounts:
    Capital stock
    Retained earnings

The method used in Exhibits 2–1 and 2–2 to (*a*) record each transaction and (*b*) prepare the financial statements would be inefficient for a business that had numerous transactions. This data collection and reporting process can be facilitated in an accounting system by establishing a separate record, called an **account,** for each item included in the financial statement elements (see the five elements and the related accounts listed above for Bass Cleaners). Let's see how an account is used.

The Account

An account is a standardized format used to accumulate data about each element in order to (*a*) facilitate **preparation** of the periodic financial statements and (*b*) to provide a continuous check on the **accuracy** of the recording of transactions.

A separate account is set up for each individual asset, liability, and owners' equity[3] (including separate accounts for each kind of revenue and expense). In most accounting systems, you will find separate accounts, individually labeled, for each **asset** (such as cash, inventory, accounts receivable, equipment, land); for each **liability** (such as accounts payable, notes payable, taxes payable); and for each element of **owners' equity** (such as capital stock, sales revenue, service revenue, and various kinds of expenses). The **Cash account** for Bass Cleaners may appear as shown in Exhibit 2–3.

Now we will discuss how accounts are used to (*a*) facilitate preparation of the financial statements and (*b*) attain accuracy in the accounting system.

a. **Keeping track of the amounts for each element**—To do this, a separate account is set up for each element that will be reported on the financial

---

[3] Owners' equity usually is designated to indicate the kind of ownership arrangement used as follows:

Corporation . . . . Shareholders' equity
Sole proprietorship . . . Owner's capital
Partnership . . . . Partners' capital

Exhibit 2–3   Account (T-account format) illustrated

Cash*				
Left or Debit Side		**Right or Credit Side**		**Acct. No. 101**
(Increases)		(Decreases)		
Investment by owners	20,000	To purchase truck		8,000
Loan from bank	5,000	Operating expenses		25,800
Cleaning revenue	40,000	Interest expense		600
Collections on accounts		Dividends declared and paid		1,800
receivable	1,000	Payment on accounts payable		500
	66,000			36,700
Balance	29,300			

* The data shown in this account were taken from Exhibit 2–1.

statements. Each account is designed so that all **increases** are entered on one side (e.g., on the left side of the Cash account in Exhibit 2–3) and all **decreases** are entered on the other side (e.g., on the right side of the Cash account in Exhibit 2–3). To illustrate the increased efficiency possible, compare the list of plus and minus amounts on the cash lines of Exhibit 2–1 with the location arrangement in Exhibit 2–3. Also, imagine thousands or millions of such increases and decreases during the year in a typical business. The Cash account shown in Exhibit 2–3 reflects a left side total of $66,000 and a right side total of $36,700; the difference, $29,300, is the ending cash balance (as reported on the balance sheet in Exhibit 2–2). When the total amount on the decrease side of the Cash account is larger than the total amount on the increase side, a cash deficit (bank overdraft) is indicated. The account system is very flexible; for example, instead of being set up in the "T-account" format shown in Exhibit 2–3, it can be set up in other formats such as the columnar form shown in Exhibit 3–4. The account system can be used with either (or a combination of) handwritten, mechanical, or computerized approaches.

b. **Providing a systematic method of checking for accuracy during the recording process**—To resolve this problem, the account was designed to provide two **equalities or balances** that may be summarized as follows:

Equalities	Basis
1. Assets = Liabilities + Owners' Equity	Algebraic relationship in the fundamental accounting model
2. Debits = Credits	Algebraic relationship between account increases and decreases

These two basic equalities may be explained as follows:

First equality—Assets = Liabilities + Owners' Equity. This method is an algebraic representation of the economic position of an entity at any point in time. By definition, it always balances and can be rearranged mathematically (e.g., Assets − Liabilities = Owners' Equity). Observe in Exhibit 2–1 that the analysis of each transaction and the cumulative effects of all transactions were always in balance in terms of this algebraic model (also shown in the balance sheet in Exhibit 2–2). Thus, the first check for accuracy listed above is applied continuously throughout the accounting process as each transaction is recorded.

Second equality—Debits = Credits. In this context, it is useful to think of an account as having two sides (i.e., parts): the **left side,** which is always called the **debit** side, and the **right side,** which is always called the **credit** side. These designations were used in Exhibit 2–3.[4]

The Debits = Credits feature in accounting has an interesting history. In 1494, Pacioli (a mathematician) first described the fundamental accounting model used today. Knowing the importance of accuracy, and after designing the T-account (similar to that illustrated in Exhibit 2–3), Pacioli applied an algebraic concept that has proven to be of great significance in minimizing errors in the accounting process. The fundamental accounting model, **Assets = Liabilities + Owners' Equity,** is an algebraic model that has mathematical equality. Pacioli added another algebraic balance feature to the basic model to minimize errors in recording increases and decreases in each account. Let's see how it was done.

Pacioli perceived that having designed the T-account with two sides to reflect increases and decreases, he could add another algebraic **balancing feature** by simply **reversing** the position in the account of the "increases" and "decreases" on the **opposite sides** of the basic accounting model. This second algebraic balance feature is still used today; it has the "+" and "−" **in reverse order** on the opposite sides of the accounting model in this way:

Assets		=	Liabilities		+	Owners' Equity	
Debit	Credit		Debit	Credit		Debit	Credit
+	−		−	+		−	+

Notice that **debit** always refers to the left side of an account and **credit** always refers to the right side of an account. Thus, debit and credit positions do not change; only the plus and minus signs change positions. The addition of this algebraic concept resulted in the second "balancing" feature, that is, **debits**

[4] Handwritten or manually maintained accounts in the formats shown here are used in small businesses. Highly mechanized and computerized systems retain the concept of the account but not this format. T-accounts are useful primarily for instructional purposes.

always should equal credits. Thus, the system used for recording increases and decreases in the accounts may be tabulated as follows:[5]

	Increases	Decreases
Assets	Debit	Credit
Liabilities	Credit	Debit
Owners' equity	Credit	Debit

Debits and Credits for Revenues and Expenses

After some practice you will become comfortable using the words **debit** and **credit** to signify changes in assets, liabilities, and owners' equity accounts. However, some persons are confused about the proper terms to reflect changes in revenue and expense accounts. Remember that owners' equity is increased by credits and decreased by debits. Revenues increase owners' equity; therefore, **revenues are recorded as credits.**

Expenses decrease owners' equity; therefore, **expenses are recorded as debits.** In other words, the debit-credit relationship for owners' equity accounts is applied to revenues and expenses, as illustrated in the following T-accounts:[6]

Expenses*		Owners' Equity		Revenue†	
Debit	Credit	Debit	Credit	Debit	Credit
(To record)		−	+		(to record)

* Decrease in owners' equity.
† Increase in owners' equity.

In summary, the balance features of the fundamental accounting model are:

1. Assets = Liabilities + Owners' Equity.
2. Debits = Credits.

The next section of this chapter illustrates the use of accounts and emphasizes application of the fundamental accounting model and its dual-balancing feature.

---

[5] Historically, and today, accountants refer to the left side as the debit side and to the right side as the credit side. For accounting purposes, the terms **debit** and **credit** have no other meanings. The words **to debit** and **to credit** should not be confused with "increase" or "decrease" as will become clear in the next few paragraphs. Contrary to what some people think, there is no implication of "goodness" attached to credits or "badness" attached to debits (or vice versa).

[6] To "charge an account" is a frequently used expression meaning to **debit** an account. Thus, the word *debit* is used as both a verb and a noun.

Transaction Analysis

Transaction analysis is a term frequently used to describe the process of studying a transaction to determine its dual effect on the entity in terms of the accounting model. Transaction analysis starts when a business document is available that indicates a completed transaction. Based upon the (*a*) nature of the transaction and (*b*) proper application of the fundamental accounting model, the effects of the transaction are recorded in the accounting system.

Application of the fundamental accounting model and accounting principles require that **accrual basis accounting** be used. This means that assets, liabilities, revenues, expenses, and the other elements should be recognized (i.e., recorded) when the transaction that caused them was completed. The related cash collected or paid at a later date is recorded as a separate transaction. For example, a sale made on the last day of Year 1, with 30-day credit terms, must be recorded in Year 1, and the cash collection must be recorded in Year 2. In contrast, **cash basis accounting,** which is not appropriate, would record the sale only in Year 2 when the cash is collected. In contrast, the concept of accrual accounting requires that revenues and expenses be measured and reported in the accounting period in which the transactions occur rather than when the related cash is received or paid.

Now, let's see how **each transaction** is subjected to transaction analysis to determine (1) its dual economic effect on the entity and (2) how that dual effect is recorded in the accounts (i.e., in terms of the fundamental accounting model).

Recall that for each transaction recorded, **two separate balances** must be maintained: (1) Assets = Liabilities + Owners' Equity, and (2) Debits = Credits.

Transaction Analysis and Recording

Bass Cleaners, Inc., will be used again to demonstrate transaction analysis and the basic recording process. We analyze each transaction (given in Exhibit 2–1) and trace the manner in which the dual effect is recorded in the accounting model by using T-accounts (rather than using the simple plus and minus signs shown in Exhibit 2–1). The transactions (repeated for convenience) are identified with letters for ready reference.

For each transaction, Exhibit 2–4 gives its (*a*) nature, (*b*) analysis, (*c*) journal entry, and (*d*) T-account effect. The **journal entry** is an accounting method of expressing the results of transaction analysis in a Debits = Credits format. Notice that for each transaction (*a*) the debits are written first, (*b*) the credits are written below all of the debits, and (*c*) the credits are indented (both words and amounts).

You should study Exhibit 2–4 carefully (including the explanations of transaction analysis). Careful study is essential to understand (*a*) application of the fundamental accounting model, (*b*) transaction analysis, (*c*) recording the dual

Exhibit 2–4 Transaction analysis, journal entries, and T-accounts illustrated, Bass Cleaners, Inc.

BASS CLEANERS, INC.

a. Received $20,000 cash invested by the four owners and in turn issued 800 no-par shares of capital stock.

Transaction analysis—This transaction increased the company's cash by $20,000, which is recorded in the **Cash** account as a debit (increase); liabilities were unaffected; and owners' equity was increased by $20,000, which is recorded in the **Capital Stock** account as a credit (increase). The journal entry (recording) in the accounting system may be summarized conveniently in what often is called a **journal entry**. This format lists the **debit** first—account name and amount—then lists the credit—account name and amount (which is indented for clarity).

Journal Entry

	Debit	Credit
(a) Cash (asset)	20,000	
Capital stock (owners' equity)		20,000

The two T-accounts would appear as follows:

Cash (asset)		Capital Stock (owners' equity)	
Debit	Credit	Debit	Credit
(a) 20,000			(a) 20,000

Dual check for accuracy—The entry meets both tests: Assets (+$20,000) = Liabilities (–0–) + Owners' Equity (+$20,000), and Debits ($20,000) = Credits ($20,000).

b. Borrowed $5,000 cash from the bank on a 12% interest-bearing note payable.

Transaction analysis—This transaction increased cash by $5,000, which is recorded in the **Cash** account as a debit (increase); liabilities were increased by $5,000, which is recorded in the **Notes Payable** account as a credit (increase); and owners' equity was not changed. The journal entry may be summarized as follows:

	Debit	Credit
(b) Cash (asset)	5,000	
Note payable (liability)		5,000

The accounts affected would appear as follows (new items are boxed):

Cash (asset)		Notes Payable (liability)	
Debit	Credit	Debit	Credit
(a) 20,000			(b) 5,000
(b) 5,000			

Dual check for accuracy—The entry meets both tests: Assets (+$5,000) = Liabilities (+$5,000) + Owners' Equity (–0–), and Debits ($5,000) = Credits ($5,000).

Exhibit 2–4 *(continued)*

---

c. **Purchased a delivery truck for cash at a cost of $8,000.**

Transaction analysis—This transaction increased the asset, **Delivery Truck,** by $8,000, which is recorded in that asset account as a debit (increase); and the cash was decreased by $8,000, which is recorded in the asset account **Cash** as a credit (decrease). Liabilities and owners' equity were not affected. The journal entry may be summarized as follows:

(*c*) Delivery truck (asset) 8,000
        Cash (asset) 8,000

The two accounts affected would appear as follows:

Delivery Truck (asset)				Cash (asset)			
	Debit		Credit		Debit		Credit
(*c*)	8,000			(*a*)	20,000	(*c*)	8,000
				(*b*)	5,000		

Dual check for accuracy—The entry meets both tests: Assets (delivery truck, + $8,000, and cash, − $8,000) = Liabilities (–0–) + Owners' Equity (–0–), and Debits ($8,000) = Credits ($8,000).

d. **Cleaning revenue earned and collected in cash, $40,000.**

Transaction analysis—This transaction increased cash by $40,000, which is recorded in the asset account **Cash** as a debit (increase); liabilities were not affected; and owners' equity was increased by $40,000 as a result of earning revenue. Owners' equity is credited (increased) for $40,000. A separate owners' equity account, **Cleaning Revenue,** is used to keep track of this particular revenue. The journal entry may be summarized as follows:

(*d*) Cash (asset) 40,000
        Cleaning revenue (owners' equity) 40,000

The two accounts affected would appear as follows:

Cash (asset)				Cleaning Revenue (owners' equity)			
	Debit		Credit		Debit		Credit
(*a*)	20,000	(*c*)	8,000			(*d*)	40,000
(*b*)	5,000						
(*d*)	40,000						

Dual check for accuracy—The entry meets both tests: Assets (+ $40,000) = Liabilities (–0–) + Owners' Equity (+ $40,000), and Debits ($40,000) = Credits ($40,000).

Exhibit 2–4 *(continued)*

e. **Cleaning revenue earned, but the cash was not yet collected, $4,000.**

Transaction analysis—This transaction increased the company's asset, **Accounts Receivable,** by $4,000, which is recorded as a debit (increase) to that account; liabilities were not affected; and owners' equity was increased by $4,000. Owners' equity is credited (increased) by $4,000 using a separate account, **Cleaning Revenue,** which is used to keep track of this particular revenue. The journal entry may be summarized as follows:

(*e*) Accounts receivable (asset)   4,000
      Cleaning revenue (owners' equity)   4,000

The effect on the two accounts would appear as follows:

Accounts Receivable (asset)		Cleaning Revenue (owners' equity)	
Debit	Credit	Debit	Credit
(*e*) 4,000		(*d*) 40,000	
		(*e*) 4,000	

Dual check for accuracy—The entry meets both tests: Assets (+$4,000) = Liabilities (–0–) + Owners' Equity (+$4,000), and Debits ($4,000) = Credits ($4,000).

f. **Expenses incurred and paid in cash, $25,800.**

Transaction analysis—This transaction decreased cash by $25,800, which is recorded in the **Cash** account as a credit (decrease); liabilities were not affected; and owners' equity was decreased by $25,800 as a result of paying expenses. Owners' equity is decreased by debiting a separate account **Operating Expenses,** which is used to keep track of this particular type of expense. The journal entry may be summarized as follows:

(*f*) Operating expenses (owners' equity)   25,800
      Cash (asset)   25,800

The effect on the two accounts would appear as follows:

Operating Expenses (owners' equity)		Cash (asset)			
Debit	Credit	Debit		Credit	
(*f*) 25,800		(*a*) 20,000	(*c*) 8,000		
		(*b*) 5,000	(*f*) 25,800		
		(*d*) 40,000			

Dual check for accuracy—The entry meets both tests.

Exhibit 2–4 *(continued)*

---

g. **Expenses incurred, but the cash not yet paid, $2,000.**

   Transaction analysis—This transaction did not affect the company's assets; liabilities were increased by $2,000, which is recorded as a credit (increase) to **Accounts Payable;** and owners' equity was decreased $2,000 by debiting a separate account, **Operating Expenses,** which is used to keep track of this particular type of expense. The journal entry summarized is:

   (*g*) Operating expenses (owners' equity)   2,000
          Accounts payable (liability)   2,000

The two accounts affected would appear as follows:

Operating Expenses (owners' equity)		**Accounts Payable (liability)**	
Debit	Credit	Debit	Credit
(*f*) 25,800			(*g*) 2,000
(*g*) 2,000			

Dual check for accuracy—The entry meets both tests.

h. **Paid cash interest incurred on note payable in (*b*) ($5,000 × 12% = $600).**

   Transaction analysis—This transaction decreased cash by $600, which is recorded as a credit (decrease) in the **Cash** account; the principal amount of the related liability ($5,000) was not changed; however, owners' equity was decreased by the amount of the interest ($600) because the payment of interest (but not the principal of the note) represents an expense. Owners' equity is decreased by debiting a separate account, **Interest Expense,** which is used to keep track of this particular type of expense. The journal entry summarized is:

   (*h*) Interest expense (owners' equity)   600
          Cash (asset)   600

The two accounts affected would appear as follows:

Interest Expense (owners' equity)		**Cash (asset)**	
Debit	Credit	Debit	Credit
(*h*) 600		(*a*) 20,000	(*c*) 8,000
		(*b*) 5,000	(*f*) 25,800
		(*d*) 40,000	(*h*) 600

Dual check for accuracy—The entry meets both tests.

Exhibit 2–4 *(continued)*

> ***i*. Depreciation expense on the truck for one year ($8,000 ÷ 5 years = $1,600).**
>
> Transaction analysis—This transaction is caused by the **internal** use (wear and tear) of an asset owned for operating purposes (rather than for resale). This use is measured in dollars and recorded as depreciation expense. Owners' equity was decreased by this expense, which is recorded as a debit to a separate account for this type of expense, **Operating Expenses** (alternatively, a separate expense account, called depreciation expense, could have been used). Assets (i.e., the delivery truck) were decreased because a part of the cost of the asset was "used up" in operations. Instead of directly crediting (decreasing) the asset account, Delivery Truck, a related **contra account, Accumulated Depreciation, Delivery Truck,** is credited so that the total amount of depreciation can be kept separate from the cost of the asset. This procedure will be explained and illustrated in detail in Chapter 9. The journal entry summarized is:
>
> (*i*) Operating expenses (owners' equity) 1,600
>   Accumulated depreciation, delivery truck
>   (contra account) 1,600
>
> The two accounts affected would appear as follows:

	Operating Expenses (owners' equity)		Accumulated Depreciation, Delivery Truck (contra account)	
	Debit	Credit	Debit	Credit
(*f*)	25,800			
(*g*)	2,000			
(*i*)	1,600		(*i*)	1,600

> Dual check for accuracy—The entry meets both tests: Assets (−$1,600) = Liabilities (–0–) + Owners' Equity (−$1,600), and Debits ($1,600) = Credits ($1,600).

[handwritten in margin: Contra acct has]

effects of each transaction, and (*d*) the dual-balancing system. Exhibit 2–4 emphasizes these important aspects of the accounting processing system. Notice that the amounts for each additional entry illustrated are shown in boxes to facilitate your study of this exhibit.

In summary, Exhibit 2–4 presented the following features of an accounting system:

1. **Collecting information about each completed transaction** that is necessary for accounting purposes.
2. **Analyzing each transaction** to determine how it affected the fundamental accounting model—Assets = Liabilities + Owners' Equity.

Exhibit 2–4 *(continued)*

j. Declared and paid cash dividends to shareholders, $1,800.

Transaction analysis—This transaction decreased the company's cash by $1,800, which is recorded in the **Cash** account as a credit (decrease); liabilities were unaffected; owners' equity was decreased by $1,800 as a result of the resources (cash) paid out of the business to the shareholders. Owners' equity is debited (decreased) by using a separate account, **Retained Earnings,** which is used to keep track of this kind of decrease in owners' equity (and certain increases explained later). Dividends declared and paid decrease owners' equity but do not represent an expense (which also decreases owners' equity), rather dividends represent a cash distribution of "earnings" to the owners. The journal entry summarized is:

(*j*) Retained earnings (or dividends paid)   1,800
        Cash (asset)   1,800

The two accounts would appear as follows:

Retained Earnings (owners' equity)				**Cash (asset)**			
Debit		Credit		Debit		Credit	
(*j*)	1,800			(*a*)	20,000	(*c*)	8,000
				(*b*)	5,000	(*f*)	25,800
				(*d*)	40,000	(*h*)	600
						(*j*)	1,800

Dual check for accuracy—The entry meets both tests.

k. Collected $1,000 cash on accounts receivable in (e).

Transaction analysis—This transaction increased the asset cash by $1,000, which is recorded as a debit (increase) in the **Cash** account; another asset, **Accounts Receivable,** was decreased, which is recorded as a credit (decrease) of $1,000. Liabilities and owners' equity were not affected because there was a change in two assets with no change in total assets. The journal entry summarized is:

(*k*) Cash (asset)   1,000
        Accounts receivable (asset)   1,000

The two accounts would appear as follows:

Cash (asset)				**Accounts Receivable (asset)**			
Debit		Credit		Debit		Credit	
(*a*)	20,000	(*c*)	8,000	(*e*)	4,000	(*k*)	1,000
(*b*)	5,000	(*f*)	25,800				
(*d*)	40,000	(*h*)	600				
(*k*)	1,000	(*j*)	1,800				

Dual check for accuracy—The entry meets both tests.

Exhibit 2–4 *(concluded)*

l. **Paid $500 cash on accounts payable in** *(g)*.

Transaction analysis—This transaction decreased cash by $500, which is recorded as a credit (decrease) in the **Cash** account; the $500 decrease in liabilities is recorded as a debit (decrease) to the **Accounts Payable** account. Owners' equity was not affected because there was no revenue or expense involved in this transaction. The journal entry summarized is:

(*l*) Accounts payable (liability)   500
　　　　Cash (asset)   500

The two accounts would appear as follows:

Accounts Payable (liability)				Cash (asset)			
Debit		Credit		Debit		Credit	
(*l*)	500	(*g*)	2,000	(*a*)	20,000	(*c*)	8,000
				(*b*)	5,000	(*f*)	25,800
				(*d*)	40,000	(*h*)	600
				(*k*)	1,000	(*j*)	1,800
						(*l*)	500

Dual check for accuracy—The entry meets both tests.

For further illustration purposes, all of the above accounts are repeated in Exhibit 3–3 with their respective balances (i.e., the total increases minus the total decreases in each account) shown in Exhibit 3–5.

3. **Recording the effects of transactions is accomplished in the "journal entry format"** commonly used in accounting as follows:

Account name (debit) xx
　　　Account name (credit)   xx

4. **Showing the effects in T-accounts** which provide for increases and decreases in each account as follows:

Assets		=	Liabilities		+	Owners' Equity	
(Debit)	(Credit)		(Debit)	(Credit)		(Debit)	(Credit)
+	−		−	+		−	+

5. **Preparing periodic financial statements** from the data accumulated in the accounts (discussed in Chapter 3).

DEMONSTRATION CASE

On January 1, 19A, an ambitious university student started the ABC Service Company. The primary purpose was to earn money to complete a university education. Completed transactions (summarized) through December 31, 19A, for ABC Service Company (a sole proprietorship) were:

 a. Invested $5,000 cash in the business.
 b. Purchased service supplies, $600; paid cash. These supplies were placed in a storeroom to be used as needed.
 c. Revenues earned, $32,000, collected in cash, except for $2,000 on credit.
 d. Operating expenses incurred, $17,000; paid cash except for $1,000 on credit.
 e. Used $500 of the service supplies from the storeroom for operating purposes.
 f. Owner withdrew $3,000 cash from the business.
 g. At year-end purchased a tract of land for a future building site. Paid cash, $2,000, and gave a $5,000, 10%, interest-bearing note payable for the balance.

Requirement 1:
Set up T-accounts for Cash, Accounts Receivable (for services on credit); Service Supplies (for supplies on hand in the storeroom); Land; Accounts Payable (for operating expenses procured on credit); Note Payable; Owner's Equity; Service Revenues; and Operating Expenses. Next, analyze each transaction, prepare journal entries, and then enter the effects on the fundamental accounting model in the appropriate T-accounts. Identify each amount with its letter given above.

Requirement 2:
Refer to the three financial statements illustrated in Chapter 1: income statement (Exhibit 1–4); balance sheet (Exhibit 1–5); and the statement of changes in financial position (Exhibit 1–6). Use the **amounts in the T-accounts,** prepared in Requirement 1, to prepare these three 19A statements for ABC Service Company. The solutions to these two requirements are shown in Exhibit 2–5.

 Preparation of the 19A **income statement** involved selection of the **account balances** for all revenues and expenses. The **income statement model** (page 60) is applied—Revenues – Expenses = Net Income.
 The 19A **balance sheet** required use of the **account balances** for **all** assets and liabilities. The **balance sheet model** (page 60) is applied—Assets = Liabilities + Owners' Equity. Notice that owner's equity includes the net income amount ($14,500) reported on the income statement because it increased owner's equity.
 The 19A statement of changes in financial position requires an analysis of the Cash account. The model for this statement (page 29)—Cash sources (inflows) from operations and financing and investing activities – Cash uses (outflows)

Exhibit 2–5 Transaction analysis, journal entries, T-accounts, and financial statements—
a demonstration case

Requirement 1—Transaction analysis and journal entries:

a. Increase cash, $5,000; increase owner's equity account, $5,000.

Journal entry:

Cash	5,000	
Owner's equity		5,000

b. Increase asset, service supplies, $600; decrease cash, $600 (supplies are not an expense until used).

Journal entry:

Service supplies	600	
Cash		600

c. Increase assets, cash, $30,000, and accounts receivable, $2,000; increase service revenues (an owner's equity account), $32,000.

Journal entry:

Cash	30,000	
Accounts receivable	2,000	
Service revenues		32,000

d. Decrease asset, cash, $16,000; increase liability, accounts payable, $1,000; increase operating expenses, $17,000 (which decreases owner's equity).

Journal entry:

Operating expenses	17,000	
Cash		16,000
Accounts payable		1,000

e. Decrease asset, service supplies, $500; increase operating expenses, $500 (which decreases owner's equity).

Journal entry:

Operating expenses	500	
Service supplies		500

f. Decrease asset, cash, $3,000; decrease owner's equity account, $3,000.

Journal entry:

Owner's equity	3,000	
Cash		3,000

g. Increase assets, land, $7,000; decrease asset, cash, $2,000; increase liability, note payable, $5,000.

Journal entry:

Land	7,000	
Cash		2,000
Note payable		5,000

Exhibit 2–5 *(continued)*

T-accounts:

Cash

(a)	5,000	(b)	600
(c)	30,000	(d)	16,000
		(f)	3,000
		(g)	2,000
Balance	13,400		

Accounts Receivable

(c)	2,000		
Balance	2,000		

Service Supplies

(b)	600	(e)	500
Balance	100		

Land

(g)	7,000		
Balance	7,000		

Accounts Payable

(d)	1,000		
		Balance	1,000

Note Payable

		(g)	5,000
		Balance	5,000

Owner's Equity Account

(f)	3,000	(a)	5,000
		Balance	2,000

Service Revenues

		(c)	32,000
		Balance	32,000

Operating Expenses

(d)	17,000		
(e)	500		
Balance	17,500		

Requirement 2—Periodic financial statements:

ABC SERVICE COMPANY
Income Statement
For the Year Ended December 31, 19A

Revenues:
    Service revenues $32,000

Expenses:
    Operating expenses 17,500

Net income $14,500

Exhibit 2–5 (concluded)

ABC SERVICE COMPANY
Balance Sheet
At December 31, 19A

Assets		Liabilities	
Cash	$13,400	Accounts payable	$ 1,000
Accounts receivable	2,000	Note payable	5,000
Service supplies	100	Total liabilities	6,000
Land	7,000		

		Owner's Equity	
		Owner's equity account ...... $ 2,000	
		Net income (Req. 2) 14,500	
		Total owner's equity	16,500
		Total liabilities and owner's	
Total assets	$22,500	equity	$22,500

ABC SERVICE COMPANY
Statement of Changes in Financial Position, Cash Basis
For the Year Ended December 31, 19A

Sources of cash (inflows):
  From operations:

Revenues	$30,000
Less: Cash used for expenses ($16,000 + $600)	16,600
Cash inflow from operations	13,400

  From financing:

Investment by owner (cash)	5,000
Total cash sources during the year (inflows)	18,400

Uses of cash (outflows):

For financing—to pay cash to owner (withdrawals)	$3,000	
For investing—to pay on land purchased	2,000	
Total cash used during the year (outflows)		5,000
Change: Increase in cash during the year		$13,400*

* Agrees with the increase in cash from a beginning zero balance to $13,400 on the balance sheet above.

---

for investing and financing activities = Net change in cash (increase or decrease). Notice two aspects of this statement:

a. **Net cash** inflow from continuing operations must be reported as the difference between cash received from revenues $30,000 (which excludes revenues on credit) and cash paid for expenses ($16,000 plus the $600 cash paid for the supplies, even though some of them have not yet been used).

    b. **Uses of cash** include the $2,000 cash paid on the $7,000 cost of the land (investing) because the remaining $5,000 was on credit, and the $3,000 withdrawn by the owner for personal use (financing).

Some Misconceptions

Some people confuse a bookkeeper with an accountant and bookkeeping with accounting. In effect, they confuse one of the parts with the whole of accounting. Bookkeeping involves the routine and clerical part of accounting and requires only minimal knowledge of the accounting model and its application. A bookkeeper may record the repetitive and uncomplicated transactions in most businesses and may maintain the simple records of a small business. In contrast, the accountant is a highly trained professional competent in the design of information systems, analysis of complex transactions and economic events, interpretation and analysis of financial data, financial reporting, financial advising, auditing, taxation, and management consulting.

    Another prevalent misconception is that all of the financial affairs of an entity are subject to precise and objective measurement each period and that the accounting results reported in the financial statements are exactly what happened that period. In contrast, accounting numbers are influenced by estimates as illustrated in subsequent chapters. Many people believe that accounting should measure and report the market value of the entity (including its assets), but accounting does not attempt to do this. To understand financial statements and to interpret them wisely for use in decision making, the user must be aware of their limitations as well as their usefulness. One should understand what the financial statements do and do not try to accomplish.

    Finally, financial statements are often thought to be inflexible because of their quantitative nature. As you study accounting, you will learn that it requires considerable **professional judgment in application** on the part of the accountant to capture the economic essence of complex transactions. Thus, accounting is stimulating intellectually; it is not a cut-and-dried subject. Rather, it calls upon your intelligence, analytical ability, creativity, and judgment. Accounting is a communication process involving an audience (users) with a wide diversity of knowledge, interest, and capabilities; therefore, it will call upon your ability as a communicator. The language of accounting uses concisely written phrases and symbols to convey information about the resource flows measured for specific organizations.

    As you study accounting and later as a decision maker, you must be wary of these misconceptions. To understand financial statements and to be able to interpret the "figures" wisely, you must have a certain level of knowledge of the concepts and the measurement procedures used in the accounting process. You should learn what accounting "is really like" and appreciate the reasons for using certain procedures. This level of knowledge cannot be gained by reading a list of the "concepts" and a list of the misconceptions. Neither can a generalized discussion of the subject matter suffice. A certain amount of involvement, primarily problem solving (similar to the requirement in mathematics courses), is essential in the study of accounting focused on the needs of the user. Therefore, we provide problems aimed at the desirable knowledge level for the user (as well as the preparer) of financial statements.

SUMMARY OF CHAPTER

This chapter discussed the **fundamental accounting model** and illustrated its application in the accounting system for a business. For accounting purposes, transactions were defined as (*a*) exchanges between the business and other individuals and organizations, and (*b*) certain events that exert a direct effect on the entity (such as a fire loss), and events caused by the passage of time (such as depreciation of a building).

Application of the model—Assets = Liabilities + Owners' Equity—was illustrated for a small business. The application involved: (*a*) transaction analysis, (*b*) journal entries, and (*c*) the accounts (T-account format).

An extended illustration, Exhibit 2–4, was presented. This exhibit demonstrated that each transaction caused at least two different accounts to be affected because the economic position of the entity in terms of the fundamental accounting model—Assets = Liabilities + Owners' Equity—always has a dual effect. This characteristic of the model is the reason its application often is referred to as a **double-entry** system.

The fundamental accounting model and the mechanics of the debit-credit concept in T-account format can be summarized as follows, where + means increase and − means decrease:

Assets		=	Liabilities		+	Owners' Equity	
Debit	Credit		Debit	Credit		Debit	Credit
+	−		−	+		−	+

Revenue (increase in owners' equity)	
Debit	Credit
	(To record)

Expenses (decrease in owners' equity)	
Debit	Credit
(To record)	

An increase in **revenue** (a credit) represents an **increase** in owners' equity. When a revenue is earned, the resources (i.e., assets) of the business are increased (or liabilities may be decreased), and because of the dual effect, owners' equity is increased by the same amount. In contrast, when an **expense** is incurred, the net resources of the business are decreased (i.e., assets are decreased and/or liabilities increased), and because of the dual effect, owners' equity is decreased by the same amount.

IMPORTANT TERMS DEFINED IN THIS CHAPTER

Account A standardized format used to accumulate data about each financial statement element. It provides for recording increases and decreases in these elements caused by transactions. *p. 61*

Accrual Basis Accounting All financial statement elements—assets, liabilities, revenues, expenses, etc.—are recognized (recorded) when the related transaction occurs. In contrast, cash basis accounting is not appropriate because it recognizes **only** cash transactions. *p. 65*

Business (Source) Document A document that evidences (supports) a business transaction. *p. 56*

Cash Basis Accounting See accrual basis accounting. *p. 65*

Debits and Credits Debit is the name for the left side of a T-account. Debits represent increases in assets and decreases in liabilities and owners' equity. Credit is the name for the right side of a T-account. Credits represent decreases in assets and increases in liabilities and owners' equity. *p. 63*

Elements of Financial Statements Items that are reported on financial statements, such as revenues, expenses, assets, liabilities, and owners' equity. *p. 57*

Journal Entry An accounting method of expressing the results of transaction analysis in a Debits = Credits format. *p. 65*

Periodic Financial Statements The financial statements that must be prepared each reporting period for external parties—balance sheet, income statement, and statement of changes in financial position. *p. 56*

Transaction An exchange between a business and one or more external parties and certain other events, such as a fire loss. *p. 55*

Transaction Analysis The process of studying a completed transaction to determine its economic effect on a business in terms of the fundamental accounting model: Assets = Liabilities + Owners' Equity. *p. 65*

QUESTIONS

1. Give (*a*) the fundamental accounting model and (*b*) define each of its elements.
2. Assume your personal financial condition at the beginning of a year is assets, $30,000; and debts, $20,000. You pay a $10,000 debt plus 12% interest for the year. Show how your personal financial condition will change at the end of the year in terms of the fundamental accounting model.

30,000·

3. Define a business transaction in the broad sense and give an example of the two different kinds of transactions.

4. Explain why owners' equity is increased by revenues and decreased by expenses.

5. Demonstrate the dual effect on the fundamental accounting model of (*a*) a cash sale of services for $1,000 and (*b*) a cash payment of $300 for office rent for the business.

6. Explain what the "separate-entity assumption" means in accounting.

7. What are the owners of a business organized as a corporation called? What is the basis for this name?

8. Explain why a "business document" is important in accounting for a business entity.

9. At December 31, 19A (end of year 1), the fundamental accounting model for YOUR Company showed the following: owners' equity, $70,000; and liabilities, $20,000.
   a. Show how YOUR Company stands in terms of the fundamental accounting model.
   b. Show the summarized balance sheet.

10. For accounting purposes, what is an "account"? Explain why accounts are used in an accounting system.

11. Explain what debit and credit mean.

12. Explain why revenues are recorded as credits and expenses as debits.

13. What is meant by the "two equalities" in accounting?

14. Complete the following matrix by entering either debit or credit in each cell.

Item	Increases	Decreases
Assets	*Debit*	*Credit*
Liabilities	*Credit*	*Deb*
Owners' equity	*Credit*	*Deb.*
Revenues		
Expenses		

15. Complete the following matrix by entering either increases or decreases in each cell.

Item	Debit	Credit
Assets		
Liabilities		
Owners' equity		
Revenues		
Expenses		

16. Briefly explain what is meant by transaction analysis.
17. Define accrual accounting. Contrast it with cash basis accounting.
18. What is a T-account? What is its purpose?
19. What is a "journal entry"?
20. Assume you and a friend started a new business called Y and M Corporation. Each of you invested $10,000. Give the effect of this transaction on the company in terms of:
    a. The fundamental accounting model.
    b. A journal entry.
    c. How it is shown in the T-accounts.
21. Complete the following tabulation:

Transaction	Assets	Liabilities	Owners' Equity
a. Investment of cash by organizers, $15,000	15,000		15000
b. Borrowed cash, $4,000	4000	4,000	4000
c. Sold goods for cash, $8,000	8000	8000	8000
d. Paid expenses, $6,000, cash	6000	6000	6000
e. Purchased equipment, $9,000, cash	9000	9,000	9000
Ending balances	19000	25000	42000

22. XR Company paid a $10,000, 12%, one-year note on the due date. Show how this transaction would affect the fundamental accounting model.

EXERCISES

E2–1   (Learning Terminology)

Match the items listed under Terminology with the descriptions by entering letters in the spaces provided.

Terminology	Description
__C__ (1) (Example) Separate-entity assumption	A. Liabilities + Owners' Equity.
__F__ (2) Business document	B. Reports assets, liabilities, and owners' equity.
____ (3) Credits	C. Accounts for a business separate from its owners.
____ (4) Assets	
____ (5) Elements of financial statements	D. Increase assets; decrease liabilities and owners' equity.
__E__ (6) Transaction	E. An exchange between an entity and other parties.
__B__ (7) Income statement	F. Evidence of a completed transaction.

Terminology	Description
_____ (8) T-account	G. Decrease assets; increase liabilities and owners' equity.
_____ (9) Balance sheet	H. Reports revenues, expenses, and net income.
_____ (10) Debits	I. Items reported on the financial statements.
	J. A standardized format used to accumulate data about each element reported on financial statements.

E2–2   (Fundamental Accounting Model—Personal)

You have just finished the university and have been working for CC Business for one month. At the start of the month your financial situation was shown in the following schedule. You are to complete the schedule by "recording" your transactions summarized in the first column and indicating your ending financial position on the last line.

Transactions	Assets	Liabilities	Owners' Equity
a. Beginning (personal items, including your rather "used" auto).	$2,000	$800	$1,200
b. Borrowed $1,000 to "get through" the first month.	1000	⊖	1000
c. Paid rent on apartment, $500.	−500	⊖	−500
d. Paid deposits with telephone and electricity companies, $200.	−200	⊖	200
e. Personal expenses; food, cleaning, etc., $700.			
f. Auto payment, $400 (including $10 interest).			
g. Trip to visit a "special" person, $300.			
h. Received a "gift" from your family, $150 cash.			
i. You gave your date a special present, $50.			
j. You received your first pay cheque (net of deductions), $1,400.			
k. Your ending financial position.			

E2–3   (Use of T-accounts; Summarize the Results)

Small Company has been operating one year (19A). At the start of 19B, its T-accounts were:

Assets:

Cash	Accounts Receivable	Land
5,000	1,000	2,000

Liabilities:

Accounts Payable		Note Payable		Income Tax Payable	
	500		400		100

Owners' Equity		Revenues		Expenses	
	7,000				

Required:

1. Enter the following 19B transactions in the T-accounts:
   a. Paid the income tax.
   b. Collected the accounts receivable.
   c. Paid the accounts payable.
   d. Revenue earned,$30,000; including 10% on credit.*
   e. Expenses incurred, $18,000; including $2,000 on credit.*
   *Hint: Each of these transactions will affect three accounts.

2. Respond to the following by using data from the T-accounts:

   a. On January 1, 19B, amounts for the following were:
      Assets, $_____ = Liabilities, $_____ + Owners' Equity, $_____.

   b. Net income for 19B was $_____.

   c. On December 31, 19B, amounts for the following were:
      Assets, $_____ = Liabilities, $_____ + Owners' Equity $_____.

3. Complete the following schedule at December 31, 19B:

Accounts	Assets	Liabilities	Owners' Equity
Cash	$	$	$
Accounts receivable			
Land			
Accounts payable			
Note payable			
Income tax payable			
Owners' equity			
Total assets	$		
Total liabilities		$	
Total owners' equity			$

E2–4   **(Learning Terminology)**
Match each item listed under Terminology with its appropriate description by entering letters in the space provided.

Terminology	Description
__D__ (1) (Example) Journal entry	A. Fundamental accounting model.
____ (2) Note payable	B. Three required periodic financial statements.
____ (3) Assets = Liabilities + Owners' Equity	C. The two equalities in accounting that aid in providing accuracy.
____ (4) Expenses	D. An accounting method of expressing the results of transaction analysis.
____ (5) Accounts payable	E. The account that is credited when money is borrowed from a bank.
____ (6) A = L + OE, and Debits = Credits	F. The account that is credited when a sale is made.
____ (7) Balance sheet, income statement, statement of changes in financial position	G. The account that is debited when an expense is incurred.
	H. The account that is debited when a credit sale is made.
____ (8) Revenues	I. The account that is credited when an expense is incurred on credit.
____ (9) Accounts receivable	J. Application of the fundamental accounting model—Assets = Liabilities + Owners' Equity.
____ (10) Double-entry system	

E2–5   **(Preparing Simple Journal Entries)**
Use the space provided to express the results of your transaction analysis for each of the following six transactions. Use only the journal entry format.

a. Example: Three investors organized XT Corporation, and each one invested $20,000 cash.

Cash ($20,000 × 3)	60,000	
Shareholders' equity		60,000

b. Borrowed $5,000 cash and signed a 10% note.
c. Earned revenues, $40,000 of which $4,000 was on credit.
d. Incurred expenses, $25,000, of which $3,000 was on credit.
e. Paid a debt, accounts payable, $1,000.
f. Collected an amount due, accounts receivable, $2,000.
g. Paid cash interest on note payable, $500.

E2–6   **(Balance Sheet, Income Statement, and Cash Flow Relationships)**
Small Corporation has been operating for one year, 19A. At the end of 19A, the financial statements have been prepared. Below are a series of independent cases based on the 19A

financial statements. For each independent case and the financial relationship it relates to, you are to supply the missing item and its amount.

Case	Data	Missing Item	Missing Amount
		Item	Amount
Example	Assets, $70,000; owners' equity, $20,000	Liabilities	$50,000
A	Revenues, $100,000; expenses, $60,000		
B	Liabilities, $30,000; owners' equity, $52,000		
C	Cash inflows, $80,000; increase in cash, $50,000		
D	Liabilities, $40,000; assets, $80,000		
E	Net income, $35,000; expenses, $60,000		
F	Net income, $20,000; revenues, $95,000		
G	Expenses, $80,000; revenues, $80,000		
H	Revenues, $80,000; expenses, $95,000		
I	Increase in cash, $20,000; cash outflows, $60,000		
J	Cash outflows, $60,000; cash inflows, $50,000		

E2-7 **(Transaction Analysis—Nonquantitative)**

For each transaction given below indicate the effect upon assets, liabilities, and owners' equity by entering a plus for increase and a minus for decrease.

Transaction	Effect on Assets	Effect on Liabilities	Effect on Owners' Equity
a. Issued shares to organizers for cash (example).	+		+
b. Borrowed cash from local bank.			
c. Purchased equipment on credit.			
d. Earned revenue, collected cash.			
e. Incurred expenses, on credit.			
f. Earned revenue, on credit.			
g. Paid cash for *(e)*.			
h. Incurred expenses, paid cash.			
i. Earned revenue, collected three-fourths cash, balance on credit.			
j. Theft of $100 cash.			
k. Declared and paid cash dividends.			
l. Collected cash for *(f)*.			
m. Depreciated equipment for the period.			
n. Incurred expenses, paid four-fifths cash, balance on credit.			
o. Paid income tax expense for the period.			

E2–8   (Understanding Transactions; Effects on Balance Sheet and Income Statement)
During its first week of operations, January 1–7, Tiny Retail Company completed eight transactions, the dollar effects of which are indicated in the following schedule:

Account	Dollar Effect of Each of the Eight Transactions								Ending Balance
	1	2	3	4	5	6	7	8	
Cash	$10,000	$15,000	$(4,000)	$80,000	$(9,000)	$(50,000)	$(11,000)	$7,000	$38,000
Accounts receivable				10,000				(7,000)	3,000
Store fixtures					9,000				9,000
Land			12,000						12,000
Accounts payable						20,000	(11,000)		9,000
Notes payable, (10%)		15,000	8,000						23,000
Capital stock	10,000								10,000
Revenues				90,000					90,000
Expenses						70,000			70,000

Required:
1. Write a brief explanation of each transaction. Explain any assumptions that you make.
2. Complete the following tabulation after the eight transactions:

> Balance sheet:
> Total assets . . . . $_____
> Total liabilities . . . . $_____
> Total owners' equity . . . . $_____
>
> Income statement:
> Total revenues . . . . $_____
> Total expenses . . . . $_____
> Net income . . . . $_____

E2–9   (Applying the Fundamental Accounting Model)
Sampson Service Company, Inc., was organized by five investors. The following transactions were completed:

a. The investors paid in $50,000 cash to start the business. Each one was issued 1,000 shares of capital stock, par value $10 per share.
b. Equipment for use in the business was purchased at a cost of $10,000, one half was paid in cash, and the balance is due in six months.
c. Service fees were earned amounting to $54,000, of which $6,000 was on credit.

d. Operating expenses incurred amounted to $33,000, of which $3,000 was on credit.

e. Cash was collected for $4,000 of the service fees performed on credit in (c) above.

f. Paid cash, $1,000, on the operating expenses that were on credit in (d) above.

g. Investor A borrowed $10,000 from a local bank and signed a one-year, 10% note for that amount.

Required:

Set up a schedule similar to the following and enter thereon each of the above transactions that should be recorded by Sampson. Transaction (a) is used as an example.

Transactions	Assets	=	Liabilities	+	Owners' Equity
a. Investment of cash in the business	Cash + $50,000				Capital stock + $50,000

After the last transaction (on the last line of the schedule), total each dollar column to prove the correctness of your solution.

E2-10   (Application of Debits and Credits; Nonquantitative)

The 12 transactions given below were completed by Duster Service Company during the year 19X:

1. The organizers paid in cash and in turn received 10,000 no-par shares of capital stock.

2. Duster borrowed cash from the local bank.

3. Duster purchased a delivery truck, paid three-fourths cash, and the balance is due in six months.

4. Revenues earned, collected cash in full.

5. Expenses incurred, paid cash in full.

6. Revenues earned, on credit (cash will be collected later).

7. Expenses incurred, on credit (cash will be paid later).

8. Declared and paid a cash dividend to shareholders.

9. Collected half of the amount on credit in (6).

10. Paid all of the credit amount in (7).

11. A spare tire was stolen from the delivery truck (not insured).

12. At the end of 19X, the delivery truck is depreciated by a dollar amount (an expense).

Required:

For each transaction given above enter in the tabulation given below, a D for debit and a C for credit to reflect the increases and decreases of the assets, liabilities, and owners' equity (separate accounts are given for owners' equity). Transaction 1 is used as an example.

Fundamental Accounting Model	Twelve Transactions											
	1	2	3	4	5	6	7	8	9	10	11	12
a. Assets	D											
b. Liabilities												
Owners' equity: c. Investments by owners	C											
d. Revenues												
e. Withdrawals (dividends)												
f. Expenses												

(Note: In some cases there may be both a D and C in the same box.)

E2–11 **(Using T-accounts; Summarizing the Results)**

Snappy Service Company, Inc., was organized and issued 10,000 no-par shares of its capital stock for $30,000 cash. The following transactions occurred during the current accounting period:

a. Received the cash from the organizers, $30,000.

b. Service fees earned amounted to $35,000, of which $25,000 was collected in cash.

c. Operating expenses incurred amounted to $23,000, of which $17,000 was paid in cash.

d. Bought two machines for operating purposes at the start of the year at a cost of $9,000 each; paid cash.

e. One of the machines was destroyed by fire one week after purchase; it was uninsured. The event to be considered is the fire. (Hint: Set up a fire loss expense account.)

f. The other machine has an estimated useful life to Snappy of 10 years (and no residual value). The event to be considered is the depreciation of the equipment because it was used for one year in rendering services.

g. Shareholder Able bought a vacant lot (land) for his own use for $5,000 of his own cash.

Required:

1. Set up appropriate T-accounts and record in them the dual effects on the fundamental accounting model of each of the above transactions that should be recorded by Snappy. Key the amounts to the letters starting with (a). Number the following required accounts consecutively starting with 101 for cash: Cash, Accounts Receivable, Machines, Accumulated Depreciation, Accounts Payable, Service Fees Earned, Operating Expenses, Fire Loss Expense, Depreciation Expense, and Capital Stock.

2. Use the data in the completed T-accounts (Requirement 1) to complete the following:

Debits = Credits:
Total debits . . . . $_____
Total credits . . . . $_____
Income statement:
Total revenues . . . . $_____
Total expenses . . . . $_____

Net income . . . . $_____
Balance sheet:
Total assets . . . . $_____
Total liabilities . . . . $_____
Total owners' equity . . . . $_____

PROBLEMS

P2–1   **(Transaction Analysis, Recording, and Reporting)**
Toni Company was organized on January 1, 19A, by J. B. Tory, S. T. Olen, R. R. Neans, and B. T. Irwin. Each organizer invested $8,000 in the company, and, in turn, each was issued 8,000 no-par shares of capital stock. To date they are the only shareholders.

During the first quarter (January–March 19A), the company completed the following six transactions (summarized and simplified for instructional purposes):

1. Collected a total of $32,000 from the organizers and, in turn, issued the shares of capital stock.
2. Purchased equipment for use in the business; paid $8,000 cash in full.
3. Purchased land for use in the business; paid $4,000 cash and gave a $6,000, one-year, 12% interest-bearing note for the balance; total cost, $10,000.
4. Earned service revenues of $40,000 of which $36,000 was collected in cash, the balance was on credit. (Hint: Two asset accounts are increased.)
5. Incurred $28,000 operating expenses of which $25,000 was paid in cash, the balance was on credit. (Hint: Three different accounts will be affected.)
6. In addition, shareholder Tory reported to the company that 500 shares of his Toni investment had been sold and transferred to shareholder Irwin for a cash consideration of $6,000.

Required:
a. Was Toni Company organized as a sole proprietorship, a partnership, or a corporation? Explain the basis for your answer.
b. What was the issue price per share of the capital stock?
c. During the first quarter, the records of the company were inadequate. You were asked to prepare the summary of transactions given above. To develop a quick assessment of their economic effects on Toni Company, you have decided to complete the tabulation that follows and to use plus (+) for increases and minus (−) for decreases for each account. The first transaction is used as an example.

| | Six Transactions—Effects | | | | | | Ending Amounts (total) |
Accounts	1	2	3	4	5	6	
Cash	$+32,000	$	$	$	$	$	$
Accounts receivable							
Land							
Equipment							
Accounts payable							
Notes payable							
Capital stock	+32,000						
Service revenues							
Operating expenses							

d. Did you include the Tory-Irwin transaction in the above tabulation? Why?

e. Based only upon the completed tabulation above, provide the following amounts (show computations):

(1) Income for the quarter.

(2) Total assets at the end of the quarter.

(3) Total liabilities at the end of the quarter.

(4) Total owners' equity at the end of the quarter.

(5) Cash balance at the end of the quarter.

(6) Net amount of cash inflow from operations, that is, from revenues and expenses combined.

(7) How much interest must be paid on the note at its maturity date?

P2–2   (Identifying Accounts for Assets, Liabilities, and Owners' Equity; Also, Usual Balance—Debit versus Credit)

Listed below are the accounts of the AAA Rental Corporation:

a. Cash.

b. Accounts receivable.

c. Capital stock (issued to shareholders).

d. Bonds payable.

e. Rent revenue.

f. Insurance premium paid in advance of use.

g. Interest revenue.

h. Investments, long term.

i. Interest expense.

j. Machinery and equipment.

k. Patents.

l. Income tax expense.

m. Property taxes payable.

n. Loss on sale of machinery.

o. Land, plant site (in use).

p. Accounts payable.

q. Supplies inventory (held for use as needed).

r. Notes payable, short term.

s. Retained earnings.

t. Investments, short term.

u. Term deposits held at bank.

v. Operating expenses.

w. Income taxes payable.

x. Gain on sale of equipment.

y. Land held for future plant site.

z. Revenue from investments.

aa. Wages payable.

bb. Accumulated depreciation.

cc. Merchandise inventory (held for resale).

Complete a tabulation similar to the following. (Enter two check marks for each account on the preceeding page.) Account *a.* is used as an example.

		Type of account		Usual balance	
			Owner's equity (including revenues and		
Account	Asset	Liability	expenses)	Debit	Credit
a.	√			√	

Etc.

P2–3   **(Transaction Analysis, Recording; Debits = Credits; Financial Statements)**
Bayside Service Company has been operating for three years. At the end of 19C, the accounting records reflected assets of $320,000 and liabilities of $120,000. During the year 19D, the following summarized transactions were completed:

a. Revenues of $160,000, of which $10,000 was on credit.

b. Issued an additional 1,000 shares of capital stock, no-par, for $10,000 cash.

c. Purchased equipment that cost $25,000, paid cash $10,000, and the balance is due next year.

d. Expenses incurred were $110,000, of which $15,000 was on credit.

e. Collected $8,000 of the credit amount in (*a*).

f. Declared and paid cash dividends to shareholders of $12,000.

g. Paid $10,000 of the credit amount in (*d*).

h. Borrowed $20,000 cash, on a 12% interest-bearing note, from a local bank (on December 31, 19D), payable June 30, 19E.

i. Cash amounting to $400 was stolen (not covered by insurance).

j. Depreciation on equipment was $600 for 19D (because of use).

Required:

1. Enter each of the above transactions in the following schedule. The first transaction is used as an example.

	Assets		Liabilities		Owners' Equity	
Transactions	Debit	Credit	Debit	Credit	Debit	Credit
Balances, January 1, 19D	$320,000			$120,000		$200,000
a. Revenues	150,000					160,000
	10,000					
b.						
Etc.						

2. Respond to the following:
   a. Why were two debits entered in the above schedule for transaction (*a*)?
   b. Complete the following at the end of 19D:

   Income statement:
   Revenues . . . . $_____
   Expenses . . . . $_____

   Net income . . . . $_____
   Balance sheet:
   Assets . . . . $_____
   Liabilities . . . . $_____
   Owners' equity . . . . $_____

   c. Explain why the dividend declared and paid is not an expense.

P2–4 **(Transaction Analysis; Recording Debits and Credits)**
Listed below is a series of accounts for Service Corporation, which has been operating for three years. These accounts are listed and **numbered** for identification. Below the accounts is a series of transactions. For each transaction indicate the account(s) that should be debited and credited by entering the appropriate account number(s) to the right of each transaction. The first transaction is used as an example.

Account No.	Account title	Account No.	Account title
1.	Cash.	10.	Wages payable.
2.	Accounts receivable.	11.	Income tax payable.
3.	Supplies inventory (on hand, pending use).	12.	Capital stock, no-par.
4.	Prepaid expense.	13.	Retained earnings.
5.	Equipment (used in the business).	14.	Service revenues.
6.	Accumulated depreciation, equipment.	15.	Operating expenses.
7.	Patents.	16.	Income tax expense.
8.	Accounts payable.	17.	Interest expense.
9.	Notes payable.	18.	None of the above (explain).

Transactions	Debit	Credit
a. Example—Purchased equipment for use in the business; paid one-third cash and gave a note payable for the balance.	5	1, 9
b. Investment of cash in the business; capital stock was issued.	___	___
c. Paid cash for salaries and wages.	___	___
d. Collected cash for services performed this period.	___	___
e. Collected cash for services performed last period.	___	___
f. Performed services this period on credit.	___	___
g. Paid operating expenses incurred this period.	___	___
h. Paid cash for operating expenses incurred last period.	___	___
i. Incurred operating expenses this period, to be paid next period.	___	___
j. Purchased supplies for inventory (to be used later); paid cash.	___	___
k. Used some of the supplies from inventory for operations.	___	___
l. Purchased a patent; paid cash.	___	___
m. Made a payment on the equipment note (*a*) above; the payment was part principal and part interest expense.	___	___
n. Collected cash on accounts receivable for services previously performed.	___	___
o. Paid cash on accounts payable for expenses previously incurred.	___	___
p. Paid three fourths of the income tax expense for the year; the balance to be paid next period.	___	___
q. On last day of current period, paid in cash for an insurance policy covering the next two years.	___	___

P2–5   **(Transaction Analysis: Recording in the Accounts)**

Listed below is a series of accounts (with identification numbers) for Silver Service Corporation.

Account No.	Account title	Account No.	Account title
1.	Cash.	20.	Capital stock, par $10 per share.
2.	Accounts receivable.	21.	Contributed surplus.
3.	Service supplies inventory.	25.	Service revenues.
4.	Trucks and equipment.	26.	Operating expenses.
5.	Accumulated depreciation.	27.	Depreciation expense.
10.	Accounts payable.	28.	Interest expense.
11.	Notes payable.	29.	Income tax expense.
12.	Income tax payable.	30.	None of the above (explain).

During 19X, the company completed the selected transactions given in the tabulation that follows:

Required:

To the right indicate the accounts (by identification number) that should be debited and credited and the respective amounts. The first transaction is used as an example.

Transactions	Debit Acct. No.	Debit Amount	Credit Acct. No.	Credit Amount
a. Example: Purchased panel truck for use in the business for $18,000; paid $10,000 cash and signed a 10% interest-bearing note for the balance, $8,000.	4	18,000	1 11	10,000 8,000
b. Service revenues earned, $150,000, of which $10,000 was on credit.				
c. Operating expenses incurred, $100,000, of which $20,000 was on credit.				
d. Purchased service supplies, $500, paid cash (placed in supplies inventory, for use as needed).				
e. Collected $8,000 of the credit amount in (*b*).				
f. Paid $15,000 of the credit amount in (*c*).				
g. Used $400 of the service supplies (taken from inventory) for service operations.				
h. Depreciation on the truck for the year, $3,000.				
i. Paid six months' interest on the note in (*a*).				
j. Income tax expense for the year, $4,000; paid three-fourths cash; balance payable by April 1 of next year.				

P2–6   **(Transaction Analysis; Note: This problem uses a spreadsheet computer program.)**

1. Use the structure and the accounts of P2-1 to record the transactions listed.
2. Sum each account across, then sum the totals down to see if the accounts balance. (Hint: The sum down should be $0 if the accounts are in balance because a credit should be entered as a minus.)
3. Below the transactions section, prepare an income statement and a balance sheet. References in the statements can be used to transfer amounts. Sum to achieve totals. Calculate EPS (Hint: EPS, 0.375).

CASES

C2–1   **(Inspection of a Balance Sheet to Evaluate Its Reliability)**

J. Doe asked a local bank for a $50,000 loan to expand his small company. The bank asked Doe to submit a financial statement of the business to supplement the loan application. Doe prepared the balance sheet shown below.

Balance Sheet
June 30, 19X6

Assets:

Cash	$ 9,000
Inventory	30,000
Equipment	46,000
Residence (monthly payments, $18,000)	300,000
Remaining assets	20,000
Total assets	$405,000

Liabilities:

Short-term debt to suppliers	$ 62,000
Long-term debt on equipment	38,000
Total debt	100,000
Owners' equity, J. Doe	305,000
Total liabilities and owners' equity	$405,000

Required:

The balance sheet has several flaws; however, there is at least one major deficiency. Identify it and explain its significance.

C2-2 **(Analyzing and Restating an Income Statement That Has Major Deficiencies; a Challenging Case)**

Allen Jenkins started and operated a small service company during 19A. At the end of the year, he prepared the following statement based on information stored in a large filing cabinet.

JENKINS COMPANY
Profit for 19A

Service fees income collected during 19A		$80,000
Cash dividends received		12,000
Total		92,000
Expense for operations paid during 19A	$58,000	
Cash stolen from cash register	300	
Supplies purchased for use on service jobs (cash paid)	1,700	
Total		60,000
Profit		$32,000

A summary of completed transactions was:

a. Service fees earned during 19A, $87,000.

b. The cash dividends received were on some Dow Jones common shares purchased six years earlier by Allen Jenkins personally.

c. Expenses incurred during 19A, $62,000.

d. Supplies on hand (unused) at the end of 19A, $200.

Required:

1. Did Jenkins prepare the above statement on a cash basis or an accrual basis? Explain how you can tell. Which basis should be used? Explain why.

2. Revise the above statement to make it consistent with proper accounting and reporting. Explain (using footnotes) the reason for each change that you make.

C2-3 **(A Challenging Analytical Case Related to Application of the Fundamental Accounting Model)**

SEC Company was organized during January 19A by T. E. Scott, W. D. Evans, and R. L. Cates. On January 20, 19A, the company issued 5,000 shares to each of its organizers. Following is a schedule of the **cumulative** account balances immediately after each of the first 10 transactions.

Accounts	Ten Transactions—Cumulative Balances									
	1	2	3	4	5	6	7	8	9	10
Cash	$75,000	$70,000	$87,000	$77,000	$66,000	$66,000	$70,000	$58,000	$55,000	$54,000
Accounts receivable			8,000	8,000	8,000	11,000	11,000	11,000	11,000	11,000
Office fixtures		20,000	20,000	20,000	20,000	20,000	20,000	20,000	20,000	20,000
Land				14,000	14,000	14,000	14,000	14,000	14,000	14,000
Accounts payable					2,000	2,000	2,000	7,000	4,000	4,000
Notes payable		15,000	15,000	19,000	19,000	19,000	19,000	19,000	19,000	19,000
Capital stock*	75,000	75,000	75,000	75,000	75,000	75,000	79,000	79,000	79,000	79,000
Revenues			25,000	25,000	25,000	28,000	28,000	28,000	28,000	28,000
Expenses					13,000	13,000	13,000	30,000	30,000	31,000

* Owners' equity.

Required:

1. Analyze the changes in the above schedule for each transaction; then explain the transaction. Transactions 1 and 2 are used as examples:

   a. Cash increased $75,000, and capital stock (owners' equity) increased $75,000. Therefore, the transaction was an issuance of the capital stock of the corporation for $75,000 cash.

   b. Cash decreased $5,000, office fixtures (an asset) increased $20,000, and notes payable (a liability) increased $15,000. Therefore, the transaction was a purchase of office fixtures that cost $20,000. Payment was made as follows: cash, $5,000; note payable, $15,000.

2. Based only upon the above schedule (disregarding your response to Requirement 1) respond to the following after transaction 10:

   a. Income statement:
   Revenues . . . . $_____
   Expenses . . . .
   Net income . . . . $_____
   b. Balance sheet:
   Total assets . . . . $_____
   Total liabilities . . . . _____
   Total owners' equity . . . . _____

C2–4   (Overview of an Actual Set of Financial Statements)

Refer to the financial statements of Consolidated-Bathurst Inc. given in Appendix B immediately preceding the Index. Answer the following questions for the 1987 annual accounting period:

1. What is the name of the company?
2. What is the beginning date and the ending date for the current reporting year?
3. What is the name of the independent PA firm (i.e., auditor)?
4. What current-year amounts are reported for the following?

   Total assets . . . . $_____.
   Total liabilities . . . . $_____.
   Total owners' equity . . . . $_____.

5. What was the definition of "Funds" used in the SCFP?
6. What current-year amounts are reported for the following?

   Change in funds (increase or decrease) . . . . $_____.

7. What years are included in the Ten-Year Financial Summary?
8. What is the name of the auditors' report?
9. What are the position titles of the two managers who signed the report "On behalf of the Board"?

C2–5   **(Nature of Transactions)**

The following article is supposed to illustrate creative accounting.

Creative accounting is manna

Harry the Bean-Counter was morose, moody and otherwise downright glum. Although corporate accountancy was his game, he had never lifted his nose out of the red ink long enough to invent his own money-making scheme.

Retirement was nearing and he had nothing to show for his years of pencil-pushing but an inadequate (meaning cheap) company pension.

Despondent, he thumbed through a copy of the 1986 Nova Scotia budget which happened to be atop the pile of paper trash on his desk. Suddenly, he swung his worn loafers off the desk and sat bolt upright. A tiny lightbulb glowed above his balding head and he whispered, "Morty Shulman, move over! Anyone *can* make a million, and you don't need a dollar to do it!"

This is what had caught his attention in the budget:

"The Government has exercised severe restraint when preparing this year's budget, and the results of our measures have been significant. If expenditures had been allowed to increase in 1986–87 based on historical trends, the deficit would have been $378.9-million. As a matter of fact, at the beginning of the budget process, original departmental requests would have resulted in an even higher deficit level. As a result of this intensive and ongoing process, the deficit will total $232.9-million. This has resulted in a 1986–87 deficit that is $146-million lower than it might otherwise have been."

Harry was captivated by the Maritime simplicity. Oh, sure, he had heard of a similar theory taught by the Wilson School of Economics in Ottawa, but he had never fully understood it until now.

After a moment of euphoria, Harry got down to business. He whipped out his corporate pencil and his corporate notepad and began to compose a five-year retirement plan.

_____

Source: Orland French, *The Globe and Mail,* April 28, 1986, p. A7.

The key lay in dealing with the inertia of those pesky "historical trends." Harry's historical trend, aided and abetted by his spree-shopping wife Ethel, was to spend everything he earned, plus a few dollars more which he called "negative consumerism cashflow." His traditional response had been a plea to spend less.

He could see now that the best approach was to plan to spend more, then not spend it. But he could not be cautious. Massive savings could only be accumulated by cancelling lavish expenditures. And the faster the expenditures were cancelled, the faster his retirement savings would grow.

Following the Nova Scotia principle, Harry calculated he could become a millionaire by the time he retired in five years.

He had always wanted a sailboat, so he wrote down, "1986, plan to buy yacht in 1987, $200,000." That would get his retirement plan off to a fast start.

Then he wrote, "1987, cancel plan to buy yacht, save $200,000, plan to buy luxury condominium in Florida in 1988, $300,000."

Harry decided he really didn't want to live in Florida, so he wrote, "1988, cancel plan to buy condominium, save $300,000, plan to buy executive mansion in 1989, $500,000."

He was halfway to his goal, without even counting the interest on his savings from the yacht and the condominium. Now he would need to furnish the house, but he hated to dip into the half-million he had already saved. He wrote, "1989, cancel plan to buy house, save $500,000, plan to buy furniture for house in 1990, $350,000."

When he realized he was planning to buy furniture for a house which he had already decided not to buy, Harry was extremely pleased with himself. This was his most creative accounting in 35 years in the business.

But it looked rather silly on paper, so he wrote, "1990, cancel plan to buy unnecessary furniture, save $350,000, plan to go on lavish, six-month world tour in 1991, $150,000."

Since Harry hated travelling, he wrote a final entry, "1991, cancel plan to go on world tour, save $150,000. Stay at home in three-bedroom suburban bungalow and look at savings in bank book every day."

In all, Harry would save $1.5-million over the next five years. He picked up the telephone and called home. "Ethel," he said, "go out and buy that fur coat you've always wanted. We're rich."

Required: What is wrong with Harry's accounting?

THREE

THE ACCOUNTING INFORMATION PROCESSING CYCLE

▽

PURPOSE

Chapter 2 emphasized the fundamental accounting model and transaction analysis. It also discussed the use of journal entries and T-accounts to record the results of transaction analysis for each business transaction. The purpose of Chapter 3 is to discuss the **accounting information cycle,** which processes financial data from the transaction to the end result—the periodic income statement, balance sheet, and statement of changes in financial position. This chapter will expand your knowledge of journal entries, accounts, and financial statements introduced in Chapter 2.

On the facing page the summary report of a familiar company, Petro-Canada, is presented. Financial results and physical operating results are disclosed.

LEARNING OBJECTIVES

1. Identify and explain the characteristics of an accounting system.
2. List and explain the six sequential phases of the accounting system.
3. Apply the six phases of the accounting information processing cycle using simple situations.
4. Prepare simple financial statements—income statement, balance sheet, and SCFP.
5. Expand your vocabulary by learning about the "Important Terms Defined in This Chapter."
6. Apply the knowledge gained from this chapter.

ORGANIZATION

1. Characteristics of an accounting system.
2. Application of the accounting information processing cycle—six sequential phases.
3. Subclassifications on the:
   a. Income statement.
   b. Balance sheet.
   c. Statement of change in financial position (SCFP).
4. Demonstration case—the accounting information processing cycle.

Petro-Canada

Products Division

■ Earnings and margins squeezed by price cutting in wholesale and retail markets

■ Focus on strengthening customer loyalty while reducing operating costs

Financial and Operating Profile

Financial	1987	1986
Revenue (millions of dollars)	4,461	4,588
Earnings (millions of dollars)	95	115
Cash generated from operations (millions of dollars)	330	346
Net capital expenditures (millions of dollars) Property, plant and equipment	122	112
Acquisitions	—	301
Average capital employed (millions of dollars)	2,757	2,846
Return on average capital employed (per cent)	3.4	4.0

Operating	1987	1986
Petroleum product sales (thousands of m³ per day)	45.6	44.4
Number of retail and wholesale marketing outlets	4,268	4,344
Refinery crude capacity (thousands of m³ per day)	64.0	64.0
Crude oil processed by Petro-Canada (thousands of m³ per day)	48.4	47.2
Refinery utilization (per cent)	76	74

Characteristics of an Accounting System

An accounting system, regardless of the size of a business, is designed to collect, process, and report periodic financial information about the entity. **Financial reports** are prepared at the end of each **reporting period,** often called the **accounting period.** For external reporting, the reporting period is one year, which may, or may not, be the calendar year (January 1 to December 31). Therefore, during each reporting period, the accounting system must systematically collect and process economic data about all of the transactions completed by the entity. This collecting and processing activity is called the **accounting information processing cycle.** It is called a cycle because it must be repeated each accounting period for the new economic data. This processing cycle involves a series of sequential phases (steps), starting with the transactions and extending, in the accounting system, through the accounting period and finally to the preparation of the required financial statements—income statement, balance sheet, and statement of changes in financial position. We will discuss the primary sequential phases in the information processing cycle in the order in which they usually are accomplished. The phases are outlined in Exhibit 3–1.

Application of the Accounting Information Processing Cycle

This section discusses the first six phases of a typical accounting information processing cycle. Each phase is discussed in order and illustrated by using Bass Cleaners, Inc. (see Exhibit 2–4). At the end of this chapter, a comprehensive demonstration case, with its solution, is given to tie all of these six phases together.

Phase 1—Collect Original Data

The initial phase in the accounting information processing cycle is the collection of original economic data about each transaction affecting the entity. Such economic data are collected continuously throughout the accounting period as transactions occur. Each transaction that involves **external** parties usually generates one or more source documents that provide essential data about that transaction. Examples are sales invoices, cash register tapes, purchase invoices, and signed receipts. Documentation must be generated **internally** for certain economic effects such as depreciation and the using up of office supplies already on hand.[1] Importantly, the original economic data (from the supporting source documents) entered into an accounting system are not generated by the accounting function but through the various **operating** functions of a business. The quality of the **outputs** of an information processing system is determined primarily by the quality (and timeliness) of the inputs of original data based on

---

[1] Recall from Chapter 2 that transactions include (*a*) events that involve an exchange between two or more separate entities (or persons) and (*b*) events that are not between entities but nevertheless have a particular economic impact on the entity being accounted for.

Exhibit 3–1 Phases of the accounting information processing cycle

SEQUENTIAL ACTIVITIES COMPLETED DURING THE ACCOUNTING PERIOD
Phases
1 **COLLECT INFORMATION** about each transaction as it occurs.
2 **ANALYZE EACH TRANSACTION** in terms of *(a)* Assets = Liabilities + Owners' Equity, and *(b)* Debits = Credits.
3 **RECORD THE ECONOMIC EFFECTS** of each transaction in the journal.
4 **TRANSFER THESE ECONOMIC** effects from the journal to the ledger.
COMPLETED AT THE END OF THE ACCOUNTING PERIOD
5 **PREPARE A TRIAL BALANCE** from the ledger.
6 **PREPARE FINANCIAL STATEMENTS.**
7–11 Other phases at end of the accounting period—discussed in Chapter 5.

transactions. Therefore, a carefully designed and controlled data collection system is essential throughout a business. The initial data collection procedure constitutes an integral and important subsystem of an accounting information processing system.

To illustrate the collection of original data, return to Bass Cleaners, Inc. (Exhibit 2–4). The first transaction was the issuance of 800 shares of capital stock for $20,000 cash. The business documents to support this transaction would be a copy of the cash receipt given to each shareholder and an internal memorandum that identifies the number of shares issued to each of the four organizers.

Phase 2—Analyze Each Transaction

This phase in the accounting information processing cycle was explained and illustrated in Exhibit 2–4 of Chapter 2. Recall from Chapter 2 that the objective of this analytical activity is to determine the **economic effects** on the entity of each transaction in terms of the basic accounting model, Assets = Liabilities + Owners' Equity, and the equality, Debits = Credits. When this analysis of a business transaction is completed, the economic effects are then formally entered into the accounting system in the Debits = Credits format.

Transaction analysis requires an understanding of the nature of business transactions, the operations of the business, and a sound knowledge of the concepts and procedures of accounting.

To illustrate, analysis of the first transaction of Bass Cleaners, Inc. (Exhibit 2–4)—the issuance of 800 shares of capital stock to the organizers for $20,000 cash—would be:

ASSETS		LIABILITIES		SHAREHOLDERS' EQUITY
Cash debit, $20,000	=	No effect	+	Capital stock credit, $20,000

Phase 3—Record Transactions in the Journal

After transaction analysis, the economic effect of each transaction is formally entered into the **accounting system** in a record known as the **journal.** The journal is a simple form used to record the economic effects of each transaction using the Debits = Credits format.

In a simple situation, after the analysis of a business transaction, it could be recorded directly in the separate accounts for each asset, liability, and owners' equity. However, in more complex situations, it is essential that the economic effects of each transaction on the accounting model be recorded in one place in **chronological order** (i.e., in order of date of occurrence). The accounting record designed for this purpose is the journal. Typically, the effects of transaction analysis are recorded first in the journal and later transferred to the appropriate accounts (refer to the various journal entries and T-accounts used for Bass Cleaners in Exhibit 2–4).

The journal contains a chronological listing of each entry for all of the transactions. The **format** of the entry in the journal for each transaction is designed to facilitate posting so that the economic effects on the accounting model and the debit and credit features are physically linked. For example, in Exhibit 2–4, the first transaction by Bass Cleaners would appear in the journal in the following format:

JOURNAL

	Debit	*Credit*
(Date) Cash	20,000	
Capital stock		20,000
To record investment of cash by owners.		

Notice that the **debit always is listed first** and the **credit is listed last and indented** to avoid incorrect identification.

The physical linking of the dual effects of each transaction in the journal contrasts with the use of separate accounts, where the debits and credits associated with each transaction must be separated physically between two or more accounts. For example, recall that the economic effects of the above entry for Bass Cleaners appear in separate accounts as follows:

Cash		**Capital Stock**	
(Date) 20,000			(Date) 20,000

The **journal** is the place of initial (or first) entry of the economic effects of each transaction. Therefore, it has been referred to as the **book of original entry.** The journal serves three useful purposes:

1. It provides for the initial and orderly listing (by date) of each transaction immediately after its transaction analysis is completed.
2. It provides a single place to record the economic effects of each transaction without further subclassifications of the data.

Exhibit 3–2 Journal illustrated

Date	Account Titles and Explanation	Folio	Debit	Credit
	Journal			Page ___1___
Jan. 1	Cash	101	20,000	
	Capital stock	301		20,000
	Investment of cash by owners			
Jan. 3	Cash	101	5,000	
	Note payable	205		5,000
	Borrowed cash on 12% note			
Jan. 6	Delivery truck	111	8,000	
	Cash	101		8,000
	Purchased delivery			
	truck for use in			
	the business			

3. It facilitates later **tracing;** checking for possible errors; and construction of each transaction, its analysis, and its recording.

Knowledge of the approximate date of a transaction often is used in tracing activities. In this regard, the journal is the only place in the accounting system where the economic effects of each transaction are linked physically and recorded chronologically.

Let's see how the journal is used in a manually maintained system. The first three transactions for Bass Cleaners have been entered in a typical journal shown in Exhibit 3–2. Recording transactions in the journal in this manner is called **journalizing,** and the entries made are called **journal entries.**

To summarize the discussion about journal entries: (1) each transaction and event is first recorded in the journal as a separate entry; (2) each entry in the journal is dated, and entries are recorded in chronological order; (3) for each transaction, the debits (accounts and amounts) are entered first, the credits follow and are indented; and (4) for each transaction, the economic effects on the accounting model and the debits and credits are linked in one entry. These features provide an "audit or tracing trail" that facilitates subsequent examination of past transactions and assists in locating errors. Also the journal is designed to simplify subsequent accounting (as will be shown later).

Phase 4—Transfer to the Ledger

As shown in Exhibit 2–4, for Bass Cleaners, a separate account was set up for each asset, liability, and owners' equity. An accounting system typically contains a large number of such accounts. Collectively, these individual accounts are contained in a record known as the **ledger.** The ledger may be organized in many ways. Handwritten accounting systems may use a loose-leaf ledger—one page for each account. In the case of a "machine" accounting system, a separate machine card is kept for each account. With a computerized accounting system, the ledger is kept on electronic storage devices, but there are still individual accounts under each system. Each account is identified by a descriptive **name** and an **assigned number** (e.g., Cash, 101; Accounts Payable, 201; and Capital Stock, 301).

Exhibit 3–3 shows the ledger for Bass Cleaners in T-account format. The ledger (i.e., all of the accounts) contains information that initially was recorded in the journal and then **posted** (i.e., transferred) to the appropriate accounts in the ledger. The transfer of information from the journal to the ledger is called posting. This transfer from the chronological arrangement in the journal to the account format in the ledger is a very important **reclassification** of the data because the ledger reflects the data classified as assets, liabilities, owners' equity, revenues, and expenses (i.e., by individual accounts) rather than chronologically.

A business using a handwritten system will record the transactions in the journal each day and **post** to the ledger less frequently, say, every few days. Of course, the timing of these **information processing activities** varies with the data processing system used and the complexity of the entity.

The T-account format shown in Exhibit 3–3 is useful for instructional purposes. However, the typical account used is the columnar format shown in Exhibit 3–4. It retains the debit-credit concept, but it is arranged to provide columns for date, explanation, folio (F), and a running balance.

To post to the ledger, the debits and credits shown in the journal entries are transferred directly, as debits and credits, to the appropriate accounts in the ledger. In both the journal (Exhibit 3–2) and the ledger (Exhibit 3–3), there is a **Folio** column for **cross-reference** between these two records. In the journal, shown in Exhibit 3–2, the numbers in the Folio column indicate the account **to which** the dollar amounts were posted (i.e., transferred). In the ledger account for Cash, the numbers in the Folio column indicate the journal page **from which** the dollar amounts were posted. Folio numbers are used in the posting phase to (a) indicate that posting has been done and (b) provide an "audit trail."

The economic data ends up in the ledger; therefore, it has been called the **book of final entry.**

Exhibit 3–3   Ledger illustrated (T-accounts)

BASS CLEANERS, INC.
LEDGER at December 31, 19A

ASSETS	=	LIABILITIES	+	OWNERS' EQUITY

Cash   101

(a)	20,000	(c)	8,000
(b)	5,000	(f)	25,800
(d)	40,000	(h)	600
(k)	1,000	(j)	1,800
		(l)	500

(Net debit balance, $29,300)

Accounts Payable   201

(l)	500	(g)	2,000

(Net credit balance, $1,500)

Capital Stock   301

		(a)	20,000

Accounts Receivable 102

(e)	4,000	(k)	1,000

(Net debit balance, $3,000)

Note Payable   205

		(b)	5,000

Retained Earnings* 310

(j)	1,800	

Cleaning Revenue   312

		(d)	40,000
		(e)	4,000

(Net credit balance, $44,000)

Delivery Truck   120

(c)	8,000	

Operating Expenses 320

(f)	25,800	
(g)	2,000	
(i)	1,600	

(Net debit balance, $29,400)

Accumulated Depreciation, Delivery Truck† 121

	(i)	1,600

Interest Expense   325

(h)	600	

Totals	$38,700	=	$6,500	+	$32,200

Note: The accounting model, Assets = Liabilities + Owners' Equity, given at the top of this exhibit and the totals at the bottom are shown for your convenience in study; they would not appear in an actual ledger.

* Retained Earnings is an owners' equity account that reports accumulated earnings minus dividends paid to date. Dividends paid reduce cash and owners' equity (Chapter 12). Dividends paid is a distribution to owners—not an expense because it does not contribute to earning revenue.

† The delivery truck is depreciated over a five-year period because that is its estimated useful life to Bass Cleaners. Depreciation refers to the "wearing out" of the truck due to use. The truck is assumed to wear out at a steady rate each year throughout its life; therefore, the annual depreciation is $8,000 ÷ 5 years = $1,600. This amount is recorded in an account called Accumulated depreciation; it is a negative, or contra, account to the Delivery Truck account. The $1,600 also is an expense for the year. For further explanation of depreciation, see Chapter 9.

Exhibit 3–4 Ledger account in columnar format illustrated

Date	Explanation	Folio	Debit	Credit	Balance

Account Title _____ *Cash* _____   Account Number __*101*__

Date	Explanation	Folio	Debit	Credit	Balance
Jan. 1	Investments	1	20,000		20,000
3	Borrowing	1	5,000		25,000
6	Truck purchased	1		8,000	17,000
7	Cleaning revenue	4	40,000		57,000
8	Operating expenses	4		25,800	31,200
10	Interest expense	5		600	30,600
15	Payments to owners	7		1,800	28,800
16	Collections on receivables	8	1,000		29,800
17	Payments on accounts payable	8		500	29,300

Phase 5—Develop a Trial Balance

At the end of the **accounting period** (also called the reporting period), to verify recording accuracy, and for subsequent processing uses, a **trial balance** is prepared directly from the ledger. A trial balance is a listing, in ledger account order, of the individual ledger **accounts** and their respective **net ending** debit and credit balances. The ending balance shown for each individual account is the difference between the total of its debits and the total of its credits. Exhibit 3–5 shows the trial balance of Bass Cleaners at December 31, 19A. It was prepared directly from the ledger accounts given in Exhibit 3–3.

A trial balance has two purposes in the accounting information processing cycle:

1. It provides a check on the equality of the debits and credits as shown in the ledger accounts at the end of the period.
2. It provides financial data in a convenient form to help in preparing the financial statements.

Phase 6—Prepare Financial Statements

At the end of the reporting period, the first four phases of the accounting information processing cycle will have been completed—data collection, analy-

Exhibit 3–5 Trial balance illustrated

BASS CLEANERS, INC.
Trial Balance
December 31, 19A

Account No.	Account titles	Net balance Debit	Credit
101	Cash . . . *Asset*	$29,300	
102	Accounts receivable	3,000	
120	Delivery truck	8,000	
121	Accumulated depreciation, delivery truck *contra account*		$ 1,600
201	Accounts payable		1,500
205	Notes payable		5,000
301	Capital stock (800 shares)		20,000
310	Retained earnings (explained later) . *income statement*	1,800	
312	Cleaning revenues		44,000
320	Operating expenses	29,400	
325	Interest expense	600	
	Totals	$72,100	$72,100

sis, journal entries, and posting to the ledger.[2] Phase 5, illustrated above, starts the end-of-period phases.

The next phase (i.e., Phase 6) is preparation of the three required financial statements—income statement, balance sheet, and statement of changes in financial position. The trial balance provides basic data that are needed to prepare the financial statements at the end of the reporting period. The 19A income statement and balance sheet for Bass Cleaners are shown in Exhibit 3–6. Notice that the amounts on these statements were taken directly from the trial balance, except for retained earnings. Retained earnings is computed as: Beginning balance, $-0- (this is Year 1 for Bass Cleaners), + Net income (from the income statement), $14,000, − Dividends paid to shareholders, $1,800, = Ending balance, $12,200.[3]

Classification of Elements Reported on the Financial Statements

External decision makers who use financial statements have varied backgrounds, education, experience, financial interests, and problems. These

---

[2] Chapter 5 will expand the accounting information cycle to include some additional activities to develop the financial statements in complex situations.

[3] Notice how much easier it is to prepare these statements from a trial balance than when the accounts are used directly (as was done in Chapter 2, Exhibit 2–2). Retained earnings, an element of shareholders' equity, will be discussed in detail later.

Exhibit 3–6 Income statement and balance sheet, Bass Cleaners, Inc.

BASS CLEANERS, INC.
Income Statement
For the Year Ended December 31, 19A

Cleaning revenues		$44,000
Expenses:		
Operating expenses	$29,400	
Interest expense	600	
Total expenses		30,000
Net income		$14,000

Earnings per share (EPS), $14,000 ÷ 800 shares = $17.50

BASS CLEANERS, INC.
Balance Sheet
At December 31, 19A

Assets

Cash		$29,300
Accounts receivable		3,000
Delivery truck	$ 8,000	
Less: Accumulated depreciation	1,600	6,400
Total assets		$38,700

Liabilities

Accounts payable		$ 1,500
Notes payable		5,000
Total liabilities		$ 6,500

Shareholders' Equity

Contributed capital:		
Capital stock, (800 no-par shares)	20,000	
Retained earnings ($14,000 − $1,800)	12,200	
Total shareholders' equity		32,200
Total liabilities and shareholders' equity		$38,700

---

decision makers include investors, creditors, employees, governmental agencies, unions, customers, and other interested parties. Often financial statements are referred to as **general-purpose financial statements** because they are prepared to serve the diverse needs of these groups.

To make financial statements clearer and more useful to the wide range of decision makers, **subclassifications** of the economic information presented are included on the financial statements. Standard subclassifications have evolved; however, they have some acceptable variations, and changes are sometimes made. Throughout this textbook the subclassifications given in the next few paragraphs will usually be used.

For continuing reference as you study the remaining chapters, the typical subclassifications on each of the three required financial statements are outlined on the next few pages. Following each outline some of the major distinctions are briefly discussed. Future chapters will discuss these subclassifications in more detail.

Subclassifications on the Income Statement

An income (or earnings) statement is subclassified as follows:

A. **Revenues**
    By type:
    Sales
    Services

B. **Expenses**
    By kind:
    Cost of goods sold (an expense)
    Operating expenses
    Administrative expenses
    Financial expenses
    Income tax expense

C. **Income before extraordinary items (A − B)**

D. **Extraordinary items (unusual and nonrecurring)**
    Gains and losses

E. **Net income (C − D)**

F. **Earnings per share (EPS)** *only to corp.*

Cost of goods sold is an expense incurred when goods or merchandise are sold. The goods or merchandise had to be purchased before they were sold. The amount paid to the supplier for the items sold is called cost of goods sold. Assume goods purchased for resale cost $40,000. If three fourths of these goods are sold for $50,000, the effect can be shown on an income statement as:

Sales revenue	$50,000
Less: Cost of goods sold ($40,000 × 3/4)	30,000
Gross margin on sales	20,000
Operating expenses:	
Etc.	

Extraordinary items are gains and losses that are (*a*) unusual in nature and (*b*) infrequent in occurrence. These items must be separately reported on the income statement. Since they seldom occur, separate reporting informs decision makers that they are not likely to recur and should not be part of the recurring factors needed to evaluate the organization.

Income tax expense is incurred by a corporation but not by a sole proprietorship or partnership.[4] Income taxes are payable each year (partially in

---

[4] The earnings of a sole proprietorship and a partnership must be reported on the **personal** income tax returns of the owners.

advance on quarterly estimates). A corporation must report income tax expense on its income statement separately for operations and extraordinary items. Both ordinary income and extraordinary gains and losses attract income taxes and thus the income tax expense for the period is separated so that it is matched with the two categories of income (or loss) on the income statement. Assume XT Corporation computed **pretax** amounts as follows: income from operations, $80,000; and an extraordinary gain, $10,000. If the income tax rate is 30%, the income statement would show the following:

Pretax income from operations		$80,000
Less: Income tax ($80,000 × 30%)		24,000
Income before extraordinary items		56,000
Extraordinary gain	$10,000	
Less: Income tax ($10,000 × 30%)	3,000	7,000
Net income		$63,000

Earnings per share relates only to the common stock of a corporation. As was mentioned in Chapter 1, not all companies with share capital have to report EPS but companies with a large number of shareholders do. It is computed by dividing income by the average number of common shares outstanding during the reporting period. If an extraordinary gain or loss is reported, these earnings per share amounts must be reported so that investors do not confuse recurring factors from unusual nonrecurring ones. Assume ART Corporation reported the following **aftertax** amounts on its income statement:

Income before extraordinary items	$100,000
Less: Extraordinary loss	20,000
Net income	$ 80,000

If 40,000 shares of common stock are outstanding, EPS should be reported as follows:

Income before extraordinary items	($100,000 ÷ 40,000 shares) =	$2.50
Extraordinary loss	($20,000 ÷ 40,000 shares) =	(0.50)
Net income	($80,000 ÷ 40,000 shares) =	$2.00

Subclassifications on the Balance Sheet

Typically a balance sheet (or statement of financial position) is subclassified as follows:

A. **Assets (by order of liquidity).**[5]
 (1) Current assets (short term)
 (2) Long-term investments and funds
 (3) Operational assets (property, plant, and equipment)
 (4) Intangible assets

---

[5] Liquidity refers to the average period of time required to convert a noncash asset to cash.

Exhibit 3–7 Typical operating cycle of a business

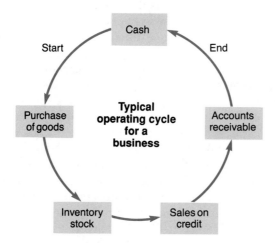

(5) Deferred charges (beyond year) long term
(6) Other (miscellaneous) assets
    Total assets

B. **Liabilities (by order of time to maturity):**

Acts P. (1) Current liabilities (short term) pay off in year
    (2) Long-term liabilities — mortgage
        Total liabilities

C. **Owners' equity (by source):**
    (1) Contributed capital (by owners) earned-div.
    (2) Retained earnings (accumulated earnings minus accumulated divi-
        dends declared)

cash, accts. reciev.

Current assets are resources owned by the entity that are reasonably expected to be realized in cash or used up within one year from the balance sheet date or during the normal operating cycle of the business, whichever is longer. The **normal operating cycle** for a merchandising company may be shown graphically as in Exhibit 3–7.

The usual current assets are cash, short-term investments, accounts receivable and other short-term receivables, inventory, and prepaid expenses (i.e., expenses paid in advance of usage).

Current liabilities are those short-term debts at the balance sheet date that are expected to be paid out of the current assets listed on the same balance sheet. Short-term liabilities are expected to be paid during the coming year or the normal operating cycle of the business, whichever is longer. Current liabilities include accounts payable, short-term notes payable, wages payable, income tax payable, and other expenses incurred (used) but not yet paid.

The difference between total current assets and total current liabilities is called **working capital.** It is a widely used measure of a company's liquidity.

current assets - current lib. = working capital
measure of company's liquidity.

Operational assets are often called property, plant, and equipment or fixed assets. This group includes those assets that have physical substance (i.e., they are tangible) and were acquired for use in **operating the business** rather than for resale as inventory items or held as investments. The assets included are buildings owned; land on which the buildings reside; and equipment, tools, furniture, and fixtures used in operating the business. Operational assets, with the exception of land, are depreciated as they are used (i.e., worn out). Because their usefulness decreases as they are used, their initial cost is apportioned to expense over their estimated useful lives. This apportionment of cost over useful life is called **depreciation.** Land is not depreciated because it does not wear out like machinery, buildings, and equipment. The amount of depreciation computed for **each period** is reported on the income statement as depreciation **expense.** The **accumulated** amount of depreciation expense for all past periods from acquisition date is **deducted** (as a contra amount) on the balance sheet from the initial cost of the asset to derive **"book or carrying value"** at the balance sheet date. To illustrate, Bass Cleaners purchased a delivery truck for $8,000. It had an estimated useful life of five years. Therefore, depreciation expense was computed as $8,000 ÷ 5 years = $1,600 depreciation expense per year. The five balance sheets developed during the five-year period would report the following:

	19A	19B	19C	19D	19E
Delivery truck	$8,000	$8,000	$8,000	$8,000	$8,000
Less: Accumulated depreciation	1,600	3,200	4,800	6,400	8,000
Book or carrying value	$6,400	$4,800	$3,200	$1,600	$ –0–

Intangible assets have no **physical existence** and have a long life. Their value is derived from the legal **rights and privileges** that accompany ownership. Examples are patents, trademarks, copyrights, franchises, and goodwill. Intangible assets usually are not acquired for resale but rather are directly related to the operations of the business.

Owners' equity, called shareholders' equity for a corporation, represents the residual claim of the owners (i.e., A − L = OE). This claim results from the initial contributions of the shareholders (contributed capital) plus retained earnings, which is the accumulated earnings of the company less the accumulated dividends declared. Thus, retained earnings represents the amount of earnings that have been left in the company for growth. Typically long-time successful companies have grown more from retained earnings than from additional contributions by investors for capital stock.

Capital stock may have a par value which is a legal amount per share. It has little or no relationship to the **market price** of the shares. When a corporation issues capital stock above the par value, the excess must be recorded in a separate account. Assume a corporation issued 6,000 shares of its capital stock, par $10 per share, for $80,000 cash. The required journal entry would be:

Cash	80,000	
Capital stock (6,000 shares × par $10)		60,000
Contributed surplus ($80,000 − $60,000)		20,000

If the corporation used the increasingly popular no-par shares the entry would be:

Cash 80,000
    Capital stock (6,000 no-par shares)   80,000

This topic will be discussed in Chapter 12.

Subclassifications on the Statement of Changes in Financial Position (SCFP)

A SCFP, cash basis, is subclassified as follows:

  A. **Sources of cash:** *(increases)*
      (1) From continuing (or primary) operations
      (2) From extraordinary items
      (3) From financing sources (e.g., borrowing)
      (4) From investing sources (e.g., sale of long-term asset)
          Total cash sources (inflows)

  B. **Uses of cash:**
      (1) For investing—for example, to purchase long-term assets
      (2) For financing—for example, to pay liabilities—to pay dividends
          Total cash uses (outflows)

  C. **Net change in cash during the period (increase or decrease)**

The classification of SCFP into Sources and Uses is somewhat more elaborate than is currently used. Financing sources and uses could be shown under the single Financing heading to yield a net source or use, and investing sources and uses could also be grouped under the heading, Investing. Pluses and minuses would disclose whether the amount is a source or use. The SCFP will be discussed in more detail in Chapter 15.

The preceding summaries of each financial statement were given to (*a*) provide an overview of financial statements and (*b*) use as a reference when you study the subsequent chapters.

DEMONSTRATION CASE

The Accounting Information Processing Cycle

We chose the case of a small business to show an actual **accounting information processing cycle** from the capture of the raw economic data during the reporting period to the financial statements prepared at the end of the accounting year. Only representative and summary transactions are used to simplify the illustration. You should study each step in the solution carefully because it reviews the discussion in Chapters 1, 2, and 3.

On January 3, 19A, M. Hall and P. Garza organized a corporation, La Paloma Apartments, to build and operate apartment complexes. At the start, each one

Exhibit 3–8 Trial balance and transactions for demonstration case

LA PALOMA APARTMENTS
Ledger Balances
July 1, 19C (start of Year 2 of rental operations)

Account No.	Account titles	Balance Debit	Credit
101	Cash	$ 18,000	
103	Accounts receivable (or rent receivable)		
105	Supplies inventory	2,000	
112	Prepaid insurance		
121	Land (apartment site)	30,000	
122	La Paloma apartment building	200,000	
123	Accumulated depreciation, apartment building		$ 10,000
125	Furniture and fixtures	60,000	
126	Accumulated depreciation, furniture and fixtures		12,000
131	Land for future apartment site		
201	Accounts payable		6,000
202	Property tax payable		
203	Income tax payable		
204	Mortgage payable, 10% (apartment building)		180,000
205	Note payable, long term, 12%		
301	Capital stock (par $10, 6,000 shares)		60,000
302	Contributed surplus		20,000
303	Retained earnings (accumulated earnings to June 30, 19C)		22,000
401	Rent revenue		
521	Utilities and telephone expense		
522	Apartment maintenance expense		
523	Salary and wage expense		
524	Insurance expense		
525	Property tax expense		
526	Depreciation expense		
527	Miscellaneous expenses		
531	Interest expense		
532	Income tax expense		
	Totals	$310,000	$310,000

(Assets, $288,000 = Liabilities, $186,000 + Shareholders' Equity, $102,000)

invested $40,000 cash and in turn received 3,000 shares of $10 par value capital stock. On that date the following entry was recorded in the journal:

January 3, 19A:

Cash	80,000	
Capital stock, par $10 (6,000 shares)		60,000
Contributed surplus		20,000

Then land was acquired for $30,000 cash, and a construction contract was signed with a builder. The first apartments were rented on July 1, 19B. The owners

Exhibit 3–8 *(concluded)*

Transactions, July 1, 19C, through June 30, 19D:

Date	Description

a. On November 1, 19C, paid $3,000 cash for a two-year insurance policy covering the building, its contents, and liability coverage. ✓

b. Rental revenue earned: collected in cash, $105,500; and uncollected by June 30, 19D, $2,000.

c. Paid accounts payable (amount owed from the prior year for expenses), $6,000.

d. Bought a tract of land, at $35,000, as a planned site for another apartment complex to be built in "about three years." Cash of $5,000 was paid, and a long-term note payable (12% interest per annum, interest payable each six months) was signed for the balance of $30,000.

e. Operating expenses incurred and paid in cash were:

Utilities and telephone expense	$23,360
Apartment maintenance expense	1,200
Salary and wage expense	6,000

f. At the end of the accounting year (June 30, 19D), the following bills for expenses incurred had not been recorded or paid: June telephone bill, $40; and miscellaneous expense, $100.

g. Paid interest for six months on the long-term note at 12% per annum. (Refer to item [*d*].) (Hint: Interest = Principal × Rate × Time.)

h. An inventory count at the end of the accounting period, June 30, 19D, showed remaining supplies on hand amounting to $400. Supplies used are classified as a miscellaneous expense by this company.

i. By the end of the accounting period, June 30, 19D, one third (8 months out of 24 months) of the prepaid insurance premium of $3,000 paid in transaction (*a*) had expired because of passage of time.

j. Depreciation expense for the year was based on an estimated useful life of 20 years for the apartment and 5 years for the furniture and fixtures (assume no residual or salvage value).

k. The property tax for the year ending June 30, 19D, in the amount of $2,700 has not been recorded or paid.

l. Cash payment at year-end on the mortgage on the apartment was:

On principal	$20,000
Interest ($180,000 × 10%)	18,000
Total paid	$38,000

m. Income tax expense for the year ending June 30, 19D, was $5,940 (i.e., a 20% average rate). This obligation will be paid in the next period.

---

decided to use an **accounting year** of July 1 through June 30 for business purposes (instead of a period that agrees with the calendar year).

It is now July 1, 19C, the beginning of the second year of rental operations; therefore, certain **accounts in the ledger** have balances carried over from the prior accounting year ended June 30, 19C. A complete list of the accounts in the ledger that will be needed for this case, their folio numbers, and the balances carried over from the previous year is given in Exhibit 3–8. **Typical transactions** (summarized) for the 12-month accounting year—July 1, 19C, through June 30, 19D—are also given in Exhibit 3–8. Instead of using dates, we will use the letter notation to the left of each transaction.

Required:

Complete the accounting information processing cycle by doing each of the following:

1. **Set up a ledger** with T-accounts that has all of the accounts listed on the trial balance given in Exhibit 3–8; include the account numbers as given. Enter the July 1, 19C, balances in each account in this manner:

Cash		101
Balance	18,000	

2. **Analyze,** then **journalize** (i.e., enter in the journal), each transaction listed above for the accounting period July 1, 19C, through June 30, 19D. Number the journal pages consecutively starting with 1.

3. **Post all entries** from the journal to the ledger; use the folio columns for account numbers.

4. **Prepare a trial balance** at June 30, 19D.

5. **Prepare an income statement** for the reporting year ending June 30, 19D. Use the following subclassifications:

> Revenue
> Operating expenses:
>   Total operating expenses
> Income from apartment operations
> Financial expense
> Pretax income
>   Income tax expense
> Net income
> EPS

6. **Prepare a balance sheet** at June 30, 19D. Use the following subclassifications:

> **Assets**
>
> Current assets
> Operational assets
> Other assets
>
> **Liabilities**
>
> Current liabilities
> Long-term liabilities
>
> **Shareholders' Equity**
>
> Contributed capital
> Retained earnings

Suggested Solution:

Requirement 1—Ledger (see pages 121 and 122):

Requirement 2—Journal (Note: Be sure you understand all of these entries):

JOURNAL   Page 1

Date	Account Titles and Explanation	Folio	Debit	Credit
a.	Prepaid insurance	112	3,000	
	Cash	101		3,000
	Paid insurance premium for two years in advance.			
	(Explanatory note: An asset account, Prepaid Insurance, is debited because a future service, insurance coverage, is being paid for in advance.)			
b.	Cash	101	105,500	
	Accounts receivable (or rent receivable)	103	2,000	
	Rent revenue	401		107,500
	To record rent revenues earned for the year, of which $2,000 has not yet been collected.			
c.	Accounts payable	201	6,000	
	Cash	101		6,000
	Paid a debt carried over from previous year.			
d.	Land for future apartment site	131	35,000	
	Cash	101		5,000
	Note payable, long term (12%)	205		30,000
	Bought land as a site for future apartment complex. (This is a second tract of land acquired; the present apartment building was built on the first tract.)			
e.	Utilities and telephone expense	521	23,360	
	Apartment maintenance expense	522	1,200	
	Salary and wage expense	523	6,000	
	Cash	101		30,560
	Paid current expenses.			
f.	Utilities and telephone expense	521	40	
	Miscellaneous expenses	527	100	
	Accounts payable	201		140
	Expenses incurred, not yet paid.			
g.	Interest expense	531	1,800	
	Cash	101		1,800
	Paid six months' interest on a long-term note ($30,000 × 12% × 6/12 = $1,800).			

Requirement 2 (continued):

JOURNAL   Page 2

Date	Account Titles and Explanation	Folio	Debit	Credit
h.	Miscellaneous expenses	527	1,600	
	Supplies inventory	105		1,600
	To record as expense supplies used from inventory during the year.			
	(Explanatory note: Supplies are bought in advance of use. Therefore, at that time they are recorded as an asset, Supplies Inventory. As the supplies are used from inventory, the asset thus used becomes an expense. Refer to Supplies Inventory account [$2,000 − $400 = $1,600].)			
i.	Insurance expense	524	1,000	
	Prepaid insurance	112		1,000
	To record as an expense the cost of the insurance that expired ($3,000 × 8/24 = $1,000).			
j.	Depreciation expense	526	22,000	
	Accumulated depreciation, apartment building	123		10,000
	Accumulated depreciation, furniture and fixtures	126		12,000
	Depreciation expense for one year.			
	Computation: Apartment: $200,000 ÷ 20 years = $10,000. Furniture and fixtures: $60,000 ÷ 5 years = $12,000.			
k.	Property tax expense	525	2,700	
	Property tax payable	202		2,700
	Property tax for the current year, not yet paid.			
l.	Mortgage payable	204	20,000	
	Interest expense	531	18,000	
	Cash	101		38,000
	Payments on principal of mortgage payable plus interest expense ($180,000 × 10%).			
m.	Income tax expense	532	5,940	
	Income tax payable	203		5,940
	Income tax for the year; payable later.			

Requirements 1 and 3—Ledger:

LEDGER

Cash   101

Date	F	Amount	Date	F	Amount
Balance		18,000	(a)	1	3,000
(b)	1	105,500	(c)	1	6,000
			(d)	1	5,000
			(e)	1	30,560
			(g)	1	1,800
			(l)	2	38,000

(Net debit balance, $39,140)

Accounts Receivable   103

(b)	1	2,000			

Supplies Inventory   105

Balance		2,000	(h)	2	1,600

Prepaid Insurance   112

(a)	1	3,000	(i)	2	1,000

Land (apartment site)   121

Balance		30,000			

La Paloma Apartment Building   122

Balance		200,000			

Accumulated Depreciation, Apartment Building   123

			Balance		10,000
			(j)	2	10,000

Furniture and Fixtures   125

Date	F	Amount	Date	F	Amount
Balance		60,000			

Accumulated Depreciation, Furniture and Fixtures   126

			Balance		12,000
			(j)	2	12,000

Land for Future Apartment Site   131

(d)	1	35,000			

Accounts Payable   201

(c)	1	6,000	Balance		6,000
			(f)	1	140

Property Tax Payable   202

			(k)	2	2,700

Income Tax Payable   203

			(m)	2	5,940

Mortgage Payable (10%) (apartment building)   204

(l)	2	20,000	Balance		180,000

Requirements 1 and 3 (continued):

Note Payable, Long Term (12%) 205							Insurance Expense			524		
Date	F	Amount	Date	F	Amount	Date	F	Amount	Date	F	Amount
			(d)	1	30,000	(i)	2	1,000			

Capital Stock		301		Property Tax Expense			525
	Balance	60,000	(k)	2	2,700		

Contributed Surplus		302		Depreciation Expense			526
	Balance	20,000	(j)	2	22,000		

Retained Earnings		303		Miscellaneous Expenses			527
	Balance	22,000	(f)	1	100		
			(h)	2	1,600		

Rent Revenue			401		Interest Expense			531
	(b)	1	107,500	(g)	1	1,800		
				(l)	2	18,000		

Utilities and Telephone Expense			521		Income Tax Expense			532
(e)	1	23,360		(m)	2	5,940		
(f)	1	40						

Apartment Maintenance Expense			522
(e)	1	1,200	

Salary and Wage Expense			523
(e)	1	6,000	

Requirement 4:

LA PALOMA APARTMENTS
Trial Balance
June 30, 19D

Account No.	Account titles	Debit	Credit
101	Cash	$ 39,140	
103	Accounts receivable (or Rent receivable)	2,000	
105	Supplies inventory	400	
112	Prepaid insurance (16 months)	2,000	
121	Land (apartment site)	30,000	
122	La Paloma apartment building	200,000	
123	Accumulated depreciation, apartment building		$ 20,000
125	Furniture and fixtures	60,000	
126	Accumulated depreciation, furniture and fixtures		24,000
131	Land for future apartment site	35,000	
201	Accounts payable		140
202	Property tax payable		2,700
203	Income tax payable		5,940
204	Mortgage payable (10%) (apartment building)		160,000
205	Note payable, long term (12%)		30,000
301	Capital stock (par $10, 6,000 shares)		60,000
302	Contributed surplus		20,000
303	Retained earnings (accumulated earnings to June 30, 19C)		22,000
401	Rent revenue		107,500
521	Utilities and telephone expense	23,400	
522	Apartment maintenance expense	1,200	
523	Salary and wage expense	6,000	
524	Insurance expense	1,000	
525	Property tax expense	2,700	
526	Depreciation expense	22,000	
527	Miscellaneous expenses	1,700	
531	Interest expense	19,800	
532	Income tax expense	5,940	
	Totals	$452,280	$452,280

Requirement 5:

LA PALOMA APARTMENTS
Income Statement
For the Year Ended June 30, 19D

Revenues:		
Rent revenue		$107,500*
Operating expenses:		
Utilities and telephone expense	$23,400	
Apartment maintenance expense	1,200	
Salary and wage expense	6,000	
Insurance expense	1,000	
Property tax expense	2,700	
Depreciation expense	22,000	
Miscellaneous expenses	1,700	
Total operating expenses		58,000
Income from apartment operations		49,500
Finance expense:		
Interest expense		19,800
Pretax income		29,700
Income tax expense		5,940
Net income		$ 23,760
EPS ($23,760 ÷ 6,000 shares)		$3.96

* Notes:
a. These amounts were taken directly from Requirement 4, the trial balance.
b. No products are sold by this business; therefore, gross margin cannot be reported.

Requirement 6:

LA PALOMA APARTMENTS
Balance Sheet
At June 30, 19D

Assets

Current assets:			
Cash		$ 39,140*	
Accounts receivable		2,000	
Supplies inventory		400	
Prepaid insurance		2,000	
Total current assets			$ 43,540
Operational assets:			
Land (apartment site)		30,000	
La Paloma apartment building	$200,000		
Less: Accumulated depreciation, building .contra. .	20,000	180,000	
Furniture and fixtures	60,000		
Less: Accumulated depreciation, furniture and fixtures . . .	24,000	36,000	
Total operational assets			246,000
Other assets:			
Land acquired for future apartment site† does not deprec.			35,000
Total assets			$324,540

Requirement 6 (continued):

Liabilities

Current liabilities:
Accounts payable	$ 140	
Property tax payable	2,700	
Income tax payable	5,940	
Total current liabilities		$ 8,780

Long-term liabilities:
Mortgage payable	160,000	
Note payable, long term	30,000	
Total long-term liabilities		190,000
Total liabilities		198,780

Shareholders' Equity

Contributed capital:
Capital stock, par $10 (6,000 shares)	$60,000	
Contributed surplus	20,000	
Total contributed capital	80,000	
Retained earnings (beginning balance, $22,000 +		
net income, $23,760)	45,760 *retained.*	
Total shareholders' equity		125,760
Total liabilities and shareholders' equity		$324,540

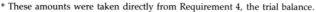

* These amounts were taken directly from Requirement 4, the trial balance.
† Classified as "other" rather than "operational" because this land is not being used currently for operating purposes.

● SUMMARY OF CHAPTER

An accounting system is designed to collect, process, and report financial information about an entity. During each period, an **accounting information processing cycle** starts with data collection and may end with the periodic financial statements if financial statements are prepared for that particular period. The phases of this sequential cycle are summarized in Exhibit 3–9. Let's briefly review the essence of this accounting cycle.

The fundamental accounting model—Assets = Liabilities + Owners' Equity—gives the basic framework for transaction analysis and recording the dual effect of each transaction. The accounting model has two balancing features that must be met for each transaction and event recorded: (1) assets must equal liabilities plus owners' equity and (2) debits must equal credits. After transaction analysis, the dual effects of each transaction are recorded first in the journal and then are posted to the ledger. The journal provides a chronological record of the transactions, and the ledger reflects a **separate account** for each kind of asset, liability, and owners' equity. Normally, asset accounts will have debit balances, whereas liability accounts will have credit balances. Owners' equity accounts normally will show credits for the capital stock and retained earnings accounts— expenses will show debit balances, and revenues will show credit balances. The accounting information processing cycle accumulates the financial data needed

Exhibit 3–9   Sequential phases of an accounting information processing cycle summarized*

Activity	**Flow of Data**

(1) Collect raw data

(capture the economic data
about each **transaction**)

Original source documents

| Invoices | Vouchers | Bills | Etc. |

(2) Analyze each transaction

(determine economic effects
of each transaction on the entity)

Transaction analysis
(effect on the enterprise
in terms of accounting
model A = L + OE)

(3) Journalize
(record the economic effects
of each transaction on the
accounting model in
chronological order)

Journal

Journal

(4) Post to the ledger

(accumulate each asset,
liability, and owners' equity
in separate accounts)

Ledger

CASH   101

(5) Develop a trial balance

(list of account balances to
facilitate preparation of
financial reports)

Trial balance

Trial balance		
Account	Debit	Credit

(6) Prepare financial statements

(to help decision makers
make better decisions)

Financial statements

| Income statement | Balance sheet | Statement of cash flows | Special reports |

* This cycle will be expanded in Chapter 5.

to develop the periodic financial statements: the income statement, balance sheet, and statement of changes in financial position (SCFP).

The chapter also gave an outline of the subclassifications on the required financial statements—income statement, balance sheet, and statement of changes in financial position.

IMPORTANT TERMS DEFINED IN THIS CHAPTER

Accounting Information Processing Cycle Sequential accounting phases used to process data from initial transaction to financial statements. *p. 102*

Accounting (or Reporting) Period Time period; usually one year; the period covered by the financial statements. *p. 102*

Accounting System Designed to collect, process, and report financial information about an entity. *p. 104*

Cost of Goods Sold An expense that represents the cost of purchasing goods and merchandise that were sold during the accounting period. *p. 111*

Current Assets Assets that are expected to be converted to cash within one year or the operating cycle if longer. *p. 113*

Current Liabilities Liabilities that will be paid by using current assets within one year or the operating cycle if longer. *p. 113*

Extraordinary Gain or Loss A gain or loss that is unusual and infrequent; separately reported on the income statement. *p. 111*

Journal Entry An original entry made in the journal in terms of: A = L + OE, and Debits = Credits. *p. 105*

Journalizing Recording transactions in the journal; original entry; chronological order. *p. 105*

Ledger Contains all of the individual accounts for assets, liabilities, and owners' equity. *p. 106*

Normal Operating Cycle of a Business Used to define current assets and current liabilities; the time from cash to purchase of inventories; to sale on credit, and back to cash. *p. 113*

Operational Assets Assets used to operate a business; not for resale; often called property, plant, and equipment. *p. 114*

Posting Transferring data from the journal to the ledger. *p. 106*

Reporting Period Same as accounting period (see above). *p. 102*

Trial Balance A list of all of the accounts in the ledger and their balances. *p. 108*

Working Capital Difference between total current assets and total current liabilities. *p. 113*

QUESTIONS

1. What is the function of an accounting system?
2. Explain the accounting information processing cycle.
3. How does a company collect the data needed for accounting purposes?
4. What is meant by transaction analysis?
5. Explain the meaning of "to debit" and "to credit."
6. Define the following terms: (*a*) accounting period and (*b*) reporting period.

7. What is the (*a*) book of original entry and (*b*) book of final entry?
8. Define the journal. What is its purpose?
9. Define the ledger. What is its purpose?
10. Explain the difference between journalizing and posting.
11. What is the purpose of the folio notations in the journal and in the ledger accounts?
12. What is a trial balance? What is its purpose?
13. What is an audit trail?
14. What is the primary purpose of subclassification of the information presented on financial statements?
15. What are the six major classifications on the income statement?
16. Define extraordinary items. Why should they be reported separately on the income statement?
17. List the six subclassifications of assets reported on a balance sheet.
18. Briefly define (*a*) current assets, (*b*) current liabilities, and (*c*) working capital.
19. What is a prepaid expense?
20. For operational assets, as reported on the balance sheet, explain (*a*) cost, (*b*) accumulated depreciation, (*c*) book value, and (*d*) carrying value.
21. What are the subclassifications of liabilities on a balance sheet?
22. Briefly explain the major subclassifications of owners' equity for a corporation.
23. What are three major subclassifications on a SCFP, cash basis?
24. Why would it be important to a user to be able to distinguish extraordinary items?

EXERCISES

E3-1 **(Phases in the Accounting Information Processing Cycle)**
Match the following phases with the descriptions of the accounting processing cycle by writing the correct letters in the blanks to the left.

Phases of the accounting information processing cycle (sequential order)

_____ Data collection
_____ Transaction analysis
_____ Journalizing
_____ Posting
_____ Trial balance
_____ Financial statements

Description of phases

A. Income statement, balance sheet, SCFP.
B. Transfer of amount for each account affected by the transaction; results in a reclassification of the data.
C. A listing of each account and its debit or credit ending balance; checks Debits = Credits.
D. Source documents that underlie each transaction.
E. A chronological record is prepared that reflects the economic effects of each transaction.
F. A careful study of each transaction and determination of its economic effects on the entity.

E3-2   (Overview of the Accounting Information Processing Cycle)
On January 1, 19A, Joe Hotstrike started the Hotstrike Electric Company (a single-owner business). During 19A, the company completed the following summarized transactions:

a. Cash invested by the owner, $20,000.

b. Service revenues earned, $80,000 (all cash).

c. Operating expenses incurred, $30,000 (all cash).

d. Cash withdrawn from the business by the owner, $4,000 per month for twelve months.

Required:
You are to process these four transactions through the accounting information processing cycle by phases as given below. (Hint: Refer to Exhibit 3–1 and the related discussions.)

Phase 1—Collect information—already done above.

Phase 2—Analysis. Write your analysis of each transaction in terms of Assets = Liabilities + Owner's Equity, and Debits = Credits.

Phase 3—Journalize each transaction.

Phase 4—Post the journal entries to the ledger. Use only the following T-accounts: Cash, Owner's Equity—Hotstrike, Service Revenues, and Operating Expenses.

Phase 5—Prepare a trial balance.

Phase 6—Prepare the following financial statements:

a. Income statement.

b. Balance sheet.

E3-3   (Write Journal Entries from T-accounts)
The following T-accounts for Ringer Service Company, Inc., show five different transactions (entries). Prepare a journal entry for each transaction and write a complete description of each one. (Hint: Notice that some transactions have two debits or two credits. Opening balances for the T-accounts are not provided.)

Cash				Accounts Payable				Capital Stock, 7,000 No-Par Shares		
(a)	70,000	(c)	9,000	(e)	1,500	(c)	2,000		(a)	70,000
(b)	20,000	(e)	1,500							
(d)	2,000	(f)	5,000							

Accounts Receivable				Note Payable				Service Revenue		
(b)	4,000	(d)	2,000			(f)	15,000		(b)	24,000

Equipment				Operating Expenses		
(f)	20,000			(c)	11,000	

E3–4   (Journalize and Compute Account Balances)

On January 1, 19A, Wilson and Young organized the WY Service Company, Inc. The completed transactions from January 1, 19A, through February 15, 19A, can be summarized as follows:

Jan. 1   Cash invested by the organizers was: Wilson, $30,000 (for 3,000 shares); and Young, $20,000 (for 2,000 shares).

   3   Paid monthly rent, $1,500.

  15   Purchased equipment for use in the business that cost $24,000; paid one third down and signed a 12% note payable for the balance. Monthly payments (24) made up of part principal and part interest are to be paid on the note.

  30   Paid cash for operating expenses amounting to $20,000; in addition, operating expenses of $4,000 were incurred on credit.

  30   Service fees earned amounted to $50,000, of which $40,000 was collected and the balance was on credit.

Feb. 1   Collected $6,000 on account for services performed in January and originally recorded as an account receivable and service revenue.

  2   Paid $3,000 on the operating expenses incurred in January and originally recorded as an account payable and operating expenses.

  15   Paid the first installment of $753 on the equipment note, including $160 interest expense.

Required:

1. Analyze and journalize each of the above transactions (refer to Exhibit 3–2 and the Demonstration Case, Requirement 2).
2. Based on your journal entries only, compute the following:
   a. Cash balance at February 15, 19A.
   b. Pretax income for the period January 1, 19A, through February 15, 19A.

E3–5   (Terminology Related to the Income Statement)

Below are terms related to the income statement. Match the terms with the definitions by writing the correct letter to the left for each term.

Terms	Brief definitions
__E__ (Example): Cost of goods sold	A. Sales revenue minus cost of goods sold.
__G__ Interest expense	B. Items that are both unusual and infrequent.
__B__ Extraordinary items	C. Sales of services for cash or on credit.
__C__ Service revenue	D. Revenues + Gains − Expenses − Losses (including EO items).
__F__ Income tax expense on operations	E. Amount of resources used to purchase the goods that were sold during the reporting period.
__I__ Income before extraordinary items	F. Income tax on revenues minus operating expenses.
__D__ Net income	G. Time cost of money (borrowing).
__A__ Gross margin on sales	H. Income divided by common shares outstanding.
__H__ EPS	
__J__ Operating expenses	

	Terms		**Brief definitions**

_K_ Pretax income from operations

I. Income before extraordinary items and the related income tax.

J. Total expenses directly related to operations.

K. Income before all income tax and before extraordinary items.

E3–6 **(Complete a Partial Income Statement with Income Tax and an Extraordinary Loss)**
Cotten Corporation (common stock, 10,000 shares outstanding) is preparing the income statement for the year ended December 31, 19D. The pretax operating income was $100,000, and there was a $30,000 pretax loss on earthquake damages to one of the plants properly classified as an extraordinary item. Total tax expense is $28,000 on the basis of a 40% tax rate on operations and on the earthquake loss.

Required:

1. Complete the following income statement:

(Already completed to here)
Pretax operating income
Less: Income tax
Income before EO items:
   Extraordinary loss
   Less: Income tax
Net income
Earnings per share

2. Why is the income tax of $28,000 separated into two parts?

E3–7 **(Ordering the Classifications on a Typical Balance Sheet)**
Following is a list of major classifications and subclassifications on the balance sheet. Number them in the order in which they normally appear on a balance sheet. (Hint: Start with Assets as No. 1.)

No.	Title
9	Current liabilities
8	Liabilities
11	Owners' equity
10	Long-term liabilities
3	Long-term investments and funds
5	Intangible assets
4	Operational assets (property, plant, and equipment)
2	Current assets
13	Retained earnings
12	Contributed capital
1	Assets
7	Other assets
6	Deferred charges

E3–8   (Terminology Related to the Balance Sheet)
Below are terms related to the balance sheet. Match the terms with the definitions by writing the correct letter to the left for each term.

Terms	Definitions
_G_ (Example) Retained earnings	A. A miscellaneous category of assets.
____ Current liabilities	B. Current assets minus current liabilities.
____ Liquidity	C. Total assets minus total liabilities.
____ Contra asset account	D. Nearness of assets to cash (in time).
____ Accumulated depreciation	E. Assets expected to be realized within one year or operating cycle, if longer.
____ Intangible assets	F. Same as carrying value; cost less accumulated depreciation to date.
____ Other assets	
____ Shares outstanding	G. Accumulated earnings minus accumulated dividends.
____ Normal operating cycle	H. Asset offset account (subtracted from asset).
____ Book value	
____ Working capital	I. Number of shares issued to shareholders.
____ Liabilities	J. Assets that do not have physical substance.
____ Operational assets	K. Items owned by the business that have future economic values.
____ Owners' equity	
____ Current assets	L. Liabilities expected to be paid out of current assets within the next year or operating cycle, if longer.
____ Assets	
____ Long-term liabilities	M. The average cash-to-cash time involved in the operations of the business.

N. Sum of the annual depreciation expense on an asset from its acquisition to the current date.

O. All liabilities not classified as current liabilities.

P. Property, plant, and equipment.

Q. Obligations to give up (pay) economic benefits in the future.

E3–9   (Classification of Investments in Common Shares on the Investor's Balance Sheet)
Tucker Manufacturing Corporation is preparing its annual financial statements at December 31, 19B. The company has two investments in shares of other corporations:

a. Common shares of X Corporation: 1,000 shares purchased for $80,000 during 19A. X Corporation is a supplier of parts to Tucker Corporation; therefore, the latter "intends to hold the shares indefinitely." The shares acquired represented 2% of the shares outstanding. X shares were selling at $95 at the end of 19B.

b. Common shares of Y Corporation: purchased 500 shares at a cost of $60 per share on August 15, 19B. Tucker made this investment to "temporarily use some idle cash that probably will be needed next year." Y shares were selling at $70 at the end of 19B.

Required:

Illustrate and explain the basis for the classification and amount that should be reported for each investment on the 19B balance sheet of Tucker Corporation.

E3–10 **(Prepare a Simple SCFP, Cash Basis)**

At the end of the annual reporting period, December 31, 19B, the records of BT Company showed the following:

a. Cash account: beginning balance, $36,000; ending balance, $22,000.
b. From the income statement:
    (1) Cash revenues $180,000
    (2) Cash expenses   135,000
c. From the balance sheet:
    (1) Additional capital stock sold: common stock, par $10; sold 2,000 shares at $15 per share.
    (2) Borrowed cash on a long-term note, $25,000.
    (3) Purchased equipment for use in the business, $110,000; paid cash, $75,000; balance on credit.
    (4) Paid a long-term note, $25,000.
    (5) Declared and paid a cash dividend, $14,000.

Required:

1. Prepare the 19B statement of changes in financial position for BT Company. Use the following captions: Sources of cash (operations, financing, investing). Uses of cash (investing, financing). Net increase (decrease) in cash during 19B.

2. Prove your answer.

PROBLEMS

P3–1 **(Journalize, Post, and Compute Account Balances)**

Kool Air Conditioning Service Company, Incorporated, has been operating for three years. I. M. Kool, the majority shareholder, built it from a one-person organization to an operation requiring 10 employees. In the past, few records were kept; however, Kool now realizes the need for a complete accounting system. The size and complexity of the business is partially indicated by the following selected transactions completed during January 19E:

Jan. 1 Purchased three new service trucks at $12,000 each; paid a third down and signed a 12% one-year, interest-bearing note for the balance. Twelve monthly payments, each including principal and interest, are to be made on the note.

     31 Service revenue earned in January amounted to $85,000, which included $5,000 on credit (due in 90 days).

     31 Operating expenses incurred in January amounted to $60,000, which included $4,000 on credit (payable in 60 days).

     31 Dividends declared and paid of $2,000 in cash to the shareholders.

     31 Paid $2,132 on the truck note, which included $240 interest.

     31 Paid 19D taxes on business property, $150; this amount was recorded in 19D as a liability (property taxes payable) and as an expense.

     31 Collected $4,400 on the services extended on credit in January.

Required:

1. Analyze and journalize each of the preceding transactions. Number the first journal page, 51; etc. (Hint: Refer to the Demonstration Case, Requirement 2.)
2. Post the journal entries to the following T-accounts. Use folio numbers.

Account No.	Account titles	Balance, January 1, 19E
101	Cash	$40,000 (debit)
102	Accounts receivable	20,000 (debit)
103	Trucks	None
104	Accounts payable	9,000 (credit)
105	Notes payable	None
106	Property taxes payable	150 (credit)
107	Retained earnings	80,000 (credit)
108	Service revenues	None
109	Operating expenses	None
110	Interest expense	None

Remaining accounts—not needed.

3. Compute the following amounts based on the above data only:
   a. Cash balance at the end of January 19E.
   b. Pretax income for the month of January 19E.

P3–2   (Complete Phase 2, Transaction Analysis, and Phase 3, Journalize)
Fast Stenographic and Mailing Service, Incorporated, was organized by three persons during January 19A. Each investor paid $11,000 cash, and each received 1,000 no-par shares. During 19A, the transactions listed below occurred (Phase 1). The letters at the left of each item will serve as the date notation.

a. Received the $33,000 investment of cash by the organizers and issued the shares.
b. Purchased office equipment which cost $6,000; paid cash.
c. Paid $400 cash for a two-year insurance policy on the office equipment for 19A and 19B (debit the asset account, Prepaid Insurance, because the premium is paid in advance on this date).
d. Purchased a delivery truck at a cost of $12,000; paid $7,000 down and signed a $5,000, 90-day, 12%, interest-bearing note payable for the balance.
e. Purchased office supplies for cash to be used in the stenographic and mailing operations, $2,000. The supplies are for future use (therefore, debit the asset account, Office Supplies Inventory—an asset account because they have not yet been used).
f. Revenues earned during the year were:

	Cash	On credit
Stenographic fees . . .	$55,000	$6,000
Mailing fees	8,000	2,000

g. Operating expenses incurred during the year were (excluding transactions [h] through [l]):

Cash	$26,000
On credit	14,000

h. Paid the $5,000 note on the panel truck. Cash paid out was for the $5,000 principal plus the interest for three months.

i. Purchased land for a future building site at a cost of $20,000; paid cash.

j. Depreciation on the truck for 19A was computed on the basis of a 5-year useful life; on the office equipment, a useful life of 10 years was assumed (compute full-year depreciation on each and assume no residual value).

k. By December 31, 19A, insurance for one year had expired. Prepaid Insurance should be decreased and an expense recorded because half of the insurance was "used" during 19A.

l. An inventory of the office supplies reflected $300 on hand at December 31, 19A. Supplies Inventory should be reduced and an expense recognized because some, but not all, of the supplies were used in 19A.

m. Income tax expense, based on a 20% rate, was $5,190 (to be paid in 19B).

Required:

1. Analyze and journalize each of the above transactions. Use the journal format illustrated in Exhibit 3–2. Write a brief explanation after each journal entry.
2. What was the balance in the cash account at the end of 19A?

P3–3 **(Complete an Income Statement with Income Tax, Extraordinary Loss, and EPS)**
Bill and Marcie Day organized the Day Hardware Company, Inc., on January 1, 19A. On that date, 20,000 shares of common stock were issued to three owners (Bill, Marcie, and a relative) for $100,000 cash.

At the end of the first year, December 31, 19A, the records kept by Marcie showed the following:

a. Merchandise sold: for cash, $200,000; on credit, $20,000.

b. Interest on debt; paid in cash, $2,000.

c. Salaries and wages paid in cash, $53,000.

d. Other operating expenses, $5,000, incurred (used) but not yet paid.

e. Cost of the merchandise sold, $100,000.

f. Services sold (all for cash), $10,000.

g. Extraordinary (EO) loss, $5,000 (subject to income tax).

h. Average corporate income tax rate on all items, 20%.

Required:

a. Complete the following income statement for the year, 19A:

Revenues
Expenses:
  Cost of goods sold
  Operating expenses
  Interest expense
Pretax income from operations
  Income tax expense
Income before EO item
  EO loss
  Less: Income tax saving
Net income
EPS

b. What was the total amount of income tax for 19A? Explain.

c. Explain why the $100,000 cash paid by the organizers is not considered to be revenue.

P3-4   (Prepare a Balance Sheet and Analyze Some of Its Parts)

Ace Jewelers is developing the annual financial statements for 19C. The following amounts were correct at December 31, 19C: cash, $41,200; accounts receivable, $49,000; merchandise inventory, $110,000; prepaid insurance, $600; investment in shares of Z Corporation (long term), $31,000; store equipment, $50,000; used store equipment held for disposal, $9,000; allowance for doubtful accounts, $800; accumulated depreciation, store equipment, $10,000; accounts payable, $43,000; long-term notes payable, $40,000; income taxes payable, $7,000; retained earnings, $80,000; and common stock, 100,000 shares outstanding, par $1 per share (originally sold and issued at $1.10 per share).

Required:

1. Based on the above data, prepare a 19C balance sheet. Use the following major captions (list the individual items under these captions):

    Assets: Current assets; long-term investments and funds; operational assets; and other assets.

    Liabilities: Current liabilities; and long-term liabilities.

    Shareholders' equity: Contributed capital; and retained earnings.

    (Hint: The balance sheet total is $280,000.)

2. What is the book or carrying value of the:
    (1) Inventory?
    (2) Accounts receivable?
    (3) Store equipment?
    (4) Notes payable (long term)?
    Explain what these values mean.

3. What is the amount of working capital?

P3-5   (Prepare the Shareholders' Equity Section of a Balance Sheet)

At the end of the 19A annual reporting period, the balance sheet of Avon Corporation showed the following:

AVON CORPORATION
Balance Sheet
At December 31, 19A
Shareholders' Equity

Contributed capital:	
Common stock, par $10; 5,000 shares outstanding . . .	$ 50,000
Contributed surplus	10,000
Total contributed capital	60,000
Retained earnings:	
Ending balance	40,000
Total shareholders' equity	$100,000

During 19B, the following selected transactions (summarized) were completed:

a. Sold and issued 1,000 shares of the common stock at $16 cash per share (at year-end).

b. Net income, $30,000.

c. Declared and paid a cash dividend on the beginning shares outstanding of $3 per share.

Required:

1. Prepare the shareholders' equity section of the balance sheet at December 31, 19B.

2. Give the journal entry to record the sale and issuance of the 1,000 shares of common stock.

P3–6 **(Complete Phase 6, Income Statement and Balance Sheet, from a Trial Balance)** Mission Real Estate Company (organized as a corporation on April 1, 19A) has completed Phase 1 (data collection), Phase 2 (analyses), Phase 3 (journal entries), and Phase 4 (posting) for the second year, ended March 31, 19C. Mission also has completed a correct trial balance (Phase 5) as follows:

MISSION REAL ESTATE COMPANY
Trial Balance
At March 31, 19C

Account titles	Debit	Credit
Cash	$ 41,000	
Accounts receivable	53,800	
Office supplies inventory	200	
Automobiles (company cars)	26,000	
Accumulated depreciation, automobiles		$ 12,000
Office equipment	2,000	
Accumulated depreciation, office equipment		1,000
Accounts payable		12,150
Income tax payable		
Salaries and commissions payable		1,000
Notes payable, long term		20,000
Capital stock (par $1; 30,000 shares)		30,000
Contributed surplus		5,000
Retained earnings (on April 1, 19B)		7,350
Dividends declared and paid during the current year	10,000	
Sales commissions earned		90,000
Management fees earned		8,000
Operating expenses (detail omitted to conserve your time)	46,000	
Depreciation expense (on autos and including $333 on office equipment)	6,000	
Interest expense	1,500	
Income tax expense (not yet computed)		
Totals	$186,500	$186,500

Required:

1. Complete the financial statements, as follows:

a. Income statement for the reporting year ended March 31, 19C. Include income tax expense, assuming a 30% tax rate. (Hint: EPS is $1.04.) Use the following major captions: Revenues; Expenses; Pretax income; Income tax; Net income; and EPS (list each item under these captions).

b. Balance sheet at the end of the reporting year, March 31, 19C. Include (1) income taxes for the current year in income tax payable, and (2) dividends in retained earnings. Use the captions that follow (list each item under these captions). (Hint: Total assets are $110,000.)

Assets

Current assets
Operational assets

Liabilities

Current liabilities
Long-term liabilities

Shareholders' Equity

Contributed capital
Retained earnings

2. Give the journal entry to record income taxes for the year (not yet paid).

P3–7   (Reporting Building, Land, and Depreciation Expense)
Tabor Company is preparing the balance sheet at December 31, 19X. The following assets are to be reported:

1. Building, purchased 15 years ago (counting 19X); original cost, $330,000; estimated useful life, 20 years from date of purchase; and no residual value.
2. Land, purchased 15 years ago (counting 19X); original cost, $25,000.

Required:

a. Show how the two assets should be reported on the balance sheet. What is the total book value of these operational assets?
b. What amount of depreciation expense should be reported on the 19X income statement? Show computations.

P3–8   (Prepare a Simple Statement of Changes in Financial Position, Cash Basis)
Sweet Bakery is preparing its annual financial statements at December 31, 19X. The income statement and balance sheet are finished. The statement of changes in financial position must be prepared. Therefore, the following cash flow data have been determined to be correct for 19X:

a. Sales and service revenues, $300,000, including $15,000 on credit and not yet collected.
b. Expenses, $256,000, including $6,000 noncash items.
c. Sold Sweet's used delivery truck for $3,000 cash (the gain on the sale was $1,000).
d. Borrowed cash, $20,000 on a three-year note payable (10% interest payable each year-end). The note was dated December 31, 19X.
e. Purchased a new delivery truck for $14,000 cash.
f. Paid a $40,000 long-term note payable.
g. Paid cash dividend of $12,000.

h. Purchased a tract of land for a future building site that cost $24,000. Paid one-third cash and signed a note payable for the balance.

i. Cash account: balance January 1, 19X, $36,000; balance December 31, 19X, $20,000.

Required:

1. Prepare the 19X statement of changes in financial position, cash basis, for Sweet Bakery. Use the following format, with appropriate details under each caption:

Heading

Sources of cash:
    From continuing operations
    From financing
    From investing
        Total sources of cash
Uses of cash:
    For investing
    For financing
Net increase (decrease) in cash

2. Prove your answer.

3. What was the major (*a*) source of cash and (*b*) use of cash?

P3–9   **(Short Problem; Completion of the First Six Phases of the Accounting Information Processing Cycle)**

Super Service Company, Inc., was started on January 1, 19A. During the first year ended December 31, 19A (end of the accounting period), the following summarized entries were completed:

Date	Transaction
a.	Issued 20,000 shares of its common stock (par $1 per share) for $60,000 cash.
b.	Purchased equipment for use in operations that cost $40,000 cash. Estimated life, 10 years.
c.	Borrowed $50,000 cash on a long-term note payable (10% interest).
d.	Revenues earned, $100,000, of which $8,000 was on credit (not yet collected at year-end).
e.	Expenses incurred (including interest on the note payable), $60,000, of which $5,000 was on credit (not yet paid at year-end).
f.	Paid cash dividend, $10,000. (Hint: Debit retained earnings.)
g.	Recorded depreciation expense. Assume no income tax.

Required:

Process the above transactions through the accounting information processing cycle by phases as follows:

Phase 1—Collect information about each transaction; already done above.

Phase 2—Analysis; write your analysis of each transaction in terms of: Assets = Liabilities + Shareholders' Equity, and Debits = Credits.

Phase 3—Journalize each transaction. Start your journal with page 1. Use the date letters for identification of transactions.

Phase 4—Post the journal entries to the ledger accounts (as you complete each journal entry or after the last journal entry). Set up the following ledger accounts and account numbers: Cash, 101; Accounts Receivable, 102; Equipment, 105; Accumulated Depreciation, 106; Accounts Payable, 201; Note Payable, Long Term, 205;

Common Stock, 301; Contributed Surplus, 302; Retained Earnings, 303; Revenues, 310; and Expenses, 315.

Phase 5—Prepare a trial balance. (Hint: Debit total is $219,000.)

Phase 6—Prepare the following 19A financial statements:
- a. Income statement. (Hint: EPS is $1.80.)
- b. Balance sheet. (Hint: Total assets are $141,000.)

P3–10   **(Comprehensive Problem: Completion of the First Six Phases of the Accounting Information Cycle)**

Able, Baker, and Cain organized ABC Realty as a corporation to conduct a real estate and rental management business. Each one contributed $20,000 cash and received 1,500 shares (par value $10 per share). They began business on January 1, 19A. The transactions listed below, representative of those during the first year (19A), were selected from the actual transactions.

Assume that these transactions comprise all of the transactions for 19A. All of the accounts needed in the ledger are given below (Phase 1). Use the letters given at the left as the date notation.

- a. Received $60,000 cash invested by shareholders and issued 4,500 shares.
- b. On January 5, 19A, purchased office equipment that cost $6,000; paid one-third cash and charged the balance (one third due in 6 months, and the remaining third is due in 12 months). Credit Accounts Payable for the amount not paid in cash.
- c. Purchased land for future office site: cost, $20,000; paid cash.
- d. Paid office rent in cash, 12 months at $200 per month (debit Rent Expense).
- e. Sold nine properties and collected sales commissions of $56,000.
- f. Paid salaries and commissions expense to salespersons amounting to $52,000 and miscellaneous expenses amounting to $1,000.
- g. Collected rental management fees, $20,000.
- h. Paid utilities, $1,400.
- i. Paid auto rental fees (auto rented for use in business), $3,600.
- j. Paid for advertising, $7,500.
- k. The estimated life of the office equipment was 10 years; assume use for the full year in 19A and no residual value.
- l. Additional commissions earned during 19A on sale of real estate amounted to $64,000 of which $14,000 was uncollected at year-end.
- m. Paid the installment of $2,000 on the office equipment (see [b] above). Assume no interest.
- n. Assume an average income tax rate of 30%; 19A tax expense of $21,450 will be paid in 19B.

Required:

1. Set up T-accounts as follows (no beginning balances because this is the first year):

Account No.	Account titles	Account No.	Account titles
101	Cash	402	Rental management revenue
102	Accounts receivable	501	Rent expense
103	Office equipment	502	Salary and commission expense
104	Accumulated depreciation, office equipment	503	Miscellaneous expense
105	Land for future office site	504	Utilities expense
201	Accounts payable	505	Auto rental expense
203	Income tax payable	506	Advertising expense
301	Capital stock, par $10	507	Depreciation expense
302	Contributed surplus	508	Income tax expense
401	Realty commission revenue		

2. Complete Phase 2 (analyze) and Phase 3 (journalize) each of the above transactions. Use the journal format shown in Exhibit 3–2. Use the letters for dates. Number the journal pages starting with 1. Write a brief explanation of each entry.

3. Complete Phase 4—Post each transaction from the journal to the ledger. Use folio cross-references when posting. You may post each entry as it is made, or wait until all of the journal entries are made.

4. Complete Phase 5—Prepare a trial balance. (Hint: The trial balance total is $224,050, including cash, $94,100.)

5. Complete Phase 6—Prepare the following 19A financial statements:
   a. Income statement—major captions:
      Revenues; Expenses; Pretax income; Income tax expense; Net income; and EPS (enter individual items under each). (Hint: EPS is $11.12.)
   b. Balance sheet—major captions:
      Assets: Current assets; Operational assets; and Other assets.
      Liabilities: Current liabilities.
      Shareholders' equity: Contributed capital; and Retained earnings.
      (Enter individual items under each.)

P3–11   (Challenging Analysis of the Amounts on an Income Statement)

Below is a partially completed income statement of WRY Corporation for the year ended December 31, 19B.

Item	Other Data	Amounts	
Net sales revenue			$200,000
Cost of goods sold			
Gross margin on sales	Average markup on sales,* 40%		
Expenses: Selling expenses			
General and admin- istrative expenses		$23,000	
Interest expense		2,000	
Total expenses			
Pretax income			
Income tax on operations			
Income before EO† items:			
EO gain		10,000	
Income tax effect			
Net EO gain			
Net income			

EPS (on common shares):
  Income before EO†
  gain
			1.00

EO gain			
Net income			

* Gross margin/net sales revenue.
† EO = Extraordinary.

Required:

Based upon the data given above, and assuming (1) a 20% income tax rate on all items and (2) 20,000 common shares outstanding, complete the above income statement. Show all computations.

CASES

C3–1   **(Analysis of Financial Statements)**

The amounts listed below were selected from the annual financial statements for Small Corporation at December 31, 19C (end of the third year of operations):

From the 19C income statement:

Sales revenue	$300,000
Cost of goods sold	(180,000)
All other expenses (including income tax)	(90,000)
Net income	$ 30,000

From the December 31, 19C, balance sheet:

Current assets	$100,000
All other assets	265,000
Total assets	$365,000

Current liabilities	$ 60,000
Long-term liabilities	79,000
Capital stock, par $10	150,000
Contributed surplus	15,000
Retained earnings	61,000
Total liabilities and shareholders' equity	$365,000

Required:

Analyze the data on the 19C financial statements of Small by answering the questions that follow. Show computations.

a. What was the gross margin on sales?

b. What was the amount of EPS?

c. What was the amount of working capital?

d. If the income tax rate were 25%, what was the amount of pretax income?

e. What was the average sales price per share of the capital stock?

f. Assuming no dividends were declared or paid during 19C, what was the beginning balance (January 1, 19C) of retained earnings?

C3–2   (Identification and Correction of Several Accounting Errors)

The bookkeeper of Careless Company prepared the following trial balance at December 31, 19B:

Account titles	Debit	Credit
Notes receivable	$ 4,000	
Supplies inventory		$ 200
Accounts payable	800	
Land	16,000	
Capital stock		20,000
Cash	7,045	
Interest revenue	200	
Notes payable		5,000
Operating expenses	19,000	
Interest expense		800
Other assets	9,583	
Service revenues		30,583
Totals	$56,583	$56,583

Required:

An independent PA (auditor) casually inspected the trial balance and saw that it had several errors. Draft a correct trial balance and explain any errors that you discover. All of the amounts are correct except "Other Assets."

C3–3   (A Complex Situation that Requires Technical Analysis of an Income Statement; Challenging)

Simon Lavoie, a local attorney, decided to sell his practice and retire. He has had discussions with an attorney from another city who wants to relocate. The discussions are at the complex stage of agreeing on a price. Among the important factors have been the financial statements on Lavoie's practice. Lavoie's secretary, under his direction, maintained the records. Each year they developed a "Statement of Profits" on a cash basis from the incomplete records maintained, and no balance sheet was prepared. Upon request, Lavoie provided the other attorney with the following statements for 19x8 prepared by his secretary:

S. LAVOIE
Statement of Profits
19x8

Legal fees collected		$92,000
Expenses paid:		
Rent for office space	$10,400	
Utilities	360	
Telephone	2,900	
Office salaries	19,000	
Office supplies	900	
Miscellaneous expenses	1,600	
Total expenses		35,160
Profit for the year		$56,840

Upon agreement of the parties, you have been asked to "examine the financial figures for 19x8." The other attorney said: "I question the figures because, among other things, they appear to be on a 100% cash basis." Your investigations revealed the following additional data at December 31, 19x8:

a. Of the $92,000 legal fees collected in 19x8, $28,000 was for services performed prior to 19x8.

b. At the end of 19x8, legal fees of $7,000 for services performed during the year were uncollected.

c. Office equipment owned and used by Lavoie cost $3,000 and had an estimated remaining useful life of 10 years.

d. An inventory of office supplies at December 31, 19x8, reflected $200 worth of items purchased during the year that were still on hand. Also, the records for 19x7 indicate that the supplies on hand at the end of that year were about $125.

e. At the end of 19x8 a secretary, whose salary is $12,000 per year, had not been paid for December because of a long trip that extended to January 15, 19x9.

f. The phone bill for December 19x8, amounting to $1,500, was not paid until January 11, 19x9.

g. The office rent paid of $10,400 was for 13 months (it included the rent for January 19x9).

Required:

a. On the basis of the above information, prepare a correct income statement for 19x8. Show your computations for any amounts changed from those in the statement prepared by Lavoie's secretary. (Suggested solution format with four column headings: Items; Cash Basis per Lavoie Statement, $; Explanation of Changes; and Corrected Basis, $.)

b. Write a comment to support your schedule prepared in (a). The purpose should be to explain the reasons for your changes and to suggest some other important items that should be considered in the pricing decision.

C3–4 **(Analysis of the Income Statement and Balance Sheet Included in an Actual Set of Financial Statements)**
Refer to the financial statements of Consolidated-Bathurst Inc. given in Appendix B immediately preceding the Index. Answer the following questions for the 1987 annual accounting period:

1. On what date did the 1987 accounting period end? How were the dollar amounts rounded?

2. Complete the following fundamental accounting model by providing the 1987 amounts for:
   Assets, $_____ = Liabilities, $_____ + Owners' Equity, $_____.

3. How much was the 1987 net sales revenue? _____.

4. What was the dual economic effect on the company of the total revenues?
   a. _____ $ _____
   b. _____ $ _____

5. What was the dual economic effect on the company of the cost of the products sold?
   a. _____ $ _____
   b. _____ $ _____

6. What was the dual economic effect on the company of the cash dividends paid?

   a. _____ $ _____

   b. _____ $ _____

7. Investment income was _____ debited; _____ credited for $ _____ , and interest expense was _____ debited; _____ credited for $ _____ .

8. Prepare a journal entry to record corporate administrative expenses assuming they were all paid in cash.

9. What amounts were reported for (*a*) long-term debt and (*b*) prepaid expenses?

10. What was the amount of depreciation expense? Prepare a journal entry to record this amount.

11. List the subclassifications that the company emphasized on the earnings statement.

12. List the subclassifications that the company emphasized in the balance sheet.

C3–5   (Accountants' Responsibilities)

The following article from *The Bottom Line* illustrates a problem the auditors encountered as a result of an omission of some necessary procedures in their audit.

Windsor auditors assessed highest negligence damages ever

Toronto: A recent Supreme Court of Ontario decision may have set a new high in judgments against auditors found guilty of professional negligence.

The decision by Mr. Justice R. E. Holland, released February 2, involved the Federal Business Development Bank as plaintiff and the Windsor, Ontario-based CA firm Morris, Burk & Co. The bank had approved a $4.5 million loan to a Windsor meat packer after relying on "negligent misrepresentations made" in the financial statements by the meat packers' auditors, S. Morris, J. Burk, B. Luborsky, D. David and P. Kale, partners of Morris, Burk.

The FBDB and the Guarantee Company of Canada initiated the action in May 1983, suing the accounting firm for damages. Although they were later joined by the National Bank, that suit was settled out of court.

Morris, Burk & Co. had been the auditor of Windsor Packing Company Ltd., which had not been able to recover from a disastrous fire in 1977. Although one of the principals tried to turn the company around by juggling the books, it went bankrupt in 1982. In the interim, serious losses were suffered in the years 1979–81, when both the inventory and accounts receivable were inflated and accounts payable understated.

"The auditors failed to discover the fraud and the audited financial statements for 1978 through 1981 and the unaudited interim statements reflected the false entries," Judge Holland wrote.

For example, at trial it was discovered that the accountants had failed to obtain a confirmation of a sizable inventory stored off the premises. That inventory, it seemed, had been falsified by about $300,000. "If Morris Burk had checked directly with Producers they would have ascertained that the inventory had been overstated by $300,000," the judge stated.

In the meantime, the FBDB had loaned Windsor Packing $1.5 million in 1979 and $4.5 million in 1981, relying on the company's financial statements. More-

Source: *The Bottom Line*, March 1988, p. 9.

over, the Guarantee Company of North America had issued a series of bonds to secure the indebtedness of Windsor Packing to the Ontario Hog Producers for $400,000 in 1982, again relying on the audited financial statements.

The judge stated that "the discrepancy between the reported and actual figures for inventory, receivables and payables was so great in 1979, 1980, and 1981 and the resulting loss so substantial that I accept without question the evidence that FBDB would not have made the $4.5 million loan if it had knowledge of the true state of accounts."

"The evidence of negligence on the part of the auditors in connection with these statements is overwhelming," the judge wrote. "Clearly, there was negligent misrepresentation in connection with these financial statements."

Expert witnesses called by the plaintiffs stated that the auditors should have obtained a confirmation of the inventory. As the judge stated: "I conclude that Morris Burk was negligent in conducting the 1978 audit in so far as the inventory at Producers was concerned. The audited financial statement was wrong. The opinion expressed was wrong. The explanation relating to the inventory was not made in accordance with generally accepted auditing standards."

The actual award of damages against the accounting firm was for $4.5 million, less any balance outstanding on the $1.5 million loan as of the date of the 1981 loan, less any payments received and less any security realized by the FBDB. The FBDB is also entitled to interest on the balance at 11% from the date of the writ of summons in May 1983. Moreover, the Guarantee Company of North America was awarded a judgment of $400,000, less the net realized security, plus interest at 11%.

Required:
1. What were the financial implications of the false financial statements issued by the company for the auditor and the creditors?
2. Given the checks present in transaction recording, present two types of entries that could be used to maintain accuracy while accomplishing the entry of the fictitious amounts on Windsor Packing Company's books. (Hint: Consider how credit sales and supplies expenses are recorded.)
3. Would damages be the most serious loss for the auditors?

FOUR

CONCEPTUAL FRAMEWORK OF ACCOUNTING AND ADJUSTING ENTRIES

PURPOSE

Chapter 3 discussed the accounting information processing cycle. That cycle rests upon a foundation of accounting concepts called the **conceptual framework of accounting.** A primary purpose of Chapter 4 is to present that framework and to explain how it is used in transaction analysis, recording, and reporting accounting information.

The other primary purpose of this chapter is to discuss the implications of accrual basis accounting related to the time-period assumption. This topic leads to discussion of a group of entries called **adjusting** entries. These entries are made at the end of each reporting period so that the revenue and matching principles can be properly applied.

On the facing page is the cover and introductory paragraph of FASB's latest statement of concepts.

LEARNING OBJECTIVE

1. Identify and explain the essential characteristics of accounting information.

2. Give an overview of the conceptual framework of accounting.

3. Use the conceptual framework as a qualitative supplement while studying the other chapters.

4. Expand your accounting vocabulary by learning about the "Important Terms Defined in This Chapter."

5. Apply the knowledge learned from this chapter.

ORGANIZATION

Part A—conceptual framework of accounting

1. Essential characteristics of accounting information.

2. Fundamental concepts of accounting assumptions, principles, elements of financial statements, and constraints.

3. Types of adjusting entries.

Part B—adjusting entries illustrated

1. Revenues.

2. Expenses.

No. 017 | December 1985

Financial Accounting Series

Statement of Financial Accounting Concepts No. 6

Elements of Financial Statements

a replacement of FASB Concepts Statement No. 3
(incorporating an amendment of
FASB Concepts Statement No. 2)

This Statement of Financial Accounting Concepts is one of a series of publications in the Board's conceptual framework for financial accounting and reporting. Statements in the series are intended to set forth objectives and fundamentals that will be the basis for development of financial accounting and reporting standards. The objectives identify the goals and purposes of financial reporting. The fundamentals are the underlying concepts of financial accounting – concepts that guide the selection of transactions, events, and circumstances to be accounted for; their recognition and measurement; and the means of summarizing and communicating them to interested parties. Concepts of that type are fundamental in the sense that other concepts flow from them and repeated reference to them will be necessary in establishing, interpreting, and applying accounting and reporting standards.

PART A—CONCEPTUAL FRAMEWORK OF ACCOUNTING

Importance of the Conceptual Framework

The prior chapters discussed the fundamental accounting model (A = L + OE), financial statements, and the accounting information processing cycle. Those discussions emphasized **applications**—the how of accounting. Part A of this chapter discusses the **conceptual framework of accounting.** The concepts are important because they (*a*) help explain the "why" of accounting, (*b*) provide guidance when new accounting situations are encountered, and (*c*) significantly reduce the need to memorize accounting procedures when learning about accounting.

Discussion of the conceptual framework of accounting is included in this early chapter for two important reasons. First, it will help you understand the reasons for particular accounting methods and approaches. Second, the conceptual framework will provide a qualitative, rather than a mechanical, understanding of accounting. Your analytical and interpretive skills will be enhanced significantly.

Finally, a word of caution. The learning objective of Part A of this chapter is to help you develop a general understanding of the concepts. You should not expect to memorize them, nor be able to realize their full effect and importance. Throughout all of the chapters the concepts will be used to support the discussions. In that way you will learn more about what the concepts mean and how they are applied in recording and reporting accounting information.

Overview of the Conceptual Framework

The conceptual framework of accounting is like a basic rule of society. It is continually modified to meet certain changing needs of society and has evolved through experience and consensus.

In Canada, the *CICA Handbook* has served as a focal point for accounting standards rather than the location of a conceptual framework. While conceptual ideas are scattered throughout the various standards, they are not organized in a manner that would justify them being termed a conceptual framework. In December 1988, the CICA Accounting Standards Committee issued a new section to the *Handbook* (numbered 1000) entitled "Financial Statement Concepts." The purpose of this new section is to present the concepts that serve as the foundation for the development and use of accounting principles that exist in general-purpose financial statements of profit-oriented enterprises. It is hoped the document will guide future accounting standards and assist preparers of accounting statements with judgments needed to apply accounting principles and in areas where standards have not been written.

Canadian accounting like the Canadian economy is influenced by what happens in the United States. While Canadian accounting, like Canada itself, does maintain a certain level of independence from the United States, CICA does use FASB's research and pronouncements as a starting point for some of its own efforts. FASB published its first statement in its *Conceptual Framework* in November 1978. Since then five more statements have been issued and one withdrawn. The comprehensive and integrated discussion in these statements does present a reasonable description of a conceptual framework for accounting. Because of the more extensive development of FASB's framework, the discussions that follow are based on the structure of the FASB's *Statements of Financial Accounting Concepts*. Reference will be made to Canadian statements to present the detailed terminology appropriate in Canada.

The FASB conceptual framework of accounting can be viewed from the perspective of (*a*) the essential **characteristics** of accounting information and (*b*) the **concepts** that make up the overall framework.

Essential Characteristics of Accounting Information

The conceptual framework of accounting starts with definitions of the **essential characteristics** that accounting information must possess. These essential characteristics are outlined in Exhibit 4–1. First, the **users** of accounting information are defined as **decision makers.** Users of financial statements are primarily decision makers defined as average, prudent investors, creditors, and others who may find such information helpful. Users are expected to have a reasonable understanding of accounting concepts and procedures (which may be one of the reasons you are studying accounting) as well as a reasonable knowledge of business and economic activities.

Exhibit 4–1   Essential characteristics of accounting information

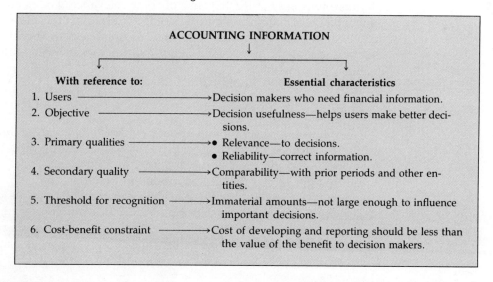

ACCOUNTING INFORMATION

With reference to:	Essential characteristics
1. Users	Decision makers who need financial information.
2. Objective	Decision usefulness—helps users make better decisions.
3. Primary qualities	• Relevance—to decisions. • Reliability—correct information.
4. Secondary quality	Comparability—with prior periods and other entities.
5. Threshold for recognition	Immaterial amounts—not large enough to influence important decisions.
6. Cost-benefit constraint	Cost of developing and reporting should be less than the value of the benefit to decision makers.

The second essential characteristic of accounting concerns the necessary **qualities of accounting information.** Accounting information must help the users make better decisions. To satisfy this objective, it must have the primary **qualitative characteristics** of relevance and reliability. **Relevance** means that accounting information must be capable of influencing decisions. To be relevant, information must have predictive and feedback value as well as be timely in its presentation to the decision maker. **Reliability** means that accounting information must be accurate, termed representatively faithful, unbiased, or neutral, and verifiable.

Also, accounting information must have a secondary qualitative characteristic called **comparability.** This means that accounting information must help users compare the information of a business entity with information about other businesses and prior time periods. Comparability is designated as a secondary characteristic because it is not as important as relevance and reliability.

The two remaining qualitative characteristics of accounting information given in Exhibit 4–1 focus on the cost of preparing accounting information. The **threshold for recognition** (often called materiality) means that accounting for a specific item (i.e., transaction) need not conform precisely to specified accounting guidelines if the amount of the item is not large enough to affect important decisions. This concept has been typically known as the materiality concept. Second, the **cost-benefit** (also called utility) **constraint** recognizes that it usually is costly to produce and report accounting information. Under this constraint, accounting should not use more resources to develop and report a specific item than its value to decision makers—to do so would clearly be uneconomic. Measurement of the cost-benefit relationship is very subjective—especially the value of the benefits.

The interaction of these qualitative characteristics will necessitate trade-offs, particularly between relevance and reliability. Different situations may necessitate more reliability at the expense of some relevance. For example, a delay in issuing financial statements may be needed to establish reliable amounts but the delay would generally mean some loss of timeliness of the information. Accounting decisions will continually involve various trade-offs among the qualitative characteristics.

Fundamental Concepts of Accounting

The fundamental concepts build upon the characteristics of accounting shown in Exhibit 4–1. The fundamental concepts of accounting provide the conceptual guidelines for application of the accounting information cycle. This cycle was introduced in Chapter 3 and is expanded in Chapter 5.

Exhibit 4–2 gives an overview of the **fundamental concepts of accounting.** Notice the five categories—assumptions, principles, constraints, elements of financial statements, and detailed practices and procedures. Because of the significance of these fundamental concepts, each category is discussed below.

Exhibit 4–2 Fundamental concepts of accounting

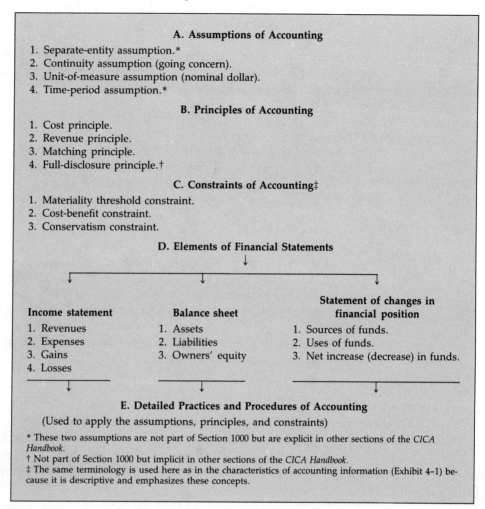

A. Assumptions of Accounting
1. Separate-entity assumption.*
2. Continuity assumption (going concern).
3. Unit-of-measure assumption (nominal dollar).
4. Time-period assumption.*

B. Principles of Accounting
1. Cost principle.
2. Revenue principle.
3. Matching principle.
4. Full-disclosure principle.†

C. Constraints of Accounting‡
1. Materiality threshold constraint.
2. Cost-benefit constraint.
3. Conservatism constraint.

D. Elements of Financial Statements

Income statement	Balance sheet	Statement of changes in financial position
1. Revenues	1. Assets	1. Sources of funds.
2. Expenses	2. Liabilities	2. Uses of funds.
3. Gains	3. Owners' equity	3. Net increase (decrease) in funds.
4. Losses		

E. Detailed Practices and Procedures of Accounting
(Used to apply the assumptions, principles, and constraints)

* These two assumptions are not part of Section 1000 but are explicit in other sections of the *CICA Handbook*.
† Not part of Section 1000 but implicit in other sections of the *CICA Handbook*.
‡ The same terminology is used here as in the characteristics of accounting information (Exhibit 4–1) because it is descriptive and emphasizes these concepts.

Assumptions of Accounting

The four assumptions are primarily based on the business environment in which accounting and the expectations that set certain limits on the way accounting information is reported.

Separate-Entity Assumption

Each business must be accounted for as an individual organization, separate and apart from its owners, all other persons, and other entities. The personal transactions of the owners are not considered as transactions of the business. A business entity usually is a sole proprietorship, partnership, or corporation or even a group of corporations (discussed in Chapter 14).

Continuity Assumption

For accounting purposes a business is assumed to have an indefinite life. This assumption is sometimes called the "going-concern assumption" because accounting assumes that a business will continue to follow its objectives in the foreseeable future.

Unit-of-Measure Assumption

Each entity will account for, and report, its financial results primarily in terms of the national monetary unit. Therefore, the financial statements of companies in Canada use the Canadian dollar. This assumption implies that the monetary unit is a stable measuring unit, without a changing value (due to inflation and deflation[1]).

Time-Period Assumption

The time-period assumption recognizes that decision makers require **periodic information** about the financial condition of a business. The periodic **reporting period** does not have to conform to the calendar year. However, the accounting information processing cycle and the primary financial statements cover one full reporting year.

All of the chapters discuss the effects of these four assumptions on accounting and financial reporting.

Principles of Accounting

The four principles of accounting are important because they provide the conceptual guidelines for application of the basic accounting model (A = L + OE). Also, they give the measurement, recording, and reporting phases of the accounting information processing cycle. They can be characterized as "how to apply" concepts.

Cost Principle

This principle defines the conceptual basis for measuring the assets, liabilities, and owners' equity (including revenues and expenses) of a business. The cost principle (also termed the historical cost principle) states that the **cash-equiv-**

---

[1] The exchange unit (Canadian dollars) changes in purchasing power due to the effects of inflation and deflation; simply put, the dollar does not always command the same amount of real goods. Thus, money does not have the most basic element of any measurement unit (i.e., a metre always is the same length); that is, uniformity is magnitude. During inflation and deflation, the monetary unit is not uniform in magnitude because one unit will command fewer, or more, real goods, respectively, than before. Chapter 17 presents the specific definitions of inflation used in practice.

alent cost should be used for recognizing (i.e., recording) all financial statement elements (discussed later). Under the cost principle, cost is **measured** as the cash paid plus the current value of all noncash considerations.

Revenue Principle

The revenue principle relates to the income statement model (Revenues − Expenses = Income). This principle specifies when revenue should be **recognized** (i.e., recorded) and how it should be measured. Revenue should be recognized when there is an inflow of net assets (assets minus liabilities) from the sale of goods or services. Revenue is **measured** as the cash received plus the current dollar value of all noncash considerations received. The revenue principle implicitly includes the concept of accrual mentioned in Chapter 2. In addition, the revenue principle satisfies the more general recognition criteria for all elements of the financial statements; namely, measurability and the probable obtaining or sacrificing of future economic benefits.

Matching Principle

This principle relates directly to the income statement (Revenues − Expenses = Income). Resources that are used to earn revenues are called **expenses.** The matching principle holds that when the period's revenues are properly recognized in conformity with the revenue principle, all of the expenses incurred in earning those revenues must be **matched** with the revenues of that period. For example, if the revenue from selling a television set is recognized in 19X, the purchase cost of the set must be recognized as an expense in 19X only. The accrual basis of accounting mentioned in Chapter 2 is implicit in the matching principle.

Full-Disclosure Principle

The periodic financial statements of a business must clearly report (i.e., disclose) all of the relevant information about the economic affairs of a business. This principle requires (*a*) complete financial statements and (*b*) notes to the financial statements to elaborate on the "numbers." The term *fair disclosure* is also commonly used to denote the essence of this principle.

Constraints of Accounting

The constraints of accounting are practical guidelines to reduce the **volume** and **cost** of reporting accounting information without reducing its value to decision makers. The constraints are materiality, cost benefit, and conservatism.

Materiality Threshold Constraint

Although items and amounts that are of low significance must be accounted for, they **do not have to be separately reported if they would not influence reasonable decisions.** Accountants usually designate such items and amounts as **immaterial.**

Cost-Benefit Constraint

The **benefits of accounting information to decision makers should be higher than the cost of providing that information.** This concept is economically sound; however, measurement of benefits is difficult.

Conservatism Constraint

Special care should be taken to **avoid (*a*) overstating assets and revenues and (*b*) understating liabilities and expenses.** This constraint produces conservative income statement and balance sheet amounts. Conservatism is applied in a manner reflected by the term **prudence.** When faced with uncertainty, if two estimates are equally likely, conservatism suggests the less optimistic one should be used. If the estimates are not equally likely, then the better of the two should be used. Care is always needed as well not to permit conservatism to create unreliable or noncomparable statements.

Elements of Financial Statements

The **elements** of financial statements are the broad classifications (e.g., assets, revenues) of information that should be reported on the required financial statements. These elements were discussed briefly in Chapter 3, which presented practical definitions of the elements. Exhibit 4–3 gives the conceptual definitions of all of the elements for each required financial statement.

Practices and Procedures of Accounting

The "practices and procedures of accounting" were listed last in Exhibit 4–2 because they primarily involve implementation of the fundamental concepts. Practices and procedures are practical and detailed guidelines. They have been developed to attain a reasonable degree of uniformity in applying the fundamental concepts. The practices and procedures of accounting are discussed in all of the chapters of this textbook. A major portion of the illustrations given in Chapter 3 involved accounting practices and procedures such as journal, ledger, trial balance, subclassifications on the financial statements, and depreciation.

Conceptual Framework Related to the Financial Statements

The conceptual framework of accounting determines how each phase of the accounting information cycle—transaction analysis, recording, and reporting—is done. **The end product—the periodic financial report—should be in conformity with the conceptual framework.** The three financial statements—the balance sheet, income statement, and statement of changes in financial position—were discussed in the preceding chapters. This section emphasizes the **relationships** among these financial statements. These three financial statements and their accompanying notes, supporting schedules, and the auditors' opinion

Exhibit 4–3   Elements of financial statements defined*

Income statement:

1. **Revenues**—Inflows of assets or settlements of liabilities from sale of goods and services that constitute the entity's **ongoing or major operations.**
2. **Expenses**—Outflows or using up of assets or incurrence of liabilities for delivery of goods or services and other activities that constitute the entity's **ongoing or major operations.**
3. **Gains**—Increases in net assets (assets minus liabilities) from **peripheral or incidental transactions,** and all other activities except those from revenues or investments by owners.
4. **Losses**—Decreases in net assets from **peripheral or incidental transactions** and other events except those from expenses or distributions to owners.

Balance sheet:

1. **Assets**—Probable future economic benefits owned by the entity as a result of past transactions.
2. **Liabilities**—Probable future sacrifices of economic benefits as a result of past transactions; involves transfer of assets or services.
3. **Owners' equity**—Residual interest of the owners after all debts are paid (i.e., Assets − Liabilities = Owners' Equity).

Statement of changes in financial position:†

1. **Sources of funds**—Cash (or cash plus short-term investments less short-term borrowings) actually received during the period.
2. **Uses of funds**—Cash (or cash plus short-term investments less short-term borrowings) actually paid during the period.

* Adapted from: FASB, *Statement of Financial Accounting Concepts No. 6,* "Elements of Financial Statements" (Stamford, Conn., December 1985); reported in FASB, *Accounting Standards: Statements of Financial Accounting Concepts 1–6* (Homewood, Ill.: Richard D. Irwin, 1989), pp. 227–28. The definitions above are consistent with those used by the *CICA Handbook.*
† Chapter 15 will provide a more complete discussion of this statement and its elements.

(see page 13) should be viewed as the entire financial report for the selected time period. This entire reporting package is necessary to meet the varied needs of a diverse population of financial statement users. Exhibit 4–4 gives the basic relationships among the three required financial statements for a reporting period, such as January 1, 1988, through December 31, 1988. The exhibit shows that the beginning balance sheet was changed to the ending balance sheet by the items reported on the income statement and statement of changes in financial position. You can see changes in the financial position of a business by comparing its balance sheets at the beginning and the end of the year.

The income statement and statement of changes in financial position are often referred to as **change** statements because they help users understand what caused the period's change in financial position. Exhibit 4–4 shows that the **income statement** explains one change in financial position—retained earnings.

Exhibit 4–4   Relationship among the three required financial statements

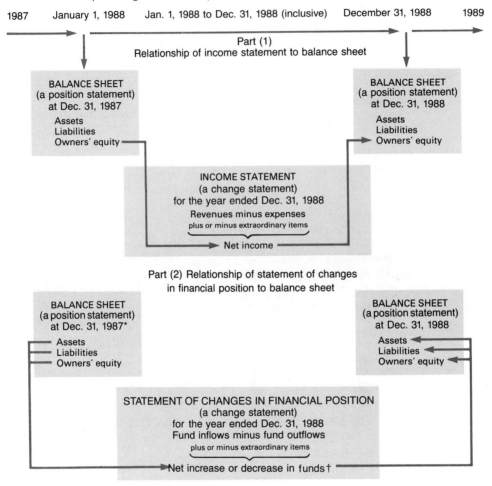

1987   January 1, 1988   Jan. 1, 1988 to Dec. 31, 1988 (inclusive)   December 31, 1988   1989

Part (1)
Relationship of income statement to balance sheet

BALANCE SHEET
(a position statement)
at Dec. 31, 1987

Assets
Liabilities
Owners' equity

BALANCE SHEET
(a position statement)
at Dec. 31, 1988

Assets
Liabilities
Owners' equity

INCOME STATEMENT
(a change statement)
for the year ended Dec. 31, 1988
Revenues minus expenses
plus or minus extraordinary items

Net income

Part (2) Relationship of statement of changes
in financial position to balance sheet

BALANCE SHEET
(a position statement)
at Dec. 31, 1987*

Assets
Liabilities
Owners' equity

BALANCE SHEET
(a position statement)
at Dec. 31, 1988

Assets
Liabilities
Owners' equity

STATEMENT OF CHANGES IN FINANCIAL POSITION
(a change statement)
for the year ended Dec. 31, 1988
Fund inflows minus fund outflows
plus or minus extraordinary items

Net increase or decrease in funds†

* The balance sheet of December 31, 1987, also is the balance sheet at the beginning of 1988.
† Funds are measured as either cash or cash plus short-term investments less short-term borrowings.

The income statement gives detailed information that "explains" net income. The **statement of changes in financial position** explains all of the changes in financial position (i.e., assets, liabilities, and owners' equity) in terms of cash inflows and cash outflows.

Thus, the three financial statements are linked in important ways. This linking often is called **articulation;** that is, an amount in one statement (e.g., net income on the income statement) is carried to another statement (e.g., the statement of retained earnings). Similarly, net income is tied to the SCFP (discussed later). Decision makers can better interpret the financial statements when they clearly understand these relationships. Understanding these relationships will be helpful as you study the remaining chapters.

Accrual Basis Accounting

The conceptual framework of accounting (Exhibits 4–1 and 4–2) requires that **accrual basis accounting** be used for the income statement and balance sheet.

Accrual basis accounting means that all **completed transactions** are recorded when they occur, regardless of when any related cash receipts or payments occur. In contrast, **cash basis accounting** means that these transactions are recorded only when the related cash is received or paid. Cash basis accounting is not in conformity with GAAP.

Accrual basis accounting requires application of the revenue and matching principles.

The revenue principle specifies that revenues are **earned** (i.e., recognized) in the period when the revenue transaction occurs, rather than when the cash is collected. Therefore, the total amount of revenues reported on the income statement for the period should include sales and services of that period collected in cash. Also included are all sales and services of the period on credit, even though the cash may be collected in the next period. Similarly, when rent (for example) is collected in advance, rent revenue should be reported on the income statement for the period in which occupancy occurred, rather than in the period of cash collection. Assume rent revenue of $1,200 is collected on December 1, 19A, for 12 months' future occupancy ending November 30, 19B. Rent revenue **earned** in 19A would be $100 and in 19B, $1,100.

To apply the **revenue principle,** the general guideline is that revenue is considered earned (realized) when the **earning process** is substantially completed. In the case of the sale of goods, the earning process is substantially completed when ownership of the goods passes from the seller to the buyer. In the case of the sale of services, the earning process is substantially completed as the services are performed (rather than when the services finally are completed in all respects). This general guideline is applied to most revenue transactions; however, there are a few exceptions that will be discussed in later chapters.

Expenses are **incurred** in the period when the goods or services are **used or consumed.** Therefore, the total amount of expense incurred should be reported on the income statement of the period. In some cases, the expense-incurring services and goods are obtained on credit whereby the cash is paid in a later period; and in other cases, the cash is paid in advance of use of the goods or services (as in the case of prepayment of a three-year insurance premium on a building). In each of these cases, the date of the cash flow is not used to determine the period in which the expense should be reported on the income statement. In contrast, individual and very small businesses sometimes use the **cash basis** for their records. That is, all revenues are considered earned only when the cash is collected. All expenses are considered incurred only when the cash is paid. This method does not conform to GAAP because it incorrectly measures revenues and expenses when their transaction dates precede or lag the related cash flow dates.

Accrual Basis Accounting and the Time-Period Assumption

The above discussion of the relationships among the three required financial statements emphasized the dating of financial statements. Each financial statement should specifically identify its **time dimension** (see Chapter 1, pages 21, 25, and 28). Exhibit 4–4 reemphasizes that the time dimension of the balance sheet is at a specific date (such as "At December 31, 19X"). In contrast, the two "change" statements cover a **specified period of time** (such as, "For the Year Ended December 31, 19X").

The life span of most business entities is assumed to be indefinite according to the continuity assumption. However, decision makers need **current** information about the entity. Therefore, the life span of an entity is divided into a series of short time periods, such as one year, for many financial reporting purposes. This division of the activities of a business into a series of equal time periods is known as the **time-period assumption.**

Because annual periods tend to be dominant in our society, the accounting period usually is 12 consecutive months. Consequently, accounting emphasizes annual financial statements. Many companies use a year that corresponds to the natural cycle of their business, such as July 1 through June 30, rather than to the calendar year.

In addition to the annual financial statements, many businesses prepare and publish quarterly financial reports for external distribution. These statements usually are called **interim reports.** In addition to annual reports, monthly financial statements often are prepared exclusively for **internal management** purposes. The monthly reports are not distributed to outsiders.

Dividing the life span of a business into short time periods, such as a year, for measurement purposes often causes complex accounting problems because **some transactions start in one accounting period and are, in effect, concluded in a subsequent period.** This continuity of the effects of a transaction may occur for all classifications. For example:

a. **Assets**—A machine that is purchased in year 19A will be depreciated over its estimated useful life, for example, 10 years.

b. **Liabilities**—A note payable is signed that requires interest payments in each of three years and payment of the principal at the end of the third year.

c. **Owners' equity**—Shares are sold in one year with a cash down payment plus two equal annual installment payments and issuance of the shares at the date of the last installment.

d. **Revenues**—Rent is collected in one year for six months in advance, and two of the occupancy periods (months) extend into the next year.

e. **Expenses**—An insurance premium on property is paid in advance for two years of future coverage.

When the effects of a transaction, such as those listed above, overlap two or more accounting periods, accrual basis accounting necessitates a **cutoff** point at each year-end. At this cutoff point the effects of the transaction must be separated between the two accounting periods. To explain—the "bottom line" on an income statement is called **net income.** Accrual basis accounting requires that both revenues and expenses be correctly measured each accounting period. The revenues of the period are determined in conformity with the revenue principle, then the expenses must be matched with the revenues that they earned. This measurement process is complicated because some revenue and expense transactions start in one period and extend over one or more future periods. Therefore, a careful cutoff of all revenues and expenses between accounting periods must be made. This cutoff is done by applying the revenue and matching principles.

The **matching principle** focuses on the measurement of expenses and the matching of them with the periodic revenues **earned** during the period. The matching principle states that all of the **expenses incurred in earning revenues** should be identified, or matched, with only those revenues.

To apply the matching principle, it is necessary to consider the **purposes** for which the expenses were incurred. If the expenses are associated with a specific revenue, as is the usual case, the expenses should be identified with the period in which that revenue was earned. Resources used in one period to earn revenues in other periods should be assigned to those other periods. Some expenses, such as general company administration and institutional advertising, do not have a direct relationship to the revenues of a specific accounting period. Therefore, such expenses, are recognized on the income statement of the period in which they were incurred.

Accrual basis accounting involves a cutoff at the end of each accounting period to satisfy the revenue and matching principles. That is, at the end of each accounting period, accounting entries must be made for those transactions whose effects extend beyond the year in which the initial transaction occurred. These entries are called **adjusting entries.**

Adjusting Entries

Adjusting entries are made to change certain account balances at the end of the accounting period. For example, assume a company purchased a machine for use in the business on January 1, 19A. The machine cost $50,000 and had an estimated useful life of five years (no residual value). On January 1, 19A (the date the transaction was completed), an asset account—Machinery—was debited (increased) for $50,000. However, by December 31, 19A (end of the first accounting period), the machine had depreciated to $40,000. Therefore, due to an internal economic event (use of the machine), an **adjusting entry** must be made to (*a*) decrease the book value of the asset by $10,000 and (*b*) record depreciation expense of $10,000.

Adjusting entries have four basic characteristics as follows:

1. An **income statement** account balance (revenue or expense) is changed.
2. A **balance sheet** account balance (asset or liability) is changed.
3. They usually are recorded at the end of the accounting period.
4. They never directly affect the Cash account.

The four different types of adjusting entries are as follows:

Revenues (revenue principle applied):

1. **Revenue collected in advance but not yet earned**—Revenue collected in advance of being **earned** must be deferred to the future period or periods in which it will be earned. In this case, cash collection **leads** (precedes) revenue recognition.

   Example: On December 1, 19A, Alpha Company collected $1,000 cash for December 19A and January 19B rent (i.e., $500 per month). On the transaction date, the company debited Cash and credited Rent Revenue for $1,000.

   Analysis on December 31, 19A: Rent revenue was earned in 19A for only one month, December; the other monthly rent will be earned in 19B; however, cash was collected in 19A for both months. Therefore, on December 31, 19A, an **adjusting entry** for $500 must be made to (*a*) decrease (debit) Rent Revenue and (*b*) increase (credit) Rent Revenue Collected in Advance. The $500 credit balance in this account must be reported on the 19A balance sheet as a **liability** because the company owes the renter occupancy for one month (January 19B).

2. **Revenue earned but not yet recorded or collected**—Revenue not collected or recorded but earned in the current accounting period should be recorded as **earned** in the current period, even though the related cash will be collected in a subsequent period. In this case, cash collection lags revenue recognition.

   Example: On December 31, 19A, Alpha Company finished two phases of a service job for a customer; the third phase will be done in January 19B. The total contract price was $1,200 (i.e., $400 per phase) cash, payable upon completion of all phases.

   Analysis on December 31, 19A: Service revenue of $800 (i.e., $1,200 $\times$ 2/3) was earned in 19A, although not yet recorded or collected. Therefore, an **adjusting entry** for $800 must be made on December 31, 19A. This entry will (*a*) increase (debit) Accounts Receivable and (*b*) increase (credit) Service Revenue because revenue for the first two phases has been earned in 19A. A receivable must be recorded because the collection of cash will be made in 19B.

Expenses (matching principle applied):

3. **Expense paid in advance but not yet incurred**—Expense paid in advance of use of the services or goods must be deferred to the future period, or periods, in which such services or goods will be used. In this case, cash payment **leads** expense recognition.

    Example: On January 1, 19A, Alpha Company paid a two-year premium of $800 for property insurance; the coverage is for 19A and 19B (i.e., $400 per year). The company recorded this transaction on January 1, 19A, as a debit (increase) of $800 to Prepaid Insurance (an asset), and a decrease (credit) to Cash.

    Analysis on December 31, 19A: On this date half of the benefit of the insurance coverage has been used. Half of the related insurance premium has expired (i.e., $800 ÷ 2 = $400); the other half remains prepaid. Therefore, on December 31, 19A, an **adjusting entry** for $400 must be made to (*a*) increase (debit) Insurance Expense and (*b*) decrease (credit) Prepaid Insurance. This entry records the $400 expense for 19A and leaves $400 in the asset account, Prepaid Insurance. Prepaid insurance is an asset because Alpha Company has an obligation from the insurance company to provide insurance coverage for 19B (the premium already has been paid).

4. **Expense incurred but not yet recorded or paid**—Expense incurred (the services or goods have been used) in the current accounting period but not yet recorded or paid (the related cash payment will be in a subsequent period) should be recorded as expense in the current period. In this case, cash payment **lags** expense recognition.

    Example: On December 31, 19A, Alpha Company employees have earned $1,000 in wages that will be paid in cash on the next payroll date January 6, 19B.

    Analysis on December 31, 19A: The company has incurred wage expense in 19A of $1,000 (the employees were helping to earn 19A revenues). Because the employees have not been paid, the company has a $1,000 liability on December 31, 19A. Therefore, an **adjusting entry** for $1,000 must be made on December 31, 19A. This entry will (*a*) debit (increase) Wage Expense and (*b*) credit (increase) Wages Payable. This liability will be reported on the 19A balance sheet and will be paid on the next payroll date, January 6, 19B.

In summary, adjusting entries usually are made at the end of each accounting period, after the regular entries are completed. At this time, the accountant must make a careful check of the records and supporting documents to determine whether there are any cases such as those listed above that need **adjusting entries.** In most cases, one or more such entries will be required. If any required adjusting entries are not made, revenue for the period may be measured incorrectly, and/or expenses may not be matched with the revenues earned during the period. In either case, the result would be an incorrect measurement of amounts on both the income statement and the balance sheet for both the current and subsequent period or periods. Adjusting entries are not unusual. They require only a knowledge and analysis of the actual facts about each item.

Terminology—Accrue and Defer

Accountants often use two technical terms in respect to adjusting entries and in a more general sense. Throughout this textbook and in many of your other courses (and in the outside environment), you will encounter the terms **accrued** (or to accrue) and **deferred** (or to defer). Definitions for accounting purposes are: Accrued, in the case of expenses, means not yet paid; in the case of revenues, not yet collected. Deferred, in the case of revenues, means collected in advance; in the case of expenses, paid in advance. To summarize:

Term	Definition	Example
1. Accrued expense.	An expense incurred; not yet paid or recorded.	Wages earned by employees but not yet paid.
2. Accrued revenue.	A revenue earned; not yet collected or recorded.	Services performed in advance of collection.
3. Deferred revenue.	A revenue not yet earned; collected in advance.	Rent collected in advance of occupancy.
4. Deferred expense.	An expense not yet incurred; paid in advance.	Insurance premium paid in advance.

PART B—ADJUSTING ENTRIES ILLUSTRATED (A CASE STUDY)

This part of the chapter continues the discussion of adjusting entries. It provides detailed illustrations and explanations of numerous adjusting entries. Our emphasis will be on the **analysis** of specific examples to determine the appropriate adjusting entry and the related entries that are made in subsequent periods. These illustrations will increase your understanding of the application of the accounting model, the measurement of periodic revenues and expenses, and the determination of income. Throughout the examples we will refer to High-Rise Apartments (organized as a corporation on January 1, 19A) and will assume that the current annual accounting period ends December 31, 19B. This case is continued in Chapter 5 to illustrate the complete accounting information processing cycle. Adjusting entries are entered in the journal and posted to the ledger accounts. All adjusting entries are recorded and dated at the end of the accounting period.

Revenue Collected in Advance (Deferred Revenue)

Businesses may collect cash and record it in advance of earning the related revenue from the sale of services or goods. The amount collected in advance is called unearned or deferred revenue. Unearned revenue must be apportioned to the period in which the services are performed or the sale is completed in conformity with the **revenue principle.** When unearned revenue has been received, an **adjusting entry** usually is required at the end of the period. This entry will recognize (1) the correct amount of revenue **earned** during the current period and (2) the remaining obligation in the future to provide the related goods or services. We will analyze one such case for High-Rise Apartments that occurs because some tenants pay their rent in the middle of each month. Each adjusting entry is letter coded for reference.

   Example: On December 11, 19B, two tenants paid rent for one month from December 11, 19B, through January 10, 19C, in the amount of $1,500. The sequence of entries recorded by High-Rise would be:

December 11, 19B—date of the transaction:

```
Cash . . . . . . . . . . . . . . . . . . . . . . . . . . . . . . . . . . . . . .    1,500
    Rent revenue . . . . . . . . . . . . . . . . . . . . . . . . .              1,500
    To record one month's rent for the period December 11, 19B,
    through January 10, 19C.
```

December 31, 19B—end of the accounting period:

   Analysis: The $1,500 cash collected included rent revenue for December 19B of $1,500 \times 20/30 = $1,000, and rent revenue collected in advance for January 19C of $1,500 \times 10/30 = $500. Therefore, an **adjusting entry** is required on December 31, 19B, to (*a*) reduce the balance in Rent Revenue by $500 and (*b*) record the obligation to furnish occupancy in 19C for one third of a month which was paid in advance of that year. This $500 is a current liability that will be paid in January 19C by providing occupancy rights.

   a. December 31, 19B (end of the accounting period)—**adjusting entry:**[2]

```
Rent revenue  . . . . . . . . . . . . . . . . . . . . . . . . . . . . . . .    500
    Rent revenue collected in advance  . . . . . . . . . . . . . . . .          500
    To adjust the accounts for revenue collected in advance as of the
    end of the current period.
```

---

   [2] The entry at collection date, December 11, 19B, could have been recorded so that it would preclude the need for an adjusting entry later:

```
Cash  . . . . . . . . . . . . . . . . . . . . . . . . . . . . . . . . . . . . .    1,500
    Rent revenue . . . . . . . . . . . . . . . . . . . . . . . . . . .              1,000
    Rent revenue collected in advance  . . . . . . . . . . . . . . .                 500
```

   Also, it could be accounted for as follows with the same end result:

December 11, 19B:

```
Cash  . . . . . . . . . . . . . . . . . . . . . . . . . . . . . . . . . . . . .    1,500
    Rent revenue collected in advance  . . . . . . . . . . . . . . .              1,500
```

December 31, 19B—adjusting entry:

```
Rent revenue collected in advance . . . . . . . . . . . . . . . . . . .    1,000
    Rent revenue . . . . . . . . . . . . . . . . . . . . . . . . . . .              1,000
```

As the above variations illustrate, the exact nature of an adjusting entry depends on how the transaction was recorded and what, if any, adjustments have been made previously. In practice, adjustments require judgment by the accountant so that they are made correctly.

The $1,000 (i.e., $1,500 − $500) rent revenue is reported on the 19B income statement. The rent revenue collected in advance of $500 is reported on the 19B balance sheet as a current liability.

January 19C:

```
Rent revenue collected in advance . . . . . . . . . . . . . . . . . . . . . . . . . .    500
    Rent revenue . . . . . . . . . . . . . . . . . . . . . . . . . . . . . . . . . . .          500
    To transfer the rent revenue from the liability account to the
    19C revenue account because it now has been earned.
```

Revenue Earned prior to Collection (Accrued Revenue)

At the end of the current accounting period, analysis may reveal that some revenue has been **earned** (in conformity with the revenue principle) but has **not yet been recorded or collected.** Such unrecorded revenue usually is called accrued revenue.

The revenue principle states that if revenue was earned in the current accounting period, it must be recorded and reported in that period along with the asset that has been created (an account receivable). This is accomplished by making an **adjusting entry** to recognize (*a*) a receivable for the amount earned but not yet collected and (*b*) the amount of revenue earned. We will analyze a typical situation for High-Rise Apartments and give the sequence of entries.

Example: On December 31, 19B, the manager of High-Rise Apartments analyzed the rental records and found that one tenant had not paid the December rent amounting to $600. The sequence of entries recorded by High-Rise would be:

b. December 31, 19B (end of accounting period)—adjusting entry:

```
Rent revenue receivable . . . . . . . . . . . . . . . . . . . . . . . . . . . . . . .    600
    Rent revenue . . . . . . . . . . . . . . . . . . . . . . . . . . . . . . . . . . .          600
    To record rent revenue earned in 19B but not collected by year-end.
```

January 19C—date of collection:

```
Cash . . . . . . . . . . . . . . . . . . . . . . . . . . . . . . . . . . . . . . . . . .    600
    Rent revenue receivable . . . . . . . . . . . . . . . . . . . . . . . . . . . . . .          600
    To record collection of receivable for 19B rent revenue.
```

The adjusting entry at the end of 19B has two measurement purposes: (1) to record rent revenue earned in 19B of $600 and (2) to record a receivable (an asset) for occupancy provided in 19B for which $600 cash will be collected in January 19C. Rent revenue receivable is reported on the December 31, 19B, balance sheet as a current asset.

Expenses Paid in Advance (Deferred or Prepaid Expense)

Often a company either pays cash or incurs a liability in one accounting period for assets purchased or services obtained that will be used in one or more future accounting periods to help earn revenues during those future periods. Such transactions create an asset because of the future benefits. The asset usually is called a **prepaid expense** (or a deferred expense). As the future periods pass, the related revenues are earned in conformity with the revenue principle. Then, as the revenues are earned, period by period, the prepaid expense amount must be apportioned to the appropriate periods in conformity with the **matching principle.**

For example, if the related revenues are earned over three accounting periods, the prepaid expense must be apportioned to each of those three periods in order to measure net income for each period.

For High-Rise Apartments we will analyze three such transactions that occurred in 19B.

Prepaid Insurance

On January 1, 19B, High-Rise paid cash of $2,400 in advance for a two-year insurance policy on the apartment building. The entries by High-Rise for this prepaid expense would be:

January 1, 19B—date of the transaction:

```
Prepaid insurance (an asset account) . . . . . . . . . . . . . . . . . . . . . . . 2,400
    Cash . . . . . . . . . . . . . . . . . . . . . . . . . . . . . . . . . . .         2,400
    To record prepayment of a two-year premium on building.
```

December 31, 19B—end of the accounting period:

Analysis: The $2,400 cash paid on January 1, 19B, was for insurance coverage for two full years; therefore, insurance expense for each of the two years will be $1,200. At the end of 19B, an adjusting entry must be made to (*a*) reduce prepaid insurance by $1,200 and (*b*) record insurance expense of $1,200 for 19B.

c. December 31, 19B (end of the accounting period)—adjusting entry:

```
Insurance expense . . . . . . . . . . . . . . . . . . . . . . . . . . . . . . . . 1,200
    Prepaid insurance . . . . . . . . . . . . . . . . . . . . . . . . . . . . . .      1,200
    To record 19B insurance expense for 12 months
    ($2,400 × 12/24 = $1,200).
```

The adjusting entry has two measurement purposes: (1) it apportions insurance expense to the current period for **matching** purposes and (2) it adjusts (reduces) the Prepaid Insurance account to the correct asset amount ($1,200) for the unexpired insurance remaining at the end of 19B. That is, at the end of 19B, the company was entitled to one more year of insurance protection (with a cost of $1,200), which is a current asset.

December 31, 19C (end of next accounting period)—adjusting entry:

```
Insurance expense . . . . . . . . . . . . . . . . . . . . . . . . . . . . . . . . 1,200
    Prepaid insurance . . . . . . . . . . . . . . . . . . . . . . . . . . . . . .      1,200
    To record 19C insurance expense.
```

This entry apportions insurance expense to 19C and reduces the prepaid insurance balance to zero because the policy term ends on December 31, 19C.

Depreciation

On January 1, 19A, a contractor finished an apartment building for High-Rise. The contract price of $360,000 was paid in cash. The building had an **estimated useful life** of 30 years and an estimated $60,000 **residual value** at the end of the 30 years. This transaction involved the acquisition of an asset (building) that may affect the financial statements for the next 30 years (including 19A). At this point, we will consider one continuing effect—depreciation. The entries by High-Rise are discussed below.

January 1, 19A—date of acquisition of the building:

Apartment building 360,000
  Cash   360,000
  To record full payment for construction cost of the building.

d. December 31, 19B (end of the accounting period)—adjusting entry:

Depreciation expense 10,000
  Accumulated depreciation, building   10,000
  To record straight-line depreciation expense for one year
  ($360,000 − $60,000) ÷ 30 years = $10,000.

The adjusting entry for depreciation expense will be repeated at the end of each year over the 30-year life of the building. The estimated amount expected to be recovered when the asset is sold or disposed of is known as the **residual value** (sometimes it is called scrap or salvage value). For computing depreciation, the cost of the asset must be **reduced** by the residual value. The difference ($360,000 − $60,000 = $300,000) is the net amount of cost to be depreciated over the estimated useful life. Thus, the annual depreciation expense on the apartment building is ($360,000 − $60,000) ÷ 30 years = $10,000.[3] The residual value of $60,000 is deducted because it is the amount of cost that is expected to be recovered at the end of the useful life (of the building) to the company.

The adjusting entry has two measurement purposes: (1) it allocates a part of the cost of the building to expense for the current period for **matching** purposes and (2) it adjusts (reduces) the amount of the asset to its undepreciated cost. The credit to Accumulated Depreciation, Building could have been made directly to the building account with the same effect. However, it is desirable, for reporting purposes, to keep the balance of the asset account Apartment Building at original cost. This is accomplished by an asset **contra,** or **offset,** account titled Accumulated Depreciation, Building. The difference between the acquisition cost and accumulated depreciation is called **book** or **carrying value.** The book or carrying value does not represent the current **market** value of the asset because

_____

[3] This example assumes straight-line depreciation; that is, an equal amount of depreciation expense is apportioned to each period. Other methods of depreciation will be discussed in Chapter 9.

accounting for depreciation is a cost allocation process rather than a market valuation process.

Supplies Inventory and Expense

High-Rise purchases maintenance supplies not for resale but for use as needed. They are kept in a small storeroom from which supplies are withdrawn as needed. On January 1, 19B, the inventory of maintenance supplies was $100; these were **unused** supplies on hand carried over from the previous year. On March 18, 19B, additional supplies were purchased for $500 and placed in the storeroom. No accounting entry is made when the supplies are withdrawn for use. To determine the amount of supplies **used** during the period, an inventory of the supplies remaining is taken at the end of the period. At December 31, 19B, the inventory of the supplies in the storeroom showed $200. The entries by High-Rise would be:

March 18, 19B—date of purchase of supplies:

Inventory of maintenance supplies (an asset)	500	
Cash		500

To record purchase of maintenance supplies for addition to inventory.

Note: This entry increases the inventory account balance from $100 to $600.

e. December 31, 19B (end of the accounting period)—adjusting entry:

Maintenance expense	400	
Inventory of maintenance supplies		400

To record the amount of supplies used from inventory:
Beginning inventory, $100 + Purchases, $500 − Ending inventory, $200 = Supplies used, $400.

Analysis: Before the adjusting entry is made, the balance in the Inventory of Maintenance Supplies account is $600 (i.e., beginning inventory, $100, plus the purchase, $500); however, the actual inventory count at this date showed $200, which means that usage of supplies was $400 (i.e., $100 + $500 − $200 = $400). The above adjusting entry is required to (*a*) reduce the inventory account by $400 (so that the asset, inventory, will be shown as $200 per the inventory count) and (*b*) to record an expense for the amount of supplies used, $400. Therefore, the 19B income statement will report supplies expense of $400. The 19B balance sheet will report a current asset—inventory of maintenance supplies—of $200.

Expenses Incurred prior to Payment (Accrued Expenses)

Most expenses are incurred and paid for during the same period; however, at the end of the accounting period there usually are some expenses that have been **incurred** (i.e., goods and/or services that already have been used) but are **not yet recorded.** Such unpaid expenses are called **accrued expenses.** These expenses must be recorded in the current period because they must be **matched** with the revenues of the current period in conformity with the matching principle. Also, the liability for those unpaid expenses must be recorded and reported on the balance sheet of the current period. These effects are recorded by using an adjusting entry. We will analyze and illustrate three such transactions, each of which required an adjusting entry by High-Rise Apartments.

Salary and Wage Expense

On December 31, 19B, the manager of High-Rise was on vacation and would return January 10, 19C. Therefore, the manager's December salary of $900 was not paid or recorded by December 31, 19B. The sequence of entries by High-Rise for the accrued salary expense (disregard employee benefits at this time) would be:

f. December 31, 19B (end of the accounting period)—adjusting entry:

Salary expense	900	
Salaries payable (or accrued salaries payable)		900
To record salary expense and the liability for December salary not		
yet paid.		

January 10, 19C—date of payment of the December 19B salary:

Salaries payable	900	
Cash		900
To record payment of a December 19B salary.		

The adjusting entry had two measurement purposes: (1) to record an expense incurred in 19B for matching with revenues and (2) to record the liability for the salary owed at the end of 19B for balance sheet purposes. The entry in 19C recorded the payment of the liability.

On December 28, 19B, a tax bill for $5,700 was received from the city for 19B property taxes. The taxes are due on February 15, 19C; therefore, they were unpaid and unrecorded at the end of 19B. The entries for High-Rise would be:

g. December 31, 19B (end of the accounting period)—adjusting entry:[4]

Property tax expense	5,700	
Property tax payable		5,700
To record 19B property taxes incurred and the related liability.		

This adjusting entry records the incurred, but unpaid, tax expense for 19B, and also the tax liability that must be reported on the 19B balance sheet.

---

[4] This is an example of a case where there may or may not be an adjusting entry. For example, assume the tax bill was received on December 5, 19B. At that date, a **current entry** probably would be made identical to the adjusting entry given above. Under these circumstances, an adjusting entry at December 31, 19B, would not be needed.

February 15, 19C—payment of the 19B liability for property tax:

Property tax payable 5,700
    Cash   5,700
    To record payment of property tax liability.

Interest Expense

On November 1, 19B, High-Rise borrowed $30,000 cash from a local bank on a 90-day note with an annual interest rate of 12%. The principal plus interest is due in three months. The entries by High-Rise are:

November 1, 19B—date of transaction:

Cash 30,000
    Note payable, short term   30,000
    To record a loan from a bank.

> **Analysis:** At December 31, 19B, the end of the accounting period, two months have passed since the note was signed. Therefore, interest expense for two months has accrued on the note because interest legally accrues with the passage of time. At year-end, there is a **liability** for interest for the two months. This expense and the related liability have not yet been recorded. Therefore, an **adjusting entry** is necessary to (*a*) debit interest expense for $600 (i.e., $30,000 \times 12\% \times 2/12 = 600) and (*b*) credit interest payable for the same amount. The adjusting and payment entries would be:

h. December 31, 19B (end of the accounting period)—adjusting entry:

Interest expense   600
    Interest payable (or accrued interest payable)   600
    To record accrued interest expense for two months on note payable
    ($30,000 \times 12\% \times 2/12 = 600).

January 31, 19C—maturity date; payment of the principal of the note and interest:

Note payable, short term 30,000
Interest payable (per adjusting entry)   600
Interest expense (19C—$30,000 \times 12\% \times 1/12$)   300
    Cash   30,900
    To record payment of principal plus interest on note payable
    at maturity date.

Recording Adjusting Entries

The preceding examples showed the application of the revenue and matching principles at the end of the accounting period by using adjusting entries. In cases when certain economic effects have not been recorded, appropriate adjusting entries are necessary to ensure that both the income statement and balance sheet will be correct. Adjusting entries are made to allocate revenue and expense among the current and one or more future periods so that expenses are properly matched with revenues each accounting period.

Adjusting entries relate to transactions that start in one period and, in effect, continue into one or more subsequent periods. Therefore, an analysis to determine whether an adjusting entry is needed, and if so, how it should be made, must be based on the sequence of related events covering the periods affected. The demonstration case at the end of this chapter illustrates how adjusting entries are influenced by particular situations.

Adjusting entries are entered first in the journal (dated the last day of the accounting period) immediately after all of the regular transactions are recorded. Then the adjusting entries are posted from the journal to the ledger accounts. Recording in the journal and posting to the ledger are necessary because adjusting entries reflect economic events, and their effects must be processed through the accounting information system and into the financial statements in the same manner as the regular transactions. These procedures are illustrated in the next chapter within the context of a complete information processing cycle.

In some instances, it is difficult to draw a clear line between regular and adjusting entries. Also, there are no reasons to make the distinction, other than the fact that adjusting entries (a) usually must be made at the **end** of the accounting period and (b) **update** certain income statement and balance sheet accounts. The important point is that adjusting entries (as well as many other entries) are necessary to appropriately measure periodic revenues and to match expenses with those revenues that were earned during the period.

DEMONSTRATION CASE

(Try to solve the requirements before proceeding to the suggested solution that follows.)

New Service Corporation is owned by three shareholders and has been in operation for one year, 19A. Cash flow and expenses are critical control problems. Minimal recordkeeping has been performed to save money. One secretary performs both the secretarial and recordkeeping functions. Because of a loan application made by the corporation, the bank has requested an income statement and balance sheet. The secretary prepared the following (summarized for case purposes):

NEW SERVICE CORPORATION
Profit Statement
Annual—December 31, 19A

Revenues:	
Service	$78,500
Expenses:	
Salaries and wages	(43,200)
Utilities	(1,800)
Miscellaneous	(4,000)
Net profit	$29,500

NEW SERVICE CORPORATION
Balance Sheet
December 31, 19A

Assets

Cash	$ 4,000
Accounts receivable	35,500
Supplies on hand	8,000
Equipment	40,000
Other assets	16,000
Total assets	$103,500

Liabilities

Accounts payable	$ 9,000
Income taxes payable	
Note payable, one year, 12%	10,000

Net Worth

Capital stock, 5,000 no-par shares	55,000
Retained profits	29,500
Total liabilities and net worth	$103,500

After reading the two statements, the bank requested that an independent PA examine them. The PA found that the secretary used some obsolete captions and terminology and did not include the effects of the following data (i.e., the adjusting entries):

a. Supplies inventory on hand at December 31, $3,000.

b. Depreciation for 19A. The equipment was acquired during January 19A; estimated useful life, 10 years, and no residual value.

c. The note payable was dated August 1, 19A. The principal plus interest are payable at the end of one year.

d. Rent expense of $3,600 was included in miscellaneous expense.

e. Income taxes; assume an average tax rate of 17%.

Required:

1. Recast the above statements to incorporate the additional data, appropriate captions, preferred terminology, and improved format. Show computations.

2. Prepare the adjusting entries (in journal form) for the additional data at December 31, 19A.

3. Comment on any part of this situation that the bank loan officer should note if it appears to be unusual.

Suggested Solution
Requirement 1:

NEW SERVICE CORPORATION
Income Statement
For the Year Ended December 31, 19A

	Amounts reported	Effects of adjusting entries*	Corrected amounts
Revenues:			
Service revenue	$78,500		$78,500
Expenses:			
Salaries and wages	43,200		43,200
Utilities	1,800		1,800
Supplies expense		*(a)* + 5,000	5,000
Depreciation expense		*(b)* + 4,000	4,000
Interest expense		*(c)* + 500	500
Rent expense		*(d)* + 3,600	3,600
Miscellaneous expense	4,000	*(d)* − 3,600	400
Total expenses	49,000		58,500
Pretax income	$29,500		20,000
Income tax expense ($20,000 × 17%)		*(e)* + 3,400	3,400
Net income			$16,600
EPS ($16,600 ÷ 5,000 shares)			$3.32

NEW SERVICE CORPORATION
Balance Sheet
At December 31, 19A

Assets

Cash	$ 4,000		$ 4,000
Accounts receivable	35,500		35,500
Supplies inventory	8,000	*(a)* − 5,000	3,000
Equipment	40,000		40,000
Accumulated depreciation		*(b)* − 4,000	(4,000)
Other assets	16,000		16,000
Total assets	$103,500		$94,500

Liabilities

Accounts payable	$ 9,000		$ 9,000
Income taxes payable		*(e)* + 3,400	3,400
Interest payable		*(c)* + 500	500
Note payable, one year, 12%	10,000		10,000
Total liabilities	19,000		22,900

Shareholders' Equity

Capital stock, 5,000 no-par shares	55,000		55,000
Retained earnings	29,500	− 29,500 + 16,600	16,600
Total liabilities and shareholders' equity	$103,500		$94,500

Note: Observe changes in captions, terminology, and format.
* The letters identify the adjustments shown under Requirement 2.

Requirement 2:
Adjusting entries at December 31, 19A:

a. Supplies expense 5,000
    Supplies inventory   5,000

    To reduce supplies inventory to the amount on hand December 31,
    19A, $3,000, and to record supplies expense, $8,000 − $3,000 =
    $5,000.

b. Depreciation expense 4,000
    Accumulated depreciation   4,000

    Depreciation for one year, $40,000 ÷ 10 years = $4,000.

c. Interest expense   500
    Interest payable   500

    To record interest expense and the interest accrued (a liability) from
    August 1 to December 31, 19A ($10,000 × 12% × 5/12 = $500).

d. Rent expense 3,600
    Miscellaneous expense   3,600

    To record rent expense in the proper account.

e. Income tax expense 3,400
    Income taxes payable   3,400

    To record income tax expense and the liability for unpaid tax
    as computed on the income statement.

Requirement 3:
The loan officer should note particularly the following:

a. The overstatement of net income by 78%; [i.e., ($29,500 − $16,600) ÷
    $16,600] and total assets by 10% [i.e., ($103,500 − $94,500) ÷ $94,500].
    This suggests either (1) an attempt to mislead or (2) a need for better
    accounting.
b. The very high amount in accounts receivable compared to cash and
    total assets. This fact suggests inadequate evaluation of credit and/or in-
    efficiency in collections.
c. The small amount of cash compared with accounts payable (a current li-
    ability).
d. Inclusion of rent expense in miscellaneous expense.
e. Inappropriate captions, terminology, and format shown in the financial
    statements.

SUMMARY OF CHAPTER

Part A of the chapter discussed the conceptual framework of accounting. Those discussions are summarized in Exhibit 4–5. This exhibit will be particularly useful as you study the other chapters.

Part B of the chapter discussed **adjusting entries** that are necessary to apply those principles. Matching expenses with revenue for the period is critical because the life span of an enterprise, although indefinite in length, must be divided into a series of short time periods (usually one year each) for the periodic financial statements.

To measure net income, the **revenue principle** states that revenues earned

Exhibit 4–5 Summary of the conceptual framework of accounting

Fundamentals	Brief explanations	Examples
USERS of financial statements (persons to whom they are directed—the audience)	Primarily decision makers who are "average prudent investors" and are willing to study the information with diligence.	Investors, creditors, including those who advise or represent investors and creditors.
OBJECTIVES of financial statements (decision usefulness)	To provide economic information about a business that is useful in projecting the future cash flows of that business.	The operations of a business are summarized in net income, which is the primary long-term source of cash generated by a business.
QUALITATIVE characteristics of financial statements (necessary to make the reported information useful to decision makers)	Characteristics that make financial statements useful, viz: 1. Relevance—affects decisions; timely presentation; has predictive and feedback value. 2. Reliability (believable)—unbiased, accurate, and verifiable. 3. Comparability—comparable with other periods and entities.	1. The financial statements are available soon after their data have been audited and present complete information. 2. Audited financial statements. 3. Use same method for merchandise inventory matching from period to period.
IMPLEMENTATION ASSUMPTIONS of financial statements (imposed by the business environment)	1. Separate-entity assumption—each business is accounted for separately from its owners and other entities. 2. Continuity (going-concern) assumption—assumes the entity will not liquidate, but will continue to pursue its objectives. 3. Unit-of-measure assumption—accounting measurements will be in the monetary unit. 4. Time-period assumption—accounting reports are for short time periods.	1. XYZ Company is a separate entity; its owners and creditors are other entities. 2. Accounting for XYZ Company will assume it will carry on its normal operations. 3. Assets, liabilities, owners' equity, revenues, expenses, etc., are measured in Canadian dollars. 4. Financial statements of XYZ Company are prepared each year.

Exhibit 4–5 *(continued)*

Fundamentals	Brief explanations	Examples
IMPLEMENTATION PRINCIPLES of accounting	1. Cost principle—Cost (cash equivalent cost given up) is the appropriate basis for initial recording of assets, liabilities, owners' equity, revenues, expenses, gains, and losses.	1. XYZ Company purchased a machine; record the cash equivalent given up, $10,000, as the historical cost of the machine.
	2. Revenue principle—The cash equivalent amount received for the sale of goods or services is recognized as earned revenue when ownership transfers or as the services are rendered.	2. Sale of merchandise for $2,000, half cash and half on credit—record sales revenue of $2,000 on date of sale.
	3. Matching principle—Revenues are recognized in conformity with the revenue principle; then all expenses incurred in earning that revenue must be identified and recorded in the period in which those revenues are recognized.	3. Sales of merchandise during the period of $100,000 are recorded as earned; the cost of those goods, $60,000, is recorded as expense of that period.
	4. Full-disclosure principle—The financial statements of an entity should disclose (present) all of the relevant economic information about that entity.	4. Report inventory on the balance sheet and explain in a note the inventory accounting policies. The disclosures should be "fair."
CONSTRAINTS OF ACCOUNTING (based on practical reasons)	1. Materiality—Amounts of relatively small significance must be recorded; however, they need not be accorded strict theoretical treatment (for cost-benefit reasons).	1. Purchase of a pencil sharpener for $4.98 (an asset) may be recorded as expense when purchased.
	2. Cost-benefit—The value of a financial item reported should be higher for the decision makers than the cost of reporting it.	2. An expense report costs $3,000; its potential cost saving is $1,000.
	3. Conservatism—Exercise care not to overstate assets and revenues and not to understate liabilities and expenses.	3. A loss and a gain are probable, but not for sure. Report the loss but not the gain.

during the period from the sale of goods or services must be identified, measured, and reported for that period. The **matching principle** states that the expenses incurred in earning those revenues must be identified, measured, and matched with the revenues earned in the period to determine periodic net income. To implement the revenue and matching principles, certain transactions and events whose economic effects extend from the current period to one or more future accounting periods, must be analyzed at the end of the accounting

Exhibit 4–5 *(concluded)*

Fundamentals	Brief explanations	Examples
ELEMENTS of financial statements (basic items reported on the financial statements)	Income statement: 1. Revenues—Inflows of assets, or settlements of liabilities from sale of goods and services that constitute the entity's ongoing or major operations.	1. Sale of merchandise for cash or on credit.
	2. Expenses—Outflows or using up of assets, or incurrence of liabilities for delivery of goods or services, and other activities that constitute the entity's ongoing or major operations.	2. Wages earned by employees paid in cash or owed.
	3. Gains—Increases in net assets from peripheral or incidental transactions, and all other activities except those from revenues or investments by owners.	3. Sale of a tract of land for a price more than its cost when acquired.
	4. Losses—Decreases in net assets from peripheral or incidental transactions and other events except those from expenses or distributions to owners.	4. Sale of a tract of land for a price less than its cost when acquired.
	Balance sheet: 5. Assets—Probable future economic benefits, owned by the entity as a result of past transactions.	5. Land, buildings, equipment, patent.
	6. Liabilities—Probable future sacrifices of economic benefits as a result of past transactions; involves transfer of assets or services.	6. Note owed to the bank; taxes owed but not yet paid; unpaid wages.
	7. Owners' equity—Residual interest of owners after all debts are paid (i.e., Assets − Liabilities = Owners' Equity).	7. Capital stock outstanding plus retained earnings.
DETAILED accounting practices and procedures (detailed measurement and recording guidelines)	1. Those related to asset and income measurement. 2. Those related to reporting accounting information. 3. Other accounting procedures.	1. Straight-line versus accelerated depreciation. 2. Separate reporting of extraordinary items (net of income tax); terminology. 3. Control and subsidiary ledgers; special journals; bank reconciliations, worksheets.

Source: Based on FASB, *Accounting Standards: Statements of Financial Accounting Concepts 1–6* (Homewood, Ill.: Richard D. Irwin, 1989).

period. This analysis is the basis for allocating their effects to the current and future periods. The allocation of some revenues and expenses to two or more accounting periods requires the use of **adjusting entries.** Adjusting entries follow the same concepts and procedures as entries for the usual transactions except that they are made at the end of the accounting period.

IMPORTANT TERMS DEFINED IN THIS CHAPTER

Accrual Basis Accounting   Record completed transactions when they occur, regardless of when the related cash is received or paid. *p. 159*

Accrue (Accrued)   An expense incurred but not yet paid; a revenue earned but not yet collected. *p. 164*

Adjusting Entries   End-of-period entries required by the revenue and matching principles to attain a cutoff between periods. *p. 161*

Cash Basis Accounting   Record only cash basis transactions; not in conformity with GAAP. *p. 159*

Conceptual Framework of Accounting   See Exhibit 4–5. *p. 176*

Conservatism Constraint   Do not overstate assets and revenues; do not understate liabilities and expenses. *p. 156*

Contra Account   An account, related to a primary account, that is an offset (or reduction) to the primary account. *p. 168*

Cost-Benefit Constraint   Accounting information should have a higher use value than the cost of reporting it. *p. 156*

Cost Principle   All assets, liabilities, and owners' equity items are recorded initially at cost. *p. 154*

Defer (Deferred)   An expense paid in advance of use; a revenue collected in advance of being earned. *p. 164*

Depreciation   Expense of using (wearing out) a building, machinery, fixtures, etc., each period of useful life. *p. 168*

Elements of Financial Statements   Major classifications on the financial statements. *p. 156*

Expenses Incurred But Not Recorded   Expenses actually incurred but not yet paid or recorded. *p. 163*

Expenses Paid in Advance   Cash paid for goods, or services, before those goods or services are used; prepaid expenses. *p. 163*

Full-Disclosure Principle   Financial statements must report all relevant information about the economic affairs of a business. *p. 155*

Interest Expense   Time value of money; the cost of borrowing money. *p. 171*

Interim Reports   Financial reports for periods of less than one year, quarterly or monthly reports. *p. 160*

Matching Principle All costs incurred to earn the revenues of the period must be identified then matched with revenue by recording as expense. *p. 155*

Materiality Constraint Items of low significance need not be separately reported. *p. 155*

Residual Value Value (estimated) of an operational asset at the end of its useful life to the business (scrap or salvage value). *p. 168*

Revenue Collected in Advance Revenue collected in cash before that revenue is earned. Precollected revenue. *p. 162*

Revenue Earned but Not Yet Collected or Recorded Revenue not yet collected, or recorded, but already earned. Accrued revenue. *p. 162*

Revenue Principle Recognize revenue in the period earned rather than when the cash is received; earning process completed. *p. 155*

Separate-Entity Assumption A business is accounted for separate and apart from its owners and all others. *p. 153*

Supplies Inventory Supplies purchased and still on hand; unused supplies at the end of period. *p. 169*

Time-Period Assumption Division of the operating activities of a business into a series of equal time periods (usually one year) for accounting purposes. *p. 154*

Unit-of-Measure Assumption Financial statements measured in terms of the monetary unit—Canadian dollars. *p. 154*

QUESTIONS

Part A: Questions 1–16

1. Briefly explain why a conceptual framework of accounting is important.
2. Explain the purpose of defining the six essential characteristics of accounting information.
3. Briefly explain the cost-benefit characteristic of accounting information.
4. An essential characteristic of accounting information that is considered to be a secondary characteristic involves what two comparisons?
5. What are the two primary characteristics of accounting information? Briefly explain each.
6. List the five categories that comprise the fundamental concepts of accounting. Briefly explain each.
7. List and briefly explain the three accounting constraints.
8. List the four elements reported on the income statement. Explain the primary difference between revenues and gains and expenses and losses.
9. Explain why the balance sheet is dated differently than the income statement and the statement of changes in financial position.
10. Explain the basic difference between accrual basis accounting and cash basis accounting.

11. What basis of accounting is required by GAAP on the (*a*) income statement, (*b*) balance sheet, and (*c*) statement of changes in financial position?

12. Briefly explain why the time-period assumption and the accrual basis of accounting require a precise "cutoff" at the end of each accounting period.

13. Briefly explain adjusting entries. List the four types of adjusting entries.

14. Explain two different types of trade-offs that are common among elements of the conceptual framework.

15. Why would CICA not have developed a conceptual framework soon after FASB did in 1978?

16. The opinion paragraph of the auditors' report for Consolidated-Bathurst in Appendix B contains two key sets of words among others: "present fairly" and "in accordance with generally accepted accounting principles." Is the amount for equipment in the balance sheet for New Service presented fairly when it is valued at historical cost less accumulated depreciation? Would selling price be fairer? How can the two quotations from the auditors' report be connected to make historical cost "fair"?

Part B: Questions 17–21

17. AB Company collected $600 rent for the period December 15, 19A, to January 15, 19B. The $600 was credited to Rent Revenue Collected in Advance on December 15, 19A. Give the adjusting entry required on December 31, 19A (end of the accounting period).

18. On December 31, 19B, Company T recorded the following adjusting entry:

    Rent revenue receivable 500
    Rent revenue   500

    Explain the situation that caused this entry and give the subsequent related entry.

19. On July 1, 19A, M Company paid a two-year insurance premium of $400 and debited Prepaid Insurance for that amount. Assuming the accounting period ends in December, give the adjusting entries that should be made at the end of 19A, 19B, and 19C.

20. Explain "estimated residual value." Why is it important in measuring depreciation expense?

21. Explain why adjusting entries are entered in the journal on the last day of the accounting period and then are posted to the ledger.

EXERCISES

Part A: Exercises 4–1 to 4–6

E4–1 **(Pair the Essential Characteristics of Accounting Information with Conceptual Designations)**
Match the essential characteristics of accounting information with the related designations by entering appropriate letters in the blanks provided.

Designations	Essential characteristics
_____ (1) Users	A. Comparability with prior periods and other entities.
_____ (2) Utility constraint	
_____ (3) Secondary quality	B. Decision usefulness—helps users make better decisions.
_____ (4) Purpose	
_____ (5) Threshold for recognition	C. Decision makers who need financial information.
_____ (6) Primary qualities	D. Relevance to decisions and reliability.
	E. Immaterial amounts—not large enough to influence important decisions.
	F. Cost of developing and reporting is less than the use-value to decision makers.

E4–2 **(Pair Financial Statements with the Elements of Financial Statements)**
Match the financial statements with the financial statement elements by entering appropriate letters in the spaces provided.

Elements of financial statements	Financial statements
_____ (1) Liabilities	A. Income statement.
_____ (2) Uses of funds	B. Balance sheet.
_____ (3) Losses	C. Statement of changes in financial position.
_____ (4) Assets	D. None of the above.
_____ (5) Revenues	
_____ (6) Sources of funds	
_____ (7) Gains	
_____ (8) Owners' equity	
_____ (9) Expenses	
_____ (10) Assets owned by proprietor	

E4–3 **(Pair Descriptive Statements with Conceptual Terms)**
Match the following brief descriptions with the terms by entering an appropriate letter in each space provided.

Term	Brief description
_____ (1) Primary users of financial statements	A. To prepare the income tax return of the business.
_____ (2) Broad objective of financial reporting	B. Separate entity, going concern, time periods, and unit of measure.
_____ (3) Qualitative characteristics of financial statements	C. Guidelines to apply the assumptions and principles.
	D. To provide financial information that is useful in projecting future cash flows.
_____ (4) Implementation assumptions	E. Relevance and reliability.
	F. Investors, creditors, and those who advise and represent them (decision makers).

Term	Brief description
_____ (5) Elements of finan-	G. Materiality, cost benefit, conservatism.
cial statements	H. Assets, liabilities, owners' equity, revenues, ex-
_____ (6) Implementation	penses, gains and losses, source of funds, use
principles	of funds.
_____ (7) Exceptions to	I. Revenue, cost, matching, full disclosure.
implementation	
principles	
_____ (8) Detailed account-	
ing practices and	
procedures	
_____ (9) None of the above	

E4–4   (Terminology Related to Adjusting Entries)
Match the following terms with the statements by entering appropriate letters in the spaces provided. There will be two answers for each term.

Term	Statements
_____ _____ (1) Accrued expense	A. A revenue not yet earned; collected in
_____ _____ (2) Deferred expense	advance.
_____ _____ (3) Accrued revenue	B. Office supplies on hand; will be used next
_____ _____ (4) Deferred revenue	accounting period.
	C. Interest revenue collected; not yet earned.
	D. Rent not yet collected; not yet earned.
	E. An expense incurred; not yet paid or
	recorded.
	F. A revenue earned; not yet collected or
	recorded.
	G. An expense not yet incurred; paid in
	advance.
	H. Property taxes incurred; not yet paid.

E4–5   (Two Simple Adjusting Entries)
Simplex Company has completed its first year of operations on December 31, 19A. All of the 19A entries have been recorded, except for the following:

a. At year-end, employees have earned wages of $6,000. These wages will be paid on the next payroll date, January 6, 19B.

b. At year-end, interest revenue of $2,000 has been earned by the company. The cash will be collected March 31, 19B.

Required:

1. What is the annual reporting period for this company under the time-period assumption?

2. Give the required adjusting entry for transactions (*a*) and (*b*) above. Give appropriate dates and write a brief explanation of each entry.

E4–6   (Pairing Transactions with Types of Adjusting Entries)
Match the following transactions with the terms by entering the appropriate letter in each blank space.

Term	Transaction
____ (1) Deferred revenue	A. At the end of the year, wages payable of $2,500 had not been recorded or paid.
____ (2) Accrued revenue	B. Supplies for office use were purchased during the year for $600 and $100 of the office supplies remained on hand (unused) at year-end.
____ (3) Deferred expense	C. Interest of $300 on a note receivable was earned at year-end, although collection of the interest is not due until the following year.
____ (4) Accrued expense	D. At the end of the year, service revenue of $1,000 was collected in cash but was not yet earned.

Part B: Exercises 4–7 to 4–14

E4–7   (Effects of Three Adjusting Entries on the Income Statement and Balance Sheet)
XT Company started operations on January 1, 19A. It is now December 31, 19A (end of the annual accounting period). The part-time bookkeeper needs your help to analyze the following three transactions:

a. On January 1, 19A, the company purchased a special machine for a cash cost of $15,000 (debited to the machine account). The machine has an estimated useful life of five years and no residual value.

b. During 19A, the company purchased office supplies that cost $400. At the end of 19A, office supplies of $100 remained on hand.

c. On July 1, 19A, the company paid cash of $300 for two years' premium on an insurance policy on the machine.

Required:
Complete the following schedule of the amounts that should be reported for 19A:

Selected Balance Sheet Amounts
At December 31, 19A

	Amount to be reported
Assets:	
Machine . . . . $	15,000
Accumulated depreciation	3,000
Carrying value	12,000
Office supplies inventory	300
Prepaid insurance	75

Selected Income Statement Amounts
For the Year Ended December 31, 19A

Depreciation expense . . . . $	3,000
Office supplies expense	300
Insurance expense	75

E4–8   **(Journalize Seven Typical Adjusting Entries)**

Rich Department Store is completing the accounting process for the year just ended, December 31, 19B. The transactions during 19B have been journalized and posted. The following data in respect to adjusting entries are available:

a. Office supplies inventory at January 1, 19B, was $120. Office supplies purchased and debited to Office Supplies Inventory during the year amounted to $360. The year-end inventory showed $80 of supplies on hand.

b. Wages earned during December 19B, unpaid and unrecorded at December 31, 19B, amounted to $1,400. The last payroll was December 28; the next payroll will be January 6, 19C.

c. Three fourths of the basement of the store is rented for $800 per month to another merchant, J. B. Smith. Smith sells compatible, but not competitive, merchandise. On November 1, 19B, the store collected six months' rent in advance from Smith for $4,800, which was credited in full to Rent Revenue when collected.

d. The remaining basement space is rented to Spears Specialty; for $360 per month, payable monthly. On December 31, 19B, the rent for November and December 19B was not collected nor recorded. Collection is expected January 10, 19C.

e. Delivery equipment that cost $21,000 was being used by the store. Estimates for the equipment were: (1) useful life five years and (2) residual value at the end of five years' use, $1,000. Assume depreciation for a full year for 19B. The asset will be depreciated evenly over its useful life.

f. On July 1, 19B, a two-year insurance premium amounting to $1,000 was paid in cash and debited in full to Prepaid Insurance.

g. Rich operates an alteration shop to meet its own needs. Also, the shop does alterations for J. B. Smith. At the end of December 31, 19B, J. B. Smith had not paid for alterations completed amounting to $450. This amount has not been recorded as Alteration Shop Revenue. Collection is expected during January 19C.

Required:

Give the adjusting entry for each situation that should be recorded in the journal of Rich Department Store at December 31, 19B.

E4–9   **(Adjusting Entries for Interest on Two Notes Receivable)**

On April 1, 19B, Davis Corporation received a $4,000, 15% note from a customer in settlement of a $4,000 open account receivable. According to the terms, the principal of the note, plus the $600 interest, is payable at the end of 12 months. The annual accounting period for Davis ends on December 31, 19B.

Required:

a. Give the journal entry for Davis for receipt of the note on April 1, 19B.

b. Give the adjusting entry required on December 31, 19B.

c. Give the journal entry on date of collection, March 31, 19C, for the principal and interest.

On August 1, 19B, to meet a cash shortage, Davis Corporation obtained a $20,000, 12% loan from a local bank. The principal of the note, plus interest expense is payable at the end of 12 months.

Required:

d. Give the journal entry for Davis on the date of the loan, August 1, 19B.

e. Give the adjusting entry required on December 31, 19B.

f. Give the journal entry on date of payment, July 31, 19C.

E4–10   (Adjusting Entries for Prepaid Insurance—Two Cases)

Kay Company is making adjusting entries for the year ended December 31, 19B. In developing information for the adjusting entries, the accountant learned that on September 1, 19B, a two-year insurance premium of $2,400 was paid.

Required:

a. What amount should be reported on the 19B income statement for insurance expense?

b. What amount should be reported on the December 31, 19B, balance sheet for prepaid insurance?

c. Give the adjusting entry at December 31, 19B, under each of two cases:

> Case 1—Assume that when the premium was paid on September 1, 19B, the bookkeeper debited the full amount to Prepaid Insurance.
>
> Case 2—Assume that when the premium was paid September 1, 19B, the bookkeeper debited Insurance Expense for the full amount.
>
> (Hint: In Case 2 be sure that after the adjusting entry, you end with the same amount in the Prepaid Insurance account as in Case 1.)

E4–11   (Adjusting Entry for Supplies Inventory)

Wise Manufacturing Company uses a large amount of shipping supplies that are purchased in large volume, stored, and used as needed. At December 31, 19B, the following data relating to shipping supplies were obtained from the records and supporting documents:

Shipping supplies on hand, January 1, 19B	$ 2,000
Purchases of shipping supplies during 19B	13,000
Shipping supplies on hand, per inventory December 31, 19B	4,000

Required:

a. What amount should be reported on the 19B income statement for shipping supplies expense?

b. What amount should be reported on the December 31, 19B, balance sheet for shipping supplies inventory?

c. Give the adjusting entry at December 31, 19B, assuming the purchases of shipping supplies were debited in full to Shipping Supplies Inventory ($13,000).

d. What adjusting entry would you make assuming the bookkeeper debited Shipping Supplies Expense for the $13,000? [Hint: In solving (c) and (d), be sure that each solution ends up with the same amount remaining in the Shipping Supplies Inventory account.]

E4–12 **(Correct Income Statement and Balance Sheet Amounts for the Effects of Three Adjusting Entries)**
On December 31, 19B, Wag Company prepared an income statement and balance sheet and failed to take into account three adjusting entries. The income statement, prepared on this incorrect basis, reflected a pretax income of $20,000. The balance sheet reflected total assets, $90,000; total liabilities, $30,000; and owners' equity, $60,000. Wag is not a corporation; therefore, it does not pay income tax. The data for the three adjusting entries were:

a. Depreciation was not recorded for the year on equipment that cost $55,000; estimated useful life, 10 years, and residual value, $5,000.

b. Wages amounting to $8,000 for the last three days of December 19B were not paid and were not recorded (the next payroll will be on January 10, 19C).

c. Rent revenue of $3,000 was collected on December 1, 19B, for office space for the period December 1, 19B, to February 28, 19C. The $3,000 was credited in full to Rent Revenue when collected.

Required:
Complete the following tabulation to correct the financial statement amounts shown (indicate deductions with parentheses):

Item	Net income	Total assets	Total liabilities	Owners' equity
Balances reported	$20,000	$90,000	$30,000	$60,000
Effects of depreciation	____	____	____	____
Effects of wages	____	____	____	____
Effects of rent revenue	____	____	____	____
Correct balances	====	====	====	====

E4–13 **(Prepare Correct Income Statement to Include Effects of Seven Adjusting Entries; Give Adjusting Entries)**
Supreme Auto Rentals, Inc., completed its first year of operations on December 31, 19A. Because this is the end of the annual accounting period, the company bookkeeper prepared the following tentative income statement:

Income Statement, 19A

Rental revenue		$102,000
Expenses:		
Salaries and wages	$26,400	
Maintenance expense	10,000	
Rent expense (on location)	8,000	
Utilities expense	3,000	
Gas and oil expense	2,000	
Miscellaneous expense (items not listed above)	400	
Total expenses		49,800
Income		$ 52,200

An independent PA reviewed the income statement and developed additional data as follows:

1. Wages for the last three days of December amounting to $600 were not recorded or paid (disregard employee benefits).

2. The telephone bill for December 19A amounting to $200 has not been recorded or paid.

3. Depreciation on rental autos, amounting to $20,000 for 19A, was not recorded.

4. Interest on a $20,000, one-year, 12% note payable dated November 1, 19A, was not recorded. The 12% interest is payable on the maturity date of the note.

5. Rental revenue includes $2,000 rental revenue for the month of January 19B.

6. Maintenance expense includes $1,000, which is the cost of maintenance supplies still on hand (per inventory) at December 31, 19A. These supplies will be used in 19B.

7. The income tax rate is 20%. Payment of income tax will be made in 19B.

Required:

a. Give the adjusting entry at December 31, 19A, for each of the additional data items. If none is required, explain why.

b. Prepare a correct income statement for 19A, assuming 10,000 shares are outstanding. Show computations.

E4–14   (Prepare Three Adjusting Entries and Recast the Income Statement and Balance Sheet)

On December 15, 19C, the bookkeeper for Seaway Company prepared the income statement and balance sheet summarized below but neglected to consider three of the adjusting entries.

	As prepared	Effects of adjusting entries	Corrected amounts
Income statement:			
Revenues	$95,000		
Expenses	(83,000)		
Income tax expense			
Income	$12,000		
Balance sheet:			
Assets			
Cash	$18,000		
Accounts receivable	26,000		
Rent receivable			
Equipment*	40,000		
Accumulated depreciation . . .	(8,000)		
	$76,000		
Liabilities			
Accounts payable	$10,000		
Income tax payable			
Owners' Equity			
Capital stock	50,000		
Retained earnings	16,000		
	$76,000		

* Acquired January 1, 19A, 10-year life, no residual value; straight-line depreciation.

Data on the three adjusting entries:

1. Depreciation on the equipment was not recorded for 19C.
2. Rent revenue earned of $1,000 for December 19C was neither collected nor recorded.
3. Income tax for 19C was not paid or recorded. The average rate was 20%.

Required:

a. Complete the two columns to the right in the above tabulation to show the correct amounts on the income statement and balance sheet.

b. Prepare the three adjusting entries (in journal form) that were omitted. Use the account titles given above.

PROBLEMS

Part A: Problems 4–1 to 4–8

P4–1 **(Pair Definitional Statements with Concepts)**
Match the following descriptive statements with the fundamental concepts of accounting by entering appropriate letters in the spaces provided.

Fundamental concepts	Descriptive statements
_____ (1) Separate-entity assumption	A. Used to apply the assumptions, principles, and constraints.
_____ (2) Continuity assumption	B. The reporting period usually is one year.
_____ (3) Unit-of-measure assumption	C. Expenses are matched with revenues period by period.
_____ (4) Time-period assumption	D. Items of low significance do not need to be reported separately.
_____ (5) Cost principle	E. Account for the business separate from owners.
_____ (6) Revenue principle	F. Report in terms of the monetary unit.
_____ (7) Matching principle	G. When to recognize inflow of net assets from the sale of goods and services that is measurable in dollars.
_____ (8) Full-disclosure principle	H. All relevant information about the financial activities must be reported.
_____ (9) Materiality threshold	I. The entity is a going concern.
_____ (10) Cost-benefit contraint	J. Financial statement elements are initially recorded at cash equivalent cost.
_____ (11) Conservatism constraint	K. Reports revenues, expenses, gains, and losses.

Fundamental concepts	Descriptive statements
____ (12) Income statement	L. Value of user benefits must exceed cost of providing the item of financial information.
____ (13) Balance sheet	M. Reports cash inflows, outflows, and net change.
____ (14) Statement of changes in financial position	N. Reports Assets = Liabilities + Owners' Equity.
	O. Do not overstate assets and revenues and do not understate liabilities and expenses.
____ (15) Practices and procedures of accounting	

P4–2   (Pair Definitional Statements with Elements of Financial Statements)
Match the following definitions with the elements of financial statements by entering the appropriate letters in the spaces provided.

Elements   Brief definitions

Income statement:

____ (1) Revenues

____ (2) Expenses

____ (3) Gains

____ (4) Losses

Balance sheet:

____ (5) Assets

____ (6) Liabilities

____ (7) Owners' equity

Statement of changes in financial position:

____ (8) Sources of funds

____ (9) Uses of funds

A. Cash received during the accounting period.

B. Probable future sacrifices of economic resources.

C. Increase in net assets from peripheral transactions.

D. Outflow of assets for delivery of goods or services.

E. Residual interest of owners.

F. Inflow of net assets from major ongoing operations.

G. Cash paid out during the period.

H. Probable future economic benefits owned by the entity.

I. Decreases in net assets from incidental transactions.

P4–3   (Pair Transactions and Events with Concepts)
Below are listed the concepts of accounting. Match each brief description of a transaction or event with a concept by entering the appropriate letter in the spaces provided. Use one letter for each blank.

Concept applied   Brief description of transaction or event

____ (1) Users of financial statements

____ (2) Objective of financial statements

Qualitative characteristics:

____ (3) Relevance

____ (4) Reliability

A. Recorded a $1,000 sale of merchandise on credit.

B. Counted (inventoried) the unsold items at the end of the period and valued them in dollars.

C. Acquired a vehicle for use in operating the business.

D. Reported the amount of depreciation expense because it likely will affect important decisions of statement users.

Concept applied	Brief description of transaction or event

Implementation assumptions:

_____ (5) Separate entity

_____ (6) Continuity

_____ (7) Unit of measure

_____ (8) Time period

Elements of financial statements:

_____ (9) Revenues

_____ (10) Expenses

_____ (11) Gains

_____ (12) Losses

_____ (13) Assets

_____ (14) Liabilities

_____ (15) Owners' equity

Implementation principles:

_____ (16) Cost

_____ (17) Revenue

_____ (18) Matching

_____ (19) Full disclosure

Constraints of accounting:

_____ (20) Materiality threshold

_____ (21) Cost-benefit constraint

_____ (22) Conservatism constraint

E. Identified as the investors, creditors, and others interested in the business.

F. Used special accounting approaches because of the uniqueness of the industry.

G. Sold and issued notes payable of $1 million.

H. Paid a contractor for an addition to the building with $10,000 cash and $20,000 market value of the shares of the company ($30,000 was deemed to be the cash equivalent price).

I. Engaged an outside independent PA to audit the financial statements.

J. Sold merchandise and services for cash and on credit during the year then determined the cost of those goods sold and the cost of rendering those services.

K. Established an accounting policy that sales revenue shall be recognized only when ownership to the goods sold passes to the customer.

L. To design and prepare the financial statements to assist the users to project the future cash flows of the business.

M. Established a policy not to include in the financial statements the personal financial affairs of the owners of the business.

N. Sold an asset at a loss that was a peripheral or incidental transaction.

O. The user value of a special financial report exceeds the cost of preparing it.

P. Valued an asset, such as inventory, at less than its purchase cost because the replacement cost is less.

Q. Dated the income statement "For the Year Ended December 31, 19B."

R. Used services from outsiders—paid cash for some and the remainder on credit.

S. Acquired an asset (a pencil sharpener that will have a useful life of five years) and recorded as an expense when purchased for $1.99.

T. Disclosed in the financial statements all relevant financial information about the business; necessitated the use of notes to the financial statements.

U. Sold an asset at a gain that was a peripheral or incidental transaction.

V. Assets, $500,000 − Liabilities, $300,000 = Owners' Equity, $200,000.

W. The accounting and reporting assumes a "going concern."

P4–4   (Convert from Cash to Accrual Basis)

The accounting records of Sly Service Company showed the following data:

	For the year		
	19A	19B	19C
Service revenue:			
Cash	$46,000	$57,000	
On credit	20,000	14,000	
19B revenue collected in 19A in advance (not included in $46,000)	2,000		
19C revenue collected in 19B in advance (not included in the $57,000)		3,000	
Expenses:			
Paid in cash	28,000	33,000	
On credit	7,000	10,000	
19B expenses paid in 19A in advance (not included in $28,000)	1,000		
19C expenses paid in advance of 19C (not included in the $33,000)		1,000	

Required:

Complete the following tabulation (show computations):

	For the year	
	19A	19B
a. Service revenue that would be reported:		
Accrual basis	$ _____	$ _____
Cash basis	$ _____	$ _____
b. Expenses that would be reported:		
Accrual basis	$ _____	$ _____
Cash basis	$ _____	$ _____

P4–5   (Restate Income Statement from Cash Basis to Accrual Basis)

Art Little Company (not a corporation) prepared the income statement given below including the two footnotes:

ART LITTLE COMPANY
Income Statement, Cash Basis
For the Year Ended December 31, 19B

Sales revenue (does not include $20,000 sales on credit because collection will be in 19C)	$100,000
Expenses (does not include $10,000 expenses on credit because payment will be made in 19C)	75,200
Profit	$ 24,800

Additional data:

a. Depreciation on operational assets (a company truck) for the year amounted to $15,000. Not included in expenses above.

b. On January 1, 19B, paid a two-year insurance premium on the truck amounting to $400. This amount is included in the expenses above.

Required:

a. Recast the above statement on the accrual basis in conformity with GAAP. Show computations and explain each change.

b. Explain why the cash basis does not measure income as well as the accrual basis.

P4-6 **(Challenging; Convert Income Statement and Balance Sheet from Cash to Accrual Basis)**

At the end of 19A, Foster Corporation prepared the following annual income statement and balance sheet:

FOSTER CORPORATION
Income Statement
For the Year Ended December 31, 19A

Revenues	$280,000
Expenses	248,000
Income before taxes	32,000
Income taxes (average rate, 30%)	9,600
Net income	$ 22,400

FOSTER CORPORATION
Balance Sheet
At December 31, 19A

Assets			Liabilities	
Cash		$ 18,000	Accounts payable	$ 8,000
Accounts receivable		22,000	Income taxes payable (This	
Inventory (by count)		76,800	is the one half unpaid)	4,800
Fixtures	$25,000		Notes payable, 12%	
Less: Accumulated			(due June 30, 19B)	20,000
depreciation	7,000	18,000	Total liabilities	32,800
Total assets		$134,800		

Shareholders' Equity	
Common stock, par $10	
5,000 shares	$50,000
Contributed surplus	10,000
Retained earnings	42,000
Total shareholders' equity	102,000
Total liabilities and shareholders' equity	$134,800

An independent audit of the above statements and underlying records showed the following:

1. Depreciation expense included in total expense was $2,000 for 19A; it should have been $2,500.

2. A tentative order was received from a customer on December 31, 19A, for goods having a sales price of $10,000 and was included in sales revenue and accounts receivable. The goods were on hand (and included in the ending inventory). It is quite likely that a sale may not materialize; the customer will decide by January 20, 19B. This tentative order should not have been recognized as a sale in 19A.

Required:

Other than these two items, the amounts on the financial statements were correct. Recast the two statements to take into account the depreciation error and the incorrect recognition of the tentative order. Show computations and assume an average income tax rate of 30%. (Hint: Revised EPS is $3.01.)

P4–7   (Prepare Four Simple Adjusting Entries)

The annual accounting year used by Jones Service Company ends on December 31. It is December 31, 19X, and all of the 19X entries have been made except the following adjusting entries:

a. On September 1, 19X, Jones collected six months' rent of $1,200 on some storage space. At that date Jones debited Cash and credited Rent Revenue for $1,200.

b. The company earned service revenue of $1,000 on a special job which was completed December 29, 19X. Collection will be made during January 19Y, and no entry has been recorded.

c. On November 1, 19X, Jones paid a one-year premium for property insurance, $600. Cash was credited and Insurance Expense was debited for this amount.

d. At December 31, 19X, wages earned by employees not yet paid, $400. The employees will be paid on the next payroll date, January 15, 19Y.

Required:

Give the adjusting entry required for each transaction. Provide a brief explanation for each entry.

P4–8   (Prepare Four Types of Adjusting Entries)

Vitro Service Company started operations on September 1, 19A. It is now August 31, 19C, end of its second year of operations. All entries for the annual accounting period have been journalized and posted to the ledger accounts. The following end-of-year entries are to be recorded:

a. Service revenue collected in advance, $1,500. On August 15, 19C, the company debited Cash and credited Service Revenues for this amount. The services will be performed during September 19C.

b. Revenue earned but not yet collected or recorded, $5,000. The company completed a large service job, which passed inspection on August 31, 19C. Collection is expected on September 6, 19C.

c. Expense paid in advance, $3,000. The company purchased service supplies on August 1, 19C, at which time Expense was debited and Cash credited for this amount. At August 31, 19C, one third of these supplies were on hand (will be used later on other jobs).

d. Expense incurred but not yet paid or recorded. The company used the consulting services of an engineer during the last two weeks of August 19C. The services have been performed, and Vitro expects to pay the $500 billing on September 15, 19C.

Required:

1. What is the accounting (i.e., reporting) year for this company? What accounting assumption supports your answer?

2. Prepare the required adjusting entry for each situation, including a brief explanation of each entry.

3. Explain the effect on net income if these entries are not made on August 31, 19C (disregard income tax).

Part B: Problems 4-9 to 4-17

P4-9 **(Give Six Adjusting Entries and Related Balance Sheet Classifications)**
Jackson Service Company is preparing the adjusting entries for the year ended December 31, 19B. On that date, the bookkeeper for the company assembled the following data:

1. On December 31, 19B, salaries earned by employees but not yet paid or recorded, $6,000.

2. Depreciation must be recognized on a service truck that cost $9,000 on July 1, 19B (estimated useful life is six years with no residual value).

3. Cash of $1,000 was collected on December 28, 19B, for services to be rendered during 19C (Service Revenue was credited).

4. On December 27, 19B, Jackson received a tax bill of $200 from the city for 19B property taxes (on service equipment) that is payable (and will be paid) during January 19C.

5. On July 1, 19B, the company paid $840 cash for a two-year insurance policy on the service truck (2 above).

6. On October 1, 19B, the company borrowed $10,000 from a local bank and signed a 12% note for that amount. The principal and interest are payable on the maturity date, September 30, 19C.

Required:

a. The bookkeeper has asked you to assist in preparing the adjusting entries at December 31, 19B. For each situation above, give the adjusting entry and a brief explanation. If none is required, explain why.

b. Based on your entries given in Requirement (a), complete the following schedule to reflect the amounts and balance sheet classifications:

Item no.	Accounts	19B amount	Assets	Liabilities	Owners' Equity
			Balance sheet classification (one check on each line)		
1	Salaries payable	$ ____	____	____	____
2	Accumulated depreciation	____	____	____	____
3	Revenue collected in advance	____	____	____	____
4	Property tax payable	____	____	____	____
5	Prepaid insurance	____	____	____	____
6	Interest payable	____	____	____	____

P4-10 **(Prepare Seven Adjusting Entries and Recompute Income to Include Their Effects)**
Slow Transportation Company is at the end of its accounting year December 31, 19B. Slow is not a corporation; therefore, it does not pay income tax. The following data that must be considered were developed from the company's records and related documents:

1. On July 1, 19B, a three-year insurance premium on equipment was paid amounting to $900 that was debited in full to Prepaid Insurance on that date.

2. During 19B, office supplies amounting to $1,000 were purchased for cash and debited in full to Supplies Inventory. At the end of 19A, the inventory count of supplies remaining on hand (unused) showed $200. The inventory of supplies on hand (unused) at December 31, 19B, showed $300.

3. On December 31, 19B, B&R Garage completed repairs on one of Slow's trucks at a cost of $650; the amount is not yet recorded and, by agreement, will be paid during January 19C.

4. In December 19B a property tax bill on real estate owned during 19B, amounting to $1,400, was received from the city. The taxes, which have not been recorded, are due and will be paid on February 15, 19C.

5. On December 31, 19B, Slow completed a hauling contract for an out-of-province company. The bill was for $7,500 payable within 30 days. No cash has been collected, and no journal entry has been made for this transaction.

6. On July 1, 19B, Slow purchased a new hauling van at a cash cost of $21,600. The estimated useful life of the van was 10 years, with an estimated residual value of $1,600. No depreciation has been recorded for 19B (compute depreciation for six months in 19B).

7. On October 1, 19B, Slow borrowed $6,000 from the local bank on a one-year, 15% note payable. The principal plus interest is payable at the end of 12 months.

Required:

a. Give the adjusting entry required on December 31, 19B, related to each of the above transactions. Give a brief explanation with each entry.

b. Assume Slow Transportation Company had prepared a tentative income statement for 19B that did not include the effect of any of the above items and that the tentative net income computed was $30,000. Considering the above items, compute the corrected net income for 19B. Show computations.

P4–11   (Compute Income Statement Amounts for Three Items and Identify Any Adjusting Entries)

The following information was provided by the records and related documents of Greene Garden Apartments (a corporation) at the end of the annual fiscal period, December 31, 19B:

Revenue:

a. Rent revenue collected in cash during 19B for occupancy in 19B (credited to Rent Revenue) $497,000

b. Rent revenue earned for occupancy in December 19B; will not be collected until 19C 8,000

c. In December 19B, collected rent revenue in advance for January 19C (credited to Rent Revenue) 6,000

Salary expense:

d. Cash payment made in January 19B for salaries incurred (earned) in December 19A 3,000

e. Salaries incurred and paid during 19B (debited to Salary Expenses) 58,000

f. Salaries earned by employees during December 19B; will not be paid until January 19C 2,000

g. Cash advance to employees in December 19B for salaries that will be earned in January 19C (debited to Receivable from employees) 4,000

Supplies used:
   h. Maintenance supplies inventory on January 1, 19B (balance on hand)   2,000
   i. Maintenance supplies purchased for cash during 19B
     (debited to Maintenance Supplies Inventory when purchased)   8,000
   j. Maintenance supplies inventory on December 31, 19B   1,500

Required:

1. In conformity with the revenue and matching principles, what amounts should be reported on Greene's 19B income statement for:

   a. Rent revenue   . . . . $ _____
   b. Salary expense . . . .   _____
   c. Maintenance supplies expense   . . .   _____

   Show computations.

2. Check the items that would need an adjusting entry at the end of 19B:
   a. ____; *b.* ____; *c.* ____; *d.* ____; *e.* ____; *f.* ____; *g.* ____; *h.* ____; *i.* ____;
   j. ____.

P4–12 **(Determine the Effect of Five Adjusting Entries on the Income Statement)**
Rapid Service Company has completed its annual financial statements for the year ended December 31, 19C. The income statement (summarized) reflected the following:

Revenues:	
Service	$95,600
Rental (office space)	2,400
Total revenues	98,000
Expenses:	
Salaries and wages	44,000
Service supplies used	2,600
Depreciation expense	2,000
Maintenance of equipment	2,000
Rent expense (service building)	8,400
Oil and gas for equipment	1,800
Insurance expense	200
Utilities expense	800
Other expenses	6,200
Total expenses	68,000
Net income	$30,000

    Rapid is a partnership; therefore, it does not pay income taxes. An audit of the records and financial statements by PA revealed that the following items were not considered:

1. Service revenue of $700 earned but not collected on December 31, 19C, was not included in the $95,600 on the income statement.

2. The $2,600 of service supplies used included $600 of service supplies still on hand in the supplies storeroom on December 31, 19C.

3. Rent revenue of $100 that was collected in advance and not yet earned by December 31, 19C, was included in the $2,400 on the income statement.

4. Property tax for 19C of $400 was billed during December 19C, but will be due and paid during January 19D (not included in the above amounts on the income statement).

5. A two-year insurance premium of $400 was paid on July 1, 19B; no premiums were paid in 19C.

Required:

a. Recast the above income statement to include, exclude, or omit each of the items identified by the PA. Use a format similar to the following:

	Amounts		Amounts that
Items	as reported	Corrections	should be reported

b. The owner of the company asked you to explain the following:
   (1) The insurance premium was paid in 19B; therefore, why was insurance expense reported in 19C?
   (2) Although the company paid no cash for depreciation expense, $2,000 was included in 19C as expense. Why was this so?

P14–13   **(Determine the Effects of Six Entries on the Income Statement and Balance Sheet)** It is December 31, 19B, end of the annual accounting period for TT Service Company. Below are listed six independent transactions (summarized) that affected the company during 19B. The transactions are to be analyzed as to their effects on the balance sheet and income statement for 19B.

a. On January 1, 19A, the company purchased a machine that cost $10,000 cash (estimated useful life five years and no residual value).
   (1) Show how the machine should be reported on the 19B balance sheet.
   (2) Show how the 19B income statement should report the effects of the machine usage.
b. On September 1, 19B, the company signed a $10,000, 12%, one-year note payable. The principal plus interest is payable on the maturity date.
   (1) Show how the liability should be reported on the 19B balance sheet.
   (2) Show how the effects of the note should be reported on the 19B income statement.
c. During 19B, service revenues of $90,000 were collected of which $10,000 was collected in advance.
   (1) Show how the $10,000 should be reported on the 19B balance sheet.
   (2) Show how the 19B income statement should report the effects of the transaction.
d. In 19B, expenses paid in cash amounted to $60,000 of which $5,000 was paid for expenses yet to be incurred (prepaid).
   (1) Show how the 19B balance sheet should report the $5,000.
   (2) Show how the income statement should report this situation.
e. In 19B, $85,000 cash revenues were collected, and in addition revenues of $5,000 were on credit.
   (1) Show how the $5,000 should be reported on the 19B balance sheet.
   (2) Show how the 19B income statement should report the revenues.
f. In 19B, expenses amounting to $56,000 were paid in cash, and in addition expenses of $3,000 were on credit.
   (1) Show how the $3,000 should be reported on the 19B balance sheet.
   (2) Show how the expenses should be reported on the 19B income statement.

P4–14 **(Analytical—Compare Two Sets of Account Balances to Determine What Adjusting Entries Were Made)**
Modern Service Company is completing the information processing cycle at the end of its fiscal year, December 31, 19B. Below is listed the correct balance for each account at December 31, 19B (*a*) before the adjusting entries for 19B and (*b*) after the adjusting entries for 19B.

| | Account balance, December 31, 19B | | | |
| | Before adjusting entries | | After adjusting entries | |
Item	Debit	Credit	Debit	Credit
a. Cash	$ 8,000		$ 8,000	
b. Service revenue receivable			400	
c. Prepaid insurance	300		200	
d. Operational assets	120,200		120,200	
e. Accumulated depreciation, equipment		$ 21,500		$ 25,000
f. Income taxes payable				5,500
g. Capital stock		70,000		70,000
h. Retained earnings, January 1, 19B		14,000		14,000
i. Service revenue		60,000		60,400
j. Salary expense	37,000		37,000	
k. Depreciation expense			3,500	
l. Insurance expense			100	
m. Income tax expense			5,500	
	$165,500	$165,500	$174,900	$174,900

Required:

a. Compare the amounts in the columns before and after the adjusting entries in order to reconstruct the four adjusting entries that were made in 19B. Provide an explanation of each.

b. Compute the amount of income assuming (1) it is based on the amounts, "before adjusting entries" and (2) it is based on the amounts, "after adjusting entries." Which income amount is correct? Explain why.

P4–15 **(Compute Effects of Adjusting Entries on the Balance Sheet and Income Statement; Two Consecutive Years)**
On January 1, 19A, four persons organized WAS Company. The company has been operating for two years, 19A and 19B. Given below are data relating to six selected transactions that affect both years. The annual accounting period ends December 31.

a. On January 1, 19A, the company purchased a computer for use in the business at a cash cost of $14,000. The computer has an estimated useful life of seven years and no residual value. It will be depreciated on a straight-line basis.

b. On September 1, 19A, the company borrowed $10,000 cash from City Bank and signed a one-year, 12%, interest-bearing note. The interest and principal are payable on August 31, 19B.

c. The company owns its office building. On October 1, 19A, the company leased some of its office space to A. B. Smith for $6,000 per year. Smith paid this amount in full on October 1, 19A, and expects to use the space for one year only. The company increased (debited) Cash for $6,000 and increased (credited) Rent Revenue for $6,000 on October 1, 19A.

d. Office supplies were purchased for use in the business. Cash was decreased (credited), and Office Supplies Inventory was increased (debited). The unused supplies at each year-end are determined by inventory count. The amounts were:

Year	Purchased	Inventory
19A	$700	$200
19B	500	300

e. Wages are paid by the company at the end of each two weeks. The last payroll date in December usually is four days before December 31. Therefore, at each year-end, unpaid wages exist that are paid in cash on the first payroll date in the next year. The wages paid in cash and wages incurred but not yet paid or recorded at each year-end were:

Year	Wages paid in cash during the year	Wages unpaid and unrecorded Dec. 31
19A	$30,000	$2,000
19B	36,000	3,000

f. On July 1, 19A, the company paid a two-year insurance premium (on the computer) of $240. At that date, the company increased (debited) an asset account— Prepaid Insurance—and decreased (credited) Cash, $240.

Required:

Complete the following schedule for 19A and 19B by entering the amounts that should be reported on the financial statements of WAS Company. Show computations.

	19A	19B
Balance sheet:		
Assets		
Computer . . . . $	_____	$ _____
Less: Accumulated depreciation	_____	_____
Carrying value	_____	_____
Office supplies inventory	_____	_____
Prepaid insurance	_____	_____
Liabilities		
Note payable, City Bank	_____	_____
Interest payable	_____	_____
Rent revenue collected in advance . . .	_____	_____
Wages payable	_____	_____
Income statement:		
Rent revenue . . . . $	_____	$ _____
Depreciation expense	_____	_____
Interest expense	_____	_____
Office supplies expense	_____	_____
Wage expense	_____	_____
Insurance expense	_____	_____

P4–16 **(A Comprehensive Bonus Problem; Prepare Six Adjusting Entries and Recast the Income Statement and Balance Sheet)**

Morris Transportation Corporation has been in operation since January 1, 19A. It is now December 31, 19A, the end of the annual accounting period. The company has not done well financially during the first year, although transportation revenue has been fairly good. The three shareholders manage the company, but they have not given much attention to recordkeeping. In view of a serious cash shortage, they asked a local bank for a $10,000 loan. The bank requested a complete set of financial statements. The 19A annual financial statements given below were prepared by a clerk and then were given to the bank.

MORRIS TRANSPORTATION CORPORATION
Year Ended **December 31, 19A**

Income Statement

Transportation revenue	$90,000
Expenses:	
Salaries	20,000
Maintenance	15,000
Other expenses	25,000
Total expenses	60,000
Net income	$30,000

E.P.S.
Inventory

Balance Sheet   *Titles*
Co. *Date* **Assets**

(no) (no)
Class, depreciation

Cash	$ 1,000
Receivables	4,000
Inventory of maintenance supplies	5,000
Equipment	30,000
Remaining assets	37,000
Total assets	$77,000

Liabilities

Accounts payable	$ 7,000

Capital

Capital stock	40,000
Retained earnings	30,000
Total liabilities and capital	$77,000

After briefly reviewing the statements and "looking into the situation," the bank requested that the statements be redone (with some expert help) to "incorporate depreciation, accruals, inventory counts, income taxes, and so on." As a result of a review of the records and supporting documents, the following additional information was developed:

1. The inventory of maintenance supplies of $5,000 shown on the balance sheet has not been adjusted for supplies used during 19A. An inventory count of the maintenance supplies on hand (unused) on December 31, 19A, showed $2,000. Supplies used are debited to Maintenance Expense.

2. The insurance premium paid in 19A was for years 19A and 19B; therefore, the prepaid insurance at December 31, 19A, amounted to $1,000. The total insurance premium was debited in full to Other Expenses when paid in 19A.

3. The equipment cost $30,000 when purchased January 1, 19A. It has an estimated useful life of five years (no residual value). No depreciation has been recorded for 19A.

4. Unpaid (and unrecorded) salaries at December 31, 19A, amounted to $1,500.

5. At December 31, 19A, hauling revenue collected in advance amounted to $3,000. This amount was credited in full to Transportation Revenue when the cash was collected earlier during 19A.

6. Assume an income tax rate of 20%.

Required:

a. Give the six adjusting entries (in journal form) required by the above additional information for December 31, 19A.

b. Recast the above statements after taking into account the adjusting entries. You do not need to use subclassifications on the statements. Suggested form for the solution:

Items	Amounts reported	Changes Plus	Changes Minus	Correct amounts
(List here each item from the two statements)				

(Hint: The correct balance sheet total is $69,000.)

c. Omission of the adjusting entries caused:
   (1) Net income to be incorrect by: $_____, __ overstated, or __ understated.
   (2) Total assets on the balance sheet to be incorrect by: $_____, __ overstated, or __ understated.

Write a brief, nontechnical report to the bank explaining the causes of these differences.

P4–17 **(Computer Spreadsheet; Financial Statements)**

Required:

1. Using the data provided in P4–12, prepare an income statement following the format given in (a) of the Required using a computer spreadsheet.

2. Using the data provided in P4–16 and following the format suggested in (b) of the Required, prepare the corrected financial statements.

CASES

C4–1 **(A Question of Full Disclosure)**

Forbes magazine (December 8, 1980, p. 57) reported the following: "One firm sold shares for a new coal mining company. The prospectus stated that the firm had acquired 15,000 acres of land with proven coal deposits. What the 'entrepreneurs' who raked in some $20 million didn't mention in the prospectus was that they had only leased surface rights to the land. So the only way they could possibly get any coal out of it was if the black stuff came popping out of its own volition."

Explanation:
A prospectus is defined in *Webster's Dictionary* (7th edition) as "A preliminary printed statement that describes an enterprise (as a business) and is distributed to prospective buyers, investors, or participants."

Required:
If the firm were to prepare a financial report for external decision makers, should they disclose the facts cited above? Give the basis for your decision.

C4–2   **(Analysis of Four Transactions of a Real Estate Company that Involve Adjusting Entries)**
Fast Company, a closely held corporation, invests in commercial rental properties. Fast's annual accounting period ends on December 31. At the end of each year, numerous adjusting entries must be made because many transactions completed during current and prior years have economic effects on the financial statements of the current and future years. This case is concerned with four transactions that have been selected for your analysis. Assume the current year is 19D.

Transaction A:
On July 1, 19A, the company purchased office equipment for use in the business that cost $12,000. The company estimates that the equipment will have a useful life of 10 years and no residual value.

 a. Over how many accounting periods will this transaction affect the financial statements of Fast? Explain.
 b. Assuming straight-line depreciation, how much depreciation expense should be reported on the 19A and 19B income statements?
 c. How should the office equipment be reported on the 19C balance sheet?
 d. Would an adjusting entry be made by Fast at the end of each year during the life of the equipment? Prove your answer.

Transaction B:
On September 1, 19D, Fast collected $18,000 rent on some office space. This amount represented the monthly rent in advance for the six-months' period, September 1, 19D, through February 28, 19E. Rent Revenue was increased (credited), and Cash was debited for $18,000.

 a. Over how many accounting periods will this transaction affect the financial statements of Fast? Explain.
 b. How much rent revenue on this office space should Fast report on the 19D income statement? Explain.
 c. Did this transaction create a liability for Fast as of the end of 19D? Explain. How much?
 d. Should an adjusting entry be made by Fast on December 31, 19D? Explain why. If your answer is yes, give the adjusting entry.

Transaction C:

On December 31, 19D, Fast owed employees unpaid and unrecorded wages of $5,000 because the payroll was paid on December 27, and between this day and year-end, employees worked three more days in December 19D. The next payroll date is January 5, 19E.

a. Over how many accounting periods would this transaction affect the financial statements of Fast? Explain.

b. How would this $5,000 affect the 19D income statement and balance sheet of Fast?

c. Should an adjusting entry be made by Fast on December 31, 19D? Explain why. If your answer is yes, give the adjusting entry.

Transaction D:

On January 1, 19D, Fast agreed to supervise the planning and subdivision of a large tract of land for a customer—J. Ray. This service job, to be performed by Fast, involved four separate phases. By December 31, 19D, three phases had been completed to the satisfaction of Ray. The remaining phase will be done during 19E. The total price for the four phases (agreed upon in advance by both parties) was $40,000. Each phase involves about the same amount of services. On December 31, 19D, no cash had been collected by Fast for the services already performed.

a. Should Fast record any service revenue on this job for 19D? Explain why. If yes, how much?

b. If your answer to (*a*) is yes, should Fast make an adjusting entry on December 31, 19D? If yes, give the entry. Explain.

c. What entry will be made by Fast when the last phase is completed, assuming the full contract price is collected on completion date, February 15, 19E?

C4–3   **(Analysis of How Alternative Ways of Recording a Transaction Affect Adjusting Entries)**

General situation: On December 1, 19A, Voss collected $4,000 cash for office space rented to an outsider. The rent collected was for the period December 1, 19A, through March 31, 19B. The annual accounting period ends on December 31.

Required:

a. How much of the $4,000 should Voss report as revenue on the 19A annual income statement? How much of it should be reported as revenue on the 19B income statement?

b. What is the amount of rent revenue collected in advance as of December 31, 19A? How should Voss report this amount on the 19A financial statements?

c. On December 1, 19A, Voss could have recorded the $4,000 collection in one of three different ways as follows:

Approach A:

Cash	4,000	
Rent revenue		4,000

Approach B:

Cash	4,000	
Rent revenue collected in advance		4,000

Approach C:

Cash 4,000		
Rent revenue	1,000	
Rent revenue collected in advance	3,000	

For each approach, give the appropriate adjusting entry (in journal form) at December 31, 19A. If no adjusting entry is required, explain why.

d. Do you believe one of the approaches shown above is better than the other two? Which one? Explain.

C4–4 **(An Overview of a Complete Set of Actual Financial Statements)**
Refer to the Consolidated-Bathurst Inc. financial statements given in Appendix B at the end of this textbook immediately preceding the Index. Answer the following questions for the 1987 annual accounting period.

1. On what date did the 1987 accounting year end? How were the dollar amounts rounded?
2. What was the name of the firm of independent PAs? What was the title of their report?
3. What is the name of the schedule in which the company implements the full-disclosure principle in the long term? How many years does it cover? What is the number of (a) employees and (b) common shareholders for 1983 through 1987?
4. What two lines on the income statement, that involve large amounts, directly reflect the matching principle? Compute the ratio between these two amounts (a cost ratio) for 1987 and 1986.
5. What categories on the balance sheet specifically refer to the cost principle?
6. How many "Notes to the Consolidated Financial Statements" were included?
7. What accounting principle was violated according to note 2? Why did the auditors not mention this violation?
8. Give the titles that the company used for the required financial statements.
9. What is the name of the discussion prepared by the management? List its major topics.

C4–5 **(Concepts)**
Accounting involves the collection, summarization and reporting of financial information. In many cases, clear-cut conclusions as to identification, measurement, and reporting decisions are not possible.

Consideration of who the users of financial statements are and their information needs should lead to an understanding of the objectives of financial reporting. These objectives, together with the consideration of the qualitative characteristics of accounting information determine, ultimately, the form and substance of the financial statements.

The figure below illustrates the essentials of a framework of accounting theory. Preparers of financial statements must relate the framework to the circumstances involved and must exercise their professional judgment.

A FRAMEWORK OF ACCOUNTING THEORY

User Orientation

Decision maker's:
    Needs
    Characteristics
    Level of knowledge
↓

Objectives

1. Provide information useful in investment and credit decisions for individuals who have a reasonable understanding of business.
2. Provide information useful in assessing future cash flows.
3. Provide information about enterprise resources, claims to those resources, and changes in them.

↓

Basic Elements of Financial Statements

    Assets
    Liabilities
    Owners' equity
    Revenues and gains
    Expenses and losses
    Earnings (net income)

↓

Qualitative Characteristics of Accounting Information

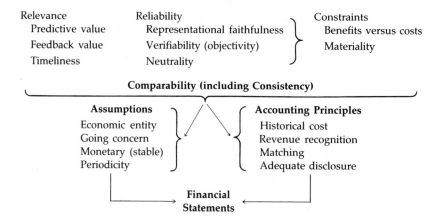

Relevance	Reliability	Constraints
Predictive value	Representational faithfulness	Benefits versus costs
Feedback value	Verifiability (objectivity)	Materiality
Timeliness	Neutrality	

Comparability (including Consistency)

Assumptions		Accounting Principles
Economic entity		Historical cost
Going concern		Revenue recognition
Monetary (stable)		Matching
Periodicity		Adequate disclosure

Financial Statements

Source: Adapted from Kieso et al., *Intermediate Accounting* (Rexdale, Ont.: John Wiley & Sons Canada Limited, 1982). Copyright © 1982. Courtesy of John Wiley & Sons Canada Limited. Reprinted by permission.

Required:

Discuss each of the following independent statements, making direct reference to the relevant components of the framework of accounting theory illustrated.

a. The existence of a variety of asset costing methods, each of which has a somewhat different effect on net income when prices are increasing or decreasing, points out that the freedom to shift from one costing method to another at will permits a wide range of possible net income figures for a given company over a given period. This in turn makes financial statements less meaningful.

b. Accounting attempts to serve many masters, a job that is not easy because the needs of one group may conflict with the needs of the others.

c. Information that is most objective may not be relevant to many decisions, and that which is most relevant may not be objective.

d. Issues of revenue and expense recognition must never be viewed in isolation from those of asset and liability valuation. They are intrinsically related. Any determination that affects reported income must necessarily affect a related balance sheet account, and vice versa.

e. At best, accounts receivable and the related revenues can never be viewed as being "accurately" presented—only "fairly" presented.

f. Any enterprise, whose securities are traded in a public market or that is required to file financial statements annually with a securities commission, is required to disclose segmented information in its financial statements. Faced with excessive costs to gather and communicate information, multinationals and diversified enterprises argue that segmented information renders redundant the information contained in consolidated financial statements.

(SMAC, Adapted)

C4-6 (Accounting Concepts)

The following article deals with differing accounting concepts and practices in Canada and the United States.

Auditors raise red flag on latest LAC annual report

Because LAC Minerals Ltd. of Toronto reports to U.S. regulatory authorities, its auditors have raised a red flag in LAC's latest annual report.

The cautionary note deals with the fact that LAC was on the losing end of a lawsuit over ownership of its Hemlo gold mine in Northern Ontario, which will be the largest in Canada when it reaches full production in 1988.

If LAC were dealing only with Canadian regulators, a warning in the auditors' report about the Hemlo mine would not be required.

In the main part of its report on LAC's 1985 financial statements, auditors Thorne Riddell use the standard language saying the report "presents fairly the financial position of the company." Beneath that is a separate note under the heading, "Comments on differences in Canadian-United States reporting standards."

Applying U.S. rules, the note says, the auditors' opinion is qualified "subject to the outcome of significant uncertainties."

The uncertainty is that a trial court judge has awarded the property to International Corona Resources Ltd. of Toronto and an appeal of that decision is to be heard in the fall.

Applying Canadian accounting standards, Thorne Riddell said, the report on

Source: Bud Jorgensen, *The Globe and Mail*, "Report on Business," April 15, 1986, p. B3.

LAC is not qualified because the uncertainty is disclosed in the financial statements.

Note 14c in the financial report summarizes the judgment and says LAC "completely disagrees with the findings and considers them to be contrary to the evidence at trial."

The U.S. rule used in the LAC annual report is what accountants call a "subject to qualification." The intent of that language is to draw attention to information in one of the footnotes, [which] usually deals with serious potential consequences for the financial statements.

William Buchanan, research director for the Canadian Institute of Chartered Accountants, said there is a provision in Canadian accounting rules for a statement from an auditor to draw attention to one of the notes. But that provision is rarely used, he said.

"The flags are in the financial statements," Mr. Buchanan said. "Why does the auditor have to flag them again?"

The U.S. rule was written because it was required by the Securities and Exchange Commission, Mr. Buchanan said. Regulatory authorities in Canada have made no similar requirement, he said.

"In this country we say: 'Look at all the footnotes,'" he said."The U.S. thing is quite illogical."

LAC's financial statement has a sentence at the bottom of each major component saying: "The accompanying notes are an integral part of these financial statements."

A sampling of U.S. corporate reports showed that it is common to use a similar note following their balance sheets and earnings statements.

Ian Hamilton, LAC senior vice-president and general counsel, said it is too soon to consider writing down LAC's asset value.

"We can't back it (the Hemlo mine) out on any basis because we don't know what the value would be," Mr. Hamilton said.

The trial judge, Ontario Supreme Court Justice R. E. Holland, set the after-tax value of the mine at about $515-million—using methods of valuation that he called "a very rough guide." He also said LAC should be paid $154-million for its development costs.

Both the value of the mine and the development costs are disputed by both sides and the figures are being challenged in appeals.

Required:

After reading the above article, answer the following questions.

1. Is accounting a universal truth? Why or why not?
2. Who was called in to try to resolve the valuation dispute at LAC? Why?
3. Are Canadian standards remiss in not requiring auditor disclosure of the uncertainty in a manner similar to that required in the United States? What about full disclosure?

INFORMATION PROCESSING IN AN ACCOUNTING SYSTEM

PURPOSE

Chapter 3 introduced the accounting information processing cycle, and Chapter 4 discussed an important phase of the cycle—adjusting entries. The purpose of Chapter 5 is to expand and complete the cycle. The expansion in this chapter involves additional phases that are performed at the end of the accounting (i.e., reporting) year. Accounting worksheets, adjusting entries, closing entries, and financial statements are emphasized. A clear understanding of this chapter will help you learn more applications of the (a) conceptual framework of accounting (Chapter 4, Part A) and (b) accounting information processing cycle.

All systems, such as information processing accounting, use some variation of an **annual** information processing cycle, as shown on the facing page. All financial statements show when this cycle starts and when it ends.

LEARNING OBJECTIVE

1. Define and explain the complete accounting information processing cycle.

2. Apply the four phases of the cycle that are performed during the accounting year.

3. Apply each of the seven phases of the cycle that are performed at the end of the accounting year.

4. Expand your accounting vocabulary by learning the "Important Terms Defined in This Chapter."

5. Apply the knowledge learned from this chapter.

ORGANIZATION

1. Data processing approaches in an accounting system—manual, mechanical, electronic.

2. Phases of the accounting information processing cycle during the accounting year.

3. Phases of the accounting information processing cycle at the end of the accounting year.

4. Interim financial statements.

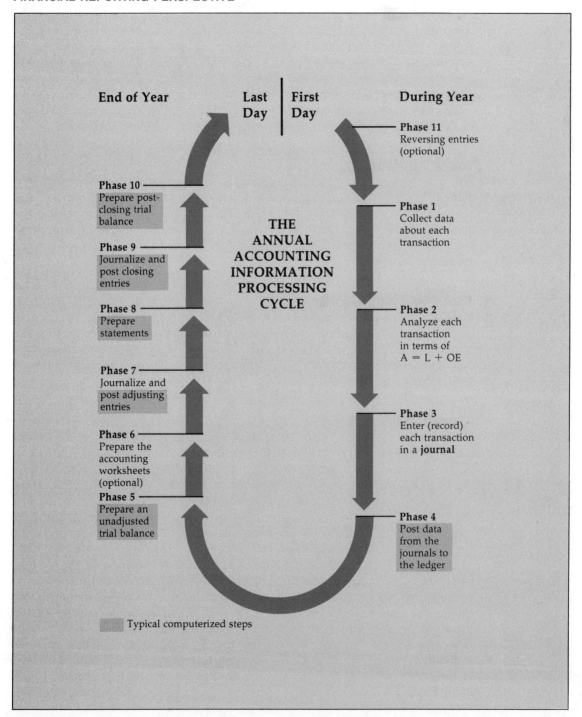

End of Year   **Last Day** | **First Day**   **During Year**

THE
ANNUAL
ACCOUNTING
INFORMATION
PROCESSING
CYCLE

Phase 11
Reversing entries
(optional)

Phase 1
Collect data
about each
transaction

Phase 10
Prepare post-
closing trial
balance

Phase 9
Journalize and
post closing
entries

Phase 2
Analyze each
transaction
in terms of
A = L + OE

Phase 8
Prepare
statements

Phase 3
Enter (record)
each transaction
in a **journal**

Phase 7
Journalize and
post adjusting
entries

Phase 6
Prepare the
accounting
worksheets
(optional)

Phase 5
Prepare an
unadjusted
trial balance

Phase 4
Post data
from the
journals to
the ledger

Typical computerized steps

Data Processing Approaches in an Accounting System

Data processing in an accounting system refers to the flow of data through the accounting information processing cycle during each accounting period. Although data processing can be time consuming and costly to the enterprise, a well-designed processing system provides an efficient flow of data from the daily transactions to the financial statements at the end of the accounting period. The processing of accounting data may be done in one of three ways, or, as is the usual case, by a combination of them. The three approaches are: manual data processing, mechanical data processing, and electronic data processing.

Manual Data Processing

With this approach, the accounting work is done by hand (i.e., manually). The manual approach is used in small entities. In large and medium-sized businesses, certain parts of the information process often are done manually. The manual approach also is used in accounting textbooks to illustrate data processing because you can see what is being done. You cannot see what is going on inside a computer.

Mechanical Data Processing

Mechanical data processing is used to record repetitive transactions that occur in large numbers. Mechanical processing of accounting data uses accounting machines that vary in type and application. These mechanical devices range from cash registers to posting machines. Although mechanical data processing is used today, it is being rapidly replaced by electronic data processing.

Electronic Data Processing

Electronic processing of accounting data uses electronic computers of varying size and sophistication. When electronic data processing is used, the use of manual and mechanical activities in an accounting system is minimal. Because of the large capability to store data and the speed with which such data can be manipulated and recalled, electronic data processing is widely used in accounting. Electronic data processing needs "hardware" and "software." The computer and equipment related to it (usually called peripheral equipment) make up the **hardware. Software** includes (*a*) the computer programs that are instructions to the computer and (*b*) other items related to the operation of the system. Electronic data processing is applied widely to such accounting problems as payrolls, billings for goods and services, accounts receivable, accounts payable, inventories, and to the preparation of detailed financial statements. Because of the rapid development of microcomputers and software "packages" for them, it is technically and economically feasible for even the smallest businesses (and individuals) to have an electronic accounting system. Supplement 5C to this chapter will elaborate on how the accounting processing cycle might appear using electronic data processing.

Exhibit 5-1 Phases of the accounting information processing cycle expanded

Phases Completed during the Accounting Period 1-4

1. **Collection of economic data** about each transaction of the entity; supported with business documents.
2. **Transaction analysis** of each current transaction (when completed) to determine the economic effects on the entity in terms of the accounting model.
3. **Journalizing** the results of the analysis of the current transactions. This phase encompasses recording the entries in chronological order in the **journal.**
4. **Posting** the current entries from the journal to the respective accounts in the **ledger.**

Phases Completed Only at the End of the Accounting Period 5-10

5. **Prepare an unadjusted trial balance** from the ledger.
*6. **Prepare an accounting worksheet** (optional, see Supplement 5B):
   a. Collection of data for adjusting entries and analysis of the data in the context of the accounting model. Enter the adjusting entries on the worksheet.
   b. Separation of the adjusted data among the income statement, balance sheet, and statement of retained earnings. Prepare SCFP worksheet (discussed in Chapter 15).
*7. **Adjusting entries** (at the end of the period):
   a. Recorded in the journal.
   b. Posted to the ledger.
8. **Prepare financial statements:**
   a. Income statement.
   b. Balance sheet.
   c. Statement of changes in financial position (SCFP; discussed in Chapter 15).
*9. **Closing** the revenue and expense accounts in the **ledger:**
   a. Recorded in the journal.
   b. Posted to the ledger.
*10. **Prepare a post-closing trial balance.**

Phase Completed Only at the Start of the Next Accounting Period 11

11. Optional **reversing entries** (see Supplement 5A).

* Phases added in this chapter to expand the cycle.

Expanding the Accounting Information Processing Cycle

This section expands, but does not change, the **accounting information processing cycle** introduced in Chapter 3. You should review those discussions (particularly Exhibit 3–9). The expansion has additional phases related to the end-of-period activities. Exhibit 5–1 shows the additional phases.

Phases Completed during the Accounting Period

The phases completed during the accounting period were discussed and illustrated in Chapter 3. For study convenience, these phases are summarized below.

Phase 1—Collection of Economic Data about Each Transaction

This phase is a continuing activity that collects **source documents** (such as sales invoices) from all of the transactions as they occur. The collection process involves all operations of the entity and a large number of employees (including nonaccountants). Source documents provide data to be analyzed and recorded in the accounting system. The source documents must be collected in a timely manner and must provide **complete and accurate data** about each transaction.

Phase 2—Transaction Analysis

This phase is an analysis of source documents to identify and measure the economic impact of each transaction on the entity in terms of the basic accounting model: Assets = Liabilities + Owners' Equity, and Debits = Credits. It requires determination of the specific asset, liability, and owners' equity accounts that should be increased and/or decreased to properly reflect the economic consequences of each transaction.

Phase 3—Journalizing

This phase involves recording by date the analysis of each transaction in the **journal** in the Debits = Credits format. Thus, the economic impacts of each transaction on the entity are recorded first in the journal in chronological order.

Phase 4—Posting

This phase involves transferring the data in the journal to the **ledger.** The ledger has separate accounts; one for each kind of asset, liability, and owners' equity. Thus, posting to the ledger reorders the data from the chronological order in the journal to the classifications in the fundamental accounting model—Assets = Liabilities + Owners' Equity. The ledger is viewed as the basic accounting record because it provides appropriately classified economic data about the entity that will be used to **complete the remaining phases** of the accounting information processing cycle (including preparation of the periodic financial statements). The beginning balances displayed in the T-accounts in Exhibit 5–2 reflect the completion of these four phases.

Phases of the Accounting Information Processing Cycle Completed at the End of the Accounting Period

The phases of the accounting information cycle discussed in Chapter 3 are expanded in this chapter to *(a)* handle large volumes of accounting data, *(b)* facilitate the end-of-period accounting activities, and *(c)* minimize accounting errors and omissions. The specific procedures associated with the remaining phases are discussed in detail in this section.

Phase 5—Unadjusted Trial Balance

At the end of the accounting period, after all current transactions have been recorded in the journal (journalized) and then posted to the ledger, a listing of all

Exhibit 5-2 Ledger accounts illustrated with adjusting and closing entries

HIGH-RISE APARTMENTS, INC.
LEDGER—19B

Cash 101	Property Tax Payable 207	Maintenance Expense 351
12,297	(g) 5,700	3,000 │ (7) 3,400
	(e) 400	

Rent Revenue Receivable 102	Income Tax Payable 208	Salary Expense 352
(b) 600	(i) 6,120	17,400 │ (7) 18,300
	(f) 900	

Prepaid Insurance 103	Interest Payable 209	Interest Expense 353
2,400 │ (c) 1,200	(h) 600	19,563 │ (7) 20,163
	(h) 600	

Inventory of Maintenance Supplies 104	Mortgage Payable 251	Utilities Expense 354
600 │ (e) 400	238,037	34,500 │ (7) 34,500

Land 110	Capital Stock 301	Miscellaneous Expenses 355
25,000	50,000	4,200 │ (7) 4,200

Contributed Surplus 302

5,000

Exhibit 5–2 *(concluded)*

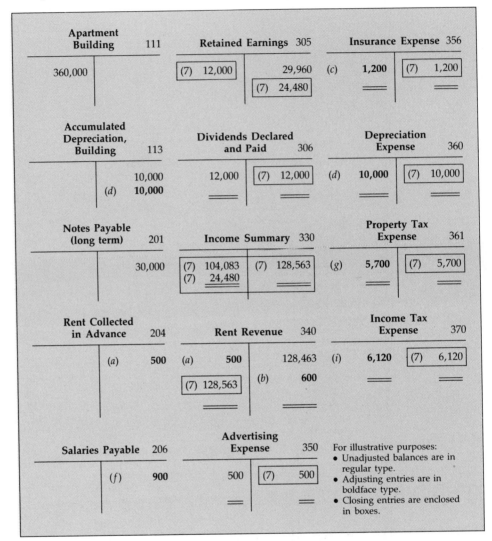

For illustrative purposes:
- Unadjusted balances are in regular type.
- Adjusting entries are in boldface type.
- Closing entries are enclosed in boxes.

ledger accounts and their balances is prepared. This listing, displayed in Exhibit 5–3, is called the **unadjusted trial balance.** This trial balance has two purposes: (*a*) it can be used to check the two accounting equalities—Assets = Liabilities + Owners' Equity, and Debits = Credits—and (*b*) it provides basic data needed to prepare the financial statements after adjusting entries are prepared.

This trial balance is called **unadjusted** because it does not include the effects of the **adjusting** entries (discussed in Chapter 4). The expanded phases—6

Exhibit 5–3   Unadjusted trial balance

HIGH-RISE APARTMENTS, INC.		
	Unadjusted trial balance December 31, 19B	
Account titles	**Debit**	**Credit**
Cash	12,297	
Prepaid insurance	2,400	
Inventory of maintenance supplies	600	
Land	25,000	
Apartment building	360,000	
Accumulated depreciation, building		10,000
Notes payable, long term		30,000
Rent collected in advance		
Mortgage payable, long term		238,037
Capital stock, par $10, 5,000 shares*		50,000
Contributed surplus		5,000
Retained earnings, Jan. 1, 19B		29,960
Dividends declared and paid	12,000	
Rent revenue		128,463
Advertising expense	500	
Maintenance expense	3,000	
Salary expense	17,400	
Interest expense	19,563	
Utilities expense	34,500	
Miscellaneous expenses	4,200	
Insurance expense		
Depreciation expense		
Salaries payable		
Property tax expense		
Property tax payable		
Interest payable		
Rent revenue receivable		
	491,460	491,460

* Average issue price per share: ($50,000 + $5,000) ÷ 5,000
share = $11. This topic is discussed in Chapter 12.

through 10—show how the adjusting entries are included in the (*a*) financial
statements and (*b*) the accounting records.

Phase 6—The Accounting Worksheet

The outline given in Exhibit 5–1 lists six different phases that are completed at
the end of the accounting period, including an **accounting worksheet.** The

worksheet may be prepared before the financial statements are prepared and before the adjusting and closing entries are recorded. The **completed worksheet provides all of the data needed to complete the remaining end-of-period phases** by bringing together in one place, in an orderly way, the (1) unadjusted trial balance, (2) adjusting entries, (3) income statement, (4) statement of retained earnings, (5) balance sheet, and (6) the closing entries (explained later).

Worksheets are a facilitating procedure. This term means they can help the completion of the adjusting and financial statement phase as well as the closing entries by organizing the general ledger trial balance in one location. The balances in the general ledger then become clearly visible to the accountant who can use the self-checks built into the worksheet procedure to prevent errors from entering the adjustment, statement, and closing phases. In addition, in interim dates during a fiscal year such as the end of a month or a quarter, the accountants may not wish to post the adjustments to the general ledger or close the accounts. Instead, they would need the effects of various adjustments to the general ledger so they can prepare accurate financial statements. A worksheet can be used to show the effects of the adjustments without actually posting the adjustments in the general ledger.

In practice, adjusting can become a reasonably routine activity. As such, accountants know what period end adjustments will be required without the need for a worksheet. A computer program can be designed to maintain the balance accuracy checks thus obviating the need for the worksheet. Thus worksheets become an optional phase whose use depends on the particular needs dictated by the situation. Supplement 5B will illustrate the preparation and use of worksheets.

Phase 7—Journalize and Post the Adjusting Entries

This phase is needed to enter the effects of the adjusting entries into the accounts. Immediately after finishing the adjusting entries, the financial statements are prepared and distributed to the users. The adjusting entries for High-Rise Apartments, with a **folio notation** to show that posting is completed, are shown in Exhibit 5–4. The ledger, with the adjusting entries posted (in boldface type for identification), is shown in Exhibit 5–2. You should trace the posting from the journal to the ledger.

Phase 8—Prepare Financial Statements

The completed adjustments provide the amounts needed to prepare the income statement, balance sheet, and statement of retained earnings. The statement of retained earnings, although not presented in previous chapters, usually is prepared by corporations. The **retained earnings statement** ties together the income statement and the shareholders' equity section of the balance sheet.

The financial statements for High-Rise Apartments, prepared directly from the general ledger, Exhibit 5–2, are shown on the next two pages. Notice that all of the figures were provided by the adjusted balances in the general ledger before closing entries are posted.

HIGH-RISE APARTMENTS, INC.
Income Statement
For the Year Ended December 31, 19B

Revenue:		
Rent revenue		$128,563
Operating expenses:		
Advertising expense	$ 500	
Maintenance expense	3,400	
Salary expense	18,300	
Interest expense	20,163	
Utilities expense	34,500	
Miscellaneous expenses	4,200	
Insurance expense	1,200	
Depreciation expense	10,000	
Property tax expense	5,700	
Total operating expenses		97,963
Pretax income		30,600
Income tax expense ($30,600 × 20%)		6,120
Net income		$ 24,480
EPS ($24,480 ÷ 5,000 shares)		$4.90

HIGH-RISE APARTMENTS, INC.
Statement of Retained Earnings
For the Year Ended December 31, 19B

Retained earnings balance, January 1, 19B	$29,960
Add net income of 19B	24,480
Total	54,440
Less dividends declared and paid in 19B	12,000
Retained earnings balance, December 31, 19B	$42,440

HIGH-RISE APARTMENTS, INC.
Balance Sheet
At December 31, 19B

Assets

Current assets:			
Cash		$ 12,297	
Prepaid insurance		1,200	
Inventory, maintenance supplies		200	
Rent revenue receivable		600	
Total current assets			$ 14,297
Operational assets:			
Land		25,000	
Apartment building	$360,000		
Less: Accumulated depreciation	20,000	340,000	365,000
Total assets			$379,297

HIGH-RISE APARTMENTS, INC.
Balance Sheet
At December 31, 19B

Liabilities

Current liabilities:		
Salaries payable	$ 900	
Property tax payable	5,700	
Interest payable	600	
Income tax payable	6,120	
Rent collected in advance	500	
Total current liabilities		$ 13,820
Long-term liabilities:		
Note payable	30,000	
Mortgage payable	238,037	
Total long-term liabilities		268,037
Total liabilities		281,857

Shareholders' Equity

Contributed capital:		
Capital stock, par $10; outstanding 5,000 shares	50,000	
Contributed surplus	5,000	
Total contributed capital	55,000	
Retained earnings (see statement of retained earnings)	42,440	
Total shareholders' equity		97,440
Total liabilities and shareholders' equity		$379,297

Phase 9—Closing Entries for the Income Statement Accounts

Chapters 2 and 3 emphasized that the revenue and expense accounts are subdivisions of retained earnings which is a part of owners' equity. The revenue, gain, expense, and loss accounts are **"income statement"** accounts. The remaining accounts are **"balance sheet"** accounts. The revenue, gain, expense, and loss accounts are often called **temporary** (or nominal) accounts because they are used to accumulate data for the **current accounting period only.** At the end of each period, their balances are transferred, or **closed,** to the Retained Earnings account. This periodic closing (or clearing out) of the balances of the income statement accounts into Retained Earnings is done by using closing entries. The closing entries have two purposes: (1) to transfer net income (or loss) to retained earnings (i.e., owners' equity), and (2) to establish a **zero balance** in each of the temporary accounts to start the next accounting period. In this way, the **income statement accounts** again are ready for their **temporary** periodic collection function for the next period.

In contrast, the **balance sheet accounts** (assets, liabilities, and owners' equity) are not closed periodically; therefore, they are often called **permanent** (or real) accounts. To illustrate, the ending cash balance of one accounting period must be the beginning Cash balance of the next accounting period. The only time a permanent account has a zero balance is when the item represented (such as machinery or notes payable) is no longer owned (or is fully depreciated) or no longer owed. The balance at the end of the period in each balance sheet account is carried forward in the ledger as the **beginning** balance for the next period.

Exhibit 5–4 Adjusting entries recorded in the journal

	HIGH-RISE APARTMENTS, INC.			
	JOURNAL			Page 6
Date 19B	Account Titles and Explanation	Folio	Debit	Credit
Dec. 31	a. Rent revenue	340	500	
	Rent collected in advance	204		500
	To adjust the accounts for revenue collected in advance (see pages 164–66).			
31	b. Rent revenue receivable	102	600	
	Rent revenue	340		600
	To adjust for rent revenue earned in 19B, but not yet collected (see page 166).			
31	c. Insurance expense	356	1,200	
	Prepaid insurance	103		1,200
	To adjust for insurance expired during 19B (see pages 167–68).			
31	d. Depreciation expense	360	10,000	
	Accumulated depreciation, building	113		10,000
	To adjust for depreciation expense for 19B (see pages 168–69).			
31	e. Maintenance expense	351	400	
	Inventory of maintenance supplies	104		400
	To adjust for supplies used from inventory during 19B (see page 169).			
31	f. Salary expense	352	900	
	Salaries payable	206		900
	To adjust for salaries earned but not yet recorded or paid (see page 170).			
31	g. Property tax expense	361	5,700	
	Property tax payable	207		5,700
	To adjust for 19B property tax incurred, but not yet recorded or paid (see pages 170–71).			
31	h. Interest expense	353	600	
	Interest payable	209		600
	To adjust for accrued interest expense for two months on note payable ($30,000 × 12% × 2/12 = $600) (see page 171).			
31	i. An adjusting entry for income tax expense is computed when the pretax income is computed thereon (see pages 219 and 230). The entry is:			
	Income tax expense	370	6,120	
	Income tax payable	208		6,120

The **closing entries** made at the end of the accounting period to transfer the balances of all of the income statement accounts is only a clerical phase. To close an account means to transfer its balance to another designated account by means of an entry. For example, an account that has a credit balance (such as a revenue account) is closed by **debiting** that account for an amount equal to its balance and crediting the account to which the balance is transferred. In the closing process, a credit balance is always transferred to another account as a credit, and a debit balance is always transferred to another account as a debit. Closing entries are **dated** the last day of the accounting period, entered in the journal in the usual Debits = Credits format, and immediately posted to the ledger.

A special summary account, called Income Summary, sometimes is used in the closing process. All of the income statement accounts—revenues, gains, expenses, and losses—are closed to Income Summary. The summarized difference is net income or net loss, which is then closed to the Retained Earnings account. The following summarized data for High-Rise Apartments (from Exhibit 5–2) is used to illustrate the Income Summary account: total revenues, $128,563, total expenses, $104,083, and net income, $24,480. The three closing entries, as they would be shown in the ledger accounts, would be as follows:

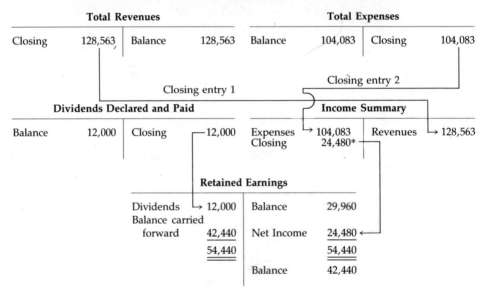

* Notice that this is the net income for the accounting period.

The detailed closing entries are shown in Exhibit 5–5. The data used in the detailed closing entries can be taken directly from the general ledger, Exhibit 5–2.

The last journal entry shown on Exhibit 5–5 closed Dividends Declared and Paid to Retained Earnings (not to Income Summary). High-Rise Apartments, Inc., declared and paid a $12,000 cash dividend to its shareholders. Dividends Declared and Paid was debited, and Cash was credited for this amount. Dividends are payments to the shareholders out of earnings. A dividend reduces

Exhibit 5–5   Closing entries recorded in the journal (source of data is Exhibit 5–2)

	HIGH-RISE APARTMENTS, INC.			
	JOURNAL			Page <u>7</u>
Date 19B	Account Titles and Explanation	Folio	Debit	Credit
Dec. 31	Rent revenue	340	128,563	
	Income summary	330		128,563
	To transfer revenues into Income Summary.			
31	Income summary ($97,963 + $6,120)	330	104,083	
	Advertising expense	350		500
	Maintenance expense	351		3,400
	Salary expense	352		18,300
	Interest expense	353		20,163
	Utilities expense	354		34,500
	Miscellaneous expenses	355		4,200
	Insurance expense	356		1,200
	Depreciation expense	360		10,000
	Property tax expense	361		5,700
	Income tax expense	370		6,120
	To transfer expense amounts into Income Summary.			
31	Income summary	330	24,480	
	Retained earnings	305		24,480
	To transfer Net Income into Retained Earnings.			
31	Retained earnings	305	12,000	
	Dividends declared and paid	306		12,000
	To transfer Dividends Declared and Paid to Retained Earnings.			

retained earnings. Therefore, the dividend account is closed to Retained Earnings.[1] Notice that the **ending** balance in the ledger account for Retained Earnings is: $29,960 + $24,480 − $12,000 = $42,440. Net income and dividends paid are included in the statement of retained earnings (see Phase 8).

After the closing process is completed, all of the temporary (i.e., the income statement) accounts have been closed to a zero balance. These accounts then are ready for reuse during the next accounting period for accumulating the revenues and expenses of the new period. When T-accounts are used, as in Exhibit 5–2, a zero balance is indicated by a double ruling on each side of the account.

———/

[1] When the dividend was declared and paid, the debit could have been made directly to Retained Earnings. In this case, the closing entry would not be made.

The permanent (i.e., balance sheet) accounts will have an **ending** balance, which is carried forward as the beginning balance for the next period. The balance carried forward in a T-account can be shown as follows:[2]

Retained Earnings			305
Dividends (19B)	12,000	Jan. 1, 19B, balance	29,960
Balance carried forward to 19C	42,440	Net income (19B)	24,480
	54,440		54,440
		Jan. 1, 19C, balance	42,440

Closing entries are not typically recorded at the end of interim accounting periods such as the end of a month or a quarter. Typically they are made only once a year at the end of the fiscal period. Thus Phase 9 is commonly skipped when interim financial statements are prepared.

Phase 10—Post-Closing Trial Balance

This phase is a clerical verification of the account balances after all closing entries have been posted. In computerized accounting systems this verification can be done automatically. In other systems it may be done with a printing calculator or an adding machine. Some accountants prefer to prepare another formal trial balance, called a **post-closing trial balance**, before starting a new period. All of the income statement accounts have been closed to Retained Earnings; therefore, the post-closing trial balance will show balances **only** for the permanent accounts classified as assets, liabilities, and owners' equity. The ending balances shown in the ledger accounts after the closing process will be the beginning balances for the next period.

Phase 11—Reversing Entries

Some accountants add an **optional phase** to the accounting information processing cycle called **reversing entries.** This phase is dated as of the first day of the next accounting period. It is used for the sole purpose of **facilitating** certain subsequent entries in the accounts. Reversing entries are related specifically to certain adjusting entries that already have been journalized and posted to the accounts. When appropriate, such adjusting entries are reversed on the first day of the next period (i.e., the debits and credits simply are reversed by the reversing entry). Reversing entries involve bookkeeping skills rather than accounting concepts and principles. Supplement 5A at the end of this chapter discusses and illustrates reversing entries for those who want to learn about this optional facilitating technique.

---

[2] Exhibit 3–4 shows the columnar format for ledger accounts that is always used. The T-account format is used only for instructional convenience.

Interim Financial Statements

Financial statements for a reporting period of less than one year are called **interim financial statements.** Such statements usually are prepared quarterly or monthly. **Monthly** financial statements almost always are for internal management uses only. In contrast, many larger companies prepare quarterly financial statements for internal management use and also present summarized versions of them to their shareholders and other external parties.

When monthly or quarterly interim financial statements are prepared, the company usually does not go through the phases of interim adjusting and closing entries. The formal phases of journalizing and posting adjusting entries typically are performed only at the end of the annual accounting period. Instead, the company prepares a worksheet to facilitate preparation of the interim financial statements. Therefore, the worksheet has another very useful purpose when interim monthly or quarterly financial statements are prepared. At the end of each interim period, an unadjusted trial balance is taken from the ledger accounts and entered directly on an interim (say, monthly) worksheet. The interim worksheet then is completed by entering the interim adjusting entries on it and extending the adjusted amounts to the Retained Earnings, Income Statement, and Balance Sheet columns. The interim statements (say, monthly) are prepared on the basis of the worksheet. In such cases, the remaining phases of the accounting information processing cycle (adjusting entries recorded, closing entries recorded, and post-closing trial balance) are not completed at the end of each interim period.

SUMMARY OF CHAPTER

This chapter discussed the accounting information processing cycle that is completed in cases where periodic financial statements are developed for both external and internal users. The cycle captures economic data on transactions as they occur and then records and processes their economic effects on the entity and communicates these effects by means of the periodic financial statements. The accounting information system must be designed to measure net income, financial position, and funds flow accurately and effectively. Such an information system also must be designed to fit the specific characteristics of the entity.

The worksheet, the closing entries, and the post-closing trial balance phases are clerical data processing procedures and do not involve any new accounting principles. The 11 phases discussed in this chapter constitute the accounting information processing cycle that is repeated each accounting period in most accounting systems.

Many adaptations of the procedures used to implement the cycle are observed in actual situations because entities have different characteristics such as size, type of industry, complexity, accounting expertise, and sophistication of the management.

The information processing activities in a particular entity can be effective in terms of the outputs (the financial statements), but unfortunately, the opposite may be true. The effectiveness of the system depends on the competence of those performing the data processing tasks and the importance attached by the management and owners to the financial measurement of operating results and financial position. In this context, the information processing system of an entity is significant to all parties interested in the entity because the end results—the financial statements—are important in decision making.

CHAPTER SUPPLEMENT 5A

Reversing Entries Illustrated

After finishing Phase 10 of the accounting information processing cycle (i.e., the post-closing trial balance), an **optional facilitating phase** may be added as Phase 11 (see Exhibit 5–1). This optional phase involves reversing entries. **Reversing entries are dated at the beginning of the next period and relate only to certain adjusting entries made at the end of the prior period.** Certain adjusting entries may be reversed on the first day of the next period solely to facilitate recording subsequent related entries. Unlike most of the prior phases in the accounting information processing cycle, reversing entries are optional and involve only bookkeeping skills rather than accounting principles or concepts.

The reversing entry phase is presented because (1) it introduces a common data processing technique used in most companies, whether the system is manual, mechanical, or computerized; and (2) a knowledge of the circumstances under which this phase may be used gives some additional insight into certain relationships in the efficient processing of accounting information.

Reversing entries are given this name because they reverse, at the start of the next accounting period, the effects of certain adjusting entries made at the end of the previous period. Reversing entries are always the opposite of the related adjusting entry. It may be desirable to "reverse" certain adjusting entries; the other adjusting entries should not be reversed.

To illustrate reversing entries and the type of situation where a reversing entry will simplify the subsequent accounting entry, assume that Day Company is in the process of completing the information processing cycle at the end of its accounting period, December 31, 19B. To place the reversing entry in context, Exhibit 5–6 presents a situation that shows (1) an adjusting entry on December 31, 19B; (2) the reversing entry that could be made on January 1, 19C; and (3) the subsequent entry on January 13, 19C, that was facilitated or simplified. To demonstrate the facilitating effect of a reversing entry, we also have presented entries in the exhibit reflecting the same situation assuming no reversing entry. You should study carefully the two sets of entries and the explanatory comments in Exhibit 5–6. The reversing entry, *c*, is shown in boldface for emphasis.

Exhibit 5–7 presents another illustration of the effects of reversing entries. It is presented to emphasize the facilitating feature of reversing entries as shown in

Exhibit 5–6 Purpose of reversing entries illustrated with wages

---

DAY COMPANY

Situation: The payroll was paid on December 28, 19B; the next payroll will be on January 13, 19C. At December 31, 19B, wages of $3,000 were earned for the last three days of the year that had not been paid or recorded.

With reversing entry	Without reversing entry

a. **The preceding adjusting entry:**

December 31, 19B, adjusting entry to record the $3,000 accrued (unpaid) wages:

Wage expense	3,000			Wage expense	3,000	
Wages payable				Wages payable		
(a liability)		3,000		(a liability)		3,000

b. **The closing entry:** The revenue and expense accounts are closed to Income Summary after the adjusting entries are completed and posted to the ledger.

December 31, 19B, closing entry:

Income summary	3,000			Income summary	3,000	
Wage expense		3,000		Wage expense		3,000

c. **The reversing entry: The information processing cycle in 19B is complete. All closing entries have been posted, and the post-closing trial balance has been verified. At this point in time, January 1, 19C, the accountant should decide whether it is desirable to reverse any of the 19B adjusting entries (i.e., any reversing entries) to simplify the subsequent related entries. Question: Would a reversing entry on January 1, 19C, simplify the entry to be made on January 13, 19C, when the wages are paid?**

January 1, 19C, reversing entry:

Wages payable			No reversing entry assumed.	
(a liability)	3,000			
Wage expense		3,000		

d. **The subsequent entry that was facilitated:** The payroll of $25,000 was completed and paid on January 13, 19C. This subsequent payment entry is to be recorded. Question: Did the reversing entry facilitate or simplify this entry?

January 13, 19C, payroll entry:*

Wage expense	25,000		Wages payable	3,000	
Cash		25,000	Wage expense	22,000	
			Cash		25,000

***** **Explanation:** Observe that when the reversing entry was used, this last entry required only one debit, contrasted with two debits when no reversing entry was made. This difference was due to the fact that the reversing entry served to (1) clear out the liability account, Wages Payable, and (2) set up a temporary **credit** in the Wage Expense account. After the last entry, to record the payment of the payroll, both accounts affected—Wage Expense and Wages Payable—are identical in balance under both approaches. If the reversing entry is not made, the company must go to the trouble of identifying how much of the $25,000 paid on January 13, 19C, was expense and how much of it was to pay the liability set up in the adjusting entry at the end of the prior period ([*a*] above).

Exhibit 5–7 Reversing entries illustrated, journal and ledger (with interest revenue)

Situation: On September 1, 19A, Company X loaned $1,200 on a one-year, 10%, interest-bearing note receivable. On August 31, 19B, the company will collect the $1,200 principal plus $120 interest revenue. The annual accounting period ends December 31.

JOURNAL	LEDGER

JOURNAL

a. September 1, 19A—To record the loan:

Note receivable 1,200
    Cash   1,200

b. December 31, 19A (end of the accounting period)—Adjusting entry for four months' interest revenue earned but not collected ($1,200 × 10% × 4/12 = $40):

Interest receivable   40
    Interest revenue   40

c. December 31, 19A—To close interest revenue:

Interest revenue   40
    Income summary   40

d. **January 1, 19B—To reverse adjusting entry of December 31, 19A:**

Interest revenue   40
    Interest receivable   40

Observe that after this entry, the Interest Receivable account reflects a zero balance and Interest Revenue reflects a debit balance of $40 (four months' interest).

e. August 31, 19B—Subsequent entry; to record collection of note plus interest for one year:*

Cash 1,320
    Note receivable   1,200
    Interest revenue   120

LEDGER

Cash

	x,xxx	(a) 9/1/19A 1,200
(e) 8/31/19B	1,320	

Note Receivable

(a) 9/1/19A	1,200	(e) 8/31/19B 1,200

Interest Receivable

(b) 12/31/19A	40	(d) 1/1/19B 40

Interest Revenue

(c) 12/31/19A	40	(b) 12/31/19A 40
(d) 1/1/19B	40	(e) 8/31/19B 120

Income Summary

		(c) 12/31/19A 40

Note: To demonstrate the facilitating feature, assume the reversing entry (d) was not made. The August 31, 19B, entry would be more complex, viz:

Cash 1,320
    Note receivable   1,200
    Interest receivable   40
    Interest revenue   80

* Observe that after this entry, the Note Receivable account has a zero balance and the Interest Revenue an $80 balance which represents eight months' interest revenue earned in 19B.

---

both the journal and ledger. The reversing entry *d,* is shown in boldface to facilitate your study.

In the above discussion we explained that certain adjusting entries could be reversed to facilitate or simplify subsequent related entries and that certain adjusting entries would **not** be reversed. How does one decide which entries may be reversed to advantage? There is no inflexible rule that will answer this question. The accountant must analyze each case and make a rational choice. In general, short-term accruals and deferrals are candidates for reversal. In the case of short-term deferrals such as prepaid insurance or supplies inventory, or rent received in advance, reversing entries are typically used when the original transaction entries are recorded in the income or expense accounts, an option discussed in Chapter 4.

The adjusting entry to record depreciation and other entries of this type should never be reversed. In these cases, the adjusting entry is not followed by a subsequent "collection or payment" entry; therefore, it would be not only pointless to reverse the adjusting entry for depreciation but would introduce an error into the accounts because the accumulated depreciation account would reflect a zero balance for the first period. Thus, many adjusting entries are not candidates for reversal. Those that are candidates are easily identified if one considers the nature of the subsequent related entry (i.e., whether there is a subsequent collection or payment).

Perhaps the most compelling reason for reversing entries is to increase the likelihood that the effects of certain adjusting entries will not be overlooked when recording the next related transaction in the following period.

CHAPTER SUPPLEMENT 5B

Worksheets Illustrated

The simplified case used in Chapter 4 (pages 164–72) for High-Rise Apartments will be used to illustrate preparations of a typical worksheet at the end of the accounting year, December 31, 19B. To make the illustration easier, two exhibits are given:

Exhibit 5–8—Worksheet format with the unadjusted trial balance and adjusting entries.

Exhibit 5–9—Worksheet completed; shows the **income statement, statement of retained earnings, and balance sheet.**

The sequential steps used to develop the worksheet are:

Step 1. Set up the worksheet format by entering the appropriate column headings. This step is shown in Exhibit 5–8. The left column shows the account titles (taken directly from the ledger). There are six separate pairs of debit-credit money columns. Notice that the last six debit-credit columns show the data for the financial statements.

Step 2. Enter the **unadjusted** trial balance as of the end of the accounting period directly from the ledger into the first pair of debit-credit columns. When all of the current entries for the period, **excluding** the adjusting entries, have been recorded in the journal and posted to the ledger, the amounts for the **unadjusted** trial balance are the balances of the respective ledger accounts. Before going to the next step, the equality of the debits and credits in the unadjusted trial balance should be tested by totaling each column (totals $491,460). When a worksheet is used, there is no need to develop a **separate** unadjusted trial balance (Phase 5) because it can be developed on the worksheet.

Step 3. The second pair of debit-credit columns, headed "Adjusting Entries," is completed by developing and then entering the adjusting entries directly on the worksheet. The adjusting entries for High-Rise Apartments shown in Exhibit 5–8 were shown (with the same letter codes) and discussed in detail in Chapter 4, Part B. To facilitate examination (for potential errors), future reference, and study, the adjusting entries usually are coded on the worksheet as illustrated in Exhibit 5–8. Some of the adjusting entries may need one or more account titles in addition to those of the original trial balance listing (see last four account titles in Exhibit 5–8). After the adjusting entries are completed on the worksheet, the equality of debits and credits for those entries is checked (totals $19,900).

The remaining steps to complete the worksheet are shown in the "Financial Statements" area of Exhibit 5–9. These steps are:

Step 4. The pair of debit-credit columns headed "Adjusted Trial Balance" is completed. Although not essential, this pair of columns helps to assure accuracy. The adjusted trial balance is the line-by-line combined amounts of the unadjusted trial balance, plus or minus the amounts entered as adjusting entries in the second pair of columns. For example, the Rent Revenue account shows a $128,463 credit balance under Unadjusted Trial Balance. To this amount is **added the credit** amount, $600, **minus the debit amount,** $500, for combined amount of $128,563, which is entered as a **credit** under Adjusted Trial Balance. For those accounts that were not affected by the adjusting entries, the unadjusted trial balance amount is carried directly across to the Adjusted Trial Balance column. After each line has been completed, the equality of the debits and credits under Adjusted Trial Balance is checked (total $509,260).

Step 5. The amount on each line, under Adjusted Trial Balance, is **extended horizontally** across the worksheet and entered (*a*) as a debit, if it is a debit under Adjusted Trial Balance, or as a credit, if it is a credit under Adjusted Trial Balance; and (*b*) under the financial statement heading (income statement, retained earnings[3], or balance sheet) on which it must be reported. You can see that (1) each amount extended across was entered under only one of the six remaining columns, and (2) debits remain debits and credits remain credits in the extending process.

Step 6. At this point, the two Income Statement columns are summed (subtotals). The difference between these two subtotals is the **pretax income (or loss).** Income tax expense then is computed by multiplying this difference by the tax rate. In Exhibit 5–9, the computation was (Pretax revenues, $128,563 − Pretax expenses, $97,963) × Tax rate, 20% = $6,120. The **adjusting entry** for income tax then was entered at the bottom of the worksheet (a "loopback").

---

[3] The statement of Retained Earnings is discussed below under Step 7.

Exhibit 5–8 Worksheet format with unadjusted trial balance and adjusting entries (already entered)

HIGH-RISE APARTMENTS, INC.
Worksheet for the Year Ended December 31, 19B

Account titles	Unadjusted trial balance Debit	Unadjusted trial balance Credit	Adjusting entries Debit	Adjusting entries Credit	Adjusted trial balance Debit	Adjusted trial balance Credit	Income statement Debit	Income statement Credit	Retained earnings Debit	Retained earnings Credit	Balance sheet Debit	Balance sheet Credit
Cash	12,297											
Prepaid insurance	2,400			(c) 1,200								
Inventory of maintenance supplies	600			(e) 400								
Land	25,000											
Apartment building	360,000											
Accumulated depreciation, building		10,000		(d) 10,000								
Notes payable, long term		30,000										
Rent collected in advance				(a) 500								
Mortgage payable, long term		238,037										
Capital stock, par $10, 5,000 shares*		50,000										
Contributed surplus		5,000										
Retained earnings, Jan. 1, 19B		29,960										
Dividends declared and paid	12,000											
Rent revenue		128,463	(a) 500	(b) 600								
Advertising expense	500											
Maintenance expense	3,000		(e) 400									
Salary expense	17,400		(f) 900									
Interest expense	19,563		(h) 600									
Utilities expense	34,500											
Miscellaneous expenses	4,200											
Insurance expense			(c) 1,200									
Depreciation expense			(d) 10,000									
Salaries payable				(f) 900								
Property tax expense			(g) 5,700									
Property tax payable				(g) 5,700								
Interest payable				(h) 600								
Rent revenue receivable			(b) 600									
	491,460	491,460	19,900	19,900								

* Average issue price per share: ($50,000 + $5,000) ÷ 5,000 shares = $11. This topic is discussed in Chapter 12.

Exhibit 5–9 Accounting worksheet completed

HIGH-RISE APARTMENTS, INC.
Worksheet for the Year Ended December 31, 19B

Account titles	Unadjusted trial balance		Adjusting entries*		Adjusted trial balance		Financial statements					
							Income statement		Retained earnings		Balance sheet	
	Debit	Credit	Debit	Credit	Debit	Credit	Debit	Credit	Debit	Credit	Debit	Credit
Cash	12,297				12,297						12,297	
Prepaid insurance	2,400			(c) 1,200	1,200						1,200	
Inventory of maintenance supplies	600			(e) 400	200						200	
Land	25,000				25,000						25,000	
Apartment building	360,000				360,000						360,000	
Accumulated depreciation, building		10,000		(d) 10,000		20,000						20,000
Notes payable, long term		30,000				30,000						30,000
Rent collected in advance				(a) 500		500						500
Mortgage payable, long term		238,037				238,037						238,037
Capital stock, par $10, 5,000 shares		50,000				50,000						50,000
Contributed surplus		5,000				5,000						5,000
Retained earnings, Jan. 1, 19B		29,960				29,960				29,960		
Dividends declared and paid	12,000				12,000				12,000			
Rent revenue		128,463	(a) 500	(b) 600		128,563		128,563				
Advertising expense	500				500		500					
Maintenance expense	3,000		(e) 400		3,400		3,400					

Worksheet (continued)

Account	Trial Balance Dr	Trial Balance Cr	Adjustments Dr	Adjustments Cr	Adjusted Trial Balance Dr	Adjusted Trial Balance Cr	Income Statement Dr	Income Statement Cr	Balance Sheet Dr	Balance Sheet Cr
Salary expense	17,400		(f) 900		18,300		18,300			
Interest expense	19,563		(h) 600		20,163		20,163			
Utilities expense	34,500				34,500		34,500			
Miscellaneous expenses	4,200				4,200		4,200			
Insurance expense			(c) 1,200		1,200		1,200			
Depreciation expense			(d) 10,000		10,000		10,000			
Salaries payable				(f) 900		900				900
Property tax expense			(g) 5,700	(g) 5,700	5,700	5,700	5,700			5,700
Property tax payable										
Interest payable				(h) 600		600				600
Rent revenue receivable			(b) 600		600				600	
	491,460	491,460	19,900	19,900	509,260	509,260	97,963	128,563		
							6,120			600
Income tax expense†			(i) 6,120				104,083	128,563		
Income tax payable				(i) 6,120			24,480		12,000	6,120
Net income‡							128,563	128,563	42,440	24,480
									54,440	54,440
Retained earnings, Dec. 31, 19B§									54,440	54,440
									399,297	399,297

* Explanation of adjusting entries is provided in Exhibit 5–4.
† Revenues, $128,563 − Pretax expenses, $97,963 = $30,600; $30,600 × tax rate, 20% = $6,120.
‡ Pretax income, $30,600 − Income tax, $6,120 = $24,480.
§ $54,440 − $12,000 = $42,440.

Income tax expense and income tax payable now can be extended horizontally to the Income Statement and Balance Sheet columns. Net income is entered as a **balancing debit** amount in the Income Statement column and as a credit (i.e., increase) in the Retained Earnings column.

Step 7. The two Retained Earnings columns are summed. The difference is the ending balance of retained earnings. This balance amount is entered as a balancing debit amount (under Retained Earnings) and also as a balancing credit amount (i.e., an addition to owners' equity). At this point, the two Balance Sheet columns should sum to equal amounts. The continuous checking of the equality of debits and credits in each pair of debit-credit columns helps to assure the correctness of the worksheet. However, the balancing feature alone does not assure that the worksheet has no errors. For example, if an expense amount (a debit) were extended to either the Retained Earnings debit column or to the Balance Sheet debit column, the worksheet would balance in all respects; however, at least two money columns would have one or more errors. Therefore, special care must be used in selecting the appropriate debit-credit columns during the horizontal extension process.[4]

The completed worksheet, Exhibit 5–9, provides the data needed to complete the remaining phases of the accounting information processing cycle as follows (summarized from Exhibit 5–1):

Phase	Phase description	Source on worksheet
7	Record adjusting entries in journal and post to ledger	Adjusting Entries columns
8	Prepare income statement	Income Statement columns
	Prepare balance sheet	Balance Sheet columns
	Prepare statement of retained earnings	Retained Earnings columns
9	Record closing entries in journal and post to ledger	Income Statement and Retained Earnings columns
10	Post-closing trial balance	Prepare from ledger and check with Balance Sheet columns

---

CHAPTER SUPPLEMENT 5C

Electronic Data Processing Illustrated

Exhibit 5–10 presents the information processing cycle described throughout this chapter. As was mentioned, the description provided in the chapter is one represented by a manual accounting system. A manual system enables the observation of each of the steps involved but at the expense of a significant amount of tedious work.

---

[4] The number of paired columns on a worksheet can be reduced by omitting both, or either, the Adjusted Trial Balance columns and the Retained Earnings columns. Also, the number of columns can be reduced further by using only one money column for each set instead of separate debit and credit columns (for example, the credits can be indicated by parentheses).

Exhibit 5-10 The accounting information processing cycle

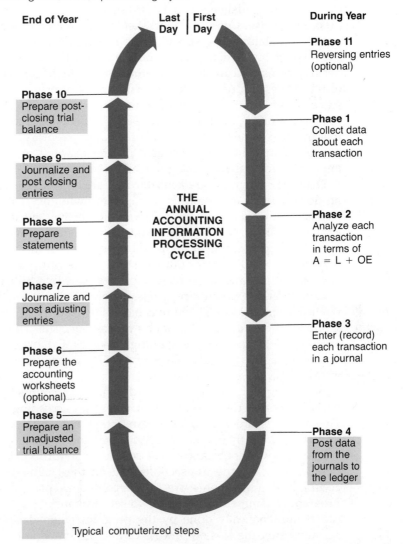

End of Year	Last Day	First Day	During Year

Phase 11
Reversing entries
(optional)

Phase 10
Prepare post-
closing trial
balance

Phase 1
Collect data
about each
transaction

Phase 9
Journalize and
post closing
entries

Phase 2
Analyze each
transaction
in terms of
A = L + OE

Phase 8
Prepare
statements

Phase 3
Enter (record)
each transaction
in a journal

Phase 7
Journalize and
post adjusting
entries

**THE
ANNUAL
ACCOUNTING
INFORMATION
PROCESSING
CYCLE**

Phase 6
Prepare the
accounting
worksheets
(optional)

Phase 5
Prepare an
unadjusted
trial balance

Phase 4
Post data
from the
journals to
the ledger

Typical computerized steps

Computerization of the processing cycle can remove some of the tedium because the computer is very good at performing repetitive tasks that have been preassigned to it. Most reasonably sized microcomputers can be assigned some of the routine activities that constitute the processing cycle. Computerized accounting information processing can be done by having various steps programmed into the computer. However, such programming can itself be tedious. Computer spreadsheets can be constructed to do some of the steps in the processing cycle. Certainly, worksheets and financial statements can effectively use the capabilities of a spreadsheet. The adjusting entries columns of a worksheet could be used to record routine transactions if necessary. Sophisticated macro commands can be programmed in spreadsheets to improve the efficiency of the processing of transactions using account numbers if desired. However, spreadsheets by themselves have not proven to be an efficient means of handling some of the steps in the processing cycle. Particularly, extensive journalizing and the details of accounts receivable, inventory, payrolls, and accounts payable that will be demonstrated in later chapters are awkward and close to impossible to deal with using spreadsheets.

Data base programs are available that are efficient organizers and processors of details such as accounts receivable, inventory, accounts payable, and payrolls. However, they are relatively ineffective and inefficient at processing adjusting entries, trial balances, and financial statements. Complete accounting information processing systems have been written in a data base language and they can be used to carry out the steps in the processing cycle for reasonably small situations and some relatively large ones that utilize large computers.

Computerized accounting packages are available on the market for prices ranging from $100 to $2,500 that have been specifically written to deal with a number of steps in the information processing cycle. The descriptions provided in Exhibit 5–11 are for the beginning packages. Extensions are available to some of the packages at additional costs. Also continuous modifications and upgrading is taking place by the developers.

Beginning with a trial balance and a chart of accounts that is numbered, these packages permit the coding of journal entries according to a displayed format. These entries are stored in a transaction file until posting is desired. The transactions are then used to update the stored balances, in effect posting, to achieve a new set of balances. The computer performs balancing checks of debits minus credits on the transactions and on the balances to assure arithmetical accuracy. If adjustments are also recorded as part of the transactions, the program can immediately prepare a set of financial statements. Closing entries can be automatically done by the program when desired. A trial balance of accounts after the closing process can be presented and used to begin the next period. Reversing entries can be recorded and posted if desired to ease the recording of transactions in the subsequent period. The steps in the processing cycle typically done as part of the computerized accounting package for small computers are highlighted in Exhibit 5–10. Notice the two matters the computer typically does not do are the analysis of transactions and their entry. Computers can collect routine data using bar codes such as you see in department stores, but someone has to specify how this data is to be treated if the routine is changed for some reason. Thus some collection and entry of data can be computerized; but in effect it has to be collected, analyzed, and entered before the computer can take over.

Exhibit 5–11 Entry-level computerized accounting systems

	Accpac Easy	Bedford	Dac-Easy	TAS Books
Functions included:				
General ledger	Yes	Yes	Yes	Yes
Accounts receivable	No (1)	Yes	Yes	Yes
Accounts payable	No (1)	Yes	Yes	Yes
Inventory	No	Yes	Yes	Yes
Job costing	No	Yes	No	No
Payroll	No	Yes	No (2)	Yes
General ledger:				
Sample chart included	Yes	Yes	Yes	Yes
Possible account numbers	1000–9998	100–599	Any 6 char.	Any 10 char.
Maximum number of accounts	2,000	500	(3)	65,000
Financial statement format	(4)	(4)	(5)	(6)
Number of accounting periods	1–13 periods	365 days	12 months	12 months
Number of years' history	1	0	2	2
Budget comparisons	Yes	No	Yes	Yes
On-line/batch posting	Batch	Automatic	Batch	Batch
Departmental accounting	Yes	No	Yes	No
Accounts Receivable:				
Number of customers	N/A	999	(3)	65,000
Open item/balance forward	—	Open item	Both	Open Item
Statements	—	Yes	Yes	Yes
User-defined aging periods	—	Yes	No	No
Accounts Payable:				
Number of suppliers	N/A	999	(3)	65,000
Create purchase orders	—	No	Yes	Yes
Inventory:				
Number of items	N/A	999	(3)	65,000
Costing method	—	(7)	3 methods	(7)
Job costing:				
Number of projects	N/A	999	N/A	N/A
Canadian payroll:				
Number of employees	N/A	999	N/A	999
Tax table updates	—	(8)	—	(9)
Other:				
Export data	Yes	Yes	Yes	Yes
Copy protected	No	No	No	No
Memory required	320K	256K	256K	256K
Network version available	No	No	No (2)	Yes
Suppliers	Computer Associate	Bedford Software	System Inc.	Accounting Solutions of Canada
Suggested price	$95.00	$249.00	$119.95	$149.00

(1) Balance forward listing only. No transaction detail maintained by system.
(2) Under development.
(3) Limited only by available disk space.
(4) Account number determines location in fixed layout statement.
(5) User-coded layout using report parameters within columnar format.
(6) User-defined format within fixed layout.
(7) Weighted average method only.
(8) Annual update service available for fee.
(9) Modified by user from Revenue Canada chart.

N/A = Not available.
Source: *The Bottom Line*, May 1988, page 21. Article written by Edward Hall.

Exhibit 5-12 Computerized accounting results

```
High-Rise Apartments
CHART OF ACCOUNTS Dec 31, 1988


ASSETS                                      LIABILITIES

  100 CURRENT ASSETS ...............H         200 CURRENT LIABILITIES ...........H
      106 Cash .....................R             221 Salaries Payable ..........R
      113 Prepaid Insurance .........R             222 Property Tax Payable ......R
      115 Inv. of Maint. Supplies ...R             223 Interest Payable ..........R
      120 Rent Revenue Receivable ...R             224 Income Tax Payable ........R
  139 TOTAL CURRENT ASSETS ..........T             225 Rent Collected in Advance .R
                                              269 TOTAL CURRENT LIABILITIES .....T
  150 OPERATIONAL ASSETS ...........H
      151 Land .......................R        270 LONG TERM LIABILITIES .........H
      152 Apartment Building .........L             271 Note Payable ..............R
      153 Acc. Dep'n, Apt. Building ..L             272 Mortgage Payable ..........R
      154 Apartment Building, net ....S        273 TOTAL L.T. LIABILITIES ........T
  159 TOTAL OPERATIONAL ASSETS .....T


                                            EQUITY

                                              300 CONTRIBUTED CAPITAL ...........H
                                                  310 Capital Stock, par $10 ....L
                                                  311 Contributed Surplus .......L
                                                  312 TOTAL CONTRIBUTED CAPITAL .S
                                                  356 Retained Earnings .........R
                                                  360 Current Earnings ..........X
                                                  365 Dividends Dec. & Paid ......R
                                              369 TOTAL EARNINGS ................T


REVENUE                                     EXPENSE

  400 REVENUE .......................H         500 OPERATING EXPENSES ...........H
      402 Rent Revenue ...............R             501 Advertising Expense .......L
  403 TOTAL REVENUE .................T             502 Maintenance Expense .......L
                                                  503 Salary Expense .............L
                                                  504 Interest Expense ...........L
                                                  505 Utilities Expense ..........L
                                                  506 Miscellaneous Expense .....L
                                                  507 Insurance Expense ..........L
                                                  508 Depreciation Expense, Apt. .L
                                                  509 Property Tax Expense .......L
                                                  515 TOTAL OPERATING EXPENSES ..S
                                                  520 Income Tax Expense .........R
                                              539 TOTAL ADMINISTRATION ..........T
```

Exhibit 5–12 *(continued)*

```
High-Rise Apartments
TRIAL BALANCE Dec 31, 1988
                                              Debits        Credits
                                            ---------      ---------

106   Cash                                  12,297.00           -
113   Prepaid Insurance                      2,400.00           -
115   Inv. of Maint. Supplies                 600.00            -
120   Rent Revenue Receivable                   0.00            -
151   Land                                  25,000.00           -
152   Apartment Building                    360,000.00          -
153   Acc. Dep'n, Apt. Building                   -        10,000.00
221   Salaries Payable                            -             0.00
222   Property Tax Payable                        -             0.00
223   Interest Payable                            -             0.00
224   Income Tax Payable                          -             0.00
225   Rent Collected in Advance                   -             0.00
271   Note Payable                                -        30,000.00
272   Mortgage Payable                            -       238,037.00
310   Capital Stock, par $10                      -        50,000.00
311   Contributed Surplus                         -         5,000.00
356   Retained Earnings                           -        29,960.00
365   Dividends Dec. & Paid                 12,000.00           -
402   Rent Revenue                                -       128,463.00
501   Advertising Expense                     500.00            -
502   Maintenance Expense                   3,000.00            -
503   Salary Expense                        17,400.00           -
504   Interest Expense                      19,563.00           -
505   Utilities Expense                     34,500.00           -
506   Miscellaneous Expense                  4,200.00           -
507   Insurance Expense                         0.00            -
508   Depreciation Expense, Apt.                0.00            -
509   Property Tax Expense                      0.00            -
520   Income Tax Expense                        0.00            -
                                            ---------      ---------
                                           491,460.00     491,460.00
```

Exhibit 5–12 displays the printout of the details of High-Rise Apartments using the Bedford computerized accounting package noted in Exhibit 5–11. The printout begins with a chart of accounts with indicators (letters) signifying the type of account, heading (H), subtotal (S), total (T), postable account (R or L), or (X), a single account for current earnings, essentially income summary. The opening trial balance is presented next, then the adjustments, the general ledger accounts, and the adjusted trial balance. Finally, the financial statements are disclosed. The printout in Exhibit 5–12 presents only enough of the capabilities of the accounting package to demonstrate the phases of the accounting cycle described in this chapter.

Exhibit 5–12 *(continued)*

High-Rise Apartments
GENERAL JOURNAL Dec 31, 1988 TO Dec 31, 1988   Page 1

Date	J#	Description		Acct	Account	Debits	Credits
12-31-88	J1	to adjust for unearned rent rev.	A	402	Rent Revenue	500.00	-
				225	Rent Collected in Advance	-	500.00
12-31-88	J2	to adjust for unearned rent rev.	A	402	Rent Revenue	500.00	-
				225	Rent Collected in Advance	-	500.00
12-31-88	J3	correcting entry for J1		402	Rent Revenue	500.00	-
				225	Rent Collected in Advance	-	500.00
12-31-88	J4	to record rent revenue receivable	B	120	Rent Revenue Receivable	600.00	-
				402	Rent Revenue	-	600.00
12-31-88	J5	to record insurance expense	C	507	Insurance Expense	1,200.00	-
				113	Prepaid Insurance	-	1,200.00
12-31-88	J6	to record annual depreciation	D	508	Depreciation Expense, Apt. Building	10,000.00	-
				153	Acc. Dep'n, Apt. Building	-	10,000.00
12-31-88	J7	to record use of main. supplies	E	502	Maintenance Expense	400.00	-
				115	Inv. of Maint. Supplies	-	400.00
12-31-88	J8	to record salaries expense	F	503	Salary Expense	900.00	-
				221	Salaries Payable	-	900.00
12-31-88	J9	to record property tax expense	G	509	Property Tax Expense	5,700.00	-
				222	Property Tax Payable	-	5,700.00
12-31-88	J10	to record interest expense	H	504	Interest Expense	600.00	-
				223	Interest Payable	-	600.00
12-31-88	J11	to record income tax expense	I	520	Income Tax Expense	6,120.00	-
				224	Income Tax Payable	-	6,120.00
						27,020.00	27,020.00

Exhibit 5–12 *(continued)*

High-Rise Apartments
LEDGER Dec 31, 1988 TO Dec 31, 1988

Account / Date / Description	Ref	J	Debits	Credits	Debit balance	Credit balance
106 Cash					12,297.00	-
113 Prepaid Insurance					2,400.00	-
12-31-88 to record insurance expense	C	J5	-	1,200.00	1,200.00	-
			0.00	1,200.00		
115 Inv. of Maint. Supplies					600.00	-
12-31-88 to record use of main. supplies	E	J7	-	400.00	200.00	-
			0.00	400.00		
120 Rent Revenue Receivable					0.00	-
12-31-88 to record rent revenue receivable	B	J4	600.00	-	600.00	-
			600.00	0.00		
151 Land					25,000.00	-
152 Apartment Building					360,000.00	-
153 Acc. Dep'n, Apt. Building					-	10,000.00
12-31-88 to record annual depreciation	D	J6	-	10,000.00	-	20,000.00
			0.00	10,000.00		
221 Salaries Payable					-	0.00
12-31-88 to record salaries expense	F	J8	-	900.00	-	900.00
			0.00	900.00		
222 Property Tax Payable					-	0.00
12-31-88 to record property tax expense	G	J9	-	5,700.00	-	5,700.00
			0.00	5,700.00		
223 Interest Payable					-	0.00
12-31-88 to record interest expense	H	J10	-	600.00	-	600.00
			0.00	600.00		
224 Income Tax Payable					-	0.00
12-31-88 to record income tax expense	I	J11	-	6,120.00	-	6,120.00
			0.00	6,120.00		
225 Rent Collected in Advance					-	0.00
12-31-88 to adjust for unearned rent rev.	A	J1	500.00	-	500.00	-
12-31-88 to adjust for unearned rent rev.	A	J2	-	500.00	-	-
12-31-88 correcting entry for J1		J3	-	500.00	-	500.00
			500.00	1,000.00		

241

Exhibit 5-12 (continued)

			Debits	Credits	Debit balance	Credit balance
271 Note Payable					—	30,000.00
272 Mortgage Payable					—	238,037.00
310 Capital Stock, par $10					—	50,000.00
311 Contributed Surplus					—	5,000.00
356 Retained Earnings					—	29,960.00
365 Dividends Dec. & Paid					12,000.00	—
402 Rent Revenue					—	128,463.00
12-31-88 To adjust for unearned rent rev.	A	J1		500.00	—	128,963.00
12-31-88 to adjust for unearned rent rev.	A	J2	500.00		—	128,463.00
12-31-88 correcting entry for J1	B	J3	500.00		—	127,963.00
12-31-88 to record rent revenue receivable		J4		600.00	—	128,563.00
			1,000.00	1,100.00		
501 Advertising Expense					500.00	—
502 Maintenance Expense					3,000.00	—
12-31-88 to record use of main. supplies	E	J7	400.00		3,400.00	—
			400.00	0.00		
503 Salary Expense					17,400.00	—
12-31-88 to record salaries expense	F	J8	900.00		18,300.00	—
			900.00	0.00		
504 Interest Expense					19,563.00	—
12-31-88 to record interest expense	H	J10	600.00		20,163.00	—
			600.00	0.00		
505 Utilities Expense					34,500.00	—
506 Miscellaneous Expense					4,200.00	—
507 Insurance Expense					0.00	—
12-31-88 to record insurance expense	C	J5	1,200.00		1,200.00	—
			1,200.00	0.00		
508 Depreciation Expense, Apt.					0.00	—
12-31-88 to record annual depreciation	D	J6	10,000.00		10,000.00	—
			10,000.00	0.00		
509 Property Tax Expense					0.00	—
12-31-88 to record property tax expense	G	J9	5,700.00		5,700.00	—
			5,700.00	0.00		
520 Income Tax Expense					0.00	—
12-31-88 to record income tax expense	I	J11	6,120.00		6,120.00	—
			6,120.00	0.00		

End

Exhibit 5–12 *(continued)*

```
High-Rise Apartments
TRIAL BALANCE Dec 31, 1988
                                             Debits        Credits
                                           ---------      ---------

106   Cash                                 12,297.00          -
113   Prepaid Insurance                     1,200.00          -
115   Inv. of Maint. Supplies                 200.00          -
120   Rent Revenue Receivable                 600.00          -
151   Land                                 25,000.00          -
152   Apartment Building                  360,000.00          -
153   Acc. Dep'n, Apt. Building                   -       20,000.00
221   Salaries Payable                            -          900.00
222   Property Tax Payable                        -        5,700.00
223   Interest Payable                            -          600.00
224   Income Tax Payable                          -        6,120.00
225   Rent Collected in Advance                   -          500.00
271   Note Payable                                -       30,000.00
272   Mortgage Payable                            -      238,037.00
310   Capital Stock, par $10                      -       50,000.00
311   Contributed Surplus                         -        5,000.00
356   Retained Earnings                           -       29,960.00
365   Dividends Dec. & Paid                12,000.00          -
402   Rent Revenue                                -      128,563.00
501   Advertising Expense                     500.00          -
502   Maintenance Expense                   3,400.00          -
503   Salary Expense                       18,300.00          -
504   Interest Expense                     20,163.00          -
505   Utilities Expense                    34,500.00          -
506   Miscellaneous Expense                 4,200.00          -
507   Insurance Expense                     1,200.00          -
508   Depreciation Expense, Apt.           10,000.00          -
509   Property Tax Expense                  5,700.00          -
520   Income Tax Expense                    6,120.00          -
                                          ----------     ----------
                                          515,380.00     515,380.00
```

Exhibit 5–12 *(continued)*

High-Rise Apartments
BALANCE SHEET Dec 31, 1988

ASSETS		
CURRENT ASSETS		
Cash	12,297.00	
Prepaid Insurance	1,200.00	
Inv. of Maint. Supplies	200.00	
Rent Revenue Receivable	600.00	
TOTAL CURRENT ASSETS		14,297.00
OPERATIONAL ASSETS		
Land		25,000.00
Apartment Building	360,000.00	
Acc. Dep'n, Apt. Building	20,000.00−	
Apartment Building, net		340,000.00
TOTAL OPERATIONAL ASSETS		365,000.00
TOTAL ASSETS		379,297.00

LIABILITIES			
CURRENT LIABILITIES			
Salaries Payable		900.00	
Property Tax Payable		5,700.00	
Interest Payable		600.00	
Income Tax Payable		6,120.00	
Rent Collected in Advance		500.00	
TOTAL CURRENT LIABILITIES			13,820.00
LONG TERM LIABILITIES			
Note Payable		30,000.00	
Mortgage Payable		238,037.00	
TOTAL L.T. LIABILITIES			268,037.00
TOTAL LIABILITIES			281,857.00
EQUITY			
CONTRIBUTED CAPITAL			
Capital Stock, par $10	50,000.00		
Contributed Surplus	5,000.00		
TOTAL CONTRIBUTED CAPITAL		55,000.00	
Retained Earnings		29,960.00	
Current Earnings		24,480.00	
Dividends Dec. & Paid		12,000.00−	
TOTAL EARNINGS			97,440.00
TOTAL EQUITY			97,440.00
LIABILITIES AND EQUITY			379,297.00

Exhibit 5–12 *(concluded)*

```
High-Rise Apartments
INCOME Dec 31, 1988

REVENUE

  REVENUE
    Rent Revenue                             128,563.00
  TOTAL REVENUE                              128,563.00
                                             ----------
TOTAL REVENUE                                128,563.00
                                             ==========

EXPENSE

  OPERATING EXPENSES
    Advertising                                  500.00
    Maintenance Expense                        3,400.00
    Salary Expense                            18,300.00
    Interest Expense                          20,163.00
    Utilities Expense                         34,500.00
    Miscellaneous Expense                      4,200.00
    Insurance Expense                          1,200.00
    Depreciation Expense, Apt.                10,000.00
    Property Tax Expense                       5,700.00
                                             ----------
  TOTAL OPERATING EXPENSES                    97,963.00
  Income Tax Expense                           6,120.00
                                             ----------
  TOTAL ADMINISTRATION                       104,083.00

                                             ----------
TOTAL EXPENSE                                104,083.00
                                             ==========

INCOME                                       24,480.00
                                             ==========
```

IMPORTANT TERMS DEFINED IN THIS CHAPTER

Accounting Information Processing Cycle   Accounting phases (steps) from the time a transaction is completed to the financial statements. *p. 213*

Closing Entries   End-of-period entries to close all revenue and expense accounts to Retained Earnings (through Income Summary). *p. 222*

Computer Hardware   Computer and other equipment used with it. *p. 212*

Computer Software   Computer programs and instructions for using an electronic computer. *p. 212*

Electronic Data Processing   Accounting process performed (in whole or in part) using electronic computers. *p. 212*

Manual Data Processing   Accounting process performed (in whole or in part) in handwriting; manually. *p. 212*

Mechanical Data Processing   Accounting process performed (in whole or in part) using machines. *p. 212*

Permanent (Real) Accounts   Permanent (or real) accounts are the balance sheet accounts; no closing entries. *p. 220*

Post-Closing Trial Balance   Trial balance prepared after all of the closing entries have been posted. *p. 224*

Reversing Entries   Recorded at beginning of next accounting period; backs out certain adjusting entries; facilitates subsequent entries. *p. 224*

Statement of Retained Earnings   Reports increases and decreases in retained earnings; ties together the income statement and balance sheet. *p. 218*

Temporary (Nominal) Accounts   Income statement accounts; closed at the end of the accounting period. *p. 220*

Unadjusted Trial Balance   A trial balance that does not include the effects of the adjusting entries. *p. 216*

Worksheet   A "spread sheet" designed to minimize errors and to provide data for the financial statements. *p. 217*

QUESTIONS

1. Distinguish among manual, mechanical, and electronic data processing. How does each relate to accounting information processing?
2. Identify, in sequence, the 11 phases of the accounting information processing cycle.
3. Contrast transaction analysis with journalizing.
4. Compare journalizing with posting.
5. How does posting reflect a change in the classification of the data?
6. Contrast an unadjusted trial balance with an adjusted trial balance. What is the purpose of each?
7. What is the basic purpose of the worksheet?

8. Why are adjusting entries entered on the accounting worksheet?

9. Why are adjusting entries recorded in the journal and posted to the ledger even though they are entered on the worksheet?

10. What is the purpose of closing entries? Why are they recorded in the journal and posted to the ledger?

11. Distinguish among (a) permanent, (b) temporary, (c) real, and (d) nominal accounts.

12. Why are the income statement accounts closed at the end of an annual accounting period but the balance sheet accounts are not?

13. What is a post-closing trial balance? Is it a useful part of the accounting information processing cycle? Explain.

14. What are reversing entries? When are reversing entries useful? Give one example of an adjusting entry that (a) should be reversed and (b) another one that should not be reversed (based on Supplement 5A).

15. Businesses in many industries have significant fluctuations in the amount of sales that are made during the months or quarters that make up their fiscal year. If prepaid insurance is assigned to expense in the period representing the expiry of the insurance policy because of the need to match expenses with revenue, how can this practice be justified when revenue is fluctuating significantly for each interim period? If prepaid insurance is felt to be insignificant, what about straight-line depreciation?

16. How should a business decide on whether to use manual, mechanical, or electronic data processing?

17. List the steps in the accounting information processing cycle that even the entry level computerized accounting packages can handle.

18. What steps in the accounting information processing cycle are not handled by the computerized accounting packages? Why is this the case?

EXERCISES

E5-1   **(Pairing Brief Descriptive Statements with the 11 Phases of the Accounting Information Processing Cycle)**

Match the descriptive statements with the phases by entering the appropriate letter in each blank provided.

Phase	Descriptive statements
_____ (1) Data collection	A. Reduces income statement accounts to zero.
_____ (2) Transaction analysis	
_____ (3) Journalizing	B. Converts chronological data to A = L + OE basis.
_____ (4) Posting	
_____ (5) Unadjusted trial balance	C. Collection of source documents.
_____ (6) Worksheet	D. Backs out certain adjusting entries.
_____ (7) Financial statements	E. Income statement, balance sheet, statement of retained earnings, and SCFP.

Phase		Descriptive statements
_____	(8) Adjusting entries recorded	F. Recording the results of transaction analysis.
_____	(9) Closing entries recorded	G. Checks equalities after the adjusting entries.
_____	(10) Post-closing trial balance	H. Determines effects of transactions on A = L + OE.
_____	(11) Reversing entries	I. Records transactions and events at the end of the accounting period that are not yet recognized properly.
		J. Checks equalities before the adjusting entries.
		K. Facilitates, in an orderly way, completion of the remaining phases of the cycle.

E5–2   (Pairing Brief Definitions with Important Terms Used in the Chapter)
Match the following brief definitions with the terms by entering the appropriate letter in each space provided.

Term		Brief definition
_____	(1) Interim financial statements	A. A "spread sheet" used to facilitate completion of the financial statements.
_____	(2) Permanent accounts	B. Computer instructions and programs.
_____	(3) Closing entries	C. Reconciles the income statement with the balance sheet at the end of each accounting period.
_____	(4) Computer hardware	
_____	(5) Statement of retained earnings	D. Recorded only on the first day of each accounting period to facilitate subsequent entries.
_____	(6) Temporary accounts	E. A computer and dot matrix printer.
_____	(7) Accounting worksheet	F. All of the income statement accounts.
_____	(8) Adjusting entries	G. Cause all temporary accounts to have a zero balance.
_____	(9) Computer software	H. Recorded to recognize items only at the end of the accounting period.
_____	(10) Folio notation	I. All of the balance sheet accounts.
_____	(11) Reversing entries	J. Prepared after adjusting entries and before closing entries to check equalities.
_____	(12) Adjusted trial balance	
_____	(13) Income summary account	K. Used to indicate that posting has been done.
_____	(14) Nominal accounts	L. Financial statements that cover less than one year.
_____	(15) Real accounts	M. A special clearing account used only during the closing process.

E5–3   **(Prepare a Simple Income Statement and Balance Sheet, Including Four Adjusting Entries, Without a Worksheet)**

Vista Company prepared the unadjusted trial balance given below at the end of the accounting year, December 31, 19B. To simplify the case, the amounts given are in thousands of dollars.

Account titles	Debit	Credit
Cash	$ 33	
Accounts receivable	27	
Prepaid insurance	4	
Machinery (10-year life, no residual value)	50	
Accumulated depreciation, machinery		$ 4
Accounts payable		6
Wages payable		
Income tax payable		
Capital stock, no-par (2,000 shares)		62
Retained earnings		10
Dividends declared and paid during 19B	3	
Revenues (not detailed)		60
Expenses (not detailed)	25	
Totals	$142	$142

Other data not yet recorded at December 31, 19B:

1. Insurance expired during 19B, $2.
2. Depreciation expense for 19B, $5.
3. Wages payable, $3.
4. Income tax rate, 20%.

Required:

(Note: A worksheet may be used but is not required.)

a. Complete the income statement and balance sheet given below for 19B.
b. Give the adjusting entries for 19B.
c. Give the closing entries for 19B.

Income Statement
For the Year Ended
December 31, 19B

Revenues (not detailed)	$ 60 000
Expenses (not detailed)	35 000
Pretax income	25 000
Income tax expense	5 000
Net income	$ 20 000
EPS	$_____

Balance Sheet
December 31, 19B

Assets		Liabilities	
Cash	$_____	Accounts payable	$_____
Accounts receivable	_____	Wages payable	_____
Prepaid insurance	_____	Income tax payable	_____
Machinery	_____	**Shareholders' Equity**	
Accumulated depreciation	_____	Capital stock	_____
		Retained earnings	_____
Total	$_____	Total	$_____

E5-4   (Determining How to Extend an Unadjusted Trial Balance to Complete a Worksheet; Uses Answer Codes)

The worksheet at December 31, 19B, for Bustle Realty Corporation has been completed through the adjusted trial balance. You are ready to extend each amount to the several columns to the right. The columns that will be used are listed below with the code letters:

Code	Columns
A	Income Statement, debit
B	Income Statement, credit
C	Retained Earnings, debit
D	Retained Earnings, credit
E	Balance Sheet, debit
F	Balance Sheet, credit

Below are listed representative accounts to be extended on the worksheet. You are to give, for each account, the code letter that indicates the proper worksheet column to the right of "Adjusted Trial Balance" to which the amount in each account should be extended. Assume normal debit and credit balances.

	Account titles	**Code**
(1)	Cash (example)	E
(2)	Inventory of office supplies	
(3)	Interest payable	
(4)	Capital stock	
(5)	Commission revenue earned	
(6)	Rent revenue collected in advance	
(7)	Salary expense	
(8)	Prepaid insurance	
(9)	Retained earnings, beginning balance (a credit)	
(10)	Building	
(11)	Mortgage payable	
(12)	Income tax payable	
(13)	Sales commissions receivable	
(14)	Accumulated depreciation on building	
(15)	Contributed surplus	
(16)	Dividends declared and paid	
(17)	Income tax expense	
(18)	Investment in bonds	
(19)	Net income amount (indicate both the debit and credit on the worksheet)	
(20)	Net loss amount (indicate both the debit and credit on the worksheet)	
(21)	Retained earnings, positive ending balance amount (indicate both the debit and credit on the worksheet)	

E5-5 **(Completing a Worksheet Starting with an Unadjusted Trial Balance)**
Miller Company is completing the annual accounting information processing cycle at December 31, 19B. The worksheet, as shown below, has been started (to simplify, amounts given are in thousands of dollars).

Account no.	Account titles	Unadjusted trial balance Debit	Credit
101	Cash	$ 20	$
102	Accounts receivable	38	
103	Inventory	22	
104	Prepaid insurance	3	
110	Equipment (10-year life, no residual value)	70	
111	Accumulated depreciation, equipment		7
119	Accounts payable		11
120	Wages payable		
121	Income tax payable		
122	Revenue collected in advance		
123	Note payable, long term (10% each December 31)		20
130	Capital stock, par $10		60
131	Contributed surplus		10
140	Retained earnings		15
141	Dividends declared and paid	8	
145	Revenues		99
146	Expenses	61	
147	Income tax expense		
	Totals	$222	$222

Data not yet recorded for 19B:

a. Insurance expense, $1.

b. Depreciation expense, $7.

c. Wages earned by employees; not yet paid, $2.

d. Revenue collected by Miller; not yet earned, $3.

e. Income tax rate, 20%.
   (Note: No accrued interest is recorded because interest is paid on each December 31.)

Required: (Supplement 5B)

Complete the worksheet in every respect (you may use account numbers instead of account titles). Set up additional column headings for Adjusting Entries, Adjusted Trial Balance, Income Statement, Retained Earnings, and Balance Sheet. Record all revenues and expenses (except income tax) in the two accounts given (145 and 146). Use a computer spreadsheet if available.

E5–6   **(Completing a Worksheet Starting with an Unadjusted Trial Balance)**

Scott Corporation, a small company, is completing the annual accounting information processing cycle at December 31, 19B. The worksheet, prior to the adjusting entries, has been started as shown below.

Account Titles	Unadjusted Trial Balance	
	Debit	Credit
Cash	$ 24,000	
Accounts receivable	14,000	
Equipment	30,000	
Accumulated depreciation		$ 9,000
Other assets	64,000	
Accounts payable		11,000
Long-term note payable		10,000
Capital stock, par $10		40,000
Contributed surplus		11,000
Retained earnings		14,000
Revenues		90,000
Expenses	53,000	
	$185,000	$185,000
Income tax expense		
Income tax payable		
Net income		

Data not yet recorded for 19B:

a. Depreciation expense, $3,000.

b. Income tax rate, 25%.

Required: (Supplement 5B)

Complete the worksheet in all respects. Set up additional column headings for Adjusting Entries, Adjusted Trial Balance, Income Statement, Retained Earnings, and Balance Sheet. Use a computer spreadsheet if available.

E5-7 **(Identifying Adjusting Entries by Comparing Unadjusted and Adjusted Trial Balances)**
Moline Service Company is in the process of completing the information processing cycle at the end of the accounting year, December 31, 19B. The worksheet and financial statements have been prepared. The next step is to journalize the adjusting entries. The two trial balances given below were taken directly from the completed worksheet.

| | December 31, 19B | | | |
| | Unadjusted Trial Balance | | Adjusted Trial Balance | |
Account Titles	**Debit**	**Credit**	**Debit**	**Credit**
a. Cash	$ 9,000		$ 9,000	
b. Accounts receivable			800	
c. Prepaid insurance	300		150	
d. Equipment	120,000		120,000	
e. Accumulated depreciation equipment		$ 21,300		$ 26,300
f. Income tax payable				3,300
g. Capital stock, 5000 no-par shares		50,000		50,000
h. Retained earnings, January 1, 19B		15,000		15,000
i. Service revenues		61,000		61,800
j. Salary expense	18,000		18,000	
k. Depreciation expense			5,000	
l. Insurance expense			150	
m. Income tax expense			3,300	
	$147,300	$147,300	$156,400	$156,400

Required:
By examining the amounts in each trial balance, reconstruct the four adjusting entries that were made between the unadjusted trial balance and the adjusted trial balance. Give an explanation of each adjusting entry.

E5-8   (Journalizing Adjusting and Closing Entries Based on a Completed Worksheet)
The accountant for Rocky Corporation has just completed the following worksheet for the year ended December 31, 19D (note the shortcuts used by the accountant to reduce the number of vertical columns on the worksheet—credits in parens, and no column for adjusted trial balance; see Supplement 5B):

Account Titles	Unadjusted Trial Balance (credits)	Adjusting Entries Debit	Adjusting Entries Credit	Income Statement (credits)	Balance Sheet (credits)
a. Cash	15,000				15,000
b. Prepaid insurance	300		100		200
c. Accounts receivable	20,000				20,000
d. Machinery	80,000				80,000
e. Accumulated depreciation	(24,000)		8,000		(32,000)
f. Other assets	13,700				13,700
g. Accounts payable	(7,000)				(7,000)
h. Rent collected in advance			200		(200)
i. Interest payable			450		(450)
j. Income tax payable			3,375		(3,375)
k. Notes payable, long term	(10,000)				(10,000)
l. Capital stock, 5000 no-par shares	(50,000)				(50,000)
m. Retained earnings	(18,000)				(18,000)
n. Revenues	(80,000)	200		(79,800)	
o. Expenses (not detailed)	60,000	100		60,100	
p. Depreciation expense		8,000		8,000	
q. Interest expense		450		450	
r. Income tax expense		3,375		3,375	
s. Net income				7,875	(7,875)
Totals	–0–	12,125	12,125	–0–	–0–

Required:

a. Prepare the adjusting entries in journal form required on December 31, 19D. Write a brief explanation with each entry. (Supplement 5B not required.)

b. Prepare the closing entries at December 31, 19D.

E5-9   (Recording Adjusting Entries in Journal Format)
For each of the 10 independent situations, give the journal entry by entering the appropriate code(s) and amounts.

Code	Account	Code	Account
A	Cash	K	Interest revenue
B	Office supplies inventory	L	Wage expense
C	Revenue receivable	M	Depreciation expense
D	Office equipment	N	Interest expense
E	Accumulated depreciation	O	Supplies expense
F	Note payable	P	Capital stock
G	Wages payable	Q	Retained earnings
H	Interest payable	R	Dividends declared and paid
I	Rent revenue collected in advance	S	Income summary
J	Service revenues	X	None of the above

| | Debit | | Credit | |
Independent Situations	Code	Amount	Code	Amount
a. Accrued wages, unrecorded and unpaid at year-end, $400 (example).	L	400	G	400
b. Service revenue collected and recorded as revenue, but not yet earned, $700.				
c. Dividends declared and paid during year and debited to Dividends account, $900. Give entry at year-end.				
d. Depreciation expense for year not yet recorded, $650.				
e. Balance at year-end in Service Revenue account, $59,000. Give the closing entry at year-end.				
f. Service revenue earned but not yet collected at year-end, $300.				
g. Balance at year-end in Interest Revenue account, $360. Give the closing entry at year-end.				
h. Office Supplies Inventory account at year-end, $550; inventory of supplies on hand at year-end, $100.				
i. At year-end interest on note payable not yet recorded or paid, $180.				
j. Balance at year-end in Income Summary account after all revenue and expense accounts have been closed, $9,900 (credit).				

E5–10   **(Based on Supplement 5A; Determining When to Use a Reversing Entry)**
Dover Company has completed the accounting information processing cycle for the year ended December 31, 19A. Reversing entries are under consideration (for January 1, 19B) for two different adjusting entries (of December 31, 19A). For case purposes, the relevant data are given in T-accounts:

Prepaid Insurance

1/1/19A Balance	600	(a) 12/31/19A Adj. entry	400

Insurance Expense

(a) 12/31/19A Adj. entry	400	(c) 12/31/19A Closing entry	400

Accrued Wages Payable

		(b) 12/31/19A Adj. entry	1,000

Wage Expense

Paid during 19A	18,000	(d) 12/31/19A Closing entry	19,000
(b) 12/31/19A Adj. entry	1,000		

Income Summary

12/31/19A Closing entries		12/31/19A	
(c)	400	Closed to Retained	
(d)	19,000	Earnings	19,400

Required:

Would a reversing entry on January 1, 19B, facilitate the next related entry for (a) Prepaid Insurance and (b) Accrued Wages Payable? Explain why.

PROBLEMS

P5–1   **(Prepare an Income Statement and Balance Sheet from an Unadjusted Trial Balance and Include the Effects of Five Adjusting Entries)**

AAA Services Company, Inc., a small service company, keeps its records without the help of an accountant. After much effort, an outside accountant prepared the following unadjusted trial balance as of the end of the annual accounting period, December 31, 19C:

Account titles	Debit	Credit
Cash	$ 30,000	
Accounts receivable	31,000	
Service supplies inventory	700	
Prepaid insurance	800	
Service trucks (5-year life, no residual value)	20,000	
Accumulated depreciation, service trucks		$ 8,000
Other assets	10,400	
Accounts payable		2,000
Wages payable		
Income tax payable		
Note payable (3 years, 10% each December 31)		10,000
Capital stock, par $1		30,000
Contributed surplus		3,000
Retained earnings		6,500
Dividends declared and paid	2,000	
Service revenues		75,000
Remaining expenses (not detailed)*	39,600	
Income tax expense		
Totals	$134,500	$134,500

* Excludes income tax expense.

Data not yet recorded at December 31, 19C:

1. The supplies inventory count on December 31, 19C, reflected $200 remaining on hand; to be used in 19D.
2. Insurance expired during 19C, $400.
3. Depreciation expense for 19C, $4,000.
4. Wages earned by employees not yet paid on December 31, $500.
5. Income tax rate, 20%.

Required:

Note: A worksheet may be used but is not required.

a. Complete the financial statements given below (show computations) for 19C to include the effects of the five transactions listed above.

b. Give the 19C adjusting entries. (Hint: Journalize the above five data items.)

c. Give the 19C closing entries. (Hint: Use the income statement column.)

(Hint: The EPS amount is $0.80.)

Income Statement
For the Year Ended December 31, 19C

Service revenues		$_____
Remaining expenses (not detailed)	$_____	
Supplies expense	_____	
Insurance expense	_____	
Depreciation expense	_____	
Remaining wage expense	_____	
Total expenses		_____
Pretax income		_____
Income tax expense		_____
Net income		$_____
EPS		$_____

Balance Sheet
At December 31, 19C

Assets

Cash	$_____
Accounts receivable	_____
Service supplies inventory	_____
Prepaid insurance	_____
Service trucks	_____
Accumulated depreciation, trucks	_____
Other assets (not detailed)	_____
Total assets	$_____

Liabilities

Accounts payable	$_____
Wages payable	_____
Income tax payable	_____
Note payable, long term	_____
Total liabilities	_____

Shareholders' Equity

Capital stock, par $1	_____
Contributed surplus	_____
Retained earnings	_____
Total shareholders' equity	_____
Total liabilities and shareholders' equity	$_____

P5–2   (Use the Ledger Balances to Explain the Adjusting Entries Recorded and to Give the Closing Entries; Answer Three Analytical Questions)

The ledger accounts of Home Service Company at the end of the second year of operations, December 31, 19B (prior to the closing entries), were as shown below. The 19B adjusting entries are identified by letters, and account numbers are given to the right of the account name.

Cash 101	Note Payable, (10%) 201	Capital Stock (Par $1) 301
Balance 20,000	Jan. 1, 19B 10,000	Balance 50,000

Inventory, Maintenance Supplies 102	Wages Payable 202	Contributed Surplus 302
Balance 500 │ (a) 400	(e) 600	Balance 6,000

Service Equipment 103	Interest Payable 203	Retained Earnings 303
Jan. 1, 19A 90,000	(b) 1,000	Balance 9,000

Accumulated Depreciation, Service Equipment 104	Revenue Collected in Advance 204	Service Revenues 304
Balance 18,000 (d) 18,000	(c) 7,000	(c) 7,000 │ Balance 220,000

Remaining Assets 105	Income Tax Payable 205	Expenses 305
Balance 42,500	(f) 6,600	Balance 160,000 (a) 400 (b) 1,000 (d) 18,000 (e) 600 (f) 6,600

Required:

a. Develop three 19B trial balances of Home Service Company using the following format:

Account No.	Unadjusted Trial Balance		Adjusted Trial Balance		Post-Closing Trial Balance	
	Debit	Credit	Debit	Credit	Debit	Credit
101						

b. Write an explanation of each adjusting entry for 19B.

c. Give the closing journal entries (do not use Income Summary).

d. What was the apparent useful life of the service equipment? What assumptions must you make to answer this question?

e. What was the average income tax rate for 19B?

f. What was the average issue (sale) price per share of the capital stock?

P5–3 **(Supplement 5B, Complete a Worksheet Starting with the Adjusted Trial Balance; Compute the Amounts for the Adjusting Entries; and Give the Closing Entries)** Avis Corporation has partially completed the following worksheet for the year ended December 31, 19E:

Account Titles	Unadjusted Trial Balance Debit	Unadjusted Trial Balance Credit	Adjusting Entries Debit	Adjusting Entries Credit
Cash	18,000			
Accounts receivable	26,000			
Supplies inventory	200			(a) 120
Interest receivable			(b) 200	
Long-term note receivable, 10%, dated Sept. 1, 19E	6,000			
Equipment (10-year life)	75,000			
Accumulated depreciation		30,000		(c) 7,500
Accounts payable		11,000		
Short-term note payable, 12% dated June 1, 19E		8,000		
Interest payable				(d) 560
Income tax payable				(e) 3,620
Capital stock, 40,000 no-par shares		42,000		
Retained earnings		7,000		
Service revenue		68,000		
Interest revenue				(b) 200
Expenses (not detailed)	40,800		(a) 120	
Depreciation expense			(c) 7,500	
Interest expense			(d) 560	
Income tax expense			(e) 3,620	
Totals	166,000	166,000	12,000	12,000

Required:

1. Use additional columns for Adjusted Trial Balance, Income Statement, Retained Earnings, and Balance Sheet; and complete the worksheet.

2. Show how the following amounts were computed in the adjusting entries:

   a. $120.

   b. $200.

   c. $7,500.

   d. $560.

3. Give the closing entries.

4. Why are the adjusting and closing entries journalized and posted?

P5–4   (Supplement 5B, Start with a Partially Completed Worksheet and Complete Phases 6–9 in Order)

Vancouver Corporation is completing the accounting information processing cycle for the year ended December 31, 19C. The unadjusted trial balance, taken from the ledger, was as follows:

Account no.	Account title	Unadjusted trial balance Debit	Credit
101	Cash	$ 43,550	
103	Accounts receivable (net)	17,000	
105	Prepaid insurance	450	
107	Interest receivable		
120	Long-term note receivable, 12%	6,000	
150	Equipment (10-year life)	100,000	
151	Accumulated depreciation, equipment		$ 20,000
170	Other assets	30,000	
201	Accounts payable		14,000
203	Wages payable		
205	Interest payable		
210	Long-term note payable, 15%		10,000
300	Capital stock, par $10		80,000
301	Contributed surplus		12,000
310	Retained earnings		34,000
311	Dividends declared and paid during 19C	8,000	
320	Service revenue		150,000
322	Interest revenue		
350	Expenses (not detailed)*	115,000	
351	Depreciation expense		
360	Interest expense		
370	Income tax expense		
207	Income tax payable		
	Totals	$320,000	$320,000

* Includes wage expense and insurance expense.

Additional data for adjusting entries:

a. Expired insurance during 19C was $150.

b. Interest on the long-term note receivable (dated September 1, 19C) is collected annually each August 31.

c. The equipment was acquired on January 1, 19A (assume no estimated residual value).

d. At December 31, 19C, wages earned but not yet paid or recorded, amounted to $3,000.

e. Interest on the long-term note payable (dated May 1, 19C) is paid annually each April 30.

f. Assume a 20% average income tax rate.

Required:

a. Phase 6—Complete a worksheet for the year ended December 31, 19C. Key the adjusting entries with letters. (Hint: Net income is $16,872.)

b. Phase 7—Write an explanation and prepare each adjusting entry.

c. Phase 8—Prepare an income statement (use two captions: Revenues and Expenses), a statement of retained earnings, and a balance sheet; use three captions only (Assets, Liabilities, Shareholders' Equity).

d. Phase 9—Give the closing entries in journal form. Explain why they must be journalized and posted to the ledger.

P5-5   **(A Comprehensive Problem to Cover Chapters 2 through 5, Starting with an Unadjusted Trial Balance and Ending with the Closing Entries)**
W&P Moving and Storage Service, Inc., has been in operation for several years. Revenues have increased gradually from both the moving and storage services. The annual financial statements prepared in the past have not conformed to GAAP. The newly employed president decided that a balance sheet, income statement, and cash flow statement would be prepared in conformity with GAAP. The first step was to employ a full-time bookkeeper and engage a local PA firm. It is now December 31, 1988, the end of the current accounting year. The bookkeeper has developed a trial balance from the ledger. A member of the staff of the PA firm will advise and assist the bookkeeper in completing the accounting information processing cycle for the first time. The unadjusted trial balance at December 31, 1988, is shown below.

Unadjusted Trial Balance
December 31, 1988

Debits		Credits	
Cash	$ 25,880	Accumulated depreciation	$ 18,000
Accounts receivable	2,030	Accounts payable	6,000
Office supplies inventory	150	Wages payable	
Prepaid insurance	600	Interest payable	
Land for future building		Revenue collected advance	
site	6,000	Income tax payable	
Equipment	68,000	Note payable (12%)	30,000
Remaining assets		Capital stock,	
(not detailed)	27,000	(20,000 no-par shares)	20,000
Salary expense	74,000	Retained earnings,	
Advertising expense	1,000	January 1, 1988	21,600
Utilities expense	1,270	Hauling revenue	106,400
Maintenance expense	6,500	Storage revenue	14,000
Miscellaneous expenses	570		
Insurance expense			
Wage expense			
Depreciation expense			
Interest expense			
Income tax expense			
Dividends declared and paid	3,000		
	$216,000		$216,000

Examination of the records and related documents provided the following additional information that should be considered for adjusting entries:

a. A physical count of office supplies inventory at December 31, 1988, reflected $40 on hand. Office supplies used are a miscellaneous expense. Office supplies purchased during 1988 were debited to this inventory account.

b. On July 1, 1988, a two-year insurance premium was paid amounting to $600; it was debited to prepaid insurance.

c. The equipment cost $68,000 when acquired. Annual depreciation expense is $6,000.

d. Unpaid and unrecorded wages earned by employees at December 31, 1988, amounted to $1,200.

e. The $30,000 note payable was signed on October 1, 1988, for a 12% bank loan; principal and interest are due at the end of 12 months from that date.

f. Storage revenue collected and recorded as earned before December 31, 1988, included $400 collected in advance from one customer for storage time to be used in 1989. (Hint: Reduce storage revenue.)

g. Gasoline, oil, and fuel purchased for the vehicles and used during the last two weeks of December 1988 amounting to $300 have not been paid for nor recorded (this is considered maintenance expense).

h. The average income tax rate is 20% which produces income tax expense of $5,600.

Required:

a. Phase 6—If Supplement 5B has been studied, enter the unadjusted trial balance on a worksheet. Enter the adjusting entries. Complete the worksheet. (Hint: The adjusted trial balance total is $230,000.)

b. Phase 7—Prepare the 1988 adjusting entries in journal form.

c. Phase 8—Prepare an income statement (use two captions: Revenues and Expenses), statement of retained earnings, and balance sheet. Use subclassifications as shown in Chapter 3, page 112. (Hint: The balance sheet total is $105,400.)

d. Phase 9—Prepare 1988 closing entries in journal form.

P5–6   **(An Alternate Comprehensive Problem to Cover Chapters 2 through 5, Starting with an Unadjusted Trial Balance and Ending with the Closing Entries)**
Charter Air Service, Incorporated, was organized to operate a charter service in a city of approximately 350,000 population. The 10 organizers were issued 7,500 shares of no-par value for a total of $75,000 cash. To obtain facilities to operate the charter services, the company rents the hangar and office space at the airport for a flat monthly rental. The business has prospered because of the excellent service and the high level of maintenance on the planes. It is now December 31, 1988, end of the annual accounting period, and the accounting information processing cycle is in the final phases. Representative accounts and unadjusted amounts selected from the ledger at December 31, 1988, are as follows:

Unadjusted Trial Balance
December 31, 1988

Debits		Credits	
Cash	$ 24,600	Accumulated depreciation,	
Prepaid insurance	6,000	aircraft	$ 60,000
Maintenance parts inventory	18,000	Notes payable, 12%	100,000
Aircraft	260,000	Capital stock,	
Salary expense	90,000	7,500 no-par shares	75,000
Maintenance expense	24,000	Retained earnings,	
Fuel expense	63,000	January 1, 1988	20,600
Advertising expense	2,000	Charter revenue	262,400
Utilities expense	1,400		
Rent expense	14,000		
Dividends declared and paid	15,000		
	$518,000		$518,000

For the 1988 adjusting entries, the following additional data were developed from the records and supporting documents:

a. On January 1, 1988, the company paid a three-year insurance premium amounting to $6,000.

b. The aircraft, when purchased on January 1, 1985, cost $260,000; and the estimated useful life to the company is approximately 10 years. The equipment has an estimated residual value of $60,000. Annual depreciation expense is $20,000. (Can you verify this amount?)

c. On July 1, 1988, the company borrowed $100,000 from the bank on a five-year, 12% loan. Interest is payable annually starting on June 30, 1989.

d. Charter revenue, on occasion, is collected in advance. On December 31, 1988, collections in advance amounted to $1,000; when collected, this amount was recorded as Charter Revenue.

e. Rent amounting to $14,000 on hangar and office space was paid during the year and recorded as Rent Expense. This included rent paid in advance amounting to $2,000 for January and February 1989. The total amount was recorded as Rent Expense in 1988.

f. The inventory of maintenance parts at December 31, 1988, showed $7,000. All parts purchased are debited to Maintenance Parts Inventory when purchased.

g. For case purposes, assume an average income tax rate of 20%, which results in income tax expense of $6,000.

Required:

a. After studying Supplement 5B, enter the above accounts and unadjusted balances from the ledger on a worksheet and complete the worksheet as required. (The following accounts should be added at the bottom of the worksheet because they will be needed for the adjusting entries: Insurance Expense, Depreciation Expense, Interest Expense, Interest Payable, Revenue Collected in Advance, Prepaid Rent Expense, Income Tax Expense, and Income Tax Payable.)

b. Based on the additional data given above, journalize the 1988 adjusting entries.

c. Phase 8—Prepare the 1988 income statement (use two captions, Revenues and Expenses), statement of retained earnings, and the balance sheet (classified as shown in Chapter 3, page 112). (Hint: The total on the balance sheet is $217,600.)

d. Phase 9—Journalize the 1988 closing entries.

P5–7 **(A Mini-Practice Set Starting with Transactions and Continuing Through a Complete Accounting Information Cycle; Simplified by Using Only 10 Basic Entries plus 5 Adjusting Entries)**

Little Service Company (a corporation) began operations on January 1, 19A. The annual reporting period ends December 31. The trial balance on January 1, 19B, was as follows (rounded to even thousands to simplify):

Account no.	Account titles	Debit	Credit
01	Cash	$ 2	$
02	Accounts receivable	6	
03	Service supplies inventory	15	
04	Land		
05	Equipment	80	
06	Accumulated depreciation, equipment		8
07	Remaining assets (not detailed to simplify)	5	
11	Accounts payable		7
12	Note payable		
13	Wages payable		
14	Interest payable		
15	Income tax payable		
21	Capital stock, 83,000 no-par shares		83
31	Retained earnings		10
35	Service revenues		
40	Depreciation expense		
41	Income tax expense		
42	Interest expense		
43	Remaining expenses (not detailed to simplify)		
50	Income summary		
	Totals	$108	$108

Transactions during 19B, summarized in thousands of dollars (the letters indicate dates):

a. Borrowed $12,000 cash on a 10% note payable, dated March 1, 19B.

b. Purchased land for future building site, paid cash, $12.

c. Revenues for 19B, $140, including $20 on credit.

d. Sold 2,000 shares of capital stock for $1 cash per share.

e. Remaining expenses for 19B, $80, including $6 on credit.

f. Collected accounts receivable, $14.

g. Purchased "remaining" assets, $10 cash.

h. Accounts payable paid, $9.

i. Purchased service supplies for future use, $10 (debit to Account No. 3).

j. Signed a $15 service contract to start February 1, 19C.

k. Declared and paid cash dividend, $15. (The accountant decided to debit Account No. 31 rather than a special account.)

Data for adjusting entries:

1. Service supplies inventory counted on December 31, 19B, $10 (debit Remaining Expenses).

2. Equipment, useful life 10 years (no residual or scrap value).

3. Accrued interest on note payable (to be computed).

4. Wages earned since the December 24 payroll; not yet paid, $16.

5. Income tax rate, 20%; payable in 19C.

Required:

Phases 1, 2, and 3—Analyze and journalize each of the 11 transactions. Give a description below each entry. Start with journal page 1 and provide a column for "Folio."

Phase 4—Set up the 20 ledger accounts. Use the following format (see page 108) (enter the beginning balances):

Cash   **Account No. 01**

Date	Explanation	Folio	Debit	Credit	Balance
19B	Beginning balance	✓			2
a	Borrowed cash	1	12		14

Note: Cash requires 10 lines; the remainder, 4 lines each.

Post the journal; use the folio columns.

Phase 5—Set up an accounting worksheet like Exhibit 5–8 and enter the unadjusted trial balance at December 31, 19B, if Supplement 5B has been studied. (Hint: The total is $249.)

Phase 6—Complete the worksheet. (Hint: Net income is $16.)

Phase 7—Journalize and post the adjusting entries.

Phase 8—Prepare the 19B income statement and balance sheet. To save time use only major captions.

Phase 9—Journalize and post the closing entries.

Phase 10—Prepare a post-closing trial balance. (Use account numbers rather than titles to save time.)

Phase 11—Identify the two reversing entries that could be made.

P5–8 **(Based on the Supplement 5A; Selecting Adjusting Entries that Often Are Reversed)**

Alvin Corporation has completed all information processing including the annual financial statements at December 31, 19D. The adjusting entries recorded at that date were as follows:

a.	Insurance expense	150	
	Prepaid insurance		150
b.	Interest receivable	200	
	Interest revenue		200
c.	Supplies expense	80	
	Supplies inventory		80
d.	Depreciation expense	2,000	
	Accumulated depreciation		2,000
e.	Wage expense	500	
	Wage payable		500
f.	Interest expense	300	
	Interest payable		300
g.	Income tax expense	4,000	
	Income tax payable		4,000

Required:

For each of the above adjusting entries indicate whether it usually would be reversed. Give the reversing entry in each instance (if none, so state) and explain the basis for your response.

P5-9   **(Computer Report)**

Ace Taxi Ltd. owns and operates a fleet of 50 automobiles. All expenses are charged to the company. After every shift, each driver records the expenses incurred for gas and oil, tires or repairs, and the unit number of the automobile. Not all of the 50 autos in the fleet need necessarily to be used during one shift. This expense report is turned in by the driver together with an account of the kilometres travelled.

Management wants a daily report in unit sequence that will provide the following information:

Unit no.	Gas oil	Tires	Repairs	Kilometres	Cost per 100 km

It is suggested that the unit number be used as a subscript for the array of data. A flowchart for the report where 999 is used as a unit number to signify the end of the array of data is shown on the following page.

Required:

Write a computer program to produce the report.

P5-10   **(Computer Program)**

The Lemon Company operates a used car lot in a medium-sized city. They have up to 200 cars at any time, and the published selling price is 20% greater than the price Lemon paid for each car.

It costs the company $5 per day to keep a car on the lot.

Salesmen are authorized to sell any car on the lot at the minimum selling price which is the original cost, plus one half of the markup, plus storage costs.

The owner wishes to know the minimum amount of profit on each car and therefore wants a daily report in unit number sequence that will provide the following information:

Unit number.
Original cost of the car.
Number of days the car has been on the lot.
Published selling price.
Minimum selling price.
Profit on each car if it were sold for the minimum selling price.

For each car on the lot, an input record is prepared daily and contains the following:

Unit number	3 digits
Original cost	5 digits (dollars only)
Number of days the car has been on the lot	3 digits

This input is not in any sequence, and a unit number of 999 signals end of data.

Required:

Write a program to produce the report. Headings are required. Variable names are to be identified through the use of REM statements.

(SMAC Adapted)

P5-11   **(Computerized Worksheet and Statements)**

Using any standard computer spreadsheet program, prepare Required (*a*) and (*c*) of P5-6.

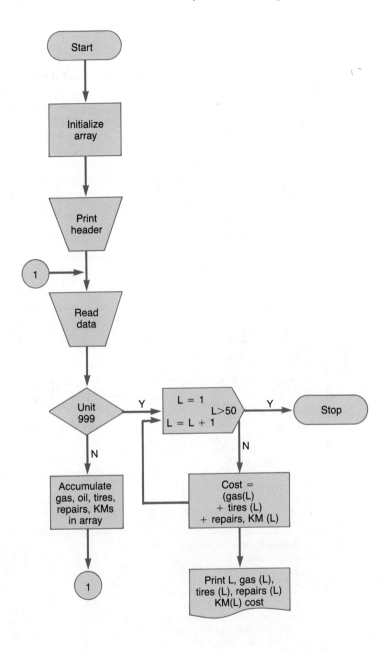

CASES

C5–1   (Analyze Some Simple Errors to Determine the Effects of Each on Income, Assets, and Liabilities)

Lax Company (not a corporation) was very careless about its financial records during its first year of operations, 19A. It is December 31, 19A, end of the annual accounting period. An outside PA examined the records and discovered numerous errors. All of those errors are described below. Assume each error is independent of the others. Analyze each error and indicate its effect on 19A and 19B income, assets, and liabilities *if not corrected*. Do not assume any other errors. Use these codes to indicate the effect of each dollar amount: O = overstated; U = understated, and N = no effect. Write an explanation of your analysis of each transaction to support your response. The first error is used as an example.

	Effect on							
	Net income		Assets		Liabilities		OE	
Independent errors	**19A**	**19B**	**19A**	**19B**	**19A**	**19B**	**19A**	**19B**
a. Depreciation expense for 19A, not recorded in 19A, $950.	O $950	N	O $950	O $950	N	N	O $950	O $950
b. Wages earned by employees during 19A, not recorded or paid in 19A, but will be paid in 19B, $200.								
c. Revenue earned during 19A, but not collected or recorded until 19B, $400.								
d. Amount paid in 19A and recorded as expense in 19A, but not an expense until 19B, $500.								
e. Revenue collected in 19A and recorded as revenue in 19A, but not earned until 19B, $600.								
f. Sale of services and cash collected in 19A. Recorded as a debit to Cash and as a credit to Accounts Receivable, $800.								
g. On December 31, 19A, bought land on credit for $9,000, not recorded until payment was made on February 1, 19B.								

Explanation of analysis of errors if not corrected:

a. Failure to record depreciation in 19A caused depreciation expense to be too low; therefore, income was overstated by $950. Also, accumulated depreciation is too low by $950, which causes assets to be overstated by $950 until the error is corrected.

C5–2   (Analytical—Prepare Adjusting and Closing Entries by Analyzing Unadjusted and Adjusted Trial Balances; Then Answer 10 Analytical Questions)

Delta Company was organized on January 1, 19A. At the end of the first year of operations, December 31, 19A, the bookkeeper prepared the following two trial balances (amounts in thousands of dollars):

Account no.	Account titles	Unadjusted trial balance Debit	Unadjusted trial balance Credit	Adjusted trial balance Debit	Adjusted trial balance Credit
11	Cash	$ 30	$	$ 30	$
12	Accounts receivable	25		25	
13	Prepaid insurance	3		2	
14	Rent receivable			1	
15	Operational assets	48		48	
16	Accumulated depreciation, operation assets				6
17	Other assets	4		4	
18	Accounts payable		11		11
19	Wages payable				2
20	Income tax payable				2
21	Rent revenue collected in advance				3
22	Note payable, 10% (dated January 1, 19A)		30		30
23	Capital stock, par $1 per share		50		50
24	Retained earnings				
25	Dividends declared and paid	2		2	
26	Revenues (total)		92		90
27	Expenses (total including interest)	71		80	
28	Income tax expense			2	
	Totals	$183	$183	$194	$194

Required:

a. Based upon inspection of the two trial balances, give the 19A adjusting entries developed by the bookkeeper (provide brief explanations).

b. Based upon the above data, give the 19A closing entries with brief explanations.

c. Answer the following questions (show computations):
   (1) How many shares of capital stock were outstanding at year-end?
   (2) What was the estimated useful life of the operational assets assuming no residual value?
   (3) What was the amount of interest expense that was included in the total expenses?
   (4) What was the balance of Retained Earnings on December 31, 19A?
   (5) What was the average income tax rate?
   (6) How would the two accounts (a) Rent Receivable and (b) Rent Revenue Collected in Advance be reported on the balance sheet?
   (7) Explain why cash increased by $30,000 during the year even though net income was very low comparatively.

(8) What was the amount of EPS for 19A?

(9) What was the average selling price of the shares?

(10) When was the insurance premium paid and over what period of time did the coverage extend?

C5–3 **(Analysis of Adjusting and Closing Entries—Related to an Actual Set of Financial Statements)**

Refer to the financial statements of Consolidated-Bathurst Inc. given in Appendix B immediately preceding the Index. Respond to the following questions for the 1987 annual accounting period. Use an Income Summary account.

1. What dates should the company use for the (*a*) adjusting entries, (*b*) closing entries, and (*c*) reversing entries?

2. Give the 1987 adjusting entry that the company made for depreciation (on continuing operations).

3. Give the closing entry for cash dividends paid.

4. Give the closing entry for net sales.

5. Give the closing entry for cost of goods sold and administrative and selling expenses.

6. Give the closing entry for net income.

7. List five accounts that would not appear on the post-closing trial balance.

8. List five accounts that would appear on the post-closing trial balance.

9. Give the entries, if any, to close (*a*) interest expense and (*b*) interest revenue (income).

10. Give the entry, if any, to close accumulated depreciation.

SIX

ACCOUNTING FOR SALES REVENUE AND COST OF GOODS SOLD

PURPOSE

The previous five chapters discussed the various phases of the information processing cycle and the conceptual framework of accounting. In this chapter, you will apply that knowledge by examining typical business transactions that involve the purchase and sale of merchandise. Net income reported on the income statement is a measure of the operating success of a business. As a result, proper recording of sales revenue and the related cost of goods sold is important to both managers and users of financial statements.

Summary data from combined income and retained earnings statements are presented on the facing page. Notice that cost of sales (also cost of goods sold) is usually a large percentage of sales revenue. Small changes in cost of sales can result in large changes in net income.

LEARNING OBJECTIVES

1. Apply the revenue principle and record sales revenue.
2. Account for credit sales and sales discounts.
3. Use the allowance method to record bad debts.
4. Apply the matching principle to record cost of goods sold.
5. Identify and explain two inventory systems.
6. Describe the cost of goods sold model.
7. Make closing entries with each of the inventory systems.
8. Expand your accounting vocabulary by learning about the "Important Terms Defined in This Chapter."
9. Apply the knowledge gained from this chapter.

ORGANIZATION

Part A—accounting for sales revenue
1. Recording sales revenue.
2. Measuring bad debt expense.
3. Sales returns and allowances.

Part B—accounting for cost of goods sold
1. Nature of cost of goods sold.
2. Inventory systems.
3. Taking a physical inventory.

Union Carbide Canada Limited

Consolidated Statement of Income and Retained Earnings

Year ended December 31 ($ thousands)	1986	1985
Sales	**$359,035**	$360,791
Cost of sales	264,493	271,563
Selling, general and administrative expenses	28,593	34,265
Depreciation	27,115	29,063
Interest	26,869	27,700
Interest capitalized during construction*	(1,153)	—
Investment and other income	(8,200)	(5,389)
	337,717	357,202
	21,318	3,589
Share of income of companies carried at equity*	6,839	7,670
Income from continuing operations before income taxes	28,157	11,259
Deferred income taxes (recovery)*	7,915	(4,764)
Income from continuing operations	20,242	16,023
Loss from discontinued operations (Note 2)	(3,896)	(15,863)
Income before extraordinary items	**16,346**	160
Extraordinary items (Note 4)	31,151	(89,801)
Net income (loss)	**47,497**	(89,641)
Retained earnings at beginning of year	144,988	242,821
	192,485	153,180
Dividends — preferred*	3,948	4,186
— common	4,010	4,006
	7,958	8,192
Retained earnings at end of year	**$184,527**	$144,988
Earnings per share (in dollars)		
Income from continuing operations	$ 0.81	$ 0.59
Income (loss) before extraordinary items	0.62	(0.20)
Net income (loss)	2.17	(4.67)

The notes on pages 13 to 18 are an integral part of this statement.

*Explained in chapters that follow.

PART A—ACCOUNTING FOR SALES REVENUE

Applying the Revenue Principle

Determination of the amount of sales revenue that should be recorded and the appropriate accounting period in which to record it sometimes presents complex problems. Sales may be for cash or on credit and may involve the trade-in of a noncash asset. Sales activities often begin in one accounting period and end in another. Problems associated with accounting for sales revenue are easier to resolve if you know the revenue principle (Exhibit 4–5). In conformity with the revenue principle, sales revenue is measured as the **market value** of the considerations (resources) received, or the market value of the item sold, whichever is more clearly determinable. Also, sales revenue should be recognized in the accounting period when ownership of the goods passes from the seller to the buyer. Problems in implementing this principle will be discussed in this part of the chapter.

Observe the income statement for Campus Corner in Exhibit 6–1. Cost of goods sold[1] (an expense) is set out separately from the remaining expenses,[2] which makes it possible to report a step difference called **gross margin on sales**.[3] The difference between net sales revenue and cost of goods sold reflects the total amount of **markup** on all goods sold during the period. It is expressed in dollars on the income statement ($40,000) and often is reported as the gross margin ratio (Gross margin on sales, $40,000 ÷ Net sales revenue, $100,000 = 0.40, or 40%). For Campus Corner, the average markup maintained on sales was 40% of sales.[4]

The column denoted percentage analysis in Exhibit 6–1 represents part of the financial statement analysis discussed more fully in Chapter 16. Besides the average markup on sales of 40%, operating expenses are shown to be 25% of net sales. This implies that 25 cents of every dollar of net sales was for selling and administrative expenses. By detailing these expenses, further analysis of the use of sales dollars would be possible. Income taxes represent 3% of net sales while net income was 12% of net sales. It should be noted that these percentages are the result of analysis of the income statement results rather than the typical disclosure of an income statement. As will be noted in Chapter 16, comparisons of these component percentages over time and to the expectations of managers can provide useful information to financial statement users.

---

[1] Similar titles sometimes used are "cost of sales" and "cost of products sold." Regardless of title, it is an **expense.**

[2] In this chapter, to simplify the illustrations, we ordinarily shall not show the detailed operating expenses. In the single step format for the income statement, revenues would be reported as above under a major caption "Revenues." However, all expenses, including cost of goods sold, would be reported under a major caption "Expenses." Therefore, in the single-step format, gross margin on sales is not reported.

[3] This often is called gross profit on sales or simply gross margin or gross profit.

[4] This percent is based on sales revenue rather than cost. The markup percent on **cost** would be $40,000 ÷ $60,000 = 66⅔%.

Exhibit 6–1 Income statement

CAMPUS CORNER
Income Statement (multiple-step format)
For the Year Ended December 31, 19F

		Amount	Percentage analysis
Gross sales		$108,333	
Less: Sales returns and allowances		8,333	
Net sales revenue		100,000	100
Cost of goods sold		60,000	60
Gross margin on sales		40,000	40
Operating expenses:			
Selling expenses (detailed)	$15,000		
Administrative expenses (detailed)	10,000	25,000	25
Pretax income		15,000	15
Income tax expense		3,000	3
Net income		$ 12,000	12
EPS ($12,000 ÷ 10,000 shares)		$1.20	

Recognizing Sales Revenue

In most cases, the seller records sales revenue when ownership of goods passes from the seller to the buyer. Under the revenue principle, the sales price (net of any discounts) is the measure of the amount of revenue that should be recorded. If the sale is for cash, the amount of revenue to be recorded simply is the amount of cash that was received. If the sale is on credit, the revenue is the **cash equivalent** of the assets to be received excluding any financing charges (i.e., interest). If the sale involves the trade-in of a noncash asset (such as the trade-in of an old car for a new car), the amount of revenue to record is the cash equivalent of the goods received, that is, the cash received plus the value of the trade-in, or what was given up, the market price of the new car, whichever is the more clearly determinable. Thus, under the revenue principle, Campus Corner would recognize a sale in 19F (i.e., when ownership passed) as follows:

a. Cash sales for the day per the cash register tapes:

```
Jan. 2  Cash ........................................ 2,000
             Sales revenue ............................       2,000
```

b. Credit sales for the day per all charge tickets:

```
Jan. 2  Accounts receivable ......................... 1,000
             Sales revenue ............................       1,000
```

Alternatively, a **separate sales revenue** account could be kept in the ledger for the sales of each department. The two journal entries above would be as follows:

Jan. 2 Cash 2,000
      Accounts receivable 1,000
          Sales, Department 1   1,000
          Sales, Department 2   1,500
          Sales, Department 3   500

Complexities of the Revenue Principle[5]

Two conditions underlie the determination of when revenue is recognized. The first is determining when the revenue is actually earned by the performance of the enterprise. The buyer may purchase the goods and take them away and in effect own the items. In this case ownership may clearly pass from the seller to the buyer. Performance is achieved so the next requirement is considered. Can a reliable estimate be made of the value of the consideration received? If cash is received, the answer is yes. If a cheque is received, the answer is maybe. If a promise to pay is received, the ultimate collectibility has to be estimated. If a reliable estimate of collectibility is available through the measurement of bad debt expense, then revenue recognition is possible because reliable measurement exists. Besides bad debts, customers may be able to return what they purchased. Sales returns and allowances can affect the measurement of the consideration received from the sale. A reliable estimate of returns outstanding when the sale is made is necessary where the amounts are material. Both bad debts and sales returns and allowances are discussed in later sections of this chapter.

Specific Exception Situations

Three specific revenue recognition situations are as follows:

1. **Long-term credit sales coupled with a relatively small down payment**—Such sales often pose the question of **risk** that full collection will not be made ultimately (i.e., a default and repossession may occur). For example, in the case of land development companies, one common practice has been to sell undeveloped land for a down payment of approximately 5% coupled with a 10- to 30-year debt payment period. Because of the number of defaults that this industry experienced, businesses should follow a practice resembling the current accounting guideline in the United States that sales revenue should not be recorded as **earned** until the period in which the total cash collected is at least 10% of the sale price.

2. **Installment sales**—Often there is a high risk of default when a company sells high-cost items of merchandise with a relatively low cash down payment and liberal credit terms (such as the sale of an

---

[5] *CICA Handbook,* Section 3400, presents many of the complexities surrounding revenue recognition. This chapter and later ones on investments will present the more common revenue recognition issues.

expensive TV set). Such situations may require application of **install-ment-sales accounting.** This method of recognition of revenue is applied when the characteristics of the sale transaction are: (1) a relatively small down payment is required; (2) the payment period is long and calls for monthly payments of principal plus interest; (3) the seller retains conditional ownership of the goods until full payment is made; and (4) bad debt losses cannot be estimated reliably. When all of these characteristics exist in combination, there is a relatively high risk that the merchandise will be repossessed because of nonpayment (default). The installment method of accounting is used in this situation. Under this method, the revenue is considered to be earned as the **cash is collected.** As a consequence, this method is close to cash basis accounting.

3. **Long-term construction contracts**—Revenue and expense recognition problems arise for the **construction contractor** when a construction contract extends across two or more accounting periods. For example, assume a building contractor signs a contract to build a large plant at a cost of $3,500,000 and the construction period is three years, starting January 1, 19A. The contractor estimates a construction cost of $3,200,000; that is, an estimated profit of $300,000. The question is: should the profit be reported as (1) earned in 19C when the project is completed or (2) allocated on an estimated basis to each of the three years? One accounting method used is called the **completed contract method.** Under this method, all of the profit is recognized as earned in the year of **completion.** This method is conservative because recognition of profit is deferred until completion when the actual profit is known. Another accounting method used for long-term construction contracts is called the **percentage-of-completion method.** It permits **allocation** of profit to each of the three construction periods based on estimates (usually based on the ratio of actual costs incurred during the period to total costs of the project) covering the three-year period. Specifically, one common form of the calculation involves the following:

$$\begin{array}{c} \text{Total} \\ \text{accrued} \\ \text{profit} \end{array} = \frac{\text{Costs incurred to date}}{\begin{array}{c}\text{Costs incurred to date} +\\ \text{Estimated costs to complete}\end{array}} \times \begin{array}{c}\text{Expected profit}\\ \text{on contract}\end{array} \tag{1}$$

$$\begin{array}{c}\text{Profit}\\ \text{recognized}\\ \text{in current year}\end{array} = \begin{array}{c}\text{Total accrued}\\ \text{profit from (1)}\end{array} - \begin{array}{c}\text{Profit accrued}\\ \text{in prior years}\end{array} \tag{2}$$

A portion of the estimated $300,000 would be recognized as profit each year during the construction period.

At the present time, a contractor is permitted to select the completed contract method of accounting for long-term construction contracts only if reliable estimates cannot be made of the progress toward completion.

Measuring Bad Debt Expense

Despite careful credit investigations, a few credit customers will not pay their bills. If an account receivable is uncollectible, the business has incurred a **bad debt expense.** Businesses that extend credit know that there will be a certain amount of bad debt losses on credit sales. An extremely low rate of bad debt losses may indicate too tight a credit policy. If the credit policy is too restrictive, many good credit customers may be turned away causing a loss of sales volume. Bad debt losses can be thought of as a necessary expense associated with generating credit sales.

In conformity with the matching principle, bad debt expense must be matched with the sale revenues that caused those losses. This requirement is difficult to implement because it may be one or more years after the sale was made before the business will know that the customer will be unable to pay.

To satisfy the matching principle, the **bad debt allowance method** is used to measure bad debt expense. The allowance method recognizes that bad debt expenses must be recorded in the year in which the sales that caused those losses were made rather than in the year that the customer is unable to pay. There is no way of knowing in advance which individual customers will not pay. Therefore, the allowance method is based upon **estimates** of the probable amount of bad debt losses from uncollectible accounts. The estimate is made in each accounting period based on the total credit sales for the period.

Estimating the probable amount of expense due to uncollectible accounts is not difficult in some situations. A company that has been operating for some years has sufficient experience to project probable future bad debt losses. New companies often rely on the experience of similar companies that have been operating for a number of years, if such information is available. Assume an analysis of accounting data on total credit sales and total uncollectible accounts for the past five years by Campus Corner indicated an average bad debt loss of 0.9% of total credit sales as follows:

Year	Bad debt losses	Credit sales
19A	$ 440	$ 54,000
19B	480	57,000
19C	620	53,000
19D	500	66,000
19E	660	70,000
	$2,700	$300,000

Aggregate: $2,700 ÷ $300,000 = 0.9% average loss rate for the five-year period 19A-E

Usually a company will adjust the average loss rate of the past to reflect future expectations. Campus Corner expects a small increase in uncollectible accounts from 19F sales; therefore, it increased the expected loss rate to 1.0%.

Assuming net credit sales in 19F of $40,000, we would record bad debt expense of $40,000 × 1% = $400 in 19F. This estimate would require the following **adjusting entry** at the end of the accounting period, December 31, 19F:

Bad debt expense	400	
Allowance for doubtful accounts (or bad debts)		400

To adjust for the estimated bad debt loss based on credit sales with an average expected loss rate of 1% ($40,000 × 1% = $400).

Bad debt expense of $400 would be reported on the 19F income statement. It would be matched with the related sales revenue for 19F, the year in which the credit was granted. The Bad Debt Expense account is closed at the end of each accounting period along with the other expense accounts. The credit in the above journal entry was made to a **contra account** titled "Allowance for Doubtful Accounts."[6] By reading the detail underlying the Accounts Receivable general ledger account as described in Supplement 6B at the end of this chapter, it should become obvious why this contra account is necessary. Accounts Receivable cannot be credited because there is no way of knowing which account receivable is involved. The balance in Allowance for Doubtful Accounts **always** is a subtraction from the balance of Accounts Receivable. The two accounts would be reported in the current asset section of the balance sheet as follows:

CAMPUS CORNER
Balance Sheet (partial)
At December 31, 19F

Current assets:		
Cash		$34,000
Accounts receivable	$100,000	
Less: Allowance for doubtful accounts	400	99,600

Allowance for Doubtful Accounts has a cumulative credit balance. It is not closed at the end of the accounting period because it is a balance sheet account. The balance of the allowance account is the total amount of the accounts receivable that is estimated to be uncollectible. The difference between the balances of Accounts Receivable and the allowance account measures the **estimated net realizable** value of accounts receivable. In the above example, the difference between the two accounts—$99,600—represents the **estimated net realizable value** of accounts receivable (also called the book value of accounts receivable).

The bad debt estimate should be based only on credit sales. Sometimes, a company bases the estimate on total sales (i.e., cash plus credit sales). This practice is illogical because (1) it is impossible to have a bad debt loss on a cash sale (except in the case of a "hot" cheque that is uncollectible), and (2) a shift in the relative proportion between cash and credit sales would affect the accuracy of the estimate. The total amount of credit sales for each period can be determined (because these transactions are recorded in Accounts Receivable as debits); therefore, there is no reason for not using credit sales as the base for the estimate. Another method of estimating bad debt expense (called aging accounts receivable) is explained in Supplement 6C.

---

[6] Other acceptable titles for this account are "Allowance for Bad Debts" and "Allowance for Uncollectible Accounts."

Writing Off a Bad Debt

When a specific customer's account receivable is determined to be uncollectible, the amount should be removed from the Accounts Receivable account with an offsetting debit to the allowance account. This entry does not record a bad debt expense because the estimated expense was recorded previously with an adjusting entry in the period of sale, and the related allowance account was established. Assume Campus Corner sold J. Doe merchandise on credit in 19D amounting to $100 (which was properly credited to the 19D Sales Revenue and debited to Accounts Receivable). At the end of 19F, Campus Corner decided that it would never collect the $100. The journal entry to record the write-off would be:

December 31, 19F:

Allowance for doubtful accounts	100	
Accounts receivable (J. Doe)		100
To write off a receivable from J. Doe determined to be uncollectible.		

Notice that the above journal entry did not affect any income statement accounts. The expense already had been recorded (when the adjusting entry was made at the end of 19D). Also, the entry did not change the **net realizable value** (i.e., the book value) of Accounts Receivable. The difference between Accounts Receivable and the allowance account is the same as before the entry:

	Before write-off	After write-off
Accounts receivable	$100,000	$99,900
Less: Allowance for doubtful accounts	400	300
Difference—estimated net realizable value	$ 99,600	$99,600

Actual Write-Offs Compared with Estimates

The amount of uncollectible accounts actually written off seldom will equal the estimated amounts previously recorded. If the accounts actually written off are less than the estimated amount, the Allowance for Doubtful Accounts will continue with a credit balance.[7] If an account is written off as bad and the customer subsequently pays it, the write-off entry should be reversed and the collection should be recorded in the usual way.

Terminology

The caption "Accounts Receivable" often appears on the balance sheet under current assets without additional descriptive terms; however, a more descriptive phrase such as "Receivables from trade customers" is preferable for some users.

---

[7] On the other hand, if the amount written off is more than the allowance balance, there will be a temporary debit balance in the allowance account. This situation will be resolved when the next adjusting entry is made. It indicates that the estimated loss rate used may be too low.

Receivables from other than the regular trade customers, such as loans to officers or employees, should not be included in the accounts receivable category. Instead, such nontrade receivables should be reported as separate items.

Sales Returns and Allowances

Many businesses let customers return unsatisfactory or damaged merchandise and receive a refund. In some cases, rather than taking back such merchandise, an adjustment may be given to the customer. To measure correctly sales revenue, returns and adjustments are recorded by reversing the original sales entry. Although the Sales account could be debited (i.e., reduced) to record these reductions in sales, a separate account "Sales Returns and Allowances" often is used. This account has an important purpose. It informs management of the volume of returns and allowances. If cash is refunded, the Cash account is credited. If a credit adjustment is given, accounts receivable of the customer must be credited. The Sales Returns and Allowances account is a contra revenue account; therefore, it is a deduction from gross sales revenue (as shown in Exhibit 6–1). Assume a customer, F. Fox, bought five new lamps from Campus Corner for $500. Fifteen days after payment, Fox returned one damaged lamp. The sequence of journal entries by Campus Corner would be:

Date of sale:

Accounts receivable (F. Fox)	500	
Sales revenue		500
To record sale.		

Date of sale return:

Sales returns and allowances	100	
Cash*		100
To record sale return, 1 unit.		

* If payment had not been made, this credit would be to Accounts Receivable.

If sales returns and allowances are a significant factor in the sales practices of a business, the above illustrations would introduce an error in the amount of revenue recognized in a given period. The practice illustrated for Campus Corner recognizes sales returns and allowances when the customer actually makes the claim which can be in another accounting period from the actual sale. To properly apply the revenue principle in a material situation, an estimate of returns and allowances is needed when the sale is made. Using past history in the same way it was done for bad debts, reliable estimates can often be made of what percentage of the sales will be returned. Assuming 8% of sales recorded for Campus Corner were expected to be returned, the entry would be as follows:

Sales returns and allowances	8,667	
Allowance for sales returns and allowances		8,667
To record the estimated returns and allowances at the point of sale		
8% × $108,333 = $8,667.		

When the customer actually makes the claim, perhaps in another accounting period, the entry for a $100 return of one unit would be:

Allowance for sales returns and allowances   100
    Cash   100
    To record the return of 1 unit for a full allowance of $100.

The actual location of the account, allowance for sales returns and allowances, depends on the nature of the sales practices used. If the original sale was a credit sale, then the Allowance account could be treated as a contra account to accounts receivable. If the sale was a cash sale, then the allowance account could be renamed as Estimated sales returns and allowances outstanding and disclosed as a current liability.

To avoid undue complications in further examples, the "nonallowance" method of recording sales returns and allowances will be followed.

Sales and Provincial Sales Taxes[8]

Most provinces in Canada collect a percentage of the sales price of defined items at the point when the sale is made. If the sales tax rate was, for example, 10% of the sales price of $90 for a lamp at Campus Corner, then the customer would pay $99 for the article. The Campus Corner acts as a collection agent for the province so the entry to record the illustrated sale would be:

Cash (or Accounts receivable)   99
    Sales revenue   90
    Sales taxes payable   9

Sales taxes payable would be a current liability. The total amount collected by the seller for a month would be remitted to the province shortly after the month end according to the rules of the province involved. Thus provincial sales taxes do not constitute a part of the revenue of the seller. Rather they represent a liability to the province imposing the tax because the seller is simply an agent for the province.

PART B—ACCOUNTING FOR COST OF GOODS SOLD

Nature of Cost of Goods Sold

Cost of goods sold is a major expense item for most nonservice businesses. Cost of goods sold (CGS) is directly related to sales revenue. Sales revenue for a product during an accounting period is the number of units sold multiplied by

---

[8] Further illustrations in this chapter will not continue to compute sales taxes so that only the essential ideas are clearly presented.

the sales price. Cost of goods sold is the same number of units multiplied by the unit cost. Revenue and expense are matched on the income statement in conformity with the **matching principle** (see Exhibit 4–5). Cost of goods sold includes the cost of all merchandise sold during the period. However, it excludes the cost of all merchandise remaining on hand at the end of the accounting period (i.e., the ending merchandise inventory).

A business will start each accounting period with a stock of merchandise on hand for resale called the **beginning inventory (BI)**. The merchandise on hand at the end of an accounting period is called the **ending inventory (EI)**. The ending inventory for one accounting period automatically becomes the beginning inventory for the next period.

During the accounting period, the beginning inventory is increased by the purchase or manufacture of more merchandise. The sum of the beginning inventory and the **purchases (P)** during the period represents the **goods available for sale** during that period. If all of the goods available for sale were sold during the period, there would be no ending inventory. Typically, not all of the goods available for sale are sold, and there is an ending inventory for the period. From these relationships, we can compute cost of goods sold as follows:

$$BI + P - EI = CGS$$

To illustrate, Campus Corner reported cost of goods sold of $60,000 (Exhibit 6–1), which was computed as follows:

Beginning inventory (January 1, 19F)	$40,000
Add purchases of merchandise during 19F	55,000
Goods available for sale	95,000
Deduct ending inventory (December 31, 19F)	35,000
Cost of goods sold	$60,000

Two Different Inventory Systems

To compute cost of goods sold, three amounts must be known: (1) beginning inventory, (2) purchases of merchandise during the period, and (3) ending inventory. The beginning inventory of one accounting period is the ending inventory of the previous period. The amount of purchases for the period is accumulated in the accounting system. The amount of the ending inventory can be determined by using one of two different inventory systems:

1. **Periodic inventory system**—Under this system, no up-to-date record of inventory is maintained during the year. An actual physical count of the goods remaining on hand is required at the **end of each period.** The number of units of each type of merchandise on hand is multiplied by the purchase cost per unit to compute the dollar amount of the ending inventory. Thus, the amount of goods on hand is not known

until the last day of the period when the inventory count is done. Also, the amount of cost of goods sold cannot be determined until the inventory count is done.

2. **Perpetual inventory system**—This system involves the maintenance of up-to-date inventory records in the accounting system during the period. For each type of merchandise stocked, a detailed record is maintained that shows (*a*) units and cost of the beginning inventory, (*b*) units and cost of each purchase, (*c*) units and cost of the goods for each sale, and (*d*) the units and cost of the goods on hand at any point in time. This up-to-date record is maintained on a transaction-by-transaction basis throughout the period. **Thus, the inventory record gives both the amount of ending inventory and the cost of goods sold amount at any point in time.**

Periodic Inventory System

The periodic inventory system requires an actual count of the goods on hand at the end of the period and valuation of the units at their purchase cost. The primary reasons for using the periodic inventory system are low cost and convenience. Consider the expense and difficulty associated with a grocery store attempting to keep track of the number of units sold and the cost of each purchase and sale for thousands of low-priced items that usually are stocked. In many stores, no record is made at the cash register of the cost and quantity of each item sold. Instead, the total sales price is entered into the cash register. The primary disadvantage of a periodic inventory system is the lack of inventory control (for purchasing purposes and detection of theft).[9]

A periodic inventory system applies the cost of goods sold computation as follows:

Model:	Beginning inventory	+	Purchases of the period	−	Ending inventory	=	Cost of goods sold
	↓		↓		↓		↓
Source:	Carried over from prior period		Accumulated in the Purchases account		Measured at end of period by physical inventory count		Computed as a residual amount

A periodic inventory system may be outlined sequentially as follows:

1. **Record all purchases**—During the period, the cost of all goods purchased is recorded in an account called Purchases (or Merchandise Purchases). A credit or cash purchase would be recorded as follows:

---

[9] Because of this important disadvantage, numerous stores now have computerized perpetual inventory systems tied in directly to the cash registers.

January 14, 19F:

Purchases 9,000
    Accounts payable (or Cash) 9,000

2. **Record all sales**—During the period, the sales price received for all goods sold is recorded in a Sales Revenue account. A credit or cash sale would be recorded as follows:

January 30, 19F:

Accounts receivable (or Cash) 8,000
    Sales revenue 8,000

3. **Count the number of units on hand**—At the end of each accounting period, the inventory account balance still shows the ending inventory amount carried over from the prior period because **no journal entries** are made to the inventory account during the period. To measure the ending inventory for the current period, a physical inventory count must be made. A physical count is needed because under the periodic inventory system, a transaction-by-transaction record is not maintained. Taking a physical inventory count is discussed later.

4. **Compute the dollar valuation of the ending inventory**—The dollar amount of the ending inventory quantities is computed by multiplying the number of units on hand by their unit purchase cost. The dollar amounts of all of the types of goods stocked are summed to determine the total ending inventory valuation for the company.

5. **Compute cost of goods sold**—After the ending inventory valuation is determined, cost of goods sold for the period is computed. The calculation of cost of goods sold for Campus Corner is shown below.

CAMPUS CORNER
Schedule of Cost of Goods Sold
For the Year Ended December 31, 19F

Beginning inventory (carried over from the last period in the
  inventory account) $40,000
Add purchases for the period (accumulated balance in the
  Purchases account) 55,000
    Goods available for sale 95,000
Less ending inventory (determined by physical count, per above) 35,000
    Cost of goods sold (as shown in Exhibit 6–1) $60,000

Perpetual Inventory System

A perpetual inventory system typically involves a large amount of clerical effort. However, the maintenance of a separate inventory record for each type of goods stocked on a transaction-by-transaction basis usually is desirable, particularly for control purposes. To minimize clerical difficulties, most perpetual inventory systems are computerized. Whether the accounting system is manual, mechanical, or computerized, the data that are recorded and reported are the same.

Exhibit 6–2   Perpetual inventory record

	PERPETUAL INVENTORY RECORD									
Item Super X				**Code** No. 33				**Minimum stock** 10		
Location Storage No. 4				**Valuation basis Cost**				**Maximum stock** 20		

		Goods Purchased			Goods Sold			Balance on Hand		
Date	Explanation	Units Rec'd	Unit Cost	Total Cost	Units Sold	Unit Cost	Total Cost	Units	Unit Cost	Total Cost
Jan. 1	Beginning inventory							8	5,000	40,000
July 14	Purchase	11	5,000	55,000				19	5,000	95,000
Nov. 30	Sale				13	5,000	65,000	6	5,000	30,000
Dec. 31	Return sale				(1)	5,000	(5,000)	7	5,000	35,000
Recap: Total purchases		11		55,000						
Total cost of goods sold					12		60,000			
Ending inventory								7		35,000

Assume, for this illustration only, that Campus Corner stocks and sells only one item, called Super X. The following events apply to 19F.

Jan. 1   Beginning inventory—8 units, at unit cost of $5,000.
July 14   Purchased—11 additional units, at unit cost of $5,000.
Nov. 30   Sold—13 units, at unit sales price of $8,333.
Dec. 31   Return sale—1 unit (returned to stock and refunded sales price).

The perpetual inventory record for the Super X item is shown in Exhibit 6–2.[10]

When the perpetual inventory system is computerized, the computer does exactly what was done manually in Exhibit 6–2; however, a computerized system does it with tremendous speed and accuracy. Computers overcome many of the difficulties associated with the perpetual system. Computers permit large, medium, and small companies to use the perpetual system.

A perpetual inventory system may be outlined sequentially as follows:

---

[10] Measuring inventories and cost of goods sold when there are different unit purchase costs is deferred to Chapter 7.

1. **Record all purchases**—During the period, the cost of all goods purchased is recorded in the **inventory** ledger account and is entered in a detailed perpetual inventory record (Exhibit 6–2). A cash or credit purchase of goods for resale would be recorded as follows:

July 14, 19F:

Inventory* (Super X, code 33)   55,000
    Accounts payable (or Cash)   55,000
* Also entered in the perpetual inventory record as shown in Exhibit 6–2.

2. **Record all sales**—During the period, each sale is recorded using **two companion journal entries.** One entry is to record the sales revenue, and the other entry is to record the cost of goods sold. A credit or cash sale would be recorded as follows (refer to data presented in Exhibit 6–2):

   a. To record the sales revenue at the sales price of $8,333 per unit:

   Accounts receivable (or Cash)   108,329
       Sales revenue (13 units @ $8,333)   108,329

   b. To record the cost of goods sold (at cost per the perpetual inventory record—Exhibit 6–2):

   Cost of goods sold*   65,000
       Inventory (13 units @ $5,000)   65,000
   * Also entered in the perpetual inventory record as shown in Exhibit 6–2.

3. **Record all returns**—During the period, the costs of both **purchase returns and sales returns** are recorded in the Inventory account and on the perpetual inventory record. The return by a customer of one unit of Super X on December 31 requires companion journal entries to reverse the two entries made on the date of sale (but only for the number of units returned). The return is recorded as follows:

   a. To record the sales return at sale price (one unit):

   Sales returns and allowances (1 unit @ $8,333)   8,333
       Accounts receivable (or Cash)   8,333

   b. To record the return of the unit to inventory at cost:

   Inventory (1 unit @ $5,000) 5,000*
       Cost of goods sold   5,000
   * This amount was provided by the perpetual inventory record; also it is restored to the perpetual inventory record as shown in Exhibit 6–2.

4. **Use cost of goods sold and inventory amounts**—At the end of the accounting period, the balance in the Cost of Goods Sold account is the amount of that expense reported on the income statement. It is not necessary to compute cost of goods sold because under the perpetual inventory system the Cost of Goods Sold account is up-to-date. Also, the inventory account shows the ending inventory amount reported on

the balance sheet. The sum of all the inventory balances in the various perpetual inventory records should equal the balance in the Inventory account in the ledger at any point in time.

When a perpetual inventory system is used, it is not necessary to take a physical inventory count in order to measure the inventory and cost of goods sold. However, because clerical errors, theft, and spoilage may occur, a physical inventory should be taken from time to time to check upon the accuracy of the perpetual inventory records. If an error is found, the perpetual inventory records and the Inventory account must be changed to agree with the physical count.

To summarize: There are two basic accounting differences between periodic and perpetual systems:

1. Inventory account:
   a. Periodic system—During the period, the balance in the Inventory account is not changed; thus, it reflects the beginning inventory amount. During the period, each purchase is recorded in the Purchases account. Therefore, the ending inventory for each accounting period must be measured by physical count, then valued (or "costed") at unit purchase cost.
   b. Perpetual system—During the period, the Inventory account is increased for each purchase and decreased (at cost) for each sale. At any point during the period, it measures the correct amount of inventory.

2. Cost of Goods Sold account:
   a. Periodic system—During the period, no entry is made for cost of goods sold. At the end of the period, after the physical inventory count, cost of goods sold is calculated as follows:

$$\text{Beginning inventory} + \text{Purchases} - \text{Ending inventory} = \text{Cost of goods sold}$$

   b. Perpetual system—During the period, cost of goods sold is recorded at the time of each sale and the Inventory account is reduced (at cost). This system directly measures the amount of cost of goods sold for the period.

The perpetual inventory system provides the following advantages over the periodic inventory system:

1. It gives up-to-date inventory amounts (units and dollar cost for each item).
2. It gives the cost of goods sold amount without having to take a periodic inventory count.

3. It gives continuing information needed to keep minimum and maximum inventory levels by appropriate timing of purchases.
4. It gives continuing information about the quantity of goods on hand at various locations.
5. It gives a basis for measuring the amount of theft.
6. It gives cost-of-goods-sold information needed to record sales at both selling price and cost.
7. It is adaptable for use by computers that quickly process large quantities of inventory data.

For these reasons there has been an increase in the use of the perpetual inventory system and a decrease in use of the periodic inventory system.

Additional Issues in Measuring Purchases

Goods purchased for resale are recorded as a purchase at the date that **ownership** passes from the seller to the buyer. Ownership usually passes when the goods are received and not when the purchase order is placed. Goods purchased should be recorded at their **cash equivalent cost** in conformity with the cost principle. Cost includes the cash equivalent price paid to the vendor (seller) plus other amounts paid for transportation and handling in order to get the goods into location and condition for intended use. Cost does not include interest paid on cash borrowed to make the purchase. Many of the problems associated with accounting for purchases are the same as those discussed in Part A of this chapter from the perspective of the seller.

Purchase Returns and Allowances

Goods purchased may be returned to the vendor if they do not meet specifications, arrive in unsatisfactory condition, or otherwise are unsatisfactory. When the goods are returned or when the vendor makes an allowance because of the circumstances, the effect on the cost of purchases must be measured. The purchaser will receive a cash refund or a reduction in the liability to the vendor for the purchase. Assume Campus Corner returned unsatisfactory goods that cost $1,000 to Company B. The return would be recorded by Campus Corner (which uses the periodic system) as follows:

Accounts payable (or Cash) 1,000
    Purchase returns and allowances* 1,000

* Inventory is credited when the perpetual inventory system is used.

Purchase returns and allowances are accounted for as a deduction from the cost of purchases.

The procedures for handling purchasing returns and allowances parallel the "nonallowance" approach to handling sales returns and allowances discussed earlier in this chapter. When items are returned, an entry is made to record the purchase return or allowance. If the amounts are material, it is possible damaged or overstocked items could exist in the inventory at the end of the period that are expected to be returned. Should an estimate be made of such items? The purchaser has the inventory and the debt until the goods are sent back. Once they are sent back, the transaction entry for the purchase allowance will be made. Unless there is some unusual delay, the timing of the return should closely follow the purchase which means the correct matching of returns and purchases occurs following the nonallowance approach. If, however, a significant claim is outstanding and can be accurately estimated at the end of the period, an entry could be made in anticipation of the return or allowance. Care would be necessary to assure that the item to be returned was excluded from the inventory records. If the claim estimate cannot be accurately determined at the end of the period, then the item would have to be held in inventory and no allowance entry would be possible. Application of the lower of cost or market practices discussed in Chapter 7 would be appropriate.

Transportation-In

The **purchase cost** of goods acquired for resale should include all freight and other transportation-in costs incurred by the purchaser. When a perpetual inventory system is used, transportation costs paid on goods purchased should be apportioned to each inventory item and included in the inventory cost amount entered in the perpetual inventory. When a periodic inventory system is used, such costs should be recorded as a debit (i.e., increase) to the Purchases account. It is difficult to apportion a freight bill to the several items it may cover. It is more practical to enter the amount of the bill in a separate account "Transportation-In," or "Freight-In." Also, for control purposes it is often useful to classify separately this significant cost. The journal entry to record a payment for transportation charges upon delivery of merchandise acquired for resale is:

Jan. 17	Transportation-in	3,000
	Cash	3,000

At the end of the accounting period, the balance in the Transportation-In account is reported as an addition to the cost of purchases.

Assuming freight-in and purchase returns, cost of goods sold may be shown as follows on the income statement when periodic inventory procedures are used:

Cost of goods sold:		
Beginning inventory		$40,000
Purchases	$53,000	
Add: Transportation-in	3,000	
Deduct: Purchase returns and allowances	(1,000)	
Net purchases		55,000
Goods available for sale		95,000
Less: Ending inventory		35,000
Cost of goods sold		$60,000

Purchase Discounts

Cash discounts must be accounted for by both the seller and the buyer (accounting by the seller is discussed in supplement 6A of this chapter). When merchandise is bought on credit, terms such as 2/10, n/30 sometimes are specified. This means that if payment is made within 10 days from date of purchase, a 2% cash discount is granted. If payment is not made within the discount period, then the full invoice cost is due 30 days after purchase. Assume on January 17, Campus Corner bought goods that had a $1,000 invoice price with terms 2/10, n/30. The purchase should be recorded on the net basis by Campus Corner as follows:[11]

January 17—date of purchase:

Purchases*	980	
Accounts payable		980

* Inventory is debited when a perpetual inventory system is used.

January 26—date of payment, within the discount period:

Accounts payable	980	
Cash		980

If for any reason Campus Corner did not pay within the 10-day discount period, the following entry would be needed:

Feb. 1	Accounts payable	980	
	Purchase discounts lost (or Interest expense)	20	
	Cash		1,000

Purchase discounts lost should be reported on the income statement as a **financial expense** along with interest expense.

Taking a Physical Inventory

A physical inventory count must be taken from time to time. When a **periodic** inventory system is used, the inventory must be counted (and costed) at the **end of each period** because the financial statements cannot be prepared without this key amount. When the perpetual inventory system is used, the physical inventory count is taken at various times during a fiscal period to test the accuracy of the perpetual inventory records.

1. **Quantity count**—The **count** of merchandise is made after the close of business on the inventory date. Normally, it would be difficult to count

---

[11] Some persons prefer to record the transaction at the date of purchase at the gross amount, that is, at $1,000. In this instance, payment within the discount period would result in credit to an account called Purchase Discounts, $20. The purchase discount credit would then be reported as a revenue, or as a deduction from purchases. This credit is not revenue and if deducted in full from purchases on the income statement would tend to misstate both inventory and purchases. In contrast, the net basis has the distinct advantage in that recording the **purchase discount lost** calls direct attention to inefficiency—failure to take the discount.

the goods accurately during business hours when sales activities are taking place. A physical count is made of all items of merchandise on hand and entered on an appropriate form. An inventory form, such as the one shown in Exhibit 6–3, may be used. Special care must be used so that all of the merchandise owned by the business is included, wherever located. Also, all items for which the business does not have legal ownership should be excluded. Sometimes, a business will have possession of goods it does not own (see discussion of consignments in Chapter 7).

2. **Inventory costing**—After the physical count of goods on hand has been completed, each kind of merchandise must be assigned a **unit cost.** The quantity of each kind of merchandise is multiplied by the unit cost to derive the inventory amount (as shown in Exhibit 6–3). The sum of the inventory amounts for all merchandise on hand is the total ending inventory amount for the business. Exhibit 6–3 presents the computation of the ending inventory shown on the income statement for Campus Corner. To determine the value of inventory, the cost principle must be applied. A problem arises if there are different unit costs for inventory items that are the same. When this situation occurs, there are several ways to identify the unit cost for inventory purposes such as the first-in, first-out (FIFO), last-in, first-out (LIFO), or average cost approaches. These alternative approaches to costing inventories are discussed in Chapter 7.

Management must deal with complex problems associated with planning and control of inventories. An excessive amount of inventory may tie up resources (i.e., cash) that could be used more economically in other ways in the business. Insufficient inventory often results in lost sales. Decisions must be made concerning maximum and minimum levels of inventory that should be kept; when to reorder; how much to reorder; and the characteristics of the items to stock, such as size, colour, style, and specifications. From the viewpoint of the investor, creditor, and other interested parties, information concerning the investment in inventory is important in decision making. Therefore, explanatory footnotes related to inventories are included in the financial reports.

Data Processing—Closing Entries for Sales Revenue, Cost of Goods Sold, and Merchandise Inventory

Closing the Sales Revenue and Bad Debt Expense Accounts

Revenue and expense accounts are **temporary** accounts that must be closed at the end of the accounting period. Sales Revenue is closed by recording a debit in that account and a credit in the Income Summary. Sales Discount Revenue is closed in the same way. Bad Debt Expense is closed by recording a credit in that account and a debit to the Income Summary. Sales Returns and Allowance (a contra revenue account) is closed by recording a credit to that account and a

Exhibit 6–3 Physical inventory form

Campus Corner
PHYSICAL INVENTORY SHEET

Date of Inventory *12/31/90* Department *4 (and last)* Taken by *M. R.*

Location	Identification of Merchandise	Quantity on Hand	Date Purchased	Unit Cost	Unit Market Price*	Unit Cost (LCM)	Inventory Amount
1	Headsets #8-16	20	12/2/90	$ 20	$ 21	$ 20	$ 400
2	Television sets #17-961	7	11/5/90	300	300	300	2,100
2	Radios #23-72	4	10/26/90	52	50	50	200
	Total Department Inventory						6,000
	TOTAL INVENTORY VALUE—ALL DEPARTMENTS				12/31/90		$ 35,000

* Replacement cost that would have to be paid if the item were being purchased on the inventory date (see lower of cost or market discussion in Chapter 7).

debit to the Income Summary. The closing entries for cost of goods sold (an expense) and the merchandise inventory amounts depend upon the inventory system (periodic versus perpetual) used.

Closing Entries When a Periodic Inventory System Is Used

When a periodic inventory system is used, there is no Cost of Goods Sold account in the ledger. The merchandise inventory account requires two directly related closing entries: (1) an entry to close the **beginning inventory** amount to the Income Summary account and (2) an entry to transfer the **ending inventory** amount from the Income Summary account to the Inventory account. A third entry is needed to close the Purchases account. Campus Corner would make closing entries for the merchandise inventories as follows:

December 31, 19F.

a. To close (transfer) the **beginning** merchandise inventory amount into Income Summary:

```
Income summary  . . . . . . . . . . . . . . . . . . . . . .  40,000
    Merchandise inventory (beginning)  . . . . . . . . . . . . . . .      40,000
```

b. To transfer the **ending** merchandise inventory amount from the Income Summary account to the Merchandise Inventory account:

Merchandise inventory (ending) 35,000
     Income summary   35,000

The effects of these two journal entries are *(a)* to replace the beginning inventory amount in the Merchandise Inventory account with the ending inventory amount, *(b)* to enter the beginning inventory amount in the Income Summary account as an **expense** (a debit), and *(c)* to remove the ending inventory amount from the Income Summary account (a credit) as a cost transfer to the asset account Merchandise Inventory.

c. In addition, the Purchases account is closed to Income Summary as follows:

Income summary 55,000
     Purchases   55,000

The reason for the two closing entries for merchandise inventories under the **periodic inventory system** can be understood if you recall that the ending inventory of the one year automatically is the beginning inventory for the next year. Also, the Inventory account balance is not changed during the year because all purchases of merchandise are entered in the Purchases account rather than in the Inventory account. Therefore, at the end of the accounting period, the beginning inventory amount ($40,000 for Campus Corner) is still in the Inventory account. It must be transferred out as an expense and be replaced with the ending inventory amount ($35,000 for Campus Corner). Notice that when the ending inventory amount is transferred out of the Income Summary, the Income Summary is decreased by the amount of cost of goods sold (beginning inventory plus purchases minus ending inventory equals cost of goods sold). After completion of these closing entries, the Merchandise Inventory, Purchases, and Income Summary accounts for Campus Corner would appear as follows:

PERIODIC INVENTORY SYSTEM

Merchandise Inventory

12/31/19E (beginning)	40,000	*(a)* To close	40,000
(b) 12/31/19F (ending)	35,000		

Purchases

12/31/19F (balance)	55,000	*(c)* To close	55,000

Income Summary

Operating expenses (not shown)		Revenues (not shown)	
(a) 12/31/19E (beginning inventory)	40,000	*(b)* 12/31/19F (ending inventory)	35,000
(c) (purchases)	55,000		

(Note that these three amounts net to $60,000, the amount of cost of goods sold.)

These closing entries, along with all the other closing entries, are shown in the demonstration case (Rote Appliance Store) at the end of this chapter.[12] This demonstration case should be studied carefully because it ties together the discussion in this chapter.

Closing Entries When a Perpetual Inventory System Is Used

When a perpetual inventory system is used, the Merchandise Inventory account and Cost of Goods Sold account always show the correct up-to-date balance. Therefore, no adjusting or closing entries are needed for the Merchandise Inventory account; it shows the ending inventory amount that will be reported on the balance sheet. Because the Cost of Goods Sold account is an expense account, it will be closed. For example, Campus Corner would record the following closing entry under the perpetual inventory system:

Retained Earnings

Income summary 60,000
   Cost of goods sold   60,000

Inventory Shrinkage   *Expense account*

Inventory shrinkage occurs because of theft, breakage, spoilage, and incorrect measurements. The measurement of inventory shrinkage is important for internal control purposes and, if large, is a major concern for investors and creditors. The dollar amount of shrinkage is reported on **internal** financial statements, but seldom are such amounts significant enough to be reported **separately** on **external** financial statements. Accurate measurement of this loss is related directly to the inventory system used.

When a **periodic inventory** is used, measurement of inventory shrinkage often is difficult, and may be impossible. The inventory, as counted at the end of the period, does not give a basis for measurement of shrinkage. An implicit assumption underlying the calculation of cost of goods sold (i.e., Beginning inventory + Purchases − Ending inventory = Cost of goods sold) is that if an item is not in ending inventory, it must have been sold. Therefore, under the periodic inventory system, cost of goods sold includes inventory shrinkage.

In contrast, a perpetual inventory system gives data on shrinkage loss. The inventory record gives both cost of goods sold and the ending inventory. These data make it possible to measure shrinkage loss. Assume the perpetual inventory records showed cost of goods sold for the period, 12 units, $60,000, and ending inventory of 7 units, $35,000. An inventory count at the end of the period showed 6 units on hand. An inventory shrinkage would be reported as 1 unit,

---

[12] There are several mechanical variations in how the closing entries can be made; all of them give the same end results. For example, some persons prefer to record the two inventory entries as adjusting, rather than closing, entries. Also, some persons prefer to use a temporary Cost of Goods Sold account in the closing process under a periodic inventory system; in this approach the two inventory amounts and purchases are first transferred to the Cost of Goods Sold account, which is then closed to Income Summary.

and the loss amount would be $5,000 (assuming no insurance recovery). The journal entry to record the shrinkage, using a perpetual inventory system, is:

Inventory shrinkage* 5,000
    Inventory   5,000

* Closed to Income Summary.

DEMONSTRATION CASE

(Try to resolve the requirements before proceeding to the Suggested Solution that follows.)

Rote Appliance Store has been operating for a number of years. It is a relatively small but profitable retail outlet for major appliances, such as refrigerators and air conditioners. Approximately 40% of the sales are on short-term credit. This case has been simplified to demonstrate information processing when there are significant selling activities (the service activities have been deleted). The case shows the application of both perpetual and periodic inventory systems with the same data. The annual accounting period ends December 31, 19D. Two independent cases will be assumed:

Case A—Perpetual inventory system.

Case B—Periodic inventory system.

The trial balance at December 31, 19D, was:

	Unadjusted trial balance			
	Case A—Perpetual inventory system used		Case B—Periodic inventory system used	
Account titles	**Debit**	**Credit**	**Debit**	**Credit**
Cash	$ 34,100		$ 34,100	
Accounts receivable	5,000		5,000	
Allowance for doubtful accounts		$ 1,000		$ 1,000
* Merchandise inventory:				
January 1, 19D			20,000	
December 31, 19D	16,000			
Store equipment	30,000		30,000	
Accumulated depreciation, equipment		9,000		9,000
Accounts payable		8,000		8,000
Income tax payable				
Capital stock, par $10		40,000		40,000
Retained earnings, January 1, 19D		9,000		9,000
Sales revenue		102,000		102,000
Sales returns and allowances	2,000		2,000	
* Cost of goods sold	60,000			
* Purchases			57,000	
* Purchase returns and allowances				1,000
Expenses (not detailed)	21,900		21,900	
Depreciation expense				
Income tax expense				
Totals	$169,000	$169,000	$170,000	$170,000

* These account balances are different between the two cases because of the effects of the two inventory systems used.

Data developed by Rote as a basis for the adjusting entries at December 31, 19D, were:

a. Credit sales in 19D were $40,000; the average loss rate for bad debts is estimated to be 0.25% of credit sales.

b. The store equipment is depreciated on the basis of an estimated 10-year useful life with no residual value.

c. On December 31, 19D, the periodic inventory count of goods remaining on hand was $16,000.

d. The average income tax rate is 20%.

e. The beginning inventory, January 1, 19D, was as shown on the trial balance (Case B).

Required:

a. Based upon the above data, complete a worksheet at December 31, 19D, similar to that shown in Exhibit 5–9 if you have studied Supplement 5B in Chapter 5. You may omit the columns for Adjusted Trial Balance. **Prepare a separate worksheet for each separate case.** Otherwise, prepare and post adjusting entries to the T-accounts for Rote Appliance.

b. Present an income statement for each case. Use a single-step format for Case A and a multiple-step format for Case B.

c. Present, in parallel columns, the closing entries for each situation at December 31, 19D.

In preparing the worksheet when a **perpetual inventory** system is used, no new complications are presented. The inventory amount is extended across the worksheet as an asset because the balance in the Inventory account reflects the ending inventory when a perpetual inventory system is used. The expense—cost of goods sold—is extended to the Income Statement debit column along with the other expenses. (See Exhibit 6–4.)

In preparing the worksheet with a **periodic inventory system,** both the beginning and ending inventory amounts must be used. First, the beginning inventory amount must be extended horizontally as a debit to the Income Statement column (because it now is an expense). A special line, "Merchandise inventory, ending" is added to the bottom of the worksheet, and the ending inventory amount is entered on this line under Income Statement, credit. This amount also is listed on the same line under Balance Sheet, debit.[13]

---

[13] There are several mechanical ways of handling the inventories on the worksheet when a periodic inventory system is used. Some accountants view the inventory entries as closing rather than adjusting entries. The various approaches arrive at the same net results, and each has its particular mechanical advantages and disadvantages.

Suggested Solution
Requirement a:

Exhibit 6–4 Worksheets compared for perpetual and periodic inventory systems

	ROTE APPLIANCE STORE									
	Worksheet, December 31, 19D									
	Case A—Assuming Perpetual Inventory System Is Used									

Account Titles	Trial Balance		Adjusting Entries*		Income Statement		Retained Earnings		Balance Sheet	
	Debit	**Credit**	**Debit**	**Credit**	**Debit**	**Credit**	**Debit**	**Credit**	**Debit**	**Credit**
Cash	34,100								34,100	
Accounts receivable	5,000								5,000	
Allowance for doubtful accounts		1,000		(*a*) 100						1,100
Merchandise inventory, Dec. 31, 19D	16,000								16,000	
Store equipment	30,000								30,000	
Accumulated depreciation		9,000		(*b*) 3,000						12,000
Accounts payable		8,000								8,000
Income tax payable				(*c*) 3,000						3,000
Capital stock, (par $10)		40,000								40,000
Retained earnings, Jan. 1, 19D		9,000						9,000		
Sales revenue		102,000				102,000				
Sales returns and allowances	2,000				2,000					
Cost of goods sold	60,000				60,000					
Expenses (not detailed)	21,900		(*a*) 100		22,000					
Depreciation expense			(*b*) 3,000		3,000					
	169,000	169,000			87,000	102,000				
Income tax expense†			(*c*) 3,000		3,000					
Net income					12,000			12,000		
			6,100	6,100	102,000	102,000	–0–	21,000		
Retained earnings, Dec. 31, 19D							21,000			21,000
							21,000	21,000	85,100	85,100

* Note that a **simplifying mechanical change** is used—the "Adjusting Entries" total is not entered until **after** the income tax is computed and entered.
† ($102,000 − $87,000) × 20% = $3,000 income tax expense.

Optional Requirement a—T-Accounts:
The account balances shown in Exhibit 6–5 are those reflected in the December 31, 19D, trial balance. Adjusting entries are set in boldface and closing entries are boxed.

Exhibit 6–4 *(concluded)*

<table>
<tr><td colspan="11" align="center">ROTE APPLIANCE STORE
Worksheet, December 31, 19D
Case B—Assuming Periodic Inventory System Is Used</td></tr>
<tr>
<th rowspan="2">Account Titles</th>
<th colspan="2">Trial Balance</th>
<th colspan="2">Adjusting Entries*</th>
<th colspan="2">Income Statement</th>
<th colspan="2">Retained Earnings</th>
<th colspan="2">Balance Sheet</th>
</tr>
<tr>
<th>Debit</th><th>Credit</th>
<th>Debit</th><th>Credit</th>
<th>Debit</th><th>Credit</th>
<th>Debit</th><th>Credit</th>
<th>Debit</th><th>Credit</th>
</tr>
<tr><td>Cash</td><td>34,100</td><td></td><td></td><td></td><td></td><td></td><td></td><td></td><td>34,100</td><td></td></tr>
<tr><td>Accounts receivable</td><td>5,000</td><td></td><td></td><td></td><td></td><td></td><td></td><td></td><td>5,000</td><td></td></tr>
<tr><td>Allowance for doubtful accounts</td><td></td><td>1,000</td><td></td><td>(a) 100</td><td></td><td></td><td></td><td></td><td></td><td>1,100</td></tr>
<tr><td>Merchandise inventory, Jan. 1, 19D</td><td>20,000</td><td></td><td></td><td></td><td>20,000</td><td></td><td></td><td></td><td></td><td></td></tr>
<tr><td>Store equipment</td><td>30,000</td><td></td><td></td><td></td><td></td><td></td><td></td><td></td><td>30,000</td><td></td></tr>
<tr><td>Accumulated depreciation, equipment</td><td></td><td>9,000</td><td></td><td>(b) 3,000</td><td></td><td></td><td></td><td></td><td></td><td>12,000</td></tr>
<tr><td>Accounts payable</td><td></td><td>8,000</td><td></td><td></td><td></td><td></td><td></td><td></td><td></td><td>8,000</td></tr>
<tr><td>Income tax payable</td><td></td><td></td><td></td><td>(c) 3,000</td><td></td><td></td><td></td><td></td><td></td><td>3,000</td></tr>
<tr><td>Capital stock, (par $10)</td><td></td><td>40,000</td><td></td><td></td><td></td><td></td><td></td><td></td><td></td><td>40,000</td></tr>
<tr><td>Retained earnings, Jan. 1, 19D</td><td></td><td>9,000</td><td></td><td></td><td></td><td></td><td></td><td>9,000</td><td></td><td></td></tr>
<tr><td>Sales revenue</td><td></td><td>102,000</td><td></td><td></td><td></td><td>102,000</td><td></td><td></td><td></td><td></td></tr>
<tr><td>Sales returns and allowances</td><td>2,000</td><td></td><td></td><td></td><td>2,000</td><td></td><td></td><td></td><td></td><td></td></tr>
<tr><td>Purchases</td><td>57,000</td><td></td><td></td><td></td><td>57,000</td><td></td><td></td><td></td><td></td><td></td></tr>
<tr><td>Purchase returns and allowances</td><td></td><td>1,000</td><td></td><td></td><td></td><td>1,000</td><td></td><td></td><td></td><td></td></tr>
<tr><td>Expenses (not detailed)</td><td>21,900</td><td></td><td>(a) 100</td><td></td><td>22,000</td><td></td><td></td><td></td><td></td><td></td></tr>
<tr><td>Depreciation expense</td><td></td><td></td><td>(b) 3,000</td><td></td><td>3,000</td><td></td><td></td><td></td><td></td><td></td></tr>
<tr><td>Merchandise inventory, Dec. 31, 19D</td><td></td><td></td><td></td><td></td><td></td><td>16,000</td><td></td><td></td><td>16,000</td><td></td></tr>
<tr><td></td><td>170,000</td><td>170,000</td><td></td><td></td><td>104,000</td><td>119,000</td><td></td><td></td><td></td><td></td></tr>
<tr><td>Income tax expense†</td><td></td><td></td><td>(c) 3,000</td><td></td><td>3,000</td><td></td><td></td><td></td><td></td><td></td></tr>
<tr><td>Net income</td><td></td><td></td><td></td><td></td><td>12,000</td><td></td><td></td><td>12,000</td><td></td><td></td></tr>
<tr><td></td><td></td><td></td><td>6,100</td><td>6,100</td><td>119,000</td><td>119,000</td><td>–0–</td><td>21,000</td><td></td><td></td></tr>
<tr><td>Retained earnings, Dec. 31, 19D</td><td></td><td></td><td></td><td></td><td></td><td></td><td>21,000</td><td></td><td></td><td>21,000</td></tr>
<tr><td></td><td></td><td></td><td></td><td></td><td></td><td></td><td>21,000</td><td>21,000</td><td>85,100</td><td>85,100</td></tr>
</table>

* Note that a **simplifying mechanical change** is used—the "Adjusting Entries" total is not entered until after the income tax is computed and entered.

† ($119,000 − $104,000) × 20% = $3,000 income tax expense.

Exhibit 6–5   Perpetual inventory system—Rote Appliance Store

Cash				Accounts Payable		
Balance	34,100					Balance	8,000

Accounts Receivable				Income Tax Payable		
Balance	5,000					Balance	0
						(c)	3,000

Allowance for Doubtful Accounts				Capital Stock		
		Balance	1,000			Balance	40,000
		(a)	100				

Merchandise Inventory				Retained Earnings		
Balance	16,000					Balance	9,000
						(7)	12,000

Store Equipment				Income Summary		
Balance	30,000			(5)	60,000	Balance	0
				(6)	28,000	(1)	100,000
				(7)	12,000		

Accumulated Depreciation, Equipment				Expenses (Not Detailed)		
		Balance	9,000	Balance	21,900	(6)	22,000
		(b)	3,000	(a)	100		

Sales Revenue				Depreciation Expense		
(1)	102,000	Balance	102,000	**Balance**	0	(6)	3,000
				(b)	3,000		

Sales Returns and Allowances				Income Tax Expense		
Balance	2,000	(1)	2,000	Balance	0	(6)	3,000
				(c)	3,000		

Cost of Goods Sold		
Balance	60,000	(5)	60,000

only an perpetual inventory system

Optional Requirement b—T-Accounts:

The account balances given in Exhibit 6–6 are those reflected in the December 31, 19D, trial balance. Adjusting entries are set in boldface and closing entries are boxed.

Exhibit 6–6 Periodic inventory system—Rote Appliance Store

Cash				Accounts Payable		
Balance	34,100				Balance	8,000

Accounts Receivable				Income Tax Payable		
Balance	5,000				**Balance**	**0**
					(c)	**3,000**

Allowance for Doubtful Accounts				Capital Stock		
		Balance	1,000		Balance	40,000
		(a)	**100**			

Merchandise Inventory				Retained Earnings		
Balance	20,000	(3)	20,000		Balance	9,000
(4)	**16,000**				(7)	12,000

Store Equipment				Income Summary		
Balance	30,000				Balance	0
				(2)	56,000	(1)	100,000
				(3)	20,000	(4)	16,000
				(6)	28,000		
				(7)	12,000		

Accumulated Depreciation Equipment		
	Balance	9,000
	(b)	**3,000**

Exhibit 6–6   *(concluded)*

Sales Revenue				Expenses (Not Detailed)			
(1)	102,000	Balance	102,000	Balance	21,900		
				(*a*)	100	(6)	22,000

Sales Returns and Allowances				Depreciation Expense			
Balance	2,000	(1)	2,000	Balance	0		
				(*b*)	3,000	(6)	3,000

Purchases				Income Tax Expense			
Balance	57,000	(2)	57,000	Balance	0		
				(*c*)	3,000	(6)	3,000

Purchase Returns and Allowances			
(2)	1,000	Balance	1,000

Adjusting Entries
December 31, 19D

	Case A		Case B	
	Perpetual inventory		Periodic inventory	
a. Expenses (estimated bad debt loss)	100		100	
Allowance for doubtful accounts		100		100
Bad debt loss estimated, $40,000 × 0.25% = $100.				
b. Depreciation expense	3,000		3,000	
Accumulated depreciation equipment		3,000		3,000
Depreciation for one year, $30,000 ÷ 10 years = $3,000.				
c. Income tax expense	3,000		3,000	
Income tax payable		3,000		3,000
Income tax for year, $15,000 × 20% = $3,000.				

Requirement b:

ROTE APPLIANCE STORE
Income Statement
For the Year Ended December 31, 19D
Case A—Perpetual Inventory System and Single-Step Format

Revenues:
Gross sales revenue	$102,000	
Less: Sales returns and allowances	2,000	
Net sales revenue		$100,000
Expenses:		
Cost of goods sold	60,000	
Expenses (not detailed for case purposes)	22,000	
Depreciation expense	3,000	85,000
Pretax income		15,000
Income tax expense ($15,000 × 20%)		3,000
Net income		$ 12,000
EPS ($12,000 ÷ 4,000 shares)		$3.00

ROTE APPLIANCE STORE
Income Statement
For the Year Ended December 31, 19D
Case B—Periodic Inventory System and Multiple-Step Format

Gross sales revenue		$102,000
Less: Sales returns and allowances		2,000
Net sales revenue		100,000
Cost of goods sold:		
Inventory, January 1, 19D	$ 20,000	
Purchases	57,000	
Purchase returns and allowances	(1,000)	
Goods available for sale	76,000	
Less: Inventory, December 31, 19D	16,000	
Cost of goods sold		60,000
Gross margin on sales		40,000
Operating expenses:		
Expenses (not detailed for case purposes)	22,000	
Depreciation expense	3,000	25,000
Pretax income		15,000
Income tax expense ($15,000 × 20%)		3,000
Net income		$ 12,000
EPS ($12,000 ÷ 4,000 shares)		$3.00

Requirement c:

Closing Entries
December 31, 19D

	Case A		Case B	
	Perpetual inventory		**Periodic inventory**	
1. Sales revenue	102,000		102,000	
Sales returns and allowances		2,000		2,000
Income summary		100,000		100,000
To transfer the revenue amounts to Income Summary.				
2. Income summary	(Not applicable)		56,000	
Purchase returns and allowances			1,000	
Purchases				57,000
To transfer purchase amounts to Income Summary.				
3. Income summary	(Not applicable)		20,000	
Merchandise inventory (beginning)				20,000
To transfer beginning inventory to Income Summary.				
4. Merchandise inventory (ending)	(Not applicable)		16,000	
Income summary				16,000
To transfer ending inventory from Income Summary.				
5. Income summary	60,000		(Not applicable)	
Cost of goods sold		60,000		
6. Income summary	28,000		28,000	
Expenses (not detailed)		22,000		22,000
Depreciation expense		3,000		3,000
Income tax expense		3,000		3,000
To transfer expense amounts to Income Summary.				
7. Income summary	12,000		12,000	
Retained earnings		12,000		12,000
To transfer net income to Retained Earnings.				

SUMMARY OF CHAPTER

This chapter discussed the measuring, recording, and reporting of the effects on income of the selling and purchasing activities of various types of business.

In conformity with the matching principle, the total cost of the goods sold during the period must be matched with the sales revenue earned during that period. The Cost of Goods Sold account measures the **cost** of merchandise that was sold while the Sales Revenue account measures the **selling price** of the same merchandise. When cost of goods sold is deducted from sales revenue for the period, the difference is called gross margin on sales. From this amount, the remaining expense must be deducted to derive income.

This chapter also discussed the effect on cost of goods sold of the beginning and ending inventory amounts. We observed that the ending inventory of one period is the beginning inventory of the next period. Two inventory systems were discussed for measuring the merchandise remaining on hand at the end of the period (ending inventory) and cost of goods sold for the period: (1) the perpetual inventory system, which is based on the maintenance of detailed and continuous inventory records for each kind of merchandise stocked; and (2) the periodic inventory system, which is based upon a physical inventory count of ending inventory and the costing of those goods in order to determine the proper amounts for cost of goods sold and ending inventory.

CHAPTER SUPPLEMENT 6A

Credit Sales and Sales Discounts

A large portion of the sales made by many businesses is on credit. When merchandise is sold on credit, the terms of payment should be definite so there will be no misunderstanding as to the amounts and due dates. Credit terms usually are printed on each credit document. Often, credit terms are abbreviated using symbols such as "n/10, EOM," which means the net amount (i.e., the sales amount less any sales returns) is due not later than 10 days after the end of the month (EOM) in which the sale was made. In other cases, **sales discounts** (often called cash discounts) are granted to the purchaser to encourage early payment. For example, the credit terms may be "2/10, n/30," which means that if cash payment is made within 10 days from the date of sale, the customer may deduct 2% from the invoice price; however, if not paid within the 10-day discount period, the full sales price (less any returns) is due in 30 days from date of sale.

Usually customers will pay within the discount period because the savings are substantial. For example, with terms 2/10, n/30, 2% is saved by paying 20 days early, which is approximately 37% annual interest.[14] Credit customers

---

[14] To determine the annual interest cost, consider the following: 2% of $1,000 = $20, the discount lost. $20 cost for 20 days on ($1,000 − $20) is ($20/$980) × (365/20) = 37% annual interest rate.

conceivably may borrow cash from a bank in order to take advantage of cash discounts. Normally the bank's interest rate is less than the high interest rate that would result from not taking cash discounts. Because the cash discount on sales almost always will be taken, the amount of sales revenue that is recorded should be based on the amount of cash that probably will be received rather than for the gross sales amount. To do otherwise would be inconsistent with the **revenue principle** which holds that sales revenue should be measured as the cash or cash equivalent received for the goods sold. Assume a sale by Campus Corner of $1,000 with terms 2/10, n/30. The sequence of journal entries is:

a. January 18, date of sale on credit:

    Accounts receivable 980
        Sales revenue   980
      Terms: 2/10, n/30 ($1,000 × 0.98 = $980).

b. January 27, date of collection if payment is made **within** the discount period (the usual case):

    Cash 980
        Accounts receivable   980

c. January 31, date of collection if payment is made **after** the discount period (the unusual case):

    Cash 1,000
        Sales discount revenue*   20
        Accounts receivable   980

    * Interest revenue sometimes is used because conceptually it is in the nature of interest revenue earned.

The conceptually preferred method for recording sales revenues, illustrated above, is called the **net method**. As an alternative, some companies use the **gross method of recording sales revenue**. Under the gross method, sales revenue is recorded without deducting the amount of the cash discount. The following journal entries would be made for a $1,000 sale if the gross method were used instead of the net method:

a. January 18, date of sale on credit:

    Accounts receivable 1,000
        Sales revenue   1,000

b. January 27, date of collection if payment is made **within** the discount period (the usual case):

    Cash 980
    Sales discounts   20
        Accounts receivable   1,000
      Terms 2/10, n/30 ($1,000 × 0.98 = $980).

c. January 31, date of collection if payment is made **after** the discount period (the unusual case):

Cash 1,000
     Accounts receivable   1,000

The Sales Discounts account (used with the gross method) may be reported as (a) a contra revenue account, or (b) an addition to selling expense. The gross method overstates both accounts receivable and sales revenue. The net method is theoretically preferable, but most companies choose the method that they believe involves the least clerical effort. However, the bookkeeping differences between the two methods are not significant.

Cash discounts are not the same as **trade discounts.** A cash discount is a price concession given to encourage early payment of an account. A trade discount is sometimes used by vendors for quoting sales prices; the amount **after** the trade discount is the sales price. For example, an item may be quoted at $10 per unit subject to a 20% trade discount on orders of 100 units or more; thus, the price for the large order would be $8 per unit.

In recent years there has been a trend toward more credit sales, particularly at the retail level. However, the use of cash discounts appears to be declining. The fairness of the practice of awarding cash discounts is subject to question because the effect is to charge the cash customers more than the credit customers who pay within the discount period. Also, the discount not taken by credit customers is a hidden financing charge that may be governed by legislation dealing with credit practices.

Extending credit usually involves an increase in the amount of bookkeeping required because detailed records must be kept for each credit customer. Some businesses have their credit sales handled by a credit card company (such as MasterCard or Visa), which charges a fee for this service. The fee paid to the credit card company is recorded as a collection expense (and not a sales discount). Supplement 6B discusses some aspects of the detailed records kept for credit customers.

CHAPTER SUPPLEMENT 6B

Data Processing; Control Accounts and Subsidiary Ledgers

Control accounts and subsidiary ledgers facilitate keeping records in situations where a large number of similar transactions occur. Their use does not involve accounting theory, principles, or standards but involves only the mechanics of data processing. The use of control accounts and subsidiary ledgers will be explained for accounts receivable; however, the procedure also is applicable in any situation that involves numerous transactions that are similar and require detailed records, such as accounts payable and operational assets.

Some businesses carry thousands of individual customers on a credit status. If a separate Accounts Receivable account was kept in the general ledger for each

Exhibit 6–7   General ledger

GENERAL LEDGER

Date 19A	Cash #101	Folio	Debit	Credit	Balance
Jan. 12		3	1 000		

	Accounts Receivable Control #102				
Jan 5		1	2 400		2 400
7		2		140	2 260
12		3		1 000	1 260

	Sales #610				
Jan 5		1		2 400	2 400

	Sales Returns #620				
Jan 7		2	140		140

customer, there would be thousands of receivable accounts in the general ledger. Instead, in most large businesses, the Accounts Receivable account is an aggregation of all of the individual customer accounts. However, to maintain adequate control, and for billing purposes, a business also must keep detailed records about each customer's account.

Most large businesses keep a **single control account** in the general ledger for Accounts Receivable and a **separate subsidiary ledger** that carries an individual account for each credit customer. Thus, in Exhibit 6–7, the **general ledger** would include Accounts Receivable as a **single control account,** and the **subsidiary ledger** (Exhibit 6–8) may include several thousand **individual receivable accounts.** The **sum** of the individual account balances in the receivable subsidiary ledger always should equal the single balance in the Accounts Receivable control account in the general ledger. The individual customer accounts, as subdivisions

Exhibit 6–8   Subsidiary ledger

SUBSIDIARY LEDGER

Adams, J. K. 102.1

Jan.	5		1	740		740
	7	*Return*	2		140	600
	12		3		400	200

Baker, B. B. 102.2

Jan.	5		1	570		570

Ford, C. E. 102.3

Jan.	5		1	340		340
	12		3		340	-0-

Moore, W.E. 102.4

Jan.	5		1	320		320
	12		3		220	100

Price, V. T. 102.5

Jan.	5		1	430		430
	12		3		40	390

Ward, B. L. 102.6

Jan.	5		1	450		450

of the control account, are subsidiary to the control account; thus they are called subsidiary ledgers.

To illustrate the use of a control account with a subsidiary ledger for Accounts Receivable, we will assume several transactions for the Mayo Department Store. Mayo uses a manual system, but control accounts and subsidiary ledgers also are used extensively with computerized systems. Credit sales could be recorded in the general journal as follows:

GENERAL JOURNAL   Page 1

Date	Account Titles and Explanation	Folio	Debit	Credit
Jan. 5	Accounts receivable	102	2,400	
	Sales revenue	610		2,400
	To record the following credit sales:			
	Adams, J. K. . . . . $ 740	102.1		
	Baker, B. B. 120	102.2		
	Ford, C. E. 340	102.3		
	Moore, W. E. 320	102.4		
	Price, V. T. 430	102.5		
	Ward, B. L. 450	102.6		
	Total $2,400			

Posting of the above journal entry to the control account in the general ledger is indicated by entering the Accounts Receivable and Sales Revenue **account numbers** in the folio column in the usual manner. Posting to the individual customer accounts in the subsidiary ledger is indicated by entering an individual customer's account number in the folio column of the journal. Thus, the total amount was posted to the control account, Accounts Receivable (a debit total of $2,400), and the several single amounts were posted to the subsidiary ledger. Note that the debit-credit-balance form is used in the Mayo subsidiary ledger rather than the T-account form that often is used for instructional purposes.

On January 7, one customer, J. K. Adams, returned some unsatisfactory merchandise purchased on January 5. Mayo accepted the goods and gave Adams credit on his account. The journal entry was:

GENERAL JOURNAL   Page 2

Date	Account Titles and Explanation	Folio	Debit	Credit
Jan. 7	Sales returns	620	140	
	Accounts receivable	102		140
	To record the return of goods:			
	Adams, J. K. $140	102.1		

The folio column shows that the above entry has been posted in total to the control account in the general ledger. Also, the single amount has been posted to the individual customer account in the subsidiary ledger.

Cash collections from customers are recorded in the journal entry given below. The folio column shows that the entry has been posted in total to the control account and each single amount to the individual customer accounts in the subsidiary ledger.

GENERAL JOURNAL   Page 3

Jan. 12	Cash	101	1,000	
	Accounts receivable	102		1,000
	To record collections on accounts as follows:			
	Adams, J. K. . . . . $ 400	102.1		
	Ford, C. E. 340	102.3		
	Moore, W. E. 220	102.4		
	Price, V. T. 40	102.5		
	Total $1,000			

The subsidiary ledger should be reconciled frequently with the control account in order to determine whether errors were made in posting. This reconciliation is accomplished by summing the balances in the subsidiary ledger to determine whether that total agrees with the total shown by the control account in the general ledger. A reconciliation schedule for Mayo follows:

MAYO DEPARTMENT STORE
Schedule of Accounts Receivable
January 28, 19A

Account		Amount
No.	Customer	(per subsidiary)
102.1	Adams, J. K.	$ 200
102.2	Baker, B. B.	120
102.4	Moore, W. E.	100
102.5	Price, V. T.	390
102.6	Ward, B. L.	450
102	Total accounts receivable (per control account)	$1,260

The subsidiary ledger total should agree with the balance in the control account. If there is disagreement, one or more errors are indicated; however, agreement does not necessarily mean there are no errors. A transaction could be posted to the wrong customer's account, and the two ledgers would still reconcile in total.

The **Sales Revenue** account also could be established as a control account. This account would be supported by a subsidiary ledger that would contain separate accounts for the sales of **each department** or for **each product.** Another common application of control accounts relates to **accounts payable** when there are numerous purchases on credit.

Control accounts are also useful when accounting for **operational assets.** For example, the Office Equipment account usually is included in the general ledger as a control account. This control account is supported by a subsidiary ledger of office equipment that has an account for each different kind of office equipment, such as copiers, typewriters, calculators, and furniture. These examples show that the control account/subsidiary ledger procedure is an important element of the accounting information processing system of most enterprises.

One advantage of the use of subsidiary ledgers in a manual system is that it facilitates the subdivision of work. A person can be trained in a short time to maintain a subsidiary ledger because a knowledge of the broad field of accounting is not needed for such routine bookkeeping tasks.

In the journal entries given above, the individual amounts relating to each individual customer account were listed in the Explanation column of the journal and then were posted to the subsidiary ledger. There are two approaches to simplifying this phase of the bookkeeping. Amounts could be transferred directly from the charge tickets to the subsidiary ledger accounts and thus avoid the detailed listing in the journal entry. This approach is used sometimes by small companies. Another simplifying approach involves the use of a related procedure known as **special journals.** This procedure is explained in Supplement 8C.

Although our illustration used a manual approach to show subsidiary ledgers, most companies apply the procedure using computers. The computer can be programmed to process credit sales, returns, collections on account, reconciliation of account balances, and a printout of monthly bills to be mailed to the customers.

CHAPTER SUPPLEMENT 6C

Aging Accounts Receivable

Usually as an account receivable gets older there is an increase in the probability that the account will be uncollectible. Therefore, an analysis of the age of accounts receivable provides management with valuable information about probable losses due to uncollectible accounts. This information is used by some companies to provide amounts needed to make the **adjusting entry** at the end of each period for estimated bad debt expense.

An aging analysis of the individual accounts receivable balances is done to **estimate** the amount of bad debts instead of estimating bad debt expense on the basis of credit sales for the period, as illustrated in this chapter. The amount estimated to be uncollectible under the aging method is the balance that should be in the account "Allowance for Doubtful Accounts" at the end of the period. The **difference** between the **actual balance** in that account and the **estimated balance** is the amount recorded as bad debt expense in the adjusting entry at the end of the period.

For example, the general ledger for Macon Appliance Store reflected the following account balances:

Accounts receivable . . . . $ 40,000 (debit balance)
Allowance for doubtful accounts . . . .   900 (credit balance)
Sales on credit for 19B 200,000

The company uses the aging method for determining the amount of the adjusting entry for bad debt **expense** that must be made at December 31, 19B. The following aging analysis of accounts receivable was completed:

Aging Analysis of Accounts Receivable, December 31, 19B						
Customer	Total	Not Yet Due	1–30 Days Past Due	31–60 Days Past Due	61–90 Days Past Due	Over 90 Days Past Due
Adams, A. K.	$ 600	$ 600				
Baker, B. B.	1,300	300	$ 900	$ 100		
Cox, R. E.	1,400			400	$ 900	$ 100
Day, W. T.	3,000	2,000	600	400		
Zoe, A. B.	900					900
Total	$40,000	$17,200	$12,000	$8,000	$1,200	$1,600
Percent	100%	43%	30%	20%	3%	4%

The management, on the basis of experience and knowledge of specific situations, can use the above analysis as a basis for realistically estimating the probable **rates of uncollectibility for each age group.** Assume the management **estimated** the following probable bad debt loss rates: not yet due, 1%; 1–30 days past due, 3%; 31–60 days, 6%; 61–90 days, 10%; over 90 days, 25%. The following estimating schedule can be prepared:

Estimate of Probable Uncollectible Accounts, December 31, 19B			
Age	Amount of Receivable	Percent Estimated to Be Uncollectible	Balance Needed in Allowance for Doubtful Accounts
Net yet due	$17,200	1	$ 172
1–30 days past due	12,000	3	360
31–60 days past due	8,000	6	480
61–90 days past due	1,200	10	120
Over 90 days past due	1,600	25	400
Total	$40,000		$1,532

The adjusting entry on December 31, 19B, is:

```
Dec. 31   Bad debt expense . . . . . . . . . . . . . . . . . . . . . . . . . . . 632
              Allowance for doubtful accounts  . . . . . . . . . . . . . . . .        632

          To adjust Allowance for Doubtful Accounts to the estimated
          balance needed.

          Computations
          Balance needed (per schedule above)  . . . . . . . . . . . . . . . . . $1,532
          Balance before adjustment (page 312) . . . . . . . . . . . . . . . .     900
                Difference—adjustment needed (increase) . . . . . . . . . . . . . $  632
```

Some persons argue that the aging method approach to estimate the amount of bad debt expense does not apply the **matching principle** as effectively as the percent-of-credit-sales method discussed in the chapter. When the estimate is based on the amount of credit sales from which uncollectible accounts ultimately will occur, bad debt expense is best matched with revenues.

The aging method is based on the ending balance in Accounts Receivable. It tends to match bad debt expense with credit sales for a number of periods. As a result, the matching principle may not be served well each period. However, the aging method produces a good measurement of the net realizable value of accounts receivable because it takes into account probable losses by actual age distribution of the amounts in each account.

IMPORTANT TERMS DEFINED IN THIS CHAPTER

Aging Accounts Receivable   Method to estimate uncollectible accounts based on the age of each account receivable. *p. 312*

Bad Debt Allowance Method   Method that bases bad debt expense on an estimate of uncollectible accounts. *p. 278*

Bad Debt Expense   Expense associated with estimated uncollectible accounts receivable. *p. 278*

Gross Margin on Sales   As a dollar amount, net sales minus cost of goods sold; as a ratio, gross margin divided by net sales revenue. *p. 274*

Gross Method to Record Revenue   Sales revenue is recorded without deducting the authorized cash discount. *p. 306*

Inventory Shrinkage   Missing inventory caused by theft, breakage, spoilage, and incorrect measurements. *p. 295*

Markup   The difference between net sales revenue and cost of goods sold. *p. 274*

Net Method to Record Revenue   Sales revenue is recorded after deducting the amount of any authorized cash discount. *p. 306*

Periodic Inventory System   Ending inventory and cost of goods sold are determined at the end of the accounting period. *p. 283*

Perpetual Inventory System A detailed inventory record is maintained continuously during the accounting period. *p. 284*

Physical Inventory Count Actual count of units in inventory. *p. 291*

Purchase Discount Cash discount received for prompt payment of an account payable. *p. 291*

Purchase Returns and Allowances A deduction from the cost of purchases associated with unsatisfactory goods. *p. 289*

Sales Discount Cash discount offered to encourage prompt payment of an account receivable. *p. 305*

Sales Returns and Allowances A contra revenue account which is associated with unsatisfactory goods. *p. 281*

Subsidiary Ledgers A group of subaccounts that provides more detail than the general ledger control account. *p. 308*

Trade Discount A discount that is deducted from list price to derive the actual sales price. *p. 307*

QUESTIONS

Part A: Questions 1–18

1. In a company that has extensive selling and purchasing activities, the **quantity** of goods included in sales revenue also must be included in a particular **expense** amount. Explain the basis for this statement.
2. Explain the difference between gross sales and net sales.
3. What is gross margin on sales? How is the gross margin ratio computed (in your explanation, assume that net sales revenue was $100,000 and cost of goods sold was $60,000)?
4. What is a sales discount? Use 1/10, n/30 in your explanation.
5. When merchandise, invoiced at $1,000, is sold on terms 2/10, n/30, the vendor must make the following entry:

   Accounts receivable . . . .
       Sales revenue . . . .

   What amounts should be used in this entry under the net method of recording sales discounts? Why is the net method preferred over the gross method?
6. A sale is made for $500; terms are 2/10, n/30. At what amount should the sale be recorded under the net method of recording sales discounts? Give the required entry with an explanation. Also, give the collection entry assuming it is after the discount period.
7. Because the actual time of cash collection is not relevant in determining the date on which a sale should be given accounting recognition, what factor is relevant?
8. Why is an estimate, instead of the actual amount of bad debts, used as a measure of periodic bad debt expense?

9. What is a contra account? Give two examples.

10. Define the book value of accounts receivable.

11. Why should estimated bad debt losses be based on credit sales rather than on total sales for the period?

12. What is the distinction between sales allowances and sales discounts?

13. What purpose is served by an aging of accounts receivable used to compute the allowance for doubtful accounts that could not be served by simply knowing the total accounts receivable balance?

14. Contrast the completed contract method with the percentage-of-completion method of recognizing revenues for long-term construction contracts.

15. The revenue principle takes precedence over the matching principle in determining when recognition is to occur on the income statement. Yet the inability to reliably estimate bad debt losses may be a reason for deferring the recognition of revenue to later periods. Why? (Hint: Consider the specifics of the revenue principle and also the definition of the value for revenue in Exhibit 4–5.)

16. Two guidelines are provided to help determine when revenue can be recognized. First, recognize revenue in the period in which the earnings process is substantially completed. Second, recognize revenue when reliable estimates are available. Relate these two guidelines to each other and state which is more general in its application. (Hint: Consider the revenue recognition examples in this chapter.)

17. The estimated bad debt losses on sales for a period are treated as an expense in the chapter as they commonly are in published financial statements. Consider carefully the valuation of revenue and justify treating estimated bad debt losses on the credit sales for a period as a contra account to sales. Why might practice ignore your argument?

18. Sales discounts can be reported as (*a*) a contra revenue account, (*b*) an addition to selling expense, or (*c*) an interest expense. If the net method is theoretically correct as indicated in the chapter, what is the correct disclosure of sales discounts? Why?

Part B: Questions 19–30

19. Define goods available for sale. How does it differ from cost of goods sold?

20. Define beginning inventory and ending inventory.

21. Briefly distinguish between the perpetual and periodic inventory systems. How does each measure (*a*) inventory and (*b*) cost of goods sold?

22. Describe the calculation of cost of goods sold under the periodic inventory system.

23. Why is it necessary to take an actual physical inventory count at the end of the period when the periodic inventory system is used?

24. Under the cost principle, at what amount should a purchase be recorded? Be specific.

25. What is the purpose of a perpetual inventory record for each item stocked?

26. What accounts are debited and credited for a purchase of goods for resale (*a*) when a perpetual inventory system is used and (*b*) when a periodic inventory system is used?

27. What accounts are debited and credited for a sale of goods on credit (*a*) when a perpetual inventory system is used and (*b*) when a periodic inventory system is used?

28. Why is there no purchases account when the perpetual inventory system is used?

29. Why is transportation-in considered to be a cost of purchasing merchandise?

30. Contrast the treatment of sales returns that are material in amount with that of purchase returns. Justify any differences in the conceptual handling of the two opposite type items.

EXERCISES

Part A: Exercises 6–1 to 6–10

E6–1   **(Pair Definitions with Terms)**
Match the following brief definitions with the terms by entering the appropriate letter in each space provided.

<table>
<tr><th>Terms</th><th>Definitions</th></tr>
<tr><td>_____ (1) Cost of goods sold</td><td>A. Analysis of the elements of individual accounts receivable according to the time elapsed after the dates of billing.</td></tr>
<tr><td>_____ (2) Trade discount*</td><td></td></tr>
<tr><td>_____ (3) Bad debt loss</td><td></td></tr>
<tr><td>_____ (4) Sales returns and allowances</td><td>B. Use of this method establishes a contra account titled "Allowance for Doubtful Accounts" which is considered a subtraction from the balance of "Accounts Receivable."</td></tr>
<tr><td>_____ (5) Gross margin on sales</td><td></td></tr>
<tr><td>_____ (6) Inventory shrinkage</td><td>C. Receivables determined to be uncollectible.</td></tr>
<tr><td>_____ (7) Aging accounts receivable</td><td>D. Synonym for gross profit.</td></tr>
<tr><td>_____ (8) Periodic inventory system</td><td>E. Method of recording revenue which, without adjusting entries, may overstate both accounts receivable and sales revenue.</td></tr>
<tr><td>_____ (9) Physical inventory count</td><td>F. The difference between the value of inventory if there were no theft, breakage, or clerical errors, and the value of inventory when it is physically counted.</td></tr>
<tr><td>_____ (10) Markup</td><td></td></tr>
<tr><td>_____ (11) Purchase returns and allowances</td><td></td></tr>
<tr><td>_____ (12) Net method to record revenue*</td><td>G. A percentage often reported as the gross margin ratio.</td></tr>
<tr><td>_____ (13) Perpetual inventory method</td><td>H. The preferred method for recording sales on credit.</td></tr>
<tr><td>_____ (14) Bad debt allowance method</td><td>I. Method where the cost of goods sold is computed periodically by relying solely on physical counts and not keeping any day-to-day records.</td></tr>
<tr><td>_____ (15) Gross method to record revenues</td><td>J. A system that keeps a continuous record that tracks inventories and cost of goods sold on a day-to-day basis.</td></tr>
</table>

Terms	Definitions
_____ (16) Sales discount*	K. A process which involves two steps: (1) a quantity count and (2) an inventory costing.
_____ (17) Subsidiary ledger	L. A cash discount received by a credit customer for prompt payment.
_____ (18) Purchase discount	M. Products returned by the customer, or a reduction in the selling price resulting in a deduction from the cost of purchases.
	N. A price concession offered by a seller to a customer for prompt payment.
	O. A contra revenue account used to record goods returned by customers.
	P. A supporting ledger that provides details for specific accounts in the general ledger.
	Q. A price concession often offered on volume orders that applies a reduction to the list price resulting in a lower invoice price.
	R. Beginning inventory + Purchases − Ending inventory.

* Applicable to Supplement 6A.

E6–2   (Analysis of Income Statement Relationships)

Supply the missing dollar amounts for the 19B income statement of Better Retail Company for each of the following independent cases:

	Case A	Case B	Case C	Case D	Case E
Sales revenue	$900	$800	$800	$?	$?
Selling expenses	?	200	80	120	180
Cost of goods sold	?	480	?	500	610
Income tax expense	?	30	30	20	40
Gross margin	400	?	?	?	390
Pretax income	100	40	?	180	?
Administrative expenses	100	?	60	100	90
Net income	80	?	120	?	80

E6–3   **(Preparation of an Income Statement Using the Gross Margin)**
The following data were taken from the records of Strickland Appliances, Incorporated, at December 31, 19D:

Sales revenue	$150,000
Administrative expenses	15,000
Distribution (selling) expenses	20,000
Income tax rate	20%
Gross margin ratio	40%
Common shares outstanding	4,000

Required:
Prepare a complete income statement for Strickland. Show all computations. (Hint: Set up side captions starting with sales revenue and ending with earnings per share; rely on the percents given.)

E6–4   **(Preparation of a Multiple-Step Income Statement)**
The following data were taken from the records of Teen Centre at December 31, 19B:

Gross margin (40% ratio)	$24,000
Selling (distribution) expenses	9,000
Administrative expenses	?
Pretax income	10,000
Income tax rate, 20%	
Common shares outstanding	4,000

Required:
Prepare a complete multiple-step income statement for Teen Centre. Show all computations. (Hint: Set up the side captions starting with sales revenue and ending with earnings per share; rely on the percents given.)

E6–5   **(Preparation of a Multiple-Step Income Statement and Analysis of Gross Margin)**
The following data were taken from the records of Burton Corporation on December 31, 19B:

Sales of merchandise for cash	$145,000
Sales of merchandise for credit	257,000
Sales returns and allowances	2,000
Selling expenses	100,000
Cost of goods sold	242,000
Administrative expenses	40,500

Items not included in above amounts:
   Estimated bad debt loss, 2% of net credit sales.
   Average income tax rate, 20%
   Number of shares of common stock outstanding,
      10,000

Required:
a. Based on the above data, prepare a multiple-step income statement. There were no extraordinary items. Include a column for percentage analysis.
b. How much was the gross margin? What was the gross margin ratio? Explain what these two amounts mean.

E6–6   (Using Percentage Analysis with an Income Statement)

The following summarized data were provided by the records of Melody's Music Store, Incorporated, for the year ended December 31, 19B:

Sales of merchandise for cash $124,000
Sales of merchandise on credit   80,000
Cost of goods sold 120,000
Distribution expenses 30,800
Administrative expenses 20,000
Sales returns and allowances   4,000

Items not included in above amounts:
Estimated bad debt loss, 1¼% of credit sales.
Average income tax rate, 20%.
Number of shares of common stock outstanding, 5,000

Required:

a. Based upon the above data, prepare a multiple-step income statement. Include a Percentage Analysis column.

b. What was the amount of gross margin? What was the gross margin ratio? Explain.

E6–7   (Recording Sales Revenue Using the Net Method, Supplement 6A)

During the months of January and February, the WNH Corporation sold goods to three customers. The sequence of events was as follows:

Jan. 6 Sold goods for $800 to J. Doe and billed that amount subject to terms 3/10, n/30.
      6 Sold goods to R. Roe for $600 and billed that amount subject to terms 2/10, n/30.
     14 Collected cash due from J. Doe.
Feb. 2 Collected cash due from R. Roe.
     28 Sold goods for $500 to B. Moe and billed that amount subject to terms 2/10, n/45.

Required:

a. Give the appropriate journal entry for each date. Assume a periodic inventory system is used and that the net method is used to record sales revenue.

b. Explain how each account balance as of February 28 should be reported, assuming that this is the end of the accounting period.

E6–8   (Using the Net Method to Record Sales Revenue, Supplement 6A)

The following transactions were selected from among those completed by Martin Retailers:

Nov. 25 Sold 20 items of merchandise to Customer A at an invoice price of $2,000 (total); terms 3/10, n/30.
     28 Sold 10 items of merchandise to Customer B at an invoice price of $4,000 (total); terms 3/10, n/30.
     30 Customer B returned two of the items purchased on the 28th; the items were defective and credit was given to the customer.
Dec. 5 Customer B paid the account balance in full.
     30 Customer A paid in full for the invoice of November 25, 19B.

Required:

a. Give the appropriate journal entry for each of the preceding transactions assuming Martin Retailers uses the periodic inventory system and records sales revenue under the net method.

b. Assume it is December 31, 19B, end of the accounting period. Show how the various account balances would be reported on the balance sheet and the income statement.

E6–9   (Accounting for Bad Debts Using the Allowance Method)

Luther Company started business on January 1, 19A. During the year 19A, the company's records indicated the following:

Sales on cash basis	$200,000
Sales on credit basis	100,000
Collections on accounts receivable	75,000

[handwritten: 200,000 300,000 = 3% = A/R 100,000 -75,000 25,000]

The manager of Luther Company is concerned about accounting for the bad debts. At December 31, 19A, although no accounts were considered bad, several customers were considerably overdue in paying their accounts. A friend of the manager suggested a 1% bad debt rate on sales, which the manager decided to use at the start.

Required:

a. You have been employed, on a part-time basis, to assist with the recordkeeping for Luther Company. The manager told you to set up bad debt expense of $3,000. Give the required entry.

b. You are concerned about how the $3,000 was determined, and the manager told you it was from another manager "who knew his business" and used 1% of sales. Do you agree with the $3,000? If you disagree, give the correct entry and explain the basis for your choice.

c. Show how the various accounts related to credit sales should be shown on the December 31, 19A, income statement and balance sheet.

E6–10   (Analysis and Evaluation of a Bad Debt Estimate)

During 19G, Joan's Ready-to-Wear Shop had sales revenue of $110,000, of which $40,000 was on credit. At the start of 19G, Accounts Receivable shows a debit balance of $80,000 and the Allowance for Doubtful Accounts, a $500 credit balance. Collections on accounts receivable during 19G amounted to $33,000.

Data during 19G:

1. December 31, 19G, an account receivable (J. Doe) of $700 from a prior year was determined to be uncollectible; therefore, it was written off immediately as a bad debt.

2. December 31, 19G, on the basis of experience, a decision was made to continue the accounting policy of basing estimated bad debt losses on 2% of credit sales for the year.

Required:

a. Give the required journal entries for the two items on December 31, 19G (end of the accounting period).

b. Show how the amounts related to accounts receivable and bad debt expense would be reported on the income statement and balance sheet for 19G. Disregard income tax considerations.

c. On the basis of the data available, does the 2% rate appear to be reasonable? Explain.

Part B: Exercises 6–11 to 6–19

E6–11   (Analysis of Income Statement Relationships)

Supply the missing dollar amounts for the 19B income statement of Janice Retailers for each of the following independent cases:

Case	Sales Revenue	Beginning Inventory	Purchases	Total Available	Ending Inventory	Cost of Goods Sold	Gross Margin	Expenses	Pretax Income or (Loss)
A	900	100	700	?	200	?	?	200	?
B	900	180	750	?	?	?	?	100	0
C	?	140	?	?	300	650	350	100	?
D	900	?	600	?	210	?	?	150	50
E	900	?	650	900	?	?	100	?	(50)

E6–12   (Finding Missing Amounts Based on Income Statement Relationships)

Supply the missing dollar amounts for the 19D income statement of Albert Company for each of the following independent cases:

	Case A	Case B	Case C
Sales revenue	6,000	6,000	?
Sales returns and allowances	150	?	100
Net sales revenue	?	?	5,920
Beginning inventory	9,000	9,500	8,000
Purchases	5,000	?	5,300
Freight-in	?	120	120
Purchase returns	40	30	?
Goods available for sale	?	14,790	13,370
Ending inventory	10,000	9,000	?
Cost of goods sold	?	?	5,400
Gross margin	?	110	?
Expenses	690	?	520
Pretax income	1,000	(500)	–0–

E6–13 **(Accounting for Sales and Purchases Using the Periodic Inventory System)**
The following transactions involving University Book Store were selected from the records of January 19B:

1. Sales: cash, $150,000; and on credit, $40,000 (terms n/30).
2. Some of the merchandise sold on credit in 1 was subsequently returned for credit, $800.
3. Purchases: cash, $80,000; and on credit, $15,000 (terms n/60).
4. Some of the merchandise purchased was subsequently returned for credit, $700.
5. Shipping costs paid in cash on the merchandise purchased, $400 (debit Freight-In).
6. Bad debt losses, on the basis of experience, are estimated to be 2% of credit sales net of sales returns and allowances.
7. An account receivable amounting to $400 was written off as uncollectible. The sale was made two years earlier.

Required:

a. Give the journal entry that would be made for each transaction, assuming the company uses a periodic inventory system.
b. Prepare an income statement for January 19B, through the caption "Gross margin on sales" and show the details of cost of goods sold. The December 31, 19A, inventory of merchandise was $75,000; and the physical inventory count of merchandise taken on January 31, 19B, amounted to $90,000.

E6–14 **(Recording Sales and Purchases Using the Net Method, Supplement 6A)**
L&L Sport Shop sells merchandise on credit terms of 2/10, n/30. A sale invoiced at $800 was made to K. Williams on February 1, 19B. L&L uses the net method of recording sales discounts.

Required:

a. Give the journal entry to record the credit sale.
b. Give the journal entry assuming the account was collected in full on February 9, 19B.
c. Give the journal entry assuming, instead, the account was collected in full on March 2, 19B.

On March 4, 19B, L&L purchased sporting goods from a supplier on credit, invoiced at $6,000; the terms were 1/15, n/30. L&L uses the net method to record purchases.

Required:

d. Give the journal entry to record the purchase on credit. Assume periodic inventory system.
e. Give the journal entry assuming the account was paid in full on March 12, 19B.
f. Give the journal entry assuming, instead, the account was paid in full on March 28, 19B.

E6–15   **(Accounting for Inventory Using the Perpetual System)**

Hill Company uses a perpetual inventory system. Because it is a small business and sells only five different high-cost items, a perpetual inventory record is maintained for each item. The following selected data relate to Item A for the month of January:

1. Beginning inventory—quantity 5, cost $77 each.
2. Purchased—quantity 4, cost $72 each; paid $20 total freight.
3. Sold—quantity 6, sales price $150 each.
4. Returns—2 sold in 3 were returned for full credit.

Required:

a. Give the journal entries for the above transactions assuming a perpetual inventory system and cash transactions.
b. Prepare the perpetual inventory record for Item A.
c. For January, give the following amounts for Item A:

> a. Sales revenue . . . . $ _____
> b. Cost of goods sold . . . . . . $ _____
> c. Gross margin on sales . . . . $ _____
> d. Ending inventory . . . . $ _____

d. Is it possible to determine if there was any inventory shrinkage? Explain.

E6–16   **(Accounting for Sales and Purchases under the Perpetual Inventory System)**

Flower Company uses a perpetual inventory system that provides amounts for the period for (a) cost of goods sold and (b) ending inventory. Physical inventory counts are made from time to time to verify the perpetual inventory records. On December 31, 19B, the end of the accounting year, the perpetual inventory record for Item No. 18 showed the following (summarized):

	Units	Unit cost	Total cost
Beginning inventory	500	$2	$1,000
Purchases during the period	900	2	1,800
Sales during the period (sales price $3.50)	800		

Required:

a. Give the journal entry to record the purchase of 900 units for cash during the period.
b. Give the journal entry to record the sales for cash during the period.
c. Assume a physical inventory count was made after the above transactions and it shows 595 units of Item No. 18 on hand. Give any journal entry required.
d. Give the following amounts for 19B related to Item No. 18:

> 1. Ending inventory . . . . units_____ $ _____
> 2. Cost of goods sold . . . . units_____ $ _____
> 3. Shrinkage loss . . . . units_____ $ _____

e. As a manager, would you investigate in this situation? How?

E6–17   **(Comparison of the Periodic and Perpetual Inventory Systems)**
During 19B, Iota Corporation's records reflected the following for one product stocked:

1. Beginning inventory . . . 1,000 units, unit cost $2
2. Purchases . . . . 8,000 units, unit cost $2
3. Sales . . . . 7,000 units, unit sales price $3
4. Purchase returns . . . . .   10 units, for $2 per unit refund from the supplier
5. Sales returns . . . .   5 units, for $3 per unit refund to the customer

Required:

a. All transactions were in cash; give the journal entries for the above transactions as-suming:

Case A—A perpetual inventory system.

Case B—A periodic inventory system.

b. How would the amount of cost of goods sold be determined in each case?

c. Would you expect the cost of goods sold amount to be the same for Case A as for Case B? Why?

E6–18   **(Use of a Worksheet; Periodic Inventory System)**
The trial balance for Mountain Store, Incorporated, at December 31, 19B (the end of the accounting year), is given below. Only selected accounts are given to shorten the case. The company uses a periodic inventory system. With the exception of the ending inventory, all of the accounts (before adjusting and closing entries) that you will need are listed in the trial balance.

Data developed as a basis for the adjusting entries at December 31, 19B, were:

a. Estimated bad debt expense for 19B was 1% of net credit sales of $12,000.

b. An inventory of store supplies on hand taken at December 31, 19B, reflected $50.

c. Depreciation on the store equipment is based on an estimated useful life of 10 years and no residual value.

d. Wages earned through December 31, 19B, not yet paid or recorded, amounted to $500.

e. The beginning inventory is shown in the trial balance. A physical inventory count of merchandise on hand and unsold, at December 31, 19B, reflected $2,000.

f. Assume an average income tax rate of 20%.

Required:
Prepare a worksheet similar to the one in the demonstration case. If desired, you may omit columns for Adjusted Trial Balance and Retained Earnings. Enter the trial balance, adjusting entries, ending inventory, and complete the worksheet. (Note: This exercise also can be done using T-accounts.)

Debits		Credits	
Cash	$ 8,000	Allowance for doubtful	
Accounts receivable	3,000	accounts	$ 150
Merchandise inventory,		Accumulated depreciation	900
January 1, 19B	4,000	Accounts payable	5,000
Store supplies inventory	250	Wages payable	
Store equipment	3,000	Income tax payable	
Sales returns	150	Capital stock, par $10	6,000
Purchases	6,000	Retained earnings	1,870
Bad debt expense		Sales revenue	13,000
Depreciation expense		Purchase returns	480
Freight-in (on purchases)	100		
Income tax expense			
Other operating expenses	2,900		
	$27,400		$27,400

E6–19 **(Use of a Worksheet; Perpetual Inventory System)**

The trial balance for Modern Appliances, Incorporated, at December 31, 19B (end of the accounting year), is given below. Only selected items have been used in order to shorten the case. The company uses a perpetual inventory system. All of the accounts you will need are listed in the trial balance.

Trial Balance
December 31, 19B

Account titles	Debit	Credit
Cash	$ 6,800	
Accounts receivable	13,000	
Allowance for doubtful accounts		$ 700
Merchandise inventory, ending	64,000	
Operational assets	40,000	
Accumulated depreciation		13,000
Accounts payable		8,000
Income tax payable		
Capital stock, 6,000 no-par shares		60,000
Retained earnings, January 1, 19B		14,300
Sales revenue		105,000
Sales returns and allowances	1,200	
Cost of goods sold	56,000	
Expenses (not detailed)	20,000	
Bad debt expense		
Depreciation expense		
Income tax expense		
	$201,000	$201,000

Additional data developed for the adjusting entries:

a. Estimated bad debt expense is 2% of net credit sales. Net credit sales for 19B amounted to $35,000.

b. The operational assets are being depreciated $4,000 each year.

c. The average income tax rate is 20%.

Required:

Prepare a worksheet similar to the one in the demonstration case. If desired, you may omit columns for Adjusted Trial Balance and Retained Earnings. Enter the trial balance, adjusting entries, and complete the worksheet. (Note: This exercise also can be done using T-accounts if desired.)

PROBLEMS

Part A: Problems 6–1 to 6–6

P6–1   (Understanding the Income Statement)

The following data were taken from the year-end records of Erbs Company. You are to fill in all of the missing amounts. Show computations.

	Independent cases	
Income statement items	Case A	Case B
Gross sales revenue	$110,000	$212,000
Sales returns and allowances	10,000	12,000
Net sales revenue	100,000	200,000
Cost of goods sold (62%)	?62,000	?120,000
Gross margin on sales	?38,000 (40%)	?80,000
Operating expenses	18,000	45,000
Pretax income	?20,000	35,000
Income tax expense (20%)	?4,000	?7,000
Income before extraordinary items	?16,000	?29,000
Extraordinary items (gain)	5,000 (loss)	5,000
Less: Income tax (20%)	1,000	?1,000
Net income	20, ?000	?24,000
EPS (10,000 shares)	2.00	? 2.40

P6–2   (Preparation of a Multiple-Step Income Statement)

Dryden Equipment Company, Inc., sells heavy construction equipment. There are 10,000 no-par shares of common stock outstanding. The annual fiscal period ends on December 31. The following condensed trial balance was taken from the general ledger on December 31, 19D:

Account titles	Debit	Credit
Cash	$ 15,000	
Accounts receivable	20,000	
Allowance for doubtful accounts		$ 1,000
Inventory, (ending)	90,000	
Operational assets	40,000	
Accumulated depreciation		12,000
Liabilities		17,000
Common stock, 10,000 no-par shares		100,000
Retained earnings, January 1, 19D		20,000
Sales revenue		208,000
Sales returns and allowances	8,000	
Cost of goods sold	110,000	
Selling expenses	37,000	
Administrative expenses	20,000	
Interest expense	3,000	
Extraordinary loss, unusual and infrequent storm damage	5,000	
Income tax expense*	10,000	
Totals	$358,000	$358,000

* Assume a 40% average tax rate on both operations and the extraordinary loss.

Required:

a. Prepare a multiple-step income statement.

b. Prepare the following ratio analyses:
   (1) Gross margin on sales ratio.
   (2) Net profit margin ratio on ordinary operations.
   (3) Return on owners' investment from ordinary operations.

c. To compute (b2) and (b3), what amount did you use as the numerator? Explain why.

d. Briefly explain the meaning of each of the three ratios computed in (b).

P6–3 (Preparation and Analysis of an Income Statement)

Stevenson Corporation is a local grocery store organized seven years ago as a corporation. At that time, a total of 10,000 shares of common stock was issued to the three organizers. The store is in an excellent location, and sales have increased each year. At the end of 19G, the bookkeeper prepared the following statement (assume all amounts are correct; also note the inappropriate terminology and format):

STEVENSON CORPORATION
Profit and Loss
December 31, 19G

	Debit	Credit
Sales		$305,000
Cost of goods sold	$169,500	
Sales returns and allowances	5,000	
Selling expenses	60,000	
Administrative and general expenses	30,000	
Interest expense	500	
Extraordinary loss	4,000	
Income tax expense (on operations, $12,000 less $1,200 saved on the extraordinary loss)	10,800	
Net profit	25,200	
Totals	$305,000	$305,000

Required:

a. Prepare a multiple-step income statement. Assume an average 30% income tax rate.

b. Prepare the following ratio analyses:

(1) Net profit margin on sales ratio from ordinary operations.

(2) Gross margin on sales ratio.

(3) Return on investment from ordinary operations; use owners' equity of $200,000.

c. In computing ratios (b1) and (b3), what amount did you use for income? Explain why.

d. Generally, it is conceded that of the three ratios in (b), return on investment has the highest information content for the typical investor. Why?

P6-4   **(Recording Sales, Returns, and Bad Debts, Supplement 6A)**
The data below were selected from the records of Baldwin Company for the year ended December 31, 19C.

Balances January 1, 19C:
Accounts receivable (various customers) $80,000
Allowance for doubtful accounts 6,000

Transactions during 19C:

1. Sold merchandise for cash, $300,000. Sold merchandise on credit terms 2/10, n/30, in the order given below with a unit sales price of $1,000 each. Use the net method to record sales revenue.

2. Sold merchandise to T. Smith; invoice price, $18,000.

3. Sold merchandise to K. Jones; invoice price, $30,000.

4. T. Smith returned one of the units purchased in (2) above, two days after purchase date and received account credit.

5. Sold merchandise to B. Sears; invoice price, $20,000.

6. T. Smith paid his account in full within the discount period.

7. Collected $72,000 cash from customer sales on credit in prior year, all within the discount periods.

8. K. Jones paid the invoice in (3) above within the discount period.

9. Sold merchandise to R. Roy; invoice price, $10,000.

10. Three days after paying the account in full, K. Jones returned one defective unit and received a cash refund.

11. Collected $5,000 cash on an account receivable on sales in a prior year, after the discount period.

12. Baldwin wrote off a 19A account of $2,500 after deciding that the amount would never be collected.

13. The estimated bad debt rate used by Baldwin is 1% of **net** credit sales.

Required:

a. Give the journal entries for the above transactions, including the write-off of the uncollectible account and the adjusting entry for estimated bad debts. Assume a periodic inventory system. Show computations for each entry. Hint: Set up T-accounts on scratch paper for Cash, Accounts Receivable by customer, Allowance for Doubtful Accounts, Sales Revenue, Sales Returns, Sales Discount Revenue, and Bad Debt Expense (this will provide the data needed for the next requirement).

b. Show how the accounts related to the above sale and collection activities should be reported on the 19C income statement and balance sheet.

P6–5   **(Comparison of the Net and Gross Methods Using the Periodic Inventory System, Supplement 6A)**
The following transactions were selected from the records of Electric Company:

July 15 Sold merchandise to Customer A at an invoice price of $4,000; terms 2/10, n/30.

20 Sold merchandise to Customer B at an invoice price of $3,000; terms 2/10, n/30.

21 Purchased inventory from Alpha Supply Company at an invoice price of $500; terms 3/10, n/45.

22 Purchased inventory from Beta Supply Company at an invoice price of $1,000; terms 1/20, n/30.

23 Received payment from Customer A, within the discount period.

25 Paid invoice from Alpha Supply Company, within the discount period.

Aug. 25 Received payment from Customer B, after the discount period.

26 Paid invoice from Beta Supply Company, after the discount period.

Required:

a. Give the appropriate journal entry for each of the above transactions. Assume that Electric Company uses the periodic inventory system and records sales and purchases using the net method.

b. Give the appropriate journal entry for each of the above transactions. Assume that Electric Company uses the periodic inventory system and records sales and purchases using the gross method.

P6–6 **(Based on Supplement 6C; Use Aging Analysis)**

Farley Equipment Company uses the aging approach to estimate bad debt expense at the end of each accounting year. Credit sales occur frequently on terms n/60. The balance of each account receivable is aged on the basis of three time periods as follows: (a) not yet due; (b) up to one year past due; and (c) more than one year past due. Use first sold, first paid to identify which sales invoice was paid where doubt may exist. Experience has shown that for each age group the average loss rate on the amount of the receivable at year-end due to uncollectibility is (a) 1%, (b) 5%, and (c) 30%.

At December 31, 19F (end of the current accounting year), the Accounts Receivable balance was $50,500 and the Allowance for Doubtful Accounts balance was $1,500. To simplify, only five customer accounts are used; the details of each on December 31, 19F, follow:

A. Able—Account Receivable

Date	Explanation	Debit	Credit	Balance
3/11/19E	Sale	15,000		15,000
6/30/19E	Collection		5,000	10,000
1/31/19F	Collection		3,000	7,000

C. Carson—Account Receivable

Date	Explanation	Debit	Credit	Balance
2/28/19F	Sale	21,000		21,000
4/15/19F	Collection		10,000	11,000
11/30/19F	Collection		3,000	8,000

M. May—Account Receivable

Date	Explanation	Debit	Credit	Balance
11/30/19F	Sale	18,000		18,000
12/15/19F	Collection		8,000	10,000

T. Tyler—Account Receivable

Date	Explanation	Debit	Credit	Balance
3/2/19D	Sale	5,000		5,000
4/15/19D	Collection		5,000	–0–
9/1/19E	Sale	12,000		12,000
10/15/19E	Collection		10,000	2,000
2/1/19F	Sale	19,000		21,000
3/1/19F	Collection		1,000	20,000
12/31/19F	Sale	1,500		21,500

Z. Ziltch—Account Receivable

Date	Explanation	Debit	Credit	Balance
12/30/19F	Sale	4,000		4,000

Required:

a. Set up an aging analysis schedule and complete it; follow the illustration given in Supplement 6C.

b. Compute the estimated uncollectible amount for each age category and in total.

c. Give the adjusting entry for bad debt expense at December 31, 19F.

d. Show how the amounts related to accounts receivable should be presented on the 19F income statement and balance sheet.

Part B: Problems 6–7 to 6–19

P6–7   **(Accounting for Cash Discounts by the Seller and the Purchaser, Supplement 6A)**
Assume the following summarized transactions between Company A, the vendor, and Company B, the purchaser. Use the letters to the left as the date notations. Assume each company uses a periodic inventory system and each uses the net method to record sales revenue and purchases.

1. Company A sold Company B merchandise for $10,000; terms 1/10, n/30.
2. Prior to payment, Company B returned $1,000 (one tenth) of the merchandise for credit because it did not meet B's specifications.

Required:
Give the following journal entries in parallel columns for each party:

a. The sale/purchase transaction.
b. The return transaction.
c. Payment in full assuming it was made within the discount period.
d. Payment in full assuming, instead, it was made after the discount period.

Use a form similar to the following:

		Co. A—Vendor		Co. B—Purchaser	
Date	Accounts	Debit	Credit	Debit	Credit

P6–8   **(Recording Sales and Purchases Using the Net Method)**
University Store, Incorporated, is a student co-op. On January 1, 19X, the beginning inventory was $200,000; the Accounts Receivable balance was $3,000; and the Allowance for Doubtful Accounts had a credit balance of $400. A periodic inventory system is used and purchases are recorded using the net method.

The following transactions (summarized) have been selected from 19X for case purposes:

1. Merchandise sales for cash	$300,000
2. Merchandise returned by customers as unsatisfactory, for cash refund	1,400
Merchandise purchased from vendors on credit; terms 2/10, n/30:	
3. May Supply Company invoice price, before deduction of cash discount	4,000
4. Other vendors, invoice price, before deduction of cash discount	115,000
5. Purchased equipment for use in the store; paid cash	1,800
6. Purchased office supplies for future use in the store; paid cash	600
7. Freight on merchandise purchased; paid cash (set up a separate account for this item)	500

Accounts payable paid in full during the period as follows:

8.	May Supply Company, paid after the discount period	4,000
9.	Other vendors, paid within the discount period	98,000

Required:

a. Prepare journal entries for each of the above transactions.

b. Give the closing entry required at December 31, 19X, for:
   (1) Beginning inventory.
   (2) Ending inventory (assume $130,000).

c. Prepare a partial income statement through gross margin on sales.

d. Explain why it was preferable to record purchases using the net method.

P6–9   (Reporting Sales Transactions on the Financial Statements)
The transactions listed below were selected from those occurring during the month of January 19D for Polo Department Store, Incorporated. A wide line of goods is offered for sale. Credit sales are extended to a few select customers; the usual credit terms are n/EOM.

1. Sales to customers:
   Cash $350,000
   On credit 30,000
2. Unsatisfactory merchandise returned by customers:
   Cash 4,000
   Credit 1,000
   Merchandise purchased from vendors on credit; terms 1/20, n/30:
3. AB Supply Company, amount billed, before deduction of cash discount 1,000
4. From other vendors, amount billed, before deduction of cash discount 120,000
5. Freight paid on merchandise purchased; paid cash (set up a separate account
   for this item) 2,000
6. Collections on accounts receivable 17,000
   The accounts payable were paid in full during the period as follows:
7. AB Supply Company, paid after the discount period 1,000
8. Other vendors, paid within the discount period 118,800
9. Purchased two new typewriters for the office; paid cash 900
10. An account receivable from a customer from a prior year amounting to
    $300 was determined to be uncollectible and was written off.
11. At the end of January the adjusting entry for estimated bad debts is to be made.
    The loss rate, based on experience, is 1% of net credit sales for the period (i.e.,
    on credit sales less credit returns).

Relevant account balances on January 1, 19D, were Accounts Receivable, $3,200 (debit); and Allowance for Doubtful Accounts, $900 (credit). Total assets at the end of the period, $250,000.

Required:

a. Prepare journal entries for the above transactions assuming a periodic inventory system is in use, and record purchases using the net method.

b. Show how the following amounts should be reported on the January 19D income statement and balance sheet. Show computations.
   (1) Bad debt expense.
   (2) Balance in accounts receivable.
   (3) Balance in allowance for doubtful accounts.

c. Explain why bad debt expense should not be debited for the $300 uncollectible account written off in January.

P6–10   **(Application of the Perpetual Inventory System)**

Air Express Distributing Company uses a perpetual inventory system for the items it sells. The following selected data relate to Item 10, a small but high-cost item stocked during the month of January 19B.

1. Beginning inventory—quantity, 70; cost, $50 each.
2. Purchases—quantity, 90; cost $48 each plus $180 for transportation on the purchases.
3. Sales—quantity, 120; sale price, $95 each.
4. Returns—Air Express accepted a return of two of the items sold in 3 because they were not needed by the customer and they had not been used.
5. At the end of January 19B a physical inventory count showed 40 items remaining on hand.

Required (assume all transactions were cash):

a. Prepare the perpetual inventory record for Item 10.
b. Give journal entries for each of the above transactions.
c. Prepare the income statement for January 19B through gross margin on sales as it related to Item 10. What was the gross margin ratio?
d. As the responsible manager, would you investigate the inventory shrinkage? How?
e. Assume that you observe quite often that the required items are out of stock. How can a perpetual inventory system be helpful in avoiding this problem?

P6–11   **(Use of the Perpetual Inventory System and Analysis of Shrinkage)**

Green Company uses a perpetual inventory system. During the month of January 19D, the perpetual inventory record for Item A, which is one of the 23 items stocked, is shown below (summarized):

PERPETUAL INVENTORY RECORD

Date	Explanation	Goods Purchased Units	Goods Purchased Total Cost	Goods Sold Units	Goods Sold Total Cost	Balance Units	Balance Total Cost
1	Beginning inventory					40	$3,200
2	Purchase (at $80 each)	20					
3	Sale (sales price $150 each)			31			
4	Purchase return (one unit)						
5	Purchase (at $80 each)	30					
6	Sales return (one unit)						
7	Sale (sales price $150 each)			29			
8	Inventory shortage (four units)						

Required:

a. Complete the perpetual inventory record.

b. Give the journal entry for each transaction reflected in the perpetual inventory record (assume transactions are cash).

c. Complete the following tabulation:

> Income statement:
> Sales . . . . $ _____
> Cost of goods sold . . . . _____
> Gross margin on sales . . . . _____
> Gross margin ratio . . . . _____
>
> Balance sheet:
> Inventory . . . . _____

d. Explain how the inventory shortage should be reported.

e. As the responsible manager, would you investigate this situation? How?

f. Assume "stockout" has been a problem. What would you recommend?

P6–12 (Comparison of Periodic and Perpetual Inventory Systems)
The following transactions, relating to one product sold by Jackson Company, were completed in the order given during January:

a. Purchased—quantity, 120; cost, $20 each.

b. Sold—quantity, 100; $35 each.

c. Purchase return—returned one of the units purchased in (a) because it was the wrong size.

d. Sales return—accepted two units from a customer that were sold in (b). The customer did not need them, and they were not damaged.

e. Inventories:

Beginning inventory, January 1—30 units at total cost of $600.

Ending inventory, January 31—per periodic inventory count, 51 units @ $20 = $1,020.

f. Cost of goods sold for January—98 units @ $20 = $1,960.

Required:

Give the journal entries that would be made for the above transactions assuming: Case A—a perpetual inventory system is used; and Case B—a periodic inventory system is used. To do this, set up the following form (assume cash transactions):

		Perpetual		Periodic	
Date	Explanation	Debit	Credit	Debit	Credit
a.	To record the purchase				
b.	To record the sale				
c.	To record the purchase return				
d.	To record the sales return				
e.	To record the closing entries for inventories				
f.	To record the closing entry for cost of goods sold				
g.	To close purchases and purchase returns				

Note: T-accounts may prove useful.

P6–13   (Completion of a Worksheet)

Quality Retailers, Inc., is completing the accounting information processing cycle for the year ended December 31, 19D. The worksheet given below has been completed through the adjusting entries. (An optional column, "Adjusted Trial Balance," may be helpful in completing the requirements.)

Required:

a. Complete the following worksheet (periodic inventory system is used). Assume an average income tax rate of 20%. (Note: This problem can be done using T-accounts only.)

b. Give the closing journal entries at December 31, 19D. Close all revenue and expense accounts to Income Summary.

QUALITY RETAILERS, INC.
Worksheet—December 31, 19D

Account Titles	Trial Balance		Adjusting Entries*		Income Statement		Retained Earnings		Balance Sheet	
	Debit	Credit	Debit	Credit	Debit	Credit	Debit	Credit	Debit	Credit
Cash	27,200									
Accounts receivable	12,000									
Allowance for doubtful accounts		300		(a) 400						
Merchandise inventory, Jan. 1, 19D	30,000									
Equipment	22,500									
Accumulated depreciation, equipment		9,000		(b) 1,500						
Other assets	20,000									
Accounts payable		8,000								
Interest payable				(c) 300						
Note payable, long term (12%)		10,000								
Capital stock (par $10)		50,000								
Contributed surplus		7,500								
Retained earnings, Jan. 1, 19D		13,000								
Dividends declared and paid (19D)	6,000									
Sales revenue		95,000								
Sales returns and allowances	1,000									
Purchases	52,000									
Freight-in	2,000									
Purchase returns and allowances		1,100								

QUALITY RETAILERS, INC. *(concluded)*

Account Titles	Trial Balance		Adjusting Entries*		Income Statement		Retained Earnings		Balance Sheet	
	Debit	Credit	Debit	Credit	Debit	Credit	Debit	Credit	Debit	Credit
Operating expenses (not detailed)	20,300									
Bad debt expense			(a) 400							
Depreciation expense			(b) 1,500							
Interest expense	900		(c) 300							
Merchandise inventory, Dec. 31, 19D ($32,000)										
	193,900	193,900								
Income tax expense										
Income tax payable										
Net income										
Retained earnings, Dec. 31, 19D										

P6–14   **(Related to Supplement 6A; Use of Subsidiary Ledgers)**

City Department Store, Incorporated, is a large department store located in a western city with a population of approximately 200,000 persons. The store carries top brands and attempts to appeal to "quality customers." Approximately 80% of the sales are on credit. As a consequence, there is a significant amount of detailed recordkeeping related to credit sales, returns, collections, and billings. The accounts receivable records are maintained manually; however, the store is considering computerizing this phase of the accounting information system. Included in the general ledger is a control account for Accounts Receivable. Supporting the control account is an accounts receivable subsidiary ledger which has individual accounts for more than 20,000 customers. For case purposes, a few accounts and transactions with simplified amounts have been selected. The case requirement is intended to indicate the nature of the data processing work that City Store plans to computerize; however, here it will be completed manually.

On January 1, 19F, the Accounts Receivable control account (No. 52), in the general ledger, shows a debit balance of $4,000 and the subsidiary ledger shows the following balances:

52.1 Akins, A. K. $400
52.2 Blue, V. R. 700
52.3 Daley, U. T. 900
52.4 Evans, T. V. 300
52.5 May, O. W. 800
52.6 Nash, G. A. 100
52.7 Roth, I. W. 600
52.8 Winn, W. W. 200

During the month of January, the following transactions and events relating to sales activities occurred (use the notation at the left for date):

a. Sales of merchandise on credit.

Akins, A. K.	$300
Blue, V. R.	250
Winn, W. W.	730
May, O. W.	140
Daley, U. T.	70
Roth, I. W.	370
Evans, T. V.	410

b. Unsatisfactory merchandise returned by customers:

Roth, I. W.	$30
Winn, W. W.	70
Akins, A. K.	20

c. Collections on accounts receivable:

Winn, W. W.	$800
May, O. W.	940
Akins, A. K.	200
Roth, I. W.	700
Blue, V. R.	750
Daley, U. T.	600

d. The account for G. A. Nash has been inactive for several years. After an investigation, the management decided that it was uncollectible; therefore, it is to be written off immediately.

e. The estimated loss rate is 2% of net credit sales (i.e., credit sales less returns for credit).

Required:

a. Set up the general ledger control account for Accounts Receivable. Also, set up the general ledger account for Allowance for Doubtful Accounts (No. 53) with a credit balance of $600. Indicate the beginning balance as "Bal." and for convenience use T-accounts for these two accounts.

b. Set up an accounts receivable subsidiary ledger; use three columns—Debit, Credit, and Balance. Enter the beginning balances with the notation "Bal."

c. Prepare journal entries for each of the above transactions.

d. Post the entries prepared in (c) to the Accounts Receivable control account, Allowance for Doubtful Accounts, and the subsidiary ledger. Use folio numbers.

e. Prepare a schedule of accounts receivable to show how much each customer owed at the end of January.

f. Show how accounts receivable and the related allowance amounts would be reported in the January balance sheet.

P6–15 **(A Review of Chapters 3, 4, 5, and 6)**
Discount Furniture Store, Inc., has been in operation for a number of years and has been quite profitable. The losses on uncollectible accounts and on merchandise returns are about the same as for other furniture stores. The company uses a perpetual inventory

system. The annual fiscal period ended December 31, 19B, and the end-of-period accounting information processing cycle has been started. The following trial balance was derived from the general ledger at December 31, 19B.

Account titles	Debit	Credit
Cash	$ 28,880	
Accounts receivable	36,000	
Allowance for doubtful accounts		$ 4,600
Merchandise inventory (ending)	110,000	
Store equipment	22,000	
Accumulated depreciation		10,000
Accounts payable		10,000
Income tax payable		
Interest payable		
Notes payable, long term (12%)		50,000
Common stock, 7,000 no-par shares		70,000
Retained earnings, January 1, 19B		11,400
Sales revenue		441,000
Sales returns and allowances	25,000	
Cost of goods sold	223,350	
Selling expenses	102,700	
Administrative expenses	49,070	
Bad debt expense		
Depreciation expense		
Interest expense		
Totals	$597,000	$597,000
Income tax expense		
Net income		

Data for adjusting entries:

a. The bad debt losses due to uncollectible accounts are estimated to be $6,000.

b. The store equipment is being depreciated over an estimated useful life of 11 years with no residual value.

c. The long-term note of $50,000 was for a two-year loan from a local bank. The interest rate is 12%, payable at the end of each 12-month period. The note was dated April 1, 19B. (Hint: Accrue interest for nine months.)

d. Assume an average 20% corporate income tax rate.

Required:

a. Based upon the above data, complete a worksheet similar to the one illustrated in the chapter for the demonstration case. If you prefer, you may omit columns for Adjusted Trial Balance and Retained Earnings. (Hint: Net income is $22,704; Note: This problem may be done using T-accounts only.)

b. Based upon the completed worksheet, prepare a multiple-step income statement and classified balance sheet.

c. Based upon the completed worksheet, prepare the adjusting and closing journal entries for December 31, 19B. Close all revenue and expense accounts to Income Summary.

P6–16 **(A Review of Chapters 3, 4, 5, and 6)**

Northwest Appliances, Incorporated, is owned by six local investors. It has been operating for four years and is at the end of the 19D fiscal year. For case purposes, certain accounts have been selected to demonstrate the information processing activities at the end of the year for a corporation that sells merchandise rather than services. The following trial balance, assumed to be correct, was taken from the ledger on December 31, 19D. The company uses a periodic inventory system.

Debits		Credits	
Cash	$ 18,000	Allowance for doubtful	
Accounts receivable	28,000	accounts	$ 600
Merchandise inventory,		Accumulated depreciation	12,000
January 1, 19D	80,000	Accounts payable	15,000
Prepaid insurance	300	Notes payable, long term (12%)	30,000
Store equipment	40,000	Common stock, 4,000	
Sales returns and		no-par shares	40,000
allowances	3,000	Retained earnings,	
Purchases	250,000	January 1, 19D	2,000
Freight-in	11,000	Sales revenue	400,000
Operating expenses	76,300	Purchase returns	7,000
	$506,600		$506,600

Additional data for adjusting entries:

a. Credit sales during the year were $100,000; based on experience, a 1% loss rate on credit sales has been established.

b. Insurance amounting to $100 expired during the year.

c. The store equipment is being depreciated over a 10-year estimated useful life with no residual value.

d. The long-term note payable for $30,000 was dated May 1, 19D, and carries a 12% interest rate per annum. The note is for three years, and interest is payable on April 30 each year.

e. Assume an average income tax rate of 30%.

f. Inventories:

Beginning inventory, January 1, 19D (per above trial balance), $80,000.

Ending inventory, December 31, 19D (per physical inventory count), $75,000.

Required:

a. Prepare a worksheet at December 31, 19D, similar to the one shown in the demonstration problem in the chapter. If you prefer, you may omit columns for Adjusted Trial Balance and Retained Earnings. To save time and space, all operating expenses have been summarized. However, you should set up additional expense accounts for depreciation, bad debts, interest, and income tax. Also, you will need additional liability accounts for interest payable and income tax payable. (Hint: Net income is $37,940; Note: This requirement may be done using T-accounts only.)

b. Based upon the completed worksheet, prepare a multiple-step income statement and classified balance sheet.

c. Based upon the completed worksheet, prepare the adjusting and closing journal entries at December 31, 19D. Close all revenue and expense accounts to Income Summary.

P6–17   (Review of Errors and Their Correction)

Shaky Corporation has applied for a significant bank loan and prior to considering the application, the bank asked you to conduct an audit for the three years the corporation has been in existence. In conducting the audit you find the following:

a. Reported net income for the three years:

1986	$16,000
1987	(4,000)
1988	24,000*

* The $24,000 net income for 1988 was picked up from the worksheet which was completed for the year. The adjusting entries as of December 31, 1988, were journalized and posted. The closing entries have not as yet been journalized. Shaky uses the periodic inventory procedure.

b. Omission of earned (uncollected) revenue at year-end was $500 in 1986, $800 in 1987, and $600 in 1988.

c. A three-year insurance policy was purchased July 1, 1986, for $1,800. The expenditure was debited to insurance expense at the time of purchase.

d. Goods in transit owned by the company had been shipped but had not arrived in time for the inventory count, which resulted in an understatement of an ending inventory of $1,200 as of December 31, 1987. The invoice was received and had been recorded in 1987.

e. Advances from customers (unearned at year-end) were included in revenue. The amounts were: $600 in 1986, $400 in 1987, and $700 in 1988.

f. Shaky used the direct write-off method of bad debts rather than the allowance method which should have been used. The following data are to be used for conversion to the allowance method and adjustment of reported net income (loss). Probable losses of outstanding accounts as of December 31, 1988, were for:

1987 accounts	$ 800
1988 accounts	2,200

Accounts had been written-off to expense as follows:

Accounts	1986	1987	1988
1986	$600	$1,800	—
1987	—	1,600	$2,400
1988	—	—	1,200

Required:

Determine the correct net income (loss) for 1986, 1987, and 1988. (Assume there was no change in income tax expense.)

	1986	1987	1988
a. Reported net income	$16,000	$(4,000)	$24,000
Effect on reported net income of:			
b.	___	___	___
c.	___	___	___
d.	___	___	___
e.	___	___	___
f.	___	___	___
Adjusted net income	___	___	___

(CGAC Adapted)

P6-18   (Computer Spreadsheet of Missing Amounts)

Required:

Using a computer spreadsheet and the data from Problem P6-1, complete the Required of the problem.

P6-19   (Computer Spreadsheet of a Worksheet)

Required:

Using a computer spreadsheet and the worksheet in Problem P6-13, complete part (*a*) of the Required for that problem.

CASES

C6-1   (Revenue Recognition)

Carbonated Beverage Ltd. (CB), was federally incorporated in 1976. In the initial years, the company produced an orange drink for sale at sporting and entertainment events in Western Canada. In 1980, operations were expanded to include sales to bars, restaurants, and fast-food outlets. To penetrate additional markets, CB started manufacturing a wide variety of soft drinks and acquired the distributorship of another company's cola syrup. Sold under the brand name "Sun Brite," the soft drink sales were only moderately successful.

In 1982, a management review indicated, that, while sales of the new soft drink line had increased, CB's cost to manufacture was also greater than that of its competitors. Much of the net income was being made on the distribution of cola syrup.

In an attempt to improve profitability, the company entered the retail market in 1983. To finance this expansion, CB obtained funds from two sources: bank loans and the issue of shares to the public. The funds were used to purchase a bottling plant in Vancouver and to provide working capital during the first year of operation. In the first year, the retail operation incurred a loss that in subsequent years became a profit.

CB continued to expand until it had a nationwide bottling and distribution network. Some bottlers it owned; some in smaller cities were independents who bottled other products as well. CB sold its own syrup to these independents.

In 1986, CB acquired a vending company's operations. By expanding these operations, CB was able to manufacture and sell vending machines as well as soft drinks through the vending machines.

The contract between CB and local operators of vending machines (CB does not operate its own machines) stipulates that local operators must sell only CB products.

The major portion of all matching sales was done using what is termed a conditional sales contract. This contract specifies an initial down payment of $350 and monthly payments of $75 per month for the next 48 months. Maintenance of machines is the responsibility of the operator.

The syrup and cups for the machines are purchased directly from CB or from local independent bottlers who in turn buy the supplies from CB. The independents receive a discount from CB sufficient to permit them to make a 20 percent markup on their cost.

During 1988, CB expects to sell 7,000 machines. Each machine costs $1,500 to manufacture. The cash sales price for those few who have the cash is $3,400.

Required:

In August 1988, you were engaged as an independent adviser. Prepare a report to the president of CB which:

a. Outlines the major accounting issues faced by the company.

b. Identifies alternative policies to deal with the issues outlined.

c. Provides recommendations on the preferred policies.

(CICA, Adapted)

C6–2   **(Accounting for Bad Debts)**

You serve as an investment adviser to a variety of clients who invest in banks. You come across the following article concerning the treatment of bad debts by banks:

Banks must now report loan losses same year they occur

The accounting rules for banks have been changed, effective immediately, to require the reporting of loan losses on income statements in the years they actually occur.

Previously, deductions for loan losses were based on a formula that averaged loan losses over the previous five years. That method had the effect of smoothing out the financial results. The new rules established by the office of the federal Superintendent of Financial Institutions will give a clearer picture of banks' actual year-end performances.

In the past, when a bank had particularly heavy losses in a given year, it did not have to absorb the total impact of those losses that same year because of the five-year averaging formula.

The accounting changes will show up in the next couple of weeks as the banks start reporting results for the first quarter, the three months ended Jan. 31. The banks have also been directed to restate their profits for the corresponding period a year earlier.

The new rules follow months of consultation between the superintendent, the banks and accountants.

"The five-year averaging formula, as a smoothing mechanism, has served the industry well," said an employee in the superintendent's office. "But, as a result of events in the last couple of years, there was widespread agreement that it was appropriate to look at the accounting for loan losses."

The averaging formula was criticized in 1986 when Mr. Justice Willard Estey released his report on the 1985 failures of the Canadian Commercial Bank and the Northland Bank, both based in Alberta.

The accounting for loan losses, based on the formula, was "one of the most confusing aspects of bank financial statements," Judge Estey wrote.

Judge Estey wrote that bond rating agencies in Canada, as a matter of course in analyzing bank results, have immediately converted "the figures to accord with ordinary accounting for bad debts and debt reserves.

"They [the bond-rating agencies] thereby penetrate the fog surrounding the existing accounting procedure."

For some years, the Bank of Montreal has distributed two sets of financial results to shareholders: one set reflecting the five-year loan-loss averaging formula, as required by

---

Source: Virginia Galt, *The Globe and Mail,* "Report on Business," February 16, 1988.

law, and the other prepared to reflect the bank's actual operating results on a current loss basis.

Bank of Montreal chairman William Mulholland has long been a proponent of setting out the losses as they occur. And, in recent years, the current loss figures have made the bank's performance look better than the official figures because it has had marked success in getting its loan losses under control.

The year-end losses reported by the major Canadian chartered banks in 1987 resulted from a special provision to increase reserves against possible defaults on loans to less-developed countries.

"In the case of the CCB, the appropriation for contingencies account declined in the financial statement for the 1984 fiscal year. At the same time, loan quality was deteriorating and management was taking additional provisions against losses.

"All but the most sophisticated readers of the financial statement would understand this to mean that the bank's financial condition was improving when, in reality, it was deteriorating. This potentially misleading accounting device is unknown in the United States and the United Kingdom."

You know that such bad debt allowances are income tax deductible for the expenses accrued and that banks have been expressing serious concerns over their exposure to Third-World loan losses in seemingly increasing amounts.

You wish to develop a response for your clients about the potential effect of this new accounting policy on their investment.

Required:

1. Would this change in accounting practices for bad debts result in a violation of the comparability principle (Exhibit 4–5)?
2. Why would banks have used the previous bad debt policy? Was it in violation of any accounting policies?
3. What effect, if any, would this new accounting policy have on your client's investments?

C6–3   (Data Base Accounts Receivable, Design and Operation)

Dental Practice: Accounts Receivable Problem

Introduction to Exercise

The purpose of this exercise is to learn how data base programs can be used to solve business data processing problems, in particular, an accounts receivable processing problem. In addition, if you have access to a data base program, you can create a small data base and use the data in this problem to answer some questions and prepare some management reports.

As an illustration consider a dental practice located in a metropolitan area in a prairie province with a population of approximately 200,000 people. Of its patients, 80% pay on credit. As a consequence, there is a significant amount of detailed recordkeeping related to recording services, billing patients, collecting cash, and writing off bad debts. The accounts receivable records are maintained manually; however, the dentists are considering computerizing this phase of the accounting information system.

Included in the general ledger is a control account for Accounts Receivable. Supporting the control account is an accounts receivable subsidiary ledger which has individual accounts for more than 2,000 patients.

Before beginning this assignment, review Supplement 6B which deals with subsidiary ledgers and Supplement 6C which deals with aging accounts receivable.

For purposes of this case, a few accounts and transactions with simplified amounts have been selected. The case requirement is intended to illustrate the nature of the data processing work that the dentists plan to computerize.

Introduction to Data Base Systems

In simplest terms, a data base is nothing more than a collection of facts. A data base program is a computer program which facilitates the creation, updating, and extraction of information from a data base that exists on a computer. Because of the way in which data base programs work, users of such programs need not be particularly concerned with how data is physically stored in computer files yet users are able to relate easily to various different types of information contained in the data base.

Prior to the development of data base programs, it was difficult to relate information that was generated for one purpose to information that was generated for another purpose. For example, it would normally be difficult to determine the cost of services rendered to individual patients unless the recordkeeping system collected and stored such data whenever services were rendered. With a data base system, if information about who performed a given service and what supplies were used is available in the patient's record, it should be relatively easy to relate this data to personnel and inventory data to compute the cost of treating a given patient.

Within organizations, data bases are used to provide management and others with the information they need to do their jobs. Data base programs make it much easier to extract such information than is possible without such programs because they facilitate the creation of files, the addition of data to those files, and the updating of that data. In addition, data base programs allow users to answer many different types of questions either through formal reports or on-line queries without having to know the location and format of stored data.

Traditional versus Data Base Programs

1. Traditional system

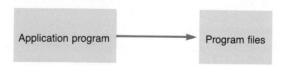

In a traditional system, each application program, for example, accounts receivable and inventory, manipulates its own data files. This means that to use any data, a program must know precisely where on the disk or tape data is stored, the format used to store it, and so on.

2. Data base system

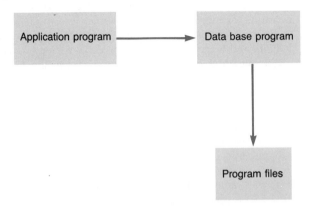

In a data base system, application programs do not directly access data. Instead, they request data from the data base system which actually stores and retrieves data. Those wishing to use specific data give the commands required by the data base system to obtain this information. The data base system handles all the details; that is, finds the data, presents it to the requestor in the desired format and so on.

Data base programs run on all types of computers. In general, those that run on microcomputers are less powerful, but easier to use than those that run on larger machines. However, as microcomputers increase in power, the data base programs that run on them are growing in power, and as individuals have grown accustomed to good user interfaces on microcomputers they have increasingly demanded and have begun to receive more user friendly programs on mainframe computers. Indeed, today, one can often find the same data base program running on both large and small computers and on many different types of machines within any given category.

Each data base program has its own method of performing the basic functions of creating files, adding or changing data, and extracting information. In most microcomputer data base programs, much of this can be done via a series of menus. However, there are generally some functions that cannot be done, or be done efficiently, using menus. To handle such situations, most data base programs have special "programming" languages which can be used to perform such functions.

General Systems Design

Before attempting to use a data base program, a number of critical issues need to be resolved. However, before considering these issues, it will be useful if one understands the basic flow of accounts receivable information through the system.

Diagram for Manual System

1. Revenue earned

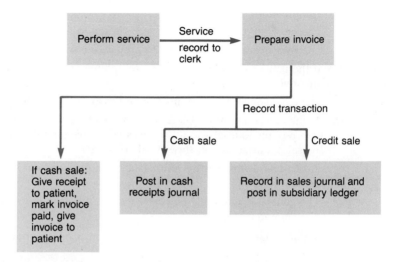

2. Monthly posting and reporting*

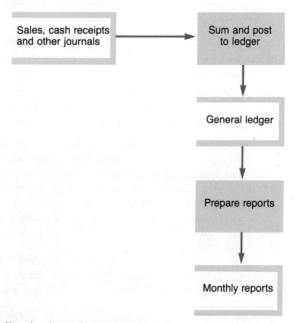

*Open boxes signify files; closed ones denote processing.

Explanation of basic data processing steps:

a. Service is rendered to patients and a record of this service is prepared by the person providing the service.

b. The record of the service provided is given to the receptionist/clerk.

c. The receptionist uses this data to prepare an invoice.

d. If the patient pays cash, then the receptionist prepares a cash receipt and marks the invoice as paid.

e. The receptionist gives the invoice and cash receipt to the patient.

f. At the end of the day: (1) services for which cash was received are posted in the cash receipts journal and (2) services which were rendered on credit are posted in the sales journal and in the subsidiary ledger.

g. At the end of the month, journals are summed and amounts are posted to the general ledger.

h. The general ledger and subsidiary ledgers are used to prepare various management reports.

In the design of a system, there are a number of important issues which need to be resolved.

1. The first of these critical issues is the determination of the information which will be required by the users of the system. The clinic will need data to answer many management questions and to:

   a. Mail statements to patients on a monthly basis.

   b. Respond to patient queries concerning the status of their accounts (this will require a subsidiary ledger such as is discussed in Supplement 6B).

   c. Determine the general ledger amount for accounts receivable.

   d. Provide various reports to the dentists (these reports should include an aging of receivables such as that which is set forth in Supplement 6C).

   In deciding on the specific information individuals will be able to obtain from the system, it is important to consider providing them with the data currently available to them as well as the additional information they would like to have.

   One must decide what data is to be included in formal reports and what data should be available to help individuals answer on-line interactive queries. In general, it is much more difficult to determine the information needed to answer interactive queries than to determine what is needed in formal reports. This is because it is very difficult to know in advance what questions individuals will ask. As individuals receive answers to a given question, they will raise additional questions for which they will also want answers. Once they use a data base system to answer given types of questions, they will inevitably want to use it to answer other types of questions.

   Requirement 1:
   For the accounts receivable example described above, what are the primary questions one might want to answer? For example, one might want to know how much each patient owes the firm. [answer 1]

2. After one has determined the information that must be produced by the system, the next step is to determine what data must be collected and processed in order for the system to generate the desired outputs.

Requirement 2:

In the accounts receivable example, what data will the dental clinic have to collect to answer the preceding questions? [answer 2]

It should be noted that it may not be possible to answer, or answer completely, some questions because of the difficulty of collecting the required input data. For example, it may not be feasible to collect some desired information for patients who pay cash.

3. After one has determined the specific information that is to be collected, one must group the various data items together in some reasonable manner. In grouping the data one will want to consider, among other things, the impact of different groupings on:

   a. Maintaining accurate data.

   b. Minimizing delays in accessing data.

   c. Maximizing the efficiency of equipment in extracting and manipulating data.

   d. Minimizing the amount of storage space that is required for the data.

   In the discussion that follows, no distinction has been made between logical and physical groupings of data even though it is often desirable to make such a distinction.

4. After one has ascertained the information the system must generate, the primary data inputs, and the basic file structures, the next task is to determine the general processing steps that are required to go from the stated inputs to the desired outputs.

   The actual processing steps required depend on, among other things, the objectives of the processing, the way in which it is to be done, the data items to be stored within the system, and the specific way in which they are to be stored. For example, if and only if individual patient account balances are kept in the system can one determine an account balance by merely looking up a given record and reading the balance. If account balances are not kept as a separate data item, then one must review all the transactions for a given patient and calculate the balance. Likewise, the processing steps required to determine the total services rendered to patients who live in a particular suburb will depend on whether patient addresses and service data are stored in one or two files.

Concrete Implementation Steps

Once the general system design issues discussed above have been resolved, one begins to make the concrete decisions that must be made in order to actually implement a system.

Step 1. The first of these steps is to define precisely each data item. One must determine:

a. The words to be used to refer to each input or calculated amount; for example, P__NAME__SUR might be used to refer to the surnames of patients.

b. The characteristics to be associated with each input or calculated amount; for example, P__NAME__SUR might be defined as a field 20 characters long and ACCT__ BAL (balance of patient's account), a calculated amount might be defined as a real number accurate to two decimal places with a maximum value of just under $10,000 and equal to the previous balance plus the debit or minus the credit that arises from the transaction being processed.

c. The file(s) where each data input, calculated amount, and so on will be stored; for example, the file that holds patient data might be called PATIENT.

The above details must be resolved in accord with the requirements of the specific data base program being used. For example, if a data base program requires that field names be no more than 12 characters long, ACCOUNT__BALANCE is too long.

After precisely defining the data items, files can be created and records entered into them. However, one would normally not enter more than a small number of data items into the system until it and all its programs have been thoroughly tested.

Requirement 3:

If you have access to a data base program, define, for use in that system, the files and data items required to computerize the clinic's accounts receivable system. [answer 3]

Step 2. Having precisely defined data inputs and set up files, one must next determine the processing steps required to convert inputs to the desired outputs. Again this specification must be in accord with the requirements of the particular data base program being used.

Included in this detailed specification will be:

a. A listing of steps users must go through in order to extract the information or generate the reports they want.

b. Programs which when called by users allow them to perform some desired function.

In setting forth the detailed processing steps, it is useful to prepare a flowchart; that is, a pictorial representation of these steps.

If you have access to a data base system and are creating a receivable system, you should prepare a detailed flowchart.

Before attempting to draw a flowchart, you should have a general idea of how a computerized receivable system works.

Diagram for Computerized System

1. Revenue earned

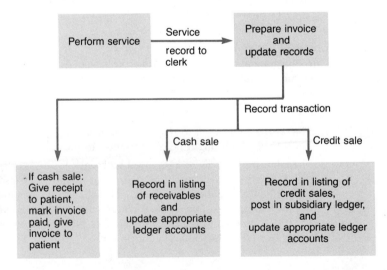

2. Monthly reporting

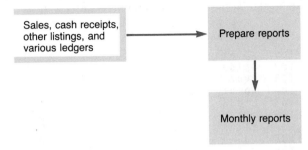

Computerized and manual data processing differ from each other in the following ways:

a. At the same time invoices are prepared, accounts can be updated; in a manual system invoices are prepared and then, later, the books are updated; in a computerized system, invoices may be prepared on the computer and records will be updated immediately.

b. When transactions are recorded, the appropriate general ledger accounts are immediately updated; in a manual system, general ledger accounts are updated at the end of the period when various journals are summed and posted.

c. Because of the above, interactive queries or reports generated at any point in time will reflect accurate account balances as of that point in time; by contrast, in a manual system, the only account balances which are apt to be correct between periodic postings are the subsidiary ledger accounts.

After deciding on the general processing steps that need to be followed, the initial set of "programs" to be used should be developed and tested.

These programs should make it possible for authorized users to:

a. Create records.
b. Update records.
c. Delete records.
d. Query the data base interactively for desired information.
e. Run programs to generate various formal reports.

If you have access to a data base program, write the programs required to generate the outputs you have specified. [answer 4]

Step 3. After the processing steps are specified, the next task is to implement the system. This involves creating any files that have not already been created and writing any "programs" which have not yet been written.

In addition to this, data must be entered into each of the files which have been created.

Listed below are some sample data, as of 30 September 1988, for selected clinic patients. (Dates are in day/month/year format.)

No.	PATIENT Last name	Initials	Beginning balance	Last payment date
101	Ahleth	D.M.	700.00	05/03/88
102	Spica	J.D.	160.00	10/08/88
103	Evpa	E.S.	625.00	15/06/88
104	Solor	T.L.	1,220.00	24/08/88
105	Lidow	J.F.	840.00	27/08/88
106	Wirec	H.C.	525.00	01/06/88
107	Elipha	S.S.	160.00	22/09/88
108	Shafo	A.B.	210.00	16/08/88
109	Unthe	K.V.	720.00	02/07/88
110	Dapro	F.W.	340.00	21/09/88
111	Cafor	K.F.	200.00	01/09/88
112	Pewa	F.C.	205.00	23/09/88
113	Falma	W.H.	170.00	16/09/88
114	Riper	A.G.	1,180.00	02/09/88
115	Hotog	C.A.	3,130.00	17/04/88
116	Dalo	M.I.	520.00	19/08/88
117	Ezebe	B.T.	1,020.00	05/08/88
118	Brone	L.C.	115.00	15/03/88
119	Mefro	F.M.	400.00	13/09/88
120	Alsha	R.Y.	110.00	14/07/88
121	Habnah	H.O.	first visit after 30 Sept. 88	
122	Drutho	S.T.	first visit after 30 Sept. 88	
123	Ansa	W.O.	first visit after 30 Sept. 88	
124	Turlit	U.M.	first visit after 30 Sept. 88	
125	Evand	H.S.	first visit after 30 Sept. 88	

These individuals had the following transactions with the clinic between 1 October 1988 and 31 December 1988:

TRANSACTION No.	Date	Type	Amount	Source Doc.	PATIENT No.	LastN.	Initials
3919	02/10/88	C	100.00	Cash rec.	110	Dapro	F.W.
3920	05/10/88	S	370.00	Pat.Rec.	102	Spica	J.D.
3921	05/10/88	C	160.00	Cash rec.	102	Spica	J.D.
3922	08/10/88	S	310.00	Cash rec.	108	Shafo	A.B.
3923	13/10/88	C	180.00	Cash rec.	111	Cafor	K.F.
3924	14/10/88	S	60.00	Pat.Rec.	104	Solor	T.L.
3925	15/10/88	C	250.00	Cash rec.	105	Lidow	J.F.
3926	18/10/88	C	360.00	Cash rec.	109	Unthe	K.V.
3927	19/10/88	D	100.00	memo	119	Mefro	F.M.
3928	20/10/88	C	500.00	Cash rec.	114	Riper	A.G.
3929	20/10/88	S	130.00	Pat. Rec.	120	Alsha	R.Y.
3930	22/10/88	C	125.00	Cash rec.	103	Evpa	E.S.
3931	23/10/88	C	200.00	Cash rec.	117	Ezebe	B.T.
3932	23/10/88	S	180.00	Pat.Rec.	121	Habnah	H.O.
3933	23/10/88	C	85.00	Cash rec.	113	Falma	W.H.
3934	28/10/88	C	160.00	Cash rec.	107	Elipha	S.S.
3935	31/10/88	C	175.00	Cash rec.	106	Wirec	H.C.
3936	08/11/88	C	205.00	Cash rec.	112	Pewa	F.C.
3937	10/11/88	C	370.00	Cash rec.	102	Spica	J.D.
3938	10/11/88	S	230.00	Pat.Rec.	102	Spica	J.D.
3939	10/11/88	C	200.00	Cash rec.	108	Shafo	A.B.

| | | TRANSACTION | | | | PATIENT | |
No.	Date	Type	Amount	Source Doc.	No.	LastN.	Initials
3940	11/11/88	S	140.00	Pat.Rec.	122	Drutho	S.T.
3941	11/11/88	C	100.00	Cash rec.	110	Dapro	F.W.
3942	12/11/88	S	90.00	Pat.Rec.	123	Ansa	W.O.
3943	13/11/88	C	250.00	Cash rec.	105	Lidow	J.F.
3944	13/11/88	C	180.00	Cash rec.	121	Habnah	H.O.
3945	13/11/88	S	220.00	Pat.Rec.	105	Lidow	J.F.
3946	17/11/88	C	125.00	Cash rec.	103	Evpa	E.S.
3947	17/11/88	C	360.00	Cash rec.	109	Unthe	K.V.
3948	20/11/88	C	500.00	Cash rec.	114	Riper	A.G.
3949	20/11/88	C	200.00	Cash rec.	117	Ezebe	B.T.
3950	20/11/88	S	90.00	Pat.Rec.	110	Dapro	F.W.
3951	20/11/88	S	130.00	Pat.Rec.	107	Elipha	S.S.
3952	22/11/88	S	175.00	Pat.Rec.	124	Turlit	U.M.
3953	22/11/88	D	80.00	memo	102	Spica	J.D.
3954	25/11/88	D	20.00	memo	111	Cafor	K.F.
3955	25/11/88	D	40.00	memo	107	Elipha	S.S.
3956	25/11/88	S	75.00	Pat.Rec.	111	Cafor	K.F.
3957	26/11/88	C	175.00	Cash rec.	106	Wirec	H.C.
3958	27/11/88	C	85.00	Cash rec.	113	Falma	W.H.
3959	30/11/88	S	40.00	Pat.Rec.	114	Riper	A.G.
3960	01/12/88	S	170.00	Pat.Rec.	109	Unthe	K.V.
3961	02/12/88	D	220.00	memo	114	Riper	A.G.
3962	03/12/88	C	300.00	Cash rec.	119	Mefro	F.M.
3963	06/12/88	D	150.00	memo	117	Ezebe	B.T.
3964	07/12/88	C	200.00	Cash rec.	108	Shafo	A.B.
3965	08/12/88	C	500.00	Cash rec.	115	Hotog	C.A.
3966	08/12/88	D	20.00	memo	110	Dapro	F.W.
3967	08/12/88	C	150.00	Cash rec.	102	Spica	J.D.
3968	08/12/88	S	260.00	Pat.Rec.	102	Spica	J.D.
3969	09/12/88	C	220.00	Cash rec.	116	Dalo	M.I.
3970	09/12/88	S	90.00	Pat.Rec.	116	Dalo	M.I.
3971	11/12/88	C	1,280.00	Cash rec.	104	Solor	T.L.
3972	13/12/88	C	100.00	Cash rec.	110	Dapro	F.W.
3973	13/12/88	S	140.00	Pat.Rec.	124	Turlit	U.M.
3974	13/12/88	S	430.00	Pat.Rec.	112	Pewa	F.C.
3975	14/12/88	C	250.00	Cash rec.	105	Lidow	J.F.
3976	17/12/88	S	190.00	Pat.Rec.	125	Evand	H.S.
3977	18/12/88	C	125.00	Cash rec.	103	Evpa	E.S.
3978	28/12/88	C	175.00	Cash rec.	106	Wirec	H.C.
3979	28/12/88	S	300.00	Pat.Rec.	106	Wirec	H.C.
3980	30/12/88	D	25.00	memo	120	Alsha	R.Y.
3981	30/12/88	C	50.00	Cash rec.	111	Cafor	K.F.
3982	31/12/88	W	700.00	memo	101	Ahleth	D.M.
3983	31/12/88	W	2,630.00	memo	115	Hotog	C.A.
3984	31/12/88	W	115.00	memo	118	Brone	L.C.

Because the information presented above may not be sufficient for you to generate all the outputs you specified in response to Requirement 1, you will probably have to modify your outputs and programs or make up additional data, such as patient addresses, to complete this exercise.

Step 4. After you have created the system, use it to generate the reports and other information you specified.

Dental Practice dBASE III PLUS Example

1. System outputs:
   a. Listing of beginning receivable balances and all transactions as well as listings for:
      (1) Beginning receivable balances.
      (2) Revenue earned.
      (3) Discounts granted.
      (4) Cash collections.
      (5) Accounts written off.
   b. Listings of all the information referred to above for individual patients or all patients meeting certain criteria.
   c. Summations of each item mentioned above.
   d. Computation of ending account balances.
   e. Counts of the number of records in each file.
   f. Counts of patients who meet certain criteria: for example, balances greater than zero.
   g. Reports showing for each patient name, transactions, and ending balance.
   h. Reports showing an aging of receivables.
2. System inputs:
   a. Account names.
   b. Subsidiary account numbers.
   c. Type of "transaction," these include:
      (1) Beginning balance.
      (2) Service revenue.
      (3) Cash collections.
      (4) Discounts.
      (5) Write-offs.
   d. Date of transaction.
   e. Amount of transaction.
   f. Source documents for transactions.
3. Organize the data into files.
      In this example, there are two files. The patient file includes basic patient information including patient number, surname, given names, account balance, and last payment date. The transaction file includes basic information about transactions including the transaction number, date, type, patient number, transaction amount, and source document for the transaction.
4. General processing steps.
      The main program, ACCOUNTS, and the functions it calls allow one to do the following:
   a. Add new patient accounts.
   b. Enter new transactions; this is done by typing a patient name; the program searches for all patients with the same last name; the user can either accept or reject the suggested accounts; if rejected, a new patient record is created; after this, the transaction is entered.
   c. Prepare an aging report based on the last date on which each patient has paid on account; both the last payment date and the balance of the patient's account appear in the patient file.

 d. Prepare a summary of each patient's transactions with the clinic; these summaries can be done for all patients or merely those who meet certain criteria; in specifying criteria, one must use the standard dBASE logical expressions.

 e. Prepare listings of transaction and patient data; two types of listings are possible: (1) formatted information for all data, which results in a report which repeats the patient data for each transaction related to that patient; and (2) unformatted information for selected fields in the file. Either of these listings can be done either for all records in the combined patient-transaction file or for any subset of the file; in specifying criteria to select records, one must use the standard dBASE logical expressions.

 f. All other tasks such as deleting records, counting or averaging various amounts, and making other queries, must be done either through the ASSIST menu or at the dBASE dot prompt; no facilities are provided in the programs to perform those functions.

5. Precisely define the data inputs and create the required data files.

 At this stage specific names are given to each of the data items, and their characteristics are determined. For example, the amount of a transaction might be given the name T__AMOUNT and defined as a real number, 10 characters wide, and accurate to two decimal places.

 The file PATIENT contains the following items:

Item	Name	Data type	Field len
Patient number	P__NUMB	Numeric	5 spaces
Patient surname	P__NAME__SUR	Character	20 spaces
Patient given names	P__NAME__GIV	Character	20 spaces
Account balance	ACCT__BAL	Numeric	10 spaces
Last payment date	LAST__PAID	Date	8 spaces

 The file TRANSACT contains the following items:

Item	Name	Data type	Field len
Transaction number	T__NUMB	Numeric	8 spaces
Transaction data	T__DATE	Date	8 spaces
Type of transaction	T__TYPE	Character	1 space
Patient number	P__NUMB	Numeric	5 spaces
Transaction amount	T__AMOUNT	Numeric	10 spaces
Source document	SOURCE__DOC	Character	10 spaces

6. Input initial data into the files.

 The beginning balance information has been entered into the file PATIENT. For each of these items, a transaction has been entered into the file TRANSACT which has "Beginning Balance" as its source document.

7. Set forth the required processing steps.

 In specifying these steps one must be precise enough so that, when followed, the desired output will be generated. In this example, the processing steps will generate the following outputs:

Aging report

Last name	Initials	Current	30+ days	60+ days	90+ days
Ahleth	D.M.	0.00	0.00	0.00	0.00
Alsha	R.Y.	0.00	0.00	0.00	215.00
Ansa	W.O.	0.00	90.00	0.00	0.00
Brone	L.C.	0.00	0.00	0.00	0.00
Cafor	K.F.	25.00	0.00	0.00	0.00
Dalo	M.I.	390.00	0.00	0.00	0.00
Dapro	F.W.	110.00	0.00	0.00	0.00
Drutho	S.T.	0.00	140.00	0.00	0.00
Elipha	S.S.	0.00	0.00	90.00	0.00
Evand	H.S.	190.00	0.00	0.00	0.00
Evpa	E.S.	250.00	0.00	0.00	0.00
Ezebe	B.T.	0.00	470.00	0.00	0.00
Falma	W.H.	0.00	0.00	0.00	0.00
Habnah	H.O.	0.00	0.00	0.00	0.00
Hotog	C.A.	0.00	0.00	0.00	0.00
Lidow	J.F.	310.00	0.00	0.00	0.00
Mefro	F.M.	0.00	0.00	0.00	0.00
Pewa	F.C.	0.00	430.00	0.00	0.00
Riper	A.G.	0.00	0.00	0.00	0.00
Shafo	A.B.	120.00	0.00	0.00	0.00
Solor	T.L.	0.00	0.00	0.00	0.00
Spica	J.D.	260.00	0.00	0.00	0.00
Turlit	U.M.	0.00	915.00	0.00	0.00
Unthe	K.V.	0.00	170.00	0.00	0.00
Wirec	H.C.	300.00	0.00	0.00	0.00
Total		1955.00	2215.00	90.00	215.00

Summary report of a patient's transactions with the clinic

Patient number: 111　　Patient name: Cafor　　　　　　　　　K.F.

Transaction number	Type	Date	Amount	Source document
1111	B	01/01/80	200.00	Beg.Bal.
3923	C	13/10/88	−180.00	Cash rec.
3954	D	25/11/88	−20.00	Memo
3956	S	25/11/88	75.00	Pat.record
3981	C	30/12/88	−50.00	Cash rec.

Account Balance & Last Payment Date　　　　25.00　　30/12/88

Unformatted listing of selected information

Rec.#	p__numb	p__name__sur	Last_paid	T_date	T_amount	Source doc.
1	101	Ahleth	05/03/88	01/01/80	−700.00	Beg.Bal.
2	101	Ahleth	05/03/88	31/12/80	−700.00	memo
17	110	Dapro	13/12/88	01/01/80	340.00	Beg.Bal.
18	110	Dapro	13/12/88	02/10/88	−100.00	Cash rec.
19	110	Dapro	13/12/88	11/11/88	−100.00	Cash rec.
20	110	Dapro	13/12/88	20/11/88	90.00	Pat.record
21	110	Dapro	13/12/88	08/12/88	−20.00	memo
22	110	Dapro	13/12/88	13/12/88	−100.00	Cash rec.
24	107	Elipha	28/10/88	01/01/80	160.00	Beg.Bal.
25	107	Elipha	28/10/88	28/10/88	−160.00	Cash rec.
26	107	Elipha	28/10/88	20/11/88	130.00	Pat.record
27	107	Elipha	28/10/88	25/11/88	−40.00	memo
29	103	Evpa	18/12/88	01/01/80	625.00	Beg.Bal.
30	103	Evpa	18/12/88	22/10/88	−125.00	Cash rec.

Rec.#	p__numb	p__name__sur	Last_paid	T__date	T__amount	Source doc.
31	103	Evpa	18/12/88	17/11/88	−125.00	Cash rec.
32	103	Evpa	18/12/88	18/12/88	−125.00	Cash rec.
45	105	Lidow	14/12/88	01/01/80	840.00	Beg.Bal.
46	105	Lidow	14/12/88	15/10/88	−250.00	Cash rec.
47	105	Lidow	14/12/88	13/11/88	−250.00	Cash rec.
48	105	Lidow	14/12/88	13/11/88	220.00	Pat.record
49	105	Lidow	14/12/88	14/12/88	−250.00	Cash rec.
61	108	Shafo	07/12/88	01/01/80	210.00	Beg.Bal.
62	108	Shafo	07/12/88	08/10/88	310.00	Pat.record
63	108	Shafo	07/12/88	10/11/88	−200.00	Cash rec.
64	108	Shafo	07/12/88	07/12/88	−200.00	Cash rec.
65	104	Solor	11/12/88	01/01/80	1220.00	Beg.Bal.
66	104	Solor	11/12/88	14/10/88	60.00	Pat.record
67	104	Solor	11/12/88	11/12/88	−1280.00	Cash rec.
68	102	Spica	08/12/88	01/01/80	160.00	Beg.Bal.
69	102	Spica	08/12/88	05/10/88	370.00	Pat.record
70	102	Spica	08/12/88	05/10/88	−160.00	Cash rec.
71	102	Spica	08/12/88	10/11/88	−370.00	Cash rec.
72	102	Spica	08/12/88	10/11/88	230.00	Pat record
73	102	Spica	08/12/88	22/11/88	−80.00	memo
74	102	Spica	08/12/88	08/12/88	−150.00	Cash rec.
75	102	Spica	08/12/88	08/12/88	260.00	Pat.record
78	109	Unthe	17/11/88	01/01/80	720.00	Beg.Bal.
79	109	Unthe	17/11/88	18/10/88	−360.00	Cash rec.
80	109	Unthe	17/11/88	17/11/88	−360.00	Cash rec.
81	109	Unthe	17/11/88	01/12/88	170.00	Pat.record
82	106	Wirec	28/12/88	01/01/80	525.00	Beg.Bal.
83	106	Wirec	28/12/88	31/10/88	−175.00	Cash rec.
84	106	Wirec	28/12/88	26/11/88	−175.00	Cash rec.
85	106	Wirec	28/12/88	28/12/88	−175.00	Cash rec.
86	106	Wirec	28/12/88	28/12/88	300.00	Pat.record

Listing of data in formatted report

No.	Name		End bal	Last pmt	Tran#	T__date		Amt.	Source doc.
101	Ahleth	D.M.	0.00	05/03/88	1101	01/01/80	B	700.00	Beg. Bal.
101	Ahleth	D.M.	0.00	05/03/88	3982	31/12/88	W	−700.00	memo
110	Dapro	F.W.	110.00	13/12/88	1110	01/01/80	B	340.00	Beg.Bal.
110	Dapro	F.W.	110.00	13/12/88	3919	02/10/88	C	−100.00	Cash rec.
110	Dapro	F.W.	110.00	13/12/88	3941	11/11/88	C	−100.00	Cash rec.
110	Dapro	F.W.	110.00	13/12/88	3950	20/11/88	S	90.00	Pat.rec.
110	Dapro	F.W.	110.00	13/12/88	3966	08/12/88	D	−20.00	memo
110	Dapro	F.W.	110.00	13/12/88	3972	13/12/88	C	−100.00	Cash rec.
107	Elipha	S.S.	90.00	28/10/88	1107	01/01/80	B	160.00	Beg.Bal.
107	Elipha	S.S.	90.00	28/10/88	3934	28/10/88	C	−160.00	Cash rec.
107	Elipha	S.S.	90.00	28/10/88	3951	20/11/88	S	130.00	Pat.rec.
107	Elipha	S.S.	90.00	28/10/88	3955	25/11/88	D	−40.00	memo
103	Evpa	E.S.	250.00	18/12/88	1103	01/01/80	B	625.00	Beg.Bal.
103	Evpa	E.S.	250.00	18/12/88	3930	22/10/88	C	−125.00	Cash rec.
103	Evpa	E.S.	250.00	18/12/88	3946	17/11/88	C	−125.00	Cash rec.
103	Evpa	E.S.	250.00	18/12/88	3977	18/12/88	C	−125.00	Cash rec.
105	Lidow	J.F.	310.00	14/12/88	1105	01/01/80	B	840.00	Beg.Bal.
105	Lidow	J.F.	310.00	14/12/88	3925	15/10/88	C	−250.00	Cash rec.
105	Lidow	J.F.	310.00	14/12/88	3943	13/11/88	C	−250.00	Cash rec.
105	Lidow	J.F.	310.00	14/12/88	3945	13/11/88	S	220.00	Pat.rec.
105	Lidow	J.F.	310.00	14/12/88	3975	14/12/88	C	−250.00	Cash rec.
108	Shafo	A.B.	120.00	07/12/88	1108	01/01/80	B	210.00	Beg.Bal.
108	Shafo	A.B.	120.00	07/12/88	3922	08/10/88	S	310.00	Pat.rec.
108	Shafo	A.B.	120.00	07/12/88	3939	10/11/88	C	−200.00	Cash rec.

No.	Name		End bal	Last pmt	Tran#	T_date		Amt.	Source doc.
108	Shafo	A.B.	120.00	07/12/88	3964	07/12/88	C	−200.00	Cash rec.
104	Solor	T.L.	0.00	11/12/88	1104	01/01/80	B	1220.00	Beg.Bal.
104	Solor	T.L.	0.00	11/12/88	3924	14/10/88	S	60.00	Pat.rec.
104	Solor	T.L.	0.00	11/12/88	3971	11/12/88	C	−1280.00	Cash rec.
102	Spica	J.D.	260.00	08/12/88	1102	01/01/80	B	160.00	Beg.Bal.
102	Spica	J.D.	260.00	08/12/88	3920	05/10/88	S	370.00	Pat.rec.
102	Spica	J.D.	260.00	08/12/88	3921	05/10/88	C	−160.00	Cash rec.
102	Spica	J.D.	260.00	08/12/88	3937	10/11/88	C	−370.00	Cash rec.
102	Spica	J.D.	260.00	08/12/88	3938	10/11/88	S	230.00	Pat.rec.
102	Spica	J.D.	260.00	08/12/88	3953	22/11/88	D	−80.00	memo
102	Spica	J.D.	260.00	08/12/88	3967	08/12/88	C	−150.00	Cash rec.
102	Spica	J.D.	260.00	08/12/88	3968	08/12/88	S	260.00	Pat.rec.
109	Unthe	K.V.	170.00	17/11/88	1109	01/01/80	B	720.00	Beg.Bal.
109	Unthe	K.V.	170.00	17/11/88	3926	18/10/88	C	−360.00	Cash rec.
109	Unthe	K.V.	170.00	17/11/88	3947	17/11/88	C	−360.00	Cash rec.
109	Unthe	K.V.	170.00	17/11/88	3960	01/12/88	S	170.00	Pat.rec.
106	Wirec	H.C.	300.00	28/12/88	1106	01/01/80	B	525.00	Beg.Bal.
106	Wirec	H.C.	300.00	28/12/88	3935	31/10/88	C	−175.00	Cash rec.
106	Wirec	H.C.	300.00	28/12/88	3957	26/11/88	C	−175.00	Cash rec.
106	Wirec	H.C.	300.00	28/12/88	3978	28/12/88	C	−175.00	Cash rec.
106	Wirec	H.C.	300.00	28/12/88	3979	28/12/88	S	300.00	Pat.rec.
*** Total ***								1610.00	

8. Enter the transaction data.

Enter all the transaction data listed above except that for transaction 3919, a $100 cash receipt from Dapro.

On the disks (available from instructors only) that accompany the text, there are a number of files which relate to the Dental Practice Accounts Receivable Problem. These files are described below.

This exercise uses two data base files. The programs included on the disk call files are called PATIENT.DBF, which has in it the basic information about patients, and TRANSACT.DBF, which has in it all transaction data.

There are two SETS of data base files included on the disk. The first set consists of TRANSACT.DBF and PATIENT.DBF. These files have in them data after having made all the transactions included in the exercise. The second set consists of TRNORG.DBF and PATORG.DBF. These files contain initial data for the Dental Practice, prior to any of the transaction information set forth in the case. In order to use these files, TRNORG.DBF should be copied to another disk and given the name TRANSACT.DBF (this file consists of the initial transaction data). PATORG.DBF should also be copied to another disk and given the name PATIENT.DBF (this file consists of the initial patient data).

There are eight programs that have been written for the accounts receivable example. In addition, there is one general program in the file BORDERS.PRG.*

The program ACCOUNTS (run by entering the command DO ACCOUNTS, file ACCOUNTS.PRG) is the main program. This program calls the program ARINIT (file ARINIT.PRG) which opens the data base files, with the appropriate index file (file ARNAMES.NDX) used by the program and sets certain default values for the

---

* This latter program comes from T. W. Carlton and C. O. Stewart, dBASE III Plus Applications Library, Que Corporation, 1986.

exercise. The ACCOUNTS program also displays the main menu which presents one with the following options:

Main menu
1. Add new patients
2. Record transactions
3. Prepare aging report
4. Create patient summary data
5. List data for selected patients

0. EXIT TO dBASE DOT PROMPT

Option 1, add new patients, runs the program ARAPPEND.PRG which allows one to create new patient records to be added to the patient file.

Option 2, record transactions, runs the program ARTRANS.PRG which allows one to enter recognized service revenue, cash collections, discounts, or to write off accounts. This program calls the screen format files ARTRANS.FMT and ARSHOREC.FMT. Should one not find an appropriate patient for a particular transaction, the program ARTRANS will call the program ARNEWPAT, in file ARNEWPAT.PRG which allows one to enter data on a new patient.

Option 3, prepare aging report, runs the program ARAGING.PRG which in turn calls the report form program ARAGING.FRM. This option prepares an aging of accounts receivable.

Option 4, create patient summary data, runs the program, ARBILLS.PRG, which presents detailed information, including all transactions, for some or all of the Dental Practice's patients. This program provides the kind of information that would be required in order to send patients bills.

Option 5, list data for selected patients, runs the program ARLIST.PRG, which uses the report form file ARLIST.FRM. Selecting this option lists a variety of data for all or selected patients.

Option 0, EXIT TO dBASE DOT PROMPT, stops the program from running and returns one to dBASE's interactive mode.

Prepared by C. Dirksen

SEVEN

COSTING METHODS FOR MEASURING INVENTORY AND COST OF GOODS SOLD

PURPOSE

Chapter 6 discussed accounting for sales revenue and cost of goods sold. You were introduced to the periodic and perpetual inventory systems. In Chapter 6, we assumed that the cost of items purchased for inventory did not change over time. In reality, however, the unit cost of inventory items often will change each time a new purchase order is placed. In this chapter, we will discuss accounting for inventory and cost of goods sold when unit costs are changing.

Accounting for inventories affects both the balance sheet (current assets) and the income statement (cost of goods sold). Most financial statements contain detailed notes concerning inventories. On the facing page, notice that Union Carbide does not include depreciation as a cost of its inventory.

LEARNING OBJECTIVES

1. Analyze the effects of inventory errors.
2. Identify what items should be included in inventory.
3. Describe and use the four inventory costing methods with the periodic and perpetual inventory systems.
4. Explain the comparability principle.
5. Apply the lower of cost or market rule.
6. Estimate ending inventory and cost of goods sold.
7. Expand your accounting vocabulary by learning about the "Important Terms Defined in This Chapter."
8. Apply the knowledge gained from this chapter.

ORGANIZATION

Part A—measuring ending inventory and cost of goods sold with a periodic inventory system
1. Inventory effects on the measurement of income.
2. Measuring inventory cost.
3. Application of the inventory costing methods with the periodic inventory system.

Part B—application of a perpetual inventory system and selected inventory costing problems
1. Application of the inventory costing methods with a perpetual inventory system.
2. Lower of cost or market; damaged goods; estimating inventory and cost of goods sold.

Union Carbide Canada Limited

Consolidated Balance Sheet

December 31 ($ thousands)	1986	1985
Assets		
Current Assets		
Accounts receivable	$ 72,908	$ 74,319
Inventories	58,761	54,446
	131,669	128,765

Notes to the Consolidated Financial Statements

Note 1
Summary of Significant Accounting Policies
Inventories

Inventory values do not include
depreciation of fixed assets and are
stated at the lower of average cost
and net realizable value.

Note 3
Supplementary Balance Sheet Detail

($ thousands)	1986	1985
Inventories		
Raw materials and supplies	$ 10,189	$ 11,036
Work in process	32,026	29,967
Finished goods	16,546	13,443
	$ 58,761	$ 54,446

PART A—MEASURING ENDING INVENTORY AND COST OF GOODS SOLD WITH A PERIODIC INVENTORY SYSTEM

Inventory Effects on the Measurement of Income

A direct relationship exists between ending inventory and cost of goods sold. When the periodic inventory system (Chapter 6) is used, items not in the ending inventory are assumed to have been sold. Thus, the measurement of ending inventory affects both the balance sheet (assets) and the income statement (cost of goods sold and net income). The measurement of ending inventory affects not only the net income for that period but also the net income for the **next accounting period.** This two-period effect occurs because the ending inventory for one period is the beginning inventory for the next accounting period. The 19A and 19B income statements for SAL Company are shown in panel A of Exhibit 7–1. The reported 19A ending inventory was $10,000. Notice that this amount is shown as the beginning inventory for 19B.

An error in measuring the 19A ending inventory would affect both 19A and 19B income. For example, if the 19A ending inventory for SAL Company should have been $11,000 (i.e., $1000 more than reported), both 19A and 19B income would be incorrect by $1,000. The restated income statements for SAL Company are shown in panel B of Exhibit 7–1. The various accounts that are affected by the $1,000 error are identified in panel C. Two generalizations can be made concerning the impact of an inventory error:

1. **In the period of the change**—An increase in the amount of the ending inventory for a period decreases cost of goods sold by the same amount, which in turn increases pretax income for that period by the same amount. A decrease in the amount of ending inventory increases cost of goods sold, which in turn decreases pretax income for that period by the same amount.

2. **In the next period**—An increase in the amount of the ending inventory for a period increases the beginning inventory for the next period. The increase in beginning inventory increases cost of goods sold, which decreases the pretax income of the **next period** by the same amount. In contrast, a decrease in the amount of the ending inventory for a period decreases cost of goods sold of the next period, which increases pretax income of the **next period** by the same amount. After applying the closing entries to the income statement accounts, the income effect of an error in Year 1 will directly affect the retained earnings for that year. However, this misstatement of retained earnings in 19A will be offset by the misstatement in 19B leaving the ending balance for 19B correctly stated. The effect of the error shown in Exhibit 7–1 on retained earnings assumes a 20% income tax rate and no dividends. As noted, the retained earnings reported in 19B is the same as the corrected amount.

Exhibit 7–1 Impact of error in measuring inventory

2 year

Panel A:

SAL COMPANY
Income Statement (as reported)

	19A	19B
Sales revenue	$100,000	$110,000
Cost of goods sold:*		
Beginning inventory	$ –0–	$10,000
Purchases	70,000	58,000
Goods available for sale	70,000	68,000
Ending inventory	10,000	–0–
Cost of goods sold	60,000	68,000
Gross margin	40,000	42,000
Expenses	35,000	35,500
Pretax income	$ 5,000	$ 6,500

* See Chapter 6: BI + P − EI = CGS.

Panel B:

SAL COMPANY
Income Statement (corrected)

	19A	19B
Sales revenue	$100,000	$110,000
Cost of goods sold:		
Beginning inventory	$ –0–	$11,000
Purchases	70,000	58,000
Goods available for sale	70,000	69,000
Ending inventory	11,000	–0–
Cost of goods sold	59,000	69,000
Gross margin	41,000	41,000
Expenses	35,000	35,500
Pretax income	$ 6,000	$ 5,500

Panel C—Comparison:

		As reported	Corrected
19A	Ending inventory	$10,000	$11,000
19A	Cost of goods sold	60,000	59,000
19A	Gross margin	40,000	41,000
19A	Retained earnings (original amounts assumed)	4,800	5,600
19A	Pretax income	5,000	6,000
19B	Beginning inventory	10,000	11,000
19B	Goods available for sale	68,000	69,000
19B	Gross margin	42,000	41,000
19B	Pretax income	6,500	5,500
19B	Retained earnings (original amounts assumed)	10,000	10,000

An error in measuring ending inventory is caused by either incorrectly counting the inventory or by using an incorrect unit cost to value the inventory. Accountants use great care in counting and valuing inventory, but errors do occur. For example, several years ago the financial statements of Lafayette Radio Electronics Corporation had the following note:

> Subsequent to the issuance of its financial statements the company discovered a computational error in the amount of $1,046,000 in the calculation of its year-end inventory which resulted in an overstatement of ending inventory.

Items Included in Inventory

Usually, inventory includes tangible property that (1) is held for sale in the normal course of business or (2) will be used in producing goods or services for sale. Inventory is reported on the balance sheet as a current asset because it usually will be used or converted into cash within one year or within the next operating cycle of the business, whichever is the longer. Because inventory is less liquid (i.e., less readily convertible to cash) than accounts receivable, it usually is listed below accounts receivable on the balance sheet.

The kinds of inventory normally held depend upon the characteristics of the business:[1]

Retail or wholesale business:

Merchandise inventory—goods (or merchandise) held for resale in the normal course of business. The goods usually are acquired in a finished condition and are ready for sale without further processing.

Manufacturing business:[2]

Finished goods inventory—goods manufactured by the business, completed and ready for sale.

Work in process inventory—goods in the process of being manufactured but not yet completed as finished goods. When completed, work in process inventory becomes finished goods inventory.

Raw materials inventory—items acquired by purchase, growth (such as food products), or extraction (natural resources) for processing into finished goods. Such items are accounted for as raw materials inventory until used. When used, their cost is included in the work in process inventory (along with other processing costs such as direct labour and factory overhead). The flow of inventory costs in a manufacturing environment can be diagrammed as follows:

---

[1] Supplies on hand usually are reported as prepaid expenses.

[2] Subsequent accounting courses present a complete discussion of inventory measurement and accounting in a manufacturing environment.

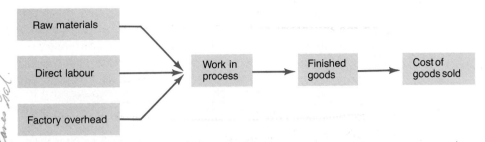

The work in process inventory includes (1) the cost of raw materials used, (2) the **direct** labour incurred in the manufacturing process, and (3) the factory overhead costs. Direct labour cost represents the earnings of employees who work directly on the products being manufactured. Factory overhead costs include all manufacturing costs that are not raw material or direct labour costs. For example, the salary of the plant surpervisor is included in factory overhead.

When counting the **physical quantity** of goods in the inventory, a company should include all items to which it has **ownership,** regardless of their locations. In purchase and sale transactions, accounting focuses on the passage of ownership. Usually when ownership passes, one party records a sale and the other party records a purchase. At this point, goods should be included in the inventory of the purchaser and not in the inventory of the seller. In a sale transaction, the basic guideline is that ownership to the goods passes at the **time intended by the parties** to the transaction. Usually, ownership passes when the seller gives the goods to the buyer; however, there are situations in which this is not the case.

The terms of sale have conditions that can affect the passage of title to the goods to the buyer. Three conditions are generally encountered either explicitly in the terms of sale or implicitly in the usual trade relations between the buyer and seller. Conditions of quantity, time, and place of delivery, if not followed by the seller, can lead to a rescinding of the contract by the buyer. Two common shorthand notations for terms which signify the relative conditions to be followed are: (1) FOB (free on board) at a location specified which signifies the seller's responsibility to place the goods on the type of transport specified and have the goods delivered at the seller's expense to the location specified, such as FOB Halifax. (2) CIF (cost, insurance, freight) signifies the seller agrees the price includes insurance in the name of the buyer, shipping, and freight to the location specified, such as CIF Ottawa.[3] The 1980 Incoterms statement by the International Chamber of Commerce of Paris, France, outlines the more generally accepted shipping terms. FOR or FOT stands for free on rail car or free on a truck at a specific departure point. FOS stands for free alongside a ship at a particular port. Ex QUAY implies port, import costs, and taxes are paid to a

---

[3] J. E. Smyth and D. A. Soberman, *The Law and Business Administration in Canada,* 4th ed. (Scarborough, Ont.: Prentice-Hall Canada, 1983), pp. 362–78.

specific port. At this point it is worth noting that the term FOB destination commonly found in accounting textbooks is no longer an accepted term by transportation authorities. CIF or C&F at port of destination is now used in place of the older term. Because the terms and conditions such as FOB, CIF, and COD (cash on delivery) are only part of the sales terms that govern the passage of title to the goods to the buyer, the accountant must be careful to understand these terms in order to appropriately record the sale. Care will be needed when these terms are encountered to read the description following FOB or CIF and so on because it is this description that determines the conditions of sale, not the abbreviations themselves.

The passage-of-ownership guideline is used to apply the revenue principle (Exhibit 4–5). Without the passage-of-ownership guideline, the financial statements could be manipulated to overstate revenue by entering **sales orders** received, regardless of whether ownership to the goods has passed to the buyer. Conversely, costs could be manipulated by not recording purchases even though ownership to the goods has passed.

When a company has possession of goods that it does not own, it should exclude those goods from the inventory. This situation often occurs when goods are on **consignment** for sale on a commission basis. The supplier (called the consignor) legally retains ownership to the goods on consignment, although the goods are in the physical possession of the party that will sell them (called the consignee). The consignor should include the goods in the ending inventory, while the consignee should exclude them from the ending inventory.

Measuring Inventory Cost

Goods in inventory are recorded in conformity with the **cost principle** as follows:

> In the case of merchandise purchased for resale, or of raw materials which are to enter into production, cost may be said to be "laid-down" cost; for example, an invoice cost (in terms of Canadian dollars) plus customs and excise duties and freight and cartage. In the case of work in process and finished goods, cost will include the laid-down cost of material plus the cost of direct labour applied to the product and ordinarily the applicable share of overhead expense properly chargeable to production.[4]

In conformity with the cost principle, indirect expenditures related to the purchase of goods, such as freight, insurance, and storage, theoretically should be included in measuring the purchase cost of the goods acquired. However, because these incidental costs often are not **material in amount** (see the materiality constraint, Exhibit 4–5), they do not have to be assigned to the inventory cost. Thus, for practical reasons, some companies use the **net invoice price** to assign a unit cost to goods and record the indirect expenditures as a separate cost which is reported as an expense.

---

[4] *CICA Handbook*, Section 3030.

Chapter 6 discussed the assignment of **dollar cost** to (a) the ending inventory and (b) cost of goods sold in situations in which unit purchase (or manufacturing) cost remained constant. This chapter expands those discussions to the typical situation in which the cost per unit of the goods stocked changes during the annual accounting period.

Chapter 6 presented two alternative inventory systems used to accumulate data to facilitate determination of (a) the ending inventory and (b) cost of goods sold. The two alternative inventory systems are:[5]

1. **Periodic inventory system**—This system accumulates total merchandise acquisition cost (including the beginning inventory). At the **end of the accounting period,** the ending inventory is measured by means of a physical inventory count of all goods remaining on hand. The units counted on hand then are valued (costed) in dollars by using appropriate unit purchase costs. The periodic inventory system measures **cost of goods sold** as a residual amount; that is:

$$BI + P - EI = CGS$$

2. **Perpetual inventory system**—This system keeps a detailed daily inventory record throughout the period for each item stocked. This record includes (a) the beginning inventory, (b) each purchase, (c) each issue (i.e., sales), and (d) a continuous (perpetual or running) balance of the inventory. This system measures cost of goods sold and ending inventory without a physical inventory count at the end of each accounting period. Under this system, the **ending inventory** can be viewed as a residual amount; that is:

$$BI + P - CGS = EI$$

In this part of the chapter, we discuss several alternative inventory costing methods using the **periodic inventory system.** Part B of this chapter discusses these methods with a perpetual inventory system.

Purpose of Inventory Costing Methods

The four generally accepted inventory costing methods commonly used are:

1. Weighted average.
2. First-in, first-out (FIFO).
3. Last-in, first-out (LIFO).
4. Specific identification. *each item had an inventory record. (high priced items not many units*

---

[5] Often a company will use one of the systems for certain items stocked and the other system for the remaining items. The choice usually depends upon such factors as the nature of the item (size), unit cost, number of units stocked, and cost to implement the system.

Exhibit 7–2 Illustrative inventory data

SUMMER RETAIL STORE
19A Illustrative Data—Beginning Inventory, Purchases, and Sales

Transactions	Symbol	Number of units	Unit cost	Total cost
Beginning inventory, January 1, 19A (carried over from last period)	BI	100	$6	$ 600
Purchases during 19A:				
January 3, first purchase	P	50	7	$ 350
June 12, second purchase	P	200	8	1,600
December 20, third purchase	P	120	9	1,080
Total purchases during 19A		370		3,030
Goods available for sale during the year . . .		470		3,630
Goods sold during 19A:				
January 6 (unit sales price, $10)	S	40		
June 18 (unit sales price, $12)	S	220		
December 24 (unit sales price, $14)	S	60		
Total sales during 19A		320		?
Ending inventory, December 31, 19A (units 470 − 320)	EI	150		?

If unit costs of items purchased for inventory did not change, there would be no need for alternative inventory costing methods. When unit costs change, an accounting method is needed to assign the various costs to units in the ending inventory and to the units that have been sold. Consider Summer Retail Store (Exhibit 7–2). The total cost of goods available for sale is $3,630. There are four different unit costs ($6, $7, $8, and $9). The amounts of ending inventory and cost of goods sold that are reported depend upon the costing method that is selected.

The four inventory costing methods are **alternative allocation methods** for assigning the total amount of goods available for sale (BI + P) between (a) ending inventory (reported as an asset at the end of the period) and (b) cost of goods sold (reported as an expense of the period). Refer to the data for Summer Retail Store given in Exhibit 7–2. The two allocated amounts were calculated using the weighted-average inventory costing method, as shown below. At this point you need to be concerned about how the two amounts were calculated.

	Units	Amount
Goods available for sale (total amount to be allocated)	470	$3,630
Cost allocation:		
Ending inventory (determined by inventory count and then costed at weighted-average unit cost)	150	1,158
Cost of goods sold (residual amount)	320	$2,472

Exhibit 7–3 Illustration of cost allocation

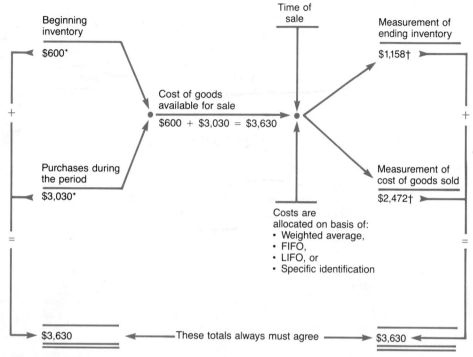

* Data from Exhibit 7–2.
† Based on the weighted-average cost method.

The amount of **goods available for sale** ($3,630) was allocated between **ending inventory** ($1,158) and **cost of goods sold** ($2,472). The sum of these two amounts (and the related units) must be the same as goods available for sale. This cost allocation procedure also is shown graphically in Exhibit 7–3.

Inventory Costing Methods Illustrated

The choice among the four inventory costing methods is not based on the physical flow of goods on and off the shelves. For most companies, the actual **physical flow** of goods is first-in, first-out (FIFO). Regardless of the physical flow of goods, a company can use any of the inventory costing methods. Generally accepted accounting principles only require that the inventory costing method used be rational and systematic. The method selected should be the one to achieve the fairest matching of costs against the revenues recognized.

A company is not required to use the same inventory costing method for all inventory items, and no particular justification is needed for the selection of one or more of the acceptable methods. However, a change in method is significant and needs special disclosures in the notes to the financial statements because such a change would violate the comparability characteristic described in Exhibit 4–5.

Weighted-Average Inventory Costing Method

The weighted-average method requires computation of the weighted-average unit cost of the goods available for sale. In a periodic inventory system, the computed unit cost is multiplied by the **number of units** in inventory to derive the total cost of ending inventory. Cost of goods sold is determined by subtracting the ending inventory amount from the amount of goods available for sale. For example, the weighted-average method would be applied by Summer Retail Store (Exhibit 7–2) as follows using a **periodic** inventory system.[6]

Step 1—Computation of the weighted-average unit cost for the period:

$$\frac{\text{Total goods available for sale—at cost}}{\text{Total goods available for sale—units}} = \frac{\$3,630}{470} = \$7.72 \left\{ \begin{array}{l} \text{Weighted-} \\ \text{average} \\ \text{cost per} \\ \text{unit for} \\ \text{the period} \end{array} \right.$$

Step 2—Allocation of the cost of goods available for sale under the periodic inventory system:

	Units	Amount
Goods available for sale (Exhibit 7–2)	470	$3,630
Ending inventory (150 units × $7.72)	150	1,158*
Cost of goods sold (residual amount)	320	$2,472†

* Reported on the balance sheet.
† Reported as an expense on the income statement. This amount can be verified as 320 units × $7.72 = $2,470 (a $2 rounding error).

The weighted-average cost method is rational, systematic, easy to apply, and not subject to manipulation. It is representative of costs during the entire period including the beginning inventory rather than of the cost only at the beginning, end, or at one point during the period.[7] Representative costs are reported on both the balance sheet (ending inventory) and the income statement (cost of goods sold).

First-In, First-Out Inventory Costing Method

The first-in, first-out method, frequently called **FIFO,** assumes that the oldest units (i.e., the first costs in) are the first units sold (i.e., the first costs out). The

---

[6] When an average cost is used, uneven unit cost amounts usually are rounded to the nearest cent. The rounded unit cost amount is used to compute the ending inventory amount which allocates any rounding error to cost of goods sold. Under the perpetual inventory system, a moving average unit cost (rather than the weighted-average unit cost) usually is used (see Part B).

[7] A weighted-average unit cost rather than a simple average of the unit costs must be used. For example, ($6 + $7 + $8 + 9) ÷ 4 = $7.50 would be incorrect because it does not consider the number of units at each unit cost.

units in the beginning inventory are treated as if they were sold first. Then the units from the first purchase are sold next, and so on until the units left in the ending inventory all come from the most recent purchases. FIFO allocates the oldest unit costs to cost of goods sold and the most recent unit costs to the ending inventory.

Often, FIFO is justified because it is consistent with the actual physical flow of the goods. In most businesses, the first goods placed in stock are the first goods sold. However, FIFO can be used regardless of the actual physical flow of goods because the objective of FIFO is to allocate costs to ending inventory and to cost of goods sold in a systematic and rational manner.

FIFO is applied by Summer Retail Store (Exhibit 7–2) as follows under a **periodic** inventory system:

	Units	Unit cost	Total cost
Goods available for sale (Exhibit 7–2)	470		$3,630
Valuation of ending inventory (FIFO):			
At latest unit costs, 150 units:			
From December 20 purchase (latest)	120	$9	$1,080
From June 12 purchase (next latest)	30	8	240
Valuation, FIFO basis	150		1,320*
Cost of goods sold (residual FIFO amount)	320		$2,310†

* Report on balance sheet.
† Report as an expense on income statement. This amount can be verified as follows: Units sold at oldest costs—100 units × $6 = $600, plus 50 units × $7 = $350, plus 170 units × $8 = $1,360, which sum to $2,310.

The FIFO method is rational, systematic, easy to apply, and not subject to manipulation. On the balance sheet, the FIFO ending inventory amount is valued on the basis of the most recent unit costs. It is likely to provide a realistic valuation prevailing at the balance sheet date. In contrast, on the income statement, cost of goods sold is at the oldest unit costs, which may not reflect the current cost of items that were sold. The significance of the impact of FIFO on the income statement (i.e., cost of goods sold and income) and the balance sheet (i.e., the ending inventory amount) depends on how much the unit costs change during the period.

Last-In, First-Out Inventory Costing Method

The last-in, first-out method, often called **LIFO,** assumes that the most recently acquired goods are sold first. Regardless of the physical flow of goods, LIFO treats the costs of the most recent units purchased as cost of goods sold. Therefore the unit costs of the beginning inventory and the earlier purchases remain in the ending inventory. The LIFO flow assumption is the exact opposite of the FIFO flow assumption.

LIFO is applied by Summer Retail Store (Exhibit 7–2) as follows under a **periodic** inventory system:

	Units	Unit cost	Total cost
Goods available for sale (Exhibit 7–2)	470		$3,630
Valuation of ending inventory (LIFO):			
At older unit costs, 150 units:			
From beginning inventory (oldest)	100	$6	$600
From January 3 purchase (next oldest)	50	7	350
Valuation, LIFO basis	150		950*
Cost of goods sold (residual LIFO amount)	320		$2,680†

* Report on balance sheet.
† Report as an expense on income statement. This amount can be verified as follows: Units sold at latest costs—120 units @ $9 = $1,080, plus 200 units @ $8 = $1,600, which sum to $2,680.

The LIFO method is rational and systematic. However, it can be manipulated by buying (or not buying) goods at the end of a period when unit costs have changed. By this action, it is possible to manipulate cost of goods sold and, hence, reported income. On the income statement, LIFO cost of goods sold is based on the latest unit costs, which is a realistic measurement of the current cost of items that were sold. In contrast, on the balance sheet, the ending inventory amount is based on the oldest unit costs, which may be an unrealistic valuation. The comparative impact of LIFO will be discussed later.[8]

Specific Identification Inventory Costing Method

When the specific identification method is used, the cost of each item sold is individually identified and recorded as cost of goods sold. This method requires keeping track of the purchase cost of each item. This is done either by (1) coding the purchase cost on each unit before placing it in stock, or (2) keeping a separate record of the unit and identifying it with a serial number. If the 40 units sold by Summer Retail (Exhibit 7–2) on January 6 were selected from the units that were purchased at $6 each, the cost of goods sold amount for that sale would be measured as 40 units × $6 = $240. Alternatively, if 20 of the units were selected from those that cost $6 each and the other 20 from those that cost $7 each, cost of goods sold would be measured as (20 units × $6) + (20 units × $7) = $260.

The specific identification method is tedious and impractical when unit costs change frequently or a large number of different items are stocked. On the other hand, when there are "big-ticket" items such as automobiles and expensive jewelry, this method is appropriate because each item tends to be different from the other items. In such situations, the selling price of an item usually is based on a markup over its cost. However, the method may be manipulated when the units are identical because one can affect the cost of goods sold and the ending

---

[8] The discussion assumes an item-by-item application of LIFO and costing of goods sold currently throughout the period. Other approaches to the computation of LIFO are possible but the results are approximately the same as the item-by-item approach used here. It should be noted, as well, that LIFO is not popular in Canada because it is not allowed for Canadian income tax computations. However, it is possible to use LIFO for book purposes while retaining one of the other methods for income tax purposes.

inventory accounts by "picking and choosing" from among the several available unit costs, even though the goods are identical in other respects. In the previous example, cost of goods sold was either $240 or $260, depending on which items were chosen for sale.

Comparison of the Inventory Costing Methods

Each of the four alternative inventory costing methods is in conformity with generally accepted accounting principles. However, each method may produce significantly different income and asset (i.e., ending inventory) amounts. To illustrate this difference, the comparative results for Summer Retail Store are as follows:

	Sales revenue	Cost of goods sold	Gross margin	Balance sheet (inventory)
Weighted average	$3,880	$2,472	$1,408	$1,158
FIFO	3,880	2,310	1,570	1,320
LIFO (end of period)	3,880	2,680	1,200	950

From the above results, we see that when unit costs are changing, each method will give different income and different inventory amounts. Notice that the difference in **the gross margin** among each of the methods is the same as the difference in the inventory amounts. The method that gives the highest ending inventory amount also gives the highest pretax income amount and vice versa. The weighted-average cost method will give pretax income and inventory amounts that are between the FIFO and LIFO extremes.

We will focus now on a comparison of the FIFO and LIFO methods because they usually represent the extreme, opposite effects. Note in the comparison above that unit costs were **increasing. When unit costs are rising, LIFO produces lower pretax income and a lower inventory valuation than FIFO. Conversely, when unit costs are declining, LIFO produces higher pretax income and higher inventory valuation than FIFO.** These effects occur because LIFO will cause the new unit costs to be reflected on the income statement whereas FIFO will cause the older unit costs to be reflected on the income statement.

Evaluation of Alternative Inventory Costing Methods

No single method of inventory costing can be considered the "best." Many accountants believe that the best inventory costing method is the one that best reflects the sales pricing policy of the company. Many companies do price units for sale in each of the ways implied by these four costing methods. Government price regulation of certain industries has restricted price increases when costs increase until inventory accumulated at lower costs has been sold. Such a pricing practice is a good example of FIFO in action. Other accountants believe that the choice of method should be based upon whether the measurement emphasis should be on the income statement or on the balance sheet. Those who believe that the income statement should be given primary emphasis tend to defend

LIFO because it matches the most recent purchase cost with current sales revenue. Those who prefer to emphasize the balance sheet tend to prefer FIFO because it reports the ending inventory on the balance sheet at the most current cost price. Because of these considerations, it is easy to understand why the accounting profession has accepted several alternative inventory costing methods.

Comparability

Different income statement and balance sheet amounts are caused by the use of different inventory costing methods. These differences in reported financial data cause problems for statement users in comparing companies that use different accounting methods. Problems also occur when an individual business changes accounting methods over time. The **comparability quality** (Exhibit 4–5) is applied to maximize comparability when accounting alternatives are permitted. The comparability quality holds that all accounting concepts, principles, and measurement approaches should be applied in a similar or consistent way from one period to the next. This characteristic is necessary to assure that the data reported in the financial statements are reasonably comparable over time. It prevents arbitrary changes from one accounting or measurement approach to another, but the comparability quality does not preclude change. Changes in accounting are permitted when they improve the measurement of financial results and financial position. Comparability is a difficult concept to define precisely and poses problems in application.

A business is not allowed to change from one inventory costing method to another from period to period. Changing from one inventory costing method to another is a major event. Such a change requires full disclosure about the reason for the change and the accounting effects.

PART B—APPLICATION OF A PERPETUAL INVENTORY SYSTEM AND SELECTED INVENTORY COSTING PROBLEMS

This part of the chapter discusses **application of each of the inventory costing methods with a perpetual inventory system.** Separate discussion of the two inventory systems is essential because:

a. The timing of the application of the inventory costing methods between the two systems causes some differences in the allocated amounts. The periodic inventory system costs inventory units at the end of the period; the perpetual inventory system costs units on a day-to-day basis.

b. The accounting entries vary between the two systems.

c. The inventory controls that are available with the two systems vary.

d. Recent developments of computers of various capabilities have encouraged a high percentage of large, medium, and even small businesses to change to the perpetual inventory system for numerous items in their inventories.

Application of the Inventory Costing Methods with a Perpetual Inventory System

A perpetual inventory system requires the maintenance of a day-to-day **perpetual inventory record** for each kind of goods or merchandise. This record shows units, unit costs, and dollar amounts for (*a*) beginning inventory, (*b*) goods received (purchases), (*c*) goods sold (issues), and (*d*) balance of goods on hand (ending inventory). Each purchase and each sale transaction is entered in the perpetual inventory record when it occurs. The perpetual inventory record is designed so that cost of goods sold and the ending inventory are measured on a perpetual or continuous basis.

In the following discussions, a **perpetual inventory record** will be shown for each of the four inventory costing methods. We will use the data for Summer Retail Store given in Exhibit 7–2. The beginning inventory of 100 units at a unit cost of $6 would have been carried over in the records from the prior period. Each purchase is recorded as follows and at the same time entered on the perpetual inventory record (see Exhibit 7–4):

Jan. 3	Inventory (50 units × $7)	350
	Cash (or accounts payable)	350

A sale generates two companion entries when a perpetual inventory system is used; one at sales price and one at cost:

Jan. 6	Cash	400
	Sales revenue (40 units × $10)	400
	Cost of goods sold (FIFO basis)	240
	Inventory (40 units × $6)	240
	From Exhibit 7–5.	

Weighted-Average Inventory Costing Method

When the weighted-average cost method is applied with a perpetual inventory system, a **moving weighted-average** unit cost is used because the cost of goods sold amount is measured and recorded at the **time of each sale.** It is impossible to use an **annual** weighted average with the perpetual system because the recording of cost of goods sold would be delayed until year-end, which is the only time an annual average unit cost can be computed.

Under the perpetual inventory system, a **new** average unit cost is computed at the time of **each purchase.** Cost of goods sold and the remaining inventory are measured at the then current moving average unit cost. A perpetual inventory record on a moving weighted-average basis for the Summer Retail Store is shown in Exhibit 7–4. The moving weighted-average unit cost was recomputed

Exhibit 7–4 Moving weighted-average method—perpetual inventory system

PERPETUAL INVENTORY RECORD

Item   Item A   Cost basis   Moving average

Location   320   Minimum level   100

Code   13   Maximum level   300

	Received (purchases)			Issued (sales)			Inventory Balance		
Date	Units	Unit Cost	Total Cost	Units	Unit Cost	Total Cost	Units	Unit Cost	Total Cost
1/1 bal.							100	6.00	600
1/3	50	7.00	350				150	6.33	950
1/6				40	6.33	253	110	6.33	696
6/12	200	8.00	1,600				310	7.41*	2,297
6/18				220	7.41	1,630	90	7.41	667
12/20	120	9.00	1,080				210	8.32*	1,747
12/24				60	8.32	499	150	8.32	1,248
Total cost of goods sold						2,382			
Total ending inventory									1,248

* New moving weighted-average unit cost computed.

three times during the period because there were three purchases. Units sold are removed from the inventory record at the current moving average unit cost. For example, the moving weighted-average unit cost was computed on the date of the first purchase as follows:

	Units	Cost
Beginning inventory	100	$600
Purchase, January 3	50	350
Totals	150	$950

Moving average unit cost:
$950 ÷ 150 units = $6.33 per unit.

The companion journal entries for the sale on January 6 would reflect sales revenue of $400 and cost of goods sold of $253 (from the perpetual inventory record) as follows:

Jan. 6   Cash 400
              Sales revenue (40 units × $10)   400

          Cost of goods sold (moving average basis) 253
              Inventory   253
          From Exhibit 7–4, 40 units × $6.33 = $253.

FIFO Inventory Costing Method

When the FIFO method is applied with a perpetual inventory system, after each issue the remaining units on hand must be "layered" by the different unit costs. These layers are called "inventory cost layers." The identification of inventory cost layers is necessary because goods are removed from the perpetual inventory record in FIFO order; that is, the oldest unit cost is taken off first. A perpetual inventory record on a FIFO basis is shown in Exhibit 7–5. Each purchase and each sale of goods is entered in the inventory record at the time of the transaction. At each transaction date, the balance column on the perpetual inventory record is restated to show the units and amount on hand for each different unit cost. At the same time, each transaction is recorded in the journal. The two companion journal entries to record the sales of June 18 are:

June 18   Cash 2,640
               Sales revenue (220 units × $12)   2,640

           Cost of goods sold (FIFO basis) 1,590
               Inventory   1,590
           From Exhibit 7–5, $360 + $350 + $880 = $1,590.

LIFO Inventory Costing Method

When the LIFO method is used with a perpetual inventory system, the inventory cost layers must be identified separately on the perpetual inventory record, as was the case with FIFO. This identification is necessary so that the units (and their costs) can be removed at the time of sale from the inventory record in the opposite order that they came in. Unit costs are removed from the perpetual inventory record at the time of each issue, which means that the **timing of costing is during the period rather than at the end of the period.** A perpetual inventory record on a LIFO basis is shown in Exhibit 7–6.

Specific Identification Inventory Costing Method

When the specific identification method is applied with a perpetual inventory system, the item-by-item choice (for entry in the perpetual inventory record and in the accounts) should be made at the time of sale. Use of the specific identification costing method with a perpetual inventory system is done in a manner like that shown in the preceding illustrations.

Exhibit 7–5 FIFO method—perpetual inventory system

PERPETUAL INVENTORY RECORD										
(heading—same as in Exhibit 7–4, except cost basis—FIFO)										
	Received (purchases)			Issued (sales)			Inventory Balance*			
Date	Units	Unit Cost	Total Cost	Units	Unit Cost	Total Cost	Units	Unit Cost	Total Cost	
1/1 bal.							100	6	600	
1/3	50	7	350				100	6	600	
							50	7	350	
1/6				40	6	240	60	6	360	
							50	7	350	
6/12	200	8	1,600				60	6	360	
							50	7	350	
							200	8	1,600	
6/18				60	6	360				
				50	7	350				
				110	8	880	90	8	720	
12/20	120	9	1,080				90	8	720	
							120	9	1,080	
12/24				60	8	480	30	8	240	
							120	9	1,080	
Total cost of goods sold						2,310				
Total ending inventory									1,320	
* Maintained by FIFO unit cost inventory layers.										

Comparison of Periodic and Perpetual Inventory Systems

There are two important implementation differences between the periodic inventory system and the perpetual inventory system:

a. The perpetual system requires more clerical effort than the periodic system. *2 journal entries*

Exhibit 7-6 LIFO method, costed currently—perpetual inventory system

	Received (purchases)			Issued (sales)			Inventory Balance*		
Date	Units	Unit Cost	Total Cost	Units	Unit Cost	Total Cost	Units	Unit Cost	Total Cost
1/1 bal.							100	6	600
1/3	50	7	350				100	6	600
							50	7	350
1/6				40	7	280	100	6	600
							10	7	70
6/12	200	8	1,600				100	6	600
							10	7	70
							200	8	1,600
6/18				200	8	1,600			
				10	7	70			
				10	6	60	90	6	540
12/20	120	9	1,080				90	6	540
							120	9	1,080
12/21				60	9	540	90	6	540
							60	9	540
Total cost of goods sold						2,550			
Ending inventory									1,080

PERPETUAL INVENTORY RECORD

(heading—same as in Exhibit 7-4, except cost basis—LIFO)

* Maintained by LIFO unit cost inventory layers.

b. The periodic system requires a year-end physical inventory; the perpetual system does not; however, for an accuracy check, it is advisable to do a physical count periodically.

In the past, most businesses used the periodic inventory system because of its relative low cost and convenience. However, recent advances in computer technology have produced a significant reduction in the cost of maintaining a perpetual inventory system. As a result, many businesses have adopted the perpetual system. The perpetual system offers the advantage of providing management with up-to-date inventory information.

The periodic and perpetual inventory systems often produce different valuations of cost of goods sold and ending inventory because of differences within the timing of the costing of cost of goods sold and inventory. The **periodic** inventory system costs ending inventory and cost of goods sold at the **end** of the accounting period. The **perpetual** inventory system costs inventory and cost of goods sold **throughout** the accounting period.

The FIFO inventory method gives identical valuations of ending inventory and cost of goods sold under both the periodic and perpetual inventory systems. The results are identical because of the basic FIFO assumption that the first goods into inventory are the first goods taken out of inventory, and that order is always maintained. Compare the following FIFO results for Summer Retail Store:

FIFO	Perpetual inventory system	Periodic inventory system
Source	Exhibit 7–5	Page 371
Ending inventory	$1,320	$1,320*
Cost of goods sold	2,310	2,310
Total goods available	$3,630	$3,630

* 150 units costing (120 × \$9) + (30 × \$8) = \$1,320.

In contrast, results typically will be different under periodic and perpetual systems when either the LIFO or the average inventory costing method is used. The results will be different under the **average cost** method because the **periodic** inventory system applies an **annual** weighted average for cost allocation whereas the **perpetual** inventory system applies a series of **moving** averages throughout the accounting period.

Results will be different under the **LIFO** method because the **periodic** inventory system allocates the most recent purchase cost to cost of goods sold at the end of the accounting period. In contrast, the **perpetual** system allocates the most recent purchase costs to cost of goods sold **during** the accounting period on the date that each sales transaction occurs.

To show the differences that can occur between LIFO and weighted average, compare the following results for Summer Retail Store:

LIFO	Perpetual inventory system	Periodic inventory system
Source	Exhibit 7–6	Page 372
Ending inventory	$1,080	$ 950
Cost of goods sold	2,550	2,680
Total goods available	$3,630	$3,630

Weighted Average		
Source	Exhibit 7–4	Page 370
Ending inventory	$1,248	$1,158
Cost of goods sold	2,382	2,472
Total goods available	$3,630	$3,630

To summarize, the four **inventory costing methods** (weighted average, FIFO, LIFO, and specific identification) are alternative methods of measuring the valuation of ending inventory and cost of goods sold. Each method assumes a different flow of unit costs during the accounting period; therefore, each method produces different results. The **periodic** and **perpetual inventory systems** are two different accounting approaches for applying the inventory costing methods to measure cost of goods sold and ending inventory. The periodic inventory system allocates costs at the end of the accounting period (using one of the four inventory costing methods). The perpetual inventory system allocates costs currently during the accounting period (again, using one of the inventory costing methods). Because of these two different timing assumptions, the two systems give different valuations of ending inventory and cost of goods sold under the weighted average, LIFO, and specific identification costing methods. Valuations are always the same under FIFO.

Selected Inventory Problems

The remaining discussions in this chapter relate to three issues that may affect the valuation of the ending inventory reported on the balance sheet and the amount of income reported on the income statement. They are (*a*) lower of cost or market (LCM) valuation, (*b*) damaged items, and (*c*) estimating the ending inventory.

Inventories at Lower of Cost or Market (LCM)

Inventories should be measured at their unit purchase cost in conformity with the cost principle. However, when the goods remaining in the ending inventory can be replaced with identical goods at a lower cost, the lower unit cost should be used as the inventory valuation. This rule is known as measuring inventories on a **lower of cost or market (LCM) basis.** It is a departure from the cost principle because of the conservatism constraint (Exhibit 4–5). The LCM basis recognizes a "holding" loss in the period in which the replacement cost of an item dropped, rather than in the period in which the item actually is sold. The holding loss is the difference between purchase cost and the subsequent lower replacement cost. To illustrate, assume that an office equipment dealer has 10 new electronic calculators in the 19B ending inventory. The calculators were bought for $450 each and were marked to sell at $499.95. At the end of the year, the same new calculators can be purchased for $400 and will be marked to sell for $429.95. The 10 calculators should be costed in the ending inventory at the lower of cost ($450) or current market ($400). The LCM basis costs the ending inventory at $400 per unit. There are several effects caused by using a replacement cost of $400 instead of the original purchase cost of $450 for the 10 calculators included in the ending inventory. By costing them at $50 per unit below their purchase cost, 19B pretax income will be $500 less (i.e., 10 × $50) than it would have been had they been costed in the inventory at $450 per unit. This $500 loss in the value of the inventory (i.e., the holding loss) was due to a decline in the replacement cost. Because the loss is included in cost of goods sold, 19B pretax

Exhibit 7–7   Effect of inventory measurement at LCM

	Inventory measured at—	
	Cost (FIFO)	**LCM**
Sales revenue	$41,500	$41,500
Cost of goods sold:		
Beginning inventory	$ 5,000	$ 5,000
Add purchases	20,000	20,000
Goods available for sale	25,000	25,000
Less ending inventory (10 calculators):		
At purchase cost of $450	4,500	
At LCM of $400		4,000
Cost of goods sold	20,500	21,000
Gross margin on sales	21,000	20,500
Expenses	15,000	15,000
Pretax income	$ 6,000	$ 5,500

income will be reduced by $500 in the period in which the replacement cost dropped (19B) rather than in the later period when the goods actually are sold. The $500 loss also reduces the amount of inventory that is reported on the 19B balance sheet. These effects are shown in Exhibit 7–7. LCM usually is applied to all inventories on an item-by-item basis rather than on the aggregate inventory as a whole.[9]

Application of lower of cost or market in practice requires careful consideration of the specific circumstances of the business. For example, consider the case of the 10 calculators presented in Exhibit 7–7. The company could be holding these calculators when a new model calculator is announced that will do everything the old ones would do but would sell for $410. The office equipment dealer decides to mark down the selling price of the inventory to $410 and pay a sales commission of $10 for each sale until the inventory is exhausted. In this case the replacement cost of the old model is not relevant to the lower of cost or market calculation because replacement will be made with new models. The market value of inventory would be net realizable value; namely, selling price of $410 less cost of selling $10 or $400. Each unit of the ending inventory would be assigned $400 net realizable value because this market value is below the cost of $450 each. Because of the assumed numbers, the effect on pretax income would

---

[9] In contrast, if the replacement cost had increased to $500 each, there would have been a **holding gain** of 10 units × $50 = $500. Generally accepted accounting principles do not permit recognition of holding gains because revenue is recognized only at date of sale of the goods. Because of the unfavourable connotations, holding gains are called windfall profits in the political arena. Chapter 17 presents a discussion of the supplementary disclosure of holding gains for inventories. In view of the various possible values for market such as replacement cost, net realizable value, or net realizable value less normal profit margin, the *CICA Handbook*, Section 3030.11, recommends disclosure of the specific market value used.

be identical to that displayed in Exhibit 7–7. In Canada, net realizable value is typically used as the market value for finished goods of manufacturing concerns and the merchandise inventory of retail and wholesale concerns. Replacement cost is typically used as market value for raw materials of manufacturing concerns when lower of cost or market valuation is applied.

Damaged and Deteriorated Goods

Merchandise on hand that is damaged, obsolete, or shopworn should not be measured and reported at original cost. Instead this merchandise should be reported at its present **net realizable value** when it is below cost. Net realizable value is the **estimated amount** that will be realized when the goods are sold in their deteriorated condition, less all repair and sale costs.

Assume a retail store has on hand two television sets that have been used as demonstrators and cannot be sold as new sets (i.e., they are shopworn). When purchased, the sets cost $300 each. Because of their present condition, realistic estimates are:

	Per set
Estimated sales price in present condition . . .	$175
Estimated repair costs of $20 and sales costs of $15	35
Estimated net realizable value	$140

Based on these estimates, the two television sets would be included in the inventory at $140 each, rather than at the original cost of $300 each. Net realizable value is used, rather than cost, because it records the loss in the period in which it occurred rather than in the period of sale. This method also avoids overstatement of the asset on the balance sheet.

If a **periodic** inventory system is used, the item is included in the ending inventory of **damaged goods** at its estimated net realizable value. The loss is reflected in cost of goods sold. However, if a **perpetual** system is used, the following entry would be made:

Inventory of damaged goods (2 × $140)	280	
Loss on damaged goods (an expense) ($600 − $280)	320	
Inventory (2 × $300)		600

The perpetual inventory record also would be changed to show this entry.[10]

---

[10] The subsequent entries may be as follows:

a. To record actual repair costs of $25:

Inventory of damaged goods	25	
Cash		25

b. As is often the case, actual repair costs, market prices, and actual selling costs differ from the estimates used to determine the inventory value. To record sale of the two sets for $360 (less actual selling costs of $15):

Cash ($360 − $15)	345	
Selling expense	15	
Inventory ($280 + $25)		305
Gain on sale of damaged goods		55

Damaged and deteriorated goods provide another example of when net realizable value would be more appropriate than replacement cost for lower of cost or market calculations.

Estimating Ending Inventory and Cost of Goods Sold

When a periodic **inventory system** is used, a physical inventory count must be taken to determine the amount of the ending inventory. Taking a physical inventory is a time-consuming task in many businesses. Therefore, physical inventories often are taken only once a year. Nevertheless, managers may want financial statements for internal use on a monthly or a quarterly basis. When a periodic inventory system is used, some businesses **estimate** the ending inventory for the monthly or quarterly financial statements rather than taking a physical inventory. The **gross margin method** is used for this purpose. The method uses an **estimated gross margin ratio** as the basis for the computation.

The gross margin ratio is computed by dividing the gross margin amount by net sales revenue. The gross margin method assumes that the **gross margin ratio** for the current period should be the same as it was in the recent past. Therefore, the average gross margin ratio from one or more prior periods is used as an estimate of the ratio for the current period. This estimated ratio then can be used to compute **estimated amounts** for (1) gross margin on sales, (2) cost of goods sold, and (3) ending inventory.

Patz Company uses the periodic inventory system and is preparing **monthly** financial statements at January 31, 19D. The accounting records give the following data:

PATZ COMPANY
Income Statement
For the Month Ended January 31, 19D

Sales revenue	$100,000*
Cost of goods sold:	
Beginning inventory	$15,000*
Add purchases	65,000*
Goods available for sale	80,000
Less ending inventory	(?0,000)
Gross margin on sales	4?,000
Expenses	30,000*
Pretax income	$?

* Provided by the accounts.

The January ending inventory is to be **estimated** rather than determined by physical count. The yearly net sales for 19C amounted to $1,000,000, and gross margin was $400,000; therefore, the actual gross margin ratio for 19C was $400,000 \div \$1,000,000 = 0.40$. Management has decided that this ratio is a realistic estimate for use during 19D. Using the 0.40 as our estimate for 19D, we can compute an **estimated** inventory valuation. The computational steps, in lettered sequence, are shown below:

PATZ COMPANY
Income Statement
For the Month Ended January 31, 19D (estimated)

		Computations (sequence a, b, c)
Sales revenue	$100,000	Per accounts
Cost of goods sold:		
Beginning inventory $15,000		Per accounts
Add purchases . . . . + 65,000		Per accounts
Goods available for sale 80,000		
Less ending inventory 20,000		c. $ 80,000 − $60,000 = $20,000
Cost of goods sold	60,000	b. $100,000 − $40,000 = $60,000*
Gross margin on sales	40,000	a. $100,000 × 0.40 = $40,000
Expenses	30,000	Per accounts
Pretax income	$ 10,000	

* Or alternatively, $100,000 × (1.00 − 0.40) = $60,000.

The balance sheet can be completed by reporting the $20,000 estimated ending inventory amount as a current asset.

The gross margin method has other uses. Auditors and accountants may use this method to test the reasonableness of the amount of the inventory determined by other means. If the current gross margin ratio has changed materially from the recent past, it may suggest an error in the ending inventory. The method also is used in the case of a casualty loss when an inventory of goods is destroyed or stolen and its valuation must be estimated for settlement purposes with an insurance company.[11]

DEMONSTRATION CASE A

(Try to resolve the requirements before proceeding to the "Suggested Solution" that follows.)

This case focuses on the effects of an error in the amount of the ending inventory. It does not introduce any new accounting concepts or procedures.

Metal Products, Incorporated, has been operating for eight years as a distributor of a line of metal products. It is now the end of 19C, and for the first time the company will undergo an audit by an independent PA. The company uses a

[11] Another method, known as the retail inventory method, is used widely to estimate the ending inventory by department stores. It is essentially the same as the gross margin method, but differs in detail. Discussion of it is deferred to more advanced courses.

periodic inventory system. The annual income statements, prepared by the company, were:

	For the year ended December 31	
	19B	**19C**
Sales revenue	$750,000	$800,000
Cost of goods sold:		
Beginning inventory	45,000	40,000
Add purchases	460,000	484,000
Goods available for sale	505,000	524,000
Less ending inventory	40,000	60,000
Cost of goods sold	465,000	464,000
Gross margin on sales	285,000	336,000
Operating expenses	275,000	306,000
Pretax income	10,000	30,000
Income tax expense (20%)	2,000	6,000
Net income	$ 8,000	$ 24,000

During the early stages of the audit, the independent PA discovered that the ending inventory for 19B was understated by $15,000.

Required:

a. Based on the above income statement amounts, compute the gross margin ratio on sales for each year. Do the results suggest an inventory error? Explain.

b. Reconstruct the two income statements on a correct basis.

c. Answer the following questions.
    (1) What are the correct gross margin ratios?
    (2) What effect did the $15,000 understatement of the ending inventory have on 19B pretax income? Explain.
    (3) What effect did the inventory error have on 19C pretax income? Explain.
    (4) How did the inventory error affect income tax expense?

Suggested Solution

Requirement a—Gross margin ratios as reported:

$$19B: \$285,000 \div \$750,000 = 0.38$$
$$19C: \$336,000 \div \$800,000 = 0.42$$

The change in the gross margin ratio from 0.38 to 0.42 suggests the possibility of an inventory error in the absence of any other explanation.

Requirement b—Income statements corrected:

	For the year ended December 31	
	19B	**19C**
Sales revenue	$750,000	$800,000
Cost of goods sold:		
Beginning inventory	45,000	55,000*
Add purchases	460,000	484,000
Goods available for sale	505,000	539,000
Less ending inventory	55,000*	60,000
Cost of goods sold	450,000	479,000
Gross margin on sales	300,000	321,000
Operating expenses	275,000	306,000
Pretax income	25,000	15,000
Income tax expense (20%)	5,000	3,000
Net income	$ 20,000	$ 12,000

* Increased by $15,000.

Requirement c:

1. Correct gross margin ratios:

$$19B: \$300,000 \div \$750,000 = 0.400$$
$$19C: \$321,000 \div \$800,000 = 0.401$$

The inventory error of $15,000 was responsible for the difference in the gross margin ratios reflected in Requirement (*a*). The error in the 19B ending inventory affected gross margin for both 19B and 19C, in the opposite direction, but by the same amount ($15,000).

2. Effect on pretax income in 19B: **Ending inventory understatement** ($15,000) caused an **understatement of pretax income** by the **same amount.**

3. Effect on pretax income in 19C: Beginning inventory **understatement** (by the same $15,000 since the inventory amount is carried over from the prior period) caused an **overstatement** of pretax income by the same amount.

4. Total income tax expense for 19B and 19C combined was the same ($8,000) regardless of the error. However, there was a shift of $3,000 ($15,000 × 20%) income tax expense from 19B to 19C.

Observation—An ending inventory error in one year affects pretax income by the amount of the error and in the next year affects pretax income again by the same amount but in the opposite direction.

DEMONSTRATION CASE B

(Try to resolve the requirements before proceeding to the suggested solution that follows.)

This case presents the effects on ending inventory, cost of goods sold, and the related accounting entries of a **periodic** inventory system compared with a **perpetual** inventory system assuming the LIFO inventory costing method is applied in each system.

Balent Appliances distributes a number of high-cost household appliances. One product, microwave ovens, has been selected for case purposes. Assume the following summarized transactions were completed during the accounting period in the order given below (assume all transactions are cash).

	Units	Unit cost
a. Beginning inventory	11	$200
b. Sales (selling price, $420)	8	?
c. Sales returns (can be resold as new)	1	200
d. Purchases	9	220
e. Purchase returns (damaged in shipment)	1	220

Required:

a. Compute the following amounts assuming application of the LIFO inventory costing method:

	Ending inventory		Cost of goods sold	
	Units	Dollars	Units	Dollars
(1) Periodic inventory system (costed at end of period)	____	_____	____	_____
(2) Perpetual inventory system (costed during period)	____	_____	____	_____

b. Give the indicated journal entries for transactions (b) through (e) assuming:
   (1) Periodic inventory system.
   (2) Perpetual inventory system.

Suggested Solution

Requirement a:

	Ending inventory		Cost of goods sold	
	Units	Dollars	Units	Dollars
1. Periodic inventory system (costed at end of the period)	12	$2,420	7	$1,540
2. Perpetual inventory system (costed during the period)	12	2,560	7	1,400

Computations:
   Goods available for sale: (11 units × $200 = $2,200) + (8 units × $220 = $1,760) = $3,960.
   1. Periodic LIFO inventory (costed at end):
      Ending inventory: (11 units × $200 = $2,200) + (1 unit × $220 = $220) = $2,420.
      Cost of goods sold: (Goods available, $3,960) − (Ending inventory, $2,420) = $1,540.
   2. Perpetual LIFO inventory (costed during period):
      Ending inventory: (8 units × $220 = $1,760) + (4 units × $200 = $800) = $2,560.
      Cost of goods sold: 7 units × $200 = $1,400.

Requirement b—journal entries:

1. Periodic Inventory System		2. Perpetual Inventory System	
b. Sales:			
Cash (8 × $420) 3,360		Cash 3,360	
Sales revenue	3,360	Sales revenue	3,360
		Cost of goods sold 1,600	
		Inventory (8 × $200)	1,600
c. Sales returns:			
Sales returns 420		Sales returns 420	
Cash (1 × $420)	420	Cash	420
		Inventory (1 × $200) 200	
		Cost of goods sold	200
d. Purchases:			
Purchases 1,980		Inventory 1,980	
Cash (9 × $220)	1,980	Cash	1,980
e. Purchase return:			
Cash 220		Cash 220	
Purchase returns	220	Inventory	220

SUMMARY OF CHAPTER

This chapter focused on the problem of measuring cost of goods sold and ending inventory when unit costs change during the period. Inventory should include all the items for resale to which the entity has ownership. Costs flow into inventory when goods are purchased (or manufactured) and flow out (as expense) when the goods are sold or disposed of otherwise. When there are several unit cost amounts representing the inflow of goods for the period, a rational and systematic method must be used to allocate unit cost amounts to the units remaining in inventory and to the units sold (cost of goods sold) so that the fairest matching is achieved. The chapter discussed four different inventory costing methods and their applications in both a perpetual and a periodic inventory system. The methods discussed were weighted-average cost, FIFO, LIFO, and specific identification. Each of the inventory costing methods is in conformity with generally accepted accounting principles. The selection of a method of inventory costing is important because it will affect reported income and the inventory valuation reported on the balance sheet. In a period of rising prices, FIFO gives a higher income than does LIFO; in a period of falling prices, the opposite result occurs.

Damaged, obsolete, and deteriorated items in inventory should be assigned a unit cost that represents their current estimated net realizable value. Also, the ending inventory of new items (not damaged, deteriorated, or obsolete) should be measured on the basis of the lower of actual cost or market (i.e., replacement cost or more commonly net realizable value).

This chapter explained another fundamental accounting concept (Exhibit 4–5) known as the comparability quality, which means that all accounting concepts, principles, and measurement approaches should be applied in a consistent manner from period to period.

IMPORTANT TERMS DEFINED IN THIS CHAPTER

Comparability Quality Accounting methods should be consistently applied from one period to the next. *p. 374*

Consignments Goods in possession of a seller but legal title is retained by the supplier. *p. 366*

Finished Goods Inventory Manufactured goods that are completed and ready for sale. *p. 364*

First-In, First-Out Inventory costing method that assumes the oldest units are the first units sold. *p. 370*

Gross Margin Method Method to estimate ending inventory based on the gross margin ratio. *p. 384*

Last-In, First-Out Inventory costing method that assumes the newest units are the first units sold. *p. 371*

Lower of Cost or Market Departure from cost principle that serves to recognize a "holding" loss when replacement cost or net realizable value drops below cost. *p. 381*

Merchandise Inventory Goods held for resale in the ordinary course of business. *p. 364*

Moving Weighted Average Weighted-average inventory costing method applied in the perpetual inventory system. *p. 375*

Net Realizable Value Estimated amount to be realized when goods are sold, less repair and disposal costs. *p. 383*

Periodic Inventory System Ending inventory and cost of goods sold are determined at the end of the accounting period; a physical inventory count must be taken. *p. 367*

Perpetual Inventory System A detailed daily inventory record is updated continuously during the accounting period; provides ending inventory and cost of goods sold. *p. 367*

Raw Materials Inventory Items acquired for the purpose of processing into finished goods. *p. 364*

Specific Identification Inventory costing method that identifies the cost of the specific item that was sold. *p. 372*

Weighted Average Inventory costing method used with a periodic inventory system that averages all purchase costs to calculate a weighted-average unit cost on an annual basis. *p. 370*

Work in Process Inventory Goods in the process of being manufactured that are not yet complete. *p. 364*

QUESTIONS

Part A: Questions 1–15

1. Assume the 19A ending inventory was understated by $100,000. Explain how this error would affect the 19A and 19B pretax income amounts. What would be the effects if the 19A ending inventory were overstated by $100,000 instead of understated?

2. Match the type of inventory with the type of business in the following matrix:

	Type of Business	
Type of Inventory	Trading	Manufacturing
Merchandise		
Finished goods		
Work in process		
Raw materials		

3. Why is inventory an important item to both internal management and external users of financial statements?

4. What are the general guidelines for deciding which items should be included in inventory?

5. In measuring cost of goods sold and inventory, why is passage of ownership an important issue? When does ownership to goods usually pass? Explain.

6. Identify the two parties to a consignment. Which party should include the goods on consignment in inventory? Explain.

7. Explain the application of the cost principle to an item in the ending inventory.

8. When a perpetual inventory system is used, unit costs of the items sold are

known at the date of each sale. In contrast, when a periodic inventory system is used, unit costs are known only at the end of the accounting period. Why are these statements correct?

9. The periodic inventory calculation is BI + P − EI = CGS. The perpetual inventory calculation is BI + P − CGS = EI. Explain the significance of the difference between these two calculations.

10. The chapter discussed four inventory costing methods. List the four methods and briefly explain each.

11. The four inventory costing methods may be applied with either a periodic inventory system or a perpetual inventory system. Briefly explain how the methods are applied in each system.

12. Explain how income can be manipulated when the specific identification inventory costing method is used.

13. Contrast the effects of LIFO versus FIFO on reported assets (i.e., the ending inventory) when (a) prices are rising and (b) prices are falling.

14. Contrast the income statement effect of LIFO versus FIFO (i.e., on pretax income) when (a) prices are rising and (b) prices are falling.

15.. The term **articulation,** defined early in Chapter 4, describes the linking together of four financial statements: income statement, statement of retained earnings, balance sheet, and the statement of changes in financial position. Using a specific example from inventories, speculate what measurement difficulties this articulation requirement might pose for the conceptual foundations of accounting. (Hint: Refer to the definition of expenses in Exhibit 4–5 and the definition of assets.)

Part B: Questions 16–27

16. What is the purpose of a perpetual inventory record? List the four main column headings and briefly explain the purpose of each.

17. When a perpetual inventory system is used, a moving weighted average is used. In contrast, when a periodic inventory system is used, an annual weighted average is used. Explain why the different averages are used.

18. The weighted-average inventory costing method usually produces different results when a perpetual inventory system is used rather than a periodic inventory system. Explain why.

19. Explain briefly application of the LCM concept to the ending inventory and its effect on the income statement and balance sheet when market is lower than cost.

20. When should net realizable value be used in costing an item in the ending inventory?

21. The chapter discussed the gross margin method to estimate inventories. Briefly explain this method and indicate why it is used.

22. Briefly explain the comparability quality. How might it relate to the inventory costing methods?

23. If you were given the task of programming a perpetual inventory into a computer, what method of inventory cost allocation would you prefer, FIFO, LIFO, or average? Why?

24. The *CICA Handbook*, Section 3030.09, suggests that the selection of the appropriate inventory cost allocation method should be made according to whether FIFO, LIFO, average, or specific produces the fairest matching of cost of goods sold with revenues.

    LIFO matches current purchase or manufacturing costs against current sales prices. Yet LIFO is not a popular method in Canada. Why?

25. Application of lower of cost and market valuation to inventory valuation is suggested as a departure from the cost principle in favour of conservation. Suggest another justification for LCM in terms of the definition of what constitutes an asset.

26. Is the use of the lower of cost and market method for valuing inventories a violation of the comparability principle? Explain.

27. Inventories of finished goods and work in process are said to include factory overhead costs. Depreciation of production facilities is a factory overhead cost yet Union Carbide inventories were described as excluding depreciation of factory fixed assets. Using the concepts of accounting stated in Exhibit 4–5, justify Union Carbide's accounting practice of excluding depreciation.

EXERCISES

Part A: Exercises 7–1 to 7–9

E7–1 (Pair Definition with Terms)

Match the following definitions with the terms by entering the appropriate letter in each space provided.

Terms	Definitions
_____ (1) Specific identification	A. Prevents arbitrary changes from one accounting or measurement approach to another from one period to another.
_____ (2) Work in process inventory	
_____ (3) Merchandise inventory	B. Goods held on this basis should be excluded from inventory because legal title still resides with the consignor.
_____ (4) Periodic inventory system	
_____ (5) Last-in, first-out	C. An account reported on the balance sheet as a current asset; represents goods completed in the manufacturing process.
_____ (6) Weighted average	
_____ (7) Finished goods inventory	D. An inventory costing method that assumes that those items which have been in inventory the longest are sold first.
_____ (8) Comparability quality	
_____ (9) Perpetual inventory system	E. Uses a ratio derived by dividing the gross margin amount by the net sales revenue to compute estimates for CGS, gross margin on sales, and ending inventory.
_____ (10) Gross margin method	
_____ (11) First-in, first-out	F. An inventory method that assumes that the units acquired most recently are sold first.

Terms	Definitions

Terms

_____ (12) Net realizable value

_____ (13) Lower of cost or market

_____ (14) Raw materials inventory

_____ (15) Moving weighted average

_____ (16) Consignment

Definitions

G. Recognizes a holding loss when replacement cost or net realizable value drops below cost.

H. The inventory of a retailer or wholesaler.

I. An inventory costing method in which a new average unit cost is computed at the time of each new purchase.

J. Estimated selling price of a product in the ordinary course of business, less reasonably predictable costs of completion and disposal.

K. Requires computation of the ending inventory by means of a physical count of the goods remaining on hand; CGS is computed as a residual amount.

L. System that maintains a detailed daily inventory record throughout the period for each item stocked and therefore does not require a physical count at the end of each accounting period.

M. Those items acquired by purchase, growth, or extraction of natural resources for further processing into finished goods.

N. An inventory costing method that may be appropriate for "big ticket" items but may be impractical when unit costs are low and unit costs change frequently.

O. An inventory costing method that weights the number of units purchased and unit costs that prevailed during the period; used in conjunction with a periodic inventory system.

P. An asset that includes the cost of raw materials used, the direct labour incurred in the manufacturing process, and factory overhead costs.

E7–2 **(Analysis of the Impact of an Inventory Error)**

Sydney Corporation prepared the two income statements that follow (simplified for illustrative purposes):

	First quarter 19B		Second quarter 19B	
Sales revenue		$11,000		$13,000
Cost of goods sold:				
Beginning inventory	$ 2,000		$ 3,000	
Purchases	9,000		10,000	
Goods available for sale	11,000		13,000	
Ending inventory	3,000		4,000	
Cost of goods sold		8,000		9,000
Gross margin		3,000		4,000
Expenses		1,000		1,000
Pretax income		$ 2,000		$ 3,000

During the third quarter it was discovered that the ending inventory for the first quarter should have been $2,500.

Required:

a. What effect did this error have on the combined pretax income of the two quarters? Explain.

b. Did this error affect the EPS amounts for each quarter? Explain.

c. Prepare corrected income statements for each quarter.

d. Set up a schedule that reflects the comparative effects of the correct and incorrect amounts on the income statement. What happens to retained earnings each quarter?

E7–3 **(Use of a Periodic Inventory System)**

Laura Fashions purchased 100 new shirts and recorded a total cost of $2,940 determined as follows:

Invoice cost	$2,000 ×3%= 60
Less: Cash discount 3%	
Shipping charges	·530
Import taxes and duties	110
Interest paid in advance (15%) on $2,000	
borrowed to finance the purchase	300
	$2,940

Give the journal entry(s) to record this purchase assuming a periodic inventory system. Show computations.

E7–4   (Use of the Four Inventory Methods)

The records at the end of January 19B for Olds Company showed the following for a particular kind of merchandise:

Transactions	Units	Total cost
Inventory, December 31, 19A	30	$390
Purchase, January 9, 19B	60	900
Sale, January 11, 19B (at $35 per unit)	50	
Purchase, January 20, 19B	35	490
Sale, January 27, 19B (at $36 per unit)	41	

Required:

Assuming a periodic inventory system, compute the amount of (1) goods available for sale, (2) ending inventory, and (3) cost of goods sold at January 31, 19B, under each of the following inventory costing methods (show computations and round to the nearest dollar):

a. Weighted-average cost.

b. First-in, first-out.

c. Last-in, first-out.

d. Specific identification (assume the sale on January 11 was "identified" with the purchase of January 9, the sale of January 27 was "identified" with the purchase of January 20, and any excess identified with the beginning inventory).

E7–5   (Comparison of Alternative Inventory Methods)

Tower Company uses a periodic inventory system. At the end of the annual accounting period, December 31, 19B, the accounting records provided the following information for Product 2:

Transactions	Units	Unit cost
1. Inventory, December 31, 19A	2,000	$20
For the year 19B:		
2. Purchase, April 11	2,000	22
3. Sale, May 1 (at $52 each)	3,000	
4. Purchase, June 1	6,000	24
5. Sale, July 3 (at $53 each)	4,000	
6. Operating expenses (excluding income tax expense), $140,000.		

Required:

a. Prepare a separate income statement through pretax income that details cost of goods sold for:

   Case A—Annual weighted average.

   Case B—FIFO.

   Case C—LIFO.

   Case D—Specific identification assuming two thirds of the first sale was "selected" from the beginning inventory and one third was "selected" from the items purchased on April 11, 19B. The second sale was "selected" from the purchase of June 1, 19B.

For each case, show the computation of the ending inventory. (Hint: Set up adjacent columns for each case.)

b. For each case, compare the pretax income and the ending inventory amounts. Explain the similarities and differences.

E7–6   **(Comparison of LIFO and FIFO)**

Use the data given in Exercise 7–4 for this exercise (assume cash transactions and a periodic inventory system).

Required:

a. Compute (1) goods available for sale, (2) cost of goods sold, and (3) ending inventory for Case A—FIFO and Case B—LIFO.

b. In parallel columns, give the journal entries for each purchase and sale transaction, assuming a periodic inventory system is used for each case. Set up captions as follows:

	FIFO		LIFO	
Accounts	Debit	Credit	Debit	Credit

c. Prepare an income statement through gross margin and explain why the FIFO and LIFO ending inventory, cost of goods sold, and gross margin amounts are different.

d. Which inventory costing method may be preferred for income tax purposes? Explain.

E7–7   **(Comparison of Cash Flow and Income Effects of LIFO and FIFO)**

During January 19B, Ford Company reported sales revenue of $425,000 for the one item stocked. The inventory for December 31, 19A, showed 7,500 units on hand with a cost of $165,000. During January 19B, two purchases of the item were made: the first was for 1,500 units at $24 per unit; and the second was for 7,600 units at $25 each. The periodic inventory count reflected 8,600 units remaining on hand on January 31, 19B. Total operating expense for the month was $84,900.

Required:

a. On the basis of the above information, complete the 19B summary income statements under FIFO and LIFO. Use a single list of side captions including the computation of cost of goods sold. Set up three separate column headings as follows: Units, FIFO, and LIFO. Show your computations of the ending inventory.

b. Which method gives the higher pretax income? Why?

c. Which method gives the more favourable cash flow effects? By how much, assuming a 20% tax rate?

E7–8   **(Comparison of Alternative Inventory Methods Using the Periodic Inventory System)**

Luther Company uses a periodic inventory system. Data for 19B were: beginning merchandise inventory (December 31, 19A), 1,600 units at $15; purchases, 6,000 units at $18; expenses (excluding income taxes), $51,800; ending inventory per physical count at December 31, 19B, 1,500 units; sales price per unit, $35; and average income tax rate of 25%.

Required:

a. Prepare income statements under the FIFO, LIFO, and weighted-average costing methods. Use a format similar to the following:

Income statement	Units	FIFO	LIFO	Weighted average
Sales revenue	————	$ ———	$ ———	$ ———
Cost of goods sold:				
Beginning inventory	———	———	———	———
Purchases	———	———	———	———
Goods available for sale	———	———	———	———
Ending inventory	———	———	———	———
Cost of goods sold	———	———	———	———
Gross margin	———	———	———	———
Expenses	———	———	———	———
Pretax income		———	———	———
Income tax expense		———	———	———
Net income		══	══	══

b. Comparing FIFO and LIFO, which method is preferable in terms of (1) net income and (2) cash flow? Explain.

c. What would be your answer to Requirement (b) assuming prices were falling? Explain.

E7–9 (Analysis of Cash Flow Effects of Alternative Inventory Methods)
Following is partial information for the income statement of Lime Company under three different inventory costing methods assuming a periodic inventory system:

	FIFO	LIFO	Weighted average
Unit sales price, $30.			
Cost of goods sold:			
Beginning inventory (480 units)	$ 9,600	$ 9,600	$ 9,600
Purchases (520 units)	13,000	13,000	13,000
Goods available for sale			
Ending inventory (530 units)			
Cost of goods sold			
Expenses, $1,200			

Required:

a. Compute cost of goods sold under the FIFO, LIFO, and weighted-average inventory costing methods.

b. Prepare an income statement through pretax income for each method.

c. Rank the three methods in order of favourable cash flow and explain the basis for your ranking.

Part B: Exercises 7–10 to 7–17

E7–10 (Use of FIFO with a Perpetual Inventory System)
United Company uses a perpetual inventory system and FIFO. The inventory records reflected the following for January 19B:

Transactions	Units	Unit cost
Beginning inventory, January 1	80	$1.00
Purchase, January 6	200	1.10
Sale, January 10 (at $2.40 per unit)	110	
Purchase, January 14	100	1.30
Sale, January 29 (at $2.50 per unit)	160	

Required:

a. Prepare the perpetual inventory record for January.

b. Give journal entries indicated by the above data for January (assume cash transactions).

c. Prepare a summary income statement for January through gross margin.

E7–11   **(Comparison of Periodic and Perpetual Inventory Systems Using LIFO)**

At the end of the accounting period, the inventory records of Egger Company reflected the following:

Transactions (in order of date)	Units	Unit cost
Beginning inventory	500	$10
1. Purchase No. 1	600	12
2. Sale No. 1 (at $23 per unit)	(700)	
3. Purchase No. 2	800	13
4. Sale No. 2 (at $25 per unit)	(500)	
Ending inventory	700	

Required:

a. Compute goods available for sale in units and dollars.

b. Compute the (1) ending inventory valuation and (2) cost of goods sold assuming a periodic inventory system under the LIFO inventory costing method.

c. For comparative purposes compute the (1) ending inventory valuation and (2) cost of goods sold assuming a perpetual inventory system under the LIFO inventory costing method. To do this prepare a perpetual inventory record and cost each sale when made. See Exhibit 7–6 for an example of a perpetual inventory record.

d. Compare the results of (b) and (c) and explain why the valuations of ending inventory and cost of goods sold are different as between the periodic and perpetual inventory systems.

E7–12   **(Analysis of the Moving Weighted-Average Cost Inventory Method)**

Use the data given in Exercise 7–4 for this exercise (assume cash transactions).

Required:

a. Prepare the perpetual inventory record for January on a moving weighted-average basis. Round to the nearest cent on unit costs and the nearest dollar on total cost. See Exhibit 7–4 for an example of a perpetual inventory record.

b. Give the journal entry to record the purchase of January 9.

c. Give the journal entry(s) to record the sale on January 11.

d. Prepare a summarized income statement through gross margin for January.

e. Explain why a moving weighted average rather than a weighted average for the period was used.

f. When the weighted-average cost method is used, would the ending inventory and cost of goods sold amounts usually be different between periodic and perpetual inventory systems? Explain why.

E7–13   **(Comparison of FIFO, Periodic and FIFO, Perpetual)**
Fairfield Company uses a perpetual inventory system and applies FIFO inventory costing. The data below were provided by the accounting records for 19B:

Transactions (in order of date)	Units	Unit cost	Total cost
Beginning inventory	125	$10	$1,250
1. Purchase No. 1	300	12	3,600
2. Sale No. 1 (at $21 each)	(275)		
3. Purchase No. 2	400	14	5,600
4. Sale No. 2 (at $23 each)	(200)		
Ending inventory	350		

Required:

a. Compute the valuation of (1) cost of goods sold and (2) ending inventory assuming a perpetual inventory system and application of the FIFO inventory costing method.

b. Give the journal entries to record transactions 1 and 2 assuming FIFO:

Case A—A perpetual inventory system.

Case B—A periodic inventory system.

Use adjacent amount columns for each system and assume cash transactions.

c. Explain why the journal entries are different between the perpetual and periodic inventory systems.

E7–14   **(Accounting for Damaged Goods under a Perpetual Inventory System)**
Contemporary Sound Company is preparing the annual financial statements at December 31, 19D. Two different types of tape recorders that were used as demonstrators remained on hand at year-end. These items will be sold as damaged (used) merchandise; therefore, they must be removed from the ending inventory of new merchandise. The company uses a perpetual inventory system. These items will be included in the inventory of damaged goods. Data on the tape recorder models are:

	Model 2—206	Model 112A
Quantity damaged	1	2
Actual unit cost	$400	$300
Regular sales price	700	500
Estimated unit market value in present condition	380	250
Estimated unit cost to sell	80	35

Required:

a. Compute the valuation of each item that should be used for 19D inventory purposes. Show computations.

b. Give the required journal entry(s) to reflect the appropriate inventory valuations in the accounts.

E7–15   (Alternative Applications of LCM)

Anderson Company is preparing the annual financial statements dated December 31, 19B. Ending inventory information about the five major items stocked for regular sale is:

Ending inventory, 19B

Item	Quantity on hand	Unit cost when acquired (FIFO)	Replacement cost (market) at year-end
A ...	50	$20	$18
B ...	100	45	45
C ...	20	60	62
D ...	40	40	40
E ...	500	10	8

Required:

a. Compute the valuation that should be used for the 19B ending inventory using the LCM rule applied on an item-by-item basis. (Hint: Set up columns for Item, Quantity, Total cost, Total market, and LCM valuation.)

b. Compute the valuation of ending inventory using the LCM rule applied to total cost and total market value of the inventory.

c. Which method (*a*) or (*b*) is preferable? Why?

E7–16   (Estimating Ending Inventory)

Reston Retail Company prepares annual financial statements each December 31. The company uses a periodic inventory system. This system requires an annual detailed inventory count of all items on the store shelves and items stored in a separate warehouse. However, the management also desires quarterly financial statements but will not take a physical inventory count four times during the year. Accordingly, they use the gross margin method to estimate the ending inventory for the first three quarters.

At the end of the first quarter, March 31, 19D, the accounting records provided the following information:

1. Beginning inventory, January 1, 19D . . . . $ 60,000

Data for the first quarter of 19D:

2. Sales revenue   405,000
3. Sales returns   5,000
4. Purchases   296,000
5. Freight-in   4,000
6. Operating expenses (excluding income tax expense) . . .   50,000
7. Estimated average income tax rate, 20%.
8. Estimated gross margin ratio, 30%.

Required:

Based on the above information prepare a detailed income statement for the first quarter of 19D. Show all computations.

E7–17   **(Estimating Inventory Based on Partial Records)**

On November 2, 19C, a fire destroyed the inventory of University Book Store. The accounting records were not destroyed; therefore, they provided the following information:

	19A	19B	19C to date of fire
Sales revenue	$120,000	$142,000	$120,000
Cost of goods sold	73,200	85,200	?
Gross margin on sales	46,800	56,800	?
Expenses	34,800	42,800	35,000
Pretax income	$ 12,000	$ 14,000	?
Ending inventory	$ 20,000	$ 22,000	?
Purchases during year	70,000	87,200	75,000

Required:

a. Based on the data available, prepare an estimated income statement for 19C up to the date of the fire. Show details for the cost of goods sold. Disregard income taxes and show computations.

b. What amount of loss on the inventory should be submitted to the insurance company? Write a brief statement in support of the amount of indemnity claimed.

PROBLEMS

Part A: Problems 7–1 to 7–7

P7–1   **(Analysis and Correction of an Error in Ending Inventory)**

The income statement for Pitts Company summarized for a four-year period shows the following:

	19A	19B	19C	19D
Sales revenue	$1,000,000	$1,200,000	$1,300,000	$1,100,000
Cost of goods sold	600,000	610,000	870,000	650,000
Gross margin	400,000	590,000	430,000	450,000
Expenses	300,000	328,000	362,000	317,000
Pretax income	100,000	262,000	68,000	133,000
Income tax expense (30%) . . .	30,000	78,600	20,400	39,900
Net income	$ 70,000	$ 183,400	$ 47,600	$ 93,100

An audit revealed that in determining the above amounts, the ending inventory for 19B was overstated by $30,000. The company uses a periodic inventory system.

Required:

a. Recast the above income statements on a correct basis.

b. Did the error affect cumulative net income for the four-year period? Explain.

c. Did the error affect cash inflows or outflows? Explain.

P7–2   **(Analysis of Possible Inventory Errors)**

Monroe Company has just completed a physical inventory count at year-end, December 31, 19B. Only the items on the shelves, in storage, and in the receiving area were counted and costed on a FIFO basis. The inventory amounted to $90,000. During the audit, the independent PA developed the following additional information:

a. Goods costing $400 were being used by a customer on a trial basis and were excluded from the inventory count at December 31, 19B.

b. Goods in transit on December 31, 19B, from a supplier, with terms CIF destination, cost, $700. Because these goods had not arrived, they were excluded from the physical inventory count.

c. On December 31, 19B, goods in transit to customers, with terms FOB shipping point, amounted to $900 (expected delivery date January 10, 19C). Because the goods had been shipped, they were excluded from the physical inventory count.

d. On December 28, 19B, a customer purchased goods for cash amounting to $1,500 and left them "for pickup on January 3, 19C." Monroe Company had paid $800 for the goods and, because they were on hand, included the latter amount in the physical inventory count.

e. Monroe Company, on the date of the inventory, received notice from a supplier that goods ordered earlier, at a cost of $2,400, had been delivered to the transportation company on December 27, 19B; the terms were FOB shipping point. Because the shipment had not arrived by December 31, 19B, it was excluded from the physical inventory.

f. On December 31, 19B, Monroe Company shipped $750 worth of goods to a customer, CIF destination. The goods are expected to arrive at their destination no earlier than January 8, 19C. Because the goods were not on hand, they were not included in the physical inventory count.

g. One of the items sold by Monroe Company has such a low volume that the management planned to drop it last year. In order to induce Monroe Company to continue carrying the item, the manufacturer-supplier provided the item on a consignment basis. At the end of each month, Monroe Company (the consignee) renders a report to the manufacturer on the number sold and remits cash for the cost. At the end of December 19B, Monroe Company had five of these items on hand; therefore, they were included in the physical inventory count at $2,000 each.

Required:

Begin with the $90,000 inventory amount and compute the correct amount for the ending inventory. Explain the basis for your treatment of each of the above items. (Hint: The correct amount is $82,750. Set up three columns: Item, Amount, and Explanation.)

P7–3   **(Use of Four Alternative Inventory Methods with the Periodic System)**

Ross Company uses a periodic inventory system. At the end of the annual accounting period, December 31, 19E, the accounting records for the most popular item in inventory showed:

Transactions	Units	Unit cost
Beginning inventory, January 1, 19E	300	$20
Transactions during 19E:		
1. Purchase, February 20	500	22
2. Sale, April 1 (at $40 each)	(600)	
3. Purchase, June 30	400	24
4. Sale, August 1 (at $40 each)	(200)	
5. Sales return, August 5 (related to transaction 4)	10	

Required:

Compute the amount of (1) goods available for sale, (2) ending inventory, and (3) cost of goods sold at December 31, 19E, under each of the following inventory costing methods (show computations and round to the nearest dollar):

a. Weighted-average cost.

b. First-in, first-out.

c. Last-in, first-out.

d. Specific identification, assuming that the April 1, 19E, sale was "selected" as being one third from the beginning inventory and two thirds of that sale from the purchase of February 20, 19E. Assume the sale of August 1, 19E, was "selected" from the purchase of June 30, 19E.

P7–4 **(Analysis and Use of Alternative Inventory Methods)**

At the end of January 19B, the records at St. John's Company showed the following for a particular item that sold at $20 per unit:

Transactions	Units	Amount
Inventory, January 1, 19B	700	$4,200
Sale, January 10	(600)	
Purchase, January 12	600	4,200
Sale, January 17	(550)	
Purchase, January 26	310	2,790
Purchase return, January 28 . . .	(10)	Out of Jan. 26 purchase

Required:

a. Assuming a periodic inventory system, prepare a summarized income statement through gross margin on sales under each method of inventory: (1) weighted-average cost, (2) FIFO, (3) LIFO, and (4) specific identification. For specific identification, assume the first sale was out of the beginning inventory and the second sale was out of the January 12 purchase. Show the inventory computations in detail.

b. Between FIFO and LIFO, which method will derive the higher pretax income? Which would derive the higher EPS?

c. Between FIFO and LIFO, which method will derive the lower income tax expense? Explain, assuming a 20% average tax rate.

d. Between FIFO and LIFO, which method will produce the more favourable cash flow? Explain.

P7-5 **(Manipulation of Income under the LIFO Inventory Method)**
Import Company sells large computers that it acquires from a foreign source. During the year 19W, the inventory records reflected the following:

	Units	Unit cost	Total cost
Beginning inventory	20	$25,000	$500,000
Purchases	30	20,000	600,000
Sales (35 units at $45,000)			

The company uses the LIFO inventory costing method. On December 28, 19W, the unit cost of the computer was decreased to $18,000. The cost will be decreased again during the first quarter of the next year.

Required:

a. Complete the following income statement summary using the LIFO method and the periodic inventory system (show computations):

Sales revenue	$_____
Cost of goods sold	_____
Gross margin	_____
Expenses	300,000
Pretax income	$_____
Ending inventory	$_____

b. The management, for various reasons, is considering buying 20 additional units before December 31, 19W, at $18,000 each. Restate the above income statement (and ending inventory) assuming this purchase is made on December 31, 19W.

c. How much did pretax income change because of the decision on December 31, 19W? Is there any evidence of income manipulation? Explain.

P7-6 **(Change in Inventory Method from FIFO to LIFO)**
Quick Stop Corporation reported the following summarized annual data at the end of 19X:

	(millions)
Sales revenue	$950
Cost of goods sold*	500
Gross margin	450
Expenses	200
Pretax income	$250

* Based on ending FIFO inventory of $150 million. On a LIFO basis this ending inventory would have been $80 million.

Before issuing the preceding statement the company decided to change from FIFO to LIFO for 19X because "it better reflects our operating results." The company has always used FIFO.

Required:

a. Restate the summary income statement on a LIFO basis.

b. How much did pretax income change due to the LIFO decision for 19X? What caused the change in pretax income?

c. If you were a shareholder, what would be your reaction to this change? Explain.

P7–7   (Comparison of LIFO and FIFO when Costs Are Rising and Falling)
Income to be evaluated under four different situations as follows:

Prices are rising:
    Situation A—FIFO is used.
    Situation B—LIFO is used.
Prices are falling:
    Situation C—FIFO is used.
    Situation D—LIFO is used.

The basic data common to all four situations are sales, 600 units for $5,600; beginning inventory, 500 units; purchases, 500 units; ending inventory, 400 units; and operating expenses, $3,000. The following tabulated income statements for each situation have been set up for analytical purposes:

	Prices rising		Prices falling	
	Situation A FIFO	Situation B LIFO	Situation C FIFO	Situation D LIFO
Sales revenue	$5,600	$5,600	$5,600	$5,600
Cost of goods sold:				
Beginning inventory	1,000	?	?	?
Purchases	1,500	?	?	?
Goods available for sale	2,500	?	?	?
Ending inventory	1,200	?	?	?
Cost of goods sold	1,300	?	?	?
Gross margin	4,300	?	?	?
Expenses	3,000	3,000	3,000	3,000
Pretax income	1,300	?	?	?
Income tax expense (30%)	390	?	?	?
Net income	$ 910			

Required:

a. Complete the above tabulation for each situation. In Situations A and B (prices rising), assume the following: beginning inventory, 500 units at $2 = $1,000; and purchases, 500 units at $3 = $1,500. In Situations C and D (prices falling), assume the opposite; that is, beginning inventory, 500 units at $3 = $1,500; and purchases, 500 units at $2 = $1,000. Use periodic inventory procedures.

b. Analyze the relative effects on pretax income and on net income as demonstrated by Requirement (a) when prices are rising and when prices are falling.

c. Analyze the relative effects on the cash position for each situation.

d. Would you recommend FIFO or LIFO? Explain.

Part B: Problems 7–8 to 7–17

P7–8 **(Analysis of Inventory Errors)**
The income statements for four consecutive years for Clark Company reflected the following summarized amounts:

	19A	19B	19C	19D
Sales revenue	$60,000	$60,000	$78,000	$65,000
Cost of goods sold	36,000	38,300	50,100	39,000
Gross margin	24,000	21,700	27,900	26,000
Expenses	15,000	16,700	17,200	15,800
Pretax income	$ 9,000	$ 5,000	$10,700	$10,200

Subsequent to development of the above amounts, it has been determined that the physical inventory taken on December 31, 19B, was understated by $4,000.

Required:

a. Recast the above income statements to reflect the correct amounts, taking into consideration the inventory error.

b. Compute the gross margin ratio for each year (1) before the correction and (2) after the correction. Do the results lend confidence to your corrected amounts? Explain.

c. What effect would the error have had on the income tax expense assuming a 20% average rate?

P7–9 **(Analysis of the Effects of Damaged Goods in Inventory)**
Quebec Company has completed taking the periodic inventory count of merchandise remaining on hand at the end of the fiscal year, December 31, 19D. Questions have arisen concerning inventory costing for five different items. The inventory reflected the following:

	Units	Original unit cost
Item A—The two units on hand are damaged because they were used as demonstrators. The company estimated that they may be sold at 20% below cost and that disposal costs will amount to $60 each. 202– 60 = 148 max.	2	$260
Item B—Because of a drop in the market, this item can be replaced from the original supplier at 10% below the original cost. The sale price also was reduced. 63.	20	70
Item C—Because of style change, it is highly doubtful that the four units can be sold; they have no scrap value.	4	20
Item D—This item no longer will be stocked; as a consequence it will be marked down from the regular sale price of $110 to $50. Cost of selling is estimated to be 20% of the original cost. ʌ	3	80
Item E—Because of high demand and quality, the cost of this item has been raised from $120 to $125; hence, all replacements for inventory in the foreseeable future will be at the latter price. no entry	15	120

The remaining items in inventory pose no valuation problems: their costs sum to $50,000.

Required:

Compute the total amount of the ending inventory including the damaged goods. List each of the above items separately and explain the basis for your decision with respect to each item.

P7-10   **(Comparison of LIFO and FIFO Using a Perpetual Inventory System)**
Waco Hardware Store uses a perpetual inventory system. This problem will focus on one item stocked, designated at Item A. The beginning inventory was 2,000 units at $4. During January, the following transactions occurred that affected Item A:

Jan. 5 Sold 500 units at $10 per unit.
     10 Purchased 1,000 units at $5 per unit.
     16 Sold 1,800 units at $12 per unit.
     18 Purchased 2,300 units for $13,800.
     24 Sold 500 units at $12 per unit.

Required (assume cash transactions):

a. Prepare a perpetual inventory record for January on (1) a FIFO basis and (2) a LIFO basis.

b. Give the journal entry(s) for each basis for the purchase on January 10.

c. Give the journal entry(s) for each basis for the sale on January 16.

d. Complete the following financial statement amounts for each basis:

		January	
		FIFO	LIFO
Income statement:			
Sales revenue	$	?	$?
Cost of goods sold		?	?
Gross margin		?	?
Expenses		12,000	12,000
Pretax income		?	?
Balance sheet:			
Current assets:			
Merchandise inventory		?	?

e. Which method gives the higher pretax income? Under what conditions would this comparative effect be the opposite?

f. Assuming a 20% average tax rate, which method would provide the more favourable cash position? By how much? Explain.

g. Which basis would you recommend for Waco? Why?

P7–11   **(Use of a Perpetual Inventory Record)**

Box Elder Company uses a perpetual inventory system. Below is a perpetual inventory record for the period for one product sold at $6 per unit.

PERPETUAL INVENTORY RECORD

Date								
a.						400		1,200
b.	800	3.30				1,200		
c.			500		1,600	700		2,240
d.	300		1,050					3,290
e.			200			800		2,632
f.			600		1,974	200		
g.	500	3.60						

Required:

1. Complete the column captions for the perpetual inventory record.
2. What inventory costing method is being used?
3. Enter all of the missing amounts on the perpetual inventory records.
4. Complete the following tabulation:

	Units	Per unit	Amount
a. Beginning inventory	_____	_____	_____
b. Ending inventory	_____	_____	_____
c. Total purchases	_____	_____	_____
d. Total cost of goods sold ...	_____	_____	_____

5. Give the journal entry(s) for date (b).
6. Give the journal entry(s) for date (c).
7. Assume a periodic inventory taken at the end of the period reflected 690 units on hand. Give any journal entry(s) required.
8. Disregard Requirement 7 and assume that on date (h), 10 units of the beginning inventory were returned to the supplier and a cash refund of $2.90 per unit was recovered. Give the required entry.

P7–12   **(Comparison of FIFO and LIFO Using a Perpetual Inventory System)**

Super Company executives are considering their inventory policies. They have been using the moving weighted-average method with a perpetual inventory system. They have requested an "analysis of the effects of using FIFO versus LIFO." Selected financial statement amounts (rounded) for the month of January 19B, based upon the moving weighted-average method, are as follows:

	Units	Amounts
Income statement:		
Sales revenue	180	$10,600
Cost of goods sold	180	5,710
Gross margin on sales		4,890
Less: Expenses		2,000
Pretax income		$ 2,890
Balance sheet:		
Merchandise inventory		$ 2,620

Transactions during the month were:

Beginning inventory 50 units at $30.

Jan. 6 Sold 40 units at $55.
    9 Purchased 100 units at $32.
    16 Sold 80 units at $60.
    20 Purchased 110 units at $33.
    28 Sold 60 units at $60.

Required:

a. Copy the above statement data and extend each item to the right by adding columns for FIFO and LIFO using a perpetual inventory system. This statement will provide one basis for analyzing the different results among the three inventory costing methods.

b. Which inventory costing method produces the highest pretax income? Explain.

c. Between FIFO and LIFO, which inventory costing method provides the more favourable cash position for 19B? Explain.

P7–13   (Use of LCM under the Periodic Inventory System)
Durwin Company prepared their annual financial statements dated December 31, 19B. The company uses a periodic inventory system and applies the FIFO inventory costing method; however, the company neglected to apply LCM to the ending inventory. The preliminary 19B income statement is summarized below:

Sales revenue		$310,000
Cost of goods sold:		
Beginning inventory	$ 40,000	
Purchases	206,000	
Goods available for sale	246,000	
Ending inventory (FIFO cost) . . .	50,000	
Cost of goods sold		196,000
Gross margin		114,000
Operating expenses		58,000
Pretax income		56,000
Income tax expense (30%)		16,800
Net income		$ 39,200

Assume you have been asked to restate the 19B financial statements to incorporate LCM. You have developed the following data relating to the 19B ending inventory:

Item		Quantity	Acquisition cost Unit	Acquisition cost Total	Current replacement unit cost (market)
A	. . .	2,000	$ 2	$ 4,000	$ 4
B	. . .	3,000	6	18,000	5
C	. . .	4,000	4	16,000	5
D	. . .	1,000	12	12,000	10
				$50,000	

Required:

a. Restate the above income statement to reflect LCM valuation of the 19B ending inventory. Apply LCM on an item-by-item basis and show computations.

b. Compare and explain the LCM effect on each amount that was changed in (a).

c. What is the conceptual basis for applying LCM to merchandise inventories?

d. What effect did LCM have on the cash flow of 19B? What will be the long-term effect on cash flow?

P7–14 **(Estimating the Amount of Inventory Damaged in a Flood for Insurance Purposes)**
On April 15, 19B, North Sea Company suffered a major flood that damaged their entire merchandise inventory. Fortunately, North Sea carried a casualty insurance policy that covered floods. The company uses the periodic inventory system. The accounting records were not damaged; therefore, they provided the following information for the period January 1 through April 14, 19B:

Merchandise inventory, December 31, 19A	$ 21,000
Transactions through April 14, 19B:	
Purchases	70,000
Purchase returns	2,000
Freight-in	1,000
Sales	103,000
Sales returns	3,000

Required:

For insurance indemnity purposes you have been asked to estimate the amount of the inventory loss. Your analysis to date indicates that (a) a 30% gross margin rate is reasonable and (b) the damaged merchandise can be sold to a local salvage company for approximately $4,000 cash.

What amount should be presented to the insurance company as a claim for insurance indemnity? Show computations.

P7-15   (Preparing an Interim Income Statement without Taking an Inventory Count)

The president of ET Company has been presented with the March 19B financial statements. They reflect data for three months as summarized below:

Income statements

	January	February	March	Quarter
Sales revenue	$100,000	$106,000	$90,000	$296,000
Cost of goods sold	61,000	59,360	?	?
Gross margin on sales	39,000	46,640	?	?
Expenses	32,000	33,500	32,000	97,500
Pretax income	$ 7,000	$ 13,140	$?	$?
Gross margin ratio	.39	.44	.42 (estimated)	
Ending inventory	$ 14,000	$ 16,000		

The company uses a periodic inventory system. Although monthly statements are prepared, a monthly inventory count is not made. Instead, the company uses the gross margin method for monthly inventory purposes.

Required:

a. Complete computations in the following tabulation to estimate the results for March.

	Amounts	Computations
Cost of goods sold:		
Beginning inventory	$16,000	From records
Purchases	51,000	From records
Goods available for sale	?	?
Ending inventory	?	?
Cost of goods sold		?

b. Complete the income statements given above (March and Quarter). Disregard income tax.

c. What level of confidence do you think can be attributed to the results for March? Explain.

d. Would you recommend continued use of the gross margin method for the company? Explain.

P7-16   (Computer Spreadsheet, Perpetual Inventory)

Required:

Using the data provided in P7-11, complete Requirements (3) and (4) of that problem using a computer spreadsheet.

P7-17   (Computer Spreadsheet, Costing Methods)

Required:

Do P7-12 using a computer spreadsheet for (a) of Required.

CASES

C7–1   **(Analysis of the Effects of a Reduction in the Amount of LIFO Inventory)**
An annual report of ALarge Oil Company contained the following footnote:

> During both 1981 and 1980, the company reduced certain inventory quantities which were valued at lower LIFO costs prevailing in prior years. The effect of these reductions was to increase aftertax earnings by $71 million, or $0.24 per share, and $74 million, or $0.25 per share, in 1981 and 1980, respectively.

Required:

   a. Explain why the reduction in inventory quantity increased aftertax earnings (net income).

   b. If ALarge Oil had used FIFO, would the reductions in inventory quantity in 1980 and 1981 have increased aftertax earnings? Explain.

C7–2   **(Analysis of the Effect of an Inventory Error Disclosed in an Actual Note to a Financial Statement)**
Several years ago, the financial statements of Lafayette Radio Electronics Corporation contained the following footnote:

> Subsequent to the issuance of its financial statements, the company discovered a computational error in the amount of $1,046,000 in the calculation of its year-end inventory which resulted in an overstatement of ending inventory.

> Assume that Lafayette reported an incorrect net income amount of $3,101,000 for the year in which the error occurred and that the income tax rate is 40%.

Required:

   a. Compute the amount of net income that Lafayette should report after correcting the inventory error. Show computations.

   b. Assume that the inventory error had not been discovered. Identify the financial statement accounts that would have been incorrect for the year the error occurred and for the subsequent year. State whether each account was understated or over-stated.

C7–3   **(Inventory Valuation)**
A&B Limited is a Canadian company engaged in a wholesaling business and currently distributes three major product lines. Over the years, the company has distributed several other product lines, only to discontinue them when the competition became too intense. During the past three years, one of its product lines, product line X, has suffered a continual decline in sales volume and has had a negative effect on the company's operating profits. At December 31, 1988, a significant portion of the inventory of product line X was about two years old.

In October 1988, management decided to discontinue distribution of product line X and, accordingly, notified the company's customers that it would continue to sell the inventory then on hand but would no longer accept orders for items which would have to be purchased from a manufacturer. After this notice was sent to the company's customers, sales volume of product line X declined even further. Therefore, management decided in early 1989 to sell this inventory in bulk to one of the company's competitors.

The company's preliminary financial position and operating results before any write-down of inventory are shown in the balance sheet and statements of retained earnings and income below.

A&B LIMITED
Balance Sheet
As at December 31, 1988

Current assets excluding inventories	$ 1,500,000
Inventories:	
Product line C	1,600,000
Other product lines	3,900,000
Fixed assets:	
Land and warehouses—net	6,000,000
	$13,000,000
Current liabilities	$ 2,500,000
Long-term debt:	
9¾% sinking fund bonds repayable at $500,000 per year	6,000,000
Deferred income taxes	1,000,000
Shareholders' equity:	
Share capital (1 million common shares)	1,000,000
Retained earnings	2,500,000
	$13,000,000

A&B LIMITED
Statement of Retained Earnings
For the Year Ended December 31, 1988

Retained earnings, beginning of year	$2,000,000
Net income	825,000
Dividends	(325,000)
Retained earnings, end of year	$2,500,000

A&B LIMITED
Statement of Income
For the Year Ended December 31, 1988

	Product lines			
	A	**B**	**C**	**Total**
Sales	$4,500,000	$3,000,000	$1,500,000	$9,000,000
Cost of sales	2,400,000	1,200,000	1,400,000	5,000,000
Gross margin	2,100,000	1,800,000	100,000	4,000,000
Direct operating expenses	400,000	300,000	200,000	900,000
	$1,700,000	$1,500,000	$ (100,000)	3,100,000

Unallocated expenses:		
Interest on long-term debt	$633,750	
Other	816,250	1,450,000
Income before income taxes		1,650,000
Income taxes (including $200,000 deferred)		825,000
Net income		$ 825,000

Note: Net income for the years ending December 31, 1984 to 1987 was $750,000, $800,000, $700,000, and $925,000, respectively.

In order to meet its debt agreement, audited financial statements must be provided to the bank by February 18, 1989. Your firm has been the auditor of the company for the last five years.

Early in 1989, when you arrive at the client's premises to finalize the audit of the December 31, 1988, financial statements, management informs you that they are attempting to sell the inventory of product line X in bulk. Management informs you that they are currently negotiating the sale with one competitor and that the asking price is $1,100,000, which they are confident they will get. They are unwilling to permit you to review any documentation supporting the current negotiations because of a commitment that they have made not to disclose the purchaser's identity. They also inform you that the only firm written offer received so far is from a second competitor and the amount of this offer is $800,000. They are prepared to provide you with a copy of this offer.

Management agrees that the inventory value for product line X is overstated and that a write-down is necessary. They argue that the value of the inventory was impaired at the beginning of 1988 and, although the formal decision to cease distribution of product line X was not made until 1988 the economic event occurred in 1987. To support their argument, they point out that most of the inventory is about two years old and must have been overvalued at the beginning of 1988 as demonstrated by the losses incurred during the year on sales of the product line.

Based on these facts, management concluded that a write-down of $500,000 (i.e., to the amount of $1,000,000 currently being negotiated) is all that is required and that the write-down should be treated as a charge against 1987 income. Management believes that this was abnormal in magnitude and nature to the company's regular business and that it pertains to the disposal of a major product line, and therefore, it should be treated as an extraordinary item. Management is prepared to make any disclosure you consider appropriate in the notes to the financial statements, but, will not change their position on these matters.

Required:
Discuss the accounting considerations in this situation and how they should affect the 1988 financial statement.

(CICA Adapted)

C7-4   **(Analysis of Inventory and Cost of Goods Sold Using an Actual Financial Statement)**
Refer to the financial statements of Consolidated-Bathurst given in Appendix B immediately preceding the Index.

Required:
a. What method does C-B use to determine the cost of its inventory?
b. Total inventory was $355,554,000 in 1987. What amount of inventory was finished goods (as opposed to raw materials and work in process)?
c. If the company had used FIFO for all of its inventory would net income have been higher or lower? If it cannot be determined, explain why.
d. What was the cost of goods sold for the year 1987?
e. What can be determined about the cost of goods sold for Canadian operations?

C7-5   **(Inventory Valuation)**

CA, the newly appointed shareholders' auditor, has just examined the inventory accounts of D Ltd., a medium-sized manufacturing company. Upon completion of his audit CA is satisfied with the determination of inventory quantities and condition, but not with the valuation and disclosure.

Management intends to show inventories on the balance sheet as follows:

Inventories, value at the lower of cost and market $500,000

CA has determined that the inventory consists of the following items:

a. Raw materials value at laid-down cost less 10% for anticipated waste during production $270,000

b. Work in process at list selling price less deductions for trade and cash discounts, normal profit, selling and administrative expense, and cost to completion 150,000

c. Finished goods at list price less deductions for trade and cash discounts, normal profit, selling and administrative expense 80,000

$500,000

The percentage deductions used in the above calculations were determined 10 years ago, and CA found that they bear little relationship to current ratios. If the average actual rates of deductions experienced in the previous two years were used to calculate the current inventories, the work in process inventory would total $225,000 and the finished goods inventory would total $200,000.

A cost ledger is maintained for cost control and price setting studies. If work in process inventories and finished goods inventories had been computed using the actual unit costs recorded in the memorandum ledger, they would have totaled $210,000 and $195,000, respectively.

Total assets of the company, using the company's valuation of total inventory, are $1,750,000.

The method of valuation proposed by management is favoured by the directors on the grounds that it has been the method used consistently for several years and that all the shareholders are aware of the method of valuation because the shares in the company are closely held.

The directors have asked CA to present a report which gives his views on the inventory valuation and disclosure.

Required:

Outline the points which CA should include in his report to the directors, including his reasons for dissatisfaction with the proposed valuation and disclosure of inventories and his comments on the arguments advanced by the directors in support of their position.

(CICA, Adapted)

C7–6   (Inventory Data Base—Design and Operation)

Inventory Data Base Case

Introduction to Case

In this exercise, you will:

1. Determine the basic informational outputs desired from an inventory system.
2. Determine the data inputs required in order to generate those outputs.
3. Determine the basic data processing steps required to generate the desired outputs from the specified inputs.
4. Create a data base and use it to generate specified outputs.

   As is frequently the case, the general ledger inventory account is a control account which is supported by a subsidiary ledger.

   This exercise deals with a manufacturing firm with more than 1,500 items in its inventory. These items are used in the following ways:

a. Raw materials put into work in process inventory.

b. Materials used in the production process as part of manufacturing overhead.

c. Materials used as general business supplies.

   As items are taken out of inventory, the cost of the goods taken out of inventory is charged to Work in Process, Manufacturing Overhead, or some other expense accounts. The company accounts for its inventories using the average cost system.

   For illustrative purposes, a few accounts and transactions have been selected. This data appears later in the exercise.

General System Design Steps

As discussed in the Chapter 6 data base exercise (pp. 344–59), in designing a system, there are a number of important issues that need to be resolved.

1. Determine the information that will be required by the users of the system.

Requirement 1:

What are the primary questions that one would want an inventory system to answer? For example, one might want to know how many units of each inventory item the firm has. [answer 1]

2. Determine the data that must be collected and processed in order for the system to generate the desired outputs.

Requirement 2:

In this inventory example, what data will the firm have to collect in order to answer the questions raised above? [answer 2]

3. Group the data items together in some reasonable manner.

Requirement 3:

Organize the data inputs you specified in Requirement 2 and design the files that will hold this data. [answer 3]

4. Determine the general processing steps that are required to go from the stated inputs to the desired outputs.

Before preparing a flowchart, one should have a general idea of how the inventory system works. Below are some simple diagrams that illustrate the essentials of such systems.

Before attempting to draw a flowchart, you should have a general idea of how a computerized receivable system works. Refer to Chapter 6 for information about this.

Diagram for Computerized System

1. Use of inventory*

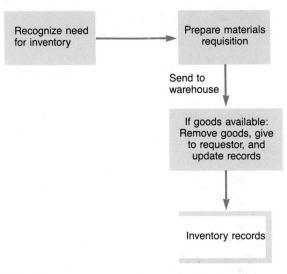

* Closed box represents processing; open box denotes a file.

2. Purchase and receipt of inventory items

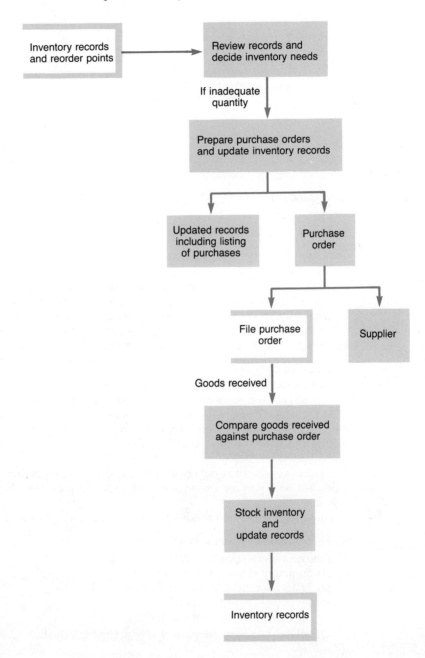

3. Monthly reporting

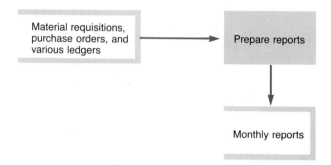

Requirement 4:

Prepare a flowchart for the inventory system.

Concrete Implementation Steps

Once the general system design issues have been resolved, one begins to make the concrete decisions that must be made in order to implement a system.

Step 1. The first of these steps is to precisely define each data item. One must determine the words to be used to refer to each input or calculated amount, the characteristics to be associated with each input or calculated amount, the file(s) where each data input calculated amount, and so on, will be stored.

Requirement 5:

If you have access to a data base program, define, for use in that system, the files and data items required to computerize the manufacturing firm's inventory system. [answer 5]

Step 2. Having precisely defined the data inputs and set up the files, next determine the steps users must go through to extract the information or generate the system's reports and write the programs that when called by users will allow them to perform some desired function.

If you have access to a data base system and are creating an inventory system, prepare a detailed flowchart for this system and write the programs that will be used by this system.

Your programs should make it possible for authorized users to:

a. Record purchases and uses of inventory.

b. Prepare various inventory reports including:
   (1) Summary of inventory items.
   (2) Ledger accounts for inventory items.
   (3) Inventory turnover report.
   (4) Listings of selected information.

c. Query the data base interactively for desired information.

Requirement 6:

If you have access to a data base program, write the required programs. [answer 6]

Step 3. After the processing steps are specified, the next task is to implement the system. This involves creating any files that have not already been created and writing any "programs" which have not yet been written.

In addition to this, data must be entered into each of the files that have been created.

Listed below are some sample data, as of 30 September 1988, for selected inventory items.

No.	Item name	Reorder point	Unit cost	Beginning inventory
2635	SOPRA	550	21.12	171
2636	OUEPH	1,180	5.64	786
2637	GILLAD	1,130	15.14	3,594
2638	NOANT	2,140	34.25	4,647
2639	WAMAK	2,170	13.92	1,473
2640	BESERV	1,740	25.87	968
2641	MOAF	1,360	19.22	82
2642	WIPRI	1,140	1.81	362
2643	LORHEL	1,120	0.60	241
2644	BELIM	1,120	36.98	2,079
2645	LAMED	2,110	36.27	4,849
2646	WOREM	2,140	18.88	1,069
2647	SWEWOR	1,140	42.24	293
2648	SAIBRA	2,050	22.81	1,473
2649	PROGAIN	2,110	78.78	70
2650	DURWOR	2,100	57.40	4,121
2651	SHABURD	2,140	47.10	3,190
2652	AMANO	1,310	46.84	830
2653	KINWHE	1,470	72.71	1,352
2654	BROYOUN	1,080	31.93	1,574
2655	GREAMO	1,180	29.84	830
2656	HABAK	1,040	54.17	3,897
2657	JUDPRO	2,140	67.18	847
2658	COMFO	1,710	24.86	867
2659	FILPOL	1,160	69.68	1,049
2660	NATJU	1,120	23.85	766
2661	HIAMS	1,060	57.56	7,737
2662	SCRITHA	1,130	72.52	7,344
2663	PHACAL	1,040	7.76	1,857
2664	LESPA	1,040	29.94	931

For these inventory items, the company had the following transactions from 1 October 1988 to 31 December 1988 (dates are in day/month/year format):

No.	Date	Type of transaction	Inventory item	Quantity	Price
2587	01/10/88	Used in WIP	2656	1,324	
2588	01/10/88	Purchase	2648	2,050	24.24
2589	01/10/88	Used in WIP	2651	1,880	
2590	03/10/88	Purchase	2662	4,810	78.35
2591	04/10/88	Expensed	2645	187	
2592	04/10/88	Purchase	2652	360	42.74
2593	05/10/88	Purchase	2646	3,520	18.23
2594	05/10/88	Purchase	2656	1,760	67.41
2595	06/10/88	Purchase	2658	3,480	23.83

No.	Date	Type of transaction	Inventory item	Quantity	Price
2596	07/10/88	Purchase	2638	5,460	33.66
2597	07/10/88	Used in WIP	2664	872	
2598	08/10/88	Purchase	2662	4,810	70.60
2599	08/10/88	Purchase	2657	1,760	58.88
2600	09/10/88	Purchase	2660	5,280	21.08
2601	10/10/88	Purchase	2637	4,680	15.68
2602	10/10/88	Purchase	2653	2,800	64.90
2603	10/10/88	Used in WIP	2656	2,800	
2604	10/10/88	Purchase	2656	1,520	63.55
2605	12/10/88	Purchase	2663	1,440	7.15
2606	12/10/88	Expensed	2660	480	
2607	12/10/88	Purchase	2650	7,020	60.84
2608	13/10/88	Purchase	2644	4,800	44.57
2609	13/10/88	Expensed	2660	324	
2610	14/10/88	Purchase	2637	5,460	16.96
2611	14/10/88	Purchase	2650	6,840	60.73
2612	15/10/88	Purchase	2652	390	42.33
2613	15/10/88	Purchase	2639	7,480	18.32
2614	15/10/88	Expensed	2651	136	
2615	16/10/88	Purchase	2641	2,460	20.57
2616	16/10/88	Used in WIP	2657	2,008	
2617	16/10/88	Purchase	2664	2,100	28.78
2618	16/10/88	Used in WIP	2658	2,388	
2619	16/10/88	Used in WIP	2656	1,148	
2620	16/10/88	Used in WIP	2654	1,052	
2621	17/10/88	Purchase	2642	5,460	1.80
2622	18/10/88	Expensed	2651	88	
2623	18/10/88	Expensed	2650	666	
2624	19/10/88	Purchase	2649	530	82.86
2625	20/10/88	Expensed	2643	112	
2626	21/10/88	Used in WIP	2639	6,936	
2627	22/10/88	Purchase	2664	1,800	33.78
2628	23/10/88	Purchase	2640	3,480	26.86
2629	25/10/88	Used in WIP	2653	2,611	
2630	25/10/88	Purchase	2650	6,840	61.86
2631	26/10/88	Purchase	2645	4,290	39.95
2632	27/10/88	Used in WIP	2661	2,340	
2633	27/10/88	Used in WIP	2650	6,588	
2634	28/10/88	Purchase	2644	5,160	40.20
2635	29/10/88	Used in WIP	2637	7,579	
2636	30/10/88	Used in WIP	2664	3,656	
2637	30/10/88	Used in WIP	2641	1,956	
2638	30/10/88	Used in WIP	2662	9,854	
2639	01/11/88	Expensed	2664	124	
2640	01/11/88	Used in WIP	2635	156	
2641	02/11/88	Used in WIP	2660	4,896	
2642	02/11/88	Used in WIP	2644	3,624	
2643	02/11/88	Purchase	2639	7,480	20.95
2644	04/11/88	Used in WIP	2650	7,794	
2645	05/11/88	Used in WIP	2646	1,516	
2646	05/11/88	Expensed	2643	120	
2647	05/11/88	Used in WIP	2652	860	
2648	06/11/88	Purchase	2637	5,330	16.76
2649	07/11/88	Expensed	2649	36	
2650	08/11/88	Used in WIP	2644	3,972	
2651	08/11/88	Used in WIP	2648	3,310	

No.	Date	Type of transaction	Inventory item	Quantity	Price
2652	09/11/88	Used in WIP	2661	3,888	
2653	10/11/88	Used in WIP	2650	6,318	
2654	10/11/88	Expensed	2662	338	
2655	10/11/88	Purchase	2647	6,020	46.22
2656	12/11/88	Used in WIP	2644	4,280	
2657	12/11/88	Purchase	2653	3,080	64.65
2658	12/11/88	Used in WIP	2649	480	
2659	13/11/88	Expensed	2648	195	
2660	13/11/88	Purchase	2650	6,840	60.17
2661	13/11/88	Used in WIP	2645	6,633	
2662	14/11/88	Used in WIP	2663	2,960	
2663	15/11/88	Purchase	2664	1,750	32.53
2664	16/11/88	Purchase	2641	2,280	20.11
2665	16/11/88	Used in WIP	2638	7,882	
2666	17/11/88	Expensed	2662	299	
2667	17/11/88	Used in WIP	2664	1,784	
2668	19/11/88	Expensed	2642	532	
2669	20/11/88	Used in WIP	2641	2,268	
2670	21/11/88	Used in WIP	2640	1,320	
2671	21/11/88	Purchase	2662	5,590	74.96
2672	21/11/88	Purchase	2653	2,520	65.65
2673	22/11/88	Purchase	2651	1,800	50.29
2674	22/11/88	Used in WIP	2652	523	
2675	23/11/88	Purchase	2651	1,800	48.15
2676	23/11/88	Used in WIP	2637	6,799	
2677	23/11/88	Expensed	2646	152	
2678	23/11/88	Used in WIP	2640	1,212	
2679	25/11/88	Expensed	2649	12	
2680	26/11/88	Purchase	2638	5,600	31.96
2681	27/11/88	Purchase	2661	2,580	47.96
2682	28/11/88	Expensed	2653	84	
2683	28/11/88	Used in WIP	2642	4,928	
2684	29/11/88	Purchase	2639	7,310	20.90
2685	30/11/88	Used in WIP	2658	1,540	
2686	30/11/88	Used in WIP	2651	1,704	
2687	30/11/88	Purchase	2649	1,390	82.55
2688	30/11/88	Purchase	2657	1,440	56.55
2689	02/12/88	Purchase	2663	1,480	8.90
2690	03/12/88	Purchase	2661	2,280	48.92
2691	04/12/88	Purchase	2637	5,070	15.44
2692	04/12/88	Used in WIP	2651	1,416	
2693	04/12/88	Purchase	2653	2,870	68.65
2694	05/12/88	Expensed	2650	198	
2695	05/12/88	Purchase	2648	2,100	22.47
2696	05/12/88	Expensed	2659	544	
2697	05/12/88	Used in WIP	2661	2,220	
2698	06/12/88	Used in WIP	2649	835	
2699	06/12/88	Used in WIP	2657	1,856	
2700	06/12/88	Expensed	2642	334	
2701	08/12/88	Expensed	2639	595	
2702	08/12/88	Used in WIP	2653	5,090	
2703	09/12/88	Used in WIP	2662	6,266	
2704	09/12/88	Purchase	2658	1,800	28.27
2705	11/12/88	Purchase	2636	3,800	5.62
2706	11/12/88	Purchase	2643	440	0.64
2707	11/12/88	Expensed	2657	68	

No.	Date	Type of transaction	Inventory item	Quantity	Price
2708	12/12/88	Purchase	2642	5,040	2.20
2709	12/12/88	Expensed	2640	72	
2710	13/12/88	Used in WIP	2637	7,345	
2711	13/12/88	Used in WIP	2649	430	
2712	13/12/88	Purchase	2645	4,290	39.73
2713	13/12/88	Used in WIP	2658	1,220	
2714	14/12/88	Used in WIP	2645	3,619	
2715	15/12/88	Used in WIP	2646	1,684	
2716	15/12/88	Used in WIP	2640	1,408	
2717	15/12/88	Used in WIP	2639	7,157	
2718	16/12/88	Expensed	2664	136	
2719	16/12/88	Used in WIP	2642	4,992	
2720	16/12/88	Used in WIP	2648	2,030	
2721	16/12/88	Purchase	2651	1,560	53.04
2722	17/12/88	Purchase	2640	2,640	29.64
2723	18/12/88	Expensed	2637	247	
2724	18/12/88	Purchase	2664	1,480	29.03
2725	18/12/88	Used in WIP	2653	4,802	
2726	18/12/88	Purchase	2649	840	78.83
2727	19/12/88	Purchase	2652	360	44.40
2728	21/12/88	Expensed	2654	96	
2729	21/12/88	Used in WIP	2647	6,022	
2730	21/12/88	Purchase	2641	4,520	20.57
2731	21/12/88	Purchase	2664	1,560	31.83
2732	21/12/88	Purchase	2658	1,480	29.94
2733	22/12/88	Used in WIP	2636	4,000	
2734	22/12/88	Expensed	2662	234	
2735	22/81/88	Purchase	2656	1,720	58.42
2736	23/12/88	Used in WIP	2650	6,444	
2737	24/12/88	Purchase	2657	1,520	56.55
2738	24/12/88	Used in WIP	2661	3,708	
2739	26/12/88	Used in WIP	2656	1,892	
2740	26/12/88	Used in WIP	2641	2,070	
2741	27/12/88	Used in WIP	2639	7,996	
2742	28/12/88	Used in WIP	2649	705	
2743	28/12/88	Used in WIP	2641	2,880	
2744	30/12/88	Used in WIP	2638	4,326	

Because the information presented above may not be sufficient for you to generate all the outputs you specified in response to Requirement #1, you will probably have to modify your outputs and programs or make up additional data, such as supplier names, to complete this exercise.

4. After you have created the system, use it to generate the reports and other information you specified.

Inventory dBASE III PLUS Example

In the design of an information system, a number of important issues must be resolved:

1. Determine the information that will be required by the users of the system.
2. Determine the data that needs to be collected and processed in order for the system to be able to generate the desired outputs.

3. Group the data together in a reasonable manner.

4. Determine the general processing steps required to go from the data inputs to the desired outputs.

5. After resolving the above-mentioned general system design issues, the first concrete implementation step is to precisely define each data item and determine the files where each data item will be stored.

6. Determine the precise steps required in order to convert the data inputs into the desired data outputs.

7. Finally, create any files that have not already been created, write any "programs" that have not yet been written, and so on; implement the system.

The way each of these issues has been dealt with in the program and data files that accompany the text is set forth below.

1. System outputs.
   a. Listing of beginning inventory balances and all transactions as well as listings for:
      (1) Inventory purchases.
      (2) Use of inventory for work in process.
      (3) Inventory items charged to expense accounts.
   b. Listings of all the information referred to above for individual inventory items or all items meeting certain criteria.
   c. Orders for any item with fewer units on hand than the reorder point.
   d. Summations of each item mentioned above.
   e. Computation of ending account balances.
   f. Counts of the number of records in each file.
   g. Counts of inventory balances that meet certain criteria, for example balances less than the reorder point.
   h. Reports showing beginning balance, transactions, and ending balance for each inventory item.
   i. Reports showing inventory turnover for each item.

2. System inputs.
   a. Name of inventory item.
   b. Identifying number for inventory item.
   c. Reorder point for item.
   d. Unit cost for inventory item.
   e. Number of units currently on hand.
   f. Transaction number for each transaction.
   g. Transaction date.
   h. Type of transaction, purchase, use in Work in Process Inventory, expense.
   i. Inventory item affected by each transaction.
   j. Cost of goods affected by a transaction; for purchases this will be the purchase price; for any use of inventory, this will be the average cost of the inventory item as it appears in the inventory record.
   k. Total amount of each transaction, the quantity times the cost.
   l. Source document for the transaction.

3. Organize the data into files.

   In this example, there are two files:
   a. The inventory file contains basic information about inventory items: identifying number and name of inventory item, reorder point, average cost of item, and quantity currently on hand.
   b. The transaction file includes basic information about transactions including the transaction number, date, type, inventory number, transaction price, quantity, and total amount, and the source document for the transaction.

4. General processing steps.

   The main program, INVENTOR, and the functions it calls allow one to do the following:
   a. Record transactions.
   b. Order merchandise.
   c. List subsidiary ledger accounts.
   d. Prepare inventory reports for all or selected inventory items, including:
      (1) Summary of goods on hand.
      (2) Summary of transactions during the period sorted by inventory item.
      (3) Inventory turnover report.
   e. List inventory and transaction data either for all or for selected items in a combined inventory-transaction file. In specifying criteria to select records, one must use standard dBASE logical expressions.
   f. All other tasks such as deleting records, counting or averaging various amounts, making other queries, and so on, must be done either through the dBASE ASSIST menu or at the dBASE dot prompt; no facilities are provided in the programs to perform such functions.

5. Precisely define the data inputs and create the required data files.

   At this stage specific names are given to each of the data items and their characteristics are determined. For example, the amount of a transaction might be given the name T AMOUNT and defined as a real number, 10 characters wide, and accurate to two decimal places.

   The file INVEN contains the following information:

Item	Name	Data type	Field len
item number	I_NUMB	Numeric	4
inventory item name	I_NAME	Character	10
reorder point	I_REORDER	Numeric	5
average cost	I_UNITCOST	Numeric	6
units on hand	I_QUANTITY	Numeric	6

   The file TRANSACT contains the following information:

Item	Name	Data type	Field len
transaction number	T_NUMB	Numeric	5
transaction date	T_DATE	Date	8
transaction type	T_TYPE	Character	1
inventory item	I_NUMB	Numeric	4
transaction price	T_PRICE	Numeric	6
trans. quantity	T_QUANTITY	Numeric	6
amount of trans.	T_AMOUNT	Numeric	10
source document	T_SOURCE	Character	10

6. Input initial data into the files.

The beginning balance information has been entered into the file INVEN. For each of these items, a transaction has been entered into the file TRANSACT which has "Beginning Balance" as its source document. In addition, the first transaction for the period has been entered into the file TRANSACT.

7. Set forth the required processing steps.

In specifying these steps one must be precise enough so that, when followed, the desired output will be generated. In this example, the processing steps will generate the following outputs.

Reports Generated by the System

Inventory turnover report:

```
                 From: 01/10/88   To: 31/12/88
           End Inventory                   Days in
 Item    Dollars    Units    Turnover    inventory
 2635      316.80      15      41.7          8.7
 2636    3,309.04     586      28.7         12.7
 2637   34,361.31   2,164     43.3          8.4
```

Summary of inventory items:

No.	Item name	Reorder	Unit price	Units on hand	Carrying value
2652	AMANO	1310	44.54	557	24808.78
2644	BELIM	1120	41.39	163	6746.57
2640	BESERV	1740	29.21	3076	89849.96
2654	BROYOUN	1080	31.93	426	13602.18
2658	COMFO	1710	28.94	2479	71742.26
2650	DURWOR	2100	60.29	3653	220239.37
2659	FILPOL	1160	69.68	505	35188.40
2637	GILLAD	1130	15.89	2164	34385.96
2655	GREAMO	1180	29.84	830	24767.20
2656	HABAK	1040	58.89	133	7832.37
2661	HIAMS	1060	50.58	441	22305.78
2657	JUDPRO	2140	56.65	1635	92622.75
2653	KINWHE	1470	66.48	35	2326.80
2645	LAMED	2110	39.13	2990	116998.70
2664	LESPA	1040	30.47	3049	92903.03
2643	LORHEL	1120	0.64	449	287.36
2641	MOAF	1360	20.53	168	3449.04
2660	NATJU	1120	21.43	346	7414.78
2638	NOANT	2140	32.52	3499	113787.48
2636	OUEPH	1180	5.62	586	3293.32
2663	PHACAL	1040	8.64	1817	15698.88
2649	PROGAIN	2110	79.53	332	26403.96
2648	SAIBRA	2050	22.48	88	1978.24
2662	SCRITHA	1130	74.25	5563	413052.75
2651	SHABURD	2140	50.88	3126	159050.88
2635	SOPRA	550	21.12	15	316.80
2647	SWEWOR	1140	46.04	291	13397.64
2639	WAMAK	2170	20.53	1059	21741.27
2642	WIPRI	1140	2.20	76	167.20
2646	WOREM	2140	18.38	1237	22736.06

```
*** Total ***
* * * *                                        1659095.77
```

Summary of Transactions

For each selected group of transactions, the following information is presented:

Item	Date	Type of trans	Source doc	Price	Quantity	Total
** Inventory item: 2636						
1102	01/01/80	B	Beg.Bal.	5.64	786	4433.04
2705	11/12/88	P	P.O.	5.62	3800	21356.00
2733	22/12/88	U	mat.reg.	5.62	−4000	−22480.00
** Subtotal **						
					586	3309.04

Subsidiary Ledger Report

For each selected group of inventory items, the following information is presented:

Item no.: 2652   Item name: AMANO

Trans no.	Date	Type	Source doc	Price	Quantity	Amount
1118	01/01/80	B	Beg.Bal.	46.84	830	38,877.20
2592	04/10/88	P	P.O.	42.74	360	15,386.40
2612	15/10/88	P	P.O.	42.33	390	16,508.70
2647	05/11/88	U	mat.reg.	44.79	−860	−38,519.40
2674	22/11/88	U	mat.reg.	44.79	−523	−23,425.17
2727	19/12/88	P	P.O.	44.40	360	15,984.00
Last Transaction Date: 19/12/88					557	24,808.78

It should be noted that the sum of the amounts may not equal the total amount of ending inventory computed on the last line of the above table by multiplying the quantity on hand at the end of the period by the unit cost in the inventory record. Any such differences are due to rounding in the computation of average cost. This error could be reduced by having the unit price data in the main INVEN file carried to more than the two decimal places that are currently used.

Listing of Selected Items

Information in a combined INVEN-TRANSACT file Items can be selected and listed. In the example that appears below, the unit cost data from the INVEN file is presented along with the transaction number, source document, transaction price, quantity, and amount are presented for one inventory item.

Record no.	I__unit cost	T__no.	T__source	T__price	T__quantity	T__amount
53	58.89	1122	Beg.Bal.	54.17	2573	139379.41
54	58.89	2587	mat.reg.	54.17	−1324	−71721.08
55	58.89	2594	P.O.	67.41	1760	118641.60
56	58.89	2603	mat.reg.	59.55	−2800	−166740.00
57	58.89	2604	P.O.	63.55	1520	96596.00
58	58.89	2619	mat.reg.	61.54	−2748	−169111.92
59	58.89	2735	P.O.	58.42	1720	100482.40
60	58.89	2739	mat.reg.	58.89	−1892	−111419.88

General Summary of Programs

The main program INVENTOR and the functions it calls allows one to:

a. Record inventory transactions.

b. Order merchandise.

c. Prepare subsidiary ledger listings for all or selected inventory items.

d. Prepare any of the following three reports or listings of selected information for all or selected inventory items:

(1) Summary report including inventory identification information, reorder point, unit price, units on hand, and total carrying value of inventory.

(2) Summary of transactions for each inventory item organized by inventory item.

(3) Inventory turnover report showing the ending inventory in both units and dollars, together with the inventory turnover ratio and the average number of days of use for inventory items which are on hand.

The ratios, inventory turnover and average days sales in inventory, represent important summary information for inventory and other managers. Given the detailed information available in the data base the following calculations are possible:

$$\frac{\text{Average use}}{\text{in units}} = \frac{\text{Inventory used in units}}{\text{Elapsed time between reports}}$$

$$\frac{\text{Days use}}{\text{in inventory}} = \frac{\text{Ending inventory in units}}{\text{Average use in units}}$$

$$\text{Turnover} = \frac{365}{\text{Days use in inventory}}$$

In recording transactions, one identifies the inventory item affected by the transaction either by name or number. The program searches a list of all inventory items for ones which have the same number or a similar name. If the system finds a possible match, the user is asked to verify the selected item. If the system is unable to find an acceptable match, a new inventory record is created for the item.

To complete the recording of a transaction, the user is asked to enter the type of transaction (a purchase, a use of the item for work in process, or an expense), the quantity involved in the transaction, its source document, and, if a purchase, the per unit purchase price.

If one attempts to remove from the inventory more items than are currently on hand, one is notified of this and forced to enter an appropriate quantity. If removing items from the inventory causes the quantity on hand to fall below the reorder point, one is notified of this.

The order merchandise module, does not actually prepare a purchase order, although it could. Instead, the program looks for all items for which the quantity on hand is below the reorder point and for each such item suggests a purchase of three times the reorder point quantity.

All other tasks such as deleting inventory records, counting or averaging various amounts, making queries which cannot be answered by any of the standard reports or listings must be done either through the ASSIST menu or at the dBASE dot prompt; no facilities are provided in the programs to perform those functions.

(Prepared by C. Dirksen)

CASH, SHORT-TERM INVESTMENTS IN SECURITIES, AND RECEIVABLES

PURPOSE

The discussions in the two preceding chapters have focused primarily on the income statement. In this chapter, the focus will shift to the balance sheet. Our discussion of balance sheet classifications will begin with the most liquid (or current) assets: cash, short-term investments, and accounts receivables. In the previous chapter, we discussed accounting for another important current asset, inventories.

A consolidated balance sheet for Inco Limited and Subsidiaries is shown on the facing page.

LEARNING OBJECTIVES

1. Identify internal control procedures for cash.
2. Perform a bank reconciliation.
3. Apply the lower of cost or market rule to short-term investments.
4. Calculate interest on receivables.
5. Account for a discounted note receivable.
6. Apply the materiality concept.
7. Expand your accounting vocabulary by learning about the "Important Terms Defined in This Chapter."
8. Apply the knowledge gained from this chapter.

ORGANIZATION

Part A—safeguarding and reporting cash
1. Internal control of cash.
2. Bank reconciliation.

Part B—measuring and reporting short-term investments
1. Definition of short-term investments.
2. Lower of cost or market rule.

Part C—measuring and reporting receivables
1. Classification of receivables.
2. Interest on receivables.

Inco Limited and Subsidiaries

Consolidated Balance Sheet (in thousands)

December 31	1985	1984	1983
Current assets			
Cash	$ 7,051	$ 6,005	$ 6,756
Marketable securities, at cost (market 1985-$14,100,000,			
1984-$13,200,000, 1983-$9,700,000)	13,579	9,287	8,996
Accounts receivable	256,640	248,826	249,925
Income tax refunds receivable	17,798	18,838	19,009
Inventories	696,995	672,576	692,733
Prepaid expenses	9,404	9,661	7,165
Total current assets	$1,001,467	$965,193	$984,584

PART A—SAFEGUARDING AND REPORTING CASH

Cash Defined

Cash is defined as money and any instrument that banks will accept for deposit and immediate credit to the depositor's account, such as a cheque, money order, or bank draft. Cash **excludes** such items as notes receivable, IOUs, and postage stamps (a prepaid expense). Cash usually is divided into three categories: cash on hand, cash deposited in banks, and other instruments that meet the definition of cash. All cash accounts are combined as one amount for financial reporting purposes, even though a company may have several bank accounts.

Many businesses receive a large amount of cash from their customers each day. Cash can be spent by anyone, so management must develop procedures to safeguard the cash that is used in the business. Effective cash management involves more than protecting cash from theft, fraud, or loss through carelessness. Other cash management responsibilities are:

1. Accurate accounting so that relevant reports of cash inflows, outflows, and balances may be prepared periodically.
2. Control to assure that enough cash is on hand to meet (*a*) current operating needs, (*b*) maturing liabilities, and (*c*) unexpected emergencies.
3. Planning to prevent excess amounts of idle cash from accumulating. Idle cash produces no revenue; therefore, it often is invested in securities to get a return (i.e., revenue) pending future need for the cash.

Internal Control of Cash

Internal control refers to those policies and procedures of an entity designed to safeguard all of the **assets** of the enterprise. Internal control procedures should extend to all assets—cash, receivables, investments, operational assets, and so on.

Because cash is the asset most vulnerable to theft and fraud, a significant number of internal control procedures should focus on cash. You have already observed internal control procedures for cash, although you may not have known it at the time. At most movie theatres, one employee sells tickets and another employee collects the tickets. It would be less expensive to have one employee do both jobs, but it would be easier for an employee to steal cash.

Effective internal control of cash should include:

Separation of functions and routines:

1. Complete separation of the **functions** of receiving cash from disbursing cash.
2. Complete separation of the **procedures** for cash receipts from cash disbursements.

3. Complete separation of (*a*) the **physical** handling of cash from (*b*) all phases of the **accounting** function.

4. Require that all cash receipts be deposited in a bank daily. Keep any cash held on hand (for making change) under strict control.

5. Require that all cash payments be made by prenumbered cheques with a separate approval of the expenditures and separate approval of the cheques in payment.

Responsibilities assigned to individuals:

6. Assign the cash receiving and cash paying responsibilities to different individuals.

7. Assign the cash handling and cash recordkeeping responsibilities to different individuals.

8. Assign the cash payment approval and cheque signing responsibilities to different individuals.

9. Assign responsibilities for the cash function and the accounting function to different individuals.

The separation of individual responsibilities and the use of prescribed policies and procedures are important phases in the control of cash. Separation of duties and responsibilities deters theft because collusion would be needed among two or more persons to steal cash and then conceal the theft in the accounting records. Prescribed procedures are designed so that the work done by one individual is checked by the results reported by other individuals.

To show how easy it is to hide cash theft when internal control is lacking, two examples are provided:

Case 1—An employee handles both cash receipts and the recordkeeping. Cash amounting to $100 was collected from J. Doe in payment of an account receivable. An employee pocketed the cash and made an entry for $100 crediting Accounts Receivable (J. Doe) and debiting Allowance for Doubtful Accounts.

Case 2—Occasionally an employee with cash payment authority would send a fictitious purchase invoice through the system. The cheque, payable to a fictitious person, was not mailed but was cashed by the employee.

In each case, the accounting records did not reveal the theft. Also, the financial statements did not provide any evidence that theft had occurred. The thefts could have been prevented with simple internal control procedures.

All cash disbursements should be made with prenumbered cheques. Cash payments should involve separate routines and responsibilities specified for (1) payment approvals, (2) cheque preparation, and (3) cheque signing. When procedures similar to these are followed, it is difficult to conceal a fraudulent cash disbursement without the collusion of two or more persons. The level of internal control, which is reviewed by the outside independent auditor, increases the reliability of the financial statements of the business.

Bank Statements to Depositors

Proper use of the bank accounts of a business can be an important internal control procedure for cash. When a business opens a bank account, a **signature card** is completed. The card shows the names and signatures of the persons authorized to sign cheques drawn against the account. By authorizing a minimum number of individuals to sign cheques, a business gains important internal control over its bank accounts.

Each month, the bank provides the depositor with a **bank statement** that lists (1) each deposit recorded by the bank during the period, (2) each cheque cleared by the bank during the period, and (3) the balance of the depositor's account. The bank statement also will show the bank charges or deductions (such as service charges) made directly to the depositor's account by the bank. The bank statement includes copies of the deposit slips and all cheques that cleared through the bank during the period covered by the statement. A typical bank statement (excluding the deposit slips and canceled cheques) is shown in Exhibit 8–1.

Example of a Bank Statement

Exhibit 8–1 lists three items that need explanation. Notice that on June 20, listed under "Cheques and Debits," is a deduction for $18 coded with "NC."[1] A cheque for $18 was received from a customer, R. Roe, which then was deposited by J. Doe Company with its bank, the Northern Bank. The bank processed the cheque through banking channels to Roe's bank. Roe's account did not have sufficient funds to cover it; therefore, Roe's bank returned it to the Northern Bank which then charged it back to J. Doe Company. This type of cheque often is called an **NSF cheque** (not sufficient funds). The NSF cheque is now a receivable; consequently, J. Doe Company must make an entry to debit Receivables (R. Roe) and credit Cash for the $18.

Notice the $6 listed on June 30 under "Cheques and Debits" and coded "SC." This is the code for **bank service charges.** The bank statement included a memo by the bank explaining this service charge (which was not documented by a cheque). J. Doe Company must make an entry to reflect this $6 decrease in the bank balance as a debit to an appropriate expense account, such as Bank Service Expense, and a credit to Cash.

Notice the $100 listed on June 12 under "Deposits" and coded "CM" for "credit memo." The bank collected a note receivable owned by Doe and increased the depositor account of J. Doe Company. The bank service charge (SC) included the collection service cost. J. Doe Company must record the collection by making an entry to debit Cash and credit Note Receivable for the $100 (assume interest on the note had been recorded).

---

[1] These codes vary among banks.

Exhibit 8–1 Example of a bank statement

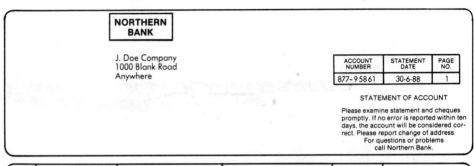

NORTHERN BANK					

J. Doe Company
1000 Blank Road
Anywhere

ACCOUNT NUMBER	STATEMENT DATE	PAGE NO.
877-9 58 61	30-6-88	1

STATEMENT OF ACCOUNT

Please examine statement and cheques promptly. If no error is reported within ten days, the account will be considered correct. Please report change of address. For questions or problems call Northern Bank.

ON THIS DATE	YOUR BALANCE WAS	DEPOSITS ADDED		CHEQUES AND DEBITS SUBTRACTED		SERVICE COST	RESULTING BALANCE
		NO.	AMOUNT	NO.	AMOUNT		
1-6-88	7 562 40	5	4 050 00	23	3 490 20	6 00	8 122 20

CHEQUES AND DEBITS			DEPOSITS	DATE	DAILY BALANCE
				1-6-88	7 562 40
			3 000 00	2-6-88	10 562 40
500 00				4-6-88	10 062 40
55 00	5 00	40 00		5-6-88	9 962 40
100 00			500 00	8-6-88	10 362 40
8 20	16 50	160 00		10-6-88	10 177 70
2 150 00	10 00		*100 00CM	12-6-88	8 117 70
7 50	15 30			16-6-88	8 094 90
35 00	1 50		150 00	17-6-88	8 208 40
40 20	15 00	6 00		18-6-88	8 147 20
*18 00NC				20-6-88	8 129 20
125 50	80 00	2 00	300 00	21-6-88	7 921 70
18 90				24-6-88	8 202 80
7 52	19 60			27-6-88	8 175 68
15 00	32 48			28-6-88	8 128 20
*6 00SC				30-6-88	8 122 20

Code:
CM—Credit Memo—Customer note collected
NC—Not sufficient funds
SC—Service charge

MEMBER F.D.I.C.   IMPORTANT: SEE REVERSE SIDE OF STATEMENT.

Cash Accounts in the Ledger

A balance sheet reports **cash** as the first current asset because it is the most liquid asset. The amount of cash reported on a balance sheet is the **total amount** of cash at the end of the last day of the accounting period. The total amount of cash reported on the balance sheet includes:

1. Cash on deposit in all chequing accounts subject to current chequing privileges (offset by any overdrafts).[2]
2. Cash on hand (not yet transmitted to a bank for deposit).
3. Cash held in all petty cash funds.

---

[2] Adjusted for deposits in transit and outstanding cheques (discussed later).

A company will have a separate account in the **ledger** for each bank account.[3] Often companies keep a small amount of **cash on hand.** Although such amounts are included in the balance of the **regular Cash account,** those amounts have not been deposited. They represent (*a*) amounts of cash received since the last deposit was made and/or (*b*) a stable amount of cash needed for making change to start the next day.

Often, a **petty cash system** is kept to make **small cash payments** (not to make change) in lieu of writing a separate cheque for each such item. This system necessitates the use of another separate cash account, usually called Petty Cash (discussed later).

Bank Reconciliation

A **bank reconciliation** is the process of comparing (reconciling) the **ending** cash balance shown in the **Cash ledger account** and the **ending** cash balance reported by the bank on the monthly **bank statement.** A bank reconciliation should be completed for each separate chequing account (i.e., for each bank statement received from each bank) at the end of each month.

Usually, the ending cash balance as shown on the bank statement does not agree with the ending cash balance shown by the related Cash ledger account on the books of the depositor. For example, the Cash ledger account at the end of June of J. Doe Company showed the following (Doe has only one chequing account):

Cash

| June 1 | Balance | 7,010.00* | June | Cheques written | 3,800.00 |
| June | Deposits | 5,750.00 | | | |

(Ending balance, $8,960.00)

* Including $200 undeposited cash held for change.

The $8,122.20 **ending cash balance** shown on the **bank statement** (Exhibit 8–1) is different from the $8,960.00 **ending book balance** of cash shown on the books of the J. Doe Company. This difference exists because (1) some transactions affecting cash were recorded in the books of depositor Doe but were not shown on the bank statement, and (2) some transactions were shown on the bank statement but had not been recorded in the books of the depositor, Doe. The most common causes of differences between the ending bank balance and the ending book balance of cash are:

1. **Outstanding Cheques**—cheques written by the depositor and recorded in the depositor's ledger as credits to the Cash account. These cheques

---

[3] Larger companies often carry one Cash control account in the ledger, which is supplemented with a series of separate cash subsidiary accounts for the depository banks. Refer to Supplement 6A.

have not cleared the bank (they are not shown on the bank statement as a deduction from the bank balance). The outstanding cheques are identified by comparing the canceled cheques returned with the bank statement and with the record of cheques (such as the cheque stubs) maintained by the depositor.

2. **Deposits in transit**—deposits sent to the bank by the depositor and recorded in the depositor's ledger as debits to the Cash account. These deposits have not been recorded by the bank (they are not shown on the bank statement as an increase in the bank balance). Deposits in transit usually happen when deposits are made one or two days before the close of the period covered by the bank statement. Deposits in transit are determined by comparing the deposits listed on the bank statement with the copies of the deposit slips retained by the depositor.

3. **Bank service charges**—an expense for bank services; listed on the bank statement. This expense must be recorded in the depositor's ledger by making a debit to an appropriate expense account, such as Bank Service Expense, and a credit to Cash.

4. **NSF Cheques**—a "bad cheque" that was deposited and must be deducted from the depositor's account. The depositor must make a journal entry to debit a receivable and credit Cash.

5. **Credit memo**—a note receivable collected by the bank for the depositor. It is recorded by making a debit to Cash and credits to Notes Receivable and Interest Revenue.

6. **Errors**—both the bank and the depositor may make errors, especially when the volume of cash transactions is large.

In view of these factors, a **bank reconciliation** should be made by the depositor immediately after each bank statement is received. A bank reconciliation is an important element of internal control and is needed for accounting purposes. To encourage bank reconciliation by depositors, many banks provide a form on the back of the bank statement for this purpose. A typical form is shown in Exhibit 8–2.

Bank Reconciliation Illustrated

The bank reconciliation for the month of June prepared by J. Doe Company to reconcile the **ending bank balance** (Exhibit 8–1, $8,122.20) with the **ending book balance** ($8,960) is shown in Exhibit 8–3. On the completed reconciliation, Exhibit 8–3, the **correct** general ledger cash balance is $9,045.00. This balance is different from both the reported bank and book balances before the reconciliation.

The format of a bank reconciliation can vary. A simple and flexible one uses a balancing format with the "Depositor's Books" and the "Bank Statement" identified separately. This format starts with two different amounts: (1) the **ending balance per books** and (2) the **ending balance per bank statement.** Space is

Exhibit 8–2 Sample form and instructions for a bank reconciliation

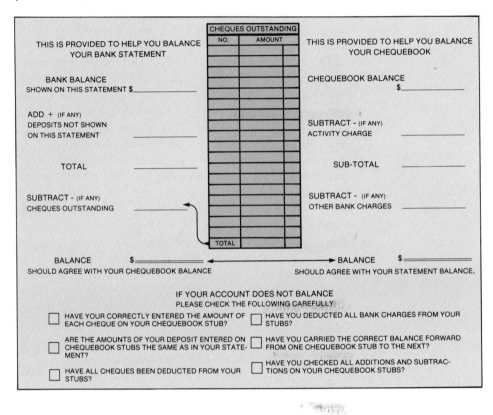

Exhibit 8–3 Bank reconciliation illustrated

J. DOE COMPANY
Bank Reconciliation
For the Month Ending June 30, 1988

Depositor's Books			Bank Statement	
Ending cash balance per books		$8,960.00	Ending cash balance per bank statement	$8,122.20
Additions:			Additions:	
Proceeds of customer note collected by bank		100.00	Deposit in transit	1,800.00
Error in recording cheque No. 137		9.00		
		9,069.00		9,922.20
Deductions:			Deductions:	
NSF cheque of R. Roe	$18.00		Outstanding cheques	1,077.20
Bank service charges	6.00	24.00		
Ending correct cash balance		9,045.00		
Less: Cash on hand		200.00		
Ending correct bank balance		$8,845.00	Ending correct bank balance	$8,845.00

provided for additions to, and subtractions from, each balance so that the last line shows the same correct cash balance (for the bank and the books). This correct balance is the amount that should be shown in the Cash account **after the reconciliation.** Notice that adjustment was made to the correct cash balance for cash in the company's hands that cannot be at the bank. The $200 cash on hand was deducted from the correct general ledger cash amount so the books can agree with the correct bank balance. In this example it is also the correct amount of cash that should be reported on the balance sheet (J. Doe Company has only one chequing account and no petty cash systems). J. Doe Company followed these steps in preparing the bank reconciliation:

1. **Identify the outstanding cheques**—A comparison of the canceled cheques returned by the bank with the records of the company of all cheques drawn showed the following cheques still outstanding (not cleared) at the end of June:

Cheque No.	Amount
101	$ 145.00
123	815.00
131	117.20
Total	$1,077.20

   This total was entered on the reconciliation as a **deduction** from the bank account. These cheques will be deducted by the bank when they clear the bank.

2. **Identify the deposits in transit**—A comparison of the deposit slips on hand with those listed on the bank statement revealed that a deposit made on June 30 for $1,800 was not listed on the bank statement. This amount was entered on the reconciliation as an **addition** to the bank account. It will be added by the bank when the deposit is recorded by the bank.

3. **Cash on hand**—On the date of the bank statement, cash on hand (i.e., undeposited cash held for making change) was $200. This amount is included in the company's Cash account but was not included in the bank statement balance (it was not deposited). Therefore, it must be entered on the reconciliation as a deduction to the book balance (or as an addition to the bank balance as it would be if deposited) so the books can agree with the bank.

4. **Record bank charges and credits:**
   a. Proceeds of note collected, $100—entered on the bank reconciliation as an **addition** to the book balance; it already has been included in the bank balance. A journal entry is needed to debit Cash and credit Note Receivable and Interest Revenue.
   b. NSF cheque of R. Roe, $18—entered on the bank reconciliation as a **deduction** from the book balance; it has been deducted from the

bank statement balance. A journal entry is needed to credit Cash to debit a receivable account.

   c. Bank service charges, $6—entered on the bank reconciliation as a **deduction** from the book balance; it has been deducted from the bank balance. A journal entry is needed to credit Cash and to debit an expense account.

5. **Determine the impact of errors**—At this point J. Doe Company found that the reconciliation did not balance by $9. Because this amount is divisible by 9, they suspected a transposition. (A transposition, such as writing 27 for 72, always will cause an error that is exactly divisible by 9.) Upon checking the journal entries made during the month, they found that a cheque was written for $56 to pay an account payable. The cheque was recorded in the company's accounts as $65. The incorrect entry made was a debit to Accounts Payable and a credit to Cash for $65 (instead of $56). Therefore, $9 (i.e., $65 − $56) must be **added** to the book cash balance on the reconciliation; the bank cleared the cheque for the correct amount, $56. The following correcting entry must be made in the accounts: Cash, debit $9; and Accounts Payable, credit $9.

Note in Exhibit 8–3 that the "Depositor's Books" and the "Bank statement" parts of the bank reconciliation now agree at a **correct bank balance** of $8,845. This amount will be reported as part of the $9,045 cash on a balance sheet prepared at the end of the period.

A bank reconciliation as shown in Exhibit 8–3 accomplishes two major objectives:

1. Checks the accuracy of the bank balance and the company cash records, which involves development of the **correct cash balance.** The correct cash balance is the amount of cash that must be in the Cash account for financial reporting purposes (i.e., the balance sheet) and the amount that would be in the bank if all cash items were recognized by the bank.

2. Identifies any previously unrecorded transactions or changes that are necessary to cause the company's Cash account(s) to show the **correct cash balance.** These transactions or changes need journal entries. The explanations given above of the development of the bank reconciliation of J. Doe Company cite such transactions and changes. Therefore, the entries shown in Exhibit 8–4, taken directly from the "Depositor's Books" part of the bank reconciliation (Exhibit 8–3), must be entered into the company's records.

Notice that all of the additions and deductions on the "Depositor's Books" side of the reconciliation need journal entries to update the Cash account. The additions and deductions on the "Bank Statement" side do **not** need journal entries because they will work out automatically when they clear the bank. The

Exhibit 8–4   Entries from bank reconciliation (Exhibit 8–3)

Accounts of J. Doe Company:

a. Cash 100
      Note receivable 100
    To record note collected by bank.

b. Accounts receivable 18
      Cash 18
    To record NSF cheque.

c. Bank service expense 6
      Cash 6
    To record service fees charged by bank.

d. Cash 9
      Accounts payable (name) 9
    To correct error made in recording a cheque payable to a creditor.

Cash account of J. Doe Company:

The Cash account prior to reconciliation was given on page 438. After the above journal entries are posted, the Cash account is as follows:

Cash (after recording results of bank reconciliation)

June 1	Balance	7,010.00	June	Cheques written	3,800.00
June	Deposits	5,750.00	June 30	NSF cheque*	18.00
June 30	Note collected*	100.00	June 30	Bank service charge*	6.00
June 30	Correcting entry*	9.00			

(Correct cash balance, $9,045.00)

* Based on the bank reconciliation.

---

cash amount reported on the balance sheet and reflected in the Cash account will be the **correct cash balance** only if the proper journal entries are made after the bank reconciliation is completed.

Cash Over and Short

Errors in handling cash inevitably occur when large numbers of cash transactions are involved. These errors cause cash shortages or cash overages at the end of the day when the cash is counted and compared with the cash records for the day. Cash overages and shortages must be recorded in the accounts. Assume that the count of cash from sales amounted to $1,347 but the cash register tapes for sales totaled $1,357—a **cash shortage** of $10 is indicated. The sales for the day should be recorded as follows:

```
Cash . . . . . . . . . . . . . . . . . . . . . . . . . . . . . . . . . . . . . . . . . . . .  1,347.00
Cash over and short . . . . . . . . . . . . . . . . . . . . . . . . . . . . . . . .    10.00
  Sales  . . . . . . . . . . . . . . . . . . . . . . . . . . . . . . . . . . . . . . . .              1,357.00
```
 To record cash sales and cash shortage.

In the case of a cash **overage,** the Cash Over and Short account is credited. Sales revenue should be recorded for the correct amount shown on the register tapes regardless of any cash overage or shortage. At the end of the period, a debit balance in the Cash Over and Short account usually is reported as miscellaneous expense. If a credit balance exists, it is reported as miscellaneous revenue.

Petty Cash

Disbursements of cash should be made by **prenumbered cheques.** However, many businesses find it inconvenient and expensive to write cheques for small payments for items such as taxi fares, newspapers, and small amounts of supplies. To avoid this inconvenience and expense, businesses often set up a **petty cash fund** to handle small miscellaneous cash payments. To set up a petty cash fund, a cheque should be drawn "Pay to the order of the Custodian of Petty Cash" for the amount needed in the fund and cashed. Small cash payments, supported by written receipts, are made from this fund, and no journal entry is made at the time of payment. When the petty cash fund gets low and at the end of each accounting period, the expenditures from the fund are summarized and a journal entry is made to reflect the payments from the fund (debits to expenses) and to record the cheque written to reimburse the fund for the total amount spent (credit to Cash). For balance sheet reporting, the amount in the Petty Cash account must be added to the other cash balances. The details of accounting for a petty cash fund are discussed in Supplement 8A.

Compensating Balances

A **compensating balance** exists when the bank requires a business to keep a minimum amount in its bank account. A compensating balance may be required by the bank explicitly (by a loan agreement) or implicitly (by informal understanding) as part of a credit-granting arrangement. Information on compensating balances is important to statement users because of two major effects on the business: (1) a compensating balance requirement imposes a restriction on the amount of cash readily available; and (2) if it arises in connection with a loan, the compensating balance increases the real rate of interest on the loan because not all of the cash borrowed can be used (i.e., the minimum must remain on deposit).

Information concerning a compensating balance must be reported in the notes to the financial statements because of its relevance to statement users.

Data Processing of Cash

Small businesses usually process cash transactions manually. In contrast, large businesses write cheques and process cash information using computers. However, recent developments with microcomputers and software have brought computer processing of cash information within the cost-benefit range of small and medium-sized businesses. Essentially, the basic data activities of accounting are the same whether manual, mechanical, or computerized approaches are used. For most instructional situations, the basic characteristics of accounting information processing are best illustrated with a manual system.

Supplement 8B presents an information processing procedure known as **special journals.** Two of these special journals relate to information processing of cash inflows (i.e., cash receipts journal) and cash outflows (i.e., cash payments journal).

PART B—MEASURING AND REPORTING SHORT-TERM INVESTMENTS

Most businesses hold extra cash in addition to the minimum required for normal daily transactions. This extra cash may be held to meet unexpected needs or may be the result of normal seasonal variations in the level of business operations. Cash that is deposited in most chequing accounts does not earn interest. A company can earn revenue by investing such idle cash in short-term investments. These investments include term deposits sold by local banks, commercial paper (short-term debt issued by corporations), bonds, and capital stock. Investments in commercial paper, bonds, and shares can often be quickly converted into cash because they can be sold on stock exchanges such as the Montreal Stock Exchange.

When bonds of another company are acquired, the purchaser becomes a creditor of the issuing company because bonds represent debt owed by the other company similar to a long-term note payable. As the holder of a bond, the investor is entitled to receive interest on the principal of the bond and the principal if held to maturity. In contrast, when shares of capital stock are purchased as an investment, the purchaser becomes one of the owners of the company that issued the shares. As an owner, the shareholder receives dividends when they are paid by the other company. Most capital stock confers voting rights, which means a shareholder can exercise some **control** over the issuing company. The degree of control depends upon the number of voting shares owned by the shareholder in relation to the total number of such shares outstanding.

Investments made by one company in the shares or bonds of another company may be either (1) short-term investments (also called marketable securities or temporary investments) or (2) long-term investments. This chapter discusses the measurement and reporting of short-term investments; long-term invest-ments are discussed in Chapter 13.

Short-Term Investments Defined

To be classified as a short-term investment, a security must meet a twofold test of (1) marketability and (2) an expected short-term holding period. **Marketability** means that the security must be readily converted into cash or it must be traded regularly on the market so that it easily can be converted to cash. Short-term investments usually must be listed on an established stock exchange. A short-term holding period means that it must be the **intention** of the management to convert the investment into cash in the near future for normal operating purposes.[4] Short term refers to the longer of the normal operating cycle of the business or one year as specified in the definition of current assets. The distinction between short-term and long-term investments is important because (1) accounting for the two types of investments is different; and (2) short-term investments are classified as a current asset, and long-term investments are classified as a noncurrent asset.

Measurement of Short-Term Investments

In conformity with the **cost principle,** short-term investments are initially recorded at their acquisition cost. Cost includes the market price paid plus all additional costs incurred to buy the security. Assume that in December, Brown Corporation purchased 1,000 shares of Artic Telephone & Telegraph (AT&T) for $56,000, including all broker's fees, transfer costs, and taxes related to the purchase. This transaction is recorded in Exhibit 8–5.

Short-term investments are reported at the **lower of cost or market** (LCM) on the balance sheet (lower of cost or market is discussed in the next section). The **current market value** of the short-term investment should be shown parenthetically. For example, at the end of the accounting period, December 31, 19A, Brown Corporation would report the short-term investment of AT&T shares, assuming a market value **above** cost of $57 per share, as shown in Exhibit 8–5.

When either a cash dividend or interest is received, Cash is debited for the amount received, and a revenue account, such as Investment Revenue, is credited for the same amount. Assume Brown Corporation received a cash dividend of $0.70 per share on the AT&T common stock on February 2, 19B. This transaction would be recorded by Brown as shown in Exhibit 8–5.

When a short-term investment is sold, the difference between the sale price and the original cost of the security is recorded as a gain, or loss, as shown in

---

[4] We shall see later that long-term investments also include marketable securities. Thus, the basic distinction between short-term and long-term investments hinges primarily on the intention of management in respect to their expected disposal date. As a result, the same kind of security may be a short-term investment in one company and a long-term investment in another company, depending upon the intentions of the respective managements.

Exhibit 8–5 Accounting for short-term investments illustrated

---

December 1, 19A—Purchase of 1,000 shares of AT&T common stock for $56,000 including all transfer costs:

Short-term investments (1,000 shares at $56)	56,000	
Cash		56,000

December 31, 19A (end of the accounting period)—On this date the AT&T shares were selling at $57 (i.e., **above** acquisition cost).*

Balance sheet at December 31, 19A:

Current assets:

Cash (assumed amount)		$62,000
Short-term investments at cost (current market value, $57,000)		56,000

February 2, 19B—Received a quarterly cash dividend on the AT&T shares of $0.70 per share: *does not affect the value of shares.*

Cash (1,000 shares × $0.70 per share)	700	
Investment revenue		700

April 5, 19B—Sold 250 shares of the AT&T shares at $58 per share (cash):

Cash (250 shares at $58)	14,500	
Short-term investments (250 shares at $56)		14,000
Gain on sale of investments		500

rev ' [handwritten note next to Gain on sale]

* See next section on LCM when the market price is **less** than the acquisition price.

Exp if loss [handwritten note]

Exhibit 8–5. If multiple purchases exist for the same security, average cost would typically be used to determine cost.

When a company owns short-term equity securities in several other companies, the securities held are referred to collectively as a **short-term portfolio of equity securities.** If debt securities also are held, they are considered to be a separate **portfolio** of **debt securities.** Each portfolio of short-term investments is managed (i.e., acquired, held, and sold) with the objective of maximizing the return while minimizing the risk. Thus, each **investment portfolio** is accounted for as a whole rather than as a number of separate investments.

Short-Term Investments Valued at Lower of Cost or Market (LCM)

Accounting for short-term investments is usually in conformity with the cost principle. There is an important exception related **only** to equity securities. The exception occurs when the **current** market value of the **short-term portfolio of equity securities** drops below the recorded acquisition cost.[5]

---

[5] *CICA Handbook*, Section 3010, suggests the use of market for this situation but does not specify how market should be applied. It should be noted here that LCM is applicable to investments in debt securities as well as shares.

Chapter 7 discussed the lower of cost or market (LCM) basis for inventory. The same rule applies to the **short-term portfolio of equity securities.** When market value drops below cost, a short-term portfolio of equity securities loses a part of its value as a short-term source of **cash.** The drop in value is viewed as an **unrealized loss** that should be recognized in the period in which the price drop occurred. However, an unrealized holding gain is **not** recorded when the current market value is **above** the acquisition cost. The LCM basis is an exception to the **cost principle** because the **conservatism exception** (see Exhibit 4–5) overrides the cost principle.

For short-term investments at the end of the accounting period, any difference between their cost and a **lower** end-of-period market value is recorded as a debit to an **expense** account called Unrealized Loss on Short-Term Investments and a credit to an **asset contra** account called Allowance to Reduce Short-Term Investments to Market. This entry records the holding (market) loss as an expense in the period in which the market dropped and revalues the short-term investment on an LCM basis.

At the end of 19B, Brown Corporation (Exhibit 8–5) still owned 750 shares of the AT&T common stock acquired at $56 per share (i.e., total cost is $42,000). At the end of 19B, the AT&T stock was selling on the stock exchange at $55 per share, which was $1 per share less than its cost. Therefore, the LCM rule must be applied. An **unrealized** loss of $750 must be recorded and reported as shown in Exhibit 8–6.

The illustration given in Exhibit 8–6 involved only one stock (AT&T) in the investment portfolio. Often the portfolio includes several different equity securities. In such cases, LCM is applied by comparing the **total portfolio cost and the total portfolio market** value rather than on an item-by-item basis. Even though the *CICA Handbook* is silent on this point, it is reasonable to expect the portfolio basis would be used in Canada. To illustrate, assume Cox Company has three separate shares, A, B, and C, in its short-term **investment portfolio.** The measurement at the end of the accounting period would be derived as follows:

Security	Acquisition cost	Current market
A Company common shares . . .	$10,000	$ 9,000
B Company preferred shares . . .	23,000	22,000
C Company common shares . . .	7,000	8,000
Total portfolio	$40,000	$39,000

Under the LCM basis, the Short-Term Investments account of Cox Company would be written down to $39,000 by recognizing a $1,000 unrealized loss as follows:

Unrealized loss on short-term investments 1,000
    Allowance to reduce short-term investments to market 1,000

The LCM rule is applied to the total portfolio because the portfolio typically is managed as a single investment instead of as several individual investments

Exhibit 8–6 Recording and reporting short-term equity investments at LCM

Entries:

December 31, 19B (end of accounting period)—AT&T common shares held as a short-term investment; 750 shares, cost $56, current market, $55 per share.

Unrealized loss on short-term investments	750*	
Allowance to reduce short-term investments to market		750

Computation:
Cost (750 shares at $56)	$42,000
Market (750 shares at $55)	41,250
Unrealized loss	$ 750

Financial statements:

Balance sheet at December 31, 19B:

Current assets:
Short-term investments (at cost)	$42,000	
Less: Allowance to reduce short-term investments		
to market	750	$41,250

or alternatively:

Current assets:
Short-term investment, at LCM (cost $42,000)	$41,250

Income statement for year ended December 31, 19B:

Expenses:
Unrealized loss on short-term investments	$750

contra account

with different objectives. The use of the allowance to reduce short-term investments to market (a contra account) reflects this wholistic view in how the procedures are carried out using the allowance account.

When investments that were written down to a lower market (i.e., LCM) are **sold,** the realized gain or loss is the difference between the sale price and the original cost regardless of any balance in the allowance account. Any balance in the allowance account at the end of the accounting period is adjusted (up or down) to reflect any difference between total portfolio cost and a lower total portfolio market of the short-term investments held at the end of the accounting period.

Assume that Cox Company sold all of the portfolio on January 15, 19C, for $39,400 cash. This transaction would be recorded as follows.

Cash	39,400	
Loss on sale of short-term investments	600	
Short-term investments (at cost)		40,000

Note: At the end of the period, the allowance to reduce short-term investments to market must be adjusted.

Term Deposits

In recent years, one common short-term investment strategy to employ idle cash has been to deposit the money for a fixed period of time. A "term deposit" is an investment contract an investor may purchase from a bank for cash. The contract specifies (1) a limited period of time for the investment, such as 90 days, 6 months, 1 year, and so on; and (2) a guaranteed interest rate. Generally, the larger the amount of the deposit (the amount invested), the higher the interest rate. The interest rate also tends to be higher for longer time periods to maturity. These term deposits and similar commercial paper often are used for the short-term employment of idle cash because of the relatively high interest return and the liquidity factor.

Term deposits require that at the end of the accounting period an **adjusting entry** be made for any accrued interest earned but not yet collected. Term deposits are accounted for separately from cash. The interest earned is reported on the income statement as **investment revenue.** For external reporting purposes, term deposits are reported on the balance sheet as a current asset as shown here:

Current assets:
Cash $200,000
Term deposit   300,000

Adjusting Entries for Investment Revenue

At the end of the accounting period, **no adjusting entry is made for dividend revenue** on shares held as an investment because dividends (1) do not accrue on the basis of time and (2) are not paid unless formally declared by the board of directors of the issuing corporation. In contrast, when term deposits, bonds, or other **debt securities are held, an adjusting entry is needed** for accrued interest revenue because interest is a legal liability that increases in amount with the passage of time. Accrual of interest is illustrated in Chapter 4 and in Part C of this chapter.

Term deposit adjusting   debit a/R   credit revenue.

PART C—MEASURING AND REPORTING RECEIVABLES

Receivables Defined

Receivables include all claims of the entity against other entities or persons for money, goods, or services. *(owed to you)* In most businesses there are two types of receivables and special (nontrade) receivables. Either type may include both short-term receivables and long-term receivables. For example, a balance sheet may report the following receivables:

(normal)
AIR

Current assets:
  Trade accounts receivable $40,000
    Less: Allowance for doubtful accounts . . .   3,000 $37,000
  Trade notes receivable, short term   5,000
  Special receivables:
    Due from employees   400
    Equipment note receivable, short term . . .   600
  Long-term investments:
    Note receivable, long term   10,000
    Special receivable, long term   8,000
  Other assets:
    Utility deposits   2,000
    Due from company officers   1,000

factoring AIR) (selling

Trade Receivables

Trade receivables include **accounts receivable** and trade notes receivable. Either may be short term or long term, although the latter is rare. Trade receivables arise from the normal operating activities of the business, that is, from the sale of merchandise and/or services.

Trade accounts receivable and the contra account, Allowance for Doubtful Accounts, were discussed in Chapter 6.

Many businesses **sell** their accounts receivable instead of holding them until they are collected. Factoring is a term used for the **sale** of accounts receivable to a financial institution, which usually occurs on the date that the goods and/or services are sold. Factoring is used widely because the company immediately receives the cash for sales. The rate of interest for factoring arrangements is high. A discussion of the detailed accounting involved for factoring is included in advanced accounting courses.

Special Receivables

Special (or nontrade) receivables arise from transactions other than the normal sale of merchandise and/or services. Special receivables may be short term or long term and should be given descriptive titles. They should not be included in the caption "Accounts receivable." Other than for appropriate classification on the balance sheet, special receivables seldom involve unusual accounting problems.

Notes Receivable *(Saleable)*

Notes receivable may be either **trade** notes or **special** notes receivable, depending upon the source of the note. A note is an unconditional promise in writing (i.e., a formal document) to pay (1) a specified sum of money on demand or at a definite future date known as the maturity or due date and (2) specified interest at one or more future dates. The person who signs a note is called the **maker.**

The person to whom payment is to be made is known as the **payee.** The maker views the note as a "note payable," whereas the payee views the note as a "note receivable." A note involves two distinctly different amounts: (1) **principal,** which is the amount that the interest rate is based upon; and (2) **interest,** which is the specified amount charged for use of the principal. The **face amount** of a note is the amount that is payable at maturity.

Interest Calculations on Notes

Interest represents the cost of using money over time. To the payee of a note, interest is **revenue;** while to the maker it is **expense.** The formula for computing interest is:

Principal × Annual rate of interest × Fraction of year = Interest amount

Interest rates are quoted on an **annual basis** and, therefore, must be restated for time periods of less than one year. Thus, the interest on a $10,000, 12%, 90-day note is calculated as follows:

$$\$10,000 \times 12\% \times 93/365 = \$306$$

Note: 90 + 3 days or grace

When a note specifies a number of days, the exact days must be counted on the calendar to determine the due date and then related to the number of days in the year.[6]

All commercial notes have interest, either explicitly or implicitly, because money borrowed or loaned has a value that cannot be ignored.[7]

Accounting for Notes Receivable

Notes receivable usually arise as a result of a business selling merchandise or services. Although most businesses use open accounts (i.e., accounts receivable), those selling high-priced items on credit often require notes from their customers. To illustrate, assume Jackson Company received a $10,000, 12%,

---

[6] For simplicity throughout this book, interest dates are given in a manner that avoids the needless counting of exact days on a calendar. Most lending institutions use 365 days in the calculations. Interest rates will be yearly rates. Canadian law adds three days of grace to the usual term of the note.

[7] An **interest-bearing note** explicitly specifies a stated rate of interest (such as 12%) on the face of the note, and the interest is to be paid in addition to the **face amount** of the note. In contrast, a **noninterest-bearing note** does not explicitly state an interest rate on the note because the interest charge is included in the face amount of the note (i.e., the interest is implicit).

interest-bearing note from a customer as a result of the sale of goods; the payee would record it on the date of the sale as follows:

Notes receivable (trade)	10,000	
Sales revenue		10,000

To record 90-day, 12%, interest-bearing note received from customer.

When **collection** is made at **maturity date** 93 days later the entry to record the principal amount and the interest would be:

Cash	10,306	
Notes receivable (trade)		10,000
Interest revenue		306

To record collection of a 90-day, 12%, interest-bearing note receivable of $10,000 plus interest ($10,000 × 12% × 93/365 = $306).

Default of a Note Receivable

A note receivable that is not collected at maturity is **dishonoured** or **defaulted** by the maker. Immediately after default, an entry should be made by the payee transferring the amount due from the Notes Receivable account to a special account such as Special Receivable—Defaulted Trade Notes. The maker is responsible for both the unpaid principal and the unpaid interest. The receivable account should reflect the full amount owed to the payee. If the above note receivable was defaulted by the maker, the entry made by the payee is:[8]

Special receivable—defaulted trade notes	10,306	
Notes receivable (trade)		10,000
Interest revenue		306

To record the principal and interest earned on defaulted note.

Special Receivable—Defaulted Trade Notes is reported as a current or non-current asset depending upon the probable collection date.

Discounting a Note Receivable

Many businesses prefer a note receivable rather than an open account receivable from customers involved in large purchases on credit. The primary reasons are (1) the note provides formal evidence of the receivable; and (2) notes, if negotiable, often can be sold to a financial institution, such as a bank, to get needed cash

---

[8] From date of default, the amount due at that date (principal plus interest) continues to draw interest either at the stipulated rate or the legal rate as specified by the law of the province. However, the wording of the revenue principle would suggest a question about the propriety of recognizing the interest revenue before collection is made when there is a reasonable probability that collection will not be made. See Chapter 6.

before the maturity date. Selling a note receivable to a financial institution frequently is called **discounting** a note receivable.

A negotiable instrument is one that can be transferred by the endorsement of the payee (there are other technical legal requisites for negotiability). The most common negotiable instrument is a cheque. Notes and a number of other instruments can be transferred by endorsement. An endorsement may be made by signature of the holder in which case it is said to be "with recourse." "With recourse" means that the endorser is liable for repayment if the maker defaults, as in the case of a NSF cheque. An endorsement may be made without recourse by writing this phrase on the instrument before the endorsement signature. **Without recourse** means that the endorser cannot be held contractually liable in the case of default by the maker. Most banks, businesses, and individuals will not accept endorsements without recourse. As a result, financial institutions can rely on both the maker and the endorser. An endorsement with recourse makes the endorser **contingently liable.** If the maker does not pay the note at maturity, the endorser pays. The **full-disclosure principle** (Exhibit 4–5) requires that such contingent liabilities be reported as a note to the financial statements.

The sale of a note receivable gives the payee immediate cash and causes the transfer of the asset (note receivable) to the lender. Often there will be a difference between the interest rate specified on the note and the interest rate charged by the purchaser of the note.

For example, assume that Jackson Company held a $10,000, 10%, 90-day interest-bearing note receivable for 30 days, then sold it to the Northern Bank at an interest rate of 12%. The bank's interest rate is applied to the **maturity value** of the note (that is, the principal amount of the note **plus** the amount of interest due at maturity). The bank's rate of interest is applied to the number of days the bank will hold the note (in this case, 63 days). Computation of the amount of cash the bank will pay for the note is:

Discounting a note receivable:
Note: Principal, $10,000; annual interest rate, 10%; term, 90 days.
Discounted: Thirty days after date; discount rate, 12% per year.

Principal amount	$10,000.00
Plus: Interest due at maturity ($10,000 × 10% × 93/365)	255.00*
Maturity value—amount subject to discount rate	10,255.00*
Less: Discount—interest charged by bank ($10,255 × 12% × 63/365)	212.00*
Cash proceeds—amount the bank pays for the note	$10,043.00*

* Rounded.

The discounting or sale of the above note receivable is recorded by the payee (Jackson Company) as follows:[9]

---

[9] The credit of $43 to Interest Revenue may be explained as follows: Had the note been held to maturity, the payee would have earned $255 interest revenue; however, the bank charged interest amounting to $212. The difference is $43, which is the net interest earned by the payee for holding it 30 of the 93 days. The discount rate is applied to the maturity value of the note because that is the amount the bank will advance, less the interest required by the bank.

Cash 10,043.00
    Notes receivable (trade) 10,000.00
    Interest revenue 43.00
  To record discounting of note receivable.

Even though the note was sold, the bank has recourse against the endorser in case of default by the maker. Therefore, Jackson Company must disclose a **contingent liability** in a note to the financial statements similar to the following:

Note: At December 31, 19B, the company was contingently liable for notes receivable discounted in the amount of $10,255.

Constraints to Accounting Principles

The preceding chapters used the terms **materiality** and **conservatism**. The conservatism constraint was cited earlier as the reason for using the LCM rule in measuring inventory (Chapter 7) and short-term investments (Chapter 8). The terms **materiality** and **conservatism** modify the accounting principles listed in Exhibit 4–5. That exhibit lists three constraints to accounting principles: (1) materiality, (2) conservatism, and (3) cost benefit.

Although compliance with the fundamental accounting assumptions and principles is essential, the benefits of absolute compliance with concepts sometimes are offset by practical considerations. Under certain **limited conditions,** a constraint may be permitted to override one or more of the other principles. The accounting constraints are:

1. **Materiality**—The fundamental accounting principles must be followed without exception for each transaction when the amount involved in the transaction is **material** (i.e., significant) in relationship to its overall effect on the financial statements. All amounts must be accounted for, but **immaterial amounts need not be accorded theoretically correct treatment.** For example, a pencil sharpener that cost $8 and has a five-year estimated life need not be depreciated under the matching principle. The $8 may be expensed in the period of acquisition because the amount involved is not material. The clerical cost alone of recording depreciation over the five-year period would exceed the cost of the asset. Also, the $1.60 annual depreciation expense would not affect any important decisions by statement users.

2. **Conservatism**—If more than one accounting alternative is acceptable for a transaction, the one having the **least favourable immediate effect on income or owners' equity usually should be selected.** For example, the LCM basis is used in measuring the amount of short-term investments and merchandise inventory. In this case, conservatism overrides the cost principle so that an unrealized loss (but not a gain) that occurs before the asset is sold is recorded and reported.

3. **Cost benefit**—This is a general utility constraint. It specifies that the cost of preparing and reporting accounting information should not exceed the value of the benefits of that information to the users of financial statements.

DEMONSTRATION CASE

(Try to resolve the requirements before proceeding to the suggested solution that follows.)

Dotter Equipment Company has been selling farm machinery for more than 30 years. The company has been quite successful in both sales and repair services. A wide range of farm equipment, including trucks, is sold. The company policy is to seek "high volume and quality service, at the right price." Credit terms with varying conditions are typical. Although most of the credit granted is carried by several financial institutions, Dotter will carry the credit in special circumstances. As a result, the company occasionally accepts a promissory note and keeps it to maturity. However, if a cash need arises, some of these notes may be sold (i.e., discounted) to the local bank with which Dotter has its chequing account. This case focuses on two farm equipment notes that were received during 19D. By following these notes from date of sale of farm equipment to final collection, we can see the various measurement problems posed and the accounting for them. The accounting period ends December 31, 19D.

The series of transactions in respect to the two notes follows:

Equipment Note No. 1:

19D

Jan. 15   Sold a farm tractor to S. Scott for $20,000 and received a 25% cash down payment plus a $15,000 equipment note receivable for the balance. The note was due in nine months and was interest-bearing at 12% per annum. A mortgage on the tractor was executed as a part of the agreement.

Apr. 15   The Scott equipment note was sold to the local bank at the 13% per annum discount rate. Dotter endorsed the note, with recourse, and the proceeds were deposited in Dotter's chequing account.

Oct. 15   Scott paid the bank the face amount of the note plus the interest, $15,000 + ($15,000 × 0.12 × 9/12) = $16,350. (As mentioned in footnote 6, for simplicity of exposition, days of grace will not be used in illustrations.)

Required:

a. Give appropriate journal entries for Dotter Equipment Company on each of the three dates. Show the interest computations and give an explanation for each entry.

b. Assume that instead of payment on October 15, 19D, S. Scott defaulted on the note. When notified by the bank, Dotter paid the note and interest in full. Give the appropriate entry for this assumption and one for the further assumption that Scott later paid Dotter in full on December 1, 19D.

Equipment Note No. 2:

19D

Oct. 1   Sold a farm truck to B. Day for $7,000; received a down payment of $1,000 and set up an account receivable for the balance; terms n/30.

Nov. 1   Day came in and wanted an extension on the account receivable "until he sold some equipment." After some discussion it was agreed to settle the account receivable with a six-month, 12%, interest-bearing note. Day signed the $6,000 note and a mortgage on this date.

Dec. 31   End of the accounting period. An adjusting entry is required.

19E

Jan. 1   Start of the new accounting period.

May 1   On this due date, Day paid the face amount of the note plus interest in full. The note was marked paid, and the mortgage was canceled by Dotter.

Required:

c. Give appropriate journal entries on each date, including any adjusting entries at year-end and the entry on maturity date. Omit closing entries at year-end. Explain what could be done on January 1, 19E, to simplify subsequent accounting. Provide a brief explanation with each entry.

Suggested Solution

The solutions for Requirements (*a*), (*b*), and (*c*) are given in Exhibit 8–7 and 8–8 on pages 456–57.

SUMMARY OF CHAPTER

This chapter discussed cash, short-term investments, and receivables. Cash is the most liquid of all assets, and it flows continually into and out of a business. As a result, cash presents some of the most critical control problems facing the managers. Also, cash may be of critical importance to decision makers who rely on financial statements for relevant information. The measurement and reporting of cash includes such problems as controlling and safeguarding cash, reconciling bank balances, accounting for petty cash, and recording the cash inflows and outflows.

The use of short-term investments to employ idle cash was discussed. Mar-

Exhibit 8–7 Accounting for discounted and defaulted notes receivable illustrated

---

Requirement *a*—Equipment Note No. 1:

January 15, 19D—Note executed:

Cash	5,000.00	
Equipment notes receivable	15,000.00	
Sales revenue		20,000.00

Sale of tractor to S. Scott for cash and equipment note; terms
of note, nine months, 12% interest, including a mortgage.

April 15, 19D—Note discounted:

Cash	15,287.25	
Equipment notes receivable		15,000.00
Interest revenue		287.25

Discounted Scott equipment note receivable at bank discount
rate of 13%.

Proceeds computed:

Principal amount	$15,000.00
Interest to maturity ($15,000 × 12% × 9/12)	1,350.00
Maturity value	16,350.00
Discount ($16,350 × 13% × 6/12)	(1,062.75)
Cash proceeds	$15,287.25

October 15, 19D—Maturity date of note:
   No entry required; Scott paid the bank that owned the note. During the period from
      April 15, 19D, until the note was paid, Dotter was contingently liable for the note
      because of the possibility that Scott would default.

Requirement *b*—Note defaulted:

October 15, 19D—Under the assumption that Scott defaulted on the note on due date,
      Dotter would have to pay the principal plus interest in full.

Special receivable (defaulted note—S. Scott)	16,350.00	
Cash		16,350.00

Scott note defaulted; payment to bank of the $15,000 principal
plus interest ($15,000 × 12% × 9/12 = $1,350).

December 1, 19D—Scott paid Dotter the full amount of the note plus interest.

Cash	16,350.00	
Special receivable (defaulted note, S. Scott)		16,350.00

Payment received in full on Scott note in default.

Note: In most provinces, Dotter could have assessed Scott interest at the **legal** rate on the $16,350
amount overdue; in this case, there would be a credit to Interest Revenue.

---

ketability and the length of the expected holding period are fundamental in the classification of an investment as short term as opposed to long term. Short-term investments are accounted for in conformity with the **cost principle;** however, in conformity with the conservatism constraint, the LCM rule is applied to the short-term investment portfolio of **equity securities** at the end of each account-

Exhibit 8–8 Accounting for interest accrual on notes receivable illustrated

Requirement c—Equipment Note No. 2:

October 1, 19D—Sale:

Cash	1,000	
Accounts receivable	6,000	
Sales revenue		7,000

Sold truck to B. Day; terms of the receivable, n/30.

November 1, 19D—Note executed:

Equipment notes receivable	6,000	
Accounts receivable		6,000

Settled account receivable with a six-month, 12%, interest-bearing note.

December 31, 19D—Accrual (end of accounting period):

Interest receivable	120	
Interest revenue		120

Adjusting entry for two months' interest accrued at 12% on Day equipment note ($6,000 \times 12\% \times 2/12 = \$120$).

January 1, 19E—Start of next accounting period:

No entry is required on this date; however, a **reversal** of the adjusting entry could be made to facilitate the subsequent entry when the interest is collected on April 30, 19E. The **optional reversing entry** would be (see Chapter Supplement 5A):

Interest revenue	120	
Interest receivable		120

Reversing entry on Day note.

April 30, 19E—Maturity date (assuming **no** reversing entry was made on January 1, 19E):

Cash $6,000 + ($6,000 \times 12\% \times 6/12)$	6,360	
Note receivable (principal amount)		6,000
Interest revenue ($6,000 \times 12\% \times 4/12$)		240
Interest receivable		120

ing period. **Debt securities** held as short-term investments are accounted for at **cost** (not LCM). Long-term investments are discussed in Chapter 13.

Receivables include trade receivables (usually called accounts receivable), special receivables, and notes receivable. Each of these should be accounted for separately. Interest calculations and discounting of notes receivable were discussed.

The chapter emphasized the importance of careful measurement of these liquid assets and the importance of examining their characteristics before classifying them as current assets for reporting purposes. Financial statement users often are faced with decisions in which these liquid assets are critical; therefore, they should be measured properly and reported adequately.

CHAPTER SUPPLEMENT 8A

Petty Cash

A petty cash fund is established to avoid the inconvenience and cost of writing cheques for the many small payments that occur daily in some businesses. This supplement discusses the detailed accounting and recordkeeping for a petty cash fund (also called an imprest fund).

Establishing the Petty Cash Fund. To establish a petty cash fund, a cheque should be written for the estimated amount needed to meet the expected payments, say, for an average month. The cheque, made payable to "the Custodian of Petty Cash," is cashed. The money is kept in a safe place under the direct control of a **designated individual** known as the **custodian.** The entry to set up a **separate Cash account** and to record the initial cheque would be:

Petty cash 100
    Cash   100
    To record establishment of a petty cash fund.

Disbursements from the Petty Cash Fund. The custodian should keep a perpetual record of all disbursements and the amount of cash on hand. No entry is made in the regular ledger accounts at the time each payment is made from the petty cash fund. Instead, the custodian keeps a separate **petty cash record** in which each disbursement is recorded when made. This record is supported by documentation, such as a signed bill, voucher, or receipt for each payment made. As an internal control feature, occasional surprise audits of the fund, and the records of disbursements should be conducted. "Borrowing" from the fund by the custodian or others should not be allowed. Careless handling of petty cash often leads to theft.

Replenishment of the Petty Cash Fund. When the amount of cash held by the custodian gets low, and at the end of each accounting period, the fund should be reimbursed (or replenished) with an amount of cash sufficient to restore it to the original amount (to $100 in the example). Reimbursement is made by having the custodian submit the petty cash record and the supporting documents to the accountants. On the basis of these records, a cheque to "the Custodian of Petty Cash" is written for the amount of cash needed for replenishment which is the same as the sum of the expenditures reported by the custodian. The cheque is cashed, and the money is given to the custodian, which increases the cash held by the custodian to the original amount ($100 in the example). A journal entry is made to credit Cash for the amount of the cheque and to debit expenses. The petty cash documents turned in by the custodian provide the underlying support for this journal entry.

    To illustrate, assume that by the end of the month there was $8.50 petty cash on hand. This means that cash expenditures by the custodian were $91.50 for the month. Assuming a cash shortage of $5.09, the bills, vouchers, and receipts accumulated by the custodian should equal this amount. These documents provide support for the additional cheque to petty cash for $91.50.

The detailed data for recording the replenishment cheque in the following journal entry are based on the supporting documents:

Telephone expense	12.40
Office supplies expense	6.32
Postage expense	21.45
Delivery expense	6.33
Travel expense	14.87
Repair expense, office equipment	15.00
Miscellaneous expense	10.04
Cash shortage expense	5.09
Cash	91.50

Notice that the Petty Cash account is debited **only** when the petty cash fund is first established and when the fund amount is increased on a permanent basis. The Petty Cash account shows a stable balance at all times ($100 in the above example). Expense accounts, not Petty Cash, are debited, and the **regular** Cash account is credited when the fund is replenished. Therefore, there will be no further entries in the Petty Cash account once it is established unless management increases or decreases the original amount on a permanent basis. The fund must be replenished (*a*) when the balance of cash in the fund is low, and (*b*) always at the end of the accounting period, whether low or not. Replenishment at the end of the accounting period is necessary to (*a*) record the expenses incurred by the fund up to the date of the financial statements and (*b*) have the amount of petty cash on hand that is shown in the Petty Cash account. The petty cash fund should be subject to rigid internal control procedures to remove all temptations to misuse it.

CHAPTER SUPPLEMENT 8B

Special Journals

In the preceding chapters, the **general journal** was used to record all transactions in chronological order (i.e., by order of date). The general journal can be used to record any transaction. However, it is inefficient if used for recording transactions that occur frequently, such as credit sales, credit purchases, cash receipts, and cash payments. The **general journal** is inefficient in three ways: (1) the same journal entry must be recorded repeatedly (except for changed amounts), (2) a large number of journal entries must be posted to the ledger, and (3) division of labour is difficult with a single journal. Special journals are designed to reduce these inefficiencies.

No new accounting principles or concepts are involved with special journals. They involve only the mechanics of data processing. Special journals should be designed to meet a special need when a particular type of data processing problem arises. We will limit this discussion to the four special journals that often are used: credit sales, credit purchases, cash receipts, and cash payments.

Credit Sales Journal.   This journal is designed to accommodate **only credit sales.** Cash sales are entered in the cash receipts journal (explained on page 463). Recall that the journal entry to record a credit sale (assuming a periodic inventory system) is:[10]

```
Jan. 3   Accounts receivable (customer's name) . . . . . . . . . . . . . . . . . . .  100
            Sales  . . . . . . . . . . . . . . . . . . . . . . . . . . . . . . . . . . . . . .       100
         To record credit sales; Invoice No. 324; terms n/30.
```

The credit sales journal is designed to simplify (1) recording this kind of entry and (2) subsequent posting to the ledger. The design of a credit sales journal is shown in Exhibit 8–9. Notice the **saving** in space, time, and accounting expertise required to journalize a credit sale.

Posting the Credit Sales Journal.   Posting the special credit sales journal involves two distinct phases. First, the **individual charges** (i.e., debits) must be posted daily to the customers' individual accounts in the accounts receivable subsidiary ledger. This task may be divided among several employees. Second, periodically (usually weekly or monthly), the **totals** are posted to the **general ledger** accounts—Accounts Receivable (debit) and Sales Revenue (credit). There is a significant saving in time compared with posting each transaction to the general ledger.

Posting on a daily basis to the **subsidiary ledger,** as shown in Exhibit 8–9, is indicated in the folio column by entering the account number for each individual customer. Daily posting to the subsidiary ledger is necessary because customers may, on any day, want to pay the current balance of their accounts.

The second phase in posting the sales journal is to transfer to the general ledger the total credit sales for the month. Thus, the $1,200 total will be posted to the general ledger as (1) a debit to the Accounts Receivable **control account** and (2) a credit to the Sales Revenue account. This posting is shown in Exhibit 8–9; note in the credit sales journal that two ledger account numbers were entered for the $1,200 total to indicate the posting procedure.

The credit sales journal can be adapted readily to fill special needs. For example, sales taxes could be recorded by adding a column headed "Sales Taxes Payable," and separate sales columns can be added to accumulate sales by department or product. You should observe the following efficiencies: (1) recording in the credit sales journal is much less time consuming than separately entering each credit sale in the general journal, (2) posting is reduced by transferring the **total** to the general ledger instead of posting separate debits and credits for each sales transaction, (3) the opportunity for division of labour, and (4) additional information (such as sales revenue by department) can be recorded easily.

---

[10] For instructional purposes, we will utilize simplified amounts, a limited number of transactions and customers, T-accounts, and a manual system. In many companies these procedures are computerized.

Exhibit 8–9 Credit sales journal and accounts receivable subsidiary ledger illustrated

CREDIT SALES JOURNAL				Page 9	
Date	**Customer**	**Terms**	**Invoice Number**	**Folio**	**Amount**
Jan. 3	Adams, K. L.	n/30	324	34.1	100
4	Small, C. C.	n/30	325	34.6	60
6	Baker, C. B.	n/30	326	34.2	110
10	Roe, R. R.	n/30	327	34.5	20
11	Mays, O. L.	n/30	328	34.3	200
16	Roe, R. R.	n/30	329	34.5	90
18	Null, O. E.	n/30	330	34.4	30
20	Baker, C. B.	n/30	331	34.2	180
21	Small, C. C.	n/30	332	34.6	150
31	Null, O. E.	n/30	333	34.4	260
	Total				1,200
	Posting				(34) (81)

ACCOUNTS RECEIVABLE SUBSIDIARY LEDGER

Adams, K. L.			34.1
Jan. 3	9	100	

Baker, C. B.			34.2
Jan. 6	9	110	
20	9	180	290

Mays, O. L.			34.3
Jan. 11	9	200	

Null, O. E.			34.4
Jan. 18	9	30	
31	9	260	290

Roe, R. R.			34.5
Jan. 10	9	20	
16	9	90	110

Small, C. C.			34.6
Jan. 4	9	60	
21	9	150	210

GENERAL LEDGER

Accounts Receivable (control)			34
Jan. 31	9	1,200	

Sales Revenue			81
	Jan. 31	9	1,200

Credit Purchases Journal.   Following the same pattern as described above, a credit purchases journal may be designed to record the entry common to all purchases on credit:

Jan. 8   Purchases* 392
             Accounts payable, C. B. Smith   392
         To record purchase on credit from C. B. Smith, Purchase Order
         No. 139; invoice dated January 5, 19B; terms 2/10, n/30. Recorded
         net of discount, $400 × 0.98 = $392.

         * This debit assumes a periodic inventory system; if a perpetual system is used, this account
         would be Merchandise Inventory.

Only credit purchases are recorded in the credit purchases journal. Cash purchases are entered in the cash payments journal as illustrated later. The design of a purchases journal is as shown in Exhibit 8–10.

Notice that purchases are recorded net of the purchase discount (as explained in Chapter 6). The cash payments journal will be used to record the subsequent payment of cash for the purchase including situations where the purchase discount is lost.

Exhibit 8–10 was not completed in detail for illustrative purposes because it follows the same pattern already shown for the credit sales journal. Daily posting would involve transfer to the creditors' individual accounts in the **accounts payable subsidiary ledger.** Periodically, the total would be posted to the **general ledger** as (1) a debit to the Purchases account and (2) a credit to the Accounts Payable control account. The efficiencies cited for the sales journal also are realized by a purchases journal.

Cash Receipts Journal.   All cash receipts can be recorded in the cash receipts journal, but no other transactions can be recorded in it. The design of a special journal to accommodate **cash receipts** is more complex because there are many

Exhibit 8–10   Credit purchases journal illustrated

CREDIT PURCHASES JOURNAL						Page 4
Date	Creditor's Account	Purchase Order No.	Date of Invoice	Terms	Folio	Amount
Jan. 8	Smith, C. B. Etc.	139	Jan. 5	2/10, n/30	51.8	392
	Total					784
	Posting					(6) (51)

Exhibit 8–11 Cash receipts journal illustrated

			DEBITS	CREDITS				
Date		Explanation	Cash	Account Title	Folio	Accounts Receivable	Sundry Accounts	Cash Sales
Jan	2	Cash sales	1,237					1,237
	3	Cash sales	1,482					1,482
	4	Sale of land	2,500	Land	43		2,000	
				Gain on sale of land	91		500	
	4	Cash sales	992					992
	6	Invoice #324	100	Adams, K. L.	34.1	100		
	6	Cash sales	1,570					1,570
	10	Bank loan, 12%	1,000	Notes payable	54		1,000	
	15	Invoice #328	200	Mays, O. L.	34.3	200		
	26	Cash sales	1,360					1,360
	31	Invoice #326	110	Baker, C. B.	34.2	110		
	31	Cash sales	1,810					1,810
		Totals	12,361			410	3,500	8,451
		Posting	(12)			(34)	(NP)	(81)

CASH RECEIPTS JOURNAL Page _14_

different accounts that are **credited individually** when the Cash account is debited. To resolve this problem, more than one **credit** column is needed to record the various credits. The number and designation of the debit and credit columns depend upon the character of the repetitive cash receipts transactions in the particular business.

A typical cash receipts journal with some usual transactions recorded is shown in Exhibit 8–11. Notice that there are separate debit and credit sections. Each column is used as follows:

1. **Cash debit**—This column is used for **each** debit to cash. The column is totaled at the end of the month and posted as one debit amount to the Cash account in the general ledger. The posting number at the bottom indicates the total was posted to account number "12," which is the Cash account.[11]

2. **Accounts Receivable credit**—This column is used to enter the individual amounts collected on trade accounts which must be posted to the individual customer accounts in the **accounts receivable subsidiary**

---

[11] This design assumes that the company correctly records credit sales at net of discounts. If credit sales are recorded at "gross," then a Sales Discount debit column also would be needed in this special journal.

ledger (as indicated by the posting numbers in the folio columns). The **total** of this column is posted at the end of the month as a credit to the Accounts Receivable **control** account in the general ledger as indicated by the posting number "34."

3. **Sundry Accounts credit**—This column is used for recording credits to all accounts other than those for which special credit columns are provided (in this example Accounts Receivable and Sales Revenue). The titles of the accounts to be credited are entered under the column "Account Title." Because the Sundry Accounts column represents a number of **accounts,** the **total** is not posted; rather, each individual amount must be posted as a credit directly to the indicated general ledger account. Account numbers entered in the related folio column indicate the posting.

4. **Cash Sales credit**—This column is used to record **all cash sales.** The total at the end of the month is posted as a credit to the Sales Revenue account in the general ledger.

Posting the cash receipts journal involves the same two phases explained previously for the credit sales and credit purchases journals. The **daily posting** phase involves posting the individual credits to the accounts receivable subsidiary ledger. The **second phase** involves posting the totals periodically to the accounts in the general ledger, with the exception of the column total for "Sundry Accounts," as explained above.

The individual accounts shown in the "Sundry Accounts" column can be posted daily or at the end of the month. Posting through January is indicated by account code numbers in the illustrated cash receipts journal.

The representative entries shown in the illustrated cash receipts journal are summarized in Exhibit 8–12, in **general journal form,** for convenience in assessing the increased efficiencies of the cash receipts journal approach in journalizing and posting a large number of individual cash transactions.

Other debit and credit columns can be added to the cash receipts journal to accommodate repetitive transactions that also involve cash receipts.

Cash Payments Journal. The special cash payments journal (often called the cheque register) is designed to accommodate efficiently the recording of **all cash payments.** Only cash payments can be recorded in the cash payments journal. The basic credit column is for Cash; columns for debits are incorporated into the format to accommodate repetitive transactions that involve cash payments. The cash payments journal also must include a column for "Sundry Accounts, Debits" to accommodate the nonrecurring transactions involving cash payments for which a special debit column is not provided.

A typical cash payments journal with some usual transactions recorded is shown in Exhibit 8–13. Notice that there are separate debit and credit sections. Each column illustrated is used as follows:

Exhibit 8–12 Journal entries for cash receipts

Jan.	2	Cash	1,237
		Sales revenue	1,237
		To record total cash sales for the day.	
	3	Cash	1,482
		Sales revenue	1,482
		To record total cash sales for the day.	
	4	Cash	2,500
		Land	2,000
		Gain on sale of land	500
		To record sale of land for $2,500 that originally cost $2,000.	
	4	Cash	992
		Sales revenue	992
		To record total cash sales for the day.	
	6	Cash	100
		Accounts receivable	100
		To record total collection of K. L. Adams account for Invoice No. 324 (no discount).	
	6	Cash	1,570
		Sales revenue	1,570
		To record total cash sales for the day.	
	10	Cash	1,000
		Notes payable	1,000
		To record bank loan, 90-day, 12%.	
	15	Cash	200
		Accounts receivable	200
		To record collection of O. L. Mays account for Invoice No. 328 (no discount).	
	26	Cash	1,360
		Sales revenue	1,360
		To record total cash sales for the day.	
	31	Cash	110
		Accounts receivable	110
		To record total collection of C. B. Baker account for Invoice No. 326 (no discount).	
	31	Cash	1,810
		Sales revenue	1,810
		To record total cash sales for the day.	

Exhibit 8–13 Cash payments journal illustrated

			CREDITS	DEBITS					
Date	Cheque No.	Explanation	Cash	Account Title	Folio	Accounts Payable	Sundry Accounts	Cash Purchases
Jan 2	101	Purchased mdse.	1,880					1,880
4	102	Invoice #37	2,970	Ray Mfg. Co.	51.3	2,970		
5	103	Jan. rent	1,200	Rent expense	71		1,200	
8	104	Purchased mdse.	250					250
10	105	Freight on mdse.	15	Freight in	63		15	
14	106	Invoice #42	980	Bows Supply Co.	51.1	980		
15	107	Paid note, plus	2,200	Notes payable	54		2,000	
		interest		Interest expense	79		200	
20	108	Insurance premium	600	Prepaid insurance	19		600	
26	109	Purchased mdse.	2,160					2,160
29	110	Invoice #91 – after	500	Myar Corp.	51.2	490		
		discount period		Discount lost	80		10	
31	111	Wages	1,000	Wage expense	76		1,000	
		Totals	13,755			4,440	5,025	4,290
		Posting	(12)			(51)	(NP)	(61)
Feb 1		Etc.						

CASH PAYMENTS JOURNAL   Page 16

1. **Cash credit**—This column is for **every credit** to the Cash account. The column is totaled at the end of the month and posted as a credit to the Cash account in the general ledger.

2. **Accounts Payable debit**—This column is used to enter the individual amounts paid on accounts payable. The individual amounts are posted as debits to the **accounts payable subsidiary ledger** (as indicated by the account numbers under folio), and the total at the end of the month is posted as a debit to the Accounts Payable control account in the general ledger.

3. **Sundry Accounts debit**—This column is used to record all accounts debited for which special columns are not provided (in this example Accounts Payable and Purchases are provided). The titles of the accounts to be debited are entered under the column "Account Titles." Because this column represents a number of accounts, the total cannot be posted; rather, each individual amount is posted as a debit directly to the indicated general ledger account.

4. **Cash Purchases debit**—All cash purchases are entered in this column. The total at the end of the month is posted as a debit to the Purchases account in the ledger.

Posting the cash payments journal involves two phases: (1) **daily posting** of the individual credit amounts to the **accounts payable susidiary ledger;** and (2) **periodic posting** of the totals to the **general ledger,** with the exception of the total of "Sundry Accounts." The posting of the individual amounts in the "Sundry Accounts" column can be done during the period, say, daily.

The illustrative transactions entered in the cash payments journal (Exhibit 8–13) were:

Jan. 2 Issued Cheque No. 101 for cash purchase of merchandise costing $1,880.

4 Issued Cheque No. 102 to pay account payable owed to Ray Manufacturing Company within the discount period. Discount allowed, 1%; Invoice No. 37, $3,000.

5 Issued Cheque No. 103 to pay January rent, $1,200.

8 Issued Cheque No. 104 for cash purchase of merchandise costing $250.

10 Issued Cheque No. 105 for freight-in on merchandise purchased, $15.

14 Issued Cheque No. 106 to pay account payable owed to Bows Supply Company within the discount period. Discount allowed, 2%; Invoice No. 42, $1,000.

15 Issued Cheque No. 107 to pay $2,000 note payable plus 10% interest for one year.

20 Issued Cheque No. 108 to pay three-year insurance premium, $600.

26 Issued Cheque No. 109 for cash purchase of merchandise costing $2,160.

29 Issued Cheque No. 110 to pay account payable to Myar Corporation; terms 2/10, n/30; Invoice No. 91, $500. Therefore, accounts payable to Myar was credited for $490 at the purchase date (see Chapter 6). The payment was made after the discount period; hence, the full invoice price of $500 was paid and purchase discount lost of $10 was recorded.

31 Issued Cheque No. 111 to pay wages amounting to $1,000.

Additional debit and credit columns can be added to the cash payments journal to accommodate other repetitive transactions involving cash disbursements.

Many companies control expenditures with a **voucher system** rather than using the credit purchases and the cash payments journals. A voucher system is adaptable to computerized accounting and gives tight control mechanisms on the sequence of events for each transaction from incurrence until final cash payment. The voucher system is explained and illustrated in Chapter 10.

In summary, special journals do not involve new accounting principles or concepts. Rather, they represent a mechanical technique designed to increase efficiency in the data processing cycle. Special journals are not standardized. They should be designed to fit each situation. For example, a small business can have a single journal called a synoptic journal to incorporate all of the functions of the cash receipts, sales, purchases, and cash payments journals. Although a manual approach has been illustrated for instructional purposes, many companies have computerized the procedures represented by special journals. In computerized systems, essentially the same mechanics illustrated for the manual system are accomplished by the computer.

IMPORTANT TERMS DEFINED IN THIS CHAPTER

Bank Reconciliation   Process of verifying the accuracy of both the bank statement and the cash accounts of the business. *p. 436*

Bank Statement   Monthly report from a bank that shows deposits recorded, cheques cleared, and running bank balance. *p. 434*

Cash   Money and any instrument that banks will accept for immediate increase in depositor's chequing account. *p. 432*

Cash Over and Short   Difference between the amount of cash held at a particular time and the amount the cash records call for. *p. 441*

Compensating Balances   Exists when a bank requires that a specified minimum cash balance must be maintained in the depositor's account. *p. 442*

Conservatism   When more than one alternative is acceptable in accounting, use the one that has the least short-term favourable effect on income and owners' equity. *p. 453*

Constraints to Accounting Principles   Implementation principles may be modified in application for (*a*) immaterial amounts, (*b*) conservatism, and (*c*) cost benefit constraint. *p. 453*

Contingent Liability   An endorser (on a negotiable instrument) is liable for its payment if the maker defaults; a contingent liability exists for the endorser. *p. 453*

Default of Note Receivable   Failure of the maker (payor) of a note to pay it by its maturity date. *p. 451*

Deposits in Transit   Deposits made by a depositor that have not yet been reported on the bank statement. *p. 437*

Discounting a Note Receivable   Sale of a note receivable to another party prior to its maturity date. *p. 451*

Internal Control   Policies and procedures of a business designed to safeguard the assets of the business. *p. 432*

Investment Portfolio   A group of securities (shares or bonds) held as an investment; grouped to be accounted for as one unit. *p. 445*

Lower of Cost or Market   Valuation of an investment at either (*a*) original cost or (*b*) current market whichever is lower. *p. 444*

Materiality   Small amounts involved in transactions must be recorded; however, the theoretically correct way may (but need not) be followed; use a simple accounting approach. *p. 453*

Negotiable Instrument   A formal (written) instrument that specifies the terms of a debt; it is **transferable by endorsement**. *p. 452*

Notes Receivable A written promise that requires another party to pay the business under specified conditions (amount, time, interest). *p. 449*

Outstanding Cheques Cheques written by a depositor that have not yet been cleared (cashed) by the depositor's bank. *p. 436*

Petty Cash A small amount of cash set aside for making small cash payments instead of writing cheques. *p. 442*

Receivables, Short-Term Short-term notes and accounts owed to the business by regular trade customers. *p. 448*

Short-Term Investment An investment that (*a*) is marketable and (*b*) will have a short-term holding period. *p. 444*

Special Receivables Receivables that arise from transactions other than merchandise and services sold. *p. 449*

Term Deposit An investment contract that can be purchased from banks; specifies amount, time, and interest rate. *p. 448*

Trade Receivables Another name for accounts receivable; open accounts owed to the business by trade customers. *p. 449*

Unrealized Loss Difference between original purchase cost of an investment and its current market value, if market value is **lower,** there is an unrealized loss (if not sold). *p. 446*

QUESTIONS

Part A: Questions 1–6

1. Define cash in the context of accounting and indicate the types of items that should be included and excluded. Identify typical categories of cash.
2. Summarize the primary characteristic of an effective internal control system for cash.
3. Why should cash-handling and cash-recording activities be separated? How is this separation accomplished?
4. What are the purposes of a bank reconciliation? What balances are reconciled?
5. Briefly explain how the total amount of cash reported on the balance sheet is computed.
6. What is the purpose of petty cash? How is it related to the regular Cash account?

Part B: Questions 7–12

7. Define a short-term investment. What is the twofold test for classification of an investment as short term?
8. Is a marketable security always classified as a short-term investment? Explain.
9. How does the cost principle apply in accounting for short-term investments in (*a*) debt securities and (*b*) equity securities?
10. What is the rationale for application of the LCM rule to the short-term investment portfolio of equity securities?

11. Explain the purpose of the Allowance to Reduce Short-Term Investments to Market account.

12. The revenue recognition principle (as discussed in Chapter 6) was defined to provide guidance as to when revenue should be recognized in the income statement. Indicate how a company should record interest on a note defaulted on by its customer using this principle.

Part C: Questions 13–21

13. Distinguish between accounts receivable and special receivables.

14. Define a promissory note indicating the designation of the parties and explain what is meant by principal, maturity date, face amount, and interest rate.

15. Distinguish between an interest-bearing and noninterest-bearing note.

16. What is a negotiable note?

17. What is a defaulted note? Who is responsible for its payment? Explain.

18. What is meant by discounting a note receivable?

19. What is a contingent liability? How does one arise in respect to a note receivable?

20. Identify and briefly explain the three accounting constraints related to the implementing accounting principles.

21. Short-term investments by most companies are valued at the lower of cost or market while accounts receivable are valued at their realizable amount. What is the difference in nature between these two classifications of assets that might warrant the difference in the two valuations?

EXERCISES

Part A: Exercises 8–1 to 8–8

E8–1 **(Pair Definition with Terms)**
Match the following brief definitions with the terms by entering the appropriate letter in each space provided.

Terms	Definitions
___ (1) Bank statement	A. An analysis that explains any differences existing between the cash balance shown by the depositor and that shown by the bank.
___ (2) Short-term investment	
___ (3) Cash over and short	B. Provided by the bank to the depositor each month listing deposits, cheques cleared, and running balance.
___ (4) Petty cash	C. Examples of this, by definition, are currency, cheques, money orders, or bank drafts.
___ (5) Compensating balances	D. Account to record errors that occur inevitably when a large number of cash transactions is involved.
___ (6) Contingent liability	
___ (7) Bank reconciliation	E. Required minimum cash balances on deposit.

Terms	Definitions

Terms

_____ (8) Special receivables
_____ (9) Internal control
_____ (10) Cash
_____ (11) Conservatism in accounting
_____ (12) Materiality
_____ (13) Deposits in transit
_____ (14) Notes receivable
_____ (15) Discounting a note receivable
_____ (16) Negotiable instrument
_____ (17) Outstanding cheques
_____ (18) Default of note receivable

Definitions

F. Selecting the accounting method that yields the most pessimistic immediate financial results.

G. A potential liability that depends on a future event arising out of a past transaction.

H. A note receivable not collected at maturity.

I. Deposits recorded in the depositor's ledger as debits to cash that have not been recorded by the bank.

J. Selling a negotiable note receivable before its maturity date to obtain cash.

K. Methods and procedures concerned with the accuracy of financial records.

L. An exception to accounting principles that says that amounts not material must be accounted for but need not be accorded theoretically correct treatment.

M. The most common example of this is a cheque.

N. Promissory notes that are evidence of a debt and state the terms of payment.

O. Cheques not listed on the bank's statement.

P. Currency used for disbursements that are usually relatively minor and conveniently made from cash on hand.

Q. A temporary investment in marketable securities.

R. Receivables, short or long term, that arise from transactions other than the sale of goods and/or services.

E8–2   (Reporting Cash When There Are Several Bank Accounts)

Modern Furniture Corporation has manufacturing facilities in several cities and has cash on hand at several locations as well as in several bank accounts. The general ledger at the end of 19A showed the following accounts: Petty Cash—Home Office, $500; City Bank—Home Office, $57,300; Cash Held for Making Change, $1,000 (included in the regular Cash Account balance); Petty Cash—Location A, $100; National Bank—Location A, $4,458; Petty Cash—Location B, $200; West Bank—Location B, $864; Petty Cash—Location C, $100; East Bank—Location C, $965; and Metropolitan Bank—Term Deposit, $8,700; and postdated cheques held that were received from two regular customers, $600.

The four bank balances given represent the current cash balances as reflected on the bank reconciliations.

Required:

What cash amount should be reported on Modern Furniture's 19A balance sheet? Explain the basis for your decisions on any questionable items.

E8–3   (Analysis of Items to Determine Correct Cash Balance)

Lakeview Company prepared a December 31, 19B, balance sheet that reported cash, $7,489. The following items were included in the reported cash balance:

Balance per bank statement at City Bank 4,934*
a. A deposit made to the local electric utility 500
b. Postage stamps on hand 80
c. Cheque signed by a customer, returned NSF 30
d. Petty cash on hand 150
e. IOUs signed by employees 80
f. Cheque signed by the company president for an advance to him; to be held until he
   "gives the word to cash it." 1,500
g. Money orders on hand (received from customers) 45
h. A signed receipt from a freight company that involved a $10 overpayment to them.
   They have indicated "a cheque will be mailed shortly." 10
i. A money order obtained from the post office to be used to pay for a special purchase
   upon delivery; expected within the next five days 160

Total cash shown on the 19B balance sheet $7,489

* Items not considered: deposit in transit, $500; cheques outstanding, $175; and cash held for making change, $100 (all included in the regular Cash account).

Required:

a. The reported cash balance is not correct. Compute the correct cash amount that should be reported on the balance sheet. Give appropriate reporting for any items that you exclude. (Hint: Set up a form similar to the above.)

b. Assume the company carries two cash accounts in the general ledger—Cash and Petty Cash. What is the correct balance that should be reflected in each cash account at December 31, 19B (end of the accounting period)? Show computations.

E8–4   (Bank Reconciliation, Entries, and Reporting)

Howard Company has the June 30, 19B, bank statement and the June ledger accounts for cash, which are summarized below:

Bank Statement

	Cheques	Deposits	Balance
Balance, June 1, 19B			$ 4,900
Deposits during June		$17,000	21,900
Cheques cleared through June . . .	$17,700		4,200
Bank service charges		75	4,125
Balance, June 30, 19B			4,125

Cash

June 1	Balance	4,900	June	Cheques written	18,100
June	Deposits	19,000			

Petty Cash

June 30	Balance	200	

Required:

a. Reconcile the bank account. A comparison of the cheques written with the cheques that have cleared the bank show outstanding cheques of $900. Cash on hand (for making change) on June 30 is $500 (included in the Cash account). Some of the cheques that cleared in June were written prior to June. There were no deposits in transit carried over from May, but there is a deposit in transit at the end of June.

b. Give any journal entries that should be made as a result of the bank reconciliation.

c. What is the balance in the cash account after the reconciliation entries?

d. What total amount of cash should be reported on the balance sheet at June 30?

E8–5 **(Bank Reconciliation, Entries, and Reporting)**

The September 30, 19D, bank statement for Witt Company and the September ledger accounts for cash are summarized below:

Bank Statement

	Cheques	Deposits	Balance
Balance, September 1, 19D			$ 5,100
Deposits recorded during September . . .		$27,000	32,100
Cheques cleared during September	$27,300		4,800
NSF cheque—J. J. Jones	80		4,720
Bank service charges	100		4,620
Balance, September 30, 19D			4,620

Cash

Sept.	1	Balance	5,300	Sept.	Cheques written	27,800
Sept.		Deposits	29,500			

Petty Cash

Sept. 30	Balance	450

Cash on hand for making change (included in the Cash account) on September 1 and September 30 amounted to $200. There were no outstanding cheques and no deposits in transit carried over from August; however, there are deposits in transit and cheques outstanding at the end of September.

Required:

a. Reconcile the bank account.

b. Give any journal entries that should be made as a result of the bank reconciliation.

c. What should be the balance in the Cash account after the reconciliation entries?

d. What total amount of cash should Witt report on the September 30 balance sheet?

E8–6 **(Bank Reconciliation with an Overage or Shortage)**

The March 31, 19C, bank statement for Star Company and the March ledger accounts for cash are summarized below:

Bank Statement

	Cheques	Deposits	Balance
Balance, March 1, 19C			$ 8,600
Deposits during March		$28,000	36,600
Note collected for depositor			
(including $100 interest)		1,060	37,660
Cheques cleared during March . . .	$32,200		5,460
Bank service charges	35		5,425
Balance, March 31, 19C			5,425

Cash

Mar. 1	Balance	8,320	Mar.	Cheques written	32,500
Mar.	Deposits	31,000			

Petty Cash

Mar. 31	Balance	200

A comparison of March deposits recorded with deposits on the bank statement showed deposits in transit of $3,000. Outstanding cheques at the end of March were determined to be $900. Cash on hand (not petty cash) for making change (included in the Cash account) was $300 at March 31.

Required:

a. Prepare a bank reconciliation for March. The bank figures have been verified as correct.

b. Give any journal entries that should be made by Star based on the reconciliation.

c. What amount should be shown as the ending balance in the Cash account after the reconciliation entries? What total amount of cash should be reported on Star's balance sheet at the end of March?

E8–7   (Bank Reconciliation, Entries, and Analysis)

In comparing the monthly bank statement for Pitman Enterprises with the cash ledger, the following items were found to reconcile the difference:

1. Bank service charge of $8.

2. Cheque No. 0178 written in payment to a supplier for $175 was inadvertently recorded in the ledger at $157.

3. Three cheques written in the month had not yet cleared the bank. The total amount was $448.

4. The deposit made on the last day of the month for $2,650 was not included on the bank statement.

5. The bank collected a note for $980 which included $80 interest for Pitman Enterprises.

6. A cheque written by Pitman Holdings, a sister company, had been charged against this bank account in the amount of $320.

7. A customer cheque was returned NSF with the bank statement. The cheque had been made out for $28. There was a $5 fee charged by the bank for this.

Required:

a. Prepare a journal entry to record each of the reconciling items where necessary in Pitman's books. Also indicate where no entry is required.

b. If the cash ledger had an unadjusted ending balance of $6,161, what was the ending balance per the bank statement?

c. Briefly explain why it is necessary to do a bank reconciliation upon receipt of the bank statement.

(SMAC Adapted)

E8–8   **(Bank Reconciliation)**

The cash in the bank account of the Hughes Co. at September 30, 1988, indicated a balance of $4,309.70 after all deposits and cheques had been posted. The bank statement indicated a balance of $4,063.10 on September 30, 1988. Comparison of the bank statement and the accompanying canceled cheques with the records revealed the following reconciling items:

1. Cheques outstanding:
   No. 711—$499.36;
   No. 735— 207.62;
   No. 732— 261.27.
2. On September 30, 1988, the company made a night deposit of $1,411.25.
3. Bank charges for the month of September amounted to $3.60.
4. The bank had deducted a $300 cheque written by R. B. Little from the company account during September.
5. A note from J. D. Large was collected by the bank on the company's behalf, but was not recorded in the company records. The note was for $500.

Required:

a. Prepare a bank reconciliation for the Hughes Co. for the month of September 1988.

b. Prepare data journal entries to adjust the accounts at September 30, 1988. Narratives are not required.

(SMAC Adapted)

Part B: Exercises 8–9 to 8–12

E8–9   **(Recording and Reporting Short-Term Investments)**

In July 19B, White Company had accumulated excess cash that would not be needed for 10 to 15 months. To employ the idle cash profitably, the management decided to purchase some shares as a short-term investment. The following related transactions occurred:

19B
July 30   Purchased 5,000 shares of the common stock of Sharp Corporation. The cash price, including fees and transfer costs, was $20,000.
Dec. 15   Received a cash dividend of $0.40 per share on the Sharp shares.
      30   Sold 1,000 of the Sharp shares at $5 per share.

Required:

a. Give the journal entries that White Company should make on each date for this short-term investment. The accounting period of White Company ends on December 31.

b. Show how this short-term investment should be reported on the balance sheet at December 31, 19B. Assume the market value of the Sharp stock was $5 per share on December 31, 19B.

E8–10   **(Recording and Reporting a Single Equity Security)**

Danbury Company purchased some common shares of Bay Corporation as a short-term investment. The following related transactions occurred:

19B

Feb. 1   Purchased 10,000 shares of Bay Corporation common for $60,000 cash.
Aug. 15   Received a cash dividend on the Bay common stock of $0.30 per share.
Dec. 30   Sold 3,000 shares of the Bay common at $5.80 per share.
     31   End of the accounting year. Bay common stock was selling at $5.75 per share.

Required:

a. Give the journal entries for Danbury Company on each date (including December 31) for the investment in Bay common shares. Danbury Company had no other short-term investments.

b. Show how the effects of this short-term investment should be reported on the financial statements at December 31, 19B.

c. Give the entry on January 15, 19C, assuming the remaining shares were sold at $5.50 per share.

d. Explain what Danbury Company should do about the allowance account on December 31, 19C, assuming no short-term investments are held on that date.

E8–11   **(Recording and Reporting a Short-Term Investment in Several Securities)**

During March 19B, Meigs Company acquired 200 shares of common stock in each of three corporations at the following costs: Corporation A, $8,000; Corporation B, $6,000; and Corporation C, $12,000. At the end of the annual accounting period, December 31, 19B, the quoted market prices per share were Corporation A, $40; Corporation B, $25; and Corporation C, $61.

Required:

a. Give the journal entry for Meigs to record the acquisition of these short-term investments.

b. Give the entry to record cash dividends of $1,800 received on the short-term investments in November 19B.

c. Give the entry to reflect the investments at LCM at December 31, 19B. Show computations.

d. Show how the investments would be reported on the financial statements at December 31, 19B.

e. Give the entry on January 5, 19C, assuming all of the shares were sold for $24,000 cash.

f. Give an entry required at December 31, 19C, assuming no short-term equity investments are held at that time (disregard any closing entries).

E8–12   **(Accounting for an Investment in a Debt Security)**

On October 1, 19B, Johnson Company purchased a debt security as a short-term investment for $25,000 cash. The security (due in 12 months) earned 8% annual interest on its principal amount of $25,000, payable on the date of maturity. At the end of the annual accounting period (December 31), the same security could be purchased for $25,100 cash.

Required:

a. Give all of the journal entries for Johnson Company on the following dates and provide an explanation for each date:
    (1) October 1, 19B.
    (2) December 31, 19B.
    (3) September 30, 19C.

b. Show how the security would be reported on the 19B financial statements.

Part C: Exercises 8–13 to 8–16

E8–13 **(Accounting for a Credit Sale through Accounts Receivable, to Notes Receivable, to Final Collection)**
Approximately 40% of the merchandise sold by King Company is sold on credit. Accounts receivable that are overdue, if material in amount, are "converted" to notes receivable when possible. The related transactions during 19B were:

Jan. 10   Sold merchandise on account to B. A. Cable for $10,000; terms n/30.
Mar. 1   The account was unpaid. King Company asked Cable to sign a six-month, 10%, interest-bearing note for the account. Cable executed the note on this date.
Aug. 31   Cable paid the principal of the note plus interest.

Required:

a. Give the journal entry that King should make on each of the three dates.

b. Give the journal entry that should be made on September 1, 19B, assuming Cable defaulted.

c. Give the journal entry assuming the default in (*b*) and also that Cable paid the note in full on September 15, 19B (no additional interest was paid).

E8–14 **(Accounting for a Credit Sale with a Note Payable)**
Pyle Company sells a line of products that has a high unit sales price. Credit terms are traditional in the industry. Pyle frequently takes a promissory note for the sale price. The accounting year ends December 31. The transactions and events were:

19B
  Dec. 1   Sold merchandise to B. T. Hamm on a three-month, 12%, interest-bearing note for $10,000.
       31   End of accounting year.

19C
  Jan. 1   Start of new accounting period.
  Mar. 1   Collected the note plus interest.

Required:

a. Give the journal entries for Pyle Company at each of the four dates; if none, so state.

b. With respect to the note, what item(s) and amount(s) should be reported on the 19B income statement?

c. With respect to the note, what item(s) and amount(s) should be reported on the balance sheet at December 31, 19B?

E8–15   **(Accounting for a Defaulted Note)**

Sidney Company frequently sells merchandise on a promissory note. These notes frequently are sold (i.e., discounted) to the local bank to obtain cash needed before maturity date. The following transactions relate to one note:

19B

Apr. 1   Sold merchandise for $9,000 to R. C. Day; took a six-month, 12%, interest-bearing note.

June 1   Discounted the note at the local bank at a 10% discount rate.

Oct. 1   Due date of the note plus interest.

Required:

a. Give the journal entries of the three dates, assuming Day paid the bank for the note on due date.

b. Give the journal entry on October 1, 19B, assuming Day defaulted on the note and Sidney Company had to make payments plus a $50 protest fee. This protest fee will be charged to Day.

c. Give the journal entry Day paid in full on October 5, 19B (no additional interest was paid).

E8–16   **(Based on Supplement 8A—Accounting and Reporting Petty Cash)**

On January 1, 19B, Moncton Company established a petty cash fund of $300 by writing a cheque to "J. Wright, Petty Cash." The fund was assigned to J. Wright, an employee, to administer as custodian. At the end of January, $60 cash remained in the fund. Signed receipts for expenditures during January were summarized as follows: postage, $63; office supplies, $28; transportation, $101; newspapers, $34; and miscellaneous (coffee for the office), $14.

Required:

a. Give the journal entry to establish the petty cash fund on January 1, 19B.

b. Give the journal entry to replenish the fund on January 31, 19B.

c. What balance would be shown in the Petty Cash account in the ledger at January 31? Explain.

d. How would petty cash be reported on the balance sheet at January 31, 19B?

e. Explain how the petty cash fund affected the January 19B income statement?

f. Assume it is January 5, 19C, and the management has decided to decrease the petty cash fund to $250. Give the required journal entry.

PROBLEMS

Part A: Problems 8–1 to 8–5

P8–1   **(Analysis of Internal Control)**

Pedernales Company has one trusted employee who, as the owner said, "handles all of the bookkeeping and paperwork for the company." This employee also is responsible for counting, verifying, and recording cash receipts and payments, such as making the weekly bank deposit, preparing cheques for major expenditures (signed by the owner), making small expenditures from the cash register for daily expenses, and collecting accounts receivable. The owners asked the local bank for a $25,000 loan. The bank asked that an audit be performed covering the year just ended. The independent auditor (a local PA), in a private conference with the owner, presented some evidence of the following activities of the trusted employee during the past year:

1. Cash sales sometimes were not entered in the cash register, and the trusted employee pocketed approximately $40 per month.
2. Cash taken from the cash register (and pocketed by the trusted employee) was replaced with expense memos with fictitious signatures (approximately $10 per day).
3. A $500 collection of an account receivable of a valued out-of-town customer was pocketed by the trusted employee and was covered by making a $500 entry as a debit to Sales Returns and a credit to Accounts Receivable.
4. A $700 collection on an account receivable from a local customer was pocketed by the trusted employee and was covered by making a $700 entry as a debit to Allowance for Doubtful Accounts and a credit to Accounts Receivable.

Required:

a. What was the approximate amount stolen during the past year?

b. What would be your recommendations to the owner?

P8–2 **(Prepare a Bank Reconciliation and Related Journal Entries)**
The bookkeeper at Rapid Growth Company has not reconciled the bank statement with the Cash account, saying, "I don't have time." You have been asked to prepare a reconciliation and review the procedures with the bookkeeper.

The April 30, 19D, bank statement and the April ledger accounts for cash showed the following (summarized):

Bank Statement

	Cheques	Deposits	Balance
Balance, April 1, 19D			$23,550
Deposits during April		$38,000	
Note collected for depositor			
(including $90 interest)		1,090	62,640
Cheques cleared during April . . .	$44,700		17,940
NSF cheque—A. B. Cage	140		17,800
Bank service charges	50		17,750
Balance, April 30, 19D			17,750

Cash

Apr.	1	Balance	23,050	Apr.	Cheques written	44,500
Apr.		Deposits	42,000			

Petty Cash

Apr. 30	Balance	200	

A comparison of cheques written before and during April with the cheques cleared through the bank showed outstanding cheques of $600 at the end of April. No deposits in transit were carried over from March, but there was a deposit in transit at the end of April. Cash on hand, held for change, at the end of April was $300 (included in the regular Cash account).

Required:

a. Prepare a detailed bank reconciliation for April.

b. Give any required journal entries as a result of the reconciliation. Why are they necessary?

c. What were the balances in the cash accounts in the ledger on May 1, 19D?

d. What total amount of cash should be reported on the balance sheet at the end of April?

P8–3   (Compute Outstanding Cheques and Deposits in Transit; Prepare a Bank Reconciliation and Journal Entries)

The August 19B bank statement for Zork Company and the August 19B ledger accounts for cash are given below.

Bank Statement

Date	Cheques	Deposits	Balance
Aug. 1			$16,000
2	$ 300		15,700
3		$7,000	22,700
4	400		22,300
5	200		22,100
9	900		21,200
10	300		20,900
15		9,000	29,900
21	700		29,200
24	21,000		8,200
25		8,000	16,200
30	800		15,400
30		2,180*	17,580
31	75†		17,505

* $2,000 note collected plus interest.
† Bank service charge.

Cash

		Cheques written:	
Aug. 1 Balance	15,250	Aug. 2	300
Deposits:		4	900
Aug. 2	7,000	15	850
12	9,000	17	550
24	8,000	18	800
31	6,000	18	700
		23	21,000

Petty Cash

Aug. 31 Balance	400

Cash on hand for making change at the end of August is $150 (included in the regular Cash account). Outstanding cheques at the end of July were $200, $400, and $300. There were no deposits in transit at the end of July.

Required:

a. Compute the deposits in transit at the end of August.

b. Compute the outstanding cheques at the end of August.

c. Prepare a bank reconciliation for August.

d. Give any journal entries that should be made as a result of the bank reconciliation by Zork Company. Why are they necessary?

e. After the reconciliation journal entries are posted, what balances would be reflected in the cash accounts in the ledger?

f. What total amount of cash should be reported on the August 31, 19B, balance sheet?

P8–4 **(Compute Outstanding Cheques and Deposits in Transit; Prepare Bank Reconciliation)**

The December 31, 19B, bank statement for Myles Company and the December 19B ledger accounts for cash are given below.

Bank Statement

Date	Cheques	Deposits	Balance
Dec. 1			$41,000
2	$400, 150	$16,000	56,450
4	7,000, 80		49,370
6	120, 180, 1,500		47,570
11	900, 1,200, 90	21,000	66,380
13	450, 700, 1,900		63,330
17	17,000, 2,000		44,330
23	40, 23,500	36,000	56,790
26	1,800, 2,650		52,340
28	2,200, 4,800		45,340
30	13,000, 1,890, 200*	19,000	49,250
31	1,650, 1,200, 28‡	6,360†	52,732

* NSF cheque, J. Doe, a customer.
† Note collected, principal, $6,000 plus interest.
‡ Bank service charge.

Cash

Dec. 1 Balance	55,850	Cheques written during December:		
Deposits:		40	5,000	2,650
Dec. 11	21,000	13,000	4,800	1,650
23	36,000	700	1,890	2,200
30	19,000	4,400	1,500	7,000
31	18,000	1,200	120	150
		180	80	450
		17,000	23,500	2,000
		90	900	1,900
		1,800	1,200	

Petty Cash

Dec. 31 Balance	150	

The November 19B bank reconciliation showed the following: Correct cash balance at November 30, $55,700; deposits in transit on November 30, $16,000; and outstanding cheques on November 30, $400 + $900 = $1,300. At the end of December 19B, cash held on hand for making change was $150 (included in the regular Cash account).

Required:

a. Compute the deposits in transit December 31, 19B.

b. Compute the outstanding cheques at December 31, 19B.

c. Prepare a bank reconciliation at December 31, 19B.

d. Give any journal entries that should be made as a result of the bank reconciliation made by Myles Company. Why are they necessary?

e. After the reconciliation journal entries, what balances would be reflected in the cash accounts in the ledger?

f. What total amount of cash should be reported on the December 31, 19B, balance sheet?

P8–5   (Bank Reconciliation)

Information concerning the banking operations of the Arrow Corporation for the month of December 1988 is presented below.

1. The ledger account for cash showed a balance on December 31, 1988 of $2,944.

2. Cash in the amount of $5,351 was deposited with the bank on December 31, 1988, but did not appear on the December bank statement.

3. The December bank statement showed a closing balance of $608.

4. Enclosed with the bank statement was a credit memo indicating that a noninterest-bearing note had been collected by the bank from F. Richard in the amount of $2,846 less a collection charge of $6.

5. The following December cheques had not been paid by the bank: No. 711 for $378; No. 690 for $256; and No. 599 for $104.

6. Cheque No. 605 for office supplies in the amount of $76 had been erroneously entered in the records as $67.

7. A debit memo was included with the canceled cheques indicating that $354 had been deducted for monthly interest on a bank loan.

8. Included with the December bank statement was a $200 cheque drawn by J. Fitz, a customer of Arrow corporation. The cheque was marked NSF. It had been included in the deposit of December 20 and had been charged back against the company's account on December 29.

Required:

a. Prepare a bank reconciliation for the Arrow Corporation for the month of December 1988.

b. Prepare journal entries *with* narratives, to adjust the accounts at December 31, 1988.

(SMAC Adapted)

Part B: Problems 8–6 to 8–8

P8–6   **(Accounting for a Portfolio of Short-Term Investments: Use of LCM)**
Heather Company usually acquires common shares as a short-term investment. This problem focuses on the purchase of three different common shares during 19B. The annual accounting period ends December 31. The sequence of transactions was:

19B
Apr. 2 Purchased (with cash) the following common shares as a short-term investment:

Corporation	Number of shares	Total price per share
X	300	$50
Y	400	70
Z	200	90

Sept. 8 Received a cash dividend of $4 per share on Corporation Z shares.
Dec. 30 Sold the shares of Corporation Y for $76 per share.
   31 Quoted market prices on this date were Corporation X shares, $53; Corporation Y shares, $75; and Corporation Z shares, $80.

Required:
a. Give the journal entry for Heather Company on each date.
b. How would the effects of these investments be shown on the 19B income statement and the balance sheet at December 31, 19B?
c. What was the amount of the 19B unrealized loss? Explain what this means.
d. Assume it is December 31, 19C, and that all of the X and Z shares still are held and that their market values per share are X, $51; and Z, $80. Give the required LCM entry. (Hint: Leave the correct balance in the Allowance account.)

P8–7   **(Accounting for Short-Term Investments in Debt Securities)**
On July 1, 19D, CAL Corporation purchased, as a short-term investment, 10 $1,000, 10% bonds of Lowe Corporation at par (i.e., at $1,000 each). The bonds mature on June 30, 19G. Annual interest is payable on June 30 each year. The accounting period for CAL Corporation ends on December 31.

Required:
a. Give the journal entries required for CAL Corporation on the following dates (if no entry is required, explain why): July 1, 19D, and December 31, 19D.
b. At the end of 19D, the bonds were quoted on the market at $975 each. Give any LCM basis journal entry required on December 31, 19D. If none is required, explain why.
c. Show how this investment should be reported on the 19D balance sheet and income statement.
d. Give the journal entry required on June 30, 19E.

P8–8   **(Accounting for Short-Term Investments in Equity and Debt Securities; Use of LCM)**

Superior Manufacturing Company produces and sells one main product. Demand is seasonal, and the unit sales price is high. Superior's accounting year ends December 31. Typically, in the busy months of the demand cycle, the company collects large amounts of cash, which is not needed during the slow months. The company often purchases short-term investments to earn a return on idle cash. Recently, the company purchased 1,000 shares of common stock in each of the two other corporations—Corporations A and B. The prices per share, including fees and related costs, were A, $30 and B, $70. In addition, Superior purchased a $10,000 bond of James Corporation. The bond pays 9% annual interest on each March 31. The bond was purchased for $10,000 cash (i.e., at par).

The sequence of transactions was:

19B

Apr.   1   Purchased the common stock and the bond. (Hint: Account for the shares and bond portfolios separately.)

Oct.   3   Received a cash dividend of $1 per share on the shares of Corporation B.

Nov. 30   Sold 600 shares of Corporation A at $26 per share and 600 shares of Corporation B at $75 per share.

Dec. 31   End of the accounting period. The market prices on this date were A shares, $31; B shares, $68; and the James bond, $100 (i.e., at par). (Hint: Do not overlook accrued interest.)

Required:

a. Give the journal entries for Superior at each of the four dates given above. Omit any closing entries.

b. Show how the effects of the investment should be reported on the balance sheet at December 31, 19B.

c. What items and amounts should be reported on the 19B income statement?

Part C: Problems 8–9 to 8–11

P8–9   **(Accounting for Accounts Receivable and Notes Receivable)**

Watertown Company sells approximately 80% of its merchandise on credit; terms n/30. Occasionally, a note will be received as a part of the collection process of a delinquent account. The annual accounting period ends December 31. The sequence of transactions was:

Note No. 1:

19B

Feb. 15   Sold merchandise for $5,000 to A. B. Lee; received $3,000 cash, and the balance was debited to Accounts Receivable.

Apr.   1   Received a 12%, interest-bearing note in settlement of the overdue account of Lee. The note is due in four months.

July   31   Due date for note; Lee defaulted.

Oct.   1   Lee paid the defaulted note plus interest, plus 8% interest on the defaulted amount for the period July 31–October 1.

Note No. 2:

19B

Oct. 1 Sold merchandise for $3,000 to J. K. Pope on account.

Nov. 1 Received a 12%, interest-bearing note in settlement of the overdue account from Pope. The note is due in three months.

Dec. 31 End of accounting period.

19C

Jan. 1 Start of new accounting period.

    30 Maturity date of the note. Pope paid the principal plus interest.

Required:

a. Note No. 1—Give the journal entries for Watertown Company on each date. Show interest calculations. Omit any closing entries.

b. Note No. 2—Give the journal entries for Watertown Company on each date. Show interest calculations. Omit any closing entries.

c. Note No. 2—How much interest revenue should be reported on the 19B income statement of Watertown Company?

d. Note No. 2—How will this note affect the 19B balance sheet of Watertown Company?

P8–10 **(Accounting for Notes Receivable, Including Discounting)**
Formex Company sells heavy machinery. Credit terms are customary and usually involve promissory notes and a mortgage on the machinery sold. The annual accounting period ends December 31. The transactions involving notes were:

Note No. 1:

19B

Feb. 1 Sold equipment to W. D. Fort for $40,000; received a $16,000 down payment and a four-month, 12%, interest-bearing note for the balance.

Mar. 1 Sold the note to the local bank at a 10% discount rate.

June 1 Due date of the note plus interest; Fort paid the note and interest in full.

Required:

a. Give the journal entry for Formex Company on each of the three dates. Show interest computations. Assume that Fort paid the bank the principal plus interest on the due date.

b. Give the journal entry on the due date, June 1, 19B, assuming instead that Fort defaulted on the note and Formex paid the local bank the face amount of the note plus interest and a $25 bank fee termed a protest fee.

c. How much interest revenue should be reported on the 19B income statement for Note No. 1?

Note No. 2:

19B

Dec. 11 Sold equipment to W. T. Owens for $30,000; received $5,000 cash down payment and a three-month, 12%, interest-bearing note for the balance.

    31 End of accounting period.

19C

Jan. 1 Start of new accounting period.

Mar. 1 Due date of the principal plus interest; Owens paid the note plus interest in full.

Required:

d. Give the journal entry for Formex Company on each of the four dates (omit any closing entries). State any assumptions you make.

e. How much interest revenue (Note No. 2) should be reported on the 19B income statement?

f. Show how Note No. 2 should be reported on the balance sheet at December 31, 19B.

P8–11   **(Based on Supplement 8B—Use of Control Accounts and Subsidiary Ledgers)**
New Company completes a variety of transactions each year. A number of them are repetitive in nature; therefore, the company maintains five different journals: general, credit sales, credit purchases, cash receipts, and cash payments. Selected transactions are listed below that are to be appropriately entered in these journals. To shorten this problem, amounts have been simplified and the number of transactions limited. All credit sales and credit purchases are recorded net of discount.

Selected transactions are listed below (use the letter to the left in lieu of the date and use the letter *v* for the last day of the period):

a. Sold merchandise to K. K. May at invoice cost of $250; terms 2/10, n/20; Invoice No. 38.

b. Received merchandise from Sable Company at invoice cost of $300; credit terms 1/10, n/20; Purchase Order No. 17.

c. Sold merchandise to B. B. Wise for $200 on credit; terms 2/10, n/20; Invoice No. 39.

d. Received merchandise from Rex Supply Company at an invoice cost of $200 on credit; terms 1/10, n/20; Purchase Order No. 18.

e. Sold merchandise to A. B. Cox for $750 cash.

f. Received merchandise from Baker Manufacturing Company at a cost of $360; paid cash (number the cheques consecutively starting with No. 81).

g. Purchased an operational asset (machinery) at a cost of $5,000; gave a 90-day, 12%, interest-bearing note payable for the purchase price.

h. Sold a tract of land for $9,000 that previously was used by the company as a parking lot and originally cost $4,000; collected cash.

i. Collected the account receivable from B. B. Wise within the discount period; Invoice No. 39.

j. Paid $600 for a three-year insurance policy on operational assets.

k. Obtained a $5,000 bank loan; signed a one-year, 12%, interest-bearing note payable.

l. Paid the account payable to Rex Supply Company within the discount period.

m. Paid monthly rent, $1,200.

n. Sold merchandise for cash, $1,400.

o. Purchased merchandise for cash, $980.

p. Sold merchandise on credit to C. C. Coe for $700; terms 2/10, n/20; Invoice No. 40.

q. Purchased merchandise on credit from Stubbs Company at an invoice cost of $400; terms 2/10/, n/30; Purchase Order No. 19.

r. Collected the account receivable from K. K. May after the discount period.

s. Paid the account payable to Sable Company after the discount period.

t. Paid monthly salaries, $2,400.

u. By year-end, six months of the prepaid insurance had expired.

Use the following general ledger account code numbers for posting: Cash, 11; Accounts Receivable, 14; Prepaid Insurance, 16; Machinery, 17; Land, 19; Accounts Payable, 21; Notes Payable, 22; Purchases, 31; Purchase Discounts Lost, 33; Sales Revenue, 41; Sales Discount Revenue, 43; Expenses, 51; and Gain on Sale of Operational Assets, 53. For journals, use the following page numbers: General, 15; Credit Sales, 18; Credit Puchases, 14; Cash Receipts, 21; and Cash Payments, 34.

Required:

1. Draft a format for each of the five journals, including a general journal, following the illustrations included in Supplement 8B. Include folio columns.

2. Set up separate T-accounts for each of the general ledger accounts listed above.

3. Set up separate T-accounts (with account numbers) for the subsidiary ledgers as follows:

Accounts receivable (14)	**Accounts payable (21)**
Coe—14.1	Sable—21.1
May—14.2	Stubbs—21.2
Wise—14.3	Rex—21.3

4. Enter each transaction in the appropriate journal.

5. Indicate all postings to the subsidiary ledgers by entering appropriate account numbers in the folio columns.

6. Total each money column in the special journals and indicate all postings to the general ledger accounts by entering the account code numbers in the folio columns and below total amounts posted. Use the account code numbers given above.

CASES

C8–1   (Analysis and Evaluation of Internal Controls)

Hall Manufacturing Company is a relatively small local business that specializes in the repair and renovation of antique jewelry, brass objects, and silverware. The owner is an expert craftsman. Although a number of skilled workers are employed, there is always a large backlog of work to be done. A long-time employee, who serves as clerk-bookkeeper, handles cash receipts, keeps the records, and writes cheques for disbursements. The cheques are signed by the owner. Small amounts are paid in cash by the clerk-bookkeeper, subject to a month-end review by the owner. Approximately 100 regular customers regularly are extended credit that typically amounts to less than $500. Although credit losses are small, in recent years the bookkeeper had established an Allowance for Doubtful Accounts, and all write-offs were made at year-end. During January 19E (the current year), the owner decided to start construction as soon as possible of a building for the business that would provide many advantages over the presently rented space and would have space usable for expansion of facilities. As a part of the considerations in financing, the financing institution asked for "19D audited financial statements." The company statements never had been audited. Early in the audit, the independent PA found numerous errors and one combination of amounts, in particular, that caused concern.

There was some evidence that a $1,500 job completed by Hall had been recorded as a receivable (from a new customer) on July 15, 19D. The receivable was credited for a $1,500 cash collection a few days later. The new account never was active again. The auditor also observed that shortly thereafter three write-offs of Accounts Receivable balances had been made to Allowance for Doubtful Accounts as follows: Jones, $250; Adams, $750; and Coster, $500; all of whom were known as regular customers. These write-offs drew the attention of the auditor.

Required:

a. What caused the PA to be concerned? Explain. Should the PA report the suspicions to the owner?

b. What recommendations would you make in respect to internal control procedures for this company?

C8–2   (Analysis of Cash, Short-Term Investments, and Receivables Using an Actual Financial Statement)

Refer to the financial statements of Consolidated-Bathurst Inc. in Appendix B immediately preceding the Index.

Required:

a. Is it possible to determine the causes of the decrease in cash and short-term investments during 1987?

b. How much cash was invested in additions to property, plant, and equipment?

c. Evaluate the adequacy of the reporting of short-term investments.

d. Explain the meaning of $344,800 shown on the SCFP for 1987.

e. What type of investment (short or long term) was sold in 1987 that was not sold in 1986?

C8–3   (Computer System; Internal Control)

Your audit client, Quebec Furniture Ltd. (QFL), which employs 250 people and manufactures furniture has recently acquired a minicomputer to replace its two mechanical bookkeeping machines. The bookkeeping machines are being used for all accounting operations, including the preparation of journals and ledgers and various documents such as sales invoices, purchase orders, cheques, and customer statements. QFL has also contracted with a local programming firm to provide a complete set of standardized accounting programs designed for small manufacturing firms. This set of computer programs performs the following functions:

1. Customer order entry.

2. Customer shipments and invoicing.

3. Accounts receivable and customer remittances.

4. Sales analysis.
5. Purchase order entry.
6. Receipts from vendors and vendor invoice processing.
7. Accounts payable and cash disbursements.
8. Inventory control.
9. Production scheduling and reporting.
10. Cost accounting.
11. Payroll.
12. Fixed assets.
13. General ledger and financial statements.
14. Generalized information retrieval and report writing.

The minicomputer has just been delivered and the programming firm's representatives are working on the installation of the set of standardized accounting programs. The minicomputer hardware consists of three visual display terminals with attached keyboards, a 150-line/minute printer, a 50-million byte magnetic disk drive, a 10-million byte magnetic tape cassette drive, and a 64,000-byte central processing unit. The minicomputer vendor's system software resides in 32,000 bytes of primary storage in the central processing unit and consists of a real-time program scheduler, an input/output control program, a BUSINESS BASIC language interpreter, and various utility programs for common data processing purposes (sort, merge, and copy data files, list programs, etc.).

The minicomputer hardware and the programming firm's software are designed so that all data input will be submitted through the keyboards attached to the visual display terminals. These terminals will also be used to call for information to be displayed on the terminal screen, to initiate the execution of computer programs which produce reports based on the data in the computer files, and to enter new programs or changes to existing programs. Data submitted to the microcomputer will either be processed immediately against master file records maintained on the magnetic disk drive or stored temporarily on the magnetic disk drive for subsequent batch processing against master file data.

The magnetic disk drive, which contains a fixed disk pack will also contain the accounting programs being supplied by the programming firm. The magnetic tape cassette drive will serve as the means of providing backup copies of the data and programs stored on the fixed magnetic disk pack.

The set of accounting programs are "standardized models" and must be tailored to each specific user firm's requirements. The tailoring process consists of modifying the programs:

1. To print outputs in a format desired by the user.
2. To insert various terms and tax rates applicable to the user (e.g., sales on a 2%, 10, net 30).
3. To insert the user's account codings and additional custom programs desired by the user.

These programs are written in BUSINESS BASIC, a high-level computer programming language noted for its simplicity. The generalized information retrieval and report writing feature allows a nonprogrammer to enter simple English-like commands through a visual display terminal to extract information and print exception reports based on any selection parameters specified by the user.

The only office staff at QFL are five clerical and bookkeeping personnel. There is no qualified accountant as QFL has relied on your firm for assistance in all accounting matters. Management consists of the owner/manager, a production manager, and several production foremen. Your firm has provided monthly accounting services leading to the preparation of monthly financial statements. The bookkeeping machine operator is being trained to be the senior data entry operator and to handle the relatively simple operations of turning on the minicomputer, setting up forms on the printer, and backing up data files and programs on the magnetic disk to magnetic tape cassette. QFL's owner/manager hopes that the use of a minicomputer will allow the firm to reduce the office staff to three: a senior data entry operator, a junior clerk, and a secretary/receptionist.

One of the main reasons why QFL's owner/manager decided to buy this minicomputer was that its operation would not require the hiring of any full-time computer people. Both he and the senior bookkeeping machine operator have attended a five-day course on programming and operating the equipment which he believes will be sufficient for either him or the operator to make any simple program changes that may be required at a future date. He plans to rely on the programming services firm for any major program changes that may be required in the future.

Required:

Discuss any significant control problems that may be created by the introduction of the minicomputer at QFL and recommend to the owner/manager steps to reduce their significance.

(CICA Adapted)

C8–4   (Computer System Design)

Cape Briton Supplies Ltd. (CBS), a client of yours, has recently installed a computerized sales/order entry system. The controller of CBS, Mr. Byte, has been reading articles and reports concerning computer fraud. He is concerned that the new system does not have appropriate controls to minimize the risks to the company. He has asked you to review the system in the normal course of your audit engagement.

CBS is a wholesale distributor of building products. It has a head office, three separate sales branches, and four separate warehouse locations. Each warehouse has significant inventory levels and approximately 2,500 different items. Annual sales are $80 million and the accounts receivable balance is $25 million. There are 5,000 customer accounts.

A schematic of the hardware configuration is outlined in Exhibit 1.

The central processor is located at the head office and includes a megabyte of storage with supporting disk drive capacity, telecommunication interface, tape drives, master printer, and master terminal. Other terminals are located in the following sites:

> Accounting department—2
> Order desk: Head office—3
>   Branches—2 at each sales branch for a total of 6
> Warehouses—1 at each of 4 warehouses

Printers are located in each warehouse for the printing of shipping documents as well as in the accounting department and in the computer room.

Historically, the computer operations at CBS have been well controlled. A review of the existing environment or general computer controls has revealed that controls over implementation, program and data files, physical operations, and the operating system are adequate.

Exhibit 1 Schematic of hardware configuration

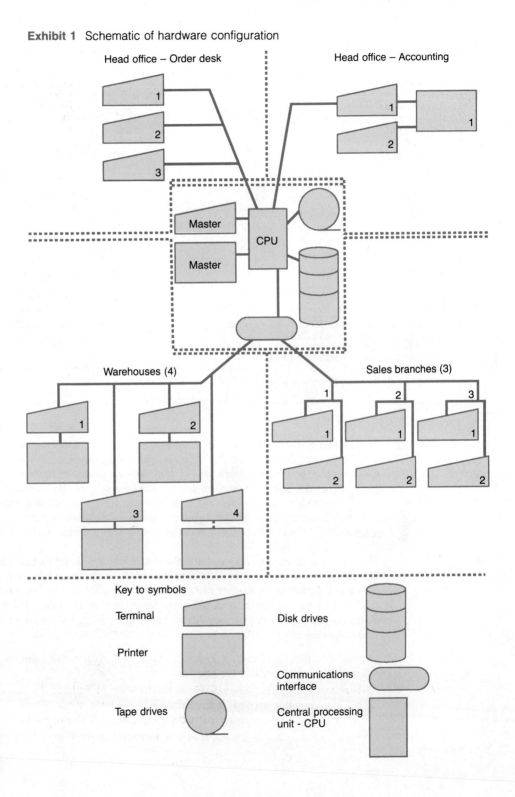

Exhibit 2 Accounts receivable file layout

Field name	No. of characters and field characteristics	Description
1. Acc-Number	9(10)	Customer number
2. Division	9(2)	Sales branch
3. Cust-Name	X(25)	Name
4. Address	X(50)	Address
5. Credit-Lim	9(7)	Credit limit
6. Total-Due	S9(7)V99	Total A#R
7. Current-Bal	S9(7)V99	
8. Bal-30-60	S9(7)V99	
9. Bal-60-90	S9(7)V99	Age of invoices on file
10. Bal-Over-90	S9(7)V99	
	S9(7)V99	
11. Invoice-No.*	9(5)	Individual invoice number
12. Invoice-Date	9(6)	Date of invoice
13. Invoice-Amt	S9(7)V99	Amount of invoice
14. Credit-No.*	9(5)	Credit note number
15. Credit-Date	9(6)	Date of credit note
16. Credit-Amt	S9(7)V99	Amount of credit note
17. Unallocated-Cash	S9(7)V99	Cash not matched with invoices

Note: S—Designates that the field is signed.
      V—Represents a decimal point.
      X—Indicates an alphanumeric field.
      9—Indicates a numeric field.
      *—File contains as many items as exist that are not matched with cash.
For example, 9(6) represents a numeric field of six characteristics.

The system was designed to speed up the order entry processing/shipping function, and improve inventory and accounts receivable management.

Clerks at the terminal locations take orders over the phone or from salesmen's written orders. The clerks call a "menu" to the screen and prepare the required order. Input includes customer numbers, product numbers, quantity, special shipping instructions, and branch location code. The computer edits the input data for correct format, valid dates, valid customer, product, and location codes, credit limits, and inventory availability.

The accounts receivable file contains the data elements listed in Exhibit 2.

For all orders clearing the edits, a sales order is produced in two copies at the warehouse location. A computer file of outstanding sales orders is created. The warehouse clerks take the orders and fill them. One copy of the sales order serves as the packing slip. The other copy is sent in accounting for filing by customer number.

The following action results when edit checks are not successful.

1. Invalid product, customer or location codes, and invalid dates are immediately identified to the operator for reentry.

2. Where the product is not available at the location identified, the inventory file of other locations is searched. If the product is available at the alternate location, a sales order is produced with instructions to ship only the relevant item.

3. Where inventory is not available at any location, a record is created in the back-

order file and a printout of the order is sent to the purchasing department for follow-up.

4. Where the credit limit is exceeded, the order is printed out in the accounting department for credit override approval.

When an order is complete and shipped, the warehouse clerk keys in this fact in the warehouse terminal and the order is flagged as shipped on the outstanding sales order file.

In the case of partial shipments from a warehouse, the clerk codes the order as partial and indicates items shipped. This is noted on the outstanding order file and when these items have been shipped, the program changes the code on the outstanding order file to read complete.

For orders for which inventory is not available, a back order is created and identified on the outstanding order file. When all items other than the back-order items are keyed in as shipped, the program codes the order complete and it enters the billing cycle.

At the end of each day, the outstanding order file is processed and all shipments coded complete enter the billing program which creates an invoice and updates the accounts receivable and sales files.

When goods are received at a warehouse, the warehouse clerk enters the data. The system searches the back-order file and immediately creates sales orders for the items in back order. It then follows the normal processing cycle.

The inventory file contains the data elements described in Exhibit 3. The warehouse clerks have access through terminals to inventory files and are encouraged to make adjustments to the records through the terminals, if in filling an order they find inventory overages or shortages. Cyclical counts of inventory are carried out by designated warehouse clerks who adjust records as required through the terminals. In order to carry out the credit checks at the input stage of the sales order system, the program accesses the price file, prices the order, and calculates the total. It then accesses the receivable file to obtain the current balance, adds the order value, and compares the total to the credit limit. To save processing time, only orders in excess of $200 are subject to the credit check.

If a customer account is not on file, as determined at the edit stage, the order is printed out at the accounting office printer, and a credit investigation is done by credit clerks. When the customer is approved for credit, the credit clerk goes to the terminal and creates the customer file with the appropriate credit limit. The order is sent back to the sales order clerks for processing in the normal fashion.

The credit manager can approve sales over the credit limit. He receives these sales order copies and reviews them. When he authorizes a sale over the credit limit, he signs the order copy and resubmits it to the sales order clerks. With a special code, they bypass the credit check and the order is processed normally.

At the end of each week, the outstanding order file is processed and a printout is produced. On Monday morning, the warehouse managers review the oustanding list.

Payments on account are received by a cash receipts clerk who takes an adding machine tape of the receipts and codes the tapes for customer number. She prepares a bank deposit slip in duplicate, and gives the payments and original deposit slip to a messenger who makes the bank deposit. She then enters the payments by customer number into the terminal for updating of the receivables file. Independently, another clerk checks the stamped bank deposit slip to the adding machine tape to ensure all receipts were deposited. A daily cash listing is printed on the accounting office printer so that the cash receipts clerk can respond to any customer queries.

Exhibit 3 Inventory file layout

Field name	No. of characters and field characteristics	Description
1. Product-Number	9(10)	Individual item identification code
2. Warehouse-Code	9(2)	Warehouse location
3. Product-Group	9(2)	
4. Production-Description	X(40)	
5. Date-Cost	9(6)	Last date cost changed (YYMMDD)
6. Recent-Cost	S9(6)V99	Most recent unit cost
7. Prior-Cost	S9(6)V99	Previous unit cost
8. Selling-Price	S9(6)V99	Current selling price
9. Data-Selling Price	9(6)	Date of last selling price change (YYMMDD)
10. Quantity-On-Hand	S9(6)	Inventory in warehouse
11. Quantity-On-Order	S9(6)	Inventory on order
12. Economic-Order	S9(6)	Economic order quantity
13. Order-Point	S9(6)	Minimum stock level#reorder level
14. Quantity-Previous-Y#E	S9(6)	Closing inventory previous year (units)
15. Current-Year's-Sales-Units	S9(6)	Number of units sold current year
16. Previous-Year's Sales	S9(7)V99	Total sales previous financial year
17. Previous-Year's-Sales-Units	S9(6)	Total units sold previous financial year
18. Date-Last-Count	9(6)	Last cyclical count date (YYMMDD)
19. Adjustment-Last-Count	S9(7)V99	Adjustment on last cyclical count
20. Net-Adjustment-Year	S9(7)V99	Net adjustments made during the year
21. Date-Last-Receipt	9(6)	Date of last receipt (YYMMDD)
22. Quantity-Last-Receipt	S9(6)	Quantity received on last receipt
23. Supplier-Number	9(8)	Designated supplier
24. Date-Last-Shipment	9(6)	Date of last shipment (YYMMDD)
25. Quantity-Last-Shipment	S9(6)	Quantity shipped in last sale

Note: S—Designates that the field is signed (i.e., positive or negative).
　　　V—Represents a decimal point.
　　　X—Indicates an alphanumeric field.
　　　9—Indicates a numeric field.

At month end, the following reports are printed:

> Accounts Receivable Aged Trial Balance
> Sales Analysis: By warehouse
> 　　　　　　　　By salesman
> 　　　　　　　　By product
> Inventory Adjustment listing
> Cash Receipts listing

These listings are used to update general ledger control accounts. Accounts receivable are reconciled to the general ledger by a clerk who is independent of the accounts receivable, inventory, and cash receipts functions.

Required:

Identify the control weaknesses in the sales/order entry and cash receipts system as described and suggest ways in which the company might correct the weaknesses.

(CICA Adapted)

C8–5   **(Computer Program for Bank Reconciliation)**

Required:

Write a computer program to solve Problem P8–4. Your program should result in a bank reconciliation report which should resemble the following:

```
RECONCILIATION OF BANK STATEMENT
BANK BALANCE                        52732
DEPOSITS IN TRANSIT                 18000
OUTSTANDING CHEQUES                -10300
CASH ON HAND                          150
BANK ERRORS                             0
TRUE BALANCE                        60582

RECONCILIATION OF BOOK CASH BALANCE
BOOK BALANCE                        54450
NOTES COLLECTED                      6360
SERVICE CHARGE                        -28
NSF CHEQUES                          -200
BOOK ERRORS                             0
TRUE BALANCE                        60582
DIFFERENCE                              0
```

If the computer language you use allows you to make the report look better than the one presented above, then do improve on it.

There are many different ways by which a computer could prepare a report like this one. The computer could get its data from a file or, in the BASIC language, from READ and DATA statements. Alternatively, the computer could prompt the user for each piece of information needed.

You should seriously consider the pros and cons of these various alternatives.

The objective is to write a simple program which will help someone who does not know much about bank reconciliations to use the computer to prepare such a report. Therefore, the program should be written to solve the problem by prompting the user for input.

Here are some hints to help write the program:

1. Study the material in the text to determine the major items that should appear in a bank reconciliation.

2. For each item for which data has to be entered into the computer, for example, the cash balance according to the bank statement, write an appropriate prompt to the terminal screen and ask for the desired information.

3. Store the information received in response to prompts in appropriate variables.

4. Organize the information received from the user of the program into the proper format and print out the bank reconciliation.

5. In writing your program, it is not necessary to have it allow the user to correct a bank reconciliation that does not balance; it is acceptable to require that the program's user reenter all the requested information; however, you should give some thought to how you might allow the user to correct various values in the statement that may have been incorrectly entered into the computer.

After solving Problem P8–4 using your program, solve Problem P8–3 using the same program.

(Prepared by C. Dirksen)

OPERATIONAL ASSETS— PROPERTY, PLANT, AND EQUIPMENT; NATURAL RESOURCES; AND INTANGIBLES

PURPOSE

The operation of a business requires a combination of assets classified on a balance sheet as current, investments and funds, operational, and other. The purpose of this chapter is to discuss operational assets. These assets usually are called property, plant, and equipment and intangible assets (sometimes fixed assets). **Operational assets are the noncurrent assets that a business retains more or less permanently (not for sale) to carry on its ongoing operations.** Operational assets include land, buildings, equipment, fixtures, natural resources, and certain intangible assets (such as a patent). Operational assets are important in carrying out normal profit-making activities.

On the facing page, notice how St. Laurence Cement reports the operational assets in its balance sheets and also provides related supplementary disclosure notes. The specifics of the intangible assets will be discussed in later chapters.

LEARNING OBJECTIVES

1. Define, classify, and explain the nature of operational assets.
2. Apply the cost principle to measure and record operational assets.
3. Apply the matching principle to record and report depreciation and depletion.
4. Define, record, and amortize intangible operational assets.
5. Expand your accounting vocabulary by learning about the "Important Terms Defined in This Chapter."
6. Apply the knowledge gained from this chapter.

ORGANIZATION

Part A—property, plant, and equipment, including depreciation

1. Measuring and recording acquisition cost.
2. Depreciation concepts and methods.
3. Effects of depreciation on the financial statements.
4. Depreciation and cash flow.

Part B—repairs and maintenance, natural resources, and intangible assets

1. Repairs and maintenance, and additions.
2. Natural resources and depletion.
3. Intangible operational assets and amortization.
4. Disposal of operational assets.

ST. LAWRENCE CEMENT

CONSOLIDATED BALANCE SHEET

As at December 31, 1986 (thousands of dollars)

	1986	1985
Assets		
Current assets		
Accounts receivable	$128,197	$111,170
Inventories	74,874	65,713
Prepaid expenses	2,307	2,991
	205,378	179,874
Investments and other assets	9,349	9,296
Fixed assets	339,880	339,542
Intangible assets	15,064	18,293
	$569,671	$547,005

NOTES TO CONSOLIDATED FINANCIAL STATEMENTS

1. Significant accounting policies

d) Fixed assets are depreciated over their estimated useful lives using the straight-line method. Quarries are depleted on the basis of tonnes extracted. The Company adjusts depreciation in accordance with established criteria to reflect variations from normal utilization.

e) The excess of the cost of purchased businesses over the fair value of net assets at dates of acquistion is being amortized on a straight-line basis over twenty years.

3. Fixed assets

	1986 Cost	1986 Net book value	1985 Cost	1985 Net book value
Land and quarries	$ 42,842	$ 32,475	$ 41,150	$ 32,303
Buildings and structures	185,579	104,019	184,032	109,213
Machinery and equipment	303,831	158,193	295,187	165,505
Transportation equipment	94,030	34,722	80,277	24,218
Other	16,852	10,471	15,776	8,303
	$643,134	$339,880	$616,422	$339,542

Year ended December 31, 1986 (tabular amounts are expressed in thousands of dollars)

4. Intangible assets

	1986	1985
Unamortized cost in excess of net assets of business acquired	$11,463	$12,348
Unamortized bond discount and expense	636	752
Deferred loss on translation of long-term debt	2,965	5,193
	$15,064	$18,293

Classification of Operational Assets

The combination of assets held by a business is reported on the balance sheet. Operational assets have different characteristics depending on the nature of the business. Therefore, operational assets are classified as follows:

1. **Tangible operational assets**—the operational assets that have **physical substance;** that is, they are tangible. This classification usually is called property, plant, and equipment. There are three kinds of tangible operational assets:
    a. Land—held for use in operations; it is **not** subject to depreciation.
    b. Buildings, fixtures, equipment; subject to **depreciation.**
    c. Natural resources; subject to **depletion.**
2. **Intangible operational assets**—the operational assets that do not have physical substance that are held by the business because of the **use rights** they confer to the owner. Examples are patents, copyrights, franchises, licenses, and trademarks. Intangible assets are subject to periodic **amortization.**

Accounting Concepts Applied to Accounting for Operational Assets

The life span of operational assets owned by a business varies from 2 years to 5, 10, 20, or more years. Therefore, the following accounting concepts usually must be applied (refer to Exhibit 4–5, page 176):

1. **Cost principle**—at purchase date, each operational asset is measured and recorded at its **cash-equivalent** cost.
2. **Matching principle**—during the period from acquisition date to disposal date, the expense of using each asset is measured and recorded in a way to match this expense with the revenues that the asset helped to earn.
3. **Recognition of gain or loss** (elements of financial statements)—at disposal date of operational assets.

Parts A and B will discuss these three application problems.

PART A—PROPERTY, PLANT, AND EQUIPMENT, INCLUDING DEPRECIATION

Measuring and Recording Acquisition Cost

Under the **cost principle,** all reasonable and necessary costs incurred in **acquiring** an operational asset, **placing** it in its operational setting, and **preparing** it for use, **less** any cash discounts, should be recorded in a designated asset account. Cost is measured as the **net cash equivalent** amount paid or to be paid. **Acquisition** cost can be readily determined when an operational asset is purchased for cash. The acquisition cost of a machine on January 1, 19A, may be measured as follows:

Invoice price of the machine	$10,000
Less: Cash discount allowed ($10,000 × 2%)	200
Net cash invoice price	9,800
Add: Transportation charges paid by purchaser	150
Installation costs paid by purchaser	200
Sales tax paid ($10,000 × .08)*	800
Cost—amount debited to the Machinery account	$10,950

* Assumed.

The seller agreed to give a 2% discount for immediate cash payment. Otherwise, the full invoice price ($10,000) must be paid. Even if the $200 discount is not taken, it still is deducted because the extra amount paid is a cost of credit; it is recorded as interest expense. Notice that the cost includes transportation, installation, and sales tax. The journal entry to record the purchase of this machine is:[1]

January 1, 19A:

Machinery	10,950	
Cash		10,950

When an operational asset is purchased and a **noncash** consideration is included in part, or in full, payment for it, the cash equivalent cost is measured as any cash paid plus the **current market value** of the noncash consideration given. Alternatively, if the market value of the noncash consideration given cannot be determined, the current market value of the asset purchased is used for measurement purposes. Assume a tract of timber (a natural resource) was acquired by Fast Corporation. Payment in full was made as follows: $28,000 cash plus 2,000 shares of Fast Corporation capital stock (nopar).[2] At the date of the purchase, Fast stock was selling at $12 per share. The cost of the tract would be measured as follows:

Cash paid	$28,000
Market value, noncash consideration given	
(2,000 shares no-par stock × $12)	24,000
	52,000
Title fees, legal fees, and other costs paid in cash	
(incidental to the acquisition)	1,000
Cost—amount debited to the asset account	$53,000

---

[1] If the invoice is not paid immediately, this entry would be:

Machinery	10,950	
Interest expense	200	
Liability, equipment purchase		10,000
Cash ($150 + $200 + $800)		1,150

[2] See Chapter 12 for discussion of capital stock.

The journal entry to record the acquisition of this natural resource is:

January 1, 19A:

Timber tract (No. 12)	53,000	
Cash		29,000
Capital stock, no par (2,000 shares × $12)		24,000

When land is purchased, all of the incidental costs paid by the purchaser, such as title fees, sales commissions, legal fees, title insurance, delinquent taxes, and surveying fees, should be included in the cost of the land. Because land is **not** subject to depreciation, it must be recorded and reported as a separate operational asset.

Sometimes, an **old** building or used machinery is purchased for operational use in the business. Renovation and repair costs incurred by the purchaser **prior to use** should be debited to the asset account as a part of the cost of the asset. Ordinary repair costs incurred **after** the asset is placed in use are normal operating expenses when incurred.

Basket Purchases of Assets

When two or more kinds of operational assets are acquired in a single transaction and for a single lump sum, the cost of each kind of asset acquired must be **measured and recorded separately.** When a building and the land on which it is located are purchased for a lump sum, at least two separate accounts must be established. One is for the building (which is subject to depreciation), and one is for the land (which is not subject to depreciation). Therefore, the single sum must be apportioned between the land and the building on a **rational** basis.

Relative market value of the several assets at the date of acquisition is the most logical basis on which to allocate the single lump sum. Appraisals or tax assessments often have to be used as indications of the market values. Assume Fox Company paid $300,000 cash to purchase a building suitable for an additional plant and the land on which the building is located. The separate, true market values of the building and land were not known; therefore, a professional appraisal was obtained that showed the following estimated market values: building, $189,000; and land, $126,000 (apparently the buyer got a good deal). The apportionment of the $300,000 purchase price and the journal entry to record the acquisition are shown in Exhibit 9–1.

Under limited conditions during the construction period of an operational asset, interest cost may be included in acquisition cost. This topic is discussed in Supplement 9A.

Government Assistance

Governments at all levels in Canada provide assistance to businesses in a variety of forms. Low-interest loans, tax write-offs, forgivable loans, property tax reductions, sales tax rebates, subsidies to reduce various operating costs, and cash grants to reduce the construction or acquisition cost of fixed assets are some

Exhibit 9–1 Recording a basket purchase of assets

Situation:

Fox Company purchased a building and the related land for $300,000 cash. Estimated current market values: building, $189,000; and land, $126,000.

Allocation of acquisition cost:

Asset	Appraised value Amount	Ratio	Apportionment of lump-sum acquisition cost Computation	Apportioned cost
Building	$189,000	0.60*	$300,000 × 0.60 =	$180,000
Land	126,000	0.40†	300,000 × 0.40 =	120,000
	$315,000	1.00		$300,000

* $189,000 ÷ $315,000 = 0.60.
† $126,000 ÷ $315,000 = 0.40.

Entry to record the acquisition:

Plant building	180,000	
Land—plant site	120,000	
Cash		300,000

common examples. To account for such a complex array of assistance can present difficulties for the accountant. Careful analysis of each case is required.

Two general rules can help guide the accountant. Grants or rebates that reduce operating expenses of the current period should be treated as such. Assistance that reduces the cash cost of acquiring or constructing fixed assets should reduce the cost of the fixed asset and correspondingly reduce the subsequent depreciation.[3] Sales tax rebates and loans, when the company has become eligible for forgiveness, are treated in the same way as a cash grant.

The receipt of a federal government cash grant of $50,000 by Fox (see Exhibit 9–1) would be accounted for as follows:

Grant receivable from government of Canada	50,000	
Plant building		30,000
Land—plant site		20,000
To record the approved grant of $50,000 allocated 60% to buildings and 40% to land.		

[3] *CICA Handbook,* Section 3800.26, permits an alternative treatment for assistance involved in the acquisition of fixed assets. Further elaboration will not be presented because the effect is also to reduce depreciation expense and this alternative is not commonly used in Canada. *Financial Reporting in Canada,* 17th ed. (Toronto, Ont.: Canadian Institute of Chartered Accountants, 1987), p. 48.

Cash 50,000

    Grant receivables from

       government of Canada   50,000

    To record the receipt of the cheque from the government.

Matching Costs with Revenues Generated from Operational Assets

In conformity with the **matching principle,** the costs of using an operational asset must be matched with revenues earned each accounting period. These **use costs** are called (1) depreciation, depletion, and amortization (discussed in Part A of this chapter); and (2) repairs and maintenance (discussed in Part B).

Nature of Depreciation, Depletion, and Amortization

For **accounting purposes** (not income tax purposes), an operational asset that has a limited useful life represents the **prepaid cost** of a bundle of **future** services or benefits that will help earn future revenues.[4] The **matching principle** (Exhibit 4–5) requires that the acquisition cost of operational assets (other than land) be **allocated** as expense to the periods in which revenue is earned as a result of using those assets. Thus, the acquisition cost of this kind of operational asset is matched in a systematic and rational manner in the future with the future revenues to which it contributes by way of services and benefits. As suggested by a careful reading of the words systematic and rational, depreciation rules have to be consistently followed according to the requirements of the comparability principle (Exhibit 4–5) and the method should have a rationale. What rationale is used in selecting a particular depreciation method is left to arguments within the matching principle. Further refinement of this rationale, beyond what is possible with matching is yet to be seen.

Three different terms are used to identify the allocation of the **use-costs** required by the matching principle. These terms are:

1. **Depreciation**—the systematic and rational allocation of the acquisition cost of **tangible** operational assets, other than natural resources, to future periods in which the assets contribute services or benefits to help earn revenue. Example—depreciation of the $10,950 cost of a machine over its estimated useful life of 10 years and no residual value (see page 499). The accounting year ends December 31, and it is the end of 19B (the second year after purchase):[5]

---

[4] A careful distinction must be maintained between depreciation for accounting purposes (prescribed by GAAP) and for income tax (prescribed by tax laws and regulations). As suggested earlier with inventories, income taxes affect the cash flows of the business while depreciation is a noncash expense. In addition, depreciation rules prescribed for income tax purposes have and do influence what accounting allocation rules are used. Usually income tax must be paid by corporations, not by sole proprietorships and partnerships.

[5] Adjusting entries made at the end of 19A would be the same as the following three entries because the allocation shown uses a straight-line assumption.

December 31, 19B (adjusting entry):

Depreciation expense ($10,950 ÷ 10 years) 1,095
    Accumulated depreciation, machinery   1,095

2. **Depletion**—the systematic and rational allocation of the acquisition cost of **natural resources** to future periods in which the use of those natural resources contributes to revenue. Example—depletion of the $53,000 cost of timber tract over the estimated period of cutting based on a "cutting" rate of approximately 20% per year (see page 499):

December 31, 19B (adjustment entry):

Depletion expense ($53,000 × 20%) 10,600
    Timber tract (No. 12)   10,600

Note: A contra account could be used, such as Accumulated Depletion.

3. **Amortization**—the systematic and rational allocation of the acquisition cost of **intangible** operational assets to future periods in which the benefits contribute to revenue. Example—amortization of the $8,500 purchase cost of a patent over its estimated economic useful life to the entity of 17 years:

December 31, 19B (adjusting entry):

Patent expense ($8,500 ÷ 17 years) 500
    Patents   500

Note: A contra account, such as Accumulated Patent Amortization, could be used for the credit.

The three terms—depreciation, depletion, and amortization—relate to the same basic objective; that is, the allocation of the acquisition cost of an operational asset to the future periods in which the benefits of its use contribute to earning revenue.

The amounts of depreciation, depletion, and amortization measured and recorded during each period are reported as expenses for the period. The amounts of depreciation, depletion, and amortization **accumulated since acquisition** date are reported on the balance sheet as deductions from the assets to which they pertain. An operational asset, such as the machine illustrated above, would be reported on the balance sheet (at the end of the second year in the example) as follows:

Balance Sheet
At December 31, 19B

Property, plant, and equipment:
  Machinery $10,950
    Less: Accumulated depreciation 2,190 $8,760*

or

Machinery (less accumulated depreciation, $2,190) . . . $8,760*

* Called book value or carrying value.

We stress that the amounts for operational assets reported on the balance sheet do not represent their market values at the balance sheet date. Rather, the amounts are called book, or carrying, values. The **book, or carrying value,** of an operational asset is its acquisition cost, less the accumulated allocation to expense of that cost from acquisition date to the date of the balance sheet. Recording and reporting depreciation is a process of **cost allocation.** It is not a process of determining the current market value of the asset. Under the **cost principle,** the cost of an operational asset is measured and recorded at acquisition date at its current market value. The cost is not remeasured on a market value basis at subsequent balance sheet dates. Instead, the acquisition cost is reduced by the accumulated expense allocation for depreciation, depletion, or amortization.

Depreciation Concepts

Tangible operational assets, except land, are subject to depreciation because they have limited economic lives. Usually, land is not subject to depreciation because it does not wear out and is not considered to be scrap.

Tangible operational assets (except land) decrease in economic utility to the user because of a number of **causative factors,** such as wear and tear, the passage of time, effects of the elements (such as the weather), obsolescence (i.e., becoming out-of-date), technological changes, and inadequacy. These causative factors always affect such assets during the periods in which the assets are being used to earn revenues. These causative factors serve as the basis for the matching rationale when selecting depreciation methods. Thus, under the **matching principle,** at the end of each accounting period an **adjusting entry** is needed to record these expense-causing factors. In developing the adjusting entry, accounting principles require the use of a rational and systematic allocation to match the acquisition cost of tangible operational assets with the revenue earned each period.[6]

Because of the wide diversity of operational assets subject to depreciation and the varying effects of the causative factors listed above, a number of **depreciation methods** have been developed that provide rational and systematic allocations.

The depreciation methods require three amounts for each asset: (1) **actual acquisition cost,** (2) **estimated net residual value,** and (3) **estimated useful life.** Of these three amounts, two are **estimates** (residual value and useful or service life). Therefore, the periodic amount of depreciation expense that is recorded and reported is an **estimate.** Depreciation expense may be measured as follows:

---

[6] *CICA Terminology for Accountants,* 3d ed. (Toronto, Ont.: Canadian Institute of Chartered Accountants, 1983), p. 52, defines depreciation accounting as "an accounting procedure in which the cost or other recorded value of a fixed asset less estimated residual (if any) is distributed over its estimated useful life in a systematic and rational manner. It is a process of allocation, not valuation." CICA Accounting Standards Committee, "Property, Plant, and Equipment," *Exposure Draft,* May 1989, para. 27, also uses the term "rational and systematic" to describe depreciation.

Acquisition cost	$625
Less: Estimated residual value	25
Amount to be depreciated over useful life . . .	$600
Estimated useful life	3 years
Annual depreciation expense: $600 ÷ 3 = . . .	$200

Estimated residual value[7] must be deducted from acquisition cost to compute depreciation. It represents that part of the acquisition cost that is expected to be recovered by the user upon disposal of the asset at the end of its estimated useful life to the entity. **Residual value** is the total estimated amount to be recovered **less** any estimated costs of dismantling, disposal, and selling. Disposal costs may approximately equal the gross residual amount recovered. Therefore, many depreciable assets are assumed to have no residual value. It is important to realize that the estimated net residual value is not necessarily the value of the asset as salvage or scrap. Rather, it may be the value to another user at the date on which the **current owner** intends to dispose of it. A company whose policy is to replace all trucks at the end of three years normally would use a higher estimated residual value than would a user of the same kind of truck whose policy is to replace the trucks at the end of five years.

Estimated useful or service life should be seen as the useful **economic** life to the **present owner** rather than as the total economic life to all potential users. In the example above, for accounting purposes, one owner would use a three-year estimated useful life, whereas the other would use a five-year estimated useful life.

Estimates are necessary to allocate a known cost amount (the acquisition cost of an operational asset) over a number of future periods during which the asset will contribute to the earning of revenues. The allocation must be made at the end of each accounting period. To defer all cost allocations until the date of disposal of an operational asset that is "used up" would not be very useful in the measurement of periodic income.

The determination of the estimated useful life of an operational asset must conform to the **continuity assumption** (see Exhibit 4–5). This assumption holds that the business will continue as a going concern; that is, that the business will continue indefinitely to pursue its commercial objectives (it will not liquidate in the foreseeable future). This assumption prevents a business from estimating the life of an operational asset to be less than its potential life to the particular business because of some conjecture that the business will liquidate in the near future.

---

[7] Residual value also is called scrap value or salvage value; however, "residual value" is a more descriptive term because the asset may not be scrapped or sold as salvage upon disposition—a subsequent buyer may renovate it and reuse it for many years. CICA Accounting Standards Committee, "Property, Plant, and Equipment," *Exposure Draft*, May 1989, para. 36–37, suggests the need for regular reviews of residual values, useful lives, and allocation methods, at least every five years.

Depreciation Methods

The depreciation methods commonly used for **accounting purposes** are discussed in this section. The different depreciation methods are the same in concept; each method allocates a portion of the cost of a depreciable asset to each of a number of future periods in a systematic and rational manner. Nevertheless, each method allocates to each accounting period a different portion of the net cost to be depreciated. The discussions that follow will define, illustrate, and evaluate the following depreciation methods:[8]

1. Straight-line (SL).
2. Productive-output (PO) (units of production).
3. Accelerated depreciation (AC).
   a. Sum-of-the-years' digits (SYD).
   b. Declining balance (DB).
4. Capital cost allowance (CCA).

The common set of facts and notations shown in Exhibit 9–2 will be used to illustrate these methods.

Exhibit 9–2 Illustrative data for depreciation

DEP CORPORATION	Symbols	Illustrative amounts
Acquisition cost of a particular operational asset (a productive machine)	C	$625
Estimated net residual value at end of useful life	RV	$ 25
Estimated service life:		
Life in years	N*	3
Life in units of productive output	P*	10,000
Depreciation rate	R	
Dollar amount of depreciation expense per period	D	

* Lowercase letters will be used for the current period. The accounting period ends December 31.

---

[8] *Financial Reporting in Canada*, 17th ed. (Toronto, Ont.: Canadian Institute of Chartered Accountants, 1987), p. 157 reports 238 of 293 companies surveyed use either a straight-line method or a straight-line method in combination with some other method. Of 293, 68 use some form of accelerated depreciation.

Sum-of-the-years' digits is not a popular method of depreciation in Canada. It is discussed in this chapter so it can be used for illustrative purposes. Only one company reported its use.

Depreciation methods that result in increasing amounts of depreciation each year will be illustrated in more advanced courses. The so-called sinking fund and annuity methods are used in some industries, real estate being a prime example. Six companies reported their use from the set of companies examined in *Financial Reporting in Canada*.

Straight-Line (SL) Method

Under the straight-line (SL) method, an **equal portion** of the acquisition cost less the estimated residual value is allocated to each accounting period during the estimated useful life. Thus, the annual depreciation expense is measured as follows (refer to Exhibit 9–2):

$$D = \frac{C - RV}{N} \text{ or } D = \frac{\$625 - \$25}{3 \text{ years}} = \$200 \text{ depreciation expense per year}$$

A depreciation schedule for the entire useful life of the machine is:

Depreciation Schedule—Straight-Line Method

Year	Periodic depreciation expense	End of year Balance in accumulated depreciation	End of year Book value
At acquisition . . .			$625
1	$200	$200	425
2	200	400	225
3	200	600	25
	$600		

The adjusting entry for straight-line depreciation expense on this machine is the same for each of the three years of the useful life:

	Year 1		Year 2		Year 3	
Adjusting entry						
Depreciation expense	200		200		200	
Accumulated depreciation, machinery		200		200		200

Notice that (*a*) depreciation expense is a constant amount for each year (often called a fixed expense), (*b*) accumulated depreciation increases by an equal amount each year, and (*c*) book value decreases by the same amount each year. This is the reason for the designation, straight line.

Evaluation. The straight-line method is simple, rational, and systematic (i.e., logical, stable, consistent, and realistically predictable from period to period). It is appropriate when the asset is used at about the same rate each period. It implies an approximately equal decline in the economic usefulness of the asset each period. For these reasons, it is used more often than all of the other methods combined (see footnote 8).

Productive-Output Method

The productive-output (PO) method relates acquisition cost less estimated residual value to the estimated productive output. Therefore, a depreciation rate per **unit of output** is computed as follows (refer to Exhibit 9–2):

$$R = \frac{C - RV}{P} \text{ or } R = \frac{\$625 - \$25}{10,000 \text{ units}} = \$0.06 \text{ depreciation rate per unit of output}$$

Assuming 3,000 units of actual output from the illustrative machine in Year 1, depreciation expense for Year 1 would be:

$$D = R \times p \quad \text{or} \quad D = \$0.06 \times 3,000 = \$180 \text{ depreciation expense}$$

Assuming actual output is 5,000 units in Year 2 and 2,000 units in Year 3, the depreciation schedule is:

Depreciation Schedule—Productive-Output Method

| | Periodic depreciation expense | | | End of year | |
Year	Actual units	Rate	Amount	Balance in accumulated depreciation	Book value
At acquisition . . .					$625
1	3,000 ×	$0.06	$180	$180	445
2	5,000 ×	0.06	300	480	145
3	2,000 ×	0.06	120	600	25
			$600		

The adjusting entry for productive output depreciation at the end of each year is:

	Year 1	Year 2	Year 3
Adjusting entry			
Depreciation expense	180	300	120
Accumulated depreciation, machinery	180	300	120

Notice that depreciation expense, accumulated depreciation, and book value vary from period to period directly with the periodic outputs. When the productive-output method is used, depreciation expense is said to be a **variable** expense.

Evaluation. The productive-output method, sometimes called the units-of-production method, is based upon the assumption that the revenue-generating benefits derived each period from a depreciable asset are related directly to the periodic **output** of the asset. Many accountants believe that such equipment as a machine should be depreciated on the basis of units produced each period (i.e., based on a measure of output) rather than on the passage of time as is assumed by the straight-line method. These accountants believe that many productive assets contribute to the earning of revenues only when they are used productively, not because time has passed.

The productive-output method is simple, rational, and systematic. It is appropriate if **output** of the asset can be measured realistically, and the output is homogeneous in nature. For example, a kilometre flown by an aircraft would be considered homogeneous while service provided by a shopping centre building varies over time. Also, it is appropriate when the economic utility of the asset to the entity decreases with productive use rather than with the passage of time. Also, when the productive use varies significantly from period to period, a more realistic **matching** of expense with revenue is attained. Despite these conceptual and practical advantages, it is not widely used, primarily because of the problems associated with measuring output (see footnote 8).

Accelerated Depreciation—Concepts

Accelerated depreciation (AC) means that in the early years of the useful life of an asset, depreciation expense amounts should be higher, and correspondingly lower in the later years. Accelerated depreciation is supported by the following arguments:

1. A depreciable asset is more efficient in the early years than in the later years. Thus the service it provides is greater in its early years than it is in later years.
2. Repair costs increase in later years; therefore, **total use-cost** per period should include decreasing depreciation expense to "offset" the increasing repair expense each period.

Exhibit 9–3 shows the relationship between accelerated depreciation expense, repair expense, and total use expense for DEP Corporation.

There are several variations of accelerated depreciation; however, the two accelerated methods illustrated are the sum-of-the-years'-digits method and the declining-balance method.

Sum-of-the-Years'-Digits (SYD) Method

Under this method depreciation expense is computed for each accounting year by multiplying the acquisition cost, less estimated residual value, by a fraction that is successively **smaller** each year. Each of the decreasing fractions is determined by using the sum of the digits that make up the estimated useful life as the denominator. The numerator is the specific year of life in **inverse order.**

Exhibit 9–3 Relationship between accelerated depreciation expense, repair expense, and total use expense

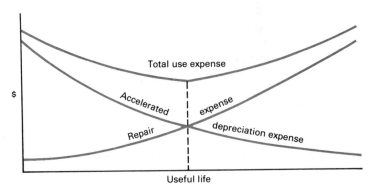

Using the data given in Exhibit 9–2, the computations are:

1. Compute the annual depreciation fraction:
    Denominator—Sum of digits in useful life:[9] 1 + 2 + 3 = 6

    Numerators—Digits (specific year of life) in inverse order: 3, 2, 1.

    Depreciation fractions—Year 1, ³⁄₆; Year 2, ²⁄₆; Year 3, ⅙ (total, %).
2. Compute annual SYD depreciation and related balances based on the data given in Exhibit 9–2:

Depreciation Schedule—Sum-of-the-Years'-Digits Method

Year	Computations	Periodic depreciation expense	Balance in accumulated depreciation (End of year)	Book value (End of year)
At acquisition . . .				$625
1	$600 × ³⁄₆ =	$300	$300	325
2	600 × ²⁄₆ =	200	500	125
3	600 × ⅙ =	100	600	25
Total		$600		

---

[9] The denominator (i.e., sum of the digits) can be computed by using the formula:

$$SYD = n\left(\frac{n+1}{2}\right)$$

For example, a five-year life would be:

$$SYD = 5\left(\frac{5+1}{2}\right) = 15$$

The adjusting entry for SYD depreciation expense by year is:

	Year 1	Year 2	Year 3
Adjusting entry			
Depreciation expense 300		200	100
Accumulated depreciation, machinery	300	200	100

Notice that, compared to straight-line results (page 507), depreciation expense under the SYD method is higher in the earlier years and lower in the later years. The total amount of depreciation expense over the entire life of the asset is the same under both methods.

Evaluation. The SYD method is used because it produces a significant accelerated effect, and it is simple to apply, rational, and systematic. However, the SYD method is criticized because it often does not relate depreciation expense to use or output. In such cases, its conformity to the **matching** principle is questionable. Footnote 8 states that it is not widely used.

Declining-Balance (DB) Method

There are several variations of the declining-balance method. One variation is based upon an acceleration rate applied to the straight-line rate. The **declining-balance (DB) rate** is found by (1) computing the straight-line rate, ignoring residual value, then (2) multiplying that straight-line rate by a **selected acceleration rate.** Assuming a five-year estimated useful life, the SL rate, excluding residual value, is

$$1 \text{ period of life} \div 5 \text{ total periods} = 20\%$$

Computation of the DB rate for three different acceleration rates (for illustrative purposes):

SL rate (excluding RV)	×	Selected acceleration rate	=	DB depreciation rate
Case A 20%	×	200% or 2.00	=	40% or 0.40
Case B 20%	×	175% or 1.75	=	35% or 0.35
Case C 20%	×	150% or 1.50	=	30% or 0.30

Computation of DB depreciation expense is illustrated below using the data given in Exhibit 9–2 and assuming a **selected acceleration rate** of 150%:

1. To compute the DB acceleration rate:

SL rate (ignoring residual value) = 1 year $\div$ 3 years = 33.3%, or 0.333.
150% acceleration DB rate = 33.3% × 1.50 = <u>50%, or 0.50.</u>

2. Depreciation schedule—declining-balance (DB) method:

Year	Computations	Periodic depreciation expense	Balance in accumulated depreciation	Book value
At acquisition . . .				$625
1	0.50 × $625 =	$313	$313	312
2	0.50 × 312 =	156	469	156
3	0.50 × 156 =	78	547	78*

Columns "Balance in accumulated depreciation" and "Book value" are grouped under the heading "End of year".

* This must be the computed amount, but it cannot be less than the estimated residual value (in this illustration, not less than $25). If necessary, depreciation in Year 3 would be reduced accordingly.

The adjusting entry for DB depreciation at each year-end is:

Adjusting entry	Year 1	Year 2	Year 3
Depreciation expense	313	156	78
Accumulated depreciation, machinery	313	156	78

Evaluation. This method began because it was acceptable for income tax purposes prior to the introduction of Capital Cost Allowance in 1948. In addition, the method is still used for income tax purposes in the United States. The method is criticized because the **selected acceleration rate** is subjectively determined for accounting purposes.

Capital Cost Allowance

All depreciable assets are, for income tax purposes, grouped into one of a number of classes. Each class of assets is permitted a maximum capital cost allowance rate. Commonly the classes use the diminishing balance method of calculating the maximum yearly deduction for tax purposes. Estimated residual values are ignored for these calculations. These rates vary at the present time from a high of 100% to a low of 4% depending upon the type of property, the date of acquisition, and the type of business.[10] To illustrate, the following table presents a few common classes and their rates:

Class	General type of asset	Rate (%)
3	Brick building	5
8	Equipment	20
10	Automobiles	30

Because the capital cost allowance method is a readily available declining-balance method for income tax determinations, it is often used for computing

---

[10] Currently the income tax regulations permit a maximum of 50% of the allowable capital cost allowance to be deducted in the year of acquisition regardless of the date the asset is acquired during the year.

depreciation expense for accounting purposes. Care is needed if it is used for accounting purposes, however, because some CCA rates are used as economic incentives by the government and thus produce unreasonable accounting depreciation.

Capital cost allowance (CCA) is computed by multiplying the **CCA rate** (illustrated above) by the **undepreciated capital cost of the asset** (i.e., its current book value) ignoring residual value. Because the estimated residual value is ignored, the undepreciated balance of the asset at the end of the last year of its life may be **higher or lower** than the residual value.

Computation of CCA expense is illustrated below using the data given in Exhibit 9–2 and assuming class 8, equipment rate.

To compute CCA tax expense (Year 1):
Current carrying value of the asset, $625 × .20 × ½ = $62.50.

The effects of the CCA method are illustrated in the following schedule:

Depreciation Schedule—Capital Cost Allowance Method

Year	Computations	Periodic CCA	End of year—undepreciated capital cost (book value)
At acquisition . . .			$625.00
1	.20 × $625 × ½	$ 62.50	562.50
2	.20 × $562.50	112.50	450.00
3	.20 × $450	90.00	360.00*

* For income tax purposes, the undepreciated capital cost of $360 would be added to the cost of the new machine acquired to replace the old one and capital cost allowance would be continued on the new total. The effect of this treatment is to depreciate the $360 after the asset has been sold. If the class of assets was empty (no assets acquired or remaining) the $360 less the residual value of $25 would be a tax expense in Year 3. For accounting purposes, a loss on disposal of $360 − $25 would be appropriate although such a large loss would suggest the use of the CCA rate is inappropriate.

If CCA were used for accounting purposes, the adjusting entry for depreciation at each year-end would be:

	Year 1	Year 2	Year 3
Adjusting entry			
Depreciation expense	62.50	112.50	90.00
Accumulated depreciation, machinery	62.50	112.50	90.00

Which Depreciation Method Should Be Used?

To date, the accounting profession has not provided definitive guidelines for selection of a depreciation method that would be preferable for each type of depreciable asset. Therefore, each of the several methods can be characterized as an acceptable alternative for financial reporting purposes. That is, any of the above depreciation methods may be used regardless of the characteristics of the operational asset and the way it is used. Exhibit 9–4 further shows the differences among the three most commonly used depreciation methods.

Exhibit 9–4 Depreciation methods compared (DEP Corporation)

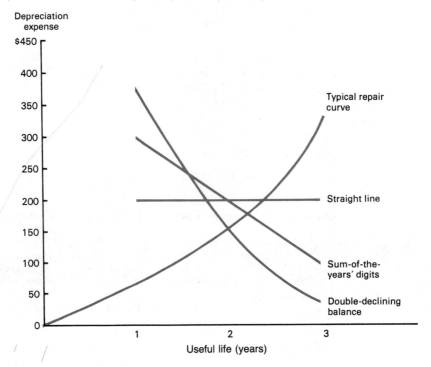

GAAP requires that the depreciation method selected must be "rational and systematic." Also, it should reliably measure net income of the company considering the circumstances in which the asset is used. Thus, it is usual for a company to use more than one depreciation method. The selection of a method of depreciation is important. It has a significant impact on net income and amounts reported on the balance sheet for operational assets. Exhibit 9–4 compares depreciation amounts under each method discussed above.

Effects of Depreciation on the Income Statement

Depreciation is an expense on the income statement so pretax income depends on the depreciation approach used for accounting purposes (refer to Exhibit 9–5, Panel B). Capital cost allowance is used to calculate the income taxes payable to the government (refer to Exhibit 9–5, Panel C). The differences between the taxes calculated using the accounting depreciation and the taxes calculated using capital cost allowance is accounted for as an income tax allocation. This difference represents one of the major timing differences that must be accounted for as part of the tax allocation procedures to be discussed in Chapter 10.

Exhibit 9–5 Illustration of depreciation effects on net income and cash flow

Panel A—Data assumed (refer to Exhibit 9–2):

Revenues (all cash): Year 1, $5,000; Year 2, $6,000; Year 3, $7,000.

	Year 1	Year 2	Year 3
Depreciation expense:			
SL (straight line)	$ 200	$ 200	$ 200
SYD	300	200	100
Remaining expenses (all cash)	2,800	3,300	3,800
Income tax rate, 20%.			

Panel B—Income statements comparing SL and SYD:

	Year 1		Year 2		Year 3	
Accrual basis	SL	SYD	SL	SYD	SL	SYD
Revenues (cash)	$5,000	$5,000	$6,000	$6,000	$7,000	$7,000
Depreciation expense (noncash) . .	(200)	(300)	(200)	(200)	(200)	(100)
Remaining expenses (cash)	(2,800)	(2,800)	(3,300)	(3,300)	(3,800)	(3,800)
*Pretax income	2,000	1,900	2,500	2,500	3,000	3,100
†Income tax expense (20%)	(400)	(380)	(500)	(500)	(600)	(620)
Net income	$1,600	$1,520	$2,000	$2,000	$2,400	$2,480

* Amounts differ between SL and SYD because of the depreciation expense.
† Income tax expense is computed on the basis of pretax income.

Panel C—Depreciation effects on cash flow comparing SL and SYD:

	Year 1		Year 2		Year 3	
Cash flow basis	SL	SYD	SL	SYD	SL	SYD
Revenues (cash)	$5,000	$5,000	$6,000	$6,000	$7,000	$7,000
Depreciation expense (noncash) . .	–0–	–0–	–0–	–0–	–0–	–0–
Remaining expenses (all cash)	(2,800)	(2,800)	(3,300)	(3,300)	(3,800)	(3,800)
*Pretax inflow	2,200	2,200	2,700	2,700	3,200	3,200
†Income tax payment	(380)	(380)	(500)	(500)	(620)	(620)
Aftertax cash inflow	$1,820	$1,820	$2,200	$2,200	$2,580	$2,580

* Same regardless of depreciation method used.
† For simplicity the example assumes SYD depreciation equals the capital cost allowance claimed for income tax purposes. The difference between taxes paid and tax expense is a tax allocation timing difference discussed in Chapter 10.

Effects of Depreciation on Cash Flow

When an operational asset is acquired, there is a cash **outflow** (i.e., payment) for its acquisition (and/or later cash outflows for any related debt). Subsequent journal entries for depreciation do not involve cash outflows because the expense lags the cash outflow already made. Therefore, depreciation expense does not represent a current cash outflow; it is a noncash expense on the income statement. However, capital cost allowance does affect cash flow each period because it **reduces** the amount of income tax that otherwise would be paid. In this way it reduces the amount of cash outflow for income tax (this reduction often is called a **tax saving** or **tax shield.**) Thus, if capital cost allowance is increased for the period the cash outflow for income tax is decreased. This cash flow effect is illustrated in Exhibit 9–5, Panel C. Observe in Panel C, for all years, that the **aftertax cash inflow** is the same under SYD as it is under SL even though Panel B shows **net income to be lower** under SYD than under SL except for the last year. In summary, as the amount of depreciation expense is increased net income is decreased. Cash inflow is increased (i.e., tax saving) as CCA is increased.

Finally, consider some misleading terminology that often is used. Analysts and others often say that "cash is provided by depreciation." Depreciation is not a source of cash, and the accumulated depreciation amount does not represent cash or a fund of cash available to replace the operational asset when it is disposed of. Accumulated depreciation is a contra asset account (not cash). Exhibit 9–5, Panel C, demonstrates that (*a*) the aftertax cash inflow (bottom line) is the result of sales to customers, less cash expenses, and (*b*) capital cost allowance reduces cash outflow because less income taxes are paid. A significant long-term effect of depreciation expense is a reduction of the cumulative balance of retained earnings. A lower balance in retained earnings in some situations possibly could reduce cash dividends. If cash dividends were reduced there would be a decrease in cash outflows.[11]

Depreciation for Interim Periods

The preceding illustrations assumed recognition of depreciation expense with an adjusting entry. Many businesses record depreciation for interim periods, such as monthly, quarterly, or semiannually. Also, a depreciable asset may be acquired or disposed of during the accounting year, which requires that depreciation expense be recognized for periods of less than one year. It is usual to compute depreciation proportionally to either the nearest month, quarter, or six-month period. Depreciation for a full month may be assumed to start or end at the nearest first of the month. For all of the methods shown, except productive output, monthly depreciation usually is determined by computing the annual amount of depreciation as shown, then dividing by 12 to obtain the monthly amount.[12] In Exhibit 9–5, sum-of-the-years'-digits (SYD) depreciation for the first year was $300. Assume the asset was acquired on August 12, 19A, with a December 31 fiscal year-end. The depreciation expense for 19A would be (nearest-month basis):

---

[11] Chapter 10 discusses the reporting implications of the use of different depreciation methods for financial reporting and tax purposes.

[12] Under the productive-output method, monthly depreciation is computed by multiplying the unit depreciation rate by the output for the particular month.

$$\frac{\$300}{12} \times 5 \text{ months} = \$125$$

Depreciation expense for 19B using SYD would include the amount for the remaining months of the first year, $175, plus 5/12 of the B amount, that is, 5/12 of $200 or $83, for a total of $258.

Depreciation expense is an estimate; therefore, small depreciation amounts should not be recognized because this would suggest a higher degree of accuracy than is warranted. Also, for this reason, depreciation expense should be rounded to the nearest amount—one, ten, hundred, or even thousand dollars—depending on the cost of the depreciable asset compared with total depreciable assets. This is in conformity with the **materiality constraint** (see Exhibit 4–5).

Changes in Depreciation Estimates

Depreciation is based on two estimates—useful life and residual value. These estimates are made at the time a depreciable asset is acquired. One, or both, of these initial estimates may have to be revised as experience with the asset accumulates. When it is clear that either estimate should be revised (to a material degree), the undepreciated asset balance, less any residual value, at that date should be apportioned, based on the new estimate, over the **remaining** estimated life. This is called a **change in estimate**.[13]

Assume the following for a machine:

Cost of machine when acquired	$33,000
Estimated useful life	10 years
Estimated residual value	$ 3,000
Accumulated depreciation through Year 6 (assuming the straight-line method is used); ($33,000 − $3,000) × 6/10	$18,000

Shortly after the start of Year 7, the initial estimates were changed to the following:

Revised estimated total life	14 years
Revised estimated residual value	$ 1,000

No entry is needed when this decision is reached. However, the **adjusting entry at the end of Year 7** would be:

---

[13] *CICA Handbook*, Section 1506, distinguishes between a change in estimate which is treated like the above example and a change in accounting policy. A change in accounting policy results in a retroactive revision. This matter will be discussed further in Chapter 12. Recent CICA Accounting Standards Committee suggestions state that if the recoverable amount falls below the net carrying amount, accumulated depreciation should be increased by a charge against income to reduce the net carrying value to recoverable value ("Property, Plant, and Equipment," *Exposure Draft*, May 1989, para. 40–41). Such a write-down is not deemed a change in estimate, as illustrated on the next page.

Depreciation expense   1,750
    Accumulated depreciation   1,750

Computation:
    Acquisition cost $33,000
    Accumulated depreciation, Years 1–6   18,000
    Undepreciated balance   15,000
        Less: Revised residual value   1,000
    Balance to be depreciated $14,000

    Annual depreciation:
        $14,000 ÷ (14 years − 6 years) . . . . $ 1,750

Under GAAP, changes in accounting estimates and depreciation methods should be made only when the new estimate or accounting method "better measures" the periodic income of the business. The **characteristic of comparability** (Exhibit 4–5) requires that accounting information reported in the financial statements should be comparable across accounting periods and among similar entities. This principle has a significant constraint on changing depreciation estimates and methods unless the effect is to improve the measurement of depreciation expense and net income.

PART B—REPAIRS AND MAINTENANCE, NATURAL RESOURCES, AND INTANGIBLE OPERATIONAL ASSETS

Repairs, Maintenance, and Additions

Subsequent to the acquisition of a tangible operational asset, related cost outlays often must be made for such items as ordinary repairs and maintenance, major repairs, replacements, and additions. The main measurement problem is determination of which expenditures should be recorded as expenses of the period when incurred, and which should be recorded as assets (i.e., as a prepayment) to be matched with **future** revenues. In this context, the term **expenditure** means the payment of cash or the incurrence of a debt for an asset or service received. The purchase of a machine or a service, such as repairs on a truck, may be for cash or on credit. In either case, there is an expenditure.

Accounting for expenditures made after the acquisition date are called revenue expenditures and capital expenditures. **A revenue expenditure is recorded as expense when incurred. A capital expenditure is recorded as an asset when incurred.**[14]

---

[14] The term **revenue** expenditure is widely used. It suggests that the expenditure is to be deducted in the current period from revenue in deriving income. However, a term such as expense expenditure would be more descriptive.

Ordinary Repairs and Maintenance

Ordinary repairs and maintenance are expenditures for normal maintenance and upkeep of operational assets that are necessary to keep the assets in their usual condition. These expenditures are recurring in nature, involve small amounts at each occurrence, and do not directly lengthen the useful life of the asset. Ordinary repairs and maintenance are **revenue expenditures.** They are recorded as expense in the accounting period in which incurred.

For example, the payment of $600 for ordinary repairs to the plant would be recorded in the current period as follows:

Repair expense	600	
Cash		600

Each expenditure made subsequent to the acquisition of an operational asset must be evaluated carefully to classify it as either a capital or revenue expenditure. The distinction between capital and revenue expenditures is essential to conform with the matching principle. The expenditures must be matched with the periodic revenues to which they relate. The purpose and nature of the expenditure is the controlling factor in its classification. For practical applications, materiality is also an important factor in determining the appropriate treatment. In the next few paragraphs we will discuss the usual types of outlays subsequent to acquisition of a tangible operational asset.

Extraordinary Repairs

Extraordinary repairs are classified as **capital expenditures;** therefore, an extraordinary repair is debited to the related asset account and depreciated over the **remaining life** of that asset. **Extraordinary repairs** seldom occur, involve large amounts of money, and increase the economic usefulness of the asset in the future because of either greater efficiency or longer life, or both. They are represented by major overhauls, complete reconditioning, and major replacements and improvements. The complete replacement of a roof on the factory building would be an extraordinary repair. Patching the old roof would be an ordinary repair.

To illustrate the accounting for extraordinary repairs, assume a machine that originally cost $40,000 is being depreciated on a straight-line basis over 10 years with no estimated residual value. At the beginning of the seventh year, a major reconditioning was finished that cost $12,700. The estimated useful life changed from 10 years to 13 years (i.e., a change in estimate). A typical sequence of entries would be:

At acquisition date:

Machinery	40,000	
Cash		40,000
Purchase of machinery.		

End of each accounting period (depreciation), Years 1 through 6:

Depreciation expense	4,000	
Accumulated depreciation, machinery		4,000

Adjusting entry to record annual depreciation ($40,000 ÷ 10 years).

Extraordinary repair—at the start of Year 7:[15]

Machinery	12,700	
Cash		12,700

Capital expenditure.

Revised annual depreciation, Years 7–13:

Depreciation expense	4,100	
Accumulated depreciation, machinery		4,100

Adjusting entry to record annual depreciation.

Computation:

Original cost	$40,000	
Depreciation, Years 1–6	24,000	
Book value remaining		$16,000
Extraordinary repair		12,700
Balance to be depreciated over remaining life		$28,700

Annual depreciation: $28,700 ÷ (13 − 6 years) = $4,100.

Additions

Additions are extensions to, or enlargements of, existing assets, such as the addition of a wing to a building. These additions are **capital expenditures;** therefore, the cost of additions should be debited to the existing account for the asset and depreciated over the remaining life of the asset to which the cost is related. However, if the life of the addition is shorter than the life of the related asset, the addition should be depreciated over its remaining useful life (less its residual value).

Natural Resources

Natural resources, such as a mineral deposit, oil well, or timber tract, are often called "wasting assets" because they are **depleted** (i.e., physically used). When acquired or developed, a natural resource is measured and recorded in the accounts in conformity with the **cost principle.** As a natural resource is used up, its acquisition cost, in conformity with the **matching principle,** must be appor-

---

[15] Some accountants prefer to debit the related asset account, as illustrated above, only when the major repair increases the efficiency above normal. In contrast, when it is estimated that only the useful life is extended, those accountants instead would debit the related accumulated depreciation account. This distinction usually is not made because it is difficult to apply practically. Also, subsequent book value and depreciation expense would be the same regardless of which account is debited because the remaining book value to be depreciated would be the same in either instance.

tioned among the various periods in which the resulting revenues are earned. The term **depletion** describes the process of periodic cost allocation over the period of use of a natural resource. A **depletion rate** per unit of the resource produced is computed by dividing the total acquisition and development cost (less any estimated residual value, which is rare) by the **estimated units** that can be withdrawn economically from the resource. The depletion rate, thus computed, is multiplied each period by the **actual** number of units withdrawn during the accounting period. This procedure is the same as the productive-output method of calculating depreciation (see page 508).

To illustrate accounting for a natural resource, assume that a gravel pit was developed that cost $80,000. A reliable estimate was made that 100,000 cubic metres of gravel could be economically withdrawn from the pit. The **depletion rate per unit** is computed as follows (assuming no residual value):

$80,000 ÷ 100,000 cubic metres = $0.80 per cubic metre (depletion rate per unit)

Assuming 5,000 cubic metres of gravel were actually withdrawn and sold during the year, depletion expense for the first year would be recorded by making the following adjusting entry.[16]

Depletion expense	4,000	
Gravel pit		4,000

Depletion for the year, 5,000 cubic metres × $0.80 = $4,000.

At the end of the first year, this natural resource should be reported as follows:

Balance Sheet

Operational assets:
    Gravel pit (cost, $80,000 − $4,000 accumulated depletion) $76,000

Since it is difficult to estimate the recoverable units from a natural resource, the depletion rate often must be revised. This is a **change in estimate;** therefore, the undepleted acquisition cost is spread over the estimated remaining recoverable units by computing a new depletion rate. Assume in Year 2 that the estimate of recoverable units remaining was changed from 95,000 to 150,000 cubic metres. The depletion rate to be applied to the cubic metres of gravel withdrawn in Year 2 would be:

($80,000 − $4,000) ÷ 150,000 cubic metres = $0.51 per cubic metre

---

[16] Consistent with the procedure for recording depreciation, an Accumulated Depletion account may be used. However, as a matter of precedent, the asset account itself usually is credited directly for the periodic depletion. Either procedure is acceptable. The same is true for intangible operational assets, discussed in the next section.

When buildings and similar improvements are built for the development and exploitation of a natural resource, they should be recorded in separate asset accounts and **depreciated**—not depleted. Their estimated useful lives cannot be longer than the time needed to exploit the natural resource unless they have a significant use-value after the resource is depleted.

Intangible Operational Assets

An intangible operational asset, like any other asset, has value because of certain rights and privileges conferred by law upon the owner of the asset. However, an intangible asset has **no material or physical substance** as do tangible assets such as land and buildings.[17] Examples of intangible operational assets are patents, copyrights, franchises, licenses, trademarks, and goodwill. The acquisition of an intangible asset usually requires the expenditure of resources. For example, an entity may buy a patent from the inventor. An intangible asset should be measured and recorded in the accounts of the entity at its cash-equivalent cost in conformity with the **cost principle.** Subsequently, it is recorded at cost less accumulated amortization.

Each kind of intangible operational asset should be recorded in a separate asset account when acquired. Assume that on January 1, 19A, Mason Company bought a patent from its developer, J. Doe, at a cash price of $17,000. The acquisition of this intangible asset is recorded as follows:

January 1, 19A:

Patents	17,000	
Cash		17,000
Bought a patent from J. Doe.		

Under the cost principle, although an intangible right or privilege may have value, it is not recorded unless there has been an identifiable expenditure of resources to acquire or develop it. The demise of a competitor's patent may cause the company's patent to be more valuable. This increase in value would not be recorded because there was no expenditure of resources that caused the increase in value.

Research and development (R&D) costs are separated into two types: research and development. Research costs are expenses even though they may result in a patent or a product which has future value. Development costs, on the other hand, can be capitalized as an asset if a set of criteria can be satisfied which indicate they have future value.[18]

---

[17] Intangible operational assets often are called intangible assets.

[18] The criteria that must be met in order to capitalize development costs are set forth in *CICA Handbook,* Section 3450.21. They are technical feasibility, management intention to develop, a defined future market, and adequate resources available or obtainable to carry out the development.

Amortization of Intangible Operational Assets

Intangible operational assets normally have limited lives; however, they seldom have a residual value. Intangible assets have a limited life because the **rights or privileges** that help earn revenues terminate or disappear. Therefore, in conformity with the **matching principle,** the acquisition cost of an intangible operational asset must be written off over its estimated economic life. This systematic write-off is called **amortization.**

An intangible asset may be amortized by using any "systematic and rational" method that reflects the actual expiration of its economic usefulness. However, the **straight-line** method is used almost exclusively. The primary intangible assets are discussed below.

Patents

A patent is an exclusive right, recognized by law, that enables the owner to use, manufacture, and sell the subject of the patent, and the patent itself. A patent that is **purchased** is recorded at its cash-equivalent cost. An **internally developed** patent is recorded at only its registration and legal cost. **GAAP does not permit** the capitalization of its research costs. In conformity with the **matching principle,** the capitalized cost of a patent must be amortized over the **shorter** of its economic life or its remaining legal life (of the 17 years from date of grant). Assume the patent acquired by Mason Company had an estimated 10-year remaining economic life. At the end of 19A, the **adjusting entry** to record amortization for one year would be (see footnote 13):

December 31, 19A:

Patent expense	1,700	
Patents		1,700

    Adjusting entry to record amortization of patent over the estimated
    economic life of 10 years ($17,000 ÷ 10 years = $1,700).

The amount of patent amortization expense recorded for 19A is reported on the income statement as an operating expense. The patent would be reported on the December 31, 19A, balance sheet as follows:

    Intangible assets:
        Patents (cost, $17,000, less amortization) $15,300

Copyrights

A copyright is similar to a patent. A copyright gives the owner the exclusive right to publish, use, and sell a literary, musical, or artistic piece of work for a period not exceeding 50 years after the author's death. The same principles, guidelines, and procedures used in accounting for and reporting the cost of patents also are used for copyrights. Currently the Parliament of Canada is studying changes in copyright legislation so accountants have to be continually aware of the implications of such changes on their accounting practices.

Franchises and Licenses

Franchises and licenses frequently are granted by governmental and other units for a specified period and purpose. A province may grant one company a franchise to operate a bus service, or a company may sell franchises, such as the right for a local outlet to operate a Kentucky Fried Chicken restaurant. Franchises and licenses usually require an investment by the franchisee to acquire them; therefore, they represent intangible operational assets that should be accounted for as shown above for patents.

Leaseholds

Leasing is a common type of business contract. For a consideration called rent, the owner (or lessor) extends to another party (the lessee) certain rights to use specified property. Leases may vary from simple arrangements, such as the month-to-month lease of an office or the daily rental of an automobile, to long-term leases having complex contractual arrangements. The rights granted to a lessee frequently are called a **leasehold.**

Long-term leases sometimes require a lump-sum advance rental payment by the lessee. In such cases, the lessee should record the advance payment as a debit to an intangible asset account (usually called Rent Paid in Advance or Leaseholds). This cost should be amortized to expense over the contractual life of the lease. Total rent expense includes the amortization of the leasehold. Therefore, the annual amortization is debited to Rent Expense. Assume Favour Company leased a building for its own use on January 1, 19A, under a five-year contract that required in addition to the monthly rental payments of $2,000, a single payment in advance of $20,000. The advance payment is recorded as follows:

January 1, 19A:

Leasehold (or Rent paid in advance)	20,000	
Cash		20,000
Rent paid in advance.		

At the end of each year, 19A through 19E, the following **adjusting entry** is made to amortize the cost of this intangible asset:[19]

December 31, 19A:

Rent expense	4,000	
Leasehold		4,000
Adjusting entry to record amortization of leasehold over five years ($20,000 ÷ 5 years = $4,000).		

---

[19] This discussion presumes an **operating** type of lease. In some cases a lease is, in effect, a sale/purchase agreement. Such leases, known as capital leases, involve complex accounting problems that are discussed in Chapter 10.

The $2,000 monthly rental payments would be debited to Rent Expense when paid each month. Thus, the 19A income statement would report rent expense of $28,000 [i.e., ($2,000 × 12) + $4,000 = $28,000]. The December 31, 19A, balance sheet would report an asset, Leasehold, of $16,000 (i.e., Cost, $20,000 − Amortization, $4,000 = $16,000).

Leasehold Improvements

In most cases, when buildings, improvements, or alterations are built by the **lessee** on leased property, such assets legally belong to the owner of the property at the end of the lease. The lessee has full use of such improvements during the term of the lease. Therefore, the cost should be recorded as an intangible operating asset, Leasehold Improvements. These expenditures should be amortized over the estimated useful life of the related improvement or the remaining life of the lease, whichever is shorter.

Goodwill

Often when a successful business is sold, the price will be higher than the market values of its recorded assets less its liabilities. A business may command a higher price because an intangible operational asset called goodwill is attached to a successful business.

Goodwill represents the potential of a business to earn above a normal rate of return on the recorded assets less the liabilities. Goodwill arises from such factors as customer confidence, reputation for dependability, efficiency and internal competencies, quality of goods and services, and financial standing. From the date of organization, a successful business continually builds goodwill. In this context, the goodwill is said to be "internally generated at no identifiable cost." On the other hand, when a business is purchased as an entity, the purchase price may include a payment for any goodwill that exists at that time. **In conformity with the cost principle, goodwill is recorded as an intangible operational asset only when it actually is purchased at a measurable cost.**

Assume Richard Roe purchased the University Men's Store on January 1, 19A, for $200,000 cash. At the date of purchase, the recorded assets had a total **market value** of $160,000, comprised of the market values of inventory, $110,000; fixtures, $35,000; prepaid rent, $1,000; and remaining assets, $14,000. Roe did not accept any of the store's liabilities. The purchase is recorded by Roe as follows:

January 1, 19A:

Inventory	110,000	
Furniture and fixtures	35,000	
Prepaid rent	1,000	
Remaining assets	14,000	
Goodwill	40,000	
Cash		200,000

Purchase of University Men's Store.

The intangible asset—goodwill—must be amortized to expense over its estimated economic life not to exceed 40 years.[20] Assuming a 40-year economic life, the amortization for 19A is recorded in an **adjusting entry** as follows:

December 31, 19A:

Goodwill amortization (expense)	1,000	
Goodwill		1,000

Adjusting entry to record goodwill amortization for one year based on 40-year economic life ($40,000 ÷ 40 years = $1,000).

Many other kinds of intangible operational assets are reported in financial statements. Examples are formulas, processes, and film rights. These types are accounted for, and reported, in a manner similar to that shown above.

Deferred Charges

An asset category called **deferred charges** occasionally is reported on the balance sheet. A deferred charge, like a prepaid expense, is an **expense paid in advance.** That is, goods or services were acquired that will be used later to earn future revenues. A deferred charge is a **long-term** prepaid expense. Therefore, it cannot be classified as a current asset. A prepaid expense is a short-term prepayment, and for this reason, it is classified as a current asset. Thus, the only difference between the two is time. For example, $1,000 expended for a five-year debt issue at the start of Year 1 would be reported as follows at the end of Year 1:

Income statement:
  Debt expense ($1,000 ÷ 5 years) $200
Balance sheet:
  Deferred charges:
    Unamortized debt issue costs ($1,000 × 4/5) . . . 800

Common examples of deferred charges are debt issuance costs (Chapter 11), start-up costs, organization costs, and plant rearrangement costs. In conformity with the **matching principle,** deferred charges are amortized to expense each period over the future periods benefited.

Disposal of Operational Assets

Operational assets may be disposed of in two ways: **voluntarily** by sale, trade-in, or retirement; or **involuntarily** as a result of a casualty, such as a storm, fire, or accident. Whatever the nature of the disposal, the cost of the asset and any

---

[20] *CICA Handbook*, Section 1580.58, suggests this treatment for goodwill arising on the purchase of one company by another company (called a business combination). Chapter 14 will discuss this issue in more detail. The treatment of goodwill in a more general setting such as the one illustrated above is not mandated in the *CICA Handbook* but would likely follow the rules for business combinations. The 40-year maximum has recently been proposed to extend to all intangibles (CICA Accounting Standards Committee, "Property, Plant, and Equipment," *Exposure Draft*, May 1989, para. 28).

Exhibit 9–6   Disposal of an operational asset

Panel A—Situation of Bye Company:

January 1, 19A—Purchased a heavy-duty truck for $38,000 cash; estimated useful life eight years and $6,000 residual value (straight-line depreciation).

December 31—End of accounting year.

June 30, 19D—The truck was wrecked, and the insurance company paid a claim of $21,000 (i.e., the replacement cost of the truck at the date of the wreck).

Panel B—Entries during the life of the truck:

January 1, 19A—To record purchase of the truck:

Truck 38,000		
Cash		38,000

December 31—To record annual depreciation 19A–19C:

	19A	19B	19C
Depreciation expense 4,000		4,000	4,000
Accumulated depreciation	4,000	4,000	4,000

Computation: ($38,000 − $6,000) ÷ 8 years = $4,000.

Panel C—June 30, 19D—Entries on date of disposal (wreck):

1. To record depreciation for six months (to date of wreck):

Depreciation expense 2,000	
Accumulated depreciation	2,000

Computation: $4,000 × 6/12 = $2,000.

2. To record the involuntary disposal of the asset and the insurance indemnity:

Cash (insurance indemnity) 21,000	
Accumulated depreciation ($4,000 × 3) + $2,000 14,000	
Casualty loss on operational assets 3,000	
Truck	38,000

Panel D—Reporting (by year):

	19A	19B	19C	19D
Income statement (for the year):				
Depreciation expense	$ 4,000	$ 4,000	$ 4,000	$2,000
Loss on disposal				3,000
Balance sheet (at December 31):				
Truck	$38,000	$38,000	$38,000	$ –0–
Accumulated depreciation	(4,000)	(8,000)	(12,000)	–0–
Book value	$34,000	$30,000	$26,000	$ –0–

accumulated depreciation, depletion, or amortization must be removed from the accounts at the date of disposal. The difference between any resources received upon disposal of an operational asset and the **book or carrying value** of the asset at the date of disposal is a **gain or loss on disposal of operational assets.** This gain (or loss) is reported on the income statement. However, it is not revenue (or expense) because it is from "peripheral or incidental" activities rather than from normal operations (see Exhibit 4–5 for the distinction between revenues and gains). Assume a machine is sold for $3,500 cash when the account balances showed Machine, $10,000; and Accumulated Depreciation, Machine, $7,000 (i.e., a book value of $3,000). The entry to record this disposal is:

Cash	3,500	
Accumulated depreciation, machine	7,000	
Machine		10,000
Gain on disposal of operational asset		500

Gain computed:

Sale price	$3,500
Book value at date of sale ($10,000 − $7,000)	3,000
Difference, gain	$ 500

Disposals of operational assets seldom occur on the last date of the accounting period. That is, the depreciation, depletion, or amortization must be updated to the date of disposal. Therefore, the disposal of a depreciable operational asset usually requires two entries: (1) an adjusting entry to update the depreciation expense and accumulated depreciation accounts, and (2) a disposal entry to remove all related account balances and to record a disposal gain or loss. Exhibit 9–6 illustrates a typical disposal. Panel A gives the situation, Panels B and C show the journal entries, and Panel D presents the reporting of a disposal.

A gain or loss on disposal occurs because (1) depreciation expense is based on estimates that may differ from actual experience, and (2) depreciation is based on original cost, not current market values.

DEMONSTRATION CASE

(Resolve the requirements before proceeding to the suggested solution that follows.)

Diversified Industries has been operating for a number of years. It started as a residential construction company. In recent years it expanded into heavy construction, ready-mix concrete, sand and gravel, construction supplies, and earth-moving services.

The transactions below were selected from those completed during 19D. They focus on the primary issues discussed in this chapter. Amounts have been simplified for case purposes.

19D

Jan. 1   The management decided to buy a building that was about 10 years old. The location was excellent and there was adequate parking space. The company bought the building and the land on which it was situated for $305,000 cash. A reliable appraiser provided the following market values: land, $126,000; and building, $174,000.

   12   Paid renovation costs on the building of $38,100.

June 19   Bought a third location for a gravel pit (designated No. 3) for $50,000 cash. The location had been carefully surveyed. It was estimated that 100,000 cubic metres of gravel could be removed from the deposit.

July 10   Paid $1,200 for ordinary repairs on the building.

Aug. 1   Paid $10,000 for costs of preparing a new gravel pit for exploitation.

December 31, 19D (end of the annual accounting period)—the following data were developed as a basis for the adjusting entries:

a.   The building will be depreciated on a straight-line basis over an estimated useful life of 30 years. The estimated residual value is $35,000.

b.   During 19D, 12,000 cubic metres of gravel were removed and sold from gravel pit No. 3. Use an Accumulated Depletion account.

c.   The company owns a patent right that is used in operations. On January 1, 19D, the Patent account had a balance of $3,300. The patent has an estimated remaining useful life of six years (including 19D).

Required:

1.   Give the journal entries for the five transactions completed during 19D.

2.   Give the adjusting entries on December 31, 19D.

3.   Show the December 31, 19D, balance sheet classification and amount for each of the following items: land, building, gravel pit, and patent.

Suggested Solution:
Requirement 1—Entries during 19D:

January 1, 19D:

Land (building site)	128,100	
Building	176,900	
Cash		305,000

Allocation of cost (based on appraisal):

Item	Appraisal value	Percent		Computation		Allocation
Land	$126,000	42	×	$305,000	=	$128,100
Building	174,000	58	×	305,000	=	176,900
Totals	$300,000	100				$305,000

January 12, 19D:

Building	38,100	
Cash		38,100

Renovation costs on building prior to use.

June 19, 19D:

Gravel pit (No. 3)	50,000	
Cash		50,000

Purchased gravel pit; estimated production, 100,000 cubic metres.

July 10, 19D:

Repair expense	1,200	
Cash		1,200
Ordinary repairs.		

August 1, 19D:

Gravel pit (No. 3)	10,000	
Cash		10,000
Preparation costs.		

Requirement 2—Adjusting entries:

December 31, 19D:

a. Depreciation expense, building 6,000

      Accumulated depreciation   6,000

    Computation:
      Cost ($176,900 + $38,100) $215,000
        Less: Residual value   35,000
      Cost to be depreciated $180,000

    Annual depreciation: $180,000 ÷ 30 years = $6,000.

b. Depletion expense 7,200

      Accumulated depletion, gravel pit (No. 3)   7,200

    Computation:
      Cost ($50,000 + $10,000) $60,000
      Depletion rate:
        $60,000 ÷ 100,000 cubic metres = $0.60
      Depletion expense: $0.60 × 12,000 cubic metres = $7,200

c. Patent expense 550

      Patent   550

    Computation:
      $3,300 ÷ 6 years = $550.

Requirement 3—Balance sheet, December 31, 19D:

Assets

Operational assets:

Land		$128,100
Building	$215,000	
Less: Accumulated depreciation	6,000	209,000
Gravel pit	60,000	
Less: Accumulated depletion	7,200	52,800
Total operational assets		$389,900
Intangible assets:		
Patent ($3,300 − $550)		2,750

SUMMARY OF CHAPTER

This chapter discussed accounting for operational assets. These are the noncurrent assets that a business retains for long periods of time for use in the course of normal operations rather than for sale. They include tangible assets and intangible assets. At acquisition, an operational asset is measured and recorded in the accounts at cost. Cost includes the cash equivalent purchase price plus all reasonable and necessary expenditures made to acquire and prepare the asset for its intended use.

An operational asset represents a bundle of future services and benefits that have been paid for in advance. As an operational asset is used, this bundle of future services gradually is used to earn revenue. Therefore, in conformity with the **matching principle,** cost (less any estimated residual value) is allocated to periodic expense over the periods benefited. In this way, the expense associated with the use of operational assets is matched with the revenues earned. This allocation process is called **depreciation** in the case of property, plant, and equipment; **depletion** in the case of natural resources; and **amortization** in the case of intangibles.

Three methods of depreciation are used widely: straight-line, productive-output, and accelerated.

Expenditures related to operational assets are classified as:

1. **Capital expenditures**—those expenditures that provide benefits for one or more accounting periods beyond the current period; therefore, they are debited to appropriate asset accounts and depreciated, depleted, or amortized over their useful lives; or

2. **Revenue expenditures**—those expenditures that provide benefits during the current accounting period only; therefore, they are debited to appropriate current expense accounts when incurred.

Ordinary repairs and maintenance costs are revenue expenditures. Extraordinary repairs and asset additions are capital expenditures.

Operational assets may be disposed of voluntarily by sale or retirement, or involuntarily through casualty, such as storm, fire, or accident. Upon disposal, such assets must be depreciated, depleted, or amortized up to the date of disposal. The disposal transaction is recorded by removing the cost of the old asset and the related accumulated depreciation, depletion, or amortization amount from the accounts. A gain or loss on disposal of an operational asset will result when the disposal price is different from the book value of an old asset. Special rules apply to the trade-in of an asset as all, or part, of the consideration given for another asset (trade-ins are discussed in Supplement 9B).

SUPPLEMENT 9A

Capitalization of Interest as a Cost of Operational Assets

When an operational asset is purchased and a loan is incurred as all, or part, of the payment, periodic interest on the debt is recorded and reported as **interest expense** during the term of the loan. However, *FASB Statement 34* provides an exception to this principle. The exception is that interest cost **must be capitalized** as a part of the cost of acquiring assets that require a lengthy period of time to get them ready for their intended use. In such cases, interest on the average expenditures incurred during the construction or acquisition period is recorded as a part of the cost of the operational asset. Interest is included in the cost of the asset (*a*) **only** during the construction or acquisition period and (*b*) not in excess of total interest cost incurred by the entity during the period. It is not necessary that the debts of the company be related to the construction of the operational asset.[21]

To illustrate capitalization of interest during construction, assume that on January 1, 19A, Byers Corporation signed a contract that required Dow Construction Company to build a new plant building at a contract price of $1,000,000. The construction period started March 1, 19A, and the building was substantially complete and ready for its intended use on December 31, 19A (end of the 10-month construction period). Byers Corporation was required to make the following quarterly cash progress payments on the contract during 19A:

---

[21] FASB, *Statement of Financial Accounting Standards No. 34*, "Capitalization of Interest Cost (Stamford, Conn., October 1979). Under this *Statement*, interest cannot be capitalized for assets that are (1) in use or ready for their intended use, or (2) not used in the earnings activities of the entity. *Statement 34* specifies the qualifying assets as follows: "Assets that are constructed or otherwise produced for an enterprise's own use (including assets constructed or produced for the enterprise by others for which deposits or progress payments have been made)."

CICA Handbook, Section 3850, concerning the capitalization of interest, suggests only that the amount of interest charged to operational assets should be disclosed. Rules are not provided as to the determination of the appropriate amount.

Date of payment	Amount
a. March 31, 19A	$ 120,000
b. June 30, 19A	220,000
c. September 30, 19A	480,000
d. December 31, 19A	180,000
Total	$1,000,000

To make the progress payments, Byers Corporation borrowed 60% of each payment from a financial institution at 10% annual interest; the remaining cash needed was from within Byers Corporation. Total interest cost incurred by Byers during the period was $70,000 (at an average rate of 10%).

Upon completion, December 31, 19A, Byers Corporation should reflect the following acquisition cost in the operational asset account, Plant Building:

Contract price (paid in full)		$1,000,000
Add interest during the construction period:		
a. $120,000 × 10% × 9/12	$ 9,000	
b. $220,000 × 10% × 6/12	11,000	
c. $480,000 × 10% × 3/12	12,000	
d. $180,000—no interest	–0–	32,000*
Total acquisition cost		$1,032,000

* Note that this amount was not based on the specific borrowings of 60% but on the expenditures. This amount cannot exceed the $70,000 total interest cost for the period (19A).

FASB Statement 34 provides the following guidelines that must be observed.

1. Interest is capitalized **only** during the construction or acquisition period.
2. Interest is computed on the average **expenditures** during the construction period.
3. The applicable **borrowing interest rate** for the company is used.
4. Interest is computed **regardless of the source** of the funds (which may be borrowed or obtained from normal operations of the entity).
5. Interest added to the cost of the operational assets **cannot exceed** the total amount of total interest cost incurred by the entity in that period (for all purposes).

SUPPLEMENT 9B

Trading in Assets

It is not unusual when acquiring an asset to trade in another asset. Although there may be a direct trade of two assets, the typical case involves the trading in of an old asset plus the payment of cash for the difference (often called boot). In such transactions, the asset acquired must be recorded in the accounts and the old asset is removed from the accounts.

Accounting for the exchange of one asset for another asset depends on two factors:[22]

1. Whether the two assets are similar or dissimilar.
2. Whether cash for the difference (boot) is paid or received.

The trading in of an old truck for a newer truck would involve similar assets. In contrast, the trading in of a plot of land for a new truck would involve dissimilar assets.

The basic principle for recording the exchange of assets can be stated as follows: If the assets exchanged are similar, the exchange should be recorded on a "book value" basis because there is no completed earning process.[23] If the assets exchanged are dissimilar, the exchange should be recorded on a "market value" basis because there is a completed earning process (for the old asset).

Exhibit 9–7 illustrates accounting for the acquisition of an asset when another asset is given as a trade-in. Four independent cases are illustrated:

Case	Situation
A . . .	Similar assets are exchanged; no cash boot is paid.
B . . .	Dissimilar assets are exchanged; no cash boot is paid.
C . . .	Similar assets are exchanged; cash boot is paid.
D . . .	Dissimilar assets are exchanged; cash boot is paid.

The four cases shown in Exhibit 9–7 explain the exchange of assets. Sometimes the terms of the transaction involving a trade-in also include the **receipt** of cash boot, in which case the recording becomes more complex.

Under the cost principle, an asset, when acquired, never should be recorded at an amount greater than its market value (i.e., its cash equivalent price). In some cases, this constraint will reduce a gain (or increase a loss) on disposal.

In the illustration in Exhibit 9–7, the market value of old Asset O was $200 in excess of its book value [i.e., $2,200 − ($5,000 − $3,000)]. Therefore, in Cases B and D (relating to dissimilar assets), this amount was recorded as a gain. In contrast, if the market value of old Asset O had been $1,900 (i.e., $100 below book value), a loss of $100 would be reported in Cases B and D. A loss would be recorded for Cases A and C (similar assets) when the market value of either asset is below book value because it indicates an impairment of value.

---

[22] *APB Opinion 29,* "Accounting for Nonmonetary Transactions" (New York, May 1973), specifies the appropriate accounting for transactions that involve the exchange of assets when either or both of these factors are present. The *CICA Handbook* is silent on this point.

[23] In the case of an exchange of similar productive assets, because the asset acquired performs essentially the same productive function as the asset given up, the exchange is only one step in the earning process. The earning process in these situations is completed when the goods or services are sold that the similar productive assets helped to produce. In contrast, in the case of an exchange of dissimilar productive assets, the earning process is completed because the productive function of the productive asset given up is terminated. The asset acquired serves a different economic purpose for the entity and begins a new earning process of its own.

Exhibit 9–7 Trading in used assets illustrated

Situation of Company T:

Transaction: Company T acquired Asset N and traded in Asset O. At the date of the transaction, the accounts of Company T reflected the following:

Asset O:

Cost when acquired	$5,000
Accumulated depreciation	3,000
Estimated market value	2,200

Asset N:

Market value	2,250

Case A—Similar assets are exchanged; **no** cash boot paid.

Principle applied: The asset acquired is recorded at the **book value** of the asset traded in.

Asset N	2,000	
Accumulated depreciation, Asset O	3,000	
Asset O		5,000

Case B—Dissimilar assets are exchanged; **no** cash boot paid.

Principle applied: The asset acquired is recorded at the **market value** of the asset traded in.

Asset N	2,200	
Accumulated depreciation, Asset O	3,000	
Asset O		5,000
Gain on disposal of operational asset		200

Case C—Similar assets are exchanged; $60 cash boot is **paid.**

Principle applied: The asset acquired is recorded at the **book value** of the asset traded in **plus the cash boot** paid.

Asset N ($2,000 + $60)	2,060*	
Accumulated depreciation, Asset O	3,000	
Asset O		5,000
Cash		60

* This amount cannot exceed the market value of the asset acquired, $2,250.

Case D—Dissimilar assets are exchanged; $60 cash boot is **paid.**

Principle applied: The asset acquired is recorded at the **market value** of the asset traded in **plus the cash boot** paid.

Asset N ($2,200 + $60)	2,250*	
Accumulated depreciation, Asset O	3,000	
Asset O		5,000
Cash		60
Gain on disposal of operational assets		190

* This amount cannot exceed the market value of the asset acquired, $2,250.

IMPORTANT TERMS DEFINED IN THIS CHAPTER

Accelerated Depreciation Higher depreciation expense in early years, and lower in later years of an operational asset. *p. 509*

Acquisition Cost Net cash equivalent amount paid for an asset. *p. 498*

Amortization Systematic and rational allocation of the cost of an intangible operational asset over its useful life. *p. 503*

Basket Purchase Acquisition of two or more assets in a single transaction for a single lump sum. *p. 500*

Book (or Carrying) Value Acquisition cost of an operational asset less accumulated depreciation, depletion, or amortization. *p. 504*

Capital Cost Allowance The method of charging operational assets against revenue for income tax purposes; tax depreciation. *p. 512*

Capital Expenditures Expenditures that are debited to an asset account; the acquisition of an asset. *p. 518*

Capitalization of Interest Interest expenditures included in the cost of an operational asset; interest capitalized during construction period. *p. 532*

Copyrights Exclusive right to publish, use, and sell a literary, musical, or artistic work. *p. 523*

Declining Depreciation An accelerated depreciation method based upon a multiple of the straight-line rate; it disregards residual value. *p. 511*

Deferred Charges An expense paid in advance of usage of the goods or services; long-term prepayment. *p. 526*

Depletion Systematic and rational allocation of the cost of a natural resource over the period of exploitation. *p. 503*

Depreciation Systematic and rational allocation of the cost of property, plant, and equipment (but not land) over its useful life. *p. 502*

Estimated Useful Life Estimated service life of an operational asset to the present owner. *p. 505*

Extraordinary Repairs Major, high cost, and long-term repairs; debited to an asset account (or accumulated depreciation); a capital expenditure. *p. 519*

Goodwill Acquisition cost of the purchase of a business that is in excess of the market value of the other assets of the business purchased. *p. 525*

Government Assistance Amounts provided by various governments to assist businesses usually in the form of operating expense reductions or fixed asset cost reductions. *p. 500*

Intangible Operational Assets Assets used in the operations of a business that have special rights but not physical substance. *p. 498*

Leasehold Improvements Expenditures by the lessee on leased property that have use value beyond the current accounting period. *p. 525*

Leaseholds Rights granted to a lessee under a lease contract that have been paid for. *p. 524*

Natural Resources   Mineral deposits, timber tracts, oil, and gas. *p. 520*

Operational Assets   Tangible and intangible assets owned by a business and used in its operations. *p. 496*

Productive-Output Depreciation   Cost of an operational asset is allocated over its useful life based upon the periodic output related to total estimated output. *p. 508*

Repairs and Maintenance   Expenditures for normal operating upkeep of operational assets; debit expense for ordinary repairs. *p. 519*

Residual Value   Estimated amount to be recovered, less disposal costs, at the end of the estimated useful life of an operational asset. *p. 505*

Revenue Expenditures   Expenditures that are debited to an expense account; the incurrence of an expense. *p. 518*

Straight-Line Depreciation   Cost of an operational asset is allocated over its useful life in equal periodic amounts. *p. 507*

Sum-of-the-Years'-Digits Depreciation   Cost of an operational asset is allocated over its useful life based upon a fraction when the denominator is the total of all of the useful years and the numerator is the year of life in inverse order. *p. 509*

Tangible Operational Assets   Assets used in the operations of a business that have physical substance. *p. 498*

QUESTIONS

Part A: Questions 1–16

1. Define operational assets. Why are they considered a "bundle of future services"?
2. What are the classifications of operational assets? Explain each.
3. Relate the cost principle to accounting for operational assets.
4. Describe the relationship between the matching principle and accounting for operational assets.
5. Define and illustrate the book value of a three-year-old operational asset that cost $11,500, has an estimated residual value of $1,500, and an estimated useful life of five years. Relate book value to carrying value and market value.
6. Under the cost principle, what amounts usually should be included in the acquisition cost of an operational asset?
7. What is a "basket purchase"? What measurement problem does it pose?
8. Distinguish between depreciation, depletion, and amortization.
9. In computing depreciation, three values must be known or estimated; identify and explain the nature of each.
10. Estimated useful life and residual value of an operational asset relate to the current owner or user rather than to all potential users. Explain this statement.
11. What kind of a depreciation-expense pattern is provided under the straight-line method? When would its use be appropriate?

12. What kind of depreciation-expense pattern emerges under the productive-output method? When would its use be appropriate?

13. What are the arguments in favour of accelerated depreciation?

14. Explain how monthly depreciation should be computed when the sum-of-the-years'-digits method is used for an asset having a 10-year life.

15. When an asset is acquired by giving up a noncash asset (noncash consideration), the preferred value for the new asset is the market value of the noncash asset rather than the market value of the asset purchased. Why?

16. What accounting principle could justify treating a government grant received for the construction of a new building as a reduction of the asset value recorded?

Part B: Questions 17–29

17. Distinguish between capital expenditures and revenue expenditures.

18. Distinguish between ordinary and extraordinary repairs. How is each accounted for?

19. Over what period should an addition to an existing operational asset be depreciated? Explain.

20. Define an intangible operational asset.

21. What period should be used to amortize an intangible operational asset?

22. Define goodwill. When is it appropriate to record goodwill as an intangible operational asset?

23. Distinguish between a leasehold and a leasehold improvement.

24. Over what period should a leasehold improvement be amortized? Explain.

25. Compare the accounting for a prepaid expense with accounting for a deferred charge.

26. When an operational asset is disposed of during the accounting period, two separate entries usually must be made. Explain this statement.

27. Why are ordinary repair costs incurred prior to the use of an asset debited to the asset account while ordinary repair costs incurred after the asset is placed in use are debited to operating expenses?

28. Why are research costs expensed while development costs may be capitalized?

29. Why are purchases of assets where a trade-in is used treated differently than a straight cash purchase of an asset?

EXERCISES

Part A: Exercises 9–1 to 9–8

E9–1   (Pair Allocation Terms with Assets)
For each asset listed below, enter a code letter to the left to indicate the allocation terminology for each asset. Use the following letter codes:

Allocation Term

A—Amortization   P—Depletion

D—Depreciation   N—None of these

Assets

_____ (1) Patent (example)   _____ (11) Copyright
_____ (2) Land   _____ (12) Investment in common shares
_____ (3) Building   _____ (13) Mineral deposit
_____ (4) Cash   _____ (14) Machinery
_____ (5) Oil well   _____ (15) License right
_____ (6) Trademark   _____ (16) Deferred charge
_____ (7) Goodwill   _____ (17) Inventory of goods
_____ (8) Stamps   _____ (18) Timber tract
_____ (9) Franchise   _____ (19) Tools
_____ (10) Plant site in use   _____ (20) Gravel pit

E9–2   **(Pair Brief Definitions with Terms)**
Match the definitions given below with the terms by entering the code letters in the blanks provided.

Terms

_____ (1) Acquisition cost (example)
_____ (2) Depreciation
_____ (3) Straight-line depreciation
_____ (4) Productive-output depreciation
_____ (5) Tangible operational assets
_____ (6) Natural resource
_____ (7) Useful life
_____ (8) Depletion
_____ (9) Basket purchase
_____ (10) Book value
_____ (11) SYD depreciation
_____ (12) Residual value

Definitions

A. Assets used in operations; have physical substance.
B. Declining expense; numerator year of life in inverse order.
C. Use cost is the same amount per year during useful life.
D. Estimated recovery less costs of disposal.
E. Cash equivalent amount.
F. Periodic expense fluctuates with actual output.
G. A timber tract.
H. Estimated productive life to the current user.
I. Systematic allocation of the cost of a natural resource.
J. Must allocate a single purchase cost to two or more assets.
K. Systematic allocation of the cost of a tangible operational asset.
L. Acquisition cost minus accumulated allocation of original cost.

E9–3   **(Record Asset Acquisition and Straight-Line Depreciation; Basket Purchase)**
Tony Company bought a building and the land on which it is located for a total cash price of $197,000. Also, Tony paid transfer costs of $3,000. Renovation costs on the building were $16,000. An independent appraiser provided market values of building, $145,152; and land, $56,448.

Required:

a. Apportion the cost of the property on the basis of the appraised values. Show computations.

b. Give the journal entry to record the purchase of the property, including all expenditures. Assume that all transactions were for cash and that all purchases occurred at the start of Year 1.

c. Give the journal entry to record straight-line depreciation at the end of one year assuming an estimated 20-year useful life and a $24,000 estimated residual value.

d. What would be the book value of the property at the end of Year 2?

E9–4   (Apply Cost Principle and Record Straight-Line Depreciation)
A machine was purchased by Mason Company on March 1, 19A, at an invoice price of $15,000. On date of delivery, March 2, 19A, Ryan Company paid $10,000 on the machine, and the balance was on credit at 12% interest. On March 3, 19A, $150 was paid for freight on the machine. On March 5, installation costs relating to the machine were paid amounting to $750. On October 1, 19A, Ryan Company paid the balance due on the machine plus the interest.

Required (round all amounts to the nearest dollar):

a. Give the journal entries on each of the above dates through October 19A.

b. Give the adjusting entry for straight-line depreciation at the end of 19A, assuming an estimated useful life of 10 years and an estimated residual value of $1,900. Depreciate to the nearest month. The accounting period ends December 31, 19A.

c. What would be the book value of the machine at the end of 19B?

E9–5   (Compute Depreciation for Four Years Using Four Different Depreciation Methods)
Vista Corporation bought a machine at a cost of $2,700. The estimated useful life was four years, and the residual value, $300. Assume that the estimated productive life of the machine is 60,000 units and each year's production was Year 1, 24,000 units; Year 2, 20,000 units; Year 3, 10,000 units; and Year 4, 6,000 units.

Required:

a. Determine the amount for each cell in the following schedule. Show your computations, and round to the nearest dollar.

Year	Depreciation Expense			
	Straight Line	Productive Output	Sum-of-the-Years' Digits	20% Capital Cost Allowance
1				
2				
3				
4				
Totals				

b. Assuming the machine was used directly in the production of one of the products manufactured and sold by the company, what factors might be considered in selecting a preferable depreciation method in conformity with the matching principle?

E9–6   (Compute Depreciation and Book Value for Two Years Using Four Depreciation Methods)

XIT Company bought a machine for $35,000. The estimated useful life was five years, and the estimated residual value, $5,000. Assume the estimated useful life in productive units is 60,000. Units actually produced were Year 1, 12,000; and Year 2, 11,000.

Required:

a. Determine the appropriate amounts to complete the schedule below. Show computations, and round to the nearest dollar.

Method of depreciation	Depreciation expense		Book value at end of	
	Year 1	Year 2	Year 1	Year 2
Straight-line	___	___	___	___
Productive-output	___	___	___	___
Sum-of-the-years' digits	___	___	___	___
20% capital cost allowance method for depreciation	___	___	___	___

b. Which method would result in the lowest EPS for Year 1? For Year 2?

E9–7   (Monthly Depreciation Using Two Depreciation Methods; Effect on Income Statement)

Stoner Company acquired, and paid for, a machine that cost $5,300 on July 1, 19B. The estimated useful life is four years, and the estimated residual value is $500. The accounting period ends December 31.

Required:

a. Compute monthly depreciation expense for July 19B and July 19C assuming (a) the straight-line method and (b) the SYD method.

b. Assume cash revenues of $50,000 and cash expenses of $30,000 for the year 19B and an income tax rate of 30%. Complete the following tabulation for 19B:

	Straight Line	Sum-of-the-Years' Digits
Revenues		
Expenses		
Depreciation expense		
Pretax income		
Income tax expense		
Net income		

c. Which method produced the higher net income? By how much? Why do the net incomes differ (use amounts)?

E9–8   (Record and Explain Change in Useful Life and Residual Value)

Belt Company owns the office building occupied by its administrative office. The office building was reflected in the accounts on the December 31, 1987, balance sheet as follows:

```
Cost when acquired  . . . . . . . . . . . . . . . . . . . . . . . . .  $250,000
Accumulated depreciation (based on straight-line
    depreciation, an estimated life of 30 years,
    and a $40,000 residual value)  . . . . . . . . . . . . . . . .   105,000
```

During January 1988, on the basis of a careful study, the management decided that the total estimated useful life should be changed to 25 years (instead of 30) and the residual value reduced to $35,000 (from $40,000). The depreciation method will not be changed.

Required:

a. Give the adjusting entry (or entries) related to depreciation at the end of 1988. Show computations.

b. Explain the basis for the entry (or entries) that you gave in (*a*).

Part B: Exercises 9–9 to 9–22

E9–9   (Identify Capital and Revenue Expenditures)

For each item listed below, enter the correct letter to the left to show the type of expenditure. Use the following:

Type of Expenditure	Transaction
A—Capital expenditure	— (1) Paid $500 for ordinary repairs.
B—Revenue expenditure	— (2) Paid $6,000 for extraordinary repairs.
C—Neither	— (3) Addition to old building; paid cash, $10,000.
	— (4) Routine maintenance; cost, $300; on credit.
	— (5) Purchased a machine, $6,000; gave long-term note.
	— (6) Paid $2,000 for organization costs.
	— (7) Paid three-year insurance premium, $600.
	— (8) Purchased a patent, $3,400 cash.
	— (9) Paid $10,000 for monthly salaries.
	— (10) Paid cash dividends, $15,000.

E9–10   (Pair Brief Definitions with Terms)

Match the definitions given below with the terms by entering the code letters in the blanks provided.

Terms	Definitions
_H_ (1) Patents (example)	A. Cash paid or received when operational assets are exchanged.
____ (2) Goodwill	B. Ownership right to publish, use, or sell a literary, musical, or artistic work.
____ (3) Leaseholds	
____ (4) Amortization	

Terms		Definitions

Terms
_____ (5) Copyrights
_____ (6) Capitalization of interest
_____ (7) Intangible operational assets
_____ (8) Deferred charges
_____ (9) Ordinary repairs and maintenance
_____ (10) Additions (to assets)
_____ (11) Leasehold improvements
_____ (12) Franchise
_____ (13) Gain (loss) on disposal of an operational asset
_____ (14) "Boot" involved in the exchange of operational assets
_____ (15) Extraordinary repairs

Definitions

C. An expense paid in advance that represents a long-term payment.

D. Long-term, major, high-cost repairs.

E. Price paid for a business in excess of the market value of the net assets.

F. Assets used in the operations of a business because of their special rights.

G. Rights granted to a lessee that have been paid for.

H. An exclusive to use, manufacture, and sell a right that is protected by law.

I. Time cost of money allocated as a part of the cost of an operational asset.

J. A right granted by a governmental or business entity to offer services or products under a contract.

K. Costs expended by a lessee on leased property (e.g., a building on leased land).

L. Difference between consideration received and book value of an operational asset disposed of.

M. Systematic and rational allocation of the cost of an intangible asset.

N. Normal low cost, regularly recurring expenditures for upkeep of operational assets.

O. Extensions to, or enlargements of, an operational asset; a capital expenditure.

E9–11 **(Record Depreciation, Repairs, and Amortization)**

Ontario Company operates a small manufacturing facility as a supplement to its regular service activities. At the beginning of 19L, an operational asset account for the company showed the following balances:

> Manufacturing equipment $70,000
> Accumulated depreciation through 19K . . . 48,400

During 19L, the following expenditures were incurred for repairs and maintenance:

1. Routine maintenance and repairs on the equipment . . . $1,000
2. Major overhaul of the equipment 6,400

The equipment is being depreciated on a straight-line basis over an estimated life of 15 years and a $4,000 estimated residual value. The annual accounting period ends on December 31.

Required:

a. Give the adjusting entry for depreciation on the manufacturing equipment that was made at the end of 19K. Starting with 19L, what is the remaining estimated life?

b. Give the journal entries to record the two expenditures for repairs and maintenance during 19L.

c. Give the adjusting entry that should be made at the end of 19L for depreciation of the manufacturing equipment assuming no change in the estimated life or residual value. Show computations.

E9–12   **(Record Depreciation; Extraordinary Repairs; Change in Estimated Useful Life and Residual Value)**

At the end of the annual accounting period, December 31, 19C, the records of Wang Company reflected the following:

> Machine A:
> Cost when acquired $34,000
> Accumulated depreciation . . .   12,000

During January 19D, the machine was renovated, including several major improvements at a cost of $8,000. As a result, the estimated life was increased from 8 years to 10 years, and the residual value was increased from $2,000 to $5,500.

Required:

a. Give the journal entry to record the renovation. How old was the machine at the end of 19C?

b. Give the adjusting journal entry at the end of 19D to record straight-line depreciation for the year.

c. Explain the rationale for your entries in (*a*) and (*b*).

E9–13   **(Record Acquisition and Depletion of a Natural Resource)**

In February 19A, ACE Extractive Industries paid $500,000 for a mineral deposit. During March, $220,000 was spent in preparing the deposit for exploitation. It was estimated that 800,000 total cubic metres could be extracted economically. During 19A, 50,000 cubic metres were extracted. During January 19B, another $80,000 was spent for additional developmental work. After conclusion of the latest work, the estimated remaining recovery was increased to one million cubic metres over the remaining life. During 19B, 35,000 cubic metres were extracted.

Required:

Give the appropriate journal entry on each of the following dates:

a. February 19A, for acquisition of the deposit.

b. March 19A, for developmental costs.

c. Year 19A, for annual depletion assuming the company uses a contra account (show computations).

d. January 19B, for developmental costs.

e. Year 19B, for annual depletion (show computations).

E9–14   **(Record Acquisition, Amortization, and Reporting of Three Different Intangible Assets)**

Reo Manufacturing Company had three intangible operational assets at the end of 19F (end of the accounting year):

1. Patent—purchased from J. Ray on January 1, 19F, for a cash cost of $4,260. Ray had registered the patent five years earlier on January 1, 19A. Amortize over the remaining legal life.

2. A franchise acquired from the local community to provide certain services for 10 years starting on January 1, 19F. The franchise cost $26,000 cash.

3. On January 1, 19F, the company leased some property for a five-year term. Reo immediately spent $4,800 cash for long-term improvements (estimated useful life, eight years, and no residual value). At the termination of the lease, there will be no recovery of these improvements.

Required:

a. Give the journal entry to record the acquisition of each intangible asset. Provide a brief explanation with the entries.

b. Give the adjusting journal entry at December 31, 19F, for amortization of each intangible. Show computations. The company does not use contra accounts.

c. Show how these assets, and any related expenses, should be reported on the financial statements for 19F.

E9–15 **(Record a Patent, Copyright, and Goodwill and Amortize Each)**
Bebie Company acquired three intangible operational assets during 19F. The relevant facts were:

1. On January 1, 19F, the company purchased a patent from J. Doe for $4,800 cash. Doe had developed the patent and registered it on January 1, 19A. Amortize over the remaining legal life.

2. On January 1, 19F, the company purchased a copyright for a total cash cost of $12,000, and the remaining legal life was 25 years. The company executives estimated that the copyright would have no value by the end of 20 years.

3. Bebie Company purchased a small company in January 19F at a cash cost of $150,000. Included in the purchase price was $20,000 for goodwill; the balance was for plant, equipment, and fixtures (no liabilities were assumed). Amortize the goodwill over the maximum period permitted.

Required:

a. Give the journal entry to record the acquisition of each intangible.

b. Give the adjusting journal entry that would be required at the end of the annual accounting period, December 31, 19F, for each intangible. The company uses contra accounts. Include a brief explanation and show computations.

c. What would be the book (carrying) value of each intangible asset at the end of 19G?

E9–16 **(Record and Amortize Rent Paid in Advance, Leasehold Improvements, and Periodic Rent)**
WT Company conducts operations in several different sites. In order to expand into still another city, the company obtained a 10-year lease, starting January 1, 19D, on a downtown location. Although there was a serviceable building on the property, the company had to build an additional structure to be used for storage. The 10-year lease required a $10,000 cash advance rental payment, plus cash payments of $2,000 per month

during occupancy. During January 19D, the company spent $60,000 cash building the structure. The new structure has an estimated life of 12 years with no residual value (straight-line depreciation).

Required:

a. Give the journal entries for WT Company to record the payment of the $10,000 advance on January 1, 19D, and the first monthly rental.

b. Give the journal entry to record the construction of the new structure.

c. Give any adjusting entries required at the end of the annual accounting period for WT Company on December 31, 19D, in respect to (1) the advance payment and (2) the new structure. Show computations.

d. What is the total amount of expense resulting from the lease for 19D?

E9–17   (Reporting Intangible Assets on the Balance Sheet)

Doe Company is in the process of preparing the balance sheet at December 31, 19B. The following are to be included:

Prepaid insurance	$ 300
Long-term investment in common shares of	
X Corporation, at cost (market $10,600)	10,000
Patent (at cost)	3,400
Accumulated amortization, patent	1,000
Accounts receivable	24,000
Allowance for doubtful accounts	700
Franchise (at cost)	1,000
Accumulated amortization, franchise	600
Land—site of building	40,000
Building	400,000
Accumulated depreciation, building	160,000

Required:

Show how each of the above assets would be reflected on Doe Company's balance sheet at December 31, 19B. Use the following subcaptions: Current assets, Investments and funds, Tangible operational assets, and Intangible operational assets. The company uses the "accumulated" accounts as listed above.

E9–18   (Record the Disposal of an Asset at Three Different Assumed Sale Prices)

Daly Company sold a small truck that had been used in the business for three years. The records of the company reflected the following:

Delivery truck	$25,000
Accumulated depreciation	20,000

Required:

a. Give the journal entry for disposal of the truck assuming the sale price was $5,000.

b. Give the journal entry for the disposal of the truck assuming the sale price was $5,400.

c. Give the journal entry for the disposal of the truck assuming the sale price was $4,400.

d. Summarize the effects of the disposal of the asset under the three different situations above.

E9–19 **(Record the Disposal of an Operational Asset; Compute Estimated Life)**
The records of Manitoba Company on December 31, 19D, showed the following data about a particular machine:

> Machine, original cost $27,000
> Accumulated depreciation . . . 16,000*
>
> * Based on a six-year estimated useful life, a
> $3,000 residual value, and straight-line de-
> preciation.

On April 1, 19E, the machine was sold for $10,700 cash. The accounting period ends on December 31.

Required:

a. How old was the machine on January 1, 19E? Show computations.

b. Give the journal entry, or entries, related to the sale of the machine.

E9–20 **(Record Accident and Insurance Indemnity on an Operational Asset)**
On August 31, 19C, a delivery truck owned by Prince Corporation was a total loss as a result of an accident. On January 1, 19C, the records showed the following:

> Truck (estimated residual value, 10% of cost) $10,000
> Accumulated depreciation (straight-line, two years) . . . 3,000

The truck was insured; therefore, Prince Corporation collected $6,300 cash from the insurance company on October 5, 19C.

Required:

a. Based on the data given, compute the estimated useful life and the estimated residual value of the truck.

b. Give all of the journal entries with respect to the truck from January 1 through October 5, 19C. Show computations.

E9–21 **(Based on Supplement 9B)**
Trade Company owned a particular machine (designated Machine O for case purposes) which no longer met the needs of the company. On December 31, 19F, the records reflected the following:

> Machine O:
> Original cost $60,000
> Accumulated depreciation . . . 34,000

On January 3, 19G, the company acquired another machine (Machine N) and traded in Machine O. On this date, a reliable estimate of the market value of Machine O was $30,000.

Required:

a. Give the journal entry by Trade to record the transaction completed on January 3, 19G, for each of the following independent cases:
   Case A—The machines were similar, and no cash difference was paid or received by Trade.
   Case B—The machines were dissimilar, and no cash difference was paid or received by Trade.

b. For each case, explain the underlying reason for the amount that you recorded as the cost of Machine N.

E9–22   **(Based on Supplement 9B)**
Use the facts and requirements given in Exercise 9–21 except that for each case assume Trade Company paid a $2,000 cash difference (boot). The market value of Machine N was $32,200.

PROBLEMS

Part A: Problems 9–1 to 9–7

P9–1   **(Apply the Cost Principle to Determine the Cost of an Operational Asset)**
On January 1, 19A, Flye Company bought a machine for use in operations. The machine has an estimated useful life of 10 years and an estimated residual value (given below). The expenditures given below were provided by the company:

a. Invoice price of the machine, $60,000.
b. Less: Cash discount of 3% on all cash paid by January 10.
c. Freight paid by the vendor per sales agreement, $1,000.
d. Flye incurred installation costs, $1,500.
e. Payment of the $60,000 was made by Flye on January 15, 19A, as follows:

Flye common stock, par $1; 3,000 shares (market value, $4 per share).
Note payable, $30,000, 10% due April 16, 19A (principal plus interest).
Balance of the invoice price settled with cash.

Required:
Compute the cost of the machine that Flye should record. Explain the basis you used for any questionable items.

P9–2   **(Basket Purchase Allocation; Record Cost and Depreciation—Three Methods)**
Bush Company bought three used machines from J. Doe for a cash price of $48,000. Transportation costs on the machines were $2,000. The machines immediately were overhauled, installed, and started operating. The machines were different; therefore, each had to be recorded separately in the accounts. An appraiser was employed to estimate their market values at date of purchase (prior to the overhaul and installation). The book values shown on Doe's books also are available. The book values, appraisal results, installation costs, and renovation expenditures were:

	Machine A	Machine B	Machine C
Book value—Doe	$6,000	$10,000	$7,000
Appraisal value	7,200	24,400	8,400
Installation costs	300	500	200
Renovation costs prior to use . . .	1,000	600	400

Required:

a. Compute the cost of each machine by making a supportable allocation. Explain the rationale for the allocation basis used.

b. Give the journal entry to record the purchase of the three machines assuming all payments were cash. Set up a separate asset account for each machine.

c. Give the entry to record depreciation expense at the end of Year 1, assuming:

		Estimates	
Machine	Life	Residual value	Depreciation method
A	6	$1,300	Straight line
B	4	1,600	SYD
C	5	1,100	200% DB

P9–3   (Compute and Record Depreciation Using Four Methods; Explain Effect of Depreciation on Cash Flow and EPS)

Bye Company bought a machine that cost $34,375. The estimated useful life is-10 years, and the estimated residual value is 4% of cost. The machine has an estimated useful life in productive output of 110,000 units. Actual output was Year 1, 15,000; and Year 2, 12,000.

Required:

a. Determine the appropriate amounts for the table below. Show your computations.

Depreciation method	Depreciation expense		Book value at end of	
	Year 1	Year 2	Year 1	Year 2
Straight line	$ _____	$_____	$_____	$_____
Productive output	_____	_____	_____	_____
Sum-of-the-years' digits ...	_____	_____	_____	_____
200% declining balance ...	_____	_____	_____	_____

b. Give the adjusting entries for Years 1 and 2 under each method.

c. In selecting a depreciation method, some companies assess the comparative effect on **cash flow** and **EPS**. Briefly comment on the depreciation methods in terms of effects on cash flow and EPS.

P9–4   (Compute Depreciation Expense and Accumulated Depreciation for Four Depreciation Methods; Also a Change in Useful Life and Residual Value)

On January 1, 19A, AA Company bought a special heavy-duty truck that cost $28,500. The truck has an estimated five-year life and a $6,000 residual value. Estimated total distance travelled by disposal date is 50,000 kilometres. Actual kilometres were: Year A, 12,000; Year B, 14,000; Year C, 16,000; Year D, 6,000; and Year E, 3,000.

Required:

a. Complete the following comparative depreciation schedule:

Depreciation Method	Year A	B	C	D	E

1. Straight line (SL):
  Depreciation expense
  Accumulated depreciation
2. Sum-of-the-years' digits (SYD):
  Depreciation expense
  Accumulated depreciation
3. Productive output (PO):
  Depreciation expense
  Accumulated depreciation
4. Declining balance, 150% (DB):
  Depreciation expense
  Accumulated depreciation
	$	$	$	$	$

b. The interim depreciation expense for January 19A would be: SL, $_____;
SYD, $_____; PO, $_____; DB, $_____.

c. Assume that at the start of 19D, the estimates were changed; total life, seven
years; residual value, $4,000. Give all related entries for 19D, for the SL method.

P9–5   (Compute and Analyze Net Cash Flow)

Stable Corporation bought an operational asset on January 1, 19A, at a cash cost of
$34,000. The estimated useful life is five years, and the estimated residual value is $4,000.
Assume a constant 30% income tax rate; all paid in cash.

The company is deciding whether to use either straight-line (SL) depreciation or class
10, 30% CCA, for both accounting and income tax purposes. The five-year projected all-
cash incomes (before depreciation and income tax) are shown in the second column
below.

Schedule to Compare Projected SL and CCA Results

Year	Income (all-cash) before Depreciation and Income Tax	Depreciation Expense (dollars) SL	CCA	Income Tax Expense (dollars) SL	CCA	Net Income (dollars) SL	CCA	Net Cash Inflow (dollars) SL	CCA
1	$ 40,000	$ 6,000	$ 5,100	$10,200	$10,470	$ 23,800	$ 24,430	$ 29,530	$ 29,530
2	40,000								
3	40,000								
4	40,000								
5	40,000								
Totals	$200,000	$30,000		$51,000		$119,000		$148,118	

Required:

a. Complete the above schedule. Round to the nearest dollar. (Hint: Use the total line to prove your computations.)

b. Respond to each of the following items, based on your answers in (*a*):
   (1) Total depreciation under each method.
   (2) Explain the periodic depreciation amounts of SL versus CCA.
   (3) Total income tax under each method.
   (4) Explain the periodic income tax amounts of SL versus CCA.
   (5) Total net income under each method.
   (6) Explain the periodic net income under each method.
   (7) Total cash flow under each method.
   (8) Explain the periodic cash flow amounts in terms of CCA and SL.

P9–6 **(Analyze and Give Entries Related to a Change in Estimated Life and Residual Value)**

Tirpo Company owns an existing building that was built at an original cost of $500,000. It is being depreciated on a straight-line basis over a 20-year estimated useful life and has a $60,000 estimated residual value. At the end of 19H, the building had been depreciated for a full eight years. In January 19I, a decision was made, on the basis of new information, that a total estimated useful life of 30 years, and a residual value of $82,000 would be more realistic. The accounting period ends December 31.

Required:

a. Compute (1) the amount of depreciation expense recorded in 19H and (2) the book value of the building at the end of 19H.

b. Compute the amount of depreciation that should be recorded in 19I. Show computations.

c. Give the adjusting entry for depreciation at December 31, 19I.

P9–7 **(This Problem Relates to Supplement 9A; It Requires Computation of Interest that Could Be Capitalized on an Operational Asset)**

On January 1, 19A, Stonewall Corporation bought land at a cost of $120,000 and paid transfer fees of $6,000. Clearing the land and planning for the building construction was started immediately. Construction of an office building for company use was started on April 1, 19A. The company borrowed about 80% of the funds to purchase the land and construct the office building at a 12% interest rate. The remaining cash needed was paid from company funds. Total interest cost for 19A was $36,000. The company made the following cash expenditures at the dates indicated:

January 1, 19A, down payment on the land (20%)	$ 24,000
January 1, 19A, transfer costs on the land	6,000
March 1, 19A, fees for preliminary surveys and work prior to start of construction	12,000
Progress payments to contractor for construction costs:	
May 31, 19A, No. 1	200,000
August 31, 19A, No. 2	300,000
November 30, 19A, No. 3 (end of the construction period)	200,000

Required:

a. Compute the cost of the tangible operational asset with separate amounts for the land and building. Assume the construction period started on April 1, 19A. Show computations.

b. How much interest should be reported on the 19A income statement?

Part B: Problems 9–8 to 9–16

P9–8 **(Recording Repairs and an Addition)**

Case Company made extensive repairs on its existing building and added a new wing. The existing building originally cost $360,000; and by the end of 19J (10 years), it was half depreciated on the basis of a 20-year estimated useful life and no residual value. During 19K, the following expenditures were made that were related to the building:

1. Ordinary repairs and maintenance expenditures for the year, $7,500 cash.
2. Extensive and major repairs to the roof of the building, $21,000 cash. These repairs were completed on June 30, 19K.
3. The new wing was completed on June 30, 19K, at a cash cost of $150,000. The wing had an estimated useful life of 10 years and no residual value.

Required:

a. Give the journal entry to record each of the 19K transactions.
b. Give the adjusting entry that would be required at the end of the annual account-ing period, December 31, 19K, for the building after taking into account your entries in (*a*) above. Assume straight-line depreciation. The company computes de-preciation based on the nearest month.
c. Show how the assets would be reported on the December 31, 19K, balance sheet. (Hint: Depreciation expense for 19K is $27,000.)

P9–9 **(Analyze, Record, Give Adjusting Entries, and Compute Book Value Related to Five Different Intangible Operational Assets)**

NFLD Company has five different intangible operational assets to be accounted for and reported on the financial statements. The management is concerned about the amortiza-tion of the cost of each of these intangibles. Facts about each intangible are:

1. **Patent**—The company purchased a patent at a cash cost of $26,000 on January 1, 19E. The patent had a legal life of 17 years from date of registration with the Pa-tent Office, which was January 1, 19A. Amortize over the remaining legal life.
2. **Copyright**—On January 1, 19E, the company purchased a copyright for $15,000 cash. The legal life remaining from that date is 30 years. It is estimated that the copyrighted item will have no value by the end of 25 years.
3. **Franchise**—The company obtained a franchise from X Company to make and dis-tribute a special item. The franchise was obtained on January 1, 19E, at a cash cost of $10,000 and covered a 10-year period.
4. **License**—On January 1, 19D, the company secured a license from the city to oper-ate a special service for a period of five years. Total cash expended to obtain the license was $8,000.
5. **Goodwill**—The company started business in January 19C by purchasing another business for a cash lump sum of $400,000. Included in the purchase price was "Goodwill, $80,000." NFLD executives stated that "the goodwill is an important long-term asset to us." Amortize over the maximum period permitted.

Required:

a. Analyze each intangible asset and give the journal entry to record each of the five acquisitions.

b. Give the adjusting entry for each intangible asset that would be necessary at the end of the annual accounting period, December 31, 19E. Provide a brief explanation and show computations. If no entry is required for a particular item, explain the basis for your conclusion.

c. Give the book value of each intangible on January 1, 19G. (Hint: The total book value for the five intangibles is $119,000.)

P9–10   **(Record the Purchase of a Business Including Goodwill; Depreciation of Assets, Acquired and Amortization of Goodwill)**
On January 1, 19A, Investor Corporation was organized by five individuals to purchase and operate a successful business known as Kampus Korner. The name was retained, and all of the assets, except cash, were purchased for $300,000 cash. The liabilities were not assumed by Investor Corporation. The transaction was closed on January 5, 19A, at which time the balance sheet of Kampus Korner reflected the book values shown below:

KAMPUS KORNER
January 5, 19A

	Book value	Market value*
Accounts receivable (net)	$ 30,000	$ 30,000
Inventory	180,000	175,000
Operational assets (net)	19,000	50,000
Other assets	1,000	5,000
Total assets	$230,000	
Liabilities	$ 80,000	
Owners' equity	150,000	
Total liabilities and owners' equity	$230,000	

* These values for the assets purchased were provided to Investor Corporation by an independent appraiser.

As a part of the negotiations, the former owners of Kampus Korner agreed not to engage in the same or similar line of business in the same general region.

Required:

a. Give the journal entry by Investor Corporation to record the purchase of the assets of Kampus Korner. Include goodwill. (Hint: Record the assets at market value in conformity with the cost principle.)

b. Give the adjusting entries that would be made by Investor Corporation at the end of the annual accounting period, December 31, 19A, for:
   (1) Depreciation of the operational assets (straight line) assuming an estimated remaining useful life of 20 years and no residual value.
   (2) Amortization of goodwill assuming the maximum amortization period is used.

P9–11   **(Record the Disposal of Three Operational Assets)**
During 19K, Hammer Company disposed of three different assets. On January 1, 19K, prior to their disposal, the accounts reflected the following:

Assets	Original cost	Residual value	Estimated life	Accumulated depreciation (straight line)
Machine A . . .	$20,000	$2,000	10 years	$12,600 (7 years)
Machine B . . .	35,400	3,000	9 years	21,600 (6 years)
Machine C . . .	65,200	6,400	14 years	46,200 (11 years)

The machines were disposed of in the following ways:

Machine A—Sold on January 1, 19K, for $6,400 cash.

Machine B—Sold on May 1, 19K, for $13,200; received cash, $3,200, and a $10,000 interest-bearing (12%) note receivable due at the end of 12 months.

Machine C—On July 2, 19K, this machine suffered irreparable damage from an accident. On July 10, 19K, it was given to a salvage company at no cost. The salvage company agreed to remove the machine immediately at no cost. The machine was insured, and $18,000 cash was collected from the insurance company.

Required:

Give all journal entries related to the disposal of each machine. Explain the accounting rationale for the way that you recorded each disposal.

P9–12   (Analyze Five Transactions to Give Original Entry and Any Related Depreciation and Amortization Adjusting Entries)

During the 19X5 annual accounting period, Baker Company completed the following transactions:

1. On January 10, 19X5, paid $6,000 for a complete reconditioning of each of the following machines acquired on January 1, 19X1 (total cost, $12,000):

    Machine A—Original cost, $23,000, accumulated depreciation to December 31, 19X4, $16,000 (straight line, $3,000 residual value).

    Machine B—Original cost, $28,000, accumulated depreciation, $12,000 straight line, $4,000 residual value).

2. On July 1, 19X5, purchased a patent for $14,000 cash (estimated useful life, seven years).

3. On January 1, 19X5, purchased another business for cash $50,000 including $12,000 for goodwill. No liabilities were assumed by Baker.

4. On September 1, 19X5, constructed a storage shed on some land leased from J. Doe. The cost was $14,400; the estimated useful life was 10 years with no residual value. Baker Company uses straight-line depreciation. The lease will expire at the end of 19X8.

5. Total expenditures during 19X5 for ordinary repairs and maintenance was $4,500.

6. On July 1, 19X5, sold Machine A for $7,000 cash.

Required (compute depreciation to the nearest month):

a. For each of the above transactions, give the entry (or entries) that should be made during 19X5.

b. For each of the above transactions, give any adjusting entry that should be made at December 31, 19X5.

P9–13   **(A Challenging Analytical Problem; Five Different Situations Are Analyzed—Two Involve Accounting Errors, One Involves a Basket Purchase, and One Involves Some Noncash Payments; Related Entries Are Required)**
It is the end of the annual accounting period, December 31, 19F, for Modern Company. The following items must be resolved before the financial statements can be prepared:

1. On January 1, 19F, a used machine was bought for $5,000 cash. This amount was properly debited to an operational asset account, Machinery. Prior to use, cash was expended for (*a*) overhauling the machine, $600, and (*b*) installation, $150; both of these amounts were debited to Expense. The machine has an estimated remaining useful life of five years and a 10% residual value. Straight-line depreciation will be used.

2. A small warehouse (and the land on which it is located) was purchased on January 1, 19F, at a cash cost of $40,000 which was debited in full to an operational asset account, Warehouse. The property was appraised for tax purposes near the end of 19E as follows: warehouse, $21,250; and land, $8,250. The warehouse has an estimated remaining useful life of 10 years and a 10% residual value; 200% declining-balance depreciation will be used.

3. During the year 19F, usual recurring repair costs of $1,200 were paid. During January 19F, major repairs (on the warehouse purchased in [2] above) of $1,000 were paid. Repair expense was debited $2,200, and Cash was credited.

4. On June 30, 19F, the company purchased a patent for use in the business at a cash cost of $2,040. The patent was dated July 1, 19A. The Patent account was debited for the full amount.

5. On December 31, 19F, the company acquired a new truck that had a list price of $15,000 (estimated life, five years; residual value, $2,000). The company paid for the truck with cash, $7,000, and issued to the seller 600 shares of its own no-par capital stock. The market value of the stock was $12 per share. This purchase has not been recorded.

Required:

a. Give the journal entry or entries that should be made to correct the accounts at December 31, 19F, before the adjusting entries are made. If none is required, so state.

b. Give the adjusting journal entries at December 31, 19F, after the corrections in Requirement (*a*) above have been made.

P9–14   **(A Challenging Problem; Focuses on the Cash Flow Effects of Income Tax for Straight-Line Depreciation versus Accelerated Depreciation)**
On January 1, 19A, Brown Corporation bought a special machine for use in the business for $33,000. The machine has a three-year useful life and a residual value of $3,000. The company is considering using either the straight-line (SL) method or class 8, 20% CCA, for depreciating the machine. Assume an average income tax rate of 30% (for both accounting and income tax purposes) and that it is paid in full in cash.

Requirement a:

Prepare an analysis of the effects of SL versus CCA depreciation on the projected financial statements and cash flows over the life of the machine (19A–19C). You have

decided to complete the following schedules—one set based on straight-line depreciation
and another set based on 20% CCA:

	Year 1	Year 2	Year 3
Income statements:			
Revenues (all cash)	$90,000	$95,000	$99,000
Expenses (all cash)	(60,000)	(62,000)	(63,000)
Depreciation expense			
Pretax income			
Income tax expense			
Net income			
EPS (5,000 shares)			
Balance sheets:			
Operational assets:			
Machine			
Accumulated depreciation			
Book value			
Cash flows:			
Revenues			
Expenses			
Depreciation expense			
Income tax			
Net cash inflow			

Requirement b:

Complete the following summary of **relevant comparisons** based upon your answer to
Requirement (*a*):

Items Compared	Year 1		Year 2		Year 3		Total (each method)
	SL	CCA	SL	CCA	SL	CCA	
1. Net income							
2. Machine, book value							
3. Net cash inflow							

Requirement c:

List, and explain, any generalizations that you can make about the three items summarized in Requirement (*b*): (1) net income, (2) book value, and (3) net cash inflow.

Requirement d:

Which method would you recommend? Explain the basis for your recommendation.
Instructional note: This problem assumes a constant income tax rate in order to focus on
the different effects of SL versus CCA depreciation. Also, the time period is limited to a
three-year useful life only to reduce the computational burden.

P9–15 **(This Problem Relates to Supplement 9B; Record the Sale of an Operational Asset under Two Assumptions: All Cash and Exchange)**

Quick Manufacturing Company operates a number of machines. One particular group of machines has five identical machines acquired on the same date. At the beginning of 19G, the operational asset account for the five machines showed the following:

> Machinery (Type A, five machines) . . . . $200,000 40,000 ea
> Accumulated depreciation (Type A machines) . . . 108,000*
>
> * Based on 10-year estimated useful life and $4,000 residual value per machine and straight-line depreciation.

One of the machines (Type A) was disposed of on September 1, 19G.

Required:

a. How old were the Type A machines at January 1, 19G? Show computations.

b. What was the book value of the machine sold (at date of disposal)? Show computations. The company computes depreciation to the nearest full month.

c. Give all journal entries to record the disposal of the machine under two independent assumptions:

(1) It was sold outright for $14,000 cash.

(2) It was exchanged for a new similar machine having a "quoted" price of $47,000; however, it was determined that it could be purchased for $44,000 cash. The old machine was traded in, and $30,000 was paid in cash. Assume the machines were similar. No reasonable market value was determinable for the old machine.

P9–16 **(This Problem Relates to Supplement 9B; Record Exchanges of Similar and Dissimilar Machines, with and without a Cash Difference)**

Mason company owned a particular machine (designated Machine O for case purposes) which no longer met the needs of the company. On December 31, 19F, the records reflected the following:

> Machine O:
> Original cost $30,000
> Accumulated depreciation . . . 17,000

On January 3, 19G, the company acquired another machine (Machine N) and traded in Machine O. On this date, a reliable estimate of the market value of Machine O was $15,000.

Required:

a. Give the journal entry by Mason to record the transaction completed on January 3, 19G, for each of the following independent cases:

Case A—The machines were similar, and no cash difference was paid or received by Mason.

Case B—The machines were dissimilar, and no cash difference was paid or received by Mason.

For each case, explain the underlying reasons for the amount that you recorded as the cost of Machine N.

b. Use the facts and requirements given above, except that for each case assume Mason paid a $1,000 cash difference and that the market value of Machine N was $16,100.

CASES

C9–1   **(Comprehensive Case; Involves Computation and Evaluation of Cash Flow Effects for 10 Years for Three Different Depreciation Methods)**
Slick Corporation acquired a large machine for use in its productive activities at a cash cost of $189,000. The machine was acquired on January 1, 19A, at which time its estimated useful life was 500,000 units of output over a period of 10 years. The estimated residual value was $24,000. Assume a 40% income tax rate for Slick for both accounting and income tax purposes.

The management of Slick is considering using either straight-line (SL), productive-output (PO), or sum-of-the-years' digits (SYD) depreciation. The management also is developing a 10-year profit plan. The 10-year projected all-cash incomes (before depreciation and income tax) are shown in the first column below.

Required:

a. Complete the following tabulation (round to nearest $1):

Year	Income (all-cash) before Depreciation and Income Tax		Depreciation Expense (dollars)			Income Tax Expense (dollars)			Net Income (loss) (dollars)		
	Units	Dollars	SL	PO	SYD	SL	PO	SYD	SL	PO	SYD
1	70,000	96,500	16,500	23,100	30,000	32,000	29,360	26,600	48,000	44,040	39,900
2	75,000	103,400									
3	80,000	102,300									
4	75,000	103,400									
5	60,000	82,700	16,500	19,800	18,000	26,480	25,160	25,880	39,720	37,740	38,820
6	60,000	82,700									
7	50,000	69,000									
8	20,000	27,600	16,500	6,600	9,000	4,440	8,400	7,440	6,660	12,600	11,160
9	8,000	11,000									
10	2,000	2,400	16,500	660	3,000	(5,640)	696	(240)	(8,460)	1,044	(360)
Total	500,000	681,000	165,000	165,000	165,000	206,400	206,400	206,400	309,600	309,600	309,600

   b. List and explain any generalizations that you can make from the columns for (1) depreciation expense, (2) income tax expense, and (3) net income.

   c. Which method would you recommend in this situation? Explain the basis for your recommendation.

C9–2   **(Analysis of Intangibles)**

Every Friday afternoon, the audit staff of the firm of TD & Co., Chartered Accountants, meets to discuss various technical and professional client matters. These meetings are used for training, planning audits, or discussing the results of audit work.

   CL Ltd., a new client, was the subject of discussion at one of these meetings. Roy Gray, an audit manager with TD & Co., had made several visits to CL. During these visits, Jeff Jax, the president, had explained the operations of his company at some length. He had also described some of CL's accounting practices, including its revenue recognition policies. At this Friday afternoon meeting, Gray relayed portions of his conversations with Jax and provided background information on the company.

   CL, a favourite of the investment community, is a public company with shares listed on Canadian stock exchanges. Its shares, originally issued at $4.50 five years ago, have recently been trading in the $25 to $30 range. Jeff Jax owns 65% of the voting shares of CL.

   Five months ago, Jax approached the senior partner of TD & Co. and stated that he had heard of the firm's excellent reputation and wanted the firm as auditor. Jax indicated that CL was growing quickly and that he wanted TD & Co. to handle all financial affairs for both CL and Jax personally.

   Jax indicated that due to the significance of debt financing, maintaining good relations with CL's various lenders was important. He did not want any difficulties with them resulting from disputes over the financial statements. Also, Jax made it clear that he wanted to maintain the company's rising profit picture. He said it correctly portrayed the growth and innovation of the company and facilitated further expansion.

   CL manufactures the hardware and develops the software for Computo, a full line of microcomputers for home and small office applications. Even though CL is faced with strong competition from the well-known products of Tandy, Apple, IBM, and others, Jax expects great expansion ahead through franchising and special contracts.

   CL operates five company stores in three major cities. In order to expand into more cities and increase its share of the market, CL sells store franchises. The number of franchise stores dealing exclusively in the Computo line is growing quickly. The franchisee is granted the exclusive right to the Computo name and products for a store in a specific area. CL is required to supply advice on store location, and to provide technical training, advertising, and other specified franchise support activities. Each store handles only the Computo line of microcomputer products, but noncompeting lines of electronic merchandise can also be carried.

   New, advanced products with good consumer acceptance are continually emerging as a result of the major expenditures on research and development during the past few years. CL's revenues were growing as the following financial statement excerpts indicate:

	Year Ended December 31, 1988	Year Ended December 31, 1987
	($000)	($000)
Sales of franchises	$4,520	$2,459
Sales of equipment	2,896	2,270
Continuing fees	898	549
Software and other sales . . .	3,066	1,781

Franchises are sold for a franchise price ranging from $80,000 to $150,000 depending on store location. Terms of payment include a down payment and a series of notes payable to CL with terms ranging from 5 to 10 years. The notes bear interest at rates significantly below the market rate at the time the agreement is signed. The financial arrangements are intended to help the new franchisees become established. CL recognizes the franchise price as revenue when contracts with franchisees are signed. Jax stated that the notes receivable are recorded by CL at face value to conform to generally accepted accounting principles.

Continuing fees are charged as a percentage of each franchisee's monthly sales of the Computo line. These fees are recorded on an accrual basis each month when reports are received from the franchisees. Revenue from both equipment and software sales is recognized when shipments are made from CL's plant.

In common with other growing firms, CL has a large proportion of its financing in the form of debt (is highly leveraged) and owes slightly over $10 million at an average interest rate of nearly 17%. A substantial part of the proceeds from this debt was used to finance research and development activities. A second major portion was used to finance two special projects. The remainder was used to finance the manufacturing assets for the Computo line.

In 1988, research costs and development costs other than interest, were close to $2 million each. CL had capitalized nearly 90% of the total $4 million to match these costs with the applicable future revenues. In addition, CL capitalized the interest on the debt applicable to the research and development expenditures. In Jax's opinion, all these costs would have a highly beneficial effect on CL in the future.

Jax was uncertain about what accounting policy he should use for the interest charges on debt relating to CL's two new special projects. He thought these interest charges probably should be capitalized because the benefits and revenues would flow in a future period.

One project is the design and construction by CL's engineers of a manufacturing facility for a line of video games. This project has been under way for nine months and will be completed in the next fiscal year. Production and marketing of the video games will commence immediately upon completion of the facility. The other project is the manufacturing of a large number of special-design, computerized components for Canadian Armed Forces equipment. All of the design costs and about 30% of the production costs will be incurred in this fiscal year. Delivery of the components will be made next year.

The interest on the debt related to the manufacturing assets for the Computo line was expensed because Jax said that it would not benefit future periods.

Considerable discussion of CL's financial and accounting affairs took place during the Friday afternoon meeting. Gray closed the meeting by summarizing the issues raised and requesting you to prepare a written report on the accounting issues. He asked you to recommend and justify the accounting policies that should be followed.

Required:
Prepare the report for Roy Gray on the accounting issues you believe are important for him to consider.

(CICA Adapted)

C9–3   (Computer Spreadsheet; Analysis of Cash Flow Effects)
Use the information provided in C9–1 and the form of the table presented therein to prepare a computer spreadsheet to analyze the following questions.

Required:

a. Assume the machine can be classified as class 8, 20% declining balance, for income tax purposes. Assume also the machine is not replaced at the end of its life. What would be the cash flow for Years 1 to 10?

b. Assume the marketing department decides to adjust the sales price downward in Year 6 and subsequent years by 15% which in turn is expected to increase the sales volume by 20%. To assist computations, assume the costs per unit will change in exact proportion to the change in sales price and that the life of the machine is limited by its production.

   What is the effect of this marketing decision on cash flows using the class 8 capital cost allowance assumption in order to compute income taxes?

C9–4 (Analysis of Some Amounts Related to Property, Plant, and Equipment Reported on Actual Set of Financial Statements)
Refer to the financial statements of Consolidated-Bathurst, Inc. given in Appendix B immediately preceding the Index. Respond to the following questions for 1987.

1. What amount was reported in 1987 for "accumulated depreciation"?
2. What methods of depreciation were used?
3. What total amount of depreciation expense was reported for 1987?
4. Give your explanation of why depreciation expense was added to net income in the computation of "cash flow from operations" on the SCFP.
5. Were any deferred charges reported on the balance sheet? If deferred charges are not reported separately, what amount on the balance sheet would include them?
6. How much interest did the company capitalize?
7. What were the amounts of (a) total interest and (b) interest expense reflected on the income statement?
8. What segment (line of business) of the company had the greatest amount of identifiable assets at year-end 1987?
9. What segment (line of business) of the company had the greatest amount of income before income taxes?
10. Which quarter of 1987 reported the greatest net income?
11. How much did the company spend for property, plant, and equipment during 1987?
12. What percent of property, plant, and equipment has been depreciated?
13. Does the company own any intangible operational assets?

TEN

MEASURING AND REPORTING LIABILITIES

PURPOSE

A business generates or receives resources from three sources: (*a*) capital contributed by owners, (*b*) income from operations, and (*c*) borrowing from creditors. **Creditors** provide resources by making cash loans and by selling property, goods, and services on credit. For users of financial statements, the liabilities reported on the balance sheet and the related interest expense reported on the income statement are important factors in evaluating the financial performance of a business. The purpose of this chapter is to discuss the measurement, recording, and reporting of liabilities and the related interest expense.

Notice on the facing page how one prominent company, Petro-Canada, reports its debts and provides a supplementary disclosure note. Long-term debt, deferred credits, and pensions will be disclosed in Chapter 11.

LEARNING OBJECTIVES

1. Define and classify liabilities.

2. Record and report current liabilities.

3. Apply income tax allocations.

4. Record and report contingent liabilities.

5. Apply the concepts of the future and present values of a single amount.

6. Apply annuity concepts to liabilities.

7. Expand your accounting vocabulary by learning the "Important Terms Defined in This Chapter."

8. Apply the knowledge gained from this chapter.

ORGANIZATION

Part A—measuring, accounting, and reporting liabilities
1. Liabilities defined and classified.

2. Measuring liabilities.

3. Short-term liabilities.

4. Long-term liabilities.

Part B—future value and present value concepts
1. Concepts.

2. Future and present values of a single amount.

3. Future and present values of annuities.

4. Ordinary annuities and annuities due compared.

Petro-Canada

CONSOLIDATED BALANCE SHEET
As at December 31,1987 (stated in millions of dollars)

	1987	1986
Liabilities and Shareholder's Equity		
Current Liabilities:		
Short-term notes payable	$ 313	$ —
Accounts payable and accrued liabilities	864	933
Current portion of long-term debt	6	13
Outstanding cheques less cash	—	88
	1,183	1,034
Long-term Debt (Note 6)	744	805
Deferred Credits (Note 7)	190	198
Deferred Income Taxes*	1,633	1,469

NOTES TO CONSOLIDATED FINANCIAL STATEMENTS
December 31,1987 (stated in millions of dollars)

Note 11: Income Taxes

The provision for income taxes of $227 million (1986-$249 million) represents an effective rate of 51.6% (1986-57.8%) on earnings before income taxes of $440 million (1986-$431 million). The computation of the provision, which requires adjustment to earnings before income taxes for non-taxable and non-allowable items, is as follows:

	1987	1986
Earnings before income taxes	$ 440	$ 431
Add (deduct)		
Royalties and other payments to provincial governments	160	169
Federal allowances		
Resource allowance	(144)	(127)
Tax depletion	(36)	(39)
Petroleum and Gas Revenue Tax	—	38
Non-deductible depreciation, depletion and amortization	99	81
Non-taxable gains	(10)	(21)
Equity in earnings of affiliates	(25)	(18)
Other	(8)	(8)
Earnings as adjusted before income taxes	$ 476	$ 506
Canadian Federal income tax at 46.6% (1986-47.8%) applied to earnings as adjusted	$ 222	$ 242
Provincial and other income taxes, net of federal abatement	9	12
Provincial income tax rebates	(4)	(5)
Provision for income taxes	$ 227	$249

Note 18: Commitments and Contingencies

(a) Commitments
The Corporation has leased property and equipment under various long-term operating leases for periods up to 2008. The minimum annual rentals for non-cancellable operating leases are estimated at $73 million in 1988, $49 million in 1989, $49 million in 1990, $40 million in 1991, $36 million in 1992 and $17 million per year thereafter until 2008.
(b) Contingencies
The Corporation is involved in litigation and claims associated with normal operations. Management is of the opinion that any resulting settlements would not materially affect the financial position of the Corporation.

*Author's note: In the future, the term should be "Future Income Tax Liability" (instead of Deferred Income Taxes) because of a change in CICA financial reporting requirements.

PART A—MEASURING, RECORDING, AND REPORTING LIABILITIES

Liabilities Defined and Classified

Liabilities are **defined** as probable future sacrifices of economic benefits.[1] Liabilities **arise** from present obligations of an entity to transfer assets or provide services to other entities in the future as a result of past transactions or events. Liabilities often are called debts or obligations.

Usually a business has several kinds of liabilities and a wide range of creditors. Therefore, the users of financial statements must rely on those statements for relevant information about the kinds and amounts of liabilities owed by the entity. The accounting model, along with an audit by an independent PA, gives the user reliable evidence that all liabilities are identified, properly measured, and fully reported in conformity with the **full-disclosure principle.** To meet these requirements, liabilities usually are classified as follows:

1. Current liabilities:
   a. Accounts payable.
   b. Short-term notes payable.
   c. Other short-term obligations.
2. Long-term liabilities:
   a. Long-term notes payable and mortgages.
   b. Bonds payable.
   c. Other long-term obligations.

Bonds payable will be discussed in Chapter 11. The other classifications will be discussed and illustrated in this chapter.

Measuring Liabilities

Usually a liability involves the payment of two different amounts: (*a*) the **principal** of the debt and (*b*) the **interest** on the principal. Assume that you borrowed $1,000 cash on January 1, 19A, and signed a $1,000 note payable that specified 10% interest and a time to maturity (repayment) of one year. You would receive $1,000 cash and repay $1,100 ($1,000 principal plus $100 interest). This liability would be measured and recorded on January 1, 19A, at its principal amount. The transaction would be recorded as follows:

---

[1] FASB, *Statement of Financial Accounting Concepts No. 3,* "Elements of Financial Statements of Business Enterprises" (Stamford, Conn., December 1980).

CICA Handbook, Section 1000, entitled "Financial Statement Concepts," para. 19, suggests that liabilities have two essential characteristics:
   i) They embody a duty or responsibility to others that entails settlement by future transfer or use of assets at a specified or determinable date, on occurrence of a specified event, or on demand; and
   ii) The transaction or event obligating the enterprise has already occurred.

January 1, 19A:

Cash 1,000
     Note payable   1,000

Liabilities are measured in conformity with the **cost principle.** When initially incurred, the amount of a liability is equivalent to the current market value of the resources received when the transaction occurred. In most cases, liabilities are measured, recorded, and reported at their **principal** amounts. This amount usually is the same as the face amount or maturity value.[2] However, there are two important exceptions to the general case:

1. **Noninterest-bearing notes**—Some notes do not specify a rate of interest, but there is **implicit** interest in the transaction. Assume you borrow $1,000 cash on January 1, 19A, and agree to repay $1,100 in one year. You sign a $1,100 note that does not specify an interest rate (called a noninterest-bearing note). The difference between the cash you repay and the cash you borrow ($1,100 − $1,000 = $100) is implicit interest expense.

2. **Liabilities with an unrealistic interest rate**—In some cases, the **stated** interest rate is higher or lower than the **market** interest rate for the transaction.[3] For example, the stated rate on the above note may have been 6%, although its market rate was 10%. Measuring liabilities with a market interest rate that differs from the stated interest rate requires application of present value concepts (discussed in Part B of this chapter).

In most cases, the stated and effective interest rates for liabilities will be the same; in these cases, the liabilities are measured at their **principal** amounts. Notes payable usually specify a stated rate of interest on the principal. This kind of note is called an **interest-bearing note.**

Current Liabilities

Current liabilities are defined as **short-term obligations that will be paid within the current operating cycle of the business or within one year of the balance sheet date, whichever is longer.** This definition presumes that current liabilities will be paid with assets that are classified as current assets on the same balance sheet.[4]

---

[2] The principal amount of a debt does not include interest because interest is an expense that is incurred only after a debt is incurred.

[3] The market rate of interest is called the **going** or **effective** rate of interest. As discussed later, interest expense is based on the market rate, rather than the stated rate, when the two rates are different.

[4] Current assets and current liabilities were defined and discussed in Chapter 2. Current assets are defined as cash and other resources reasonably expected to be realized in cash or sold or consumed within one year from the date of the balance sheet or during the **normal operating cycle,** whichever is longer.

An important financial relationship is the dollar difference between total current assets and total current liabilities. This difference is called **working capital.** The relationship between current assets and current liabilities also is measured as a ratio called the **current ratio** (or the working capital ratio). The current ratio is computed by dividing total current assets by total current liabilities. Assume the balance sheet for Nova Company on December 31, 19B, reported total current assets of $900,000 and total current liabilities of $300,000. The amount of working capital would be $900,000 − $300,000 = $600,000. The current ratio would be $900,000 ÷ $300,000 = 3.00, or 3 to 1. A current ratio of 3 to 1 means that at the balance sheet date there were $3 of current assets for each $1 of current liabilities. These relationships often help creditors and others in assessing the ability of a company to meet its short-term obligations.[5]

Current liabilities include trade accounts payable, short-term notes payable, accrued expenses (such as wages payable, taxes payable, and interest payable), cash dividends payable, the current portion of long-term debt, and revenues collected in advance (also called deferred or unearned revenues).

Accounts Payable

Trade accounts payable are created by purchases of goods for resale and services received in the normal course of business. The term **accounts payable** is used in accounting to mean trade accounts payable. Typical journal entries for an account payable are:

March 6, 19B (purchase on credit; terms 2/10, n/30; periodic inventory system):

Purchases	980	
Accounts payable		980
Purchase of merchandise on credit; terms 2/10, n/30. (Invoice price, $1,000 × 0.98 = $980.)		

March 11, 19B (payment of liability):[6]

Accounts payable	980	
Cash		980
Payment of account payable within the discount period.		

Accrued Expenses

Accrued expenses (also called accrued liabilities) arise when expenses have been incurred but have not yet been paid or recorded at the end of the accounting

---

[5] Interpretation of financial ratios is discussed in Chapter 16.

[6] In case of payment **after** the discount period, the entry would be (see Chapter 6):

Accounts payable	980	
Purchase discounts lost (or Interest expense)	20	
Cash		1,000

period. These liabilities are recorded as **adjusting entries.** To illustrate a typical accrued expense, assume that on December 31, 19B, the annual amount of property taxes for 19B was $1,600, which had not been paid or recorded. At the end of the accounting period, December 31, 19B, the expense and related liability must be recorded and reported. However, the amount will not be paid until January 15, 19C.[7] Therefore, the following **adjusting entry** must be made:

December 31, 19B (adjusting entry):

Property tax expense 1,600
    Property taxes payable   1,600
    Adjusting entry to record property taxes incurred in 19B not yet
    recorded or paid.

The entry in 19C for payment of the above liability would be:

January 15, 19C:

Property taxes payable 1,600
    Cash   1,600
    Payment of liability for property taxes accrued in 19B.

Payroll Liabilities

When employees perform services, the employer incurs an obligation that is not satisfied until the employees are paid on a weekly or monthly payroll basis. In previous chapters, accounting for wage and salary expense was simplified by disregarding payroll taxes and payroll deductions; we will now discuss these additional complications.

In addition to the obligation to the employee for salary or wages, the employer incurs other liabilities that are related directly to the payment of salaries and wages. These additional liabilities usually arise as a result of federal and provincial laws and contractual obligations (such as pension plans and union dues). Some of these liabilities are paid by the **employees** through the employer (as payroll deductions); others must be paid by the **employer** and thus are additional expenses to the business.

The take-home pay of most employees is considerably less than the gross salary or wages because of **payroll deductions** for such items as employee income taxes withheld, Canada Pension Plan (CPP) that must be paid by the employee, and other employee deductions such as insurance and union dues. The employer is required to pay the amounts, deducted from the wages, to the designated governmental agencies and other organizations such as the union. From the date of the payroll deduction until the date of payment to the agencies

---

[7] If these property taxes already had **been paid** (i.e., Expense debited and Cash credited), there would be no accrued liability to record at year-end. If these taxes **already had been recorded but not paid** (i.e., Expense debited and Taxes Payable credited), there would be no need to make an adjusting entry at year-end.

or organizations, the employer must record and report the **current liabilities** that are owed to the designated taxing agencies and other parties. A typical journal entry for a $100,000 payroll would be as follows:

```
Salaries expense  . . . . . . . . . . . . . . . . . . . . . . . . . . . . . . . . .   60,000
Wages expense  . . . . . . . . . . . . . . . . . . . . . . . . . . . . . . . . . .   40,000
    Liability for income taxes withheld—employees  . . . . . . . . . . .           21,000
    Liability for union dues withheld—employees  . . . . . . . . . . . .              400
    Unemployment insurance withheld  . . . . . . . . . . . . . . . . .             2,350
    CPP contributions withheld  . . . . . . . . . . . . . . . . . . . . .           1,455
    Cash (take-home pay)  . . . . . . . . . . . . . . . . . . . . . . . .          74,795
```
To record the payroll including employee deductions (see Supplement 10A).

In addition to the payroll taxes that the **employees** must pay through the employer, the **employer** is required by law to pay additional specified payroll taxes, such as the employer's share of the Canada Pension Plan and Unemployment Insurance (UI). These taxes constitute an operating expense for the business. Therefore, a second entry related to the payroll is needed to record the payroll taxes to be paid by the employer. A typical entry, related to the above payroll, would be as follows:

```
Payroll tax and benefits expense  . . . . . . . . . . . . . . . . . . . . . .   5,545*
    Unemployment insurance payable ($2,350 × 1.4)  . . . . . . . . . . . .          3,290
    Canada Pension Plan payable  . . . . . . . . . . . . . . . . . . . . .          1,455
    Worker's compensation payable . . . . . . . . . . . . . . . . . . . . .           800
```
Employer payroll taxes for (the particular) payroll.

* Total payroll expense: $100,000 + $5,545 = $105,545.

The five current liabilities recorded in the two entries immediately above will be paid in the near future when the company remits the requisite amounts of cash to the appropriate taxing agencies and other parties. Details involved in payroll accounting are discussed and illustrated in Supplement 10A to this chapter. Payroll accounting does not entail any new accounting concepts or principles; however, a significant amount of clerical detail is involved.

Deferred Revenues

Deferred revenues (often called unearned revenues or revenues collected in advance) arise when revenues are collected during the current period that will not be earned until a **later** accounting period (see Chapter 4).

Deferred revenues create a liability because cash has been collected but the related revenue has not been earned by the end of the accounting period. Therefore, there is a **current obligation** to render the services or to provide the goods in the future. For example, on November 15, 19B, rent revenue of $6,000 was collected. This amount was recorded as a debit to Cash and a credit to Rent Revenue. At the end of 19B, $2,000 of this amount was for January 19C rent. Thus, there is a current liability of $2,000 for deferred rent revenue that must be recognized. The sequence of entries for this case would be as follows:

November 15, 19B (collection of rent revenue):

Cash 6,000
      Rent revenue   6,000
  Collection of rent revenue.[8]

December 31, 19B (adjusting entry for unearned rent revenue):

Rent revenue 2,000
      Rent revenue collected in advance (deferred revenue)   2,000
  Adjusting entry to record unearned rent revenue at the end of
  the accounting period.

Estimated Liabilities

Coupons

Coupons represent a promotional device used by all types of companies. Bottle caps, clippings from various publications, labels, and package inserts all represent a liability on the part of the issuer to redeem those coupons that are submitted by the customer. To determine the estimated liability, two factors need to be considered: What is the cost of the incentive to the company per coupon? What proportion of the coupons issued will actually be redeemed by customers?

On December 1, 19A, Kampus Korner issued 1,000 coupons to its customers for a $5 credit toward the purchase of supplies made during the period January 3, 19B, to January 31, 19B, with the purchase of $50 of books. The coupon can only be redeemed against a single merchandise purchase during this period. Past experience with such promotions suggests a 60% redemption will be made for the full amount of the coupon. The average markup, based on selling price for the articles covered by the coupon, is 20%. Kampus Korner has a fiscal year ending December 31, 19A.

Kampus Korner will require an adjusting entry on December 31, 19A, to reflect the promotional expense associated with the sale of books and the obligation to redeem the coupons. The entry would be:

Promotional expense 2,400
      Liability for outstanding coupons   2,400
  $1,000 \times \$5 \times (1 - 0.20) \times 0.60 = \$2,400.$

The calculation determines the cost of each $5 coupon by multiplying it by the cost percentage $(1 - 0.20)$. The redemption estimate of 0.60 is then applied to the cost to ascertain the cost of the expected redemptions.

---

[8] On November 15, 19B, the $6,000 credit could have been made to Rent Revenue Collected in Advance. In that case the adjusting entry to give the same results on December 31, 19B, would be:

Rent revenue collected in advance 4,000
      Rent revenue   4,000

During January 19B, redemption of 620 coupons would be recorded as follows:

Liability for outstanding coupons 2,400
Promotional expense 80
    Inventory* 2,480
    20 × $5 × (1 − 0.20) = $80 (additional cost).

* The cost of inventory purchased by customers with the coupon. The additional 20 coupons represented a deviation from the original estimate.

Warranties and Service Contracts

Many items are sold that require the seller to repair or replace defective items. A variation of the common warranty is a service contract where for a fee the company will repair the article free of charge according to the terms of the contract.

To illustrate a warranty, assume Kampus Korner will replace defective books returned to the store during the first month of a term. Assume books sold in December 19A amounted to 3,000 volumes at an average price of $50. The defective books are returned by Kampus Korner to the publisher for an 80% refund of the cost price to Kampus. Kampus management estimates a 15% defective level among its book sales. The average markup on books is 10% of the sales price. The year-end estimated warranty costs would be recorded as follows:

Book replacement expense 4,050
    Liability for replacement of books 4,050
    [3,000 × 0.15 × $50 × (1 − 0.10)] × (1 − 0.80) = $4,050.

The estimate of defective sales (3,000 × 0.15 × $50) is converted to cost by multiplying by the cost percentage (1 − 0.10). This amount, the cost of defects, is converted to the cost to Kampus Korner by removing the recoveries from the book publisher (0.80) by multiplying by (1 − 0.80). When a book is returned in January, the following entry would occur:

Receivable from book publisher 36
Liability for replacement of books 9
    Book inventory 45
    $45 × 0.80 = $36; $45 × (1 − 0.80) = $9; $50 × (1 − 0.10) = $45.

Service contracts would be more likely to occur on computer sales. For a fee of say $100, computers sold by Kampus Korner would be serviced by company personnel. If 200 contracts were sold the following entry would be made:

Cash 20,000
    Unearned service contract revenue 20,000
    200 × $100 = $20,000.

To recognize the revenue on the service contract, the company has to estimate the pattern of claims over the term of the contract. Usually more claims occur during the early part of the contract than later. If 20% of the claims are expected in January then the entry for revenue would be:

```
Unearned service contract revenue  . . . . . . . . . . . . . . . . . . . . . .   4,000
    Service contract revenue  . . . . . . . . . . . . . . . . . . . . . . . . . .          4,000
    0.20 × $20,000 = $4,000.
```

The cost of this revenue would be the labour and materials needed for each claim submitted by customers.

Long-Term Liabilities

Long-term liabilities include all obligations of the entity not classified as current liabilities. Long-term liabilities often are incurred when purchasing operational assets or borrowing large amounts of cash for asset replacements and major expansions of the business. Long-term liabilities usually are represented by long-term **notes payable** or **bonds payable.** A long-term liability often is supported by a mortgage on specified assets of the borrower **pledged** as security for the liability. A mortgage has a separate document that is appended to the note payable. A liability supported by a mortgage is a **"secured** debt." An **unsecured** debt is one for which the creditor relies primarily on the integrity and general earning power of the borrower.

Long-term liabilities are reported on the balance sheet (immediately following current liabilities) under a separate caption "Long-term liabilities." As a long-term debt approaches the maturity date, the part of it that is to be paid from current assets is reclassified as a current liability. For example, a five-year note payable of $50,000 was signed on January 1, 19A. Repayment is in two installments as follows: December 31, 19D, $25,000; and December 31, 19E, $25,000. The December 31, 19B, 19C, and 19D balance sheets would report the following:

```
December 31, 19B:
    Long-term liabilities:
        Note payable  . . . . . . . . . . . . . .   $50,000
December 31, 19C:
    Current liabilities:
        Maturing portion of long-term note  . . .   25,000
    Long-term liabilities:
        Long-term note  . . . . . . . . . . . . .   25,000
December 31, 19D:
    Current liabilities:
        Maturing portion of long-term note  . . .   25,000
```

Notes payable may be either short term or long term. A short-term note payable usually has a maturity date within one year from the balance sheet date. Short-term notes often arise as a result of borrowing cash or from purchasing merchandise or services on credit. Bonds payable (discussed in Chapter 11) always are long-term liabilities, except for any currently maturing portion as shown above for the long-term note payable.

Notes Payable

A note payable (short term or long term) is a written promise to pay a stated sum at one or more specified future dates. A note payable may require a single-sum repayment at the due or maturity date or it may call for installment payments (called an annuity). Consider the purchase of a sailboat for $3,000, with a $1,000 cash down payment and a note payable for the balance. The note specifies 12 equal monthly payments that include principal and interest.

Notes payable require the payment of interest and the recording of interest expense. Interest expense is incurred on liabilities because of the **time value of money.** The word **time** is significant because the longer borrowed money is held, the larger is the total dollar amount of interest expense. Thus, one must pay more interest for a two-year loan of a given amount, at a given **interest rate,** than for a one-year loan. To the **borrower, interest is an expense;** whereas to the **lender (creditor), interest is a revenue.** Interest rates usually are quoted on an **annual** basis.

To calculate interest, three variables must be considered: (1) the principal, (2) the interest rate, and (3) the duration of time. Therefore, the interest formula is:

$$\text{Interest} = \text{Principal} \times \text{Rate} \times \text{Time}$$

Accounting for an Interest-Bearing Note

On November 1, 19A, Baker Company borrowed $10,000 cash on a six-month, 12%, interest-bearing note payable. The interest is payable at the maturity date of the note. The computation of interest expense would be: $10,000 \times 12\% \times \frac{6}{12}$ = $600. This note would be recorded in the accounts as follows:

November 1, 19A:

```
Cash . . . . . . . . . . . . . . . . . . . . . . . . . . . . . . . . . . . . . . . . . . . .  10,000
      Note payable, short term  . . . . . . . . . . . . . . . . . . . . . . . . . . .            10,000
   Borrowed on short-term note; terms, six months at 12% per annum;
   interest is payable at maturity.
```

Interest is an expense of the period when the money is used (unpaid); therefore, it is measured, recorded, and reported on a **time basis** rather than when the cash actually is paid or borrowed. This concept is based on legal as well as economic considerations. For example, if the $10,000 loan cited above were paid off in two months instead of in six months, interest amounting to $10,000 \times 12\% \times \frac{2}{12}$ = $200 would have to be paid.

The **adjusting entry** for accrued interest payable would be made at the end of the accounting period on the basis of time expired from the last interest date or from the date of the note. Assume the accounting period for Baker Company ends December 31, 19A. Although the $600 interest for the six months will not be paid until April 30, 19B, two months' unpaid interest (i.e., November and December 19A) must be **accrued** by means of the following adjusting entry by Baker Company:

December 31, 19A:

```
Interest expense . . . . . . . . . . . . . . . . . . . . . . . . . . . . . . . . . . . . . . . .   200
   Interest payable . . . . . . . . . . . . . . . . . . . . . . . . . . . . . . . . . . . . . . .        200
   Adjusting entry to accrue two months' interest ($10,000 × 12% × 2/12
   = $200).
```

At maturity date the payment of principal plus interest for six months would be recorded as follows:[9]

April 30, 19B:

```
Notes payable, short term . . . . . . . . . . . . . . . . . . . . . . . . . . . . .   10,000
Interest payable (per prior entry) . . . . . . . . . . . . . . . . . . . . . . .      200
Interest expense ($10,000 × 12% × 4/12) . . . . . . . . . . . . . . . . . .      400
   Cash ($10,000 + $600 interest) . . . . . . . . . . . . . . . . . . . . . .            10,600
   To record payment of note payable including interest.
```

Accounting for a note payable is the same whether it is classified as a current or as a long-term liability. Accounting for a note payable also is the same regardless of the purpose for which the note was executed.

Accounting for a Noninterest-Bearing Note

A noninterest-bearing note includes the interest amount in the face of the note. This causes a difference in the accounting entries. For example, if the Baker note above was noninterest-bearing, its face amount would be $10,600 (i.e., the principal amount plus interest). The journal entries would be:

November 1, 19A (date of note):

```
Cash . . . . . . . . . . . . . . . . . . . . . . . . . . . . . . . . . . . . . . . . . . . .   10,000
Discount on note payable . . . . . . . . . . . . . . . . . . . . . . . . . . . . . .      600
   Note payable (noninterest-bearing) . . . . . . . . . . . . . . . . . . . . . .            10,600
```

December 31, 19A (adjusting entry):

```
Interest expense ($10,000 × 12% × 2/12) . . . . . . . . . . . . . . . . . .      200
   Discount on note payable . . . . . . . . . . . . . . . . . . . . . . . . . . . . .            200
```

April 30, 19B (maturity date):

```
Note payable (noninterest-bearing) . . . . . . . . . . . . . . . . . . . . . .   10,600
Interest expense ($10,000 × 12% × 4/12) . . . . . . . . . . . . . . . . . .      400
   Discount on note payable ($600 − $200) . . . . . . . . . . . . . . . . .            400
   Cash . . . . . . . . . . . . . . . . . . . . . . . . . . . . . . . . . . . . . . . . . . .            10,600
```

The 19A balance sheet will report the note at $10,200 (i.e., Face amount, $10,600 − Unamortized discount, $400).

---

[9] This journal entry assumes no reversing entry was made on January 1, 19C. (See Supplement 5A.) If a reversing entry of the accrual had been made on January 1, 19C, the payment entry would have been:

```
Notes payable, short term . . . . . . . . . . . . . . . . . . . . . . . . . . . . . . .   10,000
Interest expense . . . . . . . . . . . . . . . . . . . . . . . . . . . . . . . . . . . . . .      600
   Cash . . . . . . . . . . . . . . . . . . . . . . . . . . . . . . . . . . . . . . . . . . . .            10,600
```

Deferred Income Tax Allocations[10]

The preceding chapters discussed income taxes paid by corporations. Income tax expense is reported on the income statement, and income tax payable is reported as a liability on the balance sheet. In addition to income tax payable, most corporate balance sheets report another tax item called **future income taxes.**

The concept of future income tax is that **income tax expense** should be based on the **taxable income** reported on the income statement. However, **income tax payable** necessarily must be based on the taxable income shown on the **tax return** (i.e., as specified in the tax laws). Often there is a difference between the time when certain revenues or expenses (which affect income taxes) appear on the income statement and when they appear on the tax return. Thus, a future income tax amount will occur whenever there is a **timing difference** between when a taxable revenue or tax-deductible expense appears on the income statement and when it appears on the tax return. Future income taxes are created only by a timing difference. Future income taxes will "reverse" or "turn around" because the taxable items will appear on both the income statement and tax return but in different periods. Consider a $10,000 taxable revenue that is reported on the 19A income statement but not on the 19A tax return. This timing difference will cause the recording of a future income tax liability in 19A. In 19B, when the $10,000 taxable revenue is reported on the tax return (but not on the income statement), the future income tax amount is reduced to zero (i.e., it "reverses"). Likewise, when a tax-deductible expense is on the income statement and the tax return in different periods, a timing difference must be accounted for. Accounting for future income taxes is illustrated in Exhibit 10–1.

Observe in Exhibit 10–1 that income tax expense for Web Corporation (on the income statement) does not agree with income tax payable on the balance sheet in years 19A and 19C. However, the totals for the three years agree ($27,000).

The difference between "income tax expense" on the income statement and "income tax payable" on the balance sheet in Exhibit 10–1 was due in this example to a single expense—depreciation. Web Corporation purchased a depreciable asset at the beginning of 19A that cost $12,000 and had a useful life of three years with no residual value. The company used straight-line depreciation in its accounts (and on its income statement) and capital cost allowance on its tax

---

[10] CICA Accounting Standards Committee in November 1988 issued a proposed new treatment for income tax allocations. The major effect of the change for material presented in this text is a change in the terminology used for balance sheet disclosure of the income tax effects of timing differences. The terms **future income tax asset** and **future income tax liability** are proposed as a replacement for the terms **deferred income tax charge (debit)** and **deferred income tax credit.** While more far-reaching effects of the proposed change are beyond the scope of this book, it is important to note the new proposal makes the treatment of timing differences between accounting and taxable incomes closer to the definitions of assets and liabilities than were those of deferred tax debits and credits used previously. However, no attempt to use the time value of money (present values) in valuing these assets or liabilities is contemplated in the exposure draft. Discussion from this point in the text will use the new terminology where possible.

Exhibit 10–1 Future income taxes illustrated

Situation—Web Corporation:

a. Depreciation—Straight-line depreciation on income statement and capital cost allowance on income tax return:

	19A	19B	19C
Income statement:			
Income before depreciation expense and before income tax expense	$34,000	$34,000	$34,000
Depreciation expense	4,000	4,000	4,000
Pretax income	30,000	30,000	30,000
Income tax expense (30%)	9,000	9,000	9,000
Net income	$21,000	$21,000	$21,000
Balance sheet (December 31):			
Liability:			
Income tax payable	$ 9,300	$ 8,400	$ 9,300
Future income tax		300Dr*	300Cr*

*Cumulative balance (as an asset or liability).

Computation of income tax and income tax payable as reported above:

a. Depreciation expense computed:

Year	Straight-line depreciation (for income statement)	Capital cost allowance— amounts assumed (for tax purposes)
19A	$4,000	$3,000
19B	4,000	6,000
19C	4,000	3,000

b. Computation of tax **expense** as reported on the income statement:

	19A	19B	19C
Income before depreciation expense and before income tax expense	$34,000	$34,000	$34,000
Less: Depreciation expense (straight line)	4,000	4,000	4,000
Amount subject to tax	30,000	30,000	30,000
Income tax expense (30%)	$ 9,000	$ 9,000	$ 9,000 ←

c. Computation of income tax **payable** as reported on the tax return:

	19A	19B	19C	
Income before depreciation expense and before income taxes	$34,000	$34,000	$34,000	Compare these
Less: Capital allowance	3,000	6,000	3,000	amounts*
Amount subject to tax	31,000	28,000	31,000	
Income tax **payable** (30%)	$ 9,300	$ 8,400	$ 9,300 ←	

Entries to record income taxes:

	19A		19B		19C	
Income tax expense (from income statement)	9,000		9,000		9,000	
Income tax payable (from tax return)		9,300		8,400		9,300
Future income tax (the difference)	300			600	300	

return. This timing difference caused a difference between income tax expense and income tax payable as shown in Exhibit 10–1.

Future Income Tax is recorded when a difference exists between income tax expense and income tax payable. Web Corporation would record future income tax each year as shown in Exhibit 10–1.

The $300 Future Income Tax amount for 19A would be classified as an asset on the balance sheet, the $300 cumulative future income tax for 19B would be classified as a liability, and no amount of future income tax would be reported in 19C. This effect occurred because the disadvantage (of capital cost allowance being $1,000 less than depreciation) in 19A was reversed in 19B when the capital cost allowance became $2,000 greater than the depreciation expense. The cumulative net balance of $300 credit in 19B was again reversed in 19C. Recall that regardless of the method of depreciation used, only the cost of the asset (less any residual value) can be depreciated for accounting purposes ($12,000 in the example above). Also, this illustration demonstrates what has been noted before—the potential economic advantage or disadvantage of capital cost allowance over straight-line depreciation is only the time value of money. That is, the tax savings resulting from using extra capital cost allowance in early years can be invested to earn a certain return during 19C.

Future tax amounts often are very large. For example, Consolidated-Bathurst reported a deferred income tax balance of $295,834,000 which represented 13% of their total assets.

It is possible to have a debit balance in future income taxes, but such a situation is not typical because the tax law usually does not require "early" tax payments. If the future income tax account has a debit balance, it would be reported under assets on the balance sheet as a prepaid expense (if short term) or other asset (if long term).

Section 3470 of the *CICA Handbook*, "Corporate Income Taxes," specifies that future income tax shall be recorded **only** when there is a timing difference between the income statement and the tax return. A timing difference occurs only when an item of revenue or expense will be included on **both** the income statement and the tax return in different years so that the deferred tax effect automatically will reverse (as illustrated in Exhibit 10–1). Another type of difference between the income statement and tax return amounts is called a **permanent difference.** A permanent difference does not create a future income tax because the revenue or expense appears on either the income statement or the tax return, but not both. For example, part of capital gains which is not taxed is included on the income statement of the recipient, but is not reported on the recipient's income tax return as income for tax purposes.

On the balance sheet, the total amount of future income tax must be reported in part in the current liability (or asset) section and in part in the long-term liability (or asset) section depending upon the classification of the specific asset that gave rise to the deferred tax amount. Thus, the future income tax amount for Web Corporation would be classified as noncurrent because it was related to a noncurrent asset.

This discussion of future income taxes was presented so that you will understand the nature of future income tax reported on the balance sheets of most medium and large corporations. Income tax payable (as a liability) is easy to comprehend; however, many statement users have had difficulty understanding the other tax item—deferred (future) income tax.

The conceptual nature of future taxes has been a complex matter that has been debated for years among practitioners and academics. The justification for deferred (future) taxes in the professional pronouncements was the need to match income tax expense with the accounting income that was earned in a fiscal period. The conceptual difficulty was that the resulting balance sheet-deferred tax debits and credits could not be easily justified as assets or liabilities. The result of this difficulty was to have deferred charges or credits that were classified as assets or liabilities yet did not satisfy the criteria of an asset or a liability such as the ones set out in Exhibit 4–5. The proposed new treatment of future income tax should help alleviate some of the conceptual difficulties, because the treatment of the tax timing effects is more consistent with the conceptual nature of assets and liabilities than were the previous deferred tax balances.

Contingent Liabilities

A contingent liability is defined as a potential liability that has arisen because of an event or transaction that **already has occurred.** However, its conversion to an effective liability depends on the occurrence of one or more **future events** or transactions (i.e., a future contingency). A contingent liability also causes a **contingency loss.** For accounting purposes, contingencies are classified as follows:[11]

a. **Likely**—the chance that future event or events will occur is high.

b. **Unlikely**—the chance of occurrence of the future event or events is slight.

At the end of the accounting period, the company must determine whether the **amount** of any contingent liability can be "reasonably estimated." The general accounting guidelines are: (1) a contingent liability that is both likely and can be **reasonably estimated** must be **recorded** and reported in the financial statements, (2) a contingent liability that is likely but cannot be reasonably estimated must be **disclosed** in a note in the financial statements. Unlikely material contingent losses should also be disclosed. For example, during 19B, Baker Company was sued for $200,000 damages based on an accident involving one of the trucks owned by the company. The suit is scheduled to start during March 19C. Whether there is an effective (i.e., enforceable) liability at the end of 19B (end of the accounting period) depends upon a future event—the decision of the court at the end of the trial.

---

[11] *CICA Handbook,* Section 3290, "Contingencies."

Case A. Baker Company and its legal counsel determines that (1) it is likely that damages will be assessed, and (2) a reasonable estimate is $150,000. Therefore, Baker must make the following entry:

December 31, 19B:

Loss due to accident 150,000
     Estimated liability due to accident 150,000

The loss is reported on the 19B income statement, and the liability is reported on the 19B balance sheet. A note would disclose that the loss could potentially be $50,000 more than the best estimate recorded.

Case B. Baker Company determines that (1) it is likely that damages will be assessed, and (2) a reasonable estimate cannot be made. Therefore, Baker must disclose the contingency by a note in the 19B balance sheet similar to the following:

> The company was sued for $200,000 based on an accident involving a company vehicle. Legal counsel believes that the suit lacks merit; however, it is reasonably possible that some damages will be assessed. The amount cannot be reasonably estimated at this date. The trial is scheduled for March 19C.

The amount recorded for a likely contingent liability is the best estimate from a range of possible losses or the minimum amount (a rather unconservative practice) if no best estimate is available. The remainder of the potential loss should be disclosed in a footnote. Contingent gains are also possible. Conservative recording for such gains is applied in that likely contingent gains are recorded as a footnote until the asset is actually received or a liability reduced. Footnote disclosure of contingencies should include the existence of the contingency, its nature, the estimated amount or the fact that an estimate is not possible, and how the subsequent settlement will be accounted for.

Controlling Expenditures with a Voucher System

The purchase of merchandise, services, and operational assets often requires that either a short-term or long-term liability be recorded. Therefore, a large number of cash payments on liabilities are made in a business. In most companies, control over cash expenditures prevents the misapplication of cash in the cash disbursement process. In a very small business, it is possible for the owner to give personal attention to each transaction and to make each cash payment. This personal attention may assure that the business is getting what it pays for, that cash is not being disbursed carelessly, and that there is no theft or fraud involving cash.

As a business grows and becomes more complex, the owner or top executive cannot devote personal attention to each transaction involving the processing of cash disbursements. In such cases, these activities must be assigned to various employees. The assignment of these responsibilities to others creates a need for systematic and effective procedures for the control of cash expenditures. This facet is important in the internal control of a well-designed accounting system.

Chapter 8 discussed the essential features of effective **internal control.** The emphasis was on the control of cash receipts. Similar internal control procedures were discussed for cash disbursements: the separation of duties, disbursement of cash by cheque, petty cash, and two special journals—the purchases journal and the cash disbursements journal. In larger companies and in computerized accounting systems, the method usually used for maintaining control over cash expenditures is the **voucher system.** This system replaces the cash disbursements journal that was explained in Supplement 8B.

A voucher system establishes strict control over those transactions that create a legal obligation for an **expenditure of cash.** The system requires that a **written authorization,** called a **voucher,** be approved by one or more designated managers at the time each such transaction occurs. An approved voucher is required regardless of whether the transaction involves the purchase of merchandise or services, the acquisition of operational assets, the payment of a liability, or an investment. The system permits cheques to be issued only in payment of properly prepared and approved vouchers. Cheque writing is kept separate from the voucher-approval, cheque-approval, and cheque-distribution procedures.

The voucher system requires that every obligation be supported by a previously approved voucher and that each transaction be recorded when incurred. The incurrence of each obligation is treated as an independent transaction. Also, each payment of cash is treated as another independent transaction. This sequence of voucher approval, followed by payment by cheque, is required even in strictly cash disbursement transactions. A **cash** purchase of merchandise for resale would be recorded under the voucher system as follows:

1. To record the incurrence of an obligation (with a periodic inventory system):

Purchases	1,000	
Vouchers payable		1,000

2. To record payment of the obligation by cheque (immediately thereafter):

Vouchers payable	1,000	
Cash		1,000

In a voucher system, the account designated **Vouchers Payable** replaces the account entitled Accounts Payable; but the designation on the balance sheet continues to be "Accounts Payable." The incurrence entries (1 above) are entered in a **voucher register,** and the payment entries (2 above) are entered in a **cheque register.**

The primary objective of the voucher system is to have continuous control over each step in an expenditure from the incurrence of an obligation to the final disbursement of cash to satisfy the obligation. Thus, each transaction that leads to a cash payment, and the cash payment itself, are reviewed systematically. Then it is subjected to an approval system based on separately designated responsibilities. Supplement 10B discusses and illustrates the **mechanics** of the voucher system.

PART B—FUTURE VALUE AND PRESENT VALUE CONCEPTS

Concepts

The measuring and reporting of liabilities, when they are first recorded in the accounts and during the periods they are outstanding, often involve application of the concepts of present value and future value. These concepts also are used in measuring the effects of long-term investments in bonds, leases, pension plans, and sinking funds. In accounting, most of these applications involve either measurement of a liability or a receivable, or the establishment of a fund of cash to be used in the future for some special purpose (such as for the retirement of debt).

The concepts of future value (FV) and present value (PV) focus on the time value of money, which is another name for interest. The **time value of money** refers to the fact that a dollar received today is worth more than a dollar received one year from today (or at any other future date). If a dollar received today can be invested at 10%, it will increase to $1.10 in one year. In contrast, if the dollar is to be received one year from today, the opportunity to earn the $0.10 interest revenue for the year is lost. The difference between the $1 and $1.10 is interest that can be earned during the year. Interest is the cost of the use of money for a specific period of time, just as rent represents the cost for use of a tangible asset for a period of time. Interest may be specified (i.e., stated explicitly), as in the case of an interest-bearing note. Also, it may be unspecified, as in a noninterest-bearing note (but interest is still paid; i.e., it is implicitly incurred).

To illustrate, Company A bought a machine for $20,000. Company A will pay the $20,000 at the end of two years. There is an implied interest rate of 12% (which is the market rate of interest). The $20,000 to be paid represents the current cash equivalent amount of the debt **plus** the interest that will be paid during the two years. In conformity with the **cost principle,** the machine account should be debited for the present value (current cash equivalent cost, excluding interest) of the debt, or $15,944 (see page 591).

There are four different types of problems related to the time value of money; they are identified in Exhibit 10–2. Each type of problem is based on the interest formula that was discussed in Part A of this chapter.

$$\text{Interest} = \text{Principal} \times \text{Rate} \times \text{Time}$$

In **future value** problems, you will be given the amount of cash (principal) to be invested at the current date and you will be asked to use the basic interest formula to calculate the amount of principal plus interest that will be available at some **future date.** In contrast, **present value** problems involve a rearrangement of the basic interest formula. In present value problems, you will be given the amount that will be available at some **future date** (principal plus interest), and you will be asked to calculate the **current** cash equivalent of that amount.

Exhibit 10–2 Four types of future and present value problems

Payment or Receipt	Symbol	
	Future Value	Present Value
Single amount	f	p
Annuity (equal payments or receipts for a series of equal time periods)	F	P

Tables are used to avoid the detailed arithmetic calculations that are required in future value and present value computations. Tables 10–1 through 10–4 (pages 582–85) give values for each of the four types of problems for different periods of time (*n*) and at different rates of interest (*i*). The values given in the tables are based on payments of $1. If a problem involves payments other than $1, it is necessary to multiply the value from the table by the amount of the payment.[12] We will examine each of the four types of present value and future value problems.

Future and Present Values of a Single Amount

Future Value of a Single Amount (f)

The future value of a single amount (i.e., the principal) is the sum to which that amount will increase at *i* interest rate for *n* periods. The future sum will be the **principal plus compound interest.** The future value concept is based on compound interest. Therefore, the amount of interest for each period is calculated by multiplying the interest rate by the principal plus any interest that accrued in prior interest periods but was not paid out.

To illustrate, on January 1, 19A, $1,000 was deposited in a savings account at 10% annual interest, compounded annually. At the end of three years, that is, on December 31, 19C, the $1,000 originally deposited would increase to $1,331 as follows:

Year	Amount at start of year	+	Interest during the year	=	Amount at end of year
1	$1,000	+	$1,000 × 10% = $100*	=	$1,100
2	1,100	+	1,100 × 10% = 110	=	1,210
3	1,210	+	1,210 × 10% = 121	=	1,331

* Rounded.

[12] Present value and future value problems assume cash flows. The basic concepts are the same for cash inflows (receipts) and cash outflows (payments). Thus, there are no fundamental differences between present value and future value calculations for cash payments versus cash receipts.

Table 10–1 Future value of $1, $f = (1 + i)^n$

Periods	2%	3%	3.75%	4%	4.25%	5%	6%	7%	8%
0	1.	1.	1.	1.	1.	1.	1.	1.	1.
1	1.02	1.03	1.0375	1.04	1.0425	1.05	1.06	1.07	1.08
2	1.0404	1.0609	1.0764	1.0816	1.0868	1.1025	1.1236	1.1449	1.1664
3	1.0612	1.0927	1.1168	1.1249	1.1330	1.1576	1.1910	1.2250	1.2597
4	1.0824	1.1255	1.1587	1.1699	1.1811	1.2155	1.2625	1.3108	1.3605
5	1.1041	1.1593	1.2021	1.2167	1.2313	1.2763	1.3382	1.4026	1.4693
6	1.1262	1.1941	1.2472	1.2653	1.2837	1.3401	1.4185	1.5007	1.5869
7	1.1487	1.2299	1.2939	1.3159	1.3382	1.4071	1.5036	1.6058	1.7138
8	1.1717	1.2668	1.3425	1.3686	1.3951	1.4775	1.5938	1.7182	1.8509
9	1.1951	1.3048	1.3928	1.4233	1.4544	1.5513	1.6895	1.8385	1.9990
10	1.2190	1.3439	1.4450	1.4802	1.5162	1.6289	1.7908	1.9672	2.1589
20	1.4859	1.8061	2.0882	2.1911	2.2989	2.6533	3.2071	3.8697	4.6610

Periods	9%	10%	11%	12%	13%	14%	15%	20%	25%
0	1.	1.	1.	1.	1.	1.	1.	1.	1.
1	1.09	1.10	1.11	1.12	1.13	1.14	1.15	1.20	1.25
2	1.1881	1.2100	1.2321	1.2544	1.2769	1.2996	1.3225	1.4400	1.5625
3	1.2950	1.3310	1.3676	1.4049	1.4429	1.4815	1.5209	1.7280	1.9531
4	1.4116	1.4641	1.5181	1.5735	1.6305	1.6890	1.7490	2.0736	2.4414
5	1.5386	1.6105	1.6851	1.7623	1.8424	1.9254	2.0114	2.4883	3.0518
6	1.6771	1.7716	1.8704	1.9738	2.0820	2.1950	2.3131	2.9860	3.8147
7	1.8280	1.9487	2.0762	2.2107	2.3526	2.5023	2.6600	3.5832	4.7684
8	1.9926	2.1436	2.3045	2.4760	2.6584	2.8526	3.0590	4.2998	5.9605
9	2.1719	2.3579	2.5580	2.7731	3.0040	3.2519	3.5179	5.1598	7.4506
10	2.3674	2.5937	2.8394	3.1058	3.3946	3.7072	4.0456	6.1917	9.3132
20	5.6044	6.7275	8.0623	9.6463	11.5231	13.7435	16.3665	38.3376	86.7362

However, we can avoid the detailed arithmetic by referring to Table 10–1, **Future value of $1** (f). For $i = 10\%$; $n = 3$, we find the value 1.331. Therefore, we can compute the balance at the end of Year 3 as $1,000 × 1.331 = $1,331. The increase of $331 was due to the time value of money. It would be interest revenue to you and interest expense to the savings institution. A convenient format to display the computations for this problem is: $1,000 × $f_{i=10\%;\ n=3}$ (Table 10–1; 1.3310) = $1,331. The table value for the future value of $1 always will be greater than $1. Exhibit 10–3 gives a summary of this future value concept.

Present Value of a Single Amount (p)

Present value of a single amount is the value now (i.e., at the present time) of an amount to be received at some date in the future. It is the **inverse** of the future value concept. To compute the present value of a sum to be received in the future, the sum is subjected to compound **discounting** at i interest rate for n

Table 10–2 Present value of $1, $p = \dfrac{1}{(1 + i)^n}$

Periods	2%	3%	3.75%	4%	4.25%	5%	6%	7%	8%
1	0.9804	0.9709	0.9639	0.9615	0.9592	0.9524	0.9434	0.9346	0.9259
2	0.9612	0.9426	0.9290	0.9246	0.9201	0.9070	0.8900	0.8734	0.8573
3	0.9423	0.9151	0.8954	0.8890	0.8826	0.8638	0.8396	0.8163	0.7938
4	0.9238	0.8885	0.8631	0.8548	0.8466	0.8227	0.7921	0.7629	0.7350
5	0.9057	0.8626	0.8319	0.8219	0.8121	0.7835	0.7473	0.7130	0.6806
6	0.8880	0.8375	0.8018	0.7903	0.7790	0.7462	0.7050	0.6663	0.6302
7	0.8706	0.8131	0.7728	0.7599	0.7473	0.7107	0.6651	0.6227	0.5835
8	0.8535	0.7894	0.7449	0.7307	0.7168	0.6768	0.6274	0.5820	0.5403
9	0.8368	0.7664	0.7180	0.7026	0.6876	0.6446	0.5919	0.5439	0.5002
10	0.8203	0.7441	0.6920	0.6756	0.6595	0.6139	0.5584	0.5083	0.4632
20	0.6730	0.5534	0.4789	0.4564	0.4350	0.3769	0.3118	0.2584	0.2145

Periods	9%	10%	11%	12%	13%	14%	15%	20%	25%
1	0.9174	0.9091	0.9009	0.8929	0.8850	0.8772	0.8696	0.8333	0.8000
2	0.8417	0.8264	0.8116	0.7972	0.7831	0.7695	0.7561	0.6944	0.6400
3	0.7722	0.7513	0.7312	0.7118	0.6931	0.6750	0.6575	0.5787	0.5120
4	0.7084	0.6830	0.6587	0.6355	0.6133	0.5921	0.5718	0.4823	0.4096
5	0.6499	0.6209	0.5935	0.5674	0.5428	0.5194	0.4972	0.4019	0.3277
6	0.5963	0.5645	0.5346	0.5066	0.4803	0.4556	0.4323	0.3349	0.2621
7	0.5470	0.5132	0.4817	0.4523	0.4251	0.3996	0.3759	0.2791	0.2097
8	0.5019	0.4665	0.4339	0.4039	0.3762	0.3506	0.3269	0.2326	0.1678
9	0.4604	0.4241	0.3909	0.3606	0.3329	0.3075	0.2843	0.1938	0.1342
10	0.4224	0.3855	0.3522	0.3220	0.2946	0.2697	0.2472	0.1615	0.1074
20	0.1784	0.1486	0.1240	0.1037	0.0868	0.0728	0.0611	0.0261	0.0115

periods. In compound discounting, the interest is subtracted rather than added (as in compounding). To illustrate, today is January 1, 19A, and you will receive $1,000 cash on December 31, 19C; that is, three years from now. With an interest rate of 10% per year, how much would the $1,000 be worth today; that is, what is its present value (today, on January 1, 19A)? We could set up a discounting computation, year by year, that would be the **inverse** to the tabulation shown above for the future value.[13] However, to facilitate the computation, we can refer to the **Present value of $1 table** (p), Table 10–2. For $i = 10\%$; $n = 3$, we find

---

[13] The detailed discounting would be as follows:

Periods	Discounting, inverse with reciprocal	Present value*
1	$1,000 × 1/1.10	= $909.10
2	$909.10 × 1/1.10	= 826.40
3	$826.40 × 1/1.10	= 751.30

* Verifiable in Table 10–2, with roundings.

Table 10–3 Future value of annuity of $1 (ordinary), $F = \dfrac{(1 + i)^n - 1}{i}$

Period rents*	2%	3%	3.75%	4%	4.25%	5%	6%	7%	8%
1	1.	1.	1.	1.	1.	1.	1.	1.	1.
2	2.02	2.03	2.0375	2.04	2.0425	2.05	2.06	2.07	2.08
3	3.0604	3.0909	3.1139	3.1216	3.1293	3.1525	3.1836	3.2149	3.2464
4	4.1216	4.1836	4.2307	4.2465	4.2623	4.3101	4.3746	4.4399	4.5061
5	5.2040	5.3091	5.3893	5.4163	5.4434	5.5256	5.6371	5.7507	5.8666
6	6.3081	6.4684	6.5914	6.6330	6.6748	6.8019	6.9753	7.1533	7.3359
7	7.4343	7.6625	7.8386	7.8983	7.9585	8.1420	8.3938	8.6540	8.9228
8	8.5830	8.8923	9.1326	9.2142	9.2967	9.5491	9.8975	10.2598	10.6366
9	9.7546	10.1591	10.4750	10.5828	10.6918	11.0266	11.4913	11.9780	12.4876
10	10.9497	11.4639	11.8678	12.0061	12.1462	12.5779	13.1808	13.8164	14.4866
20	24.2974	26.8704	29.0174	29.7781	30.5625	33.0660	36.7856	40.9955	45.7620

Period rents*	9%	10%	11%	12%	13%	14%	15%	20%	25%
1	1.	1.	1.	1.	1.	1.	1.	1.	1.
2	2.09	2.10	2.11	2.12	2.13	2.14	2.15	2.20	2.25
3	3.2781	3.3100	3.3421	3.3744	3.4069	3.4396	3.4725	3.6400	3.8125
4	4.5731	4.6410	4.7097	4.7793	4.8498	4.9211	4.9934	5.3680	5.7656
5	5.9847	6.1051	6.2278	6.3528	6.4803	6.6101	6.7424	7.4416	8.2070
6	7.5233	7.7156	7.9129	8.1152	8.3227	8.5355	8.7537	9.9299	11.2588
7	9.2004	9.4872	9.7833	10.0890	10.4047	10.7305	11.0668	12.9159	15.0735
8	11.0285	11.4359	11.8594	12.2997	12.7573	13.2328	13.7268	16.4991	19.8419
9	13.0210	13.5975	14.1640	14.7757	15.4157	16.0853	16.7858	20.7989	25.8023
10	15.1929	15.9374	16.7220	17.5487	18.4197	19.3373	20.3037	25.9587	33.2529
20	51.1601	57.2750	64.2028	72.0524	80.9468	91.0249	102.4436	186.6880	342.9447

* There is one rent each period.

the present value of $1 is 0.7513. The $1,000, to be received at the end of three years, has a **present value** (today) of $1,000 × 0.7513 = $751.30. The difference (i.e., the discount) of $248.70 is the time value of money; it is the interest. A convenient format to display the computations for this problem is: $1,000 × $p_{i=10\%;\ n=3}$ (Table 10–2; 0.7513) = $751.30. The table value for the present values of $1 will always be less than $1. The concept of the present value of $1 is summarized in Exhibit 10–3.

Future and Present Values of an Annuity

An annuity means that instead of a single amount, there is a **series of consecutive payments** (often called rents) characterized by:

Table 10-4 Present value of annuity of $1 (ordinary), $P = \dfrac{1 - \dfrac{1}{(1 + i)^n}}{i}$

Period rents*	2%	3%	3.75%	4%	4.25%	5%	6%	7%	8%
1	0.9804	0.9709	0.9639	0.9615	0.9592	0.9524	0.9434	0.9346	0.9259
2	1.9416	1.9135	1.8929	1.8861	1.8794	1.8594	1.8334	1.8080	1.7833
3	2.8839	2.8286	2.7883	2.7751	2.7620	2.7232	2.6730	2.6243	2.5771
4	3.8077	3.7171	3.6514	3.6299	3.6086	3.5460	3.4651	3.3872	3.3121
5	4.7135	4.5797	4.4833	4.4518	4.4207	4.3295	4.2124	4.1002	3.9927
6	5.6014	5.4172	5.2851	5.2421	5.1997	5.0757	4.9173	4.7665	4.6229
7	6.4720	6.2303	6.0579	6.0021	5.9470	5.7864	5.5824	5.3893	5.2064
8	7.3255	7.0197	6.8028	6.7327	6.6638	6.4632	6.2098	5.9713	5.7466
9	8.1622	7.7861	7.5208	7.4353	7.3513	7.1078	6.8017	6.5152	6.2469
10	8.9826	8.5302	8.2128	8.1109	8.0109	7.7217	7.3601	7.0236	6.7101
20	16.3514	14.8775	13.8962	13.5903	13.2944	12.4622	11.4699	10.5940	9.8181

Period rents*	9%	10%	11%	12%	13%	14%	15%	20%	25%
1	0.9174	0.9091	0.9009	0.8929	0.8850	0.8772	0.8696	0.8333	0.8000
2	1.7591	1.7355	1.7125	1.6901	1.6681	1.6467	1.6257	1.5278	1.4400
3	2.5313	2.4869	2.4437	2.4018	2.3612	2.3216	2.2832	2.1065	1.9520
4	3.2397	3.1699	3.1024	3.0373	2.9745	2.9137	2.8550	2.5887	2.3616
5	3.8897	3.7908	3.6959	3.6048	3.5172	3.4331	3.3522	2.9906	2.6893
6	4.4859	4.3553	4.2305	4.1114	3.9975	3.8887	3.7845	3.3255	2.9514
7	5.0330	4.8684	4.7122	4.5638	4.4226	4.2883	4.1604	3.6046	3.1611
8	5.5348	5.3349	5.1461	4.9676	4.7988	4.6389	4.4873	3.8372	3.3289
9	5.9952	5.7590	5.5370	5.3282	5.1317	4.9464	4.7716	4.0310	3.4631
10	6.4177	6.1446	5.8892	5.6502	5.4262	5.2161	5.0188	4.1925	3.5705
20	9.1285	8.5136	7.9633	7.4694	7.0248	6.6231	6.2593	4.8696	3.9539

* There is one rent each period.

1. An equal amount each interest period.
2. Interest periods of equal length (year, semiannual, or month).
3. An equal interest rate each interest period.

Examples of annuities include: equal monthly payments on an automobile or a home, equal yearly contributions to a savings account, and equal monthly retirement benefits received from a pension fund.

Future Value of an Annuity (F)

The future value of an annuity includes **compound interest** on each payment (i.e., rent) from its payment date to the end of the term of the annuity. There-

Exhibit 10–3 Overview of future and present value determination

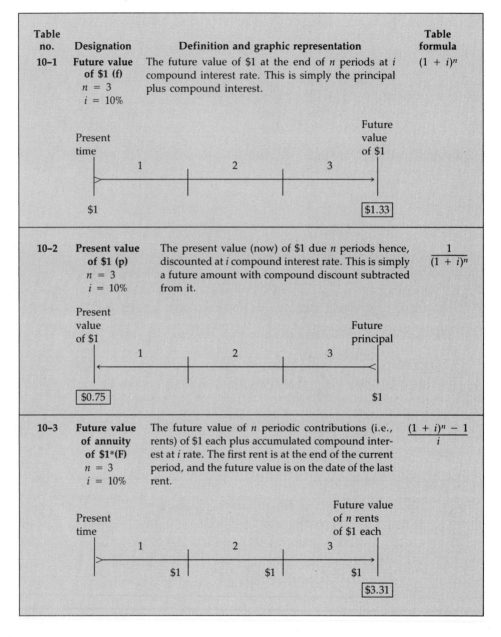

Table no.	Designation	Definition and graphic representation	Table formula
10–1	**Future value of $1 (f)** $n = 3$ $i = 10\%$	The future value of $1 at the end of n periods at i compound interest rate. This is simply the principal plus compound interest.	$(1 + i)^n$

Present time .... Future value of $1

1   2   3

$1 $1.33

| 10–2 | **Present value of $1 (p)** $n = 3$ $i = 10\%$ | The present value (now) of $1 due n periods hence, discounted at i compound interest rate. This is simply a future amount with compound discount subtracted from it. | $\dfrac{1}{(1 + i)^n}$ |

Present value of $1 .... Future principal

1   2   3

$0.75 $1

| 10–3 | **Future value of annuity of $1*(F)** $n = 3$ $i = 10\%$ | The future value of n periodic contributions (i.e., rents) of $1 each plus accumulated compound interest at i rate. The first rent is at the end of the current period, and the future value is on the date of the last rent. | $\dfrac{(1 + i)^n - 1}{i}$ |

Present time .... Future value of n rents of $1 each

1   2   3

$1 $1 $1

$3.31

fore, each payment will accumulate less interest than the prior payments only because the number of periods (n) that it accumulates interest will be less. To illustrate, you decide to deposit $1,000 cash in a savings account each year for three years at a 10% interest per year (i.e., a total principal of $3,000). The first $1,000 deposit is made on December 31, 19A; the second one on December 31,

Exhibit 10–3 *(concluded)*

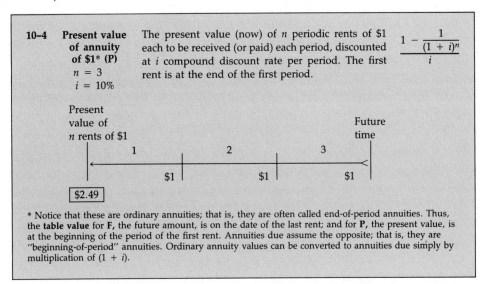

| 10–4 | **Present value of annuity of \$1* (P)** $n = 3$ $i = 10\%$ | The present value (now) of n periodic rents of \$1 each to be received (or paid) each period, discounted at i compound discount rate per period. The first rent is at the end of the first period. | $\dfrac{1 - \dfrac{1}{(1 + i)^n}}{i}$ |

Present
value of
n rents of \$1   Future
time

       1   2   3

     \$1   \$1   \$1

$\boxed{\$2.49}$

* Notice that these are ordinary annuities; that is, they are often called end-of-period annuities. Thus, the **table value** for **F**, the future amount, is on the date of the last rent; and for **P**, the present value, is at the beginning of the period of the first rent. Annuities due assume the opposite; that is, they are "beginning-of-period" annuities. Ordinary annuity values can be converted to annuities due simply by multiplication of $(1 + i)$.

19B; and the third and last one on December 31, 19C. How much would you have in the savings account at the end of Year 3, that is, immediately after the third deposit on December 31, 19C? In this case, the first \$1,000 deposit would draw compound interest for two years (for a total principal and interest of \$1,210); the second deposit would draw interest for one year (for a total principal and interest of \$1,100); and the third deposit would draw no interest because it was made on the day that the balance is computed. Thus, the total amount in the savings account at the end of three years would be \$3,310 (\$1,210 + \$1,100 + \$1,000). We could use Table 10–1 values to compute the interest on each deposit to derive the future value of this annuity. However, we can refer to Table 10–3, **Future value of annuity of \$1 (F)** for $i = 10\%$; $n = 3$, we find the value 3.3100. Therefore, the total of your three deposits (of \$1,000 each) would have increased to \$1,000 × 3.31 = \$3,310 by December 31, 19C. The increase of \$310 was due to the time value of money; it is interest revenue to you on the \$3,000 principal. A convenient format for this problem is: \$1,000 × $F_{i=10\%;\ n=3}$ (Table 10–3, 3.3100) = \$3,310. The table value for the future value of an annuity of \$1 will always be greater than the sum of its rents. This concept is summarized in Exhibit 10–3.

Present Value of an Annuity (P)

The present value of an annuity is the value now (i.e., the present time) of a series of equal amounts (i.e., rents) to be received each period for some specified number of periods in the future. It is the **inverse** of the future value of an annuity explained above. It involves compound **discounting** of each of the equal periodic amounts.

To illustrate, it now is January 1, 19A, and you are to receive $1,000 cash on each December 31, 19A, 19B, and 19C. How much would the sum of these three $1,000 future amounts be worth now, on January 1, 19A (i.e., the present value), assuming an interest rate of 10% per year? We could use Table 10–2 values to calculate the discounting of each rent as follows:

Year	Amount	Value from Table 10–2 $i = 10\%$		Present Value
1	$1,000	× 0.9091 ($n = 1$)	=	$ 909.10
2	1,000	× 0.8264 ($n = 2$)	=	826.40
3	1,000	× 0.7513 ($n = 3$)	=	751.30
		Total present value		$2,486.80

However, the present value of this annuity can be more easily computed by using one PV amount from Table 10–4 as follows:

$$\$1,000 \times P_{i=10\%;\ n=3} \text{ (Table 10–4; 2.4869)} = \$2,487 \text{ (rounded)}$$

The difference of $513 (i.e., $3,000 − $2,487) is interest. The present value of an annuity of $1 will always be less than the sum of its rents. This concept is summarized in Exhibit 10–3.

Interest rates and interest periods

Notice that the preceding illustrations assumed annual interest rates and annual periods for compounding and discounting. While interest rates almost always are quoted on an annual basis, interest compounding periods often are less than one year (such as semiannually or quarterly). When interest periods are less than a year, the values of n and i must be restated to be consistent with the length of the interest period. To illustrate, 12% interest compounded annually for five years requires use of $n = 5$ and $i = 12\%$. If compounding is quarterly, the interest period is one quarter of a year (i.e., four periods per year), and the quarterly interest rate would be one quarter of the annual rate (i.e., 3% per quarter); therefore, 12% interest compounded quarterly for five years requires use of $n = 20$ and $i = 3\%$.

There are two kinds of annuities, called ordinary annuities and annuities due. The only difference between them is the timing of the periodic rents. **Ordinary annuities** assume that the periodic rents are made at the **end of each interest period.** This chapter illustrates ordinary annuities only. **Annuities due** assume that the periodic rents are made at the **beginning of each interest period.** Therefore, an annuity due involves one more interest period (but the same number of rents) as an ordinary annuity. Therefore, the **table value** for an annuity due can be readily computed as: Ordinary annuity value (Table 10–3 or 10–4) × (1 + i) = Annuity due value. Ordinary annuities (often called end-of-period annuities) and annuities due (often called beginning-of-period annuities) may be compared as shown in Exhibit 10–4. The homework for this chapter uses only ordinary annuities unless specifically mentioned otherwise.

Exhibit 10–4 Ordinary annuities and annuities due compared

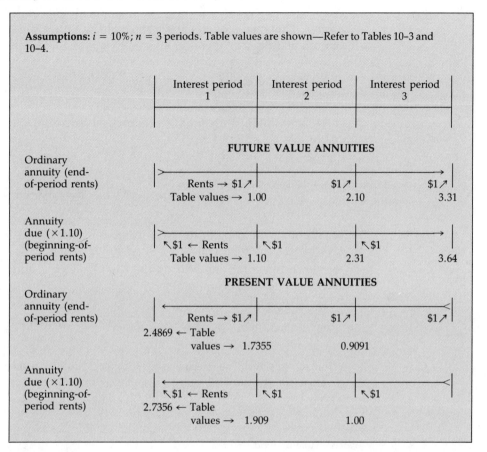

Assumptions: $i = 10\%$; $n = 3$ periods. Table values are shown—Refer to Tables 10–3 and 10–4.

DEMONSTRATION CASES

Accounting Applications of Future and Present Values

There are many transactions when the concepts of future and present value must be used for accounting measurements. Four such cases are presented below.

Case A. On January 1, 19A, Company A set aside $200,000 cash in a special building fund (an asset) to be used at the end of five years to construct a new building. The fund is expected to earn 10% interest per year, which will be added to the fund balance each year-end. On the date of deposit the company made the following entry:

January 1, 19A:

Special building fund 200,000
    Cash 200,000

Required:

1. What will the balance of the fund be at the end of the fifth year?

    Answer: This case requires application of the future value of a single amount as follows:

    $$\$200,000 \times f_{i=10\%;\ n=5} \text{ (Table 10–1; 1.6105)} = \underline{\$322,100}$$

2. How much interest revenue was earned on the fund during the five years?

    Answer:

    $$\$322,100 - \$200,000 = \underline{\$122,100}$$

3. What entry would be made on December 31, 19A, to record the interest revenue for the first year?

    Answer: Interest for one year on the fund balance is added to the fund and recorded as follows:

    December 31, 19A:

Special building fund	20,000	
Interest revenue ($200,000 $\times$ 10%)		20,000

4. What entry would be made on December 31, 19B, to record interest revenue for the second year?

    Answer:

    December 31, 19B:

Special building fund	22,000	
Interest revenue		22,000
($200,000 + $20,000) $\times$ 10% = $22,000.		

Case B. On January 1, 19A, Company B bought a new machine that had a list price of $20,000. A $20,000, two-year noninterest-bearing note payable was signed by Company B. The $20,000 is to be paid on December 31, 19B. The market interest rate for this note was 12%.

Required:

1. The company accountant is preparing the following journal entry:

    January 1, 19A:

Machinery	?	
Note payable (noninterest-bearing)		?

    What amount should be recorded in this entry?

    Answer: This case requires application of the present value of a single amount. In conformity with the **cost principle,** the cost of the machine is its current cash equivalent price, which is the present value of the future payment. The present value of the $20,000 is computed as follows:

$$\$20{,}000 \times p_{i=12\%;\; n=2} \text{ (Table 10–2; 0.7972)} = \underline{\$15{,}944}$$

Therefore, the journal entry is as follows:

January 1, 19A:

Machinery	15,944	
Note payable (noninterest-bearing)		15,944

2. **What journal entry would be made at the end of the first and second years for interest expense?**

   Answer: Interest expense for each year on the amount in the Note Payable account would be recorded in an adjusting entry, as follows:

December 31, 19A:

Interest expense	1,913	
Note payable (noninterest-bearing)		1,913

   $\$15{,}944 \times 12\% = \$1{,}913.$

   Note: The note payable would be reported on the 19A balance sheet as $15,944 + $1,913 = $17,857.

December 31, 19B:

Interest expense	2,143	
Note payable (noninterest-bearing)		2,143

   ($15,944 + $1,913) × 12% = $2,143.

3. **What journal entry should be made on December 31, 19B, to record payment of the debt?**

   Answer: At this date the amount to be paid is the balance of Note Payable, which is the same as the maturity amount on the due date, that is, $15,944 + $1,913 + $2,143 = $20,000.[14]

---

[14] The following entries also could be made with the same results:

January 1, 19A:

Machinery	15,944	
Discount on note payable	4,056	
Note payable		20,000

December 31, 19A:

Interest expense ($15,944 × 12%)	1,913	
Discount on note payable		1,913

At the end of 19A, the liability would be reported at net as $20,000 − $2,143 = $17,857.

December 31, 19B:

Interest expense ($17,857 × 12%)	2,143	
Note payable (special)	20,000	
Cash		20,000
Discount on note payable		2,143

The journal entry to record full payment of the debt would be:

December 31, 19B:

Note payable	20,000	
Cash		20,000

Case C. Company C will make five equal annual payments of $30,000 each with a financial institution to accumulate a debt retirement fund. The payments will be made each December 31, starting December 31, 19A. The fifth and last payment will be made December 31, 19E. The financial institution will pay 8% annual compound interest, which will be added to the fund at the end of each year.

Required:

1. What entry should be made to record the first payment?

    Answer:

    December 31, 19A:

Debt retirement fund	30,000	
Cash		30,000

2. What will be the balance in the fund immediately after the fifth and last payment (i.e., on December 31, 19E)?

    Answer: This case requires application of future value of an annuity as follows:

    $$\$30,000 \times F_{i=8\%; \; n=5} \text{ (Table 10–3; 5.8666)} = \underline{\underline{\$175,998}}$$

3. What entries would be made at the end of 19B?

    Answer:

    a. Interest for one year on the fund balance is added to the fund and recorded as follows:

    December 31, 19B:

Debt retirement fund	2,400	
Interest revenue ($30,000 × 8%)		2,400

    b. The second payment would be recorded as follows:

    December 31, 19B:

Debt retirement fund	30,000	
Cash		30,000

4. What is the amount of interest revenue that should be recorded at the end of 19C?

    Answer: Interest would be computed on the increased fund balance and recorded as follows:

    $$(\$30,000 + \$2,400 + \$30,000) \times 8\% = \underline{\underline{\$4,992}}$$

December 31, 19C:

Debt retirement fund	4,992	
Interest revenue		4,992

5. Prepare a **fund accumulation** schedule that shows the entry for each deposit and the increasing balance in the fund.

Fund Accumulation Schedule

Date	Cash payment (cr)	Interest revenue (prior balance × 8%) (cr)	Fund increase (dr)	Fund balance
12/31/19A	$ 30,000		$ 30,000	$ 30,000
12/31/19B	30,000	$ 30,000 × 8% = $ 2,400	32,400(a)	62,400 (b)
12/31/19C	30,000	62,400 × 8% = 4,992	34,992	97,392
12/31/19D	30,000	97,392 × 8% = 7,791	37,791	135,183
12/31/19E	30,000	135,183 × 8% = 10,815	40,815	175,998
Total	$150,000	$25,998	$175,998	

Computations:
  (a) $30,000 + $2,400 = $32,400, etc.
  (b) $30,000 + $32,400 = $62,400, etc.

Case D. On January 1, 19A, Company D bought a new machine that cost $40,000. The company was short of cash so it executed a $40,000 note payable, to be paid off in three equal annual installments. Each installment includes principal plus interest on the unpaid balance at 11% per year. The equal annual installments are due on December 31, 19A, 19B, and 19C. The acquisition was recorded as follows:

January 1, 19A:

Machinery	40,000	
Note payable		40,000

Required:
  1. What is the amount of each annual installment?

   Answer: The $40,000 is the amount of the debt today. Therefore, $40,000 is the present value of the debt, $i = 11\%$ and $n = 3$. This is an **annuity** because payment is made in three equal installments. The amount of each equal annual payment is computed by **dividing** the amount of the debt by the present value of an annuity of $1 as follows:

$$\$40,000 \div P_{i=11\%;\ n=3} \text{ (Table 10–4; 2.4437)} = \underline{\$16,369}$$

  2. What was the total amount of interest expense in dollars?

   Answer:

$$\$16,369 \times 3 = \$49,107 - \$40,000 = \underline{\$9,107}$$

3. What journal entry should be made at the end of each year to record the payment on this $40,000 note payable?

    Answer:

    a. To record the first installment payment on the note:

    December 31, 19A:

    ```
    Note payable . . . . . . . . . . . . . . . . . . . . . . . . . . . . .   11,969
    Interest expense ($40,000 × 11%) . . . . . . . . . . . . . . .    4,400
        Cash (computed above) . . . . . . . . . . . . . . . . . .              16,369
    ```

    b. To record the second installment payment on the note:

    December 31, 19B:

    ```
    Note payable . . . . . . . . . . . . . . . . . . . . . . . . . . . . .   13,285
    Interest expense [($40,000 − $11,969) × 11%] . . . . . . . .    3,084
        Cash (computed above) . . . . . . . . . . . . . . . . . .              16,369
    ```

    c. To record final installment payment on the note:

    December 31, 19C:

    ```
    Note payable . . . . . . . . . . . . . . . . . . . . . . . . . . . . .   14,746
    Interest expense  . . . . . . . . . . . . . . . . . . . . . . . . . .    1,623
        Cash (computed above) . . . . . . . . . . . . . . . . . .              16,369
    ```

    Interest: ($40,000 − $11,969 − $13,285) × 11% = $1,623
    (rounded to accommodate rounding errors).

4. Prepare a **debt payment schedule** that shows the entry for each payment and the effect on interest expense and the unpaid amount of principal each period.

Debt Payment Schedule

Date	Cash payment (cr)	Interest expense (prior balance × 11%) (dr)	Principal decrease (dr)	Unpaid principal
1/1/A				$40,000
12/31/A . . .	$16,369	$40,000 × 11% = $4,400	$11,969(a)	28,031(b)
12/31/B . . .	16,369	28,031 × 11% = 3,084	13,285	14,746
12/31/C . . .	16,639	14,746 × 11% = 1,623*	14,746	–0–
Total . . .	$49,107		$9,107	$40,000

* To accommodate rounding error.
Computations:
(a) $16,369 − $4,400 = $11,969, etc.
(b) $40,000 − $11,969 = $28,031, etc.

Notice in the debt payment schedule that of each successive payment an increasing amount is payment on principal and a decreasing amount is interest expense. This effect occurs because the interest each period is based on a lower amount of unpaid principal. When an annuity is involved, schedules such as this one often are essential.

SUMMARY OF CHAPTER

Liabilities are obligations of either a known or estimated amount. Detailed information about the liabilities of an entity is important to many decision makers, whether internal or external to the enterprise, because liabilities represent claims against the resources of an entity. Decision makers often may not be able to identify the kinds and amounts of liabilities without reliable financial statements. The existence and amounts of liabilities sometimes are easy to conceal from outsiders. The accounting model and the verification by an independent PA are the best assurances that all liabilities are disclosed.

Current liabilities are obligations that will be paid from the resources reported on the same balance sheet as current assets. They are short-term obligations that will be paid within the coming year or within the normal operating cycle of the business, whichever is longer. All other liabilities (except contingent liabilities) are reported as **long-term liabilities.** A **contingent liability** is a potential claim due to some event or transaction that has happened, but whether it will materialize as an effective liability is not certain because that depends upon some future event or transaction. At the end of the accounting period, a contingent liability must be recorded (as a debit to a loss account and a credit to a liability account) if (*a*) it is likely that a loss will occur, and (*b*) if the amount of the loss can be estimated reasonably. Other contingent liabilities are disclosed in the notes to the financial statements together with potential losses that are not recorded in the accounts.

Future and present value concepts often must be applied in accounting for liabilities. These concepts focus on the time value of money (i.e., interest). Future value is the amount that a principal amount will increase in the future due to compound interest. Present value is the amount that a future principal amount will decrease due to compound discounting. Future and present values are related to (*a*) a single amount (of principal) or (*b*) a series of equal periodic amounts of principal (called annuities). Typical applications of future and present values are to: create a fund, determine the cost of an asset, account for notes payable, and account for installment debts and receivables.

CHAPTER SUPPLEMENT 10A

Payroll Accounting[15]

Payroll accounting does not involve any new accounting concepts or principles, but payroll accounting deserves additional discussion because of the necessity to pay employees for their services promptly and correctly. In addition, detailed

---

[15] This section of the chapter was revised by E. Scott.

payroll accounting is necessary to fulfill legal requirements under federal and provincial laws with respect to withholdings for income taxes, Canada or Quebec Pension Plan, and unemployment insurance. Further, the management of an enterprise, for planning and control purposes, needs detailed and accurate cost figures for wages and salaries. Frequently, salaries and wages constitute the largest category of expense in an enterprise. As a consequence of the large amount of detailed recordkeeping that is required, payroll accounting is often computerized, including the production of individual cheques for the employees.

A detailed payroll record must be maintained for each employee. The payroll record varies with the circumstances in each company; however, it must include for each individual such data as social insurance number, number of dependents (for income tax withholding), rate of pay, a time record (for hourly paid employees), deductions from gross pay, and so on.

To understand payroll accounting, a distinction must be made between (1) payroll deductions and taxes that must be paid by the **employee** (i.e., deducted from the employee's gross earnings); and (2) payroll taxes that must be paid by the **employer.** Both types of payroll amounts must be transmitted to the governmental unit or other party to whom the amounts are owed. Payroll taxes and deductions apply only in situations where there is an employer-employee relationship. Independent contractors that are not under the direct supervision of the client, such as outside lawyers, independent accountants, consultants, and building contractors, are not employees; hence, amounts paid to them are not subject to payroll taxes and related deductions.

An employee usually receives take home pay that is much less than the gross earnings for the period. This is due to two types of payroll deductions:

1. Required deductions for taxes that must be paid by the employee as specified by provincial and federal laws.
2. Optional deductions authorized by the employee for special purposes.

Required Deductions.   There are three categories of taxes that the employee must pay and thus must be deducted from the employee's gross earnings; they are income taxes, Canada or Quebec Pension Plan contributions, and unemployment insurance premiums. The employer must remit the total amount deducted to the appropriate government agency.

Employee income taxes.   Practically every employee must prepare an annual federal income tax return. Wages and salaries earned during the year must be reported on the income tax return as income. Federal and Quebec laws require the employer to deduct an appropriate amount of income tax each period from the gross earnings of each employee. The amount of the deduction for income tax is determined from a tax table (provided by the Revenue Canada, Taxation) based upon the earnings and number of exemptions (for self and dependents) of the employee. The amount of income tax withheld from the employee's wages is recorded by the employer as a current liability between the date of deduction and the date the amount withheld is remitted to the government.

Employee Canada Pension Plan contributions. The Canada Pension Plan provides retirement and disability benefits for those who have contributed to the plan over their working life. Funding comes from contributions by both employees and employers at the rate of 1.8% of "annual pensionable earnings" from each party.[16] The employer is required to make the appropriate deductions from employees each pay period and then make remittances to the federal government.

Employee unemployment insurance premiums. The Federal Unemployment Insurance Act also requires that employers deduct premiums from employees on the basis of 2.35% of their "insurable earnings" (with the employer adding an additional contribution).[17] Eligibility for benefits is based on a "record of employment" form provided by the employer.

For each of the three types of payroll taxes described above, the total amount withheld must be paid to Revenue Canada, Taxation by the 15th day of the month following the month in which the remuneration was paid, except large employers must make bimonthly remittances. Remittance forms to accompany each payment are provided by Revenue Canada, Taxation.

To identify the amounts withheld for each employee, an annual statement (T4 Summary) is filed with Revenue Canada on or before February 28, covering the preceding calendar year. Individual statements (T4 Supplementary) are provided to each employee at the same time.

The Province of Quebec similarly requires separate withholding, reporting, and remittance for provincial income tax and the Quebec Pension Plan.

Optional Deductions. Many companies encourage programs of voluntary deductions from earnings by employees. Typical of these voluntary deductions are savings funds, insurance premiums, charitable contributions, supplementary retirement programs, repayment of loans, share purchase plans, and the purchase of Canada savings bonds. The employer agrees to make these deductions, subject to employee authorization, as a matter of convenience to the employees. The amounts deducted are remitted in a short time to the organization or agency in whose behalf the deduction was authorized. Another type of deduction is for

---

[16] Annual "pensionable earnings" in 1988 are those earnings in excess of $2,600 up to a maximum of $26,500. Monthly contributions, for example, by the employee are 1.8% of actual earnings for the month less 1/12 of the $2,600, and are determined from tables provided by Revenue Canada, Taxation. Once the maximum contributions have been made, no further contributions are required in the year for that employee.

Individuals who are "self-employed" (in business as proprietors or partners) must make both the employee's and employer's share of the contributions annually.

[17] "Insurable earnings" in 1988 are those annual earnings up to $29,380. If earnings are $5,876 or less annually ($489.66 monthly), they are exempt. Deduction tables are provided showing the amount of deductions for various amounts of earnings. (The maximum and minimum earnings are prorated by the length of the period in these tables.)

union dues as specified in the union contract. In some cases, this deduction may not be voluntary on an individual basis. The employer is required to remit the deductions, along with the employee list, to the union each month. Where the employer also agrees to contribute amounts, an employee benefits expense is incurred.

Accounting for Employee Deductions. The employer must maintain detailed and accurate records of all deductions from the earnings of each employee. From the employer's viewpoint, the employee deductions are **current liabilities** from the date of the payroll deduction to the date of remittance to the government or other entity.

To illustrate the basic accounting entry to be made for the payment of a payroll and the accrual of liabilities for the **employee** deductions, assume that Real Company accumulated the following data in the detailed payroll records for the month of January 19B:

> Gross earnings:
> Salaries $60,000
> Wages (hourly paid employees) 40,000
> Income taxes withheld 21,000
> Union dues withheld 400
> Unemployment insurance withheld . . . 2,350
> Canada Pension Plan contributions
> withheld 1,455

The entry to record the payroll and employee deductions would be:

January 31, 19B:

Salaries expense	60,000	
Wage expense	40,000	
Liability for income taxes withheld—employees		21,000
Liability for union dues withheld—employees		400
Unemployment insurance payable		2,350
CPP contributions payable		1,455
Cash (take-home pay)		74,795
Payroll for January, including employee payroll deductions.		

Employer-Paid Payroll Taxes. Remember that the payroll taxes illustrated above are those levied on the **employees.** The employer simply serves as a tax collector with respect to them. Specific payroll taxes also are levied on the employer. These taxes represent **operating expenses** of the business. The liability for these taxes is extinguished when the taxes are remitted to the designated agencies of the provincial and federal governments. Usually, three different payroll taxes must be paid by the employer—Canada Pension Plan, unemployment insurance, and provincial worker's compensation.

> *Employer Canada Pension Plan contributions.* As previously noted, the employer must match the employee's contributions to the Canada or Quebec Pension Plan by equal amounts.

Employer unemployment insurance premiums. The employer must also contribute to the unemployment insurance fund. The employer's premium is 1.4 times the amount of the employee's premiums in most cases.

Worker's compensation. Provincial legislation requires employers to pay insurance premiums on behalf of employees who may be injured or disabled in work-related activities. The premiums are paid to a provincial board which administers the program, and the amount of premium depends upon such factors as the type of employment, the amount of pay, and the claims experience.

Accounting for Employer Payroll Taxes. Payroll taxes paid by the employer are debited to an expense account and credited to a current liability when the payroll is paid each period. To illustrate, the January entry for the employer's payroll taxes for Real Company would be as follows assuming a worker's compensation premium of $800:

Payroll and benefits expense	5,545*	
Unemployment insurance payable ($2,350 × 1.4)		3,290
Canada Pension Plan payable		1,455
Worker's compensation payable		800
To record employer payroll taxes.		
*Total payroll expenses, $100,000 + 5,545 = $105,545.		

When the taxes are remitted to the governments, the liability accounts are debited and Cash is credited.

CHAPTER SUPPLEMENT 10B

The Voucher System

The voucher system is designed to attain strict control over cash expenditures from the point an obligation is incurred (by means of purchase of merchandise for resale, services, operational assets, investments, etc.) through the payment of cash. The incurrence of an obligation and the payment of cash to satisfy it are viewed as separate and independent transactions. When a voucher system is used, an account called **Vouchers Payable** replaces the account called **Accounts Payable** in the ledger. Similarly, a **voucher register** and a **cheque register** replace the purchases journal and the cash disbursements journal, respectively (see Supplement 8B).

The basic document in the voucher system is the **voucher.** A voucher is a form, prepared and used within the business, on which a transaction is (1) summarized and supported, (2) approved, (3) analyzed for recording, and (4) approved for payment. Thus, it is a comprehensive document that follows a transaction from the transaction date to the final cash payment. A voucher is prepared for **each** transaction involving the payment of cash, such as the purchase of assets, the use of services, the incurrence of expenses, and the payment of debt. The form of a voucher varies between companies because it is designed to meet the specific internal requirements of the individual company. For control purposes, all voucher forms and cheques should be numbered consecutively when printed.

After approval, each voucher is entered in the voucher register numerically. The voucher register is designed to record the basic data from the voucher, including the accounts to be debited and credited.

To illustrate the mechanics of a voucher system, we will follow a purchase of merchandise for resale through the system from the **order date** to the final cash payment date. Each step in the sequence may be illustrated and explained as follows:

19A

Jan. 10   Merchandise ordered from Box Supply Company, cost $1,000; terms n/15. A purchase order is prepared and approved.

12   Merchandise ordered from Box Supply Company on January 10 is received; invoice is received. Voucher No. 47 is drawn, and the purchase order is attached (see Exhibit 10–5). Goods are checked for quantity and condition; a receiving report is prepared.

12   Receiving report and invoice are sent to accounting department; they are attached to the voucher. Voucher is approved, and then recorded in the voucher register (see Exhibit 10–6).

26   Voucher is approved by designated manager for payment on January 27 and sent to the disbursements department; Cheque No. 90 is prepared.

27   Cheque No. 90 is signed by treasurer and mailed.

28   The accounting department enters Cheque No. 90 in the cheque register (see Exhibit 10–7); enters payment notation in the voucher register (see Exhibit 10–6); and files the voucher in the **Vouchers Paid File.**

For illustrative purposes, two more transactions are recorded in the voucher register, one of which is unpaid.

At the end of the month the voucher register and the cheque register are totaled, and the equality of the debits and credits is verified. Posting to the ledger from these two special journals follows the same pattern as for the special journals explained in Supplement 8B. Posting involves two separate phases:

1. **Current posting**—During the period, and even daily, the details in the Voucher Register columns are posted to (*a*) the selling expense subsidiary ledger (under the selling expense control); (*b*) the administrative expense subsidiary ledger (under the administrative expense control); and (*c*) other accounts to be debited. No current posting is required from the cheque register as illustrated.

2. **Monthly posting**—The totals from the voucher register, except for the "Other Accounts to Be Debited," are posted at the end of each month. The account number to which each total is posted is entered below the

Exhibit 10–5 Voucher format

| | | | Voucher No. ___47___ |

MAY DEPARTMENT STORE
Kingston, Ontario

Date of Voucher _____January 12, 19A_____   Date Paid _____January 27, 19A_____

Pay to _Box Supply Company_   Cheque No. _____90_____

　　　　1119 Brown Street

　　　　Ottawa, Ontario

For the following goods or services (attach all supporting documents):

Date Incurred	Terms	Explanation of Details	Amount
Jan. 12	*n/15*	*Merchandise, Dept. 8*	*1,000.00*
		Invoice No. 17-8132	
		Receiving Report No. 123	
		Net payable	*1,000.00*

Approvals:

　　Voucher Approval:　　Date _1/12/A_　　Signature _R. C. Roe_

　　Payment Approval:　　Date _1/26/A_　　Signature _A. B. Doe_

Accounting Analysis:

Account Debited:	Acct. No.	Amount
Purchases	*91*	*1,000.00*
Office Supplies		
Sales Salaries		
Operational Assets		
Etc.		
Total, Voucher Payable Credit *41*		*1,000.00*

Exhibit 10–6   Voucher register

Date	Vou. No.	Payee	Payment Date	Cheque No.	Vouchers Payable (Credit)	Purchases (Debit)	Selling Expense Control Account Code	Folio	Amount (Debit)	Adm. Expense Control Account Code	Folio	Amount (Debit)	Other Accounts to Be Debited Account Name	Folio No.	P	Amount (Debited)
Jan 12	47	Box Supply Co	1/27	90	1,000.00	1,000.00										
Jan 14	48	John Day-salary	1/15	89	600.00		64	✓	600.00							
Jan 31	98	Capital Nat'l Bank-note			2,160.00								Notes payable	44	✓	2,000.00
													Interest expense	82	✓	160.00
		Totals			27,605.00	14,875.00			7,410.00			3,160.00				2,160.00
		Posting notations			(41)	(91)			(60)			(70)				(✓)

Exhibit 10–7   Cheque register

Date	Payee	Voucher No. Paid	Cheque No.	Vouchers Payable (Debit)*	Cash (Credit)*
Jan. 15	John Day	48	89	600.00	600.00
27	Box Supply Co.	47	90	1,000.00	1,000.00
31	Totals			18,751.00	18,751.00
	Posting notation			(41)	(11)

* These two columns could be combined.

amount. The column for "Other Accounts to Be Debited" was posted individually; hence, the total should not be posted. The totals from the cheque register are posted to the accounts at the end of each month as shown by the account numbers entered below the total.

The balance in the ledger account Vouchers Payable is reported on the balance sheet as a liability and is designated as Accounts Payable on the balance sheet. The amount should be allocated and classified between current and long-term liabilities, depending on due dates.

The Vouchers Payable account is a control account. Its balance represents all of the **unpaid** vouchers for any given time. The total of all vouchers in the **Unpaid Voucher File** must agree with the balance of the Vouchers Payable account; therefore, the Vouchers Payable account replaces the Accounts Payable control account in the ledger (see Supplement 6A).

In studying the mechanics of the voucher system, you should not overlook its most important aspect—the high degree of **internal control** attained through formalization of the sequence of acquiring operational assets, services, and merchandise, and in making the cash payments. The internal control feature rests on (1) clear-cut separation and designation of specific approval responsibilities, (2) a prescribed routine for carrying out these responsibilities, and (3) accounting for the results.

Although a manual approach was illustrated, these routines can be adapted easily for the computer. A computer program can be designed to accomplish the same steps and procedures illustrated above. Most companies have a computerized voucher system to attain a high degree of control over expenditures and to accelerate the processing of a large volume of transactions, including cash disbursements.

CHAPTER SUPPLEMENT 10C

Lease Liabilities

For accounting purposes, leases are classified as operating leases and capital leases.

1. **Operating lease**—a short-term lease in which the owner (called the lessor), for a stated rental, grants the user (called the lessee) the right to use property under specified conditions. The **lessor** is responsible for the costs of ownership (such as taxes, insurance, and major maintenance). The **lessee** pays a monthly rental (and usually the utilities). The lease of an automobile on a daily basis and office space on a monthly basis are typical operating leases. When the monthly rent is paid, the lessor records rent revenue and the lessee records rent expense. Any unpaid rent is a current liability for the lessee and a current asset for the lessor.

2. **Capital lease**—a long-term, noncancelable lease contract in which the lessor transfers most of the **ownership rights** to the **lessee** during the lease term.

Significantly different accounting approaches are required for operating leases than for capital leases. Because of the importance of these differences, the *CICA Handbook*, Section 3065, established three criteria to differentiate capital leases from operating leases. If **any one** of the three criteria is met by the lease contract, the lease **must** be accounted for as a **capital** lease by the lessee; all other leases must be accounted for as **operating** leases. The three criteria for a **capital lease** may be summarized as follows: (1) ownership of the leased property is transferred to the lessee by the end of the lease term either by the terms of the lease contract or what is termed a bargain purchase option, (2) the lease term is at least 75% of the estimated useful life of the leased asset, and (3) the present value of the minimum lease payments is at least 90% of the market value of the leased asset on the date of the lease contract.[18]

The three criteria provide the basis for establishing whether or not the transaction is "in substance" a purchase of an asset. If the accountant deems the transaction to be "in substance" a purchase by the lessee, then the transaction is recorded in the same way as the purchase of a long-term asset with the money received from a long-term loan. Such a practice provides a classic illustration of a victory of "substance" over "form" because a lease is a lease in form, not a purchase.

Typical operating and capital leases are shown in Exhibit 10–8. On January 1, 19A, Daly Construction Company must acquire a heavy-duty machine ready to operate. The machine has a cash price of $100,000, and it has a five-year estimated useful life and no residual value. In the face of a serious cash problem, Daly's top management is considering three alternative ways of acquiring the machine: (a) purchase by signing a note for the full purchase price, (b) lease the machine on an **operating** lease, and (c) lease the machine on a **capital** lease. The basic entries for each alternative are given in Exhibit 10–8. Let's examine each alternative.

Alternative a. Purchase the machine and sign a two-year interest-bearing note; 15% interest and principal payable each month-end (i.e., 24 equal payments). On January 1, 19A, Daly would record the purchase at cost and a liability as illustrated in Exhibit 10–8. Equal monthly payments of principal plus interest ($4,849) are to be made; the journal entry to record the first payment is illustrated in Exhibit 10–8. Under this alternative Daly would own the machine. Therefore, Daly would record depreciation expense and all other expenses incurred, such as maintenance, insurance, and taxes.

Alternative b. Lease the machine on a month-to-month **operating lease** at a monthly rental of $6,000 (as determined by the lessor), payable at the first of each month. Under this alternative Daly would not own the machine. Therefore, the only journal entries to be recorded by Daly would be for the monthly rental payments as illustrated in Exhibit 10–8. Under this alternative Daly would have to continue lease payments as long as the machine is used and would never own the machine.

Alternative c. Lease the machine on a three-year **capital lease.** The contract requires Daly to pay 36 first-of-month rentals of $3,289, computed by the **lessor** to earn 12% on the $100,000 cash equivalent price. Also, Daly must pay most of the "ownership" costs such as maintenance, insurance, and taxes. The lessee learned that the rental of $3,289 was based on 12% interest; therefore, the **lessee** computed the **present value** of the future lease rentals as follows:

---

[18] *CICA Handbook,* Section 3065, also specifies the rules for determining how the lessor should account for a lease. This topic will be discussed in advanced courses.

Exhibit 10–8 Operating lease and capital lease compared

Situation:

Daly Construction Company intends to acquire a heavy-duty machine that will cost $100,000 cash equivalent price. Estimated useful life of the machine is five years and no residual value. Daly is considering three alternatives: (a) purchase by signing note, (b) rent on an operating lease, and (c) rent on a capital lease.

Alternative a:

On January 1, 19A, purchased the machine for $100,000 and signed a two-year, 15% note that requires equal month-end payments (24) of $4,849.

Journal entries:

Purchase, January 1, 19A:

Machinery	100,000	
Note payable, long term		100,000

Payment on note, January 31, 19A:

Interest expense ($100,000 × 1¼%)	1,250	
Note payable ($4,849 − $1,250)	3,599	
Cash (per note)		4,849

Alternative b:

Lease on a month-to-month **operating lease;** first-of-month rental payments of $6,000, as required by lessor.

Journal entries:

January 1, 19A:

Machinery rental expense	6,000	
Cash (per lease agreement)		6,000

Alternative c:

Lease on a **capital lease** that requires a first-of-month payment of $3,289 for 36 months (the implied interest rate is 12%). Daly is required by the lease to pay all ownership costs.

Journal entries:

January 1, 19A—Inception date of the lease (record as a purchase):

Machinery (under capital lease)	100,000	
Liability, capital lease		100,000

Computation:
Present value = Payments × Table 10–4 ($i = 1\%$; $n = 36$) × $(1 + i)$*
= $3,289 × 30.107505 × (1 + 0.01) = $100,000 (rounded)

Liability, capital lease	3,289	
Cash		3,289

To record the first payment.

January 31, 19A:

Interest expense	967	
Liability, capital lease		967

($100,000 − $3,289) × 0.01.

February 1, 19A:

Liability, capital lease	3,289	
Cash		3,289

To record the second payment.

* This value is given for illustrative purposes. Table 10–4 does not contain values for 36 periods. $(1 + i)$ is used because of an annuity due.

Present value = Rents (payments) × (Table 10–4, $i = 1\%$; $n = 36$) × $(1 + i)$

= $3,289 × 30.107505 × (1 + .01)$ (given; Table 10–4 does not contain values for 36 periods)

= $100,000 (rounded)

In accounting, a **capital lease** is equivalent to a sale of the asset by the lessor to the lessee. Daly (the lessee) would record a purchase of the machine on the date of the lease contract for $100,000 (its present value).

On January 1, 19A, Daly would debit machinery and credit a lease liability for $100,000 as shown in Exhibit 10–8. Each of the 36 first-of-the-month lease payments would be recorded. Interest will be accrued. Exhibit 10–8 shows entries at the inception of the lease (i.e., a "purchase" of the machine is recorded) and the first payment on January 1, 19A, and the interest accrual. Note carefully the fact that rents are typically paid at the beginning of a period.

Because Daly is assumed to "own" the machine during the lease term, Daly will record depreciation expense and all other "ownership" expenses incurred, such as maintenance, insurance, and taxes. Under this alternative, Daly will own the machine after the last rental payment with no further obligations to the lessor.

The above example does not suggest which alternative is the "best" for Daly. Such a determination would need more information than given. Rather, it is intended to differentiate between the required accounting approaches for an operating lease versus a financial lease. The basic difference requires the application of **present value** determination for **capital lease.**

IMPORTANT TERMS DEFINED IN THIS CHAPTER

Accrued Expenses Expenses that have been incurred but have not yet been paid or recorded at the end of the accounting period; a liability. *p. 566*

Annuities Due Beginning-of-period annuities; payments are assumed to be on the first day of each interest period. *p. 588*

Annuity A series of periodic cash receipts or payments that are equal in amount each interest period. *p. 584*

Capital Lease A lease that is viewed as a purchase/sale for accounting purposes. *p. 603*

Contingent Liability Potential liability that has arisen as the result of a past event; not an effective liability until some future event occurs. *p. 577*

Current Liabilities Short-term obligations that will be paid within the current operating cycle or one year, whichever is longer. *p. 565*

Deferred Revenues Revenues that have been collected but not earned; a liability until the goods or services are provided. *p. 568*

Future (deferred) Income Tax Difference between income tax expense and income tax liability; caused by timing differences; may be a liability or an asset. *p. 574*

Future Value The sum to which an amount will increase as the result of compound interest. *p. 580*

Interest-Bearing Note A note that explicitly gives a stated rate of interest. *p. 565*

Liabilities Probable future sacrifices of economic benefits that arise from past transactions. *p. 564*

Long-Term Liabilities All obligations that are not properly classified as current liabilities. *p. 571*

Noninterest-Bearing Note A note that does not explicitly state a rate of interest but has implicit interest; interest is included in the face amount of the note. *p. 565*

Operating Lease A rental agreement between a lessor and lessee that is not viewed as a purchase/sale in accounting. *p. 603*

Ordinary Annuities End-of-period annuities; payments are assumed to be on the last day of each interest period. *p. 588*

Permanent Difference An income tax difference that does not cause future taxes. *p. 576*

Present Value The current value of an amount to be received in the future; a future amount discounted for compound interest. *p. 580*

Time Value of Money Interest that is associated with the use of money over time. *p. 580*

Timing Difference An income tax difference that causes future (deferred) taxes; will reverse or turn around in the future. *p. 574*

Working Capital The dollar difference between total current assets and total current liabilities. *p. 566*

Working Capital (current) Ratio The ratio of total current assets divided by total current liabilities; also known as the current ratio. *p. 566*

QUESTIONS

Part A: Questions 1–16

1. Define a liability. Distinguish between a current liability and a long-term liability.
2. How can external parties be informed about the liabilities of a business?
3. Liabilities are measured and reported at their current cash equivalent amount. Explain.
4. A liability is a known obligation of either a definite or estimated amount. Explain.
5. Define working capital. How is it computed?

6. What is the current ratio? What is another name for the current ratio? How is the current ratio related to the classification of liabilities?

7. Define an accrued liability. What kind of an entry usually reflects an accrued liability?

8. Define a deferred revenue. Why is it a liability?

9. Define a note payable. Distinguish between a secured and an unsecured note.

10. Distinguish between an interest-bearing note and a noninterest-bearing note.

11. Define future income tax. Explain why future income tax "reverses, or turns around," in subsequent periods.

12. What is a contingent liability? How is a contingent liability reported?

13. Explain the primary purpose of a voucher system.

14. Compute 19A interest expense for the following note: face, $6,000; 10% interest; date of note, April 1, 19A.

15. Compare the conceptual valuation rules for accounts receivable with those of accounts payable.

16. Long-term debt due within one year that will be paid from current assets is classified as a current liability. Depreciation that will be used next year to produce inventory is not recorded until next year. Conceptually justify the difference in the treatment of these two items.

Part B: Questions 17–27

17. Explain the time value of money.

18. Explain the basic difference between future value and present value.

19. If you deposited $10,000 in a savings account that would earn 10%, how much would you have at the end of 10 years? Use a convenient format to display your computations.

20. If you hold a valid contract that will pay you $10,000 cash 10 years hence and the going rate of interest is 10%, what is its present value? Use a convenient format to display your computations.

21. What is an annuity?

22. Complete the following schedule:

Concept	Symbol	Table Values		
		$n = 4; i = 5\%$	$n = 7; i = 10\%$	$n = 9; i = 15\%$
FV of $1				
PV of $1				
FV of annuity of $1				
PV of annuity of $1				

23. If you deposit $1,000 for each of 10 interest periods (ordinary annuity) that would earn 10% interest, how much would you have at the end of period 10? Use a convenient format to display your computations.

24. You purchased an XIT auto for $20,000 by making a $5,000 cash payment and six semiannual installment payments for the balance at 10% interest. Use a convenient format to display computation of the amount of each payment.

25. What is a lease liability?

26. What is meant by a capital lease?

27. The Halifax Capitals Hockey Ltd. obtains a new ice machine by leasing the machine from a supplier under terms that require its disclosure as a capital lease. The team also hires a star player for a substantial salary on a five-year contract. Why would the ice machine be treated differently for accounting purposes than the employee contract?

EXERCISES

Part A: Exercises 10–1 to 10–11

E10–1 **(Pair Definitions with Terms)**
Match the brief definitions given below with the terms by entering the code letters in the blanks provided.

Term	Brief definition (or statement)
_B_ (1) Liabilities (example)	A. Provides resources to a business by selling its goods and services on credit.
___ (2) Interest expense	B. Probable future sacrifices of economic benefits.
___ (3) Current ratio	C. The two major classifications of liabilities on a balance sheet.
___ (4) Full-disclosure principle	D. All liabilities must be reported in conformity with this principle.
___ (5) Interest-bearing note	E. A liability requires the payment of these two different amounts.
___ (6) Secured debt	F. Interest payable on a noninterest-bearing note.
___ (7) Short term and long term	G. Current assets divided by current liabilities.
___ (8) Deferred revenues	H. A liability that represents trade accounts payable only.
___ (9) Principal and interest	I. A liability that is supported by a mortgage on specified assets.
___ (10) Working capital	J. A note that does not specify a stated rate of interest but interest nevertheless is paid.
___ (11) Noninterest-bearing note	K. Unearned revenues or revenues collected in advance.
___ (12) Accounts payable	L. Principle × Rate × Time, related to a liability.
___ (13) Accrued expenses	M. Expenses incurred by the end of the period but not yet recorded or paid.
___ (14) Creditors	N. Current assets minus current liabilities.
___ (15) Implicit interest	O. A note that specifies a stated rate of interest on the principal amount.

E10–2   **(Pair Definitions or Statements with Terms)**
Match the brief definitions with the terms by entering the code letters in the blanks provided.

	Term		Brief definition (or statement)
E	(1) A timing dif-ference (example)	A.	Amount of the difference between income tax expense and income tax payable.
___	(2) A permanent tax difference	B.	A potential liability from an event that has already happened but depends on a future event.
___	(3) A contingent lia-bility that must be recorded as a loss and a liability	C.	A contingent liability that is unlikely or cannot be reasonably estimated.
		D.	A system used to attain control over cash expenditures.
___	(4) Voucher system	E.	A future income tax item that will "reverse or turn around."
___	(5) Contingent liability	F.	A liability that is not supported by a mortgage on specific assets.
___	(6) Future income tax	G.	All liabilities are measured in conformity with this principle.
___	(7) Working capital ratio	H.	A contingent liability that is likely and can be reasonably estimated.
___	(8) A contingent lia-bility that must be reported only in a footnote	I.	Current assets divided by current liabilities.
		J.	An income tax difference that will never "reverse or turn around."
___	(9) An unsecured debt		
___	(10) Cost principle		

E10–3   **(Compute Owners' Equity, Working Capital, and Interest Expense; Provide an Adjusting Entry)**
Rath Corporation is preparing its 19B balance sheet. The company records show the following related amounts at the end of the accounting period, December 31, 19B.

Total current assets	$160,100
Total all remaining assets	665,000
Liabilities:	
Note payable (10%, due in 5 years)	24,000
Accounts payable	50,000
Income tax payable	15,000
Liability for withholding taxes	2,000
Rent revenue collected in advance	3,000
Bonds payable (due in 15 years)	200,000
Wages payable	5,000
Property taxes payable	1,000
Note payable, 12% (due in 6 months) . . .	8,000
Interest payable	100

Required:

a. Compute total owners' equity.

b. Compute (1) working capital and (2) the current ratio (show computations).

c. Compute the amount of interest expense for 19B on the 10% note. Assume it was dated October 1, 19B.

d. Give any adjusting entry required for the 10% note payable on December 31, 19B.

E10–4 **(Accounting for, and Reporting, Accrued Expenses and Deferred Revenue)**
During 19B, the two transactions given below were completed by RV Company. The annual accounting period ends December 31.

1. Wages paid and recorded during 19B were $120,000; however, at the end of December 19B, there were three days' wages unpaid and unrecorded because the weekly payroll will not be paid until January 6, 19C. Wages for the three days were $4,000.

2. On December 10, 19B, the company collected rent revenue of $1,500 on office space that it rented to another party. The rent collected was for 30 days from December 10, 19B, to January 10, 19C, and was credited in full to Rent Revenue.

Required:

a. Give (1) the adjusting entry required on December 31, 19B, and (2) the January 6, 19C, journal entry for payment of any unpaid wages from December 19B.

b. Give (1) the journal entry for the collection of rent on December 10, 19B, and (2) the adjusting entry on December 31, 19B (compute rent to the nearest 10 days).

c. Show how any liabilities related to the above transactions should be reported on RV's balance sheet at December 31, 19B.

E10–5 **(Accounting for an Interest-Bearing Note Payable through Its Time to Maturity)**
On November 1, 19A, Modesto Company borrowed $60,000 cash from the City Bank for working capital purposes and gave an interest-bearing note with a face amount of $60,000. The note was due in six months. The interest rate was 10% per annum payable at maturity. The accounting period ends December 31.

Required:

a. Give the journal entry to record the note on November 1.

b. Give any adjusting entry that would be required at the end of the annual accounting period.

c. Give the journal entry to record payment of the note and interest on the maturity date, April 30, 19B.

E10–6 **(Record a Payroll, Including Deductions)**
Corning Manufacturing Company has completed the payroll for January 19B, reflecting the following data:

Salaries and wages earned	$80,000
Employee income taxes withheld	11,000
Union dues withheld	1,100
Canada Pension Plan contributions withheld	1,356
Unemployment insurance premiums withheld	1,880
Private pension plan contributions withheld	3,360

The employer was required to pay the following additional amounts for the January payroll:

Canada Pension Plan	1,356
Unemployment insurance	2,632
Worker's compensation	700
Matching share to private pension plan	3,360

Required:

a. Give the journal entry to record payment of the payroll.

b. Give the journal entry to record employer payroll taxes.

c. Give the journal entry in February 19B to record payment of all payroll liabilities by the employer.

d. What was the amount of additional labour expense to the company due to tax laws and benefit contracts? Explain. What was the employees' take-home pay? Explain.

(Revised by E. Scott)

E10–7   (Accounting for Accounts Payable and an Interest-Bearing Note Payable)
Victor Company sells a wide range of goods through two retail stores that are operated in adjoining cities. Most purchases of goods for resale are on invoices with credit terms of 2/10, n/30. Occasionally, a short-term note payable is used to obtain cash for current use. The following transactions were selected from those occurring during 19B:

1. On January 10, 19B, purchased merchandise on credit, $20,000; terms 2/10, n/30. Record at net (see Chapter 6); the company uses a periodic inventory system.

2. On March 1, 19B, borrowed $60,000 cash from Town Bank and gave an interest-bearing note payable: face amount, $60,000; due at the end of six months, with an annual interest rate of 12% payable at maturity.

Required:

a. Give the journal entry for each of the above transactions. Record purchases and accounts payable at net.

b. Give the journal entry if the account payable of January 10, 19B, was paid within the discount period.

c. Give the journal entry if the account payable of January 10, 19B, was paid after the discount period.

d. Give the journal entry for the payment of the note payable plus interest on its maturity date.

E10–8   (Accounting for a Noninterest-Bearing Note Payable)
On September 1, 19A, Foxy Company borrowed $20,000 and signed a one-year note payable for $22,400. The accounting period ends December 31.

Required:

a. What kind of note was involved? Explain.

b. How much interest was paid? What was the implicit interest rate?

c. Give the required entries (if any) on the following dates: September 1, 19A, December 31, 19A, and October 31, 19B. Assume that reversing entries are not used.

E10–9   (Accounting for a Future Income Tax Credit)
The comparative income statements of Rowan Corporation at December 31, 19B, showed the following data (summarized and excluding income taxes):

	Annual income statement for	
	19A	19B
Sales revenue . . .	$50,000	$61,000
Expenses	40,000	48,000
Pretax income . . .	$10,000	$13,000

Included on the 19B income statement given above was an expense of $7,000 that was deductible on the income tax return in 19A rather than in 19B. Assume an average tax rate of 20%.

Required:

a. For each year compute (1) income tax expense, (2) income tax payable, and (3) any future tax.

b. Give the journal entry for each year to record income tax, including any future tax.

c. Show how the income tax liabilities should be reported on the balance sheet for each year assuming the tax is paid the following April.

E10–10   **(Accounting for a Future Income Tax Debit)**
The comparative income statement for Nader Corporation for the years ended December 31, 19A, and 19B, provided the following data (summarized and excluding income taxes):

	Annual income statement for	
	19A	19B
Revenues	$90,000	$94,000
Expenses	75,000	78,000
Pretax income . . .	$15,000	$16,000

Included on the 19B income statement given above was a revenue item of $7,000 that was included on the income tax return for 19A rather than in 19B. Assume an average income tax rate of 20%.

Required:

a. For each year, compute (1) income tax expense, (2) income tax payable, and (3) future income tax. (Hint: Future income tax will have a debit balance for 19A.)

b. Give the journal entry for each year to record income tax, including any future tax.

c. Show how income tax would be reported on the balance sheet each year if the tax is paid the following April.

E10–11   **(Accounting for Future Income Tax and Analysis of the Related Cash Flows)**
Green Corporation reported the following income statement data (summarized):

	Income statement for year ended December 31		
	19A	19B	19C
Revenues	$150,000	$150,000	$150,000
Expenses (including depreciation) . . .	110,000	110,000	110,000
Pretax income	$ 40,000	$ 40,000	$ 40,000

Depreciation expense included on the income statement was computed as follows:

Machinery cost (acquired on January 1, 19A), $60,000; estimated useful life, three years, no residual value; annual depreciation (straight-line) $60,000 ÷ 3 years = $20,000.

The company uses CCA, Class 8, 20% on the income tax return and has an average income tax rate of 30%.

Required:

a. For each year, compute (1) income tax expense for the income statement and (2) income tax payable for the tax return (show computations).

b. Give the journal entry for each year to record income tax including any future income tax.

c. What kind of "tax difference" was involved? Explain.

Part B: Exercises 10–12 to 10–21

E10–12 **(Pair Definitions with Terms)**
Match the brief definitions given below with the terms by entering the code letters in the blanks provided.

	Term		Brief definition (or statement)
C	(1) Interest (example)		A. Future value of a single amount at 10% interest for five interest periods.
___	(2) Principal × Rate × Time		B. A series of consecutive equal rents each interest period.
___	(3) $f_{i=10\%;\ n=5} = 1.6105$		C. Time cost of using money.
___	(4) Balance in a fund for $i = 8\%; n = 4$		D. Present value of a series of equal rents at 10% interest for five periods.
___	(5) $P_{i=10\%;\ n=5} = 3.7908$		E. Formula for computing interest.
___	(6) Ordinary annuity		F. A beginning-of-period annuity.
___	(7) $F_{i=10\%;\ n=5} = 6.1051$		G. Value today of a single future amount.
___	(8) Annuity		H. $30,000 × $f_{i=8\%;\ n=4}$ (1.3605) = $40,815.
___	(9) Future value of 1		I. An end-of-period annuity.
___	(10) Table value for an annuity due		J. Future value of a series of equal rents at 10% interest for five periods.
___	(11) Annuity due		K. Value in the future of a single present amount.
___	(12) $p_{i=10\%;\ n=5} = 0.6209$		L. Present value of a single amount at 10% interest for five interest periods.
___	(13) Balance in a fund with equal rents for $i = 8\%; n = 4$		M. $20,000 ÷ $P_{i=12\%;\ n=3}$ (2.4018) = $8,327.
___	(14) Present value of 1		N. Table value of an ordinary annuity × (1 + i).
___	(15) Periodic payments on a debt, $i = 12\%; n = 3$		O. $5,000 × $F_{i=8\%;\ n=4}$ (4.5061) = $22,531.

E10–13   **(Application of the Four Kinds of Present and Future Values)**
On January 1, 19A, Hyper Company completed the following transactions (assume a 12% annual interest rate):

1. Deposited $20,000 in a fund (designated Fund A).
2. Established a fund (designated Fund B) by making six equal annual deposits of $3,000 each.
3. Established a fund (designated Fund C) by depositing a single amount that will increase to $60,000 by the end of Year 7.
4. Decided to deposit a single sum in a fund (designated Fund D) that will provide 10 equal annual year-end payments of $10,000 to a retired employee (payments starting December 31, 19A).

Required (show computations and round to the nearest dollar):
a. What will be the balance of Fund A at the end of Year 9?
b. What will be the balance of Fund B at the end of Year 6?
c. What single amount must be deposited in Fund C on January 1, 19A?
d. What single sum must be deposited in Fund D on January 1, 19A?

E10–14   **(Accounting for a Savings Account; a Single Amount)**
On January 1, 19A, you deposited $12,000 in a savings account. The account will earn 8% annual compound interest, which will be added to the fund balance at the end of each year. You recorded the deposit as follows:

Savings account 12,000	
Cash	12,000

Required (round to the nearest dollar):
a. What will be the balance in the savings account at the end of 10 years?
b. What is the time value of the money in dollars for the 10 years?
c. How much interest revenue did the fund earn in 19A? 19B?
d. Give the journal entry to record interest revenue at the end of 19A and 19B.

E10–15   **(Compute Deposit Required and Account for a Single-Sum Savings Account)**
On January 1, 19A, Parent decided to deposit an amount in a savings account that will provide $40,000 four years later to send Offspring to Super University. The savings account will earn 9%, which will be added to the fund each year-end.

Required (show computations and round to the nearest dollar):
a. How much must Parent deposit on January 1, 19A?
b. Give the journal entry that Parent should make on January 1, 19A.
c. What is the time value of the money for the four years?
d. Give the journal entry Parent should make on (1) December 31, 19A, and (2) December 31, 19B.

E10–16   **(Accounting for a Savings Account with Equal Periodic Payments)**
On each December 31, you plan to deposit $1,000 in a savings account. The account will earn 8% annual interest, which will be added to the fund balance at year-end. The first deposit will be made December 31, 19A (end of period).

Required (show computations and round to the nearest dollar):

a. Give the required journal entry on December 31, 19A.

b. What will be the balance in the savings account at the end of the 10th year (i.e., 10 deposits)?

c. What is the time value of money in dollars for the 10 deposits?

d. How much interest revenue did the fund earn in 19B? 19C?

e. Give all required journal entries at the end of 19B and 19C.

E10–17   **(Accounting for a Savings Fund with Periodic Rents)**
You have planned to take a trip around the world upon graduation, four years from now (now it is January 1, 19A). Your grandfather wants to deposit sufficient funds for this trip in a savings account for you. On the basis of a budget, you estimate the trip now would cost $11,000. To be generous, your grandfather decided to deposit $2,800 in the fund at the end of each of the next four years, starting on December 31, 19A. The savings account will earn 7% annual interest, which will be added to the savings account at each year-end.

Required (show computations and round to the nearest dollar):

a. Give the required journal entry on December 31, 19A, to record the first deposit in your records.

b. How much money will you have for the trip at the end of Year 4 (i.e., after four deposits)?

c. What is the time value of the money for the four years?

d. How much interest revenue did the fund earn in 19A, 19B, and 19C?

e. Give the journal entries at the end of 19B and 19C. Yes, you left on January 1, 19E.

E10–18   **(Valuation of an Asset Based on Present Value)**
You have the chance to purchase the royalty interest in an oil well. Your best estimate is that the net royalty income will average $35,000 per year for five years. There will be no residual value at that time. Assume the cash inflow is at each year-end and that, considering the uncertainty in your estimates, you expect to earn 20% per year on the investment.

Required (show computations and round to the nearest dollar):

a. What should you be willing to pay for this investment on January 1, 19A?

b. Give the required journal entry (cash paid in full for the royalty interest) on January 1, 19A.

c. Give the required journal entries on December 31, 19A, assuming the net cash received was 20% above your estimate. Assume the cost of the royalty interest is depleted on a straight-line basis.

E10–19   **(Accounting for Interest-Bearing and Noninterest-Bearing Notes Compared)**
Assume you needed to borrow $3,600 cash for one year. The City Bank charges 12% interest per annum on such loans. Answer the following questions (show computations):

Required:

a. What would be the face amount of the note assuming the bank agreed to accept an interest-bearing note?

b. What would be the face amount of the note assuming the bank insisted on a non-interest-bearing note?

c. Give the journal entries to record the note in (*a*) and (*b*). Set the entries in parallel columns.

d. Give the journal entries at date of maturity in (*a*) and (*b*).

E10–20   **(Contingencies)**

The accounting staff of Valhalla Limited, a pharmaceuticals company, is busy preparing the 1988 financial reports. The staff is aware that a lawsuit has been filed against the company by a farmer, alleging that one of Valhalla's products has caused birth defects in several of his lambs. The farmer seeks damages in the amount of $250,000. One of three outcomes is possible. First, the farmer may win, and the courts will assess the full $250,000 against the company. Second, the farmer may win, but it is impossible to estimate how much the courts will assess. Third, the suit may be without merit and will be thrown out of court. The accounting staff is concerned with the correct reporting and disclosure of this lawsuit.

Required:

a. Define contingency.

b. Assume that the necessary preconditions exist for the first alternative outcome. Explain how the financial statements would be affected, providing full details and journal entries, if required.

c. Assume that the necessary preconditions exist for the second alternative outcome. Explain how the financial statements would be affected, providing full details and journal entries, if required.

d. Assume that the necessary preconditions exist for the third alternative outcome. Explain how the financial statements would be affected, providing full details and journal entries, if required.

(CGAC Adapted)

E10–21   **(Leases)**

The Hadfield Corporation entered into a lease for manufacturing equipment from the Crosbie Corporation, on January 1, 1988. The terms of the lease provided for yearly payments, in advance, of $27,500 for 10 years. The yearly payments include $2,500 maintenance costs. At the end of the lease, Crosbie Corporation plans to reclaim the equipment which is expected to last one more year. Crosbie Corporation estimated the residual value at $17,000, but did not disclose this information to the Hadfield Corporation. The Crosbie Corporation purchased the asset at its fair market value. The interest rate implicit in the lease is 10%, and Hadfield Corporation's incremental borrowing rate is 12%.

Required:

a. Provide the journal entries required to account for the lease in the accounts of Hadfield Corporation in 1988. Assume adjusting journal entries are made only at year-end.

b. Calculate the current and long-term portion of the lease liability of Hadfield Corporation at December 31, 1988.

(CGAC Adapted)

PROBLEMS

Part A: Problems 10–1 to 10–9

P10–1   **(Record and Report Five Current Liabilities)**
Allen Company completed the transactions listed below during 19B. The annual accounting period ends December 31, 19B.

Jan.   8   Purchased merchandise for resale at an invoice cost of $12,000; terms 2/10, n/60. Record at net (see Chapter 6); assume a periodic inventory system.

17   Paid invoice of January 8.

Apr.   1   Borrowed $60,000 from the National Bank for general use; executed a 12-month, 10%, interest-bearing note payable.

June   3   Purchased merchandise for resale at an invoice cost of $20,000; terms 1/20, n/30; record at net.

July   5   Paid invoice of June 3.

Aug.   1   Rented two rooms in the building owned by Allen and collected six months' rent in advance amounting to $4,800. Record the collection in a way that will not require an adjusting entry at year-end.

Dec.   20   Received a $500 deposit from a customer as a guarantee to return a large trailer "borrowed" for 30 days.

31   Wages earned but not paid on December 31 of $8,000 (disregard payroll deductions). The payroll will not be paid until January 3rd.

Required:
a. Prepare journal entries for each of the above transactions.
b. Prepare all adjusting entries required on December 31, 19B.
c. Show how all of the liabilities arising from the above transactions would be reported on the balance sheet at December 31, 19B.

P10–2   **(Accounting for an Interest-Bearing Note, with Adjusting Entries)**
On April 1, 19A, Ravina Company bought equipment for $150,000. A cash down payment of $50,000 was made. A $100,000 interest-bearing note (including a mortgage on the equipment) was given for the balance. The note specified 12% annual interest. Two payments on principal of $50,000 each, plus interest on the unpaid balance on March 31, 19B, and March 31, 19C, are required—these will be unequal cash payments. The accounting period ends December 31.

Required:
a. Give all of the related journal entries for the terms of this note. Do not use reversing entries.
b. Show how the liabilities should be reported on Ravina's 19A and 19B balance sheets.

P10–3   **(Accounting for Interest-Bearing and Noninterest-Bearing Notes, Including Adjusting Entries)**
During 19A, Billings Company completed two transactions that involved notes payable. The accounting period ends December 31. The company does not use reversing entries.

May 1, 19A—Borrowed $36,000 cash and signed a one-year, interest-bea.ing note. The interest rate specified on the note was 10%. The principal and interest ai e payable on the maturity date, April 30, 19B.

September 1, 19A—Borrowed $30,000 cash and signed a six-month, noninterest-bearing note for $31,500. The note did not give a stated rate of interest. The face amount is payable at maturity date, February 28, 19B.

Required:

a. Give all of the entries related to the $36,000 note from May 1, 19A, through April 30, 19B.

b. Give all of the entries related to the $31,500 note from September 1, 19A, through maturity date, February 28, 19B.

c. Show how the liabilities related to the two notes should be reported on the 19A balance sheet.

P10–4   **(Purchase of a Noncash Asset with a Noninterest-Bearing Note, Including Adjusting Entries)**

On August 1, 19A, Brewer Company purchased a machine that cost $23,000. The company paid cash of $5,000 and signed a six-month, noninterest-bearing note with a face amount of $19,080. The note did not specify a stated rate of interest. The accounting period ends December 31.

Required:

a. Compute the implicit rate of interest.

b. Give all entries related to the note from August 1, 19A, through the maturity date, February 1, 19B. Do not use reversing entries.

c. Show how the note should be reported on the 19A balance sheet.

P10–5   **(Record and Report Five Liabilities Including an Interest-Bearing Note and a Noninterest-Bearing Note)**

Saxon Company completed the transactions listed below during 19A. The annual accounting period ends December 31.

May	1	Purchased an operational asset (fixtures) for $40,000; paid $10,000 cash and signed a 12-month, 10%, interest-bearing note payable for the balance.
June	5	Purchased an operational asset (machine) at an invoice cost of $12,000; terms 3/10, n/60.
	14	Paid invoice of June 5.
Sept.	1	Collected rent revenue on office space rented to another company; the rent of $6,000 was for the next six months. Record the collection in a way to avoid an adjusting entry at the end of 19A.
Nov.	1	Borrowed $30,000 cash and signed a noninterest-bearing note for $31,800. The note matures on April 30, 19B.
Dec.	31	Received a tax bill for property tax for 19A in the amount of $1,800; the taxes are payable no later than March 1, 19B.

Required:

a. Give the 19A journal entries for each of the above transactions.

b. Prepare any required adjusting entries on December 31, 19A.

c. Show how all liabilities arising from the above transactions would be reported on the 19A balance sheet.

P10–6   **(Future Income Tax; Two Differences; Entries; Restate Comparative Income Statement to Include Income Tax)**

Radney Company is preparing comparative statements at December 31, 19B. The records show the following summarized income statement data, exclusive of income tax expense:

	19A	19B
Revenues	$180,000	$190,000
Expenses	(110,000)	(129,000)
Extraordinary item	(10,000)	4,000
Income before income tax	$ 60,000	$ 65,000

Included in the 19B revenues of $190,000 is a revenue item of $20,000 that was included on the income tax return for 19A. Also, included in the 19B expenses of $129,000 was an expense item of $6,000 that was deducted on the income tax return for 19A. Assume an average 20% income tax rate. There were no future income taxes on the extraordinary items.

Required:

a. What kind of "tax difference" is represented by the two items? Explain.

b. For each year, compute (1) income tax expense, (2) income tax liability, and (3) future income tax.

c. Give the journal entry for each year to record income tax, including any future income taxes.

d. Restate the above comparative income statement, including the appropriate presentation of income tax for each year. (Hint: Allocate income tax expense between operations and extraordinary items.)

P10–7   **(Income Tax Timing Difference and Permanent Difference; Comprehensive Problem)**

At December 31, 19A, the records of Laymon Corporation provided the following pretax information:

1. Revenues $150,000
2. Expenses (including $13,000 depreciation expense) 113,000
3. Depreciation expense was computed as follows for income statement purposes:
     Operational asset cost (acquired January 1, 19A) 52,000
     Four-year useful life (no residual value):
         Depreciation expense per year (straight-line, $52,000 ÷ 4 years) 13,000
4. Extraordinary loss (fully income tax deductible) 10,000
5. The revenues given in (1) include $5,000 tax free.
6. Assume an average income tax rate of 20% on both ordinary income and extraordinary gain.
7. Class 8, 20% capital cost allowance is used for income tax purposes.

Required:

a. Compute income tax expense.

b. Compute income tax payable on the tax return.

c. Give the journal entry to record income tax including any future income tax.

d. Prepare an income statement.

e. What kind of "tax differences" were involved? Explain the basis for your treatment of them.

P10–8 **(Based on Supplement 10A: Accounting for Payroll Costs)**

Tappen Company has completed the salaries and wages payrolls for March 19A. Details provided by the payroll were:

	March 1–15	March 16–31
Salaries and wages earned*	$100,000	$100,000
Employee income taxes withheld	21,000	21,000
Union dues withheld	—	2,000
Insurance premiums withheld	900	—
Canada Pension Plan contributions	1,712	1,712
Unemployment insurance premiums withheld each payroll period	2.35%	

* Subject in full to payroll taxes.

Required:

a. Give the journal entries to record the payrolls for March 15 and 31, including employee deductions. Show computations.

b. Give the journal entries to record the employer's payroll taxes for each payday.

c. Give combined journal entries to reflect remittance of amounts owed to governmental agencies and other organizations within 10 days of each payday.

d. What was the total labour cost for Tappen Company for March? Explain. What percentage of the March total payroll was take-home pay? Explain.

(Revised by E. Scott)

P10–9 **(Based on Supplement 10B: Application of a Voucher System to Control Cash Expenditures)**

Holt Company uses a voucher system to control cash expenditures. The following transactions have been selected from December 19B for case purposes. The accounting year ends December 31.

Design a voucher register and a cheque register similar to those shown in Supplement 10B. The transactions that follow will be entered in these two special journals.

Dec. 2 Purchased merchandise from AB Wholesalers for resale, $2,000; terms 2/10, n/30; record purchases at net and assume a periodic inventory system (see Chapter 6); Invoice No. 14; start with Voucher No. 11.

7 Approved contract with Ace Plumbing Company for repair of plumbing, $450; account, Building Repairs, No. 77.

11 Paid Voucher No. 11; start with Cheque No. 51.

22 Purchased store supplies for future use from Crown Company; Invoice No. 21 for $90; account, Store Supplies Inventory, No. 16.

23 Advertising for pre-Christmas sale, $630; bill received from Daily Press and payment processed immediately; account, Advertising Expense, No. 54.

31 Monthly payroll voucher, total $2,500; $1,500 was selling expense (Sales Salaries, No. 52), and $1,000 was administrative expense (Administrative Salaries, No. 62). The voucher was supported by the payroll record; therefore, one

voucher was prepared for the entire payroll. The voucher was approved for immediate payment. Six cheques with conservative numbers were issued.

Required:

a. Enter the above transactions in the voucher register and the cheque register.

b. Total the special journals and check the equality of the debits and credits. Set up T-accounts and post both registers. Complete all posting notations. The following accounts may be needed:

Account titles	Account No.
Cash	01
Store supplies inventory	16
Vouchers payable	30
Purchases	40
Selling expense control	50
Subsidiary ledger:	
Sales salaries	52
Advertising expense	54
Administrative expense control . . .	60
Subsidiary ledger:	
Administrative salaries	62
Building repairs	77

c. Reconcile the Vouchers Payable account balance with the Unpaid Vouchers File at the end of December.

Part B: Problems 10–10 to 10–21

P10–10   (Application of Four PV and FV Concepts)

On January 1, 19A, Vail Company completed the following transactions (use a 10% annual interest rate for all transactions):

1. Deposited $40,000 in a debt retirement fund. Interest will be computed at six-month intervals and added to the fund at those times (i.e., semiannual compounding). (Hint: Think carefully about *n* and *i.*)

2. Established a plant addition fund of $200,000 to be available at the end of Year 5. A single sum will be deposited on January 1, 19A, that will grow to the $200,000.

3. Established a pension retirement fund of $500,000 to be available by the end of Year 6 by making six equal annual deposits each year-end, starting on December 31, 19A.

4. Purchased a $100,000 machine on January 1, 19A, and paid cash, $20,000. A three-year note payable is signed for the balance. The note will be paid in three equal year-end payments starting on December 31, 19A.

Required (show computations and round to the nearest dollar):

a. In transaction 1 above, what will be the balance in the fund at the end of Year 4? What is the total amount of interest revenue that will be earned?

b. In transaction 2 above, what single sum amount must the company deposit on January 1, 19A? What is the total amount of interest revenue that will be earned?

c. In transaction 3 above, what is the required amount of each of the six equal annual deposits? What is the total amount of interest revenue that will be earned?

d. In transaction 4 above, what is the amount of each of the equal annual payments that must be paid on the note? What is the total amount of interest expense that will be incurred?

P10–11   **(Accounting for a Fund; Fund Accumulation Schedule and Entries)**
On January 1, 19A, Fast Company decided to accumulate a fund to build an addition to its plant. Fast will deposit $200,000 in the fund at each year-end, starting on December 31, 19A. The fund will earn 8% interest which will be added to the fund at each year-end. The accounting period ends December 31.

Required:

a. What will be the balance in the fund immediately after the December 31, 19C, deposit?

b. Complete the following fund accumulation schedule:

Date	Cash Payment	Interest Revenue	Fund Increase	Fund Balance
12/31/19A				
12/31/19B				
12/31/19C				
Total				

c. Give Fast's journal entries on December 31, 19A, 19B, and 19C.

d. The plant addition was completed on January 1, 19D. The total cost was $670,000. Give the entry assuming this amount is paid in full to the contractor.

P10–12   **(Accounting for a Plant Fund; a Single Amount)**
River Company will build another plant during 19C estimated to cost $900,000. At the present time, January 1, 19A, the company has excess cash, some of which will be set aside in a savings account to defray $700,000 of the plant cost. The savings account will earn 10% annual interest which will be added to the savings account each year-end.

Required (show computations and round to the nearest dollar):

a. What single amount must be deposited in the savings account on January 1, 19A, to create the desired amount by the end of 19C?

b. What will be the time value of the money by the end of 19C?

c. How much interest revenue will be earned each year (19A through 19C)?

d. Give the following journal entries:
   (1) Establishment of the fund.
   (2) Interest earned at each year-end.
   (3) Use of the fund and other cash needed to pay for the plant (completed December 31, 19C, at a cost of $940,000).

P10–13   **(Accounting for a Debt Retirement Fund; a Single Amount)**

On January 1, 19A, Reston Company set aside a fund to provide cash to pay off the principal amount of a $90,000 long-term debt that will be due at the end of five years. The single deposit will be made with an independent trustee. The fund will earn 7% annual interest which will be added to the fund balance at each year-end.

Required (show computations and round to the nearest dollar):

a. How much must be deposited as a single sum on January 1, 19A, to pay off the debt?

b. What is the time value of the money in dollars for the five years?

c. How much interest revenue will the fund earn in 19A? 19B?

d. Give the journal entries for Reston Company to record:
   (1) The deposit on January 1, 19A.
   (2) The interest revenue for 19A and 19B (separately).
   (3) Payment of the maturing liability at the end of the fifth year.

e. Show how the effects of the fund will be reported on the 19B income statement and balance sheet.

P10–14   **(Accounting for a Debt Fund; Equal Periodic Rents)**

On December 31, 19A, Cuellar Company set aside, in a fund, cash to pay the principal amount of a $120,000 debt due on December 31, 19D. Cuellar Company will make four equal annual deposits on each December 31, 19A, 19B, 19C, and 19D. The fund will earn 8% annual interest, which will be added to the balance of the fund at each year-end. The fund trustee will pay the loan principal (to the creditor) upon receipt of the last fund deposit. Cuellar's accounting period ends December 31.

Required (show computations and round to the nearest dollar):

a. How much must be deposited each December 31? (Hint: Use Table 10–3.)

b. What will be the time value of the money in dollars for the fund?

c. How much interest revenue will the fund earn in 19A, 19B, 19C, and 19D?

d. Give Cuellar's journal entries on the following dates:
   (1) For the first deposit on December 31, 19A.
   (2) For all amounts at the end of 19B and 19C.
   (3) For payment of the debt on December 31, 19D.

e. Show how the effects of the fund will be reported on the December 31, 19B, income statement and balance sheet.

P10–15   **(Debt Paid in Equal Installments; Debt Payment Schedule and Entries)**

On January 1, 19A, Big Company sold a new machine to Small Company for $40,000. A cash down payment of $10,000 was made by Small Company. A $30,000, 12% note was signed by Small Company for the balance due. The note is to be paid off in three equal installments due on December 31, 19A, 19B, and 19C. Each payment is to include principal plus interest on the unpaid balance. The purchase was recorded by Small as follows:

January 1, 19A:

Machine	40,000	
Cash		10,000
Note payable		30,000

Required (show computations and round to the nearest dollar):

a. What is the amount of the equal annual payment that must be made by Small Company? (Hint: Use Table 10–4.)

b. What was the time value of the money, in dollars, on the note?

c. Complete the following debt payment schedule:

Date	Cash Payment	Interest Expense	Principal Decrease	Unpaid Principal
1/1/19A				
12/31/19A				
12/31/19B				
12/31/19C				
Total				

d. Give the journal entries for each of the three payments.

e. Explain why interest expense decreased in amount each year.

P10–16 **(Payment for Auto in Equal Periodic Installments; Prepare Debt Payment Schedule; Entries)**
On January 1, 19A, you bought a new Super-Whiz automobile for $15,500. You paid a $6,000 cash down payment and signed a $10,000 note, payable in four equal intallments on each December 31, the first payment to be made on December 31, 19A. The interest rate is 14% per year on the unpaid balance. Each payment will include payment on principal plus the interest.

Required:

a. Compute the amount of the equal payments that you must make. (Hint: Use Table 10–4.)

b. What is the time value of the money in dollars for the installment debt?

c. Complete a schedule using the format below.

DEBT PAYMENT SCHEDULE

Date	Cash Payment	Interest Expense	Reduction of Principal	Unpaid Principal
1/1/19A				
12/31/19A				
12/31/19B				
12/31/19C				
12/31/19D				
Total				

d. Explain why the amount of interest expense decreases each year.

e. Give the journal entries on December 31, 19A, and 19B.

P10–17　**(Accounting for a Noninterest-Bearing Note; Time to Maturity, Two Years)**
On January 1, 19A, Design Furniture Company borrowed $40,000 cash from Montreal Financial Corporation. Design signed a two-year noninterest-bearing note. The note plus all interest is payable on the maturity date December 31, 19B. The market rate of interest for this risk level was 12%. The accounting period ends December 31.

Required (show computations and round all amounts to the nearest dollar):

a. Compute the face amount of the note.

b. Give Design's journal entries at the following dates:
   (1) January 1, 19A, date of loan.
   (2) December 31, 19A, end of accounting period.
   (3) December 31, 19B, end of accounting period.
   (4) December 31, 19B, maturity date.

c. Show how Design should report this note on its December 31, 19A, balance sheet.

P10–18　**(Warranty Claims, Tax Allocation)**
Jane Makula was hired on January 1, 1988, by Orion Computers to market their latest line of desk-top machines. Because of the uncertainty of the project, she agreed to accept as compensation a share of the profits if such occur. The agreement was that Jane would receive 10% of the profits on the yearly sales, which was to be paid to her in cash on February 1 of the following year. Profit is defined as accounting income before income tax and Jane's bonus. Assume an income tax rate of 40% and that the above compensation plan is deductible for tax purposes.

For the year ended December 31, 1988, accounting income before income tax expense and before Jane's compensation was $500,000. Depreciation expense for the year was $80,000. Capital cost allowance for 1988 is $150,000. Orion provides a warranty against defects and has estimated this amount to be 2% of sales, which is not deductible for tax purposes. Sales were $1,000,000 for 1988 and, although no machines were returned for repairs in 1988, it is assumed that they will be in the future. Tax laws allow a deduction only for warranty claims actually paid in the year.

Required:

a. Calculate Jane's compensation for 1988.

b. Calculate accounting income after tax.

c. Calculate income for tax purposes (taxable income).

d. Prepare the journal entry to record 1988 income taxes.

e. Prepare the journal entry used by Orion Computers to record warranty expense for 1988.

f. Assuming $18,000 was spent in 1989 on warranty claims, prepare the journal entry.

(CGAC Adapted)

P10–19　**(Warranty Claims, Tax Allocation)**
Wecha Corporation sells a line of products that carries a three-year warranty against defects. Based on industry experience, the estimated warranty costs related to dollar sales are: the first year after sale—2% of sales; second year after sale—4% of sales; and third

year after sale—5% of sales. Sales and actual warranty expenditures for the first three-year periods were as follows:

	Cash sales	Actual warranty expenditures
1986	$ 90,000	$ 1,000
1987	110,000	5,000
1988	130,000	10,000

Warranty expense is an item which could result in timing differences. For accounting purposes, an estimated warranty expense appears on the income statement, whereas the tax expense is the amount actually paid.

Required:

a. Give all necessary entries for the three years for sales and warranties. Do not pre-pare the income tax entries in this part. Use the following format.

	1986		1987		1988	
Account	DR	CR	DR	CR	DR	CR

b. Assume a tax rate of 40% and net income of: 1986, $20,000; 1987, $30,000; 1988, $40,000. Prepare a journal entry for each of the three years to record income tax expense using tax allocation methods. Warranty estimates are not tax deductible. Actual warranty costs are tax deductible.

(CGAC Adapted)

P10–20   **(Computer Spreadsheet, Fund Accumulation)**

Required:
Use the data in P10–11 to complete (b) of that problem with a computer spreadsheet.

P10–21   **(Computer Spreadsheet, Debt Repayment Schedules)**

Required:

a. Use the data in P10–15 to complete (c) of the required using a computer spreadsheet.

b. Modify the computer spreadsheet in (1) to answer (c) of the required for P10–16.

CASES

C10–1   **(Accounting for Warranty Expense and Warranty Liability; a Challenging Case)**
Hi-Fi Retailers sells television sets, stereos and other related items. This case relates to stereos. During 19A, Hi-Fi sold stereos for $180,000 cash; the related cost of goods sold was $70,000. Each stereo is guaranteed for one year for defective parts. In case of a defective part, the part is replaced and the labour cost of replacing it involves no cost to the customer. Experience by the manufacturer shows that the average cost to make good the warranty is approximately 5% of cost of goods sold. The company uses a perpetual inventory system and the accounting period ends December 31.

Actual expenditures for warranties (i.e., replacement parts and labour) during 19A was $2,700. During 19A, this amount was debited to an account called Warranty Expense and credited to Cash. Stereo sales were much higher during December than in any other prior month.

Required:

a. Give the two summary journal entries for the company to record the sales of stereos during 19A.

b. Explain why the company debited the actual 19A warranty expenditures to warranty expense.

c. Explain the nature of any liability that the company should record at the end of 19A related to the warranties.

d. Compute the estimated amount of any warranty liability that exists at December 31, 19A.

e. Give any entry needed based on your answer to Requirement (d).

f. Show how warranty expense and any warranty liability should be reported in the 19A income statement and balance sheet.

C10-2   **(Hidden Interest in a Real Estate Deal; PV)**

Slick Doe, a home builder, distributed an advertisement that offered "a $120,000 house with a zero interest rate mortgage for sale." If the purchaser made monthly payments of $2,000 for five years ($120,000 ÷ 60 months), there would be no additional charge for interest. When the offer was made, mortgage interest rates were 12%. Present value for $n = 60$, and $i = 1\%$ is 44.9550.

Required:

a. Did Slick Doe actually provide a mortgage at zero interest?

b. Estimate the true price of the home that was advertised. Assume that the $2,000 monthly payment was based on an implicit interest rate of 12%.

C10-3   **(Based on Supplement 10C; Alternative Choices Involving Leases; Challenging)**

Several years ago, Rapid Service Company borrowed $10 million from First Canadian Bank. At the time the loan was approved, Rapid Service agreed not to borrow any additional money from any other sources until at least half of the First Canadian loan was repaid. As a result of continued growth, Rapid Service must acquire a large computer during the current year. Unfortunately, Rapid Service does not have sufficient cash to purchase the computer or to repay the loan to First Canadian. You have been engaged as a consultant to Rapid Service. The president of Rapid Service, Allison Payne, described the problem during your first meeting:

The computer can be purchased from Super Computer Company for $500,000, but we don't have the cash and the bank won't let us borrow any more money. However, the computer company has agreed to lease the computer to us on a 10-year lease, which is the expected useful life of the computer (no residual value). Annual lease payments of $81,372 would be paid based on an interest rate of 10%. I think that this lease deal will solve our problem because we will not violate our agreement with First Canadian as long as we don't report any additional debt on the balance sheet. We must work this out without recording any debt. What do you think?

To help the president understand the required accounting treatment, the president should consider three alternatives as follows:

Alternative No. 1—Rapid Service can purchase the computer but would have to borrow $500,000 with a note payable to the computer company at 10% interest for 10 years. Annual year-end payments for principal and interest amount to $81,372.

Alternative No. 2—Rapid Service could rent the computer on a monthly lease basis. The terms of the lease cause it to be considered an operating lease. Annual rent payments would be $125,000 at each year-end for 10 years.

Alternative No. 3—Rapid Service could acquire the computer on a long-term lease basis. At the expiration date of the lease, the computer would be retained by Rapid for no additional cost. The terms of the lease cause it to be accounted for as a capital lease. The lease payments would be $81,372 for 10 years.

Required:

a. Assume that the computer was acquired on January 1, 19D, which is the beginning of the accounting period. Prepare journal entries to record the acquisition of the computer by Rapid Service under each of the three alternatives.

b. Assume Rapid Service makes cash payments under each alternative on December 31 of each year. Prepare the required journal entries on December 31, 19D (include adjusting entries, if required). Rapid Service uses straight-line depreciation for all assets.

c. Would the capital lease alternative, described by the president, permit Rapid Service to acquire the computer and conform to GAAP? Would a capital lease violate the agreement with the bank?

d. What are the primary problems of Alternatives 1 and 2?

C10–4 **(Leases)**

TS Limited, a well-known public company, operates a chain of department stores across Canada. These stores are in leased premises in shopping centres. TS Ltd. is required to file annually with several provincial securities commissions. The company has a long history of marginal profitability.

Management personnel are paid bonuses calculated as a percentage of the excess of net income in the financial statements over the budgeted net income. Budgets are approved by the board of directors.

The company has entered into certain contractual arrangements, including bank loan agreements, promissory notes, and mortgages. These arrangements have restrictions as to the amount of debt permitted in relation to shareholders' equity. At December 31, 1985, the company's most recent year-end, the company came close to being in default of the debt/equity restrictions.

TS Ltd. had a store in premises leased from Suburban Shopping Centres Limited (SSC) and accounts for the contract as a capital lease. In 1988, SSC paid TS Ltd. $3 million and agreed to renovate the exterior of TS Ltd.'s store. In exchange, TS Ltd. agreed: (1) to renovate the interior of the store; (2) to pay an additional $180,000 rent per annum for the remaining 12 years of the lease; and (3) to allow SSC to further develop the centre including the rental space to one of TS Ltd.'s competitors.

TS Ltd.'s auditors, CW & Co., became aware of this transaction during the interim audit in September 1988. At that time, a dispute arose between CW & Co. and the management of TS Ltd. with respect to the appropriate accounting treatment for the transaction. This dispute ultimately led to the replacement of CW & Co. by another firm of auditors, GA & Co. GA & Co. agreed to accept management's viewpoint and in March 1986, rendered an opinion on the December 31, 1988, financial statements. The statements showed that TS Ltd. had a net income of $1 million for the 1988 fiscal year. A note to the financial statements stated the following:

> The gain on disposition of a leasehold right arose as a result of a payment received from a lessor in exchange for the company's agreement to allow the expansion of a shopping centre in which it operates a department store. In November 1988, the company filed with the securities commissions reporting a change in independent public accountants. The company's former auditors, CW & Co., disagreed with the company's method of accounting for the transaction and were of the opinion that the gain should be amortized to income over the remaining term of the lease. Management, with the concurrence of the audit committee of the board of directors and the company's current auditors, GA & Co., believes its accounting treatment (i.e., recognizing the gain immediately) is preferable based on the substance of the transaction and the intent of the parties. Had the accounting treatment suggested by the company's former auditors been followed, net income for 1988 would have been $1.6 million ($.50 per share) less than reported.

The company's 1988 statement filed with the securities commissions stated the following:

> Under an amendment to a capital lease, the lessor of a shopping centre in which the company operates a store, developed plans to expand the shopping centre to become an integrated regional mall. The company consented to this development in exchange for $3 million. Further, the amendment provided that the lessor refurbish the exterior of the company's store and the company agreed to proceed diligently to alter, modernize, and refixture the interior of the store. No amount to be expended was specified. As a result of the lessor's enhancement of the centre and refurbishing of the exterior of the store, the company agreed to pay an increase in rent of $180,000 per annum for the remaining 12 of the original 30 years of the lease term (such increased rental does not apply to subsequent renewal option periods). Management concluded that the appropriate accounting treatment was to recognize income of approximately $1.6 million in the 1988 fiscal year, representing the difference between the $3 million and the present value of the increased rental. The present value was calculated using the implicit rate of the original lease which was 8 percent. The lease obligation and asset were recorded at that rate several years ago. This accounting treatment was ratified by the audit committee of the board of directors of the company.

In support of its accounting treatment, TS Ltd.'s management argued that the use of an 8% implicit interest rate resulted in conservative recognition of income. Had the 18% current borrowing rate been used, the gain on disposition would have been $2.1 million. Furthermore, they suggested that a complete note disclosure would ensure that its accounting treatment was acceptable.

A financial analyst suggested that a third alternative might have better described the true nature of the transaction. It could be considered to consist of two separate events. The first event is the selling of an exclusive right for $3 million. The second event is the improvement of the exterior of TS Ltd.'s store by the lessor, in return for higher rentals over the next 12 years. This view may be summarized by the following journal entries.

Cash	3,000,000	
Gain on disposition of leasehold right		3,000,000
To record the sale of an exclusive right.		
Leased asset, capitalized	1,400,000	
Present value of lease obligation		1,400,000
To record an increase in future lease payments as a result of the lessor's improvements to the exterior of the store.		

Required:

Discuss the accounting issues involved in this situation. Assess the various viewpoints involved as part of the discussion.

(CICA Adapted)

C10–5   (Leases, Taxes, Contingencies)

The junior accountant of Blast-off Ltd., a federally incorporated manufacturing company, has prepared the following *draft* financial statements for review by the company controller:

Statement of Income and Retained Earnings
For the Year Ended December 31, 1988
(in thousands)

Sales		$100,000
Cost of goods sold		50,000
Gross profit		50,000
Operating expenses:		
Selling	$ 18,000	
General and administrative	12,000	30,000
Net income before income taxes		20,000
Income tax expense (50%)		10,000
Net income		10,000
Retained earnings beginning of year		24,600
		34,600
Dividends declared current year		4,600
Retained earnings end of year		$ 30,000
Earnings per share		$1.00

Balance Sheet
As at December 31, 1988
(in thousands)

Assets

Current:		
Cash	$ 1,900	
Accounts receivable	5,000	
Inventories	12,000	
Prepayments	100	$ 19,000
Fixed (net):		
Land	30,000	
Plant	400,000	
Equipment	200,000	630,000
Other:		
Patent (net)		7,000
Total assets		$656,000

Liabilities and Shareholders' Equity

Current liabilities:

Accounts payable	$ 14,850	
Accrued liabilities	150	
Estimated warranty liabilities	1,000	$ 16,000

Long-term liabilities:

12% bonds payable	250,000	
Future income taxes	20,000	270,000
Total liabilities		$286,000

Shareholders' equity:

Common stock—issued and outstanding, 10,000,000 shares	$340,000	
Retained earnings	30,000	
Total shareholders' equity		370,000
Total liabilities and shareholders' equity		$656,000

While reviewing these financial statements, the controller made note of the following points:

1. The Future Income Taxes account included the following:
    a. Taxes on the excess of CCA claimed over depreciation booked, to December 31, 1988, amounted to $20,500,000.
    b. Taxes on the excess of the estimated warranty liabilities expensed over the actual warranty costs, to December 31, 1988, amounted to $500,000.

2. The Land account was reduced by $5,000,000 on July 1, 1988, when land being held for future use was sold for $6,200,000. The gain of $1,200,000 was included in general and administrative expenses. The company intends to treat the gain as a capital gain for income tax return purposes. Capital gains are taxed at full rates on ¾ of the gain. The remainder is not taxed.

3. The company had been involved in prolonged litigation with a competitor over an infringement of Blast-off's patent. At the inception of the litigation five years ago, the competitor ceased manufacturing and selling the product. The lawsuit was settled in 1988 with Blast-off being awarded a $500,000 settlement. Upon receipt of the settlement on July 6, 1988, the junior accountant debited cash and credited sales each for $500,000. Revenue Canada has advised that receipts of this type are taxable at Blast-off's current tax rate, which is 50%.

4. On January 1, 1988, the company entered into a 10-year noncancellable lease on a machine with an estimated life of 10 years and with no salvage value at the end of that time. The machine will become the property of the lessee at the end of the lease term. The fair market value of the machine on January 1, 1988, was $1,000,332. The annual lease payment, payable in advance, amounted to $148,000. The first payment was made at the inception of the lease, January 1, 1988, and was charged immediately to general and administrative expense. The lessor's implicit interest rate was 10%, which is the same as Blast-off's incremental borrowing rate. The machine would have been depreciated on the straight-line basis, if owned. It qualifies for class 8 (rate 20%) capital cost allowance.

Required:
Determine the accounting adjustments that will be required under Canadian generally accepted accounting principles. Describe any financial reporting implications of the adjustments.

(SMAC Adapted)

C10–6 **(Analysis of Liabilities Reported on an Actual Set of Financial Statements)**
Refer to the financial statements of Consolidated-Bathurst given in Appendix B immediately preceding the Index. Answer the following questions for the 1988 annual accounting period.

1. What were the (*a*) current liabilities, (*b*) long-term debt, and (*c*) any other noncurrent liabilities reported on the balance sheet?

2. How much cash was paid on (*a*) long-term debt and (*b*) other noncurrent liabilities?

3. Refer to the notes to the financial statements and complete the following:

   Total long-term debts listed . . . $_____
   Less: Current portion . . . . . . $_____
   Total long-term debt . . . . $_____

4. Explain the reason for subtracting the "current portion" in Question 3 above.

5. Did the company disclose any contingent liabilities or other commitments? Explain.

6. Did the company disclose any lease liabilities? Explain.

ELEVEN

MEASURING AND REPORTING BONDS PAYABLE AND OTHER LONG-TERM LIABILITIES

PURPOSE

Chapter 10 discussed current liabilities and the concepts of future and present value. This chapter discusses long-term liabilities, with emphasis on bonds payable. Long-term liabilities are an important source of funds that are primarily used to pay for noncurrent assets. Bonds are long-term debt instruments. When bonds are issued (i.e., sold), they represent an investment for the buyer and a liability for the issuer. Accounting for bonds involves some complexities. The purpose of this chapter is to discuss measuring, recording, and reporting the financial effects of bonds payable and other long-term liabilities.

Notice on the facing page how Petro-Canada reports its industrial development bonds and its unamortized discount. These Notes to Consolidated Statements are a continuation of the illustration used in Chapter 10.

LEARNING OBJECTIVES

1. Define and classify bonds payable.
2. Record and report bonds payable, with discount and premium amortization.
3. Record and report bond sinking funds.
4. Account for debt retirement funds.
5. Expand your accounting vocabulary by learning about the "Important Terms Defined in This Chapter."
6. Apply the knowledge gained from this chapter.

ORGANIZATION

Part A—fundamentals of measuring, recording, and reporting bonds payable
1. Characteristics of bonds payable.
2. Interest rates on bonds.
3. Accounting for bonds sold at par, discount, and premium.
4. Advantages and disadvantages of issuing bonds.
5. Financial leverage.

Part B—additional problems in accounting for bonds payable
1. Accounting for bonds sold between interest dates.
2. Accounting for bonds with different interest and accounting period dates.
3. Bond sinking funds.
4. Effective-interest amortization of bond discount and premium.

Petro-Canada

NOTES TO CONSOLIDATED FINANCIAL STATEMENTS
December 31, 1987 (stated in millions of dollars)

Note 6: Long-Term Debt

	Maturity	1987	1986
In Canadian dollars			
8.25% unsecured notes	1993	$ 11	$ 14
Other		—	1
In United States dollars			
7.25% unsecured debentures (U.S. $200 million)	1996	260	276
8.25% unsecured debentures (U.S. $200 million)	2016	260	276
LIBOR less 0.8% unsecured notes (U.S. $125 million)	1995	162	173
9% unsecured notes (U.S. $30 million)	1995	39	52
7.75% unsecured notes (U.S. $14 million)	1993	18	19
8.45% unsecured notes		—	7
		750	818
Less current portion		6	13
		$ 744	$ 805

Repayment of long-term debt

The minimum repayment of long-term debt in each of the next five years is as follows:
1988-$6 million   1989-$6 million   1990-$6 million   1991-$7 million   1992-$7 million

Note 7: Deferred Credits

	1987	1986
Advances on future natural gas deliveries	$ 118	$ 129
Long-term liabilities	39	69
Translation adjustment on long-term debt	33	—
	$ 190	$ 198

Note 14: Pension Plans

Effective January 1, 1987 the Corporation adopted prospectively the Canadian Institute of Chartered Accountants' new recommendations on accounting for pension costs and obligations. Prior to 1987 the Corporation charged to earnings an amount equal to that funded. The effect of this change was to increase 1987 net earnings by $6 million.

The Corporation's plans are defined benefit plans with the benefits generally based upon years of service and average salary during the final years of employment. They are funded by the Corporation based upon the advice of an independent actuary.

Plan Status as at December 31	1987	1986
Actuarial value of assets	$ 394	$ 351
Pension obligation	382	352
Net pension asset (obligation)	$ 12	$ (1)

The net pension asset (obligation) is amortized to earnings over the expected average remaining service life of the employees covered by the plans, which is currently 12 years.

1987 pension funding and expense amounted to $32 million and $17 million respectively.

PART A—FUNDAMENTALS OF MEASURING, RECORDING, AND REPORTING BONDS PAYABLE

Characteristics of Bonds Payable

Funds needed for long-term purposes, such as the acquisition of high-cost machinery or the construction of a new plant, often are obtained by issuing long-term debt instruments. These instruments usually are long-term notes payable (discussed in Chapter 10) and bonds payable. Bonds payable may be **secured** by a mortgage on specified assets, or the bonds may be **unsecured.** Bonds usually are issued in denominations of $1,000 or $10,000, and sometimes in denominations of $100,000. They usually are negotiable (i.e., transferable by endorsement). The bonds of some large companies are bought and sold by investors on the major stock exchanges.[1] Bonds are also sold by private placement to institutional investors such as pension plans. (Supplement 11A discusses pension plan accounting.) A typical **bond certificate** is shown in Exhibit 11–1.

The **principal** of a bond is the amount (*a*) payable at the maturity date and (*b*) on which the periodic cash interest payments are computed. The principal is specified on the bond certificate (see Exhibit 11–1), and it does not change. It is also called the **par value, face amount,** and maturity value. A bond will always specify a **stated rate of interest,** which also is specified on the bond certificate. The stated rate of interest typically does not change. A bond will specify that **periodic cash interest payments** must be paid—usually annually or semiannually. Each periodic interest payment is computed as **principal times the stated interest rate.** The selling price of a bond does not affect the periodic **cash** payments for interest. For example, a $1,000, 8% bond would always pay cash interest of (*a*) $80 on an annual basis, or (*b*) $40 on a semiannual basis.

A bond may sell at its par value, at a discount (below par), or at a premium (above par). The selling price of a bond is **determined by the difference between its stated interest rate and its market rate of interest.** The market rate of interest is the interest rate that investors (i.e., bond buyers) require to adequately compensate them for the risks related to the bonds. If the stated and market rates are the same, a bond will sell at par; if the market rate is higher than the stated rate, a bond will sell at a discount; and if the market rate is lower than the stated rate, the bond will sell at a premium. These relationships will always prevail because (*a*) the periodic cash interest payment is fixed, (*b*) the market rate of interest is set by the investors, and (*c*) the price paid for the bond must earn the market rate of interest for the investors (this is discussed further in the next section).

---

[1] Bonds also are issued by governmental units, such as federal and provincial governments, cities, and by other nonprofit institutions. The discussions in this chapter apply to both types, although we will focus mainly on those issued by corporations.

Exhibit 11-1 Typical bond certificate

$1000

DEBENTURE

$1000

DEBENTURE
75- C1262

CANADA — PROVINCE OF NOVA SCOTIA

THE CITY OF HALIFAX

DEBENTURE

GENERAL PURPOSES — 1975

Issued under authority of Chapter 193 of the Revised Statutes of Nova Scotia, 1967,
and of a resolution passed by the City Council of The City of Halifax on the 23rd day of
April, A.D. 1975.

THE CITY OF HALIFAX

WILL PAY IF UNREGISTERED TO THE BEARER HEREOF, OR IF REGISTERED TO THE REGISTERED
HOLDER HEREOF, THE SUM OF

ONE THOUSAND DOLLARS

IN LAWFUL MONEY OF CANADA AT THE OFFICE OF THE CITY TREASURER OF THE CITY OF
HALIFAX, AT HALIFAX, NOVA SCOTIA, OR AT THE PRINCIPAL OFFICE OF THE ROYAL BANK OF
CANADA IN ANY OF THE CITIES OF HALIFAX, NOVA SCOTIA; SAINT JOHN, NEW BRUNSWICK;
MONTREAL, PROVINCE OF QUEBEC; TORONTO, ONTARIO ; WINNIPEG, MANITOBA; AND
VANCOUVER, BRITISH COLUMBIA; IN CANADA, AT THE OPTION OF THE HOLDER IN

TEN YEARS (1st MAY, 1985)

FROM THE DATE HEREOF, AND WILL PAY INTEREST UPON THE SAID SUM AT THE RATE OF
— NINE AND THREE-QUARTERS PER CENTUM PER ANNUM —
PAYABLE HALF-YEARLY AT THE SAID OFFICES, AT THE OPTION OF THE HOLDER UPON THE
FIRST DAYS OF MAY AND NOVEMBER IN EACH YEAR, UPON PRESENTATION AND SUR-
RENDER OF THE COUPONS HERETO ATTACHED.

ISSUED AT HALIFAX IN THE COUNTY OF HALIFAX THIS FIRST DAY OF MAY, A.D. 1975.

City Clerk

Mayor

Special Characteristics of Bonds

Each bond issue has characteristics that are specified in the bond indenture. The issuing company often will add special characteristics to a bond issue to make the bond more attractive to investors. Bonds may be classified in different ways, depending on their characteristics. Typical bond characteristics and their related classifications are shown in Exhibit 11–2.

Measuring Bonds Payable and Interest Expense

The accounting approach used to account for bonds payable is based primarily on the **cost** and **matching principles.** When a bond is issued (i.e., sold), the proceeds include the net cash received, plus the market value of any noncash resources received. In conformity with the **cost principle,** bonds payable are recorded at their **issue price,** which is their **current cash equivalent amount.** The cash equivalent amount is equal to the present value of all future payments using the market rate of interest.

Interest Rates on Bonds

A bond specifies its **stated** interest rate, which is multiplied by the bond principal, or par, amount to determine the **cash** interest paid each interest period. This cash payment is unaffected whether the bond sold at par, at premium, or at a discount.

In contrast, the **market** rate of interest is determined by competitive forces in the financial markets. It is the agreed rate that borrowers (bond issuers) are willing to pay and lenders (investors) are willing to accept on their money, taking into consideration the perceived level of risk involved. Market rates tend to fluctuate daily, but the stated rate of interest is fixed by contract for the life of the bond. As a result, the market price of a bond is affected by changes in the market rate of interest. The market rate of interest also is called the **effective** or **yield** rate.

The **cash flows** related to a bond for the bond issuer can be summarized as follows:

1. Cash **received** at issuance date = Market price of the bond (plus any accrued interest since the last interest date, discussed in Part B).
2. Cash **paid** at each interest date = Par value of the bond × Stated rate of interest.
3. Cash **paid** at maturity date = Par value.

When a bond is **issued at par,** the issuer receives **cash** equal to both the par value and market value of the bond. Also, in this case both the stated and market rates of interest are the **same.** When a bond is **issued at a discount,** the issuer receives **less cash** than the par value of the bond. In this case, because the cash interest payments are unaffected by either the market interest rate or the selling price, the market rate of interest will be **higher** than the stated rate of

Exhibit 11–2 Bond characteristics and classifications of bonds

Bond classification	Bond characteristic
1. On the basis of the collateral (assets):	
a. Unsecured bonds (often called **debentures**).	*a.* Bonds that do **not** include a mortgage or pledge of specific assets as a guarantee of repayment at maturity.
b. Secured bonds (often designated on the basis of the type of asset pledged, such as a real estate mortgage).	*b.* Bonds that include the pledge of specific assets as a guarantee of repayment at maturity.
2. On the basis of repayment of principal:	
a. Ordinary or single-payment bonds.	*a.* The principal is payable in full at a single specified maturity date in the future.
b. Serial bonds.	*b.* The principal is payable in installments on a series of specified maturity dates in the future.
3. On the basis of early retirement:	
a. Callable bonds.	*a.* Bonds that may be called for early retirement at the option of the **issuer**.
b. Redeemable bonds.	*b.* Bonds that may be turned in for early retirement at the option of the **bondholder**.
c. Convertible bonds.	*c.* Bonds that may be converted to other securities of the issuer (usually common shares) at the option of the **bondholder**.
4. On the basis of the payment of interest:	
a. Registered bonds.	*a.* Payment of interest is made by cheque and mailed **direct** to the bondholder whose name must be on file (i.e., in the bond register).
b. Coupon bonds.	*b.* Bonds with a printed coupon attached for each interest payment. The bondholder "clips" the coupon on the interest date and deposits it in a bank like a cheque, or mails it to the issuing company. Then the company mails the interest cheque direct to the person and address shown on the completed coupon. The interest rate on coupon bonds often is called the **coupon rate**.

interest. When a bond is **issued at a premium,** the issuer receives **more cash** than the par value. Because, in this case, the cash interest is unaffected by either the market rate of interest or the selling price, market rate of interest will be **less** than the stated rate of interest.

Each interest period bond interest expense is measured, recorded, and reported in conformity with the **matching principle.** At the end of each period, the amount of interest unpaid must be accrued and reported as expense so that it will be matched with the revenues in the period in which it was incurred. The measurement and reporting of interest on bonds is similar to interest on notes receivable and notes payable. However, when bonds are issued at a premium or discount, an additional measurement problem occurs because (*a*) interest expense is based on the market rate of interest and (*b*) interest paid, or payable, is based on the stated rate of interest.

Accounting for Bonds Illustrated

Accounting and reporting for bonds payable are illustrated in Exhibit 11–3, for three different cases: (1) bonds issued at par, (2) bonds issued at a discount, and (3) bonds issued at a premium. In each of these cases the bonds are sold on the authorization date, January 1, 19A.

Bonds Sold at Par

Bonds sell at their par value when buyers (investors) are willing to invest in them at the stated interest rate on the bond. For example, on January 1, 19A, Mason Corporation issued $400,000 of the bonds payable and received $400,000 in cash. The bonds were dated to start interest on January 1, 19A. The entry by Mason Corporation to record the issuance of these bonds is given in Exhibit 11–3, Case A.

Subsequent to the sale of the bonds, interest at 5% (i.e., 10% per year) on the par value of the bonds must be paid each June 30 and December 31 until maturity. The entries to record the interest payments during 19A are given in Exhibit 11–3, Case A.

At the end of the accounting period, December 31, 19A, the financial statements must report bond interest expense and a long-term liability, as shown in Exhibit 11–3, Case A.

In this case, Mason Corporation received $1,000 cash for each $1,000 bond sold and will pay back $1,000, principal + ($50 × 20 semiannual interest payments) = $2,000. The $1,000 difference is the amount of interest expense for the 10 years; therefore, the interest cost was $100 per year and the market or effective rate of interest was $100 ÷ $1,000 = 10% per year. The stated rate called for on the bond also was 10%.

The $1,000 cash that Mason Corporation received when each bond was sold is the present value of the future cash flows associated with the bond (refer to Chapter 10, Part B) computed as follows:

	Present value
a. Principal: $1,000 × $p_{n=20;\ i=5\%}$ (Table 10–2; 0.3769)	$ 377
b. Interest: $50 × $P_{n=20;\ i=5\%}$ (Table 10–4; 12.4622)	623
Issue (sale) price of one Mason bond	$1,000

Exhibit 11–3 Accounting for bonds payable illustrated

Situation:

Mason Corporation approved a bond issue on January 1, 19A: bonds payable authorized, 500 bonds, $1,000 par per bond, 10% interest (payable semiannually each June 30 and December 31), maturity in 10 years on December 31, 19J. Mason's accounting period ends December 31.

Case A—Bonds issued at par:

On January 1, 19A, Mason issued 400 bonds at par (i.e., an effective rate of 10%) for $400,000 cash.

Entries during 19A:

January 1, 19A—To record issuance of the bonds at par:
Cash (400 bonds × $1,000) 400,000
    Bonds payable (400 bonds) 400,000

Interest payments during 19A:

	June 30, 19A	December 31, 19A
Bond interest expense	20,000	20,000
Cash ($400,000 × 5%)	20,000	20,000

Financial statement for 19A:

Income statement:
Bond interest expense . . . . $ 40,000

Balance sheet:
Long-term liabilities:
  Bonds payable, 10% (due December 31, 19J) 400,000

Case B—Bonds issued at a discount:

On January 1, 19A, Mason issued 400 ($400,000 par) of the bonds at an effective interest rate of 12% (i.e., at price of 88.5) for $354,000 cash.

Entries during 19A:

January 1, 19A—To record issuance of the bonds at a discount:
Cash (400 bonds × $885) 354,000
Discount on bonds payable [400 bonds × ($1,000 − $885)] 46,000*
    Bonds payable (400 bonds × $1,000) 400,000*

* Note: In effect, the bonds are recorded at their **issue price** because the liability is reported on the balance sheet at the net amount of these two balances.

Interest payments during 19A:

	June 30, 19A	December 31, 19A
Bond interest expense (cash interest plus amortized discount) .	22,300	22,300
Discount on bonds payable, straight-line amortization		
($46,000 ÷ 20 periods)	2,300	2,300
Cash ($400,000 × 5%)	20,000	20,000

Financial statements for 19A:

Income statement:
Bond interest expense ($22,300 × 2) . . . . $ 44,600

Balance sheet:
Long-term liabilities:
  Bonds payable, 10%, due December 31, 19J $400,000
    Less unamortized discount . . . . 41,400* 358,600†

Exhibit 11–3 *(concluded)*

Or, alternatively:

Bonds payable, 10%, due December 31, 19J
(maturity amount, $400,000, less unamortized discount) . . . .   358,600†

* $46,000 − $2,300 − $2,300 = $41,400.
† This amount is called the carrying value or net liability.

Case C—Bonds issued at a premium:

On January 1, 19A, Mason issued 400 ($400,000 par) of the bonds at an effective interest rate of 8½% (i.e., at a price of 110) for $440,000 cash.

Entries during 19A:

January 1, 19A—To record issuance of the bonds at a premium:
Cash (400 bonds × $1,100)   440,000
    Premium on bonds payable [400 bonds × ($1,100 − $1,000)]   40,000
    Bonds payable (400 bonds × $1,000)   400,000

Interest payments during 19A:

	June 30, 19A	December 31, 19A
Bond interest expense (cash interest less amortized premium)	18,000	18,000
Premium on bonds payable, straight-line amortization ($40,000 ÷ 20 periods)	2,000	2,000
Cash ($400,000 × 5%)	20,000	20,000

Financial statements for 19A:

Income statement:
Bond interest expense ($18,000 × 2) . . . . $ 36,000

Balance sheet:
Long-term liabilities:
  Bonds payable, 10% (due December 31, 19J) $400,000
  Add unamortized premium . . . .   36,000*   436,000†

Or, alternatively:
Bonds payable, 10%, due December 31, 19J (maturity amount, $400,000,
plus unamortized premium) . . . .   436,000†

* $40,000 − $2,000 − $2,000 = $36,000.
† This amount is called the carrying value or net liability.

Payment of principal (face) amount at maturity date (all three situations):

December 31, 19J:

Bonds payable   400,000
    Cash   400,000

When the effective rate of interest is equal to the stated rate of interest, the present value of the future cash flows associated with a bond **always** will equal the bond's par amount.

Bonds Sold at a Discount

Bonds sell at a discount when the buyers (investors) are willing to invest in them only at a market rate of interest that is **higher** than the stated interest rate on the bonds. Case B assumes that capital market established a 12% market rate of interest for the 10-year Mason bonds (Exhibit 11–3). The bonds have a stated rate of 10%, payable semiannually. Therefore, the bonds sold at a **discount.** At a 12% market rate, how much cash would a $1,000 bond of Mason Company generate if sold on January 1, 19A? To compute the cash issue (sale) price of one bond requires computation of its present value, at the **market rate,** of the two future cash flows specified on the bond: (*a*) the principal ($n = 20$, $i = 6\%$) and (*b*) the cash interest paid each semiannual interest period ($n = 20$, $i = 6\%$). Thus, the cash issue (sale) price of one Mason bond is computed as follows (refer to Chapter 10, Part B):

	Present value
a. Principal: $1,000 \times p_{n=20;\ i=6\%}$ (Table 10–2; 0.3118)	$312
b. Interest: $50 \times P_{n=20;\ i=6\%}$ (Table 10–4; 11.4699)	573
Issue (sale) price of one Mason bond	$885*

* Thus, the issue price was 88.5. Discount: $1,000 − $885 = $115.

The cash issue price of the 400 bonds issued by Mason would be $354,000 (i.e., 400 bonds × $885).

When a bond is sold at a discount (i.e., $115 discount per bond in the above example), the Bonds Payable account is credited for the par or maturity amount and the **discount is recorded as a debit to Discount on Bonds Payable.** The issuance of 400 of the bonds of Mason Company at a cash sale amount of $885 per bond (i.e., a 12% market rate) is recorded as shown in Exhibit 11–3, Case B.

The journal entry to record the issuance of the bonds (Exhibit 11–3) shows the discount in a separate contra liability account (Discount on Bonds Payable) as a **debit.** The discount must be given special treatment on the income statement to measure interest expense. Also, the balance sheet reports the bonds payable at their **carrying value** (maturity amount less any **unamortized** discount).

Measuring and Recording Interest on Bonds Issued at a Discount

In Exhibit 11–3, Case B, the issue price of each bond was $885 (discount $115). During the 10-year term of the bonds, Mason must make 20 semiannual cash interest payments of $50 each (i.e., $50 × 20 = $1,000 total interest) and at maturity pay back the $1,000 cash principal. Therefore, in addition to the cash interest of $1,000, $115 more cash per bond is paid back than was borrowed (i.e., $1,000 − $885). This $115 discount on each bond causes the yield or effective rate to be 12% (instead of the 10% stated on the bonds). The discount is an adjustment of the amount of interest expense that will be **reported** each accounting period on the income statement. Bond discount represents an **increase in bond interest expense.** To give accounting effect to bond discount in periods subsequent to issuance, the $46,000 debit to Discount on Bonds Payable (Exhibit 11–3, Case B) must be apportioned to each semiannual interest period as an increase in bond interest expense from the date of issuance to maturity date. There are two methods for doing this: (1) **straight-line amortization** and (2) **effective-interest amortization.** Straight-line amortization is easy to compute. The effective-interest method is discussed in Part B of this chapter.

Straight-Line Amortization.   To amortize the $46,000 bond discount over the period from date of issuance to maturity date on a straight-line basis, an equal dollar amount is allocated to each interest period. The Mason bonds have 20 six-month interest periods. Therefore, the computation would be $46,000 ÷ 20 periods = $2,300 amortization on each semiannual interest date. The interest payment on the bonds during 19A would be recorded as shown in Exhibit 11–3, Case B.

Conceptually, it can be argued that unamortized bond discount and unamortized bond premium should be disclosed as presented in Exhibit 11–3; that is, as a contra account to bonds payable or as an addition (adjunct) account to the par (face) amount. This disclosure implies the net liability should always equal the present value of all future cash payments using the market rate of interest existing when the bond was issued if the effective-interest method of amortization is used. If the straight-line method of amortization is used, the net liability will only approximate this present value. The *CICA Handbook* is silent on the disclosure of premiums, but Section 3070 permits the disclosure of bond discounts as a deferred charge in the asset section of the balance sheet. The apparent lack of concern about the rules of disclosure is likely to result from the fact that careful consideration of the stated or coupon rate of interest in terms of the market rate will cause the discount or premium to be small relative to the proceeds from the bond issue.

Each succeeding year the unamortized discount will **decrease** by $4,600; therefore, the net liability will **increase** each year by $4,600. At the maturity date of the bonds, the unamortized discount (i.e., the balance in the Discount on Bonds Payable account) will be **zero.** At that time the maturity or face amount of the bonds and the current net liability amount will be the same (i.e., $400,000).

While bond discount amortization is treated as an addition to interest expense for the period, income tax laws place restrictions on the timing and the amount of a deduction that may be claimed as an expense in computing income tax for the year. While the provisions are somewhat technical, the effect is to create a timing difference (see Chapter 10, a future income tax asset) for the amount of the bond amortization recorded for accounting purposes if the discount is small. For tax purposes the discount can be claimed as an expense only in the year the principal is paid. If the discount is too large, only three quarters of the discount can be expensed when the principal is paid at maturity or at redemption. This rule would create a permanent tax allocation difference for the one quarter that is disallowed as a deduction and a timing tax allocation difference for the remainder.

Bonds Sold at a Premium

Bonds sell at a premium when the buyers (investors) are willing to invest in bonds at a market or yield rate of interest that is **lower** than the stated interest rate on the bonds. For example, the capital market established an 8½% market rate of interest for the 10-year Mason bonds (Exhibit 11–3, Case C, stated rate, 10%, payable on semiannual basis), which means the bonds sold at a **premium.** The cash issue (sale) price of one Mason bond is computed as follows (refer to Chapter 10, Part B):

	Present value
a. Principal: $1,000 × $p_{n=20;\ i=4\frac{1}{4}\%}$ (Table 10–2; 0.4350)	$ 435
b. Interest: $50 × $\mathbf{P}_{n=20;\ i=4\frac{1}{4}\%}$ (Table 10–4; 13.2944)	665
Issue (sale) price of one Mason bond	$1,100

The cash issue price (110) of the 400 bonds issued by Mason would be $440,000 (i.e., 400 bonds × $1,100).

When a bond is sold at a premium ($100 premium per bond in the above case), the Bonds Payable account is credited for the par amount, and the **premium is recorded as a credit to Premium on Bonds Payable.** The issuance of 400 of the bonds of Mason Company at a cash sale price of $1,100 each (i.e., at an 8½% market rate) is recorded as shown in Exhibit 11–3, Case C.

Measuring and Recording Interest Expense on Bonds Issued at a Premium

The premium of $40,000 recorded by Mason must be apportioned to each of the 20 interest periods. Either the effective-interest method or the straight-line method may be used. Using the straight-line method, the amortization of premium each semiannual interest period would be $40,000 ÷ 20 periods = $2,000. Therefore, the payments of interest on the bonds during 19A would be recorded as shown in Exhibit 11–3, Case C.[2]

In the journal entry to record the sale and issuance of the bonds by Mason, the premium was recorded in a separate account, **Premium on Bonds Payable, as a credit.** The premium **decreases** interest expense. Therefore, in each period a

---

[2] The amount of interest expense recorded each semiannual period may be confirmed as follows:

Cash paid out by the borrower:	
Par amount of bonds at maturity	$400,000
Interest payments ($20,000 × 20 periods)	400,000
Total cash payments	800,000
Cash received by the borrower	440,000
Total interest expense over 10 years	$360,000
Interest expense per semiannual period ($360,000 ÷ 20 periods)*	$ 18,000

* Alternatively, $20,000 cash interest − $2,000 premium amortization = $18,000.

Exhibit 11-4   Amortization of bond discount and premium compared

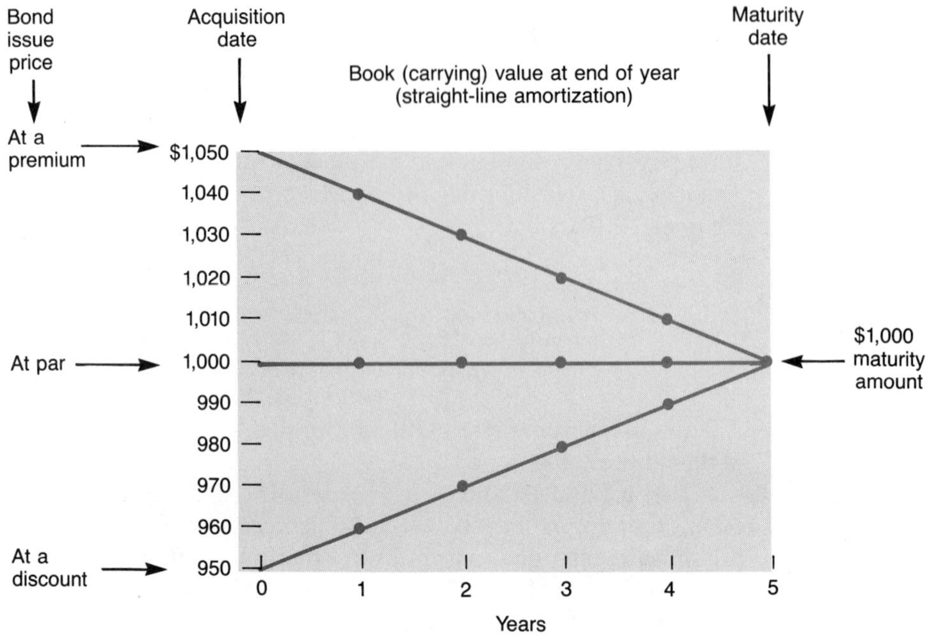

portion of it is amortized to interest expense. Notice in Exhibit 11-3, Case C, that Bond Interest Expense was reduced by $2,000 each semiannual period. At the end of 19A, the financial statements of Mason Company would report interest expense and bonds payable as shown in Exhibit 11-3, Case C.

When straight-line amortization of bond premium is used, **interest expense** is computed as the cash, or accrued, interest amount **minus** the periodic amount of premium amortized (see Exhibit 11-3).

At maturity date, after the last interest payment, the bond premium of $40,000 will be fully amortized, and the maturity or face amount of the bonds and the current net liability of the bonds will be the same (i.e., $400,000). At maturity, December 31, 19J, the bonds will be paid off in full, resulting in the same entry whether the bond was originally sold at par, a discount, or a premium.

Bond premium amortizations are treated as a reduction of interest expense for accounting purposes. For income tax purposes, they are ignored when computing the income tax payable by the corporation. Therefore, tax allocation (see Chapter 10) would treat the premium amortization as a permanent difference between the accounting income and the taxable income. This treatment implies the credit for the bond premium amortization is not included when computing income tax expense for the income statement.

The effect of amortization of bond discount and bond premium on a $1,000 bond is shown graphically in Exhibit 11-4.

The above discussion focused on the fundamental issues in measuring and reporting bonds payable. This discussion provided the background essential to understand the economic impact of bonds payable on the issuing company and its reporting on the periodic financial statements. The next part of the chapter discusses some complexities often encountered in accounting for bonds payable.

Advantages of Issuing Bonds

A corporation often uses long-term debt to obtain additional cash rather than selling its capital stock. The primary advantages of using bonds rather than capital stock are:

1. Ownership and control of the company are not diluted—in contrast to shareholders, bondholders do not participate in the management (by voting) and accumulated earnings of the company.
2. Cash payments to the bondholders are limited to the specified interest payments and the principal of the debt.
3. The **net interest cost** of borrowed funds often is less because interest expense reduces taxable income. Dividends paid to shareholders are not tax deductible.
4. **Positive financial leverage** often occurs. This occurs when the **net interest rate** on debt is less than the interest rate earned by the company on its total assets. For example, if a company borrows funds for an aftertax interest rate of 5.4% and earns 15% on its total assets, the difference, 9.6%, is called positive financial leverage because the company earns more on total invested funds than it pays out to borrow funds. Therefore, the shareholders had a significant benefit because of the relatively low cost of the borrowed cash. **Financial leverage is measured as the difference between the return on shareholders' equity and the return on total assets.**

Financial Leverage Illustrated

Exhibit 11–5 shows two comparative cases for Spicewood Corporation to illustrate the cause and economic effects of financial leverage. Case A assumes that the company has total assets of $500,000, which were provided in full by shareholders (i.e., it has no debt). In contrast, Case B assumes that of the total amount of assets, $300,000 was provided by shareholders and the remaining $200,000 was provided by creditors (i.e., debt). For illustrative purposes, the other variables are held constant in order to demonstrate the cause and economic effects of using debt to help finance a business.

In Exhibit 11–5, Case A, return on shareholders' equity is 15%, and the return on total assets also is 15%. When there is **no debt,** as in Case A, these two rates will **always** be the same.

Exhibit 11–5 Effects of financial leverage

SPICEWOOD CORPORATION

	Case A: No debt	Case B: Debt, $200,000, 9%

Balance sheet:

Total assets . . . . $500,000 . . . . $500,000
Total debt (9% interest) . . . . .   –0–   200,000

Shareholders' equity
(10,000 shares) . . . . $500,000   (6,000 shares) $300,000

Income statement:

Revenues . . . . $300,000 . . . . $300,000
Operating expense . . . . (175,000) . . . . (175,000)
Income tax
($125,000 × 40%) . . . . (50,000) . . . . (50,000)
Interest expense   ($200,000 × 9% = $18,000) –
(net of income tax) . . . . . .   –0–   ($18,000 × 40% = $7,200)   (10,800)
Net income . . . . $ 75,000 $ 64,200

Analysis:

a. Return on shareholders'
   equity ($75,000 ÷ $500,000) . . . 15%   ($64,200 ÷ $300,000) 21%
b. Return on total assets   ($64,200 + $10,800 = $75,000)
   ($75,000 ÷ $500,000) . . . . 15%   ÷ $500,000* 15%
c. Financial leverage
   [a] – [b]† . . . . –0–   (21% – 15%) 6%
d. EPS ($75,000 ÷ 10,000
   shares) . . . . $7.50   ($64,200 ÷ 6,000 shares) $10.70

* Interest on debt, net of income tax, is added back to derive total return to all fund providers (also see Chapter 16).
† Also see discussion of financial leverage in Chapter 16.

Now examine Case B, where $200,000 of debt is introduced. The return on shareholders' equity is 21%, and it is 15% on total assets. When debt is introduced, these two rates usually are different—only because of the debt.

This difference of 6% (i.e., 21% − 15%) is a measure of **financial leverage** because it measures the effect on owners' equity. Financial leverage may be positive (i.e., favourable to shareholders) or negative. In this case the financial leverage is **positive** because the rate of return on shareholders' equity (21%) is **higher** than the return on total assets (15%).

Notice in Exhibit 11–5, Case B, that to compute return on total assets, net income is increased by interest expense (net of income tax). This increase in net income is necessary because the denominator (total assets) includes resources provided by both owners and creditors. Therefore, the numerator must include the total return (i.e., net income plus the net-of-tax return provided to creditors).

The computation in Exhibit 11–5, Case B, is:

$$\frac{\$64,200 + (\$18,000 \times 60\% = \$10,800) = \$75,000}{\$500,000} = \underline{\underline{15\%}}$$

Disadvantages of Issuing Bonds

The primary disadvantages of using bonds are that (*a*) the required interest payments must be made each interest period, and (*b*) the large principal amount must be paid at maturity date. Sound financing of a business requires a realistic **balance** between the amounts of debt (including bonds payable) and owners' equity (i.e., common and preferred shares and retained earnings). In Case A, there was no debt, which is the most conservative position. In Case B, the $200,000 of debt was 40% of total assets employed (not an unusual case). However, if Spicewood Corporation had $400,000 debt, the 80% debt to total assets would be considered too high in most cases. It would be considered too high because interest payments to bondholders are **fixed charges.** Interest payments legally must be paid each period, whether the corporation earns income or incurs a loss. In contrast, dividends usually are paid to shareholders only if earnings are satisfactory. Each year, some companies go bankrupt because of their inability to make their required interest payments to creditors. Negative financial leverage can result if the overall earnings rate is less than the average aftertax interest rate on debt.

PART B—ADDITIONAL PROBLEMS IN ACCOUNTING FOR BONDS PAYABLE

This part of the chapter discusses four problems commonly encountered in accounting for bonds payable. These problems are (1) accounting for bonds sold between interest dates, (2) adjusting entries for accrued bond interest, (3) bond sinking funds, and (4) effective-interest amortization.

Accounting for Bonds Sold between Interest Dates

Although bonds may be sold on an interest date, market factors often cause them to be sold **between interest dates.** The exact amount of interest stated on the bond certificate for each interest date will be paid, regardless of whether a bond is sold on an interest date or between interest dates. Therefore, when bonds are sold between two interest dates, the investor (i.e., the buyer) must pay the interest that has **accrued since the last interest date** in addition to the market price of the bond. The amount of the next interest payment will be for a **full interest period;** therefore, the accrued interest is returned to the buyer. The net effect is that the investor will realize interest revenue only for the number of months the bonds were held from the date of sale. Similarly, the issuing

Exhibit 11–6 Accounting for bonds sold between interest dates

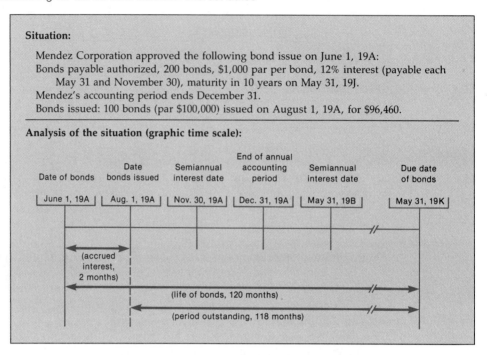

Situation:

Mendez Corporation approved the following bond issue on June 1, 19A:
Bonds payable authorized, 200 bonds, $1,000 par per bond, 12% interest (payable each
    May 31 and November 30), maturity in 10 years on May 31, 19J.
Mendez's accounting period ends December 31.
Bonds issued: 100 bonds (par $100,000) issued on August 1, 19A, for $96,460.

Analysis of the situation (graphic time scale):

Date of bonds	Date bonds issued	Semiannual interest date	End of annual accounting period	Semiannual interest date	Due date of bonds
June 1, 19A	Aug. 1, 19A	Nov. 30, 19A	Dec. 31, 19A	May 31, 19B	May 31, 19K

(accrued interest, 2 months)

(life of bonds, 120 months)

(period outstanding, 118 months)

corporation will incur interest expense for the same period. This case presents
two complexities in accounting for bonds: (1) the amount of accrued interest
charged to the buyer must be included in the journal entry of the issuer to record
the sale of bonds; and (2) any premium or discount must be amortized by the
issuer over the remaining period that the bonds will be outstanding; that is, the
period from date of sale to date of maturity of the bonds.

In this section, we will illustrate the four problems in accounting for bonds
with data for Mendez Corporation, given at the top of Exhibit 11–6. Mendez
Corporation issued bonds on August 1, 19A, which was two months after the
date of the bonds (June 1, 19A). The time scale given in Exhibit 11–6 will be
helpful in analyzing the effect of different dates on the accounting for the bond
issue.

On August 1, 19A, date of the issuance of the 100 bonds, Mendez Corporation would receive cash for the sale price of the bonds, plus two months' accrued
interest (June 1, 19A, to July 31, 19A), computed as follows (refer to the bond
time scale, Exhibit 11–6):

Market price (for 100 bonds)	$96,460
Add accrued interest for 2 months (June and July):	
$100,000 × 12% × 2/12	2,000
Total cash received	$98,460

Exhibit 11–6 *(concluded)*

Current 19A entries for bonds sold between interest dates:

August 1, 19A—Issuance of the bonds (par $100,000) for $96,460 plus two months'
     accrued interest prior to issuance date, $2,000.

Cash ($96,460 + $2,000)	98,460	
Discount on bonds payable ($100,000 − $96,460)	3,540	
Bonds payable (100 bonds × $1,000 par)		100,000
*Bonds interest expense ($100,000 × 12% × 2/12)		2,000

* This could be Bond Interest Payable.

November 30, 19A—First interest payment (issue date to maturity date, 118 months):

Bond interest expense (cash paid + amortized discount)	6,120	
Discount on bonds payable (straight-line;		
$3,540 × 4/118 mos.)		120
Cash ($100,000 × 6%)		6,000

Adjusting entry (end of the accounting period):

December 31, 19A—For 1 month interest since last interest date:

Bond interest expense ($1,000 + $30 amortization)	1,030	
Discount on bonds payable (straight-line;		
$3,540 × 1/118 mos.)		30
Bond interest payable ($100,000 × 12% × 1/12)		1,000

T-accounts for 19A:

Bond Interest Expense				Discount on Bonds Payable			
11/30/19A	6,120	8/1/19A	2,000	8/1/19A	3,540	11/30/19A	120
12/31/19A	1,030					12/31/19A	30

(Balance 12/31/19A, $5,150; close to In-
come Summary and report on income
statement.)

(Balance 12/31/19A, $3,390; report on bal-
ance sheet as a deduction (contra) to
Bonds payable.)

The bond investors must pay two months of accrued interest to Mendez
because the bond **indenture** (contract) requires that Mendez pay a full six
months of interest on the next interest date (i.e., November 30). On the first
interest date, the bonds will have been outstanding for only four months
(August 1 through November 30). Therefore, on November 30, 19A, the investors have earned four months' interest revenue, and the issuer (Mendez) has
incurred four months' interest expense. Payment by the investor to the issuer of
two months, accrued interest when the bonds are purchased is an offset that
causes interest to be adjusted to a four-month basis for both the investor and the
issuer.

The journal entry for the issuer, Mendez Corporation, to record the issuance of the 100 bonds payable is shown in Exhibit 11–6. In that entry, Bond Interest Expense was credited for $2,000 accrued interest collected because that amount will be refunded to the investor when the next interest payment is made. Conceptually, interest payable could be credited for the $2,000 if the interest payment debits were split into two elements—a debit to interest payable of $2,000, and the remainder to interest expense. However, it is expedient that the interest payment be recorded as a credit to Cash and a debit to Bond Interest Expense (Exhibit 11–6).

The $3,540 recorded in the Discount on Bonds Payable account is amortized over the **period outstanding** of 118 months. Therefore, straight-line amortization would be $3,540 ÷ 118 months = $30 per month. The entry to record the first interest payment would include **amortization of discount** only for the four months that the bonds have been outstanding. The first interest payment would be recorded as shown in Exhibit 11–6.

After journal entries are made to record the collection of accrued interest (August 1, 19A) and the payment of interest (November 30, 19A), the Bond Interest Expense account will have a debit balance of $4,120. This amount is equivalent to four months' interest (i.e., $100,000 × 12% × 4/12 = $4,000) plus four months' amortization of discount (i.e., $30 × 4 = $120). The Bond Interest Expense account would appear as follows:

Bond Interest Expense

11/30/19A	6,120	8/1/19A	2,000

(Balance, 11/30/19A, $4,120)

Adjusting Entry for Accrued Bond Interest

In Chapter 10, we discussed the **adjusting entry** that must be made for any interest expense accrued on a note payable since the last interest payment date. The same adjustment procedure must be applied to bonds payable. However, in the case of bonds, the adjusting entry must include **both the accrued interest and amortization of any bond discount or premium.** For example, Mendez Corporation (Exhibit 11–6) recorded an interest payment on November 30, 19A. Therefore, on December 31, 19A, there is accrued interest for one month. Bond discount also must be amortized for one more month. The adjusting entry at December 31, 19A, is shown in Exhibit 11–6.

After the adjusting entry is posted on December 31, 19A, the Bond Interest Expense account will have a debit balance of $5,150. This amount represents interest expense for the five months that the bonds have been outstanding during 19A (August 1 to December 31). The Bond Interest Expense account for

19A is shown at the bottom of Exhibit 11–6. The ending balance of $5,150 can be verified as follows:

Interest: $100,000 × 12% × 5/12 . . . . . . $5,000
Add discount amortized: $30 × 5   150
Total interest expense for 19A $5,150

Bond Interest Expense is closed to Income Summary at the end of the accounting period and is reported on the 19A income statement. The Bond Discount account for 19A is reported on the balance sheet as follows:

Long-term liabilities:
    Bonds payable $100,000
        Less: Discount on Bonds payable . .   3,390
        Carrying value . . . . $ 96,610

Bond Sinking Funds

On the maturity date of bonds payable, the issuing company must have available a large amount of cash to pay off the bondholders. A demand for a large amount of cash might place the issuing company in a financial strain. To avoid this situation, some companies create a separate **cash fund** by making **equal** annual **contributions** over a period of time in advance of the bond maturity date. This separate cash fund is called a **bond sinking fund.** A bond sinking fund is an asset that is invested pending the due date of the bonds. It is reported on the balance sheet under the caption "Investments and funds."

A bond sinking fund also reduces the risk of nonpayment for the bondholders. It assures them that funds will be available for retirement of the bonds at their maturity date. Each cash contribution to the fund is deposited with an **independent trustee** (a designated third party such as a bank or another financial institution). The trustee invests the funds and adds the fund earnings to the fund balance each year. Interest earned on a sinking fund is recorded as an increase in the fund balance (a debit) and as interest revenue (a credit). Thus, a bond sinking fund has the characteristics of a savings account as shown in Chapter 10, Part B. At the maturity date of the bonds, the balance of the fund is used to pay the bondholders. Any excess cash is returned to the issuing corporation, or in the case of a deficit, it is made up by the issuer.

Exhibit 11–7 illustrates a bond sinking fund for Mendez Corporation. The fund will be built up over the last five years that the bonds are outstanding by making five equal annual deposits each May 31, starting in 19F. The sinking fund contributions will be deposited with City Trust Co., as trustee, which will pay 8% annual interest on the fund balance each May 31. The amount of each deposit required can be calculated using the time value of money concepts discussed and illustrated in Chapter 10, Part B. If the fund earned no interest, each deposit would have to be $20,000 (i.e., $100,000 ÷ 5 contributions =

Exhibit 11–7 Accounting for a bond sinking fund

Situation:

Mendez Corporation plans to accumulate a bond sinking fund sufficient to retire the $100,000 bond issue outstanding on maturity date, May 31, 19J (see Exhibit 11–6). Five equal annual deposits are to be made on each May 31, starting in 19F. Expected earning rate on the fund is 8%.

Computation of periodic deposits ($n = 5$, years F through J; $i = 8\%$):

Computation (application of future value of annuity of $1):

Future value = Periodic payment $\times$ $F_{n=5;\ i=8\%}$

Substituting:

$100,000 = ? \times 5.8666$ (Table 10–3)

Periodic payment = $100,000 \div 5.8666

= $ 17,046

Entries—for first year of the fund and the second deposit:

May 31,19F—To record the first deposit by Mendez:

Bond sinking fund	17,046	
Cash (computed above)		17,046

May 31, 19G—To record interest revenue for one year added to the fund:

Bond sinking fund (notice, not the cash account)	1,364	
Interest revenue ($17,046 $\times$ 8%)		1,364

May 31, 19G—To record the second deposit by Mendez:

Bond sinking fund	17,046	
Cash (computed above)		17,046

Entry at maturity date (May 31, 19J) to retire the bonds:

Bonds payable	100,000	
Bond sinking fund		100,000

Sinking fund accumulation schedule (Deposits, $17,046; $n = 5$; $i = 8\%$):

Date	Cash Deposit (Credit Cash)	Interest Revenue (Credit)	Fund Increase (Debit Fund)	Accumulated Fund Balance
5/31/19F	17,046[a]		17,046	17,046
5/31/19G	17,046	$17,046 $\times$ 8% = 1,364[b]	18,410[c]	35,456[d]
5/31/19H	17,046	35,456 $\times$ 8% = 2,836	19,882	55,338
5/31/19I	17,046	55,338 $\times$ 8% = 4,427	21,473	76,811
5/31/19J	17,046	76,811 $\times$ 8% = 6,143*	23,189	100,000
Totals	85,230	14,770	100,000	

* Rounded $2 to accommodate prior rounding errors.
[a] Computed above.
[b] Interest earned on beginning balance in the fund each period at 8 percent.
[c] Periodic deposit ($17,046) plus interest earned ($1,364) = $18,410 (etc.)
[d] Prior balance ($17,046) plus increase in fund ($18,410) = $35,456 (etc.).
Note: This is an ordinary annuity, i.e., end-of-period contributions.

$20,000). Instead of $20,000, the annual deposit required is **less** than $20,000 because the interest earned each year will be added to the fund balance. The $17,046 required annual deposit was computed as shown in Exhibit 11–7.[3]

The journal entries for May 31, 19F, and 19G, for the sinking fund are shown in Exhibit 11–7. Notice that the fund is increased by both the annual deposits and the accumulation of interest. Identical journal entries with different interest amounts would be made for each of the five years of the accumulation period. The interest amounts increase each year because of the increasing balance in the fund. At the maturity date of the bonds, payment will be made to the bond-holders using the cash accumulated in the sinking fund. The journal entry to retire the bonds payable is shown in Exhibit 11–7.

Often it is useful to prepare a fund accumulation schedule as shown in Exhibit 11–7. Notice that the schedule provides data for (1) the entry on each interest date and (2) the buildup of the fund to maturity date.

Some bond indentures for sinking fund bonds will permit the organization to use the cash placed in the sinking fund to buy the bonds of the issuing organization on the open market. The bonds would then be canceled and the bond liability reduced correspondingly. Such an approach would mean that the sinking fund would not be an asset because each purchased bond can be offset against the outstanding liability using what is termed the **right of offset.** The accounting entries for such a procedure will be discussed in advanced courses.

Effective-Interest Amortization of Bond Discount and Premium

Amortization of bond discount and premium, using the straight-line method, was discussed in Part A (page 644). Another method is called **effective-interest amortization.** This method uses the **present value** (Chapter 10, Part B) to compute the periodic amortization amounts. The concept underlying the effective-interest method is that **interest expense each period is the unpaid balance of the liability multiplied by the effective interest rate (not the stated rate) for the bonds.**

The straight-line approach is permitted when the difference in periodic amortization results between the two methods is not material in amount. Conceptually, the effective-interest method is similar to the debt repayment which was discussed in Chapter 10. Each equal payment made on the debt has two parts: (1) a payment of principal and (2) a payment of interest.

Exhibit 11–8 shows an application of the effective-interest method. The sale price of the West Corporation bonds is the present value of the future cash flows associated with the bonds. The difference between the total par value of the bonds ($10,000) and the present value of the bonds ($8,558) is the discount ($1,442) which must be amortized over the life of the bonds. First, the journal entry to record the issuance of the bonds is shown in Exhibit 11–8.

---

[3] A company also may restrict, or appropriate, an equivalent amount of retained earnings as a dividend restriction. Restrictions of retained earnings by a corporation are discussed in Chapter 12.

Exhibit 11–8 Effective-interest amortization on bond discount

---

Situation: West Corporation sold 10, $1,000 bonds as follows:

Bonds payable authorized (10 bonds at $1,000 par each)	$10,000
Date printed on each bond	January 1, 19A
Maturity date (five-year term from January 1, 19A)	December 31, 19E
Interest, **cash payable per annum** each December 31, 8%	$800
Issued (sold) all of the bonds	January 1, 19A
Market interest rate	12%
Sale price (at a discount)	$8,558*
End of the accounting period for West	December 31

* Issue price computed as follows:
$10,000 × $p_{n=5;\ i=12\%}$ (Table 10–2; 0.5674) = $5,674
$800 × $P_{n=5;\ i=12\%}$ (Table 10–4; 3.6048)   =   2,884
                                                $8,558

Entry to record issuance (sale) of the bonds at a discount:

January 1, 19A:

Cash (computed above)	8,558	
Discount on bonds payable ($10,000 − $8,558)	1,442	
Bonds payable (10 bonds × $1,000 par)		10,000

Bond payment schedule, effective-interest amortization:

(a) Date	(b) Cash Interest Paid on Each Interest Date ($10,000 × 8%)	(c) Interest Expense (based on beginning unpaid liability at market rate of 12%)	(d) Effective-Interest Amortization (increase of liability)*	(e) Net Liability (unpaid balance)
1/1/19A				8,558
12/31/19A	800	8,558 × 12% = 1,027	227	8,785
12/31/19B	800	8,785 × 12% = 1,054	254	9,039
12/31/19C	800	9,039 × 12% = 1,085	285	9,324
12/31/19D	800	9,324 × 12% = 1,119	319	9,643
12/31/19E	800	9,643 × 12% = 1,157	357	10,000
Subtotal	4,000	5,442	1,442	
12/31/19E	10,000†		(10,000)	–0–

* Adjusts the net liability to the maturity amount.
† Payment of principal.

When the effective-interest amortization method is used, the amount of interest expense and the amount of discount or premium that is amortized **change** each interest period. The amount of cash interest paid does not change because it is based on the stated rate of interest that is stated on the bond. The

Exhibit 11–8 *(concluded)*

Periodic entries to record interest paid and discount amortization, December 31:					
	19A	**19B**	**19C**	**19D**	**19E**
Bond interest expense	1,027	1,054	1,085	1,119	1,157
Discount on bonds payable	227	254	285	319	357
Cash	800	800	800	800	800

Financial statements:

	19A	**19B**	**19C**	**19D**	**19E**
Income statement:					
Bond interest expense	$1,027	$1,054	$1,085	$1,119	$1,157
Balance sheet:					
Bonds payable (maturity amount, $10,000) minus unamortized discount	8,785	9,039	9,324	9,643	–0–

amounts for each journal entry to record the payment of interest must be recomputed for each interest period. An organized approach to this computation is based on the preparation of a **debt payment schedule.** Notice that for each period, the first computation is interest expense (Exhibit 11–8, col. c). It is computed by using the **effective-interest rate**. The schedule provides the amortization and interest expense amounts that must be recorded each interest period, as shown in Exhibit 11–8. The journal entries to record periodic interest are based on the amounts in the debt payment schedule. The journal entries for West Corporation are illustrated in Exhibit 11–8.

The effective-interest amortization method is preferred conceptually because it multiplies the **unpaid liability balance** by the effective interest rate to compute periodic interest expense. The amortization amount then is computed as the difference between interest expense and the cash interest paid. For example, West Corporation borrowed $8,558 on January 1, 19A, at a market interest rate of 12%. The interest expense for the first year should be $1,027 (i.e., 12% × $8,558 = $1,027) which is the amount recorded in the journal entry for 19A, in Exhibit 11–8. In contrast, if the straight-line method had been used, the amortization of the bond discount would have been $288 (i.e., $1,442 ÷ 5 = $288), and interest expense would have been $1,088 (i.e., $288 + $800 = $1,088). Exhibit 11–9 pictorially presents the behaviour of the unamortized liability balance over the five years.

The net liability measured and reported on the balance sheet under the effective-interest method is the present value of the remaining cash flows associated with the bond, which is the conceptually preferred amount. The straight-

Exhibit 11–9 Amortization of bond discount* and premium compared using the effective-interest method

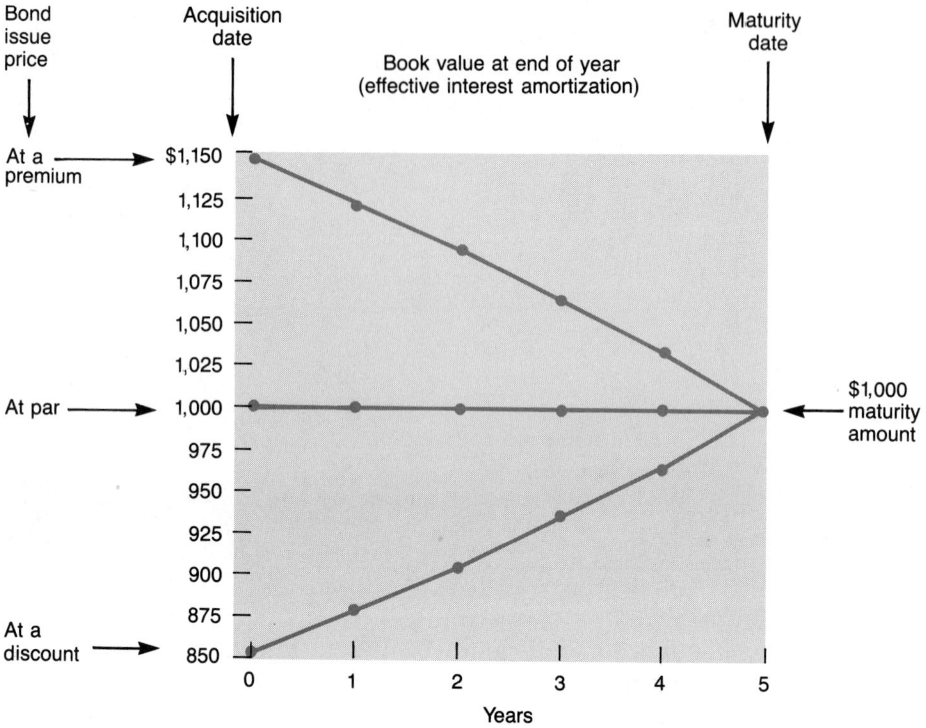

* Based on Exhibit 11–8. Premium example assumed.

line method approximates this amount and is acceptable if there is not a material difference between the two amounts.

To summarize, effective-interest amortization conceptually is superior to straight-line amortization. For each period, consistent with the issue price of the bonds, it measures (1) the true amount of interest expense each period on the income statement and (2) the true current net carrying amount of the bonds outstanding (net liability) on the balance sheet each period. In contrast, straight-line amortization gives approximations of these amounts and can be used only when the difference between the two methods is deemed not material (refer to threshold for recognition, materiality). In such cases, straight-line amortization often is used because it is less complex.

DEMONSTRATION CASE

(Try to resolve the requirements before proceeding to the suggested solution that follows.)

To raise funds to build a new plant, the management of Reed Company issued bonds. A bond indenture was approved by the board of directors. Some provisions in the bond indenture and specified on the bond certificates were:

> Par value of the bonds ($1,000 bonds) $600,000
> Date of bond issue—February 1, 19A, due in 10 years on January 31, 19K.
> Interest—10% per annum, payable 5% on each July 31 and January 31.

All of the bonds were sold on June 1, 19A, at 102½, plus accrued interest. The annual accounting period for Reed Company ends on December 31.

Required:

a. How much cash was received by Reed Company from the sale of the bonds payable on June 1, 19A? Show computations.

b. What was the amount of premium on the bonds payable? Over how many months should it be amortized?

c. Compute the amount of amortization of premium per month and for each six-month interest period; use straight-line amortization. Round to the nearest dollar.

d. Give the journal entry on June 1, 19A, to record the sale and issuance of the bonds payable.

e. Give the journal entry for payment of interest and amortization of premium for the first interest payment on July 31, 19A.

f. Give the adjusting entry required on December 31, 19A, at the end of the accounting period.

g. Give the optional reversing entry that could be made on January 1, 19B.

h. Give the journal entry to record the second interest payment and the amortization of premium on January 31, 19B.

i. Show how bond interest expense and bonds payable are reported on the financial statements at December 31, 19A.

Suggested Solution

Requirement a:

Sale price of the bonds: ($600,000 × 102.5%)	$615,000
Add accrued interest for four months (February 1 to May 31)	
($600,000 × 10% × 4/12)	20,000
Total cash received for the bonds	$635,000

Requirement b:

Premium on the bonds payable ($600,000 × 2.5%)	$ 15,000
Months amortized: From date of sale, June 1, 19A, to maturity date,	
January 31, 19K (120 months − 4 months)	116 months

Requirement c:

Premium amortization: $15,000 ÷ 116 months = $129 per month, or $774 each six-month interest period (straight-line).

Requirement d:
June 1, 19A (issuance date):

Cash (per Requirement [a] above) 635,000		
Premium on bonds payable (per Requirement [b] above)		15,000
Interest expense (per Requirement [a] above)		20,000
Bonds payable		600,000

To record sale of bonds payable at 102½ plus accrued interest for four months, February 1 to May 31, 19A.

Requirement e:
July 31, 19A (first interest payment date):

Bond interest expense ($30,000 − $258) 29,742		
Premium on bonds payable ($129 × 2 months) 258		
Cash ($600,000 × 5%)		30,000

To record payment of semiannual interest and to amortize premium for two months, June 1 to July 31, 19A.

Requirement f:
December 31, 19A (end of the accounting period):

Bond interest expense 24,355		
Premium on bonds payable ($129 × 5 months) 645		
Bond interest payable ($600,000 × 10% × 5/12)		25,000

Adjusting entry for five months' interest accrued plus amortization of premium, August 1 to December 31, 19A.

Requirement g:
January 1, 19B (reversing entry):

Bond interest payable 25,000		
Premium on bonds payable		645
Bond interest expense		24,355

Reversing entry; optional.

Requirement h:
January 31, 19B (second interest date and assuming reversing entry [g] was made):[4]

Bond interest expense 29,226		
Premium on bonds payable (per Requirement [c]) 774		
Cash ($600,000 × 10% × 6/12)		30,000

To record payment of semiannual interest and to amortize premium for six months.

---

[4] If no reversing entry was made on January 1, 19B, this entry would be:

Bond interest payable 25,000		
Premium on bonds payable 129		
Bond interest expense 4,871		
Cash		30,000

Requirement i:
Interest expense reported on the 19A income statement should be for the period outstanding during the year (i.e., for seven months, June 1 through December 31). Interest expense, per the above entries, is $29,742 + $24,355 − $20,000 = $34,097; or alternatively, ($600,000 × 10% × 7/12 = $35,000) − ($129 × 7 months = $903) = $34,097.

Income statement for 19A:
Interest expense	$ 34,097

Balance sheet, December 31, 19A:
Long-term liabilities:		
Bonds payable, 10% (due January 31, 19K)	$600,000	
Add unamortized premium*	14,097	614,097

* $15,000 − ($258 + $645) = $14,097.

SUMMARY OF CHAPTER

This chapter discussed bonds payable, which represent a primary way to obtain funds to acquire long-term assets and to expand a business. An important advantage of bonds payable is that the **cost** of borrowing the funds—interest expense—is deductible for income tax purposes which reduces the interest cost to the business.

Bonds may be sold at their par (or face) amount, at a premium, or at a discount, depending upon the stated interest rate on the bonds compared with the market (or yield) rate of interest that the bond buyers demand and the issuer will accept. In each case, bonds are measured, recorded, and reported at their current cash equivalent amount. The price of a bond varies based on the relationship between the market and stated rates of interest. If the market rate is higher than the stated rate on the bond, the bonds will sell at a discount. Conversely, if the market rate is lower than the stated rate on the bond, the bonds will sell at a premium.

Discounts and premiums on bonds payable are adjustments of the cash interest payments made by the issuing company during the term of the bonds. Therefore, discount or premium on bonds payable is amortized to interest expense over the period outstanding from issue date to maturity date.

To assure that funds are available to retire bonds payable at maturity, a company may set aside cash in advance by means of periodic contributions to a bond sinking fund. Such a fund is like a savings account. The bond sinking fund usually is administered by an independent trustee. Interest earned on the fund balance is added to the fund each period. At the maturity date of the bonds, the fund is used to pay the bondholders. The fund is reported on the balance sheet under the caption "Investments and funds." Interest earned on the fund is reported on the income statement as "Interest revenue."

CHAPTER SUPPLEMENT 11A

Pensions

One employee benefit that creates significant accounting problems and challenges is employee pensions. A private pension is an amount paid to an employee upon retirement or at death out of funds accumulated by the employer and perhaps the employee. Canada Pension (Chapter 10) payments are similar but the funds are accumulated by the employee in the hands of the Federal Government or the Quebec Government in the case of Quebec pensions. The concern from an accounting perspective is the employer's portion of a private **pension plan**. The employee contributions and contributions to government plans are treated like other withholdings from payroll discussed in Chapter 10.

The employer contributions are placed with a trustee and invested by that trustee in a manner similar to a sinking fund. When an employee retires, the accumulated contributions are paid according to the rules of the pension agreement. Employees who leave before death or retirement receive a defined amount from the **fund**.

Accounting for pensions is concerned with establishing the pension benefit expense and the associated balance sheet disclosures for any liabilities or assets of the plan. In the simplest case, what the employer pays to the plan is the expense for the employer. Unfortunately, the simplest case is not the only situation the accountant has to face.

Two distinct types of pension plans exist. The least common is a **defined contribution plan**. As the name implies, what the employer must contribute is fixed, usually as a percentage of the compensation paid, but the amount the employee receives upon retirement depends upon how much the fund earns. Because the contributions at the time of employment are fixed in amount according to a formula, the accounting is straightforward. Pension expense is accrued according to what it is calculated to be. Payments are debited against the accrual and essentially the accounting is finished. Disclosure of the details of the plan is desirable but not mandatory.[5]

The more complex and common type of pension plan is a **defined benefit pension plan**. As the name implies, the amount of pension benefits an employee will receive is defined in amount or as a formula based on employee earnings close to retirement. The accounting problem is to determine what the expense is this year for something that will be paid years in the future. An actuary, a specialist in making such projected calculations, determines what the cash contributions should be in the current year to accumulate to the estimated benefits if certain assumptions are satisfied. Periodic actuarial reviews establish the accuracy of the assumptions and determine the adjustments needed to conform to the revised assumptions. Asset and/or liability disclosure on the employer's balance sheet also must be determined. Thus from an accounting

---

[5] *CICA Handbook*, Section 3460, "Pension Cost and Obligations," para. 75.

perspective, the amounts other than the cash payments specified by the actuary are based on estimates of what the future may bring both in terms of what the contributions to the trustee will earn and what will be paid to employees when they leave, die, or retire. Questions concern what is the expense in this accounting period, what is the liability or asset that should be recorded on the balance sheet, and what disclosures should be made, particularly for a defined benefit pension plan. An additional complication also occurs at the initiation of pension plans. It is common that pension benefits be given for past service when a plan is established. The accounting costs for these past services, termed **past service pension costs**, have to be matched to future accounting periods, contrary to what is implied in their name. The justification is that they are additional benefits for future work of employees.[6]

Exhibit 11–10 provides an illustration of the accounting aspects of pensions. Memoranda records are kept on pension fund assets deposited with a trustee and the actuarily determined accrued benefits for the pension plan. The **accrued benefits** represent the present value of the pension benefits accrued as a result of work performed to the date of its calculation. A set of calculations is made for both the assets and the accrued benefits based on the expected returns, contributions made by the employer and contributions paid by the plan to employees. At the end of a defined period of time, usually the year, the actual amounts are determined—the accrued benefits by the actuary, the assets according to their market values. The differences between the actual amounts and the expected amounts are experience gains or losses resulting because expectations did not occur. (See calculations A and B in Exhibit 11–10.)

The expense accrual for the period is calculated by the accountant based on the accrual for service specified by the actuary, adjusted for interest earned on the pension fund assets less interest expense on the accrued benefits. Included as well is the amortization of experience gains or losses. Journal entry (2) in Exhibit 11–10 records the expense in the accounts. The cash contribution to the pension fund trustee is recorded according to the amount the actuary tells the company to pay the fund. Journal entry (1) in Exhibit 11–10 records the illustrated amount.

Financial statement disclosure is illustrated in Exhibit 11–10. Also, the illustrated notes for Petro-Canada displayed on page 635 reflect one company's implementation of Canadian standards. Pension expense is customarily included with salaries and wages expense so it may not be evident to a reader. Pension accrual will appear as an asset or liability depending on the balance in the account.

Conceptual accounting issues for pensions are involved and complex even for professional accountants. First, what should be the liability (assets) shown on the balance sheet; the pension accrual or the accrued benefits less the pension fund assets? At this juncture, professional standards in North America have decided on the legalistic answer, the pension accrual, because it is legalistic and

---

[6] Accounting for past service costs is discussed in advanced courses.

Exhibit 11–10 Pension plan illustration

Data for X Company:

Actuarially determined accrued benefits, January 1, 19A $1,000,000
Pension fund assets at market value, January 1, 19A $1,000,000
Expected rate of return for 19A 12%
Convenient assumption: No outstanding pension obligations resulting from unfunded past service
  costs or for any other reason.
Events for year 19A:
  Actuarially determined expense accrual for year . . . . $ 50,000
  Total contributions to fund made in 12 equal monthly installments . . . . $ 48,000
  Pension benefits paid—Assume July 1, 19A . . . . $ 20,000
  Market value of pension fund assets, December 31, 19A $1,150,000
  Accrued benefits, actuarially determined, December 31, 19A $1,100,000

Records Needed:

a. Memoranda in T-account form

Pension Fund Assets		**Accrued Benefits**	

Open balance 19A
    1,000,000
		Open balance 19A
		    1,000,000	

Net change
  (Calculation B)
    149,680
		Net change
		  (Calculation A)
		    101,800	

End balance 19A
    1,149,680
		End balance 19A
		    1,101,800	

Open balance 19B
    1,150,000
		Open balance 19B
		    1,100,000	

b. General ledger accounts

Pension Expense		**Pension Accrual**	
(2) 50,120		Open balance 19A 0	
	(1) 48,000	(2) 50,120	
(To be closed with other income accounts at end of 19A.)		End balance 19A 2,120	

c. Journal entries

(1) Pension accrual 48,000
        Cash 48,000
     One entry of $4,000 at the end of each month; total $48,000 for 19A.

(2) Pension expense 50,120
        Pension accrual 50,120
     To record expense accrual according to Calculation C.

Exhibit 11–10 *(concluded)*

Balance Sheet:
Pension fund obligation (Note) $2,120
Income statement:
Salaries and wages (include $50,120 in pension expense)
SCFP cash flow from operations (include only $48,000 cash outflow)

Note:
Accrued pension benefits $1,100,000
Pension fund assets   1,150,000
Excess contributions . . . . $ 50,000

Other details of the type of pension plan and amortization of experience gains and losses would be specified.

Calculations:

A. Calculation of accrual benefits balance, December 31, 19A:
Balance January 1, 19A $1,000,000
Interest accrued at 12% for 1 year   120,000
Less: Interest saved on benefits paid
$20,000 \times .12 \times 1/2$ . . . .   (1,200)
Add: Interest accrued on current expense
$50,000 \times .12 \times 1/2$ (accrued evenly throughout year)   3,000
Less: Benefits paid in 19A . . . .   (20,000)
Expected balance of accrued benefits $1,101,800
Actuarially determined balance (used as beginning balance for 19B)   1,100,000
Experience gain (amortized to years 19B and subsequent) . . . . $ 1,800

B. Calculation of pension fund assets, December 31, 19A:
Balance January 1, 19A $1,000,000
Interest accrued at 12% for 1 year   120,000
Less: Interest lost on benefits paid
$20,000 \times .12 \times 1/2$ . . . .   (1,200)
Add: Interest earned on current contributions
$48,000 \times .12 \times 1/2$ 2,880
Add: Contributions for 19A   48,000
Less: Benefits paid in 19A . . . .   (20,000)
Expected balance in pension fund $1,149,680
Market value of pension assets (used as beginning balance for 19B)   1,150,000
Experience loss (amortized to years 19B and subsequent) . . . . $ (320)

C. Calculation of pension expense:
Accrual for service . . . . $ 50,000
Interest on accrued benefits:
Calculation A: $120,000
                   (1,200)
                    3,000
                   ───────   121,800
Less: Interest earned on pension fund assets:
Calculation B: $120,000
                   (1,200)
                    2,880
                   ───────   (121,680)
Amortization of experience gain or loss on accrued benefits (see Calculation A)   0
Amortization of experience gain or loss on pension fund assets (see Calculation B)   0
Expense for 19A . . . . $ 50,120

more reliably measured than the memoranda amounts. Also the notes do disclose the pension fund assets and the accrued benefits. Some accountants believe that the professional stance is a compromise between the earlier cash-oriented approach and full recording of the pension assets offsetting the accrued benefits. The second issue is a less visible one. It involves how to allocate the pension expense over the life of employee service. Some suggest a form of straight-line allocation, termed level contribution method, while others used an increasing charge-type method, termed the accrued benefits approach. Canadian standards have adopted the accrued benefits, increasing-charge type, allocation approach based on the argument that it better matches pension costs to revenue in a given period. Amortization of experience gains or losses is consistent with the treatment used for revision of estimates for fixed assets so little argument exists for this third factor. Valuing pension fund assets at market is different than the treatment of other investments, but the direction of accounting standards for investments is towards market.[7]

IMPORTANT TERMS DEFINED IN THIS CHAPTER

Actuarial Accrued Benefits A specialist determined present value of expected pension benefits. *p. 663*

Bond Certificate The bond document; an example is given in Exhibit 11–1. *p. 636*

Bond Discount A bond that is sold for less than par is sold at a discount; the difference between selling price and par. *p. 643*

Bond Premium A bond that is sold for more than par is sold at a premium; the difference between selling price and par. *p. 645*

Bond Principal The amount payable at the maturity of the bond; face amount. *p. 636*

Bond Sinking Fund A cash fund accumulated for payment of a bond upon maturity. *p. 653*

Callable Bond A bond that may be called for early retirement at the option of the issuer. *p. 639*

Convertible Bond A bond that may be converted to other securities of the issuer (usually common shares). *p. 639*

Coupon Rate of Interest The stated rate of interest on coupon bonds. *p. 639*

Debenture An unsecured bond; no assets are specifically pledged to guarantee repayment. *p. 639*

Defined Benefit Pension Plan Amount of employee benefits is fixed; employer expense has to be determined by an actuary. *p. 662*

Defined Contribution Pension Plan Amount of employer expense is fixed; employee benefits can vary. *p. 662*

---

[7] Chapter 13 will discuss investment valuation further.

Effective-Interest Amortization   Theoretically preferred method to amortize a bond discount or premium; interest expense is based on the effective-interest rate. *p. 655*

Effective-Interest Rate   Another name for the market rate of interest on a bond when issued; also called the yield rate. *p. 638*

Face Amount   Another name for principal or the principal amount of a bond. *p. 636*

Financial Leverage   Use of borrowed funds to increase the rate of return on owners' equity; occurs when the interest rate on debt is lower than the earnings rate on total assets. *p. 647*

Indenture   A bond contract that specifies the legal provisions of a bond issue. *p. 651*

Market Interest Rate   Current rate of interest on a debt when incurred; also called yield or effective rate. *p. 638*

Net Interest Cost   Interest expense, less any income tax savings associated with interest expense. *p. 647*

Par Value   Another name for bond principal or the maturity amount of a bond. *p. 636*

Past Service Pension Cost   Costs of pension benefits to employers for work before plan established; a future expense. *p. 663*

Pension Fund   Pension plan assets deposited with a trustee. *p. 662*

Pension Plan   A contract to pay employees after retirement. *p. 662*

Redeemable Bond   Bond that may be turned in for early retirement at the option of the bondholder. *p. 639*

Stated Rate   The rate of cash interest per period specified in the bond contract. *p. 636*

Straight-Line Amortization   Simplified method to amortize a bond discount or premium. *p. 644*

Trustee   An independent party appointed to represent the bondholders. *p. 653*

Yield Interest Rate   Another name for the market rate of interest on a bond. *p. 638*

QUESTIONS

Part A: Questions 1–14

1. What are the primary characteristics of a bond? For what purposes are bonds usually issued?
2. What is the difference between a bond indenture and a bond certificate?
3. Distinguish between secured and unsecured bonds.
4. Distinguish among callable, redeemable, and convertible bonds.
5. Distinguish between registered and coupon bonds.

6. From the perspective of the issuer, what are some advantages of issuing bonds, as compared with issuing common shares?

7. As the tax rate increases, the net cost of borrowing money decreases. Explain.

8. Explain financial leverage. Can financial leverage be negative?

9. At the date of issuance, bonds are recorded at their current cash equivalent amount. Explain.

10. What is the nature of the discount and premium on bonds payable? Explain.

11. What is the difference between the stated interest rate and the effective interest rate on a bond?

12. Distinguish between the stated and effective rates of interest on a bond (*a*) sold at par, (*b*) sold at a discount, and (*c*) sold at a premium.

13. Why are bond discounts and premiums amortized over the outstanding life of the related bonds payable rather than the period from the date of the bonds to their maturity date?

14. What is the carrying value of a bond payable?

Part B: Questions 15–18

15. Why is the lender (i.e., the purchaser of a bond) charged for the accrued interest from the last interest date to the date of purchase of the bonds?

16. If a 10-year bond dated January 1, 19A, is sold on April 1, 19B, how many months is used as the period outstanding for amortizing any bond premium or discount?

17. What is a bond sinking fund? How should a bond sinking fund be reported in the financial statements?

18. Explain the basic difference between straight-line amortization and effective-interest amortization of bond discount or premium. Explain when each method should, or may, be used.

EXERCISES

Part A: Exercises 11–1 to 11–7

E11–1 **(Pair Definitions with Terms)**
Match the brief definitions given below with the terms by entering the code letters in the blank spaces provided.

	Term		Brief definition (or statement)
_D_	(1)	Secured bonds (example)	A. Amount payable at due date (other than interest).
____	(2)	Principal of a bond	B. An individual or company that is engaged by bond issuers to sell bonds.
____	(3)	Stated interest rate on a bond	
____	(4)	Trustee (related to a bond issue)	C. Arises when a bond is sold for less than its par amount.
____	(5)	Par value of a bond	D. Bond supported by a mortgage on specified assets.

Term	Brief definition (or statement)
____ (6) Bond premium	E. Same as the face or maturity amount of a bond.
____ (7) Carrying value of a bond	F. The amount of cash interest that must be paid regardless of its issue price.
____ (8) Bond indenture	G. An independent party appointed to represent bondholders.
____ (9) Underwriter	H. Same as the market or yield rate of interest on a bond.
____ (10) Bond discount	I. Arises when a bond is sold for more than its par amount.
____ (11) Financial leverage	J. A contract that specifies the legal provisions of a bond issue.
____ (12) Primary disadvantage of bonds payable	K. Present value of the future cash flows related to a bond.
____ (13) Present and par value of a bond are the same	L. A bond sold at its par value.
____ (14) Effective-interest rate	M. Issue price of a bond less any amortized premium or plus any amortized discount.
____ (15) Bond issue or selling price	N. Net interest rate on debt is different from interest rate earned on total assets.
	O. Cash payments of interest and principle required, regardless of income or loss.

E11–2 (Pair Bond Characteristics with Bond Classifications)

Match the following bond characteristics with the bond classifications by entering the answer codes in the spaces provided.

Bond classification	Bond characteristics
__E__ (1) Serial bonds (example)	A. Bonds with parts attached that are turned in to receive interest.
____ (2) Unsecured bonds	B. Bonds that are retired early upon request of the issuer.
____ (3) Convertible bonds	C. The principal amount is payable at a single maturity date.
____ (4) Ordinary bonds	D. Bonds that may be turned in for early retirement at the option of the bondholders.
____ (5) Coupon bonds	E. Principal amount is payable in installments.
____ (6) Redeemable bonds	F. Do not include a mortgage on specific assets.
____ (7) Registered bonds	G. Bonds that include pledged assets to assure payment at maturity.
____ (8) Callable bonds	H. Bonds that may be exchanged for other securities at the option of the bondholder.
____ (9) Secured bonds	I. Interest payments are made by cheque directly to the bondholders on each interest date.

E11-3   **(Compute Issue Prices of Bonds for Three Cases; Record Bond Issuances)**
Felix Corporation is planning to issue $300,000, five-year, 10% bonds. Interest is payable semiannually each June 30 and December 31. All of the bonds will be sold on January 1, 19A. The bonds mature on December 31, 19E.

Required (round to the nearest 10 dollars):
a. Compute the issue (sale) price on January 1, 19A, for each of the following three independent cases (show computations):

Case A—The market (yield) rate is 10%.
Case B—The market (yield) rate is 8%.
Case C—The market (yield) rate is 12%.

b. Give the journal entry to record the issuance for each case.

E11-4   **(Record Bond Issue and First Interest Payment, with Discount; Verify Issue Price)**
On January 1, 19A, Century Corporation sold a $300,000, 7% bond issue for $279,872 (8% market rate). The bonds were dated January 1, 19A, and pay interest each December 31. The bonds mature 10 years from January 1, 19A.

Required:
a. Give the journal entry to record the issuance of the bonds.
b. Give the journal entry to record the interest payment on December 31, 19A. Assume straight-line amortization.
c. Show how the bond interest expense and the bonds payable should be reported on the December 31, 19A, annual financial statements.
d. Verify the sale price of $279,872 (show computations).

E11-5   **(Record Bond Issue and First Interest Payment, with Premium; Show Reporting and Verify the Issue Price)**
Star Corporation sold a $150,000, 10% bond issue on January 1, 19A, for $159,626 (at a market rate of 9%). The bonds were dated January 1, 19A, and interest is paid each December 31. The bonds mature 10 years from January 1, 19A.

Required (round to the nearest dollar):
a. Give the journal entry to record the issuance of the bonds.
b. Give the journal entry for the interest payment on December 31, 19A. Assume straight-line amortization.
c. Show how the bond interest expense and the bonds payable should be reported on the December 31, 19A, annual financial statements.
d. Verify the issue (sale) price (show computations).

E11-6   **(Analysis to Determine Bond Issue Price and Stated Interest Rate; Entries for Issuance and Interest)**
FAB Corporation had $200,000, 10-year, coupon bonds outstanding on December 31, 19A (end of the accounting period). Interest is payable each December 31. The bonds were issued (sold) on January 1, 19A. The 19A annual financial statements showed the following:

Income statement:
Bond interest expense (straight-line amortization) . . . . $ 18,600
Balance sheet:
Bonds payable (net liability)   194,600

Required (show computations):

a. What was the issue price of the bonds? Give the issuance entry.

b. What was the coupon rate on the bonds? Give the entry to record 19A interest.

E11–7   **(Cash Borrowed; Analyze Financing Cost (Net of Tax) and Determine Financial Leverage)**
On January 1, 19A, Snappy Corporation borrowed $120,000 on a three-year note payable. The interest rate is 10% per annum, payable each year-end. The company computed its return on total assets [i.e., Net income ÷ (Liabilities + Owners' Equity)] to be 20%. The average income tax rate for the company is 40%.

Required:

a. What amount of interest would be paid for 19A?

b. Considering the effect of income tax, what would be the net interest cost and the net interest rate (net of income tax)?

c. Would financial leverage be present in this situation? Explain.

d. List two primary advantages to Snappy Corporation in favour of the note payable versus selling more of its unissued capital stock to obtain needed funds.

Part B: Exercises 11–8 to 11–15

E11–8   **(Accrued Interest on Bond Issue Date; Record Issuance; Reporting at Year-End)**
Yukon Corporation authorized the issuance of $300,000, 9%, 10-year bonds. The bonds are dated January 1, 19A. The interest is payable each June 30 and December 31.

On September 1, 19A, the company issued (sold) $200,000 of the bonds at 96 plus any accrued interest. The accounting period ends December 31.

Required:

a. How much cash did Yukon Corporation receive on September 1, 19A? Show computations.

b. Give the journal entry to record the issuance.

c. How much interest expense should be reported on the 19A income statement? Use straight-line amortization.

d. Show how the bonds should be reported on the 19A balance sheet.

E11–9   **(Accrued Interest on Bond Issue Date; Straight-Line Amortization; Reporting)**
White Corporation issued the following bonds:

Bonds payable authorized $60,000
Date on each bond . . . .   Jan. 1, 19A
Maturity date (10 years) . . . .   Dec. 31, 19J
Interest, 10% per year, payable each December 31.

White sold all of the bonds on March 1, 19A, and received $62,180 cash which included the accrued interest.

Required:

a. What was the amount of accrued interest and the discount or premium on issuance date?

b. Over what period of time should the discount or premium be amortized?

c. What would be the amortization amount per month assuming straight-line amortization?

d. Give the journal entry to record the issuance.

e. Give the journal entry on first interest payment date.

f. What amount should be reported as interest expense for 19A?

g. What amount of net liability should be shown on the balance sheet at December 31, 19A?

E11–10   **(Accrued Interest on Issuance Date; Recording and Reporting Issuance and Interest)**

Dopuch Corporation issued $10,000, 9% bonds dated April 1, 19A. Interest is paid each March 31. The bonds mature in three years on March 31, 19D. The bonds were sold on June 1, 19A, for $9,660 plus any accrued interest. The accounting period ends each December 31.

Required:

a. Give the journal entry to record the bond issuance on June 1, 19A.

b. Give the adjusting entry required on December 31, 19A. Use straight-line amortization.

c. What amount of interest expense should be reported on the income statement for 19A?

d. Show how the bonds should be reported on the balance sheet at December 31, 19A.

e. Give the journal entry to record the first interest payment on March 31, 19B.

E11–11   **(Accounting and Reporting for a Bond Sinking Fund; Compute the Annual Contribution Needed)**

Tower Corporation has a $100,000 bond issue outstanding that is due four years hence. It wants to set up a bond sinking fund for this amount by making five equal annual contributions. The first contribution will be made immediately and the last one on the due date (i.e., an ordinary annuity). The corporation will deposit the annual contributions with a trustee who will increase the fund at the end of each year at 8% on the fund balance that existed at the beginning of the year.

Required:

a. Compute the required annual contribution (rent) to the fund.

b. Give the journal entry for the first and second contributions, including interest.

c. Show how the effects of the fund would be reported on the financial statements at the end of the second year.

d. Give the entry to pay the bondholders at maturity date assuming the bond sinking fund has the exact amount needed.

E11–12 **(Accounting and Reporting for a Bond Sinking Fund; Fund Accumulation Schedule; Entries)**
Small Company has a $90,000 debt that will be due at the end of three years. The management will deposit three equal year-end amounts of $27,723 in a debt retirement fund (i.e., an ordinary annuity). The fund balance will earn 8% interest which will be added to the fund at each year-end.

Required:
a. Prepare a fund accumulation schedule similar to Exhibit 11–7. Round to the nearest dollar and show computations.
b. Give the journal entry(s) at the end of the second year to record the increase in the fund.
c. Show how the $27,723 was computed.
d. Did the earnings on the fund increase the balance of the company's cash account? Explain.

E11–13 **(Analyze a Bond Amortization Schedule; Reporting Bonds Payable)**
Jolly Corporation issued a $1,000 bond on January 1, 19A. The bond specified an interest rate of 8% payable at the end of each year. The bond matures at the end of 19C. It was sold at a market rate of 9% per year. The following schedule was completed:

	Cash	Interest	Amortization	Balance
Jan. 1, 19A (issuance) . . .				$ 975
End of Year A	$80	$88	$8	983
End of Year B	80	88	8	991
End of Year C	80	89	9	1,000

Required:
a. What was the issue price of the bond?
b. Did the bond sell at a discount or a premium? How much was the premium or discount?
c. What amount of cash was paid each year for bond interest?
d. What amount of interest expense should be shown each year on the income statement?
e. What amount(s) should be shown on the balance sheet for bonds payable at each year-end (for Year C, show the balance just before retirement of the bond)?
f. What method of amortization was used?
g. Show how the following amounts were computed for Year B: (1) $80, (2) $88, (3) $8, and (4) $991.
h. Is the method of amortization that was used preferable? Explain why.

E11–14 **(Prepare a Debt Payment Schedule with Effective-Interest Amortization; Entries)**
Butle Company issued a $10,000, 11%, three-year bond on January 1, 19A. The bond interest is paid each December 31. The bond was sold to yield 10% (issue price, $10,249).

Required:
a. Complete a bond payment schedule. Use the effective-interest method.
b. Give the interest and amortization entry at the end of 19A, 19B, and 19C.
c. Show how the $10,249 issue price was computed.

E11–15 **(Pensions, Supplement A)**
Blue Ltd. approved the establishment of a noncontributory pension plan on January 1, 1988. An actuarial firm recommended an 8% rate as adequate to fund the pension liability. The normal annual pension cost is expected to be $160,000 and is to be fully funded each year by semiannual payments of $80,000 on June 30 and December 31.

Required:

a. Calculate the amounts which Blue Ltd. must report on its balance sheet and its income statement with respect to the pension plan for its fiscal years ending December 3, 1988, and 1989. Include all computations.

b. What is the problem with this plan?

(CGAC Adapted)

PROBLEMS

Part A: Problems 11–1 to 11–6

P11–1 **(Bonds Issued at Par, Discount, and Premium Compared; Entries and Reporting)**
To get cash to purchase operational assets, Solect Corporation, whose annual accounting period ends on December 31, issued the following bonds:

Date of bonds: January 1, 19A.

Maturity amount and date: $100,000 due in 10 years (December 31, 19J).

Interest: 11% per annum payable each December 31.

Date sold: January 1, 19A.

Required:

a. Give the journal entry to record the issuance and the first two interest payments under each of three different independent cases (assume straight-line amortization):

Case A—The bonds sold at par.

Case B—The bonds sold at 96.

Case C—The bonds sold at 104.

b. Provide the following amounts to be reported on the 19A financial statements:

	Case A	Case B	Case C
1. Interest expense	$ ____	$ ____	$ ____
2. Bonds payable	____	____	____
3. Unamortized premium or discount	____	____	____
4. Net liability	____	____	____
5. Stated rate of interest	____	____	____
6. Cash interest paid	____	____	____

c. Explain why items 1 and 6 in Requirement (b) are different.

P11–2 **(Compute Issue Price of Bonds; Record Issuance and Interest Payments; Reporting)**

Ward Company issued bonds with the following provisions:

Maturity value: $300,000.

Interest: 11% per annum payable semiannually each June 30 and December 31.

Terms: Bonds dated January 1, 19A, due five years from that date.

The annual accounting period for Ward ends December 31. The bonds were sold on January 1, 19A, at a 10% market rate.

Required:

a. Compute the issue (sale) price of the bonds (show computations).

b. Give the journal entry to record issuance of the bonds.

c. Give the journal entries at the following dates (use straight-line amortization): June 30, 19A; December 31, 19A; and June 30, 19B.

d. How much interest expense would be reported on the income statement for 19A? Show how the liability related to the bonds should be reported on the December 31, 19A, balance sheet.

P11–3 **(A Comprehensive Analysis of the Issuance of Bonds at Par, Discount, and Premium; No Entries)**

On January 1, 19A, Beckwith Corporation sold and issued $100,000, 8%, five-year bonds. The bond interest is payable annually each December 31. Assume the bonds were sold under three separate and independent cases: Case A, at par; Case B, at 95; and Case C, at 105.

Required:

a. Complete a schedule similar to the following for each separate case assuming straight-line amortization of discount and premium. Disregard income tax. Give all dollar amounts in thousands.

	At Start of 19A	At End of 19A	At End of 19B	At End of 19C	At End of 19D	Prior to Payment of Principal	Payment of Principal
						At End of 19E	
Case A—Sold at par (100): Pretax cash inflow	$	$	$	$	$	$	$
Pretax cash outflow							
Interest expense on income statement							
Net liability on balance sheet							

| | At Start of 19A | At End of 19A | At End of 19B | At End of 19C | At End of 19D | At End of 19E | |
						Prior to Payment of Principal	Payment of Principal
Case B—Sold at a discount (95): Pretax cash inflow							
Pretax cash outflow							
Interest expense on income statement							
Net liability on balance sheet							
Case C—Sold at a premium (105): Pretax cash inflow							
Pretax cash outflow							
Interest expense on income statement							
Net liability on balance sheet							

b. For each separate case, calculate each of the following:
   (1) Total pretax cash outflow.
   (2) Total pretax cash inflow.
   (3) Difference—net pretax cash outflow.
   (4) Total pretax interest expense.

c. (1) Explain why the net pretax cash outflows differ among the three cases.
   (2) For each case, explain why the net pretax cash outflow is the same amount as total interest expense.

P11–4   (Analysis of Differences among Bonds Issued at Par, Discount, and Premium; Issuance and Interest Entries)

Southwick Corporation sold a $200,000, 8% bond issue on January 1, 19A. The bonds pay interest each December 31, and will mature 10 years from January 1, 19A. For comparative study and analysis, assume three separate cases. Use straight-line amortization, and disregard income tax unless specifically required.

   Case A—The bonds sold at par.
   Case B—The bonds sold at 97.
   Case C—The bonds sold at 103.

Required:

a. Complete the following schedule to analyze the differences among the three cases.

	Case A (par)	Case B (at 97)	Case C (at 103)
1. Cash inflow at issue (sale) date			
2. Total cash outflow through maturity date			
3. Difference—total interest expense			
Income statement for 19A:			
4. Bond interest expense, pretax			
Balance sheet at December 31, 19A:			
Long-term liabilities:			
5. Bonds payable, 8%			
6. Unamortized discount			
7. Unamortized premium			
8. Net liability			
9. Stated interest rate			
10. Total interest expense, net of income tax (40% tax rate)*			

* Assume discount expensed for tax purposes at maturity.

b. Give the journal entries for each case on January 1, 19A, and December 31, 19A (excluding closing entries).

c. For each case, explain why the amounts in items 3, 4, and 10 of Requirement (*a*) are the same, or different.

P11–5   **(Computation and Explanation of Financial Leverage)**

The 19A financial statements of Little Corporation provided the following data:

Balance sheet:

Total assets	$100,000
Total liabilities (10% interest)	60,000
Total shareholders' equity	40,000

Income statement:

Total revenues	$150,000
Total expenses (including pretax interest)	135,000
Pretax income	15,000
Income tax ($15,000 × 20%)	3,000
Net income	$ 12,000

Required (round to nearest percent):

a. Compute the following:
   (1) Return on shareholders' equity.
   (2) Return on total assets.
   (3) Financial leverage.

b. Is the financial leverage positive or negative? Explain.

P11–6   **(Compute, Interpret, and Compare Financial Leverage for Two Companies in the Same Industry)**

The information given below is from the 19B annual financial statements of two competing companies in the same industry. Each company had 50,000 shares of common stock outstanding.

	Thousands of dollars	
	Company A	Company B
Balance sheet:		
Total assets	$900	$900
Total liabilities (10% interest)	400	600
Income statement:		
Total revenues	480	421
Total expenses (including income tax)	300	400
Income tax rate	40%	20%

Required:

a. Complete a tabulation similar to the following (show computations):

Item	Company A	Company B
Earnings per share		
Return on shareholders' equity		
Return on total assets		
Financial leverage		

b. Interpret and compare the financial leverage figures for the two companies.

Part B: Problems 11–7 to 11–15

P11–7   (Recording and Reporting Bonds Issued between Interest Dates)

On January 1, 19A, NWT Corporation authorized $500,000, five-year, 10% bonds payable. The bonds are dated January 1, 19A, and pay semiannual interest each June 30 and December 31. The accounting period ends December 31.

On March 31, 19A, $300,000 of the bonds were sold at 103.

Required (round to the nearest dollar):

a. Give the journal entry to record the issuance of the bonds on March 31, 19A.

b. Give all of the interest entries (excluding closing entries) required during 19A. Use straight-line amortization.

c. Give the amounts that should be reported on the 19A financial statements for:
   (1) Interest expense.
   (2) Bonds payable.
   (3) Unamortized discount or premium.
   (4) Net liability.

d. What would be the 19A aftertax net interest cost (dollars) assuming a 30% income tax rate?

P11–8   (Bonds Sold at Par, Discount, and Premium between Interest Dates; Compare Cash Flows and Reporting)

Cody Corporation authorized a $300,000, 10-year bond issue dated July 1, 19A. The bonds pay 8% interest each June 30. The accounting period ends December 31. Assume the bonds were sold on August 1, 19A, under three different cases as follows:

Case A—Sold at par.

Case B—Sold at 98.

Case C—Sold at 102.

Required:

Complete a schedule for Cody Corporation similar to the following assuming straight-line amortization. Show computations.

	Case A par	Case B 98	Case C 102
1. Cash received at issuance (sale) date	$_____	$_____	$_____
2. Cash received for accrued interest at issuance date . . .	_____	_____	_____
3. Amount of premium or discount at issuance date	_____	_____	_____
4. Stated rate of interest (annual)	_____%	_____%	_____%
5. Net cash interest paid during 19A	$_____	$_____	$_____
6. Interest expense reported for 19A	_____	_____	_____
7. Bonds payable reported at end of 19A	_____	_____	_____
8. Unamortized premium or discount reported at end of 19A	_____	_____	_____
9. Net liability (carrying value) reported at end of 19A . . .	_____	_____	_____
10. Interest payable reported at end of 19A	_____	_____	_____

P11–9   **(Recording and Reporting Bonds Issued between Interest Dates and the Interest Period Not at the End of the Accounting Year)**
Fisher Corporation issued bonds with the following provisions and dates:

Maturity amount: $100,000

Interest: 8%, payable each December 31

Dates: Bonds dated January 1, 19A
       Bonds sold, $60,000 at 104 on May 1, 19A
       End of accounting period, June 30
       Maturity date, December 31, 19E (5 years)

Required (round to the nearest dollar):
a. Give the journal entry to record the issuance of the bonds.
b. Give all 19A entries related to the interest on the bonds. Use straight-line amortization and exclude closing entries.
c. Complete the following for the year ending June 30, 19A:

                Income statement:
                  Interest expense
              Balance sheet:
                Current liabilities:
                Long-term liabilities:

P11–10   **(Recording and Reporting Bonds Issued between Interest Dates and Interest Period Not at the End of the Accounting Period)**
In order to expand to a new region, Uplands Manufacturing Company decided to build a new plant and warehouse. Approximately 60% of the resources required would be obtained through a $600,000 bond issue. The company developed and approved a bond indenture with the following provisions:

      Date of bonds . . . . March 1, 19A, due in 10 years
      Amount authorized . . . . . . $600,000 (par amount)
      Interest . . . . 10% per annum, payable 5%
                           each Feb. 28 and Aug. 31

The annual accounting period ends on December 31. The bonds were issued (sold) on May 1, 19A, at 102.36.

Required:

a. How much cash was received by Uplands on May 1, 19A?

b. What was the amount of the premium? Over how many months will it be amortized?

c. Give journal entries, if any, at each of the following dates: May 1, 19A; August 31, 19A; December 31, 19A; and February 28, 19B. Do not use a reversing entry on January 1, 19B.

d. As to the financial statements for December 31, 19A:
   (1) How much interest expense should be reported on the income statement?
   (2) Show how the liabilities related to the bonds should be reported on the balance sheet.

P11–11   **(Accounting for a Bond Sinking Fund; Compute Deposits; Entries)**
On December 31, 19F, Steady Company had outstanding bonds of $120,000 par (8% annual interest payable each December 31). The bonds will mature at the end of 19J. Anticipating the maturity date, the maturity amount, and some possible miscellaneous related costs, Steady Company decided to accumulate a bond sinking fund of $122,102 so that cash will be available to pay the bonds on maturity date. Steady will make five equal annual deposits on December 31, 19F, G, H, I, and J. The trustee will handle the fund and will increase its balance by 10% at each year-end starting in 19G.

Required:

a. Compute the amount of each of the five equal deposits that Steady Company must make to accumulate $122,102.

b. Give the journal entry to record the first deposit by Steady Company (December 31, 19F).

c. Prepare a fund accumulation schedule for the five annual deposits.

d. Give the journal entry that Steady Company should make on December 31, 19G.

e. Assume it is December 31, 19J.
   (1) Give the journal entry that Steady Company should make to record the payment of the bond principal.
   (2) What balance remains in the bond sinking fund? What disposition should Steady Company make of this amount?

P11–12   **(Accounting for Bonds and Related Bond Sinking Funds; Compute Fund Deposits)**
On January 1, 1972, Regina Corporation issued $500,000, 6% bonds due at the end of 20 years (December 31, 1991). The bonds specified semiannual interest payments on each June 30 and December 31. The bonds originally sold at par. Also, the bond indenture called for the establishment of a bond sinking fund to be accumulated over the last five years by making five equal annual deposits on each December 31, starting in 1987. Interest on the fund balance at 8% will be added to the fund at year-end.

Required:

a. Give the journal entry for issuance of the bonds on January 1, 1972.

b. Give the journal entry for the semiannual interest payment on the bonds on June 30, 1987.

c. Give the journal entry on December 31, 1987, for the first $85,228 contribution of cash to the sinking fund. Show how this amount was computed.

d. Give the sinking fund entry that will be made at the end of 1988.

e. Prepare a fund accumulation schedule.

f. Give the journal entry to record retirement of the bonds at maturity assuming the total bond sinking fund accumulation is $500,000.

P11–13 **(Effective-Interest Amortization of Bond Premium; Analysis of a Prepared Amortization Schedule)**

Foster Corporation issued bonds and received cash in full for the issue price. The bonds were dated and issued on January 1, 19A. The stated interest rate was payable at the end of each year. The bonds mature at the end of four years. The following schedule has been completed:

Date	Cash	Interest	Amortization	Balance
Jan. 1, 19A				$5,173
End of Year 19A	$350	$310	$40	5,133
End of Year 19B	350	308	42	5,091
End of Year 19C	350	305	45	5,046
End of Year 19D	350	304	46	5,000

Required:

a. What was the maturity amount of the bonds?

b. How much cash was received at date of issuance (sale) of the bonds?

c. Was there a premium or a discount? If so, which and how much?

d. How much cash will be disbursed for interest each period and in total for the full life of the bond issue?

e. What method of amortization is being used? Explain.

f. What is the stated rate of interest?

g. What is the effective rate of interest?

h. Show how the following amounts for 19C were computed: (1) $350, (2) $305, (3) $45, and (4) $5,046.

i. What amount of interest expense should be reported on the income statement each year?

j. Show how the bonds should be reported on the balance sheet at the end of each year (show the last year immediately before retirement of the bonds).

k. Why is the method of amortization being used preferable to other methods? When must it be used?

P11–14 **(Pensions, Supplement A)**

Bermuda Company adopted a pension plan early in Year 19A. The plan was to be administered by an insurance company and stipulated that the payment by Bermuda to the insurance company would consist of the amounts that follow:

1. Payments for current service cost based on the number of employees, their birth-dates, and the earnings rate that the insurance company is able to earn on the pension fund investments. These payments will be based on payroll data for the latest year and will be paid in two installments: $33,000 on June 30 of each year

and the balance (as determined on December 31 of each year) on January 5 of the following year. These amounts also represent current service costs for each year.

2. The payments made to the insurance company during the first two years of the pension plan are listed below:

	Current service cost	
Year	Jan. 5	June 30
19A	$ –0–	$33,000
19B	37,010	33,000
19C	36,050	–0–

Payments by the insurance company to retired employees for the first two years were:

Sept. 30, 19A—$7,390

July 31, 19B—$9,177

The estimated expected working lives for all employees at the end of 19A was 35 years, 19B was 33 years. These lives are to be used to amortized experience gains or losses.

3. The inventory of fund assets at the end of 19A was $31,000 and at the end of 19B, $85,000. The accrued benefits at the end of 19A were determined to be $100,000, and at the end of 19B, $143,000. Interest rates were assumed to be 7% in both years.

Required:
Determine the various disclosures required by Bermuda for both 19A and 19B.

P11–15   (Bond Amortization; Computer Spreadsheet)

GR Corporation authorized a 10-year bond dated January 1, 19A, that has an annual coupon rate of interest of 9% payable each June 30 and December 31. On January 1, 19A, $200,000 were issued for $194,000.

Required:
Using a computer spreadsheet package determine the following:

a. The effective rate of interest.

b. The amortization schedule for the 10 years using the effective-interest method of amortization.

c. How much the company would have to deposit at the beginning of Year 8 to pay off the bonds at the end of Year 10 assuming the original effective interest rate was still in effect and if the effective-interest rate was 15% per year.

(Hint: If your spreadsheet package does not contain interest functions, use the formulas in Chapter 10.)

CASES

C11–1   (Demonstration of Financial Leverage; Computation and Interpretation)

The financial statements of New Corporation for 19A showed the following:

Income Statement

Revenues	$200,000
Expenses	(139,000)
Interest expense	(1,000)
Pretax income	60,000
Income tax (40%)	(24,000)
Net income	$ 36,000

Balance Sheet

Assets	$150,000
Liabilities (average interest rate, 10%)	$ 10,000
Common stock, 10,000 no par	100,000
Retained earnings	40,000
	$150,000

Notice in the above data that the company had a debt of only $10,000 compared with common stock outstanding of $100,000. A consultant recommended the following: debt, $60,000 (at 10%) instead of $10,000, and common stock outstanding of $50,000 (5,000 shares) instead of $100,000 (10,000 shares). That is, the company should have more debt and less owner contributions to finance the business.

Required (round to nearest percent):

a. You have been asked to develop a comparison between the (1) actual results and (2) results had the consultant's recommendation been followed. To do this you decided to develop the following schedule:

Item	Actual results for 19A	Results with an increase in debt of $50,000
a. Total debt	_____	_____
b. Total assets	_____	_____
c. Total shareholders' equity	_____	_____
d. Interest expense (total at 10%)	_____	_____
e. Net income	_____	_____
f. Return on total assets	_____	_____
g. Earnings available to shareholders:		
(1) Amount	_____	_____
(2) Per share	_____	_____
(3) Return on shareholders' equity	_____	_____
h. Financial leverage	_____	_____

b. Based upon the completed schedule in (a), provide a comparative analysis and interpretation of the actual results and the recommendation.

C11–2   (Theoretical—Straight-Line versus Effective-Interest Methods of Amortizing Bond Discount and Premium)

Tumbleweed Corporation manufactures electronic equipment. The board of directors of the company authorized a bond issue on January 1, 19A, with the following terms:

Maturity (par) value: $500,000.

Interest: 9% per annum payable each December 31.

Maturity date: December 31, 19E.

The bonds were sold at an effective interest rate of 13%.

Required:

a. Compute the bond issue price. Explain why both the stated and effective-interest rates are used in this computation.

b. Give the entry to record this bond issue.

c. Assume Tumbleweed used the straight-line approach to amortize the discount on the bond issue. Compute the following amounts for each year (19A–19E):
   (1) Cash payment for bond interest.
   (2) Amortization of bond discount or premium.
   (3) Bond interest expense.
   (4) Interest rate indicated (Item 3 ÷ $500,000).
   (5) The straight-line rate is theoretically deficient when interest expense, (4) above, is related to the net liability (i.e., carrying value of the debt). Explain.

d. Assume instead that Tumbleweed used the effective-interest method to amortize the discount. Prepare an effective-interest bond amortization schedule similar to Exhibit 11–8 in the text.

   The effective-interest method provides a constant interest rate when interest expense is related to the net liability. Explain by referring to the bond amortization schedule.

e. Which method should be used by Tumbleweed to amortize the bond discount?

C11–3   (Bond Valuation)

In some parts of the world, companies issue "zero coupon" bonds. For example, bonds with a face value (maturity value) of $400,000 due in 1996 (eight years after issuance) were issued early in 1988. At the time the bonds were sold to the public, similar bonds paid a 15% effective (true) interest. A discussion of such bonds might state, "It's easy to see why corporations like to sell bonds that don't pay interest. But why would anybody want to buy that kind of paper (bond)?"

Required:

a. Explain why an investor would buy "zero coupon" bonds. If investors could earn 15% on similar investments, how much should they be willing to pay for such a bond with a par value of $1,000 (due eight years after issuance)?

b. Assume that the bonds were sold on May 1, 1988, the first day of the term (life) of the bond issue. Give the journal entry to record the sale of the bonds for cash.

c. Assume that the accounting period for the company ends on December 31 each year. Give the journal entry required on December 31, 1988, to record accrued interest expense. If none is required, state why.

C11–4   (Bond Valuation)

MB Mining Limited is a federally incorporated company with shares traded on Canadian stock exchanges. The company has a number of public issues of bonds outstanding and a bond indenture that contains restrictions regarding the ratio of shareholders' equity. In addition, top executives of MBM receive bonuses based upon net income measured in accordance with generally accepted accounting principles.

MBM operates several silver mines in Canada. In 1980, 3.6 million ounces of silver were produced at the mines. Independent mining engineers have estimated that as of January 1, 1981, the company's proven and probable silver reserves are about 24.3 million recoverable ounces.

In April 1981, MBM issued to the public $25 million of 8½% silver-indexed bonds due April 15, 1996. The bonds were issued at par. Each $1,000 face value bond is payable at maturity in $1,000 cash or 50 ounces of silver at the holders' option. The bonds are secured by an agreement entitling the trustee to receive, upon default, and on behalf of the bondholders, 3.7% of the annual mining production of MBM, Limited to not more than an aggregate of 50 ounces of silver per outstanding bond.

The transaction may be viewed as an issuance of convertible debt. Debt securities are often issued with a conversion feature which permits the holder to convert a bond into a predetermined number of shares of common stock, whereas MBM bonds permit the holders to convert a bond into a predetermined number of ounces of silver. This option on silver allowed MBM to issue the bonds initially at a substantially higher price than it could have obtained for a bond with an 8½% interest rate but without the option on silver. Major considerations in deciding how MBM should account for the proceeds from the issuance of the convertible debt are:

1. The valuation of the liability at the date of issuance and subsequently.
2. The measurement of interest expense in each period the debt is outstanding.
3. The treatment of the bond retirement at maturity.

One possibility for accounting for the bonds at issuance, though not one proposed by management, is to view the convertible debt as possessing the characteristics of both a debt and an option on silver. Consistent with this view, a portion of the proceeds could be allocated to the call option and credited to a separate account. The amount so allocated would be a measure of the excess of the fair value of the bond liability expected at maturity over its par value. The remainder of the proceeds would be allocated to the debt. To reflect the bond liability at its par value, the recording of a bond discount would be required. The amount assigned to the options could be measured as the excess of the amount received for the bonds over the estimated price that could have been obtained for similar bonds without the option on silver since estimation can be made with reasonable accuracy. The amount recorded in the deferred credit account would be included in the liabilities of the company's balance sheet. The following entry reflects this interpretation (all amounts are hypothetical):

Cash	1,000	
Discount on silver-indexed bond	300	
Silver-indexed bond payable		1,000
Deferred credit—option on silver		300
To record the issuance of one silver-indexed bond.		

Consistent with this method, the bond discount would be amortized to interest expense in each year the debt is outstanding. The deferred credit would be adjusted upward or downward each year to reflect changes in the fair value of the option on silver because of changes in the market price of silver. Any such adjustment would be charged or credited to interest expense in each year.

The entry at maturity, assuming the market price of silver is $40 per ounce, at that time, is as follows (all amounts are hypothetical):

Silver-indexed bond payable	1,000	
Deferred credit—option on silver	1,000	
Revenue from the sale of silver		2,000
To record the delivery of 50 ounces of silver to the trustee to satisfy the debt obligation on one silver-indexed bond.		

Alternatively, the management of MBM has proposed another method to record the silver-indexed bond in a manner consistent with a "debt only" view of the transaction. The bonds would be recorded at their face value. Interest expense reported in each period would reflect the coupon rate of interest. If bondholders elect to take silver as payment at maturity, management proposes to record the delivery to the trustee as a sale of silver at $20 per ounce.

This method would result in the following journal entry at maturity (all amounts are hypothetical):

Silver-indexed bond payable 1,000
    Revenue from the sale of silver   1,000
    To record the delivery of 50 ounces of silver to the trustee to satisfy the
    debt obligation on one silver-indexed bond.

Under management's proposed method, MBM would realize, at maturity, a loss or profit from the delivery of silver depending on whether or not the cost of producing silver exceeds $20 per ounce at maturity. If the market price of silver at maturity falls below $20 per ounce, bondholders will take cash rather than silver to satisfy the debt obligation, so that all of the company's silver production would be sold in the normal course of operation.

The silver-indexed bonds of MBM reflect an unusual and unique response to inflation—namely, providing bondholders with a hedge against inflation. As inflation continues at or near double-digit rates, we are likely to see an increased number of debt obligations similar to that of MBM which are convertible into various commodities such as silver, gold or oil, all of which give the bondholder the opportunity to share in the appreciation of nonmonetary assets over long periods of time. These types of complicated option contracts are likely to put considerable pressure and strain on transaction or exchange-based accounting, since such transactions or exchanges may effectively be held open for many years.

Required:

Discuss the accounting treatment of the bonds of MBM Ltd.

(CICA Adapted)

C11–5   **(Liability Valuation)**

The following article published in *The Globe and Mail* discusses the concept of SCAN.

Hees finds financial tool to replace troubled perps

The financial explorers at Hees International Corp. have announced their discovery of another new security in the uncharted territory between debt and equity.

The Toronto-based merchant banker—a financial and management services company that serves as the public parent of the Edper Bronfman empire—has replaced a public debenture issue with a new form of convertible debt that will shift $150-million into shareholders' equity.

This, in turn, will increase Hees' capital base to almost $1.5-billion, several of its managing partners said in introducing the new instrument.

Source: Kimberley Noble, *The Globe and Mail*, "Report on Business," August 29, 1987, p. B1.

Called a subordinated convertible auction note, or SCAN, the security came out of in-house efforts by the financial whiz kids at Hees to find an attractive alternative they could offer holders of a problematic issue of perpetual floating-rate notes.

Known as "perps," the perpetual floating-rate notes have been in trouble in Canada since the bottom fell out of the London-based market last winter. The secondary market for these debentures has dried up almost completely, leaving Canadian institutional investors holding billions of dollars in unsellable paper.

Debenture holders—institutional investors who bought the original issue in $100,000 blocks last year—approved the switch on Thursday.

Hees has designed a form of financing that falls somewhere between selling off pieces of the company as common shares and piling on debt. Finding such an instrument has been one of its on-going goals. The SCAN is the second instrument Hees has added to its repertoire since the federal Government's white paper on tax reform signalled the demise of the preferred share issue, a previous Hees' favorite.

The other new instrument is the adjustable-rate convertible debenture, or ARC, which has a return linked to the issuer's common share dividend. Companies controlled by Edward and Peter Bronfman's Edper Investments Ltd. of Toronto have raised $575-million during the past 10 months with this product.

The SCAN, which Hees' managing partner George Myhal called "the first of its kind, internationally unique," and investment analyst Donna Pulcine-Toth of Lévesque Beaubien and Co. Inc. described as "very innovative," is subordinated debt similar to the floating-rate notes it replaced.

Convertible into common shares at $32 (Hees common closed at $25.12 on the Toronto Stock Exchange yesterday), the SCAN is designed to pay an increased return to investors when capital markets are unsettled, but match the company's common share dividend when the share price is higher than the conversion rate.

Like the notes they replace, the SCANs mature in 2085, 99 years from the date of issue. Interest on the previous debt floated at the higher of either the prime rate plus seven-eighths of a percentage point, or the short-term money market rate (such as the Banker's Acceptance rate) plus 40 basis points. The rate paid on SCAN starts out at 9½ per cent, but will change according to bids submitted at a semi-annual auction.

Current and potential holders will submit bids, and the notes will be given to those who will accept the lowest rate of return and redistributed upward until they are all gone. Those who don't bid low enough could be forced to sell the securities.

The highest accepted bid then becomes the rate of return.

Extending this system to the SCANs should enable the company to get the return it pays to debt holders down to as low as 2 or 3 per cent, Mr. Myhal said. As Hees' share price rises, investors anxious to hold on to their SCANs are expected to accept a lower rate of return.

You are contemplating the accounting procedure needed to account for a SCAN issue by your employer.

Required:

How would a liability representing the SCAN issue be valued on a balance sheet?

C11–6   **(Pension Theory, Supplement A)**

For organizations with defined benefit pension plans, the actuary's estimate of the organization's obligation to accumulate promised pension benefits is sometimes disclosed. The market value of pension plan assets available to satisfy that obligation may also be disclosed in the notes to financial statements. Within accounting circles, there is considerable debate as to the appropriate disclosure of pension information in an organization's financial statements. Consider, for example, the following conversation, which took place at a social gathering, between the chief financial officer (CFO) of a large corporation and a financial analyst (FA) from a brokerage firm:

FA: I'm sick and tired of having to adjust liabilities on the balance sheet for footnote liabilities such as the pension obligation! The obligation is that of the organization, not the pension fund, and it belongs, along with related plan assets, on the organization's balance sheet.

CFO: I was under the impression that it was the extent of disclosure, not the form, that mattered to you analysts.

FA: That's not the point. A balance sheet must be complete to be useful. It seems to me that the pension obligation meets any reasonable definition of a liability, and it belongs on the balance sheet along with other liabilities. Besides, some users might be misled because they expect the balance sheet to contain all liabilities.

I also object to the games some organizations play with pension amounts in their income statements. A few years ago, one organization I know took a revaluation gain, amounting to 90% of profit for that year, immediately into income.

CFO: I have some concerns about putting the pension obligation on the balance sheet. For one thing, the pension fund is a separate legal entity. Take my organization for example. We have agreed with our union to work towards a goal of having the plan, which is currently underfunded, fully funded by 1995. Our only obligation is to make contributions to the pension fund as suggested by the actuary in order to achieve our funding objective.

For another thing, I believe that the obligation is too soft a number to warrant balance sheet recognition along with other liabilities. There are many uncertainties related to measurement. For example, consider our plan formula, which provides for an annual post-retirement pension benefit of 2% of the employee's career average earnings for each year of service, to be paid each year beyond retirement until death. All payments are fully indexed to cost-of-living increases after retirement.

And one more thing. How is our auditor supposed to be able to express an opinion as to whether the obligation on the balance sheet is fairly presented? That means a lot of hours spent with the actuary, hours that our organization will have to pay for! Things are much simpler for the auditor when the obligation appears in a footnote only.

FA: The need to make estimates about the future is not unique to pensions. I wonder whether the claim about uncertainties related to measurement is just an excuse you executives use to conceal your real concerns.

CFO: Well, to be honest, our organization does have concerns about the economic consequences resulting from putting the pension obligation and the plan assets on the balance sheet. Our stock price could be adversely affected, not to mention our credit rating, borrowing capacity, and management compensation contracts.

FA: It seems that the controversy regarding pension accounting continues!

Required:

Discuss the issues raised in the above conversation.

(CICA Adapted)

C11–7   **(Pension Disclosure, Supplement A)**

The following article from *The Globe and Mail* discusses some ongoing pension plan problems.

Dominion case creates worries on pension funds

The battle over $38-million worth of surplus money removed from the pension fund of Dominion Stores Ltd. has caused many Canadians to wonder if the same thing could happen to their own pension plans.

Regulators and pension consultants are swamped with inquiries at a time when new federal and provincial legislation is approaching its finished form after two years of wrangling.

Toronto-based Dominion Stores withdrew $62-million of surplus funds after unilaterally changing its plan to permit such a move.

Several employees and the Retail, Wholesale and Department Store Union are disputing $38-million of that withdrawal in separate actions. An Ontario divisional court trial is to decide who owns the money.

Publicity about the case has caused people to express their concern about withdrawals of pension fund surpluses to federal and provincial officials.

As a result, the topic was added to the agenda of a recent meeting of federal and provincial finance ministers. Officials at both levels are studying the issue in preparation for renewed discussions.

Many pension plans have made extraordinary gains in the past several years because of high interest rates and strong stock market performances.

The returns have exceeded the expectations of the actuaries who designed the pension funds' contribution and benefit levels, and many funds now have more money than they need to pay the prescribed benefits to retired workers.

Surpluses can also be generated when circumstances change from the actuarial assumptions used when contribution and benefit levels were set.

For example, Dominion Stores is closing many of its stores, putting hundreds of people out of work. As a result, it needs less money in its pension fund to provide benefits for its remaining staff.

Ironically, Dominion used the disputed $38-million to help cover the costs of closing the stores.

Lately, a rash of companies have moved to withdraw extra money and use it for corporate purposes, including Inco Ltd., which withdrew $105-million last spring, and Noranda Inc., which took a $75-million surplus from its plan in September. Both companies are based in Toronto.

In Ontario alone, companies removed more than $187-million in the first nine months of the current fiscal year, which ends on March 31, and $177-million in the previous year, in contrast to the $2.7-million total for fiscal 1981.

(In the United States, employers may withdraw pension surpluses only if they terminate their pension plans. U.S. plans, like those in Canada, have re-

---

Source: Patricia Lush, *The Globe and Mail,* "Report on Business," March 24, 1986, pp. B1, B3.

cently built up substantial surpluses. Last year, 8,674 U.S. plans were terminated, more than double the number ended in 1980.)

Employees think the surpluses should be used to improve pensions. They see pensions as deferred wages and note the erosion of pensions' real buying power in inflationary times. Some have fears, usually unfounded, that the withdrawals will jeopardize their retirement benefits.

The companies argue that they have to bear the risk if their plans fail to generate enough funds in lean times, so they should be able to withdraw the surpluses in more prosperous times.

Pension plans are either contributory (the employees pay into the fund) or non-contributory (the plan is financed entirely by the employer). In all cases, employers are required to contribute unless the plan is overfunded.

In the Dominion Stores case, according to testimony in the Supreme Court of Ontario, the plan was contributory for 35 years, with employees putting in 5 per cent of their basic pay, until 1979 when the company assumed responsibility for the fund.

Dominion's contributions after that move are not known, but company reports filed with the Ontario Pension Commission show that it paid nothing in 1983 and 1984.

New federal and Ontario laws are likely to be passed this summer and similar changes to the regulations of several other provinces are expected to follow. Regulators have been working for more than two years to achieve uniformity in pension laws across the country.

Saskatchewan intends to change its pension act. Manitoba (and, to a lesser degree, Alberta) has expressed willingness to move toward uniformity. Nova Scotia is likely to follow Ontario's lead.

"It is not possible to get cookie-cutter uniformity," but more similarity among the provinces' regulations would be of significant assistance to companies that operate in several jurisdictions, said an Ontario Treasury official who asked that his name not be used.

Imperial Oil Ltd. of Toronto, for example, has employees across the country and so has "one pension plan marching to nine different drummers."

Substantial progress has been made in the drive to achieve uniformity, but the question of companies withdrawing surpluses remains a sticking point.

Federal regulations and those of eight provinces (British Columbia and Prince Edward Island have no pension legislation) allow companies to withdraw pension surpluses when plans are being wound up. All except Quebec allow such withdrawals from continuing pension plans.

But guidelines specifying the circumstances under which such withdrawals may be made differ from province to province, and many of the rules are unclear, an Ontario Treasury official said.

Manitoba, for example, allows companies to take the surpluses in their pension plans if they provide some sort of inflation protection for the plans' beneficiaries.

The new Ontario act sets out clearly for the first time a policy on the withdrawal of surpluses, according to the Ontario Treasury official. He expressed the hope that the new rules will eliminate the confusion that has existed and perhaps prevent disagreements such as the Dominion Stores case.

The Ontario law is also to include provisions for portability (allowing departing employees to take their pension interests to their new jobs) and vesting (the funds or benefits become the property of the member) after two years.

In addition, minimum contributions from employers will be stipulated. As a result, the costs of financing and running company-sponsored pension plans are expected to rise.

David Stouffer, pension consultant with William M. Mercer Ltd. of Toronto, estimates that employers' contributions in two typical plans would jump by 15 per cent and 38 per cent. Generally, employers' costs will increase by 0.5 to 0.75 per cent of the payroll, he said.

Concern is being expressed that some companies will decide to wind up their plans rather than bear the higher costs.

But Donald Coxe, research director for Gordon Capital Corp. of Toronto, disagrees. He said the healthy returns achieved by most plans in recent years will more than make up for the added costs resulting from the new legislation, although "certainly, the reforms will drain away a lot of the surpluses."

However, the legislation goes a long way toward eliminating the existing unfairness and removing some of the worries, he added.

Required:

a. How would accounting rules help to disclose withdrawals of surplus money from pension plans?

b. Could more disclosure be made? How?

C11–8   **(Analysis of the Reporting of Bonds Payable on an Actual Set of Financial Statements)**

Refer to the financial statements of Consolidated-Bathurst given in Appendix B immediately preceding the Index. Answer the following questions for the 1987 annual accounting period.

1. Did the company report any bonds payable on the balance sheet? Explain.

2. How much cash was provided (or used) from bonds payable? Explain what this means.

3. Refer to the notes to the financial statements and identify all bonds payable included in long-term debts.

4. Are any of the bonds (or indentures) supported by a bond sinking fund?

5. What balance sheet amounts (or footnote disclosure) exist for Consolidated-Bathurst pensions?

6. What obligations exist for capital leases at December 31, 1987? What amount is recorded for leased assets at December 31, 1987?

TWELVE

MEASURING AND REPORTING OWNERS' EQUITY

PURPOSE

A business receives funds from a variety of sources. In the two previous chapters, we discussed accounting for funds provided by creditors (i.e., liabilities). In this chapter, we will examine measuring and reporting funds provided by the owners of a business. Accounting for owners' equity is affected by the type of business organization and appears somewhat differently on the balance sheets of sole proprietorships, partnerships, and corporations. However, given the same set of transactions, the total amount of owners' equity on a given date will be the same (except for income tax effects) for every type of business. This chapter's primary focus is on the corporate form because it is the most prominent type of business entity.

Owners are particularly interested in the accounting for a company's capital stock. The facing page shows how dividend policy and value of shares will affect investors' cash flows.

LEARNING OBJECTIVES

1. Describe the basic nature of a corporation.
2. Compare and contrast the various types of capital stock.
3. Record transactions involving treasury stock.
4. Account for dividends on common and preferred stock.
5. Record stock dividends and stock splits.
6. Measure and report retained earnings.
7. Expand your accounting vocabulary by learning about the "Important Terms Defined in This Chapter."
8. Apply the knowledge gained from this chapter.

ORGANIZATION

Part A—shareholders' equity
1. Nature and structure of a corporation.
2. Accounting for various types of capital stock.
3. Treasury stock.

Part B—accounting for dividends, retained earnings, and unincorporated businesses
1. Dividends defined.
2. Dividends on preferred stock.
3. Stock dividends and stock splits.
4. Reporting retained earnings.
5. Unincorporated businesses.

Petro-Canada

Liabilities and Shareholder's Equity	1987	1986
Capital (Note 9)	$ 4,161	$ 4,161
Deficit	(289)	(450)
	3,872	3,711

CONSOLIDATED STATEMENT OF RETAINED EARNINGS
For the year ended December 31, 1987 (stated in millions of dollars)

	1987	1986
Retained Earnings (Deficit) at Beginning of Year	$ (450)	$ (519)
Net earnings before dividends on redeemable preferred shares	213	182
Dividends on redeemable preferred shares	(41)	(59)
Exchange adjustment on redemption of redeemable preferred shares	(11)	(54)
Retained Earnings (Deficit) at End of Year	$ (289)	$ (450)

NOTES TO CONSOLIDATED FINANCIAL STATEMENTS
December 31, 1987 (stated in millions of dollars)

Note 8: Redeemable Preferred Shares

The redeemable preferred shares, which were issued by a subsidiary to a group of Canadian chartered banks, are floating rate, cumulative and non-voting. Cumulative dividends, payable quarterly, are, at the option of the subsidiary, based on a percentage of either the United States Base Rates or the London Inter-Bank Offered Rates of the banks. At December 31, 1987, the dividend rate was approximately 4.4% per annum. The shares are redeemable, at the option of the subsidiary, at one hundred dollars U.S. per share, plus accured dividends. In 1987 the subsidiary exercised its option to redeem 779,000 shares (1986-850,000 shares) for a consideration of U.S. $78 million (1986-U.S. $85 million). In 1986 the subsidiary repurchased an additional 1,728,000 shares for a consideration of U.S. $172 million. At December 31, 1987, 7,093,000 shares were outstanding.

Subsequent to December 31, 1987 the Corporation gave notice of its intention to redeem the shares by April 11, 1988. The funds for this redemption are to be provided by additional debt.

Note 9: Capital

Authorized

(a) 71,188 common shares with a par value of one hundred thousand dollars each, and

(b) Preferred shares issued to the Government of Canada provided that the amount of such shares together with any loans received, and outstanding, from the Consolidated Revenue Fund of the Government of Canada is not in excess of one billion dollars. These shares have a par value of one dollar each, are redeemable at par at the option of the Corporation, carry no stated rate of dividend and are non-cumulative.

Issued (to the Government of Canada):

	Number of Shares	Consideration
Common Shares		
Balance at beginning and end of year	31,883	$ 3,188
Preferred Shares		
Balance at beginning and end of year	972,771,853	973
Total Capital at Beginning and End of Year		$ 4,161

PART A—SHAREHOLDERS' EQUITY

Nature of a Corporation

A corporation is a separate legal entity that is created by law. It has many of the same rights and duties as individuals. A corporation may be owned by a number of persons and perhaps other business entities. Ownership in the corporation is evidenced by shares of capital stock. The life of a corporation is indefinite and is not affected by changes in the group of individuals, or other entities, that own it.

In terms of volume of business, the corporation is the dominant type of business organization in Canada. This popularity can be attributed to three important advantages that a corporation has over the sole proprietorship and the partnership. First, the corporate form facilitates the bringing together of large amounts of funds through the sale of ownership interests (capital stock) to the public. Second, it facilitates the transfer of separate ownership interests because the shares can be transferred easily to others. Third, it provides the shareholder with limited liability.[1]

The corporation is the only business form that is recognized in law as a separate legal entity. As a distinct entity, the corporation enjoys a continuous existence separate and apart from its owners. It may own assets, incur liabilities, expand and contract in size, sue others, be sued, and enter into contracts independently of the shareholder owners.

Structure of a Corporation

Ownership of a corporation is evidenced by shares of **capital stock** that are freely transferable without affecting the corporation. The owners of a corporation are known as **shareholders** or **stockholders.**

The federal government and all provinces have laws that govern the organization and operation of limited companies incorporated within their jurisdiction. The specific provisions vary from act to act. To form a corporation in the majority of Canadian provinces and federally, an article of incorporation is filed by the incorporators or their representatives, which results in the receipt of a **charter** from the jurisdiction. This charter is called a certificate of incorporation. Other

---

[1] In case of insolvency of a corporation and in the absence of any special agreement the creditors have recourse for their claims only to the assets of the corporation. Thus, the shareholders stand to lose, as a maximum, only their equity in the corporation. In contrast, in the case of a partnership or sole proprietorship, creditors have recourse to the personal assets of the owners if the assets of the business are insufficient to meet the outstanding debts of the business. Lending institutions often take personal as well as corporate guarantees when making loans to corporations. Such special agreements extend the liability of owners beyond their share contributions.

jurisdictions use terms such as letters patent or memorandum of association for the charter.

The charter sets forth the name, objectives, type of shares to be issued, and any restrictions on the transfer of shares. Bylaws are used to clarify the detailed relationships among various classes of shareholders and to specify other specific rules governing the operation of the company. The governing body of a corporation is the board of directors, a body elected by the shareholders.

When a person acquires shares of capital stock, a **share certificate** is issued as evidence of an ownership interest in the corporation. The certificate states the name of the shareholder, date of purchase, type of share, number of shares represented, and characteristics. Exhibit 12–1 shows a share certificate for 100 common shares. The back of the certificate has instructions and a form to be completed when the shares are sold or transferred to another party.

Exhibit 12–1   Common share certificate

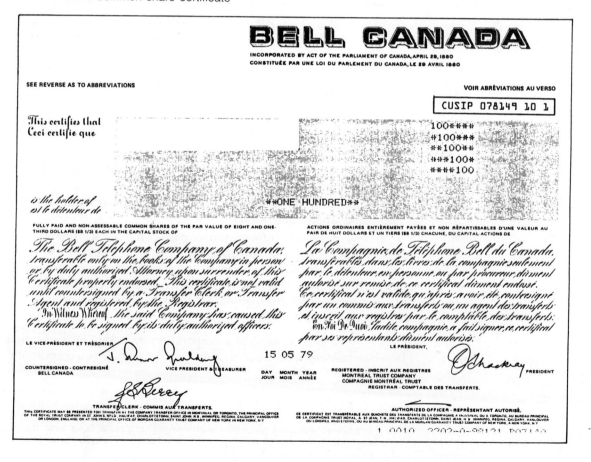

Exhibit 12–2 Typical organizational structure of a corporation

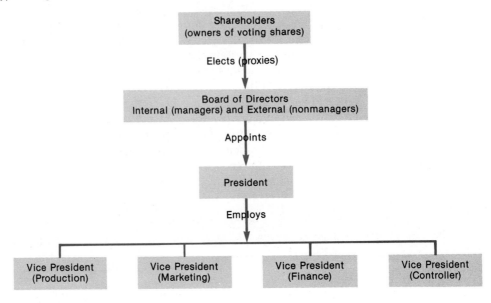

Shareholders, in the absence of special agreement, have the following basic rights:

1. Vote in the shareholders' meeting (or by proxy) on major issues concerning management of the corporation.[2]
2. Participate proportionately with other shareholders in the distribution of profits of the corporation.
3. Share proportionately with other shareholders in the distribution of corporate assets upon liquidation.
4. Right to receive minimum information as part of the annual financial statements and to inspect certain specified documents such as the minute book of shareholders' meetings, the register of share transfers, the charter, the bylaws, and register of shareholders and directors. Formal court procedures are required to permit examination of the accounting books and records of the company.

Shareholders exercise their control of a corporation by voting in the annual meeting of the shareholders. The usual organizational structure of a corporation is shown in Exhibit 12–2.

-----

[2] A voting proxy is a written authority given by a shareholder that gives another party the right to vote his or her shares in the annual meeting of the shareholders. Typically, proxies are solicited by, and given to, the president of the corporation.

Issued and Outstanding Capital Stock

Accounting for, and reporting of, capital stock involve the terms: issued and outstanding shares of capital stock. Subsequent to the granting of the charter, the number of shares issued and the number of shares outstanding are determined by the share transactions of the corporation. Exhibit 12–3 defines and illustrates the three terms usually used in respect to corporate shares.

Types of Capital Stock

All corporations must issue **common stock (shares)** which may be viewed as the "normal" shares of a corporation because they have voting rights. A corporation may issue preferred shares that grant **preferences** that the common shareholders do not have. These preferences usually specify, as a minimum, that the preferred shareholders must receive their dividends **before** any dividends can be declared or paid to the common shareholders. Because of the important differences between common and preferred shares, they are identified separately in accounting and reporting (and on the stock exchanges).

In addition, companies may have various classes of shares, simply called Class A, Class B, and so on, which contain various rights and privileges. For ease of description, the terms **preferred** and **common** will be used in subsequent

Exhibit 12–3 Issued and outstanding shares

Definition	Illustration
Issued number of shares: The total cumulative number of shares that has been issued to date by the corporation.	To date, Tye Corporation sold and issued **30,000** shares of its capital stock.
Subscribed number of shares: Shares sold on credit and not yet issued.	Tye Corporation sold 1,000 shares on credit; the shares will be issued when the sale price is collected in full. Subscribed shares = 1,000.
Outstanding number of shares: The number of shares currently owned by shareholders.	Tye Corporation: Outstanding shares **30,000***

* Observe that outstanding shares and issued shares are the same (i.e., 30,000 shares) in this situation. Treasury stock (i.e., shares that have been issued then subsequently repurchased by the issuing corporation) will be presented later. When treasury stock is held, the number of shares issued and the number outstanding will differ by the number of shares of treasury stock held (treasury stock is included in "issued" but not in "outstanding").

The province of Manitoba is the only Canadian province currently requiring the authorization of the number of shares in the charter before they can be issued.

discussions. Common shares may be viewed conveniently as the "usual" or "normal" shares of the corporation. In contrast, preferred shares (if issued) are distinguished because they grant certain **preferences** that the common shares do not have.

Common Stock

When only one class of stock is issued, it must be common. It has voting rights and often is called the **residual equity** because it ranks **after** the preferred stock for dividends and assets distributed upon liquidation of the corporation. Common stock does not have a fixed dividend rate (as does most preferred stock). As a result, common stock may pay higher dividends and have significant increases in market value. Common stock may be either par value or no-par value.

Par Value and No-Par-Value Stock

Many years ago, all capital stock had to specify a par value. Par value is a **nominal** value per share established for the shares in the charter of the corporation and is printed on the face of each share certificate. Shares that are sold by the corporation to investors above par value are said to sell at a **premium;** whereas, shares sold below par are said to sell at a **discount.** In recent years, the laws of essentially all jurisdictions have been changed to forbid the initial sale of shares by the corporation to investors below par value.[3] Originally, the concept of par value was established as protection for creditors by specifying a permanent amount of capital that could not be withdrawn by the owners as long as the corporation existed. Par value has no relationship to market value. The original idea that it represented protection for creditors was ill conceived. Today, par value, when specified, only identifies the stated or **legal capital** of the corporation (otherwise, it has no particular significance).

The par value concept was ineffective in protecting either creditors or shareholders. For that reason, all jurisdictions in Canada permit **no-par-value** shares.[4] No-par-value common shares do not have an amount per share specified in the charter. They may be issued at any price without concern for a **discount or premium.** No-par-value shares avoid giving the impression of a market value. When no-par shares are used by a corporation, the legal, or stated, capital is as defined by the law.

When par value shares are used, the par value typically is set at a very low amount (such as $1 per share) and the issuing (selling) price is set much higher (such as $10 per share). This arrangement reduces the possibility of a discount.

---

[3] Our discussions concerning the sale of capital stock refer to the **initial** sale of the shares by the corporation rather than to later sales between investors as is the common situation in the day-to-day transactions of the stock markets. Because the sale of shares by a corporation at a discount no longer is legal, no further discussion of it is included. The sale of shares among **individuals** is not recorded in the accounts of the corporation.

[4] In Canada, about half of the provinces permit the use of both par and no-par shares. Ontario and most of the Western provinces along with the Canada Business Corporations Act deem all issues to be no par.

The term **legal capital** is defined by the law of incorporation. While it varies, legal capital usually is viewed as the par value of the shares outstanding (in the case of par value shares), or as either the stated value set by the company or the amount for which the shares were sold originally (in the case of no-par value shares). We shall see later that legal capital usually cannot be used as the basis for dividends. The share certificate shown in Exhibit 12–1 represents par value common (par $8.33).

Preferred Stock

When stock other than common stock is issued, the additional classes are called **preferred stock.** A sample preferred share certificate is presented in Exhibit 12–4. Preferred stock has some characteristics that make it different from the common stock. The usual characteristics of preferred stock are:

1. Dividend preferences.
2. Conversion privileges.
3. Asset preferences.
4. Nonvoting specifications.

Exhibit 12–4   Sample of preferred share certificate

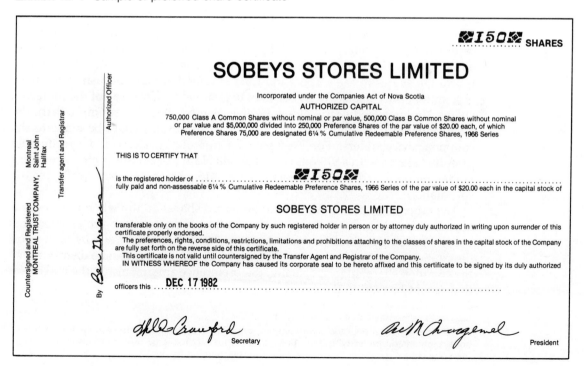

Preferred shares have both favourable and unfavourable characteristics.[5] For example, the nonvoting characteristic is an unfavourable characteristic. Preferred shares may be no-par value, although typically it has a par value. Most preferred shares have a fixed dividend rate. For example, the charter of Tye Corporation may specify "nonvoting, 6% **preferred stock,** 10,000 shares, par value $10 per share" in addition to the common stock. In this situation, the annual preferred dividend would be 6% of par, or $0.60 per share. In contrast, if the preferred shares are no-par value, the preferred dividend would be specified as $0.60 per share.

A corporation may choose to issue more than one class of shares to (1) obtain favourable control arrangements from its own point of view, (2) issue shares without voting privileges, and (3) appeal to a wide range of investors by offering preferred shares with special provisions.

The dividend preferences of preferred shares take precedence over the common shares, up to a specified limit. Dividend preferences will be discussed in Part B of the chapter. The other features of preferred shares are explained below.

Convertible Preferred Shares

Convertible preferred shares provide preferred shareholders the option to exchange their preferred shares for shares of **common** stock of the corporation. The terms of the conversion will specify dates and a conversion ratio. A charter could read: "Each share of preferred stock, at the option of the shareholder, can be converted to two shares of common stock anytime after January 1, 19A."

Asset Preferences of Preferred Shares

Two **asset preferences** usually are specified on preferred shares. One preference is provided with preferred shares that are **callable** or redeemable. At the option of the issuing corporation, holders of callable preferred shares can be required to return the shares to the corporation for a specified amount of cash. The call or redemption price usually is higher than the par value. Upon call of the preferred shares, the preferred shareholders receive cash equal to, but no more than, the asset preference of their shares before any distributions could be made to the common shareholders. For example, a corporate charter could specify that preferred shares with a $10 par value are callable at $15. At this preference rate, a holder of preferred shares would receive $15 per share upon "call" by the corporation.

The other asset preference on the preferred shares occurs when the corporation **dissolves** (e.g., in the case of termination of operations). Preferred shares usually have a specified preference amount per share that must be paid upon dissolution to the preferred shareholders before any assets can be distributed to the common shareholders. Usually, the preference amount also is the maximum that would be paid to the preferred shareholders.

---

[5] A majority of corporations issue only common stock. Often large corporations tend to have both common and preferred in their financial structures. Some large companies also issue more than one class of preferred stock in addition to the common stock.

Nonvoting Specifications on Preferred Shares

Nonvoting preferred shares are customary, even though the nonvoting feature may be considered undesirable to the investors. This feature denies the preferred shareholder the right to vote at shareholder meetings. It is one method for obtaining capital without diluting the control of the common shareholders.

In summary, preferred shares benefit the investor because of dividend, conversion, and asset preferences (to the extent that they are specified). However, preferred shares have the disadvantages of the nonvoting feature and upper dividend limits. In contrast, common shares are not constrained on dividend limits, asset limits on dissolution, and voting rights. If the corporation is profitable, common shares are more attractive to investors than preferred shares. Preferred shares are less risky than common shares because of the dividend, conversion, and asset preferences.

Accounting for, and Reporting of, Capital Stock

Accounting for shareholders' equity is based upon a **concept of sources.** Under this concept, owners' equity from different sources is recorded in different accounts and reported separately in the shareholders' equity section of the balance sheet. The two basic sources of shareholders' equity are:

1. **Contributed capital (often called paid-in capital)**—the amount invested by shareholders through the purchase of shares from the corporation. Contributed capital has two distinct components: (*a*) stated capital—par or stated value derived from the sale of capital stock; and (*b*) additional contributed capital—amounts derived from the sale of shares in excess of par or stated value. This often is termed **contributed surplus.**

2. **Retained earnings**—the **cumulative** amount of net income earned since the organization of the corporation less the cumulative amount of dividends paid by the corporation since organization.

Sale and Issuance of Par Value Shares

When par value shares are sold for cash, three accounts are affected: (1) cash is debited for the sale price, (2) the par value amount is credited to an appropriately designated contributed capital account for each type of share, and (3) any difference between the sale price and the par value of the shares is credited to a separate additional contributed capital account entitled "Contributed Surplus." The par value is recorded in a separate account because it represents legal capital.

The sale of par value common and preferred shares is shown in Exhibit 12–5. Notice in the first journal entry that the preferred and common stock accounts were credited for the **par value** of the shares sold. The differences between the sale prices and the par values were credited to two capital-in-excess-of-par accounts. Tye Corporation recognized **two** different sources of shareholders'

Exhibit 12–5 Sale and issuance of par value capital stock

Situation of Tye Corporation:

Type of shares authorized:
 Preferred stock, 6% par $10.
 Common stock, par $1.

Sale and issuance for cash:

Preferred stock, 1,000 at $12.
 Common stock, 30,000 at $5.

Cash (1,000 × $12) + (30,000 × $5)	162,000	
Preferred stock (1,000 × par $10)		10,000
Common stock (30,000 × par $1)		30,000
Contributed surplus, preferred [(1,000 × ($12 − $10)]		2,000
Contributed surplus, common [30,000 × ($5 − $1)]		120,000

Sale and issuance for services:

Issued 100 shares of preferred stock for legal services when the shares were selling at $12.

Legal expense	1,200	
Preferred stock (100 × par $10)		1,000
Contributed surplus, preferred [100 × ($12 − $10)]		200

Reporting on the financial statements:

Balance sheet—shareholders' equity:
 Contributed capital:
 Preferred stock, 6%, par $10; issued and outstanding,

1,100 shares	$ 11,000	
Common stock, par $1; issued and outstanding,		
30,000 shares	30,000	
Contributed surplus:		
Preferred shares	2,200	
Common shares	120,000	
Total contributed capital		$163,200
Retained earnings (illustrated later)		

Income statement:

Legal expense		1,200

equity—preferred and common stock—and each source was subdivided between the par value and the excess received over par.[6]

Capital Stock Sold and Issued for Noncash Assets and/or Services

Often **noncash** considerations, such as buildings, land, machinery, and services (e.g., attorney fees), are received in payment for capital stock issued. In these

---

[6] Contributed surplus sometimes is called premium on capital stock or paid-in capital in excess of par.

cases, the assets received (or expenses incurred in the case of services) should be recorded by the issuing corporation at the **market value** of the shares issued at the date of the transaction in accordance with the **cost principle.** If the market value of the shares issued cannot be determined, then the market value of the consideration received should be used. Assume Tye Corporation issued 100 shares of preferred stock for legal services when the shares were selling at $12 each. The second journal entry given in Exhibit 12–5 records this transaction. Notice that the value of the legal services received is assumed to be the same as the value of the shares that were issued.

Reporting Shareholders' Equity

The **full disclosure principle** requires that the major classifications of shareholders' equity be reported separately. Also, the subdivisions of each of these major classifications must be reported. Exhibit 12–5 shows the typical reporting of **contributed capital** and its subdivisions. Notice the separation of each type of stock and of par values and amounts in excess of par. Also, notice that the number of **shares** of each kind issued and outstanding is reported.

Sales and Issuance of No-Par Capital Stock

No-par shares do not have a specific dollar amount designated in the charter of the corporation. However, the laws of all jurisdictions specify how legal capital must be determined. There are two typical specifications, depending upon the particular jurisdiction that issued the charter, that affect the way the sale and issuance of no-par shares is recorded, viz:

1. The corporation, in its bylaws, must specify a **stated** value per share as legal capital. This stated value is a substitute for par value.
2. The corporation must record the **total** proceeds received from each sale and issuance of no-par shares as legal capital (the more common approach today).

Recall that **legal** capital is credited to the capital stock account (e.g., common or preferred shares). Any excess of sale price over legal capital is credited to a separate account (e.g., Contributed Surplus, No-Par Common, or Preferred, Shares).

Exhibit 12–6 illustrates the sale and issuance of no-par capital stock.

Treasury Stock

Treasury stock is a corporation's own capital stock that was sold, issued, **reacquired** subsequently and still held by the corporation. Treasury stock frequently is purchased for sound business reasons, such as to obtain shares needed for employee bonus plans, to remove fractional shares that are outstanding, to settle a claim against the corporation, or to have shares on hand for use in the

Exhibit 12–6   Sale and issuance of no-par capital stock

Situation of Sun Corporation:

Type of shares: common, no par.
Issued and sold—60,000 shares at $6 per share (cash).

Sale and issuance:

Case A—The provincial law requires that the corporation set a **stated** value per share to
represent legal capital for no-par shares. The company's charter specified a stated
value of $0.50 per share.

Cash (60,000 × $6)	360,000	
Common stock, no par (with stated value of $0.50)		
(60,000 × $0.50)		30,000
Contributed surplus 60,000 × ($6.00 − $0.50)		330,000

Case B—The provincial law requires that the total proceeds be recorded as legal capital.

Cash	360,000	
Common stock, no par		360,000

acquisition of other companies. Treasury stock, while held by the issuing corporation, has no voting, dividend, or other shareholder rights.[7]

When a corporation purchases its own capital stock, the assets (usually cash)
of the corporation and the shareholders' equity are reduced by equal amounts.
When treasury stock is sold, the opposite effects occur. Purchases of treasury
stock are recorded by debiting its cost to a shareholders' equity account called
Treasury Stock (by type of stock) and crediting Cash. Because the Treasury Stock
account has a debit balance, it often is referred to as a **negative** (or contra)
shareholders' equity account. When treasury stock is sold, the Treasury Stock
account is credited at cost and Cash is debited. Usually the purchase and sale
prices of treasury stock are different, necessitating recognition of the difference
in an appropriately designated **contributed capital** account in the entry to record
the sale.[8]

Accounting for, and reporting of, treasury stock are illustrated in Exhibit
12–7. Observe in the first journal entry that the **Treasury Stock** account is
debited for the **cost** of the treasury stock purchased ($3,600). The second journal
entry credits the Treasury Stock for the **cost** of the 100 shares of treasury stock

---

[7] Section 32 of the Canada Business Corporation Act (1984) states that a company shall not
purchase its own shares . . . "if there are reasonable grounds for believing that (*a*) the corporation is, or would after the payment be, unable to pay its liabilities as they become due; or (*b*) the
realizable value of the corporation's assets would after the payment be less than the aggregate of
its liabilities and stated capital of all classes."

[8] *CICA Handbook,* Section 3240.20, states that if the proceeds from the subsequent resale are
less than the carrying amount of the treasury stock, the difference is first debited to any previously created contributed surplus and then to retained earnings to the extent necessary. In no
case are these differences to appear on the income statement.

Exhibit 12–7 Accounting for, and reporting of, treasury stock

---

Situation of May Corporation on January 1, 19B:

MAY CORPORATION
Summarized Balance Sheet
January 1, 19B

Assets		Shareholders' Equity		
Cash	$ 30,000	Contributed capital:		
Other assets	70,000	Common shares, par $10, authorized 10,000 shares, issued 8,000 shares		$ 80,000
		Retained earnings		20,000
Total assets	$100,000	Total shareholders' equity		$100,000

Purchase of treasury stock:

On January 2, 19B, May Corporation purchased 300 of its own outstanding shares of common stock at $12 per share.

Treasury stock, common (300 shares at $12 per share)	3,600	
Cash		3,600

(Note: This transaction reduces both assets and shareholders' equity by $3,600.)

Sale of treasury stock:

On February 15, 19B, May sold one third of the treasury stock at $13 per share.

Cash (100 shares at $13)	1,300	
Treasury stock, common (100 shares at cost, $12)		1,200
Contributed surplus, treasury stock transactions		100

(Note: This transaction increases both assets and shareholders' equity by $1,300.)

Reporting treasury stock:

MAY CORPORATION*
Summarized Balance Sheet
February 15, 19B

Assets		Shareholders' Equity		
Cash	$27,700	Contributed capital:		
Other assets	70,000	Common shares, par $10, authorized 10,000 shares, issued 8,000, of which 200 shares are held as treasury stock		$ 80,000
		Contributed surplus, treasury stock transactions		100
		Total contributed capital		80,100
		Retained earnings		20,000
		Total		100,100
		Less cost of treasury stock held		2,400
Total assets	$97,700	Total shareholders' equity		$ 97,700

* Reflects the additional effects of the two transactions given above.

sold. A corporation is not permitted by GAAP to increase its income or retained earnings by buying or selling its own shares. Therefore, in Exhibit 12–7, upon resale of the 100 shares of treasury stock, **contributed surplus** was increased by $100, which was the difference between cost and sales price of the treasury shares sold [i.e., 100 shares $\times$ ($13 − $12)]. Observe that this difference was **not** recorded as a gain as would be done for the sale of an asset (such as investments in marketable securities). The basic accounting concept is that "gains or losses" on transactions involving a corporation's own shares are balance sheet **(shareholders' equity)** items and not income statement items. Therefore, the balance sheet of May Corporation, presented at the bottom of Exhibit 12–7, reports "Contributed surplus, treasury stock transactions" of $100.

The Treasury Stock account never has a credit balance, although owners' equity accounts normally carry a credit balance. The balance in the Treasury Stock account reflects a **contraction** of shareholders' equity; thus, it is a **negative** equity account. The debit balance in the Treasury Stock account represents the acquisition **cost** of the treasury stock still held at the date of the balance sheet. Observe this deduction on the balance sheet at the bottom of Exhibit 12–7.[9] That balance sheet reports the number of shares as:

Classification	Shares
Issued*	8,000
Treasury shares	−(200)
Outstanding*	7,800

*Different by the number of treasury shares held.

The purchase and/or resale of treasury stock does not affect the number of shares of **unissued** (or issued) stock; however, the number of shares of **outstanding** stock is affected. The only difference between treasury stock and unissued shares is that treasury stock has been sold at least once and recorded in the accounts.

To illustrate the **resale** of treasury stock at a price **less than cost,** assume that an additional 50 shares of the treasury stock were resold by May Corporation on April 1, 19B, at $11 per share; that is, $1 per share below cost. The resulting entry would be:

April 1, 19B:

Cash	550	
Contributed surplus, treasury stock transactions	50	
Treasury stock, common (50 shares)		600
Sold 50 shares of treasury stock at $11 per share; cost, $12 per share.		

Note that the difference between sale price and cost was debited to the same contributed surplus account to which the difference in the preceding journal entry (Exhibit 12–7) was credited. Retained Earnings would be debited for some

---

[9] For the purpose of computing earnings per share, treasury stock should not be treated as outstanding shares (*CICA Handbook*, Section 3240.23).

or all of the amount of the difference only if there were an insufficient credit balance in the account Contributed Surplus, Treasury Stock Transactions.

Where a restriction does not exist as to how many shares may be issued by the corporations (no authorized maximum capital stock), treasury stock could be immediately canceled so no balance exists in the Treasury Stock account after the shares are purchased. Only if there are restrictions on the number of shares that can be issued would there be any reason to hold treasury shares for reissue. As was mentioned earlier in this chapter, it is common today that the number of authorized shares is unlimited so no need exists to hold treasury shares for reissue. Entries to record this alternative treatment are simply the reverse of the entries used to issue shares. If contributed surplus is insufficient to absorb the debit when shares are canceled, the additional amount required would be debited to retained earnings. For example, the entry to record May Corporation treasury stock purchase in Exhibit 12–7 would be:

```
Common shares . . . . . . . . . . . . . . . . . . . . . . . . . . . . . . . . 3,000
Retained earnings . . . . . . . . . . . . . . . . . . . . . . . . . . . . . .     600
    Cash . . . . . . . . . . . . . . . . . . . . . . . . . . . . . . . . . . . . . . .          3,600
        300 × ($12 − $10).
```

Essentially legal requirements of the incorporating jurisdiction determine the applicable alternative accounting treatment.

PART B—ACCOUNTING FOR DIVIDENDS AND RETAINED EARNINGS AND UNINCORPORATED BUSINESSES

Dividends Defined

Usually a dividend is a distribution of cash to shareholders by a corporation. Dividends can be paid in assets other than cash or in capital stock of the corporation. Dividends must be approved by the board of directors of the corporation (i.e., a dividend declaration) **before** they can be paid. Without a qualifier, the term **dividend** means a **cash** dividend, which is the most common type. A dividend distribution of the corporation's own shares is called a **stock dividend.** Dividends usually are stated in terms of dollars per share, or as a percent of par value.

The declaration and payment of a **cash dividend** reduces the assets (cash) and the shareholders' equity (retained earnings) by the total amount of the dividend. Exhibit 12–8 illustrates the declaration and payment of a cash dividend. Observe that assets and shareholders' equity **both** were reduced by the amount of the cash dividend ($12,400).

Dividends from the Perspectives of the Investor and the Issuer

An **investor** acquires shares of a corporation with the expectation of earning a future economic return on the investment, usually in future cash inflows. The investor's future cash inflows from the share investment come from two sources:

Exhibit 12–8 Declaration and payment of a cash dividend

Situation prior to cash dividend (Box Corporation):

Cash	$ 20,000	
Remaining assets	135,000	
Liabilities	(35,000)	$120,000

Shareholders' equity:

Preferred stock, 6%, par $20, shares outstanding, 2,000	$ 40,000	
Common stock, par $10, shares outstanding, 5,000	50,000	
Retained earnings	30,000	$120,000

Dividend declaration:

"On December 1, 19E, the Board of Directors of Box Corporation hereby declares an annual cash dividend of $2 per share of the common stock and 6% per share on the preferred stock to the shareholders on date of record, December 10, 19E, payable on December 30, 19E."

Journal entries:*

December 1, 19E:

Retained earnings (or Dividends declared which is closed to		
Retained earnings)	12,400	
Dividends payable (a current liability)		12,400

   Declaration of a cash dividend:
   Preferred stock (2,000 shares × par $20 × rate 6%) = $ 2,400.
   Common stock (5,000 shares × $2)   = 10,000.

December 30, 19E:

Dividends payable	12,400	
Cash		12,400
Payment of dividend liability.		

Effects of the cash dividend on the balance sheet:

Cash	$ 7,600	
Remaining assets	135,000	
Liabilities	(35,000)	$107,600

Shareholders' equity:

Preferred stock	$ 40,000	
Common stock	50,000	
Retained earnings	17,600	$107,600

* These two entries could be combined into one journal entry on the date of payment, as a debit to Retained Earnings and a credit to Cash of $12,400 because they were in the same accounting year.

---

(1) periodic cash inflows in the form of dividends on the shares and (2) a cash inflow at the time the shares are sold. The investor anticipated that the sum of the present values of these two cash inflows will be greater than the original investment in the shares. The investor views cash dividends as revenue; that is, the return **on** the investment. The other cash inflow includes a return **of** the

investment (from sale of the shares) and will usually result in a **realized gain or loss,** depending on whether the investor sells the shares above or below their acquisition price. The amounts and frequency of dividends paid by a corporation have an effect on the market price of the shares.

The primary financial objective of a corporation is to earn income on the resources provided by shareholders and creditors. The ability to attract and retain resources from present and potential investors depends in good measure upon the income record of the company. The earnings of a corporation may be retained in the business for corporate expansion or paid to the shareholders as dividends. One of the significant decisions faced by the board of directors of a corporation is how much of the earnings should be retained and how much should be distributed to the shareholders as dividends each year.

Exhibit 12–8 demonstrated that a cash dividend reduces both assets (cash and shareholders' equity (retained earnings). There are two fundamental requirements for the payment of a cash dividend:

1. **Sufficient retained earnings**—The corporation has accumulated a sufficient amount of retained earnings to cover the amount of the dividend. The legal position in Canada is unclear as to what could happen if a dividend were declared without the existence of retained earnings. It is possible, however, for a corporation to amend formally its charter in order to change the stated capital which in turn could be used to cancel the negative retained earnings (called a deficit). As a matter of financial policy, and to meet growth objectives, corporations seldom disburse more than 40% to 60% of the average net income amount as dividends.

2. **Sufficient cash**—The corporation must have access to cash sufficient to pay the dividend and, in addition, adequate cash to meet the continuing operating needs of the business.

The Canada Business Corporations Act (1984), Section 40, states:

A corporation shall not declare or pay a dividend if there are reasonable grounds for believing that
a.   the corporation is, or would after the payment be, unable to pay its liabilities as they become due; or
b.   the realizable value of the corporation's assets would thereby be less than the aggregate of its liabilities and stated capital of all classes.

The mere fact that there is a large **credit** in the Retained Earnings account does not indicate sufficient cash to support a cash dividend. The cash generated in the past by earnings represented in the Retained Earnings account may have been expended to acquire inventory, purchase operational assets, and/or pay liabilities. Consequently, there is no necessary relationship between the balance of retained earnings and the balance of cash on any particular date (simply, retained earnings is not cash).

Exhibit 12–8 indicated a cash balance of $20,000 and a balance in retained earnings of $30,000. In this example, it appears that cash may be the constraining factor on dividends. Some companies overcome this cash constraint (at least temporarily) by borrowing cash to pay cash dividends. The balance in retained earnings is a more inflexible constraint because retained earnings cannot be borrowed.

Dividends on Preferred Shares

Recall that preferred shares give certain rights that have precedence over the rights of common shareholders. The primary distinguishing characteristics of preferred shares are dividend preferences. The **dividend preferences** may be classified as follows.[10]

1. Current dividend preference.
2. Cumulative dividend preference.
3. Participating dividend preference.

Preferred shares may have one or a combination of these three dividend preferences. The charter and the share certificates of the corporation must state the distinctive features of the preferred shares.

Current Dividend Preference on Preferred Shares

Preferred shares always carry a **current dividend preference.** It requires that if any dividends are declared, the current preferred dividend must be declared and paid before any dividends can be declared and paid on the common shares. When the current dividend preference is met (and no other preference is operative), dividends then can be paid to the common shareholders. The current dividend preference on par value preferred shares is a specified percent of the par value.

Declared dividends must be **allocated** between the preferred and common shares. First, the preferences of the preferred shares must be met then the remainder of the total dividend can be allocated to the common shares. Exhibit 12–9, Case A, illustrates the allocation of the **current dividend** preference under four different assumptions concerning the **total** amount of dividends to be paid.

Cumulative Dividend Preference on Preferred Shares

Cumulative preferred shares have a preference that states if all or a part of the specified current dividend (e.g., 6% in Exhibit 12–9) is not paid in full, the unpaid amount becomes **dividends in arrears.** Thus, when the preferred shares are cumulative, the amount of any preferred dividends in arrears must be paid before any common dividends can be paid. In any one year, preferred shares

---

[10] A dividend preference does not mean that dividends will be paid automatically. Dividends are paid only when **formally declared** by the corporation's board of directors. Thus, the declaration of a dividend is discretionary. A typical dividend problem involves the allocation of a total amount of dividends declared between the preferred share and common share as illustrated in the next section.

Exhibit 12–9 Dividends on preferred shares

Case A—Current dividend preference only:

Preferred stock outstanding, 6%, par $20; 2,000 shares = $40,000 par.
Common stock outstanding, par $10; 5,000 shares = $50,000 par.

Allocation of dividends between preferred and common shares assuming **current dividend** preference only:

		Amount of dividend paid to shareholders of	
Assumptions	Total dividends paid	6% preferred stock (2,000 shares at $20 par = $40,000)*	Common stock (5,000 shares at $10 par = $50,000)
No. 1	$ 1,000	$1,000	–0–
No. 2	2,000	2,000	–0–
No. 3	3,000	2,400	$ 600
No. 4	18,000	2,400	15,600

* Preferred dividend preference, $40,000 × 6% = $2,400; or 2,000 shares × $1.20.

Case B—Cumulative dividend preference:

Preferred and common stock outstanding—same as above. Dividends in **arrears** for the two preceding years.

Allocation of dividends between preferred and common stock assuming **cumulative** preferred stock:

		Amount of dividend paid to shareholders of	
Assumptions (dividends in arrears, 2 years)	Total dividends paid	6% preferred stock (2,000 shares at $20 par = $40,000)*	Common stock (5,000 shares at $10 par = $50,000)
No. 1	$ 2,400	$2,400	–0–
No. 2	7,200	7,200	–0–
No. 3	8,000	7,200	$ 800
No. 4	30,000	7,200	22,800

* Current dividend preference, $40,000 × 6% = $2,400; dividends in arrears preference, $2,400 × 2 years = $4,800; and current dividend preference plus dividends in arrears = $7,200.

cannot receive total dividends in excess of the current year dividend preference plus all dividends in arrears. However, arrears of cumulative dividends are not a form of liability until they are declared. Of course, if the preferred shares are **noncumulative,** dividends never can be in arrears. Therefore, any dividends passed (i.e., not declared) are lost permanently by the preferred shareholders. Because preferred shareholders are not willing to accept this unfavourable feature, preferred shares usually are cumulative.

The allocation of dividends between **cumulative** preferred shares and common shares is illustrated in Exhibit 12–9, Case B, under four different assumptions concerning the **total** amount of dividends to be paid. Observe that the dividends in arrears are paid first, next the current dividend preference is paid, and, finally, the remainder is paid to the common shareholders.

Some preferred shares may provide dividends that are greater than the required minimum amount. Participating preferred shares are discussed in Supplement 12A.

Stock Dividends

The board of directors may vote to declare and issue a stock dividend instead of a cash dividend. A **stock dividend is a distribution of additional shares of a corporation's own capital stock on a pro rata basis to its shareholders at no cost.** Stock dividends usually consist of common shares issued. **Pro rata basis** means that each shareholder receives additional shares equal to the percentage of shares already held. A shareholder with 10% of the outstanding shares would receive 10% of any additional shares issued as a stock dividend. Therefore, a stock dividend does not change the proportionate ownership of any shareholder. It does not involve the distribution of any assets (e.g., cash) of the corporation to the shareholder, and it does not affect the **total** shareholders' equity of the issuing corporation. Assume King Corporation has outstanding 100,000 shares of common stock, par $5, originally sold at $8 per share. The board of directors voted to declare and issue a 10% common stock dividend (i.e., 10,000 shares) when the market value of the common stock was $11 per share. The entry by King Corporation to record the declaration and issuance of this stock dividend would be:[11]

```
Retained earnings (10,000 shares × $11) . . . . . . . . . . . . . . . . . . . . . . 110,000
     Common stock, par $5 (10,000 shares × $5) . . . . . . . . . . . . . .          50,000
     Contributed surplus, common stock:
       10,000 shares × ($11 − $5) . . . . . . . . . . . . . . . . . . . . . . . .          60,000
  Common stock dividend of 10% distributed when the market value per
  share was $11.
```

Observe in the above entry that **retained earnings** was **decreased** by $110,000 and that **contributed capital** (i.e., common stock and contributed surplus) was

---

[11] Some accountants prefer to debit an account called Stock Dividends Distributed, which is closed to Retained Earnings at the end of the period. The effect is the same. As an alternative, some accountants may wish to make an entry at the declaration date as follows:

```
Retained earnings  . . . . . . . . . . . . . . . . . . . . . . . . . . . . . . . . . . 110,000
     Stock dividend payable  . . . . . . . . . . . . . . . . . . . . . . . . . . .          110,000
```

Stock dividend payable is a separate contributed capital account. It would not be a liability because no assets will be used to settle the item. The amounts would need to be estimated at the declaration date. The subsequent payment entry would be:

```
Stock dividend payable . . . . . . . . . . . . . . . . . . . . . . . . . . . . . . . . 110,000
     Common stock  . . . . . . . . . . . . . . . . . . . . . . . . . . . . . . . . .          50,000
     Contributed surplus  . . . . . . . . . . . . . . . . . . . . . . . . . . . . . .          60,000
```

increased by $110,000; assets and liabilities were unaffected. Therefore, the stock dividend did **not** change total shareholders' equity—it only changed some of the balances of the accounts that comprise shareholders' equity. This process of transferring an amount from retained earnings to contributed (i.e., permanent) capital often is called **capitalizing earnings** because it reduces the amount of retained earnings available for future dividends.

After a stock dividend, each **shareholder** has the same **proportionate** ownership of the corporation as before, and no additional assets are received by the shareholders (only more shares to represent the same total value previously held). Because more shares now represent the same "value," the **market** price per share should drop proportionately.

Observe in the previous journal entry, the amount that was transferred from Retained Earnings to Contributed Capital was the **current market value** of the shares issued as a stock dividend. The use of the market value amount is considered appropriate when the stock dividend is "small"; that is, when it is less than 25% of the previously outstanding shares. In those cases where a stock dividend is "large" (i.e., more than 25%), the amount transferred should be the total par value of the shares issued.

Reasons for Stock Dividends

Stock dividends often serve useful purposes for both the corporation and the individual shareholder. The two primary purposes of a stock dividend are:

1. **To maintain dividend consistency**—Many corporations prefer to declare dividends each year. In the case of a cash shortage, the dividend record may be maintained by issuing a stock dividend. Stock dividends tend to satisfy the demands of shareholders for continuing dividends and yet avoid the demand on cash. Also, a stock dividend is not considered as revenue to the shareholder for income tax purposes.

2. **To capitalize retained earnings**—A stock dividend is used to transfer retained earnings to permanent capital and thus remove such earnings from cash dividend availability. When a corporation consistently retains a large percent of its earnings for growth, the related funds often are invested permanently in long-term assets such as plant and other property. Therefore, it is realistic to transfer those accumulated earnings to permanent capital. A stock dividend is a convenient approach to capitalize retained earnings.

Stock Splits

Stock splits are **not** dividends. They are (*a*) similar to a stock dividend, (*b*) often confused with a stock dividend, and (*c*) quite different from a stock dividend in their impact upon the shareholders' equity accounts. In a stock split, the **total** number of shares is increased by a specified amount, such as a two-for-one split. In this instance, each share held is called in, and two new shares are issued in its place. Typically, a stock split is accomplished by **reducing the par or stated value per share** of all shares so that the **total** par or stated value (in dollars) of all shares is unchanged. For example, assume 1,000 shares of $20 par value stock were outstanding before a two-for-one split. This stock split would involve reducing the par value of each new share to $10 and the issuance of 2,000 shares of $10 par value stock. In contrast to a stock dividend, a stock split does **not** result in a transfer of retained earnings to contributed capital. No transfer is needed because the reduction in the par value per share compensates for the increase in the number of shares. The primary reason for a stock split is to **reduce the market price per share,** which tends to increase the market activity of the shares. Sometimes a corporation wants to **reduce** the number of shares outstanding. One way to do this is to implement a **reverse** stock split. A stock dividend requires a journal entry while a **stock split does not require a journal entry.**

In both a stock dividend and a stock split the shareholder receives more shares but does not disburse any additional assets to acquire the additional shares.

The **comparative effects** of a stock dividend versus a stock split may be summarized as follows:

	Shareholders' equity		
	Before a stock dividend or split	After a 100% stock dividend	After a two-for-one stock split
Contributed capital:			
Number of shares outstanding	30,000	60,000	60,000
Par value per share	$ 10	$ 10	$ 5
Total par value outstanding	300,000	600,000	300,000
Retained earnings	650,000	350,000	650,000
Total shareholders' equity	950,000	950,000	950,000

Dividend Dates

The preceding discussions assumed that a dividend was paid immediately after its declaration by the board of directors. Typically, there is a time lag between declaration and payment. A typical dividend declaration is as follows:

On November 20, 19B, the Board of Directors of XY Corporation hereby declares a $0.50 per share cash dividend on the 200,000 shares of no-par common stock outstanding. The dividend will be paid to shareholders of record at December 15, 19B, on January 15, 19C.

This declaration specifies **three important dates:**

1. **Declaration date—November 20, 19B:** This is the date on which the board of directors officially approved the dividend. As soon as a public announcement of the declaration is made, it is irrevocable. Therefore, a **dividend liability** is created when a dividend is declared. On the date of declaration, XY Corporation would record the following journal entry:

November 20, 19B:

Retained earnings (or Dividends declared) 100,000
    Dividends payable   100,000
    Cash dividend declared: 200,000 shares × $0.50 = $100,000.

The December 31, 19B, balance sheet would report **Dividends Payable as a current liability.**

2. **Date of record—December 15, 19B:** This date follows the declaration date, usually by about one month, as specified in the declaration. It is the date on which the corporation prepares the list of current shareholders based on the **shareholder records.** The dividend is payable only to those names listed on the record date. Thus, share transfers between investors reported to the corporation before this date result in the dividend being paid to a new owner. Changes reported **after** this date result in the dividend being paid to the old owner; the new owner will receive all subsequent dividends. No journal entry would be made on this date.

3. **Date of payment—January 15, 19C:** This is the date on which the **cash** is disbursed to pay the dividend liability. It follows the date of record as specified in the dividend announcement. The entry to record the cash disbursement by XY Corporation would be as follows:

January 15, 19C:

Dividends payable 100,000
    Cash   100,000
    To pay the liability for a cash dividend declared and recorded
    on November 20, 19B.

For instructional purposes this time lag may be ignored because it does not pose any substantive issues. Also, when all of the three dates fall in the same accounting period, a single entry on the date of payment may be made in practice for purely practical reasons.

Shareholder Records

A corporation must keep a record of each shareholder. The record includes at least the name and address of each shareholder, number of shares owned, certificate numbers, and dates acquired. This record is known as the **shareholders' subsidiary ledger**. The Capital Stock account is the **control account** in the general ledger for this subsidiary ledger. Sales of shares by a shareholder to others must be reported to the corporation so that new share certificates can be issued and the shareholders' subsidiary ledger can be changed. Dividends are sent only to the names and addresses shown in the shareholders' subsidiary ledger on the date of record. Large corporations with thousands of shareholders usually pay an independent **transfer agent** to handle the transfer of shares, to issue new share certificates, and to maintain the equivalent of a shareholder's subsidiary ledger.

An important record that must be kept by all corporations is called the **minute book.** This is an official record of the actions taken at all meetings of the board of directors and of the shareholders. The independent auditor is required to inspect the minute book as a part of the audit program. Often, it is used as evidence in lawsuits and in income tax litigation.

Reporting Retained Earnings

The preceding chapters emphasized that the income statement reports two income amounts: (1) income before extraordinary items and (2) net income (i.e., after extraordinary items). The *CICA Handbook,* Section 3480, defines **extraordinary items** as those transactions and events that meet three criteria; that is, to be classified as extraordinary, a gain or loss must be (1) not typical of the normal business activities, (2) not expected to occur regularly, and (3) not considered as recurring factors in any evaluation of ordinary operations of the enterprise. Extraordinary items are set out separately on the income statement to enable statement users to focus on the usual and frequent results; that is, income **before** extraordinary items because it is more reflective of future earnings and cash inflow than is net income (i.e., after extraordinary items). Some examples would be:

1. The discontinuance, or substantial change in, a business programme that resulted in the sale of a property or segment of the business, or the sale of a long-term investment.
2. A government expropriation of properties.
3. Acts of God such as hurricanes, floods, and similar catastrophic events.

In some previous chapters we discussed the statement of retained earnings. Although not a required statement, it usually is presented to conform with the **full disclosure principle.** Because retained earnings is one of two basic components of shareholders' equity, users of financial statements need sufficient disclosures to understand the causes of changes in the amount of retained earnings. A typical statement of retained earnings is shown in Exhibit 12–10.

The statement of retained earnings shown in Exhibit 12–10 reports two items that have not been discussed: (1) prior period adjustments and (2) restrictions on retained earnings.

Prior Period Adjustments

This category of events is defined in the *CICA Handbook,* Section 3600, as adjustments having all four of the following characteristics:

a. Are specifically identified with and directly related to the business activities of particular prior periods.
b. Are not attributable to economic events occurring subsequent to the date of the financial statements for such prior periods.

Exhibit 12-10   Statement of retained earnings

FERRARI CORPORATION
Statement of Retained Earnings
For the Year Ended December 31, 19C

Retained earnings balance, January 1, 19C		$226,000
Prior period adjustment:		
Deduct adjustment for correction of prior accounting error		
(net of income tax)		10,000
Balance as restated		216,000
Net income for 19C		34,000
Total		250,000
Deduct dividends declared in 19C:		
On preferred stock	$ 6,000	
On common stock	12,000	18,000
Retained earnings balance, December 31, 19C (see Note 5)		$232,000

Note 5. Restriction on retained earnings; total, $100,000.
  The bonds payable indenture requires that retained earnings be restricted in accordance with an agreed schedule. The schedule amounts for 19B and 19C total $100,000.

c. Depends primarily on decisions or determinations by persons other than management or owners.

d. Could not be reasonably estimated prior to such decisions or determinations.

Prior period adjustments must be reported on the statement of retained earnings as an **adjustment of the beginning balance of retained earnings** (not on the income statement). Prior period adjustments should be recorded in specially designated gain and loss accounts, which are closed at the end of the period **directly** to the Retained Earnings account. Examples of prior period adjustments would be corrections of **accounting errors** made in a prior period, retroactive application of a change in an accounting policy, settlements of income taxes, and settlements of claims from litigation.[12] Exhibit 12-10 illustrates reporting of a prior period adjustment.[13] Observe that prior period adjustments are defined and reported quite differently than extraordinary items.

---

[12] The first two of these examples may seem somewhat outside the four characteristics. Errors should be rare but can happen, and the treatment of changes in accounting policy is necessary to ease the effect on current income and to improve comparability among annual reports.

[13] The tax effects of such prior period adjustments are part of procedures related to income tax allocations discussed in Chapter 10. The specific term for these tax amounts is "intraperiod tax allocations."

Restrictions on Retained Earnings

Often corporations have restrictions on retained earnings. Such a **restriction temporarily removes the restricted amount of retained earnings from being available for dividends.** When the restriction is removed, the amount that was restricted is available for dividends and other "uses" of retained earnings. Restrictions on retained earnings may be voluntary or involuntary. The restriction reported on Exhibit 12–10 is involuntary; it was imposed by **contract.** On occasion, the management or the board of directors may voluntarily establish a restriction on retained earnings for expansion of the business. The amount of retained earnings restricted for this purpose often is called "Retained earnings appropriated for earnings invested in plant and equipment." This restriction can be removed by the management or board of directors at any time.

The **full disclosure principle** requires that restrictions on retained earnings be reported on the financial statements. The approach most widely used is by note, as illustrated in Exhibit 12–10.

A practice used widely in past years, but now used less often, was to set up a special retained earnings account for each appropriation. Such accounts, somewhat illogically, often were called reserves. A journal entry to establish a "reserve" for the restriction of retained earnings by Ferrari Corporation (Exhibit 12–10) would be:

Retained earnings	100,000	
Reserve for bonds payable		100,000

In preparing the statement of retained earnings, Ferrari Corporation could list the "reserve" account on the statement of retained earnings, and Note 5 would be unnecessary. When the restrictions are removed, the above entry is reversed.

An appropriation (or restriction) of retained earnings is **not cash.** Observe in the above entries that cash was not affected; the **only** effect was to remove a specific amount of retained earnings from dividend availability. In order to set aside cash for a special purpose, cash is credited and a **fund** account (e.g., building construction fund) is debited. Such fund accounts are assets similar to a savings account. Thus, there is no necessary relationship between appropriations of retained earnings and cash.

Accounting and Reporting for Unincorporated Businesses

There are three forms of business organizations: **corporations** (i.e., shares owned by a number of individuals), **sole proprietorships** (i.e., one owner), and **partnerships** (i.e., two or more owners). The fundamentals of accounting and reporting for unincorporated businesses are the same as for a corporation except for **owners' equity.** Typical account structures for the three forms of business organizations are outlined in Exhibit 12–11.

Accounting for sole proprietorships and partnerships is discussed in Supplement 12B.

Exhibit 12–11 Comparative account structures among types of business entities

TYPICAL ACCOUNT STRUCTURE		
Corporation (shareholders' equity)	**Sole Proprietorship** (owner's equity)	**Partnership** (partners' equity)
Capital stock Contributed surplus	Doe, capital	Able, capital Baker, capital
Retained earnings	Not used	Not used
Dividends paid	Doe, drawings	Able, drawings Baker, drawings

Income summary
    (closed to
    Retained Earnings)
	Income summary
	    (closed to
	    Doe, Capital)
		Income summary
		    (closed to Able, Capital,
		    and Baker, Capital)

Revenues, expenses, gains, and losses	Same	Same
Assets and liabilities	Same	Same

DEMONSTRATION CASE

(Try to resolve the requirements before proceeding to the "Suggested Solution" that follows.)

This case focuses on the organization and operations for the first year of Shelly Corporation, which was organized on January 1, 19A. The Canada Business Corporations Act specifies that the legal capital for no-par stocks is the full sale amount. The corporation was organized by 10 local entrepreneurs for the purpose of operating a business to sell various operating supplies to hotels. The charter **authorized** the following capital stock:

Common stock, no-par value shares.
Preferred stock, $5; no par (cumulative, nonparticipating, nonconvertible, and nonvoting; liquidation value, $110).

The following summarized transactions, selected from 19A, were completed on the dates indicated:

1. Jan.   Sold a total of 7,500 shares of no-par common stock to the 10 entrepreneurs for cash at $52 per share. Credit the No-Par Common Stock account for the total sales amount.

2. Feb.   Sold 1,890 shares of preferred stock at $102 per share; cash collected in full.

3. Mar.   Purchased land for a store site and made full payment by issuing 100 shares of preferred stock. Early construction of the store is planned. Debit Land (store site). The preferred shares are selling at $102 per share.

4. Apr.   Paid $1,980 cash for organization costs. Debit an intangible asset account entitled "Organization Cost."

5. May   Issued 10 shares of preferred stock to A. B. Cain in full payment of legal services rendered in connection with organization of the corporation. Assume the preferred shares are selling regularly at $102 per share. Debit Organization Cost.

6. June   Sold 500 shares of no-par common stock for cash to C. B. Abel at $54 per share.

7. July   Purchased 100 shares of preferred stock that had been sold and issued earlier. The shareholder was moving to another province and "needed the money." Shelly Corporation paid the shareholder $104 per share.

8. Aug.   Sold 20 shares of the preferred stock at $105 per share.

9. Dec. 31   Purchased equipment for $600,000; paid cash. No depreciation expense should be recorded in 19A.

10. Dec. 31   Borrowed $20,000 cash from the City Bank on a one-year, interest-bearing note. Interest is payable at a 12% rate at maturity.

11. Dec. 31   Gross revenues for the year amounted to $129,300; expenses, including corporation income tax but excluding amortization of organization costs, amounted to $98,000. Assume that these summarized revenue and expense transactions were paid in cash. Because the equipment and the bank loan transactions were on December 31, no related adjusting entries at the end of 19A are needed.

12. Dec. 31   Shelly Corporation decided that a "reasonable" amortization period for organization costs, starting as of January 1, 19A, would be 10 years. This intangible asset must be amortized to expense. Give the required adjusting entry for 19A.

Required:
  a. Give appropriate journal entries, with a brief explanation for each of the above transactions.
  b. Give appropriate closing entries at December 31, 19A.
  c. Prepare a balance sheet for Shelly Corporation at December 31, 19A. Emphasize full disclosure of shareholders' equity.

Suggested Solution

Requirement a—Journal entries:

1. January 19A:

Cash	390,000	
No-par common stock (7,500 shares)		390,000
Sale of no-par common shares ($52 × 7,500 shares = $390,000).		

2. February 19A:

Cash	192,780	
Preferred stock, $5, no par (1,890 shares)		192,780
Sale of preferred shares ($102 × 1,890 shares = $192,780).		

3. March 19A:

Land (store site)	10,200	
Preferred stock, $5, no par (100 shares)		10,200
Purchased land for future store site; paid in full by issuance of 100 shares of preferred stock. The market value is, $102 × 100 shares = $10,200.		

4. April 19A:

Organization cost	1,980	
Cash		1,980
Paid organization cost.		

5. May 19A:

Organization cost	1,020	
Preferred stock, $5, no par (10 shares)		1,020
Organization cost (legal services) paid by issuance of 10 shares of preferred stock. The implied market value is, $102 × 10 shares = $1,020.		

6. June 19A:

Cash	27,000	
No-par common (500 shares)		27,000
Sold 500 shares of the no-par common stock ($54 × 500 shares = $27,000).		

7. July 19A:

Preferred stock, $5, no par, (100 shares at $104)	10,400	
Cash		10,400
Purchased 100 shares of preferred stock ($104 × 100 shares = $10,400).		

Note: A somewhat more sophisticated entry to reflect the $2 extra payment would be as follows:

Retained earnings	200	
Preferred stock	10,200	
Cash		10,400

8. **August 19A:**

Cash (20 shares at $105)	2,100	
Preferred stock, $5, no par		2,100

Sold 20 shares of preferred stock at $105.

9. **December 31, 19A:**

Equipment	600,000	
Cash		600,000

Purchased equipment.

10. **December 31, 19A:**

Cash	20,000	
Note payable		20,000

Borrowed on one-year, 12%, interest-bearing note.

11. **December 31, 19A:**

Cash	129,300	
Revenues		129,300
Expenses	98,000	
Cash		98,000

To record summarized revenues and expenses.

12. **December 31, 19A:**

Expenses	300	
Organization cost		300

Adjusting entry to amortize organization cost for one year
($1,980 + $1,020) ÷ 10 years = $300.

Requirement b—Closing entries:

13. **December 31, 19A:**

Revenues	129,300	
Income summary		129,300
Income summary	98,300	
Expenses ($98,000 + $300)		98,300
Income summary	31,000	
Retained earnings		31,000

($129,300 − $98,300 = $31,000.)

Requirement c:

SHELLY CORPORATION
Balance Sheet
At December 31, 19A

Assets

Current assets:

Cash		$ 50,800
Tangible assets:		
Land	$ 10,200	
Equipment (no depreciation assumed in the problem)	600,000	610,200
Intangible assets:		
Organization cost (cost, $3,000 less amortization, $300)		2,700
Total assets		$663,700

Liabilities

Current liabilities:

Note payable, 12%		$ 20,000

Shareholders' Equity

Contributed capital:

Preferred stock, $5, no par; issued 1,920 shares	$195,700	
Common stock, no-par value, issued and outstanding 8,000 shares	417,000	
Total contributed capital	612,700	
Retained earnings	31,000	
Total shareholders' equity		643,700
Total liabilities and shareholders' equity		$663,700

SUMMARY OF CHAPTER

This chapter discussed accounting for owners' equity for corporations. Sole proprietorships and partnerships are discussed in Supplement 12B. Except for owners' equity, accounting basically is unaffected by the type of business organization. Accounting for owners' equity is based upon the concept of **source;** each specific source of owners' equity should be accounted for and reported separately. The two basic sources of owners' equity for a corporation are contributed capital and retained earnings. Separate accounts are kept for each type of capital stock.

The earnings of a corporation that are not retained in the business for growth and expansion are distributed to the shareholders by means of dividends. Dividends are paid only when formally declared by the board of directors of the corporation. A cash dividend results in a decrease in assets (cash) and a commensurate decrease in shareholders' equity (retained earnings). In contrast, a stock dividend does not change assets, liabilities, or total shareholders' equity. A stock dividend results in a transfer of retained earnings to the permanent or contributed capital of the corporation by the amount of the stock dividend. Therefore, a stock dividend affects only certain account balances within shareholders' equity. A stock split affects only the par value of the stock and the number of shares outstanding; the individual equity account balances are not changed. Frequently a corporation purchases its own shares in the marketplace. Shares previously issued by the corporation and subsequently reacquired are known as **treasury stock** as long as they are held by the issuing corporation. The purchase of treasury stock is viewed as a contraction of corporate capital, and the subsequent resale of the treasury stock is viewed as an expansion of corporate capital if the law does not require them to be immediately canceled.

CHAPTER SUPPLEMENT 12A

Participating Dividend Preference on Preferred Shares

Preferred shares may be nonparticipating, fully participating, or partially participating. Participation relates to the dividends that can be paid on preferred shares **after** dividends in arrears and **after** the current dividend preference.

Most preferred shares are **nonparticipating,** as shown in Exhibit 12–9. Preferred shares that are **participating** may be either noncumulative or cumulative.

Fully participating and **noncumulative** preferred shares receive a first priority for the current dividend preference; then a matching proportionate amount is allocated to the common shares; any remaining balance of the total dividend is allocated on a proportionate basis to the preferred and common shares as shown in Exhibit 12–12, Case A.

Fully participating and **cumulative** preferred shares receive a first priority on both dividends in **arrears** and the current dividend preference. After those preferences are satisfied, a proportionate amount is allocated to the common shares; any remaining balance of total dividends to be paid is allocated on a proportionate basis to the preferred and common shares as shown in Exhibit 12–12, Case B.

Partially participating preferred shares essentially are the same as fully participating. However, the participating preference in excess of the current dividend rate is limited to a stated percent of par. For example, the corporate charter may read, "and partially participating only up to an additional 2 percent." Fully participating and partially participating preferred share preferences are rare.[14]

CHAPTER SUPPLEMENT 12B

Accounting for Owners' Equity for Sole Proprietorships and Partnerships

A sole proprietorship is an unincorporated business owned by one person. The only owner's equity accounts needed are (1) a capital account for the proprietor

---

[14] Textbooks for more advanced courses in accounting contain additional discussion and illustrations of the participating features and the payment of a dividend in assets other than cash, such as property and shares of other corporations being held as an investment.

Exhibit 12–12 Dividends on participating preferred shares

Situation (Box Corporation; refer to Exhibit 12–8):

Preferred stock, 6%, par $20; shares outstanding, 2,000 = $40,000.
Common stock, par $10; shares outstanding, 5,000 = $50,000.
Dividends in arrears for the two previous years.

Allocation of dividends between preferred and common shares assuming fully participating:

	6% preferred stock (total par, $40,000)	**Common stock (total par, $50,000)**	**Total dividends paid**
Assumptions (dividends in arrears, two years)			
Case A—Preferred stock is fully participating and noncumulative (two years in arrears). Total dividends			
paid, $7,200: Current dividend ($40,000 × 6%)	$ 2,400		$ 2,400
Equivalent amount to common ($50,000 × 6%)		$3,000	3,000
Subtotal			5,400
Full participation—balance allocated in ratio of par values:			
($40,000/$90,000) × ($7,200 − $5,400)	800		800
($50,000/$90,000) × ($7,200 − $5,400)		1,000	1,000
Totals	$ 3,200	$4,000	$ 7,200
Case B—Preferred stock is fully participating and cumulative (two years in arrears). Total dividends			
paid, $16,500: Arrears ($2,400 × 2 years)	$ 4,800		$ 4,800
Current preference ($40,000 × 6%)	2,400		2,400
Equivalent amount to common ($50,000 × 6%)		$3,000	3,000
Subtotal			10,200
Full participation—balance allocated in ratio of par:			
($40,000/$90,000) × ($16,500 − $10,200)	2,800		2,800
($50,000/$90,000) × ($16,500 − $10,200)		3,500	3,500
Totals	$10,000	$6,500	$16,500

(e.g., J. Doe, Capital), and (2) a drawing (or withdrawal) account for the proprietor (e.g., J. Doe, Drawings). The **capital account** of a sole proprietorship is used for two purposes: to record investments by the owner and to accumulate the periodic income or loss. Thus, the **Income Summary** account is closed to the capital account at the end of each accounting period. The **drawing account** is used to record withdrawals of cash or other assets by the owner from the business. The drawing account is closed to the capital account at the end of each accounting period. The capital account reflects the cumulative total of all investments by the owner, plus all earnings of the entity, less all withdrawals of resources from the entity by the owner. In most respects, the accounting for a sole proprietorship is the same as for a corporation.

Exhibit 12–13 presents the recording of selected transactions and the owner's equity section of the balance sheet of Doe Retail Store to illustrate the accounting for and reporting of **owner's equity** for a sole proprietorship.[15]

There are two more differences between accounting for corporations and sole proprietorships. A sole proprietorship does not pay income taxes. Therefore, the financial statements of a sole proprietorship will not reflect income tax expense or income taxes payable. The net income of a sole proprietorship is taxed when it is included on the **personal** income tax return of the owner. Also, because an employer/employee contractual relationship cannot exist with only one party involved, a "salary" to the owner is not recognized as an expense of a sole proprietorship. The salary of the owner is accounted for as a distribution of profits (i.e., a withdrawal).

Owners' Equity for a Partnership.   The Partnership Acts of most provinces, define a partnership as "an association of two or more persons to carry on as co-owners of a business for profit." The partnership form of business is used by small businesses and professionals, such as accountants, doctors, and lawyers. A partnership is formed by two or more persons reaching mutual agreement about the terms of the partnership. The law does not require an application for a charter as in the case of a corporation. The agreement between the partners constitutes a **partnership contract** that should be in writing. The partnership agreement should specify such matters as division of periodic income, management responsibilities, transfer or sale of partnership interests, disposition of assets upon liquidation, and procedures to be followed in case of the death of a partner. If the partnership agreement does not specify on these matters, the laws of the resident province will be binding. The primary advantages of a partnership are (1) ease of formation, (2) complete control by the partners, and (3) no income taxes on the business itself. The primary disadvantage is the unlimited liability of each partner for the liabilities of the partnership.

As with a sole proprietorship, accounting for a partnership follows the same underlying fundamentals of accounting as any other form of business organization, **except for those entries that directly affect owners' equity.** Accounting for partners' equity follows the same pattern as illustrated earlier for a sole proprietorship, except that separate partner capital and drawings accounts must be established for **each** partner. Investments by each partner are credited to the partner's capital account. Withdrawals from the partnership by each partner are debited to the respective drawings account. The net income for a partnership is divided between the partners in the **profit ratio** specified in the partnership agreement. The Income Summary account is closed to the respective partner capital accounts. The respective drawings accounts also are closed to the partner capital accounts. Therefore, after the closing process, the capital account of each

---

[15] Alternatively, the balance sheet may reflect only "J. Doe, capital, December 31, 19A, $156,000," with a supplemental or supporting **statement of owner's equity** that would be the same as shown in the exhibit.

Exhibit 12–13 Accounting and reporting of owner's equity for a sole proprietorship

Selected entries during 19A:

January 1, 19A:

J. Doe started a retail store by investing $150,000 of personal savings. The journal entry for the business would be as follows:

Cash	150,000	
J. Doe, capital		150,000

Investment by owner.

During 19A:

Each month during the year, Doe withdrew $1,000 cash from the business for personal living costs. Accordingly, each month the following journal entry was made:

J. Doe, drawings	1,000	
Cash		1,000

Withdrawal of cash by owner for personal use.

Note: At December 31, 19A, after the last withdrawal, the drawings account will reflect a debit balance of $12,000.

December 31, 19A:

Usual journal entries for the year, including adjusting and closing entries for the revenue and expense accounts, resulted in an $18,000 **credit balance** in the Income Summary account (i.e., $18,000 net income). The next closing entry will be:

Income summary	18,000	
J. Doe, capital		18,000

Closing entry to transfer net income for the year to the owner's equity account.

December 31, 19A:

The journal entry required on this date to close the drawings account would be:

J. Doe, capital	12,000	
J. Doe, drawings		12,000

Closing entry to transfer drawings for the year to the capital account.

Balance sheet December 31, 19A (partial):

Owner's Equity

J. Doe, capital, January 1, 19A	$150,000	
Add: Net income for 19A	18,000	
Total	168,000	
Less: Withdrawals for 19A	12,000	
J. Doe, capital, December 31, 19A		$156,000

Exhibit 12–14 Accounting for and reporting of partners' equity

---

Selected entries during 19A:

January 1, 19A:

AB Partnership was organized by A. Able and B. Baker on this date. Able contributed $60,000 and Baker $40,000 cash in the partnership and agreed to divide net income (and net loss) 60% and 40%, respectively. The journal entry for the business to record the investment would be:

Cash	100,000	
A. Able, capital		60,000
B. Baker, capital		40,000
Investment to initiate a partnership.		

During 19A:

It was agreed that in lieu of salaries, Able would withdraw $1,000 and Baker $650 per month in cash. Accordingly, **each month** the following journal entry for the withdrawals was made:

A. Able, drawings	1,000	
B. Baker, drawings	650	
Cash		1,650
Withdrawal of cash by partners for personal use.		

December 31, 19A:

Assume the normal closing entries for the revenue and expense accounts resulted in a $30,000 **credit balance** in the Income Summary account (i.e., $30,000 net income). The next closing entry would be:

Income summary	30,000	
A. Able, capital		18,000
B. Baker, capital		12,000

Closing entry to transfer net income to the respective capital accounts. Net income divided as follows:

A. Able, $30,000 × 60% = $18,000
B. Baker, $30,000 × 40% =   12,000

Total $30,000

December 31, 19A:

The journal entry required to close the drawings account would be:

A. Able, capital	12,000	
B. Baker, capital	7,800	
A. Able, drawings		12,000
B. Baker, drawings		7,800

Closing entry to transfer drawings for the year to the respective capital accounts.

Exhibit 12–14 *(concluded)*

After the closing entries the partners' accounts would reflect the following balances:

Income summary	–0–
A. Able, drawings	–0–
B. Baker, drawings	–0–
A. Able, capital	$66,000
B. Baker, capital	44,200

Reporting partners' distribution of net income and partners' equity:

Income statement for the year ended December 31, 19A:

Net income .... $ 30,000

Distribution of net income:
A. Able (60%) $18,000
B. Baker (40%) 12,000
$30,000

Balance sheet December 31, 19A:

Partners' Equity

A. Able, capital $66,000
B. Baker, capital 44,200

Total partners' equity $110,200

A separate statement of partners' capital similar to the following customarily is prepared to supplement the balance sheet:

AB PARTNERSHIP
Statement of Partners' Capital
For the Year Ended December 31, 19A

	A. Able	B. Baker	Total
Investment, January 1, 19A	$60,000	$40,000	$100,000
Add: Additional investments during the year	–0–	–0–	–0–
Net income for the year	18,000	12,000	30,000
Totals	78,000	52,000	130,000
Less: Drawings during the year	12,000	7,800	19,800
Partners' equity, December 31, 19A	$66,000	$44,200	$110,200

partner reflects the cumulative total of all investments of the individual partner, plus the partner's share of all partnership earnings, less all withdrawals by the partner.

Exhibit 12–14 presents selected 19A journal entries and partial financial statements of AB Partnership to illustrate the accounting for and reporting of the distribution of income and partners' equity.

The financial statements of a partnership follow the same format as a corporation, except (1) the income statement includes an additional section entitled "Distribution of net income," (2) the partners' equity section of the balance sheet is detailed for each partner in conformity with the full disclosure principle, as illustrated in Exhibit 12–14, (3) there is no income tax expense or income taxes payable because partnerships do not pay income tax (each partner must report his or her share of the partnership profits on the individual tax return), and (4) salaries paid to partners are not recorded as expense but are treated as a distribution of earnings (i.e., withdrawals).

IMPORTANT TERMS DEFINED IN THIS CHAPTER

Authorized Shares The type or maximum number of shares of the corporation that can be issued as specified in the charter. *p. 697*

Charter of a Corporation The legal articles of incorporation by the jurisdiction that creates a corporation; specifies purpose and capital. *p. 694*

Common Stock The basic, normal, voting shares issued by a corporation; not preferred shares; residual equity. *p. 697*

Convertible Preferred Shares Preferred shares that are convertible, at the option of the holder, to common shares. *p. 700*

Cumulative Dividend Preference Preferred share preference that dividends not declared for a particular year cumulate as a subsequent preference. *p. 710*

Current Dividend Preference The basic dividend preference on preferred shares for a particular year. *p. 710*

Dividend Dates:

Declaration Date dividend declared; entry for cash dividend; dividends payable. *p. 714*

Record Date on which the shareholders are individually identified to receive a declared dividend. *p. 715*

Payment Date on which a cash dividend is paid to the shareholders of record; cash is disbursed. *p. 715*

Dividends in Arrears Dividends on cumulative preferred shares that have not been declared in prior years. *p. 710*

Issued Shares Total shares that have been issued; shares outstanding plus treasury shares held. *p. 697*

Legal or Stated Capital Defined by law; usually par value; provides a "cushion" for creditors; cannot be used for dividends. *p. 698*

Minute Book An official record of the actions of the board of directors of a corporation. *p. 716*

No-Par-Value Shares Shares of capital stock that have no par value specified in the corporate charter. *p. 698*

Outstanding Shares Shares, in total, that are owned by shareholders on any particular date. *p. 697*

Partnership An unincorporated business owned by two or more persons. *p. 718*

Par Value Nominal value per share of capital stock; specified in the charter; basis for legal capital. *p. 698*

Preferred Stock Shares that have specified rights over the common shares. *p. 699*

Prior Period Adjustments Amounts debited or credited directly to retained earnings resulting from correction of accounting errors. *p. 717*

Restrictions on Retained Earnings Temporary removal of some or all of the balance of retained earnings from dividend availability. *p. 718*

Share Certificate Evidence of the number of shares held by an investor; ownership interest. *p. 695*

Shareholders' Subsidiary Ledger A record, usually maintained by a transfer agent, of the names, addresses, and shares owned, of all the shareholders. *p. 715*

Share Transfer Agent An individual or organization appointed by a corporation to transfer shares and maintain shareholders' records. *p. 715*

Sole Proprietorship An unincorporated business owned by only one person (one owner). *p. 718*

Stock Dividends Distribution of additional shares to current shareholders on a proportional basis at no cost; decreases retained earnings. *p. 707*

Stock Splits The total number of shares is increased by a specified ratio; issued at no cost; does not change proportional ownership of each shareholder; does not decrease retained earnings. *p. 713*

Treasury Stock A corporation's own shares that have been issued, then reacquired and still held by that corporation. *p. 704*

Unissued Shares Shares of a corporation that have never been issued. *p. 697*

QUESTIONS

Part A: Questions 1–10

1. Define a corporation and identify its primary advantages.
2. What is the charter of a corporation?
3. Explain each of the following terms: (*a*) authorized capital stock, (*b*) issued capital stock, and (*c*) outstanding capital stock.
4. Distinguish between common stock and preferred stock.
5. Explain the distinction between par value shares and no-par-value capital stock.
6. What are the usual characteristics of preferred shares?
7. What are the two basic sources of shareholders' equity? Explain each.
8. Owners' equity is accounted for by source. What is meant by source?
9. Define treasury stock. Why do corporations acquire treasury stock?
10. How is treasury stock reported on the balance sheet? How is the "gain or loss" on treasury stock which has been sold reported on the financial statements?

Part B: Questions 11–21

11. What are the two basic requirements to support a cash dividend? What are the effects of a cash dividend on assets and shareholders' equity?
12. Distinguish between cumulative and noncumulative preferred stock.
13. Define a stock dividend. How does it differ from a cash dividend?
14. What are the primary purposes in issuing a stock dividend?
15. Identify and explain the three important dates in respect to dividends.
16. Define retained earnings. What are the primary components of retained earnings at the end of each period?
17. Define prior period adjustments. How are they reported?
18. What is meant by restrictions on retained earnings?
19. Using the legal rules for when a dividend can be declared as specified in the chapter, does a restriction of retained earnings hinder the payment of dividends? If not, what purpose could be served by such a reserve of retained earnings?
20. Realizable value of assets is part of one of the legal restrictions of when a company is entitled to purchase its own shares or to declare a dividend. Which accounts on a traditional balance sheet would not reflect such realizable values for purposes of these calculations? What might be done to determine their realizable values?
21. Because a person who operates a small business could incorporate a limited company or operate as a sole proprietorship, the net income reported for the same operations would be different. What constitutes the difference and why would a prospective buyer of such a business be concerned?

EXERCISES

Part A: Exercises 12–1 to 12–7

E12–1   **(Pair Definition with Terms)**
Match the following brief definitions with the terms by entering the appropriate letter in each space provided.

Term	Description
_____ (1) Stock dividends	A. Specified by the corporate charter, the maximum number of shares of capital stock the corporation can issue.
_____ (2) Dividends in arrears	
_____ (3) Authorized shares	B. The class of shares that is issued when only one kind is issued.
_____ (4) No-par-value stock	C. Provides the option of being exchanged for common shares.
_____ (5) Common stock	
_____ (6) Declaration date	D. Requires that if dividends are not paid in full, the unpaid amount of dividends accumulates.
_____ (7) Stock splits	
_____ (8) Cumulative dividend preference	E. The date on which the board of directors officially approves a dividend.

Term	**Description**
_____ (9) Record date	F. The date on which the corporation prepares a list of those owning outstanding shares.
_____ (10) Issued shares	
_____ (11) Par value	G. The date cash dividends are disbursed.
_____ (12) Legal or stated capital	H. The accumulated unpaid preferred stock dividends.
_____ (13) Payment date	I. Shares in hands of shareholders.
_____ (14) Treasury stock	J. Par value.
_____ (15) Convertible preferred shares	K. Shares that cannot be sold at a premium or discount.
_____ (16) Preferred shares	L. Nominal value per share established in the charter of the corporation.
_____ (17) Prior period adjustment	M. Shares whose characteristics usually include: dividend preferences, conversion privileges, asset preferences, and nonvoting specification.
	N. Correction of an error in the financial statements of a prior period that must be reported on the statement of retained earnings.
	O. A board of directors may declare and issue this instead of a cash dividend; it decreases retained earnings.
	P. Similar to a stock dividend but does not decrease retained earnings.
	Q. Capital stock reacquired which reduces cash and shareholders' equity by equal amounts.

E12–2   **(Preparing the Shareholders' Equity Section of the Balance Sheet)**

Janex Corporation was organized in 19A to operate an engineering service business. The charter authorized the following capital stock: common stock, par value $10 per share, unlimited number of shares. During the first year, the following selected transactions were completed:

1. Sold and issued 5,000 shares of common stock for cash at $25 per share.
2. Issued 500 shares of common stock for a piece of land that will be used for a facilities site; construction began immediately. Assume the shares were selling at $27 per share at the date of issuance. Debit land.
3. Sold and issued 1,000 shares of common stock for cash at $27 cash per share.
4. At year-end, the Income Summary account reflected a $7,000 loss. Because a loss was incurred, no income tax expense was recorded.

Required:

a. Give the journal entry required for each of the transactions listed above.

b. Prepare the shareholders' equity section as it should be reported on the year-end balance sheet.

E12–3   **(Analysis of Transactions Affecting Shareholders' Equity)**

Reed Corporation was organized in January 19A by 12 shareholders to operate an air conditioning sales and service business. The charter issued by the province authorized the following capital stock:

Common stock, $1 par value shares.

Preferred stock, $10 par value, 8%, nonparticipating, noncumulative shares.

During January and February 19A, the following share transactions were completed:

1. Collected $30,000 cash from each of the 12 organizers and issued 1,000 shares of common stock to each of them.
2. Sold 8,000 shares of preferred stock at $30 per share; collected the cash and immediately issued the shares.

Required:

a. Give the journal entries to record the above share transactions.

b. Net income for 19A was $35,000; cash dividends declared and paid at year-end were $15,000. Prepare the shareholders' equity section of the balance sheet at December 31, 19A.

E12–4   (Issuing Common and Preferred Stock)

Sound Systems, Incorporated, was issued a charter on January 15, 19A, that authorized the following capital stock:

Common stock, no-par shares.

Preferred stock, 6%, $10 par value shares.

During 19A, the following selected transactions were completed in the order given:

1. Sold and issued 30,000 shares of the no-par common stock at $30 cash per share.
2. Sold and issued 4,000 shares of preferred stock at $21 cash per share.
3. At the end of 19A, the Income Summary account had a credit balance of $15,000.

Required:

a. Give the journal entry indicated for each of the above transactions.

b. Prepare the shareholders' equity section of the balance sheet at December 31, 19A.

E12–5   (Shareholders' Equity Transactions, Including Noncash Consideration)

Datalife Corporation obtained a charter at the start of 19A that authorized no-par common stock and preferred stock of par value $10. The corporation was organized by five individuals who "reserved" 51% of the common stock shares for themselves. The remaining shares were to be sold to other individuals at $50 per share on a cash basis. During 19A, the following selected transactions occurred:

1. Collected $20 per share cash from four of the organizers and received two adjoining lots of land from the fifth organizer. Issued 3,000 shares of common stock to each of the five organizers and received title to the land.
2. Sold and issued 5,000 shares of common stock to an "outsider" at $50 cash per share.
3. Sold and issued 4,000 shares of preferred stock at $15 cash per share.
4. At the end of 19A, the Income Summary account, after income taxes, reflected a credit balance of $30,000.

Required:

a. Give the journal entries indicated for each of the transactions listed above.

b. Prepare the shareholders' equity section of the balance sheet at December 31, 19A.

c. Explain the basis that you used to determine the cost of the land.

E12–6 **(Finding Missing Amounts from the Shareholders' Equity Section)**
The shareholders' equity section on the December 31, 19D, balance sheet of Halifax Corporation was:

Shareholders' Equity

Contributed capital:
Preferred stock, par value $30, ___?___ issued and outstanding . . .	$150,000
Common stock, no par; issued and outstanding 7,000 shares	630,000
Contributed surplus, preferred	7,150
Contributed surplus treasury stock transactions	2,000
Retained earnings	40,000

Required:

Complete the following statements and show your computations.

a. The number of shares of preferred stock issued and outstanding was

_____.

b. The average sale price of the preferred shares when issued was $_____ per share.

c. Have the treasury stock transactions (1) increased corporate resources _____; or (2) decreased resources _____? By how much?

_____.

d. Total shareholders' equity is $_____.

e. What was the average issue price of the common shares? $_____.

E12–7 **(Accounting for Treasury Stock Transactions)**
The balance sheet (summarized) of Pope Corporation reflected the information shown below at December 31, 19B:

POPE CORPORATION
Balance Sheet
At December 31, 19B

Assets		Liabilities	
Cash	$100,000	Current liabilities	$ 60,000
All other assets	412,000	Long-term liabilities	80,000
			140,000
		Shareholders' Equity	
		Contributed capital:	
		Common stock, par $20;	
		outstanding 12,000	
		shares	240,000
		Contributed surplus	72,000
		Retained earnings	60,000
	$512,000		$512,000

During the next year, 19C, the following selected transactions affecting shareholders' equity occurred:

Feb. 1   Purchased in the open market, 500 shares of Pope's own common stock at $40 cash per share.

July 15   Sold 100 of the shares purchased on February 1, 19C, at $41 cash per share.

Sept. 1   Sold 20 more of the shares purchased on February 1, 19C, at $38 cash per share.

Dec. 15   Sold an additional 80 of the treasury shares at $35 per share.

31   The credit balance in the Income Summary account was $31,140.

Legislation requires that treasury stock be held in a separate account until it is resold.

Required:

a. Give the indicated journal entries for each of the five transactions.

b. Prepare the shareholders' equity section of the balance sheet at December 31, 19C.

Part B: Exercises 12–8 to 12–13

E12–8   **(Comparing Various Types of Preferred Shares)**
The records of Quality Plumbing Supply Company reflected the following balances in the shareholders' equity accounts at December 31, 19H:

Common stock, par $5 per share, 30,000 shares outstanding.

Preferred stock, 6%, par $10 per share, 3,000 shares outstanding.

Retained earnings, $150,000.

On September 1, 19H, the board of directors was considering the distribution of a $42,000 cash dividend. No dividends were paid during 19F and 19G. You have been asked to determine the total and per share amounts that would be paid to the common shareholders and to the preferred shareholders under three independent assumptions (show computations):

a. The preferred shares are noncumulative and nonparticipating.

b. The preferred shares are cumulative and nonparticipating.

c. The preferred shares are cumulative and fully participating (solve this assumption only if Supplement 12A is assigned for study).

d. Give the journal entry to record dividends separately for preferred and common shares under each assumption.

e. Explain why the dividends per share of common stock were less for each assumption than for the preceding assumption.

f. What factor would cause a more favourable per share result to the common shareholders?

E12–9   **(Recording Dividends)**
Rye Corporation has the following capital stock outstanding at the end of 19B:

Preferred stock, 8%, par $20, outstanding shares, 6,000.

Common stock, par $5, outstanding shares, 20,000.

On October 1, 19B, the board of directors declared dividends as follows:

Preferred stock, the full cash preference amount; payable December 20, 19B.

Common stock, a 10% common stock dividend (i.e., one additional share for each 10 held), issuable December 20, 19B.

On December 20, 19B, the market prices were: preferred shares, $50, and common shares, $20.

Required:

a. Give any required journal entry(s) to record the declaration and subsequent payment of the dividend on the preferred shares.

b. Give any required journal entry(s) to record the declaration and issuance of the stock dividend on the common shares.

c. Explain the comparative overall effect of each of the dividends on the assets, liabilities, and shareholders' equity of Rye Corporation.

E12–10 **(Analysis of Stock Dividends)**
On December 31, 19E, the shareholders' equity section of the balance sheet of Hyde Park Corporation reflected the following:

Common stock, par $10; shares outstanding, 20,000 . . . $200,000
Contributed surplus   15,000
Retained earnings   103,000

On February 1, 19F, the board of directors declared a 15% stock dividend to be issued April 30, 19F. The market value of a share on February 1, 19F, was $16. The market value will be capitalized.

Required:

a. Give any required journal entry(s) to record the declaration and issuance of the stock dividend.

b. For comparative purposes, prepare the shareholders' equity section of the balance sheet (1) immediately before the stock dividend and (2) immediately after the stock dividend. (Hint: Use two amount columns for this requirement.)

c. Explain the effects of this stock dividend on the assets, liabilities, and shareholders' equity.

E12–11 **(Preparation of a Statement of Retained Earnings)**
The following account balances were selected from the records of Comed Corporation at December 31, 19E, after all adjusting entries were completed:

Common stock, par $5, issued 119,500 shares   597,500
Contributed surplus   280,000
Bond sinking fund   70,000
Dividends declared and paid in 19E   24,000
Retained earnings, January 1, 19E   90,000
Correction of prior period accounting error (a debit, net of income tax)   10,000
Income summary for 19E (credit balance)   45,000

Required:
Based on the above data, prepare (*a*) the statement of retained earnings for 19E and (*b*) the shareholders' equity section of the balance sheet at December 31, 19E. (Hint: Total shareholders' equity is $978,500.)

E12–12   (Preparing the Statement of Retained Earnings)

The data given below were selected from the records of Stonewall Corporation at December 31, 19B.

Common stock, par $2; issued and outstanding 109,000 shares	218,000
Preferred stock, 6%, par $10; issued and oustanding 15,000 shares . . .	150,000
Contributed surplus:	
Common stock	230,000
Preferred stock	120,000
Dividends declared and paid during 19B	24,000
Net income for 19B	64,000
Retained earnings balance, January 1, 19B	130,000
Prior period adjustment (gain, net of income tax)	10,000
Extraordinary loss (unusual and infrequent, net of income tax)	22,000

Required:

a. Prepare a statement of retained earnings for the year December 31, 19B.

b. Prepare the shareholders' equity section of the balance sheet dated December 31, 19B. (Hint: Total shareholders' equity is $892,000.)

E12–13   (Comparison of Stock Dividends and Splits)

On July 1, 19B, Brodnik Corporation had the following capital structure:

> Common stock, par $2, 20,000 issued.
> Contributed surplus, $60,000.
> Retained earnings, $120,000.

Required:

a. The number of outstanding shares is _____.

b. Total shareholders' equity is _____.

c. Assume the board of directors declared and issued a 20% stock dividend (i.e., one new share for each five shares already owned) when the shares were selling at $11 each. Give any required journal entry(s). If none is required, explain why.

d. Disregard the stock dividend in (c) above. Assume that the board of directors voted a six-to-five stock split (i.e., a 20% increase in the number of shares). The market price prior to the split was $11 per share. Give any required journal entry(s). If none is required, explain why.

e. Complete the following comparative tabulation followed by comments on the comparative effects:

Item	Before Dividend and Split	After Stock Dividend	After Stock Split
Common stock account	$	$	$
Par per share	$2	$	$
Shares outstanding	#	#	#
Contributed surplus	$ 60,000	$	$
Retained earnings	$120,000	$	$
Total shareholders' equity	$	$	$

PROBLEMS

Part A: Problems 12–1 to 12–5

P12–1   **(Preparation of the Shareholders' Equity Section of the Balance Sheet)**
Alliance Corporation received its charter during January 19A. The charter authorized the following capital stock:

Preferred stock, 6%, par $10.
Common stock, par $2.

During 19A, the following transactions occurred in the order given:

1. Issued a total of 60,000 shares of the common stock to the six organizers at $5 per share. Alliance collected cash in full from five of the organizers, and legal services were received from the other organizer in full payment for the shares. The shares were issued immediately.
2. Sold 3,000 shares of the preferred stock at $22 per share. Collected the cash and issued the shares immediately.
3. Sold 2,000 shares of the common stock at $7 per share and 1,000 shares of the preferred stock at $30. Collected the cash and issued the shares immediately.
4. Total revenues for 19A, $206,000, and total expenses (including income tax), $140,000.

Required:
a. Give all of the journal entries required for the above items including closing entries.
b. Prepare the shareholders' equity section of the balance sheet at December 31, 19A.
c. What was the average issue price of the common stock?
d. Explain the basis you used to value the legal services in the first journal entry.

P12–2   **(Analysis of Transactions Affecting Shareholders' Equity)**
Xenia Corporation began operations in January 19A. The charter authorized the following capital stock:

Preferred stock, 6%, $10 par.
Common stock, no par.

During 19A, the following transactions occurred in the order given:

1. Issued 20,000 shares of the no-par common shares to each of the three organizers. Collected $8 cash per share from two of the organizers and received a plot of land, with a small building thereon, in full payment for the shares of the third organizer and issued the shares immediately. Assume that 20% of the noncash payment received applies to the building.
2. Sold 4,000 shares of the preferred shares at $15 each. Collected the cash and issued the shares immediately.
3. Sold 200 shares of the preferred stock at $16 and 1,000 shares of the no-par common stock at $10 per share. Collected the cash and issued the shares immediately.

4. Operating results at the end of 19A, were as follows:

Revenue accounts $160,000
Expense accounts, including income taxes . . .   115,000

Required:

a. Give the journal entries indicated (including closing entries) for each of the above transactions.

b. Prepare the shareholders' equity section of the balance sheet at December 31, 19A.

c. Explain what you used to determine the cost of the land and the building in the first journal entry.

P12–3   **(Comparison of Par and No-Par Shares)**
Myles Company was issued a charter in January 19A. During 19A, the following selected transactions occurred in the order given:

1. Sold 10,000 shares of common stock for cash at $70 per share. Collected the cash and issued the shares immediately.

2. Acquired land to be used as a future plant site; made payment in full by issuing 500 shares. Assume a market value per share of $70.

3. At the end of 19A, the Income Summary account reflected a credit balance of $40,000.

Two independent cases are assumed as follows for comparative study purposes:

Case A—Assume the common stock was $30 par value per share. The provincial law specifies that par value is legal capital.

Case B—Assume the common stock was no par and that the total sale price is credited to the Common Stock, No-Par account because the provincial law specifies this amount as legal capital.

Required:
For each independent case:

a. Give the journal entries for each of the three transactions.

b. Prepare the shareholders' equity section of the balance sheet at December 31, 19A.

c. Should total shareholders' equity be the same amount among the two independent cases? Explain.

d. Should the noncash asset (land) be recorded at the same cost under each of the two independent cases? Explain.

P12–4   **(Analysis of Shareholders' Equity Transactions)**
Mika Company obtained a charter from the province in January 19A. Authorized were $1 par value common shares. The shareholders comprised 20 local citizens. During the first year, the following selected transactions occurred in the order given:

1. Sold 80,000 shares of the common stock to the 20 shareholders at $5 per share. Collected the $400,000 cash and issued the shares.

2. During the year, one of the 20 shareholders needed cash and wanted to sell the shares back to Mika. Accordingly, the corporation purchased the investor's 5,000 shares at $7 cash per share. Common shares were immediately canceled.

3. Two months later, 1,000 of the shares were sold to another individual at $7.25 cash per share.

4. An additional 2,000 shares of the common stock were sold at $6.90 cash per share.

5. On December 31, 19A, the end of the first year of business, the Income Summary account reflected a credit balance of $28,550.

Required:

a. Give the indicated journal entry for each of the above items.

b. Prepare the shareholders' equity section of the balance sheet at December 31, 19A.

c. What dollar effect did the treasury stock transactions have on the assets, liabilities, and shareholders' equity of Mika Corporation? Explain.

P12–5   **(Analysis of Shareholder Transactions Including Noncash Consideration)**
Centex Manufacturing Company was granted a charter that authorized the following capital stock:

Common stock, no-par shares. Assume the no-par shares are not assigned a stated value per share.

Preferred stock, 6%, par $10 shares.

During the first year, 19A, the following selected transactions occurred in the order given:

1. Sold 20,000 shares of the no-par common stock at $30 cash per share and 3,000 shares of the preferred stock at $22 cash per share. Collected cash and issued the shares immediately. For the no-par shares, credit the full selling price to the Common Stock account.

2. Issued 1,000 shares of preferred stock as full payment for a plot of land to be used as a future plant site. Assume the shares were selling at $22.

3. Purchased 1,000 shares of the no-par common stock sold earlier; paid cash, $26 per share. The common shares were immediately canceled.

4. Sold 1,000 common shares. The sale price was $29 per share.

5. Purchased 200 shares of the company's own preferred shares at $24 cash each. These shares were immediately canceled.

6. At December 31, 19A, the Income Summary account reflected a credit balance of $21,200.

Required:

a. Give the journal entries indicated for each of the above transactions.

b. Prepare the shareholders' equity section of the balance sheet at December 31, 19A, end of the annual accounting period.

Part B: Problems 12–6 to 12–12

P12–6   **(Comparison of Stock and Cash Dividends)**
Annapolis Equipment Company had the following shares outstanding and retained earnings at December 31, 19E:

Common stock, $10 par, outstanding 20,000 shares $200,000
Preferred stock, 6%, $20 par, outstanding 5,000 shares . . .   100,000
Retained earnings   240,000

The board of directors is considering the distribution of a cash dividend to the two groups of shareholders. No dividends were declared during 19C or 19D. Three independent cases are assumed:

Case A—The preferred shares are noncumulative and nonparticipating; the total amount of dividends is $36,000.

Case B—The preferred shares are cumulative and nonparticipating; the total amount of dividends is $18,000.

Case C—Same as Case B, except the amount is $58,000.

Required:

a. Compute the amount of dividends, in total and per share, that would be payable to each class of shareholders for each case. Show computations.

b. Give the journal entry to record the cash dividends declared and paid in 19E for Case C only. Assume that the declaration and payment occurred simultaneously on December 31, 19E.

c. Give the required journal entry assuming, instead of a cash dividend, the declaration and issuance of a 10% common stock dividend on the outstanding common shares. Assume the market value per share of common shares was $20.

d. Complete the following comparative schedule including explanation of the comparative differences.

	Amount of Dollar Increase (Decrease)	
Item	Cash Dividend—Case C	Stock Dividend
Assets	$	$
Liabilities	$	$
Shareholders' equity	$	$

P12–7   **(Recording Dividends)**
Value Manufacturing Company has outstanding 50,000 shares of $5 par value common stock and 15,000 shares of $10 par value preferred stock (8%). On December 1, 19B, the board of directors voted an 8% cash dividend on the preferred shares and a 20% common stock dividend on the common shares (i.e., for each five shares of common stock held,

one additional share of common stock is to be issued as a stock dividend). At the date of declaration, the common stock was selling at $30 and the preferred at $25 per share. The dividends are to be paid, or issued, on February 15, 19C. The annual accounting period ends December 31.

Required:

a. Give any journal entry(s) required to record the declaration and payment of the cash dividend.

b. Give any journal entry(s) required to record the declaration and issuance of the stock dividend.

c. Explain the comparative effects of the two dividends on the assets, liabilities, and shareholders' equity (1) through December 31, 19B, (2) on February 15, 19C, and (3) the overall effects from December 1, 19B, through February 15, 19C. A schedule similar to the following might be helpful:

	Comparative Effects Explained	
Item	**Cash Dividend on Preferred**	**Stock Dividend on Common**
1. Through December 31, 19B: Assets		
Etc.		

P12-8   (Analysis of Shareholders' Equity Transactions Including Treasury Stock)

The accounts of Federated Corporation reflected the following balances on January 1, 19C:

Preferred stock, 5%, $50 par value, cumulative shares;	
issued and outstanding 2,000 shares	$100,000
Common stock, $10 par value; outstanding 20,000 shares	200,000
Contributed surplus, preferred	5,000
Contributed surplus, common	10,000
Retained earnings	200,000
Total shareholders' equity	$515,000

The transactions during 19C relating to the shareholders' equity are listed below in order:

1. Purchased 200 shares of preferred stock at $150 per share. These shares were immediately canceled.

2. The board of directors declared and paid a cash dividend to the preferred shareholders only. No dividends were declared during 19A or 19B. The dividend was sufficient to pay the arrears plus the dividend for the current year.

3. The board of directors declared a 1-for-10 (i.e., 10%) common stock dividend on the outstanding common shares. Market value of $20 per share is to be capitalized.

4. Net income for the year was $80,000.

Required:

a. Give the journal entry for each of the above transactions, including the closing entries. Show computations.

b. Prepare a statement of retained earnings for 19C and the shareholders' equity section of the balance sheet at December 31, 19C. (Hint: Total shareholders' equity is $551,500.)

c. Explain the comparative effects on assets and shareholders' equity of the (1) cash dividend and (2) the stock dividend.

P12-9   (Preparing the Shareholders' Equity Section of the Balance Sheet)

EMBA Company is completing its year-end accounting, including the preparation of the annual financial statements, at December 31, 19E. The shareholders' equity accounts reflected the following balances at the end of the year, 19E:

Common stock, par $10, shares outstanding 50,000	$500,000
Contributed surplus	50,000
Retained earnings, January 1, 19E (credit)	300,000
Cash dividends declared and paid during 19E (debit)	30,000
Income summary account for 19E (credit balance; after tax)	60,000

The following selected transactions occurred near the end of 19E; they are not included in the above amounts:

1. During 19D, EMBA Company was sued for $85,000, and it was clear that the suit would be lost. Therefore, in 19D, EMBA should have debited a loss and credited a liability for this amount. This journal entry was not made, and the accounting error was found in 19E. (Hint: Credit Liability for Damages.) Disregard any income tax effects.

2. The board of directors voted a voluntary restriction on retained earnings of $100,000. It is to be designated as "Earnings appropriated for plant expansion" effective for the 19E financial statements.

Required:

a. Give the appropriate journal entries for the events listed immediately above. If no entry is given, explain.

b. Prepare a statement of retained earnings for 19E and the shareholders' equity section of the balance sheet at December 31, 19E. (Hint: The ending balance of shareholders' equity is $795,000.)

P12–10   **(Preparation of the Statement of Retained Earnings)**
Fred Company has completed all of the annual information processing at December 31, 19D, except for preparation of the financial statements. The following account balances were reflected at that date:

FRED COMPANY
Adjusted Trial Balance
December 31, 19D

	Debit	Credit
Cash	$ 57,000	
Accounts receivable (net)	58,000	
Merchandise inventory, December 31, 19D	120,000	
Long-term investment in Company Y	20,000	
Bond sinking fund	40,000	
Land	20,000	
Buildings and equipment (net)	738,000	
Other assets	29,200	
Accounts payable		$ 86,000
Income tax payable		18,000
Bonds, payable, 7%, payable December 31		100,000
Preferred stock, par $10		99,900
Common stock, par $5		660,000
Contributed surplus, preferred		5,100
Contributed surplus, common		19,900
Retained earnings, January 1, 19D		163,300
19D net income		40,000
19D cash dividends on preferred	26,000	
19D common stock dividends distributed (10,000 shares) . . .	70,000	
19D, discovered an accounting error made in 19A in recording a purchase of land (the correction required a net credit to land of $14,000)	14,000	
	$1,192,200	$1,192,200

Note: Retained earnings is restricted in an amount equal to the bond sinking fund per the provisions of the bond indenture.

Required:
Prepare a statement of retained earnings for 19D and a classified balance sheet at December 31, 19D. (Hint: Total shareholders' equity is $878,200.)

P12-11 **(Evaluation of an Inaccurately Prepared Statement)**

The bookkeeper for Careless Company prepared the following balance sheet:

CARELESS COMPANY
Balance Sheet
For the Year 19W

Assets

Current assets	$ 45,000
Fixed assets (net of depreciation reserves, $70,000) . . .	125,000
Other assets	50,000
Total debits	$220,000

Liabilities

Current liabilities	$ 32,000
Other debts	25,000

Capital

Stock, par $10	60,000
Stock premium	30,000
Earned surplus	58,000
Treasury stock (500 shares)	(10,000)
Reserve for treasury stock	10,000
Correction of prior year error (a credit, net)	7,000
Cash dividends paid during 19W	(12,000)
Net profit for 19W	20,000
Total credits	$220,000

Required:

a. List all of the deficiencies you can identify in the above statement. Assume the amounts given are correct.

b. Prepare a statement of retained earnings for 19W.

c. Recast the above balance sheet in good form; focus especially on shareholders' equity.

P12-12 **(Based on Supplement 12B—Comparison of Shareholders' Equity Sections for Alternative Forms of Organization)**

Assume for each of the three independent cases below that the annual accounting period ends on December 31, 19W, and that the Income Summary account at that date reflected a debit balance of $30,000 (i.e., a loss).

Case A—Assume that the company is a **sole proprietorship** owned by Proprietor A. Prior to the closing entries, the capital account reflected a credit balance of $70,000 and the drawings account a balance of $6,000.

Case B—Assume that the company is a **partnership** owned by Partner A and Partner B. Prior to the closing entries, the owners' equity accounts reflected the following balances: A, Capital, $50,000; B, Capital, $45,000; A, Drawings, $7,000; and B, Drawings, $6,000. Profits and losses are divided equally.

Case C—Assume that the company is a **corporation**. Prior to the closing entries, the shareholders' equity accounts showed the following: Capital Stock, $20 par, outstanding 4,000 shares; Contributed Surplus, $2,000; and Retained Earnings, $40,000.

Required:

a. Give all of the closing entries indicated at December 31, 19W, for each of the separate cases.

b. Show how the owners' equity section of the balance sheet would appear at December 31, 19W, for each case.

CASES

C12-1   **(Finding Missing Amounts)**

At December 31, 19E, the records of Lone Star Corporation provided the following selected and incomplete data:

> Common stock, par $10 (no changes during 19E):
>   Shares issued __?__ issue price $12 per share; cash collected in full, $1,800,000.
>   Shares held as treasury stock, 2,000 shares—cost $15 per share.
> Net income for 19E, $176,000.
> Dividends declared and paid during 19E, $74,000.
> Bond sinking fund balance, $20,000.
> Prior period adjustment—correction of 19B accounting error, $18,000 (a credit, net of income tax).
> Retained earnings balance, January 1, 19E, $180,000.
> Extraordinary gain (net of income tax), $22,000.

Required:

a. Complete the following tabulation:
   Shares issued _____.
   Shares outstanding _____.

b. The balance in the Contributed Surplus account appears to be $_____.

c. EPS on net income is $_____.

d. Dividend paid per share of common stock is $_____.

e. The bond sinking fund should be reported on the balance sheet under the classification _____.

f. Net income before extraordinary items was $_____.

g. The prior period adjustment should be reported on the _____ as an addition _____ or a deduction _____.

h. Treasury stock should be reported on the balance sheet under the major caption _____ in the amount of $_____.

i. The amount of retained earnings available for dividends on January 1, 19E, was $_____.

j. Assume the board of directors voted a 100% stock split (the number of shares will double). After the stock split, the par value per share will be $_____ and the number of outstanding shares will be _____.

k. Assuming the stock split given in (j) above, give any journal entry that should be made. If none explain why.

l. Disregard the stock split (assumed in [j] and [k] above). Assume instead that a 5% stock dividend was declared and issued when the market price of the common stock was $15. Give any journal entry that should be made.

C12–2   (Comprehension Review of Variety of Accounting Issues)

Independent Grape Growers (IGG) is a partnership of grape growers in Canada. IGG is currently divided into 125 partnership units. The partnership was formed in January 1987, at which time units were allocated at a unit cost of $10,000 each to the various partners based on their projected grape harvest.

In February 1987, the partnership signed a 10-year building lease, bought equipment and supplies, and hired its first employees. Your employer, CA, was auditor for its first fiscal period ended June 30, 1987. There were no sales or sales-related expenses in this period. No depreciation was recorded because, according to management, the assets had not yet been used for productive purposes. No significant accounting policies had been adopted for the 1987 fiscal period.

Your employer, CA, has been reappointed auditor for the year ended June 30, 1988. He has also been engaged to develop an accounting system, to select suitable financial accounting policies, and to offer any other advice he feels would benefit IGG and its partners.

You have been asked to prepare a report for CA on the special engagement. Your report should identify and analyze the important issues and provide recommendations.

In August 1988, you visited IGG's offices and obtained the information in Exhibit 1.

Required:
Prepare the report requested by CA.

Exhibit 1   Information on IGG

---

1. The partners deliver their grapes to IGG where they are graded. Based on the grading, the decision is made as to which grapes will be sold fresh and which will be processed into grape juice, frozen concentrated juice, grape jelly, wine, or other products. IGG sells the fresh grapes to other wineries and to grocery chains. The harvest and fresh grape sales occur in late summer but IGG sells its processed items throughout the year.

2. Partners are credited with 80% of the market value of their harvest when they deliver it to IGG. Actual cash disbursement of this amount is to be made in installments of one third each on the following December 31, March 31, and June 30.

    The partners are to receive a cash payment on September 30 for their share of IGG's income for the previous fiscal year. For purposes of the computation of this payment, IGG's partners want to use the annual financial statement income figure. However, they would like accounting policies that give consideration to the cyclical nature of their activities and cash flows as well as those of IGG. They do not want to make any withdrawals that will reduce the capital that is needed to maintain the business.

3. Partnership units can be sold only with the approval of the other partners. The value of partnership units is determined based on the June 30 financial statement results. New partners are admitted on this date.

4. Seventy percent of the partners are privately owned limited companies. The remainder are individuals.

5. Managers are entitled to bonuses totaling 15 percent of the operating income of the partnership. Bonuses are allocated to individual managers through a point system based on their past experience and performance.

6. IGG borrows funds when inventories and receivables are high, during the autumn and winter periods. The bank requires unaudited quarterly financial statements and audited annual financial statements. IGG's loan was at its highest level of $12.5 million in early January 1988. The current interest rate is 13% per annum. The loan is secured by inventories, receivables, and the guarantees of the partners.

7. IGG operates from a building that houses the facilities for processing, warehousing, wine storage, and administration.

Exhibit 1 *(concluded)*

8. The employees are not unionized. Because of the seasonal nature of the processing activity, extensive use is made of temporary employees.

9. There are three physically separate departments: juice, jelly, and wine. Raisins, pie fillings, and other products are processed in the jelly department. Much of the processing is mechanized. Each department has separate storage facilities in the warehouse.

10. IGG's wines will be aged for no more than two years before sale to government liquor stores. Specialized processing equipment is used in winemaking.

11. A portion of sales of nonwine products is made on long-term contracts to grocery chains. For these contracts, cash is usually not received until 120 days after delivery. Other customers pay in cash or within 30 days. IGG's managers project a steady increase in the number of noncontract customers over the next five years.

12. The market for jams and jellies was weak at June 30, 1988. Customers were offering to buy at $4 per kilogram, but IGG would not sell below its estimated cost of $6 per kilogram. In August, 1988, the offering price had dropped to $3.50 per kilogram.

13. Extracts from the audited financial statements of IGG at June 30, 1988, are as follows:

    a. Packaging materials, jars, boxes and similar products on hand . . . . $ 186,230

    b. Inventories:

        Wine (1,500,000 bottle equivalent) $2,000,000

        Jams and jellies (100,000 kilograms) 600,000

        Raisins (800,000 kilograms) 1,120,000

        Pie fillings (200,000 kilograms) 410,000

        Juice (800,000 litres) 400,000

        Sugar (100,000 kilograms) 70,000

    c. Prepaid lease . . . . $ 10,000

    d. Unearned revenue. Deposit on sale of 150,000 kilograms of raisins at $1.00 per kilogram,

        to be delivered in November 1988 . . . . $ 25,000

    e. Bonus payable to managers . . . . $ 210,000

    f. Forgivable loan of $800,000 from the provincial government on September 1, 1987, for establishing IGG and creating 10 permanent jobs. Provided certain conditions are met, one fifth of the loan principal is forgiven on September 1 of each year from 1988 to 1992. Interest at 10 percent per annum is payable on September 1 each year . . . . $ 800,000

    g. Balance due to partners for grape harvest $7,462,000

    h. Interest and storage charges related to wine inventory currently on hand . . . . $ 317,600

    i. Cost of printing discount coupons for IGG brand juice (mailed to households in June and July 1988) . . . . $ 12,000

(CICA Adapted)

C12–3   **(Comprehensive Review; Disclosure Issues)**

Delta Ltd. (Delta) is incorporated under the Canada Business Corporations Act. In 1987 the board of directors decided to sell the Printing and Binding Division of the company and concentrate its efforts in its two other divisions: Book Publishing, and a new Educational Technology Division. An offer was received for the assets and liabilities of the Printing and Binding Division, and the sale became effective in late January 1988. Delta's financial year ends on December 31.

For the past 20 years Delta had been a public company, with preferred shares listed on a Canadian stock exchange. Its bonds were also publicly traded. On receipt of the offer in 1987 for the assets and liabilities of the Printing and Binding Division, the board began rethinking certain aspects of the status of the company. After several meetings the board decided that Delta would become a private company, and would therefore call in its bonds for redemption and its preferred shares for cancellation. The necessary legal negotiations were commenced with the provincial securities commissions, the Department of Consumer and Corporate Affairs, the stock exchange, and the holders of the bonds and preferred shares.

The board decided to change the company's status from public to private because the company would gain greater privacy and tax benefits, and it would be easier to reach agreement on the company's future direction. During their discussions on the change in status, some board members argued that the financial disclosure required of private companies is less extensive than that required of public companies. In their opinion, not only is the distribution of the financial statements of a private company such as Delta restricted to a relatively small group, but the financial information that must be disclosed is less extensive. While readily acknowledging that the change in status would restrict the distribution of Delta's financial statements, other directors maintained that disclosure requirements will not change significantly.

The bonds were redeemed in January 1988. The preferred shares were bought on the open market in several transactions during January and February and were canceled in February 1988. On March 7, 1988, Delta became a private company.

During January 1988, the majority shareholder, Mr. Richards, bought out all the majority holders of Delta's common shares.

It is now April 1988. Mr. Richards has engaged you, CA, to help Delta adjust efficiently and effectively to being a private company with two divisions. He wants you to prepare a report that includes your recommendations on financial accounting, management accounting and control, tax and other related matters. You have assembled the information shown in Exhibit 2.

Required:
Prepare the report requested by Mr. Richards.

Exhibit 2 Information Assembled by CA

---

1. Audited financial statements for the year ended December 31, 1987, were made available to interested parties in February 1988. An annual meeting has not yet been scheduled for the calendar year 1988; the previous meeting was held in May 1987.
2. The legal costs incurred in dealing with the various governmental and stock exchange officials amounted to $70,000.
3. The bonds had to be redeemed at a 2% premium that amounted to $80,000.
4. Some of the preferred shares were bought on the open market in early January 1988 at a price that was $60,000 less than their recorded book value. But, after discussions with the securities commissions, it is not clear that Delta is entitled to this sum of $60,000; they may have to pay it to sellers of the shares. The remaining preferred shares, also purchased on the open market, were bought at a price that was $75,000 above their book value.
5. The buyer of the Printing and Binding Division agreed to hire most of Delta's production employees, but not the office staff. Thus, Delta had to dismiss some employees and retire a few early. Severance pay amounted to $200,000.
6. The company's actuary checked into the funding needed for a work force of reduced size. The actuary has estimated that the pension plan is overfunded by about $350,000. This situation has arisen because it

Exhibit 2 *(concluded)*

had been assumed that 60% of all new employees would stay with the company the necessary six years to qualify for a pension. However, as a result of selling the division, Delta does not have to provide a pension for those who worked for the company for less than six years. Delta has decided to leave the $350,000 in the pension fund. Accordingly, it does not have to make payments to the fund over the next few years.

7. The sale of the Printing and Binding Division has reduced Delta's assets to about $3 million, and annual revenues from $15 million to $6 million.

8. In January 1987, prior to its sale, the Printing and Binding Division's revenue was $820,000, and cost of goods sold was $430,000. The Division incurred other expenses of $170,000.

9. The Educational Technology Division is relatively new to Delta. Its activities involve the coordination of franchise operations for a foreign manufacturer of computer and video equipment. Delta has been granted the entire Canadian territory. The company is required to develop software programs that meet the educational needs of Canadians.

Franchising is effective as it facilitates the development of specific market segments. Each franchisee is responsible for developing specialized software for its market segment. During 1987, six franchisees were signed up, but no cash was received, nor were services performed because the computer equipment from the foreign manufacturer was not scheduled to be delivered until April 1988. During 1987, $120,000 spent on software development was capitalized by Delta. Thus far in 1988, an additional $180,000 has been spent by Delta on software development; the sum is currently in a temporary ledger account awaiting distribution to appropriate accounts.

10. Delta sells franchises for a total price of $200,000 each, with payments due equally over five years. One half of the sum must be paid to the foreign manufacturer. To date in 1988, Delta has received $240,000, representing payments by the six franchisees at $40,000 each. It also operates four franchises itself.

11. The Educational Technology Division has no management reporting system at present. In addition to the activities described above, its operations consist of:
    a. Ordering equipment from the foreign manufacturer in sufficient quantity and at suitable times. Some equipment will be shipped directly to the franchisees by the manufacturer.
    b. Invoicing franchisees for equipment purchases, initial franchise fees ($40,000 per year), monthly franchise fees (to cover advertising, promotion, and other services) and loan guarantee fees. (Delta is willing to guarantee bank loans to a few franchisees in order to help develop software. Any loan losses are in turn "guaranteed" to be repaid to Delta by the foreign manufacturer.)
    c. Paying Delta sales staff for (i) signing up new franchisees; (ii) finding customers for the equipment and software sold where Delta is its own franchisee; and (iii) signing up organizations that will develop software.
    d. Developing software for the equipment. Where possible, Delta has been trying to sign contracts whereby a third party develops the software, and Delta markets it for a fee. At the present time five such contracts exist.

12. The Book Publishing Division has used the following accounting policies in the years to December 31, 1987:
    a. Revenue is recognized when books are shipped to book stores. Each store is allowed to return up to 20% of purchases made in the past 12 months.
    b. Inventory is valued at the lower of printing and binding cost or net realizable value.
    c. Depreciation is charged in the accounts on a straight-line basis.
    d. Bonuses to employees and royalties to authors are expensed in the year that they are paid, which is normally the year after the period to which they relate. Sales employees receive bonuses for the net sales in their territory. Editorial staff receives bonuses for successful publications.

13. The Book Publishing Division has signed eight new authors to produce manuscripts in 1988 and 1989.

14. The senior management of Delta was paid a salary plus a bonus of preferred shares in the period to December 31, 1987. The plan was canceled when the company became private. Senior management of Delta is now seeking a new remuneration and incentive program.

(CICA Adapted)

C12–4   **(Analysis of Shareholders' Equity Using an Actual Financial Statement)**
Refer to the financial statements of Consolidated-Bathurst Inc. given in Appendix B immediately preceding the Index.

Required:

a. How many shares of common stock were purchased during 1987? What was the average cost per stock of common stock purchased during 1987?

b. How many shares of common stock were issued at the end of 1987? How many shares were authorized?

c. Has the company issued any preferred shares? How many?

d. How many shareholders own stock in the company?

e. Prepare the journal entry to record the dividends for 1987.

THIRTEEN

MEASURING AND REPORTING LONG-TERM INVESTMENTS

PURPOSE

One corporation may invest in the capital stock of another for a variety of reasons. Often the investment is for a short term, designed to earn a return on idle funds (see Chapter 8). Some investments in other corporations are for the long term. These may be designed to provide the investing corporation with significant influence or control over the other corporation. Long-term investments that do not provide the investor with control are discussed in this chapter, as well as investments in the bonds of another corporation. These investments are always designed to provide a return on idle funds, because bond investments never provide the investor with the ability to influence the other corporation (i.e., bonds do not have voting rights).

   Accounting for long-term investments in securities is more complex than for short-term investments. The facing page shows how a note is often included in the financial statement to provide additional information about the investment.

LEARNING OBJECTIVES

1. Explain and use the cost and equity methods.

2. Account for bonds purchased at par; at a discount; at a premium.

3. Record bonds purchased between interest dates.

4. Use the straight-line and effective-interest amortization methods.

5. Expand your accounting vocabulary by learning about the "Important Terms Defined in This Chapter."

6. Apply the knowledge gained from this chapter.

ORGANIZATION

Part A—long-term investments in equity securities (shares)

1. Cost method—no significant influence.

2. Equity method—significant influence but no control.

Part B—long-term investments in debt securities (bonds)

1. Bonds purchased at par.

2. Bonds purchased at a discount.

3. Bonds purchased at a premium.

4. Bonds purchased between interest dates.

5. Effective-interest amortization on bonds.

Total Erickson Resources Ltd.

4. Long-Term Investments	1987	1986
(a) Ranchmen's Resources Ltd. (i)		
1,119,700 (1986-819,700) class A,		
common, non-voting shares	$ 13,516,785	$ 9,931,785
50,000 class D, common, voting shares	800,000	800,000
Share of income (losses)	(12,137,131)	(12,545,132)
Provision for permanent impairment	(3,563,700)	(3,563,700)
Dividends	(840,100)	(690.100)
Shares, on equity basis	(2,224,146)	(6,067,147)
Convertible Debentures		
1% convertible debenture, due July 16, 2001, convertible into class A, common, non-voting shares at $12.50 per share*	33,483,215	37,068,215
2% convertible debenture, due July 16, 2001, or on notice on March 31, 1993, 1996, or 1999, convertible into class A, common, non-voting shares at $9.25 per share*	2,200,000	2,200,000
	33,459,069	33,201,068
(b) Trans-Canada Resources Ltd. (note 2)	—	1,562,357
(c) Other	277,354	1
	277,354	1,562,358
	$ 33,736,423	$ 34,763,426

*Subject to adjustment made pursuant to anti-dilution provisions.

(i) The Company is obligated to convert the balance of the 1% and 2% convertible debenture into class A common shares of Ranchmen's by April 1988. Upon that conversion the Company will have a 53% equity interest and a 44.2% voting interest in Ranchmen's.

At December 31, 1987, the Company has a 44.2% (1986-44.2%) voting and 23.45% (1986-19.66%) equity interest in Ranchmen's before considering the effect of converting the debentures into shares and the proposed acquisition of the shares of Canadian Oil and Gas Fund Ltd. described below.

(ii) Kristian Ross, an officer and director of the Company, has entered into an agreement to acquire, subject to certain conditions, the controlling interest in Canadian Oil and Gas Funds Ltd., ("COGF"). COGF holds the controlling interest in Ranchmen's. Under the terms of the Agreement, this individual has agreed to cause Ranchmen's, following the acquisition of the interest in COGF, to hold certain shareholders' meetings to consider and vote on certain resolutions which, if passed, will convert the non-voting shares of Ranchmen's into voting shares. If these resolutions are passed, the Company will hold, on a fully diluted basis, the largest single equity interest in Ranchmen's. In connection with the Agreement, the Company has entered into a further agreement by which the Company has agreed to purchase, on demand, all of the shares of COGF acquired for approximately $4,700,000 cash, provided that at the date of demand COGF does not hold any voting shares in Ranchmen's.

PART A—LONG-TERM INVESTMENTS IN EQUITY SECURITIES (SHARES)

A company may invest in the equity securities (either common or preferred shares) of one or more other corporations for various reasons. Some of the reasons are to earn a return on excess cash; exercise influence or control over the other company; attain growth through sales of new products and new services; and gain access to new markets and new sources of supply. An entity may acquire capital stock of a corporation by purchasing outstanding shares from other shareholders for cash (or other assets); or if the investor is a corporation, by exchanging some of its own capital stock for outstanding capital stock of the other corporation.

When one company purchases **outstanding** shares of another company, the transaction is between the acquiring company and the **shareholders** of the other company (not the other company itself). The original investor and the purchaser record the effects of the transaction in their respective records. The accounting of the other company is not affected because the shares that were purchased were accounted for when they were issued.

The investor may acquire **some or all** of the outstanding shares of the other company (often called the **investee**). If the purpose of the investment is to gain influence or control, the investor will acquire **common** stock because it has voting rights. The number of outstanding shares of a corporation acquired by another entity usually depends upon the objectives of the investor. For measuring and reporting purposes, **three different levels of ownership** are recognized. The three levels are related to the percentage of the outstanding shares of **voting** capital stock owned by the investor.

Measuring Long-Term Investments in Voting Common Shares

Accounting for long-term investments in voting shares involves measuring the amount of the investment (reported on the balance sheet) and the periodic investment revenue (reported on the income statement). In conformity with the cost principle, at the dates of acquisition of the shares, long-term investments in the voting shares of another company are measured and recorded as the total consideration given to acquire them. This total includes the market price, plus all commissions and other purchasing costs. Subsequent to acquisition, accounting for long-term investments depends upon the relationship between the investor and the investee company. The relevant characteristic of the relationship is the extent to which the investing company can exercise **significant influence or control over the operating and financial policies** of the other company. Significant influence and control are related to the number of voting shares owned of the investee company in proportion to the total number of such shares outstanding.

For measuring and reporting long-term investments in the voting shares of another company, *CICA Handbook*, Section 3050, distinguishes between the two terms, **significant influence** and **control**, essentially as:

1. **Significant influence**—the ability of the investing company to have an important impact on the operating and financing policies of another company in which it owns voting shares. Significant influence may be indicated by (*a*) membership on the board of directors of the other company, (*b*) participation in the policy-making processes, (*c*) material transactions between the two companies, (*d*) interchange of management personnel, or (*e*) provision of technical information. In the absence of a clear-cut distinction based upon these factors, **significant influence is presumed** if the investing company owns at least 20% but not more than 50% of the outstanding voting shares of the other company.

2. **Control**—the ability of the investing company to determine the operating and financing policies of another company in which it owns voting shares. For all practical purposes, **control is assumed** when the investing company owns more than 50% of the outstanding voting shares of the other company.

The three levels of ownership that relate to the measuring and reporting of long-term investments in voting capital stock are as follows:

Level of ownership	Measuring and reporting approach
1. Neither significant influence nor control	Cost method
2. Significant influence but not control	Equity method
3. Control	Consolidated statement method

Each of these approaches is outlined in Exhibit 13–1. The first two are discussed in this chapter, and the third is discussed in Chapter 14.

Cost Method

The **cost method** of accounting must be used when the number of shares of **voting** capital stock of a corporation does not give the investing corporation the ability to exercise significant influence or control. Under the cost method, the investment is recorded at the acquisition date in conformity with the cost principle, as shown in Exhibit 13–2. Subsequent to acquisition, the investment amount is reported at the **lower of cost or market** (LCM). Cash dividends declared by the investee corporation are reported by the investor as "Revenue from investments" in the period declared.

CICA Handbook, Section 3050, requires that long-term investments accounted for under the cost method be valued at LCM after acquisition. Thus, at the end of each accounting period, the long-term investments, accounted for under the cost method, must be reviewed as to whether or not a permanent impairment of value has occurred. If so, then a write-down in the carrying value of the investment is required. Obvious indicators of a permanent decline in value would be the bankruptcy of the investee, an agreement by the investor to sell at a loss, a prolonged period where the market value of the security is less than the

Exhibit 13–1 Measuring and reporting long-term investments in voting shares of another company

Status of ownership	Method	Measurement at date of acquisition	Measurement after date of acquisition	
			Investment	Revenue
1. **Investor can exercise no significant influence or control.** Presumed if investor owns less than 20% of the outstanding voting shares of the investee company.	Cost method	Investor records the investment at cost. Cost is the total outlay made to acquire the shares.	Investor reports the investment on the balance sheet at LCM.	Investor recognizes revenue each period when dividends are declared by the investee company. A realized gain or loss is recognized when the investment is sold.
2. **Investor can exercise significant influence, but not control,** over the operating and financing policies of the investee company. Presumed if the investor owns at least 20%, but not more than 50%, of the outstanding voting shares of the investee company.	Equity method	Same as above.	Investor measures and reports the investment at cost **plus** the investor's share of the earnings (or less the losses) and **minus** the dividends received from (i.e., declared by) the other company. (Dividends received are not considered revenue. To recognize dividends as revenue, rather than as a reduction in the investment, would involve double counting.)	Investor recognizes as revenue each period the investor's proportionate share of the earnings (or losses) reported each period by the investee company.
3. **Investor can exercise control** over the operating and financing policies of the investee company. Control is presumed if the investor owns more than 50% of the outstanding voting shares of the investee company.	Consolidated financial statement method	Same as above.	Consolidated financial statements required each period (discussed in Chapter 14).	

Exhibit 13–2 Cost method of measuring and reporting long-term investments in equity securities

Situation:

Able Corporation purchased the following long-term investments on February 1, 19A:

Baker Corporation common stock (no par), 1,000 shares at $12 per share (represents 10% of the outstanding shares).

Cox Corporation, 5% preferred stock (par $20), nonvoting, 500 shares at $40 per share (represents 10% of the outstanding shares).

February 1, 19A, to record the acquisition:

Long-term investment	32,000	
Cash		32,000

Computations:
Baker common stock, 1,000 shares × $12 = $12,000
Cox preferred stock 500 shares × $40 = 20,000
    Total acquisition cost $32,000

November 30, 19A, cash dividends declared (payable in January 19B) as follows: Baker common stock, $1 per share; Cox preferred, 5% of par.

Dividends receivable	1,500	
Revenue from investments		1,500

Computations:
Baker common stock (1,000 shares × $1)   = $1,000
Cox preferred stock (500 shares × $20 × 5%) =   500
    Total dividends $1,500

December 31, 19A, end of the accounting period, quoted market prices: Baker common shares, $13, Cox preferred shares, $36.

Loss on long-term investments	2,000	
Long-term investments—Cox		2,000

	Shares	Market Dec. 31, 19A	Acquisition cost	Market Dec. 31, 19A
Baker common stock	1,000	$13	$12,000	$13,000
Cox preferred stock	500	36	20,000	18,000
			$32,000	$31,000

LCM: $20,000 − $18,000 = $2,000 (on Cox assuming loss is permanent).

January 15, 19B, received cash for the dividends of Baker and Cox Corporations (declared on November 30, 19A).

Cash	1,500	
Dividends receivable		1,500

June 15, 19B, sold 300 shares of the Cox preferred at $41.

Cash (300 shares × $41)	12,300	
Long-term investments (300 × $36)		10,800
Gain on sale of investment		1,500

Exhibit 13–2 *(concluded)*

November 30, 19B, cash dividends declared (payable December 30, 19B) as follows:
Baker common stock, $0.90 per share; Cox preferred stock, 5% of par.

Dividends receivable 1,100
   Revenue from investments   1,100

Computations:
Baker common stock, 1,000 shares × $0.90 = $ 900
Cox preferred stock, 200 shares × $20 × 5% =   200

Total dividends $1,100

December 30, 19B, received cash for the dividends of Baker and Cox Corporations (declared on November 30, 19B).

Cash 1,100
   Dividends receivable   1,100

December 31, 19B, end of the accounting period, quoted market prices: Baker common share, $11, Cox preferred share, $43.

Loss on long-term investment 1,000
   Long-term investment—Baker   1,000

Computations:

	Shares	Market Dec. 31, 19B	Carrying	Market Dec. 31, 19B
Baker common shares	1,000	$11	$12,000	$11,000
Cox preferred shares	200	43	7,200	8,600
			$19,200	$19,600

LCM: $12,000 − $11,000 = $1,000. Reduction in Baker assuming the decline is permanent.

December 31, 19A, and 19B, reporting on the **income statement** and **balance sheet** (partial):

	19A	19B
Income statement:		
Revenue from investments	$ 1,500	$ 1,100
Loss from long-term investments	(2,000)	(1,000)
Gain on sale of investment		1,500
Balance sheet:		
Current assets:		
Dividends receivable	1,500	
Investments and funds:		
Investments in equity securities*	$30,000	$18,200

*Include a note to disclose breakdown.

carrying value, and severe or continued losses. The question of whether or not the market is compared to the carrying value security by security or by portfolio is not explicitly dealt with in the Canadian pronouncement. Implicitly, however, the pronouncement discusses specific investments so a security by security comparison would be warranted. If a company had a long-term portfolio of securities, professional judgment could suggest the use of the portfolio approach. Comparison of the market value for the portfolio to the cost of the portfolio would permit the offsetting of a decline in the value of one security against the rise in another. Care is necessary here because a nontemporary decline in the value of a single security in a portfolio is a permanent event that may represent a permanent loss in the value of the portfolio. For illustrations and problems, the individual security approach will be used.

When long-term securities are sold, the difference between the sale price and carrying value is recorded and reported as a **realized** gain or loss. It should be noted that if the investment had been written down to market because of a permanent decline in value, it should not be increased if for some reason the market later increased. Any gain subsequently realized is recognized only when the investment is sold.

Application of the cost method is illustrated in Exhibit 13–2. The journal entry to record the acquisition of a long-term investment is in accordance with the **cost principle.** Observe that on November 30, 19A, dividend revenue was recorded on the date that cash dividends were **declared.**

In Exhibit 13–2, the investments are valued at LCM on December 31, 19A, the end of the accounting period. Observe that LCM is applied individually to each investment. For illustration purposes the decline is assumed to be permanent for the Cox preferred shares. The investment was written down to LCM, from cost ($20,000) to market ($18,000), and a loss of $2,000 was recorded.

On June 15, 19B, 300 Cox shares were sold. The journal entry to record the sale removes the shares sold from the investment account at the carrying value. The difference between the original carrying value of shares ($10,800) and the sale price ($12,300) is recorded as a **realized** gain of $1,500.

Exhibit 13–2 presents the reporting effects of the cost method on the income statement and the balance sheet. The income statement is affected by dividend revenue and gains or losses on the investments.

The journal entries given in Exhibit 13–2 reflect application of the cost principle at the date of acquisition and application of LCM subsequent to that time. The investment is carried continuously at LCM, and dividend revenue is recognized from the investment **only** in periods in which dividends are declared.

The fact that Able Corporation purchased 10% of the outstanding voting common shares of Baker Corporation and 10% of the outstanding preferred shares of Cox Corporation had absolutely no effect on the accounting and reporting by either Baker or Cox Corporations.

Equity Method

The equity method must be used when significant influence (but no control) exists. This influence is presumed to be sufficient to permit the transfer of dividends when the investor decides but it is insufficient to justify the purchase of the investee, a necessity for consolidation. Thus, the equity method recognizes a proportionate share of the reported income of the investee company as revenue for the investor. Dividends from the investee company are not recognized as income for the investor.

The concept underlying the equity method is that the investor has earned income from the investment equivalent to its ownership share. This income is recorded as a debit to the investment account and a credit to investment revenue. Dividends from the investee company are treated as a return of a part of the investment. Under the equity method, dividends are recorded as a debit to cash and a credit to the investment account.[1] If dividends were recorded as revenue, there would be a double counting of the proportionate share of income and the distribution of that income.

Application of the equity method is shown in Exhibit 13–3.[2] The illustration is based on the assumption that Crown Corporation (the investor company) purchased 3,000 shares (or 30%) of the outstanding common stock of Davis Corporation (the investee company) at a cash price of $120 per share. The equity method must be used because Crown Corporation purchased 30% of the outstanding voting shares of Davis Corporation. The first journal entry in Exhibit 13–3 shows how the investment would be recorded by Crown Corporation.

When the investee corporation reports income (or loss), the investor company records its percentage share (i.e., equity) of the investment revenue. The second entry by Crown Corporation (the investor company) given in Exhibit 13–3 recognizes its proportionate share of the net income of Davis Corporation.

In Exhibit 13–3, the proportionate share of the net income of Davis Corporation was recorded by Crown Corporation as revenue and as an **increase** in the investment account. When a dividend is received, it is necessary to avoid double-counting the income from the investee company; therefore, the dividend from the investee company is recorded as a debit to Cash and as a **credit to the investment account.** This entry reflects the fact that a dividend represents the conversion of a part of the investment account balance to cash.

The investment and revenue accounts of the investor company, Crown Corporation, are shown in Exhibit 13–3. The financial statements for Crown also are shown in Exhibit 13–3.

The term LCM is not technically appropriate for equity investments. If,

---

[1] When a cash dividend is declared in one year and paid in the following year, the dividend is recognized by the investor when declared by debiting Dividends Receivable (a current asset) instead of Cash. Subsequently, when the cash is received, the Cash account is debited and Dividends Receivable is credited. In contrast, dividends declared and paid in the same year may be recorded by the investor on the payment date as a debit to Cash and credit to the investment account. This procedure is true for both the cost method and the equity method.

Because the revenue from such investments is the net of revenue and expenses of the investee and net of certain expenses of the investor, the term investment income rather than the investment revenue might be more descriptive.

[2] This example assumes that the investment was purchased at "book value." The accounting procedures for other situations are more complex. They involve asset write-ups and write-downs and, perhaps, the recognition of "goodwill." This chapter presents the fundamentals without unnecessary complexity. More advanced accounting courses devote considerable attention to these complexities.

Exhibit 13–3 Equity method of measuring and reporting long-term investments in equity securities

---

Situation:

  Crown Corporation (the investor company) purchased 3,000 shares of the outstanding common stock of Davis Corporation (the investee company) on January 15, 19E, at a cash cost of $120 per share. At date of purchase, Davis Corporation had outstanding 10,000 shares of common stock (par $100 per share).

Analysis:

  The equity method must be used by Crown Corporation because it now owns between 20% and 50% of the outstanding voting shares of the investee company.

January 15, 19E, to record the acquisition:

  Investment in common shares, Davis Corporation (3,000 shares) . 360,000
    Cash   360,000
    Purchased 3,000 shares (30%) of the common stock of Davis
    Corporation at $120 per share.

December 31, 19E, end of the accounting period, Davis Corporation reported net income of $50,000. On this date, Crown Corporation recognized its proportionate share as follows:

  Investment in common shares, Davis Corporation 15,000
    Revenue from investments   15,000
    To record the proportionate share of 19E income reported by
    Davis Corporation ($50,000 × 30% = $15,000). The credit often
    is called Equity in Earnings of Partially Owned Company.

December 31, 19E, Davis Corporation declared and paid immediately a $10,000 cash dividend, of which 30% (i.e., $3,000) was received by the investor, Crown Corporation. Crown Corporation recorded its share of the dividend as follows:

  Cash   3,000
    Investment in common shares, Davis Corporation   3,000
    To record the receipt of a cash dividend from Davis Corporation ($10,000 × 30% = $3,000).

---

however, a substantial and permanent decline in the market price of the investment occurred, a write-down from equity value to market would appear appropriate. However, this write-down cannot be termed the use of lower of "cost" or market because the investment is recorded at equity, not cost. Thus the LCM term should be lower of equity or market although the LCM term is often used because of its popularity.

Financial statements must disclose the method used to account for long-term investments. Also, regardless of whether the cost or the equity method is used, the original cost, current market value, and carrying value of the investment should be disclosed.

The cost and equity methods represent a compromise on the part of the accounting profession. Many accountants believe that all marketable securities

Exhibit 13–3 *(concluded)*

December 31, 19E, the investment and revenue accounts of Crown Corporation for the year 19E would be as follows (based upon the above entries):

Investment in Common Shares, Davis Corporation

1/15/E	Purchased 3,000 shares	360,000	12/31/E	Proportionate share of dividends of Davis Corporation	3,000
12/31/E	Proportionate share of 19E income of Davis Corporation	15,000			

(debit balance, $372,000)

Revenue from Investments

		12/31/E	Revenue from Davis Corporation 15,000

December 31, 19E, reporting by Crown Corporation (investor) on the **income statement** and **balance sheet** (partial):

Income Statement
For the Year Ended December 31, 19E

Revenue from investments . . . . $ 15,000

Balance Sheet
At December 31, 19E

Investments and funds:
  Investment in common shares, Davis Corporation, equity basis
  (cost, $360,000; market, $369,000)* $372,000

* Market is measured as the number of shares owned multiplied by the actual market price per share on the balance sheet date. Decline in market is assumed not to be permanent.

should be reported at their **current market values** at each balance sheet date. Under this approach, which is not currently acceptable, both dividends received and changes in the market value of the shares since the last period would be reported as revenue (or loss) on the income statement. Accountants who support this approach believe that it meets most closely the objective of reporting the **economic consequences** of holding an investment in marketable securities. The **cost method** measures only the dividends received by the investor as revenue, but dividends may have no relationship to the earnings of the investee company for the period. The cost method does not reflect the earnings pattern of the investee company. The **equity method** overcomes this deficiency; however, it does not reflect the economic impact of market changes in the investment shares held. The effect of such market changes is significant to the investor. At present, all three approaches listed in Exhibit 13–1 are acceptable to the accounting profession.

PART B—LONG-TERM INVESTMENTS IN DEBT SECURITIES (BONDS)

In Chapter 11 we discussed bonds as long-term liabilities of the issuing corporation. This part of the chapter discusses bonds of another company held as a **long-term investment.** Bonds offer significantly different investment risks and returns than capital stock. Bonds have a stated rate of interest (which determines the amount of cash that will be received on each interest date) and a specified maturity value (which will be received in cash at maturity date). Shareholders receive cash dividends only when they are declared by the board of directors. Dividends tend to vary with the profitability of the corporation. Bondholders, in general, have no voting rights.

Similar to capital stock, bonds are bought and sold in the regular security markets. The market price of bonds fluctuates **inversely** with changes in the **market rate** of interest because the **stated rate** of interest remains constant over the life of the bonds (see Chapter 11). If the market rate of interest increases, bond prices fall.

Measuring and Reporting Bond Investments

Investors may buy bonds at their date of issuance or at subsequent dates during the life of the bonds. Regardless of the timing of the bonds' acquisition, at the end of each accounting period the investor must measure the (1) cost, adjusted for the cumulative amount of discount or premium that has been amortized; and (2) interest revenue earned.

At the date of acquisition, a bond investment is recorded in conformity with the **cost principle.** The purchase cost, including all incidental acquisition costs (such as transfer fees and broker commissions), is debited to an investment account such as "Long-Term Investment, Bonds of Beta Corporation." The amount recorded is the **current cash equivalent amount.** This amount may be the same as the maturity amount (if acquired at par), less than the maturity amount (if acquired at a discount), or more than the maturity amount (if acquired at a premium).[3] Usually the premium or discount on a bond investment is not recorded in a separate account as is done for bonds payable (Chapter 11). The investment account shows the current book or carrying amount. However, the bond investment account can be debited at par, and a separate discount or premium account can be used with the same results.

If a bond investment was acquired at par, the book value remains constant over the life of the investment because there is no premium or discount to be amortized. In this situation, revenue earned from the investment each period is measured as the amount of cash interest collected (or accrued).

---

[3] Fees, commissions, and other incidental costs decrease the discount, or increase the premium; therefore, they are amortized over the remaining period to maturity. Alternatively, such costs sometimes are recorded separately and amortized on the same basis as the discount or premium.

When a bond investment is purchased at a discount or premium, measurement of the book value of the investment after date of acquisition necessitates adjustment of the investment account balance from acquisition cost to maturity amount each period over the life of the investment. This adjustment is the periodic amortization of the discount or premium. The periodic amortization is made as a debit to the investment account if there is a discount, or as a credit if there is a premium.

When a bond investment is acquired at a discount or premium, the revenue from interest each period is measured as the cash interest collected (or accrued) plus or minus the periodic amortization of discount or premium. As was illustrated in Chapter 11 for bonds payable, bond discount or premium may be amortized by using either the straight-line or effective-interest method. The former is simpler, whereas the latter is conceptually preferable. In the following paragraphs, we will assume straight-line amortization; effective-interest amortization is explaineed at the end of this part.

In contrast to long-term investments, discount or premium is not amortized on bonds held as a **short-term** investment because the bonds will not be held to maturity.

After the date of acquisition, interest revenue must be accrued (by means of an adjusting entry) for periods between the last date on which interest revenue was collected and the end of the accounting period. The procedure for accruing interest expense and interest revenue was discussed in several prior chapters.

One of the complications created by bond premiums and discounts on long-term investments in bonds comes about because of the treatment of these differences for income tax purposes. Ordinary minor discounts and premiums would be treated as capital gains and losses for income tax purposes in the period when the bonds mature or are sold. Thus the amortization of premiums or discounts for accounting purposes would not be included in computing taxable income. To account for this difference in timing two income tax allocation adjustments (Chapter 10) are necessary: (1) one quarter of the amortization in each period is treated as a permanent difference in the future (deferred) tax calculation and (2) three quarters are treated as a timing difference. The permanent difference represents the quarter of the capital gain or loss that is not taxed. Treatment of substantial discounts and various accounting options for recording interest revenue for taxation purposes are left to advanced courses. (See Exhibit 13–5 for an illustration of the journal entries for future taxes on the bond discount amortization.)

Accounting for Bonds Illustrated

On July 1, 19E, Roth Company purchased $10,000, 8%, 10-year bonds in the open market. The bonds were issued originally on July 1, 19A, and mature on June 30, 19J. The 8% interest is paid each June 30.[4] Roth Company's annual

---

[4] Bonds usually pay interest semiannually. Annual interest is used in this illustration to reduce the number of repetitive entries. The concepts are applied the same way in either case.

accounting period ends December 31. The sequence of journal entries made by Roth Company during 19E are illustrated under three different purchase cost assumptions as follows:

Assumption	Exhibit
1. Bond investment purchased at par (100)	13–4
2. Bond investment purchased at a discount (98)	13–5
3. Bond investment purchased at a premium (102)	13–6

Bonds Purchased at Par

When bond investors accept a rate of interest on a bond investment that is the **same** as the stated rate of interest on the bonds, the bonds will sell at par (i.e., at 100). Bonds that sell at par will not cause a premium or discount. Exhibit 13–4 illustrates the recording and reporting of an **investment** in bonds purchased at par.

Bonds Purchased at a Discount

When bond investors demand a rate of interest that is higher than the **stated rate,** bonds will sell at a **discount.** When a bond is purchased at a discount, the investor receives the periodic interest payments stated in the bond contract plus the maturity value, which is a greater amount than the initial cash invested. A discount increases the interest revenue earned on a bond investment. Assume that on July 1, 19E, Roth Company purchased a $10,000, 8% bond issued by Baker Company for $9,800 cash. The bond will mature in five years (in 19J). Interest of $10,000 × 8% = $800 will be collected annually.

Although $800 cash is collected each year, the annual revenue **earned** from the investment is $840. The additional $40 is due to amortization of the discount. Analysis of the interest revenue, using straight-line amortization, is as follows:

```
Cash inflows from the investment:
  Annual interest collected, July 1, 19E through June 30, 19J
    ($10,000 × 8% × 5 years) . . . . . . . . . . . . . . . . . . . . . . $ 4,000
  Collection of bond at maturity date, June 30, 19J . . . . . . . . . .   10,000    $14,000

Cash outflow for the investment:
  July 1, 19E—purchase of bond  . . . . . . . . . . . . . . . . . . . .              9,800
    Difference—net increase in cash (the total interest revenue
      earned)  . . . . . . . . . . . . . . . . . . . . . . . . . . . . .            $ 4,200

Revenue from investment per year: $4,200 ÷ 5 years = $840
(assuming straight-line amortization).
```

Exhibit 13–5 illustrates the recording and reporting of a bond investment purchased at a discount.

When a bond is purchased, it is recorded at cost. Therefore, when a bond is purchased at a discount, the investment account balance at the purchase date will be less than the maturity value. Through **amortization** of the discount, the balance of the investment account is **increased** each period so that the book value will be the same as the par amount on the maturity date. Amortization of

Exhibit 13–4 Bonds purchased at par

Situation:

   On July 1, 19E, Roth Company purchased $10,000, 8%, 10-year bonds of Ellsworth Company for cash, $10,000 (i.e., at par). The bonds were issued originally on July 1, 19A, and mature June 30, 19J. Interest is paid each June 30. Roth's accounting period ends December 31.

July 1, 19E, to record purchase of bond investment at par (100):

   Long-term investment, bonds of Ellsworth Company 10,000
      Cash   10,000
      Purchased at par, $10,000 maturity value, 8% bonds of Ellsworth
      Company. (Note: Because the bonds were purchased on an in-
      terest date, there was no accrued interest.)

December 31, 19E, adjusting entry at end of the accounting period (and each year
   through maturity date):

   Bond interest receivable   400
      Revenue from investments*   400
      Adjusting entry to accrue six months' interest revenue on
      Ellsworth Company bonds ($10,000 × 8% × 6/12 = $400).

   * Alternate titles are Interest Revenue and, sometimes, Interest Income.

June 30, 19F, to record annual interest (and each year until maturity):[a]

   Cash ($10,000 × 8%)   800
      Bond interest receivable (from December 31 entry)   400
      Revenue from investments   400
      Receipt of annual interest payment on the Ellsworth
      Company bonds.

June 30, 19J, maturity date of the bonds; to record cash received for face (maturity)
   amount of the bond investment:[b]

   Cash 10,000
      Long-term investment, bonds of Ellsworth Company   10,000
      Retirement of bonds at maturity date (assumes last interest
      receipt already recorded).

December 31, 19E, Roth Company's **income statement** and **balance sheet** (partial):

Income statement for the year ended December 31, 19E:
   Revenue from investments . . . . $ 400

Balance sheet at December 31, 19E:
   Current assets:
      Bond interest receivable . . . . $ 400
   Investments and funds:
      Investment in bonds, at cost (market, $10,125)   10,000

Notes: *a.* This entry presumes that there was no reversal on January 1, 19F, of the prior adjusting
          entry. A reversing entry is optional because it serves only to facilitate the subsequent entry
          (see Chapter 5).
       b. Because the bond investment was purchased at par, there was no premium or discount to
          be amortized.

Exhibit 13–5 Bonds purchased at a discount

Situation:

Exactly the situation given in Exhibit 13–4, except that on July 1, 19E, Roth Company purchased $10,000 of bonds of Baker Company for $9,800 (i.e., at 98), rather than at par.

July 1, 19E, to record purchase of bond investment at a discount rate (98):

Long-term investment, bonds of Baker Company (at cost)	9,800	
Cash		9,800

Purchased $10,000 maturity value, 8% bonds of the Baker Company at 98.

Note: This entry records the investment at its cost; that is, net of any discount or premium. Some accountants prefer to record it at gross as follows with the same end result:

Long-term investment	10,000	
Discount on long-term investment		200
Cash		9,800

December 31, 19E, end of accounting year; to record adjusting entry for interest revenue and amortization of discount on bond investment (and each year until maturity):

Bond interest receivable ($10,000 × .08 × 6/12)	400	
Long-term investment, bonds of Baker Company (amortization: $40 × 6/12)	20	
Revenue from investments		420

Adjusting entry to (1) accrue interest revenue for six months and (2) amortize discount on the bond investment for six months (July 1 to December 31); $200 ÷ 5 years = $40 amortization per year.*

* Income tax expense	6	
Future income taxes		6

(3/4 × 20 × .40) Adjustment to record the future income taxes on the bond discount amortization assuming a 40% tax rate.

This entry could be made each time the interest is accrued or in practice when the future income taxes are calculated.

June 30, 19F, to record cash interest received and to amortize discount on bond investment (and each year until maturity):

Cash ($10,000 × .08)	800	
Long-term investment, bonds of Baker Company (amortization: $40 × 6/12)	20	
Bond interest receivable (from December 31 entry)		400
Revenue from investments		420

Receipt of annual interest on Baker Company bonds and amortization of discount for six months (January 1 to June 30).

June 30, 19J, maturity date; to record cash maturity amount received:

Cash	10,000	
Long-term investment, bonds of Baker Company		10,000

Retirement of bonds at maturity (assumes last interest-receipt already recorded).†

† Future income taxes	60	
Income taxes payable		60

(3/4 × 200 × .40 = $60) Adjustment to record the liability for the income tax on the capital gain when the bond matures assuming an income tax rate of 40 percent.

In practice this entry would be included with the remainder of the future income tax items.

Exhibit 13–5 *(concluded)*

December 31, 19E, long-term investment account for 19E–19J:

Long-Term Investment, Bonds of Baker Company

July 1, 19E At acquisition	9,800	June 30, 19J Retirement	10,000
Yearly amortizations by:			
Dec. 31, 19E	20		
31, 19F	40		
31, 19G	40		
31, 19H	40		
31, 19I	40		
June 30, 19J	20		
	10,000		10,000

December 31, 19E, **income statement** and **balance sheet** for year 19E (partial)

Income statement for the year ended December 31, 19E:
Revenue from investments . . . . $ 420

Balance Sheet at December 31, 19E:
Current assets:
  Bond interest receivable . . . . $ 400

Investments and funds:
  Investment in bonds, at amortized cost (market, $10,125) 9,820
Long-term liabilities:
  Future income taxes (see * footnote) . . . . $ 6

the discount each period increases the amount of interest revenue earned. The amount of discount amortized each period is debited to the investment account and credited to Interest Revenue.

In Exhibit 13–5, each year Roth Company must amortize a part of the discount ($10,000 − $9,800 = $200), so that the total discount is amortized over the remaining life of the bond investment. Using straight-line amortization, the amount of discount amortized each full year will be $200 ÷ 5 years = $40 per year.

The balance of the long-term investment account will increase from cost at date of purchase to par value at maturity date because of the amortization of the bond discount. This effect is recorded in Roth's investment ledger account shown in Exhibit 13–5.[5] Also shown in Exhibit 13–5 is 19E financial statement information for Roth Company.

---

[5] Observe that the amortization of discount or premium on bond investments conceptually is the same as the amortization discussed and illustrated in Chapter 11 in the issuer's accounts. Here, we are looking at the other side of the transaction. A minor procedural difference may be noted. In Chapter 11, premium or discount was recorded in a separate account; in this chapter, the **net amount** (i.e., the cost) was recorded in the investment account. Either procedure can be

Bonds Purchased at a Premium

When bond investors are willing to invest at a rate of interest that is **less** than the **stated rate** of interest on bonds, the bonds will sell at a **premium.** When bonds are purchased at a premium, the investment account is debited for an amount greater than the par or maturity value of the bonds. Therefore, the premium must be **amortized** over the **remaining life** of the bonds as a **decrease** in the balance of the investment account so that the investment account balance will be the par value on maturity date. The amortization is similar to the procedure illustrated for a discount, except that each period the investment account is credited and the premium amortization **decreases** interest revenue.

Assume Roth Company purchased Garden Company bonds on July 1, 19E, for $10,200 cash. The bonds have an 8% interest rate and mature in five years from that date, on June 30, 19J. Using straight-line amortization, the cash outflow and inflows for this investment may be analyzed to illustrate the effect of the premium on interest revenue as follows:

Cash inflows from the investment:
Annual interest collected, July 1, 19E, through June 30, 19J
  ($10,000 × 8% × 5 years) . . . . $ 4,000
June 30, 19E, collection of bond at maturity 10,000 $14,000

Cash outflow for the investment:
July 1, 19J—purchase of bond   10,200

Difference—net increase in cash (the total interest
  revenue earned) . . . . $ 3,800

Revenue from investment, per year: $3,800 ÷ 5 years = $760.

Exhibit 13–6 presents the journal entries and financial statements for the investor, Roth Company.

Bonds Purchased between Interest Dates

Investors usually purchase bonds between the interest dates specified on the bonds. In these situations, the investor must pay the amount of **interest accrued** since the last interest date in addition to the purchase price of the bond. The bond market operates in this manner because the seller of the bond is entitled to interest from the last interest date to the date of the sale transaction; but on the next interest payment date, the new owner will receive interest for the full period between interest dates, regardless of the purchase date. Assume Hayes Company purchased a $1,000 bond, 12% interest, payable 6% each March 31 and September 30. The bond was purchased on June 1, 19F, at 100 plus any accrued interest. The purchase of this bond investment is recorded by Hayes Company as follows:

---

used in either situation with the same results. Common practice follows the procedures illustrated in the respective chapters. Tax allocations entries are, however, different because of the various income tax rules associated with the premium and discount of the issuer.

Exhibit 13–6   Bonds purchased at a premium

Situation:

   Exactly the same situation given in Exhibit 13–4, except that on July 1, 19E, Roth Company purchased $10,000 of bonds of Garden Company for $10,200 (i.e., at 102), rather than at par.

July 1, 19E, to record purchase of bond investment at a premium (102):

   Long-term investment, bonds of Garden Company (at cost) 10,200
      Cash   10,200
      Purchased $10,000 maturity value, 8% bonds of Garden
      Company at 102.

December 31, 19E, end of accounting year; to record adjusting entry for interest revenue and amortization of premium on bond investment (and each year until maturity):

   Bond interest receivable ($10,000 × 8% × 6/12)   400
      Long-term investment, bonds of Garden Company
         (amortization: $40 × 6/12)   20
      Revenue from investments   380
      Adjusting entry to (1) accrue interest revenue for six months
      and (2) amortize premium on the investment for six months
      (July 1 to December 31); $200 ÷ 5 years = $40 amortization
      per year.

June 30, 19F, to record cash interest received and to amortize premium on bond investment (and each year until maturity):

   Cash ($10,000 × 8%)   800
      Bond interest receivable (per December 31 entry)   400
      Long-term investment, bonds of Garden Company
         (amortization: $40 × 6/12)   20
      Revenue from investments   380
      Receipt of annual interest revenue on Garden Company bonds
      and amortization of premium for six months (January 1 to June
      30).

June 30, 19J, maturity date; to record cash maturity amount received:

   Cash 10,000
      Long-term investment, bonds of Garden Company   10,000
      Retirement of bonds at maturity (assuming the last interest
      receipt has been recorded).

December 31, 19E, **income statement** and **balance sheet** for year 19E (partial):

Income statement for year ended December 31, 19E:
   Revenue from investments . . . . $ 380

Balance sheet at December 31, 19E:
   Current assets:
      Bond interest receivable . . . . $ 400
   Investments and funds:
      Investment in bonds, at amortized cost (market, $10,225)   10,180

June 1, 19F:

Long-term investment, 12% bond 1,000
Revenue from investments ($1,000 × 12% × 2/12)*   20
   Cash [$1,000 + ($1,000 × 12% × 2/12)]   1,020
   Purchase of a $1,000, 12% bond as a long-term investment at
   100 plus accrued interest for two months, March 31, 19F (last interest
   date) to June 1, 19F (date of purchase).

* Alternatively, an account, Bond Interest Receivable, could have been debited on June 1 for $20 and then credited for that amount on September 30. The net effect would have been the same. When the end of the accounting period falls between the purchase date and the next interest date, such a procedure may be less complex.

Hayes Company debited the long-term investment account for the cost of the investment, which **excludes** the accrued interest. The $20 accrued interest was paid in cash by Hayes Company. However, it will be returned to Hayes Company at the next interest date, September 30, 19F. At that time, Hayes Company will receive the full amount of cash interest for six months, although it has owned the bond for only four months (i.e., June 1 to September 30, 19F).

The journal entry to record the first interest collection after the purchase is:

September 30, 19F:

Cash   60
   Revenue from investments   60
   Collected interest for six months on bond investment
   ($1,000 × 6% = $60).

After these two entries are posted, the Revenue from Investments account on the books of Hayes Company will reflect $40 interest earned for the four months since purchase as follows:

Revenue from Investments

6/1/19F	20	9/30/19F	60

(balance, $1,000 × 12% × 4/12 = $40 credit)

Sale of a Bond Investment

A long-term investment in bonds is accounted for with the expectation that the bonds will be held to maturity. This expectation is the basis for amortizing any premium or discount over the period from the date of purchase to the maturity date. However, the bonds may be sold prior to their maturity date. When an investor sells bonds prior to maturity, the difference between the sale price and the book value of the bonds is recorded as a "Gain (or Loss) on the Sale of Investments."

Assume Carson Corporation has two $1,000 12% bonds of Drake Company that are being held as a long-term investment. Each bond was purchased at 104. The long-term investment account was debited for $2,080. Because of amortization of bond premium to January 1, 19F, the investment account balance is

$2,040. On that date one of the bonds was sold at 100. The entry by Carson Company to record the sale is:

```
Cash . . . . . . . . . . . . . . . . . . . . . . . . . . . . . . . . . . . . . . . . . . . . 1,000
Loss on sale of investments . . . . . . . . . . . . . . . . . . . . . . . . . . .        20
      Long-term investment, Drake Company bonds . . . . . . . . . . . . . .              1,020
   Sale of long-term investment.
```

Effective-Interest Amortization on Bond Investments

Effective-interest amortization of the discount or premium on a bond investment is similar to the procedures discussed for bonds payable in Chapter 11. This method of amortization is conceptually preferable because (1) interest revenue is measured correctly each period for income statement purposes, and (2) the book value of the investment is measured correctly for balance sheet purposes at the end of each accounting period. Assume that on January 1, 19A, Farmer Company purchased a five-year, $10,000, 8% bond of Research Corporation as a long-term investment. The purchase price, based on a 12% effective-interest rate, was 85.58. Therefore, the cash paid was $8,558 (a $1,442 discount). The bonds have a stated rate of interest of 8% per year, payable each December 31. The acquisition was recorded by Farmer Company as follows:[6]

```
Long-term investment, Research Corporation bonds
   (maturity amount $10,000) . . . . . . . . . . . . . . . . . . . . . . . . . . . . 8,558
      Cash . . . . . . . . . . . . . . . . . . . . . . . . . . . . . . . . . . . . . . . . .       8,558
   Purchase of long-term investment.
```

Farmer Company used the effective-interest amortization method to amortize the bond discount. The journal entries for a bond investment are the same regardless of the amortization method used, except for some of the **amounts** in the periodic interest entries.

Computation of effective-interest amortization is shown in Exhibit 13–7. Notice that the effective rate of interest of 12%, rather than the stated rate of 8%, is used to compute the interest revenue amounts.

The first column in Exhibit 13–7 shows the cash inflow each period for interest (based on the stated rate). The second column shows the interest revenue that should be reported on the income statement each period (based on the effective rate). The third column shows the amount of the discount that is amortized (which is the difference between the interest revenue earned and the amount of cash received). The last column shows the book value of the investment (i.e., the unamortized principal) that should be reported on the balance sheet at the end

---

[6] Given the effective rate of 12%, the price of the bonds can be determined from a bond table or computed as follows:

$$\$10,000 \times P_{n=5,\ i=12\%} = \$10,000 \times .5674 \text{ (Table 10–2)} \quad \$5,674$$
$$\$800 \times P_{n=5,\ i=12\%} = \ \ \$800 \times 3.6048 \text{ (Table 10–4)} \quad \underline{2,884}$$
$$\text{Bond price } (PV \text{ of future cash flows)} \quad \underline{\underline{\$8,558}}$$

Exhibit 13–7 Schedule of effective-interest amortization

Date	Cash Interest Received Each Interest Date	Interest Revenue (based on beginning balance of investment)	Amortization (increase investment)*	Net Investment
1/1/19A (acquisition)				8,558
12/31/19A	800	8,558 × 12% = 1,027	227	8,785
12/31/19B	800	8,785 × 12% = 1,054	254	9,039
12/31/19C	800	9,039 × 12% = 1,085	285	9,324
12/31/19D	800	9,324 × 12% = 1,119	319	9,643
19/31/19E	800	9,643 × 12% = 1,157	357	10,000
Totals	4,000	5,442	1,442	

Note: This example is identical to the illustration of the issuer's situation shown in Exhibit 11–8. Computation of the sale price of the bonds at an effective rate of 12% is shown in footnote 6.

* Adjusts the net investment balance to the maturity amount.

of each period. The entry for interest revenue each period can be taken directly from the schedule (Exhibit 13–7):

	Year 1	Year 2	Etc.
Cash	800	800	
Long-term investment	227	254	
Revenue from investments	1,027	1,054	

Conceptually, the effective-interest method derives the true interest revenue earned during each period and the correct book value of the investment at the end of each period. The straight-line approach gives only approximations of these amounts. Straight-line amortization often is used because it is simple to apply, and the different amounts of premium or discount amortized each period are not material.

DEMONSTRATION CASE

(Try to resolve the requirements before proceeding to the "Suggested Solution" that follows.)

Howell Equipment Corporation sells and services a major line of farm equipment. Both sales and service operations have been profitable. At the beginning of 19S, the company had excess cash. At that time, the management decided to invest in some securities of two of the manufacturers that supply most of the equipment purchased by Howell for resale. The annual accounting period ends on December 31.

This case focuses on the two long-term investments purchased in 19S. One investment was in equity securities, and the other in debt securities. The transactions were:

19S

a. Jan.   1   Purchased 2,000 common shares of Dear Company at $40 per share. This was 1% of the shares outstanding.

b. Aug.   1   Purchased $100,000, 9% bonds payable of the Massey Company at 102, plus any accrued interest. The bonds pay semiannual interest each May 31 and November 30. The bonds mature on May 31, 19X (i.e., five years from June 1, 19S). Brokerage fees were $900.

c. Nov. 30   Received semiannual interest on Massey Company bonds. Uses straight-line amortization.

d. Dec. 28   Received $4,000 cash dividend on the Dear Company shares.

e. Dec. 31   Adjusting entry for accrued interest on the Massey Company bonds.

f. Dec. 31   The current market price of the Dear shares is $39 and $103 for the Massey bonds.

g. Dec. 31   Closed Revenue from Investments to Income Summary.

Required:

a. Give the journal entry for each of the above transactions.

b. Show how the two investments, the accrued interest receivable and the related revenue, should be reported on the balance sheet and income statement at December 31, 19S.

Suggested Solution

Requirement a:

a. **January 1, 19S:**

Long-term investment, common shares of Dear Company (2,000 shares)	80,000	
Cash		80,000

Purchased 2,000 common shares Dear Company at $40 per share.

b. **August 1, 19S:**

Long-term investment, bonds of Massey Company	102,900	
Revenue from investments ($100,000 × 9% × 2/12)	1,500	
Cash		104,400

Purchased $100,000 bonds of the Massey Company.

Computations:
Cost ($100,000 × 1.02) + $900 = $102,900
Accrued interest for 2 months
$100,000 × 9% × 2/12   =   1,500
Total cash paid $104,400

c. November 30, 19S:

Cash	4,500	
Long-term investment, bonds of Massey Company . . .		200
Revenue from investments		4,300

Record interest receipt and amortization.

Computations:
Semiannual interest: $100,000 × 4½% = $4,500
Amortization of premium:
$2,900 ÷ 58 months = $50*
per month; $50 × 4 months = 200
Revenue from investments $4,300

* August 1, 19S, to May 31, 19X = 58 months remaining life.

d. December 28, 19S:

Cash	4,000	
Revenue from investments		4,000

Received dividend on Dear Company shares.

e. December 31, 19S:

Interest receivable	750	
Long-term investment, bonds of Massey Company . . .		50
Revenue from investments		700

Adjusting entry for accrued interest and premium
amortization for one month on Massey Company bonds.

Computations:
Accrued interest receivable:
$100,000 × 9% × 1/12 = $750
Amortization of premium:
$50 × 1 month = 50
Revenue from investments $700

f. December 31, 19S:

Loss on long-term equity investment	2,000	
Long-term investment Dear Company common shares		2,000

To record LCM on Dear shares:
2,000 shares × ($40 − $39) = $2,000.

Note: Entry assumes the decline was permanent and substantial.

g. December 31, 19S:

Revenue from investments	7,500	
Income summary		7,500

Closing entry: $4,300 − $1,500 + $4,000 + $700 = $7,500.

Requirement b:

HOWELL EQUIPMENT CORPORATION
Balance Sheet (partial)
At December 31, 19S

Current assets:
Interest receivable . . . . $ 750

Investments and funds:
2,000 Common Shares of Dear Company, at LCM
(cost, $80,000) . . . . $ 78,000*
Bonds of Massey Company, at amortized cost
($100,000 maturity value; market, $103,000) . . . .   102,650†   180,650

*Cost of equity securities . . . . $ 80,000
Less: Write-down to reduce long-term
equity investment to LCM   2,000
Equity investment at LCM . . . . $ 78,000

†Cost of debt securities $102,900
Less: Amortization of premium
($200 + $50)   250
Debt investment at amortized cost $102,650

HOWELL EQUIPMENT CORPORATION
Income Statement (partial)
For the Year Ending December 31, 19S

Revenue from investments . . . . $ 7,500
Loss on write-down of long-term investment
to market—Dear Company common shares . . . . . . ($2,000)

SUMMARY OF CHAPTER

This chapter discussed the measuring and reporting of two types of long-term investments: capital stock (equity securities) and bonds (debt securities) of another company. An investor may acquire a part or all of the outstanding capital stock of a corporation by **purchase** of its shares or if the investor is a corporation, by **exchange** of its own shares for shares in the other company. The measuring and reporting of long-term investments in the capital stock of another company are determined by the percent of shares owned in relation to the total number of shares outstanding.

If the ownership level of **voting** shares is less than 20%, or if the ownership is of nonvoting shares, the **cost method** must be used. Under this method, the investment amount reported by the investor is based on the lower of cost or market, and investment revenue is recognized on the basis of dividends declared by the investee corporation.

If the ownership is at least 20% but not more than 50%, the **equity method** must be used. Under this method, the investment is recorded at cost by the investor at date of acquisition. Each period thereafter, the investment amount is increased (or decreased) by the proportionate interest in the income (or loss) reported by the investee corporation and decreased by the proportionate share of the dividends declared by the investee corporation. Each period, the investor recognizes as revenue its proportionate share of the income (or loss) reported by the investee company.

If there is a controlling interest—that is, more than 50% ownership of the outstanding voting shares is held by the investor—the financial statements of the affiliated companies (investor and investee) are **consolidated.** This subject is discussed in Chapter 14.

An investor may purchase the bonds (i.e., debt securities) of another entity as a long-term investment. In contrast to capital stock, bonds are a liability of the issuing company; therefore, bonds (1) have a specified maturity date and maturity amount, (2) require the payment of a stated rate of interest at regular specified interest dates, and (3) do not confer voting rights. At the date of purchase, a long-term investment in bonds is recorded at cost, which may be at par, at a discount, or at a premium. When purchased at a premium or a discount, amortization of the premium or discount over the **remaining life** of the bonds is required. The periodic amortization adjusts (1) the balance of the investment amount so that the book value will be the same as the par value on the maturity date and (2) the interest revenue which is reported on the income statement.

IMPORTANT TERMS DEFINED IN THIS CHAPTER

Control The ability of an investor to determine the operating and financing policies of another company (the investee). *p. 757*

Cost Method Method used by investor if less than 20% of the voting shares of the investee company is owned by the investor. *p. 757*

Discount A bond that is purchased for less than par value is purchased at a discount; the difference between cost and par of a bond. *p. 767*

Effective Interest The real or true rate of interest; also called the market rate of interest. *p. 774*

Equity Method Method used by investor if 20% to 50% of the voting shares of the investee company is owned by the investor. *p. 761*

Premium A bond that is purchased for more than par value is purchased at a premium; the difference between cost and par of a bond. *p. 771*

Significant Influence The ability of an investor to have an important impact on the operating and financing policies of another company (the investee). *p. 756*

Stated Interest Rate The annual rate of cash interest specified in the bond contract. *p. 765*

QUESTIONS

Part A: Questions 1–11

1. Explain the difference between a short-term investment and a long-term investment.

2. Match the following:

   Measurement method:
   _____ Cost method.
   _____ Equity method.
   _____ Consolidation.

   Level of ownership of the voting capital stock:
   a. More than 50% ownership.
   b. Less than 20% ownership.
   c. At least 20% but not more than 50%.

3. Explain the application of the cost principle to the purchase of captial stock in another company.

4. Under the cost method, when and how is revenue measured by the investor company?

5. Under the equity method, why is revenue measured on a proportionate basis by the investor company when income is reported by the other company, rather than when dividends are declared?

6. Under the equity method, dividends received from the investee company are not recorded as revenue. To record dividends as revenue would involve double counting. Explain.

7. Match the following items that relate to the long-term investment amount reported on the balance sheet of the investor company:

   Measurement method:
   _____ Cost method.
   _____ Equity method.

   Explanation of balance in the investment account:
   a. LCM.
   b. Original cost plus proportionate part of the income of the investee, less proportionate part of the dividends declared by investee.

8. Why might the lower of cost or market rule in accounting for long-term investments require that the decline of market below cost to be permanent (nontemporary) to justify a write-down to market when for temporary investments such a requirement is not required?

9. What income statement classifications could be used to disclose the gain or loss from the sale or write-down of a long-term investment? Why?

10. The equity method of valuing investments is neither cost nor market. How can such an exceptional valuation be justified when no other asset seems to use such a hybrid approach?

11. How would you justify the portfolio approach to the application of lower of cost or market to long-term investments over the individual security approach?

Part B: Questions 12–17

12. Explain the difference between an equity security and a debt security.

13. Explain why interest revenue must be accrued on a long-term investment in bonds but not on a long-term investment in capital stock.

14. Under what conditions will a bond sell at (*a*) par, (*b*) a discount, and (*c*) a premium?

15. Distinguish between a long-term investment in bonds and a long-term investment in the capital stock of another company.

16. Why is it necessary to amortize premium or discount that arises from the purchase of a long-term bond investment above or below par? Over what period should the premium or discount be amortized?

17. When a bond investment is purchased between interest dates, the purchaser must pay accrued interest plus the purchase price of the bond. Explain why the accrued interest must be paid.

EXERCISES

Part A: Exercises 13–1 to 13–6

E13–1   **(Pair Definitions with Terms)**
Match the following brief definitions with the terms by entering the appropriate letter in each space provided.

Term	Brief description
_____ (1) Significant influence	A. Assumed when the investing company owns more than 50% of the outstanding voting shares of another company.
_____ (2) Discount	
_____ (3) Control	B. Accounting treatment prescribed when an investing company does not have significant influence or control over the other company.
_____ (4) Effective interest	
_____ (5) Equity method	
_____ (6) Stated interest rate	C. Occurs when the stated interest rate is less than the market rate.
_____ (7) Premium	
_____ (8) Cost method	D. Market rate of interest.
	E. Accounting treatment prescribed when an investing company has significant influence, but not control over the other company.
	F. Occurs when the stated interest rate is more than the market rate.
	G. Presumed if the investing company owns 20% to 50% of the outstanding voting shares of the other company.
	H. When this rate matches a bond investor's required rate of return, the bond will sell at par value.

E13–2   (Compare Primary Characteristics of Cost and Equity Methods)

Company P purchased a certain number of the outstanding voting shares of Company S at $15 per share as a long-term investment. Company S had outstanding 10,000 shares of no-par value. On a separate sheet complete the following matrix relating to the measurement and reporting by Company P after acquisition of the shares of Company S.

Questions	Method of Measurement	
	Cost Method	Equity Method
a. What is the applicable level of ownership by Company P of Company S to apply the method?	Percent	Percent
For (*b*), (*e*), (*f*), and (*g*) that follow, assume: Number of shares acquired of Company S Net income reported by Company S in the first year Dividends declared by Company S in the first year Market price at end of first year, Company S shares, $13.50.	1,000 $40,000 $15,000	3,000 $40,000 $15,000
b. At acquisition, the investment account on the books of Company P should be debited at what amount?	$	$
c. On what basis should Company P recognize revenue earned on the shares of Company S? Explanation required.		
d. After acquisition date, on what basis should Company P change the balance of the investment account in respect to the shares of Company S owned (other than for disposal of the investment)? Explanation required.		
e. What would be the balance in the investment account on the books of Company P at the end of the first year?	$	$
f. What amount of revenue from the investment in Company S should Company P report at the end of the first year?	$	$
g. What amount of unrealized loss should Company P report at the end of the first year?	$	$

E13–3   (Identification of the Use of Proper Method to Account for a Long-Term Investment in Equity Securities)

During 19B, Eli Company acquired some of the 60,000 outstanding shares of the common stock, par $10, of Cox Corporation as a long-term investment. The accounting period for both companies ends December 31. The following transactions occurred:

19B

July   2   Purchased 9,000 shares of Cox common stock at $20 per share.

Dec. 31   Received the 19B annual financial statement of Cox Corporation that reported net income of $40,000.

   31   Cox Corporation declared and paid a cash dividend of $0.50 per share.

   31   Market price of Cox common shares was $19 per share.

Required:

a. What accounting method should Eli Company use? Why?

b. Give the required journal entries for Eli Company for each transaction. If no entry is required, explain why.

c. Show how the long-term investment and the related revenue should be reported on the 19B financial statements of Eli Company.

E13–4   (Recording and Reporting a Long-Term Investment in an Equity Security)

Black Company acquired some of the 40,000 shares of outstanding common stock (no par) of Noe Corporation during 19E as a long-term investment. The annual accounting period for both companies ends December 31. The following transactions occurred during 19E:

19E

Jan. 10   Purchased 16,000 common shares of Noe at $30 per share.

Dec. 31   Received the 19E financial statement of Noe Corporation which reported net income of $80,000.

   31   Noe Corporation declared and paid a cash dividend of $1.25 per share.

   31   Market price of Noe shares was $30 per share.

Required:

a. What method of accounting should Black Company use? Why?

b. Give the journal entries by Black Company for each of the above transactions. If no entry is required, explain why.

c. Show how the long-term investment and the related revenue should be reported on the 19E financial statements of Black Company.

E13–5   (Identify and Use the Proper Method to Account for a Long-Term Investment in an Equity Security)

During 19H, Steven Company purchased some of the 100,000 common shares, par $5, of Salt Marine, Inc., as a long-term investment. The annual accounting period for each company ends December 31. The following transactions occurred during 19H.

19H

Jan.   7   Purchased 15,000 common shares of Salt Marine at $15 per share.

Dec. 31   Received the 19H financial statement of Salt Marine, which reported net income of $70,000.

   31   Salt Marine declared and paid a cash dividend of $2 per share.

   31   Market price of Salt Marine shares was $18 per share.

Required:

a. What method of accounting should Steven Company use? Why?

b. Give the journal entries for Steven Company for each of the above transactions. If no entry is required, explain why.

c. Show how the long-term investment and the related revenue should be reported on the 19H financial statements of Steven Company.

E13–6   (Identify and Use the Proper Method to Account for a Long-Term Investment in an Equity Security)

Use the same situation for Steven Company and the data given in Exercise 13–5, **except** for the January 7, 19H, transaction. Assume it was as follows:

19H
Jan. 7   Purchased 30,000 common shares of Salt Marine at $15 per share.

(The data for December 31 are unchanged.)

Required:

a. What method of accounting should Steven Company use? Why?

b. Give the journal entries for Steven Company for each transaction (refer also to transactions given in Exercise 13–5). If no entry is required, explain why.

c. Show how the long-term investment and the related revenue should be reported on the 19H financial statements of Steven Company.

Part B: Exercises 13–7 to 13–15

E13–7   (Accounting for a Debt Security from Purchase Date to Maturity Date)

On July 1, 19A, AB Company purchased at par a $10,000, 9%, 20-year bond of CD Corporation as a long-term investment. The annual bond interest is payable each year on June 30. The accounting period for AB Company ends December 31. At the date of purchase, the bond had five years remaining before maturity.

Required:
Give the journal entries on the books of AB Company for the following transactions:

a. July 1, 19A, acquisition date.

b. December 31, 19A.

c. June 30, 19B.

d. Maturity date of the bond, June 30, 19F.

E13–8   (Accounting for a Debt Security from Purchase Date to Maturity Date)

On April 1, 19A, Rover Company purchased at par ten $1,000, 9%, 10-year bonds of HI Corporation as a long-term investment. The bond interest is payable semiannually each March 31 and September 30. The accounting period for Rover Company ends on December 31. At the date of purchase, the bonds had six years remaining to maturity.

Required:
Give the journal entry for each of the following dates in the accounts of Rover Company in respect to the long-term investment: April 1, 19A; September 30, 19A; December 31, 19A; March 31, 19B; and the maturity date.

E13–9   (Recording an Investment in Bonds)

On February 1, 19A, Jones Company purchased at par a $15,000, 10%, 30-year bond of Lam Corporation as a long-term investment. The bond interest is payable semiannually each January 31 and July 31. The accounting period for Jones Company ends December 31. At the date of purchase, the bonds had four years remaining to maturity.

Required:

Give all journal entries required in the accounts of Jones Company for the period February 1, 19A, through January 31, 19B, and on the maturity date.

E13–10   **(Compare Bonds Sold at Par; at a Discount; at a Premium)**

On July 1, 19B, Tiana Company purchased three different bonds as long-term investments. Data about the three bonds and the purchase prices are:

Bond designation	Par of bond	Annual interest	Payable semiannually	Remaining years to maturity	Market purchase price*
A	$1,000	10%	Dec. 31 and	7	$1,000
B	1,000	9	June 30	10	960
C	1,000	12	each year	5	1,050

* These amounts do not include any accrued interest.

Required:

a. Give the journal entries to record separately the purchase of each bond.

b. Give the journal entries to record separately collection of interest on the first interest date after purchase. Use straight-line amortization of any discount or premium.

c. Give the journal entries to record separately the maturity of each bond.

E13–11   **(Entries and Reporting for a Debt Security Using Straight-Line Amortization)**

On May 1, 19B, Artic Company purchased $9,000 maturity value bonds of Opel Corporation at 96.25 (plus any accrued interest) as a long-term investment. The bond interest rate is 10% per annum payable 5% each April 30 and October 31. The bonds mature in four years from May 1, 19B.

Required:

a. Give the journal entries for Artic Company on May 1, 19B; October 31, 19B; and December 31, 19B (adjusting entry for accrued interest). Use straight-line amortization and round all amounts to the nearest dollar.

b. Show how this long-term investment and the related revenue should be shown on the December 31, 19B, annual financial statements of Artic Company. (Hint: Include the investment, interest receivable, and revenue.)

E13–12   **(Entries and Reporting for a Debt Security Using Straight-Line Amortization)**

On May 1, 19B, Slow Company purchased $10,000 of the 8% bonds of Cook Corporation, at 112 (plus any accrued interest) as a long-term investment. The bonds pay interest each April 30 and October 31. The bonds mature in five years on April 30, 19G.

Required:

a. Give the journal entries for Slow Company on May 1, 19B; October 31, 19B; and December 31, 19B (adjusting entry for accrued interest). Use straight-line amortization and round to the nearest dollar.

b. Show how this long-term investment should be shown on the December 31, 19B, annual financial statements of Slow Company.

E13–13   **(Entries and Reporting for a Debt Security Purchased between Interest Dates; Straight-Line Amortization)**
On March 1, 19B, Erbs Corporation purchased $6,000 of the 12% bonds of TU Corporation as a long-term investment. The bonds pay interest each June 30 and December 31. The bonds mature in 10 years on December 31, 19K. The purchase price was $6,236, plus any accrued interest.

Required:
a. Give the journal entry by Erbs Corporation to record the purchase on March 1, 19B.
b. Give the journal entry to record the interest received on June 30 and December 31, 19B. Use straight-line amortization.
c. What was the amount of interest revenue in 19B? At what amount should the bond investment be reported on the balance sheet at December 31, 19B?

E13–14   **(Analysis of an Effective-Interest Amortization Schedule)**
On January 1, 19A, Cotton Company purchased, as a long-term investment, a $3,000 bond of Devons Company for $2,922 (plus any accrued interest). The bond had a stated interest rate of 7%, payable each January 1. The bond matures in three years on December 31, 19C. Cotton Company uses effective-interest amortization. The amortization table given below was developed.

Date	Cash inflow	Interest revenue	Investment change	Investment balance
January 1, 19A . . .				$2,922
End year 19A	$210	$234	$24	2,946
End year 19B	210	236	26	2,972
End year 19C	210	238	28	3,000

Required:
a. How much was the discount or premium?
b. What was the total cash outflow and the total cash inflow over the life of this investment? What does the difference represent? Explain.
c. How much interest revenue should be recognized on the income statement each year and in total?
d. What amounts should be reported on the balance sheet each year? For the last year give the amounts just prior to collection of the maturity amount.
e. What was the effective rate of interest per year? Show computations.
f. Show how the four different amounts that are listed on the line 19B were computed.
g. Show how the price of the bond of $2,922 was computed.

E13–15   **(Prepare an Effective-Interest Amortization Schedule; Entries and Reporting)**
On January 1, 19A, Indian Company purchased, as a long-term investment, a $10,000 par value, 12% bond issued by Jackson Corporation. The bond pays interest each year on December 31 and has five years remaining life to maturity from January 1, 19A. The accounting period for Indian Corporation ends December 31.

The bond was purchased to yield a 10% effective rate of interest; therefore, the price of the bond was computed as follows:

$$\$10,000 \times P_{n=5;\ i=10\%}\ (0.6209) = \$\ 6,209$$
$$\$1,200 \times P_{n=5;\ i=10\%}\ (3.7908) = \underline{4,549}$$
$$\text{Sales price} \dots \dots \dots \quad \underline{\underline{\$10,758}}$$

Required:

a. Give the journal entry for Indian Company to record the purchase of the bond on January 1, 19A.

b. Prepare a schedule of effective-interest amortization.

c. Give the journal entries for the collection of interest on the bond investment during 19A and 19B.

d. Complete the following schedule (show computations):

	December 31	
	19A	**19B**
Income statement:		
Revenue from bond investment . . . $ _____		$ _____
Balance sheet:		
Bond-interest receivable	_____	_____
Long-term investment, bond of Jackson Corporation	_____	_____

PROBLEMS

Part A: Problems 13–1 to 13–5

P13–1   **(Identify, Record, and Report Using the Proper Method to Account for an Equity Investment)**

During January 19A, Quick Company purchased 10,000 shares of the 100,000 outstanding common shares (no-par-value) of Eleven Corporation at $40 per share. This block of shares was purchased as a long-term investment. Assume the accounting period for each company ends December 31.

Subsequent to acquisition, the following data were available:

	19A	19B
Income reported by Eleven Corporation at December 31	$60,000	$70,000
Cash dividends declared and paid by Eleven Corporation during the year	25,000	30,000
Market price per share of Eleven common on December 31	37	39

Required:

a. What accounting method should be used by Quick Company? Why?

b. Give the journal entries for Quick Company for each year (use parallel columns) for the following (if none, explain why):

(1) Acquisition of Eleven Corporation shares.

(2) Net income reported by Eleven Corporation.

(3) Dividends received from Eleven Corporation.

(4) Market value effects at year-end.

c. Show how the following amounts should be reported on the financial statements for Quick Company for each year:

(1) Long-term investment.

(2) Loss.

(3) Revenues.

P13–2 **(Identify, Record, and Report Using the Proper Method to Account for Two Different Equity Investments)**

During January 19A, John Corporation purchased the shares listed below as long-term investment:

Corporation	Capital Stock	Number of shares Out-standing	Purchase	Cost per share
M	Common (no par)	80,000	12,000	$10
N	Preferred, nonvoting (par $10)	10,000	4,000	15

The account period of each company ends on December 31.

Subsequent to acquisition, the following data were available:

	19A	19B
Net income reported at December 31:		
Corporation M	$20,000	$25,000
Corporation N	30,000	38,000
Dividends declared and paid per share during the year:		
Corporation M common stock	$ 1.00	$ 1.10
Corporation N preferred stock	0.20	0.30
Market value per share at December 31:		
Corporation M common stock	8.00	8.00
Corporation N preferred stock	15.00	16.00

Required:

a. What accounting method should be used by John for the M common stock? N preferred stock? Why?

b. Give the journal entries for John Corporation for each year in parallel columns (if none, explain why) for each of the following:

(1) Purchase of the investments.

(2) Income reported by Corporations M and N.

(3) Dividends received from Corporations M and N.

(4) Market value effects at year-end.

c. For each year, show how the following amounts should be reported on the financial statements for 19A:

(1) Long-term investment.

(2) Loss.

(3) Revenues.

P13–3   **(Compare Methods to Account for Various Levels of Ownership of Voting Stock)**
Company S had outstanding 20,000 shares of common stock, par value $15 per share. On January 1, 19B, Company P purchased some of these shares at $20 per share. At the end of 19B, Company S reported the following: income, $40,000; and cash dividends declared and paid during the year, $15,000. The market value of Company S shares at the end of 19B was $17 per share.

Required:

a. For each case given below (in the tabulation), identify the method of accounting that should be used by Company P. Explain why.

b. Given the journal entries for Company P at the dates indicated below for each of the two independent cases. If no entry is required, explain why. Use the following format:

Tabulation of items	Case A— 2,000 shares purchased	Case B— 8,000 shares purchased
1. Entry to record the acquisition at January 1, 19B.	_____	_____
2. Entry to recognize the income reported by Company S for 19B.	_____	_____
3. Entry to recognize the dividends declared and paid by Company S for 19B.	_____	_____
4. Entry to recognize market value effect at end of 19B.	_____	_____

c. Complete the following schedule to show the separate amount that should be reported on the 19B financial statements of Company P.

	Dollar amounts	
	Case A	Case B
Balance sheet:		
Investments and funds	_____	_____
Income statement:		
Revenue from investments . . .	_____	_____
Loss from investments	_____	_____

d. Explain why assets, shareholders' equity, and revenues are different between the two cases.

P13–4   **(Compare the Cost and Equity Methods)**
Orban Company purchased, as a long-term investment, some of the 100,000 shares of the outstanding common stock of Towns Corporation. The annual accounting period for each company ends December 31. The following transactions occurred during 19E.

19E

Jan. 10 Purchased common shares of Towns at $10 per share as follows:

Case A—10,000 shares.

Case B— 30,000 shares.

Dec. 31 Received the 19E financial statements of Towns Corporation; the reported net income was $80,000.

31 Received a cash dividend of $0.30 per share from Towns Corporation.

31 Market price of Towns shares, $8 per share.

Required:

a. For each case, identify the accounting method that should be used by Orban. Explain why.

b. Give the journal entries for Orban Company for each case for the above transactions. If no entry is required, explain why. (Hint: use parallel columns for Case A and Case B.)

c. Give the amounts for each case that should be reported on the 19E financial statements of Orban Corporation. Use the following format:

	Case A	Case B
Balance sheet (partial):		
Investments and funds:		
Investment in common shares, Towns Corporation . . .	————	————
Income statement (partial):		
Revenue from investments	————	————

P13–5 **(Compare the Cost and Equity Methods)**
Sub Corporation had outstanding 200,000 shares of no-par common. On January 10, 19B, Par Company purchased a block of these shares in the open market at $20 per share. At the end of 19B, Sub Corporation reported net income of $210,000 and cash dividends of $0.50 per share. At December 31, 19B, the Sub shares were selling at $18 per share. This problem involves two separate cases:

Case A—Par Company purchased 30,000 shares of Sub common.

Case B— Par Company purchased 60,000 shares of Sub common.

Required:

a. For each case, identify the accounting method that should be used by Par Company? Explain why.

b. For each case, in parallel columns, give the journal entries for Par Company for each of the following (if no entry is required, explain why):
   (1) Acquisition.
   (2) Revenue recognition.
   (3) Dividends received.
   (4) Market value effects.

c. For each case show how the following should be reported on the 19B financial statements of Par Company:
   (1) Long-term investments.
   (2) Market effects.
   (3) Revenues.

d. Explain why the amounts reported (in Requirement [c]) are different between the two cases.

Part B: Problems 13–6 to 13–11

P13–6 **(Compare Accounting for Equity Securities with Accounting for Debt Securities)**
On January 1, 19B, Ace Company purchased $60,000, 11% bonds of Bye Company as a long-term investment, at 100 (plus any accrued interest). Interest is payable annually on December 31. The bonds have six years to maturity from December 31, 19A. The annual

accounting period for Ace Company ends December 31. In addition, on January 2, 19B, Ace Company purchased in the market 5% of the 10,000 shares of outstanding common stock of Bye Company at $30 per share.

Required:

a. Give the journal entry for Ace Company to record the purchase of the bonds on January 1, 19B.

b. Give the journal entry to record the purchase of the common shares on January 2, 19B.

c. Give the journal entry assuming a cash dividend of $3 per share was declared and received on the Bye stock on December 28, 19B.

d. Give the journal entry for the receipt of the interest on the Bye bonds on December 31, 19B.

e. Show how the long-term investments and the related revenues should be reported on the 19B annual financial statements of Ace Company. Market price of Bye shares was $31 at the end of 19B.

P13–7 **(Reporting Bond Investments Using Straight-Line Amortization of the Discount)**
On May 1, 19B, Moon Company purchased $30,000, 8% bonds of Taylor Company as a long-term investment. The interest is payable each April 30 and October 31. The bonds have four years to maturity from May 1, 19B. The bonds were purchased at 95 (plus any accrued interest). In addition, brokerage fees of $540 were paid by Moon Company.

Required:

a. Give the 19B journal entries for Moon Company on the following dates:

May 1 Purchase.
Oct. 31 First interest date. Use straight-line amortization.
Dec. 31 Adjusting entry for accrued interest at the end of the annual accounting period.

b. Show how the investment, interest receivable, and related revenue should be reported on the 19B annual financial statements of Moon Company.

c. Give the journal entry at the maturity date of the bonds.

P13–8 **(Reporting for a Debt Security Using Straight-Line Amortization of a Bond Premium)**
On June 1, 19B, Fred Company purchased $30,000, 12% bonds of Gray Company, as a long-term investment. The interest is payable each April 30 and October 31. The bonds have five years to maturity from the issue date, May 1, 19B. The bonds were purchased at 105 (plus any accrued interest). In addition, Fred Company paid brokerage fees of $270. The annual accounting period for Fred Company ends December 31.

Required:

a. Give the journal entries for Fred Company on the following dates:

June 1 Purchase plus any accrued interest.
Oct. 31 First interest date. Use straight-line amortization.
Dec. 31 Adjusting entry for accrued interest.

b. Show how the investment, interest receivable, and related revenue should be reported on the 19B annual financial statements of Fred Company.

c. Give the journal entry at the maturity date of the bonds, April 30, 19G.

P13-9   **(Compare Entries and Reporting for Bonds Purchased at Par; at a Discount; at a Premium)**

During 19A, Akers Company purchased the following bonds of Jackson Corporation as a long-term investment:

	Series A	Series B	Series C	Series D
Maturity amount	$10,000	$10,000	$10,000	$10,000
Date purchased	7/1/19A	7/1/19A	7/1/19A	9/1/19A
Interest per annum	8%	7%	9%	9%
Interest dates, annual	June 30	June 30	June 30	June 30
Maturity date	6/30/19F	6/30/19F	6/30/19F	6/30/19F
Purchase price*	100	95	106	100

* Plus any accrued interest.

Required:

a. Give the journal entries to record separately the purchase of the long-term investments.

b. Give the adjusting entries of Akers Company for December 31, 19A, assuming this is the end of the accounting period. Give a separate journal entry for each series. Use straight-line amortization.

c. Give the journal entry of Akers Company for each separate series that should be made on June 30, 19B, for collection of the first interest payment.

d. Complete the following schedule to show the amounts that should be reported on the 19A financial statements (show each series separately):

Income statement (19A):
Revenue from investments . . . . $ _____

Balance sheet (at December 31, 19A):
Long-term investment, bonds of Jackson Corporation . . . $ _____

P13-10   **(Analyze Effective-Interest Amortization; Prepare Schedule and Entries)**

On January 1, 19A, Austin Corporation purchased $50,000, 9% bonds of Briton Company to yield an effective rate of 10%. The bonds pay the interest on June 30 and December 31 and will mature on December 31, 19C.

This long-term investment was recorded by Austin Corporation as follows:

January 1, 19A:

Long-term investment, Briton Company bonds 48,730
    Cash   48,730

Computations:
Principal—$50,000 $\times$ $p_{n=6;\ i=5\%}$ (0.7462)   = $37,310
Interest—$2,250 $\times$ $P_{n=6;\ i=5\%}$ (5.0757)   = 11,420
    Bond price $48,730

Required:

a. What were the stated and effective rates of interest?

b. What was the amount of the discount or premium? What would be the amount of discount or premium amortization each interest period assuming straight-line amortization?

c. Prepare a schedule of effective-interest amortization similar to Exhibit 13–7.

d. Give the journal entries to record interest (including amortization) on June 30 and December 31, 19A, assuming (1) straight-line and (2) effective-interest amortization.

e. Explain when it is appropriate to use each method of amortization.

P13–11   (Computer Spreadsheet for Amortization Schedule)

Required:

a. Using the data from P13–10, prepare a computer spreadsheet to display Requirement c.

b. Calculate directly the amount of the net investment at 6/30/19B independent of the schedule in Requirement a.

CASES

C13–1   (Analyze the Financial Effects of the Cost and Equity Methods)

On January 1, 19B, Emerson Company purchased 40% of the outstanding common shares of Reed Corporation at a total cost of $780,000. On December 31, 19B, the investment in Reed Corporation was reported by Emerson as $950,000, but Emerson did not purchase any additional Reed shares. Emerson Company received $100,000 in cash dividends from Reed. The dividends were declared and paid during 19B. Emerson used the equity method to account for its investment in Reed. The market price of Reed shares increased during 19B.

Required:

a. Explain why the investment account balance increased from $780,000 to $950,000 during 19B.

b. What amount of revenue from the Reed investment was reported by Emerson during 19B?

c. If Emerson used the cost method, what amount of revenue from the Reed investment should have been reported in 19B?

d. If Emerson used the cost method, what amount should be reported as the investment in Reed Corporation on the December 31, 19B, Emerson Company balance sheet?

C13–2   (Analyzing and Understanding Effective-Interest Amortization)

On January 1, 19A, Evans Corporation purchased, as a long-term investment, a bond of Fable Corporation. The following schedule was prepared based on the investment (table captions have been omitted intentionally):

January 1, 19A . . .				$10,339
End year 19A	$800	$724	$76	10,263
End year 19B	800	718	82	10,181
End year 19C	800	713	87	10,094
End year 19D	800	706	94	10,000

Required:
Respond to the following questions in respect to the investment by Evans Corporation:

a. What was the maturity amount of the bond?

b. What was the acquisition price of the investment?

c. Give the journal entry that Evans corporation should make at acquisition date.

d. Was the bond acquired at a premium or discount? How much?

e. What was the stated rate of interest per year? Show computations.

f. What method of amortization apparently will be used? Explain.

g. What was the effective rate of interest?

h. What were the total cash inflow and total cash outflow on the investment? What does the difference represent? Explain.

i. How much interest revenue should be reported each period on the income statement? How does this amount relate to the difference in (h)?

j. What amount will be reported on the balance sheet at the end of each year? (Show the amount for year 19D just prior to collection of the maturity amount.)

k. How were the amounts in each of the four columns of the above schedule computed? Use year 19B to demonstrate the computations.

l. Why is the method of amortization being used conceptually preferable?

C13–3   **(Investment Valuation and Disclosure)**
Your client, ABC Ltd., owns 15% of the shares of Y Co. Ltd. The 1988 pretax net income of ABC Ltd. is $1 million and its shareholders' equity is $3 million.

The investment in Y Co. Ltd. is carried on the balance sheet of ABC Ltd. (as of December 31, 1988) at $250,000, which represents original cost. Y Co. Ltd. has incurred significant losses in the past few years. A current appraisal by a qualified business valuator indicates that the current market value of 100% of the issued and outstanding shares of Y Co. Ltd. is $1 million. You are also aware that an investor who held 20% of the shares of & Co. Ltd. recently sold those shares for $180,000.

Your client, ABC Ltd., insists that the shares be shown at their original cost of $250,000 but is willing to expand disclosure.

Required:
In the situation above:

a. Outline, with reasons, possible deviations (if any) from generally accepted accounting principles. State your assumptions.

b. Outline the minimum note disclosure which you consider adequate in the circumstances. What additional disclosure would be desirable?

(CICA Adapted)

C13–4   **(Analysis of the Cost and Equity Methods Using an Actual Financial Statement)**
Refer to the financial statements of Consolidated-Bathurst Inc. given in Appendix B immediately preceding the Index.

Required:

a. Does the company consolidate all of its subsidiaries? If not, why and what method is used?

b. How much of the company's 1987 income is associated with investments accounted for under the equity method?

c. If the company used the cost method instead of the equity method for certain of its investments, would you expect the company's income to increase or decrease? Why?

d. The company does not consolidate the "equity companies" shown in footnote 8. Explain why.

e. Assume MacMillan Bathurst Limited, a 50% owned associated company, increased its dividend payment from $1 million to $1.5 million. What impact would the increase have on C-B's income?

f. What happened to the investment in Sulbath Exploration Ltd.? What was the effect on the 1987 income?

FOURTEEN

CONSOLIDATED STATEMENTS— MEASURING AND REPORTING

PURPOSE

The previous chapter discussed accounting for long-term investments when one company owns less than 50% of the voting shares of another corporation. This chapter discusses those situations in which one corporation has a controlling influence over another corporation as the result of owning more than 50% of the outstanding voting shares of the other corporation. Often, when a corporation has a controlling influence in another corporation, the financial statements for each corporation are combined into a single set of financial statements, an accounting process called consolidation. Most large companies prepare consolidated financial statements, and understanding the process is important for accounting majors and anyone who uses financial statements.

   A typical note describing the consolidation process is given on the facing page.

LEARNING OBJECTIVES

1. Identify necessary criteria for consolidated statements.

2. Specify appropriate use of the pooling and purchase methods.

3. Apply the pooling and purchase methods.

4. Compare the pooling and purchase methods.

5. Expand your accounting vocabulary by learning about the "Important Terms Defined in This Chapter."

6. Apply the knowledge gained from this chapter.

ORGANIZATION

Part A—acquiring a controlling interest
1. Criteria for consolidated statements.

2. Pooling of interests.

3. Purchase method.

Part B—Reporting consolidated operations after acquisition
1. Impact of pooling and purchase methods after acquisition.

2. Comparison of pooling and purchase methods.

Total Erickson Resources Ltd.

NOTES TO CONSOLIDATED FINANCIAL STATEMENTS

For Years Ended December 31

1. Significant Accounting Principles

(a) Principles of Consolidation:

The consolidated balance sheet includes the accounts of the Company, its wholly-owned subsidiaries, Total Eastcan Explorations Ltd. ("Total Eastcan"), Agnes & Jennie Mining Company Ltd., AJM Metals Ltd., Erickson Gold Mining Corp., Mount Skukum Gold Mining Corporation, and Nu-Energy Oil and Gas Inc., its 94.7% interest in Table Mountain Mines Limited, and its 51.4% interest in Trans-Canada Resources Ltd. ("Trans-Canada"). Trans-Canada was acquired effective October 31, 1987 (note 2).

The Company accounts for its 37% interest in the Mount Skukum Joint Venture in a proportionate consolidation basis.*

Effective June 30, 1985, the Company acquired all of the outstanding shares of Total Eastcan in exchange for shares issued from treasury. Since this transaction resulted in the former shareholder of Total Eastcan owning the majority of the Company's issued shares, the exchange was treated for accounting purposes as an acquistion by Total Eastcan of the assets and business of the Company. Accordingly, the net assets of Total Eastcan were included in the balance sheet at their previous net book values, while those of the Company were included at their fair values on June 30, 1985, which exceeded their book values by $18,000,000.

*Author's note: Joint ventures are a form of corporate partnership where two or more companies join together for a particular endeavor. Equity investment accounting and a special form of consolidation, termed proportionate consolidation, is used to account for joint ventures. Proportionate consolidation techniques are beyond the scope of this book.

PART A—ACQUIRING A CONTROLLING INTEREST

Criteria for Consolidated Financial Statements

A **parent** and **subsidiary** relationship exists when a company owns more than 50% of the outstanding voting shares of another corporation. The investing corporation is known as the parent company, and the other corporation is called a subsidiary. Both corporations are **separate legal entities.** Each company has its own accounting system, and each prepares its own financial statements. However, because of their special relationship, they are viewed as a **single economic entity** for financing reporting. Because the parent and subsidiary are viewed as a single economic entity, the parent company (but not the subsidiary) is required to prepare **consolidated financial statements.** The individual financial statements of the parent and each of its subsidiaries are combined by the parent company into one overall or consolidated set of financial statements. The consolidated financial statements report on the single economic entity. Each of the three required statements—balance sheet, income statement, and statement of changes in financial position—is consolidated by the parent company.

There are a number of operating, economic, and legal advantages to the parent-subsidiary relationship. Therefore, most large corporations, and many medium- and small-sized corporations, have a controlling interest in one or more other corporations. For example, a department store chain may acquire a controlling interest in many of the companies that manufacture the products it sells. As a result, the chain is assured of getting the quality and quantity of product it wants at the price it wants to pay.

Consolidated financial statements are prepared when two basic elements exist. These two basic elements are control and accounting compatibility.

Control is presumed to exist when one investor owns more than 50% of the outstanding voting shares of an entity. Nonvoting shares are not included in the determination of control because they do not provide the investor with any ability to influence the policies of the subsidiary. Effective control may not exist even though an investor owns more than 50% of the voting shares. This situation may occur when the subsidiary is located in a foreign country where **governmental restrictions** prevent the parent company from exercising meaningful control. In circumstances where control is lacking, consolidated statements are not appropriate.

Accounting compatibility means that the operations of the affiliated companies are related so that one complements the other. The operations of an automobile manufacturer are compatible with the operations of a company that manufactures spark plugs. On the other hand, a manufacturing company and a bank lack compatibility and should not be consolidated.

Consolidated statements are not prepared when an investor lacks either (*a*) meaningful control or (*b*) accounting compatibility with the other company. In such situations, the investment is reported as a long-term asset on the balance sheet of the parent as "Investment in unconsolidated subsidiary." The investment is accounted for under the **equity method** as discussed in Chapter 13 and is not consolidated.

Consolidated statements affect only the **reporting** by the parent company of the financial results of the parent and its subsidiaries. The accounting for each subsidiary company is not affected. The fact that a parent company owns a controlling interest has no effect on the accounting of a subsidiary. At the end of the accounting period, the subsidiary prepares its own financial statements. Also, the parent company accounts for its own operations in the normal manner and prepares its own financial statements at the end of each period.

When consolidation is appropriate, the financial statements of the parent and the subsidiaries are prepared in the normal manner and then are combined by the parent company on an **item-by-item basis.** Thus, the consolidated statement concept does not affect the recording of transactions by the parent and subsidiaries. It affects only the **reporting phase** of the combined entity represented by the parent company and its subsidiaries.

Methods of Acquiring a Controlling Interest

One corporation may acquire a controlling interest in another corporation either (*a*) by creating a new corporation and **retaining** more than 50% of the voting shares of the new entity or (*b*) by **acquiring** more than 50% of the outstanding voting shares of an existing corporation. Both ways of acquiring a controlling interest are used widely. A parent company may acquire the voting capital stock of an existing corporation in either of two ways:

1. **Exchanging shares of the parent company for more than 50% of the outstanding voting capital stock of the subsidiary (owned by the shareholders of the subsidiary)**—If certain additional criteria are met, this type of acquisition is called a **pooling of interests.** In this situation, the shareholders of the subsidiary give up their subsidiary shares and become shareholders of only the parent company.

2. **Purchasing by the parent, using cash, other assets, or debt, of more than 50% of the outstanding voting shares from the shareholders of the subsidiary**—This type of acquisition is known as a **combination by purchase.** In this situation, the shareholders of the subsidiary sell more than 50% of their voting shares and are not shareholders of either the parent or the subsidiary.[1]

The pooling and purchase methods have different impacts on the consolidated financial statements. In the next few paragraphs, we will discuss the

---

[1] There is a distinction between a pure combination by pooling of interest and a pure purchase. However, a controlling interest may be acquired in part by a share exchange and in part by a cash purchase. In these "nonpure" situations, a rigid list of criteria must be met to qualify as a pooling of interest (see footnote 2); otherwise, the combination must be accounted for as a combination by purchase.

Exhibit 14-1   Illustrative data for consolidation

COMPANY P AND COMPANY S
Separate Balance Sheets
January 1, 19A, Immediately before Acquisition

		Company P		Company S
Assets				
Cash		$205,000		$ 35,000
Accounts receivable (net)*		15,000		30,000
Receivable from Company S		10,000		
Inventories		170,000		70,000
Plant and equipment (net)*		100,000		45,000
Total assets		$500,000		$180,000
Liabilities and Shareholders' Equity				
Liabilities:				
Accounts payable		$ 60,000		$ 20,000
Payable to Company P				10,000
Shareholders' equity:				
Common stock, Company P (par $6)	$300,000			
Common stock, Company S (par $10)			$100,000	
Retained earnings	140,000	440,000	50,000	150,000
Total liabilities and shareholders' equity		$500,000		$180,000

* Accounts receivable, less the allowance for doubtful accounts; and plant and equipment, less accumulated depreciation. The net amounts are used to simplify the example. The end results will be the same as they would have been had the separate control accounts been used.

consolidation process and the effects of the alternative methods of acquiring a controlling interest. Throughout the chapter we will use a continuing example to illustrate the consolidation process. We will use data for Company P (the parent) and Company S (the acquired subsidiary) shown in Exhibit 14–1.

Pooling of Interests Method

When one corporation acquires more than 50% of the voting shares of another corporation by **exchanging** shares, the shareholders of the two corporations have pooled their ownership interests. This transaction is not viewed as a purchase/sale transaction, and as a result, the cost principle is **not** applied to pooling of interests acquisitions.[2] After a pooling of interests, the consolidated

---

[2] *CICA Handbook*, Section 1580, suggests that a pooling is a situation in which no party to the combination can be identified as an acquirer in the exchange of voting shares. Such combinations are considered rare even when voting shares are exchanged. If one group of prior shareholders holds more than 50% interest in the combined company, that group would normally be the acquirer. Other factors such as the composition of the board of directors, or active participation in management may signify the acquirer.

statements reflect the book values of each company, as shown on their respective financial statements and not the market value of the assets of the subsidiary on the date of the exchange of shares.

To illustrate the consolidation process, we will combine the two separate balance sheets shown in Exhibit 14–2 into a single **consolidated balance sheet.** Basically, consolidation involves combining the balances in each account on the financial statements of the parent and subsidiary companies. The result is the consolidated financial statements that would appear if there were a **single entity.** When the parent company consolidates the balance sheets shown in Exhibit 14–2, the consolidated balance sheet will report a cash balance of $240,000 (i.e., $205,000 + $35,000). During consolidation, some accounts are **eliminated** (or adjusted) to avoid including amounts that would not be reported if only a single entity existed. For example, the balance sheet of Company P shows a receivable from Company S of $10,000, and the balance sheet of Company S shows a payable to Company P of $10,000. During consolidation,

Exhibit 14–2 Balance sheets immediately after acquisition (pooling of interests method)

COMPANY P AND COMPANY S
Separate Balance Sheets (pooling of interests method)
January 1, 19A, Immediately after Acquisition

	Company P	Company S
Assets		
Cash	$205,000	$ 35,000
Accounts receivable (net)	15,000	30,000
Receivable from Company S	10,000	
Inventories	170,000	70,000
Investment in Company S (100%)	150,000*	
Plant and equipment (net)	100,000	45,000
Total assets	$650,000	$180,000
Liabilities and Shareholders' Equity		
Accounts payable	$ 60,000	$ 20,000
Payable to Company P		10,000
Common stock, Company P	360,000*	
Common stock, Company S		100,000
Contributed surplus from pooling of interests	90,000*	
Retained earnings, Company P	140,000	
Retained earnings, Company S		50,000
Total liabilities and shareholders' equity	$650,000	$180,000

* Amounts changed from preacquisition balance sheets given in Exhibit 14–1. Entry made by Company P is:

Investment in Company S	150,000	
Common stock, Company P		60,000
Contributed surplus from pooling		
of interests		90,000

these accounts must be eliminated (which means that they will not be reported on the consolidated balance sheet). The consolidated balance sheet is prepared as if a single entity existed, and it would not be proper to report an amount that the entity owed to itself.

Two items must be eliminated when the balance sheets shown in Exhibit 14–2 are consolidated under the pooling of interests method:

a. The debit balance of $150,000 in Company P's investment account will be replaced on the consolidated balance sheet with the assets (less the liabilities) of Company S. To prevent double counting, the investment account must be eliminated. The credit balance of $100,000 in the Company S common stock account is owned by Company P. It is an intercompany item that must be eliminated. Finally, the difference between the balances in the investment account and the common stock account of Company S ($150,000 − $100,000 = $50,000) must be eliminated from Contributed Surplus from Pooling of Interests (on Company P's books). This elimination is necessary because it is an intercompany amount. These three eliminations are made by Company P to avoid double counting. They can be summarized as follows:[3]

	Eliminations	
	Consolidated assets	Consolidated shareholders' equity
Investment account—decrease	−$150,000	
Common stock, Company S—decrease		−$100,000
Contributed surplus from pooling of interests—decrease (for the difference)		− 50,000

b. Company P shows a receivable of $10,000 from Company S, and the accounts of Company S show this as a payable to Company P. This amount is called an **intercompany debt.** When the two balance sheets are combined into a single consolidated balance sheet, intercompany debt must be eliminated because there is no external debt or receivable for the combined entity. Thus, the following elimination must be made when the two balance sheets are combined:

	Eliminations	
	Consolidated assets	Consolidated liabilities
Receivable from Company S—decrease . . .	− 10,000	
Payable to Company P—decrease		−$10,000

---

[3] This tabulation also can be viewed in the debit/credit format as follows:

Common stock, Company S	100,000	
Contributed surplus from pooling of interests	50,000	
Investment in Company S		150,000

It is important to note that this elimination entry is not recorded in the formal records of Company P but is used for consolidation purposes only.

Exhibit 14–3 Preparation of consolidated balance sheet (pooling of interests method)

COMPANY P and Its Subsidiary, COMPANY S (100% owned)
Consolidated Balance Sheet (pooling of interests method)
At January 2, 19A, Immediately after Acquisition

	Separate balance sheets			Consolidated balance sheet
	Company P*	Company S*	Eliminations*	
Assets				
Cash	$205,000	$ 35,000		$240,000
Accounts receivable (net)	15,000	30,000		45,000
Receivable from Company S	10,000		(b) – 10,000	–0–
Inventories	170,000	70,000		240,000
Investment in Company S	150,000		(a) – 150,000	–0–
Plant and equipment (net)	100,000	45,000		145,000
Total assets	$650,000	$180,000		$670,000
Liabilities				
Accounts payable	$ 60,000	$ 20,000		$ 80,000
Payable to Company P		10,000	(b) – 10,000	–0–
Shareholders' Equity				
Common stock, Company P	360,000			360,000
Common stock, Company S		100,000	(a) – 100,000	–0–
Contributed surplus from pooling	90,000		(a) – 50,000	40,000
Retained earnings, Company P	140,000			190,000
Retained earnings, Company S		50,000		
Total liabilities and shareholders' equity	$650,000	$180,000		$670,000

* A worksheet usually is used to derive the consolidated amounts. See Supplements 14A and 14B.

The balance sheets of Company P and Company S are shown separately in Exhibit 14–3. In the last column, these balance sheets are combined on a line-by-line basis, after deducting the "Eliminations," to develop the "Consolidated balance sheet." In an external consolidated financial statement, only the last column—the "Consolidated balance sheet" (and not the "Separate balance sheets")—would be reported by the parent company.

Review the "Consolidated balance sheet" by the pooling of interests method shown in the last column of Exhibit 14–3. Notice the following measurement procedures: (1) the amounts on each line for the consolidated assets, liabilities, and shareholders' equity are the **combined book values** of the parent and the subsidiary as were shown on the separate balance sheets; (2) the intercompany amounts for investment, subsidiary common stock, a part of contributed surplus from pooling, and the intercompany debt are eliminated; and (3) the **consoli-**

dated retained earnings amount is the sum of the two separate retained earnings amounts ($140,000 + $50,000 = $190,000).[4]

The $100,000 balance shown in the capital stock account of Company S is eliminated because it is an intercompany item (all of the capital stock is owned by Company P). Retained earnings of Company S is not eliminated because it is not an intercompany item. The old shareholders of Company P plus the former Company S shareholders (who are now shareholders of Company P) have dividend claims on the **total** of retained earnings for the combined unit.

Purchase Method

The preceding discussion considered the pooling of interests method (an exchange of shares). In contrast, when a corporation pays cash to acquire the shares of another corporation, a **purchase** transaction takes place.[5] The purchase of assets must be recorded in conformity with the **cost principle.** Thus, on the acquisition date, the investment account for the parent company must be measured at cost, which is the **market value of the acquired shares at date of purchase** (i.e., the cash or cash equivalent paid).

To illustrate a combination by **purchase,** we will use the balance sheets of Companies P and S as given in Exhibit 14–1. Assume that on January 2, 19A, Company P **purchased** from shareholders 100% of the outstanding voting shares of Company S for $165,000 and paid cash. On this date, Company P would make the following journal entry in its accounts:

January 2, 19A:

Investment in shares of Company S (10,000 shares, 100%) 165,000
    Cash   165,000
    Acquisition by purchases.

Note that Company P paid $165,000 cash for 100% of the owners' equity of Company S, although the **total book value** of the shareholders' equity of Company S that was purchased was only $150,000. The reasons for the purchase price being different from the book value are varied. Goodwill (discussed in Chapter 9) could have been purchased. Inflation, and the use of the cost principle, represent other possibilities. Chapter 17 will present a more complete discussion of these two factors. Changes in interest rates over time can affect the value of liabilities. In general, a difference between book value and current value at the time of purchase of a company should be expected.

---

[4] The pooling of interests method also requires that all comparative statements presented for prior years must be restated as if consolidated statements had been prepared.

[5] Refer to footnote 2. In some instances, exchanges of shares do not qualify for the pooling method. In these instances, the purchase method must be used.

Exhibit 14-4 Preparation of a consolidated balance sheet (purchase method)

COMPANY P and Its Subsidiary, COMPANY S (100% owned)
Consolidated Balance Sheet (purchase method)
At January 2, 19A, Immediately after Acquisition

	Separate balance sheets				Consolidated balance sheet
	Company P*	Company S*	Eliminations*		
Assets					
Cash	$ 40,000	$ 35,000			$ 75,000
Accounts receivable (net)	15,000	30,000			45,000
Receivable from Company S	10,000		(b) −	10,000	–0–
Inventories	170,000	70,000			240,000
Investment in Company S	165,000		(a) −	165,000	–0–
Plant and equipment (net)	100,000	45,000	(a) +	5,000	150,000
Goodwill†			(a) +	10,000	10,000
Total assets	$500,000	$180,000			$520,000
Liabilities					
Accounts payable	$ 60,000	$ 20,000			$ 80,000
Payable to Company P		10,000	(b) −	10,000	–0–
Shareholders' Equity					
Common stock, Company P	300,000				300,000
Common stock, Company S		100,000	(a) −	100,000	–0–
Retained earnings, Company P	140,000				140,000
Retained earnings, Company S		50,000	(a) −	50,000	–0–
Total liabilities and shareholders' equity	$500,000	$180,000			$520,000

* A worksheet usually is used to derive the consolidated amounts. See Supplements 14A and 14B.
† A title preferred by most accountants is "Excess of purchase price over the current value of the net assets of the subsidiary" rather than "Goodwill." However, the length of this term causes the shorter term to be used extensively.

Thus, Company P paid $15,000 more than "book value." In consolidating the two balance sheets, this $15,000 difference must be taken into account as explained below.

This purchase by Company P will have no effect on the accounting and reporting by the subsidiary Company S because the shares were sold (and cash was received) by the shareholders of Company S (and not by Company S itself).

After the above journal entry is posted to the accounts of Company P, the two separate balance sheets would be changed as shown in the first two columns of Exhibit 14–4. Compare these two columns with Exhibit 14–1, and you will see that for (a) Company P cash decreased by $165,000 and the investment increased by the same amount and (b) Company S accounts are unchanged.

Observe the consolidated balance sheet under the **purchase method** shown in Exhibit 14–4. The two separate balance sheets for Companies P and S were combined immediately after acquisition to develop the consolidated balance sheet. The consolidation process for a purchase is similar to consolidation for a pooling of interests (as illustrated in Exhibit 14–3). There are two intercompany items that require eliminations like those shown for the pooling of interests method. Notice, however, one item differs significantly. The two eliminations are:

a. The P Company investment account balance of $165,000 represents **market value** at the date of acquisition. It must be eliminated against the shareholders' equity of the subsidiary, which is at **book value.** Company P paid $15,000 more than book value (i.e., $165,000 − $150,000) to acquire Company S for two reasons: (1) The plant and equipment owned by Company S had a market value of $50,000 at acquisition (compared with the book value of $45,000 reported by Company S), and (2) Company S had developed a good reputation with its customers which increased the overall value of Company S. The difference between the cost and the book value of the investment may be analyzed as follows:

Purchase price for 100% interest in Company S . . .		$165,000
Net assets purchased, value at market:		
Book value, $180,000	$180,000	
Less liabilities assumed	30,000	
Net book value	150,000	
Market value increment of plant and		
equipment	5,000	
Total market value purchased		155,000
Goodwill purchased		$ 10,000

Company P paid $165,000 cash for Company S, which had net assets (total assets minus liabilities) with a **market** value of $155,000. Therefore, the goodwill of Company S cost $10,000. **Goodwill** is the amount that an investor paid for the good reputation, customer appeal, and general acceptance of the business that an acquired company had developed over the years. All successful companies have some amount of goodwill. Its "value" is never known except when a business is purchased, as it was in this case. To eliminate the Company P investment account and the owner's equity accounts of Company S, the following five steps must be completed:

1. Increase the plant and equipment of Company S from the book value of $45,000 to market value of $50,000; the increase is $5,000.
2. Recognize the $10,000 goodwill purchased as an asset.
3. Eliminate the investment account balance of $165,000.
4. Eliminate the Company S common stock balance of $100,000.
5. Eliminate the Company S retained earnings balance of $50,000.

These five steps are implemented as follows:[6]

| | Eliminations | |
	Consolidated assets	Consolidated shareholders' equity
Plant and equipment—increase	+$ 5,000	
Goodwill—increase	+ 10,000	
Investment—decrease	− 165,000	
Common stock, Company S—decrease		−$100,000
Retained earnings, Company S—decrease		− 50,000

b. The intercompany debt must be eliminated:

| | Eliminations | |
	Consolidated assets	Consolidated liabilities
Receivable from Company S—decrease	−$10,000	
Payable to Company P—decrease		−$10,000

When the purchase method is used, the balance of Retained Earnings of the subsidiary at acquisition is eliminated. In contrast, under the pooling of interest method, Retained Earnings balance is not eliminated. This elimination is made with the purchase method because the retained earnings of the subsidiary were in effect paid to the former shareholders of Company S when they were bought out for cash.

The accounts of Company S are not affected by a purchase because the transaction was between the parent and the former shareholders of the subsidiary.

The two "Separate balance sheets" are shown in Exhibit 14–4. After eliminations, they are combined on a line-by-line basis to develop the "Consolidated balance sheet" of Company P shown in the last column. In an external consolidated financial statement of Company P, only the "Consolidated balance sheet" shown in the last column (and not the "Separate balance sheets") would be reported.

To reemphasize, when the purchased method is used, the **market values** at date of acquisition of the subsidiary's assets are added on an item-by-item basis to the **book values** of the parent.

---

[6] This tabulation also can be viewed in the debit-credit format as follows (see supplements):

Plant and equipment	5,000	
Goodwill	10,000	
Common stock, Company S	100,000	
Retained earnings, Company S	50,000	
Investment, Company S		165,000

Comparison of the Effects on the Balance Sheet of Pooling versus Purchase Methods

To examine the differences in balance sheet amounts that arise when the pooling of interests method is used versus the purchase method, we can compare several of the consolidated amounts shown in Exhibits 14–3 and 14–4 as follows:

	Acquisition method		
	Pooling method	Purchase method	Difference
1. Cash	$240,000	$ 75,000	$(165,000)
2. Plant and equipment (net)	145,000	150,000	5,000 *
3. Goodwill		10,000	10,000 *
4. Common stock Company P	360,000	300,000	(60,000)
5. Contributed surplus from pooling ...	40,000		(40,000)
6. Retained earnings Company P	190,000	140,000	(50,000)*

* These three amounts reflect the basic differences between the two methods (see footnote 7).

The $165,000 difference in cash was the purchase price of the subsidiary (under the pooling method, only shares were exchanged). The $100,000 difference in the amount of common stock is due to the effect of issuing shares under pooling of interests rather than paying cash when the purchase method is chosen.[7] The plant and equipment amount is higher when the purchase method is used because the purchase method requires application of the cost principle. Under the cost principle, the **market value** at date of acquisition rather than book value must be recognized for the assets of the subsidiary. Usually, goodwill arises in purchase but not pooling of interests. These higher amounts for assets under the purchase method mean higher expenses will be reported on the income statements in the future periods. In this case, depreciation expense and amortization expense for goodwill will be higher. Finally, under the pooling of interests method, the reported retained earnings amount is higher because the amount of retained earnings of the subsidiary must be added to that of the parent as shown in Exhibit 14–3.

When the pooling of interests and purchase methods are compared, three items usually stand out on the consolidated balance sheet:

1. Operational assets almost always are valued higher under the purchase method because they are recorded at market rather than at the subsidiary's book values.

---

[7] In the example of the purchase method, the subsidiary shares were purchased by Company P for cash without borrowing, or without selling unissued shares. Had Company P borrowed the $165,000, the cash position would have been unaffected; however, there would have been an increase in debt by the same amount. Alternatively, Company P could have sold the 10,000 shares of its common stock for $165,000 cash and then purchased the 10,000 shares of Company S with that cash. In this scenario, the cash position and the contributed capital accounts would have been the same under both methods.

2. Goodwill often is recorded under the purchase method but never is recorded under the pooling of interests method.

3. Retained earnings is lower under the purchase method because only the parent company's Retained Earnings balance is reflected, while under the pooling of interests method, Consolidated Retained Earnings balance always is the sum of the parent and subsidiary retained earnings.

Conceptually a purchase reflects the application of the cost principle. The cost principle is applied with all purchase transactions; thus assets and liabilities of S have to reflect their cost to P. Pooling, on the other hand, does not have an acquirer so the cost principle cannot be involved. P has not acquired S in a pooling situation so book values are combined. The question standard setters had to face was whether or not the economic reality of the two situations could really be distinguished so as to justify the difference in accounting treatment. In general, they have suggested the circumstances should be rare when such a distinction can be made.

Part B will discuss other significant effects that are reflected on the consolidated income statement of the parent company.

PART B—REPORTING CONSOLIDATED OPERATIONS AFTER ACQUISITION

The preceding discussions focused on the effects of the consolidation process on the consolidated balance sheet immediately after acquisition. Consolidation has important effects on the income statement and for accounting periods subsequent to the year of acquisition. Exhibit 14–5 presents the consolidated income statement and balance sheet for Company P and its subsidiary, Company S, after one year of operations. Observe that the amount of net income that is reported will differ depending on whether the pooling of interests or purchase method is used. The underlying data and consolidation procedures used to derive these two financial statements are shown in Exhibit 14–10 (Supplement 14A) and Exhibit 14–11 (Supplement 14B). Compare the financial statements shown in these exhibits to get an overview of the effect of consolidation on the income statement.

The primary objective of Part B is to discuss the impact of the pooling of interests and purchase methods on reporting consolidated results after acquisition.

The Impact of the Pooling and Purchase Methods One Year after Acquisition

Recall that at the date of acquisition, the plant and equipment shown on the balance sheet of Company S had a market value of $5,000 in excess of book value. These assets are being depreciated by Company S over a remaining life of 10 years. Also, the acquisition of Company S resulted in the recognition of

Exhibit 14–5 Consolidated financial statements under the pooling and purchase methods one year after acquisition

COMPANY P and Its Subsidiary, COMPANY S (100% Owned)
Consolidated Financial Statements
Pooling and Purchase Methods Compared
At December 31, 19A, One Year after Acquisition

	Consolidated statements	
	Pooling method	Purchase method
Income statement (for the year ended December 31, 19A):		
Sales revenue	$ 510,000	$ 510,000
Expenses:		
Cost of goods sold	(279,000)	(279,000)
Expenses (not detailed)	(156,500)	(156,500)
Depreciation expense	(14,500)	(15,000)
Amortization expense (goodwill)		(500)
Income tax expense	(26,000)	(26,000)
Net income (carried to retained earnings)	$ 34,000	$ 33,000
Balance sheet (at December 31, 19A):		
Assets		
Cash	$ 271,500	$ 106,500
Accounts receivable	46,000	46,000
Inventories	250,000	250,000
Plant and equipment (net)	130,500	135,000
Goodwill		9,500
Total assets	$ 698,000	$ 547,000
Liabilities		
Accounts payable	$ 74,000	$ 74,000
Shareholders' Equity		
Common stock	400,000 *	300,000
Retained earnings	190,000	140,000
Add: Net income (from above)	34,000	33,000
Total liabilities and shareholders' equity	$ 698,000	$ 547,000

* Includes contributed surplus from pooling of interests, $40,000.

$10,000 goodwill when the purchase method was used. This goodwill will be amortized over the next 20 years.[8]

A comparison of the impact of the pooling method and the purchase method

---

[8] *CICA Handbook*, Section 1580.58, states that goodwill that is not permanently impaired should be amortized using the straight-line method over its estimated life but not to exceed 40 years.

Exhibit 14–6 Comparison of pooling of interests and purchase methods one year after acquisition

	Acquisition approach		
	Pooling method	Purchase method	Difference
Income statement:			
1. Depreciation expense	$ 14,500	$ 15,000	$ 500*
2. Amortization expense (goodwill)		500	500*
3. Net income	34,000	33,000	$ 1,000*
Balance sheet:			
4. Cash	271,500	106,500	$165,000
5. Plant and equipment (net)	130,500	135,000	(4,500)
6. Goodwill		9,500	(9,500)
7. Total	698,000	547,000	$151,000
8. Common stock	360,000	300,000	$ 60,000
9. Contributed surplus from pooling of interests	40,000		40,000
10. Retained earnings	224,000	173,000	51,000
11. Total	698,000	547,000	$151,000

* Basic difference on the income statement.

on the consolidated statements of Company P after one year of operations is shown in Exhibit 14–6.

The comparison in Exhibit 14–6 shows that 11 amounts were different because of the alternative consolidation methods. Net income was $1,000 less under the purchase method because **additional** depreciation expense and amortization expense (goodwill) must be recognized in consolidation when the assets of the subsidiary are recorded at their market values on the date of acquisition. The causes of the $1,000 difference are:

	Items	Difference
a. Depreciation expense on pooling of interests method (based on parent and subsidiary assets at book value)	$14,500	
Add depreciation on the increased asset amount of the subsidiary (to market value from book value, $5,000 ÷ 10 years)	500	$ 500
Depreciation expense on purchase method (based on parent assets at book value and subsidiary assets at market value)	$15,000	
b. Amortization expense on the intangible asset, goodwill, of $10,000, which is to be amortized over the next 20 years ($10,000 ÷ 20 years)		500
(There is no goodwill recognized under pooling of interests.)		
Total of the differences		$1,000

When the purchase method is used, net income will be less because of the additional expenses that must be recognized in each year subsequent to acquisition. Businesses usually do not like this unfavourable impact of the purchase method.

The $151,000 difference in the balance sheet totals shown in Exhibit 14–6 is caused by the (1) different way in which the shares were acquired (shares exchanged versus cash payment) and (2) accounting measurements implicit in each of the two methods. These differences may be explained as follows:

Cash—The $165,000 difference reflects the cash price paid for the shares of the subsidiary purchased under the purchase method instead of the exchange of shares under pooling of interests (see footnote 7).

Plant and equipment (net)—This difference reflects the effects of including the plant and equipment of the subsidiary at book value under the pooling of interests method compared with including them at **acquisition** market value under the purchase method. The $4,500 difference in plant and equipment may be explained as follows:

Difference between market value and book value of subsidiary assets at date of acquisition	$5,000
Deduct depreciation on the difference for one year ($5,000 ÷ 10 years)	500
Difference: Operational assets (higher under purchase method) . . .	$4,500

Goodwill—Goodwill often is recognized under the purchase method (and amortized over 40 years or less); it is not recognized under pooling of interests.

Common stock—The common stock of Company P is greater by $60,000 under a pooling of interests because of the issuance of shares in exchange for the shares of Company S. Note that this amount is the same as it was at acquisition.

Contributed surplus from pooling of interests—This amount arises only under pooling of interests as a result of the exchange of shares. In consolidation, a part or all of it is eliminated.

Retained earnings—Retained earnings is $51,000 more under the pooling of interests method than under the purchase method. This difference is due to two factors:

Amount of retained earnings eliminated:		
Under pooling of interests method	$ –0–	
Under purchase method	50,000	$50,000
Amount of consolidated net income:		
Under pooling of interests method	34,000	
Under purchase method	33,000	1,000
Difference: Retained earnings (higher under pooling of interests method)		$51,000

The pooling of interests method usually is preferred by the management of acquiring companies because it (1) requires little or no disbursement of cash, other assets, or the creation of debt; (2) results in a higher net income reported on the consolidated income statement than does the purchase method; (3) reports higher retained earnings; and (4) is susceptible to manipulation, which was evidenced by numerous abuses prior to the issuance of *CICA Handbook,*

Section 1580. However, in the opinion of many persons, the opportunities for manipulation of net income are significant deficiencies of the pooling of interests method. Three fairly common manipulative practices of the past were:

1. **Instant earnings**—Assume Company P acquired Company S through a pooling of interests. At the acquisition date, Company S owned a factory that had a book value of $100,000 and a market value of $600,000. Following the pooling of interests method, the $100,000 book value of the factory was reported on the consolidated balance sheet as an asset. During the next year the factory was sold for the $600,000 market value. The result was a reported gain on the sale of operational assets of $500,000 (disregarding income taxes), even though a factory that cost $600,000 was sold for $600,000. This transaction was called, in a derogatory way, "instant earnings." The reported gain would significantly increase **net income** and EPS and often caused the price of the shares of Company P to rise. At the higher share prices, shares were sold to the public and/or used for another round of mergers following the same pattern. Many persons believe that there was no economic gain because the cost of the plant to the acquiring company was the market value of the shares given in exchange (and that it should have been recorded at this cost amount). If the assets were recorded at acquisition cost, no gain would be reported when the plant was sold for $600,000.

2. **Escalating EPS**—This term refers to what was a common practice of seeking out smaller successful companies to acquire through a pooling of interests, so that their earnings could be **added** to those of the parent. Thus, by the simple expedient of year-end pooling acquisitions, the acquiring company could escalate net income and EPS reported on the consolidated income statement. This action became a favourite way to "doctor" net income and EPS at year-end.

3. **Tricky mixes**—This situation represented the ultimate in misleading and illogical accounting. It was referred to as "part-purchase, part-pooling of interests accounting." In acquiring another company by pooling, a corporation often found a number of shareholders of the other company who would not accept shares in exchange; they wanted cash immediately. It might work out that two thirds of the shares of the subsidiary would be acquired by exchange of shares, and the remaining third would be purchased for cash. In order to derive some of the "reporting benefits" of pooling of interests accounting, two thirds of the acquisition would be accounted for as a pooling and one third as a purchase—thus part-purchase, part-pooling accounting. This mixture of accounting approaches not only was theoretically untenable but also was misleading. It was stopped by *CICA Handbook*, Section 1580.

The "merger movement" in the 1960s came under considerable criticism because pooling of interests accounting often was used in situations that were, in substance, purchases. In response to extensive criticism, the accounting professions in both Canada and the United States restricted the application of pooling to rare types of combinations. The conceptual argument against the pooling of interests method is that it ignores the market values on which the parties traded shares and substitutes, in violation of the cost principle, the book values carried in the accounts of the subsidiary. The practical argument against the pooling of interests method is that it leads to abuses such as those cited above.

The primary arguments in favour of the pooling of interests method of reporting are (1) it avoids the problems of measuring the market value of the different assets of the subsidiary at acquisition date; (2) it avoids the necessity of recognizing goodwill, then having to amortize it as an expense in future periods; and (3) the exchange of shares is not a purchase/sale transaction but, rather, is a joining of common interests and risks. Many accountants predict that the standard setters eventually will eliminate the pooling of interests method.

DEMONSTRATION CASE

On January 1, 19A, Connaught Company purchased 100% of the outstanding voting shares of London Company in the open market for $85,000 cash. On the date of acquisition, the market value of the operational assets of London Company was $79,000.

Required:

    a. Was this a combination by pooling of interests or by purchase? Explain.

    b. Give the journal entry that should be made by Connaught Company at date of acquisition. If none is required, explain why.

    c. Give the journal entry that should be made by London Company at date of acquisition. If none is required, explain why.

    d. Analyze the acquisition to determine the amount of goodwill purchased.

    e. Should the assets of London Company be included on the consolidated balance sheet at book value or market value? Explain.

Suggested Solution

    a. The purchase method should be used because the shares of the subsidiary were acquired for cash.

    b. January 1, 19A:

Investment in subsidiary	85,000	
Cash		85,000

    c. London Company would not record a journal entry related to the purchase of shares by Connaught Company. The transaction was between

Connaught and the shareholders of London Company. The transaction did not directly involve the London Company.

d. Purchase price for London Company $85,000
Market value of net assets purchased   79,000
Goodwill . . . . $ 6,000

e. Under the purchase method, the assets of London Company should be included on the consolidated balance sheet at their market values as of the date of acquisition. The cost principle applies because a purchase/sale transaction is assumed when the combination is accounted for as a purchase. When the pooling of interests method is used, the assets of the subsidiary are reported on the consolidated balance sheet at their book value.

SUMMARY OF CHAPTER

Consolidated financial statements are required in most situations when one corporation owns more than 50% of the outstanding voting shares of another corporation. The concept of consolidation is based upon the view that a parent company and its subsidiaries constitute one economic entity. Therefore, the separate income statements, balance sheets, and statements of changes in financial position should be combined each period on an item-by-item basis as a single set of consolidated financial statements.

Ownership of a controlling interest of another corporation may be accounted for as either a pooling of interests or combination by purchase. The measurement of amounts reported on the consolidated financial statements is influenced by these two different accounting methods.

The pooling of interests method usually is used when the parent company exchanges its own voting shares for a controlling interest in the voting shares of the subsidiary. In this situation, there is no purchase/sale (exchange) transaction. Rather, there was a joining of interests by exchanging shares and the cost principle is not applied. Therefore, in preparing consolidated statements under the pooling interests method, the book values of each related company are added together. Acquisition market values are disregarded.

Under the purchase method, the parent company usually pays cash and/or incurs debt to acquire the voting shares of the subsidiary. In these circumstances, a purchase/sale transaction has been completed, and the acquisition is accounted for in conformity with the cost principle. Therefore, the assets of the subsidiary must be measured at their acquisition market values when combined with the statements of the parent company.

The differences between the pooling of interests and purchase methods are summarized in Exhibit 14–7. The acquisition of a controlling interest **does not** affect the accounting and reporting of the subsidiary companies (the subsidiary companies do not prepare consolidated statements).

Exhibit 14–7 Summary of differences between the pooling of interests and purchase methods

Item	Pooling of Interests	Purchase
1. Measuring and recording at date of acquisition by the parent company.	Acquisition is accomplished by exchanging shares. A purchase/sale transaction is not assumed; therefore, the cost principle is **not** applied. The investment account is debited for the **book value** of the subsidiary shares acquired.	Acquisition usually is accomplished by purchasing the shares with cash and/or debt. A purchase/sale transaction is assumed; therefore, the cost principle is applied. On acquisition date, the investment account is debited for the **market value** of the resources acquired.
2. Goodwill.	Goodwill is not recognized by the parent company.	Goodwill is recognized by the parent company to the extent that the purchase price exceeds the sum of acquisition market values of the assets (less the liabilities) of the subsidiary.
3. Method of aggregating or combining by the parent company to derive the consolidated balance sheet.	Assets and liabilities (less any eliminations) of the subsidiary are added, at **book value,** to the book values of the parent.	Assets and liabilities (less any eliminations) of the subsidiary are added, at their acquisition **market values,** to the book values of the assets and liabilities of the parent.
4. Method of aggregating or combining by the parent company to derive the consolidated income statement.	Revenues and expenses as reported by each company, less any eliminations, are aggregated.	Revenues as reported, less any eliminations, are aggregated. Expenses, plus additional depreciation and amortization of goodwill, less any eliminations, are aggregated.
5. Eliminations.	Eliminate all intercompany debts, revenues, and expenses. Eliminate investment account on parent's books and owners' equity of the subsidiary, excluding retained earnings.	Eliminate all intercompany debts, revenues, and expenses. Eliminate the investment account on parent's books and common stock and retained earnings of the subsidiary.
6. Usual comparative effects on the consolidated financial statements.	Expenses—lower Net income—higher EPS—higher Assets—higher cash Noncash assets—lower Liabilities—same Capital stock—higher Retained earnings—higher	Expenses—higher Net income—lower EPS—lower Assets—lower cash Noncash assets—higher Liabilities—same Capital stock—lower Retained earnings—lower

CHAPTER SUPPLEMENT 14A

Consolidation Procedures—100% Ownership

This supplement discusses in more depth the measurement procedures used in preparing consolidated financial statements. To accomplish this objective, we use a **consolidation worksheet** because it brings the underlying concepts and measurement procedures into sharp focus. The worksheet should be viewed as a learning device and not something only to be mastered mechanically. The worksheet and the entries made on it are **supplemental** to the ledger accounts of the parent company. **The worksheet entries are not recorded in the ledger accounts under any circumstances because the worksheet is an analytical device only.** The example for Company P and its subsidiary, Company S, given in Exhibit 14–1, will be continued for all of the illustrations in this supplement.

Developing Consolidated Statements for Periods Subsequent to Acquisition. At the end of each accounting period after acquisition, a consolidated balance sheet, income statement, and statement of changes in financial position must be prepared by the parent company. A single worksheet can be used to prepare both a consolidated balance sheet and consolidated income statement for accounting periods subsequent to acquisition.

Recall that on January 2, 19A, Company acquired 100% of the outstanding shares of Company S. Assume that it is now December 31, 19A. After operating for a year, each company prepared its separate income statement and balance sheet as shown in Exhibit 14–8. Two sets of financial statements are shown for Company P; the first is based on the assumption that Company S was acquired through an exchange of shares (pooling of interests), and the second is based on the assumption that Company S shares were acquired with cash (purchase).

At the end of 19A, the following additional data were available to Company P:

a. The balance in Investment in the Company S account of $165,000 was the same as at the date of acquisition; the balance of Retained Earnings of Company S at acquisition was $50,000.

b. At date of acquisition, January 2, 19A, the plant and equipment of Company S had an acquisition market value of $5,000 above book value and goodwill purchased amounted to $10,000.

c. Intercompany debt owed by Company S to Company P was $6,000 at the end of 19A.

d. The plant and equipment owned by Company S had a 10-year remaining life from January 1, 19A, for depreciation purposes. The company uses straight-line depreciation.

e. Goodwill is to be amortized from January 1, 19A, over 20 years on a straight-line basis.

f. During December 19A, Company S declared and paid a $10,000 cash

Exhibit 14–8 Illustrative data for consolidated financial statements subsequent to acquisition (100% ownership)

COMPANY P AND COMPANY S
Separate Financial Statements for 19A (unclassified)

At December 31, 19A

	Company P		Company S
	Exchange of shares	Purchase with cash	
Income statement (for 19A):			
Sales revenue	$400,000	$400,000	$110,000
Revenue from investments			
(dividend from Company S)	10,000	10,000	
Cost of goods sold	(220,000)	(220,000)	(59,000)
Expenses (not detailed)	(130,000)	(130,000)	(26,500)
Depreciation expense	(10,000)	(10,000)	(4,500)
Income tax expense	(20,000)	(20,000)	(6,000)
Net income	$ 30,000	$ 30,000	$ 14,000
Balance sheet (at December 31, 19A):			
Cash	$226,000	$ 61,000	$ 45,500
Accounts receivable (net)	18,000	18,000	28,000
Receivable from Company S	6,000	6,000	
Inventories	185,000	185,000	65,000
Investment in Company S			
(by purchase, at cost)	150,000*	165,000*	
Plant and equipment (net)	90,000	90,000	40,500
	$675,000	$525,000	$179,000
Accounts payable	$ 55,000	$ 55,000	$ 19,000
Payable to Company P			6,000
Common stock (par $10)	360,000	300,000	100,000
Contributed surplus from pooling of interests . . .	90,000		
Beginning retained earnings*	140,000	140,000	50,000
Dividends declared and paid during 19A			(10,000)
Net income for 19A (per above)	30,000	30,000	14,000
	$675,000	$525,000	$179,000

* Balance at date of acquisition.

dividend to Company P. Each company made the following journal entry in its accounts:

Company P		Company S	
Cash 10,000		Dividends declared	
Revenue from		and paid 10,000	
investments . .	10,000	Cash	10,000

A consolidated income statement and balance sheet must be prepared at the end of 19A. These statements were shown in Exhibit 14–5, assuming (1) pooling of interests method and (2) purchase method. A separate consolidation work-sheet for each method will be discussed.

Pooling of interests method—Income statement and balance sheet. This worksheet (Exhibit 14–9) has side captions for each income statement and balance sheet account, and column headings for the parent company, the subsidiary company, eliminations, and the **Consolidated Balances.** The amounts entered in the first two columns are taken directly from the separate 19A financial statements prepared by the parent and the subsidiary (as given in Exhibit 14–8).

The worksheet is designed so that the eliminations are entered in debit and credit format. This format provides an excellent check on the accuracy of the work. Remember that the elimination entries are **worksheet entries only;** they are never entered into the accounts of either the parent or the subsidiary. Consolidated statements represent a **reporting approach** that does not affect the ledger accounts of either the parent or the subsidiaries.

To complete the worksheet, the elimination entries must be entered. Then, each line is accumulated horizontally to derive the consolidated amount in the last column.

Under the pooling of interests method, there are three elimination entries that must be made on the worksheet:

a. Eliminate the investment in Company S with offsets to the accounts for (1) Common Stock, Company S, and (2) Contributed Surplus from Pooling. These eliminations can be accomplished using the following intercompany elimination entry on the worksheet (which is shown in a journal entry format):

<pre>
Common stock, Company S   100,000
Contributed surplus from pooling of interests   50,000
     Investment in Company S   150,000
</pre>

b. Eliminate the intercompany debt of $6,000 owed by Company S to Company P. These two eliminations can be accomplished by means of the following intercompany elimination entry on the worksheet:

<pre>
Payable to Company P   6,000
     Receivable from Company S   6,000
</pre>

c. During the year, Company S declared and paid dividends amounting to $10,000. Because Company P owned 100% of the outstanding shares, all of the dividends were paid to Company P. This intercompany item must be eliminated. The Revenue from Investments account of Company P is debited on the worksheet, and the Dividends Declared and Paid account of the subsidiary is credited for $10,000. Observe that separate lines are set up on the worksheet for dividends and net income. This is done for convenience and clarity. The worksheet entry for these two eliminations is:

<pre>
Revenue from investments   10,000
     Dividends declared and paid (Retained earnings,
          Company S)   10,000
</pre>

Exhibit 14–9 Consolidation worksheet (pooling of interests method; 100% ownership)

COMPANY P and Its Subsidiary, COMPANY S
Consolidation Worksheet (pooling of interests) for the Balance Sheet
and Income Statement December 31, 19A (100% ownership)

Items	Statements Company P	Statements Company S	Intercompany Eliminations Debit	Intercompany Eliminations Credit	Consolidated Balances
Income statement:					
Sales revenue	400,000	110,000			510,000
Revenue from investments	10,000		(c) 10,000		
Cost of goods sold	(220,000)	(59,000)			(279,000)
Expenses (not detailed)	(130,000)	(26,500)			(156,500)
Depreciation expense	(10,000)	(4,500)			(14,500)
Income tax expense	(20,000)	(6,000)			(26,000)
Net income (carried down)	30,000	14,000			34,000
Balance sheet:					
Cash	226,000	45,500			271,500
Accounts receivable (net)	18,000	28,000			46,000
Receivable from Company S	6,000			(b) 6,000	
Inventories	185,000	65,000			250,000
Investment in Company S	150,000*			(a) 150,000	
Plant and equipment (net)	90,000	40,500			130,500
	675,000	179,000			698,000
Accounts payable	55,000	19,000			74,000
Payable to Company P		6,000	(b) 6,000		
Common stock, Company P	360,000*				360,000
Common stock, Company S		100,000	(a) 100,000		
Contributed surplus from pooling	90,000*		(a) 50,000		40,000
Beginning retained earnings, Company P	140,000				140,000
Beginning retained earnings, Company S		50,000			50,000
Dividends declared and paid during 19A		(10,000)		(c) 10,000	
Net income, 19A (from above; not added across)	30,000†	14,000†			34,000†
	675,000	179,000	166,000	166,000	698,000

Explanation of eliminations:
(a) To eliminate Investment in Company S against Common Shares of Company S and Contributed Surplus from Pooling of Interests.
(b) To eliminate the intercompany debt.
(c) To eliminate the intercompany revenue and dividends (paid by the subsidiary to the parent).

* These amounts are based upon the pooling of interests method. The parent would have made the following journal entry at acquisition date:

Investment in Company S 150,000
    Common stock, Company P   60,000
    Contributed surplus from pooling of interests   90,000

† Carried down from above.

Purchase method—Income statement and balance sheet. Under the purchase method, a few more eliminations are needed because of the use of acquisition market values for the subsidiary. The intercompany eliminations on the worksheet (Exhibit 14–10) under the purchase method are:

a. Eliminate the investment account against the subsidiary owners' equity accounts. This elimination entry will be the same each year because it is based upon the values recognized at the date of acquisition. The $15,000 difference between the purchase price and the book value must be allocated to the subsidiary company's assets (including goodwill). The **worksheet** entry is as follows (illustrated in a journal entry format):

Common stock, Company S	100,000	
Retained earnings, Company S	50,000	
Plant and equipment	5,000	
Goodwill	10,000	
Investment in Company S		165,000

b. Eliminate the intercompany debt of $6,000 with the following entry on the worksheet:

Payable to Company P	6,000	
Receivable from Company S		6,000

c. Because the plant and equipment amount for Company S was increased by $5,000 to reflect acquisition market value, additional depreciation must be recorded on the $5,000 increment. The depreciation reflected on the statements of Company S is based on original acquisition cost and does not include this $5,000 increase to market value. Therefore, the worksheet entry must be:

Depreciation expense (Company S)	500	
Plant and equipment (Company S)		
(or accumulated depreciation)		500

$5,000 ÷ 10 years = $500.

d. Goodwill must be amortized over a realistic period not longer than 40 years. Company P decided to use a 20-year life. $10,000 goodwill was recognized in entry (a) above. This amount must be amortized. Therefore, the worksheet entry to accomplish this effect is:

Amortization expense (goodwill)	500	
Goodwill		500

$100,000 ÷ 20 years = $500.

e. During the year, Company S declared and paid dividends amounting to $10,000. Because Company P owned 100% of the outstanding shares, all of the dividends were paid to Company P. This intercompany item must be eliminated. The Revenue from Investments account of Company P must be debited on the worksheet, and the Dividends Declared and Paid account of the subsidiary credited for $10,000. Observe that

Exhibit 14–10 Consolidation worksheet (purchase method; 100% ownership)

COMPANY P and Its Subsidiary, COMPANY S
Consolidation Worksheet (by purchase) for the Balance Sheet
and Income Statement
December 31, 19A (100% ownership)

Items	Statements Company P	Statements Company S	Intercompany Eliminations Debit	Intercompany Eliminations Credit	Consolidated Balances
Income statement:					
Sales revenue	400,000	110,000			510,000
Revenue from investments	10,000		(e) 10,000		
Cost of goods sold	(220,000)	(59,000)			(279,000)
Expenses (not detailed)	(130,000)	(26,500)			(156,500)
Depreciation expense	(10,000)	(4,500)	(c) 500		(15,000)
Amortization expense					
(goodwill)			(d) 500		(500)
Income tax expense	(20,000)	(6,000)			(26,000)
Net income (carried down)	30,000	14,000			33,000
Balance sheet:					
Cash	61,000	45,500			106,500
Accounts receivable (net)	18,000	28,000			46,000
Receivable from Company S	6,000			(b) 6,000	
Inventories	185,000	65,000			250,000
Investment in Company S					
(at cost)	165,000			(a) 165,000	
Plant and equipment (net)	90,000	40,500	(a) 5,000	(c) 500	135,000
Goodwill			(a) 10,000	(d) 500	9,500
	525,000	179,000			547,000
Accounts payable	55,000	19,000			74,000
Payable to Company P		6,000	(b) 6,000		
Common stock, Company P	300,000				300,000
Common stock, Company S		100,000	(a) 100,000		
Beginning retained earnings,					
Company P	140,000				140,000
Beginning retained earnings,					
Company S		50,000	(a) 50,000		
Dividends declared and paid					
during 19A		(10,000)		(e) 10,000	
Net income, 19A (from above;					
not added across)	30,000*	14,000*			33,000*
	525,000	179,000	182,000	182,000	547,000

* Carried down from above.
Explanation of eliminations:
  (a) To eliminate the investment account against the subsidiary shareholders' equity and to allocate the difference between purchase price and book value purchased to the appropriate accounts.
  (b) To eliminate the intercompany debt.
  (c) To record additional depreciation for one year on the asset increase resulting from the acquisition.
  (d) To record amortization for one year on the goodwill recognized.
  (e) To eliminate intercompany revenue and dividends (paid by the subsidiary to the parent).

separate lines are set up on the worksheet for dividends and net income. This procedure is for convenience and clarity. The worksheet entry for these eliminations is:

Revenue from investments 10,000
   Dividends declared and paid (retained earnings,
     Company S) 10,000

After all of the intercompany eliminations have been entered on the worksheet, the consolidated financial statement amounts are determined by accumulating each line horizontally to derive the balances in the last column. The balances in the last column of the worksheet are classified in the normal manner in preparing the consolidated income statement and balance sheet.

CHAPTER SUPPLEMENT 14B

Consolidation Procedures—Less than 100% Ownership

When the parent company owns a controlling interest that is less than 100%, most of the consolidation procedures are the same as the procedures for 100% ownership. Certain eliminations differ because they are based upon the **proportionate** ownership level. When the parent company does not own 100% of the subsidiary, there will be a group of shareholders of the subsidiary company called the **minority shareholders.** Their interest in the subsidiary is not affected by the parent's interest. The minority shareholders' interest must be accorded appropriate measurement and reporting on the consolidated financial statements. **Minority interest** includes the minority shareholders' proportionate share of both the earnings and the shareholders' equity of the subsidiary.

To illustrate consolidated statements with a minority interest, we will adapt the data for Company P and Company S given in Exhibit 14–1. Assume that on January 2, 19A, Company P purchased 80% of the 10,000 shares of outstanding capital stock of Company S for $132,000 cash.[9] At acquisition date, Company P recorded the purchase of the 8,000 shares of capital stock as follows:

Investment, shares of Company S (80% ownership) 132,000
   Cash 132,000
   Acquisition of 8,000 shares (80%) of the capital stock of Company S at
   $16.50 per share.

On the acquisition date, the owners' equity for Company S showed the following amounts: capital stock, $100,000; and retained earnings,$50,000 (total owners' equity was $150,000). Company P paid $132,000 cash for 80% of the owners' equity of Company S. The book value of the investment was $120,000 ($150,000 × 80%). Thus, Company P paid $12,000 more than the book value of

---

[9] Because Company P has obviously acquired Company S, the purchase method will be used.

Company S. The market value of the subsidiary company's plant and equipment was $5,000 more than its book value. Therefore, of the $12,000 cost in excess of book value that P Company paid, $4,000 (i.e., $5,000 × 80%) was for the greater market value of the plant and equipment. The remaining amount, $8,000, was for **goodwill.** The analysis of the purchase transaction, at date of acquisition, follows:[10]

Purchase price for 80% interest in Company S	$132,000
Net assets purchased, valued at market:	
Book value, $120,000 + market value increment of	
plant and equipment, $5,000 × 80% = ...	124,000
Goodwill purchased	$ 8,000

On December 31, 19A, both companies had completed one year's operations as affiliated companies. Each company has prepared the separate 19A financial statements shown in Exhibit 14–11.

Additional data developed by Company P for the consolidation worksheet:

a. Investment account balance of $132,000 to be eliminated against 80% of shareholders' equity of subsidiary.

b. Plant and equipment of Company S to be increased by $4,000 to market value (i.e., the increment acquired by Company P). Goodwill will be recognized, $8,000 (see analysis of purchase transaction above).

c. Company S owed Company P $6,000 on December 31, 19A.

d. The plant and equipment is being depreciated on a straight-line basis over a remaining life of 10 years by Company S (no residual value).

e. Goodwill will be amortized over 20 years.

f. Company S declared and paid $10,000 cash dividends on December 15, 19A.

The consolidation worksheet under the purchase method is shown in Exhibit 14–12. It is the same as the worksheet shown in Exhibit 14–10 for 100% ownership, except for elimination entries (a), (c), (d), and (e). These intercompany eliminations differ only in **their amounts. They have been reduced to the 80% ownership level.**

On the worksheet, the minority interest (20%) is designated with an "M." In the income statement portion of the worksheet, 20% of the **subsidiary** net income (i.e., $2,800) is coded "M," and the remainder ($30,400) is identified with the parent. The amount of income attributable to the minority is removed from the consolidated net income so that revenues and expenses can be left to reflect

---

[10] Some accountants believe that the plant and equipment difference should be 100% (i.e., $5,000) rather than 80% (i.e., $4,000). This difference in opinion has not been resolved; however, it appears that most companies currently use the lower amount. In Canada, *CICA Handbook*, Section 1580, requires the use of the lower amount.

Exhibit 14–11   Illustrative data for consolidation (less than 100% ownership)

COMPANY P AND COMPANY S
Separate Financial Statements for 19A

	Company P	Company S
Income statement (for 19A):		
Sales revenue	$400,000	$110,000
Revenue from investments (dividends from Company S)	8,000	
Cost of goods sold	(220,000)	(59,000)
Expenses (not detailed)	(130,000)	(26,500)
Depreciation expense	(10,000)	(4,500)
Income tax expense	(20,000)	(6,000)
Net income	$ 28,000	$ 14,000
Balance sheet (at December 31, 19A):		
Cash	$ 92,000	$ 45,500
Accounts receivable (net)	18,000	28,000
Receivable from Company S	6,000	
Inventories	185,000	65,000
Investment in Company S (80%, at cost)	132,000	
Plant and equipment	90,000	40,500
	$523,000	$179,000
Accounts payable	$ 55,000	$ 19,000
Payable to Company P		6,000
Common stock, par $10	300,000	100,000
Beginning retained earnings	140,000	50,000
Dividends declared and paid during 19A		(10,000)
Net income for 19A (from above)	28,000	14,000
	$523,000	$179,000

the full amounts of the consolidated entity. Notice that the minority shareholders do not share in the income of the parent company. On the worksheet, the income amounts are carried down to the retained earnings section of the balance sheet. The 20% of subsidiary shareholders' equity owned by the minority shareholders was not eliminated as an intercompany item. Therefore, it is carried across as minority interest and coded "M." Aside from these adaptations, the Consolidated Balances column is completed as previously explained.

The consolidated income statement and balance sheet, based on the data in the Consolidated Balances column of the worksheet, are shown in Exhibit 14–13. The **minority interest** share of net income is identified separately on the income statement. Also, the minority interest share of shareholders' equity is identified separately on the balance sheet as a special caption between liabilities and shareholders' equity rather than as illustrated in Exhibit 14–13.

Exhibit 14–12 Consolidation worksheet (purchase method; less than 100% ownership)

	Statements		Intercompany Eliminations		Consolidated Balances
COMPANY P and Its Subsidiary, COMPANY S Consolidation Worksheet (by purchase) for the Balance Sheet and Income Statement December 31, 19A (80% ownership)					
Items	**Company P**	**Company S**	**Debit**	**Credit**	
Income statement:					
Sales revenue	400,000	110,000			510,000
Revenue from investments	8,000		(e) 8,000		
Cost of goods sold	(220,000)	(59,000)			(279,000)
Expenses (not detailed)	(130,000)	(26,500)			(156,500)
Depreciation expense	(10,000)	(4,500)	(c) 400		(14,900)
Amortization expense (goodwill)			(d) 400		(400)
Income tax expense	(20,000)	(6,000)			(26,000)
Net income	28,000	14,000			33,200
Carried down:					
Minority interest ($14,000 × 20%)					2,800 M*
Parent interest income					30,400

Exhibit 14–12 *(concluded)*

Items	Statements Company P	Statements Company S	Intercompany Eliminations Debit		Intercompany Eliminations Credit		Consolidated Balances
Balance sheet:							
Cash	92,000	45,500					137,500
Accounts receivable (net)	18,000	28,000					46,000
Receivable from Company S	6,000				(b)	6,000	
Inventories	185,000	65,000					250,000
Investment in Company S (at cost)	132,000				(a)	132,000	
Plant and equipment (net)	90,000	40,500	(a)	4,000	(c)	400	134,100
Goodwill			(a)	8,000	(d)	400	7,600
	523,000	179,000					575,200
Accounts payable	55,000	19,000					74,000
Payable to Company P		6,000	(b)	6,000			
Common stock, Company P	300,000						300,000
Common stock, Company S		100,000	(a)	80,000			20,000 M
Beginning retained earnings, Company P	140,000						140,000
Beginning retained earnings, Company S		50,000	(a)	40,000			10,000 M
Dividends declared and paid during 19A		(10,000)			(e)	8,000	(2,000)M
Net income, 19A (from above; not added across)	28,000	14,000					2,800 M 30,400
	523,000	179,000		146,800		146,800	575,200

M—Minority interest.

* The minority interest in the earnings of the subsidiary is unaffected by the consolidation procedures of the parent company. Thus, the minority interest in the earnings is $14,000 × 20% = $2,800. This amount is subtracted from consolidated income to derive the amount of consolidated income identifiable with the controlling interest. The two separate amounts then are carried down to the balance sheet section.

Explanation of eliminations:
(a) To eliminate the investment account against 80% of the owners' equity of the subsidiary and to allocate the difference between purchase price and book value to the appropriate accounts.
(b) To eliminate the intercompany debt.
(c) To record depreciation for one year on the asset increase resulting from the acquisition.
(d) To amortize goodwill recognized (one year).
(e) To eliminate intercompany revenue arising from dividends declared and paid by the subsidiary.

Exhibit 14–13 Consolidated financial statements (with minority interest)

COMPANY P and Its Subsidiary, COMPANY S
Consolidated Income Statement (purchase method)
For the Year Ended December 31, 19A

Sales revenue		$510,000
Cost of goods sold		279,000
Gross margin		231,000
Less:		
Expenses (not detailed)	$156,500	
Depreciation expense	14,900	
Amortization expense (goodwill)	400	
Income tax expense	26,000	197,800
Consolidated net income		33,200
Less: Minority interest in net income		2,800
Controlling interest in net income		$ 30,400

EPS ($30,400 ÷ 30,000 shares) = $1.013

COMPANY P and Its Subsidiary, COMPANY S
Consolidated Balance Sheet (purchase method)
At December 31, 19A

Assets

Current assets:		
Cash	$137,500	
Accounts receivable (net)	46,000	
Inventories	250,000	$433,500
Tangible operational assets:		
Plant and equipment (net)		134,100
Intangible operational assets:		
Goodwill (or excess of market value over cost of assets of subsidiary)		7,600
Total assets		$575,200

Liabilities

Current liabilities:		
Accounts payable		$ 74,000
Minority interest		30,800

Shareholders' Equity

Contributed capital:		
Common stock, par $10; 30,000 shares outstanding	$300,000	
Retained earnings	170,400	
Total		470,400
Total liabilities and shareholders' equity		$575,200

* $20,000 + $10,000 + $2,800 − $2,000 = $30,800.

IMPORTANT TERMS DEFINED IN THIS CHAPTER

Accounting Compatibility The operations of affiliated companies complement each other. *p. 798*

Consolidation The accounting process of combining financial statements from related companies into a single set of financial statements. *p. 798*

Control Presumed to exist when more than 50% of the voting shares of an entity is owned by one investor. *p. 798*

Goodwill The amount that was paid for the good reputation and customer appeal of an acquired company. *p. 806*

Minority Interest The proportionate share of both the earnings and the contributed capital of the subsidiary that is not "owned" by the parent. *p. 823*

Parent Company The company that has a significant investment in a subsidiary company. *p. 798*

Pooling of Interests An acquisition that is completed by exchanging parent company shares for subsidiary voting shares. *p. 800*

Purchase An acquisition which is completed by purchasing subsidiary company voting shares for cash. *p. 804*

Subsidiary The company that is owned by a parent company as evidenced by more than 50% of the voting shares. *p. 798*

QUESTIONS

Part A: Questions 1–11

1. What is a parent-subsidiary relationship?
2. Explain the basic concept underlying consolidated statements.
3. What two basic elements must be present before consolidated statements are appropriate?
4. The concept of consolidated statements relates only to reporting as opposed to preparing and posting journal entries in the ledger accounts. Explain.
5. What is pooling of interests?
6. What is a combination by purchase?
7. The investing corporation debits a long-term investment account when it acquires a controlling influence in another corporation. In the case of a pooling of interests, describe how to determine the amount that is debited to the investment account.
8. What are intercompany eliminations?
9. Explain why the investment account must be eliminated against shareholders' equity when consolidated statements are prepared.

10. Explain why the "book values" of the parent and subsidiary are aggregated on consolidated statements when there is a pooling of interests, but acquisition market values of the subsidiary assets are used when the combination is by purchase.

11. Why is goodwill not recognized in a pooling of interests? Why is it recognized in a combination by purchase?

Part B: Questions 12–18

12. Explain why additional depreciation expense usually must be recognized on consolidation when the combination was by purchase.

13. What is goodwill?

14. Explain why pooling of interests was more popular in the merger movement than combination by purchase.

15. Explain the basis for each of the following statements:
    a. Pooling of interests, given the same situation, reports a higher net income than combination by purchase.
    b. The cash position, other things being equal, usually is better when the combination is by pooling of interests than when the combination is by purchase.
    c. Pooling of interests, other things being equal, reports a higher amount of retained earnings than does combination by purchase.

16. What reason might have been used to justify the decision to make 40 years the maximum life over which goodwill can be amortized?

17. If a corner store has established an excellent reputation in a community, it would likely have above-ordinary income and therefore goodwill.

    Using the analogy of purchase and pooling, explain the apparent general rule as to when goodwill can be recognized?

18. Why might the accounting profession restrict the recognition of goodwill on the financial statements only to certain situations?

EXERCISES

Part A: Exercises 14–1 to 14–5

E14–1 **(Pair Definition with Terms)**
Match the following brief definitions with the terms by entering the appropriate letter in each space provided.

Term	Brief description
_____ (1) Subsidiary	A. Required because a parent and subsidiary are considered one economic entity.
_____ (2) Accounting compatibility	B. Ownership of voting shares provides more than significant influence.
_____ (3) Purchase	C. A requirement for consolidating financial statements when one company owns more than 50% of another company.
_____ (4) Minority interest	
_____ (5) Control	
_____ (6) Consolidation	

Term	Brief description
_____ (7) Pooling of interests	D. An amount whose "value" is never known except when a business is purchased.
_____ (8) Goodwill	E. Only comes into existence when there is less than 100% ownership by the parent company.
_____ (9) Parent company	F. The company that owns more than 50% of the outstanding voting shares of another corporation.
	G. This transaction often is not viewed as a purchase/sale transaction; therefore, the cost principle is not applied.
	H. In this transaction, the purchase of a controlling interest in another company is recorded under the cost principle.
	I. The company that is owned by another company.

E14–2 **(Preparation of a Consolidated Balance Sheet)**

On January 2, 19A, Company P acquired all of the outstanding voting shares of Company S by exchanging, on a share-for-share basis, its own unissued shares for Company S. Immediately after the acquisition of Company S, the separate balance sheets showed the following:

	Balances, January 2, 19A, immediately after acquisition	
	Company P	Company S
Cash	$ 38,000	$12,000
Receivable from Company S	7,000	
Inventory	35,000	18,000
Investment in Company S (100%)	60,000	
Operational assets (net of accumulated depreciation)	80,000	50,000
Total	$220,000	$80,000
Liabilities	$ 25,000	$13,000
Payable to Company P		7,000
Common stock (Company P, par $5) (Company S, par $5)	140,000	40,000
Contributed surplus from pooling of interests	20,000	
Retained earnings	35,000	20,000
Total	$220,000	$80,000

Required:

a. Is this a pooling of interests or a combination by purchase? Explain why.

b. Give the journal entry that was made by Company P to record the acquisition.

c. Prepare a consolidated balance sheet immediately after the acquisition.

d. Were the assets of the subsidiary added to those of the parent, in the consolidated balance sheet, at book value or at market value? Explain why.

e. What were the balances in the accounts of Company P immediately prior to the acquisition for (1) investment and (2) common stock? Were any other account balances for either Company P or Company S changed by the acquisition? Explain.

E14-3   **(Comparison of the Pooling and Purchase Methods)**
On January 1, 19A, Company P acquired 100% of the outstanding common stock of Company S. At date of acquisition, the balance sheet of Company S reflected the following book values (summarized):

Total assets (market value, $220,000)* . . .	$180,000
Total liabilities	30,000
Shareholders' equity:	
Common stock, par $10	100,000
Retained earnings	50,000

* One half subject to depreciation; 10-year remaining life and no residual value.

Two separate and independent cases are given below that indicate how Company P acquired 100% of the outstanding shares of Company S:

Case A—Exchanged two shares of its own common stock (par $1) for each share of Company S.

Case B—Paid $20 per share for the shares of Company S.

Required:
For each case, answer the following:

a. Was this a combination by pooling of interests or by purchase? Explain.

b. Give the journal entry that Company P should make to record the acquisition. If none, explain why.

c. Give the journal entry in the accounts of Company S to record the acquisition. If none, explain why.

d. Analyze the transaction to determine the amount of goodwill purchased. If no goodwill was purchased, explain why.

e. In preparing a consolidated balance sheet, should the subsidiary assets be included at book value or market value? Explain.

E14-4   **(Identification of the Appropriate Consolidation Method)**
On January 1, 19A, Company P purchased 100% of the outstanding voting shares of Company S in the open market for $70,000 cash. On that date (prior to the acquisition) the separate balance sheets (summarized) of the two companies reported the following book values:

	Prior to acquisition	
	Company P	**Company S**
Cash	$ 80,000	$18,000
Receivable from Company P		2,000
Operational assets (net)	80,000	60,000
Total	$160,000	$80,000
Liabilities	$ 28,000	$20,000
Payable to Company S	2,000	
Common stock:		
Company P, no par	100,000	
Company S, par $10		50,000
Retained earnings	30,000	10,000
Total	$160,000	$80,000

It was determined on date of acquisition that the market value of the operational assets of Company S was $66,000.

Required:

a. Was this a combination by pooling of interests or by purchase? Explain why.

b. Give the journal entry that should be made by Company P at date of acquisition. If none is required, explain why.

c. Give the journal entry that should be made by Company S at date of acquisition. If none is required, explain why.

d. Analyze the acquisition to determine the amount of goodwill purchased.

e. Should the assets of Company S be included on the consolidated balance sheet at book value or market value? Explain.

f. Prepare a consolidated balance sheet immediately after acquisition.

E14–5 **(Preparation of a Consolidated Balance Sheet after Acquisition)**
On January 4, 19A, Company P acquired all of the outstanding shares of Company S for $10 cash per share. At the date of acquisition, the balance sheet of Company S reflected the following:

Common stock, par $5 . . . $50,000
Retained earnings 30,000

Immediately after the acquisition, the balance sheets reflected the following:

	Balances, Jan. 4, 19A, immediately after acquisition	
	Company P	Company S
Cash	$ 13,000	$17,000
Receivable from Company P		3,000
Investment in Company S (100%), at cost	100,000	
Operational assets (net)	122,000	70,000*
Total	$235,000	$90,000
Liabilities	$ 22,000	$10,000
Payable to Company S	3,000	
Common stock, par $5	150,000	50,000
Retained earnings	60,000	30,000
Total	$235,000	$90,000

* Determined by Company P to have a market value of $78,000 at date of acquisition.

Required:

a. Was this a combination by pooling of interests or by purchase? Explain why.

b. Give the journal entry that should be made by Company P to record the acquisition.

c. Analyze the acquisition to determine the amount of goodwill purchased.

d. Should the assets of Company S be included on the consolidated balance sheet at book value or market value? Explain.

e. Prepare a consolidated balance sheet immediately after acquisition.

Part B: Exercises 14-6 to 14-7

E14-6 **(Completion of a Consolidation Worksheet)**
On January 1, 19A, Company P acquired all of the outstanding voting shares of Company S by exchanging one share of its own common stock for each share of Company S common stock. At the date of the exchange, the balance sheet of Company S showed the following:

Common stock, par $10 . . . $40,000
Retained earnings 10,000

One year after acquisition the two companies prepared their separate financial statements as shown on the following worksheet:

COMPANY P and Its Subsidiary, COMPANY S (100% owned)
Consolidated Balance Sheet and Income Statement
December 31, 19A

Items	Separate Statements Company P	Separate Statements Company S	Eliminations	Consolidated Statements
Income statement (for 19A):				
Sales revenue	96,000	42,000		
Revenue from investments	4,000			
Cost of goods sold	(60,000)	(25,000)		
Expenses (not detailed)	(17,000)	(10,000)		
Net income	23,000	7,000		
Balance sheet (at December 31, 19A):				
Cash	21,000	19,000		
Receivable from Company P		2,000		
Investment in Company S (100%)	50,000			
Operational assets (net)	59,000	47,000		
Total	130,000	68,000		
Liabilities	17,000	15,000		
Payable to Company S	2,000			
Common stock, Company P (par $10)	50,000			
Contributed surplus from pooling of interests	10,000			
Common stock, Company S (par $10)		40,000		
Beginning retained earnings, Company P	28,000			
Beginning retained earnings, Company S		10,000		
Dividend declared and paid, 19A; Company S		(4,000)		
Net income, 19A (from above)	23,000	7,000		
Total	130,000	68,000		

Required:

a. Give the journal entry that was made by Company P to record the pooling of interests on January 1, 19A.

b. Complete the Eliminations column in the above worksheet, then combine two sets of statements in the last column to develop the consolidated income statement and balance sheet. (Hint: Eliminate Revenue from Investments against Dividends Declared and Paid because this represents an intercompany transaction. The consolidated net income is $26,000.)

E14–7   (Analysis of a Consolidation Worksheet)

On January 1, 19A, Company P purchased all of the outstanding voting shares of Company S at $2.50 each. At that date the balance sheet of Company S reflected the following:

Common stock, par $1 . . . $20,000
Retained earnings 10,000

One year after acquisition each company prepared its own separate financial statements and Company P set up the following consolidation worksheet (partially completed):

Items	Separate Statements		Intercompany Eliminations		Consolidated Balances
	Company P	Company S	Debit	Credit	
Income statement (for 19A):					
Sales revenue	99,000	59,000			
Revenue from interests	6,000		(e) 6,000		
Expenses (not detailed)	(71,000)	(40,400)			
Depreciation expense .	(9,000)	(3,600)	(c) 1,200		
Amortization expense (goodwill)			(d) 400		
Net income	25,000	15,000			
Balance sheet (at December 31, 19A):					
Cash	16,000	6,000			
Receivable from Co. P		4,000		(b) 4,000	
Investment in Co. S	50,000			(a) 50,000	
Operational assets (net)	90,000	40,000*	(a) 12,000	(c) 1,200	140,800
Goodwill (amortize over 20 years)			(a) 8,000	(d) 400	
Totals	156,000	50,000			170,400
Liabilities	15,000	11,000			
Payable to Co. S	4,000		(b) 4,000		
Common stock, Co. P	80,000				
Common stock, Co. S		20,000	(a) 20,000		
Beginning retained earnings, Co. P	32,000				
Beginning retained earnings, Co. S		10,000	(a) 10,000		
Dividends declared and paid, Co. S, 19A.		(6,000)		(e) 6,000	
Net income, 19A (per above)	25,000†	15,000†			32,400†
Totals	156,000	50,000	61,600	61,600	

* Market value of the operational assets at acquisition was $12,000 above book value and their remaining useful life was 10 years.
† Carried down.

Required:

a. Give the journal entry made by Company P on January 1, 19A, to record the purchase of Company S shares.

b. Show how the $8,000 of goodwill was computed.

c. Complete the last column of the worksheet (note that under "Eliminations" debit/credit instead of +/− were used).

d. Give a brief explanation of eliminations (c), (d), and (e).

PROBLEMS

Part A: Problems 14-1 to 14-6

P14-1   **(Analysis of Acquisition and Preparation of a Consolidated Balance Sheet)**
During January 19A, Company P acquired all of the outstanding voting shares of Company S by exchanging one share of its own unissued voting common shares for two shares of Company S common stock. Immediately prior to the acquisition, the separate balance sheets of the two companies reflected the following:

	Balances immediately prior to acquisition	
	Company P	Company S
Cash	$200,000	$ 32,000
Receivable from Company P		3,000
Inventory	75,000	5,000
Operational assets (net of accumulated depreciation)	75,000	80,000
Total	$350,000	$120,000
Liabilities	$ 57,000	$ 30,000
Payable to Company S	3,000	
Common stock, Company P (par $4)	180,000	
Common stock, Company S (par $5)		50,000
Contributed surplus from pooling		
Retained earnings	110,000	40,000
Total	$350,000	$120,000

Additional data:
At the date of acquisition, the market price of Company S shares was $16 per share; there was no established market for Company P shares.

The operational assets of Company S were appraised independently at the date of acquisition at $130,000.

Required:
a. Is this a purchase or a pooling of interests? Explain why.
b. What account balances on each of the above balance sheets would be changed by the exchange of shares? List each account and amount.
c. Give the journal entry that should be made by each company to record the exchange; if no entry is required, explain why.
d. How much goodwill should be recognized? Why?
e. Prepare a consolidated balance sheet immediately after the acquisition.
f. Did you use any market values in solving the above requirements? Explain why.

P14-2   **(Analysis of Acquisition and Preparation of a Consolidated Balance Sheet)**
Assume the same facts given in P14-1 except that instead of an exchange of shares, Company P purchased from the shareholders 100% of the outstanding voting shares of Company S at a cash price of $160,000.

Required:

a. Is this a purchase or a pooling of interests? Explain why.

b. What account balances on each of the balance sheets would be changed by the purchase of the shares? List each account and amount.

c. Give the journal entry that should be made by each company to record the exchange; if no entry is required, explain why.

d. How much goodwill should be recognized? Why?

e. Prepare a consolidated balance sheet immediately after acquisition.

f. Did you use any market values in solving the above requirements? Explain why.

P14–3   (Analysis of Entry to Record Acquisition and Preparation of a Consolidated Balance Sheet)

On January 1, 19A, the separate balance sheets of two corporations showed the following:

	Balances, Jan. 1, 19A	
	Company P	Company S
Cash	$ 21,000	$ 9,000
Receivable from Company P . . .		4,000
Operational assets (net)	99,000	32,000
Total	$120,000	$45,000
Accounts payable	$ 16,000	$10,000
Payable to Company S	4,000	
Common stock, par $20	60,000	20,000
Retained earnings	40,000	15,000
Total	$120,000	$45,000

On January 3, 19A, Company P acquired all of the outstanding voting shares of Company S by exchanging one of its own shares for two shares of Company S.

Required:

a. Was this a combination by pooling of interests or by purchase? Explain why.

b. Company P made the following journal entry on its books, at the date of acquisition, to record the investment:

January 3, 19A:

Investment in Co. S	35,000	
Common stock		10,000
Contributed surplus from pooling of interests		25,000

Explain the basis for each of the three amounts in this entry.

c. Should any goodwill be recognized on the consolidated balance sheet? Explain why.

d. Prepare a consolidated balance sheet immediately after the acquisition.

P14–4   **(Analysis of Consolidation Method and Preparation of a Consolidated Balance Sheet)**

On January 2, 19A, Company P acquired all of the outstanding shares of Company S by exchanging its own shares for the shares of Company S. One share of Company P was exchanged for two shares of Company S. Immediately after the acquisition was recorded by Company P, the balance sheets showed the following:

	Balances, Jan. 2 19A, immediately	
	Company P	Company S
Cash	$ 38,000	$26,000
Receivable from Company S	6,000	
Inventory	30,000	10,000
Investment in Company S (100%)	70,000	
Operational assets (net)	90,000	50,000
Other assets	6,000	4,000
Total	$240,000	$90,000
Liabilities	$ 16,000	$14,000
Payable to Company P		6,000
Common stock, par $5	125,000	50,000
Contributed surplus from pooling of interests . . .	45,000	
Retained earnings	54,000	20,000
Total	$240,000	$90,000

Required:

a. Was this a combination by pooling of interests or by purchase? Explain why.

b. Give the journal entry that was made by Company P to record the acquisition on January 2, 19A. Explain the basis for each amount included in the entry.

c. Should the assets of Company S be included on the consolidated balance sheet at book value or market value? Explain.

d. Will any goodwill will be recognized on the consolidated balance sheet? Explain why.

e. Prepare a consolidated balance sheet immediately after acquisition.

P14–5   **(Analysis of Goodwill and Preparation of a Consolidated Balance Sheet)**
On January 5, 19A, Company P purchased all of the outstanding shares of Company S for $100,000 cash. Immediately after the acquisition the separate balance sheets of the two companies showed the following:

	Jan. 5, 19A, immediately after acquisition	
	Company P	Company S
Cash	$ 22,000	9,000
Accounts receivable (net)	14,000	6,000
Receivable from Company S	4,000	
Inventory	50,000	25,000
Investment in Company S (at cost) . . .	100,000	
Operational assets (net)	153,000	67,000
Other assets	7,000	3,000
Total	$350,000	$110,000
Accounts payable	$ 20,000	$ 16,000
Payable to Company P		4,000
Bonds payable	90,000	
Common stock, 36,000 no-par shares . .	188,000	60,000*
Retained earnings	52,000	30,000
Total	$350,000	$110,000

* 12,000 no-par shares.

The operational assets of Company S were estimated to have a market value at date of acquisition of $71,000.

Required:
a. Was this a combination by a pooling of interests or by purchase? Explain why.
b. Give the journal entry that Company P should make at the date of acquisition.
c. Analyze the acquisition to determine the amount of goodwill purchased.
d. Should the assets of Company S be included on the consolidated balance sheet at book value or market value? Explain.
e. Prepare a consolidated balance sheet immediately after acquisition.

P14–6   **(Analysis of an Acquisition and Completion of a Worksheet to Prepare a Consolidated Balance Sheet)**
On January 4, 19A, Company P purchased 100% of the outstanding common shares of Company S for $240,000 cash. Immediately after the acquisition, the separate balance sheets for the two companies were prepared as shown in the worksheet below.

COMPANY P and Its Subsidiary, COMPANY S
Consolidated Balance Sheet
January 4, 19A, Immediately after Acquisition

	Separate balance sheets			Consolidated balance sheet
	Company P	Company S	Eliminations	
Assets				
Cash	$ 80,000	$ 40,000	_____	_____
Accounts receivable (net)	26,000	19,000	_____	_____
Receivable from Company P		8,000	_____	_____
Inventories	170,000	80,000	_____	_____
Long-term investment, bonds,				
Z Company	15,000		_____	_____
Long-term investment,				
Company S	240,000		_____	_____
Land	12,000	3,000	_____	_____
Plant and equipment (net)	157,000	130,000	_____	_____
Goodwill			_____	_____
Total assets	$700,000	$280,000	_____	_____
Liabilities				
Accounts payable	$ 22,000	$ 40,000	_____	_____
Payable to Company S	8,000		_____	_____
Bonds payable, 5%	100,000	30,000	_____	_____
Shareholders' Equity				
Common stock, Company P	500,000		_____	_____
Common stock, Company S				
(par $10)		150,000	_____	_____
Retained earnings, Company P . . .	70,000		_____	_____
Retained earnings, Company S . . .		60,000	_____	_____
Total liabilities and shareholders'				
equity	$700,000	$280,000	_____	_____

It was determined at the date of acquisition that on the basis of a comparison of market value and book value, the assets as shown on the books of Company S should be adjusted as follows: (*a*) inventories should be reduced by $3,000, (*b*) plant and equipment should be increased to $148,000, and (*c*) land should be increased by $2,000.

Required:

a. Was this a combination by pooling of interests or by purchase? Explain why.

b. Give the journal entry that was made on the books of Company P to record the acquisition.

c. Analyze the acquisition transaction to determine the amount of goodwill purchased. Use data from the worksheet if needed.

d. At what amount will the assets of Company S be included on the consolidated balance sheet? Explain.

e. Complete the "Eliminations" column in the worksheet and then extend the amounts for the consolidated balance sheet.

Part B: Problems 14–7 to 14–11

P14–7   **(Analysis of Consolidation Elimination Entries and Completion of a Worksheet)**
On January 1, 19A, Company P acquired 100% of the outstanding shares of Company S
for $106,000 cash. At the date of acquisition the balance sheet of Company S showed the
following:

Total assets (including operational assets*)	115,000
Total liabilities	25,000
Common stock, par $10	60,000
Retained earnings	30,000

* Book value, $42,000; market value, $48,000 (20-year remaining life).

COMPANY P AND ITS SUBSIDIARY, COMPANY S
Consolidation Worksheet
Income Statement and Balance Sheet, December 31, 19A (100% ownership)

Items	Separate Statements Company P	Company S	Eliminations Debit		Credit		Consolidated Balances
Income statement:							
Sales revenue	80,000	47,000					
Revenue from investments	4,000		(e)	4,000			
Cost of goods sold	(45,000)	(25,000)					
Expenses (not detailed)	(15,000)	(10,000)					
Depreciation expense	(4,000)	(2,000)	(c)	300			
Amortization of goodwill			(d)	500			
Net income	20,000	10,000					
Balance sheet:							
Cash	15,000	10,000					
Accounts receivable (net)	19,000	9,000					
Receivable from Co. P		1,000			(b)	1,000	
Inventories	70,000	50,000					
Investment in Co. S (100%)	106,000				(a)	106,000	
Plant and equipment (net)	80,000	40,000	(a)	6,000	(c)	300	
Goodwill			(a)	10,000	(d)	500	
	290,000	110,000					
Accounts payable	26,000	14,000					
Payable to Co. S	1,000		(b)	1,000			
Common stock, Co. P	200,000						
Common stock, Co. S		60,000	(a)	60,000			
Beginning retained earnings, Co. P	50,000						
Beginning retained earnings, Co. S		30,000	(a)	30,000			
Dividends declared and paid during 19A, Co. P	(7,000)						
Dividends declared and paid during 19A, Co. S		(4,000)			(e)	4,000	
Net income (from above)	20,000	10,000					
	290,000	110,000	111,800		111,800		308,200

One year after acquisition the two companies prepared their December 31, 19A, financial statements. Company P developed the consolidation worksheet (partially completed) shown at the bottom of the preceding page.

Required:

a. Was this a purchase or pooling? Explain.

b. Give the journal entry made by each company to record the acquisition.

c. Complete the last column of the worksheet to develop the consolidated income statement and balance sheet.

d. How much goodwill was recognized? How was it computed?

e. Briefly explain each of the eliminations shown on the worksheet. Note that debit and credit rather than plus and minus were used in the Eliminations column.

P14–8   **(Comparison and Analysis of the Pooling of Interests and the Purchase Methods)** This problem presents the income statement and the balance sheet on a consolidated basis for Company P and its subsidiary, Company S, one year after acquisition, under two different assumptions: Case A—pooling of interests, and Case B—purchase. The two different assumptions are used so that we can compare and analyze the differences between the pooling and purchase methods.

On January 2, 19A, Company P acquired all of the outstanding common stock of Company S. At that date the shareholders' equity of Company S showed the following: Common stock, par $10, $50,000; and retained earnings, $20,000. The journal entry made by Company P to record the acquisition under each case was as follows:

Case A—Pooling of Interests method:

Investment in Company S (5,000 shares, 100%)	70,000	
Common stock, par $8		40,000
Contributed surplus from pooling		30,000

Case B—Purchase method:

Investment in Company S (5,000 shares, 100%)	80,000	
Cash		80,000

On January 2, 19A, the acquisition by purchase (Case B) was analyzed to determine the goodwill as follows:

Purchase price paid for 100% interest in Company S . . .	$80,000
Net assets purchased, value at market:	
Book value of net assets ($50,000 + $20,000 =	
$70,000 + increase of $2,000 in operational	
assets to market value)	72,000
Goodwill purchased	$ 8,000

For consolidated statement purposes the operational assets are being depreciated over 10 years remaining life, and the goodwill will be amortized over 20 years.

One year after acquisition, the two companies prepared separate income statements and balance sheets (December 31, 19A). These separate statements have been consolidated under each case as shown below.

Required:

a. Prepare a schedule of amounts that shows what items are different between each statement for Case A, compared with Case B.

b. Explain the reasons why net income is different under pooling of interests versus purchase. Use amounts from the two statements in your explanation and tell why they are different.

c. Explain why the cash balance is different between the two cases.

d. What was the balance in the account "Investment in Company S" in each case prior to its elimination? Explain.

e. Explain why the operational asset (net) amounts are different between the two cases.

f. Why is there a difference in goodwill between the two cases? Provide computations.

g. How much was eliminated for intercompany debt? Why was it eliminated?

h. What amount of "Common stock, Company S," was eliminated? Why was it eliminated?

i. Why was only $20,000 of the $30,000 of contributed surplus from pooling of interests eliminated?

j. Explain why the account "Contributed surplus in excess of par, $10,000," was not eliminated.

k. Explain why "Beginning retained earnings, Company S, $20,000," is shown under Case A (pooling) but not under Case B (purchase).

COMPANY P and Its Subsidiary, COMPANY S (100% owned)
Consolidated Income Statement and Balance Sheet
December 31, 19A

	Consolidated statements December 31, 19A	
	Pooling method (Case A)	Purchase method (Case B)
Income statement (for the year ended December 31, 19A):		
Sales revenue	$ 236,000	$ 236,000
Revenue from investments ($4,000, eliminated)		
Cost of goods sold	(112,000)	(112,000)
Expenses (not detailed to simplify)	(75,500)	(75,500)
Depreciation expense	(12,500)	(12,700)
Amortization expense (goodwill)		(400)
Net income	$ 36,000	$ 35,400
Balance sheet (at December 31, 19A):		
Assets		
Cash	$ 128,000	$ 48,000
Accounts receivable (net)	53,000	53,000
Receivable from Company S ($5,000, eliminated)		
Inventory	37,000	37,000
Investment in Company S (eliminated)		
Operational assets (net)	125,000	126,800
Goodwill		7,600
Total	$ 343,000	$ 272,400

COMPANY P and Its Subsidiary, COMPANY S (100% owned)
Consolidated Income Statement and Balance Sheet
December 31, 19A

	Consolidated statements December 31, 19A	
	Pooling method (Case A)	Purchase method (Case B)
Liabilities		
Current liabilities	$ 30,000	$ 30,000
Payable to Company P (eliminated)		
Bonds payable	50,000	50,000
Shareholders' Equity		
Common stock, Company P	140,000	100,000
Common stock, Company S (eliminated)		
Contributed surplus in excess of par	10,000	10,000
Contributed surplus from pooling of interests		
($20,000, eliminated)	10,000	
Beginning retained earnings, Company P	47,000	47,000
Beginning retained earnings, Company S	20,000	
Dividends declared and paid in 19A (eliminated)		
Net income, 19A (from income statement above)	36,000	35,400
Total	$ 343,000	$ 272,400

P14–9 **(Preparation of a Consolidated Balance Sheet and Income Statement Using a Worksheet—Based on Supplement 19A)**

On January 1, 19A, Company P purchased 100% of the outstanding shares of Company S for $98,000 cash. At that date the shareholders' equity section of the balance sheet of Company S showed the following:

Capital stock, $10 par, 5,000 shares outstanding . . . $50,000
Retained earnings 30,000
$80,000

At the date of acquisition, it was determined that the market values of certain assets of Company S, in comparison with the book values of those assets as shown on the balance sheet of Company S, should be shown by (*a*) decreasing inventories by $2,000 and (*b*) increasing equipment by $8,000.

It is now one year after acquisition, December 31, 19A, and each company has prepared the following separate financial statements (summarized):

	Company P	Company S
Balance sheet (at December 31, 19A):		
Cash	$ 52,000	$ 30,000
Accounts receivable (net)	31,000	10,000
Receivable from Company P		3,000
Inventories	60,000	70,000
Investment in Company S (at cost)	98,000	
Equipment	80,000	20,000
Other assets	9,000	17,000
	$ 330,000	$ 150,000
Accounts payable	$ 42,000	$ 30,000
Payable to Company S	3,000	
Bonds payable, 10%	70,000	30,000
Capital stock, $14,000 no-par shares	140,000	50,000 *
Beginning retained earnings	50,000	30,000
Dividends declared and paid during 19A	(10,000)	(5,000)
Net income, 19A (from income statement) . . .	35,000	15,000
	$ 330,000	$ 150,000
Income statement (for 19A):		
Sales revenue	$ 360,000	$ 140,000
Revenue from investments	5,000	
Cost of goods sold	(220,000)	(80,000)
Expenses (not detailed)	(106,000)	(44,000)
Depreciation expense	(4,000)	(1,000)
Net income	$ 35,000	$ 15,000

* 5,000 no-par shares.

Additional data during 19A:

1. Near the end of 19A, Company S declared and paid a cash dividend of $5,000.
2. The equipment is being depreciated on the basis of a 20-year remaining life (no residual value).
3. Goodwill is to be amortized over a 40-year period.

Required:

a. Give the journal entry that Company P should make to record the acquisition of the capital stock of Company S on January 1, 19A.
b. Analyze the acquisition of the shares to determine the purchased goodwill.
c. Prepare a consolidation worksheet (purchase method) for the year 19A as a basis for the 19A income statement and balance sheet. (Hint: Consolidated net income is $46,300.)
d. Prepare a consolidated income statement and balance sheet based on the data provided by the consolidation worksheet.

P14–10   (Preparation of a Consolidated Balance Sheet and Income Statement with Minority Interest—Based on Supplement 14B)

On January 1, 19A, Company P purchased 90% of outstanding voting shares of Company S for $100,000 cash. At the date of acquisition, the shareholders' equity accounts of Company S reflected the following: Capital Stock (par $10), $60,000; Contributed Surplus in Excess of Par, $10,000; and Retained Earnings, $20,000. At that date it was determined that the book value of the operational assets was $10,000 less than their market value.

It is now December 31, 19A, and each company has prepared the following separate financial statements (summarized):

	Company P	Company S
Balance sheet (at December 31, 19A):		
Cash	$ 23,000	$ 11,000
Accounts receivable (net)	57,000	13,000
Receivable from Company P		7,000
Inventories	110,000	24,000
Investment in Company S (at cost; 90% owned)	100,000	
Operational assets (net)	120,000	50,000
Other assets	6,000	5,000
	$ 416,000	$ 110,000
Accounts payable	$ 30,000	$ 8,000
Payable to Company S	7,000	
Bonds payable, 9%	80,000	10,000
Capital stock, $10 par	200,000	60,000
Contributed surplus in excess of par	4,000	10,000
Beginning retained earnings	80,000	20,000
Dividends declared and paid, 19A	(15,000)	(8,000)
Net income (from income statement)	30,000	10,000
	$ 416,000	$ 110,000
Income statement (for 19A):		
Sales revenue	$ 195,000	$ 75,000
Revenue from investments	7,200	
Cost of goods sold	(115,000)	(43,000)
Expenses (not detailed)	(52,200)	(19,500)
Depreciation expense	(5,000)	(2,500)
	$ 30,000	$ 10,000

Required:

a. Give the journal entry that Company P should make to record the acquisition of the shares of Company S.

b. Analyze the share purchase to determine the amount of goodwill purchased.

c. Prepare a consolidation worksheet (purchase method) for a balance sheet and income statement for 19A. Assume the operational assets of Company S have a 10-year remaining life and that any goodwill will be amortized over 20 years. (Hint: Consolidated net income is $31,400.)

d. Prepare an income statement and balance sheet for 19A based upon the data provided by the consolidation worksheet.

e. What is the minority interest claim to earnings and shareholders' equity at December 31, 19A?

P14–11 (Computer Spreadsheet Based on Supplement 14A)

Required:

a. Using a computer spreadsheet and the data from Problem P14–9, prepare a consolidation worksheet (purchase method) for 19A.

b. Modify the spreadsheet in Requirement (a) to reflect the consolidated results using the pooling method.

c. What happened to the net income when pooling was used?

CASES

C14-1   (Consolidation Practices)

In early September 1987, your firm's audit client, D Ltd. (D), acquired in separate transactions, an 80% interest in N Ltd. (N) and a 40% interest in K Ltd. (K). Prior to the acquisitions, both N and K were audited by other public accounting firms. D's bank and shareholders have requested that the audited consolidated financial statements of D for the year ended August 31, 1988 be available by the end of October. Your firm has been appointed the auditor of N but not of K.

All three companies are federally incorporated Canadian companies and have August 31 year-ends. They all manufacture small appliances but they do not compete with each other.

You are in charge of the audits of D and N. The partner has just received the preliminary consolidated financial statements attached (Exhibits 1 and 2) from the controller of D. He has given you the statements and requested that you provide him with a memorandum discussing the important financial accounting issues of D and its subsidiary and investee companies. The partner has requested that the memorandum also deal with any other issues which should also be brought to attention of D's management.

Exhibit 1

D LTD.
Preliminary Consolidated Balance Sheet
At August 31, 1988

Assets		Liabilities and Shareholders' Equity	
Current assets:		Current liabilities:	
Cash	$ 17,600	Bank loan payable	$ 3,000,000
Receivables	2,211,400	Accounts payable and	
Inventories		accrued liabilities	4,475,500
Finished goods at		Provision for warranty	505,500
standard cost	3,487,700		7,981,000
Raw materials at FIFO	1,062,300	Deferred income taxes	285,000
Work in process	480,000	Long-term debt of N Ltd.	
Prepaid expenses	16,000	in U.S. dollars	1,000,000
	7,275,000	Minority interest in	
Investment at K Ltd.,		N Ltd.	568,000
at equity	2,155,000	Shareholders' equity:	
Investments in other		Capital:	
companies, at cost	980,000	1,320,000 common	
Plant and equipment	14,988,500	shares	5,000,000
Less accumulated		10,000 preferred;	
depreciation	9,373,500	10%, convertible to	
	5,615,000	eight common	
Land	675,000	shares per $100	
	6,290,000	stated value	1,000,000
	$16,700,000	Retained earnings	866,000
			$16,700,000

Exhibit 1 *(concluded)*

D LTD.
Peliminary Consolidated Retained Earnings
For the Year Ended August 31, 1988

Balance, September 1, 1987	$ 618,000
Add net income	448,000
	1,066,000
Deduct dividends on preferred shares	200,000
Balance, August 31, 1988	$ 866,000

D LTD.
Preliminary Consolidated Income Statement
For the Year Ended August 31, 1988

Revenue	$14,567,800
Cost of goods sold	14,324,800
Gross profit	243,000
Selling and administrative expenses	1,345,000
	(1,102,000)
Income of K Ltd.	200,000
Loss before income taxes	(902,000)
Income tax recovery on loss	450,000
Loss before extraordinary item	(452,000)
Extraordinary gain on disposal of investments, less income taxes of $300,000 thereon	900,000
Net income	$ 448,000

D LTD.
Preliminary Consolidated Statement of Changes in
Financial Position
For the Year Ended August 31, 1988

Sources:	
From operations:	
Net income	$ 448,000
Add (deduct):	
Extraordinary item	(900,000)
Depreciation	1,317,300
Income of K Ltd.	(200,000)
	665,300
Dividend from K Ltd.	80,000
Issue of shares	4,000,000
Sale of investments	1,900,000
Other, net	165,000
Total sources of funds	$ 6,810,300
Uses:	
Acquisition of common shares of K Ltd. plus advance to K Ltd.	$ 2,450,000
Purchase of N Ltd.	4,000,000
Purchase of building and equipment	420,000
Increase in receivables	355,300
Decrease in working capital, excluding receivables	(415,000)
Total uses of funds	$ 6,810,300

Exhibit 2

N LTD.
Preliminary Balance Sheet
At August 31, 1988

Assets		Liabilities and Shareholders' Equity	
Current assets:		Current liabilities:	
Cash	$ 10,000	Accounts payable and	
Receivables	900,000	accrued liabilities	$1,220,000
Inventory, at standard		Income taxes recoverable	(18,500)
cost:		Provision for warranty	5,500
Finished goods	360,000		1,207,000
Prepaid expenses	5,000		
	1,275,000	Deferred income taxes	125,000
Fixed assets, at cost:		Long-term debt of	
Building, machinery, and		U.S. $1,000,000 due in	
equipment	7,638,000	10 equal yearly install-	
Less accumulated		ments of U.S. $100,000	
depreciation	4,331,000	commencing February	
	3,307,000	1989	1,000,000
Land	450,000	Shareholders' equity:	
	3,757,000	Common shares	1,000,000
Goodwill	60,000	Retained earnings	1,840,000
			2,840,000
Deferred research and			
development $150,000			
less $10,000 annual			
amortization to date	80,000		
	$5,172,000		$5,172,000

N LTD.
Preliminary Retained Earnings Statement
For the Year Ended August 31, 1988

Balance, September 1987	$1,850,000
Add net income	36,500
	1,886,500
Less dividends	46,500
Balance, August 31, 1988	$1,840,000

D acquired the 80 percent interest in N for $4,000,000, paid as follows:

1. $2,000,000 in cash.
2. 160,000 common shares of D recorded in the books of D at $2,000,000.

D acquired its 40% interest in K at a cost of $2,100,000 paid as follows:

1. $100,000 in cash.
2. 160 common shares of D recorded in the books of D at $2,000,000.

During the course of the audits of D and N the following information was obtained:

1. The book value of 80% of N's net assets at the date of acquisition was $2,280,000. D's management provided the following acquisition data:

Price paid in excess of the book value of the shares, at the date
of acquisition $1,720,000

Comprised of:
The excess of the current value of land over the book value . . . . $ 800,000
The excess of the current value of plant and equipment over the
book value   700,000
Adjustment for the 20% minority interest's share of the excess of the
current value of land, plant, and equipment over the book value . . . .   (300,000)
Goodwill of N written off . . . .   (48,000)
Deferred research and development expenditures written off . . . .   (72,000)
Pension liability not reduced (unfunded past service cost) . . . .   (200,000)
Unallocated excess   840,000
                                                                                $1,720,000

2. The price paid by D for its investment in K was 10% lower than 40% of the fair market value of K's net assets.

3. Five years ago, D purchased 100,000 shares of X Ltd. (X), being an 18% interest, at a cost of $780,000 and 50,000 shares of Y Ltd. (Y), being a 20% interest, at a cost of $200,000. On February 19, 1988, X declared a common stock dividend. At that date the additional shares to be received by D had a market value of $56,000. By the date of receipt of the shares in June 1985, the market value had dropped to $42,000.

4. The 20% minority shareholder in N owns a retail store which makes 30% of its purchases from N. On August 1, 1988, this shareholder leased equipment to N on a 10-year lease at $3,000 per month, with an option to renew for 5 years at $1,000 per month. At the end of the 10 years, N can purchase the asset for $40,000, or, at the end of the 15 years N can purchase the asset for $1.

5. During August 1988, K sold goods to D as follows:

Cost to K $100,000
Normal selling price . . . 125,000
Price paid by D 120,000

D had not sold these goods as of August 31, 1988.
N also sold goods to D in August 1988 and D had not sold them by August 31, 1988.

Cost to N . . . . $ 60,00
Normal selling price . . . 75,000
Price paid by D 85,000

6. For the year ended August 31, 1988, D's sales were $8,423,300 and N's sales were $6,144,500.

Required:
Prepare the memorandum requested by the partner.

(CICA Adapted)

C14–2   **(Comparison of the Pooling of Interests and the Purchase Methods)**

Some analysts believe that management would prefer to account for an acquisition under the pooling of interests method instead of the purchase method. Accounting rules do not permit management to select the method, but these analysts believe that management will structure the transaction so that it will be accounted for as a pooling. One of the alleged benefits of the pooling of interests method for management is that return on investment (net income/total assets) is usually higher under pooling. Why would you expect return on investment to be higher under pooling?

C14–3   **(Analysis of Consolidation Using an Actual Financial Statement)**

Refer to the financial statements of Consolidated-Bathurst given in Appendix B immediately preceding the Index.

Required:

a. What amount of 1987 sales revenue reported by the company is the result of transactions between companies in the consolidated group?

b. What portion of the total consolidated income was allocated to the minority interest in 1987?

c. Based on year-end investments, did the minority earn more than the equity investments of C-B?

d. Was any goodwill recorded as the result of the consolidation? If so, what amount?

e. Explain the nature of minority interest reported on the balance sheet. How is it related to the investment in equity companies?

STATEMENT OF CHANGES IN FINANCIAL POSITION

PURPOSE

Three basic statements are required for external reporting purposes—income statement, balance sheet, and statement of changes in financial position (abbreviated SCFP). This chapter will discuss the purpose of the SCFP and show how it is prepared. Two alternative methods for preparing the SCFP (the direct method and the indirect method) will be discussed.

The company identified on the facing page reports cash sources and cash uses on a two-year comparative basis.

LEARNING OBJECTIVES

1. Explain the purpose of the SCFP.
2. Identify the format and characteristics of the SCFP.
3. Classify cash flows from operating, investing, and financing activities.
4. Give examples of cash equivalents.
5. Compare the direct and indirect methods.
6. Prepare the SCFP using the direct method.
7. Prepare the SCFP using the indirect method.
8. Expand your accounting vocabulary by learning the "Important Terms Defined in This Chapter."
9. Apply the knowledge gained from this chapter.

ORGANIZATION

1. Overview of the statement of changes in financial position (SCFP).
2. Characteristics and format of the SCFP.
3. Comparison of the direct and indirect methods.
4. Preparation of the SCFP using the direct method.
5. Preparation of the SCFP using the indirect method.

Donohue Inc., and Subsidiary Companies

Year Ended December 31 (thousands of dollars)	1987	1986
CASH PROVIDED BY (USED IN):		
Operating Activities		
Net income for the year	$ 44,247	$ 24,473
Items not affecting cash		
Depreciation and depletion	34,351	33,114
Amorization of deferred exchange losses	2,037	3,368
Deferred income taxes	3,482	5,956
Minority shareholders' interest	28,793	18,307
Equity in the results of the associated company	—	1,160
	112,910	86,378
Changes in non-cash operating working capital balances	(31,631)	7,873
	81,279	94,251
Financial Activities		
Issue of common shares	227	1,777
Issue of subordinated notes to a minority shareholder of a subsidiary	21,070	—
Increase of long-term debt	16,581	113,200
Reimbursement of long-term debt	(31,153)	(41,520)
Dividends to shareholders of the Company	(11,284)	(11,227)
Dividends to minority shareholders of subsidiaries	(16,063)	(9,489)
Purchase of preferred shares	(154)	(125)
	(20,776)	52,616
Investment Activities		
Funds set aside to finance major capital projects	45,691	(41,321)
Additions to fixed assets	(33,209)	(25,098)
Construction in progress	(69,623)	(66,455)
Government grant	—	843
Investment tax credits	10,489	15,367
	(46,652)	(116,664)
Increase In Cash	13,851	30,203
Cash Position At Beginning Of Year	113,059	82,856
Cash Position At End Of Year	$126,910	$113,059

Cash position represents cash and term deposits less bank loans.

Overview of the Statement of Changes in Financial Position (SCFP)[1]

Many of us experience cash flow problems. Most businesses have this same problem from time to time. For example, a new business almost always starts with a cash flow problem which usually continues intermittently during the first five to seven years. These cash flow problems arise because the timing of cash inflows often lag the timing of cash needs. During periods of depressed economic activities, or because of ineffective planning, large businesses also may experience similar cash flow problems.

A major problem for investors, creditors, and other interested parties is that they need to realistically project the prospective (i.e., the future) cash flows of the business and hence project their own prospective cash flows.

The purpose of this chapter is to discuss the statement of changes in financial position (SCFP) that is designed to help investors, creditors, and others to project their own prospective net cash flows form investments in, and loans to, an enterprise.[2]

Purposes of the SCFP

The statement of changes in financial position (SCFP) is designed to help[3] investors, creditors, and other decision makers in two important ways:

a. To assess the **past performance** of the entity to generate, plan, and control the actual cash inflows and outflows.

b. To assess the entity's **probable future cash inflows, outflows, and net cash flows,** including its ability to meet future obligations and to pay dividends. This assessment should help the investor, or creditor, project a return on resources committed to the entity.

Consistent with the fundamental objective, the SCFP reports information concerning cash inflows and outflows of an entity classified as cash flows from: (1) operating activities, (2) investing activities, and (3) financing activities. Also, the statement reports any related investing and financing transactions that do not directly affect cash.

---

[1] Recent changes to the *CICA Handbook*, Section 1540, have proposed new titles for the SCFP such as cash flow statement of operating, financing, and investing activities, and statement of changes in cash resources. The traditional title given here is also retained to satisfy statutory requirements where necessary. For consistency SCFP will be used in this chapter.

[2] FASB, *Statement of Financial Accounting Concepts No. 1,* "Objectives of Financial Reporting by Business Enterprises" (Stamford, Conn., November 1978), states: "Since investors' and creditors' cash flows are related to enterprise cash flows, financial reporting should provide information to help investors, creditors, and others assess the amounts, timing, and uncertainty of prospective net cash inflows to the related enterprise."

[3] *CICA Handbook,* Section 1540.02, states specifically that the SCFP is intended to complement the other statements and should provide information different from other statements.

Exhibit 15–1 The basic format of an SCFP

UTEX Company

a. **Cash flows from operating activities:***
   Cash inflows (detailed) . . . . $ 60
   Cash outflows (detailed) 40

       Net cash inflow (outflow) from operating activities . . . . $ 20

b. **Cash flows from investing activities:**
   Cash inflows (detailed) 21
   Cash outflows (detailed) . . . . (30)

       Net cash inflow (outflow) from investing activities . . . . (9)

c. **Cash flows from financing activities:**
   Cash inflows (detailed) 88
   Cash outflows (detailed) . . . . (65)

       Net cash inflow (outflow) from financing activities 23

d. **Reconciliation of beginning and ending cash balance:**
   Net increase (decrease) in cash during the period 34

   Add: Beginning cash balance 42

   Ending Cash balance . . . . $ 76

* A popular alternative form of the operating activities category of the SCFP, termed the indirect method, would appear as follows:

        Net income $22
        Add (deduct) items needed to reconcile net
          income to net cash flows:
          Increase in receivables and inventory . . . (8)
          Depreciation expense 4
          Increase in payables 2
        Net cash flow from operating activities $20

Characteristics of the SCFP

The *CICA Handbook* specifies the basic format for the SCFP. An outline of this format with illustrative amounts is presented in Exhibit 15–1.

Classifications on the SCFP

To assure reasonably consistent terminology and comparability, the *Handbook* defines each major category included on the required SCFP. These definitions (with explanations) are as follows:

    a. **Cash flows from operating activities.** This classification reports both the cash inflows and cash outflows that are directly related to net income reported on the income statement. The usual cash flows under the classifications are:

Inflows—cash received from:	Outflows—cash paid for:
Customers.	Purchase of goods for resale.
Interest on receivables.	Interest on liabilities.
Dividends.	Income taxes.
Refunds from suppliers.	Salaries and wages.

A gain or loss on a nonoperating activity (e.g., the sale of excess equipment) may be "removed" from operating activities. The **full** cash effect is included in investing or financing activities, whichever is the dominant source.

The difference between the above inflows and outflows is called the **net cash inflow (outflow) from operating activities.** Typically, the net amount will be an inflow because revenues usually exceed outflows for expenses.

b. **Cash flows from investing activities.** This classification reports cash inflows and outflows that are related to the acquisition of productive facilities used by the company and other noncash assets. The **cash outflows** under this classification represent the "investments" of cash by the entity to acquire its noncash assets. The **cash inflows** under this classification occur only when cash is received back from the prior investments. Typical cash flows from investing activities are:

Inflows—cash received from:	Outflows—cash paid for:
Disposal of property and plant equipment.	Property, plant, and equipment.
Disposal of investments in securities.	Purchase of long-term investments.
Collection of a loan (excluding interest, which is an operating activity).	Lending to other parties.
Disposal of other assets used in productive activities (excluding inventories).	Other assets used in productive activities, such as a patent (excluding inventories, which are operating activities).

The difference between the above cash inflows and outflows is called **net cash inflow (outflow) from investing activities.**

c. **Cash flows from financing activities.** This classification represents both cash inflows and outflows that are related to *how cash was obtained* to finance the enterprise (including its operations). The *cash inflows* under this classification represent the financing activities used to obtain cash for the entity. The *cash outflows* occur only when cash is paid back to the owners and creditors for their prior cash-providing activities. Usual cash flows from financing activities are:

Inflows—cash received from:	Outflows—cash paid to:
Owners—issuing equity securities.	Owners for dividends and other distributions.
Creditors—borrowing on notes, mortgages, bonds, etc.	Owners for shares purchased by company.
	Payment of principal amounts borrowed (excluding interest, which is an operating expense).

The treatment of dividends is subject to differing views. Some feel it should be classified as a normal operating activity. Others suggest dividends require a separate classification. Typically, they are classified as a financing activity, the approach used in this chapter.

The difference between the above cash inflows and outflows is called **net cash inflow (outflow) from financing activities.**

   d. **Reconciling balances.** The change in cash should be reported together with a clear statement of what is classified as cash in the statement. The term **cash and its equivalents** is used as the basis for the SCFP. The components of cash and its equivalents will be discussed in the following section.

Cash and Cash Equivalents

CICA Handbook, Section 1540, requires that a SCFP explain the change during the period in **cash and cash equivalents.** Cash equivalents are defined as "temporary investments" and short-term borrowings. Cash plus temporary investments less short-term borrowings represent the pool of liquid resources readily available to the enterprise. Some judgment will be required in practice when the cash and its equivalents' pool is selected for the SCFP. Disclosure of the outcome of this decision is essential for the reader of the statement.

Comparison of the Direct and Indirect Methods

There are two alternative approaches for preparing the SCFP:

1. **Direct method** which reports the components of cash flows from operating activities as gross receipts and gross payments, such as total cash receipts from customers and total cash payments to employees. This method starts with revenues and expenses to compute net cash inflow (outflow) from operating activities. An example of a SCFP prepared under the direct method is shown in Exhibit 15–2.
2. **Indirect method** which reports only net changes in the cash flows from operating activities. This method adjusts net income to compute net cash inflow (outflow) from operating activities. An example of a SCFP prepared under the indirect method is shown in Exhibit 15–3.

Either method is acceptable.

Notice that the basic difference between the direct and indirect methods (Exhibits 15–2 and 15–3) is the way that **cash flows from operating activities** is reported (set boldface for emphasis). The two methods report the same net cash flow from each of the four classifications (A–D). Therefore, the basic difference is in the individual amounts that are shown within the classification, cash flows from operating activities.

Exhibit 15–2 Direct method—SCFP

UTEX COMPANY
Direct Method—SCFP
For the Year Ended, December 31, 19B
(in thousands)

a. **Operating activities:**
    Cash inflows:
        From customers $60
    Cash outflows:
        Payments to employees . . . . (18)
        Payments to suppliers . . . . (10)
        Administrative and selling expenses . . . . (12)
    Net cash inflow from operating activities **$20**

b. **Investing activities:**
    Cash inflows:
        From sale of plant assets   21
    Cash outflows:
        For acquisition of plant assets . . . . (30)
    Net cash outflow from investment activities . . . .   (9)

c. **Financing activities:**
    Cash inflows:
        From sale of common stock   48
        From long-term debt   40
    Cash outflows:
        For repayment of long-term debt (principal only) . . . . (46)
        For repurchase of common stock . . . . (8)
        For dividends . . . . (11)
    Net cash inflow from financing activities   23

d. Net increase (decrease) in cash during 19B   34
    Cash balance, January 1, 19B   42
    Cash balance at December 31, 19B $76

The **direct method** reports the gross cash flow amount for each revenue and expense. The direct method converts the accrual basis revenues and expenses reported on the income statement to the cash basis amounts reported on the SCFP. For example, an income statement might report revenue of $100,000 which included $75,000 cash collected from customers and $25,000 for credit sales (i.e., accounts receivable). Under the direct method, the SCFP would report cash collections from customers of $75,000.

In contrast, the **indirect method** starts with accrual basis net income and converts that amount to a cash basis. This means that under operating activities it reports only net income, changes in certain balance sheet accounts, and net cash flow from operating activities. Note, however, because the analysis begins with net income before extraordinary items, the SCFP "articulates" with the

Exhibit 15–3 Indirect method—SCFP

UTEX COMPANY
Indirect Method—SCFP
For the Year Ended, December 31, 19B
(in thousands)

a. **Operating activities:**

Net income (from the statement of income)		$22
Add (deduct) to reconcile net income to net cash inflow:		
Accounts receivable increase		(6)
Inventory increase		(2)
Depreciation expense		4
Salaries payable increase		2
Net cash inflow from operating activities		$20

b. **Investing activities:**

Cash inflows:		
From sale of plant assets	21	
Cash outflows:		
For acquisition of plant assets	(30)	
Net cash outflow from investment activities		(9)

c. **Financing activities:**

Cash inflows:		
From sale of common stock	48	
From long-term debt	40	
Cash outflows:		
For repayment of long-term debt (principal only)	(46)	
For repurchase of common stock	(8)	
For dividends	(11)	
Net cash inflow from financing activities		23

d.

Net increase (decrease) in cash during 19B		34
Cash balance, January 1, 19B		42
Cash balance at December 31, 19B		$76

income statement in the same general way the statement of retained earnings articulates with the income statement.

The remainder of this chapter discusses the direct and indirect methods. The **direct method** is discussed first because it is preferable for the following reasons:

1. It has much greater relevance for investors and creditors because it reports gross cash amounts for revenues and expenses rather than net conversion amounts.

2. It reports operations, investment, and financing activities consistently; that is, cash inflows and outflows by source under all three activities. The indirect method does this under investing and financing activities but not under operating activities.

3. It is easier to explain and understand.

Preparation of the SCFP—Direct Method

The SCFP cannot be prepared by using a trial balance, or with the worksheet that is often used to prepare the income statement and the balance sheet. We will discuss three approaches to develop the SCFP.

   a. **Schedule approach**—This approach involves a series of computations to "build up" a SCFP, piece by piece. This approach is useful primarily for very simple cases.

   b. **Spreadsheet approach** (discussed in Supplement 15A)—This approach uses a specifically designed spreadsheet that incorporates (1) summary cash flow entries for analytical purposes, (2) a complete SCFP, and (3) numerous internal checks of accuracy. This approach is widely used in practice.

   c. **T-account approach** (discussed in Supplement 15B)—This approach is typically used for instructional purposes. It provides a concise and efficient analysis of the problem that uses the analytical presentation of T-accounts to develop the information needed for the SCFP. Which of the three approaches one may wish to select depends on the complexity of the problem that uses the analytical presentation of T-accounts to develop the information needed for the SCFP. Which of the three approaches one may wish to select depends on the complexity of the problem and the purpose of the analysis. The schedule approach is usually more efficient but is more likely to result in errors in complex situations. The spreadsheet approach has more self-checking features but it is more time consuming. The T-account approach is a compromise between the other two.

The data needed to prepare a statement of cash flows are as follows:

   1. A complete income statement—used primarily in preparing cash flows from operating activities.

   2. Comparative balance sheets—used in preparing the cash flows from all activities—operating, investing, and financing.

   3. Analyses of selected accounts that reflect several different kinds of transactions and events. Individual account analyses usually are necessary because the total change amount in an account balance during the year often does not reveal the underlying nature of the cash flows.

Case data to illustrate the preparation of the SCFP are shown in Exhibit 15–4.

Schedule Approach to Develop a SCFP, Direct Method

The SCFP, direct method, for UTEX Company (Exhibit 15–2) can be developed using the schedule approach. This approach involves the following three steps:

Step 1.   Obtain an income statement and the comparative balance sheet as shown in Exhibit 15–4. Notice the net increase in the cash balance ($34). The change in the cash balance is the key check figure.

Exhibit 15–4 UTEX Company, current income statement and balance sheet (in thousands)

A. Income Statement for the Year Ended 12/31/19B:

Sales revenue	$66
Salaries expense	(20)
Cost of goods sold	(8)
Depreciation expense	(4)
Administrative and selling expenses (excluding salaries)	(12)
Net income	$22

B. Comparative Balance Sheets, 12/31/19B:

Items	12/31/19A	12/31/19B
Cash (no cash equivalents)	$ 42	$ 76
Accounts receivable	21	27
Inventory	10	12
Plant assets	82	81
Accumulated depreciation	(20)	(14)
Total assets	$135	$182
Salaries payable	$ 3	$ 5
Notes payable, long term	46	40
Common stock, no par	70	110
Retained earnings	16	27
Total liabilities and shareholders' equity	$135	$182

C. Analysis of Individual Accounts to Identify Cash Flows:*
1. Cash account—increase during 19B, $34.
2. Plant assets account:
   a. Purchased plant assets for cash, $30.
   b. Sold old plant assets for cash, $21; recorded as follows (at book value):

Cash	21
Accumulated depreciation	10
Plant assets	31

3. Long-term notes payable account:
   a. Borrowed cash, $40.
   b. Payments on note principle, $46.
4. Common stock account—repurchased 1,000 shares for $8 cash.
5. Statement of retained earnings:

Balance, 1/1/19B	$ 16
Net income for 19B	22
Cash dividend paid in cash at end of 19B	(11)
Balance, 12/31/19B	$ 27

6. Issued common stock for $48 cash.

* Source: Accounting records.

Step 2. Prepare three schedules to compute:

A—Net cash flow from operations.

B—Net cash flow from investing activities.

C—Net cash flow from financing activities.

Often the most demanding task is developing Schedule A (cash flows from operating activities). Schedule B (investing activities) and Schedule C (financing activities) are prepared by analyzing the change in each asset, liability, and equity account to identify the investing and financing cash inflows and outflows. The results of this analysis are shown in Exhibit 15–4, panel C.

Step 3.   Use the three schedules to prepare the formal SCFP (Exhibit 15–2).

The three schedules needed for UTEX Company are shown, with explanations, in Exhibit 15–5. In the following sections, we discuss the preparation of each major section of the SCFP. Exhibit 15–6 presents analytical journal entries that explain each of the calculations needed to prepare the schedules for the SCFP. Each entry is keyed to the schedule in Exhibit 15–5. Note that these entries are for analytical purposes only. They do not represent recording entries and, therefore, are not posted to the general ledger. They do not have to be used to prepare the schedule in Exhibit 15–5, but they may serve to assist in understanding the particular treatment of an item in the schedule.

Computing Net Cash Flow from Operating Activities

Under the direct method each major income statement category (i.e., revenues, gains, expenses, and losses) must be converted to a cash basis as shown in Exhibit 15–5, Schedule A. Accrual basis revenues and expenses often include **noncash** amounts. These noncash amounts cause changes in the balances of accounts receivable, inventories, and accounts payables. For example, if less cash is collected from customers than the amount of revenue recognized on the accrual basis, the balance of accounts receivable will increase. The formula under the direct method to convert amounts from the accrual basis to the cash basis for **all revenues** is:

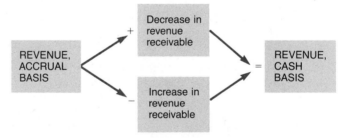

This formula applies to all revenues—service, interest, dividends, royalty, rent, and so on. Notice application of this formula to sales revenue in Exhibit 15–5, Schedule A.

The following cases illustrate use of this formula:

Case	Accounts Receivable	Revenue (accrual basis)	A	B	C	Cash basis (inflow)
A	No changes	$66	0			$66
B	Increase, $6*	66		−6		60
C	Decrease, $6	66			+6	72

* The case for UTEX Company.

Exhibit 15–5 Schedules to prepare the SCFP, direct method, UTEX Company

Schedule A. Computation of Net Cash Flow from Operating Activities (conversion of income statement from accrual to cash basis):

Items from IS and comparative balance sheet	Accrual basis	Cash Basis Change	Cash Basis Amount	Explanation
Sales revenue . . . . (a)	$66			Accounts receivable increase, $6;
Accounts receivable—increase (−); decrease (+)		−6 (g)	$60	subtracted because sales includes this amount of credit sales.
Deduct expenses:				
Salaries expense . . . . (b)	20			Salaries payable increase, $2;
Salaries payable—increase (−); decrease (+)		−2 (k)	18	subtracted because less cash was paid for salaries than was reported as salary expense on the income statement.
Cost of goods sold (c)	8			Inventory increase, $2; added
Inventory increase		+2 (h)	10	because more cash was paid to suppliers than was reported as cost of goods sold.
Administrative and selling expense (d)	12			No addition or subtraction because
Accrued expense payable— increase (−); decrease (+) .		0 (d)	12	there were no accruals; all of this expense was paid in cash this period.
Depreciation expense . . . . (e)	4	−4 (e)	0	Depreciation expense, $4; always subtracted because it is always a noncash expense.
Net income:				
Accrual basis . . . . (f)	$22			
Cash basis		(g)	$20	Reported on the SCFP (Exhibit 15–2).

Schedule B. Computation of Net Cash Flows from Investing Activities (analysis of comparative balance sheet and individual accounts):

Items from account analysis	Cash inflows (outflows)	Explanation
Purchase of plant assets	$(30) (j)	Payment in full for noncash asset.
Sale of plant assets	21 (i)	Total cash received from sale of noncash asset.
Net cash inflow (outflow) from investing activities	$(9) (g)	Reported on the SCFP (Exhibit 15–2).

Schedule C. Computation of Net Cash Flows from Financing Activities:

Items from account analysis	Cash inflows (outflows)	Explanation
Issuance of common stock	$ 48 (n)	From common stock account and cash records.
Borrowing on long-term note	40 (m)	From note payable account and cash records.
Payments on long-term note	(46) (l)	Same as above.
Repurchase of common stock	(8) (o)	From common stock account and cash records.
Paid cash dividend	(11) (p)	From statement of retained earnings and cash records.
Net cash inflow (outflow) from financing activities	$ 23 (q)	Reported on the SCFP (Exhibit 15–2).

Note: Letters key amounts presented in Exhibit 15–6.

Exhibit 15–6   Analytical entries for SCFP

Explanation of entries. It is preferable to start with the first item on the income statement and continue in order until all entries are made. The rationale for each entry is given below. For instructional convenience the following abbreviations are used: OA = operating activities, IA = investing activities, FA = financing activities. Also, entries are coded as a, b, c, and so on, for reference purposes. Notice that the entries track the original journal entries.

Enter the income statement amounts as follows:

Entry a—for revenues:
OA—From customers (a debit to cash flow)* 66
   Sales (to record)   66
* This amount is adjusted in entry g, for the effects of changes in accounts receivable.

Entry b—for expenses that require cash:
Salaries expense (to record) 28
   OA—Paid to employees (a credit to cash
      outflow)   28

Entry c—for expenses that require cash:
Cost of goods sold   8
   OA paid to suppliers (a credit to cash
      outflow)   8

Entry d—for expenses that require cash:
Administration and selling expenses (to record) 12
   OA—Paid to employees (a credit to cash
      outflow)*   12
* This amount is all cash because there were no related accruals or deferrals.

Entry e—for noncash expenses; no effect on cash flows:
Depreciation   4
   Accumulated depreciation (on the balance
      sheet)*   4
* Noncash expenses are not reported on SCFP; no OA, IA, or FA effects.

Entry f—to transfer net income to retained earnings:
Net income (i.e., income summary) 22
   Retained earnings*   22
* A noncash transfer, no OA, IA, or FA effects.

Explanation. After the above entries are made, all of the income statement accounts and some of the balance sheet accounts have been reconciled. Those reconciled can be "checked off" because no additional entries will be made to them. The entries "account" for the remaining changes in the account balances reported during the period on the balance sheet. Each entry which follows also classifies cash receipts and payments as either OA, IA, or FA. These entries can be made in any order. Therefore, we start with accounts receivable.

Entry g—to record the increase in accounts receivable:
Accounts receivable (check off; this account is now reconciled) 6
   OA—From customers*   6
* This adjusts the $66 sales revenue amount to the cash basis, $60. Notice that entry a could have been made to include the entry as follows:

From customers ($66 − $6) 60
Accounts receivable   6
   Sales   66

Exhibit 15–6 *(concluded)*

Entry *h*—to record the increase inventory:
Inventory 2
    OA—Paid to suppliers 2

Entry *i*—for the sale of old plant assets:
IA—Sale of plant assets* 21
Accumulated depreciation (to remove) 10
    Plant assets (to remove) 31
* This is the cash inflow; see analysis of plant assets, Exhibit 15–4.

Entry *j*—for the purchase of plant assets:
Plant assets 30
    IA—Purchase of plant assets* 30
* This is the cash outflow for this transaction; see analysis of plant assets.

Note: After entries *i* and *j* are made, plant assets and accumulated depreciation are fully reconciled.

Entry *k*—for increase in salaries payable:
OA—Paid to employees* 2
    Salaries payable (increase during year) 2
* This is an adjustment of salaries expense entry *b*, from the accrual to cash basis. Check off this account because it is reconciled. Notice that entry *b* could have been made to include this entry.

Entry *l*—for payment of long-term note payable:
Notes payable 46
    FA—payment on note* 46
* This is the cash outflow; see analysis of notes payable.

Entry *m*—for borrowing on note payable:
FA—borrowing on note payable* 40
    Notes payable 40
* This is the cash inflow; see analysis of notes payable; check off notes payable because it is now reconciled.

Entry *n*—for issuance of common stock:
FA—Issuance of common stock 48
    Common stock, no-par 48

Entry *o*—for repurchase of common shares:
Common shares* 8
    FA—repurchase of common shares 8
* Check off common shares because they are reconciled.

Entry *p*—for cash dividend paid:
Retained earnings* 11
    FA—payment of dividend 11
* Check off retained earnings because it is reconciled (i.e., $16 + $22 − 11 = $27).

Entry *q*—to enter, for balancing purposes only, the key check figure which is the change in cash during the period. ($20 − $9 + $23):
Cash 34
    Net increase during the year (to balance) 34
* This fully reconciles the beginning and ending cash balances ($42 + $34 = $76). Therefore, we can check off the cash account because no additional entries will be made to it.

Under accrual accounting, the total amount of an expense category may be different from the cash outflow associated with that activity. For example, the cash payments to employees may be less than the salary expense that is reported. In this case, the unpaid salary expense would cause salaries payable to increase.

The formula under the direct method, to convert from accrual basis to the cash basis for **all expenses** is:

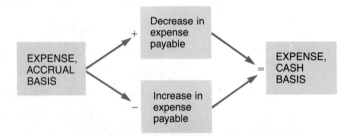

Notice application of this formula to salaries payable in Exhibit 15–5, Schedule A. The following cases illustrate use of this formula:

Case	Accounts Payable	Selling and Administrative Expense (accrual basis)	Change A	Change B	Change C	Cash basis (outflow)
A . . . . . No change*		$12	0			$12
B . . . . . Decrease, $2		12		+2		14
C . . . . . Increase, $2		12			−2	10

* The case for UTEX Company.

Noncash expenses such as bad debt expense and depreciation are reported on most income statements. Noncash expenses are not reflected on the SCFP because the entry to record those expenses does not involve a credit or debit to cash. The related cash outflow occurred when the asset was purchased, or when the debt incurred to buy it was paid.

Computing Net Cash Flow from Investing Activities

The analysis of individual accounts is provided in Exhibit 15–4, item C. The changes in the balances of all of the accounts listed on the balance sheet (Exhibit 15–4, item B) were analyzed to identify transactions that involved investing activities. In the case of UTEX Company, the analysis found that the only investing activities involved plant assets. Notice that the purchase of a plant asset and its subsequent sale are both *investing* activities; the former is a cash outflow and the latter is a cash inflow.

Computing Net Cash Flow from Financing Activities

The "financing" type of accounts for UTEX Company include notes payable, common stock, contributed surplus, if applicable, and retained earnings. An analysis of each of these accounts provided the data shown in Exhibit 15–4, item C. There are two cash inflows (issuance of common stock and borrowing) and three cash outflows (payments on debt, repurchase of common stock and cash dividends).

Preparation of the Formal SCFP

Step 3 involves preparing the SCFP based on the three schedules discussed above. The formal SCFP for UTEX Company is shown in Exhibit 15–2. The formal SCFP can be prepared using the three completed schedules (A, B, and C, in Exhibit 15–5) and the beginning and ending cash balances reported on the balance sheet.

Noncash Investing and Financing Activities

As discussed earlier in this chapter, certain transactions are important investing and financing activities but they do not have any cash flow effects. For example, the purchase of a $100,000 building with a $100,000 mortgage does not cause either the inflow or the outflow of cash. Neither does the issuance of a stock dividend.

Current accounting standards distinguish between two types of transactions when presenting an SCFP. One type is a transaction that if carefully separated would be equivalent to the receipt of cash for a financing activity and the payment of cash for investing, or vice versa. Such a transaction should be clearly reported in the SCFP as investing and financing. For example, the purchase of a building with a 100% mortgage would be disclosed as "Purchase of building by the issue of a mortgage, $100,000" under investing. In the financing category, the SCFP would show "Issue of mortgage for acquisition of building, $100,000." The second type of transaction is one that cannot be regarded as financing and investing. A stock dividend, a stock split, or a transfer to or from a retained earnings reserve is typically not disclosed in the SCFP.

Additional Problems When Preparing the SCFP

The previous discussion presented the basic concepts underlying the statement of cash flows, direct method. The UTEX Company case was developed to introduce you to the preparation of the SCFP. We will now discuss some of the additional issues that are usually encountered in developing a SCFP.

Converting Cost of Goods Sold to a Cash Basis

Cost of goods sold represents the cost of merchandise sold during the accounting period. It may be more or less than the amount of cash paid to suppliers during the period. In the case of UTEX Company (Exhibit 15–4), inventory increased from the beginning of the year to the end. Therefore, the company bought more merchandise from its suppliers than it sold to its customers. Because there is not an Accounts Payable balance on the balance sheet, UTEX Company paid more cash to its suppliers than the amount of cost of goods sold.

Typically, companies will owe their suppliers money (i.e., there will be an accounts payable balance reported on the balance sheet). In these cases, the calculation of cash payments to suppliers is somewhat more complex. In order to convert cost of goods sold, two accounts must be considered—inventory and accounts payable. Cash is required to increase inventory or to decrease accounts payable. Conversely, a decrease in inventory or an increase in accounts payable reduces cash requirements.

Cost of goods sold can be converted to a cash basis in the following manner:

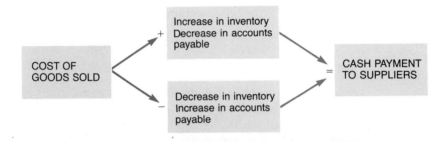

The following cases illustrate this conversion when the schedule approach is used to prepare the SCFP:

Case	Cost of goods sold (accrual basis)	Inventory change increase (decrease)	Accounts payable change increase (decrease)	Cash payments to suppliers
A	42	0	0	$42
B	42	7	0	49
C	42	(7)	0	35
D	42	0	4	38
E	42	0	(4)	46
F	42	7	(4)	53
G	42	(7)	4	31

If the spreadsheet approach is used, the entry to record the change in accounts payable is made in the same manner as the entry to record the change in inventory (illustrated in Exhibit 15–6).

Accounts Receivable and Allowance for Doubtful Accounts

The first item on the statement of cash flows, direct method, is cash inflow from revenues as shown in Exhibit 15–2 for UTEX Company (i.e., $60). The accrual basis revenue amounts reported on the income statement was converted to a cash basis as follows:

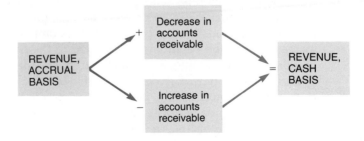

Our discussion did not consider the case when an **allowance for doubtful accounts** is needed, which is the usual case when some sales are on credit. The allowance for doubtful accounts is more complex because: (*a*) it is a contra account to accounts receivable, (*b*) it is increased for bad debt expense reported on the income statement, and (*c*) it is decreased when an uncollectible account is written off (and accounts receivable is credited for the same amount).

The accounts receivable and allowance for doubtful accounts involve three different items (entries) as follows: (*a*) the difference between total sales for the period and cash collected for sales (a cash entry), (*b*) recognition of bad debt expense (a noncash entry), and (*c*) the write-off of an uncollectible account (a noncash entry). A cash flow analysis must recognize changes due to each of these three items. This analysis can be made on the basis of net accounts receivable or gross amounts.

To illustrate, assume X Company's financial statements showed the following for 19B (in thousands):

Income statement:
    Sales revenue $60
    Bad debt expense 2
Balance sheet:
    Bad debt write-offs $1

	Balance 12/31/19A	Balance 2/31/19B	Increase (decrease)*
Accounts receivable	$ 10	$ 12	+$ 2
Allowance for doubtful accounts . . .	− 6	− 7	−1
Net	$ 4	$ 5	+$ 1

* Notice the algebraic implications.

The entry to record bad debt expense is similar to depreciation expense (entry *d*) because they are both noncash expenses. The bad debt expense entry on a spreadsheet is:

Bad debt expense   2
    Allowance for doubtful accounts   2

Notice that the entry to record bad debt expense does not include either a debit or credit to cash. Therefore, bad debt expense does not affect the SCFP under the direct method.

Now go one step further—what is the effect of a **bad debt write-off?** A write-off reduces both the allowance account and accounts receivable by the same amount. Since each account is reduced by the same amount, the difference between them remains the same as before. The write-off **does not affect cash flows.** Nevertheless, the write-off must be considered because it changes the ending balance of accounts receivable. This poses a problem because the change from the beginning to the ending balance of accounts receivable is used to compute cash flows.

The allowance for doubtful accounts contains only noncash amounts. Therefore, cash flow from sales revenue is computed under the schedule approach as:

$60 minus the $2 increase in accounts receivable minus bad debt write-offs of $1 = $57.

Alternatively, the cash flow from sales can be computed using only the net accounts receivable amounts and the bad debt expense. For example, sales revenue of $60 minus the $2 bad debt expense minus the increase in net receivables of $1 gives the cash flow of $57. Either of these two approaches will work but if the allowance for doubtful accounts or the write-offs are unavailable, the net receivable method will be the approach that must be used.

Gains and Losses

The income statement includes gains and losses from the sale of operational assets. The transactions that cause gains and losses should be classified on the SCFP as investing, or financing activities depending on their dominant characteristics. Operating activities typically generate revenues and expenses even though they are sometimes termed gains and losses in "loose" discussion. For example, if the sale of a productive asset (e.g., a delivery truck) produced a gain, it would be classified as an investing activity.

The gain or loss associated with a transaction standing alone does not reflect the complete cash flows caused by the transaction. For example, consider the following entry for Y Corporation to record the disposal of a delivery truck:

Cash	8,000	
Accumulated depreciation	4,000	
Operational assets		10,000
Gain on disposal		2,000

The inflow of cash was $8,000, but the reported gain was only $2,000. This transaction should be reported on the SCFP as an investing activity with a cash inflow of $8,000.

To prepare the SCFP, the gain of $2,000 must be removed from operating activities (i.e., net income) and the full $8,000 must be shown in the investing activities section of the statement. If the $2,000 was not removed from the operating activities section of the SCFP, it would be "counted twice" when the $8,000 was reported in the Investing Activity section. If we avoided the double-counting by only reporting $6,000 cash inflow from investing activities, we would misstate the actual effects of the transaction.

When a loss is reported on the income statement, it must also be removed when preparing the SCFP. Consider the following entry for Y Corporation to record the sale of a machine:

Cash	$25,000	
Accumulated depreciation	15,000	
Loss	5,000	
Machine		$45,000

To prepare the SCFP the loss of $5,000 must be removed from operating activities and $25,000 must be shown in the investing activities section of the statement.

Disclosure Requirements under the Direct Method

The SCFP direct method has the following disclosure requirements:

1. Disclose separately the noncash investing and financing activities.
2. Disclose the policy for determining which items are treated as cash equivalents.
3. Reconcile net income with net cash inflow (outflow) from operating activities.

The information contained in the reconciliation is similar to the information reported under the indirect method which is discussed next.

Preparation of the SCFP—Indirect Method

The indirect method of reporting cash flows has been used to some extent for more than four decades. It continues to be an acceptable and popular alternative to the direct method. Recall from Exhibits 15–2 and 15–3 that it differs from the direct method in a very important way. For operating activities, instead of reporting cash inflows from individual revenues and outflows for individual expenses, it starts with net income and reconciles net income with net cash flows from operating activities.

The direct and indirect methods require the same basic data and the same underlying concepts. Our discussion of the preparation of the SCFP under the indirect method is based on the data shown in Exhibit 15–4.

Schedule Approach

This approach involves the development of three schedules to compute net cash flow from operating, investing, and financing activities.

The adjustments used to convert accrual income to cash flow from operations are varied. Although careful analysis is needed, the following table is useful.

Item	Plus and minus adjustments to reconcile net income with net cash flow from operating activities	
	When item increases	When item decreases
Accounts receivable (trade) (net of allowance for doubtful accounts)	−	+
Accounts payable (trade)	+	−
Accrued liability and unearned revenue	+	−
Prepaid asset and accrued revenue	−	+
Inventory	−	+
Depreciation, depletion, and amortization	+	
Amortization of discount and bonds payable	+	
Amortization of premium and bonds payable	−	
Amortization of discount on bond investment	−	
Amortization of premium on bond investment	+	
Gains on the income statement	−	
Losses on the income statement	+	

Exhibit 15–7   Schedules to prepare the SCFP, indirect method, UTEX Company

Schedule A.   Computation of Net Cash Flow from Operating Activities (conversion of net income to net cash flow):

Items (see Exhibit 15–4)	Amount	Explanation
Net income, accrual basis	$ 22	From income statement.
Add (subtract) to convert to cash basis:		
Accounts receivable net of allowance for		
doubtful accounts, increase	−6 (g)	Subtract because cash inflow from sales trans- actions is less than accrual basis revenues.
Salaries payable increase	+2 (k)	Add because cash payments to employees are less than accrual basis salary expense.
Inventory increase	−2 (h)	Subtract because cash payments to suppliers are more than accrual basis of cost of goods sold.
Depreciation expense	+4 (e)	Add because depreciation expense is a non- cash expense.
Net cash inflow from operating		
activities	$ 20 (g)	Reported on the SCFP (Exhibit 15–3).

Schedule B: Computation of Net Cash Flows from Investing Activities (analysis of comparative SCFP and individual accounts):

Items from balance sheet and accounts analysis	Cash inflows (outflows)	Explanation
Purchase of plant assets	$(30) (j)	Payment in full for noncash asset.
Sale of plant assets	21 (i)	Total cash received from sale of noncash asset.
Net cash inflow (outflow) from investing		
activities	$(9) (q)	Reported on the SCFP (Exhibit 15–3).

Schedule C.   Computation of Net Cash Flows from Financing Activities:

Items from balance sheet and account analysis	Cash inflows (outflows)	Explanation
Issuance of common stock	$ 48 (n)	From common stock account and cash records.
Borrowing on long-term note	40 (m)	From note payable account and cash records.
Payments on long-term note	(46) (l)	Same as above.
Repurchase of common stock	(8) (o)	From common stock account and cash records.
Paid cash dividend	(11) (p)	From statement of retained earnings and cash records.
Net cash inflow (outflow)		
from financing activities	$ 23 (q)	Reported on the SCFP (Exhibit 15–3).

Note: Letters key amounts to analytical entries presented in Exhibit 15–6.

Exhibit 15-7 shows the three schedules that are used to prepare the SCFP with explanations. Notice that Schedules B and C are identical with those prepared using the direct method (Exhibit 15-5).

Accounting for bad debt expense in the computation of cash flow from operating activities is simpler in the indirect approach than it was under the direct approach. Recall that if the change in accounts receivable was computed net of the allowance for doubtful accounts, the calculation of revenue cash flows was as follows:

Sales, $60 − Increase in net accounts receivable, $1
  − Bad debt expense, $2
  = $57, cash flow from sales

Using the indirect approach, we begin with net income; namely, Sales $60 less Bad debt expense, $2 or $58. Therefore, if the increase in net accounts receivable is inserted in the reconciliation, −$1, the correct answer emerges, $57. Thus, accounts receivable should be treated as a net balance after the allowance for doubtful accounts is deducted. Such a treatment will permit write-offs and bad debt expense to be ignored when computing cash flows from operations using the indirect approach.

SUMMARY OF CHAPTER

The statement of changes in financial position is one of the four required financial statements. Although it has been used to some extent for several decades, *CICA Handbook*, Section 1540, established the requirements for the SCFP and prescribed a specific format.

The primary purpose of the new SCFP is to provide cash flow information in a manner that maximizes its usefulness to investors, creditors, and others in projecting future cash flows related to the enterprise.

Two different methods for reporting cash flows are permitted. They are called the direct and indirect methods. These alternative methods differ only in respect to cash flow from operating activities. Investing and financing activities are reported in exactly the same way under both methods. The direct method reports the cash inflows and outflows from the main classifications of revenues and expenses. In contrast, the indirect method reports operating activities by showing a reconciliation of net income with net cash flow from operating activities.

These approaches are available for developing the SCFP—the schedule approach, the spreadsheet approach, and the T-account approach. Both the spreadsheet approach and the T-account approach are detailed in Supplements 15A and 15B.

CHAPTER SUPPLEMENT 15A

Spreadsheet Approach to Develop a SCFP

Direct Method. The use of a spreadsheet to develop the SCFP often is more efficient than the schedule approach. The primary advantages of the spreadsheet approach are that it: (*a*) brings together all of the data that are needed; (*b*) is an organized approach that ties together all of the classifications on the SCFP; (*c*) develops the analysis in the familiar debit = credit format; and (*d*) provides continuing proofs of accuracy. Sometimes the spreadsheet is viewed as more cumbersome compared with the schedule approach but this comparison usually overlooks the advantages of using a spreadsheet when complex problems must be solved.

Exhibit 15–8 shows a completed spreadsheet for UTEX Company (based on the data given in Exhibit 15–4). Notice the following features: (*a*) it starts with the income statement and balance sheet, (*b*) it analyzes all changes between the

Exhibit 15–8 Spreadsheet to prepare the SCFP, direct method, UTEX Company, December 31, 19B (in thousands)

Items from financial statements	Beginning balances, 1/1/19A	Analysis of changes		Ending balances, 12/31/19B
		Debit	Credit	
Phase A—Analysis of income statement:				
Revenues:				
Sales	$-0-		(*a*) 66	$-0-
Expenses:				
Salaries	-0-	(*b*) 20		-0-
Cost of goods sold	-0-	(*c*) 8		-0-
Depreciation	-0-	(*d*) 4		-0-
Administrative and selling (including interest)	-0-	(*e*) 12		-0-
Net income (to retained earnings)	$-0-	(*f*) 22		$-0-
Phase B—Analysis of balance sheet:				
Cash	$ 42	(*q*) 34		$ 76
Accounts receivable	21	(*g*) 6		27
Inventory	10	(*h*) 2		12
Plant assets (analysis needed)	82	(*j*) 30	(*i*) 31	81
Accumulated depreciation	(20)	(*i*) 10	(*d*) 4	(14)
Total assets	$135			$182
Salaries payable	$ 3		(*k*) 2	$ 5
Notes payable, long term (needed analysis)	46	(*l*) 46	(*m*) 40	40
Common stock, no par	70	(*o*) 8	(*n*) 48	110
Retained earnings	16	(*p*) 11	(*f*) 22	27
Total liabilities and shareholders' equity	$135	$213	$213	$182

Exhibit 15–8 *(concluded)*

	Inflows	Outflows	Subtotals
Statement of cash flows and (outflows):			
Cash flows from operating activities:			
From customers—sales	(a) $ 66		$ 60
Accounts receivable increase		(g) $ 6	
Paid to employees—salaries		(b) 20	
Salaries payable increase	(k) 2		(40)
Paid to suppliers—cost of goods sold		(c) 8	20
Inventory increase		(h) 2	
Administrative and selling expense		(e) 12	
Cash flows from investing activities:			
Sale of plant assets	(i) 21		(9)
Purchase of plant assets		(j) 30	
Cash flows from financing activities:			
Issuance of common stock	(n) 48		
Borrowing on long-term notes	(m) 40		
Payments on long-term notes		(l) 46	23
Repurchase of common stock		(o) 8	
Paid cash dividend		(p) 11	
Net increase (decrease) during the year*		(q) 34	
Totals (to verify)	$177	$177	$ 34

* must agree with balance sheet.
Note: Letter keys are to journal entries displayed in Exhibit 15–6.

beginning and ending balances by using a series of straightforward Debit = Credit entries, (c) it provides all of the information for the SCFP, and (d) it balances throughout.

How to Prepare a Spreadsheet for the SCFP, Direct Method. The SCFP spreadsheet is easy to prepare by using an organized approach as follows:

Step 1. Set up the five money columns with the standard headings as shown in Exhibit 15–8.

Step 2. Copy the income statement (amounts in the two middle columns) and the balance sheet (amounts in the first and last money columns) exactly as shown in Exhibit 15–8.

Step 3. Immediately below the income statement and the balance sheet data, write the following side captions (leaving adequate space below each of the captions): statement of cash inflows (outflows); cash flows from operating activities; cash flows from investing activities; cash flows from financing activities; net increase (decrease) during the year and totals.

Step 4. Make debit = credit analytical entries under the two "Analysis of changes" columns. The spreadsheet is complete when the changes between the beginning and ending balances on each line are accounted for by the analytical entries.

Explanation of spreadsheet entries. It is preferable to start with the first item on the income statement and continue in order until all entries are made. The rationale for each entry is given in Exhibit 15–6. The entries on the worksheet are coded as *a, b, c,* and so on, for reference purposes. Notice that the spreadsheet entries track the original journal entries.

After entries *a* through *f* are made, all of the income statement accounts and some of the balance sheet accounts have been reconciled. Those reconciled can be "checked off" because no additional entries will be made to them. Spreadsheet entries "account" for the remaining changes in the account balances reported during the period on the balance sheet. Each entry which follows also classifies cash receipts and payments as either OA, IA, or FA. These spreadsheet entries can be made in any order; however, for instructional convenience they follow the worksheet order. Therefore, we start with accounts receivable. (See Exhibit 15–6.)

The keys entries complete the spreadsheet analysis because all accounts are reconciled. Finally, sum the two analysis columns to verify that debits = credits. Prepare the SCFP by using only the bottom part of the spreadsheet (see Exhibit 15–2). Notice that the subtotals in the lower right column of the spreadsheet tie in directly with the SCFP.

Indirect Method. When the indirect method is used, the spreadsheet does not include the income statement because the individual revenues and expenses are not analyzed to determine their respective cash flows. Instead net income is reconciled with net cash flow from operating activities. This means that the first analysis on the spreadsheet starts with net income and computes the changes in various balance sheet accounts that reconcile net income and cash flows from operating activities. It follows the pattern shown in the schedule approach (Exhibit 15–5, Schedule A). Exhibit 15–9 shows the spreadsheet for the indirect method. The remaining parts of the analysis—cash flows from operating and financing activities are the same as when the direct method is used (Exhibit 15–8).

Explanation of spreadsheet entries shown in Exhibit 15–9 using the indirect method are given below. They reconcile for all **noncash and other cash changes** that affected the net income.

Entry *a*—for net income:

Net income 22

    Retained earnings 22

    This entry is used to start the reconciliation; net income is shown as an inflow to be reconciled by the noncash reconciling entries. The credit to retained earnings reflects the effects of the original closing entry. This is the starting point for the reconciliation.

Entry *b*—for the increase in accounts receivable:

Accounts receivable 6

    Reconciling amount (deduct from net income) 6

    This entry reconciles the change in accounts receivable during the period with

Exhibit 15–9 Spreadsheet to prepare SCFP, indirect method, UTEX Company, December 31, 19B (in thousands)

Items from balance sheet	Beginning balance 1/1/19B	Analysis Debit	Analysis Credit	Ending balance 12/31/19B
Cash	$42	(*m*) 34		$ 76
Accounts receivable net of allowance for doubtful accounts	21	(*b*) 6		27
Inventory	10	(*d*) 2		12
Plant assets	82	(*g*) 30	(*f*) 31	81
Accumulated depreciation	(20)	(*f*) 10	(*e*) 4	(14)
Salaries payable	(3)		(*c*) 2	(5)
Notes payable, long term	(46)	(*j*) 46	(*c*) 40	(40)
Common stock, no par	(70)	(*k*) 8	(*h*) 48	(110)
Retained earnings	(16)	(*l*) 11	(*a*) 22	(27)
	$–0–	$147	$147	$–0–

		Inflows	Outflows	Subtotals
Statement of Cash Inflows and (Outflows):				
Reconciliation of net income to cash flow				
from operating activities:				
Net income		(*a*) $ 22		
Accounts receivable increase			(*b*) $ 6	
Salaries payable increase		(*c*) 2		
Inventory increase			(*d*) 2	
Depreciation expense		(*e*) 4		$ 20
Cash flows from investing activities:				
Sale of plant assets		(*f*) 21		
Purchase of plant assets			(*g*) 30	(9)
Cash flows from financing activities:				
Issuance of common stock		(*h*) 48		
Borrowing on long-term notes		(*c*) 40		
Payments on long-term notes			(*j*) 46	
Repurchase of common stock			(*k*) 8	
Paid cash dividend			(*l*) 11	23
Net increase (decrease) during the year			(*m*) 34	
Totals		$137	$137	$ 34

net income. It is deducted from net income because cash collections from customers were less than sales revenue.

Entry *c*—for salaries payable increase:

Reconciling amount 2

  Salaries payable   2

This entry reconciles the change in salaries payable with net income. It is added to net income because payments to employees were less than the accrual basis salary expense.

Entry *d*—for inventory increase:

Inventory 2

    Reconciling amount (deduct from net income) 2

Deduct because cash outflow for inventory was more than accrual basis
inventory included in cost of goods sold.

Entry *e*—for depreciation expense:

Reconciling amount 4

    Accumulated depreciation 4

Depreciation expense is a noncash expense. It is added back to net income
because this type of expense does not cause a cash outflow when it is
recorded.

Entry *f*—for the sale of old plant assets:

Investing activities 21

Accumulated depreciation (to remove) 10

    Plant assets (to remove) 31

This is the cash inflow; see analysis of plant assets, Exhibit 15–4.

Entry *g*—for the purchase of plant assets:

Plant assets 30

    Investing activities 30

This is the cash outflow for this transaction; see analysis of plant assets.

Entry *h*—for issue of common stock:

Financing activities 48

    Common stock, no par 48

This entry recognizes the issue of common stock which is a financing activity.
It is a cash inflow.

Entry *i*—for borrowing on notes payable:

Financing activities 40

    Notes payable 40

This is the cash inflow; see analysis of notes payable (Exhibit 15–4).

Entry *j*—for payment of long-term notes payable:

Notes payable 46

    Financing activities 46

This is the cash outflow; see analysis of notes payable.

Entry *k*—for repurchase of common stock:

Common stock 8

    Financing activities 8

This entry recognizes a cash outflow related to a financing activity. See
analysis of common stock (Exhibit 15–4).

Entry *l*—for payment of cash dividends:

Retained earnings 11

    Financing activities 11

This is a cash outflow that is associated with a financing activity. See analysis
of retained earnings.

Entry *m*—for balancing purposes:

Cash 34

    Net increase during the year 34

The net increase or decrease reported on the SCFP is the same as the change
in the cash balance during the year.

The preceding entries complete the spreadsheet analysis because all accounts are reconciled. The accuracy of the analysis can be checked by summing the two analysis columns to verify that debits = credits. The formal SCFP can be prepared directly from the spreadsheet (Exhibit 15–3).

Disclosure Requirements under the Indirect Method.   The SCFP, indirect method has seven disclosure requirements as follows:

1. Separately disclose the noncash investing and financing activities.
2. Disclose the policy for determining which items are treated as cash equivalents.
3. Reconciliation of net income with net cash inflow (outflow) from operating activities unless included in the SCFP.
4. Changes during the period in receivables, inventory, and accounts payable.
5. Clear identification of all reconciling items.

CHAPTER SUPPLEMENT 15B

T-Account Approach to SCFP

The SCFP can be prepared by using (1) a direct analysis, (2) spreadsheet analysis, or (3) a T-account analysis. The T-account analysis is used for instructional purposes, while the spreadsheet analysis is used in practice and in cases that are complex and have extensive data. The direct and spreadsheet analyses were illustrated earlier in this chapter.

This supplement presents a T-account analysis using the cash basis. The UTEX Company case given in the chapter also is used in this supplement. The T-account analysis presented in this supplement parallels the spreadsheet analysis in all ways except format. Each account is analyzed in a Debits = Credits manner, and the **analytical entries are identical** to those used in the spreadsheet analysis.

The T-account analysis to develop the SCFP, cash basis, begins by setting up **separate T-accounts for each noncash** account reported on the comparative balance sheets and then entering in each account the net change (NC) in the account balance from the beginning, and ending balance sheets (this is equivalent to Part A of the spreadsheet). Also, three T-accounts are set up to account for sources and uses of cash. These T-accounts are labeled "from normal operations," "financing," and "investing." In these three accounts, Debit = Sources and Credits = Uses. Next, the **analytical entries** are entered in the T-accounts. These entries are **identical** to those that would be entered in the spreadsheet analysis (Exhibit 15–9). The T-account analysis is shown in Exhibit 15–10.

Exhibit 15–10   UTEX Company: SCFP—cash basis: T-accounts analysis

Accounts Receivable			Inventory			Plant		
Beg. bal.	21		Beg. bal.	10		Beg. bal.	82	(f) 31
(b)	6		(d)	2		(g)	30	
End bal.	27		End bal.	12		End bal.	81	

Accumulated Depreciation			Salaries Payable			Note Payable, L. T.		
(g)	10	20 Beg. bal.			3 Beg. bal.	(j)	46	46 Beg. bal.
		(e) 4 Depr. exp.			(c) 2			(c) 40
		14 End. bal.			5 End. bal.			40 End. bal.

Common stock			Retained Earnings		
(k)	8	70 Beg. bal.	(e)	11	16 Beg. bal.
		(h) 48 Issue			(a) 22 Net inc.
		com.			
		110 End bal.			27 End bal.

Sources	From Normal Operations		Uses
(a) Net income	22	(b) 6	Increase in Acc. Receiv. bal.
(e) Depr. exp.	4	(d) 2	Increase in Inventory bal.
(c) Increase in Salaries Payable	2		
	28	8	
	20		

Sources	Financing		Uses
(c) Borrow, on long-term note	40	(j) 46 Payment of long-term note	
(h) Issue common shares	48	(k) 8 Repurchase of comm. shares	
		(e) 11 Cash dividend paid	
	88	65	
	23		

Sources	Investing		Uses
(f) Cash rec. on sale of plant assets	21	(g) 30 Purch. plant assets for cash	
		9	

Net Change in Cash: $20 + $23 − $9 = 34(M)

CHAPTER SUPPLEMENT 15C

Statement of Changes in Financial Position, Working Capital Basis

Until 1985, SCFP was mostly prepared to reflect the changes in working capital rather than the changes in cash and its equivalents. However, with the development of the conceptual framework (see Chapter 4) the emphasis was placed on the idea of relevance. Cash is what is relevant to investors and creditors, not working capital. Also confusion existed in the minds of some readers as to what was meant by working capital. As a result the switch was made to a cash-based SCFP. However, an understanding of the working capital-based statement is still useful because statements based on working capital and the working capital format for the statement can still be found in a variety of places.

The only difference between the SCFP prepared on a working capital basis and one prepared on a cash basis is how the "funds" are **measured.** This supplement discusses the sources and uses of funds in terms of **working capital** instead of cash. Compared with cash, working capital is a broader and significantly different concept of funds because it involves an arithmetical difference—**total current assets minus total current liabilities.** Thus, working capital is an abstraction because it does not represent a single asset, or group of similar assets; rather it includes total current assets and an offset—total current liabilities. It cannot be counted, handled, or used to settle receivables and payables. Because of its abstract nature, working capital often is not fully understood by statement users. Although working capital is used widely as the SCFP measurement basis, a growing use of the cash basis is evident.

To understand and interpret the SCFP prepared on the working capital basis, you should clearly understand the concept of working capital as a measurement of **funds.** As a basis for discussion, notice in Exhibit 15–4, for UTEX Company, that the comparative balance sheets reported working capital that may be tabulated as shown in Exhibit 15–11.

Exhibit 15–11   UTEX Company: SCFP—working capital basis

	December 31		Working Capital Increase (Decrease) 19A to 19B
	19A	**19B**	
Current assets:			
Cash	$42	$ 76	$34
Accounts receivable . . .	21	27	6
Inventory	10	12	2
Total current assets	73	115	42
Current Liabilities:			
Salaries payable	3	5	(2)
Total current liabilities . . .	3	5	(2)
Working capital (at end of year)	$70	$110	$40

Examination of the working capital tabulation above shows two fundamental relationships that relate directly to the SCFP working capital basis:

1. Increases in current assets and/or decreases in current liabilities **increase working capital,** and decreases in current assets and/or increases in current liabilities **decrease working capital.**

2. A transaction that affects only working capital accounts during a given period does **not** change the amount of working capital for that period because only the components of working capital are changed. The **total amount** of working capital during a given period is changed only by transactions that affect one or more **noncurrent** (i.e., nonworking capital) accounts; that is noncurrent assets, noncurrent liabilities, and owners' equity accounts. Therefore, an analysis of the **noncurrent** balance sheet accounts is used to develop a SCFP on the working capital basis.

Sources of Working Capital.   Transactions that **increase** working capital are called **sources of working capital.** These transactions involve a debit to either a current asset or current liability account and a credit to one or more **nonworking capital accounts.** The four primary sources of working capital are:

1. **From normal operations**—Net income (accrual basis) must be converted to the working capital basis. As goods and services are sold during the period, there is an inflow of cash and/or accounts receivable (both working capital items). Also, during the period, as expenses are incurred, usually there is a decrease in working capital because of cash payments and/or the incurrence of current liabilities (both working capital items). Therefore, a reported income usually results in an increase (source) of working capital. In the case of a loss, working capital usually will decrease. The conversion to working capital is done like the conversion for cash. The main difference is that the conversion adjustments that must be made affect **only nonworking capital accounts.** Because they do not include changes in current assets and current liabilities, they usually are limited to depreciation amortization, depletion, and gains and losses. For example, conversion of net income to the working capital basis is as follows:

> Income $22
> Add (deduct) to convert to working capital basis:
>   Depreciation expense   4
> Net working capital from normal operations . . . $26*
>
> * See Exhibit 15–12.

2. **Sale of capital stock for cash or short-term receivables**—A sale of capital stock is a source of working capital because cash or a short-term receivable is received for the sale price of the stock.

3. **Sale of noncurrent assets**—When a long-term investment, an operational asset, or an "other noncurrent asset" is sold, working capital is

increased by the total amount of the cash and/or short-term receivable that results from its disposition (the increased is not the amount of the disposal gain or loss).

4. **Long-term borrowing**—When a loan is obtained on a long-term basis, working capital (cash) is increased by the proceeds of the loan. In contrast, when a **short-term** loan is obtained, working capital is **not** increased because a working capital account (Cash) is increased and another working capital account (a current liability) is increased by the same amount. Because the two changes offset each other, working capital (current assets minus current liabilities) does not change. To illustrate, if UTEX Company borrowed $5,000 cash on a 90-day loan near the end of 19B, the working capital effect would be as follows:

	Before short-term loan	Effect of short-term loan	After short-term loan
Current assets	$73,000	+$ 5,000	$78,000
Current liabilities . . .	3,000	+ (5,000)	8,000
Working capital	$70,000	–0–*	$70,000

* Effect on working capital = (+$5,000) − (+$5,000) = 0.

Uses of Working Capital. Transactions that **decrease** working capital are called **uses of working capital.** These transactions involve a credit to a working capital account and a debit to a **nonworking capital account.** The three main uses of working capital are:

1. **Purchase operational assets and other noncurrent assets for cash or short-term debt**—These transactions usually require a payment of cash and, sometimes, the creation of a short-term debt. To the extent that cash is paid or short-term debt is incurred, working capital is reduced.

2. **Declare cash dividends**—This transaction causes the recognition of a current liability; therefore, working capital is reduced (used) by that amount. However, the subsequent cash payment of the dividend already declared does not reduce working capital.[4]

3. **Pay a long-term liability**—Payments on long-term notes and bonds and other long-term obligations involve an outflow of cash; therefore, they represent uses of working capital. In contrast, the payment of a **current liability does not change working capital** for the same reason explained above in respect to borrowing (source) on a short-term debt basis; that is, the two working capital effects offset one another.

---

[4] When a dividend is declared, working capital is reduced by the amount of the dividend even though payment in cash is in a later period. In this case, the dividend payable is recorded as a current liability on declaration date. The cash payment in the later period does not affect working capital at that time because equal debits and credits to working capital accounts will be made. This distinction is important only when declaration and payment dates fall in different accounting periods. The declaration and payment of a cash dividend in the same year reduces both cash and working capital for that year.

Format for the SCFP, Working Capital Basis. Exhibit 15–12 shows the SCFP, working capital basis, for UTEX Company. The original standard format for the SCFP, working capital basis, has two distinct parts (in contrast to the SCFP, cash basis, which needs only the first part):

Part A—Sources and uses of working capital
Part B—Changes in working capital during the period

Part A reports the financing activities (sources of working capital) and the investing activities (uses of working capital) during the period. Part A is the basic report. Part B lists each current asset and current liability, the resulting increases and decreases, and the net change in working capital during the period.[5] The format in Part A of the statement follows the cash basis format, except that it relates only to the sources and uses of **working capital.**

Notice that SCFP does not classify the sources and uses into investing and financing activities. This classification can easily be accomplished although such a classification scheme was not typical prior to the 1985 CICA pronouncement.

Analysis to Prepare the SCFP, Working Capital Basis. Exhibit 15–13 shows a schedule to prepare the SCFP. Compare this exhibit with Exhibit 15–7 (cash basis schedule). Notice that the working capital spreadsheet is different only in the following ways:

1. All of the working accounts are grouped on the first line called "Working capital."
2. Only the nonworking capital accounts are listed.
3. Part B captions follow the reporting format of the SCFP, working capital basis.
4. The entries in the columns "Analysis of interim entries" are limited to the nonworking capital accounts. On the cash basis worksheet the entries are related to all accounts except cash.
5. The "check" figure is the change in working capital from the beginning to the end of the accounting period.

Working Capital versus Cash Basis for the SCFP. The SCFP, working capital basis, has the following advantages over the SCFP, cash basis: (*a*) it is broader in scope because working capital includes all current assets and current liabilities; (*b*) it is easier to prepare; and (*c*) it has been used extensively in the past. In contrast, the

---

[5] Part B of Exhibit 15–12 is copied from the related comparative balance sheets. Therefore, some accountants consider Part B to be redundant. The two parts of the SCFP, working capital basis, are not called "Part A and Part B" in actual practice; this designation is used here only for instructional convenience.

Exhibit 15–12 Statement of changes in financial position, working capital basis

UTEX COMPANY
Statement of Changes in Financial Position,
Working Capital Basis
For the Year Ended December 31, 19B

Part A:

From normal operations:

Net income	$22	
Add (deduct) to convert to working capital basis (depreciation expense)	4	
Total working capital generated from normal operations		$ 26

From other sources:

Borrow on long-term note payable	40	
Issue common stock	48	
Cash received on sale of plant asset	21	
Total working capital generated from other sources		109
Total working capital generated during the period		135

Uses of working capital:

Payments on long-term note payable	46	
Repurchase of common stock	8	
Cash dividends declared and paid	11	
Purchase of plant assets for cash	30	
Total working capital used during the period		95
Net increase on working capital during the period		$ 40

Part B:

Changes in working capital during the period:

Working capital accounts	December 31 19A	December 31 19B	Working capital increase (decrease)
Current assets:			
Cash	$42	$ 76	$34
Accounts receivable	21	27	6
Inventory	10	12	2
Total current assets	73	115	42
Current liabilities:			
Salaries payable	3	5	(2)
Total current liabilities	3	5	(2)
Working capital (at end of year)	$70	$110	$40

advantages of the SCFP, cash basis, are: (*a*) cash is the primary resource of interest to decision makers because they need to project future cash flows; (*b*) cash is understood by most persons whereas working capital (being an abstract amount) often is not understood by decision makers; and (*c*) recently there has been a significant increase in the use of the cash basis.

Exhibit 15–13   Schedule to prepare SCFP, working capital basis (UTEX Company)

Part A.   Analysis of noncurrent balance sheet accounts:

Items	Balances Dec. 31, 19A	Analysis of interim entries Debit	Analysis of interim entries Credit	Ending balances Dec. 31, 19B
Debits:				
Working capital	$ 70	$40		$110
Noncurrent accounts:				
Plant assets (net)	62	5		67
Total	$132			$177
Credits:				
Note payable, long term	$ 46	6		$ 40
Common shares, no par	70		$40	110
Retained earnings	16		11	27
Total	$132	$51	$51	$177

Part B.   UTEX Company: SCFP—working capital:

Items	Income and additions	Income deductions	Subtotal
Sources of working capital:			
From normal operations:			
Net income	$ 22		Working capital from operations $26
Depreciation expense	4		

		Sources	Uses
c^1	Borrow on long-term note	40	
f	Issue common stock	48	
b^2	Cash received on sale of plant assets	21	
Uses of working capital:			
c^2	Payments on note payable		46
d	Common stock account repurchase of shares		8
e	Cash dividend declared and paid		11
b^1	Purchase plant assets for cash		30
Increase on working capital		40
		$135	$135

IMPORTANT TERMS DEFINED IN THIS CHAPTER

Cash Equivalent A short-term, highly liquid investment and a short-term borrowing. SCFP reports changes in cash and cash equivalents. *p. 859*

Cash Flows from Financing Activities Inflows and outflows related to how cash was obtained to finance the enterprise. *p. 858*

Cash Flows from Investing Activities Inflows and outflows related to the acquisition or sale of productive facilities and making or collecting long-term investments. *p. 858*

Cash Flows from Operating Activities Inflows and outflows related to earning net income. *p. 857*

Direct Method Reports components of cash flows from operating activities as gross receipts and gross payments. *p. 859*

Indirect Method Adjusts net income to compute cash flows from operating activities. *p. 859*

Noncash Expense An expense that does not cause an immediate cash outflow. For example, depreciation expense. *p. 868*

Noncash Investing and Financing Activities Transactions that do not have direct cash flow effects. Some are not reported on the SCFP. *p. 869*

QUESTIONS

1. What are the financial statements that are required in the external financial report? What does each statement report?
2. What are the main sources and uses of funds in a business?
3. What are cash equivalents?
4. Company X acquired a tract of land in exchange for a $10,000 bond payable. How does this transaction relate to the SCFP?
5. What is a direct exchange? How does a direct exchange affect the SCFP?
6. Why is the SCFP called a change statement?
7. Define the following terms. Give two examples of each.
    a. Nonfund asset accounts.
    b. Nonfund liability accounts.
8. Why is income (i.e., from normal operations) often the primary source of funds in a business in the long run?
9. In developing "sources of funds, from operations (cash or working capital)," on the SCFP, explain why depreciation, amortization of intangible assets, and depletion are added back to net income.
10. Why is the SCFP, cash basis, relevant to external statement users?
11. Explain why the SCFP, cash basis, requires the conversion of net income to another amount.

12. You are completing a SCFP, cash basis, and have the data listed below. Complete the blanks to the right.

Income (accrual basis)		$10,000
Increase in accounts receivable	$1,400	_____
Depreciation expense	1,500	_____
Amortization of patent	200	_____
Decrease in merchandise inventory	2,200	_____
Decrease in accounts payable	1,000	_____
Net cash inflow from normal		
operations for the period		$ _____

13. You are preparing a SCFP, cash basis, and have the data listed below. Complete the blanks to the right.

Income (accrual basis)		$20,000
Decrease in accounts receivable	$2,000	_____
Decrease in accounts payable	3,000	_____
Depreciation expense	8,000	_____
Gain on sale of operational asset (cash		
sale price, $3,000; book value,		
$2,000)	1,000	_____
Net cash inflow from normal operations		$ _____

14. Total sales revenue for 19B was $300,000, of which one third was on credit. The balances in accounts receivable at year's end were 19B, $15,000; and 19A, $23,000. The cash inflow from sales revenue during 19B was $_____.

15. Total expenses for 19B was $200,000, of which $10,000 was depreciation expense and $30,000 was credit (accounts payable). The balances in accounts payable at year's end were 19A, $16,000; and 19B, $12,000. The cash outflow for expenses during 19B was $_____.

16. Company X is preparing the SCFP, cash basis, for 19B. During the year, the company acquired a tract of land and paid in full by issuing 1,000 shares of its own capital stock, par $10 per share (market value $15 per share). Show how this transaction should be reported on the SCFP. Explain.

17. Should the effects of bad debts expense and the write-off of uncollectible accounts be considered when preparing a SCFP?

18. Explain why cash paid during the period for purchases and for salaries is not specifically reported on the SCFP, indirect method, as cash outflows.

19. Explain why a $50,000 increase inventory during the year must be included in developing cash flows for operating activities under both the direct and indirect methods.

20. Complete the following tabulation:

	Working capital	
Transactions	**Source**	**Use**
a. Collected an account receivable, $150	$ _____	$ _____
b. Sold land for $4,000, one half collected in cash and the balance on		
one-year note; gain, $500	_____	_____
c. Paid a bond payable, $1,000	_____	_____
d. Sold and issued common stock, $2,500 cash	_____	_____
e. Paid short-term note payable, $1,300	_____	_____

21. Complete the following tabulation:

> Income, $32,000 (accrual basis) . . . . $ _____
> Depreciation expense, $5,000 . . . . _____
> Inventory increase, $10,000 (paid cash) . . . . _____
> Working capital from normal operations . . . _____

22. Company T reported working capital at year-end of 19A, $90,000; and 19B, $75,000. During 19B, the company (*a*) paid a $5,000 short-term note and (*b*) paid a $15,000 long-term note. Disregarding interest, how much did each of these transactions change working capital during 19B? Explain.

23. Company S bought a machine that cost $30,000; payment was made as follows: cash, $10,000; short-term payable, $4,000; and long-term note payable, $16,000. How much did working capital change? Explain.

24. What are the two basic parts of a SCFP, working capital basis? Why is the second part considered redundant by some people?

25. As a statement user interested in the statement of changes in financial position, would you prefer the (*a*) cash basis or (*b*) working capital basis? Explain.

EXERCISES

E15–1   **(Pairing Definitions with Terminology)**
Match the definitions or statements with the terms by entering the appropriate letters to the left.

Term	Definition or statement
_G_ (1) Working capital (example)	A. SCFP must report only some direct exchanges both as a source and use of cash.
___ (2) Financing activities	B. Revenues reported on the income statement that did not cause fund (cash) increases.
___ (3) Noncash expenses	C. Entries made to determine sources and uses of funds.
___ (4) Noncash revenues	
___ (5) Direct exchange	D. Statement of changes in financial position.
___ (6) Liquidity	E. Cash availability; nearness to cash.
___ (7) A stock dividend	F. Depreciation, depletion, and amortization.
___ (8) SCFP, cash basis	G. Current assets minus current liabilities.
___ (9) Analytical entries	H. Transactions that cause funds (cash or working capital) to increase.
___ (10) Investing activities	
___ (11) Funds	I. A general term used to mean either cash or working capital.
___ (12) Increase (decrease) in funds during the period	J. Transactions that cause a decrease in funds (cash or working capital).
	K. Transactions that do not increase or decrease funds but must be reported on the SCFP as both a source and use of funds.
___ (13) Cash from normal operations	
___ (14) SCFP	L. Total fund inflows minus total fund outflows.
	M. SCFP basis that is more useful in projecting future cash flows.
	N. Net income is converted to this item (cash basis).

E15–2   **(Classifying transactions on the SCFP)**

For each transaction listed below, indicate how the transaction would be reported on a SCFP prepared using the direct method. Use the following notations:

OA = Operating activities
IA = Investing activities
FA = Financing activities
N = Not Reported on the SCFP

a. _____ Net income.
b. _____ Purchase of an operational asset.
c. _____ Depreciation expense.
d. _____ Collection on a long-term note receivable.
e. _____ Issuance of a stock dividend.
f. _____ Sale of a long-term investment for cash.
g. _____ Borrowed cash on a long-term note payable.
h. _____ Sale of an operational asset at a loss.
i. _____ Purchase of a long-term investment with cash.
j. _____ Exchange of common stock for an operational asset.
k. _____ Exchange of land for equipment.
l. _____ Repurchase of common stock.
m. _____ Bad debts expense.
n. _____ Payments of a cash dividend declared in a previous period.

E15–3   **(Compute Cash from Normal Operations; Use Direct Analysis)**

The 19D income statement of Coffey Company is summarized below. Additional 19D data from the 19C and 19D balance sheets are as follows:

a. Decrease in accounts receivable (for services sold) during 19D, $14,000.
b. Bought a small service machine, $6,000 (cash).
c. Increase in salaries payable during 19D, $8,000.
d. Service revenue collected in advance during 19D, $5,000.
e. Decrease in income tax payable during 19D, $7,000.

Income Statement 19D

Items	Accrual basis	Net cash inflow (outflow) from operations	
		Explanation	Amount
Service revenues	$ 60,000		
Expenses:			
Salaries	51,000		
Depreciation	11,000		
Depletion	200		
Utilities (cash)	4,000		
Remaining expenses (cash)	3,800		
Income tax	–0–		
Total expenses	70,000		
Net income (loss)	$(10,000)		

Required:

a. Complete the above income statement schedule to determine the "net cash inflow (outflow) from normal operations."

b. Because there is a net loss for 19D would you expect the net cash flow from normal operations to be negative (i.e., an outflow)? Explain.

c. Give proof of your answer to Requirement (a) by starting with the $10,000 loss and ending with your answer to Requirement (a).

E15–4   (Prepare SCFP, Cash Basis; Use Direct Analysis)

Davis Company has finished its income statement and comparative balance sheet at December 31, 19B. The following data are from those statements:

```
Net income . . . . . . . . . . . . . . . . . . . . . . . . . . . .  $32,000
Depreciation expense  . . . . . . . . . . . . . . . . . . . .    5,000
Purchase of operational assets for cash . . . . . . . . . .   26,000
Sale of long-term investment (sold at book value for
    cash, $6,000) . . . . . . . . . . . . . . . . . . . . . . . .    6,000
Inventory increase during the period  . . . . . . . . . . . .    3,000
Declared and paid cash dividends during 19B . . . . . . .    9,000
Borrowed on short-term note  . . . . . . . . . . . . . . . .   20,000
Accounts payable decrease . . . . . . . . . . . . . . . . . .    1,000
Payment of long-term note . . . . . . . . . . . . . . . . . .   30,000
Acquired land for future use; issued capital stock
    in payment (market value) . . . . . . . . . . . . . . . .   25,000
```

Required:

Prepare the SCFP, cash basis, properly classified. Use the direct analysis.

E15–5   **(Prepare SCFP, Cash Basis; Use Direct Analysis)**

Fisher Corporation has finished its 19A income statement and balance sheet. The SCFP, cash basis, must be prepared. The following 19A data have been extracted from the income statement, balance sheet, and other company records.

a. Depreciation expense, $9,000.

b. Repurchased common shares, $4,000 (cash).

c. Sold a long-term investment at book value, $6,000 (cash).

d. Declared and paid a $7,000 cash dividend during 19A.

e. Salaries recorded but unpaid on December 31, 19A, $1,000.

f. Income, accrual basis, $30,000 (from the 19A income statement).

g. Borrowed $10,000 on a one-year interest-bearing note (15% interest).

h. Service revenue recorded but uncollected on December 31, 19A, $3,000.

i. Sold 200 shares of its own common stock, no par, for $5 per share (cash).

j. Paid a $16,000 long-term note payable plus $800 interest.

k. Bought operational assets, $30,000 (cash).

Required:

a. Prepare the 19A SCFP, cash basis, for Fisher Corporation (use direct analysis).

b. Reconcile income (accrual basis) with the net increase (decrease) in cash during 19A. Use designations and amounts.

E15–6   **(Reporting Direct Exchanges on the SCFP, Cash Basis)**

The SCFP must be based on the all-resources concept. During 19B, West Corporation finished the two transactions below.

1. West acquired a large machine that had a list price of $25,000. Since West was short of cash, it paid for the machine in full by giving a $10,000, 15%, interest-bearing note due at the end of two years, and 200 shares of its capital stock, par $50 (market value $60) per share.

2. West acquired a small machine (list price $9,995). Full payment was made by transferring a tract of land that had a market value of $9,500 (this was also its book value).

Required:

For each machine show what should be reported on the SCFP, cash basis, under (a) sources of cash and (b) uses of cash. Explain the basis for your responses.

E15–7   **(Calculating Cash Receipts from Customers)**

For each independent case listed in the following schedule, calculate cash receipts from customers.

	Case A	Case B	Case C
Sales revenue	$300,000	$100,000	$150,000
Beginning accounts receivable . . .	12,000	20,000	22,000
Ending accounts receivable	15,000	11,000	22,000
Cash receipts from customers . . .	———	———	———

E15–8   **(Determining Cash Flows from the Sale of an Asset)**
During 19F, Alpha Company sold some excess equipment at a loss. The following information was collected from the company's accounting records:

From the income statement:

Depreciation expense	$ 800
Loss on sale of equipment	2,000

From the balance sheet:

Beginning equipment	10,000
Ending equipment	6,000
Beginning accumulated depreciation	2,200
Ending accumulated depreciation	2,500

No new equipment was bought during 19F.

Required:
For the equipment that was sold, determine the original cost, the accumulated depreciation on the equipment, and the cash received from the sale.

E15–9   **(Calculating Cash Flows from Operating Activities, Direct Method)**
The following information pertains to Black Company:

Sales		$100,000
Expenses:		
Cost of goods sold	$60,000	
Depreciation expense	8,000	
Salaries expense	20,000	88,000
Net income		$ 12,000
Accounts receivable increase		$ 3,000
Merchandise inventory decrease		9,000
Salaries payable increase		900

Required:
Prepare the operating activities section of the SCFP for Black Company using the direct method.

E15–10   **(Preparing the Operating Activities Section of the SCFP, Direct Method)**
The following information pertains to White Company:

Sales		$100,000
Expense:		
Cost of goods sold	$60,000	
Depreciation expense	8,000	
Salaries expense	20,000	88,000
Net income		$ 12,000
Accounts receivable decrease		$ 3,000
Merchandise inventory increase		9,000
Salaries payable decrease		900

Required:
Prepare the operating activities section of the SCFP for White Company, using the direct method.

E15–11   (SCFP Direct Method; Complete Spreadsheet, Supplement 15A)

Analysis of accounts: (*a*) purchased on operational asset, $30,000, issued capital stock in full payment, (*b*) purchased a long-term investment for cash, $10,000, (*c*) paid cash dividend, $10,000, (*d*) sold operational asset for $5,000 cash (cost, $18,000, accumulated depreciation, $16,000), and (*e*) sold capital stock, 500 shares at $11 per share cash. Complete the spreadsheet for SCFP, direct method.

Item	Balances 12/31/19A	Analysis Debit	Analysis Credit	Balances 12/31/19B
Analysis of income:				
Sales			$120,000	
Cost of goods sold		$48,000		
Depreciation		6,000		
Amortization of bond premium			300	
Wage expense		22,000		
Income tax expense		10,000		
Interest expense		7,000		
Remaining expenses		2,300		
Gain on sale of operational asset			3,000	
Net income		28,000		
Analysis of Financial Position:				
Cash	$ 19,500			$ 32,200
Accounts receivable (net)	34,000			34,000
Merchandise inventory	78,000			85,000
Investments, long-term				10,000
Operational assets	168,500			180,500
Total debits	$300,000			$341,700
Accumulated depreciation	$ 44,000			$ 34,000
Accounts payable	21,000			19,000
Wages payable	1,500			500
Income taxes payable	2,000			3,500
Bonds payable	100,000			100,000
Premium on bonds payable	4,000			3,700
Common stock, no par	120,000			155,500
Retained earnings	7,500			25,500
Total credits	$300,000			$341,700

Statement of Cash Inflows and (Outflows)

	Inflows	Outflows
Cash flows from operating activities		
Cash flows from investing activities		
Cash flows from financing activities		
Net increase (decrease) in cash		
Totals		

E15–12   (Comparison of the Direct and Indirect Methods)

To compare SCFP reporting under the direct and indirect methods, enter check marks to indicate which items are used with each method.

Cash flows (and related changes)	SCFP method Direct	SCFP method Indirect
1. Revenues from customers	___	___
2. Accounts receivable increase or decrease	___	___
3. Payments to suppliers	___	___
4. Inventory increase or decrease	___	___
5. Accounts payable increase or decrease	___	___
6. Payments to employees	___	___
7. Wages payable, increase or decrease	___	___
8. Depreciation expense	___	___
9. Net income	___	___
10. Cash flows from operating activities	___	___
11. Investing activities	___	___
12. Financing activities	___	___
13. Net increase or decrease in cash during the period	___	___

E15–13 **(SCFP Cash Flow Analysis of Cost of Goods Sold)**

The records of Jack Company showed cost of goods sold (on the income statement) of $60,000 and a change in the inventory and accounts payable balances. To demonstrate the effect of these changes on cash outflow for cost of goods sold (i.e., payments to suppliers) eight independent cases are used. Complete the following tabulation for each case:

Case	Cost of goods sold	Inventory increase (decrease)	Accounts payable increase (decrease)	Computations	Amount outflow*
A	$40,000	$-0-	$-0-	___	___
B	40,000	6,000	-0-	___	___
C	40,000	(6,000)	-0-	___	___
D	40,000	-0-	4,000	___	___
E	40,000	-0-	(4,000)	___	___
F	40,000	6,000	4,000	___	___
G	40,000	(6,000)	(4,000)	___	___
H	40,000	(6,000)	(6,000)	___	___

* This is the amount of cash paid during the current period for past and current purchases.

E15–14 **(SCFP, Indirect Method; Prepare the Reconciliation for Operating Activities)**

The data given below were provided by the accounting records of Ronald Company. Prepare the reconciliation of net income with cash flow from operations for inclusion in the SCFP, indirect method.

Net income (accrual basis), $60,000
Depreciation expense, $7,800
Decrease in wages payable, $1,200
Decrease in accounts receivable, $1,800
Increase in inventory, $2,500
Increase in long-term liabilities, $10,000
Sale of capital stock for cash, $25,000
Accounts payable increase, $4,000
Dividend paid, $10,000

E15–15   **(Calculating Cash Payments to Suppliers)**

For each independent case listed in the following schedule, calculate cash payments to suppliers.

	Case			
	A	**B**	**C**	**D**
Cost of goods sold	$20,000	$40,000	$30,000	$30,000
Beginning inventory	15,000	15,000	15,000	20,000
Ending inventory	10,000	15,000	20,000	20,000
Beginning accounts payable ...	5,000	7,000	6,000	4,000
Ending accounts payable	4,000	8,000	6,000	4,000
Cash payments to suppliers ...	_____	_____	_____	_____

E15–16   **(Comparison of the Direct and Indirect Methods)**

The following information pertains to the Vista Corporation:

Sales		$100,000
Expenses:		
Cost of goods sold	$60,000	
Salaries	8,000	
Depreciation expense	20,000	88,000
Net income		$ 12,000
Accounts receivable decrease		3,000
Merchandise inventory increase		9,000
Accounts payable increase		500
Salaries payable decrease		900

Required:

a. Prepare the cash flows from operating activities section of the SCFP for Vista Corporation using the direct method.

b. Prepare the cash flows from operating activities of the SCFP for Vista Corporation using the indirect method.

E15–17   **(SCFP, Indirect Method; Complete Spreadsheet)**

The data used in this exercise are given in Exercise 15–11.

Required:
Complete the SCFP, indirect method spreadsheet given below.

Item	Balances 12/31/19A	Analysis Debit	Analysis Credit	Balances 12/31/19B
Cash plus short-term investments	$ 19,500			$ 32,200
Noncash accounts:				
Accounts receivable (net)	34,000			34,000
Merchandise inventory	78,000			85,000
Investments, long-term				10,000
Operational assets	168,500			180,500
Total	$300,000			$341,700
Accumulated depreciation	$ 44,000			$ 34,000
Accounts payable	21,000			19,000
Wages payable	1,500			500
Income taxes payable	2,000			3,500
Bonds payable	100,000			100,000
Premium on bonds payable	4,000			3,700
Common stock, no par	120,000			155,500
Retained earnings	7,500			25,500
Total	$300,000			$341,700

Statement of cash inflows (outflows):
From operating activities:
Net income:
Conversion of net income to cash flow
from operating activities:

Cash flows from investing activities:

Cash flows from financing activities:

Net increase (decrease) in cash:

Totals

E15–18 **(Comparison of Cash versus Working Capital from Normal Operations; Use a Direct Analysis, Supplement 15C)**
Below is a tabulation that gives information about both cash and working capital for Ross Company.

Transactions	(a) Cash basis	(b) Working capital basis
Net income reported (accrual basis)	$17,000	$17,000
Depreciation expense, $2,700	___	___
Increase in wages payable, $500	___	___
Decrease in trade accounts receivable, $6,800	___	___
Increase in merchandise inventory, $9,300	___	___
Amortization of patents, $300	___	___
Increase in bonds payable, $10,000	___	___
Decrease in trade accounts payable, $7,400	___	___
Sale of unissued common stock, $5,000	___	___
Total cash generated from operations	$___	
Total working capital generated from operations		$20,000

Required:

a. Give the correct amounts for each of the blanks in the above tabulation; if none, enter a zero.

b. Compare the total of cash with the total of working capital. Why are they different?

c. Which result do you think would be of most use to statement users? Why?

E15-19   (Prepare SCFP, Working Capital Basis; Use a Direct Analysis, Supplement 15C)
Busby Company finished the income statement and the comparative balance sheet at year-end, December 31, 19B. A statement of changes in financial position must be developed. The following data are available:

	Balances at Dec. 31	
	19A	**19B**
From balance sheet:		
Current assets:		
Cash	$ 8,000	$15,000
Accounts receivable (net)	17,000	12,000
Inventory	15,000	18,000
Current liabilities:		
Accounts payable	10,000	12,000
Notes payable, short term	18,000	13,000
From income statement:		
Net income		$20,000
Depreciation expense		6,000
From other records:		
Purchase of long-term investment		15,000
Payment of long-term note		5,000
Sale of unissued capital stock		10,000
Declaration and payment of cash dividend during 19B		8,000
Purchased land for future plant site, issued		
capital stock as payment in full		25,000

Required:
Prepare a SCFP, working capital basis. Use a direct analysis.

E15–20   **(Prepare a SCFP, Working Capital Basis; Use a Direct Analysis, Supplement 15C)**
Cullen Company has never prepared a SCFP. At the end of 19B, the company book-keeper assembled the data given below (which is correct) to develop this statement:

	Balances at Dec. 31	
	19A	19B
From the balance sheet:		
Current assets:		
Cash	$ 15,000	$ 20,000
Accounts receivable (net)	24,000	17,000
Merchandise inventory	30,000	27,000
Current liabilities:		
Accounts payable	(19,000)	(15,000)
Notes payable, short term	(10,000)	(12,000)
Working capital	$ 40,000	$ 37,000

	Balances at Dec. 31
	19B
From the income statement and other sources:	
Net income	$ 21,000
Depreciation expense	4,500
Amortization of patent	500
Purchase of operational assets	(6,000)
Sale of operational assets (at book value) for cash . . .	2,000
Payment of long-term note payable	(40,000)
Issuance of bonds payable for cash	30,000
Sale and issuance of common stock for cash	10,000
Declaration and payment of a cash dividend on	
common stock during 19B	(25,000)
Difference	$ (3,000)

Required:
Prepare a SCFP, working capital basis, for 19B. Use a direct analysis.

E15–21   **(Prepare a Worksheet Analysis to Develop a SCFP, Working Capital Basis, Supplement 15C)**

Lakeland Company is developing its annual financial statements at December 31, 19B. The income statement and balance sheet are finished, and the SCFP, working capital basis, is being developed. The income statement and comparative balance sheets are summarized below:

	19A	19B
Balance sheet at December 31:		
Cash	$12,800	$10,800
Accounts receivable (net)	9,000	10,500
Merchandise inventory	6,600	5,000
Operational assets (net)	40,000	43,000
Patent	3,000	2,700
	71,400	$72,000
Accounts payable	$11,000	$ 9,000
Income tax payable	400	500
Notes payable, long term	10,000	5,000
Common stock (no par)	42,000	45,000
Retained earnings	8,000	12,500
	$71,400	$72,000
Income statement for 19B:		
Sales revenue		$60,000
Cost of goods sold		35,000
Gross margin		25,000
Expenses (including depreciation, $4,000, and patent amortization, $300)		18,000
Net income		$ 7,000

Additional data for 19B:
Purchased operational assets for cash, $7,000.
Paid $5,000 on long-term note payable.
Sold and issued common stock for $3,000 cash.
Declared and paid a $2,500 cash dividend on capital stock during 19B.

Required:

a. Based upon the above data, prepare a worksheet analysis using the SCFP, working capital basis.

b. Prepare the formal SCFP, working capital basis.

PROBLEMS

P15–1   **(Compute Cash from Normal Operations Using a Direct Analysis)**
The income statement of Josey Corporation is given below.

JOSEY CORPORATION
Income Statement for the Year Ended December 31, 19B
Accrual Basis

		Cash flow
Sales revenue (one third on credit; accounts receivable year's end—19A, $11,000; 19B, $15,000)	$300,000	$ _____
Cost of goods sold (one fourth on credit; accounts payable year's end—19A, $9,000; 19B, $8,000 (net); inventory at year's end—19A, $50,000; 19B; $45,000)	180,000	_____
Gross margin on sales	120,000	

Expenses:

Salaries and wages (including accrued wages payable at year's end—19A, $500; 19B, $300)	$44,000		
Depreciation expense	8,000		
Rent expense (no accruals)	6,000		_____
Bad debt expense	300		_____
Remaining expenses (no accruals)	11,700		_____
Income tax expense (income tax payable at year's end—19A, $2,000; 19B, $3,000)	10,000		_____
Total expenses		80,000	
Net income		$ 40,000	
Cash inflow from normal operations			$ _____

Proof of results:

Net income (accrual basis)		$40,000
Add (deduct) to convert to cash basis:		
_____		_____
_____		_____
_____		_____
_____		_____
_____		_____
_____		_____
_____		_____
_____		_____
Cash inflow from normal operations		$ _____

Note: This problem shows two different approaches to derive cash inflow from operations; the proof-of-results approach above is the one usually used because it is more direct.

Required:

a. Enter the correct cash amounts needed for cash from normal operations in the blanks provided. Use parentheses to show cash deductions, and enter a zero for no change (use direct analysis).

b. Prove your answer to Requirement (a) by starting with net income (accrual basis).

P15–2   (Complete an Analysis to Prepare a SCFP, Cash Basis)

Mason Company is developing the annual financial statements at December 31, 19B. The statements are complete except for the SCFP, cash basis. The completed comparative balance sheets and income statement are summarized below:

	19A	19B
Balance sheet at December 31:		
Cash	$ 20,000	$ 31,500
Accounts receivable (net)	26,000	25,000
Merchandise inventory	40,000	38,000
Operational assets (net)	64,000	67,000
	$150,000	$161,500
Accounts payable	$ 24,000	$ 27,000
Wages payable	500	400
Notes payable, long-term	35,000	30,000
Common stock, no par	70,000	80,000
Retained earnings	20,500	24,100
	$150,000	$161,500
Income statement for 19B:		
Sales		$ 90,000
Cost of goods sold		(52,000)
Expenses (including depreciation expense, $4,000)		(32,000)
Net income		$ 6,000

Required:

1. Set up an analysis to develop the SCFP, cash basis. Analytical entries should be made for the following:

   a. Net income—from income statement.

   b. Depreciation expense—from income statement.

   c. Bought operational assets for cash, $7,000.

   d. Paid $5,000 on the long-term note payable.

   e. Sold unissued common stock for $10,000 cash.

   f. Declared and paid a $2,400 cash dividend.

   g. Accounts receivable decrease—from balance sheets.

   h. Merchandise inventory decrease—from balance sheets.

   i. Accounts payable increase—from balance sheets.

   j. Wages payable decrease—from balance sheets.

2. Based upon the analysis completed in Requirement (*a*), prepare the formal SCFP, cash basis.

P15–3   **(Complete an Analysis to Prepare a SCFP, Cash Basis; Includes a Direct Exchange)**

Hamilton Company is developing the 19B annual report. A SCFP, cash basis, is being developed. The following spreadsheet has been set up to develop the statement:

Hamilton Company
Spreadsheet Analysis to Develop Statement of Changes in Financial Position, Cash Basis
For the Year Ended December 31, 19B

Items	Ending Balances, Dec. 31, 19A	Analysis of Interim Entries Debit	Analysis of Interim Entries Credit	Ending Balances, Dec. 31, 19B
Debits				
Cash account	$ 24,000			$ 32,200
Noncash accounts:				
Accounts receivable (net)	26,000			30,000
Inventory	30,000			28,000
Prepaid insurance	1,200			800
Investments, long term	10,800			8,000
Operational assets (net)	30,000			39,000
Patent (net)	3,000			2,700
	$125,000			$140,700
Credits				
Accounts payable	$ 21,000			$ 18,000
Wages payable	3,000			2,000
Income tax payable	1,000			1,200
Note payable, long term	25,000			20,000
Common stock, par $10	60,000			70,000
Contributed surplus	1,000			3,000
Retained earnings	14,000			26,500
	$125,000			$140,700
Sources of cash:				
Uses of cash:				
Change in cash				

Additional data for 19B:

a. Revenues, $120,000; expenses, $100,000; and net income, $20,000.

b. Depreciation expense, $3,000.

c. Amortization of patent, $300.

d. Sale of long-term investment, $2,800 cash, which was equal to its book value.

e. Purchased operational assets and issued 1,000 shares of its common stock as full payment (market value, $12 per share).

f. Declared and paid cash dividend, $7,500.

g. Increase in accounts receivable balance during the period.

h. Decrease in inventory during the period.

i. Decrease in prepaid insurance balance during the period.

j. Decrease in accounts payable balance during the period.

k. Decrease in wages payable balance during the period.

l. Increase in income tax payable balance during the period.

Required:

Complete the above spreadsheet on a cash basis. Also, show on the spreadsheet "Net cash inflow from normal operations."

P15–4 **(Complete an Analysis to Prepare a SCFP, Cash Basis; Includes a Direct Exchange and Gain on Disposal)**

Texmo Company is preparing its 19B financial statements, which include the following information:

	Comparative	
	19B	**19A**
Balance sheet:		
Cash	$ 52,000	$ 40,000
Inventory	37,000	30,000
Accounts receivable (net)	17,000	20,000
Long-term investment, shares Co. A	3,000	10,000
Machinery and equipment (net)	75,000	80,000
	$184,000	$180,000
Accounts payable	$ 11,000	$ 15,000
Income tax payable	6,000	4,000
Note payable, long term	10,000	20,000
Bonds payable	10,000	30,000
Common stock, par $10	110,000	100,000
Contributed surplus	11,000	8,000
Retained earnings	26,000	3,000
	$184,000	$180,000
Income statement:		
Revenue	$140,000	
Cost of goods sold	(65,000)	
Depreciation expense	(8,000)	
Remaining operating expenses	(29,000)	
Income tax expense	(9,000)	
Gain on disposal of machine (net of tax) . . .	1,000	
Net income	$ 30,000	

Additional data for 19B:

1. Machinery that had a book value of $10,000 was sold for $11,000 cash.

2. Long-term investment (shares of Company A) was sold for $7,000 cash, which had a carrying value of $7,000.

3. Equipment was acquired, and payment in full was made by issuing 1,000 shares of captial stock that had a market value of $13 per share.

4. Payments on debt: long-term note, $10,000; bonds payable, $20,000.

5. Declared and paid a cash dividend, $7,000.

Required:

a. Prepare either an analysis or a T-account analysis to develop a SCFP, cash basis.

b. Prepare the formal SCFP, cash basis.

P15–5 **(Prepare an Analysis to Develop a SCFP, Cash Basis; Includes a Direct Exchange)**
All-Steel Company is preparing the annual financial statements, including a SCFP, working capital basis, at December 31, 19B. The 19B comparative balance sheet and the income statement and some additional data are summarized below:

	19B	19A
Balance sheet at December 31:		
Cash	$ 21,500	$ 15,000
Accounts receivable (net)	23,000	20,000
Merchandise inventory	27,000	22,000
Prepaid insurance	300	600
Investments, long term (S Corp. shares)	12,000	
Operational assets (net)	220,000	134,000
Patent (net)	16,000	
	$319,800	$191,600
Accounts payable	$ 18,000	$ 12,000
Note payable, short term (nontrade)	10,000	18,000
Wages payable	800	1,000
Income tax payable	1,000	600
Note payable, long term	10,000	30,000
Bonds payable	100,000	
Common stock, par $10	140,000	100,000
Contributed surplus	6,000	5,000
Retained earnings	34,000	25,000
	$319,800	$191,600

Income statement for 19B:		
Sales revenue		$200,000
Cost of goods sold		126,000
Gross margin on sales		74,000
Expenses (not detailed)	$39,000	
Depreciation expense	14,000	
Amortization of patent	1,000	
Income tax expense	7,000	61,000
Net income		$ 13,000

Additional data for 19B:
1. Bought patent on January 1, 19B, for $17,000 cash.
2. Bought shares of S Corporation as a long-term investment for $12,000 cash.
3. Paid $20,000 on the long-term note payable.
4. Sold and issued 4,000 shares of common stock for $41,000 cash.
5. Declared and paid a $4,000 cash dividend.
6. Acquired a building (an operational asset) and paid in full for it by issuing $100,000 bonds payable at par to the former owner—date of transaction was December 30, 19B.

Required:
Based upon the above data, prepare a SCFP, cash basis. Use the direct method.

P15–6   **(Prepare an Analysis to Develop a SCFP; Includes a Loss on Sale of a Noncash Asset and a Direct Exchange)**

Riverside Company is preparing its 19B financial statements. The following information is given by the completed 19B comparative balance sheet and income statement:

	19B	19A
Balance sheet:		
Cash	$ 2,000	$ 10,000
Accounts receivable (net)	21,000	16,600
Inventory	25,000	17,000
Prepaid expenses	400	1,400
Operational assets (net)	68,000	59,000
Plant site	20,000	
Long-term investment	7,000	16,000
	$143,400	$120,000
Accounts payable	$ 12,000	$ 8,000
Wages payable	1,500	1,000
ST note payable (interest, December 31) . . .	3,000	6,000
LT note payable (interest, December 31) . . .	4,000	10,000
Bonds payable (interest, December 31)	50,000	30,000
Common stock, par $10	60,500	60,000
Contributed surplus	3,400	3,000
Retained earnings	9,000	2,000
	$143,400	$120,000
Income statement:		
Revenues	$135,000	
Depreciation expense	(15,000)	
Remaining expenses	(95,000)	
Loss on sale of long-term investment	(3,000)	
Net income	$ 22,000	

Additional data:

1. Purchased operational asset for cash, $24,000.
2. Sold long-term investment for $6,000 cash; carrying value, $9,000.
3. Sold 50 shares of common stock at $18 cash per share.
4. Declared and paid a cash dividend of $15,000.
5. Payment on short-term note, $3,000.
6. Payment on long-term note, $6,000.
7. Acquired plant site and issued bonds, $20,000, for full purchase price (the bonds were selling at par).

Required:

Prepare a SCFP, cash basis. Use indirect method.

P15–7 **(Prepare SCFP Using Direct Method; Includes Gain on Sale of Equipment)**
The income statement, comparative balance sheet, and additional information for Swithin Corporation for 19B appear below:

Income Statement

Revenues:

Sales	$1,300	
Gain on sale of equipment	25	$1,325

Expenses:

Cost of goods sold	600	
Advertising expense	70	
Depreciation expense	90	
Rent expense	60	
Wages expense	127	
Income tax expense	81	
Interest expense on bonds	13	1,041
		$ 284

Comparative Balance Sheet

	19B	19A
Cash	$ 210	$ 80
Accounts receivable	78	28
Merchandise inventory	258	58
Prepaid rent	14	4
Equipment	244	174
Accumulated depreciation	(72)	(12)
Total	$ 732	$ 332
Income tax payable	$ 76	$ 55
Accounts payable	120	20
Wages payable	15	10
Bonds payable	100	100
Common stock	112	112
Retained earnings	309	35
Total	$ 732	$ 332

Other information:

1. Equipment with an original cost of $50 and accumulated depreciation of $30 was sold for $45.
2. Additional equipment was purchased for cash.
3. No additional bonds were issued or retired during the year.
4. Cash dividends were declared and paid during the year.

Required:
Prepare the SCFP, cash basis. Use the direct method.

P15–8   **(Prepare SCFP Using the Direct Method; Includes a Noncash Investing and Financing Activity, Sale of Equipment at a Loss, and a Net Loss)**

The income statement, comparative balance sheet, and additional information for Wilson Corporation for 19D appear below:

Income Statement

Revenues:		
Sales		$1,000
Expenses:		
Cost of goods sold	$ 400	
Depreciation expense	30	
Rent expense	300	
Wages expense	200	
Other operating expenses	100	
Interest expense	9	
Loss on sale of equipment	5	1,044
Net loss		$ (44)

Comparative Balance Sheets

	19D	19C
Cash	$ 16	$ 80
Accounts receivable	95	115
Merchandise inventory	120	30
Prepaid rent	80	2
Equipment	280	200
Accumulated depreciation	(62)	(40)
	$ 529	$ 387
Accounts payable	$ 3	$ 10
Wages payable	8	20
Notes payable	0	0
Interest payable	5	0
Bonds payable	100	0
Common stock, no-par value	180	80
Retained earnings	233	277
Total	$ 529	$ 387

Other information:

1. Equipment was purchased during the year by issuing $100 of common stock.
2. Equipment with an original cost of $20 and accumulated depreciation of $8 was sold for $7.
3. Bonds were issued at face value during the year. Interest of $5 was accrued at year-end.
4. $50 was borrowed on a short-term note payable. The note and $4 of interest was repaid.

Required:

Prepare the SCFP, cash basis. Use the direct method.

P15-9 **(Prepare SCFP Using the Direct Method; Includes a Noncash Investing and Financing Activity, the Sale of an Asset at a Gain, and a Net Loss)**

The income statement, comparative balance sheet, and additional information for Patrick Corporation for 19C appear below:

Income Statement

Revenues:

Sales	$ 800	
Gain on sale of equipment . . .	25	$ 825

Expenses:

Cost of goods sold	$ 600	
Salaries expense	40	
Rent expense	60	
Office supplies used	30	
Patent amortization expense . .	10	
Depreciation expense	80	
Interest expense on bonds . . .	97	917
Net loss		$ (92)

Comparative Balance Sheet

	19C	19B
Cash	$ 460	$ 205
Accounts receivable	170	40
Merchandise inventory	100	400
Office supplies	7	5
Long-term investments	70	50
Operational assets	3,200	1,800
Accumulated depreciation	(660)	(600)
Patent	190	200
Total	$3,537	$2,100
Accounts payable	76	95
Rent payable	16	5
Bonds payable	1,000	0
Premium on bonds payable	37	0
Common stock, no par	1,800	1,300
Retained earnings	608	700
Total	$3,537	$2,100

Other information:

1. Equipment with an original cost of $100 and accumulated depreciation of $20 was sold for $105. Equipment costing $900 was purchased for cash.
2. Land and building valued at $600 were acquired by issuing 100 shares of common stock.
3. Bonds payable were issued during the year.
4. Long-term investments were purchased during the year.
5. Common stock was repurchased during the year in the amount of $100.

Required:

Prepare the SCFP, cash basis, using the direct method.

P15–10   **(Prepare SCFP, Indirect Method)**

Jackson Company was organized on January 1, 19A. During the year ended December 31, 19A, the company provided the following data:

Income statement:

Sales revenue	$ 75,000
Cost of goods sold	(30,000)
Depreciation expense	(2,000)
Remaining expenses	(27,000)
Net income	$ 16,000

Balance sheet:

Cash	$38,000
Accounts receivable (net)	20,000
Merchandise inventory	10,000
Machinery (net)	23,000
Total	$91,000
Accounts payable	$10,000
Accrued expenses payable	17,000
Dividends payable	4,000
Notes payable, short term	10,000
Common stock, no par	40,000
Retained earnings	10,000
Total	$91,000

Analysis of selected accounts and transactions:

a. Sold 2,000 shares of no-par common stock, at $20 per share; collected cash.

b. Borrowed $10,000 on a one-year, 9%, interest-bearing note; the note was dated June 1, 19A.

c. During 19A, purchased machinery; paid $25,000.

d. Purchased merchandise for resale at a cost of $40,000 (debited Inventory because the perpetual system is used); paid $30,000 cash, balance credited to Accounts Payable.

e. At December 31, 19A, declared a cash dividend of $6,000; paid $2,000 in December 19A; the balance will be paid March 1, 19B.

Required:

Prepare a SCFP, cash basis, using the indirect method.

P15–11   **(Prepare SCFP Using the Indirect Method; Includes a Noncash Investing and Financing Activity, and a Sale of an Asset at a Loss)**
Riverside Company is preparing its 19B financial statements. The following information is given by the completed 19B comparative balance sheet and income statement:

	19B	19A
Balance sheet:		
Cash	$ 2,000	$ 10,000
Accounts receivable (net)	21,000	16,600
Inventory	25,000	17,000
Prepaid expense	400	1,400
Operational assets (net)	68,000	59,000
Plant site	20,000	
Long-term investment	7,000	16,000
	$143,400	$120,000
Accounts payable	$ 12,000	$ 8,000
Wages payable	1,500	1,000
Short-term note payable (interest,		
December 31)	3,000	6,000
Long-term note payable (interest,		
December 31)	4,000	10,000
Bonds payable (interest,		
December 31)	50,000	30,000
Common stock, par $10	60,500	60,000
Contributed surplus	3,400	3,000
Retained earnings	9,000	2,000
	$143,400	$120,000
Income statement:		
Revenues	$135,000	
Depreciation expense	(15,000)	
Remaining expenses	(95,000)	
Loss on sale of long-term		
investment	(3,000)	
Net income	$ 22,000	

Additional data:
1. Purchased operational asset for cash, $24,000.
2. Sold long-term investment for $6,000 cash; carrying value, $9,000.
3. Sold 50 shares of common stock at $18 cash per share.
4. Declared and paid a cash dividend of $15,000.
5. Payment on short-term note, $3,000.
6. Payment on a long-term note, $6,000.
7. Acquired plant site and issued bonds, $20,000 for full purchase price (the bonds were selling at par).

Required:
Prepare a SCFP, cash basis, using the indirect method.

P15–12 **(Comparison of Cash Flows from Operating Activities Using the Direct and Indirect Methods)**

The accountants for Alpha Company just completed the income statement and balance sheet for the year, and have provided the following information:

Income Statement

Sales revenues		$15,000
Expenses:		
Cost of goods sold	$8,000	
Depreciation expense	1,000	
Salaries expense	3,000	
Rent expense	1,500	
Insurance expense	500	
Utilities expense	400	
Interest expense on bonds	780	
Loss on sale of investments . . .	100	15,280
		$ (280)

Selected Balance Sheet Accounts

	19B	19C
Merchandise inventory	$ 70	$ 95
Accounts receivable	500	400
Accounts payable	260	310
Salaries payable	30	48
Rent payable	5	3
Prepaid rent	10	6
Prepaid insurance	7	12

Other information:

The company issued $10,000, 8% bonds payable during the year. Investments costing $140 were sold for $40 during the year.

Required:

a. Prepare the cash flows from operating activities section of the SCFP, using the direct method.

b. Prepare the cash flows from operating activities section of the SCFP, using the indirect method.

P15–13 **(Computer Spreadsheet, Unconventional Use of SCFP)**

Spreadsheet Company keeps its records in somewhat of an unconventional way. It finds this approach useful because it represents one way to develop forecasted financial statements using a computer spreadsheet.

The general idea is to have a balance sheet at the beginning of the period. The activities for the fiscal period are kept in the form of a SCFP on the cash and its equivalents basis. The SCFP is then used to update the balance sheet so that a balance sheet, income statement, and statement of changes in retained earnings can be prepared.

The following is the balance sheet as at December 31, 19A.

Assets

Current assets:

Cash	$ 10,200
Accounts receivable (net)	21,400
Inventories	18,500
Prepaid insurance	700
	50,800
Property, plant and equipment	215,000
Accumulated depreciation	(21,500)
Total assets	$244,300

Liabilities

Current liabilities:

Notes payable to bank	$ 8,300
Accounts payable	9,240
Wages payable	300
Income taxes payable	460
	18,300
Long-term liabilities:	
Bonds payable at face value	110,000
Total liabilities	128,300

Shareholders' Equity

Capital stock, no par	100,000
Retained earnings	16,000
Total shareholders' equity	116,000
Total liabilities and shareholders' equity	$244,300

The following statement presents the changes in cash and its equivalents for the year 19B.

Cash from normal operations:

Net income before extraordinary items	$21,000
Income tax payable increase	10
Accounts receivable decrease	1,500
Inventory increase	(2,000)
Depreciation expense	22,500
Accounts payable increase	1,100
Wages payable decrease	(300)
Cash flow from normal operations	43,810

Financing activities:

Repayment of bonds outstanding	(20,000)
Dividends paid	(15,000)
Issue of capital stock to purchase equipment	10,000
Total financing	(25,000)

Investing activities:

Purchase of new equipment with issue of capital stock	(10,000)
Increase in cash and its equivalents	$ 8,810

Additional information obtained from the bank indicates that Spreadsheet repaid $3,000 of its bank loan during 19B.

Required (use computer spreadsheet if available):

a. Prepare a balance sheet and statement of changes in retained earnings for 19B.

b. Assuming you have access to the bank records for 19B and can obtain the following information:

Cash receipts from sales	$259,500
Cash payments for purchases	160,000
Cash payments for expenses	40,000
Cash payments for interest	10,100
Cash payments for income taxes . . .	5,590

Prepare the income statement for 19B.

P15–14 **(Critique and Recast a Deficient SCFP)**

The following statement was prepared by Old Corporation.

OLD CORPORATION
Funds Statement
December 31, 19X

Where obtained:		
Revenues	$180,000	
Accounts receivable decrease	15,000	
Expenses (including depreciation and income tax) . . .	(160,000)	
Depreciation	14,000	
Inventory increase	(6,000)	
Accounts payable increase	7,000	
Income tax payable decrease	(3,000)	
Total		$ 47,000
Sale of permanent assets (at		
book value)		17,000
Issuance of common stock for		
land		25,000
Borrowing—short-term note		40,000
Total cash received		$129,000
Where gone:		
Dividends		$ 20,000
Payment on long-term mortgage		80,000
Machinery		15,000
Land (5,000 shares of common stock)		25,000
Funds (decrease)		(11,000)
Total		$129,000

Required:

a. What was the amount of net income reported for 19X?

b. Did cash increase or decrease? Explain. How can this amount be verified independent of the SCFP?

c. Did the company give enough attention to communication of financial information to the shareholders? Explain the basis for your response.

d. Recast the above statement using a modern format and terminology.

e. What was the amount of the difference between net income and cash generated from normal operations? Why were they different?

f. Do you suspect any potential problems for this company? Explain the basis for your response.

CASE

C15–1 **(Interpreting SCFP)**

This case is based upon the 1987 financial statements of Consolidated-Bathurst, given in Appendix B immediately preceding the Index. You are to use the 1987 data to respond to the following requirements:

a. What period does the SCFP cover?

b. How does the company measure "funds" on the SCFP?

c. How much did funds increase, or decrease?

d. How much cash was retained in the business from operating activities? How was it apparently used?

e. Reconcile the SCFP with the balance sheet.

f. How were financing activities carried out? Is there something unusual in this area?

g. Does the SCFP articulate with the statement of earnings? Demonstrate.

h. How has the liquidity of C-B changed in 1987 from what it was in 1986? Comment.

USING AND INTERPRETING FINANCIAL STATEMENTS

PURPOSE

Throughout the preceding chapters, we emphasized the conceptual basis of accounting. An understanding of the rationale underlying accounting is important for both preparers and users of financial statements. In this chapter we introduce the use and analysis of financial statements. Many widely used analytical techniques are discussed and illustrated. As you study this chapter, you will see that an understanding of accounting rules and concepts is essential for effective analysis of financial statements.

Many financial analysts use ratios to help evaluate companies. Some financial statements include the results of selected ratios. As stated on the facing page, physical data regarding production, employees, or customers are often provided to statement users.

LEARNING OBJECTIVES

1. Identify the major users of financial statements and explain how they use statements.
2. Explain the objectives of ratio analysis.
3. Identify and compute 13 widely used accounting ratios.
4. Interpret accounting ratios.
5. Describe how accounting alternatives affect ratio analysis.
6. Expand your accounting vocabulary by learning about the "Important Terms Defined in This Chapter."
7. Apply the knowledge learned from this chapter.

ORGANIZATION

1. Financial reports in the decision-making process.
2. Ratio and percentage analysis.
3. Widely used ratios.
4. Interpreting ratios.
5. Impact of accounting alternatives on ratio analysis.

Triton Canada

Triton Canada marked a strong recovery in 1987 from the effects of the 1986 oil price declines: cash flow increased 47% over 1986 to $18 million; net earnings recovered to $3.1 million compared to a $17 million loss for 1986; and new equity issues drove the debt-equity ratio down to 1.1:1 from 3.3:1 in 1986.

Revenue
Revenue increased by 26% over 1986 to a record $45.5 million, with all components showing improvement. Conventional oil revenue rose 123% to $5.5 million. Heavy oil revenue increased slightly to $4.9 million from $4.4 million in 1986.

Gas production revenue showed a modest increase despite a substantial decline in gas prices, reflecting a 29% increase in production volumes. Gas transportation revenue increased 32% reflecting the increased emphasis being placed on this profit centre. Gas brokerage revenue increased to $8.3 million from $4.9 million in 1986 as Triton Canada took advantage of low spot prices to preserve its existing reserve base.

Liquidity
The dramatic improvement in Triton Canada's financial position in 1987 is clearly evident. Working capital recovered from a deficiency of $2.6 million in 1986 to a surplus of $4.4 million in 1987, a $7 million improvement. Long term obligations decreased 13%, while unused lines of credit almost tripled to $12.8 million. Combined with the effect of equity issues, this resulted in a fall in the debt-equity ratio from 3.3:1 in 1986 to 1.1:1 in 1987.

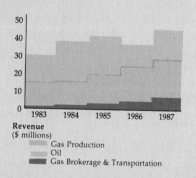

Revenue
($ millions)

- Gas Production
- Oil
- Gas Brokerage & Transportation

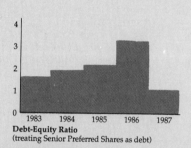

Debt-Equity Ratio
(treating Senior Preferred Shares as debt)

Operating	1987	1986	Increase (Decrease)	% Change
Gas (million cubic feet before royalty)				
Total reserves at year-end	149,664	139,105	10,559	8
Average daily production	56.2	43.7	12.5	29
Wellhead price (per thousand cubic feet)	$ 1.23	$ 1.64	$ (0.41)	(25)
Conventional oil (barrels before royalty)				
Total reserves at year-end	2,709,000	1,312,000	1,397,000	106
Average daily sales	946	437	509	116
Wellhead price (per barrel)	$ 21.21	$ 17.86	$ 3.35	19
Heavy oil (barrels before royalty)				
Total reserves at year-end	3,145,000	4,216,000	(1,071,000)	(25)
Average daily sales	911	1,157	(246)	(21)
Wellhead price (per barrel)	$ 15.49	$ 11.19	$ 4.30	38
Gross wells drilled	55	62	(7)	(11)

Financial Reports in the Decision-Making Process

The objective of financial statements is to provide information that helps users make better economic decisions. There are two broad groups of decision makers who use financial statements. One group is the management of the business who rely on accounting data to make important management decisions. The second group is "external" decision makers. This group consists primarily of investors (both present and potential owners), investment analysts, creditors, government, labour organizations, and the public. Financial accounting and the external financial reports serve a diverse group of decision makers with different information needs.

Users of financial statements are interested in three types of information:

1. **Information about past performance**—Information concerning such items as income, sales volume, extraordinary items, cash flows, and return earned on the investment helps assess the success of the business and the effectiveness of the management. Such information also helps the decision maker compare one entity with others.

2. **Information about the present condition of a business**—This type of information helps answer such questions as: What types of assets are owned? How much debt does the business owe, and when is it due? What is the cash position? How much of the earnings have been retained in the business? What are the EPS, return-on-investment, and debt/equity ratios? What is the inventory position? Answers to these and similar economic questions help the decison maker assess the successes and failures of the past; but, more importantly, they provide useful information in assessing the cash flows and profit potentials of the business.

3. **Information about the future performance of the business**—Decision makers select from among several alternative courses of action. Each course of action will cause different results. All decisions are future oriented because they do not (and cannot) affect the past. However, in predicting the probable future impact of a decision, reliable measurements of what has happened in the recent past are valuable. For example, the recent sales and earnings trends of a business are good indicators of what might be expected in the future. The primary objective of measuring past performance and the present condition of a business is to aid in predicting the future cash flows of the business. One source of information about future prospects is the management report contained in the annual report package. The report to shareholders by management (illustrated in Exhibit 16–1) commonly contains projections by management of future prospects.

Some decisions are made intuitively and without much supporting data. In such cases there is no systematic attempt to collect relevant data. Therefore, it is practically impossible to array, measure, and evaluate each alternative. Intuitive decision making is used for several reasons. The time and cost of collecting data

Exhibit 16–1 Management report—Illustration

Nineteen eighty-seven was a year of progress and achievement for Union Carbide Canada. Income before extraordinary items improved to $25.7 million, or $1.20 per share, from 1986's $16.3 million, or 62 cents a share. Sales of $421.2 million were 17 per cent higher than sales of $359.0 million the previous year.

A portion of the sales increase reflects the inclusion in 1987 results of polyethylene specialties which were recorded as a discontinued operation in 1986 after a decision had been reached to divest the polyethylene business. When the commodity segment of that business and the associated Moore Township, Ontario, manufacturing facility were sold early in the year, the specialty side of the business, serving wire and cable markets, was retained.

The sale of commodity polyethylene operations generated an extraordinary gain of $13.8 million which was partially offset by an $8.0 million writedown of an investment in Polysar Limited Third Preferred shares (see Financial Review on page 9). The difference of $5.8 million increased 1987 final net income to $31.5 million. In 1986, final net income was $47.5 million and included $31.2 million of extraordinary items.

It was the fifth successive year of solid earnings gains from continuing operations, demonstrating the strength and potential of the Company's leaner portfolio of industrial businesses that resulted from a broad 1986 restructuring. The outlook suggests the trend will be maintained in 1988. Beyond that, the Company should continue to show improved results as its major markets benefit from the liberalized trade provisions of the Canada-U.S. Trade Agreement which begin phasing in the following year.

The Board of Directors recognized the improving pattern of performance in January and increased the quarterly dividend by 50 per cent to 7.5 cents per share, or 30 cents a share on an annual basis.

Business strategies were supported in 1987 by a $34.6 million capital program, involving expansions to industrial gases capacity in Quebec, Ontario and Alberta, and the launch of a modernization program at the Company's Montreal East petrochemical complex.

After redeeming $60 million of preferred shares at mid-year, the Company subsequently completed a successful $125 million financing, utilizing the innovative concept of an equipment trust. The financing will significantly reduce borrowing costs over the next five years.

Considerable progress was achieved in introducing The Canadian Chemical Producers' Association's CAER (Community Awareness and Emergency Response) program to major facilities. The program aims to achieve greater community understanding of chemical plant operations and closer integration with the community in emergency response planning. It is a key element in a long-term CCPA program, called "Responsible Care: A Total Commitment," that pledges all 73 member companies to rigorous codes of practice to ensure control of every stage of the life cycle of chemical products.

There was one change in the Board of Directors during the year and one new senior management appointment. James C. Thackray, former Chairman of Bell Canada, retired from the Board in March after 14 years of highly valued service. In July, Allan S. Cole, formerly an Assistant Treasurer, was named Vice-President, Corporate Services.

We are pleased with the accomplishments of 1987 which, we believe, reflect Union Carbide's dedication to the basic values guiding our activities: customer service, technological leadership, people excellence, safety and environmental protection second to none and a simplified approach to the operation of our businesses.

We are also confident about the future. Our restructuring has readied us for the realities of the more competitive business environment ahead. We recognize the unsettling effect that change of this magnitude can have and are proud of Union Carbide Canada's people who have responded intelligently and energetically to the challenges.

Chairman and
Chief Executive Officer

Source: Union Carbide Canada Limited, Annual Report, 1987.

may prevent a careful analysis. Sometimes the decision maker is unsophisticated and may not understand more systematic approaches to decision making. Unsophisticated decision makers tend to oversimplify the decision-making process, disregard basic information, and often overlook the financial effects of a decision.

In contrast, sophisticated decision makers prepare a systematic analysis of each alternative. Information regarding each alternative is collected and evaluated. For most business decisions, the financial statements provide critical financial data for effective decision makers.

Financial statement users should understand what was measured and how it was measured. Even if you do not plan to major in accounting, you will use extensively the information that you have studied in this book to evaluate the data presented in the financial reports of a business. One of the objectives of the preceding chapters was to help you understand and evaluate financial statements as a decision maker.

Financial statements are general-purpose statements that are designed primarily to meet the special needs of external decision makers. Because of the varied needs of these users, supplementary financial data may be needed for many decisions.

Investors

The investor group includes current owners, potential owners, and investment analysts (because they advise investors). Investors include individuals, mutual funds, other businesses, pension funds, and institutions, such as your local university.

Most investors do not seek a controlling interest when they buy shares. Instead, they invest with the expectation of earning a return on their investment. The return on a share investment has two components: (1) dividend revenue during the investment period and (2) increases in the market value of the shares owned. When considering an investment of this type, the investor has the problem of predicting the future **income** and **growth** of the business. Investors are interested in enterprise income because it is the "source" of future dividends. They are interested in enterprise growth because it tends to cause the market value of the shares to increase. In making these predictions, the investor should consider three factors:

1. **Economywide factors**—Often the overall health of the economy will have a direct impact on the performance of an individual business. Investors should consider such data as the gross national product, productivity, unemployment rate, general inflation rate, and changes in interest rates.
2. **Industry factors**—Certain events have a major impact on each company within an industry but have only a minor impact on other companies.

For example, changes in the cost of oil products have a significant effect on the airline industry but only a minor effect on the electronics industry.

3. **Individual company factors**—These factors may be either quantifiable or nonquantifiable. Nonquantifiable factors include the introduction of a new product, a lawsuit, and changes in key personnel. Information concerning nonquantifiable factors often is presented in notes to the financial statements. Data pertaining to quantifiable factors are presented in the basic financial statements. The income statement provides significant information for the investor, such as revenue from products and services, extraordinary items, income tax impacts, net income, and earnings per share. Other relationships, such as gross margin, profit margin, and expense relationships, can be computed. Also, the balance sheet, the statement of changes in financial position, and the notes to the financial statements provide measurements of past profit performance, cash flow, and current financial position. These data constitute an important base from which predictions of future income and growth can be made. These data are particularly useful when compared with recent past periods as shown in Exhibit 16–2.

Exhibit 16–2   Illustration of comparative financial statements

PACKARD COMPANY
Comparative Income Statements (simplified for illustration)
For the Years Ended December 31, 19B, and 19A

	Year ended Dec. 31		Increase (decrease) 19B over 19A	
	19B	**19A***	**Amount**	**Percent**
Sales revenue	$120,000	$100,000	$20,000	20.0
Cost of goods sold	72,600	60,000	12,600	21.0
Gross margin on sales	47,400	40,000	7,400	18.5
Operating expenses:				
Distribution expenses	22,630	15,000	7,630	50.9
Administrative expenses	11,870	13,300	(1,430)	(10.8)
Interest expense	1,500	1,700	(200)	(11.8)
Total expenses	36,000	30,000	6,000	20.0
Pretax income	11,400	10,000	1,400	14.0
Income taxes	2,600	2,000	600	30.0
Net income	$ 8,800	$ 8,000	$ 800	10.0

* Base year for computing percents.

Exhibit 16–2 *(concluded)*

PACKARD COMPANY
Comparative Balance Sheets (simplified for illustration)
At December 31, 19B, and 19A

	At December 31		Increase (decrease) 19B over 19A	
	19B	19A*	Amount	Percent
Assets				
Current assets:				
Cash	$ 13,000	9,000	$ 4,000	44.4
Accounts receivable (net)	8,400	7,000	1,400	20.0
Merchandise inventory	54,000	60,000	(6,000)	(10.0)
Prepaid expenses	2,000	4,000	(2,000)	(50.0)
Total current assets	77,400	80,000	(2,600)	3.3
Investments:				
Real estate	8,000	8,000		
Operational assets:				
Equipment and furniture	82,500	75,000	7,500	10.0
Less: accumulated depreciation	(23,250)	(15,000)	8,250	55.0
Total operational assets	59,250	60,000	(750)	(1.3)
Other assets	1,900	2,000	(100)	(5.0)
Total assets*	$146,550	$150,000	$(3,450)	(2.3)
Liabilities				
Current liabilities:				
Accounts payable	$ 13,200	12,000	$ 1,200	10.0
Notes payable, short term	15,000	20,000	(5,000)	(25.0)
Accrued wages payable	7,200	8,000	(800)	(10.0)
Total current liabilities	35,400	40,000	(4,600)	(11.5)
Long-term liabilities:				
Notes payable, long term	7,150	10,000	(2,850)	(28.5)
Total liabilities	42,550	50,000	(7,450)	(14.9)
Shareholders' Equity				
Common stock, no par, 8,500 shares outstanding	85,000	85,000		
Retained earnings	19,000	15,000	4,000	26.7
Total shareholders' equity	104,000	100,000	4,000	4.0
Total liabilities and shareholders' equity* . . .	$146,550	$150,000	$(3,450)	(2.3)

* Base year for computing percents.

Creditors

Suppliers, financial institutions, and individuals provide long-term and short-term credit to businesses. Creditors lend money with the expectation that they will earn a return on their money and that funds will be repaid in accordance with the loan agreement. Creditors are concerned about the following:

1. Profit potential of the business because a profitable entity is more likely to meet its credit obligations.
2. Ability of the business to generate cash from recurring operations because it will be in a more favourable position to pay its debts.
3. Financial position of the business because the assets are security for the debts and the debts indicate the future demand for cash at debt maturity dates.

Creditors use the financial reports for information concerning the business. To enhance the credibility of these reports, creditors often require that the reports be audited by an independent PA.

Analysis of Financial Statements

Financial statements include a large volume of quantitative data supplemented by disclosure notes. The notes are an integral part of the financial statements and help users interpret the statements. Notes elaborate on accounting policies, major financial effects and events, and certain nonquantifiable events that may contribute to the success or failure of the firm. The notes often include supplemental schedules, such as listings of assets by geographic region or lines of business. The statements also include a letter from the chief executive officer that contains a management discussion and analysis of the operations of the company (Exhibit 16–1).

Four techniques are used to help decision makers understand and interpret the external financial statements: (1) comparative financial statements, (2) long-term summaries, (3) graphic presentations, and (4) ratio analyses.

Comparative Financial Statements

Accounting rules require the presentation of **comparative financial statements** covering, as a minimum, the current year and the immediately prior year.

Most financial statements present, side by side, the results for the current and the preceding years (similar to the statements shown in Exhibit 16–2). Analysis of comparative statements is made easier if two additional columns are added for (1) the **amount** of change for each item and (2) the **percent** of change. These data are shown in Exhibit 16–2. Often the percent of change from the prior period is more helpful for interpretative purposes than the absolute dollar amount of change. Notice on each line that the percents are determined by dividing the amount of the change by the amount for the preceding year. For example, in Exhibit 16–2, the percentage on the Cash line was computed as $4,000 ÷ $9,000 = 44.4%. The amount from the earlier years is used as the base amount.

Long-Term Summaries

In the interest of full disclosure, annual reports often give 5-, 10-, and even 20-year summaries of certain basic data, such as sales revenue, net income, total assets, total liabilities, total owners' equity, and selected ratios. Data for a series of years are important in interpreting the financial statements for the current period. Misinterpretation is likely when the statement user limits consideration to only the last one or two periods. The vagaries of business transactions, economic events, and accounting techniques are such that the financial reports for a single time period usually do not provide a sound basis for assessing the long-term potential of a business. Sophisticated financial analysts use data for a number of periods so that trends may be identified.

Care should be used in intepreting long-term summaries. Data for a period in the distant past may not be comparable because of changes in the company, industry, and environment. For example, Imperial Oil is a very different company now than it was when a gallon of gasoline sold for 25 cents.

In interpreting comparative data, the items showing significant increases and decreases should receive special attention. Analysts should identify significant **turning points,** either upward or downward, in trends for important items such as net income and cash flow. The turning points often provide indication of significant future trends. Analysts should determine the **underlying causes** for significant favourable or unfavourable changes.

Ratio and Percentage Analysis

Some amounts on financial statements, such as net income, are significant in and of themselves. Other data are more significant when expressed as a relationship to other amounts. Significant relationships can be examined through the use of an analytical tool called **ratio** or **percentage analysis.** A ratio or percent expresses the proportionate relationship between two different amounts. A ratio or percent is computed by dividing one quantity by another quantity. For example, the fact that a company earned net income of $500,000 assumes greater significance when net income is compared with the shareholders' investment in the company. Assuming that shareholders' equity is $5,000,000, the relationship of earnings to shareholder investment is $500,000 ÷ $5,000,000 = 0.1, or 10%. This ratio indicates a different level of performance than would be the case if shareholders' equity was $50,000,000. Ratio analysis helps decision makers to identify significant relationships and to compare companies more realistically than if only single amounts were analyzed.

There are two kinds of ratio analysis: (1) relationships **within one period** and (2) relationships **between periods.** Also, ratios may be computed with amounts within one statement, such as the income statement, or between different statements, such as the income statement and the balance sheet. In Exhibit 16–2, the percents of change represent a percentage analysis between periods within each statement.

Financial statement analysis is a judgmental process. No single ratio or percentage can be identified as appropriate to all situations. Each analytical situation may require the calculation of several ratios. However, there are several ratios or percentages that usually are used because they are appropriate to many situations.

Component Percentages

Component percentages are used to express each item on a particular statement as a percentage of a single **base amount** (i.e., the denominator of the ratio). Exhibit 16–3 shows a component analysis for the 19A and 19B income statements and balance sheets for Packard Company. To compute component percentages for the income statement, the base amount is **net sales revenue.** Therefore, each

Exhibit 16–3 Illustration of component percentages

PACKARD COMPANY
Income Statements (simplified for illustration)
For the Years Ended December 31, 19B, and 19A

	For the year ended			
	Dec. 31, 19B		Dec. 31, 19A	
	Amount	Percent	Amount	Percent
Sales revenue (net)*	$120,000	100.0	$100,000	100.0
Cost of goods sold	72,600	60.5	60,000	60.0
Gross margin on sales	47,400	39.5	40,000	40.0
Operating expenses:				
Distribution expenses	22,630	18.9	15,000	15.0
Administrative expenses	11,870	9.9	13,300	13.3
Interest expense	1,500	1.2	1,700	1.7
Total expenses	36,000	30.0	30,000	30.0
Pretax income	11,400	9.5	10,000	10.0
Income taxes	2,600	2.2	2,000	2.0
Net income	$ 8,800	7.3	$ 8,000	8.0

* Base amount.

Exhibit 16–3 *(concluded)*

PACKARD COMPANY
Balance Sheets (simplified for illustration)
At December 31, 19B, and 19A

	At Dec. 31, 19B Amount	Percent	At Dec. 31, 19A Amount	Percent
Assets				
Current assets:				
Cash	$ 13,000	8.9	$ 9,000	6.0
Accounts receivable (net)	8,400	5.7	7,000	4.6
Merchandise inventory	54,000	36.8	60,000	40.0
Prepaid expenses	2,000	1.4	4,000	2.7
Total current assets	77,400	52.8	80,000	53.3
Investments:				
Real estate	8,000	5.5	8,000	5.3
Operational assets:				
Equipment and furniture	82,500	56.3	75,000	50.0
Less: Accumulated depreciation	(23,250)	(15.9)	(15,000)	(10.0)
Total operational assets	59,250	40.4	60,000	40.0
Other assets	1,900	1.3	2,000	1.4
Total assets*	$146,550	100.0	$150,000	100.0
Liabilities				
Current liabilities:				
Accounts payable	$ 13,200	9.0	$ 12,000	8.0
Notes payable, short term	15,000	10.2	20,000	13.3
Accrued wages payable	7,200	4.9	8,000	5.3
Total current liabilities	35,400	24.1	40,000	26.6
Long-term liabilities:				
Notes payable, long term	7,150	4.9	10,000	6.7
Total liabilities	42,550	29.0	50,000	33.3
Shareholders' Equity				
Common stock, no par, 8,500 shares				
outstanding	85,000	58.0	85,000	56.7
Retained earnings	19,000	13.0	15,000	10.0
Total shareholders' equity	104,000	71.0	100,000	66.7
Total liabilities and shareholders' equity*	$146,550	100.0	$150,000	100.0

* Base amount.

expense is expressed as a percent of net sales revenue. On the balance sheet, the base amount is **total assets.** The percents are derived by dividing each balance sheet account by total assets.

Component percentages are useful because they reveal important proportional relationships. For example, in the income statement in Exhibit 16–3, observe that distribution expenses were 18.9% of sales revenue in 19B, compared with 15% in 19A. On the balance sheet, notice that merchandise inventory was 36.8% of total assets for 19B, compared with 40% for 19A. These changes in important relationships often suggest the need for further inquiry because they may suggest opportunities for corrective action and increased profitability.

Some Widely Used Ratios

Numerous ratios and percentages can be computed from a single set of financial statements, but only a selected number may be useful in a given situation. A common approach is to compute certain widely used ratios and then decide which additional ratios are relevant to the particular decision.

Balance sheet amounts relate to one instant in time, and income statement amounts relate to a period of time. Therefore, care should be exercised when calculating ratios that use amounts from both statements. When an income statement amount is compared with a balance sheet amount, a balance sheet **average amount** often is used to reflect changes in the balance sheet amounts. The selected balance sheet amount usually is computed as the average of the amounts shown on the beginning and ending balance sheets. When additional information is available, such as monthly or quarterly data, an average of the additional data often is more representative.

Commonly used financial ratios can be grouped into the five categories shown in Exhibit 16–4.

Tests of Profitability

Profitability is a primary measure of the overall success of a company. Indeed, it is a necessary condition for survival. Investors and creditors would prefer a **single measure** of profitability that would be meaningful in all situations. Unfortunately, no single measure can be devised to meet this comprehensive need. Tests of profitability focus on measuring the adequacy of income by comparing it with one or more primary activities or factors that are measured in the financial statements. Five different tests of profitability are explained below.

1. Return on Owners' Investment (ROI_o)

This ratio is a fundamental test of profitability. It relates income to the investment that was made by the owners to earn the income. This ratio can be used to measure the profitability of any investment, whether for a company, a project, or an individual. The return on owners' investment ratio is computed as follows:

Exhibit 16–4 Widely used accounting ratios

Ratio	Basic computation
Tests of profitability:	
1.* Return on owners' investment (ROI$_o$).	$$\frac{\text{Income}}{\text{Average owners' equity}}$$
2. Return on total investment (ROI$_t$).	$$\frac{\text{Income} + \text{Interest expense (net of tax)}}{\text{Average total assets}}$$
3. Financial leverage (ROI$_o$ − ROI$_t$).	$$\frac{\text{Return on}}{\text{owners' investment}} - \frac{\text{Return on}}{\text{total investment}}$$
4. Earnings per share.	$$\frac{\text{Income}}{\text{Average number of shares of common stock outstanding}}$$
5. Profit margin.	$$\frac{\text{Income (before extraordinary items)}}{\text{Net sales revenue}}$$
Tests of liquidity:	
6. Working capital (or current) ratio.	$$\frac{\text{Current assets}}{\text{Current liabilities}}$$
7. Quick ratio.	$$\frac{\text{Quick assets}}{\text{Current liabilities}}$$
8. Receivable turnover.	$$\frac{\text{Net credit sales}}{\text{Average net trade receivables}}$$
9. Inventory turnover.	$$\frac{\text{Cost of goods sold}}{\text{Average inventory}}$$
Test of solvency and equity position:	
10. Debt/equity ratio.	$$\frac{\text{Total liabilities}}{\text{Owners' equity}}$$
Market tests:	
11. Price/earnings ratio.	$$\frac{\text{Current market price per share}}{\text{Earnings per share}}$$
12. Dividend yield ratio.	$$\frac{\text{Dividends per share}}{\text{Market price per share}}$$
Miscellaneous ratio:	
13. Book value per share.	$$\frac{\text{Common stock equity}}{\text{Number of shares of common stock outstanding}}$$

* The numbers to the left are used in the following discussions to facilitate reference.

$$\text{Return on owners' investment} = \frac{\text{Income*}}{\text{Average owners' equity}\dagger}$$

$$\text{Packard Company, 19B} = \frac{\$8,800*}{\$102,000\dagger} = 8.6\%$$

Based on Exhibit 16–3.

* Income **before** extraordinary items should be used.

† Average owners' equity is preferable when available, that is ($100,000 + $104,000) ÷ 2 = $102,000.

Packard Company earned 8.6%, after income taxes, on the investment provided by the **owners.** Return on owners' investment is a particularly useful measure of profitability from the **viewpoint of the owners.** It relates two fundamental factors—the amount of the owners' investment and the return earned for the owners on that investment.

2. Return on Total Investment (ROI$_t$)

Another view of the return on investment concept relates income to **total assets** (i.e., total investment) used to earn income. Under this broader concept, return on total investment is computed as follows:

$$\text{Return on total investment} = \frac{\text{Income* + Interest expense (net of tax)}}{\text{Average total assets}\dagger}$$

$$\text{Packard Company 19B} = \frac{\$8,800* + (\$1,500 \times 77\%)}{\$148,275\dagger} = 6.7\%$$

Based on Exhibit 16–3.

* Income before extraordinary items should be used. This illustration assumes an average income tax rate of 23%.

† Average total assets should be used; that is ($150,000 + $146,550) ÷ 2 = $148,275.

Packard Company earned 6.7% on the **total resources it used** during the year. Under this concept, **investment** is the amount of resources provided by both owners and creditors. Return is measured as the return to both owners and creditors. To compute return on **total** investment, interest expense (net of income tax) is added back to income because interest is the return on the creditors' investment. It must be added back because it was previously deducted to derive net income. The denominator represents **total** investment, therefore, the numerator (income) must include the total return that was available to the suppliers of funds. The interest is measured net of income tax because it represents the net cost to the corporation for the funds provided by creditors.

Return on total investment reflects the combined effect of both the operating and the financing activities of a company as shown in Exhibit 16–5 (remember that total assets always equals total liabilities plus total owners' equity).

Most analysts compute the two return-on-investment ratios shown above. Return on total investment is the preferable measure of **management perform-**

Exhibit 16–5 Components of return on total investment

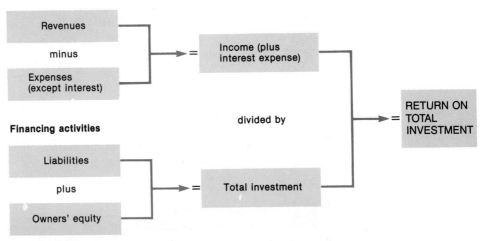

Operating activities

| Revenues |
| minus |
| Expenses (except interest) |

= Income (plus interest expense)

Financing activities

| Liabilities |
| plus |
| Owners' equity |

= Total investment

divided by

= RETURN ON TOTAL INVESTMENT

ance in using all of the resources available to the company. The return on owners' equity is relevant to the owners because it measures the return that has "accrued" to them.

3. Financial Leverage

Financial leverage is the advantage, or disadvantage, which occurs as the result of earning a return on owners' investments that is different from the return earned on total investment (i.e., $ROI_o - ROI_t$). Most companies have positive leverage. Positive leverage occurs when the rate of return on a company's investments is higher than the average aftertax interest rate on borrowed funds. Basically, the company borrows at one rate, and invests at a higher rate of return.

Financial leverage can be measured by comparing the two return-on-investment ratios as follows:

$$\text{Financial leverage} = \begin{array}{c}\text{Return on} \\ \text{owners' investment}\end{array} - \begin{array}{c}\text{Return on} \\ \text{total investment}\end{array}$$

$$\text{Packard Company, 19B} = 8.6\% - 6.7\% = 1.9\% \quad \text{(positive leverage)}$$

When a company can borrow funds at an aftertax interest rate and invest those funds to earn a higher aftertax rate of return, the difference "accrues" to the benefit of the owners. This is the primary reason that most companies obtain a significant amount of resources from creditors rather than obtaining resources only from the sale of their capital stock.

4. Earnings per Share (EPS)

This ratio evaluates profitability strictly from the common shareholders' point of view. Instead of being based on the dollar amount of the investment, it is based on the number of shares of common stock outstanding. EPS is computed as follows:

$$\text{Earnings per share} = \frac{\text{Income} - \begin{array}{c}\text{Preferred dividends}\\\text{declared}\end{array}}{\begin{array}{c}\text{Average number of shares of}\\\text{common stock outstanding}\end{array}}$$

$$\text{Packard Company, 19B} = \frac{\$8,800 - 0}{8,500} = \$1.04 \text{ per share}$$

EPS usually is computed on three amounts if extraordinary items are reported on the income statement: (1) income before extraordinary items (required), (2) extraordinary items (optional), and (3) net income (required). Of the three EPS amounts, the first one is considered the most relevant because extraordinary items are unusual and do not reoccur.

5. Profit Margin

This percent is based on two income statement amounts. It is computed as follows:

$$\text{Profit margin} = \frac{\begin{array}{c}\text{Income (before}\\\text{extraordinary items)}\end{array}}{\text{Net sales}}$$

$$\text{Packard Company, 19B} = \frac{\$8,800}{\$120,000} = 7.3\%$$

This profitability test is the percent of each sales dollar, on the average, that is profit. For Packard Company, each dollar of sales generated 7.3 cents of profit. Care must be used in analyzing the profit margin because it does not consider the amount of resources employed (i.e., total investment) to earn income. For example, the income statements of Company A and Company B may show the following:

		Company A	Company B
a.	Sales revenue	$100,000	$150,000
b.	Income	$ 5,000	$ 7,500
c.	Profit margin (b) ÷ (a)	5%	5%
d.	Total investment	$ 50,000	$125,000
e.	Return on total investment* (b) ÷ (d)	10%	6%

* Assuming no interest expense.

In this example, both companies reported the same profit margin (5%). Company A, however, appears to be performing much better because it is earning a 10% return on the total investment versus the 6% earned by Company B. The profit margin percents do not reflect the effect of the $50,000 total investment in Company A compared to the $125,000 total investment in Company B. The effect of the different amounts of investment in each company is reflected in the return on investment (ROI) percents. Thus, the profit margin omits one of the two important factors that should be used in evaluating return on the investment.

Comparing profit margins for companies in different industries is difficult. For example, profit margins in the food industry are very low while profit margins in the jewelry business are large. Both types of businesses can be quite profitable because they differ in terms of investment. Grocery stores have small margins but require a relatively small investment compared to their sales. Jewelry stores earn more profit from each sales dollar but require a large investment in relation to their sales.

Tests of Liquidity

Liquidity refers to a company's ability to meet its currently maturing debts. Tests of liquidity focus on the relationship between current assets and current liabilities. The ability of a company to pay its current liabilities is an important factor in evaluating short-term financial strength. For example, a company that does not have cash available to pay for purchases on a timely basis will lose its cash discounts and run the risk of discontinued credit by vendors. Two ratios are used to measure liquidity: the working capital (or current) ratio and the quick ratio. Recall that working capital is the difference between total current assets and total current liabilities.

6. Working Capital (Current) Ratio

This ratio measures the relationship between total current assets and total current liabilities at a specific date. It is computed as follows:

$$\text{Working capital (current) ratio} = \frac{\text{Current assets}}{\text{Current liabilities}}$$

$$\text{Packard Company, 19B} = \frac{\$77,400}{\$35,400} = 2.2 \text{ times or 2.2 to 1}$$

At year-end, current assets for Packard Company were 2.2 times current liabilities or, alternatively, for each $1 of current liabilities there were $2.20 of current assets. The working capital ratio measures the cushion of working capital maintained in order to allow for the inevitable unevenness in the flow of "funds" through the working capital accounts.[1]

7. Quick Ratio (or Acid-Test Ratio)

This ratio is similar to the working capital ratio except that it is a more stringent test of short-term liquidity. It is computed as follows:

$$\text{Quick ratio} = \frac{\text{Quick assets}}{\text{Current liabilities}}$$

$$\text{Packard Company, 19B} = \frac{\$21,400}{\$35,400} = 0.60 \text{ times or } 0.60 \text{ to } 1$$

Quick assets are readily convertible into cash at approximately their book values. Quick assets include cash, short-term temporary investments, and accounts receivable (net of the allowance for doubtful accounts). Inventories usually are omitted from quick assets because of the uncertainty of when cash will be received from the sale of inventory in the future. In unusual circumstances, if the inventory will turn to cash very quickly, it should be included. In contrast, prepaid expenses do not "convert" to cash and are excluded from quick assets. Thus, the quick or acid-test ratio is a more severe test of liquidity than is the working capital ratio.

8. Receivable turnover

Short-term liquidity often is measured in terms of **turnover** of certain current assets. Two additional ratios that measure nearness to cash are receivable turnover and inventory turnover.

Receivable turnover is computed as follows:

$$\text{Receivable turnover} = \frac{\text{Net credit sales*}}{\text{Average net trade receivables}}$$

$$\begin{array}{c}\text{Packard Company, 19B} \\ \text{(net credit sales assumed} \\ \text{to be \$77,000 for 19B)}\end{array} = \frac{\$77,000}{(\$7,000 + \$8,400) \div 2} = 10 \text{ times}$$

* When the amount of credit sales is not known, total sales may be used as a rough approximation.

---

[1] Occasionally, "working capital" is used to mean total current asssets. This usage is confusing and unnecessary because "total current assets" is more descriptive. Sometimes the term **net working capital** is used to describe the difference between current assets and current liabilities. Throughout this book, we have followed the more general use of working capital to mean the difference between current assets and current liabilities.

This ratio is called a turnover ratio because it reflects how many times the trade receivables were recorded, collected, then recorded again during the period (i.e., "turnover"). Receivable turnover expresses the relationship of the average balance in Accounts Receivable to the transactions (i.e., credit sales) that created those receivables. This ratio measures the effectiveness of the credit-granting and collection activities of the company. A high receivable turnover ratio suggests effective collection activities. Granting credit to poor credit risks and ineffective collection efforts will cause this ratio to be low. A very low ratio is obviously a problem, but a very high ratio can also be a problem. A very high ratio may indicate an overly stringent credit policy that would cause lost sales and profits.

The receivable turnover ratio often is converted to a time basis known as the average age of receivables. The computation is as follows:

$$\frac{\text{Average age of}}{\text{trade receivables}} = \frac{\text{Days in year}}{\text{Receivable turnover}}$$

$$\text{Packard Company, 19B} = \frac{365}{10} = \frac{36.5 \text{ average days}}{\text{to collect}}$$

The effectiveness of credit and collection activities sometimes is judged by the "rule of thumb" that the **average days to collect** should not exceed 1½ times the credit terms. For example, if the credit terms are 2/10, n/30, the average days to collect should not exceed 45 days (i.e., not more than 15 days past due). Like all rules of thumb, this one has many exceptions. However, an increase or decrease in the average days to collect would suggest changes in the credit policies and/or changes in collection efficiency.

9. Inventory Turnover

Inventory turnover measures the liquidity (i.e., nearness to cash) of the inventory. It reflects the relationship of the inventory to the volume of goods sold during the period. The computation is as follows:

$$\text{Inventory turnover} = \frac{\text{Cost of goods sold}}{\text{Average inventory}}$$

$$\text{Packard Company, 19B} = \frac{\$72,600}{(\$60,000 + \$54,000) \div 2} = 1.3 \text{ times}$$

The inventory "turned over" 1.3 times during the year because cost of goods sold was 1.3 times the average inventory level. Because profit normally is realized each time the inventory is sold (i.e., turned over), an increase in the ratio is usually favourable. However, if the ratio is too high, sales may be lost because of items that are out of stock. The turnover ratio often is converted to a time-basis expression called the **average days' supply in inventory.** The computation is:

$$\text{Average days' supply in inventory} = \frac{\text{Days in year}}{\text{Inventory turnover}}$$

$$\text{Packard Company, 19B} = \frac{365}{1.3} = \text{281 average days' supply in inventory}$$

Turnover ratios are used extensively because they are easy to understand. Normal (or average) inventory turnover ratios vary significantly by industry classification. Companies in the food industry (grocery stores and restaurants) have high inventory turnover ratios while companies that sell expensive merchandise (automobile dealers and high-fashion clothes) have much lower ratios.

Tests of Solvency and Equity Position

Solvency refers to the ability of a company to meet its **long-term obligations** on a continuing basis. Certain critical relationships can be identified by analyzing how a company has financed its assets and activities. The relative amount of resources provided by creditors and owners is known as a company's **equity position.** The debt/equity ratio is used to reflect the equity position of a company.

10. Debt/Equity Ratio
This ratio expresses the direct proportion between debt and owners' equity.[2] It is computed as follows:

$$\text{Debt/equity ratio} = \frac{\text{Total liabilities (i.e., creditors' equity)}}{\text{Owners' equity}}$$

$$\text{Packard Company, 19B} = \frac{\$42,550}{\$104,000} = 0.41 \text{ (or 41\%)}$$

---

[2] The relationship between debt and owners' equity alternatively may be calculated with the following two ratios:

$$\text{Owners' equity to total equities} = \frac{\text{Owners' equity}}{\text{Total equities}}$$

$$\text{Packard Company, 19B} = \frac{\$104,000}{\$146,550} = 71\%$$

$$\text{Creditors' equity to total equities} = \frac{\text{Creditors' equity}}{\text{Total equities}}$$

$$\text{Packard Company, 19B} = \frac{\$42,550}{\$146,550} = 29\%$$

This ratio means that for each $1 of owners' equity, there was $0.41 of liabilities.

Debt is risky for a company because it imposes important contractual obligations. There are (a) specific maturity dates for the principal amounts and (b) specific interest payments that must be made. Debt obligations are enforceable by law and do not depend upon the earnings of the company. In contrast, dividends for shareholders are always at the discretion of the company and are not legally enforceable until declared by the board of directors. Owners' equity is "permanent" capital that does not have a maturity date. Thus, equity capital usually is seen as much less risky than debt for a company.

Despite the risk associated with debt, most companies get significant amounts of resources from creditors because of the advantages of financial leverage. Typically, the return on company investments is higher than the aftertax interest rate paid to creditors. By accepting the risk associated with debt, management may earn a higher return for the owners because of positive financial leverage. For example, assume a company is earning 15% return on total investment, while its average interest rate on debt is 7% (net of income tax). The difference between the earnings rate on total resources (15%) and the interest paid to the creditors (7%) "accrues" to the benefit of the shareholders.[3] The shareholders benefit by the 15% earned on the resources provided by them, plus the difference between the 15% return and the 7% interest rate paid on the resources provided by the creditors. A company with a high proportion of debt is **highly levered.** The debt/equity ratio shows the balance that the management has attained between the resources provided by creditors and the resources provided by owners.

Market Tests

Several ratios have been developed to measure the "market worth" of a share. These market tests relate the current market price of a share to an indicator of the return that might accrue to the investor. The tests focus on the **current market price** of the shares because that is the amount the buyer would invest. Two market test ratios used by analysts and investors are the price/earnings ratio and the dividend yield ratio.

11. Price/Earnings (P/E) Ratio

This ratio measures the relationship between the current market price of the share and its earnings per share. Assuming a current market price of $15.60 per

---

[3] Interest expense on debt is a deductible expense on the income tax return; in contrast, dividend payments to shareholders are not deductible. Thus, in addition to the lower stated rate for debt, funds obtained by means of debt tend to be less costly because of the income tax saving. The real cost of debt in the above example depends upon the income tax rate.

share for Packard Company common stock in 19B and earnings per share of $1.04, the P/E ratio is computed as follows:

$$\text{Price/earnings ratio} = \frac{\text{Current market price per share}}{\text{Earnings per share}}$$

$$\text{Packard Company, 19B} = \frac{\$15.60}{\$1.04} = 15 \text{ (or 15 to 1)}$$

Packard shares were selling at 15 times the EPS. The P/E ratio often is referred to as the **multiple.** The P/E ratio is used as an indicator of the future performance of the shares. Analysts use the P/E ratio to predict how the share price may react to a change in the level of the company's earnings.

Sometimes the components of the P/E ratio are inverted, giving the **capitalization rate.** This is the rate at which the stock market apparently is capitalizing the current earnings. Computation of the capitalization rate on current earnings per share for Packard Company would be $1.04 ÷ $15.60 = 6.67%.

12. Dividend Yield Ratio

This ratio measures the relationship between the dividends per share paid and the current market price of the shares. Assuming dividends paid by Packard Company of $0.75 per share for 19B and a current market price per share of $15.60, the ratio is computed as follows:

$$\text{Dividend yield ratio} = \frac{\text{Dividend per share}}{\text{Market price per share}}$$

$$\text{Packard Company, 19B} = \frac{\$0.75}{\$15.60} = 4.81\%$$

This ratio measures the current dividend yield to the investor, based upon the dividends declared per share against the current market price per share. Like the P/E ratio, it is a volatile measure because the price of shares may change materially over short periods of time, and each change in market price or dividend payment changes the ratio.

Miscellaneous Ratio

13. Book Value per Share

The book value per share measures the owners' equity in terms of each share of common stock outstanding. In the case of a simple capital structure, with **only** common stock outstanding, the computation of book value per share is not difficult. To illustrate, assume Day Corporation had total owners' equity of $250,000 and 10,000 outstanding no-par common shares. The computation of book value per share would be as follows:

$$\text{Book value per common share} = \frac{\text{Total owners' equity (applicable to common shares)}}{\text{Common shares outstanding}}$$

$$\text{Packard Company, 19B} = \frac{\$250,000}{10,000 \text{ shares}} = \$25$$

Computation of book value per share is more difficult if both common and preferred shares are outstanding. In this situation, total owners' equity must be allocated between common and preferred shares. This allocation is accomplished by assigning an amount to preferred shares, based on its preferences, and, then, assigning the remaining amount of owners' equity to the common. Assume Bye Corporation had total owners' equity of $273,000; 1,000 shares outstanding of its 5% preferred stock, par $20, cumulative (no dividends in arrears for past years), and liquidation value of $22 per share; and 10,000 outstanding no-par common shares.

Allocation:
Total owners' equity		$273,000
Less equity allocated to preferred stock:		
Liquidation value (1,000 shares × $22)	$22,000	
Cumulative dividend preference for the current year		
(1,000 shares × $20 × 5%)	1,000	
Amount allocated to preferred shares		23,000
Remainder allocated to common shares		250,000

Book value per share:
Preferred, $23,000 ÷ 1,000 shares = $23
Common, $250,000 ÷ 10,000 shares = $25

Book value per share has limited significance because it has no necessary relationship to market value. Because it is a low conservative amount (historical cost basis), some analysts consider a market value below book value to imply underpriced shares.

Interpreting Ratios

The computation of any particular ratio is not standardized. Neither the accounting profession nor security analysts have prescribed the manner in which a ratio must be computed (except for earnings per share). Thus, users of financial statements should compute the various ratios in accordance with their decision objectives. Before using ratios computed by others, the user should determine the computational approach that was used. This section discusses commonly used approaches.

To interpret a ratio, it should be compared with some **standard** that represents an optimal or desirable value. For example, the return-on-investment ratio may be compared with alternative investment opportunities. Some ratios, by their characteristics, are unfavourable if they are **either** too high or too low. For example, analysis may indicate that a working capital ratio of approximately 2:1 may be considered optimal for a company. In this situation, a ratio of 1:1 may indicate a danger of being unable to meet maturing debts. A ratio of 3:1 may indicate that excess funds are being left idle rather than being employed profitably. Furthermore, an optimal ratio for one company often is not the optimal ratio for another company. Comparisons of ratios for different companies are appropriate only if the companies are indeed comparable. Differences in industry, nature of operations, size, and accounting policies make many comparisons of questionable value.

Most ratios represent **averages.** Therefore, they may obscure underlying factors that are of interest to the analyst. To illustrate, a working capital ratio of 2:1 may be considered optimal. But even an optimal working capital ratio may obscure a short-term liquidity problem if the company has a very large amount of inventory and a minimal amount of cash with which to pay debts as they mature. Careful analysis can uncover this liquidity problem. In other cases, careful analysis cannot uncover obscured problems. For example, consolidated statements include financial information about the parent and its subsidiaries. The parent company may have a high working capital ratio and the subsidiary a very low ratio. When the statements are consolidated, the working capital ratio (in effect, an average of the parent and the subsidiary) may be within an acceptable range. Obscured is the fact that the subsidiary may have a very serious liquidity problem.

Despite limitations, ratio analysis is a useful analytical tool. Financial ratios are effective in predicting bankruptcy. Exhibit 16–6 gives the working capital ratio and the debt/equity ratio for a large international corporation. Notice the deterioration of these ratios each year. In 1981, the independent auditor issued a qualified audit opinion and noted, "there are conditions which indicate that the company may be unable to continue as a going concern." In the spring of 1982, the company filed for bankruptcy. Analysts who studied the financial ratios each year probably were not surprised by the bankruptcy. After selling many of its

Exhibit 16–6 Selected financial ratios for an illustrated corporation

	19x1	19x2	19x3	19x4	19x5
Working capital ratio	1.20	0.91	0.74	0.60	0.49
Debt/equity ratio	2.03	2.45	4.88	15.67	N/A*

* In 19x5, the company reported negative owners' equity as the result of a large net loss that produced a negative balance in retained earnings. Creditors' equity exceeded **total** equities.

assets and undergoing a complete financial restructuring, the company was able to resume limited operations.

Financial analysts often use five types of "standards" against which ratios and percents are compared:

1. **Comparison of the ratios for the current year with the historical ratios for the same company**—Particular attention is given to the **trend** of each ratio over time.

2. **Comparison of the ratios for the current year with ratios of other companies for the same year**—These comparisons include the use of ratios and percents from other similar companies and from industry averages. Industry averages are published by many companies, trade associations, and governmental agencies. Exhibit 16–7 lists some popular Canadian sources of financial data.

3. **Experience of the analyst who has a subjective feel for the "right" relationships in a given situation**—These subjective judgments of an experienced and competent observer tend to be more reliable than purely mechanical comparisons.

4. **Comparison of the ratios for the current year with planned goals and objectives expressed as ratios**—Many companies prepare comprehensive profit plans (i.e., budgets) on a continuing basis that incorporate realistic plans for the future. These plans usually incorporate planned goals for significant ratios, such as profit margin, return on investment, and EPS. Internal plans seldom are available to external parties because managers are reluctant to share their business plans with competitors. Some companies have begun to experiment with methods to make this information available to users. Management comments included in annual reports (Exhibit 16–1) contain a summary of what management has to say about future prospects.

5. **Innovative comparisons, based on physical data, on such topics as the number of units produced, the number of customers, and the number of employees**—For example, a study of wages and benefits per employee over the 10-year history of Consolidated-Bathurst (available in the financial data provided in Appendix B) allows an assessment of the changes in wages over time.

Impact of Accounting on Analysis

Financial statements provide information for the average investor. Users who understand basic accounting are able to more effectively analyze the information contained in financial statements. While studying this book, you have developed an understanding of the accounting vocabulary. A knowledge of this vocabulary is necessary to understand financial statements.

Also, familiarity with the underlying accounting concepts is essential for proper analysis of statements. Some unsophisticated users do not understand the cost principle and believe that assets are reported on the balance sheet at

Exhibit 16–7 Canadian Sources of Financial Data*

Publication	Type of Information
Dun & Bradstreet's Canadian Key Directory	Business profile of top Canadian companies.
Dun & Bradstreet's Key Business Ratios	Ratio analysis of top Canadian companies.
Financial Post's *Corporation Service*	Individual companies' financial statements.
Financial Post's *Dividend Record*	Record of dividends.
Financial Post's *"Surveys of:"*	Performance of industry sectors.
Info Globe	Computerized financial data.
Moody's *Handbook of Common Stock*	Canadian companies on NYSE dividend and share performance.
Moody's *Bond Record*	Performance of corporate, convertible, government, and municipal bonds.
Moody's *Dividend Record*	List of dividends.
Toronto Stock Exchange *TSE Review*	Stock market activity of the TSE.
Blue Book of Canadian Business	Survey of individual companies.
Federal Corporation Index	Annual reports of private companies.
Bank of Canada *Annual Report*	Canada's balance of payments, bank operations.
Bank of Canada *Review*	Monetary, banking, and other financial statistics.
Consumer and Corporate Affairs *Annual Report*	Funding of consumer groups, patents, trademarks.
Consumer and Corporate Affairs *Canada Corporations Bulletin*	Statistical data on Canadian corporations.
Consumer and Corporate Affairs *Insolvency Bulletin*	Statistics on all bankruptcies.
Finance Canada Economic Review	Reviews of economic developments in Canada, main economic indicators.
Industry, Trade and Commerce *Small Business in Canada*	Statistical profile of the small business sector.
Insurance Canada *List of Securities*	Market value of all securities owned by Canadian companies.
Statistics Canada *Industrial Corporations, Financial Statistics*	Financial statements of different sectors.
Statistics Canada *Financial Institutions, Financial Statistics*	Financial statements for financial sectors.

* Other references can be found by a reference librarian.

their fair market value. We have stressed accounting concepts throughout the book because it is impossible to interpret accounting numbers without an understanding of the concepts that were used to develop the numbers.

When comparing companies, it is rare to find that they use exactly the same accounting policies. If the comparisons are to be useful, the analyst must understand the impact of various accounting alternatives. One company may use very conservative accounting alternatives such as accelerated depreciation while another may use "income maximizing" alternatives, such as straight-line depreciation. Users who do not understand the effects of accounting methods may misinterpret financial results. Perhaps the most important first step in analyzing financial statements is a review of the accounting policies that the company has selected. This information must be disclosed in a note to the statements. An example of this disclosure is shown in the annual report in Appendix B.

SUMMARY OF CHAPTER

Interpretation of amounts reported on financial statements may be enhanced by expressing certain relationships as ratios or percents. Although many ratios can be calculated, only a few will be useful for a given decision. Having selected the relevant ratios, the analyst has the problem of evaluating the results. This evaluation involves the task of selecting one or more realistic standards with which to compare the results. Four types of standards are used: (1) historical standards, (2) external standards, (3) experience, and (4) planned standards. The interpretation of ratios may suggest strengths and weaknesses in the operations and/or the financial position of the company that should be accorded in-depth investigation and evaluation.

CHAPTER SUPPLEMENT 16A

Using Financial Ratios to Forecast Financial Statements

As an accountant or business manager you may wish to apply for credit from any one of a number of financial institutions or other types of investors. Typically the application will require the use of forecasted financial statements prepared using a computer spreadsheet. To present such forecasts, revenue and expenses are estimated which in turn are combined to present forecasted income statements. However, forecasted income statements do not provide forecasted balance sheets and the statement of changes in financial position (SCFP) results. If we forecasted SCFP instead of income statements, income and balance sheet results would be missing. If we forecast each of the statements then the results would not articulate or balance. What is needed is a method to relate income results to balance sheets and cash flows in the SCFP.

The relationship needed to cause income results to articulate with balance sheets and SCFP results can be obtained from three turnover ratios:

$$\text{Accounts receivable turnover} = \frac{\text{Net sales}}{\text{Net trade receivables}}$$

$$\text{Inventory turnover} = \frac{\text{Cost of goods sold}}{\text{Inventory}}$$

$$\text{Accounts payable turnover} = \frac{\text{Purchases}}{\text{Trade accounts payable}}$$

These three ratios have been modified slightly from those presented in the main body of the chapter to facilitate computations and presentations. Average receivables and inventories could have been used but the calculations would be more complex. Accounts payable turnover is a new ratio but one whose calculations and explanation parallels the accounts receivable turnover calculation.

To illustrate the use of these ratios consider the data presented for Packard Company in Exhibit 16–2.

Assume 19B sales were forecasted to be $120,000.

Assume 19B accounts receivable turnover was forecasted to be 14.3.

The calculation of the accounts receivable balance for 19B would be:

$$\text{Accounts receivable estimate, December 31, 19B}$$
$$120{,}000 \div 14.3 = \$8{,}392$$

The actual balance was $8,400 in Exhibit 16–2. The difference resulted from rounding off the turnover ratio.

To compute the ending inventory for 19B, consider the following:

Cost of goods sold for 19B	$72,600
Estimated inventory turnover	1.34
Estimated inventory would be 72,600 ÷ 1.34 = . . .	$54,179

Again the slight difference from the amount shown in Exhibit 16–2 is caused by the rounding of the turnover.

Accounts payable at December 31, 19B requires a small amount of additional effort because the purchases amount is not disclosed. To compute 19B purchases consider the following:

Cost of goods sold for 19B	$72,600
Less: Inventory 19A	(60,000)
Add: Estimated inventory for 19B	54,179
Purchases estimated	$66,779
Estimated Accounts payable turnover	5.06

The estimated ending balance for accounts payable would be $66,779 ÷ 5.06 = $13,197

To illustrate a full integration of the sales forecast for 19B with a complete set of financial statements, the following information will be incorporated in Exhibit 16–8: The December 31, 19A balance sheet from Exhibit 16–2, the component expense percentages from 19B. Prepaid expenses will be used up in the amount of $2,000. Equipment and furniture were purchased in the amount of $7,500. Depreciation expense was $8,250. Amortization of other assets amounted to $100. Wages amounting to $7,200 were unpaid at December 31, 19B. Long-term notes payable amounting to $2,850 were paid. Dividends paid amounted to $4,000. Detailed calculations are presented in Exhibit 16–8.

Once the relationship for one year has been established, computer spreadsheets can extend these relationships in an iterative manner into future periods. Expenditures for long-term fixed assets and payments for long-term debt and dividends are discretionary decisions by management. Consultation with this group will provide the necessary information.

Exhibit 16–8 Forecasted cash flows and balance sheet—Packard Company

---

A. Estimated Income Statement:

Sales revenue (given)	$120,000
Cost of goods sold (60.5%)	72,600
Gross margin on sales	47,400
Operating expenses:	
Distribution expense (18.9%)	22,680
Administrative expenses (9.9%)	11,880
Interest expense (1.2%)*	1,440
	36,000
Pretax income	11,400
Income taxes (2.2%)*	2,640
Net income	$ 8,760

B. Estimated Statement of Changes in Financial Position:

Operating activities:	
Net income	$ 8,760
Change in accounts receivable [(120,000 ÷ 14.3) − 7,000]	(1,392)
Change in inventory [(72,600 ÷ 1.34) − 60,000]	5,821
Reduction in prepaid (given)	2,000
Depreciation expense (given)	8,250
Amortization of other assets (given)	100
Change in accounts payable [(66,779 ÷ 5.06) − 12,000]	1,197 †
Change in unpaid wages [$7,200 (given) − 8,000]	(800)
Cash flow from operations	23,936
Financing activities:	
Payment of long-term note (given)	(2,850)
Dividends paid (given)	(4,000)
Total	(6,850)
Investing activities:	
Purchase of equipment and furnitures (given)	(7,500)
Net change in cash and its equivalents (increase)	$ 9,586

Cash balance—19A	$9,000	
Less: Short-term note 19A	20,000	
Cash and equivalents	($11,000)	
Balance of cash and equivalents 19B		($1,414)‡

* These amounts can be computed in alternative ways.

† Purchases are $72,600 − $60,000 + $54,179 = $66,779.

‡ Exhibit 16–2 shows ($13,000 − $15,000) or $2,000 deficiency. The difference results because of rounding the turnovers.

Exhibit 16–8 *(concluded)*

C. Estimated Balance Sheet, December 31, 19B:

Assets

Current assets:

Accounts receivable (120,000 ÷ 14.3)	$ 8,392
Inventory (72,600 ÷ 1.34)	54,179
Prepaid expenses (4,000 − 2,000)	2,000
Total	64,571

Investments:

Real estate (same as 19A)	8,000

Operational assets:

Equipment and furniture (75,000 + 7,500)	82,500
Less: Accumulated depreciation (15,000 + 8,250)	(23,250)
	59,250
Other assets (2,000 − 100)	1,900
Total	$133,721

Liabilities

Current liabilities:

Short-term notes less cash on hand	$ 1,414
Accounts payable (66,779 ÷ 5.06)	13,197
Accrued wages payable (given)	7,200
Total	21,811

Long-term liabilities:

Notes payable, long term (10,000 − 2,850)	7,150
Total	28,961

Shareholders' Equity

Common stock, no par, 8,500 shares outstanding	85,000
Retained earnings [15,000 + 8,760 − 4,000 (given)]	19,760
Total	104,760
Total liabilities and shareholders' equity	$133,721

IMPORTANT TERMS DEFINED IN THIS CHAPTER

Common Ratios Selected ratios that are used widely. Exhibit 16–4 presents a list of 13 commonly used accounting ratios. *p. 930*

Comparative Statements Financial statements for several years; amounts are presented side by side for comparative purposes. *p. 925*

Component Percentages A percentage that expresses each item on a particular financial statement as a percent of a single base amount. *p. 927*

Long-Term Summaries Summaries of basic accounting data for many years (typically 10 years). *p. 926*

Market Tests   Ratios that tend to measure the "market worth" of a share. *p. 938*

Ratio Analysis   An analytical tool designed to identify significant relationships; measures proportional relationship between two financial statement amounts. *p. 926*

Tests of Liquidity   Ratios that measure a company's ability to meet its currently maturing obligations. *p. 934*

Tests of Solvency   Ratios that measure a company's ability to meet its long-term obligations. *p. 937*

QUESTIONS

1. What are three fundamental uses of external financial statements by decision makers?
2. What are some of the primary items on financial statements about which creditors usually are concerned?
3. Explain why the notes to the financial statements are important to decision makers.
4. What is the primary purpose of comparative financial statements?
5. Why are statement users interested in financial summaries covering several years? What is the primary limitation of long-term summaries?
6. What is the ratio analysis? Why is ratio analysis useful?
7. What are component percentages? Why are component percentages useful?
8. Explain the two concepts of return on investment.
9. What is financial leverage? How is financial leverage measured?
10. Is profit margin a useful measure of profitability? Explain.
11. Compare and contrast the working capital ratio and the quick ratio.
12. What does the debt/equity ratio reflect?
13. What are "market tests?"
14. What are the primary problems when using ratios?
15. Why is the past history of a firm as presented in the financial statements useful to persons or groups interested in the future?
16. Why is "average" owners' equity said to be preferable to period end owners' equity for computing return on owners' investment?
17. Receivable turnover uses the average of net trade receivable balances to provide a period representation of the period and balance. Would you ever want to use the period end net trade receivables rather than the average? Why?

EXERCISES

E16–1   **(Pair Definition with Terms)**
Match the following brief definitions with the terms by entering the appropriate letter in each space provided.

Term	Brief definition
_____ (1) Long-term summaries	A. Ratios and percentages calculated from financial statements to give greater insight into the profitability, liquidity, solvency, and market status of a company.
_____ (2) Market tests	
_____ (3) Common ratios	
_____ (4) Tests of solvency	B. These could be used to compare and contrast a company's financial position from year to year.
_____ (5) Comparative statements	C. If you were to compute these percentages for an income statement, the denominator would be net sales revenue.
_____ (6) Tests of liquidity	D. These documents are useful in tracking a company's progress over a long period of time.
_____ (7) Component percentages	E. Examples of these are the price/earnings ratio and the dividend yield ratio.
_____ (8) Ratio analysis	F. Used to analyze relationships both within one period and between periods.
	G. These tests focus on the relationship between current assets and current liabilities.
	H. An example of this kind of test is the debt/equity ratio.

E16–2   **(Analysis of Comparative Financial Statements Using Percentages)**
The comparative financial statements prepared at December 31, 19B, for Doan Company showed the following summarized data:

	19B	19A
Income statement:		
Sales revenue	$150,000*	$140,000*
Cost of goods sold	90,000	85,000
Gross margin	60,000	55,000
Operating expenses and interest expense	43,000	40,500
Pretax income	17,000	14,500
Income tax	5,000	4,500
Net income	$ 12,000	$ 10,000

	19B	19A
Balance sheet:		
Cash	$ 7,000	11,000
Accounts receivable (net)	12,000	14,000
Inventory	30,000	28,000
Operational assets (net)	50,000	43,000
	$ 99,000	$ 96,000
Current liabilities (no interest)	$ 14,000	$ 17,000
Long-term liabilities (10% interest)	35,000	35,000
Common stock (par $10)	40,000	40,000
Retained earnings†	10,000	4,000
	$ 99,000	$ 96,000

* One third were credit sales.

† During 19B, cash dividends amounting to $6,000 were declared and paid.

Required:

a. Complete the following columns for each item in the above comparative financial statements:

Increase (decrease)
19B over 19A

Amount   **Percent**

b. Answer the following questions:
   (1) Compute the percentage increases in sales revenue, net income, cash, inventory, liabilities, and owners' equity.
   (2) By what amount did working capital change?
   (3) What was the percentage change in the average income tax rate?
   (4) What was the amount of cash inflow from revenues for 19B?
   (5) By what percent did the average markup realized on goods sold change?
   (6) How much did the book value per share change?

E16–3   (Analysis of a Financial Statement Using Component Percentages and Selected Ratios)
Use the data given in Exercise 16–2 for Doan Company.

Required:

a. Present component percentages for 19B only.

b. Answer the following questions for 19B:
   (1) What was the average percentage markup on sales?
   (2) What was the average income tax rate?
   (3) Compute the profit margin. Was it a good or poor indicator of performance? Explain.
   (4) What percent of total resources was invested in operational assets?
   (5) Compute the debt/equity ratio. Does it look good or bad? Explain.
   (6) What was the return on owners' investment?
   (7) What was the return on total investment?
   (8) Compute the financial leverage percent. Was it positive or negative? Explain.
   (9) What was the book value per common share?

E16-4 **(Analysis of a Financial Statement Using Each Ratio Discussed in the Chapter)**
Use the data given in Exercise 16–2 for Doan Company. Use a separate sheet and complete the following tabulation for 19B only (assume a common stock price of $33 per share); compute the ratios that usually are included under each category:

Name and Computation of the Ratio (show computations)	Brief Explanation of the Ratio
A. Tests of profitability: 1. Return on owners' investment 2. Etc.	
B. Tests of liquidity: 1. Working capital ratio 2. Etc.	
C. Tests of solvency and equity position: 1. Debt/equity ratio 2. Etc.	
D. Market tests: 1. Price/earnings ratio 2. Etc.	
E. Miscellaneous ratio: 1. Book value per share	

E16-5 **(Match Each Ratio with its Computational Definition)**
Match the following by entering the appropriate letters in the blanks.

Ratio or percent

_____ (1) Profit margin
_____ (2) Inventory turnover ratio
_____ (3) Average collection period
_____ (4) Creditors' equity to total equities
_____ (5) Dividend yield ratio
_____ (6) Return on owners' investment
_____ (7) Working capital ratio
_____ (8) Debt/equity ratio
_____ (9) Price/earnings ratio
_____ (10) Financial leverage

Computation

A. Income (before extraordinary items) ÷ Net sales.
B. Days in year ÷ Receivable turnover.
C. Income ÷ Average owners' equity.
D. Income ÷ Average number of common shares outstanding.
E. Return on owners' investment − Return on total investment.
F. Quick assets ÷ Current liabilities.
G. Current assets ÷ Current liabilities.
H. Cost of goods sold ÷ Average inventory.
I. Net credit sales ÷ Average net trade receivables.
J. Creditors' equity (debt) ÷ Total equities.
K. Days in year ÷ Inventory turnover.
L. Total liabilities ÷ Owners' equity.
M. Dividends per share ÷ Market price per share.

Ratio or percent	Computation
___ (11) Receivable turn-over ratio	N. Owners' equity ÷ Total equities.
	O. Current market price per share ÷ Earnings per share.
___ (12) Average days' supply of inventory	P. Owners' equity ÷ Shares outstanding.
___ (13) Owners' equity to total equities	Q. Income + Interest expense (net of tax) ÷ Total assets.
___ (14) Earnings per share	
___ (15) Return on total investment	
___ (16) Quick ratio	
___ (17) Book value per share	

E16–6 **(Analysis of the Impact of Selected Transactions on the Working Capital Ratio, Accounts Receivable and Inventory Turnover, and Financial Leverage)**

Case A—Current assets totaled $60,000, and the working capital ratio was 1.5. Assume the following transactions were completed: (1) purchased merchandise for $3,000 of which one third was on short-term credit; and (2) purchased a delivery truck for $8,000, paid $2,000 cash, and signed a two-year interest-bearing note for the balance. Compute the cumulative working capital ratio after each transaction.

Case B—Sales for the years were $600,000 of which one half was on credit. The average gross margin rate was 40% on sales. Account balances were:

	Beginning	Ending
Accounts receivable (net) . . .	$30,000	$20,000
Inventory	20,000	16,000

Compute the turnover for the accounts receivable and inventory, the average age of receivables, and the average days' supply of inventory.

Case C—The financial statements reported the following at year-end:

Total assets	$100,000
Total debt (10% interest)	60,000
Net income (average tax rate 30%) . . .	12,000

Compute the financial leverage. Was it positive or negative?

E16–7 **(Analysis of a Financial Statement Using Ratios and Percentage Changes)**
Ryan Retail Company has just prepared the comparative annual financial statements for 19B given below:

RYAN RETAIL COMPANY
Income Statement
For the Year Ended December 31, 19B and 19A

	For the year ended	
	19B	19A
Sales revenue (one half on credit)	$100,000	$ 95,000
Cost of goods sold	48,000	46,000
Gross margin	52,000	49,000
Expenses (including $3,000 interest		
expense each year)	34,000	33,000
Pretax income	18,000	16,000
Income tax on operations (22%)	3,960	3,520
Income before extraordinary items	14,040	12,480
Extraordinary loss $3,000		
Less income tax saved 660	2,340	
Extraordinary gain	$1,000	
Applicable income tax	220	780
Net income	$ 11,700	$ 13,260

RYAN RETAIL COMPANY
Balance Sheet
At December 31, 19B and 19A

	19B	19A
Assets		
Cash	$ 47,200	$ 20,000
Accounts receivable (net) (terms 1/10, n/30)	35,000	30,000
Inventory	30,000	40,000
Operational assets (net)	90,000	100,000
Total assets	$202,200	$190,000
Liabilities		
Accounts payable	$ 60,000	$ 50,000
Income tax payable	1,500	1,000
Note payable, long term	25,000	25,000
Shareholders' Equity		
Capital stock, 8,000 no-par shares outstanding	80,000	80,000
Retained earnings	35,700	34,000
Total liabilities and shareholders' equity	$202,200	$190,000

Required (round percents and ratios to two decimal places):

a. For 19B, compute the tests of (1) profitability, (2) liquidity, (3) solvency, and (4) market. Assume the quoted price of the shares was $26.50 for 19B. Dividends declared and paid during 19B were $10,000.

b. Respond to the following for 19B:
   (1) Compute the percentage changes in sales, income before extraordinary items, net income, cash, inventory, and debt.
   (2) What appears to be the pretax interest rate on the note payable?

c. Identify at least two problems facing the company that are suggested by your responses to (*a*) and (*b*).

E16–8   **(Using Ratios to Estimate Ending Balances)**

Sales for the year amounted to $600,000 of which one half was on credit. The average gross margin rate was 40% on sales. Account balances were:

	Beginning	Ending
Accounts receivable (net)	$30,000	$20,000
Inventory	20,000	16,000

Required:

a. Compute the turnover for the accounts receivable and inventory, using the beginning balance for the year and estimate the ending balances for these two accounts.

b. How much was purchased for the year, based on your estimates in Requirement (*a*)?

PROBLEMS

P16–1   **(Analysis of a Financial Statement Using All of the Ratios Discussed in the Chapter; Emphasis on Assessing Liquidity)**

Peterson Corporation has just completed its comparative statements for the year ended December 31, 19B. At this point, certain analytical and interpretative procedures are to be undertaken. The completed statements (summarized) are as follows:

	19B	19A
Income statement:		
Sales revenue	$400,000 *	$390,000 *
Cost of goods sold	220,000	218,000
Gross margin	180,000	172,000
Operating expenses (including interest on bonds)	147,000	148,000
Pretax income	33,000	24,000
Income tax	9,000	7,000
Net income	$ 24,000	$ 17,000
Balance sheet:		
Cash	$ 5,400	$ 2,700
Accounts receivable (net)	44,000	30,000
Merchandise inventory	30,000	24,000
Prepaid expenses	600	500
Operational assets (net)	120,000	130,000
	$200,000	$187,200
Accounts payable	$ 19,000	$ 20,000
Income tax payable	1,000	1,200
Bonds payable (10% interest rate)	50,000	50,000
Common stock, 10,000 no-par shares	100,000 †	100,000
Retained earnings	30,000 ‡	16,000
	$200,000	$187,200

* Forty percent were credit sales.

† The market price of the shares at the end of 19B was $30 per share.

‡ During 19B, the company declared and paid a cash dividend of $10,000.

Required:

a. Complete a table similar to the following (show computations; round percents and ratios to two places):

Name and Computation of the 19B Ratio	Brief Explanation of the Ratio
Tests of profitability: 　1. Return on owners' investment. 　2. Etc. **Tests of liquidity:** 　1. Working capital ratio. 　2. Etc. **Tests of solvency and equity position:** 　1. Debt/equity ratio. 　2. Etc. **Market tests:** 　1. Price/earnings ratio. 　2. Etc.	

b. Answer the following questions for 19B:
   (1) Evaluate the financial leverage. Explain its meaning using the computed amount(s).
   (2) Evaluate the profit margin amount and explain how a shareholder might use it.
   (3) Explain to a shareholder why the working capital ratio and the quick ratio are different. Do you observe any liquidity problems? Explain.
   (4) Assuming credit terms are 1/10, n/30, do you perceive an unfavourable situation for the company related to credit sales? Explain.

P16-2 **(Use Ratios to Analyze Several Years of Financial Data; Identify Favourable and Unfavourable Factors; Give Recommendations to Improve Operations)**
The following information was contained in the annual financial statements of Taterwood Company, which started business January 1, 19A (assume account balances only in Cash and Capital Stock on this date; all amounts are in thousands of dollars).

	19A	19B	19C	19D
Accounts receivable (net) (terms n/30) . . . $	8	$10	$ 16	$ 22
Merchandise inventory	10	12	20	25
Net sales (¾ on credit)	40	60	100	120
Cost of goods sold	26	36	64	80
Net income (loss)	(10)	6	14	10

Required (show computations and round to two decimal places):

a. Complete the tabulation given below.
b. Evaluate the results of the three related ratios 1, 2, and 3, to identify the favourable or unfavourable factors. Give your recommendations to improve Taterwood's operations.

c. Evaluate the results of the last four ratios (4, 5, 6, and 7) and identify any favourable or unfavourable factors. Give your recommendations to improve Taterwood's operations.

Items	19A	19B	19C	19D
1. Profit margin—percent.				
2. Gross margin—ratio.				
3. Expenses as a percent of sales, excluding cost of goods sold.				
4. Inventory turnover.				
5. Days' supply in inventory.				
6. Receivable turnover.				
7. Average days to collect.				

P16–3 **(Compare Alternative Investment Opportunities Using All of the Ratios Discussed in the Chapter; Prepare Investment Recommendation)**
The 19B financial statements for Able and Baker companies are summarized below:

	Able Company	Baker Company
Balance sheet:		
Cash	$ 25,000	$ 11,000
Accounts receivable, net	30,000	17,000
Inventory	80,000	20,000
Operational assets, net	125,000	300,000
Other assets	40,000	252,000
Total assets	$ 300,000	$ 600,000
Current liabilities	$ 90,000	$ 40,000
Long-term debt (10%)	50,000	60,000
Capital stock, par $20	120,000	400,000
Contributed surplus	10,000	60,000
Retained earnings	30,000	40,000
Total liabilities and shareholders' equity	$ 300,000	$ 600,000
Income statement:		
Sales revenue (on credit) .... (⅓)	$ 600,000 (⅙)	$ 900,000
Cost of goods sold	(350,000)	(450,000)
Expenses (including interest and income tax)	(205,000)	(360,000)
Net income	$ 45,000	$ 90,000
Selected data from the 19A statements:		
Accounts receivable, net	$ 25,000	$ 19,000
Inventory	70,000	24,000
Long-term debt	50,000	60,000
Other data:		
Per share price at end of 19B (offering price)	$ 50	$ 40
Average income tax rate	30%	30%
Dividends declared and paid in 19B	$ 25,800	$ 150,400

Able and Baker companies are in the same line of business and are direct competitors in a large metropolitan area. They have been in business approximately 10 years, and each has had steady growth. The two managements have different viewpoints in many respects; however, Baker is the more conservative, and as the president said, "We avoid what we consider to be undue risks." Neither company is publicly held. Able Company has an annual audit by a PA but Baker Company does not.

Required:

a. Complete a schedule that reflects a ratio analysis of each company. Compute the 13 ratios discussed in the chapter.

b. A client of yours has the opportunity to buy 10% of the shares in one or the other company at the per share prices given above. Your client has decided to invest in one of the companies. Based on the data given, prepare a comparative evaluation of the ratio analyses (and any other available information) and give your recommended choice with the supporting explanation.

P16–4 **(Comparison of Loan Requests from Two Companies Using All of the Ratios Discussed in the Chapter)**
The 19B financial statements for Doe and Roe companies are summarized below:

	Doe Company		Roe Company
Balance sheet:			
Cash	$ 20,000		$ 40,000
Accounts receivable, net	60,000		10,000
Inventory	120,000		30,000
Operational assets, net	500,000		150,000
Other assets	155,000		54,000
Total	$ 855,000		$ 284,000
Current liabilities	$ 100,000		$ 20,000
Long-term debt (10%)	200,000		50,000
Capital stock, par $10	500,000		200,000
Contributed surplus	25,000		2,000
Retained earnings	30,000		12,000
Total	$ 855,000		$ 284,000
Income statement:			
Sales revenue (on credit) ($\frac{1}{2}$)	$ 900,000	($\frac{1}{3}$)	$ 300,000
Cost of goods sold	(522,000)		(180,000)
Expenses (including interest and income tax)	(288,000)		(84,000)
Net income	$ 90,000		$ 36,000
Selected data from the 19A statements:			
Accounts receivable, net	$ 50,000		$ 14,000
Long-term debt (10% interest)	200,000		50,000
Inventory	100,000		45,000
Other data:			
Per share price at end of 19B	$ 12.75		$ 10.50
Average income tax rate	30%		20%
Dividends declared and paid in 19B	$ 40,000		$ 13,125

These two companies are in the same line of business and in the same province but in different cities. Each company has been in operation for about 10 years. Doe Company is audited by a large accounting firm, and Roe Company is audited by a small accounting firm. Both companies received an unqualified opinion (i.e., the independent auditors found nothing wrong) on the financial statements. Doe Company wants to borrow $75,000 cash, and Roe Company needs $30,000. The loans will be for a two-year period and are needed for "working capital purposes."

Required:

a. Complete a schedule that reflects a ratio analysis of each company. Compute the ratios discussed in the chapter.

b. Assume you work in the loan department of a local bank. You have been asked to analyze the situation and recommend which loan is preferable. Based on the data given, your analysis prepared in (*a*), and any other information, give your choice and the supporting explanation.

P16–5   **(Assess the Solvency of an Actual Company Using Selected Ratios)**

The following information was contained in the actual financial statements of a large manufacturing company that currently is listed on the Toronto Stock Exchange:

Balance Sheet

	December 31 (millions of dollars)	
	19B	19A
Assets		
Current assets:		
Cash	$ 188.2	$ 123.2
Time deposits	120.8	248.8
Marketable securities	165.3	150.8
Accounts receivable (less allowance for doubtful accounts:		
19B—$34.9 millon; 19A—$16.7 million)	610.3	848.0
Inventories—at the lower of cost (substantially FIFO) or market	1,873.8	1,980.8
Prepaid insurance, taxes, and other expenses	162.3	210.2
Total current assets	3,120.7	3,561.8
Total investments and other assets	1,183.5	1,396.5
Property, plant, and equipment:		
Land, buildings, machinery, and equipment	3,733.1	3,391.3
Less accumulated depreciation	2,097.1	1,963.9
	1,636.0	1,427.4
Special tools	712.9	595.5
Net property, plant, and equipment	2,348.9	2,022.9
Total assets	$ 6,653.1	$ 6,981.2

Balance Sheet (continued)

	December 31 (millions of dollars)	
	19B	19A
Liabilities and Shareholders' Investment		
Current liabilities:		
Accounts payable	$ 1,530.4	$ 1,725.0
Accrued expenses	807.9	698.0
Short-term debt	600.9	49.2
Payment due within one year on long-term debt	275.6	12.4
Taxes on income	16.8	1.2
Total current liabilities	3,231.6	2,485.8
Total long-term debt and other liabilities	1,559.1	1,564.1
Minority interest in consolidated subsidiaries	38.3	4.8
Preferred stock—no-par value	218.7	217.0
Common stock—par value $6.25 per share	416.9	397.7
Contributed surplus	692.2	683.1
Net earnings retained	496.3	1,628.7
Total liabilities and shareholders' investment	$ 6,653.1	$ 6,981.2

Income Statement

	Year Ended December 31 (millions of dollars)	
	19B	19A
Net sales	$12,004.3	$13,669.8
Cost of goods sold	11,631.5	12,640.1
Depreciation of plant and equipment	180.6	154.0
Amortization of special tools	220.0	198.2
Selling and administrative expenses	598.5	572.1
Pension plans	260.6	262.3
Interest expense	215.4	128.9
	13,106.6	13,955.6
Loss before taxes on income	(1,102.3)	(285.8)
Taxes on income (credit)	(5.0)	(81.2)
Net loss	$(1,097.3)	$ (204.6)

Required:

a. Calculate the following ratios:
   (1) Return on owners' investment.
   (2) Return on total investment.
       (For purposes of this case, assume that the interest expense reported on the income statement is net of income taxes.)
   (3) Financial leverage.
   (4) Earnings per share.
   (5) Working capital ratio.
   (6) Quick ratio.
   (7) Inventory turnover.
   (8) Debt/equity ratio.
b. Based on your analysis of the ratios that you calculated in Requirement (a), do you think that this company will be able to continue in existence? Explain. Would you be willing to invest in this company? Explain.

P16–6   (Analysis of the Impact of Alternative Inventory Methods on Selected Ratios)
Aggressive Company uses the FIFO method to cost inventory, and Conservative Company uses the LIFO method. The two companies are exactly alike except for the difference in inventory costing methods. Costs of inventory items for both companies have been rising steadily in recent years, and each company has increased its inventory each year. Each company has paid its tax liability in full for the current year (and all previous years). Identify which company will report the higher amount for each of the following ratios. If it is not possible, explain why.

a. Working capital ratio.

b. Quick ratio.

c. Debt/equity ratio.

d. Return on owners' investment.

e. Earnings per share.

P16–7   (Forecast Financial Statements; Computer Spreadsheet)
Est. Retail Company has just prepared the comparative annual financial statements for 19B given below:

EST. RETAIL COMPANY
Income Statement
For the Years Ended
December 31, 19B, 19A

	For the year ended	
	19B	**19A**
Sales revenue (one half on credit)	$100,000	$ 95,000
Cost of goods sold		46,000
Gross margin		49,000
Expenses (including $3,000 interest expense each year)		33,000
Pretax income		16,000
Income tax on operations (22%)		3,520
Net income		12,480

EST. RETAIL COMPANY
Balance Sheet
At December 31, 19B, and 19A

	19B	**19A**
Assets		
Cash	$	$ 20,000
Accounts receivable (net)		30,000
Inventory		40,000
Operational assets (net)		100,000
Total assets		$190,000
Liabilities		
Accounts payable		$ 50,000
Income tax payable		1,000
Note payable, long term		25,000
Shareholders' Equity		
Capital stock, par $10		80,000
Retained earnings		34,000
Total liabilities and shareholders' equity		$190,000

Additional information:
Depreciation expense was $20,000 in 19B. No long-term notes payable were paid during 19B. $1,500 of income tax was unpaid at the end of 19B. $12,000 was paid in dividends during 19B. $10,000 was spent for additions to operational assets during 19B. $40,000 was in inventory, January 1, 19A.

Required:
Using a computer spreadsheet, prepare forecasts of the 19B income statement, SCFP and December 31, 19B balance sheet. (Hint: Use 19A turnovers as estimates for 19B.)

CASES

C16–1 **(Analysis of the Impact of Alternative Depreciation Methods on Ratio Analysis)**
Fast Company uses the sum-of-years'-digits method to depreciate its property, plant, and equipment, and Slow Company uses the straight-line method. Both companies use capital cost allowance for income tax purposes. The two companies are exactly alike except for the difference in depreciation methods.

Required:
a. Identify the financial ratios discussed in Chapter 16 that are **likely** to be affected by the difference in depreciation methods.
b. Which company will report the higher amount for each ratio that you have identified? If you cannot be certain, explain why.

C16–2 **(Analysis of the Impact of Business Transactions on Ratio Analysis)**
Nearly Broke Company requested a sizable loan from Second National Bank in order to acquire a large tract of land for future expansion. Nearly Broke reported current assets of $1,750,000 ($475,000 in cash) and current liabilities of $975,000. Second denied the loan request for a number of reasons including the fact that the working capital ratio was below two to one. When Nearly Broke was informed of the loan denial, the comptroller of the company immediately paid $470,000 that was owed to several trade creditors. The comptroller then asked Second to reconsider the loan application. Based on these abbreviated facts, would you recommend that Second approve the loan request? Why?

C16–3 **(Compute Accounting Ratios Based on the Actual Financial Statement)**
Refer to the financial statements of Consolidated-Bathurst Inc., given in Appendix B immediately preceding the Index.

Required:
Compute each of the 13 accounting ratios (for 1987) discussed in the chapter. If you are unable to compute a particular ratio, explain why. Assume an average price per common share of $15.

C16–4   **(Computerized Forecasted Statements)**

Windsor Clays Ltd., a federally incorporated company, began as a small pottery studio selling pottery made by the owners and by other local craftspeople. Gradually, other kinds of crafts and supplies were added, until the company became both a retailer of finished crafts and a supplier to the craftspeople. For example, the company sells the raw clay, the glaze materials, and the wheels and kilns used to make pottery, as well as selling finished pottery.

Over the years, the company has expanded to become a major regional supplier of craft raw materials and equipment. Although the retail business has grown, most of the company's revenue now comes from wholesale sales to craftspeople. The company now has four outlets, each of which has combined wholesale and retail operations. The company mixes most of its clay and glazes and performs other manufacturing and assembly work in a shop attached to its central warehouse.

In the past, essentially all the retail sales and a large portion of the wholesale sales were for cash. Therefore, the company has had low receivables. Recently, however, the company has tried to maintain its sales level by allowing more credit to wholesale customers.

Wholesale inventories have always been high in dollar value, and particularly for larger pieces of equipment, have been slow to turn over. Due to the nature of the craft business, it is necessary to carry a wide variety of inventory items.

Retail merchandise quantities are maintained at a high level. Most of this merchandise is held on consignment, and the remainder consists of items purchased from a few well-established craftspeople or produced in the company's shop.

Much of the wholesale inventory is imported from the United States and Japan. The company's margins have been severely squeezed because of recent currency fluctuations and because the recession has prevented recovery of cost increases. Crafts are considered a luxury good, so the company's retail sales and those to its wholesale customers have been hard hit. In spite of significant price reductions, sales volume has generally fallen.

During 1988, cash flow has been a problem. The company exceeded its credit limit and the bank expressed concern about the company's financial state and inability to determine its cash requirements. In an effort to alleviate the problem, several cost-cutting measures were implemented and advertising expenditures were increased to try to encourage sales. However, the company's position continued to deteriorate. The president then considered the following courses of action: reduction of inventory levels; the elimination of product lines; shift of emphasis from wholesale to retail sales; and further price reductions. He found that he was unable to evaluate any of these possibilities because the accounting system did not generate the necessary information.

The president was also considering entering into the industrial ceramics market. In industry, there is a wide variety of ceramic applications such as ceramic heat shields, decorative ceramic tiles, and electronic components. The president felt that this market would be less affected by the recession than the crafts market. In addition, the company's considerable expertise in glazes, kilns, and so on, could be used in the production of these industrial ceramic items. However, the president has some concerns about this diversification. The company lacks the marketing and production capabilities and there would be some initial costs to develop these capabilities. In addition, there is the problem of financing the diversification. He said, "It seems a vicious circle: the sales slump reduces cash flow and, therefore, reduces the company's ability to finance a diversification which could cure the slump!" Details of the venture are presented in Exhibit 1.

Exhibit 1   Information about the proposed industrial ceramics venture

The starting date for the venture would be December 1, 1988.
Anticipated annual sales volume and gross profit:

First year:	$540,000 sales and 30% gross profit.
Subsequent years:	$600,000 sales and 34% gross profit.

Anticipated inventory levels:

Raw materials:	About equal to one months' cost of goods sold.
Finished goods:	About equal to two months' cost of goods sold.

Anticipated receivables level: About two months' sales.
Manufacturing facilities:

Alternations and addition to the building will cost $168,000.
Equipment will cost $136,000.

Start-up costs (prior to January 1, 1989):

Manufacturing	$23,000
Administration	7,000
Advertising	18,000
Sales force training	4,000

Annual increases in other expenses (not included in the industrial ceramics cost of goods sold), beginning December 1, 1988.

Depreciation:

Building (alterations and addition)	$11,200
Equipment (if purchased)	13,600

Administrative expenses:

First year	6,000
Subsequent years	3,000
Advertising	15,000
Warehouse expenses	34,000

Due to the complexity of the company's problems, the president decided to approach a professional accountant for the first time. In September 1988, he called CA and requested a meeting. He informed CA of the company's background and the present situation. He provided CA with the quarterly financial statements, which had been prepared solely for the use of the bank. He expressed concern that these financial statements did not provide adequate information to enable him to make decisions. They are prepared by the company's bookkeeper in essentially the same summarized format as the annual statements which accompany the tax return. The quarterly statements for August 31, 1988, are shown in Exhibits 2 and 3. At the conclusion of the meeting, the president requested a report which addresses the matters he raised and provides analyses and recommendations.

Exhibit 2

WINDSOR CLAYS LTD.
Summarized Balance Sheets
(in $ thousands)
As of August 31, 1988

Cash	$ 43
Receivables*	116
Inventories	678
Warehouse land	24
Warehouse building	263
Equipment	92
Retail fixtures†	26
Accumulated depreciation	(182)
Other assets	14
	$1,074
Bank loans‡	$ 270
Accounts payable	281
Other liabilities*	18
11% mortgage	148
Share capital	40
Retained earnings	317
	$1,074

* Income tax amounts are included in receivables or in other liabilities.

† All of the retail store premises are leased. The leases still have several years before renewal.

‡ Interest rate at August 31, 1988 was 15%.

Exhibit 3

WINDSOR CLAYS LTD.
Summarized Income Statements
(in $ thousands)
As of August 31, 1988

Sales:
Wholesale	$2,114
Retail*	593
	2,707
Purchases*	1,689
Inventory change (beginning − ending)	(103)
Wages and salaries	435
Shop expenses	76
Warehouse expenses	128
Retail expenses	176
Advertising	52
Administrative expenses	141
Interest	52
Tax provision	(12)
	2,634
Net income (loss)	$ 73

* Consignment sales are included in retail sales, and the related
costs of goods sold are included in purchases. The ratio consignment sales to retail sales remains constant in each quarter.

Required:
Assume the role of adviser and prepare the report for the president. The report should
present a forecast of the financial position of Windsor Clays incorporating the effect of the
new proposal. You may assume the 1988 relationships will hold into the four future
periods you will include in your report.

(CICA Adapted)

C16–5   **(Interpretation of Ratios, Disclosure Issues)**
The following article discusses the issue of risk assessment using financial statements.

Statements made risk plain, Principal investigation told

Edmonton: An auditor has vigorously denied a lawyer's suggestion that his firm "badly
watered down" consolidated financial statements for a Principal Group Ltd. subsidiary in
1983.

Bruce Pennock of Touche Ross & Co. told a court inquiry into the failure of two
Principal Group subsidiaries yesterday that his company's report made it "quite plain
there is a real risk" to the viability of the larger of the two units, First Investors Corp. Ltd.

Mr. Pennock's view was hotly disputed by Sharon Harper, who represents former
Principal Group vice-president of corporate development, Christa Petracca.

Source: Matthew Fisher, *The Globe and Mail*, "Report on Business," July 5, 1988, p. B5.

Ms Harper told Alberta Court of Queen's Bench inspector William Code that the Touche Ross report was "overly optimistic. . . .

"I suggest to you that you've so badly watered down the explicit information that your own rules require you to have that nobody reading these statements could understand that there are financial difficulties with these corporations."

Mr. Pennock replied: "I completely and unequivocally disagree with you. I mean, I'm not quite sure how else to say it."

A warning about the financial health of First Investors was contained in two different places on notes attached to its 1983 financial statements, he said.

In the first paragraph of the addendum, it says the financial statements are presented on "a going concern basis."

The second-last paragraph of the six-page note prepared by Touche Ross says that if the real estate market does not improve, First Investors has an "exposure of $10-million" on its mortgages and owned properties, with an additional $4.6-million at possible risk.

Last week, Mr. Pennock told the investigation into last June's failure of First Investors and Associated Investors of Canada Ltd. that "a going concern basis" meant a company might not survive.

When the investment contract companies were closed by the Alberta Government, about 67,000 investors in Atlantic Canada and Western Canada lost about $150-million.

The sharp, 20-minute exchange between Mr. Pennock and Ms Harper was the first time in six days that the chartered accountant's evidence has been seriously challenged by any of the lawyers at the hearings.

Earlier yesterday, Mr. Pennock told Ms Harper that when auditing the books of Principal Group and its subsidiaries in 1982 and 1983 "we had a tendency to look at these entities as one." All major decisions concerning Principal Group companies were either made by or agreed to by its founder and president, Donald Cormie, Mr. Pennock added.

During his 32 days on the witness stand, Mr. Cormie stressed that he had little to do with the investment contract companies.

Mr. Pennock returns to give more evidence today. He will be followed by another auditor, Donald McCutcheon of Deloitte Haskins & Sells.

Required:

a. What ratios would typically disclose risk?

b. Are the notes to the financial statements a source of risk information?

SEVENTEEN

FINANCIAL REPORTING AND CHANGING PRICES

PURPOSE

Accounting is based on the cost principle. Our discussions in the previous chapters have been based on that principle. Some accountants question the relevancy of historical costs during a period of rapidly changing prices (e.g., inflation). This chapter discusses two alternatives to historical cost. This discussion of alternatives to historical cost is not merely theoretical; it has practical relevance for business valuations used to determine goodwill for mergers and to assist in determining the ability of a firm to be a "going concern." This chapter provides a complete understanding of these important disclosures and discusses accounting for the impact of changing prices (i.e., inflation and market value changes). Disclosure of this supplementary information is made in the Notes to the Financial Statements. Some companies have ceased disclosing the information for reasons stated on the facing page.

LEARNING OBJECTIVES

1. Identify the causes of changing prices.
2. Use price level index numbers.
3. Restate historical costs to constant dollars.
4. Identify monetary and nonmonetary items.
5. Compute the purchasing power gain (loss) on net monetary items.
6. Define three concepts of current value.
7. Prepare current cost financial statements.
8. Compute the real holding gain (loss) on nonmonetary items.
9. Expand your accounting vocabulary by learning about the "Important Terms Defined in This Chapter."
10. Apply the knowledge learned from this chapter.

ORGANIZATION

Part A—reporting the effects of general price level changes
1. Using price level index numbers.
2. Concepts underlying constant dollar (CD) restatement.
3. CD retatement procedures.
4. Overview of CD effects.

Part B—reporting current cost changes
1. Definitions of current value.
2. Concepts underlying current cost/constant dollar (CC/CD) reporting.
3. CC/CD reporting procedures.
4. Overview of CC/CD effects.
5. Reporting the effects of changing prices.

Maritime Electric Company Limited

December 31, 1987 (in thousands of dollars)

Balance Sheet (partial)	**Historical Cost**	Current Cost
Assets:		
Fixed Assets	**$125,594**	$284,983
Less: Accumulated depreciation	**41,737**	136,233
	83,857	148,750
Current Assets:		
Accounts receivable	**5,072**	5,072
Materials & supplies	**3,307**	4,013
Other	**199**	199
	8,578	9,284
Deferred charges	**586**	586
	$ 93,021	$158,620

Statement of earnings	**1987**	1987
Revenues	**$61,111**	$61,111
Operating expenses	43,209	42,939
Depreciation	4,041	8,790
Interest and preferred dividends	4,209	4,209
Financial adjustment	—	(1,344)
	51,459	54,594
Earnings before tax	9,652	6,517
Income tax	5,443	5,443
Earnings for common shareholders	4,209	1,074
Increase in provision for maintenance of operating capability	—	3,089
Financing adjustment	—	(1,344)
End of year	**$31,750**	$93,929

 Hayes-Dana Inc. Annual Report 1987

Accounting for the Effects of Inflation
In the past, a Statement of Income Adjusted for Changing Prices and Other Supplementary Data has been provided. However, inflation has had a limited impact on the Company's activities over the past few years. For this reason, combined with the fact that the preparation requires a number of assumptions and estimates, it has been decided to omit such a statement this year.

PART A—REPORTING THE EFFECTS OF GENERAL PRICE LEVEL (GPL) CHANGES

In the recent past the economy of Canada (and practically all other countries) has been affected significantly by increasing prices of most commodities and services. This fact has important, and often adverse, effects on most people because the price increases are not uniform among different goods, services, and individuals. Therefore, some groups suffer more from inflation than other groups. Also, measurements of economic events in terms of the monetary unit (dollars in Canada) become distorted. For example, from 1970 to 1987, the dollar declined in **purchasing power** (i.e., its command over real goods and services) by approximately 342%; that is, in 1987, it required $3.42 to purchase what $1 would have purchased in 1970.

Rapid and continuing increase in prices has caused users of financial statements to question the dollar measurements of assets, liabilities, revenues, and expenses reported in the traditional historical cost (HC) financial statements. In periods of inflation, HC financial statements typically aggregate amounts that include dollars of different purchasing power. This aggregation of "apples and oranges" tends to produce unrealistic measurements of accounting values. While inflation in recent years has declined to about 4.5% per year, it still has an important impact, particularly on the operational fixed assets of the business.

For financial accounting purposes, two distinctly different kinds of price changes usually are identified, viz:

1. **General price level changes**—These price level changes occur when the **average** level of the prices of commodities and services changes; that is, the purchasing power (i.e., the command over goods and services) of the monetary unit changes. Such changes are called **inflation** when the general price level increases (i.e., the purchasing power of the monetary unit decreases) and **deflation** when the general price level decreases (i.e., the purchasing power of the monetary unit increases).

2. **Specific price level changes**—These price level changes occur when the price of a **specific** commodity or service changes. Such changes cause **real value changes** if the rate of specific price level change is different than the rate of general price level changes. Part B of this chapter discusses current cost (CC), which involves the reporting of real value changes.

The impact of inflation upon HC financial statements is difficult to assess by statement users, particularly when the related price change information is not reported. Accountants, economists, and persons in business and government are not in agreement as to what should be done to make the financial statements more useful under conditions of significant price changes.

First, we will consider general price level changes. Reporting the effects of general price level (GPL) changes on financial statements requires that the traditional historical cost (HC) financial statements be **restated** from the HC basis to the latest GPL dollars, usually called **constant dollars.** This restatement requires use of general price level index numbers.[1] The resulting financial statements are known as **constant dollar** (CD) financial statements.

Using Price Level Index Numbers

Price level index numbers may be used to restate HC financial statement amounts for price changes. A **price level index** is a statistical value that expresses the relative price level of each of a series of periods. To construct a price level index, the prices of one specific item, or a group of items, for a number of periods are expressed in relative terms as a series of index numbers. A base year is selected and assigned the base index value of 100. Subsequent changes in prices are expressed in relation to this base. Two kinds of indexes are used widely:

1. **General price level (GPL) index**—A GPL index is computed on the basis of an **average** "market basket" of commodities and services.[2] An average index is computed by collecting the prices of each of the many items that make up the average market basket. Each period the average price of the basket is computed and then related to the base year index of 100. A GPL index is intended to measure **general inflation** (cheaper dollars) and **general deflation** (more expensive dollars). A GPL index is used in accounting to measure the effects of general price level changes and to restate the HC financial statements to the latest constant dollar (CD) basis. To illustrate, assume a tract of land was purchased in 1981 at a cost of $10,000 when the GPL index was 100. Assume that at the end of the current year, the land is still owned, and the GPL index is 138.2. The $10,000 cost of the land would be reported on a CD restated balance sheet at $10,000 × 138.2/100 = $13,820. The GPL increase was $3,820 (i.e., $13.820 − $10,000).

2. **Specific price level index**—A specific price level index is computed in the same manner as a GPL index except that it is related to a **single** item (or small group of homogenous items). Specific price index values often are used to estimate the current replacement cost of **specific** commodities or services. To illustrate, assume the land example given in 1 above (HC, $10,000) had a specific price index of 236.2 when acquired in 1981 and has a specific price index of 287.1 at the end of the current year. The estimated current replacement cost of the land could be computed as $10,000 × 287.1/236.2 = $12,155. This computation

---

[1] Throughout this chapter the descriptive term **restated** is used because the HC basis amounts simply are restated to current GPL or constant dollars. Alternatively, the term **adjusted** sometimes is used. It is less descriptive and suggests the notion of "adjusting" entries, which is based on a completely different concept.

[2] The two GPL series usually are the *Gross National Expenditure Implicit Price Deflator* (which is published quarterly) and the *Consumer Price Index for Urban Consumers* (CPI-U, which is published monthly). Both indexes are published by Statistics Canada. The CPI-U index is the more widely used index in accounting because of its ready availability.

Exhibit 17–1   Selected consumer price index values

	CPI-U index	
Year	**Average for the year**	**At year-end**
1970	41.0	41.1
1971	42.2	43.1
1972	44.2	45.3
1973	47.6	49.5
1974	52.8	55.6
1975	58.5	60.9
1976	62.9	64.5
1977	67.9	70.6
1978	73.9	76.5
1979	80.7	84.0
1980	88.9	93.4
1981*	100.0	104.7
1982	110.8	114.4
1983	117.2	119.6
1984	122.3	124.1
1985	127.2	129.5
1986	132.4	134.9
1987	138.2	140.5

* Base year.

Source: *The Consumer Price Index for Urban Consumers*, Statistics Canada (monthly).

indicates that the specific value of the land increased by $2,155, which was less than the GPL increase of $3,820. A specific price index does **not** measure **general** inflation; rather, it measures the change in price of the specific item to which it relates. Use of specific index numbers is illustrated in Part B of this chapter.

The pervasive history of **general inflation** (i.e., as measured by a GPL index) in recent years is reflected in the index values from the Consumer Price Index for Urban Consumers (CPI-U) presented in Exhibit 17–1.

Another application of a GPL index may be illustrated by indicating the effect of general inflation on the cost of attending a university. To illustrate: assume that in 1970 the average cost of attending "University" for two terms was $4,000 per student. Using the CPI-U index amounts given above, general inflation has increased the total cost as follows:

Year	CPI-U index (average)	Restatement computation	Average cost per student
1970 . . .	41.0		$ 4,000
1975 . . .	58.5	$4,000 × 58.5/41.0	5,707
1980 . . .	88.9	$4,000 × 88.9/41.0	8,673
1984 . . .	122.3	$4,000 × 122.3/41.0	11,932
1987 . . .	138.2	$4,000 × 138.2/41.0	13,483

The Stable Monetary Unit Assumption

One of the underlying assumptions of GAAP is the **unit-of-measure assumption** (Exhibit 4–5), which states that with many diverse items and transactions to be accounted for, it is necessary that a single unit of measure be adopted. Accounting assumes the Canadian monetary unit—the dollar—is the common denominator in the measurement process. Implicit in this assumption is that the dollar has a constant value, which is an important measurement characteristic (a "metrestick" is always one metre long!). However, during a period of inflation or deflation, the constant value assumption is not valid; the monetary unit literally becomes a "rubber" measuring unit (it stretches and contracts) as the GPL changes.

The dollar is the common denominator used for accounting measurements because it is used by the society as a measure of value. That is, the dollar will command a certain amount of real goods and services in the marketplace at a given time. Unfortunately, the dollar (or any other currency) does not maintain a stable value in terms of the real goods and services it can command.

Over time, a single dollar will command fewer goods and services in the case of inflation or, alternatively, more goods and services in the case of deflation; that is, its purchasing power changes. As a result of using the historical cost principle, transactions are recorded in the accounts and reported subsequently on the financial statements in HC basis dollars. Some of those dollar amounts (such as the cost of an old operational asset) remain in the accounts and are reported in the financial statements over many years. Thus, over a period of time, the accounting system accumulates and reports dollars that have different purchasing power, given inflation or deflation. Under HC accounting, dollars having different real values are **aggregated** on the balance sheet and **matched** on the income statement. Thus, during periods of significant inflation or deflation, the accounting amounts are apt to reflect considerable distortion from current dollars because of the effects of the changing value of the monetary unit.

To illustrate this distortion, consider a company that purchased a building for $200,000 when the GPL index was 100. Assuming straight-line depreciation, no residual value, and a 40-year life, the annual depreciation would be $5,000 per year. Let's assume that the current year is Year 30 (since acquisition) and that the current GPL index is 300. At the end of Year 30, the financial statements would show the following amounts, based on HC as recorded in the accounting system:

Balance sheet:
Operational assets:
Building (at cost) $200,000
Accumulated depreciation ($5,000 × 30 years) . . . 150,000
Carrying value $50,000

Income statement:
Depreciation expense . . . . $ 5,000

All of the amounts shown above represent dollars "valued" at acquisition date (30 years earlier). Those dollars had a purchasing power equivalent of 100 (the GPL index). With the current (GPL) index at 300, these amounts are aggregated with other dollar amounts that have different purchasing power equivalents. On the income statement, depreciation expense, expressed in dollars with one purchasing power (index 100) is matched with revenue, which is in current dollars with another purchasing power (index 300). The current GPL index of 300 means that each current dollar will command (buy) only one third (ie., 100/300) as much **real** goods and services as when the index was 100. One could **restate** the above amounts to constant dollars for the GPL change (inflation in this case). The restatement can be accomplished by multiplying the HC amount by a CD index ratio in the following manner:

$$\text{Historical cost (HC) amount} \times \frac{\text{Current period GPL index}}{\text{Transaction date GPL index}} = \text{CD restated amount}$$

The calculations and the resulting CD restated amounts for the data given above would be as follows:

Item	HC basis	CD restatement computation	CD restated amount
Balance sheet amounts:			
Operational assets:			
Building	$200,000	× 300/100 =	$600,000
Accumulated depreciation . . .	150,000	× 300/100 =	450,000
Carrying value	$ 50,000	× 300/100 =	$150,000
Income statement amount:			
Depreciation expense	$ 5,000	× 300/100 =	$ 15,000

Concepts Underlying CD Restatement of Financial Statements

Constant dollar (CD) restatement of financial statements does not involve the recording of journal entries; rather, it is a **supplementary reporting approach.** The traditional HC financial statements are prepared each period in accordance with GAAP. The HC statements continue as the basic periodic reports of the entity. When CD restatement is used, the HC basis financial statements simply are restated in current end-of-period dollars (i.e., in constant dollars). Thus, the CD restated financial statements continue to be cost basis statements except that all dollar amounts are in **constant dollars;** that is, dollars of constant purchasing power. The CD restatement computations are simple and straightforward; they involve the following three steps:

Step 1: Classify all accounts on the financial statements as either monetary or nonmonetary (defined later in the chapter). **Monetary** items are **not** restated on the CD financial statements while the **nonmonetary** items **are** restated. Exhibit 17–2 presents the classification of several accounts.

Exhibit 17–2 Classification of monetary and nonmonetary items

	Monetary	Nonmonetary
Assets		
Cash	X	
Marketable securities:		
Most common shares		X
Most bonds	X	
Accounts and notes receivable	X	
Allowance for doubtful accounts	X	
Inventories—except if valued at selling price		X
Prepaid expense:		
Claims to future services		X
Prepayments that are deposits or advance payments	X	
Long-term receivables	X	
Property, plant, and equipment		X
Accumulated depreciation		X
Patents and trademarks		X
Goodwill		X
Liabilities		
Accounts and notes payable	X	
Accured expenses	X	
Cash dividends payable	X	
Bonds payable and other long-term debt	X	
Premium or discount on bonds payable	X	
Deferred income taxes		X†
Owners' Equity		
Preferred stock (nonmonetary if not carried at a fixed redemption price)	X	
Common stock		X
Retained earnings		
This amount usually is restated as a plug or balancing amount		X

Source: Adapted from *CICA Accounting Guidelines*, "Changes in the Purchasing Power of Money," December 1974.

†*CICA Handbook*, Section 4510.47, states that deferred income taxes should be treated as nonmonetary.

Step 2: Restate each **nonmonetary** item by multiplying its HC amount by the appropriate restatement ratio (i.e., the current period GPL index divided by the GPL index that existed at the date on which the transaction was recorded).

Step 3: Calculate the purchasing power gain or loss on monetary items. This gain or loss is measured as the difference between the HC amount and the CD restated amount for each monetary item. Each of these basic steps is discussed and illustrated in the remainder of this part of the chapter.

CD Restatement—Illustrative Case

A simplified situation is used as the basis for discussing and illustrating the computations needed to develop CD restated financial statements.

Assume ACE Corporation was organized December 31, 19A, when the general GPL index was 120. The accounting period ends December 31, and the company prepares HC financial statements. Restatement of the HC financial statements of ACE Corporation to a CD restated basis is discussed and illustrated in the paragraphs to follow. Exhibit 17–3 presents the following data for ACE Corporation:

1. All transactions completed during 19A and 19B (summarized) and the GPL index at the date of each transaction.
2. Balance sheet at December 31, 19B (HC basis).
3. Income statement for the year ended December 31, 19B (HC basis).
4. Statement of retained earnings at December 31, 19B (HC basis).
5. Selected GPL index data.

Step 1—Identify Monetary and Nonmonetary Items

Restatement of HC financial statements to a CD restated basis requires that a careful distinction be maintained between two different types of items on the financial statements. These two types are known as **monetary items** and **nonmonetary items.** They cause significantly different economic effects on their holder (owner) when the real value of the monetary unit (the dollar) changes (i.e., inflation or deflation occurs).

A **monetary item** is an item that by its nature or as the result of a contract is stated in a **fixed** number of dollars and the fixed number of dollars does not change in response to changes in price levels. Thus, monetary items include cash, payables, and receivables but would not include revenues or expenses. Because inflation does not affect the amount of cash or the number of dollars to be paid or received for monetary items, these items are **not restated** on CD financial statements.

While monetary items are not restated on CD financial statements, the **purchasing power** of monetary items is affected by inflation. Consider what would happen if you left $1,000 in your wallet during a year in which the inflation rate was 20%. At the end of the year, you could buy less real goods and services with the $1,000 than you could have purchased at the beginning of the year. Your loss of purchasing power on this **asset** amounted to $200 [i.e., $1,000 − ($1,000 × 120/100)]. This $200 loss is called a purchasing power loss on monetary items.

In contrast, if you held monetary **liabilities** during a period of inflation, you would experience a purchasing power gain on monetary items because the liabilities will be paid in dollars that have less purchasing power than the dollars that were borrowed. In other words, a dollar owed through a period of inflation is still a dollar owed, although it will command fewer real goods at the end of the period.

Exhibit 17-3 Historical cost and GPL data of ACE Corporation

Summary of transactions:

Year 19A:

a. December 31, 19A: Sold and issued capital stock (no par) for $80,000 cash (GPL index, 120).

b. December 31, 19A: Borrowed $40,000 cash from a local bank; signed a $40,000 interest-bearing note due December 31, 19C (GPL index, 120).

c. December 31, 19A: Purchased equipment for use in the business at a cash cost of $60,000 (GPL index, 120).

Year 19B:

d. March 19B: Purchased land for use in the business at a cash cost of $6,350 (GPL index, 127).

e. During 19B: Purchased merchandise (evenly throughout the year) at a cash cost of $121,500 (average GPL index for 19B, 135). Assume a perpetual inventory system (average costing), cost of goods sold, $108,000, and an ending inventory of $13,500 (i.e., total, $121,500).

f. During 19B: Sales revenue, $162,000, sold evenly throughout the year (average GPL index for 19B, 135). Assume total cash collections on sales of $129,600 and accounts receivable at year-end of $32,400 (i.e., total, $162,000).

g. During 19B: Expenses paid in cash $27,000, which included interest expense and income tax expense, but excluded depreciation expense (average GPL index for 19B, 135).

h. July 1, 19B: Declared and paid a cash dividend, $2,700 (GPL average index, 135).

i. December 31, 19B: Depreciation expense on equipment (estimated five-year life and no residual value), $60,000 ÷ 5 years = $12,000.

Balance sheet, at December 31, 19B (HC basis amounts):

Assets		Liabilities	
Cash	$ 32,050	Note payable, long term	$ 40,000
Accounts receivable (net)	32,400	**Shareholders' Equity**	
Inventory	13,500		
Equipment	60,000	Capital stock (no par)	80,000
Accumulated depreciation	(12,000)	Retained earnings	12,300
Land	6,350		
Total	$132,300	Total	$132,300

Income statement, for the year ended December 31, 19B (HC basis amounts):

Sales revenue	$162,000
Cost of goods sold	(108,000)
Depreciation expense	(12,000)
Remaining expenses	(27,000)
Net income	$ 15,000

Statement of retained earnings, at December 31, 19B (HC basis amounts):

Beginning balance, January 1, 19B	$ -0-
Add: Net income of 19B	15,000
Deduct: Dividends of 19B	(2,700)
Ending balance, December 31, 19B	$12,300

GPL index data:

December 31, 19A	120
Average during 19A	110
January 1, 19B	120
Average during 19B	135
December 31, 19B	150

In summary, monetary items (i.e., monetary assets and monetary liabilities) are not restated on the CD financial statements of the current period, but their existence can cause the holder (or debtor) to incur a real gain or loss during each period of inflation. A purchasing power **gain** on net monetary items is reported (on the CD financial statements) if the purchasing power gain on monetary liabilities is more than the purchasing power loss on monetary assets. Alternatively, a purchasing power **loss** is reported if the purchasing power loss on monetary assets is more than the purchasing power gain on monetary liabilities.

Observe in Exhibit 17–4 that the three monetary items (cash, accounts receivable, and note payable) are not restated in the CD financial statements. However, a purchasing power loss on monetary items of $5,050 is reported on the CD income statement (this loss is computed in Exhibit 17–5).

Nonmonetary items include all items on the financial statements except for the monetary assets and liabilities. The basic characteristic of nonmonetary items is that they have dollar amounts that are **not** fixed in the future by their nature or by contract. The value of nonmonetary items in the marketplace tend to move up and down with inflation and deflation. For example, a tract of land purchased for $6,350 (see Exhibit 17–3) when the GPL index was 127 would **tend** to increase in market value to $7,500 as a result of an increase of the GPL price index to 150 (i.e., $6,350 \times 150/127 = $7,500). If this happened, the owner would not experience a real gain on this nonmonetary asset due to general inflation. The owner would not experience a real gain because, if the land that cost $6,350 could be sold for $7,500, the $7,500 would purchase (at the date of sale of the land) the same quantity of real goods and services that the $6,350 would have bought when the owner originally purchased the land. Of course, the land may have changed in "dollar value" more or less than the GPL, in which case there would have been a real value change (this situation is discussed later). Examples of nonmonetary items are inventories, investments in common shares, operational assets, patents, revenues, expenses, and the common stock accounts.[3]

In summary, nonmonetary items are restated on the CD financial statements, and they do not cause the holder to incur a real gain or loss as a result of changes only in the GPL.

Step 2—CD Restatement of HC Financial Statements

Now, let's return to our illustration of ACE Corporation and the three HC basis financial statements given in Exhibit 17–3. CD restatement of each HC financial statement in terms of the current GPL index of 150 is shown in Exhibit 17–4.

---

[3] Preferred shares usually are classified as a monetary item because they usually have a fixed redeemable value. In contrast, receivables and liabilities which can be settled with goods and services (rather than cash) are classified as nonmonetary items.

Exhibit 17–4 CD restatement of financial statements, ACE Corporation, year-end 19B

Items	HC basis	CD restatement computations	CD restated basis
Balance sheet, at December 31, 19B:			
Assets			
Cash	$ 32,050	Monetary, not restated	$ 32,050
Accounts receivable (net)	32,400	Monetary, not restated	32,400
Inventory	13,500	Nonmonetary, $13,500 × 150/135	15,000
Equipment	60,000	Nonmonetary, $60,000 × 150/120	75,000
Accumulated depreciation (credit)	(12,000)	Nonmonetary, $12,000 × 150/120	(15,000)
Land	6,350	Nonmonetary, $6,350 × 150/127	7,500
Total	$ 132,300		$ 146,950
Liabilities			
Note payable, long term	$ 40,000	Monetary, not restated	$ 40,000
Shareholders' Equity			
Capital stock, no par	80,000	Nonmonetary, $80,000 × 150/120	100,000
Retained earnings	12,300	Nonmonetary, plug, $146,950 − $40,000 − $100,000	6,950
Total	$ 132,300		$ 146,950
Income statement, for the year ended December 31, 19B:			
Sales revenue	$ 162,000	Nonmonetary, $162,000 × 150/135	$ 180,000
Deduct:			
Cost of goods sold	(108,000)	Nonmonetary, $108,000 × 150/135	(120,000)
Depreciation expense	(12,000)	Nonmonetary, $12,000 × 150/120	(15,000)
Remaining expenses	(27,000)	Nonmonetary, $27,000 × 150/135	(30,000)
Income from normal operations	$ 15,000		15,000
Purchasing power gain (loss) on monetary items		Computed, per Exhibit 17–5	(5,050)
Income, CD restated (common dollar)		Carry to statement of retained earnings	$ 9,950
Statement of retained earnings, at December 31, 19B			
Beginning balance, January 1, 19B	$ −0−	Nonmonetary	$ −0−
Add: Income of 19B	15,000	Nonmonetary, from restated income statement	9,950
Deduct: Dividends of 19B (debit)	(2,700)	Nonmonetary, $2,700 × 150/135	(3,000)
Ending balance, December 31, 19B	$ 12,300	Proof: check per balance sheet plug amount	$ 6,950

Exhibit 17–5 Computation of the purchasing power gain (loss) on net monetary items—ACE Corporation, year-end 19B

Items	HC basis	CD restatement computations	CD restated basis
Net monetary balances at beginning of period:			
Cash	$ 60,000		
Accounts receivable	0		
Less: Notes payable	(40,000)		
Net	20,000	$ 20,000 × 150/120	$ 25,000
Debits—increases in net monetary balances:			
Sales	162,000	162,000 × 150/135	180,000
Credits—decreases in net monetary balances:			
Purchase of land	(6,350)	6,350 × 150/127	(7,500)
Purchase of merchandise			
(108,000 + 13,500 − 0)	(121,500)		
Expenses except depreciation	(27,000)		
Dividends declared	(2,700)		
	(151,200)	151,200 × 150/135	(168,000)
Net monetary balances at end of period:			
Cash	32,050		
Accounts receivable	32,400		
Less: Notes payable	(40,000)		
Net			29,500*
	$ 24,450		24,450†
Purchasing power net loss			$ 5,050‡

Explanation:

* Subtotal of restated amount reflects net monetary items (debits in this case) that should be on hand (CD restated amount).

† Balance reflects net monetary items (debits in this case) that are on hand. No conversion is necessary if the purchasing power gain or loss is to be stated in dollars of the end of the period.

‡ Debits lost because of inflation (a loss of assets).

Restatement of the Balance Sheet

The ACE Corporation balance sheet reflects three monetary items: cash, accounts receivable, and the note payable. As explained above, these three **monetary items** were not restated because each has a fixed monetary amount in the future that is not affected by inflation or deflation. Therefore, the three monetary HC amounts were extended across on the balance sheet to the CD restatement column. In contrast, the four nonmonetary asset amounts on the balance sheet were CD restated because their market prices are free to change as a result of changes in the general price level.

Observe in Exhibit 17–4 that 10 **nonmonetary items** are restated on the CD balance sheet and income statement. Also, observe that any real gain or loss on the **nonmonetary** items is not reported on the CD financial statements (see Part B of this chapter).

Exhibit 17–4 presents the CD restatement computation for each nonmonetary item. For example, the Land account was restated as follows:

$$\begin{array}{c}\text{Historical cost} \\ \text{(HC) basis} \\ \text{amount}\end{array} \times \frac{\text{Current period GPL index}}{\text{Transaction date GPL index}} = \begin{array}{c}\text{CD} \\ \text{restated} \\ \text{amount}\end{array}$$

$$\text{Land, } \$6{,}350 \times \qquad 150/127 \qquad = \$7{,}500$$

Restatement of the Income Statement

All items on the income statement are **nonmonetary;** therefore, each item is restated. The numerator of the GPL restatement ratio is the ending GPL index, and the denominator usually is the average GPL index for the current period because it is assumed often that price changes and business transactions occurred evenly throughout the period. Observe that depreciation expense is always restated by using the same GPL index amounts used to restate the related asset (150/120 in the illustration). The only unique feature of the income statement is inclusion of the "Purchasing power gain (loss) on monetary items." This **gain or loss** must be computed separately on the monetary assets and monetary liabilities as illustrated in Step 3 (Exhibit 17–5).

Step 3—Computation of the Purchasing Power Gain or Loss on Net Monetary Items

Computation of the purchasing power gain or loss requires restatement of each monetary asset and each monetary liability. Often this is the most tedious phase of CD restatement. Monetary items that have identical numerator indexes and identical denominator indexes can be grouped for computation purposes with the same results.

Computation of the purchasing power gain (loss) on the monetary items for ACE Corporation is illustrated in Exhibit 17–5. Observe in this exhibit that the HC amount of each monetary item (first money column) is CD restated by using the appropriate numerator and denominator indexes. The net gain or loss on monetary items simply is the difference between the **ending** actual HC basis amount and the **ending** CD restated amount (i.e., for net monetary items, $24,450 − $29,500 = $5,050 loss).

The restatement of monetary items is tedious because the beginning balance of the net monetary balance sheet accounts as well as each transaction that affects these accounts must be restated with the appropriate GPL indexes. We reemphasize that **monetary** items are restated **only** for purposes of calculating the purchasing power gain or loss on net monetary items; they are **not** restated on the balance sheet.

The total purchasing power gain (loss) on monetary items ($5,050) is the algebraic sum of the purchasing power **losses on monetary assets** and the purchasing power **gains on monetary liabilities.** In the illustration, the $5,050 is a loss during a period of inflation because the monetary assets exceeded the monetary liabilities (in the opposite case, there would have been a gain). This amount is carried to the income statement (as illustrated in Exhibit 17–4) because it can be considered to represent an economic (purchasing power) gain or loss.

In summary, CD restated financial statements are prepared by restating the **nonmonetary** HC-items on the balance sheet, income statement, and statement of retained earnings. The monetary items are included in the CD financial statements at their HC basis amounts. However, the **monetary** assets and liabilities are restated separately to compute the purchasing power gain or loss on monetary items, which is reported on the income statement. The CD restated net income is carried to the CD statement of retained earnings, and the CD restated ending balance of retained earnings is reported on the CD balance sheet.[4]

Overview of CD Effects

A comparison of the two balance sheets presented in Exhibit 17–4 shows that the CD restatement increased total assets from $132,300 to $146,950 which was an 11.1% increase. In contrast, the income statement reflected a decrease in reported income of $15,000 to $9,950 which was a 34% decrease. When there is an inflationary trend, and the relationship between monetary assets and monetary liabilities remains essentially constant, **CD restated income** usually will be lower than the cost basis amount, primarily because of higher restated assets and correspondingly higher restated depreciation expense.

Having presented the concept and related procedures to derive CD restated financial statements, let us examine them in overall perspective. The HC basis financial statements rest on the unit-of-measure assumption (Chapter 4), which holds that each transaction should be measured in those dollars that "existed" at the date of each transaction. In the case of GPL changes (i.e., inflation or deflation), the HC financial statements commingle dollars that have different amounts of purchasing power. In contrast, the concept of CD restated financial statements retains the HC amounts except that they are restated in constant dollars. That is, the HC amounts are restated for the effects of changes in the purchasing power of the monetary unit (inflation or deflation) that have occurred since each transaction was recorded. This means that all nonmonetary

---

[4] In view of CD restatement on the balance sheet of only the nonmonetary items (not the monetary items), the question always arises as to why a CD balance sheet "balances." Technically, the reason is that the monetary assets and monetary liabilities are not restated on the balance sheet, but total **owners' equity** is restated. Therefore, the residual, owners' equity $(A - L = OE)$ **includes** a restatement amount for **both** the nonmonetary and monetary items. Inclusion of the purchasing power gain (loss) on monetary items on the income statement (and hence in retained earnings on the balance sheet) provides the mathematically necessary amount to bring the equation $A - L = OE$ into balance on the CD restated balance sheet.

HC dollar amounts (but not the monetary amounts) reflected in the HC statements are restated to constant (current) dollars, each having equivalent purchasing power. The CD restated income statement reports a new type of gain or loss: purchasing power gain or loss on monetary items.

Those who advocate the concept of CD restatement contend that two sets of financial statements should be presented: (1) one set prepared on the traditional HC basis, and (2) another set prepared on the CD restated basis. The primary **arguments for** presenting CD restated financial statements are (1) during periods of significant inflation or deflation, HC basis statements contain serious measurement distortions that are not presented; (2) the CD restated amounts, including the purchasing power gain or loss on monetary items, are relevant to the users of financial statements; and (3) the HC approach essentially is retained with all amounts stated in terms of dollars of the same purchasing power. In contrast, the primary **arguments against** CD restated statements are (1) two sets of financial statements (restated and not restated) potentially can confuse statement users; (2) it is difficult to justify a particular GPL price index to use for restatement purposes; (3) statement users do not find the restated amounts to be particularly useful; and (4) GPL effects and real value changes on **nonmonetary** items are not revealed separately (discussed in Part B).

CICA Handbook, Section 4510, entitled "Reporting the Effects of Changing Prices" was issued in December 1982 to apply to large publicly held companies. Compliance was requested of such companies if they satisfied either of the following two size requirements: (1) the book value of inventories plus property, plant, and equipment before deducting accumulated depreciation, depletion, and amortization of at least $50 million, or (2) total assets before accumulated depreciation, depletion, and amortization of at least $350 million at the beginning of the current accounting year.

Because Section 4510 was issued as supplementary disclosure requirements and specifically exempted real estate, banks, trust companies, and insurance companies, not all companies have complied with the suggestions. Cost of preparation, lack of mandatory disclosure, and the controversial nature of the pronouncement have all hindered its acceptance. Companies have cited the lack of coverage in the financial press as part of the evidence for a lack of relevance. The complexity of the amounts, the lack of comparability between companies in the same industry, and the lack of an audit have disturbed preparers. Certainly the lack of acceptance of these supplementary disclosures for income tax purposes has reduced the incentives to prepare this information. Certainly a reduction in inflation in recent years below double digits has reduced the demand for these supplementary disclosures.

PART B—REPORTING CURRENT COST CHANGES

Accounting academicians and professional accountants long have discussed the concept of reporting **current values** rather than HC basis amounts on the financial statements. The primary argument in favour of reporting current values is that statement users (investors, creditors, and others) are more interested in the "worth" of the assets at the date of the financial statements than in the HC amounts now reported under GAAP. The acceptance of current value accounting has been slow because opinions vary as to exactly what current value means and how it should be measured. Two basic implementation approaches are under consideration:

1. Report **current value** amounts in the financial statements instead of HC amounts. This view is that current value would be a substitute for, and not be supplementary information to, the traditional HC statements. A second view, which prevails currently, is that two different sets of financial statements should be presented each period: (*a*) one set on the traditional HC basis and (*b*) another set on the current value basis.

2. Report both current value and constant dollar in **combination.** In effect, under this approach, current values are restated so that both current value and GPL effects are reported.

In the discussions to follow, the **combination reporting approach** is assumed because it provides considerable information on both current value and GPL effects. This reporting approach is usually called the current cost/constant dollar (CC/CD) approach.

Definition of Current Value in Financial Reporting

The term **current value,** as used in financial reporting, is a general term that encompasses three different concepts of value; that is, the:

1. **Present value (value in use)**—This value represents the present value of the expected net future cash inflow attributable to an **asset** (such as inventories, equipment, and land). This concept of the valuation of an asset was discussed briefly in Chapter 10. The expected net future cash inflows are discounted to the present at an appropriate interest rate. Conceptually, this approach is superior to HC or CD; however, it is not used widely to determine "current value" in financial statements because of uncertainty in (*a*) projecting the future net cash inflow by period, and (*b*) selecting an appropriate discount rate.

2. **Net realizable value**—The net realizable value of an asset is the expected price at which the asset could be sold in its present condition, less all disposal costs. This concept of valuing an asset was discussed in Chapter 7 in respect to inventories. This asset value is used as one possible recoverable amount.[5]

3. **Current cost (CC)**—The current cost is the cost needed at the present time to acquire the amount of service embodied in the asset being

---

[5] *CICA Handbook,* Section 4510.36, specifies that current cost cannot exceed the recoverable amount of the asset. Recoverable amount can be value in use (present value) or net realizable value if the asset is to be sold.

valued, technically called its service potential. Current cost may be current reproduction cost or current replacement cost depending on the extent of technological change. Current reproduction cost is the cash needed currently to acquire a used asset of the same age, location, and condition or a depreciated new asset. Current replacement cost is the current cash cost necessary to acquire the best available asset to perform the same function as the existing asset. Because this value is the value of a new asset the amount of the current replacement cost has to be adjusted for accumulated depreciation to the current date. Current replacement cost is used where technological change has occurred.

Estimating the CC of some assets (such as a plant, because there seldom is an established market for a one-of-a-kind plant) is a complex problem. In contrast, CC may be estimated reasonably for some assets, such as merchandise inventory, because there is an established market. Primary sources for estimating CC are current price lists, prices in established markets for used items, specific price indexes, and professional appraisals.

Concepts Underlying CC/CD Financial Reporting

CC/CD financial reporting does **not** require the recording of CC/CD valuations in the accounts, although many accountants view it as a full-blown accounting and reporting method to replace the current GAAP historical cost valuation model. The discussions and illustrations that follow assume that HC basis financial statements will be reported and that CC/CD financial statements will be prepared for supplementary reporting purposes without entering the CC/CD values in the accounts.

When CC/CD financial statements are prepared, the HC amounts are converted to CC/CD amounts. Primarily, CC/CD reporting involves changes in the **nonmonetary** asset and income statement amounts. For **monetary items,** the HC carrying amounts and CC/CD carrying amounts usually will be the same. Preparation of CC/CD financial statements involves the following steps:

Step 1.   Calculation of the current cost of the ending inventory and cost of goods sold using specific price indexes.

Step 2.   Calculation of the current cost depreciation expense and gains or losses on current period disposals of fixed assets using the current cost carrying value (current cost less accumulated depreciation based on current cost) of property, plant, and equipment (pp and e) at the beginning and end of the period.

Step 3.   Calculation of the total shareholders' equity (also called net assets) on a current cost basis.

Step 4.   Calculation of the general purchasing power gain or loss on net monetary items in terms of average general price levels.

Step 5. Calculation of the nominal (unadjusted) dollar and inflation adjusted dollar (real) amount of the holding gains on inventory and property, plant, and equipment.

Step 6. Calculation of the financing adjustment applied to the holding gains calculated in Step 5 if the total of the monetary liabilities exceed the total monetary assets (see "Illustrative Case").

Step 7. Calculation of income after inclusion of the historical sales figures, the historical selling, administrative, and interest expenses, and the historical income tax expense. Include schedules for the remaining suggested disclosures.

Step 8. Present comparative information for the preceding year by adjusting the previous current cost and historical information using the year-end or average general price level information depending on the specific amount considered (generally balance sheet at year-end and income statement items at average).

Variations are possible in the exact form of the income presentation. However, all forms have essentially the same information either in the body of the income statement or in the supplementary information attached.

CC/CD Financial Reporting—Illustrative Case

The simplified situation of ACE Corporation used in Part A will be continued for the CC/CD illustrations and discussions in this part of the chapter. The HC financial statements are shown in Exhibit 17–3.

Step 1—Determine CC of Ending Inventory and Cost of Goods Sold

The first step in developing the CC/CD financial statements is to determine the current cost amount of the ending inventory and cost of goods sold. Current price lists and a record of price changes during the year are needed to develop the specific price indexes for the company. Exhibit 17–6 illustrates the application of these indexes for ACE Corporation.

Step 2—Determine Current Cost Depreciation

Exhibit 17–6 illustrates the application of specific price indexes (one method of determining current cost) to equipment. Using the average current cost amounts for equipment (no additions or disposals are presented here), the current cost depreciation is then calculated. Current cost indexes for land are not available. Appraisals by real estate experts are often used as substitutes.

Step 3—Determine Total CC Shareholders' Equity

The current cost amount of the shareholders' equity can be calculated by adding the increase in inventory and the increase in pp and e to the historical amount of the shareholders' equity. Exhibit 17–6 illustrates this computation.

Exhibit 17–6 Current cost/constant dollar data for ACE Corporation

Item	Current cost determination	CC valuation amount
Specific indexes or values for 19B	Year-end 19B inventory prices 120%. Average 19B inventory prices 108%. Year-end equipment prices 130%. Professional appraisal of land $6,985. Depreciation rate per year 20%. Depreciation accumulated one year.	
Ending inventory December 31, 19B	The specific price index at year's end of the inventory, based on CC, was 120% of HC. $13,500 × 1.20 =	16,200
Cost of goods sold	The average specific price index, based on the current cost when the goods were sold, was 108% of HC. $108,000 × 1.08 =	116,640
Equipment	The specific price index at year's end of the equipment, based on estimated current cost in new condition, was 130% of HC. $60,000 × 1.30 =	78,000
Accumulated depreciation, equipment	The equipment has a five-year useful life, no residual value, and is being depreciated on a straight-line basis. At the end of 19B, CC accumulated depreciation is one fifth of the CC amount for equipment: $78,000 × ⅕ =	15,600
Depreciation expense	The CC amount for this expense is determined by applying for depreciation rate (one-fifth) to the **average** CC amount for equipment during the year 19B. $\left(\dfrac{\$60,000 + \$78,000}{2}\right) \times \dfrac{1}{5} =$	13,800
Land	Professionally appraised at year's end.	6,985
Shareholders' equity	Increase in inventory ($16,200 − $13,500) = Increase in equipment (($78,000 − $15,600) − ($60,000 − $12,000)) = Increase in land ($6,985 − $5,350) = Historical shareholders' equity (80,000 + 12,300) = Total	$ 2,700 14,400 1,635 92,300 $111,035

Step 4—Calculation of General Purchasing Power Gain (Loss)

In Exhibit 17–5, purchasing power gain (loss) on net monetary items is calculated in terms of year-end 19B dollars (index 150). Commonly, current cost statements apply this same methodology in terms of average of 19B dollars (index 135) (Exhibit 17–7). A careful comparison of Exhibits 17–5 and 17–7 will illustrate the differences in the restated amounts.

Exhibit 17-7 Calculation of purchasing power gain or loss for ACE Corporation (using average dollars)

Item	Historical		General price level index adjustment	CD restated basis (average 19B dollars)
Net monetary assets—December 31, 19A:				
Cash	$60,000			
Less: Note payable	40,000	$ 20,000	135/120	$ 22,500
Increases:				
Sales		162,000	135/135	162,000
		182,000		184,500
Decreases:				
Land purchased		6,350	135/127	6,750
Purchases		121,500	135/135	121,500
Expenses		27,000	135/135	27,000
Dividends declared		2,700	135/135	2,700
		157,550		157,950
			Balance	26,550
Net monetary assets—December 31, 19B				
Cash	$32,050			
Accounts Receivable	32,400			
	64,450			
Notes payable	40,000	$ 24,450	135/150	22,005
Purchasing power loss (difference)				$ 4,545

Step 5—Calculation of Holding Gains or Losses

The methodology for computing holding gains or losses is illustrated in Exhibit 17–8. The approach is relatively simple to apply because it makes use of a T-account.

The amounts inserted are obtained from the historical statements and the calculations made in Steps 1 to 4. Unfortunately, however, the logic of these calculations is somewhat difficult to understand.

To understand the logic of the T-account calculation, a simple example is necessary. Assume that a business had one item of inventory on hand at the beginning of the year which had a current cost of $110. Next, the business bought another item for $115. It then sold the first item for $220 when the

Exhibit 17–8 Calculation of holding gains or losses on inventory and pp and e for ACE Corporation

Inventory

0	135/120	Inventory—Dec. 31, 19A—CC	0			
				Cost of goods sold—CC	135/135 =	
				116,640		116,640
121,500	135/135	Purchases— HC	121,500			
4,860		Calculated balance	4,860			
14,580	135/150	Inventory— Dec. 31, 19B—CC	16,200			
Holding gain— real		Holding gain— nominal				
9,720			11,340			

Land

0	135/120	Balance—Dec. 31, 19A—CC	0	Disposals		
				0	135/	0
					(Date sold)	
6,750	135/127	Purchases—HC	6,350			
6,750		Calculated balance	6,350			
6,286	135/150	Balance— Dec. 31, 19B— CC	6,985			
Holding loss— real		Holding gain— Nominal				
(464)			635			

Equipment (Net of Accumulated Depreciation)

67,500	135/120	Balance— Dec. 31, 19A—CC	60,000	Depreciation expense—CC		
				13,800	135/135	13,800
				Disposals—Net CC		
				0	135/	0
					(Date sold)	
0	135/ (Date purchased)	Purchases— —HC	0			
53,700		Calculated balance	46,200			
56,160	135/150	Balance—Dec. 31, 19A—CC	62,400			
Holding gain— real		Holding gain— nominal				
2,460			16,200			

current cost of the item was $120. The one item left over had a current cost at the year-end of $130. The nominal holding gains (unadjusted) for the two inventory items is the amount by which the current cost increased while the items were held during the year. On item 1, the current cost increased from $110 to $120, or $10. On item 2, the current cost increased from $115 to $130, or $15. The total unadjusted (nominal) holding gain was $10 + $15 or $25 for the two inventory items.

The T-account will automatically compute the holding gain or loss for this simple case and all complex cases if it is used correctly. For example,

Inventory

Balance—beg. of year CC	110		
Purchases—HC	115	Cost of goods sold—CC	120
Calculated balance	105		
Balance—end of year	130		
Difference—holding gain—nominal	25		

Exhibit 17–8 illustrates that the holding gain or loss (nominal) on land is computed in the same way as inventory. Buildings and equipment are very similar to land and inventory except depreciation expense is substituted for cost of goods sold and the balances are net of accumulated depreciation.

Real holding gains and losses represent the holding gains or losses after the effects of general inflation (general price level changes) are removed. Generally these amounts are computed in terms of average purchasing power dollars. Again the methodology to make these computations is relatively easy because it involves GPL adjusting each of the previous T-account amounts. However, the logic is difficult to understand.

Using the above inventory example, the logic is apparent. For simplicity assume the purchase of the new unit and sale of the old unit of inventory took place on July 1, 19B. The GPL adjustment would result in a cost of 135/120 × $110 = $123.75 on July 1, 19B for the unit in the beginning inventory. Therefore, general inflation resulted in a holding gain of $123.75 − $110 or $13.75. The current cost of the same item was $120 on this date. Since the specific price was only $120 there was a loss of $120 − $123.75 or $3.75 because the general price change exceeded the specific price change. The new unit was purchased for $115 on July 1 when the general index was 135. The current cost at the year-end was $130 when the general price index was 150. In terms of purchasing power on July 1, the year-end current cost was $130 × 135/150 or $117. The holding gain in excess of general inflation was $117 − $115 or $2. The real holding loss was the total of the two: loss of $3.75 less a gain of $2 or $1.75.

The T-account to calculate the real holding loss would look as follows:

Inventory

GPL amounts	GPL indexes	Nominal amounts			Nominal amounts	GPL indexes	GPL amounts
123.75	135/120	Balance—beg. of year CC	110				
				Cost of Goods Sold—CC	120.	135/135	120.
115.	135/135	Purchases—HC	115				
118.75		Calculated balance	105				
117.	135/150	Balance—end of year CC	130				
1.75 Difference		Difference	25				
—real holding loss		—nominal holding gain					

Step 6—Calculation of Financing Adjustment

The financing adjustment (sometimes called gearing adjustment) represents the portion of the holding gains (losses generally ignored) attributed to the liabilities of the firm. If an amount exists, it will be shown as a reduction of the expenses on the current cost income statement or as a separate item in the supplementary disclosures statement. Generally, the gearing adjustment is stated as $0 if holding losses are present or if the average monetary assets for the year exceed the average monetary liabilities. For ACE Corporation, monetary assets exceed the monetary liabilities so the amount is required to be $0.

The general calculation of the financing adjustment, if it exists, is as follows:

Percentage = {Average difference of (Monetary assets − Monetary liabilities) at beginning and end of year} ÷ {Total of [Average (Monetary assets − Monetary liabilities) + Average current cost shareholders' equity]}

Financing adjustment = Percentage × Nominal holding gains

Notice that all the amounts needed for these two calculations come from the earlier steps.

An example of this calculation assuming Ace had monetary liabilities in excess of its monetary assets would be as follows:

1. Assume net monetary liabilities at the beginning of the year of $25,000.
2. Assume net monetary liabilities at the end of the year of $27,000.

3. The average net monetary liabilities would then be ($25,000 + $27,000)/2 = $26,000.
4. Assume an average current cost shareholders' equity for the year of $110,000.
5. The percentage would be: $26,000/($26,000 + $110,000) = .19.
6. The financing adjustment = .19 × (11,340 + 16,200 + 635) = $5,353 if the holding gains for Ace were used. For specific problems, actual amounts would be substituted for the assumed ones in this example.

Step 7—Statement of Income and Schedules for Other Current Cost Disclosures

Exhibit 17–9 provides the disclosures of the current cost information for ACE Corporation. Different arrangements of the information are possible depending on the interpretation used by the accountant preparing the statement. For example, the nominal holding gains and the financing adjustment could be placed in the body of the income statement. Alternatively, the purchasing power gain or loss could be included in the income statement. The choice depends on what the accountant or management wants to disclose.

Step 8—Determine Comparative Amounts for Previous Year

All current cost income items are at average dollars for the current year. If current cost amounts for the previous year were available, they would be average current costs for 19A. To express 19A amounts in the same purchasing power units as 19B, it is necessary to multiply each amount by 135/Average 19A GPL index (namely 110). For the schedule of assets, the current cost amounts are in year-end purchasing power units. Therefore, 19A amounts are multiplied by 150/120 to make them comparative to the 19B amounts.

Overview of CC/CD Effects

Now that you understand the "content" of the three different sets of financial statements—HC, CD restated, and CC/CD—it is appropriate to view them in the perspective of the needs of investors, creditors, and other users of such statements, given the expectation of continuation of the current inflationary trend.

HC financial statements often are distorted during periods of significant inflation because the measuring unit (the dollar in our case) declines in purchasing power. Large changes in purchasing power result in aggregating dollars with different values (in terms of purchasing power) in the financial statements. This "adding of apples and oranges" is not very meaningful for measuring financial results. Simply stated, **HC reporting disregards both GPL and CC effects.** On the other hand, HC reporting is quite **objective** because the HC dollars recorded are those established by transactions between two or more

Exhibit 17–9 Current cost income statement and supplementary disclosures

ACE CORPORATION
Statement of Income on a Current Cost Basis
For the Year Ended December 31, 19B

Historical		Current Cost 19B		19A Restated
$162,000	Sales	$162,000	135/AVE 19A	NO O P E R A T I O N S
108,000	Cost of goods sold (Exhibit 17–6)	116,640	135/AVE 19A	
54,000	Gross margin	45,360		
27,000	Expenses other than depreciation	27,000		
12,000	Depreciation expense (Exhibit 17–6) . .	13,800		
39,000		40,800		
$ 15,000	Income before income taxes	$ 4,560		

Supplementary Information

		19B		19A Restated
	Holding gains–nominal dollars			
	Inventory (Exhibit 17–8)	$ 11,340	135/AVE 19A	NO O P E R A T I O N S
	Equipment	16,200		
	Land	635		
		28,175		

Gains caused by general inflation
$$(11,340 - 9,720) = 1,620$$
$$[635 - (-464)] = 1,099$$
$$(16,200 - 2,460) = 13,740 \qquad 16,459$$

Holding gains–real dollars		
Inventory (Exhibit 17–8)	9,720
Equipment	2,460
Land	(464)
	$ 11,716

Purchasing power gain (loss) on mone-		
tary items (Exhibit 17–7)	$ (4,545)	135/AVE 19A
Financing adjustment (Step 6)	$ 0	135/AVE 19A

Schedule of Assets on a Current Cost Basis
As at December 31, 19B

Historical 19B		Current Cost 19B		19A Restated
$ 13,500	Inventory (Exhibit 17–6)	$ 16,200		0
5,350	Land	6,985		0
48,000	Equipment (less accumulated depreciation of $15,600)	62,400	($60,000 150/120)	$ 75,000
92,300	Common shareholders' equity	111,035	($80,000 150/120)	100,000

parties with different economic interests (i.e., the buyer is motivated to buy low while the seller is motivated to sell high, and they strike a bargain).

CD restated financial statements (in contrast to HC statements) attempt to report the effects of inflation and deflation by restating the HC amounts in terms of the current GPL (i.e., in constant dollars). CD restatement retains the HC model; however, it adds two features that the HC model does not incorporate: (1) restatement of the HC amounts to constant dollars and (2) measurement of the real purchasing power gains and losses on monetary items held during periods of inflation and deflation. Thus, it fulfills its objective to resolve one of the deficiencies of HC reporting (i.e., the changing value of the measurement unit). However, it does not report CC effects. Also, some people argue that CD restated financial statements necessitate two separate sets of financial statements (e.g., HC and CD, restated). The basic argument against the two sets of financial statements is that the decision makers would be confused by an "information overload."

CC/CD financial statements attempt to correct the two basic deficiencies of HC financial statements—the GPL and CC effects. CC/CD financial statements attempt to do this by (1) reporting all amounts at their current CC values and (2) expressing the CC values in terms of constant dollars.[6] The conceptual objective of CC/CD reporting is simple: to tell decision makers the current "worth" of each item reported. This objective is important because decision makers necessarily base their decisions on (1) the current situation and (2) their predictions about the future. For example, a person considering the purchase of a 20-year-old office building would be concerned primarily about (1) its value today and (2) its potential to generate net cash inflows during the expected holding period. The fact that it cost a certain amount 20 years earlier, or that its current HC book value is another amount, should be of little, or no, concern to the potential buyer.

Although CC/CD conceptually is an ideal financial reporting model, it has a significant implementation problem; that is, attaining reliability and accuracy in determining the CC of each item at the end of each accounting period. This burden of attaining objective measurement of CC values is not easy to resolve. Of course, it may be relatively easy in some situations but extremely difficult in others. If it can be resolved so that CC values are reasonably accurate and believable, the CC/CD model should replace both HC and CD restated financial statements.

The Canadian current cost pronouncement, the main details of which were presented in this chapter, represents an attempt to correct the major deficiencies of HC statements caused by inflation while at the same time trying to avoid some of the more controversial areas of CC accounting. In addition, the pronouncement permits and even encourages flexibility so that practical experience in implementing these new practices can be obtained.

The *CICA Handbook*, Section 4510, proposes to revise two income statement

---

[6] Previous year's comparative amounts and real holding gains and losses.

items, cost of goods sold and depreciation expense. In a period of inflation, these two items are the two income statement classifications that are most distorted. Sales and operating expenses usually are the accumulated average of the current revenues and expenses for the period. Income tax expense is stated in terms of historical amounts because the taxing authorities have not adopted current cost accounting. Therefore, these last three classifications are reasonably represented by their HC income statement amounts.

Three potentially controversial items of CC income or loss are, holding gains or losses, purchasing power gain or loss, and the financing adjustment. The *Handbook* permits flexibility by suggesting that these amounts may be reported without stating whether or not they have to be included or excluded from the determination of CC net income. The user of the financial information is free to decide which of these amounts should be used to calculate CC net income. The complex topic of capital maintenance (a topic beyond the scope of this book) constitutes the basis for the decision the users are likely to make.

The CC balance sheet disclosures are restricted to three areas: inventory, property, plant and equipment net of accumulated depreciation, and shareholders' equity in total. Inventory and pp and e represent the two asset areas most affected by inflation. The shareholders' equity also would be distorted because changes in inventory and pp and e change this total if the balance sheet is to be kept in balance. However, only the total of shareholders' equity is disclosed because the decision about the internal breakdown requires a decision about the nature of capital maintenance.

Reporting the Effects of Changing Prices

Until 1987 financial reports of a number of large companies reported supplementary information about the effects of changing prices on their operations. The exhibit provided for Maritime Electric at the beginning of this chapter is typical of such disclosures. For reasons cited earlier the major portion of the companies who had disclosed changing prices information have ceased to do so in their 1987 annual reports. Certainly the judgments required to prepare current cost statements particularily have disturbed preparers. Suggestions have been made that costs of preparation exceeded the benefits. Perhaps understandability was a problem. Regardless, the technique can provide useful information for managers and specific analytical situations. Maybe when inflation resumes the benefits from inflation adjusted accounting will increase so they exceed the costs of preparation. Certainly understandability should improve as more and more future accountants and managers study the techniques for CC/CD financial statements.

IMPORTANT TERMS DEFINED IN THIS CHAPTER

CD Restatement Restatement of financial statements to reflect general price level changes. *p. 974*

Constant Dollars Dollars with constant (or equal) purchasing power. *p. 970*

CPI-U Consumer Price Index for Urban Consumers; a measure of general inflation. *p. 972*

Current Cost The cost of replacing an asset in its present operating condition. *p. 984*

GPL Index Any price index which measures general inflation. *p. 971*

Monetary Items Cash or the obligation to pay or receive a fixed number of dollars (Exhibit 17–2). *p. 976*

Nonmonetary Items All items which are not properly classified as monetary items (Exhibit 17–2). *p. 976*

Purchasing Power Gain (or Loss) The gain or loss in purchasing power that results from holding monetary items during a period of inflation (or deflation). *p. 981*

Specific Price Index Similar to a general price level index except that it is related to a single item (or a small group of homogeneous items). *p. 971*

QUESTIONS

Part A: Questions 1 to 7

1. Explain the difference between general price level changes and specific price level changes.
2. What is a price level index? Explain the difference between a general price level index and a specific price level index.
3. What happens to the "value" of a dollar during a period of inflation, and alternatively, during a period of deflation?
4. A tract of land was acquired for $15,000 when the GPL index was 150. Five years later the GPL index was 270. At what price would the land have to sell for the owner to keep up exactly with inflation? Explain.
5. Define monetary items and nonmonetary items. Give some examples of each. Explain why a careful distinction between monetary and nonmonetary items is essential when financial statements are restated on a CD basis.
6. At the beginning of the current period, the Land account reflected a balance of $18,000 (GPL index at acquisition date, 100), and the Note Payable account reflected no beginning balance but had an ending balance of $30,000 (GPL index at transaction date, 150). The GPL index at the end of the current period was 200. Compute the purchasing power gain (loss) on monetary items. Explain the nature of this gain or loss.
7. Items on the balance sheet may be either monetary or nonmonetary, while all items on the income statement are nonmonetary. Is this statement true or is it false? Explain why.

Part B: Questions 8 to 12

8. Briefly define each of the following concepts of "current value": (*a*) present value, (*b*) net realizable value, and (*c*) current cost (CC).

9. Are CC amounts usually entered into the journal and ledger? Explain.

10. Explain the nature and composition of the item "CC real holding gain (loss) on nonmonetary items." Contrast it with the "purchasing power gain (loss) on monetary items."

11. Contrast "GPL fictional changes" with "CC real value changes."

12. A tract of land was purchased on a cost of $10,000 when the GPL index was 100. At the end of Year 5, the GPL index was 240 and the appraised value of the land was $27,000. Prepare a diagram that exhibits the price change effects.

EXERCISES

Part A: Exercises 17–1 to 17–7

E17–1 **(Pair Definitions with Terms)**
Match the following brief definitions with the terms by entering the appropriate letter in each space provided.

Term	Brief definition
_____ (1) Nonmonetary items	A. When this supplementary reporting approach is used, the historical cost basis financial statements are restated in current end-of-period dollars.
_____ (2) Constant dollars	
_____ (3) Specific price index	B. Monetary units restated so as to represent the same general purchasing power.
_____ (4) CD restatement	C. A price index used to measure general inflation; Consumer Price Index—Urban Consumers.
_____ (5) Monetary items	D. Costs at present-day price levels.
_____ (6) Current cost	E. Any index intended to measure general inflation or deflation.
_____ (7) CPI-U	F. Includes cash, payables, and receivables, but not revenues or expenses.
_____ (8) GLP index	G. Includes property, plant, and equipment, and goodwill.
_____ (9) Purchasing power gain (or loss)	H. Computation of this requires restatement of each monetary asset and each monetary liability.
	I. Used to estimate the current replacement cost of specific commodities or services.

E17–2 **(Use a Price Index to Analyze Price Changes)**
During 1970, a Quality Stereo set sold for $250. Assume that each year this particular set increased in price exactly the same as the changes in the GPL index. However, in 1987 it sold for $695.

Required:

a. What was the selling price in 1975, 1980, and 1985? Use the average CPI-U index values given in the chapter and round to the nearest dollar. Show computations.

b. Analyze the change in price during 1987.

E17–3   **(CD Restatement of an Operational Asset)**
In 1970, Tower Company purchased a plant site for $23,100. Immediately thereafter, construction of a plant building was started. The building was completed in January 1971, at a cost of $336,000. The building is being depreciated on a straight-line basis assuming an estimated useful life of 30 years and no residual value.

Assume the GPL index in 1970 was 41.1, in 1975 it was 60.9, and at the end of 1987 it was 140.5.

Required:

a. Complete a schedule similar to the following:

	Amount to be reported assuming	
	HC basis	**CD restated**
Balance sheet at December 31,1987:		
Operational assets:		
Land		
Building		
Less accumulated depreciation (17 years) . . .		
Income statement for 1987:		
Depreciation expense		

Show your computations.

b. Would the CD restatement affect income tax expense for the company? Explain. Do you think it should? Explain.

E17–4   **(CD Restatement of Selected Balance Sheet Accounts and Calculation of Purchasing Power Gain [Loss] on Monetary Items)**
The balance sheet for Fargo Company, prepared on the HC basis at December 31, 19F, has been completed. Supplemental statements are to be developed on a "CD restated basis." The following four items were selected from the balance sheet:

Items	HC basis (when acquired)	GPL index (when acquired or incurred)
Receivables	$69,000	115
Investment, common shares . . .	42,000	105
Land, plant site	15,000	100
Payables	99,000	110

Note: The GPL at the end of 19F was 120.

Required:

a. Indicate which items are monetary and which are nonmonetary.

b. Set up a schedule to derive the amount that should be shown on the supplementary CD balance sheet for each item. Show computations.

c. Compute the purchasing power gain (loss) on monetary items that should be reported on the CD income statement. Show computations.

d. Explain why certain items were omitted from your computation in (c).

E17–5   **(Prepare a HC/CD Balance Sheet and Determine HC/CD Net Income)**

The items listed below were taken from the December 31, 19A, balance sheet of Environmental Systems Company (HC basis). This date is the end of the first year of operations. The GPL index at January 1, 19A, was 200, and at December 31, 19A, it was 220.

	Debits	Credits	GPL index transaction date
Cash	$ 26,000		210†
Accounts receivable (net)	45,000		210†
Investments, common shares . . .	12,000		215
Land	15,000		205
Equipment	100,000		200
Accumulated depreciation		$ 8,000	
Accounts payable		23,000	210†
Notes payable		43,000	200
Capital stock (no par)		110,000	200
Retained earnings*		14,000	
	$198,000	$198,000	

* Cash dividends declared and paid on December 31, 19A, amounted to $5,000.

† Average.

Required:

a. Prepare a CD restated balance sheet. Use a format similar to Exhibit 17–5 and round all amounts to the nearest dollar.

b. What was the amount of CD restated income for 19A? Explain.

c. Compute the amount of CD restated income from normal operations assuming the purchasing power gain on monetary items is $2,014. Show how this gain was computed.

E17–6   **(Prepare HC/CD Income Statement)**

At the end of 19A (the first year of operations), Weber Company prepared the summarized HC basis income statement shown below. At January 1, 19A, the GPL index was 220; and at December 31, 19A, it was 260.

WEBER COMPANY
Income Statement
For the Year Ended December 31, 19A

	Amount	GPL index at average transaction date
Sales revenue	$330,000	234
Cost of goods sold	(165,000)	234
Depreciation expense*	(11,000)	
Remaining expenses	(94,000)	230
Pretax income	60,000	
Income tax expense	(18,000)	260
Net income	$ 42,000	

* The related asset was acquired when the GPL index was 220.

Required:

a. Prepare a CD restated income statement. Use a format similar to Exhibit 17–5. The monetary items and their GPL indexes at transaction dates were: receivables, $32,000 (index 234), and liabilities, $16,000 (index 220). Round all amounts to the nearest dollar.

b. Prepare a CD restated statement of retained earnings assuming cash dividends of $6,000 were declared but not paid on December 31, 19A.

E17–7   (Compute Purchasing Power Gains [Losses]
December 31, 19D, the following summary data were taken from the ledger.

Transactions	GPL at transaction date	Cash	Payable
Beginning balance	118	$ 30,000	$18,000
Purchased land	125		+12,000
Sales revenue	130	+150,000	
Borrowing on note	120	+60,000	+60,000
Payment	122	−15,000	−15,000
Payment	132	−42,000	−42,000
Expenses paid	130	−90,000	
Dividends paid	132	−10,000	
Equipment purchased	120	−80,000	
Payment	125		−13,000
Ending balance		$ 3,000	$20,000

Note: GPL index numbers: January 1, 19D, 118; December 31, 19D, 132.

Required:

Compute the purchasing power gain or loss on monetary items for each account (cash and payable) separately. Round all amounts to the nearest dollar.

Part B: Exercises 17–8 to 17–10

E17–8   (Compute Purchasing Power Gain [Loss] on Monetary Items and Holding Gain [Loss] on Nonmonetary Asset)
On January 1, 19A, Sable Gas Company acquired a tract of land that cost $120,000 when the GPL was 120. Payment was made in cash, $50,000, plus a $70,000, three-year, interest-bearing note. One year later the note was still outstanding, and the GPL index was 150. The specific index, related to the land, was 100 at the beginning of 19A and was 144 at the end of 19A. The land and the note will be included on the December 31, 19A, CC/CD financial statements.

Required (show computations and round to the nearest dollar):

a. The CC/CD value for the land that should be reported on the 19A CC/CD balance sheet is $_____.

b. The purchasing power gain (loss) on the monetary liability which should be reported on the 19A CC/CD statements is $_____.

c. The CC real holding gain (loss) on the nonmonetary asset that should be reported on the 19A CC/CD statements is $_____.

d. The amount of the GPL fictional change on the land was $_____.

e. Diagram the above responses in respect to the land (not the note payable).

E17–9   **(Analysis of GPL Fictional Price Changes)**

On January 1, 19A, Lee Company purchased a machine (an operational asset) that cost $15,000. Cash paid was $10,000 and a $5,000, three-year, interest-bearing note was given to the seller. On January 1, 19A, the GPL index was 100. At the end of 19A, the Accumulated Depreciation account reflected $3,000 (i.e., straight-line depreciation; estimated life five years and no residual value). During 19A, the average GPL index was 115 and at the end of 19A the GPL index was 120. The specific price index for the machine was 110 at the beginning of 19A and 143 at the end of 19A. The machine, accumulated depreciation, and note payable will be reported on the 19A CC/CD financial statements.

Required (show computations and round to the nearest dollar):

a. Complete the following tabulation of the amounts that should be reported on the 19A financial statements:

Item	HC basis	CC/CD basis
Balance sheet:		
Machine		
Accumulated depreciation . . .		
Note payable		
Income statement:		
Depreciation expense		

b. The purchasing power gain (loss) on monetary items that should be reported on the CC/CD statements is $_____.

c. The CC real holding gain (loss) on nonmonetary items that should be reported is $_____.

d. The amount of the GPL fictional changes for machinery was $_____.

E17–10   **(Analysis of GPL Fictional Price Changes)**

Westin Company purchased merchandise for resale during 19A (the first year of operations) that cost $76,000. Payment was in cash except for an $11,400 ending balance in accounts payable. The purchases, and payments on accounts payable, occurred evenly throughout the year. The average GPL index for 19A was 190 and at the end of 19A it was 200.

The ending inventory was $15,200; therefore, cost of goods sold was $60,800. Current cost of the ending inventory was $17,000 and $68,000 for cost of goods sold (the CC cost of goods sold is based on the average cost during the year). Accounts payable, inventory, and cost of goods sold will be reported on the 19A CC/CD financial statements.

Required (show computations and round to the nearest dollar):

a. Complete the following tabulation of amounts that should be reported at the end of 19A:

Item	HC basis	CC/CD basis
Balance sheet:		
Inventory		
Accounts payable		
Income statement:		
Cost of goods sold		

b. The purchasing power gain (loss) on accounts payable that should be reported in the CC/CD disclosures is $_____.

c. The CC real holding gain (loss) on the nonmonetary items that should be reported in the CC/CD disclosures is $_____.

d. the amount of the GPL fictional changes for inventory were $_____.

PROBLEMS

Part A: Problems 17-1 to 17-6

P17-1 **(CD Restate of Selected Balance Sheet Accounts and Compute Purchasing Power Gain [Loss])**
Hill Company has prepared the annual HC basis financial statements at December 31, 19F. The company is considering the development of supplemental statements on the "CD restated basis." The following seven items were selected from the balance sheet:

Items	HC basis (when acquired)	GPL index (when acquired or incurred)
1. Cash:		
Beginning balance	$ 20,000	141.5
Debits	38,800	146*
Credits	(44,600)	147*
2. Merchandise inventory (average cost)	58,000	145
3. Accounts receivable, net	28,800	144*
4. Land (no changes during 19F)	12,000	100
5. Building, net (no changes during 19F)	157,500	105
6. Accounts payable	42,000	140*
7. Bonds payable (no changes during 19F)	88,000	110

Note: At the end of 19F the price-level index was 150. Average was 145.8.

* Average GPL index for these items.

Required:

a. Group the above items into two categories: monetary and nonmonetary.

b. Set up a schedule and compute the amount "CD restated basis" that should be shown on the CD balance sheet for each of the items. Show calculations. Round to the nearest $100 in the restatement.

c. Set up a schedule and compute the purchasing power gain or loss on cash items that will be shown on the CD restated income statement. Show calculations and round to the nearest $100.

d. Explain why some of the seven items were omitted from your computations in (c).

P17-2   **(Prepare HC/CD Balance Sheet and Income Statement)**

At the end of the first year of operations, DE Company prepared the following balance sheet and income statement (HC basis):

DE COMPANY
Balance Sheet
At December 31, 19A

Cash	$ 3,330
Accounts receivable (net)	5,650
Inventory	46,000
Operational assets (net)	55,000
Total	$109,980

Liabilities

Accounts payable	$ 3,480
Bonds payable	23,000

Shareholders' Equity

Capital stock (no par)	66,000
Retained earnings	17,500
Total	$109,980

Income Statement
For the Year Ended December 31, 19A

Revenues	$69,000
Expenses (not detailed)	(46,000)
Depreciation expense	(5,500)
Net income	$17,500

Items	GPL (when acquired or incurred)
GPL at start of year—110	
Average 115	
GPL at end of year—120	
Cash (no beginning balance)	111*
Accounts receivable (balance $5,500 at beginning of year) . . .	113*
Inventory	115
Operational assets	110
Accounts payable (no beginning balance)	116
Bonds payable (no beginning balance)	115
Revenues	115*
Expenses	115*
Depreciation expense	110
Capital stock (no par)	110

* Average GPL index for all items in the account.

Required:

a. Restate the income statement and balance sheet; use the following headings: (1) HC Basis, (2) Restatement Computations, and (3) CD Restated Basis. Round amounts to the nearest $10.

b. Explain why net income is different between the two statements; identify amounts.

c. Why were the nonmonetary items, but not the monetary, restated on the balance sheet?

d. Does the CD income statement better match expenses with revenues? Explain.

P17-3   (Prepare HC/CD Balance Sheet and Income Statement)

After operating for one year, DO Company completed the following income statement and balance sheet:

DO COMPANY
Balance Sheet
At December 31, 19A
Assets

Cash	$ 42,300*
Accounts receivable (net)	29,580
Long-term investment, common shares	7,400
Land	11,200
Plant	154,000
Accumulated depreciation	(14,000)
Total	$230,480

Liabilities

Accounts payable	$ 5,880
Bonds payable	28,000

Shareholders' Equity

Capital stock (no par)	182,000
Retained earnings	14,600
Total	$230,480

Income Statement
For the Year Ended December 31, 19A

Revenues	$ 87,000
Expenses (not detailed)	(58,400)
Depreciation expense†	(14,000)
Net income	$ 14,600

* Beginning balance, $58,800 (GPL index, 140); debits, $57,420 (GPL index, 148) credits, $73,920 (GPL index, 145.3).

† Depreciation is recorded on a straight-line basis; estimated life of the plant is 11 years and no residual value.

Items	GPL (when acquired or incurred)
GPL index at start of year—140	
GPL index at end of year—150	
GPL index average for 19A—145	
Cash	*above
Accounts receivable	141†
Long-term investment purchased, common shares	148
Land purchased	140
Plant acquired	140
Accounts payable (beginning balance $14,000)	147†
Bonds payable (unchanged during year)	140
Capital stock (no par)	140
Revenues	145†
Expenses	146†
Depreciation expense	140

† Average GPL for these amounts.

Required:

a. Restate the income statement and balance sheet with the following headings:
(1) HC Basis, (2) Restatement Computations, and (3) CD Restated Basis. Round
amounts to the nearest $10.

b. Explain why net income is different between the two statements; identify amounts.

c. Why were the nonmonetary items, but not the monetary, restated on the balance
sheet?

d. Does the CD restated income statement better match expenses with revenues? Explain.

P17–4 **(Prepare HC/CD Balance Sheet and Compute Purchasing Power Gain [Loss] on
Monetary Items)**
The transactions summarized below were completed by Sullins Company during its first
year of operations. The accounting period ends December 31. The GPL index on January
1, 19A, was 100, on December 31, 19A, it was 144, and the average for the year was 120.

> January 1, 19A: issued 10,000 shares of capital stock (no par) for $60,000 cash and
> borrowed $36,000 cash on a two-year, interest-bearing note (GPL index, 100).
> February 1, 19A: Purchased equipment for use in the business, $75,000 cash (GPL
> index, 105).
> During 19A: Purchased merchandise on credit (evenly throughout the year),
> $180,000 (GPL average index, 120).
> During 19A: Sales revenue (evenly throughout the year), $300,000, all cash (GPL
> average index, 120).
> During 19A: Paid expenses (evenly throughout the year), $80,000 (GPL average
> index, 120); includes all expenses except depreciation expense.
> During 19A: Paid accounts payable, $161,200 (GPL average index on payments,
> 124).
> December 1, 19A: Declared and paid a cash dividend of $6,900 (GPL index, 138).
> December 31, 19A: Depreciation on equipment based on estimated life of 10 years
> and a $5,000 residual value.
> December 30, 19A: Cost of goods sold, $170,000 (GPL average index for cost of
> goods sold and ending inventory, 120).

The above entries resulted in the following preclosing HC account balances at December
31, 19A (the 19A adjusting entries already have been completed).

Debits

Cash	$ 72,900
Inventory	10,000
Equipment	75,000
Cost of goods sold	170,000
Expenses	80,000
Depreciation expense	7,000
Retained earnings (dividend declared and paid)	6,900
Total	$421,800

Credits

Accumulated depreciation	$ 7,000
Accounts payable	18,800
Note payable	36,000
Capital stock (no par)	60,000
Revenues	300,000
Total	$421,800

Required:

    a. Set up a format similar to Exhibit 17–4 to derive CD restated financial statements. Enter thereon the HC basis amounts for each statement.

    b. Restate each item on each statement on a CD basis. Prepare a separate schedule similar to Exhibit 17–5 to compute the purchasing power gain or loss on monetary items. Round all amounts to the nearest dollar. (Hint: There was a $6,243 purchasing power loss.)

P17–5   **(Prepare HC/CD Balance Sheet and Compute Purchasing Power Gain [Loss] on Monetary Items)**
Small Company was organized on January 1, 19A, at which time the GPL index was 150. The accounting period ends December 31. The transactions completed during 19A were:

    a. January 1, 19A: Sold and issued 10,000 shares of capital stock (par $10) for $150,000 cash (GPL index, 150).

    b. January 1, 19A: Purchased merchandise on credit for resale, $60,000 (GPL index, 150).

    c. February 1, 19A: Purchased equipment for use in the business; paid cash, $31,000, and gave a $46,500, interest-bearing note due December 31, 19C (GPL index, 155).

    d. During 19A: Sales revenue, $180,000 (sold evenly throughout the year); one third was on credit (GPL average index, 165).

    e. During February–December 19A: Purchased merchandise on credit (evenly throughout the year) for resale, $44,000 (GPL index, 165).

    f. During 19A: Collected accounts receivable, $50,000 (average GPL index for collections, 170).

    g. During 19A: Paid accounts payable, $84,000 (average GPL index for payments, 160).

    h. During 19A: Paid expenses in cash (evenly throughout the year), $61,000 (average GPL index, 165), which included interest, income tax, and all other expenses except depreciation expense.

    i. July 1, 19A: Invested $96,000 cash for common shares of X Corporation (GPL index, 160).

    j. December 31, 19A: Declared and paid a dividend of $10,000 (GPL index, 180).

    k. December 31, 19A: Depreciation expense on equipment, $14,000.

    l. December 31, 19A: Cost of goods sold, $84,000 (average GPL index for cost of goods sold and ending inventory, 156).

The above transactions resulted in the following preclosing HC account balances (adjusting entries already have been made):

Debits

Cash	$ 38,000
Accounts receivable (net)	10,000
Inventory	20,000
Investment, common shares	96,000
Equipment	77,500
Cost of goods sold	84,000
Expenses	61,000
Depreciation expense	14,000
Retained earnings (dividend)	10,000
	$410,500

Credits

Accumulated depreciation	$ 14,000
Accounts payable	20,000
Note payable	46,500
Capital stock (par $10)	100,000
Contributed surplus	50,000
Revenues	180,000
	$410,500

Required:

a. Set up a format similar to Exhibit 17–4 to derive CD restated financial statements. Enter thereon the historical cost basis amounts for each statement. The GPL index at December 31, 19A, was 180.

b. Restate each item on each statement on a CD basis. Prepare a separate schedule similar to Exhibit 17–5 to compute the purchasing power gain or loss on monetary items. (Hint: There was a pp loss on $6,319.) Round all amounts to the nearest dollar.

P17–6 (Compute Spreadsheet Solution to HC/CD Financial Statements)

Required:

a. Prepare the solution for Problem 17–4 using a computer spreadsheet.

b. What is the purchasing power gain or loss and the net income if the year-end GPL index were 150?

c. Using the format prepared in Part A, prepare the solution for Problem 17–5.

d. What would be the purchasing power gain or loss and the net income if the investment in X Corporation had been purchased when the GPL index was 175?

Part B: Problems 17–7 to 17–11

P17–7 (Prepare CC/CD Balance Sheet and Income Statement)

The problem is based on the data given in P17–3 (DO Company). The balance sheet and income statement (HC basis) and the GPL index numbers are not changed. Current cost (CC) information is as follows:

Item	Current cost (CC) data, December 31, 19A	
Long-term investment,		
common shares	Based on stock market quotation . . .	$ 8,500
Land	Per professional appraisal	14,000
Plant (net)	Specific index, 1.10 of carrying value.	
Expenses (not detailed)	HC average and CC average the same.	

Note: GPL index data is given in Problem 17–3.

Required (show computations and round all amounts to the nearest $10):

a. Set up a schedule similar to Exhibit 17–9 to develop a CC/CD balance sheet amounts and income statement at December 31, 19A. Enter the HC data and complete the CC/CD amounts through "Income from operations." The purchasing power loss on monetary items was $2,417. Show calculations clearly.

b. Compute the CC real holding gains (losses) on nonmonetary items.

P17–8   (Prepare CC/CD Balance Sheet and Income Statement)

Modern Company began operations on January 1, 19A, at which time the GPL index was 130. The 19A balance sheet and income statement, along with relevant GPL index numbers and CC information, are given below. The 19A average GPL index was 143, and it was 156 at December 31, 19A.

	HC basis	GPL index at transaction date	CC valuations (which are different from HC) at December 31, 19A
Balance sheet:			
Assets:			
Cash	$ 14,300	143	
Accounts receivable	28,600	143	
Inventory (average)	57,200	143	Specific index, 165/143 of HC
Equipment	78,000	130	Specific index, 1.282 of HC
Accumulated depreciation . . .	(7,800)	130	Specific index, 1.282 of HC
Other assets	19,500	130	Specific index, 160/130 of HC
Total	$189,800		
Liabilities:			
Accounts payable	$ 14,300	143	
Note payable	39,000	130	
Shareholders' equity:			
Capital stock	130,000	136.84	
Retained earnings	6,500		
Total	$189,800		
Income statement:			
Revenue	$114,400	143	
Cost of goods sold	(71,500)	143	Average specific price index. 1.0577 of HC
Depreciation expense*	(7,800)	143	Based on average CC of equipment during 19A
Remaining expenses	(28,600)	143	HC and CC averages are the same
Net income	$ 6,500		

* Straight-line depreciation, 10-year estimated life and no residual value (cost, $78,000 ÷ 10 years = $7,800).

Required:

Based on the above data, the company desires to construct CC/CD disclosures as illustrated in Exhibit 17–9.

P17–9 **(Comprehensive Problem—Chapters 16 and 17)**
The following information was contained in the annual report of Large Company.

	19E	19D	19C	19B	19A
Total revenues:					
As reported	$31,729	$27,832	$20,197	$16,350	$14,263
Constant dollars	31,729	30,719	25,307	22,793	21,407
Net income from operations:					
As reported	$ 1,922	$ 1,915	$ 1,507	$ 1,076	$ 1,032
Constant dollars	1,254	1,522	1,385	1,055	1,179
Current costs	960	1,043	977	744	909
Net income from operations per share:					
As reported	$ 6.56	$ 6.54	$ 5.12	$ 3.68	$ 3.52
Constant dollars	4.28	5.20	4.70	3.61	4.02
Current costs	3.28	3.56	3.32	2.54	3.10
Cash dividends per share:					
As reported	$ 2.60	$ 2.00	$ 1.50	$ 1.40	$ 1.30
Constant dollars	2.60	2.21	1.88	1.95	1.95
Net assets at year-end:					
As reported	$10,665	$ 9,385	$ 8,369	$ 7,146	$ 6,475
Constant dollars	16,340	15,424	14,847	13,954	13,265
Current costs	21,273	21,444	20,413	17,810	17,143
Excess of increase in specific prices					
over increase due to general inflation	$ 71	$ 656	$ 965	$ 74	$ (29)
Unrealized gain from decline in purchasing					
power of net amounts owed	$ 490	$ 574	$ 537	$ 349	$ 279

Required:

a. Calculate the following:
   (1) Return on net assets for 19E: (*a*) as reported; (*b*) constant dollars; and
       (*c*) current costs (state as a percent).
   (2) Growth in revenues from 19D to 19E: (*a*) as reported; and (*b*) constant dollars
       (state as a percent).
   (3) Growth in net income from operations from 19D to 19E: (*a*) as reported;
       (*b*) constant dollars; and (*c*) current costs (state as a percent).
   (4) Profit margin for 19E: (*a*) as reported; (*b*) constant dollars; (*c*) current costs
       (state as a percent).

b. What do your calculations in Requirement (*a*) tell you about the impact of inflation
   on Large Company?

c. By studying the data presented by Large, it is possible to determine whether the
   constant dollar information is presented in average dollars for 19E or year-end dollars for 19E. Did Large use average dollars or year-end dollars?

d. Which amount is larger for Large: total monetary assets or total monetary liabilities?

P17–10 **(Computation of Cost of Goods Sold and Holding Gains)**
Regwan Ltd. is a large Canadian manufacturing company and has decided to present
current cost information in the *CICA Handbook*, Section 4510, format. They have presented you with the following information:

Opening inventory for 19B:
    14,000 units at a cost of $20 per unit.
Purchases during 19B were:

First Quarter	Cost per unit*	Sales (units)
12,000 units	$23	18,000
Second Quarter		
16,000 units	$29	20,000
Third Quarter		
18,000 units	$33	17,000
Fourth Quarter		
18,000 units	$36	13,000

* Price during the entire quarter.

At December 31, 19B, replacement cost was $38 per unit, and the net realizable value was $44 per unit for the entire fiscal period.

The Gross National Expenditure Implicit Price Deflator, a measure of the general inflation in the economy, was:

> December 31, 19A . . . 123
> Average for 19B 134
> December 31, 19B . . . 145

Required:

a. Calculate the cost of units sold, on a current cost basis.

b. Calculate the closing inventory, on a current cost basis.

c. The holding gain (or loss), both real and nominal.

d. If the net realizable value was $30 per unit during the fiscal period, how would your answers to (*a*) and (*b*) change?

P17–11   (CC Depreciation and Disclosers)

A company is considering using *CICA Handbook,* Section 4510, to guide its disclosure of current cost information on the financial statements.

	Historical Cost	
	19A	**19B**
Fixed assets	$4,500,000	$3,900,000
Accumulated depreciation . . .	1,350,000 (Note 1)	1,185,000 (Note 3)
	$3,150,000	$2,715,000
	Current Cost	
Fixed assets	$6,100,000 (Note 2)	$6,350,000

NOTES:

1. The average accumulated depreciation was 30% on the assets at December 31, 19A.

2. The appraisal estimate is gross of depreciation and is based on current reproduction cost. The assets owned by the client are not new and thus the current reproduction cost must be adjusted for depreciation.

3. There was a disposal during 19B. The cost of the asset sold was $600,000, and the accumulated depreciation on that asset was $360,000. There was a gain of $125,000 on this disposal on the income statement. Five percent depreciation was taken in 19B on the remaining assets; that is, the $3,900,000, since it is com-

pany policy not to take any depreciation on assets sold during a year. At December 31, 19A, the gross current cost of the asset sold was $721,000. The average accumulated depreciation percentage was 30.4% at December 31,19B.

Additional information:

The income statement for 19B showed depreciation expense of $195,000 which is 5% of $3,900,000.

The gross national expenditure implicit price deflator, which is a general measure of the inflation in the economy, was:

$$
\begin{aligned}
&\text{December 31, 19A} \ . \ . \ . \ 145 \\
&\text{Average for 19B} \ . \ . \ . \ . \ 156 \\
&\text{December 31, 19B} \ . \ . \ . \ 168
\end{aligned}
$$

Required:

a. Calculate the depreciation expense that would appear on the income statement. In addition, indicate any other changes that would be made to the income statement in conforming to Section 4510.

b. Prepare the disclosures for the additional CC information that would be required in the case described above.

(CGAC Adapted)

CASES

C17–1   (Theory of Monetary Items)

Frank Smith, president of Delta Corporation, has asked that you help him understand inflation accounting. During a meeting, Mr. Smith made the following comments.

I have been told that it is possible to make money by borrowing money during a period of inflation. I plan to recommend that Delta borrow $10 million, at 18% interest, on January 1, 19D, and deposit the money in Delta's chequing account (which does not pay interest). One year later, we will repay the money. The average inflation rate during 19D is expected to be 12%, consequently Delta should have a purchasing power gain on the debt. Delta will be able to use the cash from the purchasing power gain on the debt. Delta will be able to use the cash from the purchasing power gain to pay a dividend to the shareholders of the company. The only thing I don't understand is why bankers are willing to lend money during a period of inflation. If we can make money by borrowing, don't the bankers lose money by lending money?

Required:

a. Determine the amount of the purchasing power gain that Mr. Smith *expects* Delta to earn by borrowing $10 million. Will Delta actually earn the purchasing power gain that Mr. Smith expects? Explain why. Would your answer be different if the $10 million were invested in a tract of land during the year? Why?

b. Evaluate Mr. Smith's plan to use cash from a purchasing power gain on monetary items to pay a cash dividend to the shareholders.

c. Prepare a response to Mr. Smith's question concerning why bankers are willing to lend money during a period of inflation.

C17–2   **(Current Cost Theory)**

For years there has been general agreement in the Canadian business community and accounting profession that the current cost accounting model is superior to the historical cost accounting model. The fact that the primary financial statements of Canadian companies continue to be based on the historical cost accounting model demonstrates that there are strong arguments in favour of retaining this basis for general purpose financial reporting.

Required:

Discuss the reasons why the current cost accounting model has not received general acceptance as a basis for the preparation of the primary financial statements of Canadian companies.

(CICA Adapted)

OVERVIEW OF INCOME TAXES

PURPOSE

Income taxes are complex and pervasive; they affect most persons and businesses. Each individual and manager should consider the income tax implications when making economic decisions. A general knowledge of income taxes enables the decision maker to (a) recognize the importance of various income tax implications, (b) know when to seek professional assistance, and (c) carry on tax planning to minimize income taxes.

The powers of governments to tax are set out in the Canadian Constitution. Various levels of governments not only assess income taxes but also custom duties, property taxes (i.e., on real property), sales taxes (i.e., on the sale of goods and services), and excise taxes (i.e., on gasoline). Because income taxes are levied by the federal government and most provinces, the total amount exceeds any other tax. As a result, tax factors significantly affect many business and personal decisions faced by the two major groups of taxpayers: corporations and individuals.

The purpose of this appendix is to present an overview of federal income taxes applicable to individuals and corporations. This overview is designed to (a) enhance your general knowledge of the primary federal income tax provisions, (b) give you a basic understanding of income tax returns, and (c) provide an overview of the relationship between accounting income (reported on the income statement) and taxable income (reported on the income tax return).[1] The discussion in this supplement is based upon current income tax information. By the time you read this supplement, certain tax provisions discussed may not be current. However, the discussion is relevant because it deals with key concepts and terminology rather than with the numerous exceptions and detailed rules. We reemphasize that our objective is to provide a broad overview of income tax provisions rather than a highly technical view. The examples given are intended to illustrate those key concepts and termi-

nology. Parliament may change the tax rates or specific tax law which may make certain illustrations out of date but our educational objective will remain intact. To accomplish this purpose, this supplement is subdivided as follows:

Part A—income as a tax base

Part B—income taxes paid by corporations

Part C—income taxes paid by individuals

Part D—tax planning

Note: This supplement was prepared by E. Scott.

[1] Canada introduced a federal income tax in 1917 to help finance its participation in World War I. Since that time, the Canadian *Income Tax Act* has had several major revisions, and almost continuous minor changes, in the ongoing process of attempting to define a fair and equitable revenue base. At the same time it has also been an instrument through which both fiscal and social policies have been implemented, and accordingly the concepts of "income" familiar to accounting and economics have been replaced with one that is legalistic and, in some instances, startlingly different.

PART A—INCOME AS A TAX BASE

The Income Tax Act requires all taxpayers to pay taxes based on their **taxable income**—the dollar amount to which the rates are applied to determine total income taxes payable. Taxable income is determined in two major steps:

1. Determine net income (for tax purposes that is sometimes referred to as Division B income).
2. Subtract from the above a specified set of deductions (commonly called Division C deductions).

What is to be included in each of these two major items depends on the type of taxpayer. Residents and nonresidents receive different treatments and, as mentioned above, the rules for corporations are often different than those for individuals.

Net Income (For Tax Purposes)

Division B of the act provides in Section 3 a general formula for the determination of net income (for tax purposes), and supplements this with copious general and specific rules to be applied to each taxpayer's unique circumstances.

Exhibit A–1 gives an overview of the general formula and can be seen to have the following characteristics:

1. Positive net incomes and gains are brought in first (items *a* and *b*), with deductions and negative elements (losses) (items *c* and *d*) following in a particular sequence so that net income never falls below zero. (See "Division C Deductions" below.)
2. Capital gains and losses are generally handled separately (in *b*) from the noncapital net incomes or losses (in *a* and *d*), subject to a few specific exceptions. This is because only a fraction[2] of capital gains and capital losses are taxable or allowable, as explained in more detail below.
3. The noncapital net incomes or losses are further classified as to the source from which they arose—business, property, employment, and so on—to allow for differing treatments in the measurement process. (Income from business and property most closely parallels the accounting concept of net income, since these figures represent the net of revenues less allowable expenses for each source.)
4. Priority in deductions is given to a special set of items (in *c*) which an accountant would find hard to match with any particular income source. These exist for social reasons or because a special deductible status is bestowed on some capital expenditures not covered elsewhere.

---

[2] The fraction to be included is 66⅔% for the years 1988 and 1989 and 75% for 1990 and following years. This supplement will use the 66⅔% inclusion rate for subsequent discussion and illustration.

Exhibit A–1   Determination of Division B net income for tax purposes—per Section 3

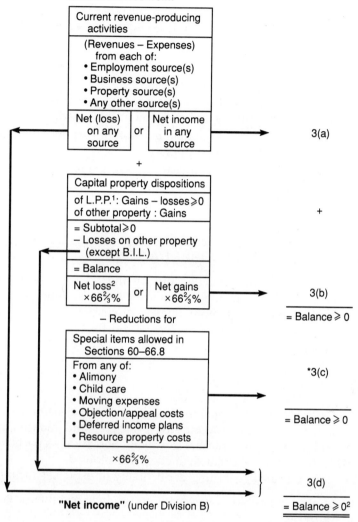

Income derives from:

Notes:

[1] If balance would have been, or is, negative (<0), the net loss may be reported in *another* taxation year as a deduction under S.3(b).

[2] If balance would have been, or is, negative (<0), the net loss may be reported in *another* taxation year as a deduction under Division C.

L.P.P. means listed personal property (collections or items of art, rare manuscripts, stamps, coins or jewelry).

B.I.L. means business investment loss (a capital loss arising on the disposition of shares or debt of a Canadian-controlled private corporation).

Division C Deductions

Further deductions are permitted after the computation of net income, so that only a portion of the net income (for tax purposes) ends up in the taxable income base and is subject to the tax. The deductions allowed under Division C exist for the following reasons:

1. To correct perceived inequitable treatment; for example, a deduction for those living in remote locations.
2. To acknowledge and promote socioeconomic goals; for example, donations by corporations and investment by Canadian individuals.
3. To minimize potential double taxation of corporate income handed on as dividends to other corporations.
4. To allow the carryover to years of positive net income the excess net losses not permitted by the net income formula in Division B.

PART B—INCOME TAXES PAID BY CORPORATIONS

Since the corporation is singled out by the act for treatment as a separate taxpayer, and since its income is primarily from the single source **business,** we will use it as a basis for a more detailed discussion.

For corporations the taxation year is the fiscal year; accrual accounting is required subject to several special rules.

Business Income

A corporation's income from business is calculated as revenues minus expenses, using generally accepted accounting principles and modifying them where a special rule may alter the normal treatment. Sometimes a particular revenue may be exempted, or a particular deduction not allowed.

The general rules governing deductibility of expenses include the following:

1. Outlays must have been made to produce revenue or have a business purpose.
2. Capital outlays are not deductible unless allowed by a specific rule (see "Capital Cost Allowance" below as an example).
3. Personal and living costs are not allowable.
4. Outlays to produce exempt income are not allowed.
5. Outlays which are not reasonable in amount or nature are not deductible.
6. Some outlays are specifically allowed, limited, or prohibited as to deductibility. (This last rule is the most difficult one because of the detailed knowledge it requires.)

The result of applying these rules and related provisions regarding revenue will produce a figure analogous (but not equal) to the accountant's "Net Income before Taxes."

Special income tax rules relating to inventories parallel those used for accounting purposes, but not completely. For example, valuation may be at lower of cost or market, reasonably determined, except that LIFO is not permitted as a measure of cost.

Another major area of difference between accounting and taxation business incomes arises because of the way the Income Tax Act provides for capital outlays. These give rise to various types of **property,** each with its own deduction rules. For example:

- a. **Capital property**—any property owned except inventory and items placed in other special property categories—no write-off until disposition.
- b. **Depreciable property**—annual write-off (as discussed in more detail below).
- c. **Eligible capital property**—usually intangibles, 75% of which is written off annually on a 7% declining balance basis. The other 25% is ignored for tax purposes.

Other categories, such as resource properties, receive various special treatments.

Capital Cost Allowance

Depreciable property is eligible for a periodic deduction familiarly described as **capital cost allowance.** Most tangible fixed assets and some intangible assets are pooled in classes prescribed in the Regulations accompanying the act. If any asset is not listed in any of the prescribed classes, it does not qualify as depreciable property. Acquisitions during the year are added to the class at their cost, and any proceeds of dispositions up to the original cost are credited to the class. Proceeds in excess of cost are treated separately as capital gains. Proceeds of disposition arise on a sale of the asset, and also may be deemed to occur in several other circumstances—for example, change of use of the asset or insurance proceeds recovered.

The annual capital cost allowance write-off is a discretionary claim and may be any amount from zero up to the maximum permitted for each class. This maximum is defined for each class by applying a specified percentage to the balance in the class at the end of the taxation year. This process continues so long as any assets of that class remain. The effect is analogous to declining balance depreciation in a group depreciation system. In early years, straight-line depreciation expense in the income statement will normally be less than capital cost allowances claimed for tax purposes. (See Exhibit A–2 for an example of capital cost allowance calculations.)

Exhibit A–2 Comparison of accounting depreciation and capital cost allowance

A. DATA—WR Limited has the following fixed assets:

Item	Land	Building	Office furniture	Auto	Delivery truck
Cost	$50,000	$400,000	$40,000	$15,000	$25,000
Useful life	n/a	30 yrs.	10 yrs.	3 yrs.	6 yrs.
Salvage	n/a	$100,000	nil	$ 9,000	$ 1,000
Depreciation method	n/a		—straight line—		

B. Calculation of depreciation expense—19X1:

Building (3⅓% of $300,000)	$10,000
Office furniture (10% of $40,000)	4,000
Auto (33⅓% of $6,000)	2,000
Delivery truck (16⅔% of $24,000)	4,000
Total	$20,000

WR LIMITED
Capital Cost Allowance Schedule
For the Year Ended December 31, 19X1

	Building (Class 3) (5%)	Office equipment (Class 8) (20%)	Motor vehicles (Class 10) (30%)	Passenger vehicles (Class 10.1) (30%)	Totals
Balance of undepreciated capital cost (UCC) at January 1, 19X1 (d)	$390,000	$36,000	$21,250	$12,750	$460,000
Add: Acquisitions at cost (a)	—	—	—	—	—
Deduct: Proceeds of dispositions (b)	—	(1,000)	—	—	(1,000)
UCC before capital cost allowance (CCA)	$390,000	$35,000	$21,250	$12,750	$459,000
CCA for 19X1 (c)	19,500	7,000	6,375	3,825	36,700
UCC December 31, 19X1	$370,500	$28,000	$14,875	$ 8,925	$422,300

Notes: It is assumed that:
(a) There were no assets acquired during the year.
(b) The $1,000 proceeds in Class 8 represents the actual proceeds of disposition for an item that had originally cost more than $1,000.
(c) Maximum possible amounts of capital cost allowances are claimed.
(d) Starting balances are given. (Note that after 1987, most buildings acquired will fall in Class 1, 4%, instead of Class 3, 5%, used above.)

Some exceptions to the declining balance pattern do occur. A few straight-line classes exist. Several rapid write-off classes exist to create an incentive to businesses to invest in certain ways. For example, Class 29, allows machinery and equipment acquired for manufacturing purposes to be written off at a higher rate than would normally apply.

There is one important exceptional rule for the regular declining balance classes. The capital cost allowances calculated on the net additions to a class (costs added less proceeds credited) are restricted to only one half the normal percentage. Other balances in the class are eligible for the full rate. This can sometimes produce the effect that depreciation expense on the books is greater than the tax write-off. (See Chapter 10 for the implications for deferred tax accounting.)

Since proceeds of disposal are credited to the class, a credit balance sometimes arises for the class at year-end. This credit balance is brought into income immediately as a "recapture" of capital cost allowance previously claimed, and the class continues with a zero balance.

When the proceeds of disposal for the *last* asset in the class are not large enough to eliminate the whole balance in the class, a **terminal loss** is claimed for the full amount of any remaining balance.

A number of other restrictive or special rules exist, requiring a more than casual knowledge of the system. Exhibit A–3 extends the calculation of capital cost allowances for WR Limited into 19X2, illustrating some of the special rules.

Investment Income—Corporations

Corporate taxpayers may also generate revenue in the form of interest and dividends; that is, income from property. For tax purposes this is called **investment income.** Net taxable capital gains by a corporation are also included with investment income.

Capital Gains and Losses

Capital gains, measured as the difference between **proceeds** and cost, can arise on the disposition of any capital property or depreciable property, but not on eligible capital property or resource property, which are covered by other special rules. Capital losses cannot occur for depreciable property because the capital cost allowance/terminal loss system takes care of dispositions where proceeds are less than cost.

In the Canadian system, capital gains were not taxed until 1972. Since then some fraction of the capital gains is included in income for tax purposes, and the same fraction of the losses is an allowable deduction. (The other portion is still ignored for tax purposes, which has the effect of taxing capital gains at a reduced marginal rate.) Generally, the allowable capital losses may only be deducted against the taxable capital gains. When an excess of allowable losses occurs in a year (net capital losses) they do not enter the calculation of Division B net income. Instead, the Division C deduction rules permit their deduction in other taxation years when net taxable capital gains occur.

A great many special rules give distinctive treatments to various types of capital property (especially personal use property) and to special circumstances; for example, where deemed dispositions occurring without an actual receipt of cash may prove onerous to the taxpayer.

Because of the more favourable treatment of capital gains, the distinction between capital amounts and revenue amounts is an important one, and the source of much disagreement between taxpayers and the taxing authorities. Numerous court decisions have tended to use indicators of the taxpayer's

Exhibit A-3

WR LIMITED
Capital Cost Allowance Schedule
For the Year Ended December 31, 19X2

	Building (Class 3) (5%)	Office equipment (Class 8) (20%)	Motor vehicles (Class 10) (30%)	Passenger vehicle (Class 10.1) (30%)	Leasehold improvement (Class 13) (straight line)	Totals
UCC, January 1, 19X2 . . .	$370,500	$28,000	$14,875	$8,925	—	$422,300
Add: Acquisitions at cost	—	3,000	—	—	$46,440	49,440
	$370,500	$31,000	$14,875	$8,925	$46,440	$471,740
Deduct: Proceeds of disposition (*a*)	—	(1,000)	(15,075)	—	—	(16,075)
UCC before CCA	$370,500	$30,000	$ (200)	$8,925	$46,440	$455,665
Recapture—100% income	—	—	200	—	—	200
CCA—Maximum (*b*) . . .	(18,525)	(5,800)	—	(2,678)	(2,322)	(29,325)
UCC December 31, 19X2 .	$351,975	$24,200	nil (*c*)	$6,247	$44,118	$426,540

Notes: It is assumed that—
  (*a*) Proceeds of disposition in each case are less than the initial "capital cost" of the item sold.
  (*b*) Maximum possible amounts of capital cost allowances are claimed. (See calculations below.)
  (*c*) Some assets remain in Class 10, so it remains "open," but with a UCC of nil following the recapture which arose when proceeds credited to the class exceeded the UCC in the class during the year.

Calculations:
  Class 8—Beginning balance: 20% of $28,000 = $5,600
      "Net additions"—Acquisitions $3,000
            Less: Proceeds   1,000
        1/2 of 20% of   2,000   200
                        $5,800

  Class 13—A straight-line class in which CCA for each year is equal to the original cost of the asset spread over the lifetime of the lease plus one renewal period. As usual, the first year allowance is only one half the normal amount. Here, a five year lease is assumed, with one renewal option for a further five years, hence 10% of $46,440 × ½ = $2,322.

intention as the deciding factor. The resulting case law provides some guidance, but each taxpayer's situation is still unique.

Division C Deductions—Corporations

Corporate taxpayers are generally permitted to reduce further their Division B net income (business income, investment income, and other sundry incomes and deductions) for three types of items:

1. **Dividends received from other taxable Canadian corporations**—to avoid double taxation when income already taxed in one corporation is moved to another corporation by way of dividends.
2. **Donations to charities and governments**—to encourage corporations in their social responsibilities. Deductible charitable donations are re-

stricted in any year to 20% of net income, but excess donations may be carried over and deducted in future years.

3. **Losses of other years**—to permit the taxpayer to use the excess business losses and net capital losses not deductible in other years. Specific matching and ordering rules govern the amount eligible in this category in any year.

The calculation of net income and taxable income of WR Limited are compared to the accounting net income in Exhibit A–4.

Tax Rates—Corporations

Revenue Canada Taxation prescribes a set of Schedules (T2–FTC) which is helpful in calculating the tax payable by a corporation. (See Exhibit A–5 for Schedule 1, page 1, which contains the major income tax calculations under Part I of the Income Tax Act).

The taxable income of corporations is subject to federal tax at the rate of 38%, less a 10% reduction for the part of the taxable income earned in a province of Canada. (This "makes room" for each of the provinces to assess their own taxes, which they do at rates up to 17% of taxable income earned in that province.)

Income earned and taxed in another country is eligible for a "foreign tax credit," to minimize or eliminate the possibility of double taxation of the same income.

Certain corporations and/or types of income are eligible for further rate reductions or dollar tax credits, and at various times some or all corporations have been subject to a surtax. Two important kinds of rate reductions are as follows:

1. The first $200,000 of business income of Canadian-controlled private corporation receives an additional rate reduction of 16%, leaving a net federal rate of 12% on that **small business** income.
2. The manufacturing and processing profits of corporations also receive a further rate reduction (but not on the income which has already earned the small business reduction).

(Similar reductions of provincial rates exist in many provinces.)

A significant dollar reduction in the tax bill may be received through the investment tax credit. This allows taxpayers to reduce their tax liabilities in lieu of receiving grants, to encourage certain types of spending (e.g., research and development, manufacturing facilities) in designated regions of the country. Political contributions have also been singled out to earn a limited tax reduction.

Several other items may enter the calculation before the total current income tax liability is determined. For example, Canadian dividends received (which escaped tax by virtue of the Division C deduction) may be subject to a (Part IV) tax at 25% which is refunded to the corporation when these dividends are distributed to its own shareholders. The result is that the effective tax rate is different for each corporation and may vary from taxation year to taxation year.

Exhibit A-4 Calculation of taxable income for a corporation

A. Normal accounting financial statements:

WR LIMITED
Condensed Income Statement
For the Year Ended December 31, 19X1

Sales		$520,000
Cost of goods sold		365,000
Gross margin		155,000
Operating and other expenses		103,700
Net income before taxes		51,300
Current taxes	$6,800	
Deferred taxes	8,200	15,000
Net income		$ 36,300

B. Additional information:

1. Beginning inventory, at LIFO cost (FIFO cost would be $124,100)	$120,000
2. Included among operating and other expenses were:	
Depreciation	20,000
Donations to charities	5,000
Political contribution (federal)	1,000
Gain on disposal of shares	(3,000)
Dividends received on shares (Canadian)	(500)
3. Capital cost allowance claimed (See Exhibit A-2)	36,700

C. Calculation of "net income" and "taxable income":

Net income per financial statements (before taxes)			$ 51,300
Add Back:	Expenses not allowed for tax purposes:		
	Depreciation	$20,000	
	Donations:		
	Charities	5,000	
	Political	1,000	$ 26,000
			77,300
Deduct:	Increase in beginning inventory value from LIFO to FIFO	$ 4,100	
	Gain on disposal of shares — 33⅓% not taxable	$ 1,000	
	Capital cost allowance	36,700	41,800
"Net income" for tax purposes (Division B)			35,500
Less:	Division C deductions for:		
	Canadian dividends received	$ 500	
	Donations to charities	5,000	5,500
"Taxable income"			$ 30,000

Exhibit A–5 T2–FTC Schedule 1 Form—Calculation of Part 1 tax for corporations

T2-FTC Schedule 1 — 1988 and subsequent years   (Rev. 88)
ORIGINAL — ATTACH TO T2 CORPORATION INCOME TAX RETURN

NAME OF CORPORATION	ACCOUNT NUMBER	FISCAL YEAR END
WR LIMITED		Day Month Year

Part I Tax on Taxable Income — All corporations

Taxable Income from the front of the T2 return. — — — — — — — — — — — — — — — — — **30,000 —** (A)

Tax at 46% of _____ | × number of days in taxation year before July 1987 / number of days in taxation year = _____
Amount (A)

Tax at 45% of _____ | × number of days in taxation year after June 1987 and before July 1988 / number of days in taxation year = _____
Amount (A)

Tax at 38% of **30,000 —** | × number of days in taxation year after June 1988 / number of days in taxation year = **202 11,400 —**
Amount (A)

Add or deduct as applicable:

Adjustments to Part I Tax per T2-FTC Schedule 1 Supplementary (To be completed by CCPC's with Investment Income,
Mutual Fund Corporations and Investment Corporations) — — — — — — — — — **208**
                                                                          Sub-total **204**

Tax at 5% of Taxable Income earned in the Nova Scotia offshore area — — — — — — — —
                                                                          Sub-total **11,400 —**

Deduct: Small Business Deduction (see below) — — — — — — — — — **4,800 —**
         Investment Corporation Deduction (section 130) — — — — **203 —**
         (Taxed Capital Gains **205** _____)
         Additional Deduction — Credit Unions (section 137) — — — **206 —**
         Federal Tax Abatement (section 124) — — — — — — — — **207 3,000 —**
         Manufacturing and Processing Profits Deduction (see below) — — — — —
                                                          Net amount **7,860 —**
Add: Corporate Surtax per form T2215   **(3%)**   **3,600 —**
                                                                      209 108 —
                                                          Sub-total **3,708 —**

Deduct: Non-Business Foreign Tax Credit per T2S-TC Part II — — — — — — — **211 —**
         Business Foreign Tax Credit per T2S-TC Part II — — — — — — — **213 —**
         Logging Tax Credit per T2S-TC Part III — — — — — — — **215 —**
         Federal Political Contribution Tax Credit — — — — — — — **217 450 —**
         (Federal Political Contributions *(per receipts attached)* **219 1,000 —**)
         Share-Purchase Tax Credit* — — — — — — — — — — — — **220 —**
         Scientific Research and Experimental Development Tax Credit* — — — — **216 —**
         Part VI Tax Credit — — — — — — — — — — — — — — **224 —**
         Investment Tax Credit per form T2038 (CORP.) — — — — — — **221 —**
         Employment Tax Credit per form T2208 — — — — — — — **222 —**
                                                                              450 —
Part I Tax Payable — (enter on front of T2 return) — — — — — — — **3,258 —**
* Attach slips.

Small Business Deduction — Canadian-controlled private corporations throughout the taxation year

Income from active business carried on in Canada per T2S(7) or T2S(7)(A) — — — — — **223 33,000 —** (A)
Taxable Income* — **225 30,000 —** (B)
Business Limit for the year** — — — — — — — — — — — — — — — — — **227 200,000 —** (C)

Small Business Deduction — Total of the following amounts:
(1) 21% of the least of _____ | × number of days in taxation year before July 1988 / number of days in taxation year = _____
    Amounts (A), (B) and (C)
(2) 16% of the least of **30,000 —** | × number of days in taxation year after June 1988 / number of days in taxation year = **231 4,800 —**
    Amounts (A), (B) and (C)

* To be reduced by: (i) for taxation years commencing before July 1988, 10/4 of the amount deductible under 126(1) if the amount determined under subparagraph 126(7)(d)(v) were determined
  without reference to subparagraph 123(1)(a)(iv); for taxation years commencing after June 1988, 10/3 of the amount deducted under 126(1).
  and (ii) for taxation years commencing before July 1988, 2 times the amount deducted under subsection 126(2); for taxation years commencing after June 1988, 10/4 of the
  amount deducted under 126(2).
** Where the corporation is associated in the year with one or more other Canadian-controlled private corporations, that portion of the Business Limit allocated to it per form T2013.

Manufacturing and Processing Profits Deduction — All corporations that have such profits

Canadian manufacturing and processing profits per T2S(27) — — — — — — — — — — **233** _____ (A)
Deduct: Least of Amounts (A), (B) and (C) per calculation
        of Small Business Deduction — — — — — — — — — — — — — — (B) _____ (C)
Taxable Income —

Deduct: (i) Least of Amounts (A), (B) and (C) per calculation of Small Business Deduction — — — _____
        (ii) Canadian Investment Income — — — — — — — _____
            Foreign Investment Income — — — — — — **449**
        Less: Net capital losses claimed on front of T2 return
        (iii) Business Foreign Tax Credit _____ × 10/4* _____
                                                                  235 _____ (D)

5% of the lesser of _____ | × number of days in taxation year before July 1987 / number of days in taxation year = _____
Amounts (A) and (B)
6% of the lesser of _____ | × number of days in taxation year after June 1987 and before July 1988 / number of days in taxation year = _____ (E)
Amounts (A) and (B)
6% of the lesser of _____ | × number of days in taxation year before July 1987 / number of days in taxation year = _____
Amounts (C) and (D)
7% of the lesser of _____ | × number of days in taxation year after June 1987 and before July 1988 / number of days in taxation year = _____
Amounts (C) and (D)
2% of the lesser of _____ | × number of days in taxation year after June 1988 and before July 1989 / number of days in taxation year = _____ (F)
Amounts (C) and (D)

Manufacturing and Processing Profits Deduction — total of Amounts (E) and (F)   **243** _____
* For taxation years commencing before July 1988, "10/4" should be read as "2".

Exhibit A–5 *(concluded)*

Refundable Portion of Part I Tax — Canadian-controlled private corporations throughout the taxation year

(1) Net Canadian Investment Income or Loss per T2S(7) — — — — — — — — — **247** 2,000 –

    Add: Net Foreign Investment Income or Loss per T2S(7) — — — — — — — **249** –   2,000 –

    Deduct: Net capital losses claimed on front of T2 return — — — — — — — —

                       (Note (1))   2,000 – (A)

(2) Canadian Investment Income per T2S(7) (Note (1)) — — — — — — — —   2,000 –

    Add: Foreign Investment Income per T2S(7) (Note (1)) ⌐ × 30% (Note (2))

    Deduct: Non-Business Foreign Tax Credit — — — — — — — — × 4 – (Note (1))

                  Sub-total   2,000 –

    Deduct: Net capital losses claimed on front of T2 return — — — — — — — —

                 (Note (1))   2,000 – (B)

(3) Taxable Income — — — — — — — — — — — — — — — — — — 30,000 –

    Deduct: Least of Amounts (A), (B) and (C) per Federal Small Business

        Deduction calculation (Note (3))   30,000 –

        Non-Business Foreign

        Tax Credit — — — — × 10/3(Note(4)) –

        Business Foreign Tax Credit × 10/4(Note(5)) –   30,000 – N/C (C)

    25% of least of Amounts (A), (B) and (C) — — — — — — — — — — **257** N/C (D)

    Part I Tax Payable (Note (6))   3,150   × 5/4 — — — — — — — 3,938 (E)

    Refundable Portion of Part I Tax — 4/5 of the lesser of Amounts (D) and (E) (Note (7)) — — **261** N/C

Note (1) If negative, enter NIL.

Note (2) For taxation years commencing before 1988 and ending after 1987, "30%" is to be read as "40%" for the number of days in taxation year that are before 1988 **over** total days in taxation year and 30% for the number of days in taxation year that are after 1987 **over** total days in taxation year.

Note (3) For taxation years commencing before July 1988, the "least of (A), (B) and (C) per Federal Small Business Deduction Calculation" is to be read as "Small Business Deduction times 4".

Note (4) For taxation years commencing before July 1988, "10/3" is to be read as "10/4".

Note (5) For taxation years commencing before July 1988, "10/4" is to be read as "2".

Note (6) Excluding the corporate surtax determined under section 123.2 (amount (B) on T2215); for taxation years commencing before 1988, "5/4" is to be read as "4/4".

Note (7) For taxation years commencing before 1988, "4/5 of the lesser of" is to be read as "the least of".

Part IV Tax on Taxable Dividends Received — Private corporations and subject corporations at any time in the taxation year

(1) Taxable Dividends subject to Part IV Tax per T2S(3) received before 1988. — — — — — — — — **404** 500 – (a)

    Deduct: Total Non-Capital and/or Farm Loss claimed for purposes of Part IV Tax per T2S(4) — — — — **406** – (b)

    Taxable Amount — — — — — — — — — — — — — — — — — — 500 – (A)

(2) Taxable Dividends subject to Part IV Tax per T2S(3) received after 1987. — — — — — — — — — **405** 500 –

    Deduct: Amount (b) above ⌐ minus Amount (a) above

    Taxable Amount — — — — — — — — — — — — — — — 500 – (B)

(3) Part IV Tax Payable —   Amount (A)   × 1/3 — (C)

                   Amount (B) 500 – × 1/4 125 – (D)   125 – (E)

(4) Part IV.1 Tax Payable, if any, on dividends subject to Part IV Tax   **418** – (F)

Total Part IV Tax Payable — Amount (E) minus Amount (F) (enter on front of T2 return)   125 –

* If negative, enter nil.

Refundable Dividend Tax on Hand — Private corporations and subject corporations at the end of the taxation year

Refundable Dividend Tax on Hand at the end of the preceding taxation year — — — — — **409**

Deduct: Dividend refund for the preceding taxation year — — — — — — — — — **410**   –

Add: Refundable Portion of Part I Tax (line 261 above) — — — — — — — — — — –

    Total Part IV Tax Payable — — — — — — — — — — — — — — — — 125 –

    Addition at December 31, 1986 of Refundable Dividend Tax on Hand

    — from form T713 (To be completed for 1988 taxation years that commenced before 1987)   **408** N/A   125 –

                        Sub-total   125 –

Deduct: Reduction at December 31, 1987 of Refundable Dividend Tax on Hand from form T763   **412**

Refundable Dividend Tax on Hand at the End of the Taxation Year — — — — — — — — **411** 125 –

Dividend Refund — Private corporations and subject corporations at the end of the taxation year

Taxable Dividends Paid in the taxation year and after 1987 per T2S(3)*   **414** 6,000 – × 1/4 1,500 –

Taxable Dividends Paid in the taxation year and before 1988 per T2S(3)*   **424** × 1/3 –

                              Total 1,500 – (A)

Refundable Dividend Tax on Hand at the end of the taxation year (line 411 above) — — — — — — — 125 – (B)

Dividend refund — Lesser of Amounts (A) and (B) (enter on front of T2 return) — — — — — — — 125 –

* Do not include capital gains dividends paid.

Form authorized by the Minister of National Revenue

Exhibit A–5 shows part of the calculation of tax for WR Limited, on the assumption that it is a "Canadian-controlled private corporation."

Payment of Tax—Corporations

A corporate taxpayer must pay installments each month of its current fiscal year toward its estimated tax bill. Final adjustments are made in the two or three months immediately following the end of the fiscal (taxation) year.

PART C—INCOME TAXES PAID BY INDIVIDUALS

The calculation of net income and taxable income for individuals has many similar rules to those followed by corporations, and some quite clear differences. The starting point is again the Section 3 formula to determine net income.

Business Income—Individuals

Individuals with business income operate as proprietors or partners. The proprietorship or partnership is not taxed directly, but rather the income of the business (calculated using the same accrual and other rules that the corporation followed) is "flowed through" and brought into the income of the owner(s) for taxing purposes. Note that the cash drawn from the business is irrelevant, and that the business financial statements do not report the income tax expense.

The taxation year for an individual is the calendar year, so it is the income of the business for its *fiscal* period ending in any calendar year that is deemed to be the owner's business income for that calendar year. The choice of a fiscal year-end thus becomes important in determining how long the taxing of the unincorporated business income may be delayed.

Income from Other Sources—Individuals

For individuals, income from investments is treated as a separate source, income from property, and includes such items as interest, dividends, and royalties. Whether rental income is business income or income from property depends on whether it is actively earned or passively collected by the individual. Generally, accrual rules apply to the determination of net income from property, but some exceptions exist which allow reporting on a cash basis or a mixed cash/accrual basis.

A special rule exists for dividends received from taxable Canadian corporations whereby 125% of the dividends received is brought into income. (This is offset in the calculation of taxes by a dividend tax credit described below.)

Investment income received during a year is reported to the taxing authority and the taxpayer by the institution making the payment on a special T5 information return (see Exhibit A–6).

Exhibit A–6 Investment income

Revenue Canada Taxation / **Revenu Canada** Impôt		**T 5** Supplementary – *Supplémentaire* Rev. 88		**STATEMENT OF INVESTMENT INCOME** **ÉTAT DES REVENUS DE PLACEMENTS**	

Dividends from Taxable Canadian Corporations
Dividendes de corporations canadiennes imposables

Year	(A) Actual Amount of Dividends	(B) Taxable Amount of Dividends	(C) Federal Dividend Tax Credit	(D) Interest from Canadian Sources	(E) Other Income from Canadian Sources
	6,000.00	7,500.00	1,000.00	1,000	
	Montant réel des dividendes	*Montant imposable des dividendes*	*Crédit d'impôt fédéral pour dividendes*	*Intérêts de source canadienne*	*Autres revenus de source canadienne*

(F) Gross Foreign Income	(G) Foreign Tax Paid	(H) Royalties from Canadian Sources	(I) Capital Gains Dividends	(J) Pension Income	(K) Amount Eligible for Resource Allowance Deduction
Année *Revenus étrangers bruts*	*Impôt étranger payé*	*Redevances de source canadienne*	*Dividendes sur gains en capital*	*Revenu de pensions*	*Montant donnant droit à la déduction en matière de ressources*

RECIPIENT: SURNAME FIRST, AND FULL ADDRESS
BÉNÉFICIAIRE: NOM DE FAMILLE D'ABORD, ET ADRESSE COMPLÈTE

Social Insurance Number
Numéro d'assurance sociale

000 000 001

➡ RICHARD, WILLIAM
1234 ANY STREET
SOMEWHERE, CANADA
XOX OXO

NAME AND ADDRESS OF PAYER (Must appear on each slip)
NOM ET ADRESSE DU PAYEUR (À inscrire sur chaque feuillet)

WR LIMITED
P.O. BOX 10,000
SOMEWHERE, CANADA

● **For Taxation Office**
● *Pour le bureau d'impôt*   1

Revenue Canada Taxation / **Revenu Canada** Impôt		**T 5** Supplementary – *Supplémentaire* Rev. 88		**STATEMENT OF INVESTMENT INCOME** **ÉTAT DES REVENUS DE PLACEMENTS**	

Dividends from Taxable Canadian Corporations
Dividendes de corporations canadiennes imposables

Year	(A) Actual Amount of Dividends	(B) Taxable Amount of Dividends	(C) Federal Dividend Tax Credit	(D) Interest from Canadian Sources	(E) Other Income from Canadian Sources
	120.00	150.00	20.00		
	Montant réel des dividendes	*Montant imposable des dividendes*	*Crédit d'impôt fédéral pour dividendes*	*Intérêts de source canadienne*	*Autres revenus de source canadienne*

(F) Gross Foreign Income	(G) Foreign Tax Paid	(H) Royalties from Canadian Sources	(I) Capital Gains Dividends	(J) Pension Income	(K) Amount Eligible for Resource Allowance Deduction
Année *Revenus étrangers bruts*	*Impôt étranger payé*	*Redevances de source canadienne*	*Dividendes sur gains en capital*	*Revenu de pensions*	*Montant donnant droit à la déduction en matière de ressources*

RECIPIENT: SURNAME FIRST, AND FULL ADDRESS
BÉNÉFICIAIRE: NOM DE FAMILLE D'ABORD, ET ADRESSE COMPLÈTE

Social Insurance Number
Numéro d'assurance sociale

000 000 001

➡ RICHARD, WILLIAM
1234 ANY STREET
SOMEWHERE, CANADA
XOX OXO

NAME AND ADDRESS OF PAYER (Must appear on each slip)
NOM ET ADRESSE DU PAYEUR (À inscrire sur chaque feuillet)

MARITIME TEL & TEL CO. LTD.
HALIFAX, N.S.
B3J 3C7

● **For Taxation Office**
● *Pour le bureau d'impôt*   1

Employment as a source of income is unique to individuals, and gets slightly different treatment. Salaries, wages, employee benefits, and fees from holding an office are included in the individual's income at their gross amount and on a cash basis for the calendar year. Employers are required to report annually such amounts along with any relevant withholdings on a T4 or T4A form (see Exhibit

Exhibit A–7 T4—Employment income

Revenue Canada Revenu Canada Taxation Impôt	T4-1988 Supplementary Supplémentaire	STATEMENT OF REMUNERATION PAID ÉTAT DE LA RÉMUNÉRATION PAYÉE	7751309

(C) EMPLOYMENT INCOME BEFORE DEDUCTIONS	(D) EMPLOYEE'S PENSION CONTRIBUTION CANADA PLAN / QUEBEC PLAN	(E) U.I. PREMIUM	(F) REGISTERED PENSION PLAN CONTRIBUTION	(G) INCOME TAX DEDUCTED	(H) U.I. INSURABLE EARNINGS	(I) C.P.P. PENSIONABLE EARNINGS	(J) EXEMPT CPP/QPP UI
30,000 :00	478:00		1,561 :00	6,570 :00		23,900:00	X
REVENUS D'EMPLOI AVANT RETENUES	DU CANADA COTISATION DE PENSION (EMPLOYÉ) / DU QUÉBEC	PRIME D'A.-C.	COTISATIONS RÉGIME ENREGISTRÉ DE PENSIONS	IMPÔT SUR LE REVENU RETENU	GAINS ASSURABLES A-C	GAINS OUVRANT DROIT À PENSIONS - R.P.C.	RPC/RRQ A-C EXONÉRATION

BOX (C) AMOUNT ALREADY INCLUDES ANY AMOUNTS IN BOXES (K), (L), (M), (N), (O), and (P) LE MONTANT DE LA CASE (C) COMPREND DÉJÀ TOUS LES MONTANTS DES CASES (K), (L), (M), (N), (O), (P)	TAXABLE ALLOWANCES AND BENEFITS AVANTAGES IMPOSABLES	(K) HOUSING BOARD AND LODGING LOGEMENT PENSION ET LOGEMENT	(L) TRAVEL IN A PRESCRIBED AREA VOYAGE DANS UNE RÉGION VISÉE PAR RÈGLEMENT	(M) PERSONAL USE OF EMPLOYER'S AUTO USAGE PERSONNEL DE L'AUTO DE L'EMPLOYEUR	(N) INTEREST FREE AND LOW INTEREST LOANS PRÊTS SANS INTÉRÊT OU À FAIBLE INTÉRÊT	(O) OTHER TAXABLE ALLOW. AND BENEFITS AUTRES AVANTAGES IMPOSABLES	(P) EMPLOYMENT COMMISSIONS COMMISSIONS D'EMPLOI

(Q) UNION DUES COTISATIONS SYNDICALES	(R) CHARITABLE DONATIONS DONS DE CHARITÉ	(S) PAYMENTS TO DPSP PAIEMENTS À UN RPDB	(T) PENSION PLAN OR DEFERRED PROFIT SHARING PLAN REGISTRATION NUMBER N° ENREGISTREMENT DE RÉGIME DE PENSION OU DE PARTICIPATION DIFFÉRÉE AUX BÉNÉFICES K 7693	(A) PROVINCE OF EMPLOYMENT N.S. PROVINCE D'EMPLOI	(B) SOCIAL INSURANCE NUMBER 000:000 :001 N° D'ASSURANCE SOCIALE

EMPLOYEE: SURNAME FIRST (in capital letters) USUAL FIRST NAME AND INITIALS AND FULL ADDRESS
EMPLOYÉ: NOM DE FAMILLE D'ABORD (en capitales) PRÉNOM USUEL ET ADRESSE COMPLÈTE
SURNAME NOM DE FAMILLE   USUAL FIRST NAME AND INITIALS · PRÉNOM USUEL

FOOTNOTES:
NOTES:

→ RICHARD, WILLIAM
1234 ANY STREET
SOMEWHERE, CANADA
XOX OXO

EMPLOYER NAME
NOM DE L'EMPLOYEUR   WR LIMITED

ACCOUNT NUMBER
NUMÉRO DE COMPTE   VGH 10001

EMPLOYEE NO.
N° DE L'EMPLOYÉ

TO BE RETURNED WITH T4-T4A SUMMARY
À RETOURNER AVEC LA T4-T4A SOMMAIRE   1

A–7).[3] All amounts received must be included unless specifically excepted, and no deductions are permitted unless they are specifically listed in Section 8 of the Income Tax Act. This list of deductions is quite short and it is often restricted to particular situations. The more common deductions allowed may be found on page 1 and at the top of page 2 of the individual tax return (see Exhibit A–8).

Sundry incomes from sources such as pensions, family allowances, unemployment insurance, and alimony are also normally reported on a cash basis. In many cases the payor is required to complete an annual information return similar to those used for investment income and employment income.

Capital Gains—Individuals

Net taxable capital gains are calculated for individuals in the same way as described above for corporations, and are treated as a separate source. Once again there must be a disposition, actual or deemed, for gains and losses to be recognized.

Individuals are subject to a number of special rules not applicable to corporations. For example, individuals other than trusts are eligible for a cumulative exemption for capital gains up to a lifetime limit of $100,000 ($66,667 of net taxable capital gains, becoming $75,000 of net taxable capital gains in 1990 and the following years). Since the exemption is operationalized by a Division C

---

[3] Other specialized information returns also exist for amounts such as payments to nonresidents and the quasi-employment income paid to fishermen.

Exhibit A-8 T1 General form (pages 1 and 2, calculation of "net income" and "taxable income")

| | Please do not use this area | ✦ | Revenue Canada Taxation | Revenu Canada Impôt | **1988** T1 GENERAL |

Federal and Nova Scotia
Individual Income Tax Return

Step 1 - Identification

Complete the following

Usual First Name and Initial | Surname, Family or Last Name (Please print)
WILLIAM | RICHARD

Present Address (Please print) *Number, Street and Apt. No., or P.O. No. or R.R. No.*
1234 ANY STREET

City
SOMEWHERE

Province or Territory | Postal Code
NOVA SCOTIA | XOX OXO

Your Social Insurance Number
000 000 001

Your Spouse's Social Insurance Number
000 000 002

On December 31, 1988, you were: Married ☒1 Widow(er) ☐2 Divorced ☐3 Separated ☐4 Single ☐5

Name of Spouse   LIL
Address of Spouse: same as mine ☒ or _____

Your Date of Birth — Day 01 Month 04 Year 1940

Have you filed an Income Tax Return before?   YES ☐   NO ☐
If "YES", please indicate for what year: 19 ___
Name on last return: same as above ☐ or _____

Your Province or Territory of Residence on December 31, 1988, was:
NOVA SCOTIA

If you were self-employed in 1988, please state province or territory of self-employment:

Address on last return: same as above ☐ or _____

If you became or ceased to be a resident of Canada in 1988, give:
Date of Entry — Day ___ Month ___   or Departure — Day ___ Month ___

Type of work or occupation in 1988   PRESIDENT
Name of present employer   WR LIMITED

If taxpayer is deceased, please give date of death: Day ___ Month ___ Year ___

Step 2 - Calculation of Total Income

Please do not use this area

		Line	Amount	
Employment Income	Employment income before deductions from Box (C) on all T4 slips (attach copy 2 of T4 slips)	101	30,000 00	⊙
	Commissions from Box (P) on all T4 slips, included in above total 102			
	Other employment income including training allowances, tips and gratuities, etc. (please specify)	104		⊙
	Total employment earnings (add lines 101 and 104)	105	30,000 00	
Pension Income	Old Age Security pension (attach copy of T4A(OAS) slip)	113		⊙
	Canada or Quebec Pension Plan benefits (attach copy 2 of T4A(P) slip)	114		⊙
	Other pensions or superannuation (attach copy 3 of T4A slips)	115		⊙
Income from Other Sources	Taxable family allowance payments (attach copy of TFA1 slip)	118	388 56	⊙
	Unemployment Insurance benefits (attach copy 2 of T4U slip)	119		⊙
	Taxable amount of dividends from taxable Canadian corporations (attach completed Schedule 4)	120	7,650 00	⊙
	Interest and other investment income (attach completed Schedule 4)	121	1,000 00	⊙
	Partnership income - limited or non-active partners only (attach completed Schedule 4) Net	122		⊙
	Rental income Gross 160 Net	126		⊙
	Taxable capital gains (attach completed Schedule 3)	127	1,333 33	
	Alimony or separation allowance income	128		⊙
	Registered retirement savings plan income (attach T4RSP slips)	129		⊙
	Other income (please specify)	130		⊙
Self-Employment Income	Business income Gross 162 Net	135		⊙
	Professional income Gross 164 Net	137		⊙
	Commission income Gross 166 Net	139		⊙
	Farming income Gross 168 Net	141		⊙
	Fishing income Gross 170 Net	143		⊙
Total Income (add lines 105 to 143 inclusive - please enter this amount on line 200 on page 2)		150	40,371 89 ➤	40,371 89

PLEASE DO NOT USE THIS AREA

| 605 | | | | | 600 | | | | |

Step 3 - Calculation of Taxable Income   2

	Total Income (from line 150 on page 1) 200			40,371 89

Deductions from Total Income

Registered pension plan contributions	207	1,561 00 ⊙	
Registered retirement savings plan contributions (attach receipts)	208	1,900 00 ⊙	
Annual union, professional or like dues (attach receipts)	212	⊙	
Child care expenses (attach form T778)	214	⊙	
Allowable business investment losses	217	⊙	
Moving expenses (from form T1-M)	219	⊙	
Alimony or separation allowance paid	220	⊙	
Carrying charges and interest expenses (attach completed Schedule 4)	221	150 00 ⊙	
Exploration and development expenses (attach completed Schedule 4)	224	⊙	
Other employment expenses (please specify)	229	⊙	
Other deductions (please specify)	232	⊙	
Add lines 207 to 232 inclusive 234		3,611 00 ▶	3,611 00

Net Income (subtract line 234 from line 200) 236   36,760 89

Add: Accumulated forward averaging amount withdrawal (from form T581)	237	
	239	36,760 89

Deductions from Net Income

Employee home relocation loan deduction (from T4 slip)	248	⊙
Stock option and shares deductions	249	⊙
Unemployment Insurance benefit repayment payable (from calculation in guide)	250	• ⊙
Limited partnership losses of other years	251	⊙
Non-capital losses of other years	252	⊙
Net capital losses of other years (1972 to 1987)	253	⊙
Capital gains deduction (from form T657)	254	1,333 33 ⊙
Northern residents deductions (from form T2222)	255	⊙
Additional deductions (as specified in guide)	256	⊙
Add lines 248 to 256 inclusive 257		1,333 33 ▶ 1,333 33

Taxable Income (subtract line 257 from line 239)   260   35,427 56

Step 4 - Calculation of Total Non-Refundable Tax Credits

Non-Refundable Tax Credits

Basic personal amount	Claim $6,000.00 300	6,000 00	
Age amount, if you were born in 1923 or earlier (if you did not receive the Old Age Security pension, attach a letter giving reasons)	Claim $3,236.00 301		
Married amount (provide details on page 3)	303	5,000 00 ⊙	
Amounts for dependent children (provide details on page 3)	304	388 00 ⊙	
Additional personal amounts (attach completed Schedule 6)	305	⊙	
Canada or Quebec Pension Plan contributions			
Contributions through employment from Box (D) on all T4 slips (maximum $478.00)	308	478 00 • ⊙	
Contribution payable on self-employment earnings (from page 3)	310	•	
Unemployment Insurance premiums from Box (E) on all T4 slips (maximum $690.56)	312	• ⊙	
Eligible pension income amount (maximum $1,000)	314	⊙	
Disability amount for self (claim $3,236.00)	316	⊙	
Disability amount for dependant other than spouse	318	⊙	
Tuition fees for self (attach receipts)	320	⊙	
Education amount for self (attach form T2202 or T2202A)	322	⊙	
Tuition fees and education amount transferred from child (attach form T2202 or T2202A)	324	1,380 00 ⊙	
Amounts transferred from spouse (attach completed Schedule 2)	326	⊙	
Medical expenses (attach receipts and complete Schedule 5) 330			
Subtract: 3% of "Net Income" (line 236 above) (maximum $1,500)			
Allowable portion of medical expenses	▶ 332	⊙	
Add lines 300 to 326 inclusive and line 332 (IF THIS AMOUNT EXCEEDS THE AMOUNT AT LINE 260, SEE "LINE 335" IN GUIDE) 335		13,246 00	
Non-refundable tax credits - 17% of line 335 or see Tax Table A instructions in Guide	338		2,252 00
Add: Charitable donations and gifts to Canada or a province (attach receipts)			
Charitable donations (attach completed Schedule 5)	340	2,600 00 ⊙	
Gifts to Canada, a province or gifts of cultural property	342	- ⊙	
Total Donations 344		2,600 00	
On the first $250 or less	250 00	the credit at 17% is 346	42 50
On the balance	2,350 00	the credit at 29% is 348	681 50

Total Non-Refundable Tax Credits (add lines 338, 346 and 348) (proceed to Step 5 on page 4)   350   2,976 00

deduction, net taxable capital gains must be calculated and included in net income for tax purposes in the usual way (see lines 127 and 254 in Exhibit A–8). Also, since the exemption is cumulative over the years, individuals realizing eligible capital gains in the year must file a return even if they have no other income and ultimately pay no tax.[4]

When an individual makes a gift, or dies, or becomes a nonresident, there is a deemed disposition of property triggering potential capital gains and losses. For gifts and bequests, some easing of the tax burden may be possible, depending upon the kind of property and who is the recipient.

Individuals are also more apt to encounter the special rules concerning **personal use property,** and three in particular are noteworthy:

1. Losses on personal use property are not deductible unless they arise on a special list of items called listed personal property such as coins, stamps, and works of art (but *not* antiques).
2. In measuring the gain or loss, both proceeds and capital cost are deemed to be at least $1,000 to avoid the necessity of accounting for nonmaterial items.
3. A full or partial exemption is provided on the disposition of a family home that has been used as a principal residence.

Another special rule of interest to individuals (but also applicable for corporations) allows most taxpayers to elect capital gains rather than income treatment on the sale of Canadian securities, even where the normal rules of intention would indicate the reason for investing was to produce an active trading profit rather than to obtain the usual passive income from property by the holding of the asset.

Deferred Income—Individuals

A special set of rules exists which allows individuals to save out of income (essentially for retirement) and delay the payment of taxes on that income until it is received.[5] Registered pension plans, registered retirement savings plans, and deferred profit sharing plans are some examples of situations where limited amounts of income may be reduced currently as funds are put into the plan. Interest earned on the plan funds is untaxed while it is registered, and the ultimate tax cost is borne only when amounts are received out of the plan.

There are enough special rules in the determination of an individual's income that it may be necessary to obtain professional assistance in situations other than the most straightforward ones.

---

[4] The capital gains exemption is increased by a further $400,000 if the property disposed of is shares of a Canadian Controlled Private Corporation, or is farm property.

[5] The whole area of retirement income planning has been under review by the government, including the taxing rules. The May 1985 budget proposals included several changes that would increase contribution limits over a five-year period, and refine eligibility requirements. After several delays, it is expected that these changes will begin to be put in place beginning in 1989.

Division C Deductions—Individuals

Individuals receive the same deductions as corporations for excess losses carried over from other years. There is no complete deduction for Canadian dividends such as corporations receive.

It is only individuals (including trusts) that can use the Division C set of deductions that are designed to allow for some sort of equity where personal and social circumstances are different. (See Exhibit A–8, page 2, for a list of these deductions from net income.)

As mentioned previously, the lifetime capital gains exemption is received as a Division C deduction by individuals. Limits are provided and eligibility restrictions exist. Schedules for the detailed calculation of each year's deduction will have to be followed.

Also among the Division C items for individuals is the employee stock option deduction which exists here simply to allow for the way related amounts were technically included in the Division B net income calculation.

Tax Calculation—Individuals

The taxable income of individuals other than trusts are subject to a **progressive** rate structure rather than the initial flat rate faced by corporations. It is considered equitable for those with larger incomes to pay proportionately more taxes. (See the bottom of part A in Exhibit A–9.)

A set of deductions from tax called **nonrefundable tax credits** allows a token deduction to everyone in lieu of actual living and personal expenses, and further provides additional deductions for age, disability, and the support of various types of dependents. The amounts of these deductions are changed from year to year to allow for inflation, and sometimes to reflect changing perceptions of what is considered **equitable**.

These credits also provide reductions for persons receiving pension income from private sources, or making payments for Canada Pension and unemployment insurance premiums, an extra deduction for disabled persons, and another for students paying tuition. There are credits for medical expenses, charitable donations, and an opportunity exists for spouses who both have positive net income to share some of these credits in a limited way. In every case, eligibility conditions and limitations on the amount of the deduction exist and must be observed. Supplementary information and structured "schedules" to assist calculations are provided with the tax return form.

Individuals, like corporations, are eligible for tax credits for foreign source income, political contributions, and certain types of investment expenditures in designated regions, as well as a number of reductions in tax arising from special circumstances.[6]

---

[6] Some individuals whose tax liability is significantly reduced by such credits may find themselves liable for an Alternative Minimum Tax, calculated at a flat rate on a modified form of the taxable income base.

Schedule 1 — **Detailed Tax Calculation** (see Guide)

Federal Income Tax — *Use the "1988 Rates of Federal Income Tax" at bottom.*

Taxable Income from line 400 on page 4 of your return   35,427 56

On the first	27,500 00	tax is	4,675 00	
On remaining	7,927 56	tax at 26 % is	2,061 17	
	Total Federal Income Tax on Taxable Income		6,736 17 ▶	6,736 17 ●

Add: Tax Adjustments (please specify; see "Line 500" in Guide)   500

Total   6,736 17

Subtract: Total Non-Refundable Tax Credits from line 350 on page 2   501   2,976 00

Federal Dividend Tax Credit - 13⅓% of Taxable amount of dividends from taxable Canadian corporations (line 120 on page 1 of your return).   502   1,020 00 ●

Minimum Tax Carry-over (see "Line 504" in Guide)   504   –   ●

Total of above credits   3,996.00 ▶   3,996 00

Basic Federal Tax 506   2,740 17

Subtract: Federal Foreign Tax Credit — make separate calculation for each foreign country. ☉

(a) Income Tax or Profits Tax paid to a foreign country   507   ●

(b) $\frac{\text{Net Foreign Income } 508}{\text{Net Income } \dagger}$ X $\left(\begin{array}{c}\text{"Basic Federal Tax" plus}\\ \text{any Dividend Tax Credit}\end{array}\right)$ =

† Net income (line 236) (or if you filed a form T581 election, use line 9 of that form - if negative, enter zero) less any capital losses of other years allowed (line 253), employee home relocation loan deduction (line 248), stock option and shares deductions (line 249) and capital gains deduction (line 254).

Deduct (a) or (b) above, whichever is less 509

Federal Tax 406   2,740 17 ✱

Federal Individual Surtax (see "Line 419" in Guide)

Basic Federal Tax (line 506)   2,740 17

Subtract: Federal Forward Averaging Tax Credit (from form T581)

Amount (A)   2,740 17

Individual Surtax - 3% of Amount (A)   510   82 20

Subtract: Additional Federal Foreign Tax Credit from Part II of form T2209   511   –

Sub Total   517   82 20

Subtract: Additional Investment Tax Credit from Section II of form T2038   518   –

Federal Individual Surtax 419   82 20 ✱

Nova Scotia Income Tax (Applicable to residents of Nova Scotia on December 31, 1988)
If you were not a resident of Nova Scotia on December 31, 1988 or if you had income from a business with a permanent establishment outside Nova Scotia in 1988, refer to the Guide.

Basic Nova Scotia Income Tax — 56.5% of Basic Federal Tax (line 506 above)   1,548 20

Subtract: Provincial Foreign Tax Credit from calculation on form T2036   –

NOVA SCOTIA TAX 423   1,548 20 ✱

✱ *Please transfer the amounts of the items indicated by an asterisk (✱) to the identically numbered lines on page 4 of the return.*

1988 Rates of Federal Income Tax

Taxable Income	Tax
$ 27,500 or less	17%
$ 27,500	$ 4,675 plus 26% on next $ 27,500
$ 55,000 or more	$ 11,825 plus 29% on remainder

Step 5 - Summary of Tax and Credits There are two methods of tax calculation (see Tax Tables in Guide).   **4**

Taxable Income from line 260 on page 2 400 **35,427 56**

TAX TABLE METHOD ONLY

Federal Income Tax from Tax Table A in Guide	401	
Subtract: Total non-refundable tax credits from line 350 on page 2	402	
Federal Tax (line 401 minus line 402 - if negative, enter zero or from line 406 on Schedule 1) 406		**2,740 17**

Subtract: **Federal political contribution tax credit** Total contributions **409** ⊙

from calculation in Guide Allowable tax credit **410**

Investment tax credit **412** •

Labour-Sponsored Funds tax credit (attach receipts) **414** •

Total of above credits 416 ▶ —

Federal tax before federal individual surtax (line 406 minus line 416 - if negative, enter zero) 417 **2,740 17**

Add: **Federal individual surtax** (look up line 406 amount on Tax Table B in Guide **or** from line 419 on Schedule 1) 419 **82 20**

Net Federal Tax 420 **2,822 37**

Add: **Nova Scotia tax** (look up line 406 amount on Tax Table B in Guide **or** from line 423 on Schedule 1) 423 **1,548 20**

Canada Pension Plan contribution payable on self-employment earnings from page 3	432	
Unemployment Insurance benefit repayment payable from calculation in Guide	433	
Recovery of child tax credit overpayment from Schedule 7	**434**	•

Total Payable (add lines 420 to 434 inclusive) 435 **4,370 57** •

— Please do not use this area —

683 ☐☐

684 ☐

Federal Credits

Child tax credit (attach completed Schedule 7)	**444**	**N/A**	•
Federal sales tax credit (attach completed Schedule 8)	**446**	**N/A**	•
Canada Pension Plan overpayment	**448**		•
Unemployment Insurance overpayment	**450**		•
Refund of investment tax credit (from form T2038-IND.)	**454**		•
Part XII.2 tax credit (attach T3 slip)	**456**		• ⊙

Provincial Credits

Nova Scotia tax credits	**464**		•

Other Credits

Total tax deducted per information slips	**470**	**6,570 00**	• ⊙
Tax paid by instalments	**476**		• ⊙
Forward averaging tax credit (from form T581)	**478**		•

Total Credits (add lines 444 to 478 inclusive) 482 **6,570 00** ▶ **6,570 00**

Subtract line 482 from line 435 and enter the difference in applicable space below.   **(2,199 43)**

A difference of less than $1.00 is neither charged nor refunded.

Refund **484** **2,199 43** •   Balance Due **485** •

Amount Enclosed •

Please attach cheque or money order **payable to the Receiver General. Do not mail cash.**
Payment is due not later than April 30, 1989.

490

I hereby certify that the information given in this return and in any documents attached is true, correct and complete in every respect and fully discloses my income from all sources.

Please sign here *William Richard*

| Telephone | | | Date | |

It is a serious offence to make a false return.

Privacy Act Personal Information Bank number RCT/P-PU-005

Name and address of any individual or firm who received compensation for the preparation of this return.

Name

Address

Telephone

Form authorized and prescribed by order of the Minister of National Revenue for purposes of Part I and Part I.1 of the Income Tax Act, Part I of the Canada Pension Plan and Part VIII of the Unemployment Insurance Act, 1971.

A most important reduction of taxes is the federal dividend tax credit on dividends received from taxable Canadian corporations. This amounts to 16⅔% of the actual dividends received (or 13⅓% of the taxable amount of dividends, after they have been grossed up 25% as described earlier). The purpose of this credit is to reduce or even eliminate the impact of the corporate taxes paid when the income was first earned by the corporation, and leave a net tax cost approximately equal to what an individual would have paid on the same business income received directly. This is referred to as the integration of corporate and personal taxes. A 3% surtax is imposed on individuals with federal tax payable.

The provinces levy their own income taxes in addition to the federal taxes. For most provinces, the reporting is done on the same return used for filing federal taxes, and the calculation is based on the basic federal tax; that is, federal taxes before any reductions except the nonrefundable tax credits, the federal dividend tax credit, and the scientific research tax credit. The province of Quebec requires the filing of a separate provincial income tax return.

The data in Exhibit A–8 draws on the previous information we have about Mr. William Richard. The form also shows that he is the president of WR Limited, is married with two sons (one of whom is eligible for Family Allowance). The other son is in the university, but he has insufficient income of his own to use his education tax credit so he has transferred it to his father.

Mr. Richard has contributed $1,900 to a registered retirement savings plan, paid $150 in carrying charges in connection with his investments, and contributed $2,600 to charities.

Exhibit A–9 shows the forms used for the calculation of tax payable by an individual. The portion designated as Schedule 1 may be bypassed by many individuals who can use precalculated tables to determine their tax liability.

In addition to the normal taxes and reductions, the federal government has provided for a child tax credit to persons who are eligible to receive Family Allowances, whether they have income taxes to pay or not. This credit is limited by the number of eligible children (receiving Family Allowance), and also by the size of the *family* income. Details are found on the income tax return filed by individuals.

A similar refundable sales tax credit is available to individuals to offset the impact of federal sales taxes on lower-income families.

Payment of Tax—Individuals

For many individuals, the tax will have been withheld, at source, by the payer of the income. Any balance would then be payable or refundable with the filing of the return on or before April 30 of the year following the taxation year.

Individuals (normally with large business or property income sources) whose taxes are over $1,000 and for whom tax is not withheld from at least 75% of their "Net Income," are required to pay installments quarterly on an estimated basis.

Both federal and provincial taxes are paid to the federal government, except for those owing to Quebec.

PART D—TAX PLANNING

Tax planning focuses on the anticipated tax consequences of future transactions. The purpose of tax planning is to avoid the unnecessary payment of taxes in the face of detailed and often complex tax rules. Tax planning to avoid tax should not be confused with tax evasion. Tax evasion involves illegal activities to reduce the tax liability, and is a criminal offence.

Minimization of the tax cost can involve:

1. Ensuring that the lowest allowable *rate* of tax is levied.
2. Deferring the payment of tax to the latest permissible time to conserve cash resources.
3. Taking advantage of opportunities and incentives permitted by the law, and avoiding the traps set for tax evaders which accidentally may catch the unwary innocent taxpayer.

Tax Planning by Business Managers

Because income tax rates are high and the related income tax law and regulations are complex, tax planning is an important consideration in many of the decisions made by the management of any business. To provide an overview of tax planning we will discuss three of the major areas that affect most business entities: (1) selecting the type of business organization, (2) financing the business, and (3) structuring transactions before they occur.

Selecting the Type of Business Organization

Sole proprietorships, partnerships, and corporations have different income tax implications for owners and managers. When starting a new business or dealing with the growth of a small business, selecting the type of business organization poses several substantive issues, one of which is the long-term income tax implications.

Annual earnings of proprietorships and partnerships are taxed at the increasing marginal rates of the owner(s), whether withdrawal or not. In contrast, corporate earnings are taxed at one or more of the flat rates applicable to corporations, partly when earned and partly when distributed, and in addition the shareholder (owner) may pay taxes on the dividends received over and above the dividend tax credit allowed.

Whether incorporating the business will increase or decrease taxes depends largely on the extent to which the dividend tax credit received against personal taxes offsets or neutralizes the tax paid in the corporation. Each case is different, and depends upon what rate the corporation pays and what income other than the business profits is being received by the owner. The salary/dividend mix from the corporation can alter these variables, and, at some levels of income, it becomes a critical part of the decision.

Other advantages may accrue to the corporate form because of incentives available only to corporate taxpayers, special provisions surrounding reorganization and disposals or dissolution of the business, and the implications for personal estate planning by shareholders—all factors requiring expert advice.

The principal disadvantage of the corporate form, apart from those cases where the taxes are higher, is the complexity of the tax rules.

Financing a Business

Basically, a business obtains funds (e.g., cash) from three sources: (1) investments by owners, (2) borrowing, and (3) earnings of the business. Often when new or additional funds are needed (e.g., for operations and expansion), the management of the company must decide between equity and debt (or some combination) as the source(s) of funds. Such decisions have important income tax implications, particularly for a corporation, because interest on debt is a fully deductible expense in computing taxable income. In comparison dividends paid to shareholders (of common and preferred shares) are not deductible. To illustrate, assume ABC Co. Limited needs $500,000 cash to acquire a new productive facility. The management is considering two alternatives:

1. **Alternative A:** Borrow the needed funds at 12% interest; the marginal income tax for the company is 40%.
2. **Alternative B:** Issue for cash, 50,000 shares of the company's cumulative 8%, preferred stock, at $10 par value per share.

The two financial alternatives can be analyzed as:

Alternative A, borrowing:

$$\$500,000 \times .12 \times (1.00 - .40) = \$36,000 \text{ aftertax cost per year}$$
$$\text{Net cost of funds: } \$36,000/\$500,000 = 7.2\%$$

Alternative B, issue capital stock:

$$\$500,000 \times .08 = \$40,000 \text{ aftertax cost per year}$$
$$\text{Net cost of funds: } \$40,000/\$500,000 = 8.0\%$$

In this case, the borrowing alternative is less costly because the interest expense is deductible from income, saving tax at the 40% marginal tax rate. However, a number of factors should be considered in making this decision. For instance, the company is legally required to make the fixed interest payments of $60,000 per year and to repay the $500,000 principal amount on the maturity date, regardless of whether the company earned income or incurred a loss. In contrast, by choosing to issue capital stock, these fixed payments may be avoided; dividends can be paid only if there are accumulated earnings (i.e., a positive balance in retained earnings); also, there is no payment on a maturity date for the shares issued. It may be helpful at this point to review the sections in Chapters 11 and 12 on (*a*) return on owner's equity, (*b*) return on total assets, and (*c*) financial leverage.

Structuring and Timing

Business transactions often can be structured and/or timed in ways to maximize their favourable, or minimize their unfavourable, income tax consequences. It is important to realize that such structuring and timing must be accomplished prior to, and not after, the transaction has been completed. Some typical transactions that can be structured or timed for this purpose are as follows:

1. Leasing versus purchase of operating assets.
2. Installment sale of capital property.
3. Allocation of the lump-sum purchase price of depreciable versus nondepreciable assets.
4. Valuation of assets and liabilities of a purchased business.
5. Timing the purchase of depreciable assets just before year-end.
6. Recognition of investment tax credit opportunities such as choice of location and type of expenditure.
7. Choice of methods of compensation for executives (tax-free versus taxable benefits).
8. The wide range of tax incentives and tax shelters.
9. Tax-free rollovers of certain types of assets by selling at the appropriate time.
10. Triggering capital gains and losses at the right time.

New (1988) and broader powers will allow the taxing authorities to change the effect of transactions where the sole purpose was to reduce taxes payable. These general antiavoidance rules (GAAR) will need intrepretation by the courts.

Tax Planning For the Individual

Individual taxpayers should also plan in order to minimize their income tax liabilities within the provisions of the tax law.

Many of the structuring and timing strategies listed above for corporations would also be considered by individuals in connection with business income. People should also be aware of additional opportunities and pitfalls that can arise in their investing and financing decisions, and in a whole group of tax provisions related to what might be called personal life events.

Investment and Financing Decisions

Individuals will try to maximize their aftertax rates of return. Probably the best return individuals can earn will be on money invested in tax-sheltered retirement savings plans. The choice between interest and dividends requires that the effect of the dividend tax credit must be considered in order to accurately compare yields. Because of the lifetime capital gains exemption, a major part of investment planning will involve the choice between investments yielding a return in the form of regular income and those yielding capital gains. Also, the timing of the realization of the gains (and/or losses) becomes very important.

Individuals should always attempt to use borrowed funds for income producing rather than personal purposes to render the interest cost tax deductible. Where personal purpose loans exist, these should be paid off first because of their higher effective aftertax cost.

Individuals have the option of reporting certain investment income on a cash or accrual basis to a limited degree. These choices may be made in ways that ease the tax burden in its amount or timing.

Personal Life Events

Several tax provisions exist which affect personal life events, including the following:

1. Retirement income planning is encouraged by the deferred income rules which allow the deduction of capital contributions and the sheltering of plan income until after retirement.
2. Splitting income among family members is sometimes possible, and helps avoid the higher marginal rates when all income is in the hands of one family member.
3. The timing and method of transferring personal and business assets to spouse or children by gift or bequest has many possibilities and requires estate planning advice.
4. Strategies that augment wealth through tax-reduced or tax-free capital gains rather than regular income should be explored.
5. Even timing marriages (and the birth of children) so that they occur close to the year-end to maximize personal tax credits has sometimes been suggested (and acted upon, other things being equal)!

Some Cautions

Individuals need to pay particular care to their reporting and payment responsibilities under the Income Tax Act, or extra costs will be incurred.

Interest penalties exist where returns are filed late, or where taxes (deductions, installment payments, or final settlements) are not remitted on time.

As well, supporting documentation for the calculation of taxable income is required to be available in the event of disagreement or tax audit. Many individuals, even in business, find this bothersome, but they should plan a document collection and filing system to avoid unnecessary tax costs.

It is evident that tax planning involves complex rules and sometimes complex strategies. Good planning will then almost always include the selection of competent professional advice.

QUESTIONS FOR DISCUSSION

1. Distinguish among the terms:
   a. Business income.
   b. Net income.
   c. Taxable income.

2. What is the taxation year for corporations? For individuals?

3. How does the Income Tax Act encourage taxpayers to pay their taxes on time? When are the payments of taxes required to be made by (a) corporations and (b) individuals?

4. In which part of the Section 3 "Net Income" formula would each of the following items appear:
   a. Wages.
   b. Rental net income.
   c. Carrying charges (allowable) on income-producing securities.
   d. Capital gain on the sale of a stamp collection.
   e. Family allowance.
   f. Capital loss on sale of Trans Canada Pipeline shares.

5. John Jones is regularly employed by Canada University at a salary of $3,000 per month. He also collected $7,500 on a consulting contract from another source. He earned $1,000 interest on deposits at his bank and received $3,000 in dividends from Lucky Strike Gold Mines Limited.

   List the information return forms that he should receive, and the basic information shown on each.

6. May income be reported on a cash basis, or must the accrual basis be used? Explain.

7. How do capital gains arise, and how are they classified by type? What is special about the taxation of capital gains?

8. Indicate which of the following business organizations is required to file a tax return: (a) sole proprietorship, (b) partnership, and (c) corporation. If no tax return is required, how is the income of the business taxed?

9. a. List six general rules governing the deductibility of expenses from business revenues to determine Net Income from business.
   b. Apply these rules to judge whether each of the following items would or would not be allowed as deductions against sales revenue:
      (1) Store supplies purchased.
      (2) Salary of $50,000 paid to a spouse for part-time work in the business.
      (3) Cost of lunch on rainy days when the owner of the business does not feel like going home.
      (4) Telephone bill for home phone on which occasional long-distance calls are made for the business.

(5) Interest on a loan to buy a delivery van for the business.

(6) Operating costs of the business owner's car which he uses to drive to and from work.

(7) Fire, theft, and public liability insurance on the store and its contents.

10. How closely does the accounting for inventory under the tax rules parallel the treatment(s) allowed under generally accepted principles?

11. What do each of the following terms mean:
    a. Capital cost allowance.
    b. Undepreciated capital cost.
    c. Recapture.
    d. Terminal loss.

12. List and briefly explain three areas in which there are differences between business accounting net income for tax purposes.

13. Business income earned by a corporation is taxed twice—once in the hands of the corporation, and again in the hands of shareholders when they receive dividends. How does the Canadian tax system try to alleviate this problem?

14. Explain the tax reasons why a corporation often prefers to obtain long-term funds by issuing bonds rather than shares of its capital stock.

EXERCISES

EA–1   Using Exhibit A–1 as a reference, compute net income for each of the following taxpayers:

	J. Smith	XYZ Co. Ltd.
Salary and benefits	$15,000	—
Net business income (loss)	(18,000)	$175,000
Net income from investments	3,000	28,000
Old-age pension	2,700	—
Capital gains (losses) at 66⅔% of actual amounts:		
Listed personal property gains	6,000	—
Other capital property gains	3,000	6,000
Listed personal property losses	(2,000)	—
Business investment loss	—	(1,000)
Other capital property losses	(9,500)	(7,000)

EA–2   Well-Stocked Co. Ltd. reported the following in its 19X3 financial statements:

	December 31	
	19X3	19X2

Balance Sheet

Merchandise inventory, at LIFO cost in 19X3, at FIFO cost in 19X2 (Note 1) $375,000 $300,000

Note 1: During the year the company changed its inventory valuation to LIFO from FIFO. The December 31, 19X3 inventory at FIFO cost was $325,000, and income has accordingly been increased by $50,000.

Required:

What effect(s) would this information have on reported net income for tax purposes?

EA-3   Down East Ltd. reported the following balances of undepreciated capital cost at the end of 19X1:

Building Class 3 (5%)	$100,000
Equipment Class 8 (20%)	20,000
Motor vehicles Class 10 (30%)	10,000

During 19X2 the following transactions occurred:

Purchased equipment—Class 8	$ 8,000
Leasehold acquired—Class 13*	40,000†
Disposed of truck for proceeds of	3,000

* The very favourable lease had three years left in its regular term and one five-year renewal option at the same low rent.
† Lump sum.

Required:
Prepare the schedule calculating the capital cost allowance that may be claimed for 19X2.

EA-4   Assume that the truck that was sold in Exercise A–3 had originally cost $11,750 and was the only asset in Class 10.

Required:
Recalculate the effect on income for tax purposes if it were sold for:

1. $3,000, as above or
2. $10,500 or
3. $12,000.

EA-5   Generosity Limited had made the following contributions and donations during 19X6, and you have been consulted to advise as to whether or not these would be deductible for tax purposes.

1. To a Pee-Wee hockey team for uniforms that had the company's name printed on them	$ 800
2. To the United Appeal	5,000
3. To a resident of the city who provided a home for stray dogs	600
4. To the New Democratic Party of Canada	1,000

Required:
In each case, indicate whether the amount is deductible:

a. In determining income.
b. In Division C to determine taxable income.
c. In Division E to determine taxes payable.
d. Not at all.

EA-6   Any Company Limited reported a net income of $250,000 and had no Division C deductions. All of the income was from nonmanufacturing business sources.

Required:

Referring to the FTC—Schedule 1 shown in Exhibit A–5, calculate the federal taxes payable if:

a. The company was a public company.

b. The company was a Canadian-controlled private corporation.

EA–7   How would your answers in (*a*) and (*b*) of Exercise A–6 change if the business income arose entirely from manufacturing activities? (A descriptive rather than a calculated answer is required.)

EA–8   Mr. E. Z. Erwin is married and has two children—a son at a university, age 18, and a 12-year-old daughter. During the summer of 19X4, the son had a temporary job and earned $2,500. Mrs. Erwin receives no income. The son's tuition and education credit base amounted to $1,460, and could not be used for himself.

Mr. Erwin's 19X4 income sources were as follows:

Salary (gross)	$25,000
Less: Income tax withheld	(4,500)
Canada Pension withheld	(478)
Unemployment insurance	(690)
Registered pension contributions	(1,022)
Net pay	$18,310
Interest on savings account	$ 300
Dividends received on Bell Canada shares	400
Family allowance (received by wife, but included as his income)	360
Proceeds of shares sold (cost 1,000)	1,600

He made the following donations:

His church	$ 520
United Appeal	420
Federal Liberal Party	100

Required:

Using the information from Exhibits A–8 and A–9 as a guide, calculate Mr. Erwin's federal income tax owing (refundable) for the 19X4 taxation year. Be sure to show clearly the calculation of: (*a*) net income, (*b*) taxable income, (*c*) federal tax payable.

PROBLEMS/CASES

PCA–1   Management of Tri-key Ltd. is contemplating the purchase of a building in which to house its expanding sales force. The company has a successful rapidly expanding business. Management is not sure whether to acquire the asset (cost $800,000, Class 1—4%) just before the 19X1 year-end, or just after the year-end.

Mr. Tristan, the president, is concerned that a purchase just before year-end would hurt its rate of return by increasing the asset base without giving the assets a chance to produce a return. Existing assets total $3 million and accounting net income averages $600,000 before taxes.

Mr. Keystone, the vice president of finance, acknowledges that problem, but feels that the cash flow tax savings could be significant in helping the company's already hard-pressed cash position, given that the $800,000 is going to be borrowed in 19X1 anyway.

Required:

a. Assuming an effective corporate tax rate of 40%, calculate the cash savings for the years 19X1 and 19X2 from the reduction of taxes associated with the extra capital cost allowances claimed if:
   (1) The building were purchased in December 19X1.
   (2) The building were purchased in January 19X2.

b. Calculate aftertax returns on investment for 19X1 under each of the conditions (1) and (2) in (a), *if* ROI were based on:
   (1) Beginning of the year assets.
   (2) Average of beginning and ending assets.

c. What would you conclude?

PCA–2 Concerns Ltd. has just completed its second year of operations, and for the first time its income statement has reported a profit.

In 19X1, a loss of $15,000 had been incurred. The 19X2 income statement showed a net income of $60,000, after taxes of $30,000 had been provided.

A review of the details of the income statement and other inquiries of management disclosed the following information:

1. Expenses included:

Depreciation expense	$240,000
Charitable donations	10,000

2. Sundry other income included:

Dividends on shares of a supplier in Toronto	2,000
Gain on the sale of unimproved land used as a parking lot	15,000

3. Maximum capital cost allowance which could be claimed in 19X2 totaled   280,000

Required:

a. Calculate for the year 19X2 the following:
   (1) Division B net income for tax purposes.
   (2) Division C deductions and taxable income.
   (3) Part I federal taxes payable, if Concerns Ltd. qualifies as a Canadian-controlled private corporation and all the income except the capital gain and dividends is business income.

b. Should the maximum amount of capital cost allowance always be claimed by a taxpayer? For example, consider the situation if Concerns Ltd. had reported a net income *before* taxes of only $30,000 in 19X2.

PCA–3 Mr. Hardy Cizion is the proprietor of the Newton Restaurant, and he is trying to decide whether or not he should incorporate this business.

In 19X7, last year, the restaurant produced for him a net income of $40,000, and he withdrew $20,000 of this for personal purposes.

He lives in a province where the provincial tax rate on corporate income is 10%, and on personal income is 50% of the federal tax.

Required:

a. Calculate the federal and provincial income taxes payable by Mr. Cizion, assuming the proprietorship business was his only source of income and his Division C deductions were nil. Nonrefundable tax credits were $1,786.

b. Assume that Newton Restaurant Limited had been incorporated. Calculate the total taxes paid by the corporation *and* Mr. Cizion personally if:

   (1) The corporation paid no dividends and he withdrew the $40,000 as salary.

   (2) The corporation paid him a salary of $20,000 and a dividend of all the remaining surplus.

   (3) The corporation paid all of its income after taxes as a dividend to Mr. Cizion.

c. Should Mr. Cizion incorporate his restaurant business now?

1987 FINANCIAL STATEMENTS OF CONSOLIDATED-BATHURST INC.

Consolidated-Bathurst Inc.

Annual Report 1987

Consolidated-Bathurst Inc.

Incorporated August 28, 1931, under the laws of Canada

Registered Office
800 Dorchester Blvd. West
Montreal, Quebec H3B 1Y9
Telephone: (514) 875-2160
Telex: 05-25165

Auditors
Touche Ross & Co.

Share listings: Con Bath
The Montreal Exchange
The Toronto Stock Exchange

Transfer Agent and Registrar
Montreal Trust Company
at Halifax, Saint John, Montreal, Toronto, Winnipeg, Regina,
Calgary and Vancouver

56th Annual Meeting
Château Champlain Hotel, Montreal
April 28, 1988 – 10:30 a.m.

Contents

Cover:
"87" was a year of record performance for Consolidated-Bathurst. It was also one of continued renewal and updating of Company facilities, exemplified by the major projects described in these pages. Other '87 milestones were noteworthy. Our earliest pulp and paper mill, the Laurentide Division at Grand-Mère, Quebec, entered its 100th year of production in 1987; it was the 20th Anniversary of the merger of Consolidated and Bathurst companies, and the larger more diversified organization's adoption of the name "Consolidated-Bathurst".

Report of the Directors

To shareholders and employees:

Last year in describing our outlook, we looked on the near term with "improved optimism". As it turned out, that description for 1987, the Company's 56th year of operations, was substantially understated. The record level of quarterly earnings that closed 1986, at $35 million, was very nearly equalled in the first quarter of 1987, and the year's succeeding quarters each posted a higher standard.

Net sales in 1987 were $2.261 billion, 12% above those of 1986, when they passed the two billion mark for the first time. Fourth quarter 1987 sales were $597 million, 14% better than the $526 million achieved in the fourth quarter of 1986.

Fuelling the year's persistent resurgence were strong demand and better prices for newsprint, market pulp and containerboard produced in Canada and the strong positive results from the Company's Bridgewater newsprint mill in the United Kingdom.

The Celgar Pulp Company mill at Castlegar, B.C., was featured last year as a key investment development of 1986 with Power Corporation and China International Trust and Investment Corporation, an agency of the Chinese Government. In 1987, the mill performed well and made a good equity contribution throughout the year.

Operating results

As summarized in the Highlights table opposite, 1987 earnings before extraordinary items for the year totalled $181.5 million, or $1.63 per common share. This was a 75% improvement over 1986 earnings of $103.7 million, or $0.87 per share, and 48% better than the Company's best previous performance, in 1980.

In contrast to extraordinary items in 1986, mainly a write-down of the Company's oil and gas investments, the extraordinary items in 1987 were a net credit of $32.9 million. This made Consolidated-Bathurst's 1987 net earnings $214.4 million, or $1.95 per share, compared with net earnings of $49.4 million, or $0.34 per share, in 1986.

Details by product sector are summarized in the segmented information presented on pages 30 and 31. Total operating earnings went up 38.5%, from $255.1 million in 1986 to $353.3 million in 1987. Those of Pulp and Paper climbed 57% to $282.5 million. This included a significant, more appropriate contribution from the Bridgewater mill, as against that mill's virtual break-even position in 1986. The total Packaging sector contribution declined by 9.3% to $68.2 million. This comprised a decline of 5.3% in Europa Carton's contribution and of 12.1% in that of CB Pak operations.

The Company's eight pulp and paper mills operated at capacity during 1987, producing 1.94 million tonnes, or 4% more than in 1986. This was in spite of an estimated loss of some 28 000 tonnes of production to a 14-day strike at the Company's three Saint-Maurice Valley mills.

In North American Packaging, a major development was the sale in August 1987 of CB Pak's equity investment in its U.S. glass container associate, Diamond-Bathurst Inc., to Anchor Glass Container Corporation of Tampa, Fla., for $114.3 million Canadian.

During the year, CB Pak's Canadian glass container subsidiary, Domglas Inc., had a lengthy strike at its Hamilton plant. While Domglas was able to maintain its sales, the strike had a severe negative impact on its earnings. Domglas operating earnings dropped 36%. In contrast, sales of Twinpak were 17% higher than in 1986 and its operating earnings were 45% better than in 1986.

CB Pak's earnings before extraordinary items in 1987 were $24.1 million, or $1.20 per share, up 11% over those of 1986. Much of this improvement was attributable to in-

creased earnings from Twinpak and from the glass tableware joint venture, Libbey-St. Clair, to higher investment income and favorable income tax adjustments. With the extraordinary gain from the sale of Diamond-Bathurst, and other items, CB Pak's net earnings in 1987 were $81 million, compared with a net in 1986 of $18 million.

Europa Carton AG, the Company's packaging affiliate in the Federal Republic of Germany, had, as expected, a difficult year in 1987. While sales declined in DM, they improved in Canadian dollars by 11%, but operating earnings declined by 17% in DM and by 5% in dollars. To improve its performance, ECA is changing the nature and emphasis of some of its operations.

Capital expenditures

Continuing to broaden its scope and renew its facilities in 1987, Consolidated-Bathurst increased its capital expenditures to $260.7 million in 1987, up 12.8% from the $231.2 million spent in 1986. The larger part of these expenditures went to pulp and paper projects, at $170.4 million, 10% above the $154.8 million spent in 1986.

Major pulp and paper mill projects included the new No. 6 Corrugating Medium Machine under construction at the Bathurst mill, the chemi-thermo-mechanical pulp mill at Belgo Division, and a new woodyard flume to handle pulpwood more efficiently at the Port Alfred Division.

Capital spending in CB Pak during 1987 was $43.6 million, 10% higher than in 1986. Expenditures included Twinpak expansions in PET plastic bottle production and various other products, and continued upgrading of Domglas facilities, including a major furnace rebuild at the Hamilton plant.

3

W.I.M. Turner, Jr.   T.O. Stangeland

In 1987, Libbey-St. Clair Inc., acquired the Ravenhead Company, a former division of United Glass and a large glass tableware producer in the United Kingdom. This virtually doubles the size and scope of Libbey-St. Clair.

At Europa Carton, capital expenditures increased by 41%, from $27.8 million to $39.2 million, with emphasis on restructuring of the company's folding carton facilities and strengthening the competitive position of ECA's Corrugated Division.

Financing

The Company's cash flow from operations was a record $360 million in 1987. There was also the additional $114 million contributed by the sale of CB Pak's investment in Diamond-Bathurst Inc. These positive factors contributed to a reduction of $95 million in the total debt of Consolidated-Bathurst and to an increase of $87 million in short-term investments. At December 31, 1987, total debt amounted to $459 million, while cash and short-term investments totalled $106 million.

In December 1987, the Company arranged term financing in the Euro-dollar debt market through a U.S. $125 million floating rate note issuance facility with a consortium of financial institutions. This facility broadens Consolidated-Bathurst's sources of financing and enables the Corporation to take advantage of attractive floating interest rates. Following the successful completion of this term financing, the revolving credit facility of Consolidated-Bathurst Inc. was reduced from U.S. $100 million to U.S. $50 million and the credit facility of Consolidated-Bathurst Pontiac Limited in the amount of U.S. $50 million was cancelled.

On January 21, 1988, Consolidated-Bathurst announced its intention to redeem on April 15, 1988, all $5.75 Second Preferred Shares, Series A, at $52 per share and U.S. $5.25 Second Preferred Shares, Series B, at U.S. $52 per share for approximately $88 million. The refinancing of these preferred shares by means of floating rate debt is expected to lower the financing charges of the Company.

4

In October 1987, the Board approved an increase in the regular quarterly dividend from 12.5¢ per share to 16¢ per share. At its January 1988 meeting, the Board approved an extra year-end dividend of 10¢ per common share, in addition to the regular quarterly dividend. This reflected the success of a year of record earnings and cash flow by the Company.

Directors and officers

Late in December, the Board lost a member and the Chairman of its Audit Committee, with the death of R.M.P. Shields, a director since April 1975. Mr. Shields, over the years, was a dedicated and consistent contributor to the Board's deliberations. His experience, good humour and irrepressible wit will be greatly missed. At the Board's meeting in January, Peter J. Saunders was appointed a director of the Corporation. Mr. Saunders is Group Finance Director of Associated Newspapers Holdings p.l.c., of London, England.

On July 1, 1987, J. Michael Dawson retired as Secretary of the Corporation, and was succeeded by Elizabeth C. Robichaud, Assistant Secretary since March 1976. Mr. Dawson had served Consolidated-Bathurst loyally and effectively during 36 years in a variety of assignments, as Secretary from 1983 and, previously, as Director of Audits, and as Controller.

Outlook

In Pulp and Paper, the momentum of improvement generated by strong demand and better product prices is expected to continue. The joint-venture Celgar Pulp Company will maintain its positive equity earnings contribution, and the return from the Bridgewater newsprint mill will continue to improve. Europa Carton's capital improvement program should also develop better returns.

The year 1987 was an outstanding one for Consolidated-Bathurst. In spite of conflicting economic predictions about the year ahead, and notwithstanding the inability of our democratic societies to seriously address even medium term problems under the duress of elections real or anticipated, we expect 1988 to be another strong year for Consolidated-Bathurst.

Last November, the Company announced that design and engineering studies will be completed in 1988 toward installation of a new groundwood specialties paper machine at our Grand-Mère mill, to be called Laurentide No. 11. This project will involve a renewal investment of some $280 million for the Company's earliest mill. During 1988, Laurentide will complete 100 years of continuous production. Ground-breaking for the new machine early in 1989 will mark an auspicious beginning to its second century.

On February 15, 1988, the Company was advised that a company formed by J.E. Souccar, President, and P.S. Echenberg, Executive Vice-President of CB Pak Inc., proposed to make a take-over bid for all the issued common shares of CB Pak. The offer, subject to obtaining satisfactory financing and the necessary regulatory approvals, is to be $25.50 per share in cash, less a special dividend of up to $3.50 which may be paid by CB Pak. Consolidated-Bathurst, which owns 16 million common shares, has agreed to tender these shares if the bid is made not later than April 15.

This sale would bring in $408 million before taxes. While increasing concentration of Consolidated-Bathurst's operations in pulp and paper, it does not involve the current large packaging components comprising our paper packaging organization in the Federal Republic of Germany nor ownership of MacMillan Bathurst Inc., Canada's largest corrugated container company.

In 1988, the Corporation enters its 21st year as Consolidated-Bathurst, the result of the merger that took place in 1967 between the Corporation, then Consolidated Paper Corporation, and Bathurst Paper Limited. We

are determined that the milestones of achievement along the way ahead will increase in their frequency and impressiveness. To that end, the continuing interest and support of Company people in our many sectors and fields of endeavour are indispensable, and we wish to assure all employees of our appreciation for their loyalty and enthusiasm, and for their contribution to Consolidated-Bathurst's progress, spirit and accomplishments in the year just past, and in those ahead.

On behalf of the Board of Directors,

W.I.M. Turner, Jr.,   T.O. Stangeland,
Chairman and   President and
Chief Executive   Chief Operating
Officer   Officer

Montreal, February 25, 1988

Directors

Pierre Arbour
President and Chief Executive Officer,
Laduboro Ltd., Montreal, Que.

Robert A. Bandeen, O.C.
President and Chief Executive Officer,
Cluny Corporation, Toronto, Ont.

Douglas A. Berlis, Q.C.
Counsel to
Aird & Berlis, Toronto, Ont.

James W. Burns
Deputy Chairman,
Power Corporation of Canada, Montreal, Que.

Pierre Côté, C.M.
Chairman,
Celanese Canada Inc., Montreal, Que.

André Desmarais
Vice-President,
Power Corporation of Canada, Montreal, Que.

Paul Desmarais, C.C.
Chairman and Chief Executive Officer,
Power Corporation of Canada, Montreal, Que.

A. Frank Knowles, C.A.
President and Chief Operating Officer,
Power Corporation of Canada, Montreal, Que.

William D. Mulholland
Chairman of the Board and Chief Executive Officer,
Bank of Montreal, Toronto, Ont.

Kenneth A. Randall
Vice-Chairman,
Northeast Bancorp, Inc., Williamsburg, Va.

The Rt. Hon. The Viscount Rothermere
Chairman,
Associated Newspapers Holdings p.l.c., London, England

Peter J. Saunders
Group Finance Director,
Associated Newspapers Holdings p.l.c., London, England

Jean Simard
Vice-President,
Simcor Inc., Montreal, Que.

T. Oscar Stangeland
President and Chief Operating Officer of the Corporation
Montreal, Que.

Peter N. Thomson
Vice-Chairman and President,
West Indies Power Corporation Limited, Nassau, Bahamas

William I.M. Turner, Jr., C.M.
Chairman and Chief Executive Officer of the Corporation
Montreal, Que.

Honorary Directors

Robert E. Morrow, Q.C.
John M. Seabrook

Officers

William I.M. Turner, Jr., C.M.
Chairman and Chief Executive Officer

T. Oscar Stangeland
President and Chief Operating Officer

Norman A. Grundy
Vice-President, International

Timothy J. Wagg
Vice-President, Finance

Jean-Jacques Carrier
Vice-President and Corporate Controller

Colin G. Fraser
Treasurer

Elizabeth C. Robichaud
Secretary

Pierre M. Richard
Assistant Secretary

Guy Dufresne
Senior Group Vice-President, North American Pulp and Paper

M. deB. Strathy
Senior Vice-President, Pulp and Paper Marketing

Bartley G. Duns
Vice-President, Pulp, Kraft and Paperboard Sales

Raymond Felx
Vice-President, Manufacturing

K. Ross Hughes
Vice-President, Newsprint Sales

Armand Legault
Vice-President, Woodlands

Ashok K. Narang
Senior Group Vice-President,
Planning, Systems and U.K. Newsprint Operations

W.B. Scott
Vice-President, U.K. Newsprint Operations

Joseph E. Souccar
Senior Group Vice-President, North American Packaging

Paul S. Echenberg
Vice-President, Plastics Packaging

Subsidiary Operations

Robert A. Nugent
President, Gillies Inc.

Michael A. Pelham
Managing Director, Bridgewater Paper Sales Limited

Ronald J. Simpson
President, Domglas Inc.

Werner Woitas
Chairman, Managing Board, Europa Carton AG

Associate Companies

Robert A. Graham
President, Libbey-St. Clair Inc.

Theodor W. Haiplik
President and Chief Executive Officer, MacMillan Bathurst Inc.

Executive Committee

Paul Desmarais, C.C., Chairman
William I.M. Turner, Jr., C.M., Vice-Chairman
James W. Burns
A. Frank Knowles, C.A.
The Rt. Hon. The Viscount Rothermere
T. Oscar Stangeland

Audit Committee

Robert A. Bandeen, O.C., Chairman
A. Frank Knowles, C.A., Vice-Chairman
Pierre Arbour
Kenneth A. Randall

Remuneration Committee

Douglas A. Berlis, Q.C., Chairman
Pierre Côté, C.M.
Paul Desmarais, C.C.

6

Financial Section

Distribution of Revenue* (millions of dollars)	1987	%	1986	%
Materials, supplies, etc.	$ 986	43	$ 905	45
Wages, salaries and fringe benefits	610	27	565	28
Fuel and power	195	8	194	9
Federal, provincial and municipal direct taxes	150	7	100	5
Depreciation	114	5	99	5
Dividends	65	3	45	2
Interest	47	2	55	3
Retained earnings (excluding extraordinary items)	113	5	57	3
	$2 280	100	$2 020	100

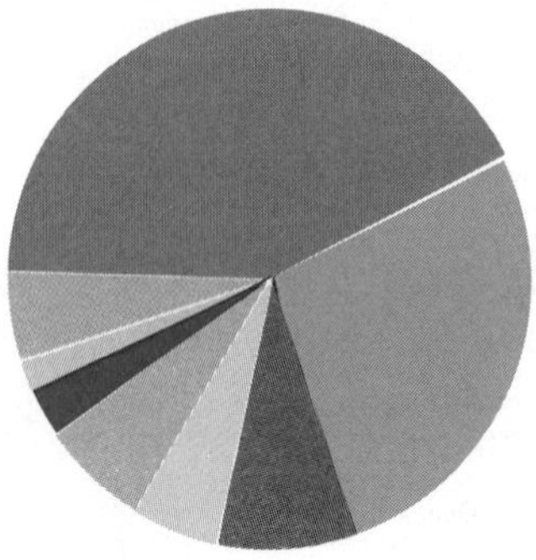

*Comprises net sales, other income and equity earnings.

Quarterly financial data

	Net sales	Earnings before extraordinary items	Earnings before extraordinary items	Dividends declared	Stock price range Low	Stock price range High
	(millions of dollars)		(per common share)		(per common share)	
1986						
First quarter	$ 454	$ 15	$0.11	$0.075	$ 9	$13⅝
Second quarter	515	25	0.21	0.075	11⅛	14⅜
Third quarter	523	29	0.25	0.075	10⅞	12⅞
Fourth quarter	526	35	0.30	0.075	$11⅝	$15⅜
	$2 018	$104	$0.87	$0.30		
1987						
First quarter	$ 533	$ 33	$0.29	$0.125	$14⅜	$23⅝
Second quarter	574	43	0.38	0.125	16½	21⅜
Third quarter	557	46	0.41	0.125	17¾	21¼
Fourth quarter	597	60	0.55	0.160	$13½	$22⅝
	$2 261	$182	$1.63	$0.535		

Financial Review

The Company's earnings before extraordinary items for 1987 were a record $181.5 million, or $1.63 per common share, representing a 75% improvement over 1986 earnings of $103.7 million, or $0.87 per share. Extraordinary items amounted to a net credit of $32.9 million, or $0.32 per share. This credit reflected gains on sales of the Company's investment in Diamond-Bathurst Inc. and of permanently closed plants in Munich, West Germany, and Burnaby, B.C., partially offset by a charge arising from the write-down of Sulbath Exploration Ltd. In 1986, there was an extraordinary charge of $54.2 million related mainly to the write-off of oil and gas investments. Consolidated-Bathurst's net earnings for 1987 were $214.4 million, or $1.95 per common share, compared with $49.4 million, or $0.34 per share, in 1986.

As a result of these improved earnings, the Company's return on common shareholders' equity increased from 12.8% in 1986 to 19.6% in 1987. Consolidated-Bathurst's net earnings margin excluding extraordinary items went up from 5.1% in 1986 to 8.0% in 1987.

Net sales in 1987 aggregated $2.261 billion, representing an increase of 12% over sales of $2.018 billion in 1986. Sales of pulp and paper products increased by 14% while those of CB Pak Inc. and Europa Carton AG rose by 7% and 11%, respectively.

Operating earnings amounted to $353.3 million, 38% higher than those of 1986. Pulp and paper operations in Canada and the United Kingdom posted substantial gains chiefly as a result of higher shipments and improved prices. These positive factors were partially offset by lower results in the packaging companies.

Cash flow from operations in 1987 totalled $360.2 million and was well in excess of capital expenditures of $260.7 million. The additional cash flow generated from the sale of the investment in Diamond-Bathurst contributed to a net increase in funds of $91 million.

The capitalization of Consolidated-Bathurst at December 31, 1987 consisted of $459 million of debt, $150 million of preferred shares and $853 million of common shareholders' equity. The debt / equity ratio of 31 / 69 at December 31, 1987 represented a considerable improvement over the ratio of 40 / 60 at the end of 1986. The Corporation's working capital improved from $339 million to $394 million in 1987; the working capital ratio, however, declined from 2.13 to 2.00 during that period. The decline was largely attributable to the increase in the current portion of long-term debt as a result of the Series I sinking fund debentures coming due on November 15, 1988 and in the accounts payable related to the capital expenditure program.

Effective January 1, 1988, Consolidated-Bathurst sold the operations of the Bridgewater Division to Bridgewater Paper Company Limited, a wholly owned subsidiary of the Corporation, and agreed to guarantee to the lessor the lease obligation related to the Bridgewater mill. This restructuring, which followed the first year of profitable operations of the U.K. newsprint operations, resulted in the designation of Bridgewater Paper Company as a self-sustaining subsidiary for purposes of translation of its financial statements in Canadian dollars. The U.K. operations were previously considered as an integrated operation of Consolidated-Bathurst. In 1988, the foreign currency translation of Bridgewater Paper Company under the current rate method will result in the deferment of the translation adjustments in the shareholders' equity section of the balance sheet.

Sales, Property and Plant, Employees, Shareholders and Shares by Country as at December 31, 1987

	Net Sales	Property & Plant – Net	Number of Employees	Number of Common Shareholders	Number of Common Shares
	(millions of dollars)				
Canada	$ 880.5	$1 023.4	11 533	11 926	85 716 970
United Kingdom	172.7	124.0	576	879	15 245 871
United States	508.7	0.1	34	377	1 001 399
West Germany	533.4	175.6	2 895	611	9 737
Other Countries	166.1	15.6	73	84	344 422
	$2 261.4	$1 338.7	15 111	13 877	102 318 399

29

Segmented Information   (millions of dollars)

Classes and major product lines

Sales to Customers		Inter-segment Sales		Net Sales		
1987	1986	1987	1986	1987	1986	
						Canadian newsprint and
$ 651.8	$ 603.6	$ —	$ —	$ 651.8	$ 603.6	groundwood specialties
196.5	157.5	—	0.6	196.5	158.1	U.K. newsprint
135.2	101.9	49.3	41.5	184.5	143.4	Market pulp
199.6	188.8	5.7	5.5	205.3	194.3	Paperboard
61.8	39.6	—	—	61.8	39.6	Lumber
1 244.9	1 091.4	55.0	47.6	1 299.9	1 139.0	Pulp and Paper
						Glass, plastic and flexible
504.6	472.4	1.3	1.2	505.9	473.6	packaging – CB Pak
502.6	451.3	—	—	502.6	451.3	Packaging – Europa Carton
1 007.2	923.7	1.3	1.2	1 008.5	924.9	Packaging
9.3	2.7	0.9	1.2	10.2	3.9	Oil and gas
—	—	(57.2)	(50.0)	(57.2)	(50.0)	Eliminations
$2 261.4	$2 017.8	$ —	$ —	$2 261.4	$2 017.8	Total operations

Inter-segment sales are accounted for at prices comparable to
market prices for similar products.

Producing geographical regions

$1 562.3	$1 409.0	$ 57.2	$ 49.4	$1 619.5	$1 458.4	Canada
196.5	157.5	—	0.6	196.5	158.1	United Kingdom
502.6	451.3	—	—	502.6	451.3	West Germany/Netherlands
—	—	(57.2)	(50.0)	(57.2)	(50.0)	Eliminations
$2 261.4	$2 017.8	$ —	$ —	$2 261.4	$2 017.8	Total operations

Canadian operations had export sales to the United States of
$508.7 (1986 $482.8), to Western Europe of $79.4 (1986 $65.5)
and to other countries of $93.6 (1986 $76.8).

*Return on Assets: Earnings before extraordinary items,
minority interest and after-tax interest, divided by total assets
after accumulated depreciation.

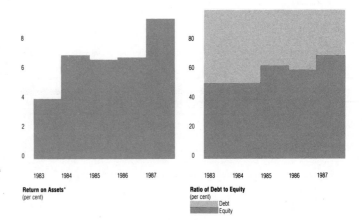

Return on Assets*
(per cent)

Ratio of Debt to Equity
(per cent)
■ Debt
■ Equity

(millions of dollars)

Operating Earnings		Depreciation		Capital Expenditures		Identifiable Assets as at December 31	
1987	1986	1987	1986	1987	1986	1987	1986
$149.5	$123.0	$ 35.4	$32.7	$ 59.3	$ 92.6	$ 669.1	$ 646.7
29.4	(0.3)	9.3	7.4	9.7	23.0	192.0	185.9
57.6	25.1	11.3	11.0	14.4	26.4	234.6	227.1
41.2	28.0	8.0	7.0	69.4	10.6	199.4	133.1
4.8	3.7	3.7	2.4	17.6	2.2	66.9	38.2
282.5	179.5	67.7	60.5	170.4	154.8	1 362.0	1 231.0
39.4	44.8	25.1	23.4	43.6	39.6	450.9	387.1
28.8	30.4	19.1	14.6	39.2	27.8	328.3	276.1
68.2	75.2	44.2	38.0	82.8	67.4	779.2	663.2
2.6	0.4	2.1	0.6	7.5	9.0	52.7	71.7
—	—	—	—	—	—	—	—
$353.3	$255.1	$114.0	$99.1	$260.7	$231.2	$2 193.9	$1 965.9

Operating Earnings		Depreciation		Capital Expenditures		Identifiable Assets as at December 31	
$295.1	$225.0	$ 85.6	$77.1	$211.8	$180.4	$1 673.6	$1 503.9
29.4	(0.3)	9.3	7.4	9.7	23.0	192.0	185.9
28.8	30.4	19.1	14.6	39.2	27.8	328.3	276.1
—	—	—	—	—	—	—	—
$353.3	$255.1	$114.0	$99.1	$260.7	$231.2	$2 193.9	$1 965.9

Corporate assets amounted to $70.8 in 1987 and $64.9 in 1986.

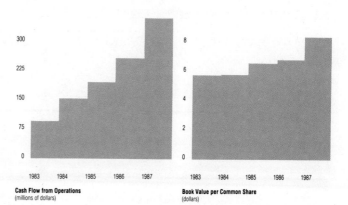

Cash Flow from Operations
(millions of dollars)

Book Value per Common Share
(dollars)

31

Consolidated Statement of Earnings for the year ended December 31, 1987		1987	1986
		(thousands of dollars)	
Net sales		$2 261 430	$2 017 834
Costs and expenses	Cost of goods sold	1 697 163	1 575 458
	Depreciation	114 020	99 132
	Administrative and selling	96 981	88 186
Operating earnings		353 266	255 058
	Interest expense – long-term	40 687	46 660
	– short-term	6 430	8 268
	Corporate administrative expense	22 679	20 975
	Other income (expense) (note 3)	2 200	(4 719)
Earnings before income taxes		285 670	174 436
	Income taxes (note 4)	112 898	72 430
Earnings before undernoted items		172 772	102 006
	Equity earnings (note 8)	16 608	6 720
	Minority interest	7 840	5 076
Earnings before extraordinary items		181 540	103 650
	Extraordinary items (note 5)	32 875	(54 233)
Net earnings		214 415	49 417
	Dividends on preferred shares	14 585	14 881
Net earnings attributable to common shareholders		$ 199 830	$ 34 536
Earnings per common share	Before extraordinary items	$1.63	$0.87
	Extraordinary items	0.32	(0.53)
	Net	$1.95	$0.34
Weighted average number of common shares outstanding – in thousands		102 379	102 244

Consolidated Statement of Retained Earnings for the year ended December 31, 1987		1987	1986
		(thousands of dollars)	
Retained earnings at beginning of year		$374 423	$371 882
Net earnings		214 415	49 417
Excess cost of purchasing common and preferred shares over stated value		(3 382)	(1 601)
Dividends	Preferred	(14 585)	(14 881)
	Common	(50 493)	(30 394)
Retained earnings at end of year		$520 378	$374 423
Dividends per share	Preferred		
	1966 Series	$1.50	$1.50
	Series A	5.75	5.75
	Series B	6.90	7.26
	Series C	2.04	2.04
	Common	$0.54	$0.30

Consolidated Statement of Changes in Financial Position for the year ended December 31, 1987

Funds provided (used)		1987	1986
		(thousands of dollars)	
Operating activities	Operating earnings	$353 266	$255 058
	Depreciation	114 020	99 132
	Interest	(47 117)	(54 928)
	Current income taxes	(48 561)	(30 700)
	Other items	(11 382)	(11 143)
	Cash flow from operations	360 226	257 419
	Decrease (increase) in accounts receivable	(47 827)	(15 069)
	Decrease (increase) in inventories	(11 008)	(5 640)
	Increase (decrease) in accounts payable and accrued liabilities	42 946	16 959
	Other items	463	5 490
	Net decrease (increase) in operating working capital	(15 426)	1 740
		344 800	259 159
Dividends	On common shares in cash	(50 493)	(29 200)
	On preferred shares	(14 585)	(14 881)
		(65 078)	(44 081)
Investing activities	Additions to property and plant	(260 756)	(231 230)
	Grants on additions to property and plant	10 550	2 780
	Increase in investments	(7 085)	(41 267)
	Other items – net	20 568	13 837
		(236 723)	(255 880)
Financing activities	Proceeds from sale of investment in Diamond-Bathurst Inc.	114 273	—
	Proceeds from sale of permanently closed plants	16 465	—
	Disposal of investments	14 777	1 560
	Issue of long-term debt	2 176	148 994
	Repayments of long-term debt	(94 623)	(78 988)
	Purchase of common and preferred shares	(5 109)	(2 863)
		47 959	68 703
Net increase in funds		$ 90 958	$ 27 901
Analysis of net change in funds	Increase in cash and short-term investments	$ 86 562	$ 9 281
	Decrease in bank loans and notes payable	4 396	18 620
		$ 90 958	$ 27 901

On behalf of the Board:

W.I.M. Turner, Jr.,
Director

T.O. Stangeland,
Director

33

Consolidated Balance Sheet as at December 31, 1987

		1987	1986
		(thousands of dollars)	
Assets			
Current assets	Cash and short-term investments	$ 106 125	$ 19 563
	Accounts receivable	317 829	270 002
	Inventories (note 6)	355 554	344 546
	Prepaid expenses	6 890	5 884
		786 398	639 995
Property and plant (note 7)	Pulp and paper mills	1 538 065	1 370 239
	Packaging plants	646 535	548 249
	Woodlands	23 487	22 765
	Oil and gas properties	37 456	40 267
		2 245 543	1 981 520
	Less accumulated depreciation	906 808	790 306
		1 338 735	1 191 214
Investments	(note 8)	109 607	172 994
Other assets	(note 9)	29 929	26 582
		$2 264 669	$2 030 785

Management's Report

The consolidated financial statements have been prepared by management on the historical cost basis in accordance with Canadian generally accepted accounting principles consistently applied and conform substantially with International Accounting Standards. These statements, which necessarily include estimates and approximations, reflect information available to February 25, 1988, and have been audited by Touche Ross & Co., Chartered Accountants, whose report is included on the next page. The financial information contained throughout the Annual Report conforms with that shown in the financial statements.

Management maintains an accounting system which incorporates extensive internal financial controls. The internal audit department performs independent appraisals of the effectiveness of these internal controls and reports its findings and recommendations to management and to the Audit Committee.

The Board appoints the members of the Audit Committee which is composed solely of outside directors. This Committee reviews the consolidated financial statements with management and the external auditors prior to submission to the Board for approval, as well as any significant recommendations of the external and internal auditors for improvements in internal controls and the actions of management to implement such recommendations.

T.J. Wagg,
Vice-President, Finance

Montreal, Quebec
February 25, 1988

34

		1987	1986
		(thousands of dollars)	
Liabilities and Shareholders' Equity			
Current liabilities	Bank loans and notes payable	$ 3 534	$ 7 930
	Accounts payable and accrued liabilities	267 151	224 205
	Taxes payable	39 393	29 059
	Dividends payable	2 497	2 542
	Current portion of long-term debt	79 888	37 350
		392 463	301 086
Long-term debt	(note 10)	375 524	508 634
Provision for German pensions		70 315	54 422
Deferred investment tax credits		66 620	54 700
Deferred income taxes		295 834	227 932
Minority interest		61 105	41 270
Shareholders' equity	Stated capital (note 11)	452 961	454 567
	Retained earnings	520 378	374 423
	Foreign currency translation adjustments	29 469	13 751
		1 002 808	842 741
		$2 264 669	$2 030 785

Auditors' Report

The Shareholders,
Consolidated-Bathurst Inc.

We have examined the consolidated balance sheet of Consolidated-Bathurst Inc. as at December 31, 1987 and the consolidated statements of earnings, retained earnings and changes in financial position for the year then ended. Our examination was made in accordance with generally accepted auditing standards, and accordingly included such tests and other procedures as we considered necessary in the circumstances.

In our opinion, these consolidated financial statements present fairly the financial position of the Corporation as at December 31, 1987 and the results of its operations and the changes in its financial position for the year then ended in accordance with generally accepted accounting principles applied on a basis consistent with that of the preceding year.

Touche Ross & Co.

Chartered Accountants

Montreal, Quebec
February 25, 1988

35

Notes to Consolidated Financial Statements
December 31, 1987

1. Summary of Significant Accounting Policies

Principles of consolidation

The consolidated financial statements include the accounts of all subsidiaries. All significant inter-company items are eliminated. Acquisitions of all subsidiaries are accounted for on a purchase basis and earnings are included in the consolidated financial statements from the date of acquisition.

Foreign currency translation

For domestic companies and integrated foreign operations, assets and liabilities are translated into Canadian dollars at exchange rates prevailing at the balance sheet date for monetary items and at exchange rates prevailing at the transaction dates for non-monetary items. Income and expenses are translated at average exchange rates prevailing during the year with the exception of depreciation which is translated at historical exchange rates. Exchange gains or losses are included in earnings except for unrealized gains or losses on translation of foreign long-term debt which are deferred and amortized over the remaining term of the related obligation. Foreign debt covered by a currency exchange agreement is translated at the guaranteed exchange rate.

For self-sustaining foreign operations, all assets and liabilities are translated into Canadian dollars at the exchange rates prevailing at the balance sheet date and all income and expenses are translated at average exchange rates prevailing during the year. Foreign currency translation adjustments are deferred in the shareholders' equity section of the balance sheet.

Inventory valuation

Pulpwood, chips, expenditures on wood operations, raw materials and supplies are stated at average cost. Work in process and finished goods inventories, the cost of which includes raw materials, direct labour and certain manufacturing overhead expenses, are stated at the lower of average cost and net realizable value. Provision is made for slow-moving and obsolete inventories.

Investments

Short-term investments are stated at the lower of cost and market. Long-term portfolio investments are stated at cost less write-downs for any permanent decline in value, when appropriate. Long-term investments over which the Corporation has significant influence are accounted for by the equity method.

Property and plant, depreciation and capitalization

Mills, plants and other properties are stated at cost. On retirement or disposal of property and plant, the Corporation removes the cost of the assets and the related accumulated depreciation. Gains or losses on disposal of assets are included in earnings.

Depreciation, calculated principally on the straight-line method, is charged to operations at rates based upon the estimated useful life of each depreciable property. The following rates apply to those assets being depreciated on the straight-line method:

	Buildings	Equipment
Pulp and paper mills	2½%	6%
Packaging plants	2–5%	8–10%

Expenditures which result in a material enhancement of the value of the facilities involved are capitalized. Maintenance and repair costs are expensed as incurred.

Grants relating to property and plant additions are deducted from the cost of the assets and depreciation is calculated on the net amount. Accruals are made for the appropriate portion of the estimated total of approved grants. Grants in respect of current expenses are included in earnings.

Interest is capitalized on major additions to property and plant involving the construction of new or materially improved manufacturing facilities. The interest cost is determined using the prime interest rates of the Corporation's principal bankers.

36

Summary of Significant Accounting Policies (continued)

Investments in shares of oil and gas companies are accounted for as described under Investments. Oil and gas expenditures by the Corporation are accounted for under the successful efforts method whereby geological, geophysical and carrying costs are expensed and exploratory drilling costs are capitalized as property and plant. When no reserves are discovered, exploratory costs are expensed. All development costs are capitalized. The amortization of capitalized costs is based on proven reserves.

Leases

Long-term leases in which the Corporation, as a lessee, retains substantially all the benefits and risks incident to ownership are accounted for as additions to property and plant. The asset value and related obligation for such capital leases is recorded at the present value of the future lease payments, using an appropriate discount rate.

Pensions

The Corporation and its subsidiaries, with the exception of Europa Carton AG, have defined benefit pension plans which are funded, trusteed and principally contributory. Europa Carton AG has unfunded defined benefit pension plans with provision being made in the financial statements for the accrued pension cost.

The cost of the benefits earned by the employees is determined using for the most part

the projected benefit method prorated on time of service. The pension expense reflects the current service cost, the interest on the actuarial surplus or unfunded liability and the amortization over the estimated average remaining service life of the employees of (i) the actuarial surplus or unfunded liability and (ii) experience gains or losses.

Income taxes

The Corporation follows the tax allocation basis in accounting for income taxes. Deferred income taxes shown in the financial statements result principally from capital cost allowance claimed for tax purposes in excess of depreciation.

Investment tax credits relating to additions to property and plant are recorded in the balance sheet in the year in which the qualifying expenditures are made. These tax credits are amortized to income on the same basis as the related property and plant are depreciated.

Earnings per common share

Earnings per common share are calculated after deducting dividends on preferred shares and using the weighted average number of common shares outstanding during the year. Common shares issuable as dividends on the Series B common shares are included as being outstanding from the dividend declaration dates.

2. Change in accounting for pension costs

Effective January 1, 1987, the Corporation adopted prospectively the recommendations of the Canadian Institute of Chartered Accountants with respect to accounting for pension costs and obligations as described under Pensions in Note 1. In previous years,

the pension costs were charged to earnings as funded except for the German pension costs which were calculated in accordance with local legislation. The new rules had no material effect on the earnings of the year.

Notes to Consolidated Financial Statements
December 31, 1987

(thousands of dollars)

3. Other income (expense)		1987	1986
	Investment income	$ 7 136	$ 3 172
	Net gain from debt retirement and disposal of property and plant	2 889	1 805
	Net translation loss on long-term debt	(7 825)	(9 696)
		$ 2 200	$ (4 719)

4. Income taxes		1987	1986
	Current	$ 48 561	$ 30 700
	Deferred	64 337	41 730
		$112 898	$ 72 430

	The Corporation's effective income tax rate is determined as follows:	1987	1986
	Combined Canadian federal and provincial income tax rate	43.7%	43.7%
	Increase (decrease) in the income tax rate resulting from:		
	Higher effective income tax rate on earnings of a foreign subsidiary	1.6	2.3
	Federal income tax surcharge	0.7	1.3
	Manufacturing and processing profits deduction	(5.2)	(4.7)
	Amortization of deferred investment tax credits	(1.0)	(1.3)
	Effect of tax-free dividends	(0.2)	(0.4)
	Miscellaneous	(0.1)	0.6
	Effective income tax rate	39.5%	41.5%

5. Extraordinary items		1987	1986
	Gain on sale of investment in Diamond-Bathurst Inc., less deferred income taxes of $15 805	$ 34 178	$ —
	Gain on sale of permanently closed plants, less income taxes of $4 805	7 165	—
	Write-down of investment in Sulbath Exploration Ltd., less income tax credits of $3 092 (1986 Nil)	(8 468)	(17 500)
	Write-off of investment in Sulpetro Limited	—	(29 944)
	Provisions for plant shutdowns, less income tax credits of $6 247	—	(6 789)
		$ 32 875	$(54 233)

(thousands of dollars)

6. Inventories

	1987	1986
Pulpwood, chips and expenditures on wood operations	$ 79 674	$ 76 392
Raw materials and supplies	133 964	126 365
Work in process and finished goods	141 916	141 789
	$355 554	$344 546

7. Property and plant

(a) Paper mill equipment held under capital leases amounted to $135 002 (1986 $134 632) less accumulated depreciation of $28 218 (1986 $17 005).

(b) Interest capitalized on major additions during 1987 was $8 461 (1986 $6 288).

8. Investments

	1987	1986
Portfolio:		
Sceptre Resources Limited		
Common shares (market value $7 758; 1986 $5 633)	$ 9 459	$ 9 459
Preferred shares (market value $4 464; 1986 $3 976)	6 984	6 984
Sulbath Exploration Ltd.	—	14 949
Other investments and advances	15 291	16 087
	31 734	47 479
Equity:		
Joint ventures		
MacMillan Bathurst Inc. (50% owned)	32 815	32 405
Power Consolidated (China) Pulp Inc. (50% owned)	21 844	25 257
Libbey-St. Clair Inc. (50% owned by CB Pak Inc.)	20 501	17 793
	75 160	75 455
Other investments	2 713	2 500
Diamond-Bathurst Inc.	—	47 560
	77 873	125 515
	$109 607	$172 994

39

Notes to Consolidated Financial Statements
December 31, 1987

(thousands of dollars)

Investments (continued)	The changes in the equity investments are summarized below:	1987	1986
	Balance at beginning of year	$125 515	$ 90 274
	Equity earnings	16 608	6 720
	Disposal of investment in Diamond-Bathurst Inc.	(47 474)	—
	Increase (decrease) in investments	(8 828)	34 739
	Dividends received	(7 948)	(2 419)
	Extraordinary item – Diamond-Bathurst Inc.	—	(3 799)
	Balance at end of year	$ 77 873	$125 515

	The combined financial statements of the equity-accounted-for companies, except for Diamond-Bathurst Inc., which was sold in 1987, are summarized below:	1987	1986
	Results of operations for the year		
	Net sales	$517 049	$382 632
	Costs and expenses	463 379	357 778
		53 670	24 854
	Earnings before income taxes		
	Income taxes	21 823	11 727
	Net earnings	$ 31 847	$ 13 127
	Financial position at December 31		
	Current assets	$168 149	$141 028
	Current liabilities	80 900	64 465
	Working capital	87 249	76 563
	Property and plant – net	124 754	116 230
	Other assets	2 654	3 437
	Long-term debt, other liabilities and shareholders' equity	$214 657	$196 230

9. Other assets		1987	1986
	Deferred translation loss (net) on long-term debt	$18 966	$17 387
	Advances to trustees under share option plans	4 643	4 950
	Deferred charges	4 274	2 033
	Unamortized long-term debt expense	2 046	2 212
		$29 929	$26 582

Of advances to trustees, $3 762 (1986 $4 246)
is owing to the trustees from officers, two of
whom are directors.

(thousands of dollars)

10. Long-term debt

		1987	1986	1987	1986
		Foreign currencies		Canadian dollars	
		(thousands)			
Consolidated-Bathurst Inc.					
Sinking fund debentures (a)					
5.85% Series A 1988	U.S. $	367	1 332	$ 477	$ 1 839
6⅛% Series B 1988	U.S. $	146	1 146	190	1 582
8¼% Series C 1993				4 442	5 692
9% Series F 1992	U.S. $	6 107	6 107	7 938	8 431
17½% Series I 1988	U.S. $	37 000	47 000	48 093	64 884
Obligations under capital leases at Bridgewater (b)	£	46 116	51 733	113 082	105 877
Revolving credit (c)	U.S. $	—	100 000	—	138 050
Note issuance facility (d)	U.S. $	—	—	—	—
Consolidated-Bathurst Pontiac Limited					
11% first mortgage sinking fund bonds, Series A, 1995				5 781	6 881
CB Pak Inc. and subsidiaries					
9½% sinking fund debentures, Series A, 1990				9 208	9 208
Revolving credit (c)				—	20 000
5⅛% Swiss bonds, 1991 (e)	SFr.	85 000	85 000	65 724	65 724
Mortgages and other				1 571	1 709
Europa Carton AG and subsidiaries					
Term bank loans, various interest rates, 1988 to 1995	DM	44 562	52 694	36 879	37 802
Reclassification of short-term borrowings (f)				157 749	69 025
Obligations under capital leases				4 251	6 764
Other				27	2 516
				455 412	545 984
Less current portion				79 888	37 350
				$375 524	$508 634

(a) The trust deeds governing the sinking fund debentures were cancelled in May 1986 in accordance with the defeasance provisions of the trust deeds. In place of the floating charge on the Corporation's assets securing these debentures, the Corporation has arranged for two major Canadian banks to guarantee the payment obligations in respect of these debentures. Since the defeasance was carried out by means of a bank guarantee, the amounts outstanding under the sinking fund debentures continue to be reported as debt in the balance sheet.

Notes to Consolidated Financial Statements
December 31, 1987

Long-term debt (continued)

(b) Under the capital lease obligation for equipment at the Bridgewater Division, the lease payments vary until March 31, 1994, with short-term U.K. interest rates and the lessor's effective tax rate in respect of the leases. Thereafter, annual lease payments will be fixed at a nominal rate based on the total cost of the leased equipment. Effective January 1, 1988, the operations of the Bridgewater Division were sold to Bridgewater Paper Company Limited, a wholly owned subsidiary of the Corporation in the United Kingdom, which also assumed the capital lease obligation. The Corporation has agreed to guarantee this obligation.

(c) The revolving credit facilities at December 31, 1987, are summarized as follows:

	Consolidated-Bathurst Inc.	Domglas Inc.
Amount of facility	Cdn./U.S. $100 000	Cdn. $20 000
Outstanding borrowings	—	—
Secured by	Unsecured	Demand debenture, Series B
Current revolving period ends	November 28, 1989	December 29, 1989

Under the revolving credit facilities, funds can be borrowed by way of direct advances or bankers' acceptances, repaid and re-borrowed during a two-year period, renewable annually. If not renewed, borrowings can, at the borrower's option, either be repaid or converted to a term loan at floating interest rates for four years in the case of Consolidated-Bathurst Inc. and ten years in the case of Domglas Inc. Effective January 26, 1988, Consolidated-Bathurst Inc. reduced its revolving credit facility from U.S. $100 000 to U.S. $50 000.

(d) On December 17, 1987, Consolidated-Bathurst Inc. arranged a U.S. $125 000 floating rate note issuance facility with a consortium of financial institutions. Under this facility, which provides direct access to the Euro-Commercial Paper Market for a minimum term of seven years, extendable annually after the second year, funds can be raised through the issue of unsecured and unsubordinated notes of the Corporation.

(e) As a result of a currency exchange agreement relating to the SFr. 85 000 principal, CB Pak Inc. is committed for fees aggregating $13 850 which are being paid and expensed over the term of the bonds. These fees guarantee a fixed exchange rate for the repayment of the bonds at maturity.

(f) Bank loans and notes payable of $157 749 at December 31, 1987, (1986 $69 025) were included in long-term debt as the Corporation intends to refinance these borrowings under its unused long-term credit facilities.

(g) As a result of an interest rate swap, Consolidated-Bathurst Inc. has fixed the interest rate at 13.1% per annum to November 1, 1992 on U.S. $50 000 of floating rate debt.

(h) Sinking fund requirements and principal payments during the next five years, based on exchange rates at December 31, 1987, are: 1988 $79 888; 1989 $28 267; 1990 $36 816; 1991 $93 395; 1992 $33 423.

(thousands of dollars)

11. Stated capital

Preferred shares

(a) Authorized
 – 6 000 000 preferred shares of which 1 027 169 are designated as 1966 Series

– unlimited number of second preferred shares, issuable in series, of which 800 000, 700 000, and 2 000 000 are designated as Series A, Series B, and Series C, respectively.

(b) Issued and outstanding

	1987		1986	
	Shares	Stated Value	Shares	Stated Value
Preferred shares – 1966 Series	699 126	$ 17 478	741 926	$ 18 548
Second preferred shares				
Series A	800 000	40 000	800 000	40 000
Series B	700 000	42 931	700 000	42 931
Series C	1 992 100	49 802	2 000 000	50 000
		$150 211		$151 479

(c) Principal features
 (i) General
  The shares are redeemable and are non-voting unless the Corporation fails to pay, in the aggregate, eight quarterly dividends. Subject to the provisions attaching to all preferred shares, the Corporation, at its option, may effect share redemptions on 30 days' notice at specific prices plus accrued dividends thereon. Unless the market price is in excess of the redemption price, the Corporation is obliged to make all reasonable efforts to purchase annually a certain number of shares of each series.
 (ii) Cumulative dividends – payable per share and quarterly on all Series
  1966 Series – $1.50 per annum
  Series A – $5.75 per annum
  Series B – U.S. $5.25 per annum
  Series C – $2.04 per annum, on or prior to December 31, 1990, and thereafter, at a rate per annum of 70% of the average prime rates of two major Canadian banks applied to $25
 (iii) Redemption
  1966 Series – at $26 per share
  Series A and
  Series B – On January 21, 1988, the Corporation announced its intention to redeem on April 15, 1988, all Series A shares at $52 per share and all Series B shares at U.S. $52 per share.

  Series C – at $25 per share on or after December 31, 1990
 (iv) Purchases for cancellation
  1966 Series – 38 686 shares annually at a cost not exceeding $26 per share. 42 800 shares were purchased in 1987 (38 700 in 1986) at a cost of $866 ($760 in 1986)
  Series A – 2% per year of the shares issued at a cost not exceeding $50 per share
  Series B – same as Series A except in U.S. dollars
   No Series A and B shares were acquired in 1987 and 1986 as the shares of each series traded above $50 per share and U.S. $50 per share, respectively, throughout this period.
  Series C – 40 000 shares annually at a cost not exceeding $25 per share up to and including December 31, 1990 and thereafter, 80 000 shares annually
   7 900 Series C shares were acquired in 1987 at a cost of $176 (nil in 1986)
 (v) Currency election
  The holders of the Series B shares may elect to receive the U.S. dollar dividend and redemption payments in the Canadian dollar equivalent thereof.

43

Notes to Consolidated Financial Statements
December 31, 1987

(thousands of dollars)

Stated capital (continued)

Common shares

(a) Authorized – unlimited number of shares

(b) Issued and outstanding

	Series A		Series B	
	Shares	Stated Value	Shares	Stated Value
Balance January 1, 1987	98 623 016	$275 208	3 643 084	$27 880
Net conversions from Series A to Series B (c)	(18 447)	(62)	18 447	62
Issued as stock dividends	—	—	244 999	—
Issued under the 1984 Employee Share Option Plan (d)	36 700	266	8 000	58
Purchased and cancelled	(237 400)	(662)	—	—
Balance December 31, 1987	98 403 869	$274 750	3 914 530	$28 000

(c) Principal features

The Series A and Series B shares are voting, inter-convertible on a share for share basis, and identical in all respects with the exception that dividends on the Series B shares are paid in the form of shares instead of cash.

(d) 1984 Employee Share Option Plan

In 1984, options were granted to a number of officers and employees to purchase, until December 31, 1989, up to an aggregate of 1 174 000 common shares of the Corporation, at $7.25 per share. As at December 31, 1987, 1 115 900 shares had been issued under this Plan.

12. Segmented information

The classes of business of the Corporation are pulp and paper, packaging and oil and gas. Information segmented by classes and major product lines and by producing geographical regions is reported on pages 30 and 31 of this report.

13. Related party transactions

Power Corporation of Canada is the major shareholder of the Corporation, owning approximately 40% of the outstanding common shares. In 1987, the Corporation had transactions with certain companies in the Power Corporation group, mainly in respect of sales of newsprint and purchases of share transfer agency, trusteeship and insurance services. Such transactions were made at market prices for similar products and services and the total value was not significant in relation to the total sales and purchases of the Corporation.

The Corporation had transactions with MacMillan Bathurst Inc., a joint venture company, in respect of sales of container-board and purchases of corrugated containers. Such transactions were made at market prices and were not significant in relation to the total sales and purchases of the Corporation.

(thousands of dollars)

14. Commitments

(a) At December 31, 1987, the future lease payments under capital and operating leases that have initial non-cancellable lease terms in excess of one year are as follows:

	Capital Leases	Operating Leases
1988	$ 29 500	$12 100
1989	26 800	6 900
1990	26 100	5 100
1991	26 100	3 700
1992	26 000	2 700
Thereafter	22 700	4 500
	157 200	$35 000
Less imputed interest	39 867	
Present value of lease payments	$117 333	

(b) At December 31, 1987, outstanding commitments for capital expenditures under purchase orders and contracts amounted to approximately $87 000.

15. Pension plans

The funded status of the pension plans of the Corporation and its subsidiaries, with the exception of Europa Carton AG, at December 31, 1987, was:

Plan assets at adjusted market values	$517 554
Actuarial projected benefit obligation	467 826
Plan assets in excess of projected benefit obligation	$ 49 728

16. Subsequent event

On February 15, 1988, the Corporation was advised that a company formed by two executives of CB Pak Inc. proposed to make a take-over bid for all the issued common shares of CB Pak Inc. The offer, subject to obtaining satisfactory financing and regulatory approvals, is to be $25.50 per share in cash, less a special dividend of up to $3.50 which may be paid by CB Pak Inc. The Corporation, which owns 16 000 000 shares of CB Pak Inc., has agreed to tender these shares if the bid is made not later than April 15, 1988.

Facilities

Pulp and Paper

☐ Woodlands Divisions
Wood harvesting, purchase of wood and chips, silviculture: *Maritimes Division* (Bathurst Area, Bathurst; Chaleurs Area, New Richmond); *Ottawa Division*, Portage-du-Fort; *Saguenay Division*, Chicoutimi; *Saint-Maurice Division*, Grand-Mère

☐ Sawmills
Dimension pine lumber, pine panelling: *Braeside*
Spruce studs: *Bathurst, Notre-Dame-du-Rosaire*
Fir and spruce lumber: *Saint-Fulgence*

– Gagnon & Frère de Roberval Inc.
Dimension spruce lumber: *Roberval*
Spruce studs: *Chibougamau Road, mile 123*

☐ Pulp, Paper and Paperboard Mills
Chemi-thermo-mechanical pulp, containerboard (corrugating medium): *Bathurst* (Bathurst Division)
Publisher newsprint: *La Baie* (Port Alfred Division), *Shawinigan* (Belgo Division)
Groundwood specialty papers, boxboard: *Grand-Mère* (Laurentide Division)
Groundwood specialty papers, kraft paper: *Trois-Rivières* (Wayagamack Division)
Containerboard (linerboard): *New Richmond* (Chaleurs Division)
Bleached kraft market pulp: *Portage-du-Fort* (Pontiac Division)
Research Centre: *Grand-Mère*

☐ U.K. Newsprint Mill
Bridgewater Paper Company Limited
Publisher newsprint: *Ellesmere Port* (Bridgewater Division)

☐ Celgar Pulp Company
(joint venture of Power Consolidated (China) Pulp Inc. and China International Trust and Investment Corporation)
Softwood kraft market pulp: *Castlegar, B.C.*

North American Packaging

☐ CB Pak Inc., *Montreal*

– Domglas Inc., *Mississauga, Ont.*

Glass containers: *Brampton, Hamilton*
Glass containers, 'Plasti-Shield' bottles: *Montreal* (Pointe Saint-Charles), *Redcliff, Alta., Scoudouc, N.B.*
Industrial glass products, glass furnace rebuilds: *Brantford*
Mould design and production: *Hamilton*
Research Centre: *Mississauga*

– Twinpak Inc., *Dorval, Que.*

Flexible Packaging Group
Multiwall paper bags, industrial plastic bags, coated and laminated products, metallized films and paper: *Brantford*
Multiwall paper bags, industrial plastic bags, plastic films: *Calgary*
Multiwall paper bags, industrial plastic bags, coated and laminated products: *Cap-de-la-Madeleine, Vancouver*

Rigid Packaging Group
Bags, food packaging systems: *Dorval*
Plastic containers, specialty closures: *Montreal, Regina*
Plastic squeeze tubes: *Granby*
PET bottles: *Calgary, Dorval, Mississauga, Moncton*

Distribution Centres
Dorval, Edmonton, Toronto, Vancouver

☐ CB Pak associate company

– Libbey-St. Clair Inc., *Mississauga, Ont.* (joint venture with Owens-Illinois, Inc.)

Glass tableware: *Wallaceburg, Ont.*; Ravenhead Company, *St. Helens, England*

☐ MacMillan Bathurst Inc., *Mississauga, Ont.* (joint venture with MacMillan Bloedel Limited)

Corrugated Container Plants:
Calgary, Edmonton, Etobicoke, Guelph, New Westminster, Pembroke, Regina, Rexdale, Saint-Laurent, St. Thomas, Town of Mount-Royal, Whitby, Winnipeg

Packaging, Europa Carton

Europa Carton AG, *Hamburg*

☐ Plants
Folding cartons: *Augsburg, Bremen, Frankfurt, Sneek (Netherlands)*
Partitions: *Heppenheim*
Corrugated containers: *Düsseldorf, Germersheim, Hamburg, Jülich, Lauenburg, Lübbecke, Neuburg, Plattling*

☐ Mills
Boxboard: *Hoya*
Containerboard (corrugating medium): *Viersen*

Waste paper collection: *Eddelak, Essen, Hamburg, Metten*

☐ Institutes
Market research: *Hamburg*
Industrial design: *Hamburg*

Laurentide –
100 years strong

On the Saint-Maurice River at Grand-Mère, the Laurentide mill has operated continuously since 1888, originally as a company in its own right, then as a division of Consolidated-Bathurst, helping to establish the community, and industry standards for pulp and paper production.

Consolidated-Bathurst's earliest continuing predecessor in pulp and paper, the Laurentide Pulp Company, was incorporated by John Forman on June 1, 1887. When its original pulp mill started up at Grand-Mère in 1888, initial daily production was 25 short tons of groundwood pulp.

In March of 1896, General Russell A. Alger, a wealthy Michigan lumber merchant, became Laurentide's controlling shareholder. He brought Sir William Van Horne and four other directors of the CPR in as members of the Laurentide Board. By the fall of 1899, they had Laurentide's capital up to $1.6 million and the mill's groundwood pulp capacity to 120 tons per day. They also had a sulphite pulp mill completed, three paper machines installed, and a mill that was turning out 40 tons per day of newsprint and 35 tons of board.

In 1900, with the addition of a fourth paper machine, newsprint production went to 75 tons per day, making Laurentide Canada's first industrial-scale producer of newsprint, and the country's largest pulp and paper mill.

George Chahoon Jr., a young papermaker of New York State was hired by Sir William to manage the mill. He came to Grand-Mère in October of 1902 and ran Laurentide for the next 29 years. At the outset, he added three more paper machines. In 1905, Mr. Chahoon engaged Canada's first professional chief forester, Ellwood Wilson. Mr. Wilson sought to farm the forest and started Canada's first commercial air service, although his primary objective for it was to map the forest more efficiently.

No. 8 and No. 9 paper machines, built by Dominion Bridge of Lachine, Que., came on stream in 1921, to increase the mill's newsprint output to 300 tons per day. By 1927, Laurentide's last annual report showed a profit of $2.8 million and no outstanding funded debt.

Like Laurentide in 1887, Consolidated Paper was born out of financial crisis, in the unfortunate timing of the efforts of Canada Power & Paper Corporation to bring together five Quebec pulp and paper companies. From Canada Power's formation in 1928, the industry's situation went from bad to worse, first, with overproduction and, later, the economic impact of the 1929 stock market crash.

A Securities Protective Committee, formed under the Chairmanship of the Hon. Charles A. Dunning to regroup Canada Power's assets, brought Consolidated Paper Corporation Limited into existence on August 28, 1931. When the Company began operations as Consolidated Paper Corporation on January 1, 1932, there was little enthusiasm that it could survive for very long.

That it did was a tribute to the close and effective management of Lamonte J. Belnap, who was hired by Mr. Dunning as Consolidated's first President, and presided over it during the succeeding three decades. Laurentide was the flagship mill of the Company during Mr. Belnap's tenure.

The sixties began a dynamic period of change for the industry. Consolidated built its first all-new paper machine, No. 10 at Laurentide, and started construction of a new market pulp mill as its Pontiac Division, at Portage-du-Fort. It also broadened into packaging, especially with the merger of Consolidated and Bathurst Paper Limited, effected during Montreal's Expo Summer of 1967. At the beginning of October of 1967, the name "Consolidated-Bathurst" was introduced.

**Challenge and achievement —
yesterday, today and tomorrow**

Through problems of the early seventies, the Company went on to meet new challenges of modernization and diversification. Paper machines were updated at various mills, a new machine installed at Wayagamack, twin-wire formers added to other machines. In 1981, a shut-down newsprint mill in the United Kingdom was acquired. It was rebuilt and modernized in 1982-83, and to supply its pulp requirements, the Bathurst mill was equipped with a new chemi-thermo-mechanical pulp mill. Laurentide, too, has seen substantial improvement over recent years, with two new supercalenders in 1980-81 to add value to its products, a new 'very high yield' sulphite pulp mill in 1981, and, in 1984, a twin-wire former for the No. 10 Paper Machine, to upgrade its product.

Laurentide will soon be the site of the largest single development project in the Company's history – the new $280 million No. 11 Paper Machine that will replace the mill's No. 8 and 9 machines. With construction to begin in the spring of 1989, Laurentide No. 11 will start up late in 1990. An appropriate recognition of Laurentide's 100th Anniversary, and of its determination to meet the relentless exigencies of the future by being world class in pulp and paper production.

Comparative Data

		1987	1986	1985
Operations (thousands of dollars)	Net sales	$2 261 430	$2 017 834	$1 727 468
	Earnings before extraordinary items	181 540	103 650	79 757
	Net earnings	214 415	49 417	77 564
	Cash flow from operations	360 226	257 419	195 823
	Additions to property and plant	260 756	231 230	175 737
	Dividends declared – common	50 493	30 394	29 695
	– preferred	$ 14 585	$ 14 881	$ 10 847
	Depreciation	$ 114 020	$ 99 132	$ 84 393
	Interest – both short and long-term	47 117	54 928	63 695
	Income taxes	112 898	72 430	40 906
	Maintenance and repair expenses	179 600	166 573	136 676
	Wages, salaries and fringe benefits	610 436	565 406	478 504
	Energy costs	$ 194 820	$ 194 041	$ 189 009
Per common share (dollars)	Earnings before extraordinary items	$ 1.63	$ 0.87	$ 0.70
	Net earnings	1.95	0.34	0.68
	Cash flow from operations	3.38	2.37	1.88
	Dividends declared	0.54	0.30	0.30
	Book value	$ 8.33	$ 6.76	$ 6.54
Per preferred share (dollars)	Dividends declared – 1966 Series	$ 1.50	$ 1.50	$ 1.50
	– Series A	5.75	5.75	5.75
	– Series B	6.90	7.26	7.20
	– Series C	$ 2.04	$ 2.04	$ —
Balance sheet (thousands of dollars)	Total assets	$2 264 669	$2 030 785	$1 862 736
	Working capital	393 935	338 909	319 630
	Property and plant – gross	2 245 543	1 981 520	1 725 656
	Accumulated depreciation	906 808	790 306	688 825
	Investments	109 607	172 994	179 385
	Long-term debt	375 524	508 634	442 030
	Provision for German pensions	70 315	54 422	39 545
	Minority interest	61 105	41 270	39 776
	Stated capital – preferred	150 211	151 479	152 447
	– common	302 750	303 088	300 139
	Retained earnings	520 378	374 423	371 882
	Foreign currency translation adjustments	29 469	13 751	(4 991)
	Total shareholders' equity	$1 002 808	$ 842 741	$ 819 477
Other data	Ratio of current assets to current liabilities	2.0 to 1	2.1 to 1	2.1 to 1
	Ratio of short and long-term debt to shareholders' equity	31/69	40/60	38/62
	*Return on assets – %	9.6	7.0	6.8
	**Return on common shareholders' equity – %	19.6	12.8	10.3
	Shares outstanding – preferred	4 191 226	4 241 926	4 280 626
	– common	102 318 399	102 266 100	101 999 614
	Number of employees	15 111	14 619	14 413
	Number of common shareholders	13 877	13 487	14 176

*Earnings before extraordinary items, minority interest and after-tax interest, divided by total assets after accumulated depreciation at the end of the period

**Earnings before extraordinary items less preferred dividends, divided by total shareholders' equity less preferred share stated capital at the end of the period

1984	1983	1982	1981	1980	1979	1978	1977
$1 622 984	$1 393 065	$1 424 284	$1 479 252	$1 389 433	$1 244 312	$1 078 843	$ 868 865
73 808	34 534	51 482	101 386	122 379	98 259	59 147	21 355
58 901	24 854	51 482	111 669	122 379	102 848	60 715	22 716
152 713	93 399	132 918	198 198	194 530	154 510	119 630	66 338
118 884	175 309	242 429	239 614	143 152	92 332	47 475	53 783
22 556	17 962	35 799	44 501	43 964	22 254	16 540	14 591
$ 10 656	$ 10 724	$ 3 979	$ 3 071	$ 3 204	$ 3 147	$ 2 057	$ 1 569
$ 72 633	$ 60 060	$ 54 509	$ 44 486	$ 42 651	$ 38 774	$ 36 022	$ 32 484
67 227	52 725	61 382	43 507	29 886	26 353	26 930	26 823
18 972	15 357	26 971	65 022	78 412	57 058	36 350	10 038
127 445	115 478	109 312	115 013	98 334	83 294	73 038	69 889
458 979	449 922	462 813	458 224	423 067	395 386	365 745	324 995
$ 195 366	$ 158 580	$ 142 792	$ 142 082	$ 104 899	$ 92 393	$ 78 059	$ 66 357
$ 0.70	$ 0.27	$ 0.53	$ 1.10	$ 1.36	$ 1.07	$ 0.65	$ 0.23
0.54	0.16	0.53	1.22	1.36	1.12	0.67	0.24
1.58	0.92	1.44	2.18	2.13	1.71	1.31	0.74
0.25	0.20	0.40	0.50	0.50	0.25	0.19	0.17
$ 5.69	$ 5.68	$ 5.73	$ 5.61	$ 4.93	$ 4.06	$ 3.20	$ 2.75
$ 1.50	$ 1.50	$ 1.50	$ 1.50	$ 1.50	$ 1.50	$ 1.50	$ 1.50
5.75	5.75	0.72	—	—	—	—	—
6.88	6.48	0.81	—	—	—	—	—
$ —	$ —	$ —	$ —	$ —	$ —	$ —	$ —
$1 675 913	$1 652 843	$1 584 570	$1 432 290	$1 136 558	$ 991 854	$ 872 944	$ 808 791
257 275	312 196	340 448	367 860	322 891	289 633	263 141	209 233
1 510 266	1 433 804	1 360 763	1 170 392	968 517	851 947	784 661	769 237
588 869	522 936	515 112	474 176	445 129	416 862	392 549	375 895
173 665	201 997	185 218	152 265	114 107	73 805	52 702	30 851
476 680	545 976	472 036	430 203	278 921	231 950	228 231	245 647
26 430	27 424	23 398	23 305	19 877	15 319	12 829	11 199
32 903	3 168	2 824	2 877	2 524	2 784	2 832	5 896
103 430	104 399	121 375	41 415	44 393	45 360	46 279	26 145
198 658	193 271	190 021	185 326	178 714	165 575	165 848	89 804
339 290	317 837	324 151	318 486	264 711	192 966	120 317	150 940
(25 044)	—	—	—	—	—	—	—
$ 616 334	$ 615 507	$ 635 547	$ 545 227	$ 487 818	$ 403 901	$ 332 444	$ 266 889
1.8 to 1	2.4 to 1	2.7 to 1	2.8 to 1	2.9 to 1	2.6 to 1	2.7 to 1	2.2 to 1
49/51	49/51	45/55	47/53	37/63	37/63	42/58	53/47
7.1	4.1	5.5	8.7	12.2	11.4	8.5	4.6
12.3	4.7	9.2	19.5	26.9	26.5	20.0	8.2
2 319 941	2 358 741	3 037 741	1 656 608	1 775 708	1 814 408	1 851 156	1 045 808
90 109 558	89 916 796	89 756 892	89 700 228	89 926 572	88 205 448	89 527 968	87 546 408
14 395	14 156	15 168	15 999	16 290	17 070	17 532	17 725
13 908	13 530	14 106	14 118	14 160	14 534	13 008	11 983

▽